Current Biography Yearbook 2022

H. W. Wilson

A Division of EBSCO Information Services, Inc.

Ipswich, Massachusetts

GREY HOUSE PUBLISHING

EIGHTY-THIRD ANNUAL CUMULATION—2022

International Standard Serial No. 0084-9499

International Standard Book No. 978-1-64265-725-8

Library of Congress Catalog Card No. 40-27432

Current Biography Yearbook, 2022, published by Grey House Publishing, Inc., Amenia, NY, under exclusive license from EBSCO Information Services, Inc.

PRINTED IN CANADA

CONTENTS

CONTENTS

LIST OF BIOGRAPHICAL SKETCHES

List Of Biographical Sketches

List Of Biographical Sketches

List Of Biographical Sketches

LIST OF OBITUARIES

List Of Obituaries

Current Biography Yearbook 2022

Current Biography® Yearbook 2022

Eric Adams

Born: September 1, 1960
Occupation: Politician

Officially sworn in as New York City's mayor in January 2022, Eric Adams has been considered by many to be a man of many nuanced parts that often appear contradictory to outside observers. For more than twenty years, he was a dedicated New York City police officer, spending several years working for the New York Police Department (NYPD) and rising to the rank of captain. However, while inside the policing system, he was one of its most outspoken critics, particularly on issues of police misconduct. For a time beginning in the late 1990s, he was a registered Republican, but he later went on to serve as a Democrat as a four-term state senator (2007–13) and two-term Brooklyn borough president (2014–21). Critical of many of the policing reforms implemented by previous mayoral administrations, during his mayoral campaign and after taking office he has prioritized addressing the city's increase in crime after decades of decline while emphasizing his desire to ensure that a return to improved public safety and tougher policing does not bring with it claims of racial profiling and injustice. In an extremely liberal city, he bested a crowded primary field of Democrats by being the most moderate. With an aim to reduce economic inequality in the city, he did not want to tax wealthier citizens or corporations, whom he believes are as much the lifeblood of New York as the working class.

"Everybody is trying to figure me out because I refuse to fit into this neat little package," he said to Juan Williams for *The Atlantic* (24 Aug. 2021). "People are saying, 'We don't know who he is.' Listen, I know New Yorkers. . . . They could care less if you call them left or right.

Those are insiders caught up in that left-and-right stuff. I am just a straight New Yorker."

EARLY LIFE AND EDUCATION

A middle child in a family that included five other children, Eric Leroy Adams was born in New York's Brooklyn borough on September 1, 1960. His parents, like many other Black Americans during that period, had relocated north from Alabama in pursuit of better economic opportunities. While his father was a butcher by trade, his mother cleaned houses, often taking on extra shifts to better provide for their family. Although his father's addiction to alcohol and womanizing caused their marriage to fail, his mother resettled the family in a new home in a Queens neighborhood, where she was also employed cooking for children at

Photo via Wikimedia Commons.
[Public domain]

a local care center. He would later credit his mother with inspiring him to work hard and unconditionally give back to others.

As a teenager, Adams became caught up in street gang activity, and at the age of fifteen he and his brother ended up held at a police precinct under a criminal trespass charge. Later, he would cite this incident, in which he has said officers subjected him to repeated kicks to his groin, as a large part of his motivation to effect change in the policing system. Around the same time, a series of police-involved killings in the area drew him to Reverend Herbert Daughtry's National Black United Front movement, through which he was encouraged to become a police officer himself to gain firsthand knowledge and bring about reform from within the institution. "I realized that every time I saw a police vehicle, every time I watched a police show, every time I heard a siren, I relived that. . . . I understood there was a demon inside me. And the only way I can get it out is for me to go in, and going in meant becoming a police officer," he explained to Terry Gross in an interview for NPR's *Fresh Air* (21 July 2016).

After graduating from Bayside High School in Queens, Adams studied at New York City College of Technology, financing the associates degree he earned partially through work as a mechanic and other odd jobs.

NYPD OFFICER

Bolstered by Daughtry's advisement and set on joining New York City's police force, in 1984 Adams graduated at the top of his class in the city's police academy. Shortly thereafter, he began working as a beat cop within the city's then independent transit police department. "I went in with such an aggressive mindset of reform because I thought that if I spent a year, a year and a half, if I survive there long, of being extremely vocal that it would start the process," he told Gross of his early mission. At the time, New York City was in the middle of a crime surge that would not begin to taper off until the 1990s.

As Adams became more entrenched in activism and committed to his everyday duties, his tenure on the force extended for much longer than he had even anticipated, with a 1993 promotion to the rank of sergeant and an appointment as the chair of the Grand Council of the Guardians, the official organization of

Black law enforcement officers in the state of New York. In 1995, the same year in which he became a part of the NYPD upon its absorption of the transit police department, Adams helped establish the group 100 Blacks in Law Enforcement Who Care. Inside and outside of the NYPD, he advocated on behalf of Black members of the force while publicly criticizing departmental issues such as the excessive use of force, the policy of stop-and-frisk, and racism. He also collaborated with the community, including helping young Black Americans understand how best to conduct themselves during police interactions. In a conversation with Jane Gross for *The New York Times* (13 Apr. 1999), he explained his philosophy regarding the importance of candidly acknowledging flawed realities. "At the academy, recruits are told that they should not see black or brown people as different, but we all do. We all know that the majority of people arrested for predatory crimes are African-American. We didn't create that scenario, but we have to police in that scenario. So we need to be honest and talk about it."

Adams further climbed the departmental ranks, earning a promotion to lieutenant around 1998 in addition to a bachelor's degree from John Jay College of Criminal Justice. During his ascent, he tried to serve as a bridge between the mostly White brass at the NYPD and Black leaders, including the Reverend Al Sharpton and Louis Farrakhan, leader of the Nation of Islam. From Adam's perspective as a police officer, he felt that the Nation of Islam had had some success in fighting crime in parts of the city; he believed that the NYPD should work in tandem with the group's leaders to prevent crime. However, many New York City leaders were uncomfortable with the anti-Semitism that Farrakhan and Sharpton often professed; in interviews Adams asserted that he did not support anti-Semitism.

Immediately following the terrorist attacks on September 11, 2001, Adams helped supervise the scene and the work of NYPD officers at the World Trade Center (WTC) towers. In 2006, he retired from the police force as a captain, having served in the department for twenty-two years.

EARLY POLITICAL CAREER

During his time with the NYPD, Adams began contemplating extending his career in public service to politics. In 1994, he attempted to enter the congressional race at the national level as a Democrat, challenging longtime seat holder Major Owens to represent New York's Eleventh Congressional District; however, he was unable to get his name on the ballot. Around 1997 he joined the Republican Party, a move he would later shift between defending and regretting. By 2001, he had returned to the Democratic fold.

Having earned a master's degree in public administration from Marist College in 2006 and proven successful in that year's election, between 2007 and 2013 Adams served in the New York State Senate, representing the Twentieth Senatorial District, which included many neighborhoods in Brooklyn. While in office he oversaw community programs focused on public safety as well as education and became the first person of color to chair the Senate's Veterans, Homeland Security, and Military Affairs Committee.

In 2013 Adams was elected to serve as Brooklyn borough president, which, while largely a ceremonial role, often serves as a training ground for politicians interested in running for mayor of New York. Reelected in 2017, in this position he advocated for the policies he would highlight in his run for mayor: school investment, economic opportunities, and improvements in public safety. Upon his swearing-in ceremony in early 2014, he emphasized combating inequality as his overall mission: "That is what I want my legacy to be: making the lives of everyday Brooklynites better," he said, as quoted by Helen Klein for the *Brooklyn Reporter* (20 Jan. 2014). As the coronavirus disease 2019 (COVID-19) pandemic hit Brooklyn and the rest of the world, in March 2020 he set up a mattress in his office and coordinated deliveries of personal protective equipment to essential workers and other citizens in need.

BECOMING MAYOR OF NEW YORK CITY

In running for New York City mayor following his announcement launching his campaign in late 2020, Adams's platform centered upon public safety and highlighted his credentials as a police officer and internal reformer. After the May 2020 murder of George Floyd, a Black man, by a White police officer in Minneapolis, Minnesota, protests took place in New York City that involved instances of violent clashes

with police at a time when the city was already facing increased violent crime. Adams stressed a tough-on-crime approach, pushing back on the notion to defund the police that many of his fellow Democrats had been urging; he argued that police misconduct was not the sole issue and that a less robust police force would have the most negative impact in communities of color, where crime rates are often higher. "You can't say 'Black lives matter' and have outrage when a police officer shoots someone . . . but ignore shootings in our city the same day when 15 people are shot," he told Williams.

Under the city's new ranked-choice voting (RCV) system, Adams emerged as the Democratic primary victor in a large field of candidates, most of whom were to the left of him politically. Among the candidates were Maya Wiley, a civil rights lawyer, and Kathryn Garcia, the former head of the city's sanitation department. "Now we must focus on winning in November so that we can deliver on the promise of this great city for those who are struggling, who are underserved, and who are committed to a safe, fair, affordable future for all New Yorkers," Adams said after his win, as quoted by Joseph Ax for *Reuters* (7 July 2021). In the November 2021 general election, he faced Republican Curtis Sliwa, the founder of the Guardian Angels, a crime-fighting group made up of unarmed civilians. Despite some spirited debates, Adams handily defeated his opponent, receiving over 65 percent of the votes.

After being sworn in on January 1, 2022, Adams vowed to combat the increase in crime by bringing back a controversial plainclothes policing unit, which had been disbanded in 2020 among accusations of excessive force. In doing so, the mayor promised to institute reforms such as greater accountability and making sure the unit treated people of color with respect. He also vowed to help the city recover from the COVID-19 pandemic, which had killed or sickened thousands of New Yorkers. "When a mayor has swagger, the city has swagger," he said, as quoted by Michelle L. Price for the Associated Press (15 Jan. 2022). "We've allowed people to beat us down so much that all we did was wallow in COVID."

PERSONAL LIFE

Adams has a son, Jordan Coleman. In 2016, upon a diabetes diagnosis, Adams switched to a plant-based diet. His book, *Healthy at Last: A Plant-Based Approach to Preventing and Reversing Diabetes and Other Chronic Illnesses*, was published in 2020.

SUGGESTED READING

Adams, Eric. "Why a Black Teen Who Was Beaten by Police Decided to Join the NYPD." Interview by Terry Gross. *Fresh Air*, NPR, 21 July 2016, www.npr.org/2016/07/21/486892032/an-african-american-police-officer-on-his-choice-to-be-a-voice-for-change. Accessed 11 Feb. 2022.

Ax, Joseph. "Eric Adams Poised to Be New York's Next Mayor." *Reuters*, 7 July 2021, www.reuters.com/world/us/new-results-expected-new-york-citys-democratic-mayoral-race-2021-07-06/. Accessed 20 Jan. 2022.

"Eric L. Adams." *NYC*, City of New York, www1.nyc.gov/office-of-the-mayor/bio.page. Accessed 20 Jan. 2022.

Gross, Jane. "Public Lives; Behind a Badge, Confronting Issues of Race." *The New York Times*, 13 Apr. 1999, www.nytimes.com/1999/04/13/nyregion/public-lives-behind-a-badge-confronting-issues-of-race.html. Accessed 11 Feb. 2022.

Klein, Helen. "Eric Adams Sworn In as Borough President, Introduces Theme of One Brooklyn." *Brooklyn Reporter*, 20 Jan. 2014, brooklynreporter.com/2014/01/eric-adams-sworn-in-as-borough-president-introduces-theme-of-one-brooklyn/. Accessed 11 Feb. 2022.

Price, Michelle L. "2 Weeks in, Does NYC Mayor Eric Adams Still Have Swagger?" Associated Press, 15 Jan. 2022, apnews.com/article/lifestyle-fires-new-york-bronx-new-york-city-979881f852691b4ef97e7f708dcd0010. Accessed 20 Jan. 2022.

Williams, Juan. "Eric Adams Is Making White Liberals Squirm." *The Atlantic*, 24 Aug. 2021, www.theatlantic.com/ideas/archive/2021/08/eric-adams-police-new-york/619869/. Accessed 20 Jan. 2022.

—*Christopher Mari*

Halima Aden

Born: September 19, 1997
Occupation: Fashion model

Even before becoming the first Muslim, hijab-wearing model in the fashion industry, Halima Aden smashed barriers everywhere she turned. She was the first hijab-wearing Muslim to be crowned homecoming queen at her high school in St. Cloud, Minnesota, and the first Somali Muslim woman to be part of the student senate at St. Cloud State University. Even though she achieved yet another first by wearing a hijab and a burkini at the 2016 Miss Minnesota USA Pageant, for her, this opportunity signified representing an entire community.

Soon, she trailblazed a path forward in the fashion industry, wearing a hijab—the traditional Muslim head covering that would come to define her career—on several of the world's runways and magazines, including *Allure*, *British Vogue*, and *Sports Illustrated Swimsuit*. Whenever Aden appeared, she propelled an imperative conversation: inclusivity in fashion.

In late 2020, Aden announced her retirement from the fashion industry, declaring that she was discontinuing her career when she realized it was in direct conflict with her identity. "Don't change yourself, change the game," she said in an interview with designer Tommy Hilfiger and Sodaba Haidare for *BBC News* (22 July 2021). "I want the girls to know, Halima took one for the team. You know, I sacrificed my career so that that they could feel comfortable to speak up in any setting."

EARLY LIFE AND EDUCATION

Somali American fashion model Halima Aden was born on September 19, 1997, in the Kakuma refugee camp, situated in the northwestern region of Kenya. The daughter of a Somali woman who had fled the civil war in her country, Aden spent her first seven years of life alongside her mother and her sister, Fadumo, in homes inside the camp made of mud, leaves, and branches that often washed away with the rain. Despite lacking toys and clothes during most of her childhood—and not always having food available in the home—Aden remembers her time at the refugee

Photo by TheOfficialPandora,
via Wikimedia Commons

a catalyst for her future career in fashion, as it pushed her to ponder: "What else? What else can I do like this?" she revealed in an interview to Maya West for *Allure* (27 Feb. 2017). Aden graduated from the high school in 2016.

MISS MINNESOTA USA PAGEANT

Following her graduation, Aden enrolled at St. Cloud State University, where she became the first Somali Muslim woman to be part of the student senate during her freshman year. She continued breaking barriers that year when she took part in the 2016 Miss Minnesota USA Pageant in November, wearing a hijab throughout the competition. When the swimsuit portion of the pageant arrived, judges saw her model a burkini—a full-body swimming costume covering the entire body except for the face, hands, and feet. The judges respected Aden's decision to wear a burkini and gave her the pass to advance to the next stage of the competition.

Aden made it to the semifinals of the competition, and while she was not crowned Miss Minnesota, for her it was more than just winning, it was about representation. Being the first woman to wear a hijab and a burkini in a Miss Minnesota USA Pageant had her continuously asking herself, "Why haven't I seen anybody dressed like me in these pageants? Why isn't that a category? Why isn't it normal?" she told West, before adding that "eventually I realized I needed to create my own category. To forget them, and just do me." And that is exactly what she did.

The Miss Minnesota competition made Aden aware that she could pursue a career in fashion while remaining unwavering in her conviction to be her true self: a Black, Muslim woman who was a refugee. This notion was confirmed when *CR Fashion Book* editor Carine Roitfeld approached a teenaged Aden and offered her her first magazine cover, despite not having any real modeling experience or an agency behind her. Her inexperience posed no issue as, when the *CR Fashion Book's* tenth issue was published in 2017, Aden was seen on the cover wearing a navy dress and her signature hijab.

A TRAILBLAZING FASHION MODEL

Much to the chagrin of her mother, who did not want Aden to become a model as it clashed with her Muslim faith, Aden signed a three-

camp fondly, where a sense of community was palpable among people coming from all over Africa. "Kakuma: a community composed of people who didn't speak the same native language or share the same religion but who found a language of understanding," Aden wrote in an article for *Glamour* (20 June 2019).

Even before leaving Kakuma at the age of seven, Aden had formed a rich foundation of empathy, gratefulness, and understanding, the pillars on which her mother taught her to build relationships with others. When Aden and her family moved to the United States and eventually settled in St. Cloud, Minnesota, it was precisely those values that allowed her to adjust to a foreign culture. "My mom didn't have the means to own a car, and I will never forget the people who stopped to offer us rides to school or to the grocery store in those winter months," she wrote in the *Glamour* article. "These were people who looked nothing like us and owed us nothing. Luckily, Minnesota is a community, too, and people invited us into the warmth."

This sense of fellowship, of being part of a community, followed her as she attended Apollo High School, where, during her senior year, Aden became the town's first hijab-wearing Muslim to be crowned homecoming queen. Representing a demographic that had never been included in such an event served as year contract with the management company IMG Models not long after partaking in Kanye West's Yeezy fashion show in early 2017. In order to devote her attention to her burgeoning career, Aden took an indefinite hiatus from her education.

Aden continued reaping success in 2017, with the young model gracing the covers of *Vogue Arabia* and *Allure Magazine* wearing a hijab for the June and July issues, respectively. That year she was also tapped by fashion outfitter American Eagle to introduce a denim hijab as part of its apparel offerings, starring in their Summer 2017 campaign wearing the garment.

In May 2018, Aden became the first model to wear a hijab on the cover of *British Vogue*, a magazine that had been in existence for over one hundred years. On the cover, she was flanked on her sides by eight other trailblazing models, including Indian Radhika Nair, African American Paloma Elsesser, and South Sudanese Adut Akech, the latter of whom was raised at Kakuma refugee camp until the age of seven, mirroring the childhood of Aden. "That out was so wild! For me to be the first hijab-wearing cover girl, that was like mind-boggling," she told Isabelle Truman in an interview for *Grazia*. "But actually finding out that Adut and I were born in the same camp—around the same age, in the same zone!—We're two young girls, leaving that world behind."

Aden, no stranger to breaking new ground in the modeling industry, next appeared on the pages of *Sports Illustrated Swimsuit* in 2019, sporting a burkini and the piece that had come to define her career as a model: a hijab. With her appearance on some of the most celebrated fashion shows and magazines, she drove the conversation about diversity and inclusion, demanding a continual talk about women's rights and the outdated standards of beauty.

However, not everything was smooth behind the scenes, as not every magazine or photographer shared nor respected her religious views. That was the case with the September 2019 issue of *King Kong* magazine, in which the young model appeared on the cover wearing bright eye shadow and a piece of jewelry that resembled a mask. While Aden thought the image was a bit too provocative, it was not until she flipped the pages and found, to her horror, the picture of a nude man, that she became very concerned. "Why would the magazine think it was acceptable to have a hijab-wearing Muslim woman when a naked man is on the next page?" she asked during an interview with Sodaba Haidare for *BBC News* (14 Jan. 2021).

ACTIVISM AND RETIREMENT FROM MODELING

In 2018, Aden became a UNICEF ambassador. Having been born and spent a large part of her childhood in a refugee camp, Aden's work with UNICEF focused on children's rights. Later that year, she returned to her birthplace, the Kakuma refugee camp, to film a popular TED Talk titled "How I Went from Child Refugee to International Model." She resigned as an ambassador, however, in 2020, stating that she did not feel the organization was doing enough to change the daily lives of the children they boasted helping.

In addition to modeling and activism, Aden took on a number of other opportunities. Joining forces with the modest fashion label Modanisa, she designed the Halima × Modanisa collection, comprising turbans and shawls, which she released at the Istanbul Modest Fashion Week in April 2019. Additional collections were released between 2020 and 2022. She also served as an executive producer for the film *I Am You* (2019), a drama based on the true story of a refugee's journey from Afghanistan.

By 2020, however, Aden's modeling career had become so demanding that she felt she had little time to spend with her family or to attend Muslim religious festivals in her hometown. Making matters worse, she had started to feel her hijab rule clashed with the industry, as, in each photo shoot, the piece was redesigned to look less and less like a hijab. She told Haidare, "I had zero excitement because I couldn't see *myself*. Do you know how mentally damaging that can be to somebody? When I'm supposed to feel happy and grateful and I'm supposed to relate, because that's me, that's my picture, that's my own picture, but I was so far removed." Not content with how her faith was being respected, or with how she and other hijab-wearing models were treated, Aden quit the fashion industry in November 2020.

When announcing her decision, Aden revealed that it was the time she spent at home in St. Cloud with her mother during the coronavirus disease 2019 (COVID-19) pandemic shutdown in early 2020 that allowed her to realize she did not want to compromise her Muslim faith. Furthermore, as the first-ever hijab-wearing model, she thought it responsible to speak about her experience of being a Black, Muslim woman in the fashion industry, in case it could inspire others. As she explained in an interview with Hilfiger after being named one of the *BBC*'s 100 Women in 2021, as quoted by Selina Denman for the *National News* (24 July 2021): "I felt great pressure being the first Muslim, hijab-wearing model in the industry and I felt a sense of responsibility for the girls who followed in my footsteps, and so I'm hoping through my exit and how vocal I have been, they're inspired to speak up on set."

SUGGESTED READING

Aden, Halima. "Born in a Refugee Camp, Model Halima Aden Is Finding Community on Her Own Terms." *Glamour*, 20 June 2019, www.glamour.com/story/halima-aden-world-refugee-day. Accessed 15 Aug. 2022.

___. "Halima Aden's Life Is Full of Firsts. But Finally, She's Not the Only One Holding the Torch." Interview by Isabelle Truman. *Grazia*, graziamagazine.com/articles/halima-aden-interview. Accessed 15 Aug. 2022.

___. "Halima Aden and Tommy Hilfiger: 'It's Not Just About Diverse Catwalks.'" Interview by Tommy Hilfiger and Sodaba Haidare. *BBC News*, 22 July 2021, www.bbc.com/news/av/world-57918698. Accessed 12 Sept. 2022.Denman, Selina. "Halima Aden: 'I Sacrificed My Career So Others Could Feel Comfortable Speaking Up.'" *The National News*, 24 July 2021, www.thenationalnews.com/lifestyle/2021/07/24/halima-aden-i-sacrificed-my-career-so-others-could-feel-comfortable-speaking-up. Accessed 15 Aug. 2022.

___. "Supermodel Halima Aden: 'Why I Quit.'" Interview by Sodaba Haidare. *BBC News*, 14 Jan. 2021, www.bbc.com/news/stories-55653029. Accessed 15 Aug. 2022.

___. "The Halima Aden Interview You've Been Waiting for." Interview by Maya West. *Allure*, 27 Feb. 2017, www.allure.com/story/halima-aden-muslim-model-interview. Accessed 15 Aug. 2022.

—*Maria del Pilar Guzman*

Akinwumi Adesina

Born: February 6, 1960
Occupation: Economist

Elected to his first five-year term in September 2015, Akinwumi Adesina became the first Nigerian president of the African Development Bank Group (AfDB), an organization that provides financial assistance to African governments and private companies that invest in countries on the African continent. The bank seeks to reduce poverty across the continent and provide funds aimed at improving the economic and social lives of everyday Africans. Founded in 1964, the AfDB has numerous national shareholders, with Adesina's native Nigeria, the United States, Egypt, Japan, South Africa, Algeria, Germany, Canada, Ivory Coast, and France being among the largest. The group's goal, as quoted from its website, is "to spur sustainable economic development and social progress in its regional member countries (RMCs), thus contributing to poverty reduction."

As president, Adesina has brought decades of experience as a developmental economist who specializes in agricultural development through free market principles. For more than thirty years, he aided struggling rural communities by helping them get access to international funding. Prior to being AfDB president, he successfully implemented policies that aided farmers as Nigeria's minister of agriculture. After beginning a second term as AfDB's president in 2020, he sought to continue to reduce poverty across the continent and to build its middle class. According to his biography on the AfDB's website, Adesina "is celebrated as one of Africa's leading development entrepreneurs based on his ability to develop and successfully execute bold initiatives that transform the lives of millions of people. His passion is to unlock wealth for African economies, end poverty, hunger and malnutrition and lift millions of Africa's poor, especially women and youth, into Africa's emerging middle class."

EARLY LIFE AND EDUCATION

Akinwumi Ayodeji "Akin" Adesina was born in Nigeria on February 6, 1960, to a farming family. He was the second son of Roland Folorunso Adesina and Eunice Adesina. He has three brothers.

Photo by Eric Roset / Africa Progress Panel,
via Wikimedia Commons

In 1981, Adesina received his bachelor's degree with first-class honors in agricultural economics from the University of Ife (now Obafemi Awolowo University) in Nigeria. Despite his first-class honors, he was told by a teacher that he would never get into Purdue University in the United States because his grades in mathematics were too weak. Undaunted, Adesina applied to Purdue and was accepted.

After moving to the United States for study, Adesina earned his master's degree in 1985 and his doctorate in agricultural economics in 1988, both from Purdue. Also in 1988, he was honored by Purdue with its outstanding PhD thesis award and won the Rockefeller Foundation Social Science Research Fellowship.

EARLY CAREER

From 1988 to 1990, Adesina served as the assistant principal economist of the International Crops Research Institute for the Semi-Arid Tropics (ICRISAT). He earned the position due to a postdoctoral fellowship with the Rockefeller Foundation. In 1990, he became the principal economist for the West African Rice Development Association (WARDA), a position he held until 1995.

From 1995 to 1998, Adesina was a senior economist and social science coordinator for the International Institute for Tropical Agriculture (IITA). He then became the associate director and regional director for the Southern Africa Office of the Rockefeller Foundation, where he remained for about ten years. While there, he developed a wide variety of programs aimed at helping impoverished and working-class Africans. One such program improved access to education; another provided philanthropy to businesspeople on the continent. Perhaps the program closest to his heart was the one that sought to develop new markets for African farmers.

In 2008, Adesina became the vice president of policy and partnerships of the Alliance for a Green Revolution in Africa (AGRA). A firm believer in the free-market system, he sought to expand access to bank financing for Africa's agricultural sector by working with African business and political leaders, as well as CEOs of the commercial banking industry. During his time with AGRA, he successfully spearheaded the procurement of more than $4 billion in financing for the agricultural sectors of several African nations—up to that time one of the largest such efforts in history.

AGRICULTURAL MINISTER

Adesina's work in helping forge private-public partnerships that aided African farmers and helped lift millions of people out of poverty brought him to the attention of the Nigerian government, which tapped him to become its minister of agriculture in 2011. Nigeria's agricultural sector had long been plagued by corruption, particularly in its fertilizer sector. Because Nigeria is the largest oil and gas producer in Africa, its agricultural sector had been neglected for more than forty years. Adesina wanted to rectify this situation, especially because agriculture employs more Nigerians than the energy field.

First, he worked at ending corruption by introducing more transparency in the fertilizer supply and distribution sector. He then asked Nigerian farmers to grow a wider variety of food crops, including cassava. In January 2013, he launched a program that provided cellular phones to millions of farmers. Because many Nigerians do not have bank accounts, the phones would be used to get the latest market information, as well as to get vouchers for fertilizer and seeds. They would also serve as an innovative electronic wallet system.

Adesina's hope was that the diversification of crops as well as better information about what foods were needed in markets would help lift more Nigerians out of poverty. The success of these efforts helped earn him widespread recognition, including being named *Forbes Africa* magazine's Person of the Year in 2013. "My goal is to make as many millionaires, maybe even billionaires, from agriculture as possible," he said while accepting the award, as quoted by the *BBC News* (3 Dec. 2013).

Four years after the rollout of the mobile phone program, fifteen million farmers were regularly using them to make decisions about their crops. Nigerian food production increased by an additional twenty-one million metric tons, and $5.6 billion in private-sector investments came into the country. The global perception of Nigerian farming began to shift from being seen as primarily one of subsistence to a viable sector of the national economy.

PRESIDENT OF THE AFRICAN DEVELOPMENT BANK GROUP

On May 28, 2015, Adesina was elected president of the AfDB. He began serving his first five-year term on September 1 of that same year. He was the eighth elected president in the AfDB's history, and the first of Nigerian ancestry. As president he has sought to expand many of the policies he implemented as agricultural minister of Nigeria to all parts of Africa in need of assistance. Some of his successful efforts as president include the procurement of a $13.7 million grant to improve the health sector in Zimbabwe; a $45 million allocation to build a bridge linking Cameroon and Chad; a $1.67 million grant to study building dams in Eswatini; and a $33 million loan to help Cabo Verde combat the coronavirus disease 2019 (COVID-19) pandemic.

Adesina's tenure has not been without controversy. In 2020, a letter written by an unnamed "Group of Concerned Staff Members of the AfDB" claimed that Adesina used the group's funds to promote himself and line his pockets. The group also said that he unfairly used his influence to give favorable treatment to Nigeria and Nigerians, and that he gave huge severance packages to ex-employees he personally favored. In April 2020 the bank's ethics board cleared him of all corruption allegations; however, US Treasury secretary Steven Mnuchin asked

for a second independent inquiry, to ensure that the reputation of the AfDB would not be besmirched. "Mnuchin's move is significant because it has now cast a limelight on governance issues and on [the] importance of an independent investigation to uphold the integrity of the AfDB," said Barbara Barungi, the bank's lead economist on Nigeria at the time, as quoted by the *BBC* (30 May 2020). "There are very few people that were willing to stick their necks out."

In the face of a second inquiry, Adesina remained confident he would again be cleared, citing a malicious level of gossip at the bank. "In spite of unprecedented attempts by some to tarnish my reputation and prejudice the bank's governance procedures, I maintain my innocence with regard to trumped up allegations that unjustly seek to impugn my honour and integrity," he wrote in a statement, as quoted by the *BBC*. "I am confident that fair, transparent and just processes that respect the rules, procedures and governance systems of the Bank, and rule of law, will ultimately prove that I have not violated the Code of Ethics of this extraordinary institution."

In July, the independent investigation cleared Adesina of all charges. On August 27, he was reelected as president, with 100 percent of the votes of its shareholders—the first such occurrence since the bank was established in 1964.

RESPONSE TO THE COVID-19 PANDEMIC

When the global COVID-19 pandemic began in late 2019, many businesses, schools, and other public events were temporarily closed by early 2020 to stop the spread of the virus. However, this also led to a sharp economic downturn. As the virus forced lockdown conditions to endure through 2020, the AfDB forecasted a 3.4 percent contraction in Africa's economy. This was a sharp reversal of its previous forecast, which had projected 3.9 percent growth before the pandemic.

Adesina continued to advocate for monetary aid to Africa in spite of the pandemic. In an opinion piece published by *CNN* (6 Apr. 2020), he wrote, "We stand ready to support Africa in the short term and for the long haul. We are ready to deploy up to $50 billion over five years in projects to help with adjustment costs that Africa will face as it deals with the knock-on effects of COVID-19, long after the current storm subsides. But more support will be needed."

PERSONAL LIFE AND AWARDS

Adesina and his wife, Grace, have two adult sons, Rotimi and Segun, and have at least one grandchild.

Throughout his long career he has received numerous accolades for his work. In addition to receiving a number of honorary doctorates from universities around the world, he was named one of the top one hundred most influential Africans by *New African* magazine (2015); he was awarded the World Food Prize (2017); he was named as *Forbes Africa*'s Person of the Year (2013) and for a second time (2019); and he was made a Grand Officer of the National Order of Merit of Tunisia (2019).

In 2019, Adesina was awarded the Sunhak Peace Prize in Seoul, South Korea. The award came with a stipend of a half-million dollars, which he dedicated to the World Hunger Fighters Foundation that he established to fight global hunger.

SUGGESTED READING

Adesina, Akinwumi. "Opinion: The Pandemic Is No Time for Fiscal Distancing." *CNN*, 6 Apr. 2020, www.cnn.com/2020/04/03/africa/adesina-fiscal-distancing-opinion/index.html. Accessed 8 Nov. 2021.

"Akinwumi Adesina: Why the US Is Targeting a Nigerian Banker." *BBC News*, 30 May 2020, www.bbc.com/news/world-africa-52831185. Accessed 8 Nov. 2021.

"Biography." *African Development Bank Group*, www.afdb.org/en/about-us/organisational-structure/the-president/biography. Accessed 8 Nov. 2021.

"Biography of Dr. Akinwumi Ayodeji Adesina—President of the African Development Bank Group." *Federal University of Agriculture, Abeokuta*, 2020, unaab.edu.ng/wp-content/uploads/2020/01/citation-Dr-Akinwumi-A-Adesina-long-version.pdf. Accessed 9 Nov. 2021.

"Dr. Akinwumi A. Adesina President African Development Bank Group." *African Development Bank Group*, www.afdb.org/fileadmin/uploads/afdb/Documents/Generic-Documents/PRST_Akinwumi_A_Adesina_Biography_EN.pdf. Accessed 9 Nov. 2021.

"Mission & Strategy." *African Development Bank Group*, 2021, www.afdb.org/en/about/mission-strategy. Accessed 9 Dec. 2021.

"Nigeria's Akinwumi Adesina Named Forbes African of the Year." *BBC News*, 3 Dec. 2013, www.bbc.com/news/world-africa-25199787. Accessed 8 Nov. 2021.

—*Chrissstopher Mari*

Nancy Ajram

Born: May 16, 1983
Occupation: Singer

Often called the "Queen of Arab Pop," Nancy Ajram is among the most popular singers in Lebanon, with a string of multiplatinum recordings to her credit and numerous endorsement deals, including a groundbreaking stint as the only female Coca-Cola spokesperson in the Arab world. She had sold more than 30 million albums by 2008 and was named a Goodwill Ambassador for the United Nations Children's Fund (UNICEF) in 2009. Ajram was introduced to a mainstream American audience in 2009, when she appeared on a special episode of the *Oprah Winfrey Show* exploring fame around the world. Winfrey hailed Ajram as "the Britney Spears of the Middle East."

Ajram went on to serve as a judge on the popular televised singing competitions *Arab Idol* (2013–17) and *The Voice Kids* (2016). By 2021 she had attracted more than 71 million followers across Facebook, Twitter, and Instagram; racked up her two-billionth view on YouTube; and been named the most-listened-to Arab female artist on the streaming service Spotify, with more than 100 million downloads. Yet, despite her undeniable popularity—and despite the fact that her stage wardrobe and dance moves are relatively tame by Western standards—Ajram has come under some fire in the Muslim world for being too provocative. Such criticism dogged her from her first hit single, "Akhasmak ah," released in 2003. The lyrics to that song, which topped the Arab pop charts for several weeks, involve a promise to a male paramour that while the singer may upset him occasionally, she will never leave him; in the video, Ajram wears a form-fitting dress and dances in a flirtatious manner. Ajram's work has reportedly been banned at times under conservative regimes in such Arab countries as Kuwait and Egypt.

EARLY YEARS AND EDUCATION

Nancy Nabil Ajram was born in the Achrafieh district of Beirut, Lebanon, on May 16, 1983, to Nabil Ajram and Rimonda Aoun. She grew up with a younger sister, Nadine, and a younger brother, Nabil Jr., who would go on to become a composer and singer. Her family are Maronite Catholics, estimated to be the largest Christian group in Lebanon in 2020 according to the Central Intelligence Agency's *World Factbook*.

Ajram began to sing from the age of eight, and she was particularly fond of older songs, such as those by the iconic Lebanese performer Nour Al-Huda, which she learned from her grandmother. (Ajram has posted videos of her and her grandmother singing together on her social media platforms.) With her father's encouragement, Ajram began performing in local talent shows, and in 1995, when she was about twelve, despite what she has described as extreme shyness, she appeared on the nationally televised show *Noujoum al-moustakbal* [*Stars of the Future*]. There she performed a song by legendary Egyptian performer Umm Kulthum and won top prize in the Tarab category, a genre of Middle Eastern music meant to elicit strong emotion in the listener. "I was too young when I started singing," she recalled to Mike MacEacheran for *The National* (12 Nov. 2011). "It was a great experience for me, but it was hard as a teenager—I had too much responsibility, more so than other children."

Ajram spent much of her teens studying music and honing her talents. Before she reached the age of eighteen, the Syndicate of Professional Artists in Lebanon, an organization established in 1993 to represent the interests of the country's singers, actors, filmmakers, and other creative professionals, had bent its rules to admit her.

MUSIC

Ajram began studying with Lebanese musician Fouad Awad. In 1998, when she was fifteen years old, she released a debut album, *Mihtagalak* [*I Need You*], but while the single of the same name received some airplay, it did not garner Ajram the attention she had hoped. Her sophomore attempt, *Sheel oyoonak anni* [*Take your Eyes Off Me*] was backed by major label

Photo by Diana Farroukh via Wikimedia Commons

EMI Music Arabia and fared somewhat better when it was released in 2001.

Ajram's real breakthrough, however, came in 2002 with the release of her next album, *Ya salam* [*How Wonderful*], created after she signed a contract with producer and manager Jiji Lamara in 2000. Lamara encouraged her to leave behind the traditional Arab folk music of her early recordings and experiment with a more pop-oriented sound. He also advised Ajram to adopt a more adult image—guidance that resulted in the mildly steamy video for "Akhasmak ah," the album's first single. Ajram next released the Egyptian-influenced *Ah w noss* [*I Mean It*], whose title track perched atop the charts for weeks in 2004.

A steady stream of other recordings followed, including, *Ya tabtab . . . wa dallaa* [Pat and pamper, 2006], the children's album *Shakhbat shakhabit* [*Scribbled Doodles*, 2007], and *Betfakkar fi eih?!* [*What Are You Thinking About?!*, 2008], which turned out to be her biggest hit to that point. Its several hit singles—including the title track, "Meen da elli nesyik," ["Who's Forgotten about You"], "Lamset eid" ["Touch of a Hand"], and "Mashi hadi" ["Walking Next to Me"]—put Ajram over the top as the Arab artist with the most number-one hits in recent memory. She also garnered her first World Music Award (WMA) for the album. As the winner of the 2008 WMA for world's best-selling Middle-Eastern artist of the year, she became the youngest Arab artist to that date ever to take home a WMA. By that time Ajram had also received many other honors, including several Murex D'or Awards, a Golden Lion, two LG Music Awards, best female Arab singer of the year recognition from the Arabian Music Awards, inclusion on Newsweek's 2005 Most Influential Arab Personalities list, and several mentions in *Arabian Business News* as one of the world's most influential Arabs and most powerful Arab singers.

Laurels continued to accrue for Ajram's subsequent albums. These included *Nancy 7* (2010), which won her a second WMA in 2011; *Super Nancy* (2012), a children's recording that debuted at number one on the HitMarker Best-Selling Albums Chart and remained there for weeks; *Nancy 8* (2014), whose lead single became the fastest-selling Arabic song in iTunes history to date and led to her third WMA; and *Nancy 9* (2017), also known as *Hassa Beek*, which perched atop the HitMarker album chart for sixteen consecutive weeks after its release. In 2015, Ajram won a lifetime achievement award at the Beirut International Awards Festival (BIAF). When not touring or in the recording studio, she served as a judge on the hit reality talent show *Arab Idol* (2013–17) and coached the young contestants on *The Voice Kids Arabia* (2016).

In 2021 the hashtag #Nancy10 began trending on social media after Ajram, who had amassed more than 71 million followers by then, began promoting the release of a new album. *Nancy 10* was also featured on billboards in New York City's Times Square courtesy of Spotify, which had announced her as the top Arab female artist in 2020, with more than 100 million downloads that year.

Ajram posted the video for the first single from *Nancy 10*, "Hobbak bi ye'wa," on Twitter without fanfare on May 28, 2021, as a surprise for fans in advance of the full release. It attracted more than a million views within twenty-four hours. In a review for *The National* (2 June 2021), Saeed wrote, "'Hobbak Bi Ye'wa' is not so much a change of direction but a welcome refresh. Composed by Walid Saad, with lyrics provided by Khaled Tajeldine, the track is a fun mélange of Egyptian pop and folk." Saad concluded: "Only time will tell if Ajram's new work can also score a perfect 10."

ENDORSEMENTS

Ajram's status as a pop star led her to numerous endorsement deals, which furthered her celebrity image. Among the products she endorsed are Nissan cars, Anlene dairy products, Huawei smartphones, Sony electronics, and Home Centre housewares. She signed her longest-running and highest-profile deal with Coca-Cola, which recognized her enormous promise and made her the soft drink's first and only female spokesperson in the Middle East in 2004. Ajram's hiring was part of a major push by the company to gain an advantage in the Middle East over rival Pepsi.

Ajram's first Coca-Cola commercial featured her song "Oul tani kida" ["Say That Again"], which she sang accompanied by a group of young people using their Coke bottles as musical instruments. It was reportedly the most expensive commercial made in the region that year and had an immediate, measurable effect on sales. Another commercial depicted two lovers arguing until Ajram approaches them, hands them two Cokes, and watches as animated hearts and flowers emerge from the opened bottles. In addition to the televised spots, the company deployed billboards with photos of her along major highways throughout the Middle East, North Africa, and the Levant, and featured her face prominently on its soda cans.

CONTROVERSIES

Ajram, like many female celebrities in the Middle East, often walked a fine line between expressing herself freely and not offending the sensibilities of religious fundamentalists or socially conservative listeners. At various points in her career her videos were censored, and Islamist officials in the governments of Kuwait and Bahrain attempted to ban her from their countries. Additionally, while she gained countless fans in Israel, her fervent support for the Palestinians in Gaza and the West Bank proved a subject of concern for conservative Israelis.

Ajram became the first woman ever to be named a UNICEF Goodwill Ambassador for the Middle East and North Africa. However, her forays into social and politically issues occasionally met with controversy. She was criticized in 2011 for posting anti-Iranian sentiments on her Facebook page; she claimed, however, that the remarks had been the work of hackers. Another controversy erupted in 2018, when she agreed to perform at a LGBTQ pride festival in Gothenburg, Sweden, but her management team asked in advance that all rainbow flags be removed from the stage and taken from audience members during her set. Many observers found her attitude hypocritical, as she had positioned herself as something of an icon to LGBTQ people in the Arab world. She exacerbated matters when she tweeted on August 22 of that year, "I would like to clarify once and for all that I respect everyone's choices without any discrimination," leading other Twitter users to point out that being gay was not a choice.

PERSONAL LIFE

In the fall of 2008 Ajram married Fadi El-Hachem, a dentist she had been dating for three years. Because the couple belonged to different Christian sects, they wed during a civil ceremony in Cyprus, attended by only close friends and family. The couple has three daughters: Mila (born in 2009, the year the readers of *Rotana Magazine* voted Ajram "Most Beautiful Mom"), Ella (b. 2011), and Lya (b. 2019).

In January 2020, an armed and masked intruder entered Ajram's family's mansion in the Keserwan district of Beirut. El-Hachem shot the man seventeen times, fatally wounding him as Ajram hid in a bathroom for safety. The intruder was later identified as Mohamed Hassan al-Moussa, an immigrant from Syria, and the gun he brandished was found to be fake. El-Hachem was charged with intentional murder, although a judge ultimately ruled that he had been acting in self-defense.

SUGGESTED READING

Ajram, Nancy. "Nancy Ajram Talks Success, Life, and Her Upcoming Album." Interview by Diyana Hakmi. *Emirates Woman*, 3 Oct. 2019, emirateswoman.com/exclusive-interview-with-nancy-ajram-about-success-life-and-upcoming-album/. Accessed 22 Dec. 2021.

Birchmeier, Jason. "Nancy Ajram." *AllMusic*, www.allmusic.com/artist/nancy-ajram-mn0000865408. Accessed 22 Dec. 2021.

Elfeqy, Salma. "Nancy Ajram Supports the LGBT+ Community after Causing a Controversy in Sweden." *Identity Magazine*, 23 Aug. 2018, identity-mag.com/nancy-ajram-supports-lgbt-community-causing-controversy-sweden/. Accessed 22 Dec. 2021.

Joseph, Sarah. "8 Things to Know about Lebanese Superstar Nancy Ajram." *Emirates Woman*, 2 Nov. 2021, emirateswoman.com/things-to-know-about-lebanese-superstar-nancy-ajram/. Accessed 22 Dec. 2021.

MacEacheran, Mike. "Family Comes First, but Nancy Ajram Intends to Keep Singing." *The National*, 12 Nov. 2011, www.thenationalnews.com/arts-culture/music/family-comes-first-but-nancy-ajram-intends-to-keep-singing-1.425144. Accessed 22 Dec. 2021.

Naguib, Maria. "Here's Why Nancy Ajram's New Hit Song Is Trending on Social Media." *Harper's Bazaar Arabia*, 4 July 2021, www.harpersbazaararabia.com/culture/celebrity/heres-why-nancy-ajrams-new-hit-song-is-trending-on-social-media. Accessed 22 Dec. 2021.

Saeed, Saeed. "*Nancy 10*: Will Nancy Ajram's New Album Speak of Past Traumas?" *The National*, 2 June 2021, www.thenationalnews.com/arts-culture/music/nancy-10-will-nancy-ajram-s-new-album-speak-of-past-traumas-1.1233671. Accessed 22 Dec. 2021.

SELECTED WORKS

Mihtagalak, 1998; *Ya salam*, 2003; *Ah w noss*, 2004; *Ya tabtab . . . wa dallaa*, 2006; *Shakhbat shakhabit*, 2007; *Betfakkar fi eih?!*, 2008; *Nancy 7*, 2010; *Super Nancy*, 2012; *Nancy 10*, 2021

—Mari Rich

Raúw Alejandro

Born: January 10, 1993
Occupation: Singer and rapper

By the end of 2021, based on the acclaim and interest surrounding the music produced for his first two albums, *Afrodisíaco* (2020) and *Vice Versa* (2021), as well as his approach to the genre, Raúw Alejandro had widely been crowned the "king of modern reggaetón." Although the musician had been working tirelessly toward such a title for years, it was the release of his single "Todo de Ti (Everything about You)" that finally earned it for him. Just weeks after its debut in May

2021, the 1980s-inspired synth sounds of "Todo de Ti" had become one of Spotify's top streamed songs while reaching number one on Billboard's Latin Airplay chart. In the year that followed, the song would be streamed hundreds of millions of times on *Spotify*, spark a TikTok trend, and turn Alejandro into a bona fide superstar. Building off of this momentum, he released more music in 2022 in the form of the EP *Trap Cake Vol. 2* while continuing to display his talents live on an international tour.

For many fans, Alejandro's appeal has been the way in which his futuristic sound, combining a mix of reggae, dancehall, and, more uniquely, R&B styles, has pushed Latin music in an exciting new direction. For others, it has been his charismatic persona. Meanwhile, Alejandro himself believed that a large part of his success had come from the way in which his onstage performances proved reminiscent of song-and-dance artists from earlier generations. He expressed this idea in his interview with Lucas Villa for *W* magazine (25 June 2021), stating, "My inspiration are all the showmen: like Prince, Michael Jackson, James Brown, and Chayanne." Continuing, he added, "When I started doing music, that was my vision since Day One. I want to be this kid that goes onstage and channels my art through my vocals and my moves."

EARLY LIFE

Raúl Alejandro Ocasio Ruiz was born on January 10, 1993, in Puerto Rico, to a father who worked in land surveying while playing guitar as a hobby and a mother who sang in choirs while employed as a government administrator. As a young boy, he lived with his family in Palma Sola—a section of a town located in a rural, mountainous northeastern part of the country. Although the electricity often went out and the house was so small that he and his older sister stayed in the same room, it was a peaceful place.

As a child, Alejandro loved music and performing, particularly singing and dancing; when he was a third grader, he even dressed up to perform a Puerto Rican bolero as part of a talent show put on by his school, and he would go on to seek out other school artistic opportunities like theater. However, despite this nascent draw to music, he was determined to become a professional soccer player. His interest in soccer began when he was seven

Photo by Bonchevip & World Latin Star Video, via YouTube/Wikimedia Commons

years old, and he became a member of a local team coached by a retired professional player. Almost obsessed with the sport, he often dreamed of the day that he could be as successful as his idol, Cristiano Ronaldo. For Alejandro, much of Ronaldo's magic was in the way that he was able to lift his family from poverty. "I liked how people loved him," Alejandro explained to Julyssa Lopez for *Rolling Stone* (20 Jan. 2022). "There used to be these videos on YouTube, with these episodes about him, and he had enough money to buy his mom a house, his family, everyone. I just wanted to be him."

Alejandro's desire to help his family was strengthened when he was twelve years old, and his parents divorced. It was then that his father moved to New York City while his mother relocated Alejandro and his sister to the city of Carolina, Puerto Rico. There, he watched his mother struggle to keep the roof of a small apartment over their heads by working long hours. At home with either his father or mother, he was exposed to a wide range of musical genres and influences. "Rock 'n' roll bands, the oldies, and the soul music—all that type of music, I learned because of my dad," he explained to Villa. "In P.R., I was raised with the reggaeton culture, and salsa, and merengue. I have all this mix of flavors from my childhood."

After his soccer skills had secured him a scholarship and he had his high school diploma in hand, Alejandro began studying at the University of Puerto Rico at Carolina. To put himself into a position where he could potentially break into the semiprofessional Premier Development League, he went to Florida in 2013. His time was spent in extensive training in addition to toiling to earn money to support himself. Although he drew enough interest to earn a brief trip to play in Europe, his lackluster performance there increased his doubts about a real professional future in the sport. He explained to Lopez that while he sustained injuries that presented obstacles, his soccer aspirations fell apart largely due to psychological reasons rather than physical ones. "When you're trying so hard to do something and it's not working out, you get frustrated. Plus, I was having economic issues, personal problems with my family, a lot of stuff," he said. "Soccer took so much time, and I wasn't seeing the light."

EARLY MUSIC CAREER

When Alejandro returned to Puerto Rico in 2014 without a soccer career, he was frustrated and depressed that he seemed stuck in a cycle of odd jobs. Having already casually dabbled in writing and recording songs that his friends had praised and encouraged him to make public online, he decided that he would seriously pursue music. Drawn to trap music while also inherently bringing in other genres such as hip-hop and R&B in a more unique twist, he regularly displayed his reggaetón-style work through the online *SoundCloud* platform in the years that followed, while building a robust, collaborative network with other up-and-coming singers.

Teaming up with similar indie musicians at the time and performing underground shows, Alejandro and others eventually began gaining some attention from more established artists as well. Then, in 2016, everything changed when his acquaintance Bad Bunny got signed to a label and entered the mainstream music industry. For Alejandro, the success of another Puerto Rican trap and reggaetón artist from the same underground scene felt like an enormous win for his own career. "It didn't matter who was breaking through first," he told Lopez. "He creates a door, an open door, to a new movement."

Indeed, Bad Bunny's rising star indirectly opened the gates for Alejandro, who was contractually brought on as an artist with Duars Entertainment in 2017. While a high-profile collaboration with Alex Rose earned him some local attention and charting recognition in 2018, his early solo efforts had gotten off to a rocky start with his new label because of the devastation caused by Hurricane Maria (2017). As such, he had to return to working in retail, including stateside, until 2019, when Duars was able to pay him to record. He ultimately put out his first EP, a seven-song collection titled *Trap Cake Vol. 1*, later that year. By that time, he had undergone intense dance training with the hopes that he could become a performer similar not only to Spanish-language Latin stars but to the likes of Chris Brown or Justin Timberlake. It was an unusual decision for a reggaetón artist—although the music genre has typically been considered dancehall, most of the singers had not been known for their own dancing, especially choreographed routines. However, having elaborate choreography and a unique sound would ultimately become traits that set Alejandro apart from other artists in the genre. As he explained to Villa, "I want to raise the bar for Latin music and put the Latin industry on a whole other level. I want to inspire other people like so many artists inspired me."

AFRODISÍACO

Further dedication resulted in a 2020 team-up with Camilo that saw the remixed version of Alejandro's song "Tattoo" peak at number seven on the Billboard Hot Latin Songs chart. The song also secured him a 2021 Latin Grammy Award for Best Urban Fusion/Performance. On November 13, 2020, Alejandro released *Afrodisíaco*. Although he had put out relatively successful singles and collaborations previous to it, in many ways *Afrodisíaco* served as his formal introduction to audiences around the world. The album received mostly positive reviews, with critics taking note of his talented take on more traditional reggaetón. In a pre-Grammy interview for *Rolling Stone* (19 Oct. 2021), also with Julyssa Lopez, Alejandro stated, "*Afrodisíaco* was inspired by reggaeton from 2003, 2004—that golden era of reggaeton. . . . It was about exploring my roots, but you could hear certain experimental details on *Afrodisíaco*, like little hints of what was coming and what might happen on the next project."

Afrodisíaco's end-of-the-year chart performance included an appearance in the third position on the Billboard Top Latin Albums chart and earned him a 2020 Best New Artist Latin Grammy trophy nomination. Although it was not a meteoric sensation and it had featured less of the musical exploration he would become noted for, the album would also go on to land him a Grammy nod for Best Música Urbana Album at the 2022 ceremony and was successful enough to put him on the radar of several bilingual American pop stars looking to make music for their Latin American audiences. Soon, Selena Gomez tapped him to be on her early 2021 single "Baila Conmigo (Dance with Me)." Christina Aguilera and Jennifer Lopez quickly followed suit.

VICE VERSA

On June 25, 2021, Alejandro released *Vice Versa*. He wrote the album with the intention of prominently demonstrating his experimental style—one that showed that he could not be contained to the confines of traditional reggaetón. Though it still maintained some of the distinct musical characteristics of the genre, the album also borrowed from styles such as R&B, pop, disco, and Brazilian funk. "I've always been that artist that goes anywhere," he said in an interview with Alexis Hodoyan-Gastelum for *Teen Vogue* (25 June 2021) as he reflected on why he has never felt tied to any one genre. "I don't like to stay in the same bubble. I like to explore."

At the time he was recording *Vice Versa*, Alejandro was listening to older electronic, funk, and synth music—a sound that inspired him and one of his longtime collaborators, Mr. NaisGai, to write the song "Todo de Ti." After giving it a 1980s vibe and ensuring that it included some live guitars and bass sounds, Alejandro knew that it was going to be a hit and had decided to make it the album's first single. The song's meteoric success led to him becoming a superstar and selling out concerts worldwide. When asked by Lopez in his pre-Grammy 2021 interview with *Rolling Stone* what he wanted *Vice Versa* to show the world about the future of reggaetón, he replied, "I want to keep showing people that you can be creative, you don't have to limit yourself, and you can make music that comes from the heart without fear." The album not only reached

number one on the Billboard Top Latin Albums chart but also made it to number seventeen on the Billboard 200.

The year 2022 saw Alejandro only continuing to rise. In addition to touring worldwide to further promote his music and extend his reach, in February he put out a new EP collection of nine tracks titled *Trap Cake Vol. 2*. Giving a memorable performance at that year's Billboard Music Awards, he had also been nominated in four categories. In September, he received eight Latin Grammy nominations.

PERSONAL LIFE

It was reported that Alejandro began dating Spanish singer and songwriter Rosalía in 2021.

SUGGESTED READING

Alejandro, Raúw. "Grammy Contenders 2022: Rauw Alejandro on Representing Puerto Rico and the 'Huge Variety' of *Vice Versa*." Interview by Julyssa Lopez. *Rolling Stone*, 19 Oct. 2021, www.rollingstone.com/music/music-latin/rauw-alejandro-interview-grammys-todo-de-ti-1233192/. Accessed 2 Sept. 2022.

___. "Rauw Alejandro Aims for GOAT Status with His New Album, *Vice Versa*." Interview by Lucas Villa. *W*, 25 June 2021, www.wmagazine.com/culture/rauw-alejandro-new-album-vice-versa-interview. Accessed 2 Sept. 2022.

___. "Rauw Alejandro Is Redefining Reggaeton." Interview by Luis Minvielle. *Range*, 25 Jan. 2022, readrange.com/rauw-alejandro-interview/. Accessed 2 Sept. 2022.

___. "Rauw Alejandro Wants to Become the Greatest Latin Performer Ever." Interview by Alexis Hodoyan-Gastelum. *Teen Vogue*, 25 June 2021, www.teenvogue.com/story/rauw-alejandro-vice-versa-interview. Accessed 15 Sept. 2022.

Lopez, Julyssa. "How Rauw Alejandro Became Reggaeton's Singing, Dancing, Feuding, Lingerie-Dodging New Superstar." *Rolling Stone*, 20 Jan. 2022, www.rollingstone.com/music/music-features/rauw-alejandro-reggaeton-todo-de-ti-dancing-rosalia-1280675/. Accessed 2 Sept. 2022.

SELECTED WORKS

Trap Cake Vol. 1, 2019; *Afrodisíaco*, 2020; *Vice Versa*, 2021; *Trap Cake Vol. 2*, 2022

—*Emily E. Turner*

Colin Allred

Born: April 15, 1983
Occupation: Politician and former football player

In November 2018, Colin Allred pulled off a stunning upset, defeating eleven-term incumbent Pete Sessions to serve as US representative for the 32nd Congressional District of Texas. The victory was especially notable because it marked a gain for the Democratic Party in a district that held Republican representation since its creation in 2003. As a result, Allred received significant attention as part of a new generation of lawmakers reshaping the US political landscape. He also drew notice for his unusual path to public office: he played professional football for four years before becoming a lawyer. "I got into civil rights law because I wanted to make a difference," he told Stephen Young in an interview for the *Dallas Observer* (2 Aug. 2017). "I really felt like going into politics was the extension of that." Allred was reelected to the House of Representatives in 2022 as his work proved popular with voters in the suburbs north of Dallas, Texas. "I want to fight every single day for the people of this area," he shared with Matthew Reyna in an interview for *Rantt* (6 May 2017). "Because I grew up with them, I am one of them, and I want to represent them."

EARLY LIFE AND EDUCATION

Colin Zachary Allred was born on April 15, 1983, in Dallas, Texas. He was raised by his mother, a teacher, in the city's northern suburbs with help from an aunt and uncle. He never met his father, who he later learned died when he was ten. Allred's mother was White, and his father was Black, which gave him early awareness of racial tensions. "To most people, when they interacted with me, I was an African American or maybe some other minority, but then I'd go home and be with my white family," Allred told Gromer Jeffers Jr. for the *Dallas Morning News* (21 Oct. 2018), noting that he faced incidents of overt racism as a boy. "I knew that whatever my family is, that's not what I am because people go on appearances. I needed to find my own identity and live my own way."

Growing up Allred attended John J. Pershing Elementary School and frequented the after-school program at the local YMCA. Much of his time in the summer was spent at Camp Grady Spruce, a YMCA overnight camp, where he participated in many outdoor activities and later volunteered and worked as a lifeguard. "I am who I am because of the Y," he later noted in a speech, as quoted on the *YMCA of Metropolitan Dallas* website.

Allred continued in the public school system through middle and high school, performing well academically and serving as president of his class. He showed an aptitude for sports, playing varsity baseball, football, and basketball for the Dallas Hillcrest High School Panthers. He received all-district honors in basketball (second team) and baseball (first team), but he especially stood out in football. As a linebacker, he helped lead the football team to consecutive district championship titles in 1999 and 2000. "He was humble, but something was driving the young man," his Hillcrest football coach, Von Harris, told Young. "I knew then he would be successful in whatever career path he chose."

COLLEGE FOOTBALL TO THE NFL

Upon graduating from high school Allred accepted a full-ride athletic scholarship to Baylor University, where he played for the Bears football team. He showed promise during his freshman year in 2001 before sitting out the 2002 season after being redshirted. Over the

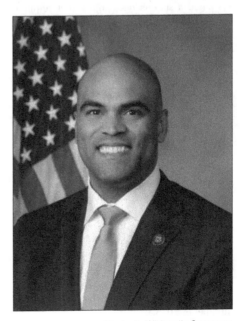

Photo via Wikimedia Commons.
[Public domain]

next three seasons he continued to improve, earning Academic All-Big 12 honors his junior year and being named team co-captain as a senior in 2005.

Despite his strong college football career, Allred was not chosen in the National Football League (NFL) Draft. After earning his bachelor's degree in history in December 2005, he planned to attend the University of California, Berkeley School of Law. However, in early 2006 he received attention from NFL teams as an undrafted free agent, and he decided to pause his law school ambitions to sign with the Tennessee Titans. Though he initially struggled to make the team's active roster, he finally made his NFL debut with the Titans in 2007, appearing in three regular-season games and one playoff contest that season. "Perseverance and determination, those are things that I take away from football," he told Reyna.

Working hard to distinguish himself, Allred ended up playing three more seasons in the NFL. In 2008, he notched nineteen total tackles in twelve regular-season appearances, helping the Titans finish with a league-best 13–3 record before being eliminated in the divisional playoff round. The following year, Allred again played in twelve games, starting in two of them, and recorded nineteen more tackles. But during the 2010 season he sustained a serious neck injury that required spinal fusion surgery, effectively ending his football career.

LAW CAREER

After retiring from the NFL, Allred reapplied to the UC Berkeley School of Law and was accepted again. At first, he thought he would pursue sports law, but he soon gravitated toward civil rights work instead. An important influence in this regard was racial justice and constitutional law professor Ian Haney López, for whom he worked as a research assistant on the book *Dog Whistle Politics* (2013). The book "delved into the way politicians from both parties used implicit racial appeals to get elected," he recalled to Renwei Chung in an interview for *Above the Law* (9 Feb. 2018). Another inspiration was President Barack Obama. Allred served as a White House intern in the Obama administration during the summer of 2013.

Allred received his JD in 2014. That same year he went to work for Battleground Texas, a groundbreaking statewide program aimed at protecting and enhancing voting rights. As regional director of the organization for the Dallas-Fort Worth area, he supervised voter-registration volunteers and poll watchers tasked with helping North Texans vote during the 2014 gubernatorial race. "If you can vote, you have a voice and can protect your own interests," he told Chung. "As attorneys, I believe we should all become voting rights activists."

In 2015, Allred was hired as an associate at the Washington, DC–based Perkins Coie law firm, where he advised political candidates and advocacy groups. A year later he joined the US Department of Housing and Urban Development (HUD) after being appointed by Obama. As special assistant to the general counsel, Allred helped enforce the Fair Housing Act as well as safeguard and bolster housing assistance programs.

ENTERING POLITICS

Through his work with HUD, Allred became increasingly enamored with public service. "The thing I most appreciated is that's it's not about you," he revealed to Brooke Hill for the *Baylor Lariat*, Baylor's student newspaper (7 Sept. 2017). "It's not about your ego, it's not about what you've done before, it's all about the American people, and I think that spirit of service really appealed to me." Though he left HUD in early 2017 with the change in presidential administration, he sought a way to get back to serving his community. He soon made the decision to enter politics with a run for Texas's 32nd Congressional seat, which covers the area of north Texas where he grew up.

Allred entered a Democratic primary field that included several experienced Obama administration officials and other notable figures. But he stood out for his local roots and his message: "I'm trying to run to represent the community that I came from and to make sure that the values that I grew up with here are being represented in Washington," he told Hill. His campaign, which balanced centrist and progressive talking points, resonated with North Texans. He finished first in the March 2018 primary by a wide margin, but because of the crowded race he did not reach the 50 percent mark and, therefore, faced a runoff against second-place finisher Lillian Salerno. With backing from the Democratic Congressional Campaign Committee, he triumphed over Salerno in May 22, earning nearly 70 percent of the vote.

During the general election campaign against longtime Republican incumbent Sessions, Allred positioned himself as an independent voice while touting a more equitable economy, affordable housing, and quality education for all children. Despite refusing corporate political action committee (PAC) money, he outraised his opponent while also earning endorsements from Obama and Dallas mayor Eric Johnson. The strategy paid off: Allred captured about 52 percent of the vote against Sessions's almost 46 percent (Libertarian candidate Melina Baker took 2 percent) in the November election, flipping the district seat to the Democratic Party for the first time. Many pundits considered the result highly significant as an indicator of Texas's increasing political competitiveness. Allred was subsequently designated copresident of his Democratic freshman representative class.

HOUSE OF REPRESENTATIVES

In January 2019, Allred was sworn into the US House of Representatives. The following month he attracted attention for taking a two-week paternity leave, which he used as a way to call for better parental leave policies nationwide. He was named to the House Veterans' Affairs Committee, the Transportation and Infrastructure Committee, and the Foreign Affairs Committee.

During his first year in office, Allred crafted a bipartisan resolution aimed at federally protecting the Affordable Care Act (ACA), also known as Obamacare, and another denouncing the attempt by the administration of President Donald Trump to legally overturn the ACA. He cosponsored more than one hundred pieces of legislation, including bills that favored voting rights and election reform, LGBTQ rights, equal pay for equal work, universal background checks, and continued US participation in the Paris Climate Agreement. Falling in line with the Democratic Party consensus on most issues, he also took part in the December 2019 vote to impeach President Trump for abuse of power and obstruction of justice.

Allred initially endorsed Julián Castro, his former HUD boss, in the 2020 presidential election before supporting eventual Democratic nominee Joe Biden. Up for reelection himself that year, Allred ran unopposed in the Democratic primary to face Republican challenger Genevieve Collins. That August he appeared as a keynote speaker during the 2020 Democratic National Convention, elevating his national profile in an election cycle dominated by the disruptions of the COVID-19 pandemic. Backed by endorsements from Biden and other high-profile Democrats, Allred successfully defended his seat in the November general election, claiming nearly 52 percent of the vote. "Texas is changing," Allred said of his ability to win in a traditionally Republican area, as quoted by Bridget Bowman for *Roll Call* (18 Aug. 2020). "Districts like mine are increasingly diverse. They do not see themselves as part of the narrow group that Donald Trump is trying to appeal to and motivate through fear and other tactics, and they're rejecting it."

On January 6, 2021, Allred was among the lawmakers trapped on the House floor when Trump supporters stormed the US Capitol in a failed effort to overturn the 2020 presidential election results. A week later, he was among the majority who voted to impeach Trump for a second time for inciting the insurrection. During his second term, Allred also supported efforts to reign in the ongoing COVID-19 pandemic and other priorities of the Biden administration, including affordable health care and prescription drugs, LGBTQ+ rights protections, and immigration reform. He remained an advocate for veterans, election security, and job creation in his district and beyond.

Allred was again unopposed in the March 2022 Democratic primary election. He faced restaurateur Antonio Swad in the general election that year.

PERSONAL LIFE

Allred married fellow attorney Alexandra Eber in 2017. The couple's first child, a son named Jordan, was born in 2019. Their second son, Cameron, was born in 2021.

SUGGESTED READING

Allred, Colin. "Berkeley Law Alum and Former NFL Player Colin Allred on Following Obama, the American Dream, and His Path Back to Dallas." Interview by Renwei Chung. *Above the Law*, 9 Feb. 2018, abovethelaw.com/2018/02/berkeley-law-alum-and-former-nfl-player-colin-allred-on-following-obama-the-american-dream-and-his-path-back-to-dallas/. Accessed 12 Sept. 2022.

___. "Meet the Former NFL Linebacker Running for Congress in Texas." Interview by Matthew Reyna. *Rantt*, 6 May 2017, rantt.com/meet-the-former-nfl-linebacker-running-for-congress-in-texas. Accessed 12 Sept. 2022.

___. *"The Dallas Observer* Q&A with Congressional Candidate Colin Allred." Interview by Stephen Young. *Dallas Observer*, 2 Aug. 2017, www.dallasobserver.com/news/dallas-observer-interview-colin-allred-9717955. Accessed 12 Sept. 2022.

Bowman, Bridget. "A Tale of Two Districts: Lamb, Allred in Convention Spotlight Highlights Democrats' Dual Strategies." *Roll Call*, 18 Aug. 2020, rollcall.com/2020/08/18/a-tale-of-two-districts-lamb-allred-in-convention-spotlight-highlights-democrats-dual-strategies/. Accessed 20 Sept. 2022.

cmccauley. "'I Am Who I Am because of the Y'—Colin Allred." *YMCA of Metropolitan Dallas*, www.ymcadallas.org/blog/i-am-who-i-am-because-y. Accessed 12 Sept. 2022.

Hill, Brooke. "Baylor Alum and Former NFL Linebacker Runs for Congress." *The Baylor Lariat*, Baylor University, 7 Sept. 2017, baylorlariat.com/2017/09/07/baylor-alum-and-former-nfl-linebacker-runs-for-congress/. Accessed 12 Sept. 2022.

Jeffers, Gromer Jr. "Colin Allred Is a Son of His Dallas District. Can He Unseat the Man Who's Represented It for Decades?" *The Dallas Morning News*, 21 Oct. 2018, www.dallasnews.com/news/2018/10/21/colin-allred-is-a-son-of-his-dallas-district-can-he-unseat-the-man-who-s-represented-it-for-decades/. Accessed 20 Sept. 2022.

—*Bertha Muteba*

Pete Alonso

Born: December 7, 1994
Occupation: Baseball player

On September 28, 2019, New York Mets player Pete Alonso hit his fifty-third and final home run of the 2019 Major League Baseball (MLB) season, breaking the MLB-wide rookie home run record in a game at the Mets' home venue of Citi Field. "I just couldn't believe it," he said afterward, as reported by Buster Olney for *ESPN* (7 Aug. 2020). "Just the positive energy, the energy that the fans were giving off, I felt the love, I felt the energy, I felt the true passion and I felt that that home run meant so much more, so much for the city of New York." In addition to breaking the rookie record, that fifty-third home run capped off an impressive rookie season for Alonso, who was subsequently named the National League's Rookie of the Year.

A dedicated baseball player since early childhood, Alonso played three seasons for the University of Florida before being drafted by the Mets in 2016. He played well for several of the Mets' minor-league affiliates over the next years and was called up to the majors at the start of the 2019 season, during which he not only showcased his skills in regular-season games but also won his first Home Run Derby. Two more solid seasons and a second Home Run Derby win followed, during which Alonso established himself as not only a rookie standout but also a strong performer in the long term. For Alonso himself, however, the attention and accolades he received had little significance on the personal level. "I'm just a normal dude who happens to play baseball," he told Bob Nightengale for *USA Today* (28 Aug. 2019). "I just want to keep being Pete Alonso, and stay true to who I am."

EARLY LIFE AND EDUCATION

Peter Morgan Alonso was born on December 7, 1994, in Tampa, Florida. The first of two sons born to Michelle and Peter Alonso, he grew up in the Tampa area. Alonso began playing baseball as a child, including in a local Little League program, and aspired to play the sport professionally one day. Though he faced bullying for his height and weight as a child, he remained committed to baseball and would later attribute his perseverance during that period and other challenging times to both stubbornness and "a very strong inner belief," as Alonso told Olney. "If you don't believe in yourself, no one else will," he explained.

Primarily a third baseman as a teenager, Alonso began his high school career at Jesuit High School, a preparatory school in Tampa. After two years, he transferred to H. B. Plant High School, a Tampa public school with

Photo by All-Pro Reels
from District of Columbia, USA,
via Wikimedia Commons

strong athletic programs. Alonso became a key member of the school's baseball team and had a particularly successful senior season, during which he scored twenty-four runs, tallied twenty-two runs batted in (RBI), and earned recognition as one of Florida's top infielders. He graduated from H. B. Plant High School in 2013.

UNIVERSITY OF FLORIDA

After graduating from high school, Alonso enrolled in the University of Florida and joined the university's Gators men's baseball team, which competed within the Division I level of National Collegiate Athletic Association (NCAA) baseball. While he had played largely as a third baseman during his high school career, he spent much of his 2014 freshman season at first base, which would later become his primary position during his early professional seasons. Alonso performed well during his first season with the Gators and was named to the Southeastern Conference All-Freshman Team.

Though hampered by injuries during his next two seasons, including a broken hand caused by a stray pitch, Alonso found further success at the collegiate level in 2015 and 2016. As a junior, he received All-American honors from several bodies, including *Baseball America* and the National Collegiate Baseball Writers

Association. He also practiced his sport during the summers, playing for collegiate summer-league teams such as the Madison Mallards and Bourne Braves.

For Alonso, his years in college were instrumental to his development as a player, helping him improve elements of his play that would prove essential to his later career. "College taught me how to put the work in in the right way and realize what I need to work on. As a freshman coming in it's like, you need to work on your hitting, you need to work everything you can a little more specialized," he explained to Mathew Brownstein in an interview for *Metsmerized Online* (9 Feb. 2017). "I was a good player throughout my life, and I was kind of more raw and toolsy. Going to college definitely helped me refine some of the things in my game." Alonso left the University of Florida after three seasons to pursue a career in professional baseball.

MINOR LEAGUES

In June 2016, the New York Mets selected Alonso in the second round of that year's MLB Draft. The sixty-fourth overall pick, he was delighted to have been drafted by the Mets and looked forward to beginning his professional career. "It was just an unbelievable experience to get drafted on the first day," he told Brownstein. "I'm extremely thankful I got drafted by such a great organization and I'm all in and I'm going to give the Mets everything I've got." Alonso signed a contract with the Mets organization later that month and in July, he reported to the minor-league team the Brooklyn Cyclones, then the Mets' short-season affiliate.

Alonso spent the next two years moving up through the ranks of the Mets' minor-league affiliates, beginning with the St. Lucie Mets. After starting his 2017 season with St. Lucie, during which time he twice earned Florida State League player of the week honors, he moved on to the Double-A Binghamton Rumble Ponies. Alonso remained with the Rumble Ponies for the start of the 2018 season before moving up to Triple-A Las Vegas 51s in June. Although he hoped to be called up by the Mets later in the season, he was unable to secure a spot on the major-league roster at that time, a disappointment that he attempted to take in stride. "It's motivation to go to the Fall League and just showcase more and showcase

I can stay consistent, not just in the season, but after," he told Mike Puma for the *New York Post* (31 Aug. 2018). "I can just continue to hit and spring training will be another opportunity to showcase myself." Alonso went on to play in the Arizona Fall League following that season, spending portions of October and November 2018 with the Scottsdale Scorpions.

ROOKIE SEASON

Having performed well in spring training prior to the 2019 MLB season, Alonso remained unsure whether he had made the Mets' roster until the last possible moment. "I'm sitting in Washington, DC, twenty-five hours before opening day, and I still don't know if I'm making the team," he recalled to Nightengale. The wait, however, made the eventual news that he had made the cut even more affecting. "I'm never going to forget that feeling as long as I live," he told Nightengale. Alonso made his debut with the Mets on March 29, 2019, in the team's season opener against the Washington Nationals.

Over the course of the 2019 season, Alonso played in 161 games and scored the ninth-most runs in the National League (NL) with 103. He led both the National League and the MLB as a whole for home runs with fifty-three, becoming one of only four active players at the time to have scored fifty or more home runs in a single season. He likewise had the opportunity to exhibit his batting skills midway through the season in the 2019 Home Run Derby, an event in which selected players compete to hit the most home runs within the allotted time. Alonso proceeded through the rounds of competition and beat Toronto Blue Jays player Vladimir Guerrero Jr. in the final round to win both the competition and a prize of one million dollars, nearly double his 2019 salary.

A substantial contributor to the Mets as a rookie, Alonso was named NL Rookie of the Month three times and was selected for the 2019 All-Star Game. "If you told me before in my rookie season that we were going to be in a playoff race, and then I'd have this individual success, it would have been kind of a pinch-me thing," he told Nightengale. "Like, really? That's it? That's what I'm walking into my first year? Really? Seriously?" Although the Mets finished the season ranked third in the NL East and narrowly missed qualifying for the playoffs, Alonso's strong rookie season continued to

garner him honors, and he became the nearly unanimous selection for NL Rookie of the Year. "To just win the award, doesn't matter if it's unanimous or not," he told the media, as reported by David Schoenfield for *ESPN* (11 Nov. 2019). "It's still such a blessing."

MILESTONES AND UNCERTAINTY

Like many other professional sports leagues, MLB was forced to adjust its 2020 schedule because of the coronavirus disease 2019 (COVID-19) pandemic, ultimately delaying the start of the 2020 season and condensing each team's schedule to sixty games. Alonso appeared in fifty-seven games during the season, recording a season batting average of .231 and fielding percentage of .982, and ranked third in the National League for home runs with sixteen. The baseball season reverted to its previous length for the 2021 season, and Alonso played in 152 games during that period, missing several games in May after spraining his hand.

While the Home Run Derby had been canceled in 2020 due to the pandemic, Alonso returned to that competition in 2021, during which he beat Trey Mancini of the Baltimore Orioles in the final round to claim his second consecutive win. "I think I'm the best power hitter on the planet," he later said, as reported by Mark Feinsand for *MLB.com* (13 July 2021). "Being able to showcase that and really put on a fun display for fans, it's truly a dream come true for me." Only the third player ever to win back-to-back Home Run Derby competitions, Alonso also made strong contributions to the Mets over the course of the season and ended 2021 ranked third in the National League for home runs with thirty-seven.

Alonso was initially set to begin his fourth major-league season in March 2022, however, a labor dispute between Major League Baseball and the MLB Players Association led to a lockout that began in December 2021. The two parties were unable to come to an agreement by the beginning of March, and the first two weeks of regular season games scheduled for April of that year were subsequently canceled. As negotiations continued, the fate of the 2022 season remained uncertain.

PERSONAL LIFE

Alonso met his wife, Haley, while playing summer-league baseball during his college years. They married in 2021. In addition to playing baseball, Alonso is a philanthropist and has donated portions of his Home Run Derby winnings to charitable organizations that address the needs of military veterans and first responders.

SUGGESTED READING

Alonso, Peter. "*MMO* Exclusive Interview: First Base Prospect, Peter Alonso." Interview by Mathew Brownstein. *Metsmerized Online*, 9 Feb. 2017, metsmerizedonline. com/2017/02/mmo-exclusive-interview-first-base-prospect-peter-alonso.html/. Accessed 7 Mar. 2022.

Carter, Scott. "College World Series: Peter Alonso Proving to Be the Key to Florida's Offense." *NCAA*, 19 June 2016, www.ncaa. com/news/baseball/article/2016-06-19/college-world-series-peter-alonso-proving-be-key-floridas-offense. Accessed 7 Mar. 2022.

Feinsand, Mark. "Re-Pete! Alonso Bops to HR Derby History." *MLB*, 13 July 2021, www. mlb.com/news/pete-alonso-wins-2021-home-run-derby. Accessed 7 Mar. 2022.

Nightengale, Bob. "Pete Alonso, Who Sets Mets' Single-Season Home Run Record, Is Living a 'Dream Come True.'" *USA Today*, 28 Aug. 2019, www.usatoday.com/story/sports/mlb/columnist/bob-nightengale/2019/08/28/pete-alonso-mets-home-run-franchise-record-dream-season/2139128001/. Accessed 7 Mar. 2022.

Olney, Buster. "'There Was No Plan B': How Pete Alonso Overcame Bullies to Become a Big League Superstar." *ESPN*, 7 Aug. 2020, www.espn.com/mlb/story/_/id/29601961/how-new-york-mets-pete-alonso-overcame-bullies-become-big-league-superstar. Accessed 7 Mar. 2022.

Puma, Mike. "Peter Alonso: I'm Disappointed but Don't Have a Beef with Mets." *New York Post*, 31 Aug. 2018, nypost.com/2018/08/31/peter-alonso-im-disappointed-but-dont-have-a-beef-with-mets/. Accessed 7 Mar. 2022.

Schoenfield, David. "Mets Slugger Pete Alonso Wins National League Rookie of the Year." *ESPN*, 11 Nov. 2019, www.espn.com/mlb/story/_/id/28060458/mets-slugger-pete-alonso-wins-national-league-rookie-year. Accessed 7 Mar. 2022.

—*Joy Crelin*

Anitta

Born: March 30, 1993
Occupation: Singer and television personality

"I don't think I have the best voice, I don't think I'm the best dancer," Brazilian singer Anitta told Raisa Bruner in an interview for *Time* (30 Sept. 2020). "I'm a person who puts in a lot of effort to learn and do things right. I'm very dedicated, very focused." Indeed, in the years following the release of her self-titled 2013 debut album, Anitta's dedication and focus enabled her to do what few other Brazilian-born singers had managed: build a dedicated fan base both within Brazil itself and outside of that country's borders, reaching listeners who spoke not only her native Portuguese but also Spanish and English. Influenced by genres such as pop, hip-hop, reggaeton, and Brazil's funk carioca, Anitta gained devoted listeners with albums such as *Bang!* (2015) and *Kisses* (2019) as well as with her collaborations with a host of popular recording artists.

Known for her highly confident public persona, Anitta offered fans a more vulnerable, behind-the-scenes look at her life in the documentary series *Vai Anitta* (2018; Go Anitta) and *Anitta: Made in Honório* (2020), which called attention to the differences between the public persona of Anitta and the human being behind that name. "Anitta is a person I call every time I need to be strong," she explained to Maria Sherman for *Nylon* (12 Apr. 2022). "If I didn't have this character that goes for it, and that I can turn off and be myself, I would be lost." Empowered by the persona she had created, Anitta set out to become an international star and in 2022 released the album *Versions of Me*, a release that, with its trilingual vocals and wide range of genre influences, embodied the multifaceted and multicultural approach for which her career had become known.

EARLY LIFE AND EDUCATION

Anitta was born Larissa de Macedo Machado on March 30, 1993, in Rio de Janeiro, Brazil. She grew up in Honório Gurgel, a neighborhood within the city. One of two children born to parents Miriam and Mauro, she has a brother, Renan, as well as an older half-brother, Felipe. A determined child from an early age, the young Anitta put her determination and ingenuity to use in securing a quality education for herself. "My dad wanted to provide a good education for me and my brother, but he didn't have the money," she explained in an interview to common collaborator, Colombian reggaeton singer J Balvin, for *Interview* magazine (27 May 2022). "The school made a competition for the 'Girl of the Spring' and whoever won would get a sponsorship to study the whole year." Though facing tough competition, including from students who had paid for professionally crafted costumes, Anitta impressed the judges with a homemade outfit she and her mother made from recycled materials. "My mom was like, 'We have no chance, let's go home.' And I said, 'No, I need to study next year for free. I'm going to win,'" she recalled to Balvin. Anitta's effort proved successful, and she went on to complete her schooling and earn a certificate in business administration.

Drawn to music and performance throughout her childhood, Anitta sang in a church choir during that period and studied both dance and English outside of school. She became a particularly devoted fan of funk carioca, a Brazilian music genre similar to hip-hop that some in Brazil considered objectionable due to its frank discussion of controversial topics. "Funk in Brazil was like hip-hop in the nineties in America—it came from the poor people's communities," Anitta explained to Sherman. "Drug trafficking, sex, guns. Society wanted to criminalize the rhythm. The rhythm is not guilty. If you change the reality of society and bring opportunity, the lyrics are going to change." Though passionate about music as a teenager, she did not initially plan to pursue a career in that field, instead taking an office job with a mining company after completing her schooling.

BECOMING ANITTA

An avid singer, Anitta first gained attention from record executives when she posted a YouTube video of herself singing in 2010. Rather than perform under her own name, she took on the stage name of Anitta, inspired by the title character of the Brazilian television series *Presença de Anita* (2001; The presence of Anita), and began to build a public persona under that name. "My character is very powerful, this girl that does everything," she later told Balvin. "But most times I'm very worried about everyone, caring about everyone,

Photo by Tony Dandrades, via Wikimedia Commons

thinking about my family and making sure everyone is good. I'm very private, so I don't let anyone know about that—it's kind of a secret. But I'm actually very much the opposite of this powerful, invincible person that I sell as an artist." Anitta signed a recording contract with Warner Music Brazil, who were impressed with her 2012 debut single "Meiga e Abusada" (Sweet and abused), and released her debut extended-play (EP) record, *Tá na Mira* (It's in Mira), not long after. Her debut full-length album, *Anitta*, was released in July 2013 and, among other tracks, featured the song "Zen," which was later nominated for the Latin Grammy Award for best Brazilian song.

In the years following her major-label debut, Anitta released the studio albums *Ritmo Perfeito* (2014; Perfect rhythm) and *Bang!* (2015) as well as *Meu Lugar* (2014; My place), a live album recorded while she was on tour in 2013 and 2014. In 2014, she also founded Grupo Rodamoinho, an entertainment group that would come to encompass a management company, record label, film production studio, and several other ventures. In addition to producing the animated series *Clube da Anittinha* (2018–21; Anittinha's club), for which Anitta provided the main character's voice, the entertainment group worked to sign and promote emerging Brazilian artists.

INTERNATIONAL ASPIRATIONS

Although Anitta found great success in Brazil during her early years as a recording artist, she was interested in expanding her reach, including into Spanish- and English-speaking markets that were unfamiliar with genres of music such as funk carioca. "I've traveled a lot to try to educate people on funk music and 'ghetto' music—favela music—coming from Brazil to other countries and other artists," she later explained to Bruner. "Funk music for example—it's also a challenge to make it play for the Latin world. So I'm matching and switching cultures and people, representatives." As part of that mission, Anitta began learning to speak and sing in Spanish, which she hoped would help give her music greater appeal among Spanish-speaking listeners, both in South America and elsewhere.

By 2015, Anitta also aspired to become a successful recording artist in the United States, something few Brazilian musicians had managed. "I knew that if I failed, everyone in my country would laugh at me," she told Griselda Flores in an interview for *Billboard* (11 May 2022). "That's what happens to everyone who tries and fails. I didn't want to become a joke. I wanted it to happen for real." To that end, Anitta began spending much of her time in Los Angeles, California, though she often returned to Brazil for performances, including her appearance during the opening ceremony of the 2016 Olympic Games in Rio de Janeiro. She signed with her first US–based management company, Shots Studios, in 2017.

NEXT MOVES

Over the next several years, Anitta worked to build a recording career that spanned three languages—Portuguese, Spanish, and English—and gained increasing notice for her collaborations with artists working within popular genres, such as J Balvin. In 2018, she starred in the Netflix documentary series *Vai Anitta*, which explored her performing and personal life. Her fourth studio album, *Kisses*, was released in 2019 and featured collaborations with several established artists, including Swedish DJ Alesso, American rapper Snoop Dogg, and Becky G, a US singer known for singing in both English and Spanish. *Kisses* went on to be nominated for the Latin Grammy for best urban music album. A second Netflix documentary series, *Anitta: Made in Honório*, debuted in December of 2020.

In addition to expanding her reach as an artist, Anitta became increasingly politically active throughout that period and was outspoken about her opposition to Brazilian president Jair Bolsonaro. Her political statements and popularity within Brazil prompted some to suggest that Anitta—though not yet old enough to hold the Brazilian presidency—run for political office in her home country. "A lot of journalists were calling me, saying, 'Are you going to listen to the people and run?'" she recalled to Julyssa Lopez in an interview for *The Guardian* (9 Aug. 2020). "I was like, 'Guys, I'm just trying to help! Wait!'" Although she did not plan to run for office at that time, Anitta worked to encourage political engagement among her Brazilian fans, promoting voter-registration efforts and political education initiatives on social media.

VERSIONS OF ME

Anitta continued her push toward international stardom in 2020 and 2021, signing a deal for international representation and performing fan outreach through social media apps such as TikTok. In September 2020, she released the single "Me Gusta" (I like it), a song performed in both English and Spanish that featured guest appearances from rappers Cardi B and Myke Towers. "Me Gusta" became Anitta's first song to appear on the US Billboard Hot 100 chart, peaking at number ninety-one. The single likewise reached the number-five position on the Billboard US Latin songs chart and also saw commercial success in Brazil and in several Spanish-speaking markets. Anitta went on to release several additional songs, including the April 2021 single "Girl from Rio," and in November of 2021 released the Spanish-language song "Envolver" (To wrap). "Envolver" proved even more successful in the United States than "Me Gusta," reaching number one on the Billboard Top Triller US chart, number seventy on the Billboard Hot 100 chart, and number three on the US Latin chart.

"Me Gusta," "Girl from Rio," "Envolver," and other songs released during that period went on to be included on the full-length studio album *Versions of Me*. Released in April 2022, the album features songs in English, Spanish, and Portuguese that deal with a wide range of themes and topics. As Anitta noted in interviews, the album's title was emblematic of her approach to music and identity. "I like being a different person every day," she told Flores. "Today I'll be romantic, tomorrow I'll be nerdy, tomorrow I'll be sad. That's what I think it is to be Anitta: to be limitless." In addition to releasing *Versions of Me* in April 2022, Anitta performed on the main stage at the Coachella Valley Music and Arts Festival that month, becoming the first Brazilian solo performer to do so.

PERSONAL LIFE

Anitta married businessman Thiago Magalhães in 2017. The couple divorced in 2018; that same year, she came out as bisexual in her docuseries *Vai Anitta*. Although she traveled often and spent much of her time in the United States as she worked to build her career there, Anitta also maintained a home in Rio de Janeiro during that period.

SUGGESTED READING

Anitta. "Anitta, Brazil's Biggest Pop Star, Doesn't Need the U.S. But Could She Make It Here Anyway?" Interview by Raisa Bruner. *Time*, 30 Sept. 2020, time.com/5890111/anitta-interview-me-gusta-brazil/. Accessed 11 July 2022.

___. "Anitta Cannot Tell a Lie." Interview by Patricia Alfonso Tortolani, *Allure*, May 2021, www.allure.com/story/anitta-cover-interview-may-2021. Accessed 11 July 2022.

___. "Anitta for President." Interview by J Balvin. *Interview*, 27 May 2022, www.interviewmagazine.com/music/anitta-for-president. Accessed 11 July 2022.

___. "Anitta's Global Vision: A Trilingual Takeover." Interview by Griselda Flores. *Billboard*, 11 May 2022, www.billboard.com/music/features/anitta-billboard-cover-story-interview-2022-1235068798/. Accessed 11 July 2022.

___. "Brazilian Pop Sensation Anitta: 'Run for President? I'm 27!'" Interview by Julyssa Lopez. *The Guardian*, 9 Aug. 2020, www.theguardian.com/music/2020/aug/09/brazilian-pop-superstar-anitta-interview. Accessed 11 July 2022.

Exposito, Suzy. "Brazil's Anitta Is Already a Global Phenom and LGBTQ Icon. Now She's Set to Conquer America." *Los Angeles Times*, 9 June 2022, www.latimes.com/entertainment-arts/music/story/2022-06-09/anitta-brazil-lgbtq-bisexual-pride. Accessed 11 July 2022.

Sherman, Maria. "At the Altar of Anitta." *Nylon*, 12 Apr. 2022, www.nylon.com/entertainment/anitta-new-album-coachella. Accessed 11 July 2022.

SELECTED WORKS

Anitta, 2013; *Ritmo Perfeito*, 2014; *Bang!*, 2015; *Kisses*, 2019; *Versions of Me*, 2022

—Joy Crelin

Ime Archibong

Born: ca. 1981
Occupation: Technology executive

As head of New Product Experimentation (NPE) at Meta, the company formerly known as Facebook, technology executive Ime Archibong became well aware that the process of developing successful new products and technologies is neither easy nor immune from failures and false starts. "For most startups, the first idea you come up with isn't likely to be the one that grows," he said, as quoted by Joel Khalili for *TechRadar* (3 Dec. 2021). "The average experience is one of a lot of pivots, a lot of tries and a lot of failures." Indeed, Archibong's own career trajectory featured its own series of pivots. A talented college basketball player who captained Yale University's Division I team, he left sports behind to pursue a career in engineering, initially working for the technology company IBM. After realizing that his interests lay more in business development than in engineering, he transitioned to a career in that field and in 2010 joined Facebook—then still a relatively new player in the technology sphere—as vice president of product partnerships.

Over the next decade, Archibong established himself as a passionate advocate both for Facebook's products and features, particularly its community-building functions, and for diversity within the company itself. "When you have people sitting around the table that have diverse backgrounds or cognitive differences in their backgrounds, better products end up getting built," he told Nikita Richardson in an interview for *Fast Company* (16 Jan. 2015). "We see this time and time again." In his role as head of NPE he championed a diverse array of new products and also led efforts to hire NPE personnel from around the world, whose perspectives and contributions he believed would be essential to Meta's continued global success.

EARLY LIFE AND EDUCATION

Ime Archibong was born in Kansas, where his parents, Chi Anyansi-Archibong and Victor Archibong, had met after emigrating separately from Nigeria, in the early 1980s. Later, his family relocated to North Carolina, where his parents both worked as professors. Growing up in Greensboro, North Carolina, he attended Bishop McGuinness Catholic High School, from which he graduated in 1999. After high school he attended Yale University, where he pursued studies in computer science and electrical engineering. Archibong was also a member of the university's varsity basketball team, which competed in the Ivy League conference of Division I National Collegiate Athletic Association (NCAA) basketball competition. A shooting guard who twice ranked among the top twenty Ivy League men's players in points scored during a season, he also captained the Yale basketball team for a portion of his college career. In 2003, he earned his bachelor's degree from the university.

Although Archibong initially hoped to pursue a career in professional basketball, connections he forged at Yale soon led him down a new path. While still in college, he met Yale graduate John Rice, who had founded the organization Management Leadership for Tomorrow with the goal of promoting racial, ethnic, and gender diversity in the corporate world. "He gave me his business card, though at the time I thought I'd play basketball professionally, so I just threw it in my bag," Archibong recalled about his encounter with Rice in an episode of the podcast *The Making of . . .* (2018), produced by Grow by Facebook in collaboration with *Vanity Fair* and Founders Forum. "Fast forward six months, when I was still on my parents' couch waiting for my basketball scholarship to come through, and John helped me land a job at IBM as a software engineer."

Archibong returned to school to complete a graduate-level program several years later, enrolling at the Stanford University Graduate School of Business amid a career transition. He earned a master's degree in business administration from that institution in 2008.

Photo by Campus Party Brasil, via Wikimedia Commons.

EARLY CAREER

Archibong launched the first phase of his professional working life with IBM in 2004, joining the illustrious technology company as a software engineer. Based in the company's office in Tucson, Arizona, he focused initially on storage technology. Remaining in that role and office until mid-2007, he then relocated to a New York–based IBM office to take a new position as a corporate strategy manager. He joined the organization's business development operations later that year in the position of advanced technology professional, a role that would see California become his long-term base.

Although Archibong enjoyed his years with IBM and would later praise the company for its emphasis on workplace diversity, he realized after several years that he did not share the same passion for IBM technology displayed by some of his colleagues. "I love technology not for technology's sake but because of how it changes the world, how human ideas affect it, and how society touches it," he told Michał Wąsowski in an interview for *Business Insider Polska* (11 May 2018). "When that became clear, it was really easy for me to say that, in the organisation I was working in at the time, I wasn't living up to my full potential." Seeking a new, more professionally fulfilling opportunity, he left IBM in late 2010.

FACEBOOK

Following his departure from IBM, Archibong secured an executive position with the social media company Facebook in November 2010. Drawn to the company by its emphasis on communication and connection as well as by its ambitious leadership, he took on the position of vice president of product partnerships, a role in which he oversaw a wide range of product offerings and initiatives. "My team works with companies like Apple, Amazon, Dropbox, Airbnb, Nike," he told Andy Gensler in an interview for *Billboard* (4 Feb. 2014), "anyone that is doing a product integration with Facebook across a bunch of different pillars." While Facebook's product offerings were initially limited to the social network of the same name, the company's products and services expanded significantly over its first decades of existence, which saw the acquisition of companies such as Instagram and WhatsApp and the development of services such as *Facebook Messenger*.

In addition to overseeing collaborations with external stakeholders, Archibong was a strong proponent of internal services such as *Facebook Groups*, a community-building feature of the *Facebook* website that he considered emblematic of the company's approach to fostering interpersonal connections. "One of the things we wanted to do as a company was back the good individuals," he explained for *The Making of . . .* "Maybe they couldn't organize a thousand-person congregation, or their neighborhood, or their sports team, until *Facebook Groups* came along. In addition to that, maybe they don't know how to be strong leaders or have the funds to invest in community work. That's the stuff we've wrestled with in the last year—creating programs, residencies, fellowships and education materials to ensure we could help this community leader bucket of people we want to serve." He also appreciated *Facebook*'s analysis of user needs and use of user feedback, which he considered essential to the design of successful products and product features.

NEW PRODUCT EXPERIMENTATION

Archibong embraced a new role at Facebook in 2019, becoming head of New Product Experimentation (NPE). As head of the NPE team, he became responsible for leading a group of workers dedicated to developing experimental new products in a manner similar to individual small start-ups. Products created and tested under the NPE umbrella would come to include applications such as the video dating app *Sparked* and the DJ application *Aux*, among many others.

Although few of the experimental products remained in long-term use, and the majority were shut down after failing to capture a substantial user base, Archibong believed that creating unsuccessful products was an essential step in the process of developing highly successful ones. Indeed, that concept was the prevailing viewpoint at Facebook, which changed its company name to Meta in late 2021. "At Meta, we've tried to create a space where people can fail, fast," Archibong explained, as quoted by Khalili. "The iterative approach to experimentation begets innovation; you have to be comfortable just putting something out there. And it's not about how often you're right, but rather when you're right, *how* right are you?"

DIVERSITY AND INNOVATION

In late 2021 Archibong and Meta announced that the NPE program, and Meta as a whole, would begin to focus more extensively on working with, and on behalf of, populations underrepresented within the Silicon Valley technology landscape, including communities living in countries outside of North America and Western Europe. For Archibong, this move was in keeping with his long-standing focus on the importance of developing products that benefit a diverse, global base of users. "If your mission is to create a world where people are more connected and people have the power to share, and you're aiming to connect everyone, you can't just stop at the folks that are here in North America or the folks that are on the internet right now, because we are actually in the minority worldwide," he once told Julia Boorstin for *CNBC* (14 Apr. 2016) about his perspective.

In addition to overseeing the creation of products geared toward global users, Archibong sought to incorporate a more diverse population of workers into Meta as well. This included graduates of historically Black colleges and universities (HBCUs) in the United States and technology workers in South Korea, among other talented candidates. He also hoped to invest in small start-ups in countries such as Nigeria, which he believed could be an otherwise overlooked source of innovative technology. "I'm very bullish on the African continent, Latin America and Asia," he said, as quoted by Khalili. "The barriers to entry are getting exponentially lower and cheaper; anyone with a design mindset can be successful—you don't even need programming skills these days. . . . In that environment, there's going to be new, innovative ideas happening in corners of the world you can't see from Silicon Valley."

PERSONAL LIFE

Archibong relocated to northern California in the 2000s, while still working for IBM, and continued to live in that region after joining Facebook. He married Lauren Baranco in 2020. In addition to leading the NPE team at Meta, he has been involved with nonprofit organizations such as Girl Effect and is an avid runner.

SUGGESTED READING

Archibong, Ime. "Facebook Turns 10: Ime Archibong on *Paper App*, Going Global, Value to Music Biz (Q and A)." Interview by Andy Gensler. *Billboard*, 4 Feb. 2014, www.billboard.com/music/music-news/facebook-turns-10-ime-archibong-on-paper-app-going-5893954/. Accessed 9 May 2022.

———. "Ime Archibong: Facebook Exec Discusses What Startups Can Learn about Diversity from IBM." Interview by Nikita Richardson. *Fast Company*, 16 Jan. 2015, www.fastcompany.com/3040635/ime-archibong-facebook-exec-discusses-what-new-tech-companies-can-learn-about-diversity-from. Accessed 9 May 2022.

———. "One of Facebook's Top Executives Tells Us 'Technology Is Dumb until a Human Touches It.'" Interview by Michał Wąsowski. *Business Insider Polska*, 11 May 2018, www.businessinsider.com/facebook-vice-president-technology-stupid-given-human-touch-2018-5. Accessed 9 May 2022.

Boorstin, Julia. "The Man Working to Connect the World for Facebook." *CNBC*, 14 Apr. 2016, www.cnbc.com/2016/04/14/the-man-working-to-connect-the-world-for-facebook.html. Accessed 9 May 2022.

Burton-Hill, Clemency, host. "The Making of Ime Archibong." *The Making of . . .*, season 1, episode 5, Grow by Facebook / Vanity Fair / Founders Forum, www.facebook.com/business/m/grow-dev/podcasts/the-making-of/ep5-ime-archibong. Accessed 9 May 2022.

Khalili, Joel. "Meta Head of Experimentation Says Failure Is His Number One Priority." *TechRadar*, 3 Dec. 2021, www.techradar.com/news/metas-head-of-experimentation-says-failure-is-his-number-one-priority. Accessed 9 May 2022.

Pupic, Tamara. "Partners in Progress: Ime Archibong, Facebook's Vice President of Product Partnerships." *Entrepreneur Middle East*, 16 Oct. 2017, www.entrepreneur.com/article/302691. Accessed 9 May 2022.

—Joy Crelin

Jonathan Bailey

Born: April 25, 1988
Occupation: Actor

On the very day that British actor Jonathan Bailey turned thirty-one, he landed the biggest role of his career: playing rakish lothario Lord Anthony Bridgerton in the Netflix historical romance series *Bridgerton*. When the Regency-era drama premiered on December 25, 2020, it became Netflix's most-watched series to date and instantly catapulted Bailey to international heartthrob status. In his native England, however, he was already a household name, having spent more than two decades on the small screen, appearing in some of Britain's most popular shows, including the crime drama *Broadchurch* (2013–15) and the Phoebe Waller-Bridge comedy *Crashing* (2016). "Jonny operates at a different voltage," Waller-Bridge told Douglas Greenwood for *GQ* (9 Mar. 2022). "Smoldering at one turn and then utterly innocent at the next, but all the time playing with this sense of untapped danger."

This quality also served him well on the stage, where he starred in several West End productions, most notably *South Downs*, *The York Realist*, *American Psycho*, and *Company*, for which he won the Laurence Olivier Award in 2019.

EARLY LIFE AND EDUCATION

Jonathan Stuart Bailey was born to Carole and Stuart Bailey on April 25, 1988, in Wallingford, Oxfordshire, England. He grew up alongside his three older sisters in the nearby village of Benson. Bailey fell in love with performing at age four, when his grandmother took him to see his first-ever play: *Oliver!* While attending Benson Church of England Primary School, Bailey made his foray into professional acting after his parents enrolled him in ballet classes at a dance studio in Henley-on-Thames. "When you joined, you automatically got represented," Bailey told Matthew Amer in an interview for *Official London Theatre* (23 Apr. 2012). "I didn't really know what was going on, but they asked me to go for an audition . . . to sing a song for a lady from the RSC." The audition landed the six-year-old his first professional job, tackling the dual role of Tiny Tim and Young Scrooge in the Royal Shakespeare Company's (RSC) 1995 production of *A Christmas Carol*.

After completing primary school in 1999, Bailey attended the Oratory School, a coed Catholic secondary school in Woodcote, Oxfordshire. He obtained his General Certificate of Secondary Education (GCSE) from the Oratory School in 2004 and gained sixth-form entry to Magdalen College School (MCS) in Oxford, where he spent the next two years studying for A-level courses and exams, in preparation for university admissions. He completed his A-levels in 2006; however, instead of pursuing a college degree, Bailey committed to his professional acting career.

CHILDHOOD PROFESSIONAL ROLES

As a child, Bailey pursued acting as a hobby, often scheduling roles around his summer vacations and Christmas holidays. In 1997, he played Gavroche in the West End revival of Andrew Lloyd Webber's *Les Misérables*. Following a one-episode appearance in the Victorian-era medical drama *Bramwell* (1997) and a small role in the made-for-television movie *Bright Hair* (1997), he costarred opposite Kate Beckinsale in the 1998 small-screen adaptation of the Lewis Carroll sequel *Alice Through the Looking Glass*.

In 2001, Bailey booked his first recurring television role on the short-lived sitcom *Baddiel's Syndrome*, in which he played the son of an acerbic architect who turns to therapy to deal with his complicated personal life. Bailey next appeared in *King John* (2003), his third RSC production, and *Ferrari* (2003), the made-for-television biopic about world-renowned Italian race car driver-turned-entrepreneur Enzo Ferrari.

Photo by See Li, via Wikimedia Commons

The following year, Bailey made his feature-film debut in *Five Children and It*, an adaptation of Edith Nesbit's classic 1902 fantasy novel of the same name about a group of siblings who encounter a mythical creature during their summer holidays in the English countryside. The live-action animated movie debuted in September 2004 at the Toronto International Film Festival.

In 2005, Bailey guest starred in *The Golden Hour*, a four-part ITV drama depicting the exploits of a helicopter emergency medical services unit. That same year, he also appeared in the television movie *Walk Away and I Stumble*.

EARLY ADULT CAREER

His first role after finishing school, in 2006, Bailey replaced actor Andrew Garfield in the West End revival of Jason Harvey's *Beautiful Thing*, in which he portrayed a gay working-class teen in love with his neighbor. Between 2007 and 2008, Bailey continued to raise his profile with appearances in the daytime soap *Doctors* (2007) and the police procedural *The Bill* (2008). He also amassed stage credits in several regional productions, including *Pretend You Have Big Buildings* (2007), *The Mother Ship* (2008), and *Girl with A Pearl Earring* (2008).

In 2009, Bailey starred in the short-lived BBC sitcom *Off the Hook*, about first-year students at a fictional UK university. After guest-starring in a 2010 episode of the detective drama *Inspector Lewis*, Bailey costarred in *Campus* (2011), another ill-fated television comedy set in the world of academia. He had greater success playing a teenage Leonardo da Vinci in the action-adventure series *Leonardo*, which aired for two seasons between 2011 and 2012 on the Children's BBC channel (CBBC).

At the same time, Bailey appeared onstage in a revival of David Hare's play *South Downs*, portraying Jeremy Duffield, a boarding-school pupil who befriends an eccentric and lonely younger student. The show enjoyed a sell-out run at Chichester Festival 2011 and a subsequent stint at London's Harold Pinter Theatre in early 2012. The performance earned Bailey an *Evening Standard* Theatre Awards nomination for Outstanding Newcomer (2012). As Bailey told Amer about acting on stage, "There's something quite dangerous about it. It doesn't feel safe. Especially if you've got a really good play like *South Downs*. It's so rich."

He then earned high-profile roles in the BBC family sitcom *Me and Mrs Jones* (2012) and the live action-animated series *Groove High* (2012).

BREAK THROUGH WITH *BROADCHURCH*

In 2013, Bailey landed a major television role, playing the investigative journalist Oliver "Olly" Stevens in the ITV mystery drama *Broadchurch*, alongside high-profile British actors David Tennant and Olivia Colman. The show's eight-episode first season revolved around the mysterious murder of a young boy, whose body is found washed ashore on the beach of a seemingly tranquil seaside town. *Broadchurch* became an instant hit with critics and audiences alike following its debut in early March. Bailey reprised the role in the show's second season, which premiered in 2015.

By this time, Bailey had returned to the stage, taking on the role of lieutenant Cassio in the Royal National Theatre's 2013 contemporary imagining of William Shakespeare's *Othello*. The same year, Bailey also appeared in an episode of the sitcom *Some Girls*, as well as two National Theatre events: a live screening of *Othello* and *National Theatre Live: 50 Years on Stage*, which highlighted performances from several notable productions that span the company's half-century. He ended 2013 by costarring opposite actor Matt Smith in the musical adaptation of *American Psycho*, which premiered in December 2013 and enjoyed a sold-out two-month run at London's Almeida Theatre.

In 2014, Bailey joined the ensemble mockumentary series *W1A*, which chronicled behind-the-scenes antics at BBC corporate headquarters. He appeared in fourteen episodes of the show across three seasons, between 2014 and 2017. Bailey next appeared in an episode of the BBC hit series *Doctor Who*, before making his lone 2014 film appearance in the big-screen adaptation of the World War I memoir *Testament of Youth*.

FIXTURE ON UK STAGE AND SCREEN

In January 2016, actor, producer, and screenwriter Phoebe Waller-Bridge—with whom he had worked on *Broadchurch*—tapped him for her first television project as writer and producer: the Channel Four sitcom *Crashing*, about the misadventures of six twenty-something roommates who serve as property guardians of an abandoned London hospital. Bailey played a bisexual womanizer who bonds with his gay male flatmate while grieving the loss of his father. Despite its popularity, the show had only one season.

Bailey then switched gears with the 2016 historical drama *The Young Messiah*, in which he costarred as power-hungry King Herod. Next came a part in the treasure hunting action-adventure miniseries *Hooten and the Lady* (2016). That fall, Bailey also returned to the stage for a revival of Jason Robert Brown's musical *The Last Five Years* (2016), which chronicles the tumultuous relationship between a budding writer and a struggling actress.

Bailey kicked off 2017 with a memorable guest appearance as actor Michaela Coel's love interest in the sitcom *Chewing Gum*. That summer, he headlined the National Theatre production of Peter Gill's *Certain Young Men*, which explored the everyday struggles faced by four same-sex couples, before returning to the Chichester Festival Theatre, where he appeared opposite Sir Ian McKellen in Jonathan Munby's production of *King Lear*, which ended its run in late October 2017.

Following his role in the biographical drama *The Mercy* (2018), starring Colin Firth and Rachel Weisz, Bailey costarred with actor Ben Batt in the play *The York Realist* (2018), written by Gill, about a forbidden same-sex romance between an assistant theater director from London and a local farmer from Yorkshire. As Bailey explained to Johanna Thomas-Carr for the *Evening Standard* (8 Feb. 2018), "I want to find stories that humanise homosexual experience and that's what Peter Gill does well. The richness comes from the detail about family and relationships and identity of where you live." The 1960s-era production premiered at the Donmar Warehouse in early February before moving to London's Sheffield Theatres in late March.

MAINSTREAM SUCCESS WITH *BRIDGERTON*

Bailey resurfaced onscreen as undercover CIA agent Lance Miller in Amazon Prime Video's summer hit *Tom Clancy's Jack Ryan* (2018). For his next project, Bailey appeared in Tony Award-winning director Marianne Elliott's gender-swapped reimagined version of Stephen Sondheim's *Company*, which opened in October 2018. Bailey's portrayal of a commitment-phobic gay man overcome with wedding-day jitters, along with his rousing rapid-fire rendition of the song "(Not) Getting Married Today," earned him the prize for Best Supporting Actor in a Musical at the Laurence Olivier Awards in early April 2019.

Bailey achieved another professional milestone later that month, when he was cast in the Netflix series *Bridgerton*, an adaptation of Julia Quinn's series of Regency-era romance novels. After initially auditioning for the part of Simon Basset, the love interest of Daphne Bridgerton, Bailey was offered the role of Daphne's eldest brother and heir to the family fortune, Anthony Bridgerton. He began filming the period drama in July, eventually wrapping up production in February 2020.

When *Bridgerton* debuted on Netflix in late December, it centered on the Bridgerton siblings' pursuit of romance amid British high-society's competitive marriage market. A season-one subplot included Anthony's ill-fated relationship with an opera singer. By January 2021, the series had been streamed by more than eighty million households worldwide, earning a season-two renewal. *Bridgerton*'s sophomore season, which premiered in March 2022, focused heavily on eligible bachelor Anthony and his love triangle with two sisters. Explaining his experience playing character, Bailey told Greenwood, "You put your life experiences into [the work]. What's most interesting is not necessarily having to talk about what that is, and keeping a sense of privacy." After posting an opening-weekend viewership record (193 million hours) for Netflix, *Bridgerton* became Netflix's most-watched English-language series.

Also in 2022, Bailey starred in the West End production of the Mike Bartlett play *Cock*, directed by Elliot, which shares the story of a gay man as he falls in love with a woman, despite being in a happy, long-term relationship with his boyfriend. The play ran from March to June 2022 and received largely positive reviews. "If you are innately someone who's outside society. . . you have that access to empathy," Bailey shared an appreciation of the experience with the play with Charlie Brinkhurst-Cuff for *The New York Times* (14 Apr. 2022). "And what comes with empathy is playfulness, because then you can see where the other person's coming from, and you can feel safe to find the joy within that."

PERSONAL LIFE

Bailey, a former London resident, moved to the county of Sussex, England, in 2020. In 2018, the notoriously private actor publicly disclosed that he is gay, with the goal of promoting diversity and LGBTQ+ representation.

SUGGESTED READING

Bailey, Jonathan. "Introducing . . . Jonathan Bailey." Interview by Matthew Amer. *Official London Theatre*, 23 Apr. 2012, officiallondontheatre.com/news/introducing-jonathan-bailey-140905/. Accessed 8 Aug. 2022.

___. "Jonathan Bailey: *Bridgerton* Has Raised the Bar for Representation." Interview by Laura Craik. *Evening Standard*, www.standard.co.uk/insider/bridgerton-jonathan-bailey-anthony-bridgerton-interview-b923366.html. Accessed 8 Aug. 2022.

Brinkhurst-Cuff, Charlie. "Jonathan Bailey Is Keeping Busy." *The New York Times*, 14 Apr. 2022, www.nytimes.com/2022/04/14/arts/television/jonathan-bailey-bridgerton.html. Accessed 8 Aug. 2022.

Greenwood, Douglas. "*Bridgerton*'s Jonathan Bailey Is Giving Us the Vapors," *GQ*, 9 Mar. 2022, www.gq.com/story/gq-hype-jonathan-bailey. Accessed 8 Aug. 2022.

Thomas-Corr, Johanna. "Jonathan Bailey on Starring in *The York Realist*, Humanising LGBT History and the Importance of Community." *Evening Standard*, 8 Feb. 2018, www.standard.co.uk/culture/theatre/jonathan-bailey-on-starring-in-the-york-realist-humanising-lgbt-history-and-the-importance-of-community-a3761256.html. Accessed 8 Aug. 2022.

SELECTED WORKS

South Downs, 2011–12; *Leonardo*, 2011–12; *Othello*, 2013; *American Psycho*, 2013; *Broadchurch*, 2013–15; *Testament of Youth*, 2014; *W1A*, 2014–17; *Crashing*, 2016; *The Young Messiah*, 2016; *King Lear*, 2017; *The Mercy*, 2018; *Company*, 2018–19; *Bridgerton*, 2020–; *Cock*, 2022

—Bertha Muteba

Gord Bamford

Born: April 17, 1976
Occupation: Country music singer-songwriter

Gord Bamford is among the most popular contemporary country musicians recording and performing in Canada. By 2022, he had been nominated for Canadian Country Music Association (CCMA) Awards twenty-six times and had also earned numerous Juno Award nominations. Additionally, he was the first two-time recipient of the Country Music Association (CMA) Global Country Artist of the Year Award.

Despite his extensive list of accolades, it took Bamford about fifteen years to have a career in which he was recognized both at home in Canada and internationally. He credits much of his success to the style of music he writes, which often celebrates small-town living and working-class communities, as well as the other songwriters with whom he collaborates. In an interview with the Australian blog *Tinsel and Tap Shoes* (9 Nov. 2016), Bamford remarked, "I've never really been a trend follower so I just stick with what I do and it's pretty simple, relatable to the blue-collar person and it seems to work. Some people want to write everything

and I don't think that's necessarily the key. I think you find the best songs that you can get that are gonna impact the person listening to it—I think that's the key."

EARLY LIFE

Gord Bamford was born on April 17, 1976, in Traralgon, Victoria, Australia, where his father, Jock Bamford, was born. His mother, a Canadian citizen, was a country singer, as was his father. For a time, the pair sang in a popular Australian country band. After they divorced when Bamford was around the age of four or five, he and his mother moved to Canada. They settled in the small city of Lacombe, in the western province of Alberta, nearby where his mother had grown up. Bamford would not see his father for many years and only began to rekindle a relationship with him in the mid-2010s, while he was on tour in Australia. Growing up with a single parent was challenging at times, and Bamford and his mother turned to organizations like the Big Brother Big Sister Foundation for support. "They really helped me out and helped her out too," he explained to Mb in an interview for *The Wire* (4 May 2016), a Canadian-based online magazine. "It's just a great organization that caters to young kids that need that mentorship."

Inspired by his mother's music career and country music legends like Willie Nelson and Merle Haggard, singing became part of Bamford's life from an early age. He performed at a variety of school and community events. Also a strong athlete, he played baseball and other sports during high school. His first foray into professional singing came in 1995, when he won the Nornet Radio Network's "Search for the Stars," a major talent show in Alberta. A year later, he recorded his first single, "Forever Starts Today," which got a lot of airplay on Canadian radio.

EARLY MUSIC CAREER

In 2000 Bamford self-released his first album, *God's Green Earth*, which he recorded in Saskatchewan, Canada, with the help of award-winning producer Bart McKay. Bamford cowrote two of the songs on the album, with the rest of the songwriting credits going to Steve Fox, Gil Grand, and other songwriters that he admired. A number of singles from the album were released, which got airplay in Canada as well as in Australia and in Europe.

In 2003 Bamford moved to Nashville, Tennessee, with the intention of working on a new album with some of the major songwriters who were based in the country music capital of the world. *Life Is Good* was released in 2004 and featured the work of several talented songwriters, including Duane Steele, who cowrote the first single, "Heroes." That song, as well as "All about Her," were widely popular on Canadian country radio, the latter of which made the Top Ten.

Over the next three years, Bamford found himself touring as an opening act for some of the biggest names in country music, including Kenny Rogers, Tim McGraw, and Terri Clark. In 2007 he released his third album, *Honkytonks and Heartaches*, which earned two nominations at the 2008 Juno Awards—one for best album and one for the single "Blame It on That Red Dress." The album garnered him enough critical and commercial acclaim to enable him to produce three new albums in fairly quick succession: *Day Job* (2010), *Is It Friday Yet?* (2012), and *Country Junkie* (2013). A single from the *Country Junkie* album, "When Your Lips Are So Close," reached the top of the country charts, becoming Bamford's first number-one hit.

By the mid-2010s, Bamford was regarded as a successful artist in the country music scene, with several hit albums under his belt; however, it was not from a lack of hard work. Reflecting on his slow and steady climb to musical success, he told Bill King in an interview for *FYI Music News* (11 Jan. 2018), "It takes so long to become a hard-ticket act. That's what everyone who's getting into music must understand. I've been at it for fifteen years and finally know that we can sell a thousand tickets a night." Further describing the gratitude he feels for his success, Bamford explained to King, "People are coming to watch your show and singing your songs, and you are interacting with them. That's the ultimate goal of the singer/songwriter. For me, it's seeing people getting into it—embracing my songs and music."

TIN ROOF AND NEON SMOKE

In 2016 Bamford's success continued when he released *Tin Roof*, which won the 2016 CCMA Album of the Year Award and was nominated for the 2016 Juno Country Album of the Year. For this album, Bamford took a new direction.

"It was a different process," he explained to *The Wire*. "Spent a lot more time making this record than I typically do but I really enjoyed it. . . . Sonically it's a little different but it's still a country record, so it makes me happy [because] that's what I like to do." The album also afforded him the opportunity to expand his fanbase and break into the Australian market. "My music is a really good fit [for Australia] and I hold dual citizenship so the story is . . . unique too," Bamford explained to the interviewer for *The Wire*. He went on tour in Australia in 2017, which gave him the chance to reconnect with his father and extended family. The experience helped strengthen Bamford's relationship with his father, who also later visited him in Nashville.

Neon Smoke, his 2018 studio album, was another hit in Canada. Although Bamford handled much of the songwriting on the album, as usual it includes songs written by others as well. The record also produced his second number-one Canadian country single, "Dive Bar." "It was a record I had my hands on from A to Z," he told King of his work on *Neon Smoke*. "I wrote a good chunk of stuff on the record and also went out and found some good songs."

COVID-19 PANDEMIC

The coronavirus disease 2019 (COVID-19) pandemic, which began in early 2020 and forced musicians around the world to cancel tours for the next several months, took a toll on Bamford. It distressed him to know that many of the people who worked with him on tour were now out of work. "It's tougher on my staff and my crew and my musicians who have been with me for ten to fifteen years," he told Eric Volmers for the *Calgary Herald* (3 June 2021). "You feel responsible for those people. That's their livelihood. That's been the biggest downfall of not being able to play." The time away from the road, however, did provide Bamford with the opportunity to write and record a considerable amount of new material, some of which was collected for his 2021 album, *Diamonds in a Whiskey Glass*. The album produced two hit singles, the title track and "Heaven on Dirt." Of the latter song, Bamford commented for *Rock n' Load* (12 July 2021), an online music review magazine, that he felt the song's message was "very powerful, especially given the times we all have been living in." He further explained, "We all live very busy lives and one of the positives of this . . . year was that we could slow down and appreciate what is important to us."

In late 2021, Bamford was finally able to play live music again—notably at a time when other musicians were canceling tours among continued COVID-19 concerns—in a tour he named the "Kick COVID in the A** Tour." He provided free COVID tests to unvaccinated attendants prior to each show, in what some critics deemed was a way to "court" anti-vaxxers. Bamford maintained people had the right to make their own choices regarding vaccination. During this period, Bamford also produced *Real Country Livin'*, a documentary video and podcast series that provided his fans with a behind-the-scenes look at his everyday life in rural Canada, with episode titles such as "Boatin'" and "Farmin.'"

PERSONAL LIFE AND CHARITABLE WORK

Bamford and his wife, Kendra, married in 2004. They have a son and two daughters. For a time in the mid-2010s, the family resided in Nashville, Tennessee, to help Bamford's career. As of mid-2021, the family lives back in Canada, in a rural area near Bashaw, Alberta.

Bamford and his family support the Gord Bamford Charitable Foundation, which they founded in 2008. By 2022, it had raised more than $4.5 million in revenue for charitable organizations such as the Big Brother Big Sister and the Make-a-Wish Foundation; events such as a Father's Day Special, a Drive-in Tour, and a Charity Gold Classic Tournament raised more than $400,000 alone. Bamford's charitable work has earned him the 4-H Canada Distinguished Alumni Award, the CCMA Humanitarian of the Year Award, and the MusicCounts Inspired Minds Ambassador Award (MIMAA). Describing the impact of these charities on his life, he told *Rock n' Load* magazine, "It's always great to get out, play music, be on stage and wake up every morning loving what I do. But probably the greatest thing I get to do is interact with a lot of these children and try to make a difference in their lives. . . . It puts it all into perspective as to why I think God put me on earth to do what I do because it's helping other people."

SUGGESTED READING

"About." *Gord Bamford*, gordbamford.com/gord/. Accessed 4 Mar. 2022.

Bamford, Gord. "A Conversation with . . . Gord Bamford." Interview by Bill King. *FYI Music News*, 11 Jan. 2018, www.fyimusicnews.ca/articles/2018/01/11/conversation-gord-bamford. Accessed 4 Mar. 2022.

___. "Interview: Gord Bamford." Interview by Mb. *The Wire*, 4 May 2016, thewiremegazine.com/interviews/186/. Accessed 4 Mar. 2022.

___. "An Interview with Gord Bamford." Interview. *Tinsel and Tap Shoes*, 9 Nov. 2016, tinselandtapshoes.com/2016/11/09/an-interview-with-gord-bamford/. Accessed 4 Mar. 2022.

"Canadian Country Star Gord Bamford Releases New Video, 'Heaven on Dirt.'" *Rock n' Load*, 12 July 2021, rocknloadmag.com/country-americana/canadian-country-star-gord-bamford-releases-new-video-heaven-on-dirt/. Accessed 8 Mar. 2022.

Volmers, Eric. "Alberta Country Artist Gord Bamford Keeps It Simple with 10th Album, Diamonds in a Whiskey Glass." *Calgary Herald*, 3 June 2021, calgaryherald.com/entertainment/music/alberta-country-artist-gord-bamford-keeps-it-simple-with-ninth-album-diamonds-in-a-whiskey-glass. Accessed 4 Mar. 2022.

SELECTED WORKS

God's Green Earth, 2000; *Life Is Good*, 2004; *Honkytonks and Heartaches*, 2007; *Country Junkie*, 2013; *Tin Roof*, 2016; *Neon Smoke*, 2018; *Diamonds in a Whiskey Glass*, 2021

—Christopher Mari

William Barber II

Born: August 30, 1963
Occupation: Minister and activist

The Reverend Doctor William J. Barber II inspires comparisons to Dr. Martin Luther King Jr. Like King, Barber is an African American pastor who became a nationally prominent social justice activist. Since 1993 he has been the pastor of Greenleaf Christian Church, a Disciple of Christ church, in Goldsboro, North Carolina. He is a past president of the North Carolina conference of the National Association for the Advancement of Colored People (NAACP) and past member of the organization's national board of directors. He has founded several social justice coalitions and organizations, including the Historic Thousand on Jones Street (HKonJ) People's Assembly Coalition, the Moral Monday alliance, Repairers of the Breach, and the Poor People's Campaign: A National Call for Moral Revival, a reboot of the1968 antipoverty campaign that King had launched a few days before he was assassinated. Asked by Pamela K. Johnson for *AARP* (21 Jan. 2020) what would top an agenda for King at this time in history, Barber responded, "Five injustices interlock to keep America from becoming what we hope it to be: poverty, systemic racism, ecological devastation, a war economy and a distorted moral narrative that tells some people God blesses all of this."

In 2018, Barber received a MacArthur Foundation Fellowship Grant as a leader of nonviolent protests against voter suppression. Of that grant, Barber told Michel Martin for National Public Radio (NPR)'s *All Things Considered* (Oct. 2018), "You want to see people have voting rights and people have health care and people treated right regardless of their race, their color, their creed, their sexuality. So a gift like this says somebody else sees what you're trying to do, and they want to be a part of you continuing to do that work." His other awards include a Franklin D. Roosevelt Four Freedoms Award and his state's highest civilian honor, the North Carolina Award, as well as *Unity Magazine*'s 2018 Walden New Thought Award.

Barber has also received hate mail and death threats for his work. Despite the threats, Barber told Martin, "I don't see any other reason for me to be alive than to work on these issues of racism and poverty and ecological devastation or economy and trying to build what I call moral analysis, moral articulation and moral action."

EARLY LIFE AND EDUCATION

William J. Barber II was born on August 30, 1963, in Indianapolis, Indiana. Both of Barber's parents were activists. In 1968, the Barber family moved from Indianapolis to North Carolina after a Black school principal there asked his parents to help integrate the staff at Washington County's White high school. Barber's father became the first Black teacher in the school's science department, while his mother became the school's first Black office manager.

Photo by Knightopia, via Wikimedia Commons

Barber attended a segregated kindergarten. By the time he reached adolescence, he was a junior official in the local chapter of the NAACP. He also became the first Black president of Washington County High School to serve a full year term. The school's custom had been to split the office with a White president, each serving part of the year.

After high school, Barber went to North Carolina Central University (NCCU), a historically Black university. Of his years there, fellow alumni Rodney Sessoms told Renee Elder for *NCCU News* (11 Nov. 2020), "Without a doubt, [Barber] had leadership qualities. People listened to him and gave credence to his ideas and words." Barber fought to establish a voting precinct on campus and protested proposed tuition changes that would hurt many of NCCU's students.

In college, Barber thought about possible career paths. He had seen the difficulties his father had endured as a minister and, not wanting to experience them himself, he initially considered law school instead. During his junior year, however, he began to heed his father's words about serving God and humanity. Barber called his father, who invited him to come home. The two drove around the eastern part of North Carolina for a couple of days on a road trip that Barber felt changed his life. He later shared some of his father's wisdom with

Tim Tyson for *Southern Cultures* (Fall 2019): "When you feel overwhelmed by your moment, go back and read the moments that people faced that are worse than yours. What courage and hope and truth did they find in that moment?" Barber preached his first sermon when he returned to campus and went on to graduate cum laude from NCCU in 1985 with a bachelor's degree in political science.

GRADUATE STUDIES AND EARLY CAREER

After NCCU, Barber pursued a Master of Divinity (MDiv) degree from Duke University, where he was a Dean scholar and a Benjamin Mays Fellow. After graduating from Duke in 1989, he continued his graduate studies and earned a Doctorate of Ministry (DMin) degree with a concentration in public policy and pastoral care from Drew University in 2003.

While in graduate school, Barber was campus minister at NCCU for the 1992–93 academic year. In 1993, Jim Hunt, then North Carolina's governor, appointed Barber to the statewide Human Relations Commission as executive director. That same year, Barber became pastor of Greenleaf Christian Church (Disciples of Christ) in Goldsboro, North Carolina. Two years later, the church did a study of a two-mile circle around the church. Discovering high unemployment and poverty rates, the church invested $1.5 million to purchase and then develop land around the church. They oversaw the building of sixty houses, a preschool, and a home for senior citizens. The church also began an after-school program and a computer lab in a community center it constructed.

Barber was active as a leader of social justice advocacy in the mid-2000s. Starting in 2005, he served as president of the North Carolina conference of the NAACP. As conference president, he pulled together 140 different organizations into the Historic Thousand on Jones Street Peoples Assembly Coalition, in 2006. The following year the coalition adopted the 14-Point People's Agenda, consisting of detailed actions that they pressed state lawmakers to include in legislation.

MORAL MONDAY MOVEMENT

As NAACP North Carolina conference president, Barber started the Moral Monday alliance in 2013. Two years before, the North Carolina General Assembly's Republican-

dominated redistricting committee submitted a plan that the NAACP and other critics condemned as unfairly, and possibly illegally, packing certain districts with Black voters to reduce their representation. The US Department of Justice approved a revised version of the plan that opponents still viewed as gerrymandering and favorable to Republican candidates in the 2012 state elections.

After North Carolina voters elected Republican governor Pat McCrory and a Republican supermajority to both state legislative houses, the governor and lawmakers started to institute voter identification requirements, limits on voting by mail, and restrictions on early voting. On Monday, April 29, 2013, Moral Monday activists met at the North Carolina statehouse to protest what Barber saw as Republican efforts to disfranchise the state's Black and low-income voters. As he told Martin, "We also want to get to where everybody 18 is automatically registered, and where voting is a holiday, and where same-day registration and early voting is something that happens in every state." Seventeen people, Barber among them, were arrested. The following Monday, more demonstrators came, and the next Monday, even more. By August 2014, the movement had branched out to eleven other states.

REPAIRING THE BREACH

In 2014, Barber founded Repairers of the Breach, a leadership development group. The group's title and mission came from Isaiah 58:12: "Your ancient ruins shall be rebuilt; you shall raise up the foundations of many generations; you shall be called the repairer of the breach, the restorer of streets to live in." At the July 2016 Democratic National Convention (DNC), Barber used Isaiah's imagery of repairing the breach as he addressed convention attendees for about ten minutes on the need for justice in a moral context. As Ari Berman reported for *Nation* (29 July 2016), Barber called for true religious faith, saying, "In my heart, I'm troubled and I'm worried about the way faith is cynically used by some to serve hate, fear, racism, and greed. Jesus, a brown-skinned Palestinian Jew, called us to preach good news to the poor, the broken, and the bruised and all those who are made to feel unaccepted."

THE POOR PEOPLE'S CAMPAIGN

On Mother's Day 2018, Barber and the Reverend Dr. Liz Theoharis launched the Poor People's Campaign: A National Call for Moral Revival. The revival, which marked the fiftieth anniversary of King's Poor People's campaign to end poverty and sought to continue his work, brought nonviolent protests to more than thirty statehouses across the country over a period of six weeks. The campaign issued its Declaration of Fundamental Rights and Poor People's Moral Agenda, which laid out demands encompassing voting rights, wealth inequality, immigration, tribal sovereignty, housing, health care, wages, education, jobs, social welfare, mass incarceration, water access, climate change, and militarization. The campaign's Declaration also critiqued the anti-poor policies of "an extremist religious and Christian nationalist agenda" that served to distract national attention from poverty and other key issues and "distort the national moral narrative" by focusing on prayer in schools, abortion, and gun rights.

Barber had worked with Theoharis at Union Theological Seminary, where he was a visiting professor and she was the director of the Kairos Center for Religions, Rights, and Social Justice. The two wanted to bring a public policy perspective, not a politically partisan one, to moral injustice around poverty. According to the campaign, poverty affected 140 million Americans in 2017, of whom 75 percent were women and children and 60 percent were Black. In an interview with Lottie Joiner for the *Crisis Magazine* in 2018, Barber said that the national conversation about ending poverty needed to focus on what was morally right to do in terms of public policy. "Our language is too puny; it's too left and right. Democrat, Republican, just constantly puts people at odds. And then issues become just simply partisan." Accordingly, the campaign did not feature speakers who were politicians or officials.

The Poor People's Campaign provided an umbrella under which the relaunch of Moral Mondays occurred in 2020. On June 20, 2020, the campaign held a Mass People's Assembly & Moral March on Washington. Though the event was largely virtual due to the coronavirus disease 2019 (COVID-19) pandemic, more than 2.5 million people tuned in on Facebook and other social media platforms.

INAUGURAL PRAYER SERVICE 2021

Barber was invited to preach the homily for the Inaugural Prayer Service in January 2021. Because of the pandemic, President Joe Biden and Vice President Kamala Harris attended from the State Dining Room. Barber's remarks included a challenge to create a Third Reconstruction, as *Time* reported (21 Jan. 2021): "We must have a Third Reconstruction. We must address the five interlocking injustices of systemic racism, poverty, ecological devastation/denial of healthcare, the war economy, and the false moral narrative of religious nationalism. These are breaches that must be addressed, and according to the text, repairing the breaches will bring revival."

PERSONAL LIFE

Barber met his wife, Rebecca McLean, during college. The couple have five children. During the 1990s, Barber was diagnosed with ankylosing spondylitis, a form of arthritis that fused his spinal vertebrae.

SUGGESTED READING

Barber II, William J. "'We Must Have a Third Reconstruction.' Read the Full Text of the Rev. William J. Barber II's Sermon at the Inaugural Prayer Service." *Time*, 21 Jan. 2021, time.com/5931343/william-barber-inaugural-prayer-service-sermon/. Accessed 14 Dec. 2021.

___. "William Barber II Reframes the Civil Rights Movement for Modern Times." Interview by Pamela K. Johnson. *AARP*, 21 Jan. 2020, www.aarp.org/politics-society/history/info-2020/william-barber-civil-rights-leader.html. Accessed 14 Dec. 2021.

___, and Tim Tyson. "Gird Up, Get Up, and Grow Up: Rev. Dr. William J. Barber II in Conversation with Tim Tyson." *Southern Cultures*, Fall 2019, www.southerncultures.org/article/gird-up-get-up-and-grow-up/. Accessed 13 Dec. 2021.

Berman, Ari. "Americans Who'd Never Heard of Reverend William Barber II Won't Be Able to Forget Him after Last Night." *The Nation*, 29 July 2016, www.thenation.com/article/archive/americans-whod-never-heard-of-reverend-william-barber-ii-wont-be-able-to-forget-him-after-last-night/. Accessed 7 Dec. 2021.

Elder, Renee. "Rev. Dr. William J. Barber II: On a Mission to Serve." *NCCU News*, NC Central University, 11 Nov. 2020, www.nccu.edu/news/rev-dr-william-j-barber-ii-mission-serve. Accessed 3 Dec. 2021.

Joiner, Lottie L. "A Moral Revolution: Fifty Years after Rev. Dr. Martin Luther King Jr. Called for a Poor People's Campaign, Rev. William Barber II Is Taking up the Mantle with a Call for a New Moral Agenda to Address Poverty." *Crisis Magazine*, vol. 125, no. 3, 2018, pp. 24–28. *Academic Search Premier*, search.ebscohost.com/login.aspx?direct=true&db=aph&AN=141816587&site=eds-live. Accessed 13 Dec. 2021.

Martin, Michel, host. "MacArthur 'Genius' Grant Winner: Rev. William J. Barber II." *All Things Considered*, NPR, 7 Oct. 2018, www.npr.org/2018/10/07/655461839/macarthur-genius-grant-winner-rev-william-j-barber-ii. Accessed 13 Dec. 2021.

SELECTED WORKS

Forward Together: A Moral Message to the Nation (with Barbara Zelter), 2014; *The Third Reconstruction: Moral Mondays, Fusion Politics, and the Rise of a New Justice Movement* (with Jonathan Wilson-Hartgrove), 2016; *Capitalism, Socialism, and the Promise of Democracy*, 2019; *We Are Called to Be a Movement*, 2020; *We Cry Justice: Reading the Bible Together with the Poor People's Campaign* (with Liz Theoharis), 2021

—*Judy Johnson*

Max Barskih

Born: March 8, 1990
Occupation: Singer and songwriter

In 2018, Stephan Rabimov wrote in an interview for *Forbes* that Ukrainian singer and songwriter Max Barskih was "one of the hottest performers capitalizing on the growing niche" of Russian-language audiences in the United States. At the time of Rabimov's writing, Barskih was best known as a 2008 contestant on the Ukrainian talent show *Fabrika Zirok 2* (*Star Factory 2*) and the winner of the best Ukrainian performer title at the 2010 MTV Europe Music Awards. Moreover, he had become one of the largest pop stars in Russia and other post-Soviet countries and had begun expanding his audience to Western countries.

Fast-forward to late February 2022, however, when Barskih—who has tens of millions of social media followers—gained new recognition as a loud and vehement opponent of Russian president Vladimir Putin's invasion of Ukraine. Barskih immediately cut short an international tour to join the Ukrainian military in response to the Soviet aggression and vowed never to record music in the Russian language again. He subsequently made what some observers considered an even greater contribution to the war effort by recording a viral single with the defiant refrain: "We attack, we don't play / Don't f—— with Ukraine."

Barskih believed that bold attitude is ingrained in his fellow citizens. "Every Ukrainian tries to help. Either physically or with moral support," he told Kristýna Jandová for *Vogue CK* (13 May 2022). "Russia is still bombing our cities, killing our civilians and trying to invade new territories. It is painful to watch, but we remain strong and believe in our victory." While he expressed some eagerness to get back to touring and making albums, he had no regrets about his career taking a back seat while hostilities raged between Russia and Ukraine. "A year ago, I was wearing sequin jackets on the stage. Now everything is green in my wardrobe," he remarked to Brian Hiatt in an interview for *Rolling Stone* (29 Apr. 2022).

EARLY YEARS

Max Barskih was born Mykola Mykolaiovych Bortnyk on March 8, 1990, in Kherson, Ukraine. He grew up in Kherson, a predominantly Russian-speaking port town in the south of Ukraine, known for its shipbuilding industry. Barskih has described his youth as a troubled one and has told tabloid journalists that he is amazed he emerged from those years intact and mentally healthy: his father was an alcoholic who could be abusive both verbally and physically, and he remembers his parents fighting constantly. Any fond memories Barskih has related to reporters are about his mother, who raised him and his two siblings almost singlehandedly. "She sacrificed much for us," he said in a Russian-language discussion translated on the site *NewsMe.com* (20 Dec. 2017). "[She] worked constantly to feed us and educate us. Was strict where necessary and supported [us] in all creative manifestations."

Photo by Okras, via Wikimedia Commons

Barskih's father left the family when Max was eleven—a change the singer has said made little difference in his life as the older man was rarely home and devoted little attention to his children. Barskih found solace in art and music, writing his first song around the age of thirteen. "Since childhood I've been listening to American music," he told Rabimov. "I listened to the 1960's music, jazz, rock-n-roll. I gained inspiration from the Western culture then I added something personal to it and created new music in my head."

As soon as he graduated from high school, Barskih left Kherson and moved to Kyiv, the capital city of Ukraine. There, he attended the Kyiv Municipal Academy of Circus and Performing Arts, where he studied vocal arts.

FABRIKA ZIROK 2

Barskih made his debut in front of a large, public audience in 2008, when he appeared as a contestant on *Fabrika Zirok 2* (*Star Factory 2*), the second season of a nationally televised talent show similar to *American Idol*. As on many such shows, *Fabrika Zirok 2* houses contestants in a luxurious apartment, and after performing in a weekly concert featuring a variety of musical genres, one is eliminated each week. Although the season-two winner was female singer Olga Tsibulska, Barskih made it to a respectable sixth-place finish

before being eliminated. The following year, he recorded his debut album, *1:Max Barskih*, which featured tracks with such titles as "Hot Girl" and "Kiss, Love, Touch." On the strength of that effort, he was named best Ukrainian act at the MTV Europe Music Awards in 2010. (That year he also appeared in *Mademoiselle Zhivago*, a short film by singer Lara Fabian that functioned, essentially, as an extended music video; it remained unreleased until 2013.)

After winning the title of singer of the year at the 2011 Baltic Music Awards, Barskih auditioned to represent Ukraine in 2012 at the Eurovision Song Contest, an annual international competition organized by the European Broadcasting Union and known for its earnest, over-the-top performances. Although he performed a version of his hit track "Dance," he was unsuccessful, and the pop diva Gaitana was chosen instead.

AN INTERNATIONAL POP STAR

Barskih had better luck in 2012 with the release of the album and video compilation *Z.Dance*, which contained four new singles and a cover of the Michael Jackson hit "Thriller." The following year, his voice became familiar even to those who were not fans of pop music when the track "I Wanna Run" was licensed by soft-drink giant Pepsi as a commercial theme song. Barskih broke new ground artistically according to many critics with the 2014 release of *According to Freud*, which contained tracks based on the psychoanalyst's work as it related to various stages in the singer's life.

By this time, Barskih had amassed a large and passionate fan base in both Ukraine and Russia. "He successfully navigates a tense pop territory," Rabimov wrote, alluding to Ukraine's contentious history with its neighbor, Russia. "In the fallout from the 2014 annexation of Crimea, many Russian and Ukrainian artists found themselves as *personas non grata* across the cultural divide. Barskih emerged as one of the few who managed to retain and grow their popularity."

Over the next several years, Barskih continued to release new albums, including *Mists* (2016) and *7* (2019), while playing hundreds of concerts annually across the post-Soviet commonwealth. Furthermore, in 2018, he mounted an international tour that took him to the United States, Canada, and the United Kingdom, where Western journalists touted him as being among the most popular, financially successful Ukrainian artists of the day. He likewise amassed hundreds of millions of views of his videos on *YouTube* from listeners all over the world. Though many of his concerts were canceled during the COVID-19 pandemic in 2020, he enjoyed the unhurried change of pace during quarantine and took time to write new songs with quieter themes. He also started a new clothing line called Nick Vangard in 2020. By 2021, when he released the infectious 1960s-influenced English-language single "Just Fly," accompanied by a colorful video filmed at the Boryspil International Airport in Ukraine, Barskih was one of the most played artists on radio stations across Russia, Ukraine, and other post-Soviet countries and seemed destined for popularity in the West.

WAR IN UKRAINE

Barskih was enjoying the success of his latest single, "Tequila Sunrise," while preparing to release a new album and performing in Kyiv on February 24, 2022, when his sister called to inform him that Russia had invaded Ukraine. He immediately cancelled his tour and left for home to usher his family to safety. "We decided to go closer to the border, and on the way we were passing all these Russian military transports and all these firefights," he recalled to Hiatt. "It was crazy. It felt like a . . . movie. I didn't sleep for two days in a row, driving."

He then returned to Kyiv, where he removed his music from all Russian streaming services, canceled contracts with Russian publishers and distributors, and began addressing his many Russian fans through social media. Their reaction was surprising to him. "I told them what was happening in Ukraine, and suddenly their love turned to hate, they started wishing me dead," he explained to Jandová.

Barskih subsequently approached military officials to ask how he could help and was advised to join the reserves. At first, fellow reservists in the communications department where he was assigned besieged him for photos and autographs, and while he was happy to be able to boost morale, their commander quickly put a stop to the practice. Although he was engaged in weapons training and other instruction, Barskih found time to create a new single, recording it in his barracks with a towel draped over his head to improve the acoustics. The video accompanying the techno-tinged track, "Don't F—— with Ukraine," features footage of Ukrainian soldiers firing missiles interspersed with scenes of civilians dancing and protesting. Deciding to no longer record music in the Russian language in protest to Putin's regime, Barskih chose to release the song in English. The singer also released the anthem "It Will Be Spring," an empowering song that aimed to unite Ukrainians, and donated money from his canceled concerts directly to the Ukrainian war effort.

Asked to comment on what might happen when the war ended, he told Hiatt: "After what I've been through and all the Ukrainians have been through, it will take lots of time to get back to normal life. I can't picture myself being onstage in, like, shiny outfits and just jumping or performing. I'm in a totally different space." Explaining that before the war, he had been living part-time in Los Angeles and practicing English, he continued, "Hopefully, since Russia is dead for me now, my journey will begin towards the European market and American market. Hopefully there is space for me as an artist."

PERSONAL LIFE

Before the Russian invasion of Ukraine in early 2022, Barskih lived in Los Angeles and Kyiv. He has been linked romantically to various women, including Ukrainian pop star Misha Romanova. When she became pregnant in 2019, unsubstantiated rumors swirled that Barskih was the father.

SUGGESTED READING

Barskih, Max. "'Don't F—— with Ukraine': How Ukrainian Pop Star Max Barskih Joined the Army and Wrote a New Anthem." Interview by Brian Hiatt. *Rolling Stone*, 29 Apr. 2022, www.rollingstone.com/music/music-features/dont-fuck-with-ukraine-max-barskih-army-russia-1344499/. Accessed 3 July 2022.

___. "Turn It Up: Max Barskih and Ukrainian Pop Diplomacy." Interview by Stephan Rabimov. *Forbes*, 14 June 2018, www.forbes.com/sites/stephanrabimov/2018/06/14/turn-it-up-max-barskih-ukrainian-pop-diplomacy/. Accessed 3 July 2022.

"International Pop Icon Max Barskih Flies to America with Soaring New Single." *Upcoming 100*, 27 Aug. 2021, www.upcoming100.com/review-detail/1757/

international-pop-icon-max-barskih-flies-to-america-with-soaring-new-single/. Accessed 3 July 2022.

Jandová, Kristýna. "Voices of Ukraine: From Pop Star to Member of the Ukrainian Army." *Vogue CZ*, 13 May 2022, www.vogue.cz/clanek/society/kristyna-jandova/voices-of-ukrajina-z-popove-hvezdy-clenem-ukrajinske-armady. Accessed 3 July 2022.

"Max Barskih for the First Time Talked about His Uneasy Childhood: I Remember How My Brother Fought with His Father." *NewsMe*, 20 Dec. 2017, newsme.com.ua/en/showbiz/chronic/3928297/. Accessed 3 July 2022.

Robinson, Kristin. "Ukrainian Artist Max Barskih Talks Pulling Music in Russia and Debuts New Song at Billboard MusicCon." *Billboard*, 13 May 2022, www.billboard.com/music/music-news/max-barskih-ukraine-musiccon-panel-recap-1235070830/. Accessed 3 July 2022.

SELECTED WORKS

1:*Max Barskih*, 2009; *Z.Dance*, 2012; *According to Freud*, 2014; *Mists*, 2016; *7*, 2019

—Mari Rich

Jon Batiste

Born: November 11, 1986
Occupation: Musician and bandleader

Jazz pianist Jon Batiste is the house bandleader of the popular late-night television program *The Late Show with Stephen Colbert*. Batiste, who is the youngest person ever to hold such a position, leads his longtime band, Stay Human, from the piano. As he told Terry Gross for an interview with National Public Radio's *Fresh Air* (26 Sept. 2018), "I think the great thing about piano is that you can create this rhythmic momentum, and it propels you. It's like a drum. But you also have tones." Prior to and during his time at *The Late Show*, Batiste also recorded his own music, releasing critically acclaimed albums like *Social Music* (2013) and *Hollywood Africans* (2018). Centered in the jazz tradition, his music blends the sounds of his hometown of New Orleans with those of rhythm and blues, funk, and pop.

The year 2021 proved to be a banner year for Batiste. Following the release of his album *We Are* (2021) and his work on the Pixar film *Soul* (2020), he was nominated for eleven Grammy Awards, becoming the musician with the highest number of nominations that year. At the April 2022 ceremony, he took home five awards, including for Album of the Year. Of his purpose and outlook on life, Batiste told Mandalit del Barco for *NPR* (25 Dec. 2020), "It's found in the things that make us all unique and [there's] never going to be another person like you in the world, ever. You're the only one. You're one of a kind. And that's beautiful."

EARLY LIFE AND EDUCATION

Jonathan Michael Batiste was born on November 11, 1986, in New Orleans, Louisiana. He grew up just outside of New Orleans, in Kenner, Louisiana, in one of the most prominent musical families in the region. At eight years of age, he began performing with his family's band, the Batiste Brothers Band, which his father, Michael, started in 1976. Batiste sang before he played an instrument and ended up as the band's lead vocalist. However, around age ten, Batiste decided he could no longer serve in that role as he found it too daunting. He began playing percussion instruments instead, and four of his cousins who were drummers taught him the basic rhythm used in much of New Orleans music, called bamboula. At age eleven, Batiste moved to the piano at his mother's suggestion. As he told Geraldine Wyckoff in an interview for *Offbeat* (Sept. 2015), "Her intuition was right. As soon as I picked up the piano it made me feel like I had found my best friend. The piano fit in a way that made me feel some sort of spiritual connection." Two years later, Batiste was playing piano professionally, performing in clubs around New Orleans.

Batiste attended the New Orleans Center for Creative Arts, a pre-professional arts training school, and St. Augustine High School in New Orleans, where freestyle rap battles took place in the courtyard during lunch. After graduating in 2004, Batiste attended the famed Juilliard School, moving to New York City at seventeen.

EARLY MUSIC CAREER

In 2005, Batiste joined with friends he met in high school and at Julliard to form the band Stay Human. They shared their music in the streets and subways of New York, mostly

Photo by Montclair Film,
via Wikimedia Commons.

playing for free. Batiste continued to explore distinctive styles of music during this period. He discovered the music of Thelonious Monk, the jazz composer and pianist, who was creating a sound Batiste wanted to create as well. He had many other influences, including artists ranging from Bach to Nina Simone. On developing his unique musical style, he told Gross, "When I was younger, I would hear other musicians, or I would start to expand my horizons on what I'd listen to and [think] . . . I want to be like that. But you can only be what you are. And that was a lesson that I had learned just by really focusing on the things that I loved." After graduating from Julliard with his master's degree in 2011, Batiste began appearing on the HBO series *Treme*, which portrayed his real-life family in New Orleans. For three seasons (from 2011 to 2013), Batiste appeared in the show as himself and also contributed compositions to it. Meanwhile, Batiste also released his first full-length album with Stay Human, titled *Social Music* (2013). It soon earned the top spot on the Billboard jazz chart, and the band toured in venues both small and large around the world. In 2014, Batiste performed on Comedy Central's *The Colbert Report*, where he was introduced to the comic Stephen Colbert for whom he would later serve as bandleader.

While promoting *Social Music*, Batiste was hired as artistic director of Harlem's National Jazz Museum. There, he created a TED-talk style program called "Jazz Is: Now!" and other educational ventures. Asked about his vision for the museum, Batiste told Jennifer Odell in an interview for *Offbeat* (Feb. 2014) that he wished to focus "on the tradition of jazz music and how to really make it become more relevant in the eyes of younger people who don't have much exposure to it." He later added codirector of the museum to his work there.

THE LATE SHOW AND MORE

In 2015, Batiste and his band joined Stephen Colbert's new late-night talk show airing on CBS, *The Late Show with Stephen Colbert*. Colbert asked Batiste to write the theme music, giving him examples of what he did not want and praising some others, including one of Batiste's own songs. Batiste gave him three options. Describing the ultimate winner, titled "Humanism," he told Gross, "I thought [it] had that kind of feeling, that nostalgia. But it was . . . more subtle, more of something that gives you an excitement. But it's not hysterical type of excitement. It's, like, intelligent excitement." In addition, Batiste helped design a stage set that broke down barriers between the band, the host, and the audience.

During his years at *The Late Show*, Batiste took on various other music projects. In 2016, he played at the opening of the National Museum of African American History and Culture in Washington, DC. He received the 2017 American Jazz Museum Lifetime Achievement Award and the ASCAP Harry Chapin Humanitarian Award that same year. Batiste also paid tribute to composer Philip Glass at the Kennedy Center Honors in 2018, playing "Opening" from Glass's composition *Glassworks*.

In 2017, the *Atlantic* magazine invited Batiste to become its music director, a role they created for him. His interpretation of "The Battle Hymn of the Republic" became the theme song for *Radio Atlantic*, the magazine's podcast. In this role, Batiste collaborated with *Atlantic* editors on various platforms, including video, print, and live events.

HOLLYWOOD AFRICANS AND SOUL

In 2018, Batiste released the album *Hollywood Africans*; the title comes from a painting by graffiti artist Jean-Michel Basquiat. (Later that year, Batiste also began creating a Broadway musical based on Basquiat's life.) The album included sounds ranging from traditional to contemporary jazz and reached number two on the Billboard jazz chart. One of the tracks was also nominated for a Grammy for Best American Roots Performance. Speaking to his composition process, he told Gross, "It's like a gumbo. You put everything in the pot. And in the moment, you just fly. You know, after you make your 100th vat of gumbo, you get a feel for where to place these things. And it's not really contrived. It just is a spirit in a moment that you follow."

After releasing two live albums in 2019 and a collaborative work with guitarist Cory Wong called *Meditations* (2020), Batiste changed direction to work on an animated feature called *Soul* (2020). Created by Pixar, the film featured the company's first Black lead, voiced by actor Jamie Foxx, as a middle-school music teacher named Joe Gardner who dreams of performing jazz on stage. Batiste not only inspired the creators of *Soul* to create such a character, including many of Batiste's theories about jazz in the film, but he also composed and performed most of the music for the film's soundtrack. In addition, the animators modeled Gardner's hands after those of Batiste. Describing the experience to del Barco, he remarked: "I was almost in tears, because you see your essence and you think: Wow, this is the first Black Pixar lead and we're putting jazz culture out there in this massive way." Batiste won an Academy Award for Best Original Score for the film, the second Black musician, after Herbie Hancock, to do so.

THE COVID-19 PANDEMIC

During the COVID-19 pandemic in 2020, Batiste alternated between activism and creating music at home, including his work on *Soul*. With many opportunities for concerts diminished, Batiste spent more time on his own work. He also referred to the time of solitude and isolation as being a kind of spiritual hibernation. As he told Andrew Chow in an interview for *Time* (12 Apr. 2021), "I don't know if I would have done the things that I did this past year had not the rhythm of everything shifted. I don't know if it's good—but I think that anything different is good when you're creative."

In June 2020, Batiste and his band led a peaceful Black Lives Matter protest against police brutality, traveling through New York City streets while playing music. He also organized and performed in outdoor concerts during the summer of 2020, held in the wake of the murder of George Floyd, and played for essential workers at the Javits Center in New York City, which had been converted into a vaccination center. "[Music] brings people together and it's used as something to transmit wisdom from generations, to pass on traditions and give people hope," Batiste told Julia Jacobs in an interview for *The New York Times* (23 Nov. 2021). "It connects us to the sacred, the divine."

Batiste emerged from the pandemic with his second studio album, *We Are* (2021), an album that leaned more pop-heavy and received high praise from critics and fans alike. Featuring hit singles "Freedom" and "I Need You," the album also included several guest appearances by jazz greats like Mavis Staples and Trombone Shorty.

THE 2022 GRAMMY AWARDS

Changes to the Grammy nomination process, in response to criticism, resulted in a landslide of nominations for Batiste's work. While for the previous two decades, an anonymous "blue-ribbon" committee decided on the four major awards, in 2021, eleven thousand voting members of the Recording Academy made the choices instead. That made it possible for contemporary musicians like Batiste who had previously been largely ignored to receive nominations.

Batiste was nominated for eleven Grammys in seven different fields. These included classical, American roots, jazz, rhythm and blues, and music for visual media and film. His album *We Are* netted eight nominations. "I've always made an effort to show that the genres are all connected, just like people in all of our lineages are connected," Batiste told Jacobs, explaining the diversity of musical genres on the album. "It just feels so great for it to be recognized on music's biggest stage." The other three nominations were for his work on *Soul*. At the ceremony, which was delayed to April 2022 due to concerns regarding a spike in COVID-19 cases, Batiste was the biggest winner of the night, taking home five awards, including Album of the Year.

PERSONAL LIFE

Batiste married writer and cancer advocate Suleika Jaouad, whom he met at band camp as a teenager, in 2022. They live outside New York City.

SUGGESTED READING

Batiste, Jon. "'In the Moment, You Just Fly': Jon Batiste Lets Loose at the Piano." Interview by Terry Gross. *National Public Radio*, 31 Dec. 2018, www.npr.org/2018/12/31/680666330/in-the-moment-you-just-fly-jon-batiste-lets-loose-at-the-piano. Accessed 20 Jan. 2022.

___. "Jon Batiste on His 11 Grammy Nominations: 'I'm So Over the Moon.'" Interview by Julia Jacobs. *The New York Times*, 23 Nov. 2021, www.nytimes.com/2021/11/23/arts/music/jon-batiste-grammy-nominations.html. Accessed 1 Feb. 2022.

___. "Jon Batiste on His Oscar-Nominated *Soul* Score and Being a 'Black Pop Star Making Black Pop Masterpieces.'" Interview by Andrew R. Chow. *Time*, 12 Apr. 2021, time.com/5953464/jon-batiste-soul-interview/. Accessed 26 Jan. 2022.

___. "Jon Batiste on the Pandemic's Impact on Touring, the Creative Arts—and His Music." Interview by Jeff Slate. *The Wall Street Journal*, 12 Dec. 2021, www.wsj.com/articles/jon-batiste-on-pandemic-impact-on-music-touring-creative-arts-11638826140. Accessed 2 Feb. 2022.

___. "Jon Batiste Talks Back." Interview by Geraldine Wyckoff. *Offbeat*, vol. 28, no. 10, Sept. 2015, pp. 69–70. *Academic Search Ultimate*, search.ebscohost.com/login.aspx?direct=true&db=asn&AN=112225768. Accessed 29 Jan. 2022.

___. "Jon Batiste Talks Back." Interview by Jennifer Odell. *Offbeat*, vol. 27, no. 2, Feb. 2014, pp. 65–66. *Academic Search Ultimate*, search.ebscohost.com/login.aspx?direct=true&db=asn&AN=94140217. Accessed 7 Apr. 2022.

Del Barco, Mandalit. "In 'Soul,' Jon Batiste's Music Helps Bring Pixar's First Black Lead to Life." *Morning Edition*, National Public Radio, 25 Dec. 2020, www.npr.org/2020/12/25/948998059/in-soul-jon-batistes-music-helps-bring-pixars-first-black-lead-to-life. Accessed 20 Jan. 2022.

SELECTED WORKS

Social Music, 2013; *Hollywood Africans*, 2018; *Soul*, 2020; *We Are*, 2021

—*Judy Johnson*

Karen Bender

Born: ---
Occupation: Novelist

Karen Bender is an American novelist best known for her short-story collection titled *Refund* (2015).

EARLY LIFE AND EDUCATION

Karen Bender was born in Los Angeles, California. She has a sister, Aimee, who is also a writer. She grew up in Los Angeles but has also lived in New York City and Iowa City, Iowa.

Bender recalls her earliest writing as stemming from a traumatic event in her childhood. When she was six years old, she was attending a child's birthday party and was struck in the head with a rock. She bled profusely and was placed at the center of the table where the birthday cake sat. Bender remembers adults clamoring around her and trying to keep blood from getting on the birthday cake. She says the turmoil of the event led her to begin writing about it while recovering at home with a large bandage on her head. She believes her innate response to the experience was to ascribe a narrative logic to the chaotic nature of the incident.

She continued to write, studying creative writing at school. She earned a Bachelor of Science (BS) degree at University of California, Los Angeles, and a Master of Fine Arts (MFA) degree at the University of Iowa. While living in Iowa City, she also attended the Iowa Writers' Workshop.

CAREER

Bender suffered from a period of intense anxiety and dropped out of college for several months at age nineteen. She lived with her grandmother and worked at a mall pizzeria. During this time, she learned of the struggles of a mentally challenged aunt and observed her grandmother's worry. She began to develop her first novel from these observations.

Bender's writing career advanced in the 1990s with the publication of her short fiction in various literary magazines and anthologies. She won the 1997 Rona Jaffe Writers' Award, recognizing women in the field of writing. She published her first novel, *Like Normal People*, in 2000. She described the process of turning the story of her aunt's hardships as both compassionate and opportunistic, likening the writing experience to that of the rock that had struck her head.

In 2002, Bender was awarded the National Endowment for the Arts grant for prose writing. At this time, Bender announced she would use the funds to write a new collection of stories titled "Anything for Money." She did not release the collection for over a decade.

In 2007, Bender teamed up with Nina de Gramont to coedit the nonfiction anthology *Choice: True Stories of Birth, Contraception, Infertility, Adoption, Single Parenthood, and Abortion*. The book includes twenty-two personal essays from a range of writers relating their experiences with all forms of reproductive choices and contraception.

A Town of Empty Rooms, Bender's second novel, was published in 2013. The novel was inspired by her family's relocation to Wilmington, North Carolina, from New York City, and their adjustment to being one of the few Jewish families in a Bible Belt town. The book focuses on the Shine family, a Jewish family who moves from New York to South Carolina, and how they navigate the cultural dissonance they experience in their new home.

Bender's work has dealt with socioeconomic issues that face American citizens, including income inequality and economic recession in the decade following the September 11, 2001, terror attacks in New York. The short-story collection that was originally intended to be released as "Anything for Money" was published in 2015 as *Refund*, which centers on these issues, following its characters as they seek to build their future amid economic hardship.

Refund was a finalist for the National Book Award for Fiction. The stories in *Refund* evolved over the years since its inception in 2002. A story with the collection's original title appears in the book. The book was also shortlisted for the Frank O'Connor International Short Story Prize.

In addition to her writing career, Bender has had a lengthy career in academia. She has taught at Hollins University, the University of North Carolina, Antioch Los Angeles, Tunghai University in Taiwan, Chatham University, the Aspen Writer's Institute, and the Iowa Summer Writer's Festival. She also taught fiction at the Writer's Voice program in New York City. Her writing draws largely from personal experience and observations about American culture. She has cited American fiction writers John Cheever and Richard Yates as influences of her style of writing and character development.

AWARDS, ACCOLADES, AND PUBLICATIONS
In addition to her National Endowment for the Arts and being a finalist for the National Book Award, Bender has won two Pushcart Prizes honoring small-press publications. Bender's short fiction has been featured in many major publications, including the *Harvard Review*, *The New Yorker*, and *Ploughshares*. She has also been anthologized in the *Best American Short Stories* and *Best American Mystery Stories* collections.

PERSONAL LIFE
Bender lives in Wilmington, North Carolina, with her husband, Robert Anthony Siegel. She met Siegel, a fellow novelist, at the Iowa Writers Workshop. They have two children.

SUGGESTED READING
Bender, Karen E. "The Accidental Writer." *The New York Times*, 25 Jan. 2013, www.nytimes.com/2013/01/27/books/review/the-accidental-writer.html. Accessed 24 Nov. 2021.

____. Like Normal People, Houghton Mifflin Harcourt; First Edition, 2000.

____. "A Q&A with Karen E. Bender, Author of the 2015 National Book Award Fiction Finalist *Refund*." Interview by Dory Athey, *Counterpoint Press*, Counterpoint, 14 Oct. 2015, www.counterpointpress.com/2015/10/. Accessed 24 Nov. 2021.

____. Refund: Stories, Counterpoint, First Edition. 2015.

____. "Talking with Karen E. Bender about *A Town of Empty Rooms*." Interview by David L. Ulin. *Los Angeles Times*, 7 Feb. 2013, www.latimes.com/books/jacketcopy/la-et-jc-talking-with-karen-e-bender-about-a-town-of-empty-rooms-20130123-story.html.

___. A Town of Empty Rooms, Counterpoint, 2013.

___. "Wonderful Strangeness: An Interview with Karen E. Bender." Interview by Kelsey Leach. *Fourth River*, Chatham University, 8 Dec. 2018, www.thefourthriver.com/blog/2019/3/8/wonderful-strangeness-an-interview-with-karen-e-bender. Accessed 24 Nov. 2021.

—*Richard Means*

Justin Bibb

Born: April 26, 1987
Occupation: Politician

On June 5, 2020, the *Cleveland Plain Dealer* published an op-ed in the wake of nationwide protests for racial justice over the murder of George Floyd by then members of the Minneapolis Police Department. "We need urgency. We can't just talk," it stated. "If the coronavirus pandemic and the recent protests have taught us anything, it's that Cleveland's comeback can't just be rooted in investments in brick-and-mortar projects. It must be rooted in investments in people." The author went on to describe the myriad problems the city was facing as one of the poorest and racially segregated in the nation before concluding, "Together, we can build a better version of Cleveland. We can be a leader if we make hard choices and act now. Cleveland can't wait."

These galvanizing words belonged to Justin M. Bibb, founder of the civic tech and entrepreneurship nonprofit Cleveland Can't Wait. Thirty-three years old at the time of his op-ed's publication, Bibb was ramping up his campaign to be elected Cleveland's fifty-eighth mayor. On January 3, 2022, just a year and a half later, he was sworn in as mayor in his most beloved childhood haven: the East 131st Street branch of the Cleveland Public Library.

In addition to being from a blue-collar Black family who witnessed the inequity and hardships endured by Cleveland's Black residents firsthand, Bibb is tech-savvy and brings eclectic professional experience with him to office having worked in nonprofits, start-ups, and the banking industry. Although these qualities have earned him a lot of criticism from his detractors, Bibb has remained undeterred. "When people are scared of something, they try to tear it down," he explained to Seth A. Richardson for the *Cleveland Plain Dealer* (11 Oct. 2021).

EARLY LIFE

Justin Morris Bibb was born on April 26, 1987, in Cleveland, Ohio, to Donald Lee Bibb and Charlene Nichols Bibb. Throughout Bibb's childhood, his father worked both as a firefighter and a policeman while his mother took on odd jobs before eventually becoming a social worker. The couple divorced when Bibb was four years old, at which time his father moved to nearby Shaker Heights. Meanwhile, Bibb and his mother moved in with his grandmother and other family members in Mount Pleasant—a neighborhood in the southeastern part of Cleveland that Bibb described to Brian Albrecht for Case Western's *Think Magazine* (1 Mar. 2022) as "tough a tough part of the city, at the height of the crack epidemic" where 60 percent of the population lived in poverty during the early 1990s.

Although his neighborhood was dangerous growing up, Bibb's family worked hard to keep him safe. To prevent drug dealers from gathering outside their house because it was on a corner lot, Bibb's grandmother collaborated with the police and organized a neighborhood block club. Additionally, his mother kept him busy with sports and music. After attending kindergarten at a public school in Cleveland, his mother sent him to Cedar Hill Christian School, a private Christian school in Cleveland Heights. In sixth grade, he decided he wanted to go to public school in Shaker Heights

Academics came easily to the young Bibb, but his transition from parochial school to a public middle school was a challenge because he did not fit in and was bullied by his classmates. "There weren't a lot of Black kids like me at Shaker at the time," Bibb said to Nick Castele for *Ideastream Public Media* (20 Oct. 2021). "I didn't know what rap really was. I don't know what Abercrombie and Fitch was. I had no idea. I was completely sheltered, so it was a culture shock for me." Eventually, his father pulled him from the school and enrolled him in the private Orange Christian Academy instead. When reflecting on the psychological and physical pain that he endured from his peers during this chapter of his life, Bibb told Richardson, "It only enhanced my identity of what I wanted to be. I wanted to be a

Photo by Michaelangelo's Photography,
via Wikimedia Commons

successful, well-credentialed Black man. That was my goal because that's what my parents raised me to be. I'm happy for the year and a half I spent there, because I think it really affirmed the path I'm on now, to be honest. It gave me the persistence I needed to survive."

Indeed, Bibb had a very clear idea of the life that he wanted for himself: one where he could be in a position to help others. In the summer between tenth and eleventh grade he fell in love with politics after being selected by Junior Statesmen of America to attend a two-month program at Georgetown University. Finally, Bibb had also become a great admirer of the man who was mayor throughout most of his childhood: Michael R. White, a Cleveland-born African American politician. White was beloved by the city for the many improvements that he made during his twelve-year tenure including building the Rock & Roll Hall of Fame and bringing the Browns back as the city's football team. By the time Bibb graduated from Trinity High School in 2005, he knew he wanted to be the mayor of Cleveland one day, too.

EDUCATION AND EARLY CAREER

In 2005, Bibb enrolled in American University (AU) in Washington, DC, where he majored in urban studies. An ambitious student, he found ways to push himself closer toward his political goals. He became president of his pre-law fraternity, Phi Alpha Delta, and, in 2007, he interned for then US senator Barack Obama. When reflecting on this formative experience years later, Bibb told Albrecht that working for Obama taught him "that your aim in life should be to do something, not just be anything. The lesson there is that it's not really about the title but about the impact; that everybody can find a way of serving."

As a junior, Bibb earned a scholarship to study public policy abroad, which he completed at the prestigious London School of Economics. When he returned to the States the following year, he started a nonprofit that provided service-learning programs for students. For his leadership in this endeavor and others, he won AU's Bruce Hughes Service Award.

Bibb was still an undergraduate when he met Jim Clifton, chief executive officer of the consulting firm Gallup, who was impressed with him. "I could just tell that Justin had unlimited potential," Clifton said, as quoted by Richardson. Clifton hired Bibb as an associate partner before he graduated from AU in 2009. As he continued to work for Gallup off and on over the next twelve years, Clifton became one of Bibb's most influential mentors.

In 2011, Bibb returned to Ohio to work for Cuyahoga County as a special assistant for education and economic development under county executive Ed FitzGerald. Bibb was vice president for corporate strategy at the private equity firm KGB Inc. in New York City for two years before returning to Cleveland to attend Case Western's law and business management schools simultaneously. His decision to pursue both a JD and an MBA stemmed from his desire to better understand city management responsibilities where the two fields intersected, like developing legislation for creating economic development tax credits.

While at Case Western, Bibb cofounded Hack Cleveland—an initiative that encouraged the creation of civic technology to help solve the social, economic, and judicial inequity that the city's Black residents were facing. Developed in response to a twelve-year-old Black boy named Tamir Rice being shot and killed by Timothy Loehmann, a twenty-six-year-old White Cleveland police officer, the initiative succeeded in earning public attention.

Throughout graduate school and immediately after, Bibb went back to working at Gallup, serving as a senior consultant and head of global cities from 2015 to 2018. After graduating with both degrees in 2018, he then worked at KeyBank from January 2019 to May 2020 as a vice president of corporate strategy. In 2019, he also took on the position of chief technology officer for Urbanova, a nonprofit designed to help mid-size cities develop and implement "smart" solutions for measuring and tracking their civic services. During this time, he launched Cleveland Can't Wait—a nonprofit that aimed to revitalize Cleveland through civic technology and entrepreneurship. He would continue working for both Cleveland Can't Wait and Urbanova throughout his mayoral campaign.

MAYORAL CAMPAIGN

In January 2021, Bibb, a Democrat, announced he was running for mayor of Cleveland, a position that is officially nonpartisan but which had been held by Democrats since 1990. Six months later, he had earned the three thousand signatures necessary to get on the primary ballot. His campaign focused on his ability to bring urgency to Cleveland's problems, collaborative governing, and a fresh, modern take on political leadership. He officially became one of seven candidates on the ballot on June 16, 2021.

Bibb's campaign was grassroots in many ways, and he spent so much time going door to door in an effort to listen to the voters and build name recognition that he lost ten pounds in the process. Some of his critics felt that he was cutting in front of more experienced candidates in a city where politicians traditionally have paid their dues in other unglamorous areas of the government before running for mayor, while other critics pointed out that he had never spent more than two years at each job. When asked how he felt about this by Richardson, Bibb said, "That's the job of being a mayor. You've got to wear multiple hats. All the experiences I've had to date have been a great proving ground to get the experience I need."

In the months leading up to the primaries, Bibb's name recognition grew thanks to endorsements from the city's main paper, the *Cleveland Plain Dealer*, several major unions, Bibb's own childhood hero—former mayor Michael R. White—and another former mayor, Jane Campbell. The mayoral primary election was held on September 14, 2021. To the media's surprise, Bibb came in first place, beating former Cleveland mayor, member of Congress, and presidential candidate Dennis Kucinich, who had been polling ahead. With the most votes, Bibb and candidate Kevin Kelley were sent to the November general election. There, Bibb handily beat Kelley with 63 percent of the vote and twelve out of the city's seventeen wards.

MAYOR OF CLEVELAND

Bibb's tenure as the city's fifty-eighth mayor got off to a rocky start. Less than two weeks after he was sworn into office, a massive snowstorm hit the city while he was out of town for a mayoral conference. Clevelanders angrily held him accountable for the fact that there were not enough snowplows or workers to help clear the roads. Bibb took responsibility for the criticism, however, and when the next storm hit there was a new online snowplow tracking system, Snowplow Tracker, that better deployed plows and offered citizens an online interface with updates on which streets had been cleared and when a plow was coming to their neighborhood.

In a newscast with Danita Harris for *News 5* (13 Apr. 2022), Bibb reflected on his first hundred days in office and how his efforts thus far to change Cleveland's status as one of the poorest, most crime-ridden cities in the country had been criticized by many of his constituents. "Voters have a right to call me out," Bibb told Harris, adding that he is the kind of person to listen to criticism and use it to make improvements. "I'm trying to move Cleveland into the twenty-first century, and that might be hard for folks to understand, but I think in the future, folks will look back and say this was the moment where we truly turned the tide."

SELECTED READING

Albrecht, Brian. "A Breath of Fresh Air." *Think Magazine*, 1 Mar. 2022, case.edu/think/spring2022/a-breath-of-fresh-air.html. Accessed 8 July 2022.

Bibb, Justin. "Cleveland Can't Wait for a Better Tomorrow: Justin Bibb." *The Cleveland Plain Dealer*, 5 June 2020, www.cleveland.com/

opinion/2020/06/cleveland-cant-wait-for-a-better-tomorrow-justin-bibb.html. Accessed 6 July 2022.

Brown, Marcia. "The Fixer." *The American Prospect*, 31 Mar. 2022, prospect.org/politics/the-fixer-justin-bibb/. Accessed 6 July 2022.

Castele, Nick. "After Jackson: Cleveland's Next Mayor—Episode 14: Justin Bibb." *Ideastream Public Media*, 20 Oct. 2021, www.ideastream.org/news/after-jackson-clevelands-next-mayor-episode-14-justin-m-bibb. Accessed 13 July 2022.

Harris, Danita. "Q-and-A: Mayor Justin Bibb Looks Back on First 100 Days in Office." *News 5 Cleveland*, 18 Apr. 2022, www.news5cleveland.com/news/local-news/cleveland-metro/q-and-a-mayor-justin-bibb-looks-back-on-first-100-days-in-office. Accessed 14 July 2022.

Naymik, Mark. "Cleveland Mayoral Candidate Justin Bibb's Resume Full of Big Job Titles and Frequent Job Changes." *WYKC Studios*, 12 Oct. 2021, www.wkyc.com/article/news/politics/elections/cleveland-mayoral-election/justin-bibb-resume-cleveland-mayoral-candidate-election/95-1a456d4a-d1e7-45f8-a43c-585ffd3f91c1. Accessed 6 July 2022.

Richardson, Seth. "A Closer Look at Justin Bibb: How a Political Newcomer Paved a Potential Path to Cleveland City Hall." *The Plain Dealer*, 22 Oct. 2021, www.cleveland.com/cityhall/2021/10/a-closer-look-at-justin-bibb-how-a-political-newcomer-paved-a-potential-path-to-city-hall.html. Accessed 6 July 2022.

—*Emily E. Turner*

Black Pumas

Occupation: Psychedelic soul band

ERIC BURTON

Born: October 7, 1989
Occupation: Songwriter, vocalist

ADRIAN QUESADA

Born: May 3, 1977
Occupation: Guitarist, producer

The year 2020 proved to be a busy year for the American psychedelic soul group Black Pumas. While most of the world was laying low due to the COVID-19 pandemic, Black Pumas were in the middle of a meteoric rise to success. After releasing their eponymous debut album in 2019, the band found themselves earning millions of plays on streaming platforms, multiple late-night talk show performances, and a Grammy nomination for best new artist. Suddenly, the Austin, Texas–based duo that began as nothing more than a casual collaboration between two artists was something of a cultural sensation. Asked to perform at such high-profile events as President Joe Biden's 2021 inauguration, they sought to use their growing fame to emphasize some positive core values. "One of our goals is unity in a time when there's a lot of divisiveness," guitarist Adrian Quesada told Roisin O'Connor in an interview for the *Independent* (23 Jan.2020). "We're not trying to make a political statement, but you look at our live show and you see these people from all different backgrounds and ethnicities and genders—it's about inclusiveness."

EARLY LIFE AND CAREER OF ADRIAN QUESADA

Black Pumas would not exist if it were not for its seasoned guitarist and producer Adrian Quesada. Considered one of the most important figures of Austin's music scene in the early twenty-first century, he played an enormous role in reinventing Latin music for new generations of listeners. Adrian Quesada was born on May 3, 1977, in Laredo, Texas, a city on the Texas–Mexico border. Despite his parents' lack of musical interest, he felt drawn to the artform at an early age. His father, a truck driver, tried to nurture his son's love of music by encouraging him to learn piano, but the young Quesada thought the instrument was uncool. Eventually they compromised, and Quesada began taking flamenco guitar lessons at age thirteen.

While growing up, Quesada was exposed to the traditional bolero rhythms of South Texas. He also became obsessed with hip-hop and would watch the show *Yo! MTV Raps* after school every day. As he got older, he discovered a deep love for funk music and alternative rock as well, and explored those sounds on his guitar.

By the time he graduated from high school in 1995, Quesada knew that he wanted to be a musician. After moving to Austin to attend the University of Texas (UT), he continued to stay close to friends from his hometown, hanging out mostly with other musicians who shared his love for both punk rock and traditional cumbia music, a style of Latin music featuring drums, flutes, accordions, and other instruments from diverse cultures. Quesada graduated from UT in the late 1990s with a degree in art and music history.

Jamming with his friends led to the development of several genre-blending Latin bands, including Brownout, Ocote Soul Sounds, Echocentrics, and Grupo Fantasma. A nine-piece Latin funk orchestra, Grupo Fantasma became popular enough to gain national acclaim in the mid-aughts. They performed with music icon Prince in 2007 and won a Grammy for best Latin rock album in 2010 for their fifth studio album, *El Existential*.

Over the next decade, Quesada continued to be prolific in his output of music with experimental sounds that paid homage to his favorite genres, including funk, soul, and cumbia. However, as time went on, he retreated further into the studio to focus on producing other people's music. "I'm not the biggest, flashiest performer," Quesada told Nancy Flores for the *Austin American-Statesman* (10 June 2011). "It's not my strong point." It seemed his time on stage was winding down—until he met Eric Burton.

EARLY LIFE AND CAREER OF ERIC BURTON

Eric Burton was born on October 7, 1989, in California's San Fernando Valley to a mother who was a dancer and a father who left when Burton was very young. He and his three siblings grew up in a family that was inherently nomadic thanks to his maternal grandmother, Mary, a missionary who had ministered all over the world. Reflecting on the constant change that defined his formative years, Burton told Kahron Spearman for the *Austin Chronicle* (21 June 2019), "If I could attribute a character or a vehicle to my family, we're like jets, built to move, to fly."

As a child, Burton was influenced by his family's creative nature. Much of his love for music came from his uncle Steve Harrison, who served as a father figure to Burton and his siblings and encouraged them to sing in the church choir and make up melodies for fun. At one point, Harrison recorded his own Christian

contemporary album and brought a young Burton with him to the studio. When Burton was a teenager in 2006, his uncle was offered an opportunity to mission at an orphanage in Alamogordo, New Mexico, so the family moved there. In New Mexico, Burton found himself becoming increasingly interested in singing and performing. He received a guitar on his eighteenth birthday from his uncle and began writing songs.

After a brief stint at New Mexico State University, where he studied early education and music composition, Burton returned to Los Angeles to help his mother, who had been suffering with health problems. He also used this time to attend open mics and busk on the Santa Monica Pier. "It was definitely a hustle and grind to wake up every day to take two buses and two trains just to get to the Santa Monica Pier," he explained to Bryan C. Parker for *Austin Monthly* (1 June 2020). "But it was the perfect place for busking."

In 2015, Burton teamed up with two friends who were also buskers and toured as a band across the southwestern and western United States. Though it was a joyful adventure that allowed him to grow musically, the band eventually parted ways. Burton ended up in Austin, and decided to stay there to pursue his solo career. He began making a stir in the city's thriving music scene, and caught the attention of a producer named Bryan Ray.

FORMING BLACK PUMAS

In 2017, Quesada was working on several tracks for a soul-influenced project but could not find anyone to record the vocals. When he asked friend Bryan Ray if he knew anyone, Ray immediately gave him Burton's contact information.

Burton had become so busy playing gigs that he completely missed the email that Quesada sent him in August 2017. When he finally went through his inbox weeks later, he dropped everything he was doing to call Quesada and sing him a song he had been working on called "Fire." Quesada was so impressed by Burton's impromptu audition that he invited him to his studio. There, the two men began tracking songs together and noticed that they had a complementary style. In late 2017, they began performing gigs in the Austin area.

On February 8, 2018, the duo performed at Austin club C-Boy's Heart and Soul to a rapturous reception. Quesada was blown away both by Burton's electric stage presence as well as the audience's response to it. According to Burton himself, while performing he sought to "take people to church," drawing on the feelings of love, connection, and being alive that he had witnessed as a child when the parishioners at his family's church would let themselves enter a different kind of consciousness while listening to sermons.

Quesada and Burton decided to keep performing together in Austin. It was clear that they had tapped into something special together, as shows started selling out and agents began approaching them about representation. Soon they began opening for the soul band St. Paul and the Broken Bones, playing in much larger venues before they had even released a single. Explaining what made their musical alchemy come together so quickly in those early days, Burton told Spencer Taylor for the *Las Cruces Sun News* (3 Jan. 2020), "It's Adrian's tight woven production and my songwriting and plaintive voice. People really enjoy the live performances. I think the live performances are our selling point for sure."

Meanwhile, for Quesada, much of what made their collaboration as a duo work from the beginning was the difference in their personalities. "He complements me because he has a way of being present, fully immersed," Quesada told Spearman. "I'm thinking about yesterday and tomorrow, and Eric is here, right now. You can throw him right in, and he will come through in a way [where I would be] overanalyzing. So I feel that's the balance, kind of a yin and yang, because both of us teeter on the edge."

After a trip to Mexico, Quesada returned to Austin and somewhat arbitrarily suggested they name the band "Black Pumas" because he liked the iconography and thought it projected a tough image. Burton agreed, and the band was officially formed.

DEBUT ALBUM RELEASED

Black Pumas' debut album was released on June 21, 2019. Titled *Black Pumas*, it comprised ten tracks, including the singles "Colors," "Black Moon Rising," and "Fire." The album received overwhelmingly positive reviews, with many critics extolling the depth, texture, and technicality of Quesada's musicianship as well as Burton's introspective songwriting and

powerful voice. For many listeners, a large part of the album's appeal was the way its sound seemed transported from a bygone time. As Stephen Thomas Erlewine wrote in his review for *Pitchfork* (1 July 2019), "The Austin-based duo don't shy away from signifiers of the past, conjuring the sounds of the late 1960s and early 1970s without succumbing to pure nostalgic pandering."

Burton, who drew comparisons to the likes of soul music icons Otis Redding and Al Green, acknowledged that the Pumas took much of their inspiration from that era. "Soul music is very central. It's by people who feel a certain way about their existence—they might not feel as accepted," he explained to O'Connor. "Adrian and I consider ourselves as sincere as possible when it comes to experiencing life today, as Americans, with the backgrounds that we come from." The album peaked at number eighty-six on the Billboard Top 200 chart. The following year, the band released a deluxe version of the album, featuring live cuts and new material.

INTERNATIONAL FAME

Thanks to the well-received release of their debut album, the duo found the momentum of their success growing steadily. After performing at the Austin-based music festival South by Southwest in early 2019, they received the Best New Band trophy at the Austin Music Awards. Then, in November of that year, they were nominated for a Best New Artist Grammy Award, up against other artists who had sold many more albums than they had. "I don't even know how we made it onto [the list]," Burton remarked to David Browne in an interview for *Rolling Stone* (21 Jan. 2020). "We feel like this is a battle against a bunch of Goliaths. It really is kind of mind-boggling."

Soon, their single "Colors"—which Burton had written over a decade earlier while living in New Mexico—had been streamed more than 100 million times on YouTube, and concerts in both the United States and Europe began to sell out. When the world shut down in 2020 because of the COVID-19 pandemic many of their tour dates were canceled, but this did not stop the band. They went on to perform on *The Tonight Show Starring Jimmy Fallon*, *Late Night with Seth Meyers*, and other talk shows. That fall, Black Pumas recorded *Capitol Cuts: Live from Studio A* at the famed Los Angeles-based studio. The album was recorded live direct to acetate—meaning it was initially only available on vinyl—and contained eight songs, including a seven-minute version of "Colors." (The album was not released until 2021.) In November 2020, the band received three more Grammy nominations: "Colors" was nominated for two Grammys, including record of the year, and the deluxe edition of *Black Pumas* was nominated for album of the year.

In January 2021, Black Pumas took part in President Joe Biden's inauguration primetime event called "Celebrating America." The band performed their hit "Colors" virtually from Austin. Later that year, they were nominated for two additional Grammys—best rock performance and best rock album—for *Capitol Cuts*, bringing their total to six Grammy nominations. As the live music industry began opening back up, the band began touring extensively. They also started work on a second album in 2021.

While the critical accolades Black Pumas received were not new for the more seasoned Quesada, Burton in particular enjoyed the newfound fame. As he remarked to Taylor, "I'm fortunate to do this music thing and not be obligated to any other job. Looking back almost moves me to tears because I spent a lot of time struggling to focus."

PERSONAL LIFE

Quesada and his wife, Celeste, have two children together. He continues to live in Austin, Texas, where he built a boutique music studio called Electric Deluxe Recorders attached to his home. He released a solo album that pays homage to Cuban ballads titled *Boleros Psicodélicos* in 2022.

Burton settled in Austin as well.

SUGGESTED READING

Erlewine, Stephen Thomas. "Black Pumas." Review of *Black Pumas*, by Black Pumas. *Pitchfork*, 1 July 2019, pitchfork.com/reviews/albums/black-pumas-black-pumas/. Accessed 13 June 2022.

Flores, Nancy. "Adrian Quesada, with Four Eclectic Bands, Helps Put Austin's Latin Scene on the Map." *Austin American-Statesman*, 10 June 2011, www.austin360.com/story/entertainment/music/2011/06/10/adrian-quesada-with-four-eclectic/6661647007/. Accessed 12 June 2022.

Parker, Bryan C. "The Wild Rise of the Black Pumas." *Austin Monthly*, June 2020, www.austinmonthly.com/the-wild-rise-of-the-black-pumas/. Accessed 12 June 2022.

Quesada, Adrian. "Black Pumas: 'We're Not Trying to Make a Political Statement.'" Interview by Roisin O'Connor. *The Independent*, 23 Jan. 2020, www.independent.co.uk/arts-entertainment/music/features/black-pumas-interview-eric-burton-adrian-quesada-album-grammys-best-new-artist-a9296311.html. Accessed 12 June 2022.

Quesada, Adrian, and Eric Burton. "Black Pumas: Rise of a Psychedelic-Soul Force." Interview by David Browne. *Rolling Stone*, 21 Jan. 2020, www.rollingstone.com/music/music-features/black-pumas-interview-grammys-935802/. Accessed 14 June 2022

Spearman, Kahron. "Black Pumas Bring Down the Hammer behind Powerhouse Singer Eric Burton." *The Austin Chronicle*, 21 June 2019, www.austinchronicle.com/music/2019-06-21/black-pumas-bring-down-the-hammer-behind-powerhouse-singer-eric-burton/. Accessed 10 June 2022.

Taylor, Spencer. "Movers and Shakers 2020: Grammy Nominee Eric Burton Honed His Musicianship in Las Cruces." *Las Cruces Sun News*, 3 Jan. 2020, www.lcsun-news.com/story/news/local/2020/01/03/black-pumas-eric-burton-grammy-nominee-honed-music-las-cruces/2760834001/. Accessed 12 June 2022.

—*Emily E. Turner*

Radha Blank

Born: September 24, 1976
Occupation: Actor and filmmaker

In 2020, Radha Blank became one of the most talked about filmmakers at the Sundance Film Festival after winning the festival's Dramatic Directing Award for her debut film, *The Forty-Year-Old Version*. When Netflix bought the distribution rights soon afterwards, the media began touting Blank as an anomaly for breaking into the industry "later" in life as a woman in her forties. For Blank, however, these designations could not have been further from the truth. Not only had she been writing and rapping since she was a child growing up in New York

City, but she had been working in television for years before filming *The Forty-Year-Old Version*.

Indeed, when examining Blank's trajectory, it becomes clear that her sudden rise to attention was backed by a long, dedicated history of creation marked by an unwillingness to compromise on the kind of art she wanted to make. For years, powerful gatekeepers had rejected her work because it did not present the Black experience in the typical Hollywood way. This did not deter Blank, however, whose beliefs on the purpose of art have always been unshakeable. "I'm not an outsider. I see myself as the people I'm writing about, but there're things that separate us. To understand those things, I have to be open," she explained in an interview with Sandra E. Garcia for the *New York Times* (21 Apr. 2022). "That's what distinguishes one artist from the next—the level of honesty with the message that's being given to them. Being an artist is also knowing that the art is bigger than you. It ain't really about you; it's about the person who experiences it."

EARLY LIFE AND EDUCATION

Radha Blank was born on September 24, 1976, in Brooklyn, a borough of New York City, into a family of creatives. Her father, Roger Blank, was a jazz drummer while her mother, Carol, was a painter and illustrator. Although both were talented and committed to their respective crafts, they struggled to make ends meet for Radha and her older brother, Ravi. As such, her father often had to take plumbing jobs while her mother split her time creating art with teaching. While growing up poor came with challenges, it also gave Blank an understanding of how creativity and ingenuity can flourish in the toughest of circumstances. "I saw my parents struggle. . . . As much as they struggled, they did it with such artistic flair," she stated in an interview with Erica Blount Danois (27 Feb. 2016) for *The Shadow League*. "Everything we did we did creatively. When the lights went out, my father figured out how to get electricity out of the streetlight. I feel like they were like my first lesson on how to create art or how to do things creatively even through all of that struggling." Blank's parents also taught her about the importance of art and how it enriches people's lives. Her mother demonstrated this by painting murals in children's hospitals and teaching art classes to everyone she could, including underserved

populations such as the deaf community, older adults, and Brazilian immigrants living in favela shanty towns.

Indeed, Blank's mother played an especially important role in her formative years. A cinephile, she introduced Blank to a wide range of filmmakers and always encouraged her daughter to find different ways to express herself. When Blank was eight and brought home a science-fiction story she had written in school about African Americans escaping racism on Earth by starting a new colony in space, her mother told her that she would be a great writer one day. She also encouraged Blank's interest in rapping. When Blank was thirteen, her mother showed her rapper and actor Queen Latifah performing on television to prove that Blank could one day do the same.

Hip-hop would ultimately become an important part of Blank's writing and artistry. "I've been rhyming since I was about ten years old," Blank told Tambay Obenson for *Indiewire* (13 Oct. 2020). "I do feel like hip-hop as an art form, you kind of have permission to brag, to live in a place of bravado and just kind of speak the truth in ways that we wouldn't ordinarily do."

When Blank was fifteen her parents divorced, and she and Ravi moved with their mother to the New York borough of Harlem. Determined not to struggle like her parents had, Blank initially decided that she would ignore her artistic inclinations and study business in school instead. While enrolled at City College, however, she discovered theater and was drawn into playwriting.

EARLY CAREER

After graduating from City College in 1997, Blank sought out acting gigs, performed standup comedy, and continued to write plays. To make ends meet, she worked as a teacher. In the early 2000s she broke into television by writing five episodes of the children's show *The Backyardigans* (2004–06) and the Nick Jr. cartoon short *Maya the Indian Princess* (2005).

In 2008, Blank was accepted into the prestigious Public Theater's Emerging Writers Group program. By the time she had completed the program she had written twelve plays, but could not find anyone to produce them. Blank explained to Alexis Soloski for the *New York Times* (8 Oct. 2020) that she would often leave meetings with producers crying because they wanted content quite different from what she created: "I wouldn't write the version of Black life that the gatekeepers value. I didn't do poverty porn. I didn't do war-torn Africa. I didn't do period pieces where people would tap dance and sing."

In 2011, Blank was able to get one play produced and staged: *Seed.* The 2010 recipient of the National Endowment of the Arts New Play Development Award, *Seed* follows a burnt-out, Harlem-based social worker named Anne struggling to navigate her career and the death of her mother. The play received mixed reviews, with some critics extolling Blank's use of hip-hop culture and verse whereas others dismissing it as "low-budget." Despite selling out its run, the play was not produced again.

Two years later, after being fired from a screenwriting job, Blank decided to create a web series about reinventing herself as a rapper named RadhaMUSprime. When her mother suddenly died, however, she found herself overwhelmed with grief and decided not to shoot the series. Several months later, a friend invited her to put on a solo show at the performance space JACK in Brooklyn and Blank accepted, hoping that expressing herself on stage would help her grieve. There she debuted *RadhaMUSprime: the 40-Year-Old Version, a Mixtape.* Essentially a hip-hop cabaret show, it allowed Blank to explore her experiences with failure while approaching the age of forty, as well as her penchant for younger men. It sparked something in her audience and so she continued performing it all over New York and later even in places as far-flung as Norway.

Around 2015 Blank relocated to Los Angeles, California, and was subsequently invited to the writers' room for the Netflix original series *The Get Down* (2016–17), which explores the rise of hip hop during the 1980s in the Bronx. Although the show produced only one season, it helped Blank get work on other television shows with primarily Black casts. In 2015, she wrote a well-received mid-season episode of the musical drama *Empire.* She then served as producer for director Spike Lee's comedy series *She's Got to Have It,* based on his 1986 film of the same name, writing three of the show's episodes between 2017 and 2019. Describing how she initially found the transition from playwriting to television writing, she told *The Shadow League,* "Working for television is very

much about collaboration. I have to check my ego. I am used to being referred to based on my work. Having to shift from this solo storyteller where I am sharing the work, sharing the burden, sharing the shine."

THE FORTY-YEAR-OLD VERSION

In addition to writing for television in the late 2010s, Blank also began reworking the ten-episode web series she had conceived before her mother's death into a feature film. Eventually the script was requested by producer Michelle Satter, who found it to be "electric" and subsequently invited Blank to join the Sundance Institute's prestigious screenwriting lab.

While at the Sundance Lab, Blank was assigned African American novelist and screenwriter Walter Mosley as her mentor. He helped her to determine what her protagonist's arc should be. Having some of the best people in the business provide her with guidance was invaluable, but equally important for Blank was the kinship she experienced with the other Sundance fellows.

Blank knew that she wanted to shoot her film in black and white, but producers balked at the idea. It was an issue that she was not willing to compromise on, however, as she felt the aesthetic was a tribute to her favorite New York-set films by directors like John Cassavetes and Spike Lee. Combined with the fact that she was unwilling to cast star actors, Blank's film remained in limbo until writer-producer Lena Waithe came on board in 2019 and helped find financing.

The 40-Year-Old Version film was ultimately shot over twenty-one days in New York City in the way that Blank had imagined. In it, she plays a version of herself also named Radha—a woman who has lost her mother and is grappling with the fact that she has not achieved success in her career the way that she wanted to. Blank described the vulnerability she felt putting herself out there in the film to Richard Phippen in an interview with *NME* (7 Oct. 2020): "It is my life on—that's my apartment, my mother's artwork, my dad's jazz playing in the background and my failures. They're tweaked and amplified to suit the narrative but I am telling on myself. It's a little scary but also liberating because I got this film out of me, and I hope it sets the tone for a really cool career as an auteur."

The film's unique aesthetic, perspective, and balance between comedy and drama proved to be a hit at the 2020 Sundance Film Festival, where it debuted. It went on to win numerous awards, including the Sundance US Dramatic Competition Directing Award, a NAACP Image Award for Outstanding Writing in a Motion Picture, and a Satellite Award for Best Picture. Critics equally praised the film, which earned a 99 percent favorable score on the review-aggregating website *Rotten Tomatoes*.

For Blank, the success of *The 40-Year-Old Version* put to rest her earlier identity as someone who had been hustling her whole life without recognition. "I want to figure out what else it is I'm supposed to be doing," she told Soloski of the potential for the next chapter of her life. "What else I could be doing. I want to figure out who else I am in the world."

SUGGESTED READING

Blank, Radha. "Defying the Note: an Interview with Radha Blank." Interview by Neila Orr. *Seen*, 1 Oct. 2020, www.blackstarfest.org/seen/read/issue-001/radha-blank-interview/. Accessed 2 Sept. 2022.

___. "Hollywood Writer Radha Blank: From a Bronx Kid to *Empire* and Beyond." Interview by Ericka Blount Danois. *The Shadow League*, 27 Feb. 2016, theshadowleague.com/hollywood-writer-radha-blank-from-a-bronx-kid-to-empire-and-beyond/. Accessed 21 Sept. 2022.

___. "It Wasn't Easy to Get a Movie about a 40-year-old Black Woman Made." Interview by Richard Phippen. *NME*, 7 Oct. 2020, www.nme.com/features/film-interviews/radha-blank-interview-40-year-old-version-2775075. Accessed 2 Sept. 2022.

___. "People Watching on a Park Bench." Interview by Sandra E. Garcia. *The New York Times*, 21 Apr. 2022, www.nytimes.com/2022/04/21/t-magazine/radha-blank.html. Accessed 2 Sept. 2022.

Obenson, Tambay. "Radha Blank Separates the Fact and Fiction of 'The Forty-Year-Old Version,' from Screenwriting to Hip Hop." *IndieWire*, 13 Oct. 2020, www.indiewire.com/2020/10/the-forty-year-old-version-netflix-fact-fiction-1202205828/. Accessed 2 Sept. 2022.

Soloski, Alexis. "A Writer-Director-Star Breaks Through. It Only Took a Lifetime." *The New York Times*, 8 Oct. 2020, www.nytimes.com/2020/10/08/movies/radha-blank-40-year-old-version.html. Accessed 2 Sept. 2022.

SELECTED WORKS
Seed, 2011; *She's Got to Have It*, 2017–2019; *The 40-Year-Old Version*, 2020

—*Emily Turner*

Gabriel Boric

Born: February 11, 1986
Occupation: Politician

When Gabriel Boric took the oath of office on March 11, 2022, at the age of thirty-six, he became the youngest person ever elected to head Chile's government as president. A member of the left-wing Social Convergence party, he was widely viewed "as the voice of a generation that is ready to break with the past," in the words of Julie Turkewitz, Pascale Bonnefoy, and John Bartlett for *The New York Times* (21 Dec. 2021). For a large segment of the population, his assumption of the nation's highest office marked a changing of the guard that had been years in the making. "Boric's win is the natural institutionalization of generational howl that has echoed throughout the country for at least a decade," The *New York Times* reporters wrote, pointing out that with the conservative, market-oriented economic systems instituted by dictator Augusto Pinochet in the 1980s still in effect, rampant social inequity had long been the norm in Chile. Boric was expected to manage a major societal metamorphosis, as he hoped to implement a new constitution and overturn the free-market models that had enabled Chile to become a top South American nation in terms of wealth and business friendliness—as well as one of the most socioeconomically unbalanced. A former prominent student protest figure whose efforts contributed to corrections of Chile's privatized education system, he vowed that as president he would revitalize public services with better funding, eliminate Pinochet's private pension plan, and raise taxes substantially on large businesses.

Although Boric secured a clear, high-margin victory amid unprecedented voter participation, opinion initially remained divided on what his election meant for the nation. "For Boric's supporters it's a long-awaited chance to transform a country that has never worked for a majority of its citizens," Ciara Nugent wrote for *Time* (17 Dec. 2021). "For his critics, it's a radical overreaction that will destroy the foundation of Chile's wealth and stability."

EARLY LIFE AND EDUCATION

Gabriel Boric Font was born on February 11, 1986, in Punta Arenas, a large Chilean city situated on the Strait of Magellan. Part of Boric's family is of Croatian descent; relatives from his father's side emigrated from the Austro-Hungarian Empire in the late 1880s to take part in the Tierra del Fuego gold rush. Boric's father, Luis Javier Boric Scarpa, worked as a chemical engineer for the state-owned energy company Empresa Nacional del Petróleo. Of Catalan descent, his mother, María Soledad Font Aguilera, was an avid community volunteer and religious movement member. In addition to Boric, his parents raised his two younger brothers, Simón and Tomás. The family was not overly enmeshed in politics; his father considered himself a centrist, and they quietly opposed Pinochet. One uncle, however, owned a radio station whose on-air personalities spoke out against the dictatorship, and on occasion death threats arrived at the family home via mail.

Boric was educated at the British School in Punta Arenas, and as a teen he began reading extensively about government and revolution. He was instrumental in revitalizing the local secondary school student union and became fascinated by the Revolutionary Left Movement, which had mostly been disbanded during Pinochet's reign. He once wrote to a minor faction still in existence that he had discovered on the Internet, but he did not receive a response.

In 2004 Boric entered law school at the University of Chile, in Santiago, where he was significantly impacted by the human-rights teachings of Professor José Zalaquett. He was elected head of the law school's student union and completed his course requirements in 2009, but he ultimately performed poorly on the final exam required for his degree and decided not to try again.

STUDENT ACTIVISM

Boric made the decision to abandon a university degree and the pursuit of a career as a lawyer,

Photo courtesy Gobierno de Chile, via Wikimedia Commons

in large part because much of his energies were spent engaged in student organizing. In 2011, the year he became president of the Federation of Students of the University of Chile (FECH), Chile's students had begun staging large demonstrations seeking qualitative systematic and structural educational (as well as overall social and economic) improvements such as greater state management and funding of public institutions, free and inclusive access, and restrictions on for-profit education models. One specific point of contention was college admissions testing that strongly favored those who could afford expensive prep courses and tutoring. Such inequities were seen as largely responsible for Chile's general lack of social mobility and high rates of income inequality. Marching in the streets and occupying school buildings for weeks at a time, the students later provoked government action aimed at closing the test-score gap and eliminating a voucher system that allowed private schools to pick from the wealthiest, best-prepared students while public schools were forced to admit everyone.

In acknowledgement of his efforts toward this movement, Boric was publicly recognized as a promising young leader. Later, he stated in a presentation given at Central European University (14 June 2017) that this period in which he was directly involved, as well as its far-reaching influence, crystalized his understanding of the necessity of political representation to actually effect change: "We needed to create our own political expression."

ENTRY INTO POLITICS

In 2013, Boric was one of a handful of student leaders who threw their hats in the ring for a seat in Chile's bicameral legislature, made up of the Chamber of Deputies (lower house) and the Senate (upper house). Boric, who had been affiliated with the political movement known as Autonomous Left, participated in the race as a prospective representative of a district including the Magallanes and Chilean Antarctic Region in the lower house. His victory was marked as notable for occurring outside of Chile's usual binomial system, which effectively excluded candidates not aligned with a major bloc.

Boric was sworn in as a member of the Chamber of Deputies in early 2014 and was one of a cohort known as the *bancada estudiantil* (student bench), who had been active in the protests of 2011. Despite scandalizing some of his new colleagues by arriving in the chamber without a tie his first day, he was assigned spots on multiple commissions, including those devoted to human rights, Indigenous peoples, and labor and social security.

In 2016, after Autonomous Left had disbanded because of internal fighting, Boric was instrumental in founding a new leftist entity, the Autonomist Movement. It joined forces with others in 2017 to form the Broad Front. That year also saw Boric run for and popularly secure reelection. In 2018, the Broad Front merged with the Libertarian Left, Socialism and Liberty, and New Democracy to form an entirely new coalition party, Social Convergence.

A TIME OF UPHEAVAL

In late 2019 unrest erupted across Chile, as hundreds of thousands of citizens took to the streets in a wave of anti-government protests that came to be known as the *estallido social* (social explosion). Although the initial impetus was an increase in public transportation fares, the demonstrators soon added the general cost of living and systemic corruption to their list of causes while emphasizing the continued effects of an extreme, unaddressed socioeconomic gap. Riots broke out all over the country, and a state of emergency was declared. Boric won the

appreciation of his constituents by speaking out against the use of armed force against the protestors, and he gained the respect of many for his willingness to reach across the aisle to search for a way to quell the situation.

In November 2019 the heads of most of Chile's political parties signed the "Agreement for Social Peace and a New Constitution," a document aimed at scrapping the Pinochet-era constitution and replacing it with one that guaranteed human rights and social justice. Although Social Convergence was not a signatory, Boric signed the agreement as an individual. Some on the far left subsequently branded him a traitor, and he was, on at least one occasion, pelted with beer and detritus during a public appearance. Still, the agreement to rewrite the constitution, overwhelmingly supported in a 2020 public referendum, was widely viewed as among the most important factors in Chile's recovery from Pinochet's reign.

PRESIDENTIAL CANDIDACY

Although Boric had angered many members of Social Convergence, the party turned to him ahead of the 2021 presidential primary. Squaring off against Daniel Jadue of the Communist Party, who had been serving as the mayor of Recoleta, Chile, Boric received more than 60 percent of the vote. He went on to face off against far-right candidate José Antonio Kast, who had attracted comparisons to Brazil's Jair Bolsonaro for his hard-line stances on issues such as crime and immigration. In an interview with Ethan Bonner and Eduardo Thomson for *Bloomberg* (19 Dec. 2021), Boric was quoted as emphasizing a need for major societal and economic change: "We need a new model of development. . . . Future historians can give the approach a name but without question it has to have social and ecological components that are far more significant than the utilitarian and material ones that guided neoliberalism." (Neoliberalism, strongly espoused by Pinochet, is characterized by unfettered free-market competition and minimal government interference.)

The first round of the general election occurred on November 21, 2021, and when the polls closed, Kast had won some 28 percent of the votes, with Boric a close second at 26 percent. As they prepared for the second round, Boric campaigned on a promise to increase the minimum wage, expand public health care, and in general dismantle Pinochet's economic model, which enriched Chile's elite at the expense of average citizens. "If Chile was the cradle of neoliberalism, it will also be its grave," he was often quoted as saying on the campaign trail.

On December 19, 2021, Boric won the runoff election with slightly over 55 percent of the vote.

PRESIDENCY

Many pundits opined that Boric's approximately 11 percent lead over Kast represented a clear mandate to enact transformative policies. He faced several challenges in doing so, however, not least of which was the ongoing global COVID-19 pandemic and its economic fallout. Also, when Boric was sworn in on March 11, 2022, the inflation rate in Chile was the highest it had been in decades. He quickly announced a $3.7 billion recovery plan, but the announcement was obscured by media-fueled controversy surrounding Interior Minister Izkia Siches, who had been accused of making false and inflammatory claims about the previous administration. Amid these issues, Boric faced growing public disapproval as his presidency began.

In an overview on Chile created under the auspices of the US Congressional Research Service (19 Apr. 2022), Peter J. Meyer and Joshua Klein outlined another major challenge, pointing out that the nation's legislature was divided nearly evenly between left-leaning and right-leaning parties. "Consequently," they wrote, "Boric faces the difficult task of negotiating legislation with centrist legislators without alienating his leftist base." Regardless of the response to his first months in office, by May 2022 the hopeful symbolism of Boric's position had earned him a place on *Time* magazine's list of the one hundred most influential people of the year.

PERSONAL LIFE

Around 2019 Boric began a relationship with anthropologist Irina Karamanos. Soccer and rock music are known as two of his personal passions. Diagnosed with obsessive–compulsive disorder (OCD) as a child, he has been open about his ongoing mental-health struggles, which at one point led him to take a brief leave of absence from the Chamber of Deputies.

SUGGESTED READING

Anderson, Jon Lee. "Can Chile's Young President Reimagine the Latin American Left?" *The New Yorker*, 6 June 2022, www.newyorker.com/magazine/2022/06/13/can-chiles-young-president-reimagine-the-latin-american-left. Accessed 7 June 2022.

Bartlett, John. "Who Is Gabriel Boric? The Radical Student Leader Who Will Be Chile's Next President." *The Guardian*, 19 Dec. 2021, www.theguardian.com/world/2021/dec/20/who-is-gabriel-boric-the-radical-student-leader-who-will-be-chiles-next-president. Accessed 16 May 2022.

Boric, Gabriel. "'We Need a New Model': Chile's President-Elect in His Own Words." Interview by Ethan Bonner and Eduardo Thomson. *Bloomberg*, 19 Dec. 2021, www.bloomberg.com/news/articles/2021-12-20/-we-need-a-new-model-chile-s-president-elect-in-his-own-words#xj4y7vzkg. Accessed 10 June 2022.

"Gabriel Boric on the Chilean Student Movement." *YouTube*, uploaded by Department of Public Policy at CEU, 14 June 2017, www.youtube.com/watch?v=M_0s8Cgd7pI. Accessed 10 June 2022.

Malinowski, Matthew, et al. "Just 46 Days in Office, Chile's Leftist Leader Runs into Trouble." *Bloomberg*, 26 Apr. 2022, www.bloomberg.com/news/articles/2022-04-26/just-six-weeks-in-chile-s-leftist-leader-is-in-big-trouble. Accessed 16 May 2022.

Meyer, Peter J., and Joshua Klein. *Chile: An Overview*. Congressional Research Service, 19 Apr. 2022, sgp.fas.org/crs/row/IF10880.pdf. Accessed 16 May 2022.

Nugent, Ciara. "The Leftist Millennial Who Could Lead One of Latin America's Wealthiest and Most Unequal Countries." *Time*, 17 Dec. 2021, time.com/6121561/gabriel-boric-chile-election/. Accessed 16 May 2022.

Turkewitz, Julie, et al. "Gabriel Boric: From Shaggy-Haired Activist to Chilean President." *The New York Times*, 21 Dec. 2021, www.nytimes.com/2021/12/21/world/americas/chile-boric.html. Accessed 16 May 2022.

—Mari Rich

Tijana Bošković

Born: March 8, 1997
Occupation: Volleyball player

In the years following her debuts in both professional volleyball and with the women's national team of Serbia, volleyball player Tijana Bošković was the recipient of many honors, including repeated recognition as most valuable player (MVP) for her contributions in major tournaments. For Bošković, however, such recognition was far less important than her in-game contributions to her teams. "My focus is always to win as a team and to help," she told the Italian website *Volley News*, as reported in English by the website of Eczacıbaşı Sports Club (31 Jan. 2022). "No matter what happens at the end, I just want to know that I am giving my best all the time." As Bošković's track record has suggested, giving her best has proven to be a successful strategy: an Olympic medalist with the Serbian national team in 2016 and 2021, she also helped her professional team, Turkey's Eczacıbaşı Dynavit, win championships on the national and international levels. Though pleased with such accomplishments, Bošković, who is left-handed and plays the position of opposite, remained focused on achieving greater things in years to come. "There is still a lot of future ahead and I can't say that I am a complete player right now," she told the Volleyball Federation of Serbia, as reported by *FIVB.com* (21 Apr. 2020). "Sure, I have far more experience than when I first appeared on the international volleyball stage, but I think even five years from now I will still be able to improve further."

EARLY LIFE AND EDUCATION

Tijana Bošković was born on March 8, 1997, in Trebinje, Bosnia and Herzegovina. Though raised in Bileća, Bosnia and Herzegovina, she would later represent the country of Serbia in international competition. An athletic child, she practiced karate for a time but soon focused primarily on the sport of volleyball, for which she was particularly well suited due to her height. "It was ideal for me to be in volleyball or basketball," she explained to *FIVB.com* (9 June 2019). "However, in my hometown there were no basketball clubs, so volleyball was the only option."

Photo by Nevanurpm,
via Wikimedia Commons

Bošković completed her primary schooling in Bileća while playing for the team ŽOK Hercegovac. In 2011, she moved to Belgrade, Serbia, at the age of fourteen to pursue volleyball opportunities and attend high school there. "Since I was fourteen years old, I had to be responsible for myself, but it did not make me feel bad, even I think it helped me grow up faster," she recalled in an interview to *WorldofVolley* (15 Nov. 2017) about that experience. She was accompanied to Belgrade by her older sister, Dajana, a fellow volleyball player who would later play professionally and represent Bosnia and Herzegovina in international tournaments. Their younger brother, Vuk, would also become a professional athlete, playing basketball professionally and on behalf of Serbia.

EARLY CAREER

In Serbia, Bošković joined the team OK Vizura, also known as OK Partizan Vizura. She played in Serbia for four seasons, during which she won a national championship with her team. In 2013, she and her teammates competed for and won the inaugural Super Cup, a championship they would go on to win again the following year.

In addition to competing at the club level, Bošković began playing for Serbia's junior national team in 2013. The team won the

European Volleyball Confederation (CEV) Women's Junior European Championship the following year, and Bošković was named MVP. She was soon called up to the senior national team and went on to compete in both the 2015 International Volleyball Federation (FIVB) Women's World Cup and the 2015 CEV European Championship, also known as EuroVolley. "To be honest, I did not expect to play," she told *FIVB.com* (2019) about those experiences. "I even joked with my friends that they would only see me during national anthems. And it was strange that I ended up being fielded on the court." Alongside her teammates, she won a silver medal at the World Cup and a bronze medal at EuroVolley, beginning her senior-level career on a strong note.

MOVE TO TURKEY

Following the end of the 2014–15 volleyball season, Bošković determined that the time had come to leave Serbia and pursue new opportunities elsewhere. "I understood that I have to take a step forward and continue to play in a stronger league and team," she explained, as reported by the website of the Eczacıbaşı Sports Club. Bošković ultimately chose to play for the Eczacıbaşı VitrA women's team, later known as Eczacıbaşı Dynavit, which was based in Istanbul, Turkey. "The club, teammates, board members and all the people were very welcoming from the first day," Bošković recalled about her arrival at Eczacıbaşı, as reported by the website of the Eczacıbaşı Sports Club. "For me as a young player it was very important to feel like home in a new environment." A team within the Sultanlar Ligi (Sultan's League), Turkey's top-level professional women's volleyball league, Eczacıbaşı also participated in international club competitions overseen by CEV and FIVB.

Over the next several years, Bošković found great success with Eczacıbaşı, winning major international competitions such as the 2016 FIVB Women's Club World Championship and the 2017–18 Women's CEV Cup. The team also proved successful on the domestic level, winning Turkey's Spor Toto Champions Cup three consecutive times between 2018 and 2020. Like many other sports leagues, the Sultan's League was disrupted significantly by the COVID-19 pandemic, which forced teams to stop competing for several months. Bošković

stayed with family in Bosnia and Herzegovina during that period but traveled back to Istanbul in time for the 2020–21 season, intent upon returning to competition. "We are hungry to win," Bošković, who was named a co-captain of the team that season, told *Volley News*, as reported by the Eczacıbaşı Sports Club.

OLYMPIC VOLLEYBALL

In addition to playing for Eczacıbaşı, Bošković remained an active member of the Serbian national team and in 2016 traveled to Rio de Janeiro, Brazil, to compete in the Olympic Games. Serbia proceeded through the preliminary round of competition before advancing to the knockout stage, during which Bošković and her teammates beat Russia in the quarterfinals and the United States in the semifinals. The team next faced China in the final round of competition but ultimately lost that round, claiming a silver medal. Bošković and her teammates went on to win a gold medal the following year at EuroVolley, and Bošković herself was named MVP of that tournament. "The feeling is incredible," she told *WorldofVolley* about that result. "As time passes, I am more aware and happier about the success we have made. To be named for the MVP is certainly a great thing for me and something that motivates me more to be a better player and get a lot more good results." Over the next two years, the Serbian national team won the 2018 FIVB Women's World Championship and the 2019 EuroVolley tournament, with Bošković earning MVP honors for both. She was likewise named the CEV female volleyball player of the year for 2017, 2018, and 2019.

Although Bošković and her teammates planned to travel to Tokyo, Japan, in mid-2020 to compete in that year's Olympic Games, the Olympics were ultimately postponed to the following year due to the ongoing pandemic. "I am sure the Olympics will be very interesting and challenging," she remarked following the postponement, as reported by *FIVB.com* (2020). "I can hardly wait to play in Japan. I am disappointed [by the postponement], but we will only have more time to prepare. The most important thing is to be healthy and we'll get out of this stronger." When the Olympics took place in 2021, Bošković and her teammates again progressed to the knockout stage, defeating Italy in the quarterfinals before losing to the United States—the eventual silver medalists—in the semifinals. The team went on to play against South Korea in the bronze medal match and won, claiming the bronze medal. While Serbia's final ranking in the tournament did not match the team's performance in 2016, Bošković put forth a particularly strong performance at the Games; having scored a total of 192 points over the competition, she achieved the highest point total of any athlete in her event and earned recognition as the tournament's best scorer.

CONTINUING SUCCESS

Following the Olympic Games, Bošković remained focused on preparing for her future competitions, in keeping with her longtime belief in the importance of sustained effort to success. "I know that behind all the medals and success there is a lot of hard work, and I am aware that if I continue to work like that, further success will come," she once explained about her mindset, as reported by *FIVB.com* (2020). "It's all about being focused, persistent, committed and disciplined."

In August and September 2021, Bošković and her Serbian teammates competed in that year's EuroVolley tournament, a portion of which was contested in Belgrade. "EuroVolley is for sure one of the most important and strongest competitions in our sport," she told Chiara Belcastro for the tournament's website. "There are many great European teams, and I think every match can be interesting to watch." The 2021 tournament was especially meaningful for Bošković because it represented her first opportunity to face off against her sister—a member of Bosnia and Herzegovina's national team—in EuroVolley, having previously only done so in club tournaments. After defeating Dajana's team and others in the pool stage of competition, Bošković and her teammates proceeded into the final rounds and ultimately claimed a silver EuroVolley medal. In addition to medaling with the national team, Bošković found further success with Eczacıbaşı over the next months and in March 2022 won the 2021–22 CEV Cup with that team, defeating the German team MTV Stuttgart in the final round of competition. In July 2022, she was ranked number twenty among all women volleyball players worldwide, according to the Volleybox website.

PERSONAL LIFE

Bošković moved to Istanbul in 2015, when she joined Eczacıbaşı. "The city is never boring," she later said of her home, as reported by the website of the Eczacıbaşı Sports Club. "There are too many nice places to discover and visit. But on the other side, as a professional athlete, I am not using the opportunity that much. My priorities on a day off is much likely to rest, recover and take care of my body."

SUGGESTED READING

Belcastro, Chiara. "A Special Day at #EuroVolleyW for the Boskovic Sisters." *CEV EuroVolley*, 19 Aug. 2021, eurovolley. cev.eu/en/articles/2021-women/a-special-day-for-boskovic-sisters/. Accessed 11 July 2022.

"Boskovic: A Privilege to Play for Serbia." *FIVB.com*, 21 Apr. 2020, www.fivb.com/en/about/news/boskovic-a-privilege-to-play-for-serbia?id=90743. Accessed 11 July 2022.

"Boskovic's Rise to Volleyball Stardom." *FIVB. com*, 9 June 2019, www.fivb.com/en/about/news/boskovics-rise-to-volleyball-stardom?id=82850. Accessed 11 July 2022.

Bošković, Tijana. "Tijana Boskovic: 'My Comfort Zone Is Inside the Court.'" *Eczacıbaşı Spor Kulübü*, 31 Jan. 2022, www. eczacibasisporkulubu.org.tr/en/news/detail/tijana-boskovic-my-comfort-zone-is-inside-the-court. Accessed 11 July 2022.

___. "Tijana Boskovic for WoV: 'I Hope That I Will Play Volleyball for a Long Time and That I Will Have a Lot of Success.'" *WorldofVolley*, 15 Nov. 2017, worldofvolley. com/interviews/91824/tijana-boskovic-for-wov-i-hope-that-i-will-play-volleyball-for-a-long-time-and-that-i-will-have-a-lot-of-success.html. Accessed 11 July 2022.

"How Tijana Boskovic and Karch Kiraly Shaped Tokyo 2020." *Volleyball World*, 12 Aug. 2021, volleyballworld.com/volleyball/competitions/olympics-2020/news/how-tijana-boskovic-and-karch-kiraly-shaped-tokyo-2020. Accessed 11 July 2022.

"Serbia's Spiking Star Tijana Boskovic Sizzles at Tokyo 2020." *International Olympic Committee*, 5 Oct. 2021, olympics.com/en/news/serbia-star-spiker-tijana-boskovic-volleyball-tokyo-2020. Accessed 11 July 2022.

—*Joy Crelin*

Katie Bouman

Born: May 9, 1989
Occupation: Engineer and computer scientist

In April 2019, Katie Bouman, then a postdoctoral fellow at Harvard University, was a key part of the team that produced the first-ever image of a black hole. The achievement was widely hailed as an incredible feat, once considered impossible. As Bouman had earlier explained to Larry Hardesty for *MIT News* (6 June 2016): "A black hole is very, very far away and very compact. [Taking a picture of the black hole in the center of a galaxy is] equivalent to taking an image of a grapefruit on the moon, but with a radio telescope." As a member of the Event Horizon Telescope (EHT) project, Bouman led the design of an algorithm—later dubbed CHIRP—that used data gleaned from a global network of radio telescopes to create the groundbreaking image.

The black hole picture generated media interest, and a photo of Bouman reacting in pure excitement as the image was created went viral itself, bringing her even more attention. She won praise from celebrities, politicians, and regular people around the world, and was soon hired as a professor at the California Institute of Technology (Caltech). Yet despite her rising profile, Bouman emphasized that she was simply one part of a complex team, as is usually the case in scientific achievement. Indeed, she stressed that even the specific subject matter of her work was not as important as the collaborative aspect. "What's cooler than black holes?" She told Hayley Hanway for the University of Michigan Electrical and Computer Engineering department website (17 Dec. 2021). "It was this idea of, okay, if we come together and think creatively, we can do something that should be impossible. We can see the invisible. I think that's what captured people and hopefully inspires people to push the boundaries in other areas, too."

EARLY LIFE AND EDUCATION

Katherine Louise Bouman was born on May 9, 1989, to parents Cristina and Charles Bouman, and grew up in West Lafayette, Indiana. She was a good student and excelled in science. "She was a super-detailed kind of kid, even when I had her in class," her eighth-grade science teacher, Phil Pusey, recalled to Dave Bangert for the Lafayette *Journal & Courier* (10 Apr. 2019). "She was always ordered and organized, lab notes were written out to super-detail." As a student at West Lafayette High School, Bouman—perhaps inspired by her father, a professor of engineering at Purdue University who studied imaging techniques—worked on imaging research with a graduate student at Purdue. She enjoyed the challenge, which involved using noise patterns to identify the source of an image. "It introduced me to this idea of there being hidden information everywhere," she told Hanway.

Bouman graduated from high school in 2007 and went on to study electrical engineering at the University of Michigan, focusing on imaging issues such as processing and reconstruction in the Michigan Research Community program. She continued to distinguish herself as a gifted thinker. Al Hero, who taught her in a design course, told Hanway that Bouman's final project was one of the best he had ever seen: "Her idea was to use a cheap camera to take a picture of a musical score—that had coffee stains or distortions or was crumpled up—and then the computer would automatically play the music on the score," he said. The project presaged her imaging a black hole. "She developed a sophisticated and elegant method that basically estimated the distortion pattern

Photo via Wikimedia Commons.
[Public domain]

that came out of these very poor lenses, and then used that estimate to correct the lens," Hero said. "She was just outstanding."

Bouman graduated with her BSE degree in 2011. She then continued her studies in electrical engineering and computer science at the Massachusetts Institute of Technology (MIT), where she was part of the Computer Science and Artificial Intelligence Laboratory (CSAIL). She earned a master's degree in 2013 and a doctorate in 2017.

CHIRP

While a graduate student at MIT, Bouman became involved in astronomical imaging. Though not technically an astronomer or astrophysicist herself, her background as an engineer using computers to analyze and understand images was highly valuable in this field, as the vast distances of space naturally make the imaging of many phenomena exceptionally difficult. Specifically, Bouman joined a diverse group of scientists studying black holes, which provided a particular imaging challenge. Black holes, predicted by Albert Einstein's general theory of relativity, are regions of space in which the gravitational pull is so strong that even light cannot escape them. Visually speaking, they are voids. One can only "see" them by their event horizon, the region that marks the boundary of a black hole. They are also highly compact and distant, so researchers long believed getting an accurate image of one would be impossible.

Bouman became a member of a sprawling project featuring scientists from CSAIL, the MIT Haystack Observatory, and the Harvard-Smithsonian Center for Astrophysics. Her work focused on developing a new algorithm that would help astronomers produce an image of a black hole using data from radio telescopes. "Radio wavelengths come with a lot of advantages," Bouman explained to Hardesty. "Just like how radio frequencies will go through walls, they pierce through galactic dust. We would never be able to see into the center of our galaxy in visible wavelengths because there's too much stuff in between." Yet for something as small and distant as a black hole, a radio telescope would need an antenna the size of the earth to capture an acceptable image. The project's solution to this problem was the Event Horizon Telescope (EHT), a network of radio telescopes across the globe

collecting data that could be coordinated to provide a more accurate picture. Still, even that data would be incomplete. Bouman's team worked to develop an algorithm that would fill the informational gaps and provide a complete image of a black hole.

Bouman called her team's algorithm Continuous High-resolution Image Reconstruction using Patch priors, or CHIRP. She and her colleagues applied complex mathematical concepts and machine learning to address the various needs of creating an image of a black hole (though CHIRP could theoretically be used in any instance of radio interferometry, a technique in which multiple signals are combined). Furthermore, CHIRP was just one of several techniques that proved integral to the EHT project. As Bouman later explained to Michelle Lou and Saeed Ahmed for *CNN* (10 Apr. 2019), "We didn't want to just develop one algorithm. We wanted to develop many different algorithms that all have different assumptions built into them. If all of them recover the same general structure, then that builds your confidence."

PORTRAIT OF A BLACK HOLE

It took Bouman and her team three years to build CHIRP, and another two years to properly evaluate it. Along the way she gave a TED Talk called "How to Take a Picture of a Black Hole" in 2016, outlining the concepts behind the algorithm and EHT. After obtaining her PhD in 2017, she took a postdoctoral fellowship at the Harvard-Smithsonian Center for Astrophysics and continued her work.

Meanwhile, in April 2017 EHT's network of radio telescopes focused on a black hole at the center of the Messier 87 (M87) galaxy, 55 million light years away. Over the course of seven days, the telescopes collected over 5 petabytes of data. The researchers then broke off into four teams, working in isolation to create images using different techniques from the same data. In a conversation with Passant Rabie for *Inverse* magazine (2 Mar. 2021), Bouman explained, "We didn't talk to each other at all about what we were getting, or if we were getting anything at all. And then after seven weeks, we came together and showed the images to each other." (Much of this process was captured in a documentary film called *Black Hole: The Edge of All We Know*, released in 2021.) The results were remarkably similar, indicating they had been successful. After further reconstruction, a final fuzzy picture of a fiery orange ring appeared on Bouman's computer screen. It was the world's first-ever actual image of a black hole. "When I first made the images, I thought that they weren't real, actually," Bouman told Rabie. "I thought that they were synthetic data that they were testing us with because it seemed too perfect."

VIRAL FAME

On April 10, 2019, the black hole image was made public and picked up as a significant story by both the scientific community and the media. Bouman also posted a photograph of her gleeful reaction to seeing the image for the first time, and it quickly went viral, inadvertently making her the public face of the achievement. The CSAIL Twitter account also made a post crediting Bouman as the leader of the team, and other media outlets and social media users picked up that message. Several politicians and other prominent figures praised Bouman, holding her up as an emblem of the contributions of women in STEM fields (which historically have often been overlooked). Another MIT post compared Bouman to Margaret Hamilton, a computer scientist who played a key role in the Apollo space program. "We had no idea the impact it would have," Bouman told Hanway of the black hole image and accompanying public response. "To see it excite people and kids about science and engineering has been amazing. It's wonderful to see younger students message me about how it inspired them to pursue careers in STEM, and how it's inspired people in other fields as well."

Yet while much of the reaction to Bouman and her work was positive, an element of controversy also arose. Some observers noted that though the media attention to Bouman was well-intentioned, borne of centuries of erasure of women, it also fed the common myth that "lone genius" scientists are solely responsible for great breakthroughs. In truth, as one of Bouman's collaborators pointed out on Twitter, as quoted by Marina Koren for the *Atlantic* (15 Apr. 2019), "big science happens in BIG teams." Bouman herself never disputed this, and indeed often emphasized that science is a team effort. But the media spun the story out of her control, revealing how the general public has been conditioned to think "that

scientific breakthroughs originate with a single mind," as Koren put it.

The backlash soon extended beyond legitimate critique of the lone genius myth, veering into outright sexism as right-wing agitators and social media trolls attempted to "debunk" Bouman's role in the EHT project and instead give credit to her colleague Andrew Chael, a White man. (Chael himself sharply rejected such claims.) Bouman became the target of a coordinated campaign of online harassment, including many fake social media accounts created in her name. This development was in turn picked up by several media outlets as proof of the enduring sexism in science and society. As Brian Resnick wrote for *Vox* (16 Apr. 2019), "the reaction to Bouman's picture reveals hostility many women scientists face all the time." Bouman herself remained silent about the backlash, however, focusing instead on the EHT team's remarkable success and the potential for future breakthroughs.

In the wake of the historic black hole image, Bouman was appointed an assistant professor of computer science at Caltech in June 2019. In 2020 she and the rest of the EHT team earned a $3 million Breakthrough Prize, and in 2021 she received the Progress Medal from the Royal Photographic Society. She also continued to work on the EHT project, which set its sights on making a video of Sagittarius A*, the black hole at the center of the Milky Way galaxy. Though Sagittarius A* is much closer than M87, it is still mind-bogglingly distant. "It's about the same size in the sky as if I had a grain of sand in New York, and I was viewing it from Los Angeles," Bouman told Rabie.

PERSONAL LIFE

Bouman married long-time boyfriend Joe Leong in Michigan in September 2018.

SUGGESTED READING

Bangert, Dave. "That First-Ever Black Hole Picture? A West Lafayette Grad Played a Big Part." *Journal & Courier*, 10 Apr. 2019, www.jconline.com/story/news/2019/04/10/first-black-hole-picture-west-lafayette-grad-played-big-part/3426430002/. Accessed 4 Feb. 2022.

Hanway, Hayley. "Katie Bouman Talks Legacy of the Black Hole Imaging Project and Favorite U-M Memories." *Electrical and Computer Engineering*, University of Michigan, 17

Dec. 2021, ece.engin.umich.edu/stories/katie-bouman-talks-legacy-of-the-black-hole-imaging-project-and-favorite-u-m-memories. Accessed 4 Feb. 2022.

Hardesty, Larry. "A Method to Image Black Holes." *MIT News*, 6 June 2016, news.mit.edu/2016/method-image-black-holes-0606. Accessed 4 Feb. 2022.

Koren, Marina. "The Dark Saga of Katie Bouman." *The Atlantic*, 15 Apr. 2019, www.theatlantic.com/science/archive/2019/04/katie-bouman-black-hole/587137/. Accessed 5 Feb. 2022.

Lou, Michelle, and Saeed Ahmed. "That Image of a Black Hole You Saw Everywhere? Thank This Grad Student for Making It Possible." *CNN*, 10 Apr. 2019, www.cnn.com/2019/04/10/us/katie-bouman-mit-black-hole-algorithm-sci-trnd/index.html. Accessed 5 Feb. 2022.

Rabie, Passant. "'To See a Black Hole, We Would Need a Telescope the Size of the Entire Earth.'" *Inverse*, 2 Mar. 2021, www.inverse.com/science/black-hole-documentary-how-did-we-image-the-invisible. Accessed 5 Feb. 2022.

Resnick, Brian. "Male Scientists Are Often Cast as Lone Geniuses. Here's What Happened When a Woman Was." *Vox*, 16 Apr. 2019, www.vox.com/science-and-health/2019/4/16/18311194/black-hole-katie-bouman-trolls. Accessed 7 Feb. 2022.

—*Molly Hagan*

Toni Breidinger

Born: July 14, 1999
Occupation: Stock car racing driver

To some observers, driving a Toyota Camry at high speeds around a track full of competing drivers might appear to be the hardest part of Toni Breidinger's career, but Breidinger herself would disagree. "Driving is the easy part," she told Alex Harrington in an interview for *Grand Tour Nation* (4 Mar. 2020). "Marketing yourself and getting sponsors is much more challenging."

A competitive driver since childhood, when she first began appearing in go-kart races, Breidinger made a name for herself in the United States Auto Club (USAC) midget car racing as a teenager, winning numerous individual races as well as a 2016 championship. She made her debut in the Automobile Racing Club of America (ARCA) Menards Series in 2018, racing late-model stock cars, but was an inconsistent presence in that series in subsequent years in part due to limited funding.

Breidinger's circumstances changed in 2022, when she began her first season racing full-time in the ARCA Menards Series, a competitive circuit often viewed as a training ground for drivers hoping to move up to National Association for Stock Car Auto Racing (NASCAR) competition.

As one of relatively few women competing in the Menards Series, she was, at times, compared to other female drivers on that circuit or to the very few women who had previously competed in NASCAR, which had no active female drivers in 2022. Breidinger, however, rejected efforts to compare her to—or pit her against—other competitors. "I . . . want to make my own name for myself, and I don't necessarily want to be in someone else's shadow or compared to someone," she told Lainey Sidell for *Paper* (15 June 2018). "I want to be the next Toni Breidinger."

EARLY LIFE AND EDUCATION

Antoinette Marie "Toni" Breidinger was born on July 14, 1999. She grew up in Hillsborough, California, alongside her twin sister, Annie. Their father, Charles, worked in construction, while their mother, Nada, was a teacher. Thanks to their father's influence, the Breidinger sisters both began racing vehicles of various types while still children. "My dad got me and my sister a go-kart when we were nine," Breidinger recalled to Harrington. "As soon as I did my first go-kart race I knew I wanted to be a race car driver. I knew I was committed to making it happen, but I'm not sure how seriously my parents took me." She and her sister raced throughout their childhoods, forming the team Breidinger Motorsports. As they grew older the sisters began to race so-called midget cars, small and lightweight vehicles that can be raced on dirt or paved tracks.

As a teenager, Breidinger began racing midget cars in competitions sanctioned by the United States Auto Club (USAC). She found significant success in USAC competition; by early 2018 she had won fourteen USAC races on paved tracks, the most by any female driver

Photo by Michaelpadluck,
via Wikimedia Commons

in USAC history up to that point. She likewise claimed the title of USAC Western HPD Pavement Midget Champion in 2016.

Breidinger attended Mercy High School in Burlingame, California, from which she graduated in 2017. By the end of high school, she had begun to transition from midget cars to late-model stock cars as a means of preparing for higher-level competition. While her sister decided to attend college to study engineering, Breidinger opted not to enroll in college and instead moved to North Carolina to pursue a career in stock car racing. "It was almost too easy of a decision," she later told Terrin Waack for *NASCAR.com* (31 Mar. 2021). "So many people were like, 'Oh my gosh, it must have been so hard.' I don't know, I just knew it would help my career. I didn't have any hesitations about it."

PROFESSIONAL RACING CAREER

Breidinger began her career in professional racing with years of prior racing experience, and she soon set multiple challenging professional goals for herself. "One of my biggest racing goals is to compete in the NASCAR cup series," she later explained in an interview for the Toyota Racing website. "I would jump at the chance to participate in Formula 1 as well which would be a dream come true as well as a challenge that I would love to try."

While those goals remained in her mind, she began her career not in NASCAR competitions but in races overseen by ARCA. In March 2018 Breidinger joined the Venturini Motorsports racing team and competed in three races in the ARCA Menards Series. She finished in tenth place in her first Menards Series race, held in June at Madison International Speedway in Madison, Wisconsin.

For a young driver such as Breidinger, pursuing a career in racing presented a number of challenges, including limited funding. The many varied tracks on which competitors race likewise represented a challenge, albeit one that she enjoyed. "Our schedule is a bit chaotic in the sense that every track is so different. You're never going to go into a track where you can apply the same things you learned from the previous one," she told Chris Rosvoglou in an interview for *The Spun* (6 May 2022). "But honestly, that's what makes it so fun and challenging."

In addition to racing late-model cars in ARCA competitions, Breidinger continued to race midget cars in USAC events during her early career. In 2019, she competed in a CARS Pro Late Model Tour event at Motor Mile Speedway in Fairlawn, Virginia, where she finished in fifteenth place while representing GMS Racing. In 2020, she competed for DLP Motorsports in Carolina Pro Late Model Series events but did not race in ARCA, as the league suffered some schedule disruptions and cancellations due to the onset of the COVID-19 pandemic.

NEW MILESTONES

In February 2021, Breidinger joined the Young's Motorsports team for which she would drive part-time in the ARCA Menards Series. Her first race of the series represented a significant milestone, as it was held at Florida's Daytona International Speedway, a prominent racing venue known for hosting the NASCAR Cup Series' prestigious Daytona 500 race. "Daytona has always been on my bucket list to race at. Every driver's dream is to race there one day," she told Alaa Elassar for *CNN* (13 Feb. 2021). "It's such a historic track. It's a step in the right direction to hopefully race in the Daytona 500 one day."

Breidinger ultimately finished the race in eighteenth place. She went on to race in four other Menards Series races with Young's

Motorsports, twice finishing in twelfth place. Though the team had announced early in the year that Breidinger would also compete in the NASCAR Camping World Truck Series in 2021, she did not race in the Truck Series during that year.

As Breidinger's profile rose due to her performance on the track, sports media increasingly focused on her status as one of the few women and the only woman of Arab descent—Breidinger is half Lebanese—competing in the ARCA Menards Series. "It's been such a big part of my life," she told Waack about her heritage. "I've always been proud of it. But also kind of nervous how people would react just because, you know, going to these short tracks, for the most part, there isn't too much diversity there. And I've heard comments in the past about other diverse people. So I was kind of apprehensive in a way, how people would take it."

While Breidinger has typically downplayed issues of gender and ethnicity in interviews, noting that each driver is simply a driver when on the track, she acknowledged her significance as a potential role model for younger competitors. "I'm honored and excited to be the first, but I don't want to be the last," she told Elassar. "I hope I can pave the way for future female Arab drivers as well."

In July 2021 Breidinger returned to Venturini Motorsports, for which she would race for the rest of the year. She finished in ninth place in the July race at Winchester Speedway in Berryville, Virginia, and again claimed ninth place in her next series race at the Illinois State Fairgrounds in Springfield, Illinois. She went on to compete in two more Menards Series races over the course of the year, as well as in two events that were part of the regional ARCA Menards Series West.

2022 ARCA MENARDS SERIES

For the 2022 racing season, Breidinger remained with Venturini Motorsports, which in January of that year announced that she had been chosen to race full-time in the ARCA Menards Series as the driver of the team's number 25 Toyota Camry. Her series began on February 19, 2022, at Daytona, where she finished the race in ninth place.

Also in February 2022, Breidinger was selected as one of the eight drivers to receive a three-year sponsorship from the Busch Light Accelerate Her Program, an initiative established to fund female drivers with the goal of reducing the gender disparities in auto racing. By April, however, she had left the program, which she characterized in a question-and-answer session on the website Reddit as a self-serving attempt by a large corporation to claim to support women in sports without truly doing so.

Following her 2022 race at Daytona, Breidinger competed in ten additional Menards Series races between February and the end of July, finishing ninth at Berlin Raceway in Marne, Michigan, and tenth at both Kansas Speedway in Kansas City, Kansas, and Pocono Raceway in Long Pond, Pennsylvania. "I'd say it has been a solid season, but I need to keep progressing," she told Rosvoglou several months into the year. She crashed twice during her first eleven races, including at the Talladega Superspeedway event in Talladega, Alabama, in April 2022. She also raced on August 6, 2022, for the Henry Ford Health 200 at Michigan International Speedway in Brooklyn, Michigan. During that race, she finished in eleventh place.

PERSONAL LIFE

In addition to racing, Breidinger spends much of her time preparing for future competitions. "When I'm not at the track I'm usually training, whether that's sim training or working out," she told *Toyota Racing*. "I really push myself to be the best that I can be and focus on where and how I can improve." She also expressed interest in restoring cars and in 2022 acquired a 1989 Jeep Wrangler for that purpose.

SUGGESTED READING

Abbas, Hassan. "Toni Breidinger: First Arab American Female Driver to Compete at NASCAR." *Arab American News*, 12 Feb. 2021, www.arabamericannews. com/2021/02/12/toni-breidinger-first-arab-american-female-driver-to-compete-at-nascar/. Accessed 8 Aug. 2022.

Breidinger, Toni. "Q&A with Toni Breidinger: Breaking Barriers, Outlook for ARCA Series, Partnership with 7-Eleven." Interview with Chris Rosvoglou. *Spun*, 6 May 2022, thespun.com/more/interviews/toni-breidinger-discusses-arca-series-breaking-barriers-latest-project. Accessed 8 Aug. 2022.

___. "Toni Breidinger." *Toyota Racing*, www.toyota.com/racing/other-series/drivers/toni-breidinger. Accessed 8 Aug. 2022.

___. "Toni Breidinger Interviewed: The Life of a Successful Female Racing Driver Explored." Interview by Alex Harrington. *Grand Tour Nation*, www.grandtournation.com/cars/toni-breidinger-interviewed-the-life-behind-a-successful-female-racing-driver/. Accessed 8 Aug. 2022.

Elassar, Alaa. "NASCAR's First Arab American Female Driver to Make Her Debut at Daytona International Speedway." *CNN*, 13 Feb. 2021, www.cnn.com/2021/02/13/us/daytona-nascar-arab-american-female-driver-toni-breidinger-trnd/index.html. Accessed 8 Aug. 2022.

Sidell, Lainey. "Beautiful People: Toni Breidinger Is Racing Full Throttle." *Paper*, 15 June 2018, www.papermag.com/beautiful-people-toni-breidinger-2578374849.html. Accessed 8 Aug. 2022.

Waack, Terrin. "A Female Inspiration." *NASCAR.com*, 31 Mar. 2021, www.nascar.com/long-form/toni-breidinger-female-driver-feature-terrin-waack/. Accessed 8 Aug. 2022.

—*Joy Crelin*

Tony Briffa

Born: 1970
Occupation: Politician

Hobsons Bay city councilor Tony Briffa is the first publicly intersex elected official in the world. In addition to being elected four times as an independent city councilor, she is also a former mayor and deputy mayor of Hobsons Bay, a suburb of Melbourne, Australia. Additionally, as a longtime advocate for intersex rights, Briffa has held executive roles in such groups as Intersex Human Rights Australia, Intersex Peer Support Australia, and the International Lesbian, Gay, Bisexual, Trans and Intersex Association (ILGA) World Intersex Committee. She has been instrumental in crafting important international documents—including the 2013 Malta Declaration, issued at the Third International Intersex Forum, and the 2017 Darlington Statement, issued jointly by Australian and New Zealand intersex organizations to outline the groups' priorities regarding human rights, education, and employment.

EARLY YEARS

Tony Briffa was born Antoinette Briffa in 1970 in the suburb of Altona, in the western region of Melbourne, along with her twin sister, Catherine, to parents of Maltese descent. Doctors assigned Briffa female at birth, even after determining that she had androgen insensitivity syndrome (AIS), a condition that results when a person is born with XY chromosomes but is unable to respond to sex hormones known as androgens. The doctors advised Briffa's parents to raise her as a girl.

During much of Briffa's childhood she was subjected to invasive tests and treatments at Melbourne's Royal Children's Hospital, and when she was seven years old, doctors surgically removed her testes. Briffa was told only that she was going to have some "tissues" taken out and imagined that the procedure would involve Kleenex. At eleven, she began hormone treatments calculated to keep her height at about five feet two inches, which was considered more feminine than the five feet ten inches she was expected to reach naturally. Because these interventions were done without her consent or court approval, later in life Briffa became a particularly staunch defender of autonomy and human rights for intersex youngsters.

"It was all a dark, shameful secret," she wrote in an article for *Intersex Day* (25 Oct. 2017). "I was made to feel like a freak and that is pretty much how I saw myself growing up. It was as if there were girls, boys, and me." Despite those travails, she had several friends and studied hard at the local Catholic schools she attended—although she sometimes found the strictures of Catholicism unfair, such as when she was denied the chance to become an altar server.

As a teen, Briffa began learning more about her condition, leading to deep feelings of loneliness and despair. "Had I not had my love of music I am not sure I would have survived," she wrote in her 2017 *Intersex Day* essay. She attended her first AIS support group at age eighteen, but she found that the discussion was dominated by doctors from the hospital where it was held, and as a result, she found little actual support or comfort there.

AVIATION ENGINEERING

Briffa earned a degree in the discipline of aviation engineering. She began her professional career in 1993 at Ansett Australia, a major Melbourne-based airline. There, she maintained airframes and engines for a variety of passenger aircraft, including the Airbus 320; Boeing 767, 737, and 727; British Aerospace 146; and Fokker 28 and 50. In 1997 she became an engineering officer at the company and was given responsibility for training other engineers, conducting reliability and warranty assessments on aircraft components, and other such tasks.

In 2002 Briffa joined Australia's Department of Defense as an airworthiness auditor and instructor, working under the auspices of the Directorate General Technical Airworthiness to ensure that safety regulations were met and that aircraft were fit to fly. She remained there until 2007, when she accepted a post as lead auditor and audit program manager in the Australian Federal Police's International Deployment Group, which is dedicated to combating transnational organized crime, participating in mandated peacekeeping operations, and contributing to border security, among other duties. In that capacity, Briffa was responsible for developing and managing the audit program and leading audits in the group's aviation and maritime sectors.

In 2014 Briffa made a move into the private sector, becoming deputy chief operating officer at the consulting firm Aviation Compliance Solutions. Beginning in early 2021, she was a quality and safety manager at Leonardo, a Melbourne-based company that supplies technology to the aerospace, national defense, and security sectors.

COMING OUT PUBLICLY

When Briffa was twenty-seven, a serious car accident left her with several broken bones and a collapsed lung. During the two years it took her to learn to walk without assistance, she decided that she no longer wanted to live the way she had been. "I wanted to make a change in the world," she wrote for *Intersex Day*. "At that point, I was no longer going to hide the fact I was intersex. Nature made me this way and I have nothing to be ashamed of. If anyone should be ashamed, it's the doctors that abused and mistreated me and my parents."

Briffa's research revealed that her endocrinologist had been giving her incomplete information about AIS, even after she became an adult, and when she asked to be given the testosterone, she would have produced naturally had she not undergone invasive surgery, the endocrinologist refused. Frustrated, Briffa agreed to appear on the nationally televised *60 Minutes* in 2000 to discuss the mistreatment of intersex children. (The request came following the highly publicized case of David Reimer, a boy who underwent a botched circumcision in Canada and was raised as a girl because of that mutilation.) She also came out publicly as intersex on the segment.

Briffa was subsequently granted testosterone treatments, and soon her voice deepened and the hair on her body grew. "I never imagined what the years ahead of me had in store," she wrote for *Intersex Day*. "There was one thing that became obvious fairly quickly though; once 'out' I would never be able to go back 'in.' The world now knew I was intersex, and that was a label that was going to stick with me in all facets of my life." Briffa appeared on *60 Minutes* once more in 2005.

ACTIVISM

After Briffa's television appearance, Briffa found herself becoming the public face of intersex rights in Australia. By then, the Internet had made it easier for individuals to find each other and organize, and she reconnected with her old hospital support group, helping it evolve into an independent and legally registered nonprofit, ASI Support Group Australia, over which she presided for a time and for which she serves as vice president.

Briffa went on to hold such offices as co-executive director and vice-chair of Intersex Human Rights Australia (formerly called OII Australia), president of Intersex Peer Support Australia, and board secretary and intersex chair of the ILGA World. "I discovered the vibrant, rich tapestry of intersex people," she wrote for *Intersex Day*. "Sadly, it was a tapestry woven with lots of shame, secrecy, misinformation, abuse, mistreatment, misunderstanding, solitude and darkness."

Despite years of advocacy, letter-writing campaigns, and sitting on various advisory boards, Briffa has noted that intersex rights are still not a given and that intersex children around the world are still being subjected to irreversible and medically unnecessary procedures. Still, in July 2021, the State of Victoria's health and equality ministries published (i) *Am Equal: Future Directions for Victoria's Intersex Community*, which described the government's plans to reform the state health system's care and support for people with intersex variations and their families. Briffa was one of three cochairs of the Victorian Intersex Expert Advisory Group, which advised the state government on the reforms outlined in (i) *Am Equal*. Of the reforms, Briffa said in the plan's introductory comments, "Addressing the human rights and treatment of Victorian children born with variations of sex characteristics has been a long time in the making, but it's important we get it right."

POLITICAL OFFICE

Not long after coming out publicly, Briffa became involved in a campaign to save a local park. That experience inspired her to run in 2004 as an independent for a seat on her local council in Hobsons Bay. Although she did not win at that time, she tried again in 2008 and became the first publicly intersex person in the world elected to public office. While her seat on the suburb's seven-person council attracted little attention, that began to change when she became deputy mayor in 2009. In 2011, she was elected mayor, and news outlets around the globe took notice, with the media touting her as the first intersex mayor in the world.

Briffa set up a website for her constituents in Hobsons Bay's Cherry Lake Ward, and within a day it had received a quarter of a million hits, many from outside the community. Although she found it difficult to keep up with the requests from journalists and letters of congratulation, she appreciated the interest and support. Even her relatively conservative and religious Maltese community voiced its approval.

Briffa, who was reelected to the council in 2012, 2016, and 2020, wrote on her official website, "Even in my 4th term I'm as excited and motivated as ever to represent our community and work to make [it] vibrant, welcoming, enjoyable, sustainable, diverse and connected." Among the accomplishments of her tenure are securing funding for upgraded parks, trails, libraries, and playgrounds; effectively addressing air quality and noise issues; and using practical measures like distributing free receptacles to increase recycling. Her most recent term coincided with the height of the COVID-19 pandemic, and she has strongly affirmed her commitment to supporting those affected and helping her ward rebuild.

PERSONAL LIFE

Briffa, who has been a justice of the peace since 2005, was married to a man from about 1989 to 1991, before coming out as a lesbian at the age of twenty-six. In September 2013, she married her partner, Manja (Sommeling) Briffa, a teacher. The ceremony took place in New Zealand because Australia then required marriage to be between a man and a woman. Four years later the law was changed, and the couple were able to repeat their vows there, with Briffa promising to be the "best husband and wife possible." Briffa had long fostered children, and the couple have a grown son and live in Briffa's hometown of Altona.

A Victorian Pride Centre ambassador and honorary fellow of Victoria University, Briffa wrote for *Adelaide Now*, "It's a challenge living in a society that's divided so clearly into men and women. But I feel very comfortable having accepted my true self and that I'm not male or female, but both. I'll continue to live as 'Tony' but I'm now at a point in my life where I can celebrate being different. Thankfully my wife, my family and my friends understand and accept all parts of me."

SUGGESTED READING

Briffa, Tony. "My Experience as the World's First Openly Intersex Mayor." *Intersex Day*, 25 Oct. 2017, intersexday.org/en/first-intersex-mayor-tony-briffa/. Accessed 23 Mar. 2022.

___. "Proud Intersex Person Tony Briffa Tells Story of Self Discovery." *Adelaide Now*, 8 Sept. 2014, www.news.com.au/lifestyle/real-life/proud-intersex-person-tony-briffa-tells-story-of-self-discovery/news-story/56036a301b2b1488fcee4b7c7b39d8aa. Accessed 23 Mar. 2022.

Cr. *Tony Briffa*, briffa.org/page/8. Accessed 14 Apr. 2022.

Daniel, Lisa "Dano," host, and Tony Briffa, guest. *Word for Word*, Joy, July 2019, joy.org.au/wordforword/2019/07/tony-briffa/. Accessed 23 Mar. 2022.

Fiest, Jenny. "Australian Politician Tony Briffa Talks about Being Intersex." *Xtra**, 10 Aug. 2013, xtramagazine.com/power/australian-politician-tony-briffa-talks-about-being-intersex-51999. Accessed 23 Mar. 2022.

Gieseke, Winston. "Intersex Mayor Elected in Australia." *Advocate*, 9 Dec. 2011, www.advocate.com/news/daily-news/2011/12/09/intersex-mayor-elected-australia. Accessed 23 Mar. 2022.

—*Mari Rich*

Quinta Brunson

Born: December 21, 1989
Occupation: Writer, comedian, and actor

From an early age, writer, comedian, and actor Quinta Brunson was inherently drawn to the immense satisfaction that comes from creative and performing arts, particularly when it involved collaboration and generating genuine laughter. Immediately setting herself apart in the entertainment industry through her authentic investment in all aspects of the creative process, she took advantage of any platforms available to showcase her humor and spark dialogue, spending several years throughout the 2010s making a name for herself with digital video content for *YouTube* and *BuzzFeed*.

Brunson's first project produced for a mainstream medium, network television, garnered widespread recognition following its premiere in late 2021. By July 2022, she had been nominated for three Emmy Awards for her contributions in writing, producing, and acting in her ABC sitcom *Abbott Elementary*. For those familiar with her work, the news of these nominations was far from surprising—not only had she been transforming the landscape of sketch and internet comedy for years, but *Abbot Elementary* had rapidly become one of the most exciting new shows of 2021. Both critics and viewers adored the series for providing warm, optimistic, and funny character-driven stories during a time when Americans were still struggling with the COVID-19 pandemic and sociopolitical unrest. Indeed, *Abbott Elementary* became so overwhelmingly popular that it was renewed within the first several weeks of being on the air, which was remarkable for a week-to-week network sitcom at a time when bingeable streaming shows reigned supreme.

When reflecting on the success of her show with Antonia Blyth in an interview for *Deadline* (14 June 2022), Brunson was grateful for the accolades but equally happy about what she was able to provide for a wide range of audiences, stating: "One of my favorite things to hear is when people say, 'My gosh, this is what I watch with my family, it's the only thing I can watch with my children.' And younger people being like, 'I've been watching it with my grandma, we both love it.' That's what I still feel you can get from network, you know? I think that's still unique to that space."

EARLY LIFE

Quinta Brunson was born on December 21, 1989, in Philadelphia, Pennsylvania. Growing up with her four older siblings, her early years were spent in a three-story house in West Philadelphia, a neighborhood that she later credited for deeply defining her identity. For work, her father served as a parking lot manager while her mother was a kindergarten teacher.

As a young child, following her time as a member of her mother's kindergarten class, Brunson took part in an offshoot, village-learning-style program at Harrity Elementary School known as Ahali. While Ahali was located in the same building as Harrity, it had a community-driven curriculum that incorporated Black history in all of its subjects. Ahali provided Brunson with a better understanding of her place in history as a Black American, which in turn strengthened her sense of identity.

Ahali instilled a love and appreciation for school in Brunson that would continue into her middle school experience. At first, she was scared to leave Ahali because it had kept her close to her mother's kindergarten class. However, her sixth-grade teacher, Mrs. Abbott, helped make the transition easier. "Mrs. Abbott has always stuck with me throughout my life," Brunson told Danielle Broadway for the *Los Angeles Times* (11 Jan. 2022). "In a way, I didn't know why she was my favorite. I couldn't put my finger on it. She just was. . . . I think it's like the Maya Angelou quote, 'People always remember how you make them feel,' and she always made me feel good." In addition to creating a safe, welcoming atmosphere for Brunson and her peers, Mrs. Abbott was extremely creative and dedicated in how she taught her curriculum. One time, she taught the kids about outer space by making a planetarium out of their classroom. She also had them organize fundraisers to earn money so they could mark completing sixth grade by taking a limousine to a nice restaurant.

Although Brunson had come to love performing through years of dancing everything from tap and jazz to ballet, and her interest in the nuances of comedy led her to entertain notions of becoming a comedic performer and writer, she worried about whether it would be possible for her to succeed in the entertainment industry. Her fears stemmed, in part, from the fact that she had seen so few Black female comedians. So, she initially tried to listen to her parents' advice and focus on pursuing a more traditional career. However, while in high school, her love for comedy and making other people laugh only continued to grow. As she told editors in an interview for *Vulture* (19 Oct. 2020), "In high school I had an obsession with comedy no matter what form. From *Martin* to *Anchorman* to Chaplin, I was obsessed." At home, she loved gathering her family together to take in a wide variety of sitcoms on TV.

EDUCATION AND EARLY CAREER

For college, Brunson decided to stay in Philadelphia and attend Temple University, where she took courses in telecommunications and advertising, beginning in 2007. While there, she became obsessed with *The Office* and *Saturday Night Live* (SNL) and, upon doing some research, learned that many of the writers and performers had studied at The Second City in Chicago. Because her boyfriend at the time was living in Chicago, she was able to take classes at the famed comedy club while visiting him. Her experience studying improv firsthand gave her the confidence she needed to pursue comedy seriously. As she told *Vulture*, "I could make my boyfriend and friends laugh, but the real testament was when I took an improv class, was effortlessly good and happy, and the teacher pulled me aside and gave me money out of her own pocket to get me to keep doing it. Someone giving you free money to do something is very motivating."

Because she was spending so much time in Chicago, her grades had begun to drop, so she opted to take a break from Temple for a semester and get a job at an Apple Store to accrue some savings. After spending a few trial months out in Los Angeles, she decided to move there permanently in 2013. Once there, she continued to work for an Apple Store and take classes at the LA Second City while also picking up odd jobs as a styling assistant. In addition to improv, she would take to the stage to present stand-up routines at open mics whenever possible and posted funny skits online that gained a great deal of attention.

SECURING A FULL-TIME GIG IN DIGITAL COMEDY

In 2014, Brunson posted a video, based on an existing stage act she had performed, titled "The Girl Who's Never Been on a Nice Date" that led to her gathering thousands of Instagram followers over the subsequent days. Encouraged, she turned it into a series and began posting installments on *YouTube*, where the videos could be longer than fifteen seconds, and steadily gained a sizeable audience. Later that same year, her keen understanding of the new frontier of internet comedy landed her a producer job with guaranteed income at BuzzFeed, creating humorous video content often focused on the experiences of being a twenty-something. By 2015, inspired by the collaborative and often conversation-provoking nature of the work, she had developed a five-episode series for BuzzFeed Motion Pictures called *Broke* while cementing her place at the company with a new development partner title.

Within the first weeks of being released, the first episode of *Broke* had gotten a million views. In April 2016, she sold the show as a twelve-episode series to YouTube Red—an achievement that validated that she could make it in the entertainment industry without having to compromise her voice or unique perspective. As she told Heather Wood Rudulph for *Cosmopolitan* (10 Oct. 2016) of the experience, "I felt like I could actually be successful at the thing I wanted to do. The best feeling was that I became part of the movement that will push new narratives into Hollywood. A lot of things people are upset about or frustrated by with Hollywood stem from the fact that the same old narrative is being sold over and over again. That's because there aren't people of color or young people as showrunners, writers, and producers."

In the years that followed, Brunson would continue to make digital content in a variety of roles. She had a series on Facebook Watch called *Quinta vs. Everything* that aired from 2017 to 2018 and created a television series pilot with Larry Wilmore and Jermaine Fowler that was ultimately not picked up. Meanwhile, as a performer, she landed roles on *iZombie* and *A Black Lady Sketch Show* in 2019 while also voicing characters in the animated series *Lazor Wulf* (2019–21), *Big Mouth* (2019–21), and *Magical Girl Friendship Squad* (2020).

ABBOTT ELEMENTARY

By 2021, Brunson was a beloved comedian among millennials and other internet comedy fans, with her online videos collectively reaching over a billion views. Moreover, her book *She Memes Well* (2021) also proved popular. However, it was the smashing success of her network sitcom *Abbott Elementary*, first airing strategically in December of that year and for which she served as a writer, producer, and star, that made her into a household name.

The idea for the sitcom had come to Brunson while she was visiting her family back in Philadelphia. At that time, her mother had been a schoolteacher for around forty years and was thinking about retirement. While waiting with her mother one evening at the school during a night designated for parent-teacher conferences, Brunson became frustrated that it was getting late, and parents were not coming in. Just minutes before the parent-teacher conferences were supposed to end, a woman who worked as a nurse showed up with her son. As Brunson watched how happy her mother was that the woman was able to make it, she realized how important teachers were to children's lives. She reflected on why she knew her mother's experience as a teacher was one she wanted to tell on television in an interview with Terry Gross for National Public Radio's *Fresh Air* (23 Feb. 2022), stating, "Despite it getting harder, despite, you know, teachers not having all the support they need, despite kids growing even more unruly than they've been in recent time. She still loved the job. . . . The beauty is someone being so resilient for a job that is so underpaid and so underappreciated because it makes them feel fulfilled."

Brunson went on to sell a sitcom about teachers to ABC, naming it *Abbott Elementary* after her beloved sixth-grade teacher. She decided to set the show in West Philadelphia and have it focus on a predominantly Black

school much like her mother's. Playing the lead character of the perpetually optimistic second-grade teacher Janine Teagues, Brunson wanted to bring attention to some of the struggles that educators in underfunded schools face in a gentle, comedic way, which she felt proved even more relatable and well received when the series finally premiered following the 2020 outbreak of the COVID-19 pandemic. The show quickly became a hit with millions of viewers and was renewed for a second season in March 2022—weeks before its finale had aired. As Brunson revealed to Quinci Legardye in an interview for *Harper's Bazaar* (31 Jan. 2022), she was not prepared for the show to be so successful so quickly: "I was expecting maybe the show finishes its first season, and then people will realize we have this great show, because that's how it goes with sitcoms a lot. To have only had a few episodes and just for it to be an abundance of support, love, conversation, and just enjoyment of the show. . . . I am just so happy, so overwhelmed." In addition to earning such plaudits as Emmy nominations, Brunson was recognized as having a major role in revitalizing the network sitcom. Another honor came with her inclusion on *Time* magazine's 2022 list of the one hundred most influential people.

PERSONAL LIFE

As of the early 2020s, Brunson had continued to reside in California, with some reports indicating that she had purchased property in late 2021 and had become engaged to marry that year.

SUGGESTED READING

Broadway, Danielle. "Quinta Brunson Was 'a Scaredy-Cat.' Then She Met the Teacher Who Inspired Her Sitcom." *Los Angeles Times*, 11 Jan. 2022, www.latimes.com/entertainment-arts/tv/story/2022-01-11/quinta-brunson-was-a-scaredy-cat-then-she-met-the-teacher-who-inspired-her-sitcom. Accessed 7 Aug. 2022.

Brunson, Quinta. "'Abbott Elementary' Creator Quinta Brunson Finds Humor and Heart in the Classroom." Interview by Terry Gross. *Fresh Air*, NPR, www.npr.org/transcripts/1082506558. Accessed 9 Aug. 2022.

___. "'Abbott Elementary' Creator Quinta Brunson on Relating to Teachers and the

Rejuvenation of Network Comedy." Interview by Antonia Blyth. *Deadline*, 14 June 2022, deadline.com/2022/06/quinta-brunson-interview-abbott-elementary-1235039597/. Accessed 7 Aug. 2022.

___. "Quinta Brunson on the Overnight Success of *Abbott Elementary*." Interview by Quinci Legardye. *Harper's Bazaar*, 31 Jan. 2022, www.harpersbazaar.com/culture/film-tv/a38940556/quinta-brunson-abbott-elementary-interview/. Accessed 7 Aug. 2022.

___. "You Can't Put Quinta Brunson in a Box." *Vulture*, 19 Oct. 2020, www.vulture.com/article/quinta-brunson-interview-comedians-you-should-know-2020.html. Interview. Accessed 7 Aug. 2022.

Rudulph, Heather Wood. "Get That Life: How I Became the Star of Your Favorite Viral BuzzFeed Videos." *Cosmopolitan*, 10 Oct. 2016, www.cosmopolitan.com/career/a4486504/quinta-brunson-buzzfeed-get-that-life/. Accessed 7 Aug. 2022.

SELECTED WORKS

Broke, 2016; *Quinta vs. Everything*, 2017–18; *A Black Lady Sketch Show*, 2019; *Abbott Elementary*, 2021–

—*Emily Turner*

Jessie Buckley

Born: December 28, 1989
Occupation: Actor and singer

For free-spirited actor and singer Jessie Buckley, life is all about savoring the experiences life has thrown her way. Enraptured by the performing arts since she was a child, she pursued her passion into adulthood, entering the BBC reality television series *I'd Do Anything* in 2008 with her sights set on the top prize: the role of Nancy in the musical production of *Oliver!* Although she did not win the show, the exposure helped her launch her career.

After *I'd Do Anything*, Buckley appeared in several theater productions, including *The Tempest* (2013) and *The Winter's Tale* (2015), in roles that she turned into a burgeoning acting career that would span both the small and silver screens. She not only appeared in the television miniseries *War and Peace* (2016) and the drama series *Taboo* (2017) but also in the

universally acclaimed HBO series *Chernobyl* (2019). Regarding film roles, she headed the critical darlings *Beast* (2017) and *Wild Rose* (2018) before taking part in the award-winning film *The Lost Daughter* (2021).

Buckley's story of her success is one of discovering the best life experiences in her craft. As she said to Jack King in an interview for *GQ* (17 Dec. 2021), "There are so many elements—that's what's so magical about making theater and film, just so many tiny, tiny little moments, between a camera, between the person you're with, where it's really like hopping into a river and anything can happen."

EARLY LIFE AND EDUCATION

Jessie Buckley was born on December 28, 1989, in Killarney, a city in County Kerry, Ireland, the first child of Tim Buckley and Marina Cassidy. Her mother was a vocal coach and professional singer, while her father ran a bed and breakfast and wrote poetry on the side. Buckley and her four younger siblings—a brother and three sisters—grew up immersed in the artistic realm. Irish dancing, singing, and acting were activities fostered by the Buckleys, who prioritized art and experiences over materialistic wealth. "Success was never based on how much you earned. It was all about how much life you could experience, and to never be scared to jump off the cliff, and learn to swim," she said to King.

For her education, Buckley attended an all-girls Catholic institution called Ursuline Secondary School, situated in County Tipperary. There, she continued preparing for her future acting career, investing her time in school theater productions, including *West Side Story* and *Chess*, in which she portrayed the male lead roles of Tony and Freddy Trumper, respectively. She also attended summer workshops held by the Association of Irish Musical Society throughout her childhood.

I'D DO ANYTHING

Taking a gap year following her completion of high school in 2007, Buckley then relocated to London, England, intent on enrolling at a drama school. However, with her plans shattered by an unwelcome rejection letter, she opted to enter the acting industry in a very modern way: as a contestant in a reality television show. The year was 2008, and the name of the BBC-produced talent competition series was *I'd Do

Photo by Montclair Film,
via Wikimedia Commons

Anything, which revolved around the search for an unknown actor who would play the role of Nancy in a West End musical production of *Oliver!* Of her experience in the show, the actor told Andrea Cuttler for *Harper's Bazaar* (12 Nov. 2020), "I was so ignorant of the rigmarole of the whole thing, which was probably the best place to be. I was more delighted that I was getting to sing and be part of a community that I thought would take a lifetime to even get a toe inside."

Although Buckley did not win *I'd Do Anything*, she earned the runner-up slot. Most importantly, the series exposed her to an incredible level of recognition and became an invaluable experience that opened doors for her in the acting world. Having signed with an agent, she considered acting programs, taking a four-week Shakespeare class at the Royal Academy of Dramatic Art (RADA) at first. When her theatrical debut arrived in late 2008, Buckley was seen on stages across England as part of the cast of the Stephen Sondheim musical *A Little Night Music*.

MORE THEATER ROLES

After her theatrical debut, a period of smaller gigs followed. Whether she was singing at jazz clubs or booking small acting roles, Buckley was happily practicing what she had learned as a child: to prioritize life experiences. "I had no

expectations and just went with whatever was in front of me that I felt drawn to," she revealed to Cuttler before continuing: "It was good to learn and try out things and fail. You take what you need to take. You can't be precious. You have to soak it all in and leave whatever is useless to you. Then it becomes your own story."

Buckley eventually made her way back to RADA, where she obtained her Bachelor of Arts degree in acting in January 2013. It was also around that time that she stepped back into the spotlight, portraying Miranda in *The Tempest* at the famous Shakespeare's Globe Theatre in London in 2012. That stage also saw Buckley make the dual role of singer Arabella Hunt and Kate her own in the play *Gabriel* by Australian playwright Samuel Adamson. When the West End production of *Henry V* premiered at the Noel Coward Theatre in September 2013, she shared the stage with seasoned actor Jude Law, who portrayed the title character, while Buckley played Princess Katharine.

After taking part in *Henry V*, which finished its run in February 2014, Buckley moved on to another Shakespeare production, *The Winter's Tale*, directed by Kenneth Branagh. She breathed life into the character of Perdita in this play, led by Judi Dench, which was later screened in cinemas beginning in November 2015.

BRANCHING OUT INTO TELEVISION AND FILM

By 2016, Buckley had turned a series of theater roles into a burgeoning acting career that would span both the small and silver screens. That year she appeared in the historical television drama series *War and Peace*, portraying the deeply religious Princess Marya Bolkonskaya. With her role in *War and Peace* praised, she next starred in the BBC television series *Taboo*, which aired in January 2017 in the United Kingdom and the United States. Playing Lorna Bow, Buckley shared the small screen with the likes of Tom Hardy and Leo Bill, among others, in an eight-episode drama that went on to earn myriad award nominations, including nods for two 2017 Primetime Emmy Awards and six 2018 British Academy Television Craft Awards.

The year 2017 was a significant year in Buckley's acting career because it also marked her first film role. Buckley won the role of the protagonist in the psychological thriller *Beast*, in which the actor played a misunderstood young woman named Moll, who starts hanging out with an alluring community outsider—who also happens to be the suspected author of murders in town. Set in the Channel Islands, the movie received a positive critical response and was nominated for a 2019 British Academy of Film and Television Arts (BAFTA) Award for outstanding British film.

When the musical drama *Wild Rose* hit theaters in the United States in 2019, audiences saw Buckley in the lead role of Rose-Lynn Harlan, a young, single mother of two from Glasgow whose dream is to make it big in the country music scene in Nashville. Using her impressive singing skills for the movie, whose soundtrack included a plethora of songs performed by her, the actor earned a nomination for a 2020 BAFTA Award for best actress in a leading role. Later that year, Buckley appeared in the universally acclaimed HBO series *Chernobyl*, a historical drama centered on the 1986 Ukrainian nuclear disaster and the cleanup efforts that followed.

Buckley found filming movies and television series challenging at times after transitioning from the world of theater. "Filming stuff is always weird," she explained to Tom Lamont for *The Guardian* (20 Mar. 2021). "You end up with a memory of an amazing communal experience [from being on set] and then over time it transcends through different hands, editing, music, grades, the director goes on his own journey with it—and ultimately it becomes something else, something greater or bigger or worse. And that's kind of hard. You can never reclaim what it was."

HIGH-PROFILE ROLES

Buckley had another successful year in 2020, as she was part of several television and film projects, including the films *Misbehaviour* and *I'm Thinking of Ending Things*. While in the comedy-drama *Misbehaviour* she portrayed 1970s activist Jo Robinson, of the newly formed women's liberation movement, in the physiological thriller *I'm Thinking of Ending Things*, her role was of a quiet young woman who is considering breaking up with her boyfriend. The two films were a testament to Buckley's multifaceted talent and, while quite different, they both earned positive reviews from critics and viewers alike.

If those films were not enough to show that Buckley was rapidly climbing the acting ladder—on both sides of the Atlantic—her appearance in the fourth season of the FX anthology series *Fargo* was bound to change that. For ten episodes, she played the hard-to-forget Oraetta Mayflower, a sweet-talking but callous nurse who takes pleasure in killing her patients.

The following year, the actor appeared in the critically acclaimed film *The Lost Daughter*, a psychological drama that marked the directorial debut of American actor Maggie Gyllenhaal. The movie narrates the story of a middle-aged college professor named Leda Caruso, played by Olivia Coleman, who, while on vacation in Greece, meets a young mother who seems dissatisfied with the life parenthood has brought for her. Through flashbacks, viewers learn about Leda's past and her feelings of being an ambivalent mother to her two daughters. With Buckley masterfully playing young Leda, it was no surprise that she earned several awards and honors, including a 2022 Academy Award nomination for best supporting actress.

After returning to her theater roots with the West End production of *Cabaret* in 2021, for which she won an Olivier Award, Buckley starred in the film *Men*. The folk horror about a young widow disturbed by a man while on holiday premiered in cinemas in mid-2022.

PERSONAL LIFE

Buckley resides in rural Norfolk, England, having bought an old house there in 2021. "It's like a person, this place, it's grown and aged," she said to Lamont, on her love of the 1600s-era house. "It has these wounds and scars."

SUGGESTED READING

Buckley, Jessie. "Jessie Buckley: 'Who Are We to Judge What Being a Good Mother Is?'" Interview by Jack King. *GQ*, 17 Dec. 2021, www.gq-magazine.co.uk/culture/article/jessie-buckley-lost-daughter-interview. Accessed 30 June 2022.

___. "Jessie Buckley and Rory Kinnear: 'I Like the Extremes of Opinion *Men* Will Instill in People.'" Interview by Adam White. *The Independent*, 1 June 2022, www.independent.co.uk/arts-entertainment/films/features/jessie-buckley-men-movie-ending-interview-b2091058.html. Accessed 30 June 2022.

Cuttler, Andrea. "Jessie Buckley Is Ready to Tell Her Own Story." *Harper's Bazaar*, 12 Nov. 2020, www.harpersbazaar.com/culture/film-tv/a34458196/jessie-buckley-fargo. Accessed 30 June 2022.

Lamont, Tom. "Jessie Buckley on Covid Filming: 'The World's Greatest Love Scene—And We Couldn't Touch!'" *The Guardian*, 20 Mar. 2021, www.theguardian.com/culture/2021/mar/20/jessie-buckley-on-covid-filming-worlds-greatest-love-scene-and-we-couldnt-touch. Accessed 30 June 2022.

SELECTED WORKS

War & Peace, 2016; *Taboo*, 2017; *Beast*, 2017; *Wild Rose*, 2019; *Chernobyl*, 2019; *Misbehaviour*, 2020; *I'm Thinking of Ending Things*, 2020; *Fargo*, 2020; *The Lost Daughter*, 2021; *Men*, 2022

—*Maria del Pilar Guzman*

Photo by All-Pro Reels, via Wikimedia Commons

Joe Burrow

Born: December 10, 1996
Occupation: Football player

Quarterback Joe Burrow quickly established himself as an exciting National Football League (NFL) star, generating much buzz as part of a new wave of talent reshaping the league. A former Ohio high school player who spent three years at Ohio State University, Burrow became a high-profile football prospect after moving to Louisiana State University (LSU) for his final two collegiate seasons, during which he won a national championship and put forth a Heisman Trophy–winning performance as a senior. He was then selected first overall by the Cincinnati Bengals in the 2020 NFL Draft, bringing high expectations that he would help revitalize the long-suffering team as a franchise quarterback.

Burrow soon lived up to the hype, showing great promise as a rookie starter even as the team as a whole continued to struggle. Although his debut season was cut short by injury, he returned in 2021 and continued to improve, taking the Bengals with him. "I think we started getting respect for our playmakers," he explained, as quoted by Bryan DeArdo for *CBS Sports* (18 May 2022). "Teams completely changed the way that they played us." Burrow ended up leading the Bengals to Super Bowl

LVI, proving that he was ready to compete at the highest level in just his second year in the NFL. Though the Bengals narrowly lost the championship to the Los Angeles Rams, the experience was nevertheless a valuable one. "You just grow and mature and understand that we're going to lose some games and have some bad days," Burrow told Conor Orr for *Sports Illustrated* (17 Aug. 2022) about the lessons he learned from his first professional playoff campaign. "You have to learn how to win and learn how to lose. You have to learn to take those losses and move on from them."

EARLY LIFE AND EDUCATION

Joseph Lee Burrow was born on December 10, 1996, in Ames, Iowa. At the time of his birth, his father, Jimmy, was coaching football at Ames High School. The family later moved to Athens, Ohio, after his father accepted a coaching staff position at Ohio University. Burrow's mother, Robin, was a school principal. In light of their father's career, Burrow and his two older brothers were immersed in football from an early age, and all three boys played the sport themselves. Burrow himself began playing as a young child and soon showed considerable skill as a quarterback, the position generally regarded as the on-field team leader. He also enjoyed watching football games and was a particular fan of the University of Nebraska Cornhuskers.

As a student at Athens High School, Burrow was a key member of the school's football team, which competed in its division's playoffs three times during his high school career. While he performed well throughout his high school career, scoring a total of 184 touchdowns over four seasons, he also experienced disappointing setbacks, including a painful state championship loss to Toledo Central Catholic High School in 2014. "I think about that game all the time," he later told reporters about the 56–52 loss, as reported by Billy Witz for the *New York Times* (13 Feb. 2022). "It was kind of a culmination of a lot of hard work and time that we put in together, and we just didn't get the job done." That experience was a formative one for Burrow, who sought to avoid similar losses as his career progressed.

COLLEGE CAREER

While still in high school, Burrow committed to attend and play football for Ohio State University, which played in the Division I (DI) Football Bowl Subdivision (FBS) of National Collegiate Athletic Association (NCAA) competition. He spent his first year at the university as a redshirt, practicing with the team and attending classes but not joining the Buckeyes' roster for games. Although Burrow did officially join the team for the next two seasons, he was considered a backup player and saw little game time, which he found disappointing. "When you don't play for three years and you're putting in the work. And you feel like you're practicing really well. And you feel like you could go out there and make plays and do what you've always done but you're not getting the opportunity to show what you can do. It's frustrating," he later told former player Chris Simms for the podcast *Chris Simms Unbuttoned*, as reported by Dave Clark for the *Cincinnati Enquirer* (24 June 2022). Overall, Burrow played in just ten games during his two active years at Ohio State and threw just two touchdowns.

In 2018, after earning a bachelor's degree in consumer and family financial services from Ohio State, Burrow enrolled in Louisiana State University (LSU), also a member of the DI FBS. In addition to pursuing graduate studies in liberal arts, Burrow had the opportunity to play two additional seasons of football at LSU, this time as the starting quarterback. He performed well as a junior in 2018 but truly excelled in his senior season, during which he completed sixty passing touchdowns, set a Southeastern Conference record for passing yards with 5,671, and helped his team achieve a perfect record during the season. He and his teammates went on to compete in and win LSU's first national championship in more than a decade, beating the Clemson Tigers in the College Football Playoff National Championship. The recipient of numerous awards while at LSU, Burrow ultimately received the 2019 Heisman Trophy as college football's most outstanding player. A member of the Southeastern Conference Academic Honor Roll during both of his years at LSU, he earned his master's degree from the university in December 2019.

NFL DRAFT AND ROOKIE SEASON

In early 2020, Burrow prepared to enter that year's NFL Draft, which was held virtually rather than in person due to the emergence of the coronavirus disease 2019 (COVID-19) pandemic. "There's definitely some disappointment," he admitted on *The Big Podcast with Shaq*, as reported by Bryan DeArdo in an interview for *CBS Sports* (15 Apr. 2020). "I was really looking forward to walking that stage, walking that red carpet, hearing my name called. But I think being at home with my family is gonna be just as good. Being drafted is being drafted." As was widely expected, the Cincinnati Bengals selected Burrow first overall, indicating the expectation that he could become a star NFL quarterback. He subsequently signed a four-year contract with the team.

Burrow immediately assumed the Bengals' starting quarterback job and made his official NFL debut in September 2020, in the team's season opener against the Los Angeles Chargers. Given his college success and lofty draft position, he received much media attention and accompanying pressure to perform. He soon showed flashes of stardom, including setting a rookie quarterback record for completed passes in his second career game. However, the Bengals continued to struggle as a team, often failing to protect Burrow from opposing defenses. That November, he took a hard hit during a game against the Washington Football Team and severely injured his left knee, cutting his promising rookie season short. He finished with ten games played, during which he compiled just a 2–7–1 record but passed for 2,688 yards and thirteen touchdowns and also scored three rushing touchdowns.

REACHING THE SUPER BOWL

Burrow spent the end of the 2020 NFL season and subsequent offseason recovering from his knee injury, a lengthy process that included careful rehabilitation. "I'm very optimistic about where I'm at and also where the team is at," he told former Bengals receiver Cris Collinsworth for the podcast *Pro Football Focus* prior to the season, as reported by Geoff Hobson for *Bengals.com* (20 Apr. 2021). "Rehab is going very, very well and lifting is going very, very well. I'm in great shape. Legs feel good, knee feels good." Although it was initially unclear whether Burrow would be ready to begin the 2021 season, that September the team announced he was cleared to play for the season opener.

As an NFL sophomore, Burrow reestablished himself as a rising star. Over the course of the 2021 season he passed for a stellar 4,611 yards with 34 touchdowns, leading the league in completion percentage and yards gained per passing attempt. In recognition of his strong performance he was twice named American Football Conference (AFC) Offensive Player of the Week and was recognized as the NFL Comeback Player of the Year by both the Associated Press and the Pro Football Writers of America.

In addition to Burrow's individual success, the Bengals as a whole fared better in 2021 than in the previous season. "We want to be one of the top offenses in the league, and we have the capacity to do that year in and year out. But . . . it's gonna take consistency of work and preparation and practice," Burrow told Albert Breer for *Sports Illustrated* (5 Sept. 2022). The team ended the regular season with a 10–7 record, winning the AFC North Division and qualifying for the playoffs. Progressing through the postseason tournament, Burrow and his teammates beat the Las Vegas Raiders to earn Cincinnati its first playoff win in over two decades, upset the first-seed Tennessee Titans, and then clinched the AFC Championship against the Kansas City Chiefs.

Earning a spot in Super Bowl LVI, Burrow and the Bengals faced off against the Los Angeles Rams, a team filled with veteran stars.

The game was close throughout, with the Bengals trailing at halftime before taking a lead into the fourth quarter. However, the Bengals continued to struggle to protect Burrow, who was sacked a Super Bowl–record seven times, and they ultimately lost, 23–20. Though disappointed, Burrow and his teammates worked to move past the defeat and prepare for the future. "We've put this behind us," he later said, as quoted by DeArdo (2022). "We lost, we had a great year, we're going forward."

2022 SEASON

Burrow's focus on his next NFL season was interrupted in July 2022, when a ruptured appendix forced him to undergo an appendectomy and miss a portion of the Bengals' training camp. However, he recovered quickly and resumed practicing with the team in mid-August. That same month he was ranked twenty-first on the player-voted list of the hundred top active NFL players.

The 2022 NFL season began in September, and Burrow hoped to build the previous year's success and lead the Bengals back to the Super Bowl. "Now, we know what it takes," he said, as reported by DeArdo (2022). "We have that experience in our back pocket going forward."

PERSONAL LIFE

In addition to football, Burrow enjoys playing video games and held weekly online gaming sessions with his friends from high school, which he credited with helping him relax throughout the NFL season. Burrow still lives with his parents at their home in Athens County, Ohio, when not playing football elsewhere.

SUGGESTED READING

Breer, Albert. "Joe Burrow Doesn't Have All the Answers, But He's Close." *Sports Illustrated*, 5 Sept. 2022, www.si.com/nfl/2022/09/05/joe-burrow-bengals-secret-success-mmqb. Accessed 12 Sept. 2022.

Burrow, Joe. "NFL Draft 2020: Joe Burrow Details His Draft Night Plans and Reveals Virtual Interview Questions." Interview with Bryan DeArdo. *CBS Sports*, 15 Apr. 2020, www.cbssports.com/nfl/news/nfl-draft-2020-joe-burrow-details-his-draft-night-plans-and-reveals-virtual-interview-questions/. Accessed 12 Sept. 2022.

Clark, Dave. "Joe Burrow: 'If You Don't Have Anything to Say, Don't Manufacture Something.'" *Cincinnati Enquirer*, 24 June 2022, www.cincinnati.com/story/sports/nfl/bengals/2022/06/23/joe-burrow-talks-chris-simms-leadership-confidence-training-diet-knee-injury-arm-strength-bengals/7718418001/. Accessed 12 Sept. 2022.

DeArdo, Bryan. "Bengals' Joe Burrow Opens Up on Super Bowl Loss, Jokes That Cincinnati Will Run the Wing-T Offense This Season." *CBS Sports*, 18 May 2022, www.cbssports.com/nfl/news/bengals-joe-burrow-opens-up-on-super-bowl-loss-jokes-that-cincinnati-will-run-the-wing-t-offense-this-season/. Accessed 12 Sept. 2022.

Hobson, Geoff. "Burrow, Back on the Run and in the Pocket, Steaming through Rehab." *Bengals.com*, 20 Apr. 2021, www.bengals.com/news/burrow-back-on-the-run-and-in-the-pocket-steaming-through-rehab. Accessed 12 Sept. 2022.

Orr, Conor. "Joe Burrow and the New Normal." *Sports Illustrated*, 17 Aug. 2022, www.si.com/nfl/2022/08/17/joe-burrow-on-new-fame-encore-super-bowl-run-daily-cover. Accessed 12 Sept. 2022.

Witz, Billy. "Joe Burrow's Last Playoff Loss Was in High School. He Still Thinks about It." *The New York Times*, 13 Feb. 2022, www.nytimes.com/2022/02/10/sports/football/bengals-joe-burrow-ohio.html. Accessed 12 Sept. 2022.

—*Joy Crelin*

Lisa Byington

Born: May 18, 1976
Occupation: Sports announcer and host

In September 2021, the National Basketball Association (NBA) team the Milwaukee Bucks announced that sports broadcaster Lisa Byington had been hired as the new play-by-play announcer whose voice would be heard on the local broadcasts of the Bucks' games. "I'm absolutely thrilled for this opportunity, and the ability to work with a first-class franchise and a championship organization like the Milwaukee Bucks," she said in a statement following her hiring, as reported by Patrick Nothaft for *MLive* (16 Sept. 2021). A longtime

broadcaster, Byington had previously made history in September 2017, when she became the first woman to serve as play-by-play announcer for a college football broadcast on the Big Ten Network (BTN). Upon making her on-air debut with the Bucks in October 2021, Byington achieved yet another first, becoming the first woman to hold a full-time play-by-play position with an NBA team.

Byington's hiring represented a significant turning point in the world of sportscasting as well as a career milestone for the announcer, who had spent the prior decades working her way up from small to major television markets. In a sports-broadcasting landscape still dominated by men, Byington had admirably forged a career for herself. However, she noted in interviews that her debut with the Bucks, though important, was just one in a series of steps toward a world in which a woman's voice in a live sports broadcast would be simply "background noise," as opposed to a novelty. "I don't know when we're going to get there," she told Nothaft for *MLive* (24 June 2021). "Maybe five years down the line, ten years down the line, twenty years down the line—but I will know that we've made ultimate progress when we start getting to that point."

EARLY LIFE AND EDUCATION

Lisa Byington was born on May 18, 1976, and grew up in Portage, Michigan, outside of Kalamazoo. Her mother, Linda, was a teacher, and her father, Bob, was a counselor who would later serve as head coach of Byington's high school basketball team. Byington cited her parents as key influences in her early life. She particularly commended her mother, who made a strong impression on her by returning to the workplace after having children. "She and my dad always told me, 'You can do whatever you want,'" Byington told Nothaft. "It was never gender-specific goals at all. They always taught me from a very young age that I could be and pursue whatever I wanted to."

An athletic teenager, Byington played both soccer and basketball while a student at Portage Northern High School and was also a member of the school's debate team. A key moment came in 1993, when her basketball team claimed a district title but subsequently lost in the state semifinals. A local news outlet reported on the semifinal loss, capturing a touching moment between Byington and her

Photo by Thebingers,
via Wikimedia Commons

father after the game. Byington was struck by the images captured. "It was amazing to see, and that was the first time I realized the impact of broadcasting," she told Scott Cacciola for *The New York Times* (14 Oct. 2021). "I always go back to that, because that's really the first moment I started thinking, 'Oh, that impacted me, and maybe someday I can impact others in the same way.'" After graduating from high school in 1994, Byington enrolled in Northwestern University in Evanston, Illinois, where she continued to play both basketball and soccer and earned academic Big Ten honors in both sports. Byington pursued a bachelor's degree in print journalism and a master's degree in broadcast journalism, completing her studies at Northwestern in 1999.

EARLY CAREER

Byington began her career in broadcasting with WBKB, a television station in the small market of Alpena, Michigan. She later moved to WLNS in Lansing, Michigan, where she worked for the better part of a decade and reported on a range of topics, from local news to high school and college sports. Moving primarily into sports broadcasting over the years, she went on to take assignments with networks such as BTN and Fox Sports. Byington worked as a freelancer for much of her second decade in broadcasting and was consequently able to take on assignments with multiple broadcasters and for an array of sports, including both college and professional sports.

Byington often worked as a sideline reporter throughout her early career, a role that often required her to conduct on-screen interviews with athletes and team personnel. She moved into play-by-play announcing after a last-minute opportunity to serve in that role for a women's basketball game emerged. "It was horrible, but I must not have screwed up enough because they kept asking me to do a bunch of different sports," she told Cacciola, recalling the challenges of jumping into that assignment with no previous play-by-play experience. Soon, she was calling play-by-plays for everything from softball and soccer to gymnastics. Byington officially joined the broadcast team for the Chicago Sky of the Women's National Basketball Association (WNBA) in 2013 and spent several seasons as a play-by-play announcer for the franchise.

MAKING HISTORY AND NEW CHALLENGES

In September 2017, Byington became the first woman to serve as a play-by-play announcer for a college football broadcast on the Big Ten Network (BTN) when she announced a game between her alma mater, Northwestern University, and Bowling Green State University. In addition to being the first woman to fill that role for BTN, she was one of very few women to have served as play-by-play announcers for the sport of football. Byington characterized that honor to David Haugh for the *Chicago Tribune* (13 Sept. 2017) as a particularly desirable sport to commentate due to its status as "America's sport." When discussing that milestone, Byington emphasized the significance her work might take on for girls and young women aspiring to become sports broadcasters. "The best advice I've gotten is don't make this about you but use it as a platform," she told Haugh. "You can count on one hand the women who have done this—and still have fingers left. So it's important for me to be a strong female role model. I didn't have a lot growing up." Byington's influence extended further in 2019, when she joined the team of play-by-play announcers for that year's International Federation of Association Football (FIFA) Women's World Cup.

While the year 2020 initially seemed to be a typical year in the realm of sports, the emergence of the coronavirus disease 2019 (COVID-19) pandemic early in the year wreaked havoc on many scheduled sporting events and shook up the broadcasting world as well. In March 2020, Byington had the unique experience of working as a sideline reporter for the final game of the National Collegiate Athletic Association (NCAA) men's basketball season, which was shut down midgame due to the pandemic. "It was really surreal," she told Ross Dellenger for *Sports Illustrated* (12 Mar. 2020). "The Big East gave us our last little taste of March Madness." Although the pandemic continued into 2021, both college and professional sporting events resumed. Byington returned to college basketball that year, becoming the first woman to serve as a play-by-play announcer in a national broadcast of the NCAA men's basketball tournament. Also in 2021, Byington joined NBC's coverage of the Summer Olympics in Tokyo, Japan, providing play-by-play announcing for soccer matches. Although she did not travel to Japan for the Games and instead broadcast her commentary from an NBC studio in Connecticut, she nevertheless appreciated the opportunity to contribute to an event as well known as the Olympics. "I think everybody has watched the Olympics in some sort of capacity, whether it's the summer or winter Olympics, and I remember watching the Olympics . . . so it's absolutely a dream come true and a bucket list broadcasting item," she told Nothaft.

MILWAUKEE BUCKS

A new opportunity for Byington emerged in 2021, when the NBA's Milwaukee Bucks began their search for a new candidate to replace longtime announcer Jim Paschke, who was retiring, as play-by-play announcer for the team's Bally Sports Wisconsin broadcasts. "My agent . . . came to me and said, 'Are you interested in this job?'" she recalled to Richard Deitsch for *The Athletic* (4 Oct. 2021). "There were other NBA jobs open—the [Philadelphia] 76ers being one of them—but we only looked at the Bucks job because I felt like it was something that matched me." Byington auditioned for the position remotely, sending in footage of her play-by-play work from an NCAA tournament game. Her work impressed the hiring team, and in September 2021, the Bucks organization announced that Byington had been hired for the position, thus becoming

the first woman to be hired as a full-time play-by-play professional for an NBA team.

For Byington, her new role represented both a major professional opportunity and an exciting challenge. Discussing the Bucks fans who might struggle to accept her voice covering their home team, Byington told Cacciola that "ultimately, I don't think of myself as a female broadcaster. I think of myself as a broadcaster, and the goal is to do the job well enough that people start thinking that way as well." Paired mainly with commentator Marques Johnson, Byington worked her first Bucks home game on October 10, 2021, during the preseason. She continued to call the play-by-play over the course of the 2021–22 NBA season, which opened on October 19 for the Bucks.

PERSONAL LIFE

Byington considered Chicago to be her home for many years. She relocated to Milwaukee, Wisconsin, after becoming the play-by-play broadcaster for the Bucks. A fitness enthusiast, she especially enjoys long bike rides and runs. Byington is the namesake of the Big Ten Conference's Lisa Byington Award, an award and professional-development program for female broadcasting students.

SUGGESTED READING

Brockway, Ella. "Lisa Byington Ready for Her History-Making March Madness Moment." *Sports Illustrated*, 16 Mar. 2021, www.si.com/college/2021/03/16/lisa-byington-march-madness-play-by-play-history. Accessed 7 Feb. 2022.

Byington, Lisa, and Kate Scott. "Meet the NBA's Pioneering New Play-by-Play Voices: Lisa Byington and Kate Scott on Their Trailblazing Paths." Interview by Richard Deitsch. *The Athletic*, 4 Oct. 2021, theathletic.com/2863466/2021/10/04/meet-the-nbas-pioneering-new-play-by-play-voices-lisa-byington-and-kate-scott-on-their-trailblazing-paths. Accessed 7 Feb. 2022.

Cacciola, Scott. "An N.B.A. Female 'First' Hopes It's Not Such a Big Deal Soon." *The New York Times*, 14 Oct. 2021, www.nytimes.com/2021/10/14/sports/basketball/lisa-byington-bucks.html. Accessed 7 Feb. 2022.

Dellenger, Ross. "Inside the Eerie Scene of College Basketball's Final Game of the

Season." *Sports Illustrated*, 12 Mar. 2020, www.si.com/college/2020/03/13/big-east-tournament-canceled-halftime-tim-brando. Accessed 7 Feb. 2022.

Haugh, David. "BTN Broadcaster Lisa Byington Braces for Historic Football Assignment." *Chicago Tribune*, 13 Sept. 2017, www.chicagotribune.com/sports/ct-lisa-byington-btn-football-haugh-spt-0914-20170913-column.html. Accessed 7 Feb. 2022.

Nothaft, Patrick. "Michigan Native Lisa Byington Becomes First Woman to Land Full-Time Play-by-Play Job in Major Men's Sports." *MLive*, 16 Sept. 2021, www.mlive.com/sports/2021/09/michigan-native-lisa-byington-becomes-first-woman-to-land-full-time-play-by-play-job-in-major-mens-sports.html. Accessed 7 Feb. 2022.

___. "Michigan Native Lisa Byington Preparing for Dream Job as Olympic Play-by-Play Announcer." *MLive*, 24 June 2021, www.mlive.com/sports/2021/06/michigan-native-lisa-byington-preparing-for-dream-job-as-olympic-play-by-play-announcer.html. Accessed 7 Feb. 2022.

—*Joy Crelin*

Rocío Caballero

Born: June 1, 1964
Occupation: Painter

Mexican painter and artist Rocío Caballero is best known for painting nightmarish images skewering structures of power. In Caballero's surreal world, men in gray suits wear pig masks and ride tricycles brandishing guns that shoot soap bubbles. Her figures are both ridiculous and terrifying in their childish disregard for the world around them. Caballero, who studied at Mexico's La Esmeralda National School of Painting in the late 1980s, began her career with works challenging constructions of gender, and later went on to exhibit her paintings and other artworks domestically and internationally. As a student, she divulged to Avelina Lésper in a Spanish-language video interview for *El Milenio* (9 Aug. 2013), that she was told she had a "masculine line." At the time this was considered a stigma for female painters, but she grew to embrace it. Caballero sees her distinctive style as a play on her surname, which means "gentleman." "I am a Gentleman, and I paint like a gentleman," she said in Spanish. Over time, Caballero moved beyond exploring notions of masculinity and femininity, adding other forms of social commentary to her work. Her most common forms are understood to be archetypal characters—Caballero variously calls them "gray goblins" or "yuppies"—representing power, dominance, and greed. In the biography written for her website (2013), Caballero's paintings are said to offer "a personal and fantastic vision of those men who can dispense with morality for the sake of a future that justifies any of their actions."

EARLY LIFE AND EDUCATION

Rocío Caballero was born in the Tepaneca neighborhood of Azcapotzalco in Mexico City, Mexico, on June 1, 1964. Her father, Jesús, was a taxi driver, and her mother, Irene, was a homemaker. Caballero was interested in art from an early age. She recalled in an interview with Pablo Llana for *Art Facto Today* (1 Sept. 2014) that, even as a child, she was said to have the "look" of a painter.

Caballero began studying for a degree in administration at the National Polytechnic School of Mexico, or IPN, but switched her focus to art in 1982. In 1985 she enrolled as a student at the La Esmeralda National School of Painting, Sculpture and Engraving. She graduated in 1990 and began teaching fine arts at a private secondary school.

FOCO GALLERY

As a student, Caballero met fellow artists Esteban Eroski, Alejandro Sánchez, and José Luis López; the four soon formed a working relationship. The small collective opened a gallery called FOCO in a garage and began to exhibit their work. FOCO and four other galleries in Mexico City formed the "Condesa Cultural Circuit," a network that sought to bring contemporary Mexican art to a broader, more diverse audience. Mónica Mayer, an artist, activist, and feminist art critic who wrote for Mexico City's daily newspaper *El Universal* (1993), noted that Caballero and her fellow artists provided for an unmet need in the Mexican art world at that time. The devastating Mexico City earthquake of 1985 had helped breed profound distrust of the Mexican government among many citizens. In this atmosphere, government-sanctioned art institutions and commercial galleries hesitated to exhibit political art. Groups like Caballero's brought this work directly to the public.

EARLY WORK

In 1993 Caballero presented her first individual exhibition in an institutional space, featuring two series of paintings entitled *Perversiones de la fe* (*Perversions of Faith*) and *Mátame y te querré siempre* (*Kill Me and I Will Always Love You*) at the José María Velasco Gallery in central Mexico City. Caballero's work in this exhibition, Mayer wrote in her review, emphasized the stark contradictions inherent in social constructions of femininity, namely the extreme contrast between "holiness and prostitution."

In 1994 Caballero presented her first exhibition in the United States, *Open Studio*, in Lexington, New York. In 1998, she mounted an exhibition called *Agua: Elemento Vivo* at the Salon of Mexican Fine Art in Mexico City. Typified by the paintings *Espíritus en el agua* (*Spirits in Water*) and *Apassionatta* (*Passionate*), the collection drew inspiration from classical mythology and featured passive, feminine forms and sea creatures submerged in water. Caballero continued this series for an exhibition, *Falta un Decir de Agua*, at the Art of Mexico gallery in Chicago, Illinois, in 1999.

GRAY GOBLINS AND *CÓDIGO GRIS*

In the early 2000s Caballero began investigating more masculine forms in her paintings. In the painting *Lesson 3: Indolence* (2004), masculine figures leap into the air, suspended above a wasteland of human bones. These figures inspired Caballero to consider a world of powerful male hedonists, playing childish games at the expense of others. Later, she would depict similar figures in gray business suits, recalling the stereotypical male business attire of the 1980s. Caballero eventually dubbed them the "gray goblins." Her "lessons series" would later be exhibited as *Código Gris* (2011), or the *Gray Code*. As Caballero explained to Lésper in Spanish, she imagined the "gray code" as a literal book of behavior—fifty visual lessons divided into five chapters—that governs the exclusive, mafia-like sect of gray goblins. It teaches that gray goblins, first and foremost, "should always be beautiful," she said. "In this first chapter comes temperance, strength, patience, the lessons they have to learn in order to become cold, cold with the

world to dominate and subdue it. They are insensitive characters, who do not know guilt or pain, they only know the game of power."

Like Caballero's previous paintings, those featuring the gray goblins engage with classical or ancient imagery, as well as other artworks. As art critic Erik Castillo, who wrote about the "Gray Code" for the Museum of Mexican Artists in 2011, noted, Caballero's *Lesson 20: Forever Galán* (2010) references Julio Galán's *Me quiero morir* (I Want to Die) (1985), and *Lesson 25: Biclón* (2010) references José Clemente Orozco's fresco, *Man on Fire* (1939). *Disertaciones de altura* (2013) offers a play on Charles Clyde Ebbets's iconic 1932 photograph "Lunch atop a Skyscraper," while *El espantapájaros* (*The Scarecrow*) foregrounds a figure in a version of Edward Hopper's *Nighthawks* (1942). In a number of the gray goblin paintings, such as *Lesson 21: Diatribe of Obedience* (2011) and *Lesson 34: Let the Pigs Come to Me* (2011), the gray goblins wear animal masks, evoking childish play but also uncertainty and danger. In the former, a male figure wearing a pig mask leans on a sword. He looms over a row of seated figures in various animal masks. In the catalogue for Caballero's 2019 retrospective *Abyss* at the National Museum of Mexican Art in Chicago, Illinois, critic Dolores Mercado wrote that the masks in the piece signify "ritual, dominance and might" but also "impunity." Their faces concealed, "they do not fear consequences."

LE BÚSQUEDA DE LA ATARAXIA

Caballero invokes esoteric symbols in other works in the Gray Code series, like *Lección 10: La búsqueda de la ataraxia* (*Lesson 10: The Search for Ataraxia*) (2010). In that painting, she arranges sleeping gray goblins, seen from above, in a spiral formation. The word "ataraxia" in the title is an ancient Greek term for an untroubled mental state, free of worry and fear. Caballero also incorporated this painting in a separate series, *Le Búsqueda de la Ataraxia* (2013), delving further into the concept. The spiral image appears again in Caballero's 2012 piece translated as *The Search for Ataraxia: Paradise*. In this painting, the gray goblins are naked and slumbering. Critic Beatriz Garduño, writing for the *Abyss* catalogue, described the figures as existing in a "collective trance" of "absolute narcissism, free of responsibilities or social conscience."

The ataraxia series, in its own provocative way, explores dreams and dreaming, central themes in much of Caballero's work. Many of her paintings feature figures either sleeping or in unguarded rest. One of her most famous and most powerful works, *Los sueños rotos* (*Broken Dreams*) (2009), depicts a woman with closed or downcast eyes. Wearing a wedding gown and a blowing veil, she stands on a barren landscape between two pink, wooden crosses. An accordion of paper figures—a recurring image in Caballero's paintings—falls from her hands. Writing for the *Chicago Tribune* (11 Dec. 2009), Lauren Viera called the piece a stark and "visually arresting" commentary on the ongoing epidemic of femicides in the Mexican border city of Ciudad Juárez. Viera, who reviewed a showing of artworks exploring the decades-long epidemic of violence against women at the National Museum of Mexican Art in Chicago, was critical of the full show's purpose and execution, but praised Caballero's work for its ability to stand on its own right.

EL REINO DE YUPPIELAND AND OTHER WORK

Over time, Caballero began to refer to her gray goblins as "yuppies," a common slang term for young, urban professionals. The childlike, or perhaps more accurately, childish, male characters in her works inhabit an unsettling dreamlike reality that Caballero calls Yuppieland. Her exhibition *News from the Kingdom of Yuppieland*, first presented in 2017, collected paintings in which the adult yuppies so familiar to Caballero's previous works appear as young children, learning the lessons that will shape them into the selfish, power-hungry people they will become. Caballero had explored this idea as early as 2009, with her painting, *Yuppy, Yuppy!*, in which the yuppies appear as teenagers. Paintings featuring the "yuppitos" became more overt later in her career. In *El Reino de Yuppieland* (2019), a laughing child with a lifted pig mask pours water on the face of a prone toy soldier. In the background, buildings drawn in a child's hand are bombed and set ablaze. In *El niño y la bestia* (*The Boy and the Beast*), a little boy holds a hyena by a chain. The boy seems unaware of what he is doing, though Caballero suggests he is practicing the dominance that will come naturally to him as an adult. In *Encrucijada* (*Crossroads*) (2019), a child wearing a bumblebee costume walks a dirt path, leaving a trail of tornadoes in his wake.

In the late 2010s, Caballero produced multiple works that spoke to a changing political iconography. In *Gotcha!* (2016), an unmasked yuppy stands in a line of masked figures. These figures wear baggy jeans, camouflage and bullet-proof vests. Casually holding automatic weapons, they evoke images of militia fighters and right-wing vigilantes. *Yuppito presidente*, also painted in 2016, depicts a magician-like man in a pig mask standing on a stool, showering three small children with confetti.

In 2021, Caballero presented an exhibition called *I Had a Dream*, in which she reproduced and updated various works, including etchings and engravings.

SUGGESTED READING

Caballero, Rocío. "El Hombre y Su Traje: Rocío Caballero [The Man and His Suit: Rocío Caballero]." Interview by Pablo Llana. *Art Facto.Today*, 1 Sept. 2014. *Google Translate*, art--facto-today.translate.goog/rocio-caballero/?_x_tr_sl=es&_x_tr_tl=en&_x_tr_hl=en&_x_tr_pto=op,sc. Accessed 7 Mar. 2022.

___. "Rocío Caballero." *Rocío Caballero*, 2013, bgmdifusion.wixsite.com/rociocaballero/biografia. Accessed 8 Mar. 2022.

___. *Rocío Caballero en* El Milenio Visto por el Arte *con Avelina Lésper.* [*Rocío Caballero in the Millennium Seen by Art with Avelina Lésper.*] *El Milenio Visto por el Arte,* 9 Aug. 2013, arte.milenio.com/artistas/18rocio/. Accessed 7 Mar. 2022.

"CCA Presents Bilingual Exhibition 'News from the Kingdom of Yuppieland.'" *Fresno State University College of Arts and Humanities,* fresnostatecah.com/2021/03/01/cca-presents-bilingual-exhibition-news-from-the-kingdom-of-yuppieland/. Accessed 23 Mar. 2022.

Garduño, Beatriz, and Dolores Mercado. *Abyss: Rocío Caballero.* National Museum of Mexican Art, Chicago, 2019, issuu.com/rociocaballero7/docs/catalogo_chicago_abyss. Accessed 23 Mar. 2022.

"Rocío Caballero." *El Milenio Visto por el Arte,* 2013 [The Millennium Seen by Art], arte.milenio.com/artistas/18rocio/. Accessed 8 Mar. 2022.

Roman, Oscar. "Rocío Caballero." *Fernanda Familiar*, 20 Aug. 2018, fernandafamiliar-soy.translate.goog/colaboradores/oscar-roman-2/rocio-caballero/?_x_tr_sl=es&_x_tr_tl=en&_x_tr_hl=en&_x_tr_pto=sc. Accessed 23 Mar. 2022.

Viera, Lauren. "Art Review." *Chicago Tribune*, 11 Dec. 2009, www.chicagotribune.com/news/ct-xpm-2009-12-11-0912090388-story.html. Accessed 8 Mar. 2022.

SELECTED WORKS

Espíritus en el agua, 1994; *Lesson 3: Indolence*, 2000; *Los sueños rotos*, 2009; *Lesson 20: Forever Galán*, 2010; *Lesson 21: Diatribe of Obedience*, 2011; *La Búsqueda de la Ataraxia*, 2013; *Gotcha!*, 2016; *El Reino de Yuppieland*, 2017, *Encrucijada*, 2019

—*Molly Hagan*

Photo by jenaragon94 via Wikimedia Commons

Jasmine Camacho-Quinn

Born: August 21, 1996
Occupation: Athlete

As track and field athlete Jasmine Camacho-Quinn prepared to compete in the Olympic Games in July 2021, focusing on her future performance, and not on the past, was of paramount importance. Five years before, she had entered the women's 100-meter hurdle event at the 2016 Summer Olympics and seemed poised to make a strong finish; however, an unfortunate series of events led to her disqualification. Her return to the Olympics, then, was a second chance to prove herself, so long as she could keep her focus. "It's basically a mind game—you tell yourself you can't do it then you're not going to be able to. Tell yourself you can, and you can," she explained to Jess Whittington for the website of *World Athletics* (25 Apr. 2021). Camacho-Quinn's strategy was an effective one: with a time of 12.37 seconds in the final round, she handily beat her opponents to claim a gold medal for Puerto Rico, only the second gold won by an athlete representing that US territory.

An accomplished hurdler since high school, Camacho-Quinn had an impressive college athletic career, winning several national titles while attending the University of Kentucky. In 2018, she left school to become a professional athlete. Her gold-medal performance at the Olympic Games, however, represented the most significant milestone of her career to that point, in large part because of her national team affiliation. "Being able to represent Puerto Rico means so much," she explained to Chris Rosvoglou for the *Spun* (19 Oct. 2021). "This year wasn't my first time representing the country, but it was my first time winning a medal for my people. That meant so much because I feel like there's nothing better than stepping out there and representing such a beautiful country. It shows what us Puerto Ricans can bring to the table, and that feeling will never go away."

EARLY LIFE AND EDUCATION

Jasmine Camacho-Quinn was born on August 21, 1996, in Charleston, South Carolina. The second of two children born to María Milagros Camacho and James Quinn, she grew up in North Charleston. The household was athletically oriented: Camacho-Quinn's parents had both been track and field athletes in college, and her older brother, Robert Quinn, played football and would go on to play professionally for several teams in the National Football League (NFL).

A gymnast early in life, Camacho-Quinn switched to track and field by the time she was in eighth grade and excelled in that sport, competing in a variety of events. In addition to the long jump and sprints of various lengths, she proved particularly skilled at the 100-meter hurdle event, in which competitors race a 100-meter distance while jumping over ten hurdles placed intermittently along the track. Demonstrating her athletic talents during her years as a student at South Carolina's Fort Dorchester High School, Camacho-Quinn began to dream of competing on the international stage and particularly of representing Puerto Rico, the US territory where her mother was born. "She wanted me to run for Puerto Rico because she never got to do it when she was younger. I wear it with pride," she told Cathal Dennehy for *Spikes* (21 May 2018) about the choice to compete for Puerto Rico rather than the United States.

COLLEGE CAREER

Following her graduation from high school in 2014, Camacho-Quinn enrolled in the University of Kentucky, having been recruited by coach Edrick Floréal. An institution with a strong athletic program, the university was home to a number of top track and field athletes, and Camacho-Quinn was able to train alongside other runners and hurdlers whom she might one day face in national or international competition. "We know that we are pretty much at the top of the world, so being able to train with each other, we can really push each other," she told Jeff Hartsell for *The Post and Courier* (29 July 2021) in a 2018 interview. "We let each other know what we need to work on."

Camacho-Quinn competed in several track and field events during her years in college, including both indoor and outdoor events, but focused primarily on the 100-meter hurdle event. She performed well in many competitions across the country. In June 2016, for example, she claimed first place in 100-meter hurdles at the National Collegiate Athletic Association (NCAA) Division I Women's Outdoor Track and Field Championships, becoming the first University of Kentucky freshman to do so. While Camacho-Quinn fell to second place in the 100-meter hurdles at the 2017 NCAA Championships, she and her teammates claimed first place in that year's 4×100-meter relay. Camacho-Quinn was also a recurring Southeastern Conference (SEC) champion during her college years, claiming SEC titles in the 60-meter and 100-meter hurdles and

the 4×100-meter relay over the course of her college career.

OLYMPIC DEBUT

Following her freshman year at the University of Kentucky, Camacho-Quinn traveled to Rio de Janeiro, Brazil, at nineteen years old to compete in the women's 100-meter hurdle event at the 2016 Summer Olympics. As she planned, she represented her mother's birthplace of Puerto Rico, which, though a US territory, competes separately from the United States in the Olympics. Already an accomplished competitor going into the event, Camacho-Quinn was optimistic about her chances of success. "I thought I had my life planned out," she later told Hartsell. "I knew if I medaled, I might not even come back to college."

Sporting events, however, can be unpredictable, and the 100-meter hurdle competition that year was no exception. After performing well in the qualifying round, placing first in her heat with a time of 12.70 seconds, Camacho-Quinn hit two hurdles with her foot during her semifinal run and collided with the final hurdle. Athletes representing the United States ultimately claimed all three medals in the event, while Camacho-Quinn, who was disqualified and unable to compete in the final round, returned home empty-handed. Devastated and embarrassed, she struggled to recover from the incident over the next several months. "It took me a while," Camacho-Quinn recalled, as reported by Hartsell. "Probably a whole semester of school. But it was a lesson for me. It was a setback, but I also kind of realized that I was not ready to grow up yet, either."

RETURN TO COMPETITION

After returning from Rio, Camacho-Quinn resumed training and competing but struggled to perform to her exacting standards. "I came back too quick," she told Dennehy. "I was really tired still so I wasn't doing everything correctly. I gained a lot of weight and I started dealing with injuries and stuff like that. I was exhausted and tired and still upset with how everything played out." By the end of the 2016–17 academic year, she decided to take the summer off from competing in order to rest and recuperate. Her decision proved to be a prudent one. Returning to the University of Kentucky for the 2017–18 school year after her summer off, Camacho-Quinn again excelled in competition. At the SEC Championships in May 2018, she completed the 100-meter hurdles in a record 12.40 seconds—the fastest time in the world that year—and went on to claim the NCAA title in 100-meter hurdles for a second time. Although she was set to complete a fourth year of college, she ultimately chose to leave school after her junior year and become a professional athlete, accepting a sponsorship from the sportswear brand Nike.

In the years after college, Camacho-Quinn competed throughout the United States as well as in Italy, France, and Qatar. Although she initially planned to return to Olympic competition in 2020 in Tokyo, Japan, the emergence of the COVID-19 pandemic that year delayed the Olympics and also limited the number of other track competitions taking place throughout the year. Camacho-Quinn resumed competing regularly in 2021, racing in World Athletics Continental Tour Gold events such as the USA Track and Field (USATF) Grand Prix, during which she placed first in 100-meter hurdles. "It's really good that I'm running consistent," she told Whittington. "I'm not really focused on trying to hit a certain time because the moment you start to focus on a certain time, that's when you mess up. I just want to get out there and run and have fun while doing it."

OLYMPIC GOLD

Postponed to mid-2021, the Tokyo Olympic Games offered Camacho-Quinn, now a more mature twenty-four years old, a new opportunity to compete on the international stage and a fresh start of sorts after the events of 2016. "My whole mindset is like 'okay, let's go out there, let's do this,' instead of dwelling on what happened in the past," she told Whittington several months prior to the competition. "I'm keeping a positive mindset and just trying to keep my body healthy to make it there." Upon entering the women's 100-meter hurdle event at the games, Camacho-Quinn achieved a time of 12.41 seconds in her qualification round and 12.26 in her semifinal performance, the latter a new Olympic record. Her strong performances qualified her to compete in the final round. During that race, she finished with a time of 12.37 seconds, which was 0.15 seconds ahead of US silver medalist Kendra Harrison and 0.18

seconds ahead of Jamaican bronze medalist Megan Tapper.

A first-time gold medalist, Camacho-Quinn was thrilled with her results, which made her only the second athlete competing for Puerto Rico to win a gold Olympic medal. (The first was 2016 women's singles tennis champion Monica Puig.) The win also meant she was the first athlete from Puerto Rico to bring home a gold for track. "I am really happy right now. Anything is possible," she told Gabriela Miranda for *USA Today* (4 Aug. 2021). "Everybody out here trained really hard for this moment. I think honestly all of us, we all should be rewarded for this. We made it." While she became the center of widespread public and media attention following the Olympics, Camacho-Quinn preferred to continue focusing on her sport rather than on her newfound celebrity. "I'm just focusing on perfecting my craft," she told Rosvoglou. "That's it, for real. I just want to be back on the track and doing what I love to do."

PERSONAL LIFE

Camacho-Quinn lives in Orlando, Florida. She remains close to her family, particularly her brother, with whom she maintains a certain degree of lighthearted competition. "Me and my brother like to trash-talk each other. We'll joke around about who won this or who did that," she told Rosvoglou. "It's never personal, it's just a way of us having fun. Robert and I know how to make fun of each other out of love."

SUGGESTED READING

Camacho-Quinn, Jasmine. "Q&A with Jasmine Camacho-Quinn: Overcoming Adversity, Partnership with Buchanan's, Winning Gold at 2020 Olympics." Interview by Chris Rosvoglou. *The Spun*, Sports Illustrated, 19 Oct. 2021, thespun.com/more/olympics/jasmine-camacho-quinn-overcoming-adversity-winning-gold-at-tokyo-olympics. Accessed 7 Jan. 2022.

Chiari, Mike. "Jasmine Camacho-Quinn, Sister of Bears DE, Sets Women's 100m Hurdles Olympic Record." *Bleacher Report*, 1 Aug. 2021, bleacherreport.com/articles/10009319-jasmine-camacho-quinn-sister-of-bears-de-sets-womens-100m-hurdles-olympic-record. Accessed 7 Jan. 2022.

Dennehy, Cathal. "Road to Redemption." *Spikes*, 21 May 2018, spikes.worldathletics.org/post/jasmine-camacho-quinn-road-to-redemption. Accessed 7 Jan. 2022.

Hartsell, Jeff. "'I'm Not Gonna Let This Race Define My Future,' Jasmine Camacho-Quinn Said after Olympic Stumble. It Hasn't." *The Post and Courier*, 29 July 2021, www.postandcourier.com/sports/im-not-gonna-let-this-race-define-my-future-jasmine-camacho-quinn-said-after-olympic/article_71f0c35a-65c1-11e8-a1d8-5ff7ce593a07.html. Accessed 7 Jan. 2022.

Mather, Victor. "Jasmine Camacho-Quinn Wins the 100-Meter Hurdles, Puerto Rico's First Gold in Track." *The New York Times*, 2 Aug. 2021, www.nytimes.com/2021/08/02/sports/olympics/jasmine-chamacho-quinn-100m-hurdles.html. Accessed 7 Jan. 2022.

Miranda, Gabriela. "Black Puerto Rican Jasmine Camacho-Quinn's Gold Medal Represents More Than a Record Win." *USA Today*, 4 Aug. 2021, www.usatoday.com/story/sports/olympics/2021/08/02/jasmine-camacho-quinn-wins-gold-puerto-rico-and-black-athletes/5452755001/. Accessed 7 Jan. 2022.

Whittington, Jess. "Consistency Is Key for Camacho-Quinn." *World Athletics*, 25 Apr. 2021, worldathletics.org/competitions/world-athletics-continental-tour/news/consistency-jasmine-camacho-quinn. Accessed 7 Jan. 2022.

—*Joy Crelin*

Photo by MDGovpics,
via Wikimedia Commons

Patrick Cantlay

Born: March 17, 1992
Occupation: Golfer

"With success, a lot of the time, people view it from afar and think, 'oh, you're suddenly successful, you've finally done the right thing,'" professional golfer Patrick Cantlay told Tom Kershaw in an interview for the *Independent* (21 Sept. 2021). "I don't really view it that way. I think it's a journey." Indeed, Cantlay's journey to success in his sport was a long one marked by notable setbacks. Having previously established himself as a talented junior golfer, he played two successful seasons of collegiate golf at the University of California, Los Angeles, before beginning his professional career in the summer of 2012. Less than a year later, however, a stress fracture in his back threatened to end his career, forcing him to sit out the majority of two PGA Tour seasons as he rehabilitated the injury.

Returning to the tour in 2017, Cantlay won his first PGA Tour event later that year, at the Shriners Hospitals for Children Open. His victory signaled a return to form for Cantlay, who would go on to win further tour events as well as international team competitions such as the 2019 Presidents Cup. The year 2021 proved particularly noteworthy, as he won several prominent tournaments and claimed the title of FedEx Cup champion as well as, ultimately, PGA Tour champion. Although such victories were undoubtedly exciting, he was pleased simply to have the opportunity to compete against the best of the best in his sport. "I play golf so I can be in those moments against the best players in the world," he told *ESPN* (5 Sept. 2021). "It's why I practice so hard. It's why I'm in love with the game, because it's that great vehicle for competition."

EARLY LIFE AND EDUCATION

Patrick Stephen Cantlay was born on March 17, 1992, in Long Beach, California. He was the first of four children born to Colleen and Steve Cantlay. He was introduced to the sport of golf at an early age and began playing the sport himself at the age of five, with the encouragement of his family. "I was fortunate to grow up in a golfing family with my grandfather and father being great players," he explained in an interview for the website of clothing brand Hugo Boss. His younger siblings would also go on to compete in the sport, with younger brother Nick making his professional debut in 2019.

As a child, Cantlay was exposed to the world of professional golf on the days he accompanied his father to the Virginia Country Club in Long Beach, a popular practice venue for players who competed on the prestigious PGA Tour. "It was good to see how they prepared and practiced, and what TOUR golf was like at a young age," he told Cameron Morfit for the website of the PGA Tour (5 Sept. 2021). "They were all really great to me. They would always take me out to play, or if I asked any questions they'd be really helpful." A skilled player himself, Cantlay went on to enroll in Servite High School, a private school with a strong golf program. He made the varsity golf team as a freshman and remained a member of that team throughout his high school career, winning the California Interscholastic Federation (CIF) State High School Boys Championship during his senior year. He was also active in amateur golf competition during his high school years and progressed to the semifinal round of the US Amateur Championship in 2010.

COLLEGIATE GOLF CAREER

After graduating from Servite High School in 2010, Cantlay enrolled at the University of California, Los Angeles (UCLA), which had a National Collegiate Athletic Association (NCAA) Division I golf program. A history major, he had a strong freshman golf season and won several awards for his performance, including the Jack Nicklaus Award for best men's collegiate golfer of the year and the Phil Mickelson Award for Division I freshman of the year. Although his decision to remain in college rather than pursue a professional golf career was surprising for some, Cantlay himself believed that maintaining his amateur status was the best course of action. "I'm not in a rush to grow up or anything," he told Gene Wojciechowski for *ESPN* (14 Aug. 2011) following his freshman year at UCLA. "I'm not really thinking about pro one way or the other right now." He then joined the 2011 US Walker

Cup team—which lost to a team representing Great Britain and Ireland—as well as the US collegiate team that beat Team Europe at the 2011 Arnold Palmer Cup. He returned to UCLA for the 2011–12 season.

In addition to competing in collegiate golf tournaments, Cantlay was active in noncollegiate amateur competition throughout his years in college and, in 2011, he placed second in the US Amateur Championship. He also competed in PGA Tour events as an amateur, forgoing any potential winnings to maintain his amateur status. Playing in five PGA Tour events in 2011, his best finish came when he tied for ninth place at the RBC Canadian Open in July. He also played in several events during his sophomore year of college, including the prestigious Masters Tournament, one of golf's four major tournaments alongside the PGA Championship, US Open, and Open Championship. An accomplished amateur competitor, he held the number-one spot in the amateur golf rankings for fifty-four weeks in a row and was awarded the 2011 Mark H. McCormack Medal as the top amateur player.

EARLY PROFESSIONAL CAREER

After his sophomore year ended in June 2012, Cantlay left both collegiate and amateur competition behind to pursue a career as a professional golfer. He competed in several PGA Tour events during the remainder of 2012 and was also active on the developmental *Web.com* Tour, later known as the Korn Ferry Tour. In September of that year, he tied for second place at the *Web.com* Tour's Chiquita Classic. The next season saw him claim his first *Web.com* Tour victory at the Colombia Championship, and he later placed second at the Hotel Fitness Championship. In May 2013, however, he suffered a back injury that was later determined to be a stress fracture. The injury forced him to step away from professional competition less than a year after making his professional debut.

The next several years were difficult for Cantlay, who played in only a few tournaments in 2013 and 2014 and did not compete at all in 2015 due to his injury, which he feared might end his career. An even more devastating moment came in 2016, when Cantlay's longtime friend and caddie Chris Roth was struck by a car and killed while out with Cantlay in California. "For a while, I couldn't care less about everything. Not just golf," he recalled to Damian Dottore for the *Los Angeles Daily News* (28 Aug. 2017). "Everything that happened in my life for a couple months didn't feel important. Nothing felt like it mattered."

RETURN TO COMPETITION

By early 2017, Cantlay decided that the time had come for him to return to competition. "I am ready to play, but we have to start slow and go from there. It is going to be fun," he told Dottore. "It has been a long time coming." Cantlay returned to the PGA Tour in February 2017 for the AT&T Pebble Beach Pro-Am, which he finished tied for forty-eighth place. A month later, however, he placed second in the Valspar Championship, signaling a return to his preinjury form. He confirmed his readiness for competition further in November of that year when he claimed his first PGA Tour win at the Shriners Hospitals for Children Open. Cantlay was a fixture on the PGA Tour during the 2017–18 season and, in addition to his Shriners win, achieved top-ten finishes in four other tour tournaments.

Cantlay played in twenty-one events on the 2018–19 PGA Tour and won the Memorial Tournament in June 2019. He also made eight other top-ten finishes, including a third-place finish at the PGA Championship and a ninth-place finish at the Masters Tournament. In December 2019, Cantlay competed for the United States at the 2019 Presidents Cup in Melbourne, Australia, where the US team claimed victory over its international counterpart. Although Cantlay planned to play regularly throughout the 2019–20 season, the season was halted in March 2020 due to the coronavirus disease 2019 (COVID-19) pandemic, and many of the events scheduled for the next several months were canceled or postponed. Cantlay returned to the tour in late June, tying for eleventh place at the Travelers Championship, and continued to play throughout the remainder of the season.

FEDEX CUP CHAMPION

The 2020–21 PGA Tour season started off strong for Cantlay, who in October 2020 claimed first place in the Zozo Championship. He continued to put forth strong performances throughout the season, including a second-place finish at the American Express and a first-place finish at the Memorial Tournament

for the second time. He went on to win the BMW Championship in August and the TOUR Championship in September of that year. His success over the course of the season, including those final three victories, earned him the title of FedEx Cup champion—the champion of the 2020–21 PGA Tour. "It's such a great honor because it's all year," Cantlay told *ESPN*. "I played really consistent all year and caught fire at the end. There's a lot of satisfaction considering all the work I've put in my whole life." His performance during the season also earned him recognition as PGA Tour player of the year, as voted on by his fellow professional golfers.

Following those victories, Cantlay again represented the United States in international competition as a member of the US team for the Ryder Cup, which was held in September 2021 after having been postponed from the previous year. "The fans at the BMW were the wildest I've seen since Covid. It felt like they were on my side and to pull off those shots, it was amazing, it made it all the more satisfying," he told Kershaw. "But from everything I've been told, the Ryder Cup is completely different. I'm expecting a much bigger stage and more excitement than I've ever felt before playing golf." Cantlay and his teammates ultimately defeated Team Europe in the tournament, claiming a Ryder Cup victory for their home country.

2021–22 PGA TOUR

Following his breakout performance on the 2020–21 PGA Tour, Cantlay took several months off from competition and did not appear in PGA Tour events during the first several months of the tour, though he expressed excitement about competing later in the season. "The major championship venues this year are off the charts. St Andrews for the British Open. I mean that's—circle that one as one I'm really looking forward to," he revealed to David Soloman in an interview for the Goldman Sachs *Talks at GS* interview series (16 Dec. 2021). "It's the home of golf, with all the history. If you could win, if there's a tournament you wanted to win that wasn't the Masters, it would be maybe the British Open at St. Andrews." He returned to competition in January 2022, placing fourth in the Sentry Tournament of Champions. He went on to place second in the WM Phoenix Open and

RBC Heritage events before winning the Zurich Classic of New Orleans in April 2022.

PERSONAL LIFE

In addition to playing golf, Cantlay enjoys playing ping pong and is an avid reader, particularly of nonfiction. "I like reading about certain people," he told Morfit, "and seeing if I can pick up anything that other successful people have done." He is the creator of the Patrick Cantlay Foundation, which has supported junior golf programs as well as charities dedicated to first responders to brushfires in Australia. When not competing elsewhere, he lives in Jupiter, Florida.

SUGGESTED READING

Cantlay, Patrick. "Interview: Patrick Cantlay." Interview. *Hugo Boss*, www.hugoboss.com/us/patrick-cantlay-interview/. Accessed 13 June 2022.

___. "Patrick Cantlay: 'Team USA Rookies Won't Be Scared at the Ryder Cup.'" Interview by Tom Kershaw. *Independent*, 21 Sept. 2021, www.independent.co.uk/sport/golf/patrick-cantlay-interview-ryder-cup-2021-b1923351.html. Accessed 13 June 2022.

___. "Patrick Cantlay, 2021 PGA TOUR Player of the Year." Interview by David Soloman. *Goldman Sachs*, 16 Dec. 2021, www.goldmansachs.com/insights/talks-at-gs/patrick-cantlay.html. Accessed 13 June 2022.

Dottore, Damian. "Patrick Cantlay Ready to Move Past Injury, Tragedy." *Los Angeles Daily News*, 28 Aug. 2017, www.dailynews.com/2017/02/06/patrick-cantlay-ready-to-move-past-injury-tragedy/. Accessed 13 June 2022.

Morfit, Cameron. "The Education of Patrick Cantlay." *PGA Tour*, 5 Sept. 2021, www.pgatour.com/news/2018/06/19/patrick-cantlay-background-rising-star.html. Accessed 13 June 2022.

"Patrick Cantlay Posts 'A Huge Win,' Capturing FedEx Cup in Dramatic Fashion at the Tour Championship." *ESPN*, 5 Sept. 2021, www.espn.com/golf/story/_/id/32156234/patrick-cantlay-posts-huge-win-capturing-fedex-cup-dramatic-fashion-tour-championship. Accessed 13 June 2022.

Wojciechowski, Gene. "Patrick Cantlay Offers Welcome Change." *ESPN*, 14 Aug. 2011, www.espn.com/espn/columns/story?columnist=wojciechowski_gene&sportCat=golf&page=wojciechowski-110822. Accessed 13 June 2022.

—*Joy Crelin*

Ana Caraiani

Born: 1985
Occupation: Mathematician

For mathematician Ana Caraiani, the field of mathematics represents not only a compelling area of academic study but also an untold number of opportunities to break new ground. "I like the intellectual freedom that comes with being a mathematician, the freedom to play around with ideas, the creativity, the possibility of using all kind of different techniques," she explained to Francesca Arici and Anna Maria Cherubini in an interview for the website *European Women in Mathematics*. The use of different mathematical techniques and exploration of a wide range of mathematical fields has long been key to Caraiani's research, much of which has focused on the Langlands program, which she and other mathematicians have described as a "grand unified theory of mathematics." A professor of mathematics who has been affiliated with institutions such as Imperial College London and Germany's University of Bonn, Caraiani has worked to build bridges between differing branches of mathematics and further the work of earlier researchers, including by attempting to prove conjectures that are key to the field. While the problems she tackles are highly challenging ones, Caraiani has long believed such challenges to be intellectually worthwhile. "You shouldn't spend all your time working on things you know how to do," she told Steve Nadis in an interview for *Quanta Magazine* (17 Nov. 2021). "It's worth taking on problems that are really hard, and maybe too hard."

EARLY LIFE AND EDUCATION

Caraiani was born in Bucharest, Romania, in 1985. Her parents, Zoe and Cornel Caraiani, were both engineers, and they introduced her to a variety of complex mathematical concepts at a young age. Encouraged by her parents, Caraiani pursued mathematics further as she grew older, studying with a former teacher who both helped her prepare to compete in mathematics contests and broadened her mathematical interests. "At least in the beginning she was training me for the competitions," Caraiani recalled in an interview for the Mathematical Sciences Research Institute (MSRI; 2004). "But as I started learning more and more, and because we were talking, I got interested in things other than competitions." In addition to undergoing private training, Caraiani attended the Liceul Teoretic "Jean Monnet," a high school in Bucharest.

As a teenager, Caraiani began to compete in the International Mathematical Olympiad, an annual event in which students who had not yet attended college or university competed to solve difficult math problems. She placed second in the 2001 competition in Washington, DC, earning a silver medal. Caraiani returned to the Olympiad in 2002 and 2003, held in Glasgow and Tokyo respectively, winning consecutive gold medals in those competitions. "It was a great experience because I travelled all over the world and met people my age from other countries who were interested in math," she told Arici and Cherubini about her years competing. In addition to providing Caraiani with the opportunity to travel, her participation in the Olympiad established her as a promising mathematics student, and she would later credit her performance in those competitions with helping her gain admission to Princeton University.

After enrolling in Princeton University in 2003, Caraiani quickly established herself as both a promising student and a strong competitor in collegiate mathematics. She was a recurring competitor in the William Lowell Putnam Mathematical Competition and ranked among the top five competitors in both 2003 and 2004, receiving the Elizabeth Lowell Putnam Prize in recognition of her performance both years. She was likewise part of Princeton's Putnam team for the 2006 competition, where the team collectively won first place. From Princeton, Caraiani was awarded the Department of Mathematics' Andrew H. Brown Prize (2006), Middleton Miller Prize (2007), and George B. Covington Prize (2007) in recognition for her mathematical accomplishments. She was also awarded the 2007 Alice T. Schafer Prize for Excellence in Mathematics by an Undergraduate Woman by the Association for Women in Mathematics.

THE LANGLANDS PROGRAM

As a senior at Princeton, Caraiani completed her senior thesis under the supervision of mathematician Andrew Wiles, who encouraged her to pursue graduate studies with fellow mathematician Richard Taylor. Based at Harvard University—where Caraiani enrolled after earning her bachelor's degree from Princeton in 2007—Taylor had previously worked with Wiles to develop a mathematical method known as the Taylor-Wiles method and was particularly known for his research related to the Langlands program. "The Langlands programme is a 'grand unified theory' of mathematics," Caraiani wrote for *EMS Magazine* (30 Apr. 2021), "a vast network of conjectures that connect number theory to other areas of pure mathematics, such as representation theory, algebraic geometry, and harmonic analysis." Named for the Canadian-born mathematician Robert Langlands, the program initially involved research into the forming of connections, also referred to as bridges, between the equations known as Diophantine equations and mathematical objects known as automorphic forms.

For Caraiani, the Langlands program represented a compelling challenge as well as an opportunity to explore her many mathematical interests. "I like all varieties of math—number theory, analysis, geometry, topology—and I realized that if I chose this area, I wouldn't have to limit myself to just one thing," she explained to Nadis. "When we work on conjectures that we don't know how to prove, we can throw everything we have at them—drawing on any relevant tool in mathematics—in the hopes of making progress." Caraiani continued to study complex mathematical concepts throughout her years at Harvard and by the end of her time there completed a thesis titled "Local-Global Compatibility and the Action of Monodromy on Nearby Cycles." She earned her doctorate from Harvard in 2012.

ACADEMIC CAREER

The recipient of a National Science Foundation (NSF) postdoctoral fellowship, Caraiani began her post-Harvard career at the University of Chicago, where she served as L. E. Dickson Instructor beginning in 2012. She moved to Princeton University in September 2013 and spent the next three years as Veblen Research Instructor, a position in which she both taught courses at Princeton and conducted mathematical research at the nearby Institute for Advanced Study (IAS). Between 2016 and 2017, Caraiani served as a Bonn Junior Fellow at the Hausdorff Center for Mathematics, part of Germany's University of Bonn, before relocating to the United Kingdom, where she became a senior lecturer and Royal Society University Research Fellow at Imperial College London in 2017. She remained at Imperial College for the next several years, working in the Number Theory Group within the Department of Mathematics, and in 2021 was promoted to full professor.

Throughout her years at Princeton, Imperial College, and other institutions, Caraiani focused on building connections between different fields of mathematical study, which she explained to Nadis would have "practical value" beyond research. "Solving a mathematical problem can be easier on one side than the other, depending on what the problem is," she told Nadis. "What often happens with a difficult problem is that you figure out something on one end and then go to the other side to do more things. In order to prove something of substance, you may end up crossing the bridges many times, so you have to be able to move freely in both directions." A particular key goal for Caraiani and her colleagues was to render methods for solving specific kinds of mathematical problems appropriate for more general uses. Papers based on Caraiani's work appeared in journals such as *Advances in Applied Mathematics*, *Algebra and Number Theory*, the *Cambridge Journal of Mathematics*, and *Compositio Mathematica*, while Caraiani herself served as an editor for the journals *International Mathematics Research Notices* (IMRN) and *La Matematica*. In recognition of her work, Caraiani won a 2018 Whitehead Prize from the London Mathematical Society and in 2020 received a European Mathematical Society (EMS) Prize.

THE TEN-AUTHOR PAPER

A particularly significant development in Caraiani's career came in 2016, when she and a group of colleagues convened for a working group at the IAS. The mathematicians sought to build upon the work of Frank Calegari and David Geraghty, who had previously developed a means to "extend the famous Taylor-Wiles method for modularity lifting to a very general

setting," as Caraiani explained to Arici and Cherubini. Calegari and Geraghty's work was based on three conjectures that would need to be proven, and proving those conjectures thus became a goal of many mathematicians working in that field. Working in collaboration with Peter Scholze, who had proven the first conjecture, Caraiani sought to prove the second. She made significant progress in that area prior to the start of the 2016 working group, which she told Arici and Cherubini had the goal of determining whether the mathematicians could "implement the Calegari-Geraghty method unconditionally, even in some very restricted settings."

The 2016 working group succeeded in proving the second conjecture and went on to write what Caraiani and her colleagues would refer to as the ten-author paper, "Potential Automorphy over CM Fields," authored by Caraiani, Scholze, Taylor, Calegari, and six other mathematicians. "One of the things that I am happiest about regarding the ten-author paper is that I think it was successful as a collaboration, mixing younger and older, more established mathematicians and the younger people especially contributed a lot," Caraiani told Arici and Cherubini about their achievement. Completed and published online in late 2018, the ten-author paper left ample openings for further work; for instance, the mathematicians had not proven the third conjecture and had instead "bypassed" it, as Caraiani told Nadis, thus leaving the task of proving the conjecture for later consideration.

NEW CHALLENGES AND OPPORTUNITIES

In the years following the completion of the ten-author paper, Caraiani continued her work on the Langlands program, for which many key issues had yet to be resolved. "I'm still interested in the third conjecture, even though we bypassed it before," she told Nadis, referring to the third of the three conjectures presented by Calegari and Geraghty. "It predicts things about related objects called Shimura varieties, which I'm really interested in and want to understand better." Caraiani continued her work initially at Imperial College London, but in 2022 was appointed Hausdorff Chair at the University of Bonn. "Bonn is one of the best places in the world to do arithmetic geometry and I am particularly excited by the chance to be colleagues with Peter Scholze, who has already had such a great impact on pure mathematics," she told the university's website (22 Feb. 2022). "In addition, I think the students in Bonn are extremely strong and I look forward to interacting with them." At the time of its announcement in February 2022, Caraiani's tenure at Bonn was set to begin in September of that year.

PERSONAL LIFE

Caraiani married Steven Sivek prior to completing her university studies. A fellow mathematician, Sivek held posts at institutions such as Princeton University and Imperial College London. Their first child, a daughter, was born following their move to the United Kingdom.

SUGGESTED READING

"Ana Caraiani: EMS Prize Winner, 8th European Congress of Mathematics." *8ECM 2020*, 2020, 8ecm.si/prizes/51. Accessed 9 May 2022.

Caraiani, Ana. "Building Mathematical Bridges: An Interview with Ana Caraiani." Interview by Francesca Arici and Anna Maria Cherubini. *EWM*, www.europeanwomeninmaths.org/ana-caraiani/. Accessed 9 May 2022.

___. "Interviews in Princeton." *Interviews with Top Finishers on the 2004 Putnam Exam*. Mathematical Sciences Research Institute, 2004, pp. 41–44, www.msri.org/activities/pastprojects/jir/Putnam_interviews.pdf. Accessed 9 May 2022.

___. "The Mathematician Who Delights in Building Bridges." Interview by Steve Nadis. *Quanta Magazine*, 17 Nov. 2021, www.quantamagazine.org/ana-caraiani-delights-in-building-mathematical-bridges-20211117/. Accessed 9 May 2022.

___. "New Frontiers in Langlands Reciprocity." *EMS Magazine*, vol. 119, 30 Apr. 2021, p. 8–16, euromathsoc.org/magazine/articles/mag-3. Accessed 9 May 2022.

Klarreich, Erica. "'Amazing' Math Bridge Extended beyond Fermat's Last Theorem." *Quanta Magazine*, 6 Apr. 2020, www.quantamagazine.org/amazing-math-bridge-extended-beyond-fermats-last-theorem-20200406/. Accessed 9 May 2022.

"Mathematician Ana Caraiani Appointed to the University of Bonn." *Uni Bonn*, 23 Feb. 2022, www.uni-bonn.de/en/news/041-2022. Accessed 9 May 2022.

—Joy Crelin

Maverick Carter

Born: ca. 1981
Occupation: Businessperson and media personality

In 2006, when basketball superstar LeBron James first entered a business partnership with Maverick Carter, many observers questioned the wisdom of James placing his business interests in the hands of a relatively inexperienced manager based simply on the pair's childhood friendship. By the 2020s, in addition to establishing himself as one of the top professional basketball players of all time, James had become an outsized social and cultural force thanks to his varied entrepreneurial and media-related ventures. Much of the credit for James's success off the court goes to Carter, who was instrumental in many of James's business ventures and deals, including a record-setting $1 billion lifetime deal with Nike. Carter also serves as CEO of the conglomerate SpringHill Company, which the two launched in 2020 after raising $100 million in capital.

The conglomerate includes SpringHill Entertainment, a media-production venture James and Carter founded in 2007; the Robot Company, a marketing agency and brand consultancy whose clients have included J.P. Morgan and Sprite; and Uninterrupted LLC, a hybrid business whose goal is to provide athletes, especially those from underserved or disenfranchised communities, with a more powerful public platform. Describing the SpringHill Company in a feature for *Bloomberg* (25 June 2020), Jason Kelly wrote, "It's part Disney storytelling power, part Nike coolness, and part Patagonia social impact."

Carter admits that he made some missteps early in his career; while he recognizes that some of the initial doubts about his abilities were well-founded, he feels he has grown in spite of it all. "The best way to learn and get information from [successful people] is to simply ask them about their successes," he told David Gelles for *The New York Times* (19 June 2020). "That has allowed me to learn and use that as fuel. . . . Even if I am underestimated, I'm fine with it. Because I go into it thinking, 'Hey, I'm here to learn and want to get information and then figure out how to apply it to my life.'"

EARLY LIFE AND EDUCATION

Maverick Carter was born in Akron, Ohio, in 1980, to Katherine Powers, a social worker, and Otis "Oldie" Carter, a high school dropout who had difficulty finding work and turned periodically to drug dealing to support himself and his family. He was incarcerated twice during Carter's youth and was rarely a presence in the family home. Still, Carter admired Otis. "You can put my dad in any situation and he's going to figure it out," Carter told Jason Whitlock for *Fox Sports* (7 Apr. 2011). "He's going to figure the people out and how to get along."

When he was sixteen, Carter decided to start selling marijuana. "I wasn't doing it because I needed the money," he recalled to Whitlock. "When you grow up where I did, it's just not a big deal at all. It's just the normal thing to do." When his mother discovered his inventory, Carter was sent to live with his grandmother, but because she ran a gambling den and after-hours bar, the environment was also not ideal for him.

Carter's mother ultimately decided to send him to St. Vincent–St. Mary High, a college preparatory school in Akron. LeBron James, whom Carter knew from his neighborhood, entered as a first-year student during Carter's senior year, and the two young men—both top players on the school's basketball and football teams—became close friends.

After graduating from high school in 2000, Carter entered Western Michigan University in Kalamazoo, Michigan, which he attended for one year before transferring to the University of Akron back in his hometown. By this time, James was showing so much promise as a high school basketball player that team scouts from the National Basketball Association (NBA) and sneaker manufacturers were coming to the city to watch him play. One Nike representative, Lynn Merritt, happened to meet Carter on a visit to Cleveland and was impressed by his drive and obvious intelligence.

Carter, who fondly remembered watching Nike commercials featuring Michael Jordan and his eponymous sneakers, subsequently accepted a sports-marketing internship at Nike. In 2003—the year James was signed to the Cleveland Cavaliers and made his NBA debut—Carter quit college to work for the company full-time as a field representative and liaison.

LRMR AND EARLY VENTURES

A few years into James's NBA career, Carter approached his old friend and asked to join the business team James was building for himself. James agreed and quickly parted ways with Aaron Goodwin, his previous agent. James and Carter's new team also included Rich Paul, an agent, and Randy Mims, as manager: the quartet of old friends eventually became known as "the four horsemen."

In 2006, Paul and Mims helped Carter and James form the management company LRMR (the initials of the partners' first names). Whitlock summed up a common reaction in the sports world: "Three young Black men with no experience, led by a twenty-three-year-old kid, were going to manage the career of the most important basketball player since Michael Jordan. How? Why?"

The group admittedly faced something of a learning curve, with the trio often failing to return phone calls or behaving unprofessionally in front of reporters, leading some observers to perceive that they were not appropriately managing themselves and, by extension, James's businesses. For example, Carter and his colleagues lent James's name to high-profile parties given in the cities the Cavaliers were playing and accepted any promotional opportunities for James, regardless of whether the opportunity was befitting a player of his stature. Still, in 2007, Carter and his partners managed to successfully launch SpringHill Entertainment, whose first project was a 2008 documentary, *More Than a Game*, which followed James and a group of his high school basketball teammates as they evolved as players.

Despite criticism and doubt from some quarters, something of a mystique began to build around Carter due to his unconventional yet often savvy approach to growing his business. For example, during a 2008 meeting with Jimmy Iovine, the chair of Interscope Records, Carter convinced the executive to give him fifteen pairs of high-end Beats headphones, a brand founded by Iovine's longtime business partner Dr. Dre, a hip-hop producer and entrepreneur. Carter then instructed James to give each of his teammates a pair of Beats, which had not yet been officially released, while the United States Olympic basketball team was traveling to the 2008 Olympic Games in Beijing China. When the team's plane landed and the players faced the international press, they had the Beats draped around their necks. The resulting photos set off frenzied demand among consumers as soon as the headphones hit the market. As LRMR had reportedly made a significant investment in Beats, this move allegedly earned James millions of dollars.

However, not all of Carter's decisions during this time had a positive influence on James's career. In 2010, Carter spearheaded a SpringHill project that was blamed for causing a public relations disaster for James and damaging his reputation. That year, James appeared in a heavily promoted ESPN television special called *The Decision*, during which James dramatically announced that he would be leaving the Cavaliers to join the Miami Heat, angering many Cleveland fans—not only with his defection to another team, but also by the manner in which the news was delivered.

Although James was largely forgiven by fans in 2014 when he returned to Cleveland and led the Cavaliers to a long-awaited championship two years later, his initial decision to play for the Heat and the associated television special generated considerable controversy. "For many, the failure of *The Decision* validated suspicions that Carter was just another star athlete's friend," Kelly wrote. "What was underappreciated at the time was that *The Decision* ushered in an era of player empowerment that's spread to other sports, as well as collegiate and high school athletics. There's virtually no athlete who doesn't feel emboldened to weigh in on just about anything on social media and demand a semblance of career control that would have been unheard of twenty years ago."

Carter also defended *The Decision*, pointing out that the ostensible "failure" did not even pose that much of a financial blow to James's business empire. "[James] was being killed in the press, and public perception was so down on him," he recalled to Jay Williams in an interview for *National Public Radio* (4 Jan.

2022). "But that year, it was weird. Like, that was the biggest year he had in jersey sales and sneaker sales. . . . So the seventeen-year-old in Houston, Texas, buying the jersey doesn't [care] what the columnist in *The New York Times* is writing."

BUILDING AN EMPIRE

In 2011, Carter negotiated a major deal in which LRMR would be integrated into Fenway Sports Management, which was involved with major sports franchises including the Boston Red Sox, Liverpool Football Club, Major League Baseball Advanced Media, Boston College Athletics, and the Professional Golf Association (PGA). In exchange, James received equity in the English Premier League and part ownership stake in the Boston Red Sox.

Carter's status rose further in 2014, when he launched Uninterrupted LLC, a digital media and management company aimed at giving athletes a way to tell their stories on a level that went far beyond stats and play-by-play commentary. The company, which also branched out into selling merchandise such as hooded sweatshirts, went on to create a 2018 documentary series that aired on *ESPN* called *More Than an Athlete*, which traces the rise of James, Carter, Paul, and Mims as businesspeople. The company was also responsible for *The Shop*, an HBO talk show that premiered in 2018 and featured James and Carter speaking with other Black celebrities, and *Kneading Dough*, an online interview series launched in 2017 with JPMorgan Chase in which athletes share financial advice.

In 2015, Carter helped James negotiate a record-setting deal with Nike that would pay James $30 million a year, or, as many sports journalists pointed out, potentially more than $1 billion over the course of his lifetime. It was the largest single-athlete guarantee up to that point and the first lifetime commitment in Nike's history.

Meanwhile, Carter and his partners at SpringHill Entertainment continued to find success in the entertainment industry. The company signed deals with Warner Brothers and other industry leaders to produce a wide variety of content, including the family sitcom *Survivor's Remorse* (2014–17), the primetime NBC game show *The Wall* (2016–), the civil rights documentary *Rise Up: The Movement*

That Changed America (2018), and *Space Jam: A New Legacy* (2021), a sequel to the original family-friendly basketball comedy *Space Jam* (1996), which starred Michael Jordan. *Space Jam: A New Legacy* featured a live-action James in the lead role interacting with animated characters from the Looney Tunes franchise.

In 2020, Carter and James reached another milestone when they attracted $100 million in capital from an investor group led by investment firm RedBird. The deal allowed SpringHill Entertainment, Uninterrupted LLC, and the Robot Company to reorganize under the umbrella of the SpringHill Company conglomerate. As Carter described it to Brooks Barnes for *The New York Times* (14 Oct. 2021), this move effectively "pour[ed] gasoline" on his and his partners' ambition to gain an even bigger foothold in the film, television, gaming, consumer product, and live event industries.

In addition to his work with SpringHill, Carter became involved with both the LeBron James Family Foundation and James's political organization, More Than a Vote, a nonprofit dedicated to fighting voter suppression in the United States. In 2018, Carter also became a board member at Live Nation, a leading ticketing and concert promotion company. "I grew up square in the middle of the hip-hop generation, right? And I think hip-hop gave me the audacity to be able to sit in that boardroom and be comfortable that I belong as a business person, but also speak the way I speak in being who I am," Carter told Gelles. "I didn't get to be on that board by being the corporate guy, wearing a suit and tie every day. I don't play golf with other people on Saturdays." Carter expanded his involvement in charity work in 2022 when he joined the board of directors of the Red Sox Foundation, a nonprofit affiliated with the Boston Red Sox.

SUGGESTED READING

Barnes, Brooks. "LeBron James's SpringHill Sells a Minority Stake to a Group Led by RedBird." *The New York Times*, 14 Oct. 2021, www.nytimes.com/2021/10/14/business/lebron-james-springhill-redbird.html. Accessed 3 June 2022.

Carter, Maverick. "A Day in the Life of Maverick Carter." Interview by Alex Bhattacharji. *The Wall Street Journal*, 12 Sept. 2018, www.wsj.com/articles/a-day-in-the-life-of-maverick-carter-1536760782. Accessed 3 June 2022.

___. "Maverick Carter on Building the LeBron James Empire." *The Limits*. Interview by Jay Williams, National Public Radio, 4 Jan. 2022, www.npr.org/transcripts/1069848572. Transcript.

Cohen, Ben. "LeBron James's Business Partner Maverick Carter Talks Talent in the NBA, Hollywood and Beyond." *The Wall Street Journal*, 11 May 2022, www.wsj.com/articles/lebron-jamess-business-partner-maverick-carter-talks-talent-in-the-nba-hollywood-and-beyond-11652280645. Accessed 3 June 2022.

Gelles, David. "LeBron James's Business Partner Now Wants to Get Out the Vote." *The New York Times*, 19 June 2020, www.nytimes.com/2020/06/19/business/corner-office-maverick-carter.html. Accessed 3 June 2022.

Kelly, Jason. "LeBron James Gets $100 Million Investment to Build Media Empire." *Bloomberg*, 25 June 2020, www.bloomberg.com/news/features/2020-06-25/lebron-james-maverick-carter-s-springhill-to-be-a-media-empire. Accessed 3 June 2022.

Whitlock, Jason. "Maverick Carter Out to Silence Critics." *Fox Sports*, 7 Apr. 2011, www.foxsports.com/stories/nba/maverick-carter-out-to-silence-critics. Accessed 3 June 2022.

—*Mari Rich*

Maia Chaka

Born: April 18, 1982
Occupation: Football referee

When Maia Chaka first started refereeing high school football games in 2007, she was determined to succeed in the largely male-dominated profession. "I've always prided myself on being different and kind of going against the grain," she admitted to Larry Rubama for the *Virginian-Pilot* (9 Oct. 2009). Within four years, Chaka was officiating Division I college football games. She moved one step closer to her ultimate goal in February 2014, with her acceptance into the National Football League's (NFL) Officiating Development Program (ODP), joining Sarah Thomas as one of the program's two female prospects.

Chaka realized her lifelong ambition in March 2021, when the NFL made her a full-time member of the league's on-field officiating crew, the second woman ever to achieve this feat. Six months later, Chaka made history by becoming the first African American woman to officiate an NFL game and third woman overall (after Thomas and Shannon Eastin) to referee a league game.

EARLY LIFE

Maia Mashariki Chaka was born at her parents' home in Rochester, New York, on April 18, 1982. She grew up as the middle child of Terry, a visual artist and executive director of the Baobab Cultural Center in Rochester, and Gerald, a counselor with the New York State Division for Youth. Chaka credited her parents, who in 1986 cofounded Kitabu Kingdom, Rochester's first Black bookstore and art gallery, with instilling in her the importance of grit and perseverance. "My parents taught me at a young age that you got to work for everything you have," she told Robert Bell for the Rochester *Democrat and Chronicle* (23 Mar. 2021). By the time that Chaka was twelve years old, she was already following in her parents' entrepreneurial footsteps. Not only was she running her own babysitting business, but she was also earning money by shoveling driveways, raking leaves, and mowing lawns.

Chaka's love affair with sports also began when she was a child. In addition to taking up swimming and gymnastics, she spent time tossing the football around with her younger brother, Anwar. Chaka, who also has an older sister, Ramisi, honed her competitive nature by challenging the neighborhood boys to basketball pickup games in her backyard. She also grew up playing tackle, or sandlot football at Aberdeen Square, a community park in Rochester, and at the local Boys and Girls Club, where she was also enrolled in tae kwon do classes. "I was always encouraged to try whatever I wanted, and I wouldn't be judged," Chaka recalled to Scott Pitoniak for the *Rochester Business Journal* (9 Mar. 2021). "If my parents saw that I had a knack and an enthusiasm for something, they fed into that. They didn't try to change me, regardless if it went against gender norms."

HIGH SCHOOL AND COLLEGE SPORTS

After struggling to find a competitive tackle football league that would enable her to continue competing at a high level, Chaka decided to focus her attention on another sport. During her four years at Edison Career and Technology High School in Rochester (1996–2000), she assumed the position of guard on the Edison Inventors girls' varsity basketball team.

Chaka received her high school diploma in 2000 after taking summer school classes that year to complete her degree. She then took a year-long hiatus from college and juggled two jobs at a mall to earn enough to pay for junior college. She also put together a highlight reel, which she sent to Bob Atwood, the women's basketball coach at Finger Lakes Community College (FLCC), a two-year, public co-ed institution located in Canandaigua, New York.

After gaining admission into FLCC, she played for the Lakers basketball squad from 2001 until 2003. During her first season (2001–02), Chaka, who appeared in twenty games, was among the team leaders in individual scoring, rebounds, and free-throw percentage and helped propel her squad to the finals of the 2002 Mid-State Athletic Conference (MSAC) tournament, where they defeated the Tompkins Cortland Community College Panthers to capture the title.

Chaka subsequently transferred to a historically Black university, Norfolk State University (NSU), in Norfolk, Virginia, where her great-aunt and great-uncle, Clara and Joe Echols, had previously taught math and coached football, respectively. While there, she pursued a Bachelor of Science (BS) degree in health, physical education, and exercise science, which included a certificate program that focused on teaching health and physical education in public schools.

Along with caring for her ailing great-aunt, Chaka supported herself financially by working for a sporting goods store, Champs Sports, and for NSU's student activities program, which involved lining the football field and scheduling officials to referee the intramural sports. While participating in the work-study program, Chaka, who spent a significant amount of time around the referees, took a crucial step toward her future profession by making the decision to serve as an on-campus referee for intramural basketball and flag football games. "I always had the itch to be around sports," she told Josiah Turner for *Andscape* (31 Mar. 2021). "And I guess that's what kind of drove me to officiate."

OFFICIATING CAREER

Following her graduation from NSU in 2006, Chaka worked as a health and physical education teacher for at-risk students at the Renaissance Academy, a public alternative high school in the Virginia Beach City Public Schools (VBCPS) district. She also became determined to pursue her newfound passion. However, after initially planning to become a basketball referee, Chaka decided, instead, to focus her attention on another competitive sport: football. She credited her crucial decision to professional mentor/coworker Shawn McMahon, who was serving as a referee within the Old Dominion Athletic Conference—the third-largest all-sport Division III conference. At his urging, she joined the Southeastern Football Officials Associations (SEFOA), a nonprofit organization whose members are assigned to oversee and mediate the sport at the public and private school levels throughout the Southside Hampton Roads area.

In 2007, Chaka embarked on her new career, officiating local junior varsity high school games. She made an immediate impression on Elisha "Cadillac" Harris, the former coach for Indian River High School in Chesapeake, Virginia. "As a coach, you can appreciate the human side of a person when a referee says, 'I may have missed that call,'" he recalled to Rubama. "She knows her craft and she cares about the game." In 2009, she served as a referee at the Virginia High School League (VHSL) championship game and as a chain crew member for Old Dominion University games. (Chain crew members are assigned to hold the vertical signal or marking poles on the sidelines.) By 2011, Chaka had made the leap from officiating at the high school level to overseeing Division I college football games. She was also designated an alternate official with Conference USA (C-USA), one of eleven conferences in the National Collegiate Athletic Association (NCAA) Division I Football Bowl Subdivision (FBS), the highest level of college football. At the time, C-USA was headed by veteran NFL referee Gerald Austin.

NFL OFFICIATING DEVELOPMENT PROGRAM

Chaka made headlines in December 2013, when she served alongside Sarah Thomas as part of the officiating crew for the Kraft Fight Hunger Bowl between the Brigham Young University (BYU) Cougars and the University of Washington Huskies. The two referees became the first-ever female officials to oversee an FBS bowl game. The following May, the pair would make history again, as the first two women to be selected for the NFL Officiating Development Program (ODP), which provides training for the country's top-performing on-field officials—and future NFL hires (once a roster spot becomes available).

As a program participant, Chaka, who was handpicked by Austin, received mentoring from other longtime referees and attended clinics and minicamps. She also officiated her first NFL preseason game, serving as a back judge during a 2014 contest between the New England Patriots and Philadelphia Eagles. (A back judge is usually positioned mid-field and oversees tight ends and nearby running backs and defenders.)

Over the next two seasons, Chaka refereed a pair of preseason contests for the Baltimore Ravens: one against the Eagles in 2015 and the other against the Indianapolis Colts in 2016. She also continued to officiate college-level games, including an October 2016 NCAA match between the Pittsburgh Panthers and the Marshall Thundering Herd as well as the 2016 Camellia Bowl.

NFL TRAILBLAZER

Between 2014 and 2017, Chaka was among the officials featured on the NFL's ODP roster. Starting in 2018, Chaka served as a line judge for the now-defunct Alliance of American Football (AAF) league. The following year she began overseeing games in the NCAA's Pacific-12 Conference football and Division I women's basketball. In March 2020, she was among the referees tapped to officiate Vince McMahon's minor football league, the XFL, whose first season was interrupted by the COVID-19 pandemic. That same year she rejoined the ODP.

In January 2021, Chaka was part of the officiating crew for the Reese's Senior Bowl, which the NFL used as a means of evaluating its ODP candidates. Two months later, she finally joined the league's officiating ranks, becoming the first Black woman hired to oversee an NFL game. Chaka made her NFL regular-season debut on September 12, 2021, serving as a line judge during the Carolina Panthers' season opener against the New York Jets. The first-year referee went on to officiate five more games in the 2021 regular season.

OTHER PURSUITS, HONORS, AND PHILANTHROPY

After teaching at the Renaissance Academy from 2006 to 2021, Chaka continued teaching as the student and program success coordinator at An Achievable Dream Academy. Chaka's accolades included Teacher of the Year (2014), I Make a Difference Awards (2014 and 2019), and being named one of Black Enterprise's 40 Under 40 in 2021. Her philanthropic efforts included founding the club Girls with Empowering Minds and Spirits (GEMS) in 2008 and starting the nonprofit Make Meaningful Change in 2022.

SUGGESTED READING

Bell, Robert. "'I Thought I Was Being Punched.' Rochester Native Maia Chaka Is NFL's First Black Female Referee." *Rochester Democrat and Chronicle*, 23 Mar. 2021, www.democratandchronicle.com/story/news/2021/03/23/maia-chaka-first-black-woman-official-nfl/4795924001/. Accessed 1 July 2022.

Chaka, Maia. "Breaking Down Barriers." Interview by Kate Andrews. *Virginia Business*, 31 May 2021, www.virginiabusiness.com/article/breaking-down-barriers/. Accessed 1 July 2022.

De la Fuente, Homero. "Maia Chaka Makes History as First Black Woman to Officiate an NFL Game." *CNN Sports*, 12 Sept. 2021, www.cnn.com/2021/09/12/sport/maia-chaka-first-nfl-black-woman-official/index.html. Accessed 1 July 2022.

Pitoniak, Scott. "Rochester Woman Makes History as NFL's First Black Female Official." *Rochester Business Journal*, 9 Mar. 2021, rbj.net/2021/03/09/rochester-woman-makes-history-as-nfls-first-black-female-official/. Accessed 1 July 2022.

Reyes, Lorenzo. "Meet Maia Chaka, the First Black Woman Ever Named to the NFL's Officiating Staff." *USA Today*, 5 Mar. 2021, www.usatoday.com/story/sports/nfl/2021/03/05/maia-chaka-nfl-official-renaissance-academy/4599337001/. Accessed 1 July 2022.

Rubama, Larry. "Football: Female Referee's Tackling the Stereotype." *The Virginian-Pilot*, 9 Oct. 2009, www.pilotonline.com/757teamz/article_b52be428-7454-5899-b712-a2b4fa5e92be.html. Accessed 1 July 2022.

Turner, Josiah. "For Maia Chaka, the NFL's First Black Female Official, Class Is Always in Session." *Andscape*, 31 Mar. 2021, andscape.com/features/maia-chaka-nfl-first-black-female-official/. Accessed 1 July 2022.

—Bertha Muteba

Rodrigo Chaves Robles

Born: June 10, 1961
Occupation: Politician and economist

Rodrigo Chaves Robles, a former World Bank economist turned conservative populist politician, was elected president of Costa Rica in April 2022. Chaves was born and raised in Costa Rica, but after earning a PhD in economics from Ohio State University, he spent nearly three decades living outside of the small country, working as an executive for the World Bank. His employment with that institution ended in 2019, when he was demoted for sexual misconduct. Resigning his position, days later he accepted a post as finance minister in Costa Rica under President Carlos Alvarado of the Citizen Action party. A scant six months later, he announced that he would run for president. His campaign was buoyed—some argue, carried—by an early endorsement from veteran Costa Rican journalist and then leader of the Partido Progreso Social Democrática (PPSD; Social Democratic Progress Party), Pilar Cisneros.

Chaves ran on the ticket of the little-known PPSD and cast himself as an underdog to frontrunner and former President José María Figueres of the dominant Partido Liberación Nacional (PLN; National Liberation Party). Chaves was not favored to win the multicandidate race; months before the election, he was polling at just two percent. Revelations about his serial sexual misconduct at the World Bank did little to derail his fledgling campaign, which was fueled by anger at Costa Rica's "corrupted elites."

Photo by Julieth Méndez -
Presidencia de la República de Costa Rica,
via Wikimedia Commons

Chaves has not proven widely popular—he took office through an election with the lowest voter turnout in over seventy years—but his populist rhetoric captured a portion of an electorate disillusioned by government corruption. Before the election, some eighty percent of Costa Ricans said that they desired political change. Chaves railed against government officials but also the structure of the government itself, suggesting that the wealthy rigged the legislature and the electoral process in their favor. Before fairly winning the election, he warned voters that the election results could be falsified—meaning, presumably, only in the case that he lost. Comparisons to former US President Donald Trump abounded and have been encouraged by Chaves himself. On his campaign website, Chaves echoed Trump's rallying cry, promising to "make Costa Rica prosperous again."

EARLY LIFE AND EDUCATION

Chaves was born Rodrigo Alberto de Jesús Chaves Robles in the El Carmen district of San José, Costa Rica, on June 10, 1961. One of eight children, he studied economics in the United States, earning a bachelor's degree and a master's degree at Ohio State University. He wrote his dissertation on credit cooperatives—

member-owned financial institutions, like credit unions—and earned a PhD in agricultural economics in 1994.

CAREER WITH THE WORLD BANK

Chaves took a job with the World Bank, working with rural businesses in dozens of countries. He served as the sector manager for the Economic Policy Unit, Latin America and the Caribbean Region from 2008 to 2011, and as the sector director for Poverty Reduction, Public Sector Reform and Economic Management, Latin America and the Caribbean from 2011 to 2013. In 2013, he was appointed country director in Indonesia, where he served through 2019. During this period, multiple women filed complaints against him, accusing him of serial sexual harassment between 2008 and 2013. In 2019, he was demoted and his salary frozen. Two days after resigning his position, he was appointed finance minister for Costa Rican President Carlos Alvarado. Chaves served in this role for just six months before launching his own campaign for president.

ALLIANCE WITH PILAR CISNEROS

Chaves joined the little-known PPSD and positioned himself as an anti-establishment candidate. His campaign was buoyed by an early endorsement from respected journalist and PPSD leader, Pilar Cisneros, who imbued the unknown politician with the gravitas of her forty-year career. Some eighty percent of Costa Ricans had never heard of Chaves before Cisneros threw her weight behind him, Iván Barrantes, a political consultant and strategist, told Esteban Arrieta for *La Republica* (3 Apr. 2022). Barrantes described Cisneros as an invaluable "key to open doors," affording Chaves access to people he would otherwise have had to spend significant time and money to reach. When his history of sexual misconduct at the World Bank surfaced in August 2021, Cisneros defended him, asking, as quoted by David Bolaños and Anatoly Kurmanaev for *The New York Times* (1 Apr. 2022), "Do you think that Pilar Cisneros would have supported a sexual harasser?" For his own part, Chaves denied and dismissed the findings, saying in a campaign video, as quoted by the *Times*, "Those who have kidnapped the nation are already showing their fear of the candidacy of Rodrigo Chaves." Given Chaves's open disdain for the press, his alliance with Cisneros was considered ironic by some. On the campaign trail, Chaves described journalists, as quoted by Douglas Marin for *Agencia EFE* (1 Apr. 2022), as "scoundrels," "liars" and "laughing stock" when the press uncovered alleged evidence that he had violated campaign finance laws.

PRESIDENTIAL CAMPAIGN

Chaves presented himself as an experienced economist and political outsider. Writing for *AP News* (8 May 2022), Javier Cordoba noted that while the former World Bank executive "is hardly a newcomer to the establishment," he was made to look like an underdog by running against "a man who was almost a symbol of it." Chaves's main opponent was veteran politician José María Figueres of the dominant PLN. Figueres had served a term as president of Costa Rica from 1994 to 1998. (To emphasize the chasm of understanding between them, Chaves liked to tell voters that his father once served as Figueres's bodyguard, but Figueres denied it and there is no evidence that this is true.) Figueres's father, José Figueres Ferrer (1907–90), served three terms as president between 1948 and 1974. Figueres's name recognition among voters seemed a boon but proved to be a hindrance; his campaign was dogged by accusations of major corruption during his earlier term.

Chaves, meanwhile, made anticorruption the centerpiece of his campaign. Taking cues from Republican populist and former US President Donald Trump, Chaves offered scathing criticism of Costa Rica's political system. He compared himself to national hero Juan Santamaría, a drummer in the Costa Rican army who martyred himself to ensure the country's sovereignty in 1856. He said that voters marching to the ballot box to vote for him was like Santamaría setting fire to the hotel where an invading army slept. Wary of the Costa Rican legislature, Chaves promised to govern by executive order and was flippant when critics expressed alarm. "They say I'm very arrogant and very dictatorial," he said, as quoted by Álvaro Murillo for *US News and World Report* (31 Mar. 2022), "but I think I tell it like it is and people don't like it."

Chaves also expressed deeply conservative views on sexuality and gender. In late March 2022 he signed a statement intent in which he promised Foro Cristiano de Asuntos Políticos (Christian Forum of Political Affairs), an evangelical Christian forum, that he would reconsider regulations allowing in vitro fertilization (IVF) and abortion, the latter of which is legal in Costa Rica, but only in cases where the life or health of the pregnant person was at risk. He vowed to eliminate the teaching of "gender ideology" in Costa Rican schools, a vague but significant attack in what has hitherto been one of the most progressive countries in Central America for LGBTQ+ rights. He also pledged to let Christian religious leaders propose candidates for ministerial posts.

PRESIDENT OF COSTA RICA

In the weeks before the election, Chaves questioned the legitimacy of Costa Rica's electoral system. He encouraged voters to bring their own pens to the polls, warning that the indelible crayons provided by the Supreme Electoral Tribunal (TSE) could be erased. Cisneros also sowed doubt in the minds of voters, saying, as quoted by Paula Ruiz for *El Observador* Costa Rica (26 Mar. 2022), "We have a powerful enemy in front of us, with a solid structure and capable of trickling down votes to take this election away from us."

Figueres won the first round of voting in February, but Chaves, surprising analysts, narrowly won the runoff election, and thus the presidency, on April 3, 2022. Although he won with 52.9 percent of the vote and a margin of 5 percent, it was hardly the triumph Chaves had sought. Voters' distaste for both candidates led to the lowest voter turnout in over seventy years; only one of every four registered voters in Costa Rica cast a ballot. Meanwhile, the president-elect's PPSD party took just ten of the legislature's fifty-seven seats, giving Chaves limited power in the legislature. Averse to coalition-building, Chaves said he planned to govern by referendum, bypassing the legislature altogether.

Chaves was sworn into office on May 8, 2022. In a speech to the nation, he doubled down on his anti-establishment rhetoric. "Not only are we going to put the house in order, we are going to rebuild it!" he said, as quoted by Cordoba, adding, "If the political class fails one more time, the country could fall apart."

As president, Chaves promised to tackle unemployment and the high cost of living—the two issues Costa Ricans said were most important to them going into the election. Chaves said that he would lower the cost of goods by executive decree but declined to specify how such a directive would work. To tackle the country's $40 billion debt—forty-two percent of Costa Rica's budget went to debt obligations in 2021—he advocated shrinking the state, deregulating businesses, and renegotiating a $1.6 billion debt-financing agreement with the International Monetary Fund (IMF). He also promised to remove tax exemptions for wealthy citizens and create a national cryptocurrency.

PERSONAL LIFE

His second wife, Signe Zeicate, is an economist from Latvia. The couple has two daughters.

SUGGESTED READING

Arrieta, Esteban. "Before Pilar Cisneros Got Involved in the Campaign, 80% of Ticos Did Not Know Rodrigo Chaves." *La Republica*, 3 Apr. 2022, www-larepublica-net.translate. goog/noticia/antes-de-que-pilar-cisneros-se-involucrara-en-campana-80-de-ticos-no-conocia-a-rodrigo-chaves?_x_tr_sl=es&_x_tr_tl=en&_x_tr_hl=en&_x_tr_pto=sc. Accessed 1 Aug. 2022.

Bolaños, David, and Anatoly Kurmanaev. "Economist Accused of Harassment Appears Set to Become Costa Rica's President." *The New York Times*, 3 Apr. 2022, www.nytimes.com/2022/04/03/world/americas/costa-rica-election.html. Accessed 17 Aug. 2022.

___. "He Was Demoted for Harassing Women. Now He's the Front-Runner for President." *The New York Times*, 1 Apr. 2022, www.nytimes.com/2022/04/01/world/americas/costa-rica-election-sexual-harassment.html. Accessed 1 Aug. 2022.

Cordoba, Javier. "Costa Rica's New Leader Takes over with a Blast at the Past." *AP News*, 8 May 2022, apnews.com/article/caribbean-central-america-costa-rica-carlos-alvarado-327d0204171eedc2c6575e0f805cf1e0. Accessed 1 Aug. 2022.

Marin, Douglas. "Rodrigo Chaves, the Controversial Economist Who Offers Change in Costa Rica." *Agencia EFE*, 1 Apr. 2022, www.efe.com/efe/america/portada/rodrigo-chaves-el-polemico-economista-que-ofrece-un-cambio-en-costa-rica/20000064-4774948. Accessed 2 Aug. 2022.

Murillo, Alvaro. "Costa Rica Ex-President Vies for Top Office Against Upstart Chaves." *US News and World Report*, 31 Mar. 2022, www.usnews.com/news/world/articles/2022-03-31/costa-rica-ex-president-vies-for-top-office-against-upstart-chaves. Accessed 1 Aug. 2022.

Ruiz, Paula. "Chaves Promises in a Religious Forum That He Will Review In vitro Fertilization Decrees and the Technical Standard for Abortion." *El Observador*, 26 Mar. 2022, observador.cr/chaves-promete-en-foro-religioso-que-revisara-decretos-de-la-fecundacion-in-vitro-y-norma-tecnica-del-aborto/. Accessed 1 Aug. 2022.

—*Molly Hagan*

Liz Chicaje

Born: December 8, 1982
Occupation: Activist

In January 2018, the sacrifices and dedication of environmental and Indigenous rights activist Liz Chicaje helped result in the elevation of the Yaguas area in Peru to the status of a national park.

A two million-acre preserve in the northeast corner of the country, home to thousands of unique wildlife species, the Yaguas area had become increasingly threatened by illegal mining and logging by the 2010s, leaving its rich biodiversity in urgent need of protection.

Luckily, Chicaje, a member of the Bora Indigenous community who grew up appreciative of the surrounding Amazonian ecosystems, recognized this need and, during her three-year tenure as the president of the Federation of Native Communities of Ampiyacu (FECONA) (2014–17), she set out to protect it, helping the park achieve official recognition in 2018.

As Chicaje told Vanessa Buschschlüter for *BBC News* (15 June 2021), "We live in the jungle, we know it better than anyone, we walk through it, so the desire to protect this territory and the people who depend on it develops naturally."

A staunch advocate of Indigenous rights and the Amazonian environment, Chicaje has earned national and international admiration, receiving both the 2019 Franco-German Prize for Human Rights and Rule of Law and the 2021 Goldman Environmental Prize.

EARLY LIFE AND WORK

Indigenous activist Liz Chicaje Churay, known professionally as simply Liz Chicaje, was born on December 8, 1982, in the Pebas district of Peru's northernmost department of Loreto, situated near the border with Colombia. She was the fifth of eleven children.

It was there, in the tucked-away village of Boras de Pucaurquillo—home to the Bora and Huitoto Indigenous communities—where Chicaje came to appreciate the area's rich Amazonian ecosystem from an early age. She often heard stories about forest protection efforts, the nearby Ampiyacu river, and the diverse flora and fauna of the region. The Bora and Huitoto communities not only relied on this ecosystem for their livelihoods, but also considered the land to be of great spiritual importance. "Many of our beloved ancestors died there due to lack of food and medicines as they tried to cross it to safety. It is a sacred place for us, and so we couldn't bear seeing it destroyed," Chicaje told Buschschlüter.

Chicaje also became aware of the traumatic history of the area's Indigenous communities. During the Amazon rubber boom of the late nineteenth and early twentieth century, many Indigenous people, including members of the Bora tribe, perished. Many Indigenous people were forced into labor, exploited, and tortured by rubber barons.

Around 1992, after Chicaje finished her elementary school education, she began working at the age of ten. Alongside her four sisters, Chicaje spent a period working as a domestic helper in Leticia, Colombia. The work required the sisters to sail along the Amazon river for two days every year and stay with Colombian families for months at a time.

While Chicaje did not give up the idea of finishing her own education, it was not until her firstborn son, Diego, commenced high school around the early 2010s that she resolved to return to school. She studied the last five years of high school with her son in Pucaurquillo. As she grew older, Chicaje also spent time working as a Sunday school teacher at her local church.

ACTIVISM AND FECONA PRESIDENCY

When she was sixteen, Chicaje began participating in Bora community meetings focused on defending Bora land against illegal logging and other threats. As time went on,

Photo by Elianalopezperez,
via Wikimedia Commons

she became increasingly concerned that the natural resources of her community's homeland were increasingly threatened by illegal mining and logging. Knowing the land was central to the culture and traditions of the surrounding Indigenous communities, Chicaje became resolute in doing what she could to protect it.

In 2013, while still working as a Sunday school teacher, Chicaje was approached by a mayoral candidate for the Pebas district who wanted Chicaje by her side to represent the Ampiyacu basin as an Indigenous councilor. After accepting the proposal, Chicaje spent the next year campaigning with the mayoral candidate, visiting the myriad Indigenous communities of the region.

While the candidate placed second in her quest to become the mayor of the Pebas district, Chicaje treasured the time she had spent on the road, as it allowed her to see firsthand the needs and political priorities of the larger Amazonian population. "We walked for a year campaigning," Chicaje told Yvette Sierra Praeli in a Spanish-language interview for *Mongabay* (30 Jan. 2019). "In this way I got to know all the communities and visualized the needs of the population."

The campaign also raised Chicaje's profile as a political activist. When the next congress of the Federation of Native Communities of Ampiyacu (or FECONA, for its acronym in

Spanish) met, Chicaje's community chose her as their representative. During that congress, FECONA elected Chicaje as the next president of the organization, which represents fourteen Bora, Huitoto, Ocaina, and Yagua communities.

Between 2014 and 2017, the years Chicaje served in the role of president, she visited wide areas of Peruvian territory, working her way along the Napo, Putumayo, and Amazon rivers.

During her three-year tenure, Chicaje deepened her knowledge of the Amazonian's biodiversity and resources while gaining wider exposure to the region's different Indigenous communities. Chicaje learned to recognize that, while all of these communities cared for the same land, each community carved out its own identity. For example, some Indigenous groups focused their work on the reforestation of the chambira palm trees while others dedicated their efforts to raising farm animals.

For her part, Chicaje committed her time and labor to projects that could ensure the communities a constant economic income, including promoting and expanding the market of local products such as black chili, starch, and farina.

CREATION OF YAGUAS NATIONAL PARK

Chicaje's most celebrated contribution during her presidency of FECONA was pushing for legal recognition of the Yaguas territory—a roughly two-million-acre wilderness in the Amazon rainforest—as an official Peruvian national park.

To accomplish this, she served as an intermediary between the Amazon communities she represented, the Peruvian Ministry of Environment, and other Indigenous organizations, including the Interethnic Association for the Development of the Peruvian Rainforest and the Regional Organization of Indigenous Peoples of the East. She was able to secure support for the park from twenty-three out of twenty-nine of the region's Indigenous communities.

As a result of her sustained efforts, the Peruvian Ministry of Environment invited Chicaje to participate in the 2017 United Nations Climate Change Conference (COP23) in Bonn, Germany, as part of Peru's official delegation. There, she advocated for the creation of the park, promising that its establishment would allow Indigenous peoples to sustain their lifestyle by hunting and fishing in a protected space. "Due to the remoteness of the area and the threats facing it, it was key to get the government involved in its protection," she said to Buschschlüter.

Her unwavering work and commitment eventually paid off; in January 2018, the Peruvian government declared the area a national park, a move celebrated by a majority of the region's Indigenous peoples. Improvements to the park began soon afterward, including the deployment of park rangers and the initiation of educational campaigns highlighting the ecological importance of the area.

The park's new status also contributed to the Peruvian government's decision to protect the area more forcefully. "Illegal loggers and gold miners were coming down the river, and it was with the help of the navy that they were driven out, and their dredges burned," Chicaje said to Buschschlüter.

INTERNATIONAL RECOGNITION AND CONTINUED ACTIVISM

Chicaje's tremendous dedication in her fight to defend the rights of Indigenous people and natural environments earned her the respect and admiration of local and international leaders. In January 2019, the French, and German ambassadors to Peru awarded Chicaje the Franco-German Prize for Human Rights and Rule of Law. The award, given to people who have contributed significantly to the protection and promotion of human rights, proved a fitting recognition of Chicaje's tireless efforts.

Soon, another major award came Chicaje's way; in 2021, she became one of the recipients of the Goldman Environmental Prize, sometimes referred to as a Nobel Prize for environmentalists. The award is granted to individuals around the world who take significant action to care for the planet. The jury chose to recognize Chicaje for her leading role in the creation of Yaguas National Park and for building strategies to ensure its ongoing protection. Although Chicaje appreciated the award, she was quick to point out that the fight to secure recognition had been a community effort. "This is a recognition that belongs to all Indigenous peoples. Achieving the Yaguas National Park has been a very intense work in which many leaders participated," Chicaje told Jack Lo Lau for *Diálogo Chino* (17 June 2021).

In the years after the end of her presidency of FECONA, Chicaje continued to be a firm, steady presence in her community. She became leader of the Pucaurquillo association of craftswomen, training her community sisters to make handicrafts from chambira, a type of palm plant. Chicaje's main goal remained protecting her ancestral homeland and the rich cultures of the area's Indigenous peoples.

She remained particularly concerned with the long-term preservation of this cultural knowledge for future generations. As she expressed to Lau, "We have to protect our customs, our language. Children no longer speak our language, minors no longer express themselves. That worries me." While concerned about this trend, Chicaje planned to take steps to address it, saying, "One of my dreams is to organize training workshops with the youth to strengthen ancestral knowledge."

PERSONAL LIFE

Chicaje and her partner, a fellow member of the Bora ethnic group, are the parents of five children: Diego, Zinedine, Matias, Job, and Cielo. Chicaje and her family practice the Christian faith.

SUGGESTED READING

Buschschlüter, Vanessa. "Liz Chicaje, Activist Whose Fight Created a National Park." *BBC News*, 15 June 2021, www.bbc.com/news/world-latin-america-57427697. Accessed 10 Sept. 2022.

Cavallito, Matteo. "Liz Chicaje Churay, Twenty Years of Struggle for Land and Biodiversity." *Re Soil Foundation*, 25 June 2021, resoilfoundation.org/en/environment/chicaje-churay-land-struggle. Accessed 10 Sept. 2022.

Chicaje, Liz. "Liz Chicaje: Una Lideresa Indígena Peruana que se Enfrentó a la Ilegalidad (Liz Chicaje: A Peruvian Indigenous Leader Who Confronted Illegality)." Interview by Yvette Sierra Praeli. *Mongabay*, 30 Jan. 2019, es.mongabay.com/2019/01/peru-liz-chicaje-indigena-contra-la-ilegalidad-yaguas. Accessed 10 Sept. 2022.

"Conoce a Liz Chicaje, la Lideresa Defensora de los Derechos Indígenas y del Ambiente (Meet Liz Chicaje, the Leading Defender of Indigenous Rights and the Environment)."

Agencia Peruana de Noticias Andina (Peruvian Andean News Agency), 24 Jan. 2019, andina.pe/agencia/noticia-conoce-a-liz-chicaje-lideresa-defensora-los-derechos-indigenas-y-del-ambiente-740260.aspx. Accessed 10 Sept. 2022.

Lo Lau, Jack. "Liz Chicaje: The Church Teacher Who Won the Goldman Prize." *Diálogo Chino*, 17 June 2021, dialogochino.net/en/climate-energy/43817-liz-chicaje-the-church-teacher-who-won-the-goldman-prize. Accessed 10 Sept. 2022.

Rodriguez, Angela. "Defensoras Ambientales: Peruanas Que Protegen la Amazonia con Vocación y Corazón (*Environmental Defenders: Peruvians Who Protect the Amazon with Vocation and Heart*)." *SPDA Actualidad Ambiental* (*SPDA Environmental News*), 11 Dec. 2020, www.actualidadambiental.pe/defensoras-de-derechos-para-ser-defensoras-debemos-tener-vocacion-esto-sale-del-corazon. Accessed 10 Sept. 2022.

"2021 Goldman Prize Winner Liz Chicaje Churay." *The Goldman Environmental Prize*, www.goldmanprize.org/recipient/liz-chicaje-churay. Accessed 10 Sept. 2022.

—*Maria del Pilar Guzman*

Sharon D. Clarke

Born: August 12, 1966
Occupation: Actor and singer

A fixture on London stages beginning in the late 1980s, actor and singer Sharon D. Clarke cemented a place for herself in the international theater world when she was finally able to bring her acclaimed portrayal of the starring role in the hit musical *Caroline, or Change* to the Broadway stage in 2021. The London production of which she had been a part since 2017 had been slated to move to Broadway in March 2020 but was postponed due to the coronavirus disease 2019 (COVID-19) pandemic declared around that time. Undeterred by this setback, she shined, as usual, upon the Studio 54 premiere in October 2021 of the play, about a Black woman named Caroline working as a maid for a White, Jewish family in the American South in 1963. While the Broadway production earned rave reviews, Clarke had already won a prestigious Olivier Award in 2019 for her performance as the play's titular character. Though it would be difficult to define Clarke's long and rich theatrical career by one role, many critics viewed Caroline as a distinguishing breakthrough for her, leading her to joke to Danny Leigh for *Vogue* (12 Feb. 2020), "I'm a 36-year overnight sensation."

Clarke made her true professional stage debut in 1988. After a brief career as a pop star, she devoted herself to the stage, originating roles in the West End musicals *We Will Rock You* (2002–04) and *Ghost* (2011–12). Also familiar to British audiences for her appearances on television shows like *Holby City* (2005–08) and *Doctor Who* (2018, 2020, 2021), she went on to play the titular role in the London revival of August Wilson's *Ma Rainey's Black Bottom* (2016) and Linda Loman in a local revival of Arthur Miller's *Death of a Salesman* from (2019, 2020). Still, she has acknowledged that playing Caroline offered her a different kind of opportunity to show the range of her talents. "It's such an amazing role; a wonderful singing role, but also there's the depth of the character. I think it made quite a few people see me in a different light. People go, 'Yes she sings,' but now they look at me as an actor, too," she related to Lisa O'Kelly in an interview for *The Observer* (13 July 2019).

EARLY LIFE AND EDUCATION

Sharon Delores Clarke was born in London on August 12, 1966. Having met as children in Jamaica, in the 1950s her parents decided to leave their home country for the United Kingdom in the hope of forging a life in an area that presented more varied opportunities. Her mother, a talented singer who served as her daughter's first vocal coach, earned a living sewing clothes while her father was employed in carpentry. As a child in the North London district of Tottenham, she was introduced to her mother's favorite classical musicals, featuring American film stars like Fred Astaire. "But there wasn't much diversity," she told Rebecca Rubin in an interview for *Variety* (7 Oct. 2021). When she saw the film version of *West Side Story* (1961), about Puerto Rican and White teenagers in New York City, she began to imagine possibilities for herself, a young Black girl, in such productions. "They were different folk, and the music was funky," she recalled to Rubin. "It showed me that musical theater was a world where I could live." Loving to sing and drawn by a friend's involvement to attend the

Photo by Linda Hartley,
via Wikimedia Commons

local Ivy Travers Dance School, from her first show, *Babes in the Wood*, at the age of six, she "was absolutely hooked" on stage performing, as she told O'Kelly.

By her teenage years, Clarke was taking classes at a drama school in Islington led by Anna Scher, learning additional performance art such as improv. Still, as she pursued acting, she also studied social work at North London College at the behest of her parents. Although she did have a natural knack and affinity for it, social work, she told O'Kelly, "was something my mum and dad wanted me to do, so I'd have something to fall back on, in case acting and singing didn't work out." However, she never needed to apply this training, as a job advertisement she came across at the college led her to an audition and subsequent position with the Battersea Arts Centre. Granted membership in the UK's Equity actors union, a rare feat without prior acting credits, she first performed as a professional actor and singer in 1984's *Southside*. Her notable professional theater debut, though, came in Derek Walcott's musical *O Babylon!* at Talawa Theatre in 1988.

MUSIC AND TELEVISION CAREERS

As Clarke appeared in theatrical productions, she also enjoyed a brief career as a pop singer. By the early 1990s, she was part of a music act called Nomad, which produced one album.

Nomad's classic groove "(I Wanna Give You) Devotion" was a top-ten hit in the United States and the United Kingdom in 1991 while the follow-up single, "Just a Groove," cracked the UK top twenty. At the same time, she had another dance hit, with a group called the F.P.I. Project, called "Going Back to My Roots" in 1989, and in 2000 she was part of a female vocal group called Six Chix, which formed to participate in the EuroVision Song Contest. Six Chix, with their song "Only the Women Know," placed second in the UK national final.

Clarke also ventured into television, playing several bit roles in shows in the late 1980s and 1990s. Most often, frustratingly for Clarke, the part offered was that of a nurse—a testament to the profoundly small pool of roles available to Black actors in the medium. "I got to the point where I genuinely thought, Okay, I just won't do telly anymore, because f—— it, I'm not just a nurse," she recalled to Leigh. A break came in 2005, when she won the role of a doctor named Lola Griffin on the BBC hospital drama *Holby City* and remained a regular on the show until 2008. "I'm very proud to have had people come up to me and say that their daughter became a doctor because of *Holby*," she told Mark Lawson for *The Guardian* (17 Jan. 2016). Beginning in 2018, she played the recurring character Grace O'Brien in season eleven of the popular *Doctor Who* television series; later, she would return for episodes in 2020 and 2021. In addition to another small-screen appearance in the 2018 thriller miniseries *Informer*, she was seen on the big screen in the 2019 films *Rocketman* and *Rocks*.

A WEST END FIXTURE

Clarke made her London West End debut in the musical *Once on This Island* in 1994. Her portrayal of Asaka, the goddess of Earth, in the original British staging earned her an Olivier Award nomination for Best Supporting Performance in a Musical. After again taking a West End stage, this time for a revival of *Guys and Dolls* (1996), she went on to portray Rose in the original West End production of *Stepping Out* the following year. After her 2000–02 run as Rafiki with the established Lyceum Theatre production of the musical adaptation of *The Lion King*, she originated the role of the Killer Queen in the West End jukebox musical *We Will Rock You* (2002 to 2004). Featuring the songs of the rock band Queen, the musical is set in a dystopian future where all music, by corporate decree, is soulless and sanitized. As the play's villain, Clarke's Killer Queen desperately tries to quash any attempts to revive the rebellious spirit of rock'n'roll. Despite generally poor critical reviews, the musical was a smash hit with audiences, and her performance earned her another Olivier Award nomination for best musical supporting role.

Between 2011 and 2012, she played the psychic medium Oda Mae Brown in the original West End staging of *Ghost*, a musical based on the 1990 film of the same name. Michael Billington, writing for *The Guardian* (19 July 2011), praised Clarke's performance while expressing distaste for the production as a whole: "Where the show sparks into life is with the emergence of Oda Mae Brown." Clarke, he wrote, "provides the show with what it mostly lacks: heart and soul." Further solidifying the power of her stage presence even outside of lead roles, this turn brought her another musical supporting role Olivier Award nomination.

The year 2013 saw Clarke appear as part of the main cast of a production of James Baldwin's 1954 play *The Amen Corner* at the National Theatre. Set in a storefront church in Harlem in the 1950s, the play revolves around the relationship between the moralizing pastor, Sister Margaret, and her estranged jazz musician husband. Clarke played Margaret's sister, Odessa, a role that brought home her first Olivier Award, for best supporting actress, in 2014. In 2016, she stepped even further into the spotlight to star in the National Theatre's British premiere of *Ma Rainey's Black Bottom*, a 1982 play by August Wilson. Taking place in Chicago in 1927, the play unfolds over the course of a recording session with the real-life blues star Ma Rainey (portrayed by Clarke) and her band. For Clarke, playing the trailblazing icon was a particular honor and high point in her career.

CAROLINE, OR CHANGE

Another star-making titular role, what would become her first on a West End stage, came for Clarke in an acclaimed revival of the musical *Caroline, or Change* that began at the Chichester Festival Theatre in 2017. Written by Tony Kushner, with music by Jeanine Tesori, the 2003 American musical is based on aspects of Kushner's own life growing up in

Lake Charles, Louisiana. Protagonist Caroline Thibodeaux is a Black maid working for the Jewish Gellman family. The musical, which takes place in 1963, explores both the personal and racial dynamics of the family. Times are dangerous and uncertain; President John F. Kennedy has recently been assassinated, and Caroline's daughter is joining the burgeoning civil rights movement. Describing Caroline as a "tour de force" in an interview with Ted Sod for the Roundabout Theatre Company's website (2020), Clarke detailed her excitement about the opportunity to take on the role: "It's very rare that you see someone of Caroline's stature at the center of a story being told. I wanted to be a part of that."

Following a subsequent stint at Hampstead Theatre, Clarke's production of *Caroline, or Change* transferred to the West End in late 2018 to exultant reviews. Shortly after the production's close in early 2019, she accepted an Olivier Award for Best Actress in a Musical. Also impressed, Kushner and Tesori began working to bring Clarke and the London production to Broadway, as Kushner recalled to Laura Collins-Hughes for *The New York Times* (20 Oct. 2021): "Both Jeanine and I felt, immediately when we saw her at Chichester: 'OK, we have to get this performance over to New York. People have to see it.'"

In the meantime, Clarke costarred in a production of Arthur Miller's classic 1949 play *Death of a Salesman* at the Young Vic in London in 2019. She played Linda Loman, wife to the titular Willy Loman. While the original play tells the story of a White salesman, the character's failure to achieve the promise of the American Dream was given new potency in this production revolving instead around a Black family. The show was briefly transferred to the West End, and in late 2020 Clarke claimed the Olivier Award for Best Actress.

Clarke's scheduled Broadway debut was delayed due to the COVID-19 pandemic. *Caroline, or Change* was in rehearsals, with only one day to go before the initial preview, when lockdowns halted live entertainment in March 2020. Rehearsals did not begin again until September 2021, but the musical finally opened on Broadway in October 2021 before closing as scheduled in January 2022. Despite Clarke's extended leave from the play, the Broadway production also won rave reviews.

PERSONAL LIFE

Clarke began dating theatre director and producer Susie McKenna in 1999. The pair had met during a production of *Cinderella* at Hackney Empire. They married in 2008 and though they live in London, they also have a house in Spain.

SUGGESTED READING

Billington, Michael. Review of *Ghost the Musical*, directed by Matt Warchus. *The Guardian*, 19 July 2011, www.theguardian. com/stage/2011/jul/19/ghost-the-musical-reviewt. Accessed 9 Mar. 2022.

Clarke, Sharon D. "Actor Sharon D Clarke: 'I'm a 30-Year Overnight Sensation!'" Interview by Lisa O'Kelly. *The Observer*, Guardian News and Media, 13 July 2019, www.theguardian. com/culture/2019/jul/13/sharon-d-clarke-interview-death-of-a-salesman-blues-in-the-night. Accessed 9 Mar. 2022.

___. "Sharon D. Clarke: An Interview." Interview by Ted Sod. *Roundabout Theatre Company*, 2020, www.roundabouttheatre. org/get-tickets/upstage-guides-current/upstage-guide-caroline-or-change/interview-sharon-d-clarke. Accessed 14 Mar. 2022.

___. "Sharon D Clarke on Making Her Broadway Debut in *Caroline, or Change* and Theater's Landmark Season for Black Artists." Interview by Rebecca Rubin. *Variety*, 7 Oct. 2021, variety.com/2021/theater/features/sharon-d-clarke-caroline-or-change-broadway-debut-1235080273/. Accessed 9 Mar. 2022.

Collins-Hughes, Laura. "For Sharon D. Clarke, a 'Big Sing' and a Big Broadway Moment." *The New York Times*, 20 Oct. 2021, www. nytimes.com/2021/10/20/theater/sharon-d-clarke-caroline-or-change.html. Accessed 10 Mar. 2022.

Lawson, Mark. "Sharon D Clarke: From *Holby City* to Siren Songs." *The Guardian*, 17 Jan. 2016, www.theguardian.com/stage/2016/jan/17/sharon-d-clarke-ma-raineys-black-bottom-interview. Accessed 9 Mar. 2022.

Leigh, Danny. "An Overnight Sensation 36 Years in the Making, Sharon D. Clarke Arrives on Broadway for *Caroline, or Change*." *Vogue*, 12 Feb. 2020, www.vogue. com/article/sharon-d-clarke-arrives-on-broadway-for-caroline-or-change. Accessed 9 Mar. 2022.

SELECTED WORKS

Once on This Island, 1994; *We Will Rock You*, 2002–04; *Holby City*, 2005–08; *Ghost*, 2011–12; *The Amen Corner*, 2013; *Caroline, or Change*, 2017–22; *Doctor Who*, 2018–21

—Molly Hagan

Patrick Collison

Born: September 9, 1988
Occupation: Entrepreneur

In 2010, Irish entrepreneur Patrick Collison and his younger brother John launched a company that would dramatically alter the trajectory of both Collison's career and the Internet as a whole. Having previously entered the world of startups as cofounders of the company Auctomatic, which they sold in 2008, the brothers next turned their attention to the realm of online payment processing. At that time, setting up a business to accept credit card payments online was a complex and time-consuming process—and unnecessarily so, in the minds of the Collisons. "The thought from our standpoint was, 'Why is there not some service you can go to, put in your basic details, your bank account information, your personal information, whatever, and click, register, activate, what have you, and now you've access to some service that will enable to you to just charge credit cards,'" Collison recalled to Kara Swisher in an interview for the *Vox* podcast *Recode Decode* (13 June 2017). The brothers soon developed such a service and went on to receive seed funding from several prominent venture capitalists for their company, which they named Stripe.

Over the next years, Stripe grew rapidly, expanding into numerous countries and enabling business to accept payments in a wide range of currencies. Although much of the media coverage of Stripe focused on its financial status—the company had an estimated valuation of $95 billion in 2021—Collison himself preferred to focus on improving Stripe's existing offerings and introducing new tools to aid companies in conducting business over the Internet. "We're not a glamorous business, just an infrastructure company that hopefully we'll be able to compound for a long time," he told Alex Konrad in an interview for *Forbes* (26 May 2022).

Photo by JD Lasica,
via Wikimedia Commons

EARLY LIFE AND CAREER

Patrick Collison was born on September 9, 1988, in Dromineer, Ireland, a small village just outside of Limerick. His mother, Lily, was a corporate trainer with a background in microbiology, while his father, Denis, was an electrical engineer. The Collisons operated an inn in the village of Dromineer during Collison's childhood, and he grew up in that village alongside younger brothers John and Tommy. He attended secondary school at Castletroy College.

Drawn to the field of computer programming from a young age, Collison developed over the years into a skilled programmer, as did his younger brother John. As a teenager, he created a programming language called Croma, a "dialect" of the language Lisp. Collison's project won him the Ireland's Young Scientist of the Year Award at age sixteen, which in turn qualified him to compete in the 2005 European Union Contest for Young Scientists, held that year in Russia. There, he won one of the contest's three second prizes, which included a monetary award. The following year, Collison traveled to the United States to study mathematics at the Massachusetts Institute of Technology (MIT). He ultimately dropped out of college before completing his studies, preferring instead to pursue entrepreneurial opportunities.

In 2007, Collison and his brother John—then just seventeen and fifteen, respectively—partnered with two other aspiring entrepreneurs to found their first company, a business that provided an auction-management solution for sellers using auction websites such as eBay. They developed the business via the accelerator Y Combinator, which offered seed money and guidance to select startups. "Through that process we sort of got familiar, somewhat, with some of the challenges of building a startup," Collison told Swisher. "In particular, we also got to meet a whole bunch of people who, themselves, were building startups, and got familiar with the challenges that they encountered." In 2008, Collison and his partners sold their company, by then known as Auctomatic, for $5 million.

STRIPE

Following the sale of Auctomatic, the Collison brothers began to think about building a new company that would shake up the online payments industry, which Collison considered to be "an unusually compelling example of an entire industry that [was] going to have its lunch eaten," as quoted by John Naughton for *The Guardian* (20 Mar. 2021). At that time, getting set up to accept credit card payments online was a complex process that was prohibitively difficult and expensive for many businesses. "We were so struck by how needlessly complicated it was and how every different payment system worked a different way and it was weeks or months of set-up complexity because of all the random needless differences that existed," he recalled to Swisher. "We thought there really should be some standardized way of handling all of this, sort of like there is for devices on Linux and Unix." The Collison brothers developed an application programming interface (API) that would enable businesses to set up their payment-processing capabilities simply by adding a few lines of code to their websites. First known as /dev/ Payments and later renamed Stripe, the company would make money by charging fees that applied to each transaction processed.

After founding Stripe in 2010, Collison and John—who would hold the roles of chief executive officer and president of Stripe, respectively—sought to acquire funding for the company from prominent venture capitalists.

One of the earliest investors was the venture capitalist Peter Thiel, who had previously cofounded the online payment service PayPal. "I remember being very critical of PayPal," Collison later said of his meeting with Thiel, as quoted by Tim Bradshaw for the *Irish Times* (19 Mar. 2021). "Halfway through the meeting I was like 'hmmm, maybe that's not the best strategy.'" Nevertheless, Thiel and several other investors decided to provide seed money for Stripe, which went on to raise an additional $18 million during its series A fundraising round in 2012.

CONTINUING GROWTH

Over the next decade, Collison and his brother worked to expand Stripe significantly, making the company's services available in numerous companies and allowing businesses to accept payment in a wide range of currencies. As Stripe established itself as a major player within the payment processing space, the company forged partnerships with other major businesses, including the social networking company Twitter; Alibaba, which operated the payment service Alipay; and Apple, which allowed for mobile payments through the service Apple Pay. "We wanted to do the Alipay deal and the Twitter partnership three years ago, but we weren't there yet," Collison told Leena Rao for *Fortune* (28 July 2015). "Now we are." In addition to building such partnerships, Collison and his colleagues focused extensively on improving the reliability of Stripe's services and limiting downtime, which could not only harm Stripe's reputation as a service provider but also prevent businesses using Stripe's services from making money. The company's work paid off, and by 2019, Stripe had an estimated valuation of $35 billion. While multiple companies reportedly offered to buy Stripe at various points in time, Collison and his brother preferred to keep the company in private hands.

Though Stripe was sometimes heralded in the press as a so-called unicorn startup—one of the rare startups to achieve a valuation of more than one billion dollars—Collison preferred to focus on Stripe's far less glamorous status as a successful infrastructure provider with long-term growth goals. "I remain a very big believer in infrastructure, and I think that Stripe is still early in its journey to unlock all sorts of entrepreneurship and economic activity that wouldn't otherwise have occurred," he told Noah Smith in an interview for *Noahpinion* (8 Mar. 2021). "Almost every week we ship an improvement that makes hundreds of thousands or millions of businesses better off—and our ability to make such improvements is growing and not shrinking with time." Stripe's valuation increased to $95 billion in early 2021. As he personally owned about fourteen percent of the company as of mid-2022, according to the Bloomberg Billionaires Index, Collison was believed to be a multibillionaire and was listed at number 214 on *Forbes* magazine's 2022 World's Billionaires List.

BEYOND PAYMENT PROCESSING

As Stripe's operations expanded, the company began to offer a number of services beyond credit card processing. Stripe Climate, for instance, enabled companies using Stripe to divert a portion of their revenue toward carbon capture projects. Stripe Atlas was designed to assist entrepreneurs in forming startups and provided guidance throughout that process, helping each user form a legal business entity, issue shares of stock to the new company's founders, and set up a Stripe payment-processing account. In 2017, the company also acquired the online community Indie Hackers, which sought to bring together independent entrepreneurs and enable them to share advice and form business partnerships with one another. "There's no shortage of attention paid to the well-funded, the sort of extravagantly venture-backed companies, but I think there's often too little attention paid to the quietly profitable, from the individual founder vantage point, highly successful private-side project or small business, and so Indie Hackers is sort of a showcase for them," Collison explained to Swisher. Stripe likewise published the software engineering magazine *Increment*, which released nineteen issues between April 2017 and November 2021, and in 2018 founded Stripe Press, a book publisher devoted to technology-related topics.

While Stripe grew substantially during the first decade of the company's existence, encompassing an array of products and building relationships with other major businesses, Collison remained convinced that further growth was likely, in part due to the continuing spread of Internet access around the world and "the explosive expansion in access to

opportunity facilitated by the Internet," as he told Smith. "Several billion people recently immigrated to the world's most vibrant city and the system hasn't yet equilibrated," he went on to explain. "In the landscape of the global commons, the internet is nitrogen fertilizer, and we still have a long way to go—economically, culturally, scientifically, technologically, socially, and everything in between." Focused on such growth, Collison believed that Stripe would remain a crucial infrastructure company going forward, enabling businesses from around the world to engage in commerce online.

PERSONAL LIFE

Collison met his wife, Swiss scientist Silvana Konermann, at the 2005 European Union Contest for Young Scientists, where she beat him to claim one of the contest's first prizes. Konermann later became an assistant professor of biochemistry at the Stanford University School of Medicine. The couple announced their engagement in 2019 and married in 2022.

SUGGESTED READING

Bradshaw, Tim. "Patrick and John Collison: Stripe's 30-Something Billionaires." *The Irish Times*, 19 Mar. 2021, www.irishtimes.com/business/technology/patrick-and-john-collison-stripe-s-30-something-billionaires-1.4515057. Accessed 8 Aug. 2022.

Browne, Ryan. "Stripe Co-Founder Says the $95 Billion Fintech Giant Is 'Very Happy' Staying Private." *CNBC*, 23 Nov. 2021, www.cnbc.com/2021/11/23/stripe-very-happy-staying-private-co-founder-john-collison-says.html. Accessed 8 Aug. 2022.

Collison, Patrick. "Full Transcript: Stripe CEO Patrick Collison on Recode Decode." Interview by Kara Swisher. *Recode Decode*, Vox, 13 June 2017, www.vox.com/2017/6/13/15794210/transcript-stripe-ceo-patrick-collison-payments-recode-decode. Accessed 8 Aug. 2022.

___. "Interview: Patrick Collison, Co-Founder and CEO of Stripe." Interview by Noah Smith. *Noahpinion*, 8 Mar. 2021, noahpinion.substack.com/p/interview-patrick-collison-co-founder. Accessed 8 Aug. 2022.

___. "The Collison Brothers Built Stripe into a $95 Billion Unicorn with Eye-Popping Financials. Inside Their Plan to Stay on

Top." Interview by Alex Konrad. *Forbes*, 26 May 2022, www.forbes.com/sites/alexkonrad/2022/05/26/stripe-exclusive-interview-collison-brothers-95-billion-plan-to-stay-on-top/?sh=53a24c725a1b. Accessed 8 Aug. 2022.

Naughton, John. "How Two Irish Brothers Started a £70bn Company You've Probably Never Heard Of." *The Guardian*, 20 Mar. 2021, www.theguardian.com/commentisfree/2021/mar/20/how-two-irish-brothers-started-a-70bn-company-stripe-john-patrick-collison. Accessed 8 Aug. 2022.

Rao, Leena. "A Billion-Dollar Startup Earns Its Stripes." *Fortune*, 28 July 2015, fortune.com/2015/07/28/stripe-payments-startup/. Accessed 8 Aug. 2022.

—*Joy Crelin*

Jon Cooper

Born: August 23, 1967
Occupation: Coach

When then-attorney Jon Cooper took on his first position as an ice hockey coach at a Michigan high school in 1999, he could not have anticipated where his newfound coaching career would take him. "I didn't get into coaching to coach in the [National Hockey League (NHL)]," he told Dan Rosen for the NHL's website (14 Apr. 2015). "I got into coaching because I loved it. I enjoyed that you get to assemble a team, and you've got one season to win a championship. I just loved that challenge." Cooper's willingness to take on new challenges took him from that first coaching job through multiple tiers of junior hockey and onward to the American Hockey League (AHL), where he coached the Norfolk Admirals to the 2012 Calder Cup championship.

A turning point in Cooper's career came in March 2013, when he was hired as head coach of the NHL's Tampa Bay Lightning. Cooper quickly helped turn the team into a perennial playoff contender. Yet they faced several painful postseason defeats, including an upset first-round elimination in the 2018–19 season after winning the Presidents' Trophy with the best record in the league. The following season, however, the Lightning broke through to win the Stanley Cup, the organization's first championship since 2004. "We went from the outhouse to the penthouse," Cooper told Joe

Smith for the *Athletic* (26 Mar. 2021) about the experience. A second consecutive Stanley Cup win in 2021 cemented the Lightning's reputation as a force within the league and garnered further acclaim for Cooper, who went on to claim his four hundredth NHL win midway through the 2021–22 season.

EARLY LIFE AND EDUCATION

Jonathan D. Cooper was born on August 23, 1967, in Prince George, British Columbia, Canada. The first of two sons born to Christine and Bob Cooper, he had dual US–Canadian citizenship through his mother, who was born in the United States. An athletic child, Cooper played multiple sports during his early life, including hockey and lacrosse. He left Prince George in tenth grade to attend Athol Murray College of Notre Dame, a boarding school in Saskatchewan with a strong hockey program. Although he was cut from the school's highest level hockey team, he played for a lower-level Notre Dame Hounds team during his years there and served as team captain for a time. Cooper also played football and lacrosse for the high school, particularly distinguishing himself in the latter. He graduated from Athol Murray College of Notre Dame in 1985.

After high school, Cooper relocated to the United States to attend Hofstra University on a lacrosse scholarship. He also played club hockey during his time at the university, from which he earned a bachelor's degree in business administration in 1989. He then worked in financial services for several years before enrolling in Michigan's Cooley Law School with the goal of becoming an attorney. Cooper went on to earn a law degree from that institution and was admitted to the Michigan bar in 1998.

EARLY COACHING CAREER

Though he was pursuing a career in law rather than in sports, Cooper returned to hockey recreationally during law school, when he was recruited by a team made up of fellow lawyers, law students, judges, and others interested in both hockey and the law. "They'd get wind of when guys with hockey backgrounds come to town," he told Ryan Satkowiak for *USA Hockey Magazine* (Oct. 2013). "I was playing hockey all the time, and it really helped me a lot because when I got out of law school, it got me jobs." One such job was a coaching position for a

Photo by TheAHL,
via Wikimedia Commons

hockey team at Lansing Catholic High School, which a friend encouraged him to take for the 1999–2000 season. "That was a special year and team. We had so much fun and success," he recalled to Neil Koepke for the *Lansing State Journal* (2 June 2015). "We were a much better team at the end of the year than we were at the start. I really enjoyed working with the kids." The Lansing Catholic team won a regional title under Cooper's leadership, beginning what would become a remarkable knack for guiding teams to championships at every level.

Balancing his legal practice as a public defender with his burgeoning coaching career, Cooper led a number of junior hockey teams over the next several years, including the Metro Jets, with which he won a title in 2002. He began coaching full time in 2003, taking a head coach position with the Texarkana Bandits of the North American Hockey League (NAHL). Cooper spent five seasons with that franchise, which, in 2006, moved to Missouri and was renamed the St. Louis Bandits. Along the way he earned NAHL Coach of the Year honors for the 2004–05 and 2007–08 seasons, and the team won championship titles in 2007 and 2008. He then took over as coach of the Green Bay Gamblers of the United States Hockey League (USHL), drastically improving the team's fortunes and leading them to a Clark Cup championship in 2010. Cooper was also

affiliated with USA Hockey during this period, collaborating with developmental teams and serving as an assistant coach for the US under-eighteen national team at the 2008 Ivan Hlinka Memorial Tournament.

AMERICAN HOCKEY LEAGUE

Cooper advanced to a new level of coaching in 2010, when he was named head coach of the Norfolk Admirals in the AHL, the second-highest level professional men's hockey league in North America. At the time of his hiring, the Admirals were the AHL affiliate of the NHL team the Tampa Bay Lightning and served as a valuable development ground for that organization. For Cooper, coaching at the AHL level was vastly different than his previous experiences with junior hockey. "I think that first year I was just trying to survive," he told Rosen. "That whole saying, you have to learn to be a pro, there's so much truth to that, for coaches too. You haven't earned the respect from the refs or the coaches when you're a rookie in pro hockey. You haven't earned anything."

In the course of two seasons with the Admirals, Cooper established himself as a strong coach at the AHL level. In the 2011–12 season he led the team to an excellent 55–18–3 record, with a notable twenty-eight-game winning streak during the regular season. In the postseason the Admirals went 15–3 and won the Calder Cup as league champions. Cooper was awarded the Louis A. R. Pieri Memorial Award in recognition of his leadership that season. The Lightning organization went on to switch its AHL affiliation from the Admirals to the Syracuse Crunch that offseason, and Cooper began the 2012–13 season with the latter team.

TAMPA BAY LIGHTNING

Partway through the Crunch's 2012–13 season, Cooper received an unexpected call from Tampa Bay Lightning management asking him to replace Guy Boucher as the NHL team's head coach. "I don't know if happy was the feeling. It was shock," he told Smith about that moment. "Like, 'Oh my God, really?'" Having accepted the offer, Cooper officially assumed his new position on March 25, 2013, and coached his first NHL game four days later.

As coach of the Lightning, Cooper faced the daunting task of revitalizing the franchise, which had won the Stanley Cup in 2004 but struggled since then, appearing in the playoffs only three times over the intervening years. The team finished out the 2012–13 season with a 5–8–3 record under Cooper and missed the postseason once more, but Cooper quickly began to show improvements in his first full season. The Lightning went 46–27–9 in 2013–14, good for second in the Atlantic Division, though they lost in the first round of the playoffs. The following season Cooper led the team to a 50–24–8 record and three playoff series victories, earning the Eastern Conference Championship. However, they lost the Stanley Cup Finals to the Chicago Blackhawks.

Cooper and the Lightning had another strong season in 2015–16, reaching the Eastern Conference Finals before falling to the eventual champion Pittsburgh Penguins. They then had a down year in the 2016–17 season, missing the postseason after finishing fifth in their division. However, the team rebounded the following season, winning the Atlantic Division with a 54–23–5 record. In the postseason they progressed to the Conference Finals, where they again lost to the eventual Stanley Cup winners, this time the Washington Capitals.

The Lighting had a historically great regular season in 2018–19 season, becoming just the third NHL team to surpass sixty wins. Their 62–16–4 record was easily the best in the league, earning the first Presidents' Trophy in franchise history. The success helped earn Cooper, who was by then the longest-tenured head coach in the NHL, a contract extension in March 2019. However, the Lighting's postseason performance proved historic in the opposite way. Entering the playoffs as heavy favorites, the team was swept by the Columbus Blue Jackets in the first round, becoming the first Presidents' Trophy winner ever to fail to record a single postseason win. Cooper later described the shocking upset to Kathryn Deen in an interview for *TAMPA Magazine* (7 Jan. 2022) as the "ultimate wake-up call for us as an organization and a team in what we needed and how we needed to commit to win."

STANLEY CUP WINNER

The 2019–20 NHL season was an unusual one due to the coronavirus disease 2019 (COVID-19) pandemic, which forced the league to suspend play in March 2020. Ultimately, a special expanded "bubble" playoff tournament was held that August, with twenty-four teams meeting under social-distancing protocols in two Canadian cities. Cooper's Lightning had once again been strong in the regular season, finishing with a 43–21–6 record, and this time they continued to thrive during the postseason. They beat the Blue Jackets and Boston Bruins before defeating the New York Islanders in the Eastern Conference Finals, setting up another trip to the Stanley Cup Finals. There the Lightning beat the Dallas Stars four games to two, securing the franchise a second championship title. "It's surreal, to be honest. You work so hard for so long. It's a lifelong dream," Cooper later told Deen about the experience. "When I was a small kid growing up in Canada, I always wanted to win the Stanley Cup. To achieve it is a thrill."

For Cooper, winning the 2020 Stanley Cup was particularly meaningful because of the Lightning's painful playoff elimination the previous year, which he believed helped the team improve. "I truly believe that you have to have failure before you have success," he explained to Smith. "You wear the bumps, you wear the bruises, you wear the heartache. You wear it on your sleeve. It keeps you up. It also drives you. We were not going to be denied." What remained to be seen, however, was whether the Lightning could replicate their performance when fueled not by failure but by success.

BACK-TO-BACK CUPS

Both delayed and condensed because of the ongoing pandemic, the 2020–21 NHL regular season began in January 2021 and ended that May, spanning only fifty-six games. Cooper led the Lightning to a 36–17–3 record, ranking third in their division but enough to qualify for the playoffs. The team went on to beat the Florida Panthers, Carolina Hurricanes, and New York Islanders to reach the Stanley Cup Finals for the second year in a row. Facing off against the Montreal Canadiens, the Lightning won the Finals four games to one, becoming only the second team to win back-to-back Stanley Cups since the introduction of the NHL's salary cap in 2005.

Having led his team to a second championship, Cooper was rewarded by the Lightning organization with a three-year contract extension in October 2021. During the 2021–22 season he continued to guide his team as one of the best in the league. On December 9, 2021, Cooper earned his four hundredth NHL win, making him the fastest head coach to reach that mark. The Lightning ranked within the top five in the standings by March 2022, prompting some to speculate that they could potentially win a third consecutive Stanley Cup. Amid such speculation, Cooper expressed confidence in his team and emphasized how supportive the fanbase had been. "[Even] before we won the Stanley Cup, we had 250-odd straight sellouts," he told Deen. "People don't realize what a hockey town Tampa has become over the years."

PERSONAL LIFE

Cooper and his wife, Jessie, have three children together. He settled in Tampa, Florida, after joining the Lightning. In addition to coaching hockey, Cooper enjoys playing golf and participated in a golf league for members of the Lightning's staff.

SUGGESTED READING

Cooper, Jon. "A Lifelong Dream Fulfilled." Interview by Kathryn Deen. *TAMPA Magazines*, 7 Jan. 2022, tampamagazines. com/jon-cooper/. Accessed 7 Mar. 2022.

___. "Jon Cooper Q&A: Stamkos, Drouin, Montreal Sweep." Interview by Luke Fox. *Sportsnet*, 31 Mar. 2015, www.sportsnet.ca/ hockey/nhl/jon-cooper-tampa-bay-lightning-coach-jonathan-drouin-steven-stamkos-montreal-canadiens-playoffs/. Accessed 7 Mar. 2022.

Encina, Eduardo A. "Lightning Coach Jon Cooper Fastest to 400 NHL Wins." *Tampa Bay Times*, 9 Dec. 2021, www.tampabay. com/sports/lightning/2021/12/09/lightning-coach-jon-cooper-fastest-to-400-nhl-wins/. Accessed 7 Mar. 2022.

Koepke, Neil. "Tampa Bay Lightning Coach Jon Cooper Began in Lansing." *Lansing State Journal*, 2 June 2015, www.lansingstatejournal.com/story/ sports/2015/06/02/jon-cooper-lansing-lightning/28349289/. Accessed 7 Mar. 2022.

Rosen, Dan. "Bet on Himself Paid Off for Lightning Coach Cooper." *NHL*, 14 Apr. 2015, www.nhl.com/news/bet-on-himself-paid-off-for-lightning-coach-cooper/c-763260. Accessed 7 Mar. 2022.

Satkowiak, Ryan. "The Road Less Traveled: Jon Cooper's Rise Up NHL Coaching Ranks." *USA Hockey Magazine*, Oct. 2013, www. usahockeymagazine.com/article/2013-10/ road-less-traveled-jon-coopers-rise-nhl-coaching-ranks. Accessed 7 Mar. 2022.

Smith, Joe. "'One of the Best Coaches Ever': How the Lightning's Patience with Jon Cooper Paid Off." *The Athletic*, 26 Mar. 2021, theathletic.com/2476498/2021/03/26/ one-of-the-best-coaches-ever-how-the-lightnings-patience-with-jon-cooper-paid-off/. Accessed 7 Mar. 2022.

—*Joy Crelin*

Spencer Cox

Born: July 11, 1975
Occupation: Lawyer and politician

Republican politician Spencer Cox was elected governor of Utah in 2020 and took office the following year. Raised in a rural farming community in Utah, Cox's rise to political prominence followed a somewhat unusual path. After completing his two-year mission for the Church of Jesus Christ of Latter-Days Saints and finishing his degree in political science, he pursued a law degree and began a lucrative career as an attorney in Salt Lake City. But he soon found himself restless to return to his family's farm and worrying that his current job was not fulfilling his desire to help people. He abruptly quit his job and returned to his hometown, where he eventually got involved in local politics. In 2012, Cox was elected to Utah's House of Representatives. Then, less than a year into his first term, he was suddenly appointed to serve as lieutenant governor of Utah. His rapid ascent from rural county politician to influential statewide figure marked him as a rising star in his home state and earned national attention as well.

Cox also stood out for his moderate views at a time of extreme partisanship in American politics. He became known as one of the few Republican leaders willing to openly criticize President Donald Trump, and at times he

Photo by Utah Reps,
via Wikimedia Commons.

split from his party on cultural issues. For example, in contrast to many conservatives, he showed notable support for LGBTQ+ rights. Cox's political style proved popular among Utahans—by 2022 he had one of the highest approval ratings of any US governor. As Gary Herbert, Cox's mentor and predecessor as governor, told Lee Davidson for the *Salt Lake Tribune* (22 Oct. 2017): "He has a personality that is conducive to bringing people together, and yet making sure principles and policies are put in place that are important and productive."

EARLY LIFE AND EDUCATION

Spencer James Cox was born on July 11, 1975, and grew up in Fairview, Utah, as the oldest of eight children. His father, Eddie Cox, was also involved in politics, serving as Sanpete County commissioner, mayor of Fairview, and later on Utah's transportation commission in addition to working for the telecommunications company CentraCom, which the Cox family had founded in the early twentieth century. Cox's parents divorced when he was ten and his father later remarried.

Living on the family farm in Fairview, Cox typically woke at 5 a.m. each morning to complete his chores before school. Family members would later characterize him as tenacious and a hard worker. For example, his father recalled that Cox once broke his

thumb before a piano recital, but insisted on performing anyway. Cox's musical interest would continue as he learned to play bass guitar and performed in a band.

Cox also showed an early interest in politics. He ran for student body president at North Sanpete High School in 1992, even crafting a humorous campaign video splicing footage of him speaking with applause shots from a presidential State of the Union address. After graduating, Cox attended Snow College in Ephraim, Utah, for a year before serving a mission to Mexico for the Church of Jesus Christ of Latter-Day Saints. He returned to Snow and graduated with an associate degree in 1996. He then completed his bachelor's degree in political science at Utah State University in 1998.

LAW CAREER

Cox was accepted to Harvard Law School, but chose to accept a scholarship from the Washington and Lee University School of Law in Lexington, Virginia. He graduated fifth in his class in 2001. Returning to Utah, Cox clerked for US District Judge Ted Stewart in Davis County. After his clerkship he accepted a job with the prestigious law firm Fabian and Clendenin in Salt Lake City and found considerable success. But he became restless living in the city and grew increasingly unsure about his career choice. He would later note that seeing a bumper sticker making fun of the negative reputation of attorneys sparked a serious moment of reflection. "Is the world a better place because of what I'm doing?" he recalled asking, as quoted by Robert Gehrke for the *Salt Lake Tribune* (16 Oct. 2013). After his wife, Abby Palmer Cox, agreed that he could be doing more fulfilling work, he decided to rethink his path.

In 2003 Cox and his growing family moved back to Fairview, where he took a job as vice president and general counsel for CentraCom, working under his father. This meant taking a steep pay cut from his earnings as a lawyer and accepting a very different life than in the city, but after careful consideration Cox felt it was the right move. His former boss, Judge Stewart, also provided some helpful advice, as Cox recalled to Doug Robinson for Salt Lake City's *Deseret News* (29 June 2014): "If you get a chance to go back home, I promise you you'll have more fulfilling opportunities to serve the community, your family and the church. You won't regret it."

EARLY POLITICAL CAREER

Soon after returning to Fairview, Cox began to get involved in local politics. He filled a vacancy on the city council in 2004, and later was elected mayor of the small rural community. In 2008 he was elected Sanpete County commissioner, and in 2012 he was elected to serve Sanpete and Juab counties in the Utah House of Representatives.

As a state legislator Cox began to develop a reputation as a moderate conservative who gave careful consideration to specific issues and was willing to vote against party lines. For example, he went against the Republican mainstream by voting for a bill banning adults from smoking in cars with children, and another barring minors from using cellphones while driving. He first began to earn statewide attention, however, in 2013 as the first Utah legislator to call for the impeachment of Utah attorney general John Swallow, a fellow Republican who was being investigated by the US Justice Department for corruption. The state House created its own investigation committee, but Cox argued that it was not enough. He won respect from many fellow lawmakers for his passionate advocacy even as a very junior legislator.

Cox had not yet completed his first year in office when Utah governor Gary Herbert named him to replace Lieutenant Governor Greg Bell, after Bell resigned to return to the private sector. The appointment of such a political novice to the position was largely met with surprise and confusion. For instance, when asked to comment about Cox at the time, a University of Utah political science professor told Lisa Riley Roche for the *Deseret News* (8 Oct. 2013), "I don't know who that is." However, Cox had worked closely with Bell, who ended up recommending him to Governor Herbert "A couple of times I said, 'Now, have you looked at Spencer Cox?'" Bell told Roche. "And when [Herbert] looked at him, he was pretty impressed."

Despite the endorsements, and the fact that the post was widely considered a stepping-stone to the governor's office, Cox hesitated to accept the appointment. "I had won the lottery in the eyes of everyone else. This was an incredible opportunity out of nowhere," he acknowledged to Robinson, but admitted that

it was also "devastating." He was anguished about disrupting the family life he had worked so hard to build. Only after confirming that he would be able to continue living in Fairview and talking through things with his family, did he take the job.

LIEUTENANT GOVERNOR

Cox was sworn in as lieutenant governor of Utah in October 2013 after being unanimously approved and confirmed. He started a routine of commuting to Salt Lake City from Fairview—a three-hour round trip. Once again, he earned a reputation for hard work and a principled approach. Cox was successfully reelected on Herbert's ticket in 2016.

That year also brought a highly contentious US presidential election, and Cox began to draw attention for his opposition to some of the extreme elements of his own party. Notably, he stated that he would refuse to vote for controversial Republican Donald Trump if he were to win the party primary. Cox called Trump "dangerous" and argued that he "represents the worst of what our great country stands for," as quoted by Davidson—risking the ire of the Republican base that coalesced around Trump and did, in fact, deliver him the Republican nomination and then the presidency. Cox did acknowledge Trump's skill in firing up his base, and he would later offer some tentative support for the president, but he remained one of the few prominent Republicans willing to criticize Trump throughout his term.

Another way Cox distinguished himself from many other Republicans was through his stance on LGBTQ+ rights. In June 2016, after a devastating mass shooting at a gay nightclub in Florida, he gave a speech that quickly went viral. In it he urged compassion for the LGBTQ+ community and apologized for his own discriminatory behavior in his youth. He also challenged the people of Utah to reflect on their empathy and bias. "How did you feel when you heard that 49 people had been gunned down by a self-proclaimed terrorist?" he said, as quoted by Davidson "That's the easy question. Here's the hard one: Did that feeling change when you found out the shooting was at a gay bar at 2 a.m.? If that feeling changed, we're doing something wrong."

Some of Cox's work as lieutenant governor further reflected his moderate stance on social issues. For example, he was appointed to lead a project called Operation Rio Grande that sought to address crime, poverty, homelessness, and addiction in downtown Salt Lake City. Part punitive and part restorative, the successful initiative cracked down on people dealing drugs, while connecting others with social services like addiction counseling and housing. "I love that we're proving that people in Utah with different backgrounds—politically, geographically—can come together on a really big problem and find common ground," he told Davidson. "It actually gives me hope for the other big problems we're facing."

GOVERNOR OF UTAH

In May 2019 Cox announced that he would run to replace Herbert, who was retiring after holding office for nearly a decade, as the governor of Utah in 2020. In the Republican primary election held in June 2020, his main opponents were Utah House Speaker Greg Hughes and popular former Utah governor, presidential candidate, and US Ambassador Jon Huntsman Jr. With Utah leaning solidly Republican, the outcome of the primary was widely expected to essentially decide the state's next governor even before the general election.

The race was complicated by the COVID-19 pandemic that emerged in early 2020. The other candidates criticized Cox over the Herbert administration's handling of the pandemic, particularly the decision to dispense with protocols safeguarding against corruption to award millions of dollars in no-bid contracts and purchase orders. Nevertheless, Cox narrowly bested Huntsman in the primary, winning with a little more than 36 percent of the vote to Huntsman's nearly 35 percent.

Cox then faced Democratic candidate Chris Peterson in the general election in November 2020. The opponents made headlines for co-releasing an ad in which they called for respect and civil disagreement in politics rather than bitter partisan enmity. As expected, Cox went on to win the election by a wide margin. In his acceptance speech, he touched on the social views that set him apart from many other Republicans: "We must be the party of civil rights. We must be the party of the downtrodden. We've given up too many of these issues to other parties," he said, as quoted by Lindsay Whitehurst for AP News (3 Nov. 2020). He was sworn into office as governor on January 4, 2021.

As governor Cox made combating the COVID-19 pandemic a priority. He sought to build public confidence in the vaccines that soon became widely available, but that proved challenging amid widespread vaccine hesitancy, especially among conservatives. Once again going against his party's line, he signed a workplace vaccine mandate, but amid political pressure in November 2021 he signed a law allowing employees to seek exemptions.

In March 2022, Cox made national headlines for vetoing a Republican-sponsored bill that would bar transgender athletes from participating in girls' school sports. He wrote a letter explaining his reasoning, including his concerns about the high rate of suicidal thoughts among trans youth, while acknowledging that the action would likely lead to political fallout—which indeed it did, as conservative pundits widely lambasted him. The Utah legislature then overrode his veto, implementing the law. "That's how it works. And that's OK," he remarked about the political process, as quoted by Katie McKellar for the *Deseret News* (21 Apr. 2022). "But I try to do the right thing for the right reasons, regardless of the consequences. And I will continue to do that."

PERSONAL LIFE

Known for his political attention to mental health issues, Cox also spoke out about his own relevant experiences. In 2018, he published an article revealing that he had struggled with suicidal thoughts as a young teenager after his parent's divorce. He credited his church and a Boy Scout leader for saving his life. A practicing Mormon, he has often spoken about how his faith impacts his life.

Cox married his high school sweetheart, Abby Palmer Cox, who trained in special education. Together they have four children: Gavin, Kaleb, Adam, and Emma Kate.

SUGGESTED READING

Davidson, Lee. "Expect Utah Lt. Gov. Spencer Cox to Do the Unexpected—Dump on Trump, Reach Out to Gays, Even Take On His Party's Right Wing." *The Salt Lake Tribune*, 22 Oct. 2017, www.sltrib.com/news/politics/2017/10/22/expect-utah-lt-gov-spencer-cox-to-do-the-unexpected-dump-on-trump-reach-out-to-gays-even-take-on-his-partys-right-wing/. Accessed 3 May 2022.

Gehrke, Robert. "How Cox Rose from Farm Boy to Lieutenant-Governor-in-Waiting." *The Salt Lake Tribune*, 16 Oct. 2013, archive.sltrib.com/article. php?id=57003071&itype=CMSID. Accessed 2 May 2022.

McKellar, Katie. "Are Utah Republicans Mad at Gov. Cox for Transgender Veto? Let Political Chips Fall, He Says." *Deseret News*, 21 Apr. 2022, www.deseret.com/ utah/2022/4/21/23035803/tucker-carlson-utah-gov-spencer-cox-transgender-sports-ban-veto-political-consequences. Accessed 11 May 2022.

Robinson, Doug. "Spencer Cox: The Lieutenant Governor Who Almost Said No." *Deseret News*, 29 June 2014, www.deseret. com/2014/6/29/20544074/spencer-cox-the-lieutenant-governor-who-almost-said-no#lt-governor-spencer-j-cox-his-wife-abby-and-their-children-gavin15-emma-kate-7-adam-10-and-kaleb-13-at-their-fairview-home-on-friday-may-30-2014. Accessed 2 May 2022.

Roche, Lisa Riley. "Gov. Herbert Names Rep. Spencer Cox New Lieutenant Governor." *Deseret News*, 8 Oct. 2013, www.deseret.com/2013/10/8/20527103/ gov-herbert-names-rep-spencer-cox-new-lieutenant-governor#utah-governor-gary-herbert-talks-about-the-resignation-of-utah-lt-governor-greg-bell-who-stepped-down-from-his-office-to-pursue-private-matters-monday-sept-16-2013-in-salt-lake-city-herbert-on-tuesday-named-rep-spencer-cox-to-replace-bell. Accessed 2 May 2022.

Rodgers, Bethany. "Utah's Incoming Gov. Spencer Cox Faces Challenges on Vaccinations, Education." *The Salt Lake Tribune*, 3 Jan. 2021, www.sltrib.com/news/ politics/2021/01/03/utahs-incoming-gov/. Accessed 11 May 2022.

Whitehurst, Lindsay. "Republican Spencer Cox Handily Wins Utah Governor Race." *AP News*, 3 Nov. 2020, apnews.com/article/donald-trump-virus-outbreak-utah-gary-herbert-c91e9b86169ef6149e62481b50378ffd. Accessed 11 May 2022.

—*Molly Hagan*

Ellen Davis

Born: ca. 1979
Occupation: Businessperson

Ellen Davis has passionately devoted decades to the world of business, adapting to evolving business landscapes and both enjoying and excelling at a variety of facets, from innovative problem-solving and devising communications strategies to initiative management and contributing to the training of the next generation of retail leadership. Specializing in the retail industry and having held a range of positions over the years, many with the National Retail Federation (NRF), she moved to the Consumer Brands Association in 2020, where she became executive vice president of industry engagement. "I've spent my entire career working for an industry that thinks about the consumer every single minute of the day—I'm so excited to take that perspective and apply a new lens to it in this role," she said, as quoted by Anne Stych for *Bizwomen* (29 Jan. 2020), about landing the job. In June 2022, she also joined the board of Soles4Souls, a nonprofit organization that recycles donated shoes and clothing for those who most need them.

By the early 2020s, Davis had become accustomed to the influx of media reports speculating on what the sustained growth in online shopping meant for retailers. As she had during previous transformative periods in her career, she continued to approach such challenges with optimism and confidence. "Retailers all recognize the customer is acting differently, spending differently, communicating differently," she explained in an interview with Bill Briggs for Microsoft's news site *Transform* (29 Jan. 2018). "It's a sophisticated challenge to solve. But a lot of executives are excited by this. I mean, nobody goes into retail who likes to do the same thing over and over again."

EARLY LIFE AND EDUCATION

Born around 1979 and raised in Galesburg, Illinois, by a farmer and a teacher, Davis and her siblings gained experience in business transactions when they contributed money gained from their sales of sweet corn toward fun trips as a family. As a child, Davis also often spent formative, influential time at the bank where her grandfather, long in the business of agricultural banking in the area, worked. Later, she would remark that she perceived resemblances between agricultural cycles and business cycles. "You have some good years and some bad years," she told Melanie D. G. Kaplan for *Georgetown Business* magazine (Fall 2016). "Some years it rains, and some it doesn't. Some things are out of your control. So you need to be adaptable in the short term and keep your eye on the long term."

When pursuing her higher education as a high school graduate, Davis initially attended Illinois Wesleyan University, concentrating in English language and literature, before transferring to Millikin University for her bachelor's in communication. In 2000, she left the institution with her degree and high honors.

EARLY CAREER AND JOINING THE NATIONAL RETAIL FEDERATION

From 2000 to 2002, Davis worked as a junior account executive at Marketing Matters. She was responsible for creatively producing marketing and public relations material that included everything from brochures to radio and television advertisements as well as direct mail pieces. In addition, she created and oversaw a campaign project for the Jefferson County Public Sewer District that lasted for almost half a year.

At the same time, Davis began honing leadership skills as she also served as an assistant project manager with J. C. Dolan and Associates from May until October 2001. Under her leadership, the marketing firm held events that promoted *Better Homes and Gardens* magazine and the iconic toy Barbie across multiple cities. As the main media point person, Davis managed both media coverage and local staff for each event.

A major step in Davis's career came when she was hired by the prominent trade association National Retail Federation (NRF), based out of Washington, DC, in late 2002 as a media relations manager, a position she would maintain for nearly a year and that would set her up for a lengthy, increasingly impactful tenure with the association as well as the retail industry as a whole. From the beginning, quotes and insights provided by her representing NRF's analysis of consumer and shopping trends appeared in both local and national

publications, including the *Washington Post* and the *New York Times*. Taking on additional responsibilities, she oversaw media content for association events and strengthened the research department. During the most active times, she might have needed to field as many as one hundred calls daily.

Indicative of the types of impressive and successful contributions she had made and would continue to make as part of the NRF, she was soon promoted to director of strategic communications in August 2003; she remained in that position until late 2005. Her duties included providing opinion pieces, speeches, and newspaper columns for NRF executives. As her career continued to flourish, her philosophy about the potential of the business world and her place in it, which she would later describe to Jeff Schmitt in an interview for *Poets and Quants for Executives* (10 June 2016), was solidified: "I believe in the power of business as a force for good, with the ability to make such a positive impact in the world."

CYBER MONDAY

While Davis's consistent progress up the NRF organizational ladder was an achievement in itself, she also became noted for being one of the people widely credited with coining the term Cyber Monday, the first Monday after Thanksgiving, while brainstorming ideas for holiday stories in 2005. Industry experts had observed a pivot to shopping online rather than fighting crowds or missing family time on the day following Thanksgiving. Seeing a need to create a term for this significant trending development, she and her team rejected ideas of Black (to mimic Black Friday), Blue (the hyperlink color), or Green (the color of money) Monday, focusing instead on the technological aspect. In addition, she found appeal in the term's lack of ambiguity. Another bonus was that in searching online at the time for the term "Cyber Monday," the team found no hits.

That Monday became the official start of online shopping day, in part because, as Davis has explained, in 2005 many people still lacked the technological capability and access at home, so they instead shopped online when they returned to work on Monday. As she told Kaplan, "It was not a campaign. We had no budget, no committee, just a couple of us sitting in a room." Continuing, she added, "But it was fun to be part of something that big in the industry." Meanwhile, she helped manage NRF's *Shop.org* resource *CyberMonday.com*. In light of the backlash in later years against keeping stores open on Thanksgiving, Cyber Monday would become an even bigger day of shopping into the 2020s.

FURTHER OPPORTUNITIES

For a brief interlude of approximately six months, from late 2005 until April 2006, Davis stepped away from the NRF and served as a managing associate with Chlopak, Leonard, Schechter and Associates. There, she increased her skills working in matters such as internet ownership and patent infringement. In April 2006, she returned to NRF as senior director of strategic communications. Her work entailed, among other tasks, developing strategies for industry crisis response as well as a variety of specific groups represented by the NRF.

In July 2008, Davis assumed the position of vice president of communications at NRF. In addition to duties such as further representing the association in the media and shepherding NRF's online media use, including of platforms such as *LinkedIn*, *Twitter*, and *Facebook* as well as a blog, she was largely responsible for the 2011 initiative Retail Means Jobs. Partially a response to the economic recession that began around 2008, this campaign entailed creating a website and sponsoring a video contest on the topic "This is Retail." While leveraging social media and advertising to attempt to broaden perceptions of what the retail industry had to offer to the economy, including beyond cashiers and clerks, she and her team also stepped-up advocacy in Washington, DC, with efforts that involved educating legislators.

Concurrent with her new role as senior vice president, Davis became the executive director of the philanthropic NRF Foundation in March 2012, putting her in a position to play an even greater part in shaping the association's increased focus not only on research but on retail job awareness, development, education, and training. The Foundation's goal is to develop next-generation talent. To that end, part of Davis's job was to convince college students with degrees in technology, finance, or marketing that retail had jobs for them. As she told *Women's Wear Daily* (12 Jan. 2018), "It doesn't take a lot to convince them once they understand what the career opportunities actually are, but there are a lot of young people who never consider a career in retail because they worked in retail once and they think they know what retail looks like."

Over subsequent years, the Foundation Honors gala, a fundraising event begun by Davis, would raise millions of dollars annually. The Foundation also established the Student Program, a nationwide event bringing together college students and retail executives for special mentorship and learning opportunities.

RISE UP

Encouraged to further her own formal training despite her experience, in 2014 Davis enrolled at Georgetown University, where she earned an Executive Master Degree in Business Administration (EMBA) from the McDonough School of Business in 2016. For her capstone project, she and a group of other graduate students went to Germany to study the socioeconomic effects of the refugee crisis. Of her EMBA, she told Schmitt, "There really aren't many moments in life where I get an opportunity to tune out everything that's happening elsewhere in order to just listen and absorb. I will miss being in the classroom, phone off, mind open, getting ready to learn something."

At work, another influential program initiated during Davis's time as the NRF's executive director was RISE Up, designed to aid workers in mastering the foundational competencies to gain employment and move into more advanced positions in retail. Begun in 2017, it offered training and credentialing modules to people who might otherwise have been unable to enter the market. Asked about the future of the retail industry amid widespread talk of a possible retail apocalypse, in an interview Davis told *Women's Wear Daily*, "The media positions retail as a battle between stores against web sites, with one destined to defeat the other. The reality is neither is going anywhere. From our perspective, it's all retail."

CONSUMER BRANDS ASSOCIATION

In March 2020, Davis shifted to the consumer packaged goods (CPG) industry trade group Consumer Brands Association (CBA), previously known as Grocery Manufacturers Association, as executive vice president of industry engagement. CBA president and CEO Geoff Freeman told the *Shelby Report* (3 Feb. 2020), "Ellen brings an incredible wealth of knowledge that will be invaluable to our new organization. She has spent the last two decades immersed in a consumer-driven industry that is also changing and being disrupted at an unprecedented speed. She's proven incredibly effective at adapting to that change to help build and evolve a successful, value-driven membership organization."

Davis began working in the areas of membership, events, and education. One of her education initiatives was CPG Speaks, a virtual leadership series offered free of charge. The information offered became even more crucial as companies tried to work around the problems created by the coronavirus disease 2019 (COVID-19) pandemic that started spreading in 2020—another challenge that Davis took head on. Within two years, the organization achieved an almost 50 percent increase in dues revenue as a result of a thirty-five percent growth in membership.

PERSONAL LIFE

Davis resides in Arlington, Virginia, with her family, which includes her husband, Chad, and two sons, Jackson and Tate. She has mentioned in interviews that some of her hobbies have included travel, especially to beaches, and writing.

SUGGESTED READING

"Cultivating the Next Generation of Retail Talent." *Women's Wear Daily*, 12 Jan. 2018, wwd.com/business-news/retail/nrf-foundation-11092104/. Accessed 11 Aug. 2022.

Davis, Ellen. "2016 Best EMBAs: Ellen Davis, Georgetown University (McDonough)." Interview by Jeff Schmitt. *Poets & Quants for Executives*, 10 June 2016, poetsandquantsforexecs.com/students/2016-best-embas-ellen-davis-georgetown-university-mcdonough/. Accessed 20 Aug. 2022.

___. "NRF Leader Eyes Retail Rejuvenation as Stores Fuse the Physical and Digital Worlds." Interview by Bill Briggs. *Transform*, Microsoft, 29 Jan. 2018, news.microsoft.com/transform/nrf-leader-eyes-retail-rejuvenation-as-stores-fuse-the-physical-and-digital-worlds/. Accessed 21 Sept. 2022.

___. "Q&A: Consumer Brands Brings Leaders Together for CPG Speaks." Interview by Audrey Altmann. *SmartBrief*, 15 Dec. 2020, corp.smartbrief.com/original/2020/12/qa-consumer-brands-brings-leaders-together-cpg-speaks. Accessed 2 Sept. 2022.

"Ellen Davis Joins Consumer Brands Association as EVP." *The Shelby Report*, 3 Feb. 2020, www.theshelbyreport.com/2020/02/03/ellen-davis-joins-consumer-brands-association-evp/. Accessed 29 Aug. 2022.

Kaplan, Melanie D. G. "Shopping Spree." *Georgetown Business*, fall 2016. *Georgetown University*, msb.georgetown.edu/news-story/shopping-spree/. Accessed 20 Aug. 2022.

Stych, Anne. "Exec Who Coined 'Cyber Monday' Moves to Consumer Brands Association." *Bizwomen*, 29 Jan. 2020, www.bizjournals.com/bizwomen/news/latest-news/2020/01/exec-who-coined-cyber-monday-moves-to-consumer.html. Accessed 25 Aug. 2022.

—*Judy Johnson*

Asha de Vos

Born: November 18, 1979
Occupation: Marine biologist

Since childhood, Sri Lankan biologist Asha de Vos has been drawn to the waters surrounding her home country and the creatures living within them. As an adult, she was particularly intrigued by the blue whales living near the island, which she determined were—unlike most blue whales—nonmigratory, year-round residents of the region. Over the course of years of research through her Sri Lankan Blue Whale Project, de Vos has sought to understand more about the whales' lifestyles and to develop a means of protecting them from threats, such as collisions with shipping vessels. She likewise works to promote greater interest in marine biology in Sri Lanka and, in 2017, launched the nonprofit organization Oceanswell, through which she conducts further work on the Sri Lankan Blue Whale Project, offers educational programs, and involves the public in Oceanswell's research through its whale photo-identification initiative. For de Vos, protecting sea life and the ocean as a whole is a group effort that will be essential to humankind's survival. "The ocean is 70 percent of our planet: we need more people working together on behalf of the oceans," she explained to Thimedi Hetti for *Frontiers* (10 Dec. 2021). "I don't want the younger generation to just inherit a planet that's broken, I want us all working alongside each other so we can all start to make the change that they want to see for their futures."

EARLY LIFE AND EDUCATION

Asha de Vos was born in Sri Lanka on November 18, 1979. She was the second of two children born to an architect father and a mother who had trained as a nurse and midwife. De Vos was an inquisitive child, and her parents encouraged her curiosity and educational pursuits. "My parents would bring me second-hand *National Geographic* magazines that I would pore over," she recalled in an interview with Bianca Fortis for *WINGS WorldQuest* (26 Mar. 2018). "I used to look through the pages and imagine that that would be me one day—going places where no one would ever go and seeing things no one would ever see." By the age of six, de Vos had developed a strong interest in the field of marine biology, and she remained drawn to that field as she completed her primary and secondary education.

Although Sri Lanka is surrounded by the Indian Ocean, marine biology was not a popular field of study there during de Vos's early life. "As an island nation, the ocean is really an extension of us, but we haven't embraced that," she told Michaela Haas in an interview for *Shondaland* (18 Aug. 2021). "I was looking out at the sea and thought, there is a whole world out there to discover." Due to a lack of marine biology programs at local universities, de Vos left Sri Lanka in 1998 to pursue studies abroad, enrolling in Scotland's University of St Andrews. She earned a bachelor's degree in marine and environmental biology from that institution in 2002 and went on to pursue graduate studies at Lincoln College Oxford, from which she earned a master's degree in integrative biosciences in 2004. Following a number of years in the workforce, de Vos enrolled in a doctoral program in environmental engineering at the University of Western Australia. She earned her doctorate from the university in 2014, having completed a thesis titled "Factors Influencing Blue Whale Aggregations off Southern Sri Lanka."

EARLY CAREER

Following her graduation from the University of St Andrews, de Vos spent time working on a

Photo by TEDx Monterey,
via Wikimedia Commons

dolphin research project in New Zealand and also served as a deckhand and science intern on the *Odyssey*—a research ship sponsored by the Ocean Alliance—during the ship's weeks off the coast of the Maldives and Sri Lanka. After completing her master's degree, she took a position with the International Union for Conservation of Nature (IUCN) in which she was tasked with presenting scientific information to government officials, a process that often proved frustrating. "I would go for government meetings where I was the only person with the knowledge that I had, and people would start talking amongst themselves because I was too young and too female for them," she told Hetti.

In addition to taking note of policymakers' reluctance to listen to young, female scientists, de Vos increasingly objected to the phenomenon of parachute science, also known as colonial science, in which researchers based outside of a particular country—often hailing from Western countries such as the United States—travel to that country to perform research but fail to engage with local scientists, ignore the relevant knowledge of local populations, and hamper existing conservation programs and research initiatives. "There's a big gaping void because they haven't engaged with or acknowledged the contributions of the local researchers," she told Hetti about the researchers engaging in parachute science. "There are people on the ground working on a problem, trying to be sensitive, understanding the political situation and local context, and foreign researchers swoop in and out, make their assumptions and ultimately advance their own careers." De Vos's observations of the negative ramifications of parachute research fueled her desire to support Sri Lankan–led research, including her own research concerning the blue whales that made the ocean surrounding Sri Lanka their home.

STUDYING BLUE WHALES

In 2008, de Vos established the Sri Lankan Blue Whale Project, a locally led research initiative focusing on the blue whales that populated the ocean near Sri Lanka. Her interest in those whales was stoked after she spotted whale feces in the area, the presence of which suggested that the whales were feeding—and subsequently producing solid waste—while in the vicinity of the country. That concept was entirely counter to the conventional wisdom about blue whales to which de Vos had been exposed during her undergraduate and graduate studies. "My textbooks and professors had taught me that large whales undertook long-range migrations between cold feeding areas and warm breeding and calving areas," she told the interviewer for *Oceanographic* magazine. "As a result, I was convinced that the blue whales we were seeing could not be feeding in Sri Lankan waters, five degrees above the equator." However, de Vos determined that the conventional understanding of whale behavior did not apply to the whales living in the ocean near Sri Lanka, which proved to be nonmigratory. "These whales had figured out how to feed in our warm tropical waters, busting all the stereotypes we had built for them," she told *Oceanographic*.

Continuing for more than a decade, de Vos's blue whale research formed the basis of her doctoral thesis as well as of her 2014 TED Talk, "Why You Should Care about Whale Poo," in which she stressed the importance of whales both to ocean ecosystems and, in their role as carbon sinks, to the wider environment. After earning her doctorate, de Vos spent two years as a postdoctoral scholar at the University of California, Santa Cruz, where she investigated ship strikes of blue whales, a major threat to those animals, before returning to Sri Lanka to continue her work there.

OCEANSWELL

In addition to performing her own research, de Vos has long hoped to encourage more Sri Lankans to enter the field of marine biology as well as to promote increased public interest in ocean conservation. To that end, de Vos in 2017 founded Oceanswell, a nonprofit organization for which she served as founder and executive director. Following its establishment, Oceanswell oversaw de Vos's existing Sri Lankan Blue Whale Project and additional research initiatives, launched educational programs to teach local scientists skills such as grant writing, and promoted public involvement in marine biology through the Sri Lankan Marine Mammal Photo-identification Database, to which members of the public could submit photographs of whale sightings and help the organization track the movement of specific whales. "This whole thing is a steep learning curve and, for me, it's a big challenge," de Vos told Fortis for *WINGS WorldQuest* about Oceanswell. "Raising funds is obviously the toughest part especially because it's not just about keeping the work going and myself afloat, but I have to create sustainability for the people I hire too." Later initiatives spearheaded by Oceanswell included the full funding of a PhD for a Sri Lankan student attending the Ocean University of Sri Lanka, which de Vos and her colleagues hoped would help contribute to the development of marine biology research in the country.

MARINE BIOLOGY AT WORK

De Vos continued her research and work with Oceanswell throughout 2020, during which the organization launched a new project to assess how the coronavirus disease 2019 (COVID-19) pandemic and virus containment measures, such as curfews, affected Sri Lankans working in the fishery industry. She was called upon to assist with an emergency situation in November of that year, when more than one hundred pilot whales stranded themselves on beaches near Panadura, Sri Lanka. In response to the mass stranding, the largest such event known to have taken place in Sri Lanka, researchers, volunteers, and navy personnel gathered to assist the whales in returning to the water. De Vos was among the scientists to assist with the effort, initially remotely while waiting for permission to break the curfew in place and later in person. "What happened was these animals had come over the reef into an area where the waves were breaking, and as pilot whales are deep-water species, navigating shallow waters is difficult for them. So in order to get them back safely, we had to guide them beyond that reef, to calmer water," she told Bhavna Mohan in an interview for the *Colombo Gazette* (9 Nov. 2020) following the incident. Using jet skis, the group managed to guide the majority of the whales to safety, and only four whale deaths were reported in the period immediately following the stranding.

For de Vos, the public response to the Panadura mass stranding spoke to the willingness of humankind to work together to solve problems, a willingness she hopes to expand through her work. "It's really important for us to highlight the community effort and also the very big collection of people from all around who—despite a curfew, despite a pandemic—came together with a lot of compassion for a species they're very, very unfamiliar with," she told Mohan. In addition to assisting during such emergencies, de Vos continued to promote marine biology education through Oceanswell and in 2021 was awarded a Tällberg-SNF-Eliasson Global Leadership Prize for her work with the organization.

PERSONAL LIFE

De Vos lives in Sri Lanka.

SUGGESTED READING

"Asha de Vos: From Dreamer to Explorer." *National Geographic*, 25 Mar. 2021, www.nationalgeographic.com/impact/article/asha-de-vos-from-dreams-to-pioneer. Accessed 7 Feb. 2022.

De Vos, Asha. "Asha de Vos Is Changing the Landscape of Marine Biology." Interview by Michaela Haas. *Shondaland*, 18 Aug. 2021, www.shondaland.com/live/technology/a37283330/asha-de-vos-is-changing-the-landscape-of-marine-biology/. Accessed 7 Feb. 2022.

___. "Coastal Heroism." Interview. *Oceanographic*, www.oceanographicmagazine.com/features/blue-whales-oceanswell-asha-de-vos/. Accessed 7 Feb. 2022.

___. "Dr. Asha de Vos to the Rescue." Interview by Bhavna Mohan. *Colombo Gazette*, 9 Nov. 2020, colombogazette.com/2020/11/09/dr-asha-de-vos-to-the-rescue-2/. Accessed 7 Feb. 2022.

___. "Women of Discovery: Q&A with Asha de Vos." Interview by Bianca Fortis. *WINGS WorldQuest*, 26 Mar. 2018, www.wingsworldquest.org/blog/2018/3/12/women-of-discovery-qa-with-asha-de-vos. Accessed 7 Feb. 2022.

Hetti, Thimedi. "Asha de Vos—Every Coastline Needs a Local Hero." *Frontiers*, 10 Dec. 2021, blog.frontiersin.org/2021/12/10/every-coastline-needs-a-local-hero/. Accessed 7 Feb. 2022.

—Joy Crelin

Elizabeth Debicki

Born: August 24, 1990
Occupation: Actor

"It's a little bit strange—the life of an actor," the Australian actor Elizabeth Debicki told Lindzi Scharf for the *Los Angeles Times* (7 June 2019). "You put your head down and you work, and when you're not working, you're still submerged under this tide of [insecurity]. In the early part of your career, it's predominantly panic. I'd worry, 'Where is the next thing coming from?'" Despite such worries, for Debicki, the "next thing" was often bigger and higher profile than the last. Introduced to international audiences in her role as socialite and golfer Jordan Baker in *The Great Gatsby* (2013), she went on to appear in major projects such as the spy film *The Man from U.N.C.L.E.* (2015) and the miniseries *The Night Manager* (2016) before entering the Marvel Cinematic Universe in *Guardians of the Galaxy Vol. 2* (2017). Later projects spanned genres from science fiction to historical drama, and in 2020, she notably costarred in one of the few major films to see a theatrical release during the first year of the coronavirus disease 2019 (COVID-19) pandemic, filmmaker Christopher Nolan's time-bending *Tenet*. "I think we're really in need of a new stimulus, new information that isn't negative—that is something artful, that captures our imagination for a period of time, that is a stimulus outside of ourselves," she told Phebe Wahl in an interview for *Modern Luxury Manhattan* (22 Oct. 2020) about her involvement with that project. "To have the opportunity to offer something for people to do that's kind of pure escapism has been lovely."

EARLY LIFE AND EDUCATION

Elizabeth Debicki was born on August 24, 1990, in Paris, France. Her parents danced ballet professionally and became acquainted when performing in France; her mother had been raised in Australia, while her father was from Poland. By the time Debicki reached the age of five her family relocated to Australia, and she grew up in a suburb of Melbourne alongside her two younger siblings. Both of her parents remained active in the performing arts following their retirement from dance, working in a dancing school and a theater, respectively. Although Debicki studied ballet and contemporary dance throughout her childhood, her parents did not encourage her to pursue a career in that field, as they were well aware how short and tumultuous a dancing career could be. "I think they wanted me to have something a little more stable in my life," she disclosed in an interview with Emma Brown for *Interview* magazine (19 Apr. 2016). "A dancer's life is as peripatetic and unstable as that of an actor's. You're freelancing yourself all the time, and a dancer's lifespan is even shorter than an actor's; once they turn 30 or 35, they have to stop."

Because of such concerns, as well as the fact that she had grown taller than the maximum height considered appropriate for a ballerina, Debicki shifted her focus to a different form of expression by her mid-teens: acting. She acted occasionally while a student at the Huntingtower School, starring as Alice in a school production of *Alice in Wonderland*. Despite receiving law school scholarships, she went on to attend, and stand out at, the Victorian College of the Arts (VCA) of the University of Melbourne. "My school was very traditional in the sense that it was very theater based," she told Brown about VCA. "It was actually quite experimental in terms of its training module and in the way it taught actors to deal with text. But I didn't have any training in film and TV." In 2010, she completed a bachelor's degree in drama.

EARLY CAREER

Debicki pursued work both on stage and on screen during the early years of her career. In 2011, she appeared in both a Melbourne Theatre Company production of the play *The Gift* and the film *A Few Best Men*. A key moment came in 2013, when she was

Photo by Gage Skidmore via Wikimedia Commons

introduced to a wider audience in the film remake of *The Great Gatsby*, having somewhat hopelessly submitted a tape of a screen test shortly after her drama school graduation and ultimately earned a role. Directed by Australian filmmaker Baz Luhrmann, the film is based on the 1925 novel by F. Scott Fitzgerald and features several major established actors, including Leonardo DiCaprio, Tobey Maguire, and Carey Mulligan. Debicki took on the role of Jordan Baker, a socialite and professional golfer who is embroiled in the film's events thanks to her friendship with Mulligan's Daisy. "I was such a baby when I made that movie," she later told Sophie Heawood for *The Observer* (12 July 2020). "This is the first time I've ever really admitted that, but I was twenty, and what did I know? I had just finished acting school, I only had the knowledge you get from your life, your own soul, and reading a lot. Not from experience. I just kind of jumped on that Baz machine." While the critical reception of *The Great Gatsby* was middling, critics appreciated Debicki's performance.

In addition to appearing in *The Great Gatsby*, Debicki earned accolades for her stage work in 2013, during which she appeared in the Sydney Theatre Company production of the play *The Maids*. She acted alongside famed Australian actors such as Cate Blanchett in the production, an experience she described to Jo

Litson in an interview for *Jo Litson: Scene and Heard* (3 June 2013) as "daunting and thrilling" as well as "surreal." Debicki went on to win the Sydney Theatre Award for Best Newcomer in recognition of her performance. She then established a stage reputation in the United States through the limited 2014 New York run of *The Maids*. Her subsequent roles included the part of Lady Macduff in the 2015 film adaptation of William Shakespeare's *Macbeth* and as the villainous Victoria in the spy film *The Man from U.N.C.L.E.*, an adaptation of the 1960s television series of the same name.

BREAKTHROUGH ROLES

Although films such as *The Great Gatsby* and *The Man from U.N.C.L.E.* helped to establish Debicki as a promising up-and-coming actor, several further credits more fully established her as an intriguing performer to watch. In 2016, she costarred in the television miniseries *The Night Manager*, based on the 1993 novel of the same name by British writer John le Carré. Playing Jed Marshall, the girlfriend of arms dealer Richard Roper (Hugh Laurie) and a woman with secrets and motivations of her own, Debicki worked with the miniseries' director, Susanne Bier, to give Jed greater depth than the character might have otherwise had, an effort that impressed le Carré himself. "He said to me, after we'd finished making the show, 'Oh, you made her so much more interesting than I did,'" she recalled to Heawood. "He really meant it, and it was very generous of him to say that." The cast and crew of *The Night Manager* received critical acclaim for their work, and the miniseries was nominated for the Emmy Award for Outstanding Limited Series, among other honors.

Increasingly in demand for casting directors, Debicki then appeared in the 2016 miniseries *The Kettering Incident*. She also returned to the theater during that period, starring in a National Theatre production of *The Red Barn* that premiered in London in late 2016. The following year saw her introduction into the hugely successful Marvel Cinematic Universe of superhero films in *Guardians of the Galaxy Vol. 2*. She enjoyed playing the role of antagonist Ayesha, although she noted that she was not particularly familiar with any of the Marvel Comics source material. "I'm still the first person to put my hand up and say I am a Marvel rookie, I'm learning everything on the fly," she told in an interview with Steve Weintraub for *Collider* (10 May 2017).

Having established herself as a versatile performer capable of portraying varied characters, Debicki took on a wide range of roles over the next several years. The diversity of her projects was particularly apparent in the year 2018, during which she took on parts in the science-fiction film *The Cloverfield Paradox*, lent her voice to an animated rabbit in the children's film *Peter Rabbit*, costarred in the heist film *Widows*, and portrayed writer Virginia Woolf in *Vita & Virginia*, among other projects. The following year she appeared in the crime thriller *The Burnt Orange Heresy*, which premiered at the 2019 Venice International Film Festival.

LATER WORK

The year 2020 was a strange one for the film industry, as the COVID-19 pandemic led to the closure of movie theaters and a shift to internet-based distribution of many films. One of the few major films to be released in theaters that year was *Tenet*, a science-fiction film written and directed by acclaimed filmmaker Nolan and featuring Debicki in the role of Kat, an art appraiser, and the estranged wife of the film's antagonist. "The scope of the movie is enormous, and it operates, as Nolan's films do, on so many layers. But I knew making it exactly what my piece of the puzzle was," she told Josh Smith for the UK edition of *Glamour* (20 Nov. 2020) about the film.

Also in 2020, it was announced that Debicki had been cast in the Netflix historical drama series *The Crown*, which follows Queen Elizabeth II and the other members of the British royal family over many decades. She was set to portray Princess Diana, who had previously been played by Emma Corrin in the fourth season of the series. The role was an exciting one for Debicki, who had been aware of Diana during her own 1990s childhood and remained fascinated by her lasting cultural influence. "She's like a symbol—like a magical person," she told Wahl. "I'm coming to understand more intimately how she existed and still exists very profoundly in collective consciousness." There was much buzz around pictures of Debicki as Diana surfacing from the set as filming for the fifth season of *The Crown* was underway in 2021. That year Debicki also had a presence in theaters once more, reprising her role as the rabbit Mopsy in *Peter Rabbit 2: The Runaway* (2021).

PERSONAL LIFE

Over the course of her career, Debicki typically spent her time moving between Los Angeles, London, and Sydney. Although some actors might prefer not to move halfway around the world for work, she largely enjoyed having the opportunity to explore new areas. "I get bored when I'm in the same place," she told Litson. "I like building a nest somewhere then dismantling it and moving on. I'm too much of a traveler I guess. I like to be in new places."

In addition to acting, Debicki served as an ambassador for the humanitarian organization Women for Women International. "Their approach is entirely about sustainability and adapting the approach depending on the group of women they're dealing with," she explained to Wahl. "It is about creating a source of sustainable income and . . . creating a community where there wasn't a community before." Alongside several other celebrity ambassadors, Debicki appeared in the Women for Women International short film *What Is Sisterhood?* (2017).

SUGGESTED READING

Debicki, Elizabeth. "Elizabeth Debicki's All-Consuming Character." Interview by Emma Brown. *Interview*, 19 Apr. 2016, www.interviewmagazine.com/culture/elizabeth-debicki-1. Accessed 7 Jan. 2022.

___. "Elizabeth Debicki Interview." Interview by Jo Litson. *Jo Litson: Scene and Heard*, 3 June 2013, jolitson.com/2013/06/03/elizabeth-debicki-interview/. Accessed 7 Jan. 2022.

___. "'Guardians of the Galaxy Vol. 2': Elizabeth Debicki on Going Gold and When She Shot THAT Scene." Interview by Steve Weintraub. *Collider*, 10 May 2017, collider.com/elizabeth-debicki-guardians-of-the-galaxy-2-adam-scene-interview/. Accessed 7 Jan. 2022.

___. "How Elizabeth Debicki Surrendered to 2020 and Prepared to Play Princess Diana." Interview by Phebe Wahl. *Modern Luxury Manhattan*, 22 Oct. 2020, mlmanhattan.com/elizabeth-debicki-tenet-crown-cover-story-interview. Accessed 7 Jan. 2022.

___. "'I Thought I Had to Be Something for Someone Else. I Was So Hard on Myself':

As Elizabeth Debicki Takes Over as *The Crown*'s Princess Diana, She Talks Body Image." Interview by Josh Smith. *Glamour*, 20 Nov. 2020, www.glamourmagazine.co.uk/article/elizabeth-debicki-interview-2020. Accessed 7 Jan. 2022.

Heawood, Sophie. "Elizabeth Debicki: 'I'm Not Interested in Being Comfortable.'" *Observer*, Guardian News and Media, 12 July 2020, www.theguardian.com/film/2020/jul/12/elizabeth-debicki-interview-im-not-interested-in-being-comfortable-spy-thriller. Accessed 7 Jan. 2022.

Scharf, Lindzi. "Elizabeth Debicki Opens Up about Her Life. Now What about That Top-Secret Project?" *Los Angeles Times*, 7 June 2019, www.latimes.com/fashion/la-ig-elizabeth-debicki-women-in-film-face-of-the-future-20190607-story.html. Accessed 7 Jan. 2022.

SELECTED WORKS

The Great Gatsby, 2013; *The Man from U.N.C.L.E.*, 2015; *The Night Manager*, 2016; *Guardians of the Galaxy Vol. 2*, 2017; *The Cloverfield Paradox*, 2018; *Peter Rabbit*, 2018, *Vita & Virginia*, 2018; *Tenet*, 2020

—*Joy Crelin*

Ariana DeBose

Born: January 25, 1991
Occupation: Actor, singer, and dancer

With the release of the film musical *West Side Story* in November 2021, the actor, singer, and dancer Ariana DeBose fulfilled a childhood dream. As a young child, she had enjoyed watching the 1961 film version of *West Side Story* and was enthralled by actor Rita Moreno's performance as the character Anita in that film—the same character DeBose would play in the 2021 adaptation. "I really liked the lady in the purple dress," she recalled to Tracy E. Gilchrist in an interview for *Out* magazine (4 Nov. 2021). "She's pretty, she sort of looks like me . . . [and] I believed I could dance like that." Over the years following her early introduction to dance, DeBose proved herself to be a skilled performer, dancing competitively and in local theater productions, which eventually led her to work as a professional performer.

Photo by Lyn Fairly Media,
via Wikimedia Commons

After making her Broadway debut in 2012 with a supporting role in *Bring It On: The Musical*, DeBose found consistent work on Broadway and in 2015 became part of the original cast of the popular musical *Hamilton*. A later project, *Summer: The Donna Summer Musical*, earned her a Tony Award nomination for best featured actress in a musical. Having made a name for herself as a stage performer, DeBose took on her largest film project to date with *West Side Story*, for which she received the Academy Award for best supporting actress. Acknowledging the importance of that role, DeBose reflected on a moment during the movie's filming to Olivia Blair in an interview for *Elle UK* (28 Mar. 2022): "I looked around and saw so many talented people all being able to be their own gorgeous-rainbow-Latino selves. And I thought, 'This is good. This is special. I'm Afro-Latina, I'm queer, I'm a woman. . . . Look at how beautiful we are!'"

EARLY LIFE AND EDUCATION

Ariana DeBose was born on January 25, 1991, in Wilmington, North Carolina. She was surrounded by creative pursuits from a young age. As a child, DeBose lived with her mother, a teacher and amateur artist, and a grandmother who encouraged her to begin studying dance. "My grandmother saw that I liked to move when music played, so she thought dance was

a good idea," she recalled to Kelly d'Amboise in an interview for the *Great Discontent* (9 June 2016). "She enrolled me in ballet, tap, and jazz, as many people do for their kids when they're three years old." Though DeBose was still very young, she soon demonstrated a talent for dance as well as a strong work ethic. "I took to it really quickly," she told d'Amboise. "I'm a competitive person, so I like being the best at things. . . . My teachers took a liking to me, and I was bitten by the bug." Hoping to pursue dance further, DeBose began training at the Dance Theater of New Bern after moving to that city with her family, and she went on to train at CC and Co. Dance Complex in Raleigh.

Following a move to Wake Forest, North Carolina, DeBose enrolled in Wake Forest-Rolesville High School, where she began to explore acting and singing in addition to dance. After playing a lead role in her first high school show, a production of the musical *Fame*, DeBose continued to pursue local theatrical opportunities. While performing in an all-county production of the musical *A Chorus Line*, she experienced a moment that reinforced her desire to pursue a career in the performing arts. "I felt like I wasn't in my body anymore," she told d'Amboise. "I've had that feeling since then, and it's like a certain transcendence. . . . I thought, 'When I feel like this, I'm doing the work I'm supposed to be doing.'" After graduating from high school in 2009, DeBose attended Western Carolina University (WCU) for a short time but soon decided to move to New York City to pursue her career. She was later inducted into the Wake County Public School System (WCPSS) Hall of Fame.

EARLY CAREER

At the age of eighteen, DeBose appeared in the sixth season of the competitive reality show *So You Think You Can Dance*, which aired in the fall of 2009. She made it into the top twenty on the show but was eliminated soon afterward. "It was my first real lesson in what showbiz actually was," DeBose recalled to Blair. "And when my time on the show ended very quickly, it was a blow, a very public brush with rejection. But the experience taught me that what other people think does not define me." Although that experience was disappointing, it did not deter DeBose, and in 2011, she originated the supporting role of Nautica in the national tour of the new production *Bring It On: The Musical*, a stage adaptation of the 2000 film of the same name about a cheerleading competition.

Remaining with the cast of *Bring It On* when the show moved to New York, DeBose made her Broadway debut with the production in 2012. She continued to work regularly on Broadway throughout the next several years, joining the ensemble of the production *Motown: The Musical* in 2013. That year she also joined the Broadway revival of the musical *Pippin*, for which she served as a member of the ensemble as well as an understudy for the role of the Leading Player.

HAMILTON

A turning point in DeBose's career came in 2013 when she was invited to join a reading of a show in development written by Lin-Manuel Miranda, a composer and playwright who had previously cowritten the music for *Bring It On: The Musical*. The production was Miranda's soon-to-be-famous hip-hop musical, *Hamilton*, about the life and eventual death of the titular American politician. "A couple members of the current cast were there, and we all read the first couple of songs that Lin had churned out," DeBose told d'Amboise about the reading. "We all knew then that it was going to be very special and that we hadn't heard anything like it." DeBose went on to appear in the Off-Broadway production of *Hamilton* in 2015 at the Public Theater and remained with the musical following its move to Broadway later that year, becoming part of its acclaimed original Broadway cast. Though seemingly an ordinary member of *Hamilton*'s ensemble, DeBose, in fact, played a special role in the production: that of the Bullet, a character who appeared whenever death was close and eventually struck Hamilton himself during his fateful duel with rival Aaron Burr.

Praised for its unique subject matter and style, and its diverse cast, *Hamilton* became a worldwide phenomenon following its move to Broadway. "It was really heartening and thrilling to watch so many people respond to the story and to the show and its music and its message," DeBose told Jeffrey Kare in an interview for *Broadway World Raleigh* (13 Dec. 2019). "People who don't frequently go to the theater were coming to the theater and bringing their friends and bringing their family members. That's really special when you can watch a work of art change the world." DeBose

remained with *Hamilton* until July 2016, when she departed to pursue new opportunities. (She would later appear in the version of the Broadway production filmed for the Disney+ streaming service in 2020, which earned the iconic musical even more acclaim.)

Following *Hamilton*, DeBose appeared in the original Broadway production of *A Bronx Tale: The Musical* in 2016 and the following year took part in the world premiere of *Summer: The Donna Summer Musical*, staged in California. Performing the character of Disco Donna, one of multiple incarnations of the famous singer to appear in the production, DeBose remained with the musical upon its move to Broadway in 2018. She was nominated for the Tony Award for best featured actress in a musical in recognition of her work.

WEST SIDE STORY

While DeBose focused on stage work throughout much of her early career, she likewise took on occasional screen projects during that period, including a 2016 episode of the television series *Blue Bloods*. She went on to costar in *The Prom* (2020), the Netflix adaptation of a musical about a queer love story, and in 2021 appeared in *Schmigadoon!*, a musical television series produced for the streaming service Apple TV+. DeBose's true screen breakthrough, however, came in November 2021 with the premiere of *West Side Story*, directed by Steven Spielberg. Based on the 1957 musical of the same name, which had also been adapted into a 1961 film, the updated version of *West Side Story* featured DeBose in the supporting role of Anita, a character previously portrayed by veteran performer Rita Moreno in the 1961 version.

West Side Story met with a positive critical reception upon its release and was nominated for numerous awards, including the Academy Award for best picture. At the Academy Awards in March 2022, DeBose was honored with the award for best performance by an actress in a supporting role, becoming the first Afro-Latina to win an Academy Award for acting as well as the first openly queer woman of color to do so. "I think it might have been one of the most validating experiences of my career, potentially my life thus far, because I was given the opportunity to say what I wanted to say," she later told Antonia Blyth in an interview for *Deadline* (18 May 2022). "I was there to represent our film, which I'm incredibly proud of, but I was also representing myself. And it was a culmination of a very long journey." In addition to her Academy Award, DeBose received a Golden Globe Award and a British Academy of Film and Television Arts (BAFTA) Award for her performance as Anita, among other honors.

OTHER PROJECTS

Following the release of *West Side Story*, DeBose appeared in a variety of other screen projects, including an episode of the animated television series *Human Resources* and the fourth season of the science-fiction series *Westworld* in 2022. "I believe in variety and I don't believe in doing the same thing twice," she told Patrick Ryan in an interview for *USA Today* (10 June 2022) about her approach to selecting projects. "I move toward projects that I find interesting, but I also want to try and make work that I feel can have even a small impact." In early 2022, it was announced that DeBose had been cast in the film *Kraven the Hunter*, based on the Marvel Comics character. Though increasingly working in film and television, DeBose remains closely connected with the theater world and in June 2022 served as host of that year's Tony Awards.

PERSONAL LIFE

Although based in New York City for much of her professional career, DeBose continues to hold ties to her home state of North Carolina. She enjoys practicing yoga, which she has identified in interviews as particularly beneficial to her work as a dancer. With *The Prom* costar Jo Ellen Pellman, DeBose founded the Unruly Hearts Initiative, an advocacy group that raises money for organizations benefitting LGBTQ youth.

SUGGESTED READING

DeBose, Ariana. "Ariana DeBose." Interview by Kelly d'Amboise. *The Great Discontent*, 9 June 2016, thegreatdiscontent.com/ interview/ariana-debose/. Accessed 8 Aug. 2022.

___. "Ariana DeBose on Hosting the Tony Awards, Why She Won't Use Her Oscar as a Toilet Paper Holder." Interview by Patrick Ryan. *USA Today*, 10 June 2022, www.usatoday.com/story/entertainment/ tv/2022/06/10/ariana-debose-interview- tony-awards-oscars/7554675001/. Accessed 8 Aug. 2022.

___. "Ariana DeBose on Portraying *West Side Story*'s Anita on Her Own Terms." Interview by Olivia Blair. *Elle*, 28 Mar. 2022, www. elle.com/uk/life-and-culture/a39351252/ ariana-debose-interview-west-side-story/. Accessed 8 Aug. 2022.

___. "Ariana DeBose Talks 'Kraven the Hunter,' 'Two and Only' and Refusing to 'Fit in a Box'—Deadline Disruptors." Interview by Antonia Blyth. *Deadline*, 18 May 2022, deadline.com/2022/05/ cannes-disruptors-ariana-debose-west-side- story-1235023474/. Accessed 8 Aug. 2022.

___. "Ariana DeBose: What You Don't Know about Me." Interview by Sarah Karmali. *Harper's Bazaar UK*, 11 Feb. 2022, www. harpersbazaar.com/uk/culture/culture-news/ a39042814/ariana-debose-video-interview/. Accessed 8 Aug. 2022.

___. "Interview: Ariana DeBose on *Hamilton*, *West Side Story*, and *The Prom*." Interview by Jeffrey Kare. *Broadway World Raleigh*, 13 Dec. 2019, www.broadwayworld.com/ raleigh/article/BWW-Interview-Ariana- DeBose-on-HAMILTON-WEST-SIDE- STORY-THE-PROM-20191213. Accessed 8 Aug. 2022.

___. . "Out100 Cover Star Ariana DeBose: 'I Am America.'" Interview by Tracy E. Gilchrist. *Out*, 4 Nov. 2021, www.out.com/ print/2021/11/4/out100-ariana-debose- interview-west-side-story-cover. Accessed 8 Aug. 2022.

SELECTED WORKS

Hamilton, 2015–16, 2020; *A Bronx Tale: The Musical*, 2016; *Summer: The Donna Summer Musical*, 2017–18; *The Prom*, 2020; *Schmigadoon!*, 2021; *West Side Story*, 2021

—Joy Crelin

David Diop

Born: February 24, 1966
Occupation: Writer and academic

David Diop, a French Senegalese writer who has also had an impact in French academia as a literature professor since the late 1990s, won the International Booker Prize in 2021 for the English translation of his second novel, *At Night All Blood Is Black* (2020). First published in French as *Frère d'âme* (translated to mean "soul brother") in 2018, the book was a best seller in France, where it won the Prix Goncourt des Lycéens. It follows the story of Alfa Ndiaye, a Senegalese soldier who fights for France in World War I, bringing to life the ignored history of soldiers from African colonized nations who were recruited and sent to armies' front lines in both world wars. In World War I, they were called *tirailleurs sénégalais*, or Senegalese riflemen, even though they came from French colonies across West Africa. On the front, soldiers like Ndiaye were given machetes, and French colonizers intentionally projected and encouraged a stereotyped image of Africans as barbaric savages to terrify enemies in battle.

Diop, who teaches eighteenth-century French literature at the Université de Pau et des Pays de l'Adour (UPPA) in southwestern France, specializes in research on European ideas about Africa and Africans. Born in Paris and raised in Dakar, Senegal, Diop is of both worlds. "What interests me are the sources of information that feed representations of the other," he told Angelique Chrisafis in an interview for the *Guardian* (18 June 2021). Indeed, his first novel, *1889, l'Attraction universelle* (2012), draws from a similar well. Set around the 1889 international exhibition in Paris, it follows a Senegalese delegation attending the event. French authorities decide to deport them, but one official "gives" them to a circus owner instead as part of a "human zoo," once a real-life form of entertainment in which colonizers put African people on display like animals. *La Porte du voyage sans retour* [The Door of the Journey of No Return], his third novel, published in France in 2021, was inspired by the story of Michel Adanson, a French naturalist who spent time in Senegal in the 1750s. While Diop has acknowledged the recognition his work has received as part of the literary "debate about silenced black voices and the reckoning with colonialism," as Simon Kuper noted for the *Financial Times* (12 June 2021), he has also emphasized that his main priority in writing is to "apprehend characters in their singularity," as he told Kuper. He added that, for example, "Alfa has a unique interiority, and isn't simply an indistinct member of a large group. That's what prejudice is: it erases distinctions."

Photo by librairie mollat, via Wikimedia Commons

EARLY LIFE AND EDUCATION

David Diop was born in Paris, France, on February 24, 1966. His mother was French and his father, in pursuit of a higher education in France at the time of their meeting, was Senegalese. "I was lucky that my French and Senegalese families both acted very warmly toward my parents. I received a lot of love from both sides," Diop told Laura Cappelle for *The New York Times* (30 May 2021). "I didn't experience my two cultural identities as a source of conflict." Born with a poetic sensibility, he has claimed that his first memory comes from when he was in utero. "I know it's impossible," he told a journalist for the *New Statesman* (6 Sept. 2021). "But I remember a dark translucent light, a reddish hue, muffled sounds. I probably reconstructed it later, but even so I like the idea of it." When he was five years old, he resettled with his family in Dakar, where he spent the rest of his childhood years. During these formative times, he gained a love of reading from his mother.

Following his high school years, Diop returned to Paris, where he received his higher education with a focus on literature at the Sorbonne. Eighteenth-century French literature and the French Enlightenment movement typified by the prolific writer Voltaire, among others, particularly captivated him. "I was drawn to their activism and commitment to human rights," he explained to Cappelle. With this literary era as his specialty, the Université de Pau et des Pays de l'Adour admitted him to its faculty in 1998 to lecture on the subject; additionally conducting research on this topic as well as Francophone literature from Black Africa, he earned his accreditation, through the submission and defense of a thesis, to supervise PhD research in 2014. Meanwhile, he had led a group formed in 2009 studying European depictions of Africa and Africans in the seventeenth and eighteenth centuries.

FRÈRE D'ÂME

Diop published his first novel, *1889, l'Attraction universelle*, in 2012. The book provides an account of a group of Senegalese delegates to the 1889 world's fair in Paris who are forced to be part of a circus that makes a spectacle of displaying African people like animals. The idea was inspired by the historical "human zoos" of the era, which, in association with prevalent racist and colonialist stereotypes, presented African people to European audiences as culturally primitive or subhuman "others" through public exhibitions.

Widespread, international attention to Diop's work would not come, however, until the publication of his second novel, *Frère d'âme*, in 2018, the "point of departure" of which, he related to Kuper, was actually many years earlier. His maternal great-grandfather served in World War I, surviving mustard gas attacks, but never wanted to discuss his time as a soldier. His silence had always intrigued his great-grandson. Later, in 1998, Diop came across a historian's collection of French soldiers' letters from World War I that immediately caught his interest. Though moved by the voices of the young men, he was also struck by the fact that any missives, of which there were only a small number, composed by soldiers recruited by the French from their West African colonies were simply "impersonal, administrative letters," as he told Chrisafis. At the time, France held several colonies in West Africa, including present-day Senegal, Mali, Niger, and Burkina Faso, but soldiers brought from these colonies to fight on the front lines in Europe were broadly referred to as *tirailleurs sénégalais*, or Senegalese riflemen. "Because I have a double cultural sensitivity," Diop explained to Chrisafis, "I wanted to find out if there were any letters written by the *tirailleurs sénégalais*."

While historians have certainly documented the *tirailleurs sénégalais*, Diop longed for stories about them like those in the majority of letters he had found, ones that expressed their lived experience of the war. Therefore, he set out to help fill that gap in representation by crafting a story that could provide the missing perspective of a Senegalese soldier.

Diop's novel is narrated by a young man named Alfa Ndiaye. Alfa and his longtime friend, Mademba Diop, are conscripted to fight for France. After Alfa witnesses his friend's agonizing death, he begins to unravel. The book is purposefully told in Alfa's voice; while it is written in French, however, Ndiaye does not actually speak French. Diop chose to convey Wolof, the Senegalese language of his youth, stylistically. "I tried to mold French," he told Cappelle, "to make it sound a little like Wolof when it's spoken in formal circumstances, using rhythm and repetition." When he set out to write the book, the author knew the language would be important to the story. In his research, he recounted in his interview with Chrisafis, he read a 1916 manual that aimed to teach French to African soldiers. French and other European colonists deemed African people ignorant and uncivilized, and the manual argued that they must be taught a cruder version of the language. "Lots of *tirailleurs* understood this was a means to infantilize them," he told Chrisafis.

As a war strategy, the French also used propaganda to project stereotyped images of *tirailleurs sénégalais* as bloodthirsty African savages and encouraged them to act associatively; to this end, the *tirailleurs* were the only group of soldiers given machetes in addition to rifles. This context is important to Ndiaye's story, which explores how, in his profound grief, he becomes increasingly obsessed with ritualized killings as well as how the other soldiers and the French officers react.

Frère d'âme became a national best seller and won the Prix Goncourt des Lycéens, a prize administered by the Ministry of National Education, Youth, and Sport that is viewed as a "younger sibling" to the Prix Goncourt and is voted by high school students.

AT NIGHT ALL BLOOD IS BLACK

Due to its popularity, *Frère d'âme* was translated into English by the American poet Anna Moschovakis and published as *At Night All Blood Is Black* in 2020. Given the importance of language in the book, translating it was a challenge. Diop praised Moschovakis's final work as more than up to the task, telling the Booker Prize Foundation, "Wolof has its own rhythm, its own unique patterns of speech, which I replicated in French. . . . The great challenge for my translator Anna Moschovakis, and her great success, was to reproduce this same rhythm in the English language, so that the reader would understand that the text is haunted by an African voice." Nigerian writer Chigozie Obioma, who reviewed the book for *The New York Times* (10 Nov. 2020), similarly praised Moschovakis's skills, writing that "the specificity and uniqueness of [the Wolof] language comes through" her translation. Obioma also described the book as "extraordinary" and dubbed Diop "a great new African writer." *At Night All Blood Is Black* won the International Booker Prize in June 2021, with Diop and Moschovakis sharing the prize equally. The honor made Diop the first French author to win the prestigious prize.

Diop's follow-up effort, published in France in August 2021, is titled *La Porte du voyage sans retour* [The Door of the Journey of No Return]. The title references the "Door of No Return," a landmark on Gorée Island, off the coast of Senegal. The island served as a port from which enslavers forcibly took millions of Africans from the continent and sold them into enslavement. The novel tells the story of a young French botanist, inspired by the historical figure Michel Adanson, who visits Senegal in the 1750s.

PERSONAL LIFE
Diop lives in France.

SUGGESTED READING
Cappelle, Laura. "He Is Senegalese and French, with Nothing to Reconcile." *The New York Times*, 30 May 2021, www.nytimes.com/2021/05/30/books/david-diop-at-night-all-blood-is-black.html. Accessed 7 Feb. 2022.

Diop, David. "International Booker Winner David Diop: 'It's War That's Savage, Not the Soldiers.'" Interview by Angelique Chrisafis. *The Guardian*, '18 June 2021, www.theguardian.com/books/2021/jun/18/international-booker-winner-david-diop-its-war-thats-savage-not-the-soldiers. Accessed 14 Feb. 2022.

___. "David Diop Q&A: 'I Don't Have a Theme Tune. I Like Songs to Take Me Away from Me.'" Interview. *The New Statesman*, 6 Sept. 2021, www.newstatesman.com/culture/2021/06/david-diop-qa-i-don-t-have-theme-tune-i-songs-take-me-away-me. Accessed 7 Feb. 2022.

___, and Anna Moschovakis. "David Diop and Anna Moschovakis on *At Night All Blood Is Black*." *The Booker Prizes*. Interview by Booker Prize Foundation, www.thebookerprizes.com/david-diop-anna-moschovakis-interview-night-all-blood-black. Accessed 7 Feb. 2022.

Kuper, Simon. "International Booker Winner David Diop on France's Colonial Legacy." *Financial Times*, 12 June 2021, www.ft.com/content/bc5df76a-f86b-4c98-b468-4529c6b44e85. Accessed 7 Feb. 2022.

Obioma, Chigozie. "In the Trenches of World War I, a Bloody Ritual Fueled by Guilt." Review of *At Night All Blood Is Black*, by David Diop, translated by Anna Moschovakis. *The New York Times*, 10 Nov. 2020, www.nytimes.com/2020/11/10/books/review/david-diop-night-blood-black.html. Accessed 7 Feb. 2022.

SELECTED WORKS
1889, l'Attraction universelle, 2012; *Frère d'âme (At Night All Blood Is Black)*, 2018; *La Porte du voyage sans retour* [The Door of the Journey of No Return], 2021

—Molly Hagan

Caeleb Dressel
Born: August 16, 1996
Occupation: Swimmer

When Caeleb Dressel first began swimming lessons as a young child, he hardly imagined that it would one day lead him to a full-time career as a swimmer, let alone one touted as the fastest in the world. "I've been swimming since I was five years old, and to be able to make a living out of it is awesome," he later told Markos Papadatos in an interview for *Digital Journal* (24 Aug. 2021). Noting that people twenty years ago did not have the same opportunities as swimmers in 2021, he went on to say, "I am in the right place at the right time with the right people in my life and the right sponsors." An accomplished swimmer in both national and international competition since his teen years, Dressel completed a successful collegiate career at the University of Florida and made his Olympic debut at the 2016 Summer Olympics in Rio de Janeiro, Brazil, serving as a key member of the United States' gold medal–winning relay teams. Repeated victories at the World Championships followed, and in 2021 he claimed a total of five gold medals and set new world records at the Olympic Games in Tokyo, Japan. Still, Dressel preferred to focus on swimming itself rather than the accolades he received, aiming for continuous improvement. "Honestly, I don't know what I would do without swimming," he told Aimee Berg for an interview in *FINA Magazine* (24 Apr. 2020). "I'm obsessed with trying to get better. Simple as that."

EARLY LIFE AND EDUCATION

Caeleb Remel Dressel was born on August 16, 1996, in Orange Park, Florida. He was one of four children born to Christina and Michael Dressel. Swimming was a popular sport in his household: Dressel's father had competed in swimming while in college, all four Dressel children were active in the sport during their early years, and Dressel's two sisters went on to swim at the college level. Dressel himself began taking swimming lessons at the age of four, though his initial experiences with the sport were not always positive. "I cried," he recalled to Karen Crouse for *The New York Times* (28 Feb. 2016). "I didn't want to learn the butterfly because it's hard. I got it right away, but I didn't want to do it." In addition to swimming, Dressel participated in sports such as soccer and football during his early life and ran track for a time at Clay High School in Green Cove Springs, Florida.

While at Clay High, Dressel also trained and swam with the Bolles School Sharks, a swimming club based at the private Bolles School in Jacksonville. He began to find success on the national level in that period, competing in events such as the 2011 Junior National Championships. He also swam in the 2012 Olympic qualifiers, although he did not qualify at that point in his career.

In 2013 Dressel competed in the senior-level National Championships, during which he placed eighth in the men's 100-meter freestyle event. That year he also competed in the

International Swimming Federation (FINA) World Junior Swimming Championships in the United Arab Emirates, where he won a gold medal in the 100-meter freestyle in addition to two silver medals and three bronze medals in other events. Though the competition was a successful one for Dressel, the increased pressure and international scrutiny he faced proved challenging for the young athlete, and he subsequently took a nearly six-month hiatus from swimming. "I had no idea if I was going to come back or not," he later told Crouse. "As a seventeen-year-old kid, people put you on this podium, and it seems like you're just a source of entertainment for people. I felt like I was swimming for other people and they'd never be satisfied." Dressel returned to swimming during his senior year at Clay High and went on to graduate in 2014.

COLLEGE CAREER

Following high school, Dressel enrolled in the University of Florida, in Gainesville, where he pursued studies in natural resource conservation and competed for the Florida Gators Division I National Collegiate Athletic Association (NCAA) swimming and diving program. An accomplished member of the Gators swim team, he earned his first NCAA title in 2015, placing first in the men's 50-yard freestyle event. Dressel became a perennial NCAA champion over the next several years, claiming two NCAA titles in 2016 and three in 2017. In 2018, his final year of NCAA eligibility, he won the men's 50-yard freestyle and 100-yard freestyle events, setting records in both, and likewise claimed NCAA titles in the 100-yard butterfly and the 200-yard freestyle relay. A frequent All-American selection, Dressel shared the College Swimming Coaches Association of America (CSCAA) Swimmer of the Year award in 2016 and 2017 and was the award's sole winner in 2018.

In addition to competing for the University of Florida, Dressel swam in major national, noncollegiate competitions during his years in college and claimed first place in the 50- and 100-meter freestyle events at the 2015 USA Swimming National Championships. He returned to the USA Swimming National Championships in 2017, claiming first place in three events and second place in another, and successfully defended those titles the following year. While Dressel's four years of NCAA eligibility ended following the 2018 season, he remained at the University of Florida to complete his studies and earned his bachelor's degree in 2019.

OLYMPIC DEBUT AND WORLD CHAMPIONSHIPS SUCCESS

Dressel made his Olympic debut at the 2016 Olympic Games in Rio de Janeiro, Brazil, where he competed in a variety of individual and team relay events. He placed sixth in the men's 100-meter freestyle event and won his first two Olympic gold medals alongside his relay teammates, winning the 4×100-meter freestyle and 4×100-meter medley relay races. The following year saw Dressel claim seven gold medals at the FINA World Championships, including medals in three individual events. He competed in the short-course FINA World Swimming Championships in 2018, winning gold medals in the 100-meter freestyle and several relay events, and that year also earned two gold medals at the Pan Pacific Swimming Championships.

In 2019 Dressel began to compete for the Cali Condors of the International Swimming League (ISL), a competitive swimming league that began operations that year. "Every part of the team is great, you get to meet new people along the way," he later told Papadatos about the experience. "This is what makes the Cali Condors so special, you really do have the team camaraderie." Dressel also found further success on the international stage that year, winning six gold medals and two silver medals at the World Championships. While his eight medals were the most won by any swimmer in a single World Championship, Dressel did not focus on his record-breaking achievement, preferring instead to concentrate on preparing for the next major competition. "I was hungry to get back in the water, to start training again and looking for ways to improve," he told *Berg*. "I don't ever want to get complacent. I know it could have been better. As soon as Worlds ended, I was already in 2020."

The year 2020, however, was characterized by uncertainty for Dressel and his fellow athletes, as the COVID-19 pandemic forced the cancellation or postponement of many scheduled competitions. This included the 2020 Olympic Games.

TOKYO OLYMPICS

Postponed due to the ongoing pandemic, the 2020 Olympics began in Tokyo, Japan, in July 2021. Dressel qualified to compete in the Games after swimming in the Olympic trials in June of that year, during which he won the men's 50-meter freestyle, 100-meter freestyle, and 100-meter butterfly events. In addition to qualifying for the US Olympic team, he was named co-captain of the men's swimming team, a position he held alongside teammate Ryan Murphy. "The whole team voted for me for this, and I didn't even vote for myself for it," he told Papadatos. "Having the honor of that captain title is something that I will be proud of for the rest of my life."

Competing in several different individual and relay events, Dressel won gold medals in two relays and won his first individual Olympic gold in the 100-meter freestyle, beating Australian swimmer Kyle Chalmers in the final race after working to overcome the stress of the initial round of competition. "Pressure is fine. It is when you turn it into stress; that is when it becomes a problem," he told Matt Butler for *I* (29 July 2021). "My first swim I felt like I was turning the pressure into stress. The semi-final and final is when I found my groove." He went on to win gold medals in the 50-meter freestyle and the 100-meter butterfly, setting a new world record in the latter event with a time of 49.45 seconds in the final race. The US team's first-place finish in the 4×100-meter medley relay likewise set a world record, with Dressel and teammates Murphy, Michael Andrew, and Zach Apple achieving a total time of 3:26.78.

LOOKING FORWARD

Dressel struggled with his mental health in the months after the Olympic Games, in part due to feeling directionless following that major competition. He also revealed in interviews that he was trying to manage his disappointment with his performance in certain Olympic events where he had not met a specific personal goal he had set for himself, even if he had won a medal. While that period was a difficult one and Dressel took a brief hiatus from swimming, he eventually returned to the sport. In April 2022, he competed in the USA Swimming International Team Trials in North Carolina where he qualified to compete in that year's World Championships.

While preparing for the World Championships, Dressel, as the reigning Olympic gold medalist in several categories, was also the subject of widespread speculation in the swimming media over whether he would defend his medals—and potentially win new ones—at the 2024 Olympic Games in Paris, France. Dressel, however, believed it was important not to assume that he was guaranteed a spot in the 2024 Games. "I very much would like to make the team, but got to get put on the team first," he said, as reported by Emily DeCiccio for *CNBC* (4 Aug. 2021). "I'm no priority over anybody in US swimming. I got to make the team first, then we can talk about Paris."

PERSONAL LIFE

Dressel met his future wife, fellow high school and collegiate swimmer Meghan Haila, when they were both in high school. They married in February 2021. When not competing elsewhere, Dressel continues to live in Florida.

SUGGESTED READING

Butler, Matt. "Caeleb Dressel: 'Weirdo Loner' Wins Gold, Sets Olympic Record and Opens Up on Managing Emotions." *i*, 29 July 2021, inews.co.uk/sport/olympics/caeleb-dressel-freestyle-gold-us-toyko-2020-emotions-1125944. Accessed 9 May 2022.

Crouse, Karen. "For a Natural, Swimming Isn't Always Easy." *The New York Times*, 28 Feb. 2016, www.nytimes.com/2016/02/29/sports/for-a-natural-swimming-isnt-always-easy.html. Accessed 9 May 2022.

DeCiccio, Emily. "Caeleb Dressel on 2024 Paris Olympics: 'I Very Much Would Like to Make the Team.'" *CNBC*, 4 Aug. 2021, www.cnbc.com/2021/08/03/caeleb-dressel-on-2024-paris-olympics-i-very-much-would-like-to-make-the-team.html. Accessed 9 May 2022.

Dressel, Caeleb. "Caeleb Dressel (USA): 'I Don't Want to Be Famous.'" Interview by Aimee Berg. *FINA Magazine*, 24 Apr. 2020, www.fina.org/news/1756593/caeleb-dressel-usa-i-dont-want-to-be-famous. Accessed 9 May 2022.

___. "How a Hiatus Helped Olympic Hopeful Caeleb Dressel Smash U.S. Records." Interview by David Gardner. *Sports Illustrated*, 22 June 2016, www.si.com/olympics/2016/06/22/olympics-rio-2016-caeleb-dressel-us-swimming-trials. Accessed 9 May 2022.

___. "Interview: Caeleb Dressel Is an Olympic Champion in the Pool and in Life." Interview by Markos Papadatos. *Digital Journal*, 24 Aug. 2021, www.digitaljournal.com/sports/interview-caeleb-dressel-is-an-olympic-champion-in-the-pool-and-in-life/article. Accessed 9 May 2022.

Rieder, David. "U.S. International Team Trials: Caeleb Dressel Pulls Away for 100 Free Title; Brooks Curry Second." *Swimming World*, 26 Apr. 2022, www.swimmingworldmagazine.com/news/u-s-international-team-trials-caeleb-dressel-pulls-away-for-100-free-title-brooks-curry-second/. Accessed 9 May 2022.

—*Joy Crelin*

Norma Dunning

Born: 1959
Occupation: Writer and educator

Norma Dunning is an award-winning Inuit author and educator. Her short story collection, *Tainna: The Unseen Ones*, won the Governor General's Literary Prize for Fiction, Canada's highest literary award, in 2021. While Dunning's mother was born and raised in Inuit ancestral lands, now the Canadian territory of Nunavut, Dunning and her siblings were raised in small towns across Quebec, far from Indigenous lands. Growing up, Dunning was unaware of her Inuit heritage. Her mother did not tell her, hoping to protect her from racism and institutional discrimination. Dunning understood the painful choice, and in fact, made it herself as a young mother, but the alienation from her ancestors rankled. Thus, she made the decision to return to school at the age of fifty. There, she embraced her Inuit identity, earning both an undergraduate and master's degree in Indigenous studies. Her research rekindled her love for poetry and storytelling, and in 2017, while working on her doctorate, Dunning published her fiction debut, *Annie Muktuk and Other Stories*. The semi-autobiographical short story collection won the Danuta Gleed Literary Award in 2018.

Dunning's work is informed by a rich and painful history, but her stories focus on contemporary Inuit people. While in many ways her characters are inseparable from their ancestral past, Dunning highlights the complexities of this relationship and seeks to dispel racist stereotypes. "I would like to trouble the perceptions of Canadian people who generally think that Inuit Canadians are standing at a seal hole with a harpoon," she explained to Sara Frizzell for *CBC News* (15 July 2017). "We are not that, we are present day people. We get up and go to work and stop at Tim Hortons." Dunning, who is also the author of the poetry collection *Eskimo Pie: A Poetics of Inuit Identity* (2020), is a professor at the University of Alberta in Edmonton.

EARLY LIFE

Norma Jean Marie Dunning was born to an Inuit family in Quebec in 1959. Her mother came from Whale Cove, now Tikiraqjuaq, in Nunavut, and endured eight years in Winnipeg at a residential school—part of a network of boarding schools run by the Canadian government and Christian churches during the twentieth century that sought to assimilate Indigenous children into Canadian society. Dunning says her mother never spoke about being Inuk. When Dunning was eight years old, she asked about her heritage. Her mother told her to tell people that she was French. "That was a way of how my mother protected us," Dunning told Kyle Muzyka for *CBC News* (28 June 2018). "If we could present as non-Indigenous children, it made our paths easier." Dunning's father was in the Canadian army, and she and her siblings grew up mostly in the remote Quebec towns where he was posted. Dunning read and wrote poetry and stories from an early age but set those interests aside to start a family as a young adult.

EDUCATION AND POSTGRADUATE RESEARCH

Dunning decided to pursue her university degree in 2009, at the age of fifty, enrolling as a student at the University of Alberta in Edmonton. She majored in Native studies and education sciences, with a minor in creative writing, and earned her bachelor's degree, with an Aboriginal Self-Governance Certification, in 2012. She began teaching courses at the university and later earned her master's degree in 2014.

Dunning wrote her master's thesis on a program called the Canadian Eskimo Identification System. From 1941 to 1978, the Canadian government made Inuit people wear identification tags in the form of a disk worn as a necklace. Although other Aboriginal groups in Canada were assigned registration numbers, Inuit were the only group to be "tagged" in this particularly demeaning way. The practice was instated in large part because government officials could not pronounce Inuit names. Dunning explored the policy from the perspective of Inuit women, including members of her own family. She was born when the system was still in practice but writes—in a 2012 essay called "Reflections of a Disk-less Inuit on Canada's Eskimo Identification System"—that neither she, nor her mother or siblings, ever received a disk. This became a serious roadblock for Dunning in 2001, when she sought to apply for Inuit beneficiary status and needed to "prove" her identity and heritage.

Dunning completed her PhD degree in 2019, writing her thesis on the academic careers of Inuit students and the difficulties of living in southern Canada, away from Arctic ancestral lands. Those challenges include navigating benefits that are provided to Inuit. "Even though some Inuit no longer live in the North, we're still members of our land claim agreement, but because we are not residing in the North, the way our funding and benefits are given out to us is very different," Dunning explained to Geoff McMaster for the University of Alberta website (24 Nov. 2021).

ANNIE MUKTUK AND OTHER STORIES

In 2017, Dunning published a book of short stories called *Annie Muktuk and Other Stories*. Many of the sixteen stories in the debut collection were developed during Dunning's time as an undergraduate creative writing student; most are inspired by her ancestors, like her grandfather, Husky Harris, who appears in the book. "Even though the work presents as fictional, there is at least . . . 95.5 percent truth in what I've written," she told Frizzell. The titular character, an Inuit woman named Annie Muktuk, appears in several stories, as does the man who loves her, Moses Henry, and his best friend. The inspiration for Annie's character, Dunning told Frizzell, came from an anthropologist's reductive assessment of the Canadian Arctic. He wrote as if Inuit women were commodities, she said, adding: "When I read it, I thought, why is it that aboriginal women are never in charge of their own sexuality? Why are we presented as women who can be used?"

The characters in the collection navigate the pain of erasure and alienation. Some, like Dunning's mother, endure the brutality of residential schools. "Strong currents of anger and courage propel the Inuit characters," Candace Fertile wrote in her review for *Alberta Views* (1 Mar. 2018). "They are survivors." Families are abandoned and women are used, but there is also tenderness, Fertile wrote. In the story "Elipsee," a woman is dying of cancer. She and her husband take a trip to a lake on the advice of a shaman. The award-winning story, Fertile wrote, "combines the love of a couple for each other with their spiritual foundations." The stories also shed light on the unique Inuit culture and traditions, including Inuit language that Dunning peppers throughout the stories and supports with a glossary. The collection earned Dunning the Danuta Gleed Literary Award for best short fiction debut by a Canadian writer in 2018. The book was translated into French in 2021.

ESKIMO PIE AND TAINNA: THE UNSEEN ONES

In 2020, Dunning published *Eskimo Pie: A Poetics of Inuit Identity*, a short book combining poetry and prose. In it, Dunning wrestles with her desire to share her work despite fears of betraying her culture and rejection from non-Inuit writers. She spoke about her experiences as an Inuit writer in her conversations with Frizzell. "In terms of the Canadian lit scene, I know other Inuit writers, they're afraid to publish and they're afraid to go through that process because we know what it's like to be colonized and you don't want your work re-colonized," she said.

In 2021, Dunning published her second collection of short stories called *Tainna: The Unseen Ones*. The six stories contained in the book explore the experiences of Inuit people living in southern Canada, an experience that is particularly important, and personal, to Dunning. "I want that visibility for us," she told Sue Carter for *Inuit Art Quarterly* (7 Dec. 2021), noting that Inuit are often asked to prove that they are authentically Indigenous by answering questions like "Do you speak your language?" and "Do you eat raw meat?" Dunning's advice to her Indigenous students, she told Carter, "is that when people question how you look, or whether or not you can speak what should have been your mother tongue, just ask them quietly, 'Why are you asking me that?'" in order to "shift the power in the conversation."

Robert J. Wiersema, who reviewed *Tainna: The Unseen Ones* for the Canadian magazine *Quill and Quire* (1 Apr. 2021), identified a common theme among the stories of "journeying between, and bridging, multiple worlds: north and south, rural and urban, living and dead." He praised the cumulative effect of the collection as a whole. "Dunning demonstrates considerable confidence in both her readers and her own skills, rarely slowing to explain, allowing the narrative to reveal connections and truths as it progresses," Wiersema wrote. As the book's subtitle suggests, the collection is full of unseen spiritual guides. In the story "Kunak," for instance, a young boy suffers the disappearance of his grandfather. As an adult, he becomes homeless and struggles with alcohol abuse, unaware that his grandfather's spirit is with him. In the dark satire "Panem et Circenses," the "unseen" is revealed in the vicious racism of an Inuit woman's friends. Other stories are about the epidemic of violence against Indigenous women. In the title story, a man discovers the body of a young woman surrounded by Canada geese, "sitting in a circle with their necks pointing outwards. Sitting like bison do when protecting their young against aggressors." The story unravels the history of the woman's life as she journeys with two spirits to another land. In another story, Dunning returns to the character of Annie Muktuk from her previous collection, who has managed to find peace through art. *Tainna* won the prestigious Governor General's Literary Prize for Fiction in 2021.

PERSONAL LIFE

Though Dunning laments her severed connection to her heritage as a child, she told Shelagh Rogers of *CBC Radio* (11 Sept. 2021) that she did not let her own three sons identify as Inuit for similar reasons. "Once a child self-identifies within the grade school system, they often end up being coded. I know how that system works," she said. "Also, when they were very small and we moved here to Edmonton, we were extremely poor and we were living in Edmonton housing. So that was another strike against [us]. . . . So I never, ever allowed them to identify."

In addition to her children, Dunning has several grandchildren. She lives in Edmonton, where in 2015, she helped found a group for Inuit living in the city called Edmontonmiut. As the vice president of that group in 2020, Dunning led a successful campaign to change the name of a local football team from the Edmonton Eskimos to the Edmonton Football Team. She is on the faculty of the education department at the University of Alberta.

SUGGESTED READING

Dunning, Norma. "Inuk Author Norma Dunning Explores Life, Death and Identity Erasure with Story Collection *Tainna*." Interview by Shelagh Rogers. *CBC Radio*, 11 Sept. 2021, www.cbc.ca/radio/thenextchapter/full-episode-sept-11-2021-1.6169801/inuk-author-norma-dunning-explores-life-death-and-identity-erasure-with-story-collection-tainna-1.6169809. Accessed 29 Apr. 2022.

___. "Norma Dunning's 'Tainna' Wins Governor General's Literary Award." Interview by Sue Carter. *Inuit Art Quarterly*, 7 Dec. 2021, www.inuitartfoundation.org/iaq-online/norma-dunning-s-tainna-wins-governor-general-s-literary-award. Accessed 30 Apr. 2022.

Fertile, Candace. Review of *Annie Muktuk and Other Stories*, by Norma Dunning. *Alberta Views*, 1 Mar. 2018, albertaviews.ca/annie-muktuk/. Accessed 29 Apr. 2022.

Frizzell, Sara. "'What Inspired Her Was Getting Mad': Inuk Writer Tells Family's Stories in New Collection." *CBC News*, 15 July 2017, www.cbc.ca/news/canada/north/norma-dunning-inuit-stories-annie-muktuk-1.4203698. Accessed 29 Apr. 2022.

McMaster, Geoff. "'We Live Everywhere': Inuk Author Sends Up Settler Stereotypes in Short Stories." *University of Alberta*, 24 Nov. 2021, www.ualberta.ca/folio/2021/11/we-live-everywhere-inuk-author-sends-up-settler-stereotypes-in-short-stories.html. Accessed 3 May 2022.

Muzyka, Kyle. "Edmonton's Indigenous Writers Finally Being Heard, Inuk Author Says." *CBC News*, 28 June 2018, www.cbc.ca/news/canada/edmonton/norma-dunning-annie-muktuk-1.4725275. Accessed 29 Apr. 2022.

Wiersema, Robert J. Review of *Tainna: The Unseen Ones*, by Norma Dunning. *Quill and Quire*, 1 Apr. 2021, quillandquire.com/review/tainna-the-unseen-ones/. Accessed 29 Apr. 2022.

SELECTED WORKS

Annie Muktuk and Other Stories, 2017; *Eskimo Pie: A Poetics of Inuit Identity*, 2020; *Tainna: The Unseen Ones*, 2021

—Molly Hagan

Laurent Duvernay-Tardif

Born: February 11, 1991
Occupation: Physician and football player

For veteran Canadian offensive lineman Laurent Duvernay-Tardif, the path to the National Football League (NFL) was an unconventional one. After being introduced to the sport in his early teens, Duvernay-Tardif never pursued football seriously until he attended McGill University's medical school. There, the six-foot-five player earned the nickname "Dr. Kill" for arriving for practice still dressed in his scrubs. His intense, physical style; his impressive size; and athleticism eventually garnered him attention from NFL scouts.

With his sixth-round selection in the league's 2014 Draft, Duvernay-Tardif became the tenth player from Canada—and second McGill player, behind Randy Chevrier—to enter the NFL. Despite not playing as a rookie, Duvernay-Tardif spent the subsequent three years firmly entrenched in the Kansas City Chiefs offense while continuing to study medicine at McGill—a feat that received plaudits from teammates. "To be a doctor and a football player . . . it shows the work ethic and dedication he's had in his life," Kansas City quarterback Patrick Mahomes told Mel Woods for *HuffPost* (31 Jan. 2020).

In 2018, Duvernay-Tardif became the first active NFL player to graduate from medical school. Less than two years later, he became the first doctor to play in and win a Super Bowl. Within months, Duvernay-Tardif had traded the offensive line for the COVID-19 pandemic front lines, forfeiting his 2020 season to volunteer at a Canadian long-term care facility. For his on-and-off-the-field exploits, Duvernay-Tardif, a 2021 inductee into Canada's Walk of Fame, has received the Muhammad Ali Sports Humanitarian Award (2021), at the Excellence in Sports Performance Yearly Awards (ESPYs); the Sports Illustrated Sportsperson of the Year award (2020); the Lou Marsh Trophy (2020);

and the Chevalier of the Ordre national du Québec (2019).

EARLY LIFE AND EDUCATION

Laurent Duvernay-Tardif was born on February 11, 1991, to Guylaine Duvernay and François Tardif in Québec City, Québec. His paternal grandfather, Guy Tardif, had served in the National Assembly of Québec and as a cabinet minister in the 1970s and 1980s.

Duvernay-Tardif enjoyed an adventurous childhood in the eastern Montreal suburb of Mont-Saint-Hilaire, Québec, spending time at the family-owned vineyard that produced wine sold at trade shows and farmers markets. At age ten, he set sail with his family along the Atlantic Coast and around the Caribbean Sea. During the year-long voyage, Duvernay-Tardif and his younger sisters, Marilou and Delphine, were "boatschooled" by both parents, as he described it to New York Jets team reporter Ethan Greenberg in December 2021; his mother taught humanities while his father, a former agriculture instructor, managed the sciences.

Duvernay-Tardif was first introduced to American football as a teen, when he joined the Richelieu Pirates, an amateur youth squad in the Montréal-Métro Football League. During the 2004–05 season, Duvernay-Tardif played defensive end and occasionally served as a kicker and offensive lineman. He subsequently embarked with his family on another yearlong sailing trip. Upon his return, he resumed his high school studies at Collège Saint-Hilaire and explored other sports (badminton and soccer) before rejoining the Pirates in 2007.

DUAL PASSIONS: MEDICINE AND FOOTBALL

In 2008, Duvernay-Tardif entered Montreal's private Collège André-Grasset for a pre-university program unique to Québec, the Collège d'enseignement général et professionnel (CEGEP; college of general and vocational education), that combines senior year of high school with a year of undergraduate study. At André-Grasset, he made the Phénix football squad as a walk-on. His enthusiasm for the sport grew during the two years he spent serving as the Phénix's defensive lineman. "I loved the contact, I loved the strategy and I loved that I was pretty good at it," Duvernay-Tardif penned in a *Players' Tribune* essay (8 July 2017). The stint at André-Grasset also helped

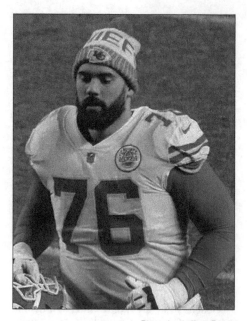

Photo by Jeffrey Beall, via Wikimedia Commons.

him uncover a passion for science, which eventually led him to enroll in medical school after graduating from André-Grasset in 2010. "Initially I was interested in engineering, but after looking into it, I realized that while I loved the scientific and logical aspects of engineering, I craved the ability to have a social impact," he also recalled for the *Players' Tribune*. "That's why medicine called to me."

Despite knowing very little English, Duvernay-Tardif attended McGill University's medical program, after jotting down the incorrect date and missing the entrance exam deadline for the French-speaking medical schools. To keep up with coursework, he relied on a pocket dictionary while observing class recordings at half speed. The first-year medical student was equally determined playing defense for McGill's football team.

After starting three of six games during the 2010 season, Duvernay-Tardif transitioned to the offense in 2011 while juggling hospital shifts, sometimes sleeping in the locker room to avoid missing early morning practices. He was designated team co-captain, most valuable player (2012), and most outstanding offensive player (2012). He amassed other honors, including the J. P. Metras Trophy (2013) as Canadian university football's top lineman and McGill male athlete of the year (2013–14). He was also named to the Canadian Interuniversity

Sport (CIS) Football All-Canadian Team (2012 and 2013) and the Réseau du sport sportif du Québec (RSEQ) Conference All-Star Team (2012 and 2013).

NFL ROOKIE TO STARTER

In 2014, Duvernay-Tardif, the top-ranked Canadian football prospect, set his sights on a professional career. Following an invite to Florida's annual East-West Shrine Game, an all-star showcase for top NFL prospects, he auditioned for scouts from four Canadian Football League clubs and nine NFL teams in late March. Two months later, Kansas City made him their sixth-round draft pick. With this selection, Duvernay-Tardif became the first Québec native, second McGill University player, and tenth Canadian university player to be drafted in the NFL. He subsequently signed a four-year, $2.34 million contract with a $100,000 signing bonus. Following the preseason, he was rendered inactive and left off the team's final roster. He spent his 2014 rookie season familiarizing himself with American football and the team's offensive playbook, as well as by watching footage. During the off-season, Duvernay-Tardif, who had one year remaining in medical school, completed the first of his three four-month clinical training rotations.

When the 2015 roster was announced, Duvernay-Tardif was designated as the starting right guard. With his aggressive physical style of play during team practices, the medical student quickly proved his toughness to his skeptical teammates. "People learned more about me and realized I'm not a nerd," he explained to Adam Teicher for *ESPN* (31 Aug. 2016). "I'm just a guy who loves [football] and has a passion for medical school." Under head coach Andy Reid, he started thirteen games for Kansas City, second-place finishers in the American Football Conference (AFC) West, with an 11–5 regular-season record. Duvernay-Tardif made his postseason debut against the Houston Texans in the 2015–16 Wild Card playoffs, which Kansas City won 30–0, but suffered a concussion during the first half. During the off-season, he did his medical school rotation in internal and emergency medicine.

CONTRACT EXTENSION AND MEDICAL DEGREE

Duvernay-Tardif returned to action in September 2016, during his team's season-opening 33–27 win over the San Diego Chargers. After being sidelined for two games with a high-ankle injury, he started the remaining thirteen games for Kansas City, whose 12–4 record clinched the AFC West division title—their first since 2010. His 2016–17 season ended following his team's loss to the Pittsburgh Steelers (18–16) in the AFC Divisional Playoffs. In February 2017, a year before Duvernay-Tardif was set to become an unrestricted free agent, Kansas City offered him a five-year, $41.25 million extension. At the time, Duvernay-Tardif was conducting a geriatric rotation at Montreal's Royal Victoria Hospital.

By September 2017, Duvernay-Tardif was back in Kansas City's starting lineup. After appearing in the team's first three regular-season games, he sustained a left knee sprain in the first quarter of their October 2 victory (29–20) against the Washington, DC, NFL team. Duvernay-Tardif was sidelined for a month before returning to the offense during Kansas City's 28–17 loss to the Dallas Cowboys. While the team ended the 2017 season with a 10–6 regular-season record and second straight AFC West division title, their postseason was short-lived, following the Tennessee Titans' 22–21 comeback victory during the AFC Wild Card game in January 2018. Four months after his team's disappointing finish, Duvernay-Tardif reached a long-awaited milestone, finally earning his doctorate in medicine and master's in surgery from the McGill University Faculty of Medicine.

In early August, Duvernay-Tardif suffered his second concussion during a team practice. After more than two weeks, he was cleared to return to training camp and was added to the team's roster for the 2018 season. He was back on the sidelines on October 9, however, following a fractured fibula and torn ankle ligaments during the team's 30–14 win against the Jacksonville Jaguars. He remained on injured reserve (IR) until mid-January 2019, as Kansas City claimed a third consecutive AFC West division and the AFC divisional game. He was inactive for the 2019 AFC Championship, which the team lost in overtime (37–31) to the New England Patriots.

SUPER BOWL AND PANDEMIC

Fully recovered, Duvernay-Tardif showed up to Kansas City's mandatory minicamp in June 2019 before attending training camp a month later. By late August, he was among the team's roster for the upcoming 2019–20 season, starting fourteen of their sixteen regular-season games. (He spent two games sidelined with an ankle injury.) For the fourth straight year, the Chiefs captured the AFC West, after amassing a 12–4 record. As a starter in the divisional playoffs, Duvernay-Tardif helped his team notch a twenty-point comeback victory (51–31) against the Houston Texans. He next appeared on the starting offensive line for the AFC Championship game, in which Kansas City defeated the Tennessee Titans 35–24 to advance to the Super Bowl, against San Francisco, in February 2020. Following Kansas City's 31–20 win, Duvernay-Tardif made history, becoming the first physician and first Québec-born player to win the Super Bowl.

The team's Super Bowl victory was overshadowed by the coronavirus disease 2019 (COVID-19) pandemic in late March. Amid this global pandemic, which created a health-care worker shortage, Duvernay-Tardif spent nearly three months performing nursing and orderly duties at CHSLD Gertrude-Lafrance, an extended-care facility in Québec. He also served on the players' association task force responsible for establishing the NFL's COVID-19 safety measures. In late July 2020, prior to the start of training camp, Duvernay-Tardif announced that he would opt out of the upcoming season to continue caring for CHSLD Gertrude-Lafrance's non-COVID patients, including feeding and bathing them as well as administering intravenous drips and medications. Another challenging task involved transferring those who tested positive from the facility's low-risk yellow zone to the high-risk, COVID-infected red zone.

RETURN TO KANSAS CITY, TRADE TO THE JETS

In September, while working at CHSLD Gertrude-Lafrance, Duvernay-Tardif enrolled in online nutrition, epidemiology, and biostatistics courses at Harvard University's T. H. Chan School of Public Health. During his absence from Kansas City, the team nearly went undefeated during the regular season, compiling a league-best 14–2 record to clinch a fifth consecutive division title and berth in the divisional playoffs, where they defeated the Cleveland Browns 22–17. After dominating the Buffalo Bills (38–24) in the 2020 AFC Championship, Kansas City advanced to their second straight Super Bowl, before losing to the Tampa Bay Buccaneers 9–31.

In May 2021, Duvernay-Tardif announced that he would be rejoining Kansas City. However, when he arrived at training camp in late July, he found himself vying with rookie Trey Smith and fellow veteran Kyle Long for the starting right guard position. Duvernay-Tardif's comeback was delayed in early August, after he sustained a broken hand during practice. Along with missing the preseason, he remained sidelined for the first half of the regular season before approving a trade to the New York Jets by the November 2 deadline.

Duvernay-Tardif subsequently started seven games with the Jets, who finished the 2021–22 season with a 4–13 record. After resolving his medical licensing issues in Canada, Duvernay-Tardif, a first-time free agent, hoped to play in 2022 but ultimately envisioned another calling. "I love both (football and medicine) but I also think it's important to build a career that you can do for a long time and medicine is that," he shared with Pat Hickey for the *Montreal Gazette* (21 Jan. 2020).

PERSONAL LIFE

Along with his longtime girlfriend, Florence-Agathe Dubé-Moreau, Duvernay-Tardif established an eponymous foundation that encourages physical activity and creativity in children. The couple, who live in Montreal, Québec, also share a passion for collecting predominantly Canadian and Québécois contemporary art. In 2018, Duvernay-Tardif realized a long-standing wish: traveling to the Olympics, which he attended as a reporter, rather than just as a spectator. "He needs to push his limits," Dubé-Moreau shared with Ben Baskin for *Sports Illustrated* (11 Sept. 2018). "That's really central, the core of who Laurent is."

SUGGESTED READING

Baskin, Ben. "Laurent Duvernay-Tardif, M.D.: How the Chiefs Guard Earned His Medical Degree While Protecting His QB." *Sports Illustrated*, 11 Sept. 2018, www.si.com/ nfl/2018/09/11/laurent-duvernay-tardif-chiefs-mcgill-university-medical-school. Accessed 12 May 2022.

Cassata, Cathy. "Meet the NFL Player Who May Soon Be Your Doctor." *Healthline*, 10 Sept. 2018, www.healthline.com/health-news/meet-the-nfl-player-who-may-soon-be-your-doctor. Accessed 12 May 2022.

Deshaies, Antoine. "We Already Saw That Duvernay-Tardif Was An Exceptional Guy," *Ici-Radio Canada*, 30 Jan. 2020, ici-radio--canada-ca.translate.goog/recit-numerique/452/laurent-duvernay-tardif-super-bowl-football-chiefs-podium?_x_tr_sl=fr&_x_tr_tl=en&_x_tr_hl=en&_x_tr_pto=sc. Accessed 12 May 2022.

Duvernay-Tardif, Laurent. "Le Docteur." *The Players' Tribune*, 8 July 2017, www.theplayerstribune.com/articles/le-docteur-laurent-duvernay-tardif-kansas-city-chiefs. Accessed 12 May 2022.

___. "Wine, Bakers and Sailors: 40-Yard Stroll Featuring Laurent Duvernay-Tardif." Interview by Ethan Greenberg. *New York Jets YouTube Channel*, 14 Dec. 2021, www.youtube.com/watch?v=86yX8zbkodM. Accessed 18 May 2022.

Teicher, Adam. "Chiefs' Laurent Duvernay-Tardif Leads Rare Life as Football Player, Future Doctor." *ESPN*, 31 Aug. 2016, www.espn.com/blog/kansas-city-chiefs/post/_/id/17958/chiefs-laurent-duvernay-tardif-leads-rare-life-as-football-player-future-doctor. Accessed 12 May 2022.

Woods, Mel. "Canadian Laurent Duvernay-Tardif Set to Be First Doctor to Play in Super Bowl." *HuffPost*, 3 Feb. 2020, www.huffpost.com/archive/ca/entry/canadian-super-bowl-doctor-laurent-duvernay-tardif_ca_5e34a936c5b6f26233294718. Accessed 17 May 2022.

—Bertha Muteba

Cathy Engelbert

Born: 1964
Occupation: Business executive

In 2019 Cathy Engelbert became the commissioner of the Women's National Basketball Association (WNBA), the longest-running women's professional sports league in the United States. "One of the reasons I think I was hired [was] to come in with the business acumen and look at what I've been calling my three pillars: the economics, growing the revenue base, and fan and player experience," she explained to Geoff Magliocchetti in an interview for *Elite Sports NY* (6 Oct. 2019). Engelbert was referring to the business acumen she gained during her thirty-three-year tenure at Deloitte, one of the so-called "Big Four" professional-services firms. After joining Deloitte directly out of college in 1986, she steadily rose through the ranks and was named chief executive officer (CEO) in 2015, making her the first female CEO at any of the Big Four firms. "When I became the first woman CEO [of Deloitte], I had no idea what a big deal it was going to be," she told Vicky Valet for *Forbes* (3 Apr. 2018). "I got hundreds of handwritten letters from grandfathers to CEOs to college students to deans of universities saying, 'Cathy, you inspire me.'"

Those leadership skills thus proved invaluable during Engelbert's early years at the helm of the WNBA, as she led the organization through the COVID-19 pandemic, among other challenges. Meanwhile, after her first two years as commissioner, the league had already made major gains, including increasing viewership on *ESPN* by nearly 50 percent and signing new high-profile sponsors such as Google. "I'm seeing a transformation before my eyes," she remarked to Sean Gregory in an interview for *Time* (15 May 2022), referring to the WNBA's progress. "We're starting to be seen as a bold progressive, sports media and entertainment property. We embody diversity and stand for social justice and the power of women."

EARLY LIFE AND EDUCATION
Catherine "Cathy" Engelbert, born in 1964, grew up in a large family in Collingswood, a suburb of Philadelphia in southern New Jersey. Her father, Kurt, was an information technology (IT) professional who worked three jobs at times to support Engelbert, her five brothers, and her two sisters. Her mother, Margaret, worked in medical administration. Before his IT career, however, Engelbert's father, who stood six feet, five inches tall, had attended St. Joseph's University in Philadelphia, playing on the school's basketball team under legendary coach Jack Ramsay in the 1950s; at one point he had been drafted by the Detroit Pistons. "You might say I had no choice but

Photo by Caty001nj,
via Wikimedia Commons

to play basketball with [that] kind of DNA or pedigree," Engelbert joked to Magliocchetti.

Indeed, the entire family grew up as avid basketball fans. Their home had a rickety basketball hoop mounted over the garage, and Engelbert and her brothers regularly engaged in two-on-two games, a practice she has credited with allowing her to shine as a player at Collingswood High School. In addition to basketball, she played tennis and lacrosse, and she also excelled academically, landing in the top ten of her graduating class. That drive to compete, she has said, was a natural result of coming from such a large family. Reflecting on how her upbringing affected her, she explained to *Lehigh News* (29 June 2015) that "the competitiveness and the leadership that you get in a family of eight, competing literally for things like cereal and snacks" had a huge impact on her drive to succeed.

Engelbert has also credited Title IX, the civil rights law passed in 1972 prohibiting gender-based discrimination in any school program receiving federal funding, with allowing her to compete. "I'm a huge beneficiary of Title IX," she asserted to Magliocchetti. "I think that's an interesting kind of thing to look back in history and say what Title IX did for us, people like me who were able to play three sports in high school and two in college."

Engelbert was recruited by Lehigh University, in nearby Bethlehem, Pennsylvania, to play lacrosse in 1982. While there, she also tried out as a walk-on for the basketball team, then coached by Hall of Famer Muffet McGraw. She ultimately captained both teams and graduated in 1986 with a bachelor's degree in accounting.

EARLY CAREER AT DELOITTE

As a senior at Lehigh, Engelbert attended a university career fair, where she interviewed with Deloitte, which provides auditing, consulting, financial advisory, risk management, tax, and other related services to a massive roster of clients, including many Fortune 500 companies, around the world. Hired to start immediately after graduation in 1986, she was assigned to the company's Philadelphia office.

At the time, culture at the Big Four firms was strongly male-dominated, and only 7 percent of Deloitte's senior staff were women. Fortuitously, the company had embarked on a drive to boost the hiring and promotion of female professionals, and Engelbert found willing mentors and supporters there. After six years in Philadelphia, she moved north and worked in both the Connecticut and New York City–area offices of Deloitte. In 1998, she was named a partner.

RISE TO CEO

Following the passage of the Sarbanes-Oxley Act in 2002, which tightened regulations on the US accounting industry, Engelbert came to be viewed as a leading expert on derivative financial instrument accounting—a type of accounting that focuses on weighing different risks, such as those associated with commodities and interest rates—as well as on issues involving the pharmaceutical and life sciences industries. Thus, she found herself in great demand as a conference speaker and author of articles for professional publications over the next decade. In 2014—having served variously as a national managing partner, deputy national professional practice director, and quality risk manager for financial accounting and reporting services—she became the chair and CEO of Deloitte and Touche LLP, the US–based accounting, auditing, and risk advisory subsidiary of the company.

In 2015, Engelbert was named CEO of Deloitte as a whole. (At Deloitte, CEOs are elected by the board every four years.) That post put her in charge of about seventy thousand employees and almost $15 billion in annual revenue. Over the course of her four-year tenure in the top spot, she focused significant effort on adopting emerging technologies like artificial intelligence, blockchain, and cloud computing, but she did not neglect the human side of the business. She has told interviewers that among her proudest achievements were implementing a sixteen-week family-leave policy and encouraging what she called a "culture of courage," in which employees felt free to speak about any aspect of work at Deloitte that concerned them.

By the time Engelbert left in 2019, revenues had grown by more than 30 percent, and the company had made major strides toward diversity and gender parity, with well over 40 percent of new hires belonging to a previously underrepresented group. Despite her success, as she explained to Ryan Lawrence for *08108 Magazine* (13 Mar. 2020), she desired "to do something different, something where I would have a broad women's leadership platform, and something I had a passion for."

WNBA

On May 15, 2019, National Basketball Association (NBA) commissioner Adam Silver announced that Engelbert would be stepping into a new role as commissioner of the WNBA. She was the first WNBA head to hold a commissioner's title; previously, the league's leaders held the title of president. The change had been made, officials explained, to signal that the WNBA—typically less highly regarded than the NBA—was a major league in its own right and that Engelbert was on a par with the heads of other pro sports leagues in the United States. As commissioner, Engelbert made an immediate impact, effecting improvements such as increased player salaries, improved maternity leave, and new travel and health benefits. "If you're trying to transform a league and lift women and women in sports, you've got to get long-term labor peace, and that's what we did," she told Lawrence. Additionally, she became an outspoken advocate of issues of social justice, about which many WNBA players were also vocal.

However, Engelbert also encountered numerous stressful situations during her first full year. Foremost among those stressors was the COVID-19 pandemic, which shut down live sports events for a period of several months in 2020. Eventually, under Engelbert's leadership, the league devised a solution that involved holding the entire 2020 season inside a "bubble" at IMG Academy in Bradenton, Florida, from which eighty-seven games were nationally televised. "Usually in the business world, you tackle a problem, you handle it, you get past it, you learn from it. With the coronavirus, every day is the start of a new day with the virus and its potential impact on us," Engelbert told Mechelle Voepel for *ESPN* (2 Oct. 2020). "We will evolve out of this, but it's the challenge of a lifetime for live sports." In another COVID-related triumph, by mid-2021, even without a mandate in place, 99 percent of its players had been vaccinated, making the WNBA the first major North American sports league to reach near-total vaccination rates.

Other challenges emerged during Englebert's early years as commissioner, including a battle over whether wealthier franchises should be allowed to charter flights to away games— Engelbert ruled that the practice would not be allowed unless funds were made available to all franchises, to level the playing field—and debates over whether there should be more than 12 teams and 144 roster spots available for the large pool of talented hopefuls. (Engelbert has argued for expansion of the league.)

Then, in early 2022, another crisis erupted when Brittney Griner, a Phoenix Mercury center and seven-time WNBA All-Star recipient who also plays on a Russian-based team, was imprisoned in Russia on suspicions that she was smuggling cannabis. Engelbert skillfully managed the fallout from the incident, regularly assuring the press that the league fully supported Griner and was collaborating with officials to have her released. She also lifted roster and salary caps so that the Mercury could attract a replacement player until Griner returned home, and she ordered every WNBA court to be festooned with the player's initials and jersey number in her honor. In addition to winning praise for her handling of such challenges, Englebert was applauded for attracting outside financial investment aimed at reducing the disparities between the NBA and WNBA in player salary and media attention.

PERSONAL LIFE

With her husband, an Army veteran, Engelbert has a daughter, Julia, and a son, Thomas. They live in Berkeley Heights, New Jersey. She chairs Catalyst, a nonprofit advocating for women in the workplace, and she was a founding member of CEO Action for Diversity and Inclusion, a group committed to advancing social equity and addressing systemic barriers to health care, technology, public safety, and voting rights.

A skilled recreational golfer, Engelbert became a member of the US Golf Association's Executive Committee in 2021, and she has also sat on the boards of McDonald's Corporation and Royalty Pharma.

SUGGESTED READING

Engelbert, Cathy. "'An Absolutely Unimaginable Situation.' WNBA Commissioner Cathy Engelbert Addresses Brittney Griner Arrest." Interview by Sean Gregory. *Time*, 15 May 2022, time.com/6175832/wnba-cathy-engelbert-commissioner-interview/. Accessed 31 May 2022.

———. "Deloitte CEO Cathy Engelbert: Lessons on Leadership." Interview by Zack Friedman. *Forbes*, 27 Feb. 2018, www.forbes.com/sites/zackfriedman/2018/02/27/deloitte-ceo-cathy-engelbert-leadership/?sh=63cdfb231dd6. Accessed 10 May 2022.

———. "WNBA Commissioner Cathy Engelbert Talks NJ, Family, and the NY Liberty." Interview by Geoff Magliocchetti. *Elite Sports NY*, 6 Oct. 2019, elitesportsny.com/2019/10/06/wnba-commissioner-cathy-engelbert-talks-nj-family-and-the-ny-liberty-esny-exclusive/. Accessed 10 May 2022.

"The Game Changer." *Lehigh News*, 29 June 2015, www2.lehigh.edu/news/the-game-changer. Accessed 10 May 2022.

Lawrence, Ryan. "Hoop Dreams." *08108 Magazine*, 13 Mar. 2020, 08108collingswood.com/2020/03/13/hoop-dreams/. Accessed 10 May 2022.

Valet, Vicky. "'Your Career Is Not Linear': Deloitte CEO Cathy Engelbert on Her Rise to the Top." *Forbes*, 3 Apr. 2018, www.forbes.com/sites/vickyvalet/2018/04/03/your-career-is-not-linear-deloitte-ceo-cathy-engelbert-on-her-rise-to-the-top/?sh=1e94f78b7893. Accessed 10 May 2022.

Voepel, Mechelle. "How Commissioner Cathy Engelbert Saved the 2020 WNBA Season." *ESPN*, 2 Oct. 2020, www.espn.com/wnba/story/_/id/30018211/how-commissioner-cathy-engelbert-saved-2020-wnba-season. Accessed 10 May 2022.

Withiam, Hannah. "'She Wants to Be an Impetus for Change': How Cathy Engelbert's Journey Positioned Her to Become WNBA Commissioner." *The Athletic*, 17 July 2019, theathletic.com/1081523/2019/07/17/she-wants-to-be-an-impetus-for-change-how-cathy-engelberts-journey-positioned-her-to-become-wnba-commissioner/. Accessed 10 May 2022.

—*Mari Rich*

Lauren Esposito

Born: November 29, 1981
Occupation: Arachnologist

"One of the really great things about studying arachnids is that they are old," arachnologist Lauren Esposito told Kevin Schultz for the *San Francisco Chronicle* (25 Dec. 2015). "In studying the history of such an ancient group, we can understand things such as what happens when climate changes." As assistant curator and Schlinger Chair of Arachnology at the California Academy of Sciences, Esposito is responsible not only for studying arachnids such as scorpions, the primary focus of her research, but also for managing the institution's collection of specimens. This includes leading outreach and educational initiatives that she hopes will address the public's fears of arachnids and create greater public awareness of the valuable information that can be gleaned by studying them.

In addition to working for the California Academy of Sciences, Esposito cofounded the 500 Queer Scientists campaign, a visibility initiative highlighting the work of queer-identified individuals working in scientific fields. She also cofounded the nonprofit Islands and Seas, an organization that established an environmentally friendly field laboratory in Baja California, and sought to offer educational programs on the environment and conservation to local youth. An accomplished field researcher herself, Esposito is deeply aware of the importance of protecting natural environments and the diverse array of creatures within them. "We're in a biodiversity crisis, the largest extinction event ever documented," she explained to Zoë Beery in an interview for *Bustle* (30 Nov. 2020). "Whether we preserve what we have determines our ability as humans to live on earth, and to preserve it, and so we need to document it. Preventing it from disappearing is how we can prevent ourselves from disappearing."

EARLY LIFE AND EDUCATION

Lauren Alyse Esposito was born in El Paso, Texas, on November 29, 1981. Her mother was a wildlife biologist who later began a career in STEM education, while her father was a veterinarian. Esposito grew up in El Paso, where she developed an interest in insects, arachnids, and other small creatures at a young age. "I loved digging in the garden and turning over rocks to look for worms and 'bugs' as a kid," she later recalled in an interview for *Untamed Science*. "My mom claims that I would proudly bring her live cockroaches that I found outside." The young Esposito also enjoyed exploring the outdoors while visiting grandparents who lived in the Bahamas, beginning what would become an enduring fascination with species native to the Caribbean.

After graduating from El Paso High School, Esposito enrolled in the University of Texas at El Paso in 1998. Though initially a pre-med student, she developed an interest in field biology while taking a class that included a field research project and, while completing a summer internship at the American Museum of Natural History (AMNH), was introduced to the form of arachnids that would soon become the focus of her research: scorpions. Esposito worked as a teaching assistant and assistant biology instructor during her years at the University of Texas and earned a bachelor's degree cum laude in biology from that institution in 2003.

Hoping to pursue her studies in arachnology further, Esposito moved to New York City and enrolled in a graduate program that was a partnership between the AMNH's Richard Gilder Graduate School and the Graduate Center of the City University of New York (CUNY). She completed a master's degree in biology in 2010 and the following year earned a doctorate in biology with the dissertation "Systematics and Biogeography of the New World Scorpion Genus *Centruroides* Marx,

Photo by Arachnerds,
via Wikimedia Commons

1890 (Scorpiones: Buthidae)." In addition to serving as an adjunct professor at CUNY during that period, Esposito served for a time as manager and later site master of the scorpion laboratory at AMNH. She also spent substantial time performing research in the field, traveling throughout the United States as well as to countries such as Jamaica, Aruba, and the Dominican Republic.

CALIFORNIA ACADEMY OF SCIENCES

The recipient of a postdoctoral fellowship in biology from the National Science Foundation (NSF), Esposito moved to California after completing her doctorate and took a postdoctoral position at the Evolab at the Essig Museum of Entomology, University of California, Berkeley. She remained in that position until mid-2014, when she began a yearlong stint as a middle school science curriculum and apps developer with Berkeley's Lawrence Hall of Science Learning Design Group. The following year, Esposito moved to the California Academy of Sciences, a museum and research institute based in San Francisco's Golden Gate Park. "I'd been trained as a museum scientist since I was nineteen years old, and all I wanted to do is museum science," she later told the institution's website. "The Academy, with its opportunities for community engagement and outreach, was always at the top of my list." Esposito took on the title of assistant curator and Schlinger Chair of Arachnology at the California Academy of Sciences in September of 2015.

In her role as an assistant curator, Esposito was responsible in part for overseeing the collections of arachnid specimens at the institution. "These collections have been made by countless researchers over hundreds of years, and represent a window in time and space," she told *Untamed Science*. In addition, Esposito continued to perform research and share her knowledge with both fellow arachnologists and the public. "I lead expeditions to the far-flung corners of the earth to try to document the species of arachnids that we share the earth with," she explained to *Untamed Science*. "An equally important aspect of my job is communicating science through education programs, lectures, and outreach all over the world." Educational programs offered by the academy include hands-on arachnid laboratory sessions as well as science activities for children to complete independently. Aware that fear of scorpions and other arachnids is prevalent in society, Esposito also worked to dispel that fear, noting at times that very few of the spiders and scorpions native to the United States are actually dangerous to humans.

SCORPION RESEARCH

Over the course of her career in arachnology, much of Esposito's research has focused on scorpions, a diverse population of arachnids that can help researchers better understand phenomena such as evolution, biodiversity, and climate change. "I'm really interested in big questions about how life evolved on earth and what it means for us," she explained to Beery. "Scorpions are an amazing way to study that because they have been around for 450 million years. They've been incredibly successful at adapting to conditions on earth and keeping up with the pace of evolution."

In addition to studying the scorpion specimens in the California Academy of Sciences' collections, Esposito at times embarked on field research expeditions to regions such as the Caribbean and South America with the goal of identifying and describing new species of scorpion. "The Caribbean in general is pretty well trodden," she told the academy's website. "As one of the most biodiverse regions on Earth, we think we have a pretty good sense of what's there, but we actually don't." In 2017, Esposito and a group of colleagues published their descriptions of three previously unknown species—*Ischnotelson peruassu, Physoctonus striatus,* and *Rhopalurus ochoai*—found in South America.

ISLANDS AND SEAS

Alongside her work at the California Academy of Sciences, Esposito operated the nonprofit organization Islands and Seas, which she had founded in 2013 with former AMNH colleague Eric Stiner. "The academic system evaluates people on how often they publish and get grants, but we believed that scientists should also be valued for things like mentorship, outreach and conservation outcomes," she explained to Beery about the origins of the project. "We wanted to do something that directly made the world better." Dedicated to research, education, and conservation, Islands and Seas was founded with the goal of establishing multiple small field stations in locations around the world. Designed to be minimally disruptive to the environment, the field stations would serve as home bases for visiting researchers and also host educational programs for local populations, including youth programs on conservation and scientific training programs for older participants.

For Esposito, Islands and Seas tied into her longstanding belief in the importance of protecting natural habitats and educating others about the importance of scientific research. "I feel a personal sense of responsibility to be a steward for the planet and do my best to document what's here and figure out how not to lose it," she explained to Schultz about her worldview. The organization established its first field facility in San Juanico, Mexico, in Baja California. Located near a national reserve area as well as a biodiverse coastline, the site featured a camp and field laboratory to which Esposito and Stiner could travel with groups of interested participants. The organization also purchased a boat to serve as a research vessel and began work on a field guide to local wildlife.

500 QUEER SCIENTISTS

In 2018, Esposito and a group of colleagues founded the 500 Queer Scientists campaign, which sought to increase the visibility of queer individuals working in scientific fields. Inspired by the existing organization 500 Women Scientists, to which Esposito had previously contributed, the 500 Queer Scientists website (*500queerscientists.com*) presented profiles of scientists in which they discussed their careers and share information about their individual experiences in science. The project was a particularly important one for Esposito, who was inspired to create it after realizing that she was the first openly queer person to fill a California Academy of Sciences curator position and that she had at times struggled with feelings of isolation during her early career. "We began with 50 brave and proud scientists willing to tell their story, and in the past three years have grown to more than 1,500 stories from across the globe, across the STEM spectrum, and across the spectrum of identities that our community encompasses," she wrote for the California Academy of Sciences' website several years after the campaign's debut. "I can proudly say that I am no longer alone!" *500 Queer Scientists.com* received extensive media coverage following its launch, and a total of more than 1,700 people had shared their stories on its website by August 2022. In addition to cofounding 500 Queer Scientists, Esposito also joined the organization EntoPOC, which worked to increase the visibility of people of color working in entomology and to help more people of color to enter that field, including by providing young entomologists with paid memberships in relevant professional societies.

PERSONAL LIFE

Esposito moved to California with her partner after accepting a position at Berkeley, settling in San Francisco. She has two children. In addition to spending time exploring the outdoors while leading research expeditions, Esposito enjoys hiking as a recreational activity.

SUGGESTED READING

"Arachnologists Discover Three New Species of Club-Tailed Scorpions." *Sci News*, 28 July 2017, www.sci.news/biology/three-new-species-club-tailed-scorpions-05083.html. Accessed 8 Aug. 2022.

Esposito, Lauren. "Arachnologist Lauren Esposito Is on a Mission to Empower Queer Scientists." Interview by Zoë Beery. *Bustle*, 30 Nov. 2020, www.bustle.com/rule-breakers/arachnologist-lauren-esposito-is-on-a-mission-to-empower-queer-scientists. Accessed 8 Aug. 2022.

___. "How One Entomologist Has Created Community for LGBTQ+ Scientists." *Entomology Today*, 30 June 2022, entomologytoday.org/2022/06/30/lauren-esposito-entomologist-created-community-lgbtq-scientists/. Accessed 8 Aug. 2022.

___. "Lauren Esposito—Scorpion Biologist." *Untamed Science*, untamedscience. com/entomologists/lauren-esposito-entomologist/. Interview. Accessed 8 Aug. 2022.

___. "New Science: Lauren Esposito." *California Academy of Sciences*, www.calacademy.org/new-science/lauren-esposito. Accessed 8 Aug. 2022.

"Lauren Esposito." *California Academy of Science*, www.calacademy.org/learn-explore/science-heroes/lauren-esposito. Accessed 8 Aug. 2022.

Schultz, Kevin. "World's Only Female Scorpion Expert on Lookout for New Species." *San Francisco Chronicle*, 25 Dec. 2015, www.sfchronicle.com/bayarea/article/World-s-only-female-scorpion-expert-on-lookout-6720569.php. Accessed 8 Aug. 2022.

—*Joy Crelin*

Jim Fitterling

Born: ca. 1961–62
Occupation: Business executive

Jim Fitterling is the chairman and chief executive officer (CEO) of Dow Inc., the international industrial chemical company best known for producing a wide variety of chemicals and plastics. Dow employs more than fifty-four thousand people across the globe and has offices in more than 160 countries. Under Fitterling's leadership, the company posted sales of more than $39 billion in 2020.

Fitterling, who has worked for Dow since 1984, has endeavored to change the company's public image since he became CEO in 2018 and chairman in 2020. Historically, the company has often been associated with the abundance of plastic pollution in the world, and at one time was well-known for creating napalm, one of the most dangerous substances used during the Vietnam War. Fitterling has sought to place Dow at the forefront of global ecological issues and sustainability by seeking a market-based solution to climate change and ensuring the recycling of plastic, which he contends has the lowest CO_2 footprint of all packaging materials on the market. Moreover, he has overseen efforts to make Dow more devoted to equity by recruiting the top minds in the field of engineering, regardless of their backgrounds. Fitterling said during an interview with Jeff Green for *Bloomberg* (20 Mar. 2019), "I've put a lot of my life into the company, and I understand the company really well, and I know what it takes to deliver good financial results."

EARLY LIFE AND EDUCATION

Little has been published about Fitterling's early life. James Ray Fitterling was born in Missouri and received his education at the University of Missouri (Mizzou) in Columbia, Missouri. While attending the university's engineering program from 1979 to 1983, he was active in the FarmHouse fraternity, where he was athletic chair, treasurer, and president, and was the chair of the Board of Elections for the Missouri Students Association. He also played trumpet with the Marching Mizzou.

Upon earning his Bachelor of Science degree in mechanical engineering, Fitterling received a job offer from Dow Chemical, located in Midland, Michigan. "Thirty-three years ago, I sat where you're sitting now—just a kid from a small Missouri farm town with a degree in mechanical engineering and a job offer from Dow Chemical," he recalled in his 2016 commencement speech for the School of Engineering at the University of Missouri. "And like you, I had no idea what the future would bring. But I can tell you this: It has been a terrific experience, and I am thankful every day that I am an engineer."

MOVING UP THE CORPORATE LADDER

Dow Chemical was founded in 1897 by Herbert Henry Dow, who had immigrated to the United States from Canada because the area around Midland was rich in bromine, a chemical used to make medicines, photographs, and other products. Throughout its long history, Dow has made several familiar household items, including Saran Wrap and Styrofoam, as well as a wide variety of plastic products still used today. It also made napalm, an incendiary chemical

used to devastating effect by the US military during the Vietnam War (1955–75).

For the first decade of his employment at Dow, Fitterling worked in Dow Chemical Company's sales, marketing, and supply chain section. From 1994 to 1998, he served as commercial director of Dow Liquid Separations at Dow Pacific. He then became global business director of Dow Liquid Separations and president and CEO of Dow's FilmTec Corporation, a thin-film membrane manufacturer, holding both of those positions until 2000. Next moving overseas, he became the general manager of Dow Thailand and managing director of SCC–Dow Group.

From 2000 to 2005 Fitterling was the CEO of the OPTIMAL Group, an affiliate of Petronas, a Malaysian national oil and gas company, and the Dow Chemical Company. He then served as Dow's business vice president of polyethylene from 2005 to 2007. Promoted to Dow's president of basic plastics in 2007, he then went on to serve as Dow's vice president of corporate development.

In 2010, Fitterling became an executive vice president, where he oversaw Dow's investments in feedstocks, energy, chemicals, hydrocarbons, plastics, and corporate development. In 2014, he was named vice chairman of business operations. In this position, he was in charge of Dow's investment strategy, supply chain, business services, environmental health and safety, and sustainability groups. He also had charge of several Dow businesses, including Dow Packaging and Specialty Plastics, Dow Elastomers, Dow Electrical and Telecommunications, as well as Dow's polyurethanes, epoxy, chemicals, hydrocarbons, and energy units. The following year, he became Dow's president and chief operating officer (COO), serving through February 2018.

During Fitterling's tenure as Dow's president and COO, Dow Chemical merged with DuPont in 2017 to become DowDuPont, a holding company formed for the purpose of eventually spinning off its divisions into separate public companies. Following the merger, he served concurrently as chief operating officer of DowDuPont's material science division from September 2017 through March 2019. Fitterling was named chief executive officer-elect of Dow in March 2018, becoming CEO that July when Andrew N. Liveris retired from the position.

LEADING DOW

In April 2019, Dow Inc., was spun off from DowDuPont into a public company, the parent company of Dow Chemical. In his position as CEO and, since April 2020, chairman, Fitterling has advocated for the usefulness of many of Dow's products, including plastic. In an interview with Jim Cramer for *CNBC* (28 Oct. 2021), in which Cramer questioned Dow's creation of plastics, Fitterling remarked, "I think what you have seen around the world is plastics have helped deliver fresh food, medicines . . . any number of things to a growing economy and a growing population and growing middle class." In 2019 Dow, at his direction, became a founding member of the Alliance to End Plastic Waste (AEPW), which seeks to create circular economies in which plastic is always recycled.

On Dow Investor Day on October 6, 2021, Fitterling announced that the corporation was launching a line of "fully circular plastic solutions" in 2022 as part of Dow's long-standing commitment to sustainability. "Sustainability has been a business imperative for us for more than 30 years. Our path toward zero-carbon emissions began in the early 2000s; and, last year, we announced our intent to be carbon neutral by 2050. Since 2005, we have already reduced our CO_2 emissions by 15%, and the announcements we made today will take us to ~30% total by 2030."

As one of the world's largest chemical manufacturers, Dow consumes a significant amount of electricity and natural gas. While the corporation is committed to achieving a zero-carbon footprint over the long term, Fitterling has publicly stated that he has reservations about some of the green-energy proposals coming from Congress and the administration of President Joe Biden. In 2021, for example, he questioned how Congress would be able to pay for a move to zero-carbon emissions if it restricted using natural gas, which is seen by many as a cleaner petrochemical. He believes that the administration's plan to get to 100 percent clean-energy sources by 2035 is not feasible with the current levels of technology. "It's not incrementally more expensive than what we do today, it's much more expensive than what we do today, and the challenge . . . is the government has to figure out how to pay for it," Fitterling told Christopher M. Matthews and Timothy Puko for *The Wall Street Journal*

(27 Aug. 2021). "What we have to do is create a clear rationale for this move to zero carbon, and start to get some economics behind it." In other interviews, Fitterling has stressed the need for the world to adopt environmental policies like those in Canada, a country that is building an infrastructure to capture CO_2 emissions in addition to creating emission caps and trading systems.

Because Dow makes considerable use of freshwater in its factories around the world, Fitterling has also sought to strengthen Dow's commitment to ensuring clean water for generations to come. As he explained in a presentation for the Water Resilience Coalition, of which Dow is a founding member: "Dow is implementing natural, long-term solutions that improve water security in water-stressed areas to lower pollution in groundwater and build coastal resilience against storms. These actions to restore, manage and protect natural ecosystems have increased the resilience of our business operations while also providing broader environmental, social and economic benefits."

ACCOLADES AND ASSOCIATIONS

Throughout his extensive career, Fitterling has received numerous accolades for his leadership in business and his community. In 2016, he was inducted into the Great Lakes Bay Region Junior Achievement Hall of Fame. A year later, the American Institute of Chemical Engineers (AIChE) presented him with the Doing a World of Good Medal. In 2018, he received the College of Engineering Alumni Award from the Mizzou Alumni Association and was named the number one LGBT+ Executive on the "OUTstanding in Business" list published annually by INvolve. The following year he joined the Out Leadership Global Advisory Board. In 2021, he was inducted into the OUTstanding Hall of Fame.

In addition to his advocacy and leadership at Dow, Fitterling is in leadership positions with the boards of directors of several companies and associations. He is chair of the National Association of Manufacturers, a former chair and current board member for the American Chemistry Council, and a board member for 3M, Catalyst, the US–China Business Council, the Business Roundtable, and the Detroit Economic Club.

PERSONAL LIFE

While posted in Hong Kong in 1994, Fitterling met the man who became his longtime partner and spouse. For the first thirty years of his career at Dow, no one apart from a few close friends knew that he was gay—even though Dow has earned a perfect score for its inclusive LGBTQ+ policies from the Human Rights Campaign Foundation's Corporate Equality Index since 2005. A cancer diagnosis in 2008 made him reevaluate the way he had been living his life, however. "I was going through several surgeries, a year's worth of chemo," he recalled to Green. "I started to look around and say, you know, I'm going to have to make some changes in my life. And one day I was thinking about a lot of stresses that I needed to reduce, and one of them was trying to live two different lives." At that point, he decided to come out to his close colleagues. In 2014, he came out at a company event for National Coming Out Day and married his husband the following year. Fitterling lives in Midland, Michigan.

SUGGESTED READING

"Dow Chemical President, MAE Alumnus Delivers Commencement Address." *MU College of Engineering*, University of Missouri, 19 Dec. 2016, engineering. missouri.edu/2016/12/dow-chemical-president-mae-alumnus-delivers-commencement-address/. Accessed 4 Jan. 2022.

Fitterling, Jim. "CNBC Transcript: Dow Chairman and CEO Jim Fitterling Speaks with CNBC's Jim Cramer Live During CNBC's ESG Impact Conference Today." Interview by Jim Cramer. *CNBC*, 28 Oct. 2021, www.cnbc.com/2021/10/28/cnbc-transcript-dow-chairman-and-ceo-jim-fitterling-speaks-with-cnbcs-jim-cramer-live-during-cnbcs-esg-impact-conference-today.html. Transcript. Accessed 21 Jan. 2022.

___. "Further Growth, More Sustainable Future." *Dow Corporate*, 6 Oct. 2021, corporate.dow.com/en-us/seek-together/investor-day-2021.html. Accessed 3 Jan. 2022.

Green, Jeff. "How Dow Chemical Got Woke." *Bloomberg*, 20 Mar. 2019, www.bloomberg.com/news/features/2019-03-20/how-dow-chemical-got-woke. Accessed 3 Jan. 2022.

Matthews, Christopher M., and Timothy Puko. "Dow CEO Warns of Price Tag on Clean-Energy Plans." *The Wall Street Journal*, 27 Aug. 2021, www.wsj.com/articles/dow-ceo-warns-of-price-tag-on-clean-energy-plans-11630056602. Accessed 3 Jan. 2022.

"Profiles in Leadership: Dow & Jim Fitterling." *Water Resilience Coalition*, UN Global Impact and Pacific Institute, ceowatermandate.org/resilience/profiles-leadership/profiles-in-leadership-dow-jim-fitterling/. Accessed 4 Jan. 2022.

—*Christopher Mari*

Colt Ford

Born: August 27, 1969
Occupation: Musician

Although Colt Ford grew up with a love for music, it was sidelined early on by his love of sports, particularly golf, and his perception of the greater financial stability available in building a career off his skills on the golf course rather than risking navigating the often-luck-based music industry. He spent several years of his adult life as a professional golfer—one of his contemporaries was Phil Mickelson—and golf club teacher. After collaborating as a writer here and there musically with artists/producers such as Jermaine Dupri, and meeting Shannon Houchins, a producer credited with shaping the modern country-rap sound, in the early 1990s, Ford eventually shifted gears. In addition to cofounding an independent record label in the 2000s, he began recording the kind of songs he had always loved to write and fully devoted himself to a music career.

Though country singers and rappers had parlayed before, Ford's music succeeds in marrying the genres in one artist. His song "Dirt Road Anthem," cowritten and recorded for his 2008 debut album, *Ride through the Country*, brought hip-hop beats to mainstream country music when it became a massive radio hit in 2011 in the hands of country star Jason Aldean. Jon Caramanica, a music critic for *The New York Times* (17 Apr. 2019), described Aldean's cover of "Dirt Road Anthem" as an important turning point in the immersion of rap into country music. "[Aldean] catapulted rapping to the center of the country conversation: His [version] was a No. 1 Hot Country

Songs hit and made it plain that hip-hop was an inevitable—and surprisingly welcome—influence on the genre."

This boost from Aldean gave Ford's music career a momentum that has continued into the 2020s—a lucky break for the Georgia-born golfer. He has released several studio albums, including the country chart–topping *Declaration of Independence* in 2012 and 2019's *We the People*. "I've lived two dream jobs," he told Jeff Shain for *Morning Read* (5 Feb. 2019). "I don't want to ever let go, if I can help it."

EARLY LIFE AND PRO GOLF CAREER

Colt Ford was born Jason Farris Brown on August 27, 1969, and grew up in Athens, Georgia. From an early age, he loved sports—his father, who owned a used-car company, also worked as a baseball coach—and excelled at baseball and golf. Attending Clarke Central High School, he played golf at the junior level, achieving regional titles as well as being named a high school All-American golfer. Motivated to have the potential to earn at least a stable living through the game, he continued to hone his golf game as a student first at Central Alabama Community College and then at the University of Georgia before going on to turn professional, competing on various mini-tour circuits. "I played for a long time," he told Kevin Prise for the *PGA Tour* website (15 May 2015). "I was lucky to make a living playing golf for about 7 or 8 years, then I became a teaching pro." Among his former students is four-time (as of 2021) PGA Tour winner Kevin Kisner.

COMMITTING FULLY TO A MUSIC CAREER

Ford might have been content to continue teaching golf, but the recession beginning around 2007 forced him to reconsider his plans. Along with a friend, he had recently launched a business, traveling with clients to golf courses abroad, but the venture had stalled. Ford turned again to music, which he has often called his "first love," but had felt would be, as opposed to golf, a riskier career venture: "You've got to have some talent, and God gave me some," he explained to Shain. "But there's a lot of luck involved, too." During his developmental years he had listened to classic country acts while writing lyrics of his own before he had even turned ten. In high school, he fell in love with

Photo by Dj virt, via Wikimedia Commons

the hip-hop group Run-DMC and made an album with a local producer. He would continue to write and work in music, even as he later began to focus on his career as a golfer. This included meeting, working with, and learning from producer Dupri for several years in the 1990s, contributing as a writer on projects for acts like Kris Kross. It was this connection to Dupri that fostered Ford's longtime friendship and business relationship with hip-hop record producer Houchins, who had become involved with Dupri's So So Def Recordings and would be considered instrumental in country-rap evolution. Around 2006, Ford teamed up with Houchins to establish a record label called Average Joes Entertainment.

Ford and Houchins were interested in making country music infused with rap but were concerned that a mainstream space and audience in country did not really exist yet for the unique genre. "Now, you're talking about a guy who's sold 40 million records as a producer," Ford explained to Bob Doerschuk for the *Moultrie Observer* in Georgia (16 July 2011), referring to Houchins as he discussed their efforts to get their label, headquartered in Nashville, off the ground. "And when we get to Nashville, everyone is looking at us like we're just a couple of bums on the street."

RIDE THROUGH THE COUNTRY AND CHICKEN AND BISCUITS

Meanwhile, Ford had yet to record his own music according to his authentic style that he had more recently embraced melding country with hip-hop. However, having attended many of its events, he wrote a song for the sports organization Professional Bull Riders (PBR). PBR's CEO, whom he was friends with, loved it, and "Buck 'Em" became PBR's official anthem for the season. The hip-hop song—and debut of the artist's "Colt Ford" persona—motivated him to write and record his first album, *Ride through the Country*, in 2008.

One of the album's featured tracks, a collaboration with singer-songwriter Brantley Gilbert called "Dirt Road Anthem," proved to be one of Ford's most influential early songs. Written by Ford and Gilbert, it was inspired by the rural roads of Athens. Country singer Aldean recorded a cover of "Dirt Road Anthem" that was included on his album *My Kinda Party* (2010), and in 2011 it served as one of its singles. His version was a top-ten mainstream hit that reached number one on the Billboard Country Airplay chart, was nominated for a Grammy Award, and secured some of the highest digital song sales numbers—which helped make Ford's *Ride through the Country* a grassroots hit and earned him, as one of the song's writers, a 2011 Country Music Association Award nomination for Song of the Year. Responding to the success of "Dirt Road Anthem," Ford told Jewly Hight for *Rolling Stone* (8 July 2014), "We didn't have any idea that we would write a song that would be that monumentally big. . . . We were just writing about what we liked." At the same time, Average Joes' list of signed artists such as Montgomery Gentry had continued to grow.

Chicken and Biscuits (2010), Ford's acclaimed second album, cracked the top ten of the Billboard Top Country Albums chart. As he remained committed to his honest style as well as collaborating with other artists despite radio play, the album features stars like Darryl Worley, Randy Houser, and James Otto. The song "Ride On, Ride Out" features Darryl "DMC" McDaniels of Run-DMC, a hero of Ford's who became a Ford fan. To maintain momentum, he performed several live shows, and he would continue to do so in the future, as it is an aspect of the job that he has particularly enjoyed.

EVERY CHANCE I GET AND DECLARATION OF INDEPENDENCE

Ford's third album, *Every Chance I Get* (2011), includes guest appearances by Eric Church, Luke Bryan, Nappy Roots, and Tim McGraw, with the latter collaborating on the popular song "Twisted." Other notable songs on the record, which climbed the Top Country Albums chart even higher to number three, include the title track, its only solo and the first one to feature Ford singing.

The year 2012 saw the release of *Declaration of Independence*, Ford's first number-one album on the Top Country Albums chart. It features another eclectic lineup of guests including Kix Brooks of Brooks and Dunn, Wanya Morris of Boyz II Men, and Darius Rucker, the former lead singer of Hootie and the Blowfish who subsequently launched a country career. Aldean joins in on "Drivin' Around Song," which evokes "Dirt Road Anthem." Though the album also yielded Ford's first country top-forty single, "Back," featuring country singer Jake Owen, in interviews around its release Ford expressed some frustration in his songs' continued lack of radio airplay. Proud of his output and citing the fact that many of his fans were "diehard country people," he told Billy Dukes for *Taste of Country* (23 Aug. 2012), "I just want a chance to be heard, you know? I just want the same chance everyone else has. I know I don't sound like everybody else, but I shouldn't, should I?"

FURTHER ALBUMS AND ENTERTAINING DURING A PANDEMIC

Ford released his fifth album, *Thanks for Listening*, in 2014. With Ford still attracting high-profile figures for his projects, the album features country music veteran Keith Urban as well as reality television star Willie Robertson of *Duck Dynasty*. The album's lead single was "The High Life," featuring Chase Rice, but commentators and Ford himself took note of the more somber "Workin' On," about a man coming to terms with his vices and his past. The release of *Thanks for Listening* coincided with the publication of a comic book series called *Average Joes*, in which Ford and other Average Joes labelmates are superheroes who fight crime.

Over the course of the next three years, Ford toured and put out a compilation album. *Love Faith Hope*, his sixth studio album, with guests the likes of Toby Keith and Brad Paisley, was released in 2017 while his seventh album, *We the People*, was released in 2019. The latter's title was intended to inspire unity at a time of profound political division. The titular song, a bluesy rock banger, invites people to come together. "When I first heard this song, I knew it was the right song to record and release considering all the division in our country right now," Ford told Chris Parton for *Sounds Like Nashville* (9 May 2019). "'We the People' is not a political song—it's a song about enjoying one another, finding a way to get along, finding a way to have fun, finding a way to continue to build this country and this world into a better place." Guests on the album include Mitchell Tenpenny and Jimmie Allen.

Even as Ford made a name for himself as a musician, his passion for golf also remained, and in addition to having taken part in several celebrity events throughout the years, in late 2020 he tentatively returned to professional golf, playing two tournaments on the PGA Champions Tour. Because the coronavirus disease 2019 (COVID-19) pandemic declared in early 2020 and its associated virus control measures such as lockdowns and physical distancing meant that he had been forced to abstain from, and then severely limit, live performances, in interviews he expressed particular excitement about having the chance to participate in the golf events. While 2020 saw the release of an expanded version of *Chicken and Biscuits* with a few new tracks, in 2021 he reported working on more of his own music while also helping Average Joes artists with production in between performing on tour as pandemic conditions allowed. In November 2021, he put out the EP *Keys to the Country*, consisting of six new collaborative tracks.

PERSONAL LIFE

Ford and his wife, Jessica, have two children. In 2021, he reported that he had undergone surgery to remove a cancerous spot on one of his eyes.

SUGGESTED READING

Caramanica, Jon. "A History of Country-Rap in 29 Songs." *The New York Times*, 17 Apr. 2019, www.nytimes.com/2019/04/17/arts/music/country-rap-playlist.html. Accessed 15 Dec. 2021.

Doerschuk, Bob. "Colt Ford: Talking Country." *The Moultrie Observer*, 16 July 2011, updated 28 July 2014, www.moultrieobserver.com/news/local_news/article_685c5c22-e49d-5313-a0e2-2e80ac969f58.html. Accessed 14 Dec. 2021.

Ford, Colt. "Colt Ford Interview: 'Declaration of Independence' Is His Best Record, but May Be His Last." Interview by Billy Dukes. *Taste of Country*, 23 Aug. 2012, tasteofcountry.com/colt-ford-declaration-of-independence-interview/. Accessed 15 Dec. 2021.

___. "Colt Ford on Beating the Country Odds and Thanking His Fans." Interview by Jewly Hight. *Rolling Stone*, 8 July 2014, www.rollingstone.com/music/music-country/colt-ford-on-beating-the-country-odds-and-thanking-his-fans-243751/. Accessed 15 Dec. 2021.

___. "Q&A: Ford on His Transition from Pro Golfer to Country Music Star." Interview by Kevin Prise. *PGA Tour*, 15 May 2015, www.pgatour.com/korn-ferry-tour/news/2015/05/15/colt-ford-bmw-charity-pro-am.html. Accessed 14 Dec. 2021.

Parton, Chris. "Colt Ford Calls for 'Party' Unity in Rocking New Single, 'We the People.'" *Sounds Like Nashville*, 9 May 2019, www.soundslikenashville.com/music/colt-ford-wethepeople-exclusive-premiere/. Accessed 14 Dec. 2021.

Shain, Jeff. "Colt Ford Plays Familiar Tune at Pebble." *Morning Read*, Sports Illustrated, 5 Feb. 2019, www.si.com/golf/news/feature-2019-02-05-colt-ford-plays-familiar-tune-at-pebble. Accessed 15 Dec. 2021.

SELECTED WORKS

Ride through the Country, 2008; *Chicken and Biscuits*, 2010; *Declaration of Independence*, 2012; *Thanks for Listening*, 2014; *We the People*, 2019; *Keys to the Country*, 2021

—*Molly Hagan*

Thomas Forster

Born: 1986
Occupation: Ballet dancer

When the coronavirus disease 2019 (COVID-19) pandemic forced performance venues throughout the United States to close in early 2020, ballet dancer Thomas

Forster wondered what that interruption to his performing schedule would mean for his career. A longtime dancer with the American Ballet Theatre (ABT) who was promoted from corps de ballet member to soloist in 2015, Forster had been experiencing a career upswing prior to the pandemic and had been scheduled to dance prominent roles in the company's upcoming productions. The cancellation of the ABT's scheduled seasons, then, put his work on hold for an uncertain amount of time—a concerning prospect for a dancer who, already in his thirties, was considered to be approaching the final years of his performing career. "There was definitely a moment when I thought, 'Wait, can I still do this?'" he recalled to Marina Harss for *The New York Times* (20 Oct. 2021). His concern, however, proved unnecessary: promoted to principal dancer with the ABT in September 2020, he returned to the stage as venues reopened in 2021, taking on increasingly high-profile roles in ballets such as *Giselle*. He also made his debut as an author during that period, publishing the children's book *My Daddy Can Fly!* in late 2021. Scheduled to dance at major venues such as the Metropolitan Opera House during the ABT's 2022 summer season, Forster expressed appreciation for his continued opportunities to exhibit his skills as a performer. "I'm just trying to work as hard as I can and enjoy it for what it is," he told Harss.

EARLY LIFE AND EDUCATION

Thomas Alfred Forster was born in London, England, in 1986. One of three children, he grew up in the Penge area of southeast London. As a young child, he aspired to take karate classes to emulate his personal heroes, the cartoon characters the Teenage Mutant Ninja Turtles; however, he was unable to enroll in martial arts due to his age. "Apparently I was too young, so my mom signed me up for ballet classes instead," he told *ALL ARTS* (16 Sept. 2021). In those classes, at a small ballet school located in a church, he was the only boy, and he was occasionally teased for his participation. Still, he continued with the lessons, initially viewing ballet as a means of strengthening his legs in preparation for future karate study. However, he soon demonstrated a talent for dance, and instructor June Lowdell encouraged him to pursue ballet further. With the support of his parents, he auditioned for

London's Royal Ballet School Junior Associate program at the age of eight and successfully secured a spot in the program, with which he trained for several years. There, he was enamored to find the classes filled with boys like himself pursuing the art of dance.

Upon aging out of the Junior Associate program, Forster was unable to secure a spot in the Royal Ballet School's Lower School and was thus forced to consider other options for his secondary education and continuing ballet training. "The schools were good where I was in London, but the education I could have got through going to a ballet school would have been so much higher, so Mum told me to audition for these boarding schools," he explained to *OfficialLondonTheatre.com* (20 Aug. 2013). He ultimately enrolled at Elmhurst School for Dance at the age of eleven and spent five years at that institution, later known as Elmhurst Ballet School. He went on to join the Royal Ballet School's Upper School in 2002. While a student at the Upper School, he visited the United States with a school group and caught the attention of the American Ballet Theatre (ABT), which subsequently offered him a position in its Studio Company. He graduated from the Upper School in 2005.

AMERICAN BALLET THEATRE

After completing his studies at the Upper School, Forster relocated to New York City, having accepted the offer to join the ABT Studio Company. "It was absolutely incredible—a young British boy getting a chance to live in New York? I jumped at the chance!" he recalled to Alice York for *Sheridan Road* magazine (2 Apr. 2019). "I was very lucky to be chosen and am so grateful." An ensemble made up of dancers in their late teens and early twenties, the Studio Company exists for the purpose of training talented young performers who might go on to become members of the main ABT company. In addition to completing extensive training and rehearsals, the group also performs and tours, giving its dancers valuable professional experience. Forster quickly made an impression at ABT, in part because of his size. At six foot three, he is unusually tall for a dancer, which has proved challenging at times. "It takes me a little longer to find myself," he explained to *Ballet News* (15 Feb. 2011). "Each person matures differently but I definitely feel being tall, there's so much resistance when you jump . . . and you really have to focus on what you're doing [or] otherwise you'll fall on the floor."

The year 2007 marked a turning point for Forster, who joined the main ABT company as an apprentice early in the year and was then promoted to the corps de ballet—members of the company who do not perform the roles set aside for higher ranked dancers such as soloists—by year's end. "It's a great company, everyone is so friendly," he later told *Ballet News* about the ABT. "The ballet masters and mistresses are really nice and they're there to help. It's just a nice atmosphere to work in, and you definitely feel self-improvement." Early ABT productions in which he appeared included the 2007 world premiere of *From Here on Out*, choreographed by the dancer and choreographer Benjamin Millepied, and the ABT premiere of *Baker's Dozen*, in which he played a featured role. He would continue to appear in several ABT premiere productions over the next years, including the 2012 production of *Blue Pas de Deux* at the Metropolitan Opera House, and in 2013 he created a role—that is, served as the first dancer to perform a particular role—in the new ballet *Aftereffect*.

SOLOIST

As a longtime member of the ABT's corps de ballet, Forster enjoyed having the opportunity to dance in a wide range of productions and did not focus on progressing through the ranks of his company. "I feel everyone wants to be principal or soloist but for me, honestly, I just want to be the best I can be," he told *Ballet News*. "I do get a lot of satisfaction from being given something and then taking it on and improving and doing it well. If something comes my way, great, if not then at least I've done my best." Nevertheless, he was promoted to soloist in 2015, a rank that would enable him to play more prominent roles in the company's productions.

Over the next several years, Forster appeared in numerous major productions, including the production *Seven Sonatas* (2016), *Thirteen Diversions* (2017), and the world premieres of *Garden Blue* and *Harlequinade* (2018). Though perhaps best known for performing in New York, he was also part of the ABT's 2019 residency at Chicago's Auditorium Theatre, during which he danced multiple parts in the ballet *Whipped Cream*.

PERSONAL TRAINER

While Forster found success as a dancer throughout his years with the ABT, he struggled at times with injuries, which he attributed in part to a problem with his shoulder joint. "I'm super loosey-goosey," he explained to Harss. "When I was young, every time I would lift a partner above my head, my left shoulder would subluxate, not a full dislocation, but it would pop in and out." In addition to undergoing surgery around 2007 to address his shoulder pain, he developed an interest in forms of exercise beyond dance itself, which he found to be essential to improving his overall physical conditioning.

Hoping to help other ballet dancers build strength, endurance, and mobility, Forster pursued studies in personal training and received full certification from the National Academy of Sports Medicine in 2017. "Ballet class doesn't give you great stamina," he told *Dance Magazine* (17 Feb. 2019), "so you need to do something else to really build that so when you have to do a variation that's fifteen minutes long and you're absolutely exhausted, your body can handle it." In the years after completing his certification program, he worked as a trainer for several ABT dancers and taught body conditioning classes at the ABT's Jacqueline Kennedy Onassis School.

PRINCIPAL DANCER

In early 2020, the COVID-19 pandemic necessitated the closure of most major performance venues, including New York City's Metropolitan Opera House. As a result, the ABT canceled many of its productions scheduled for that year, including a planned production of *Swan Lake* in which Forster was set to play a major role. Though he was initially concerned about his future with the company, his worries were alleviated somewhat in September 2020, when the ABT promoted him to principal dancer—the highest level of dancer in the company. He returned to in-person performance for the ABT fall 2021 season, which saw the company stage a number of works at New York's David H. Koch Theatre. In October of that year, he performed the role of Count Albrecht in the ABT production of the ballet *Giselle*. He received extensive critical acclaim for his performance, although Forster himself preferred to focus on the experience rather than the accolades. "I'm really at the last stage of my career, and I'm just enjoying every moment," he told Harss.

A new milestone in Forster's career came in November 2021 with the release of his debut children's book, *My Daddy Can Fly!* Cowritten with author and dancer Shari Siadat and illustrated by Jami Gigot, *My Daddy Can Fly!* features a child protagonist based on Forster's own son and seeks both to inspire boys to dance and to dispel stereotypes about male ballet dancers. "The message I want the book to share is that whatever you want to do as a young person, work hard and go for it," Forster told April Deocariza for *Pointe* (9 Nov. 2021). Forster himself was set to take that advice in 2022, during which he was scheduled to dance in several of the ABT's touring engagements, including a March production of *Don Quixote* at the John F. Kennedy Center for the Performing Arts in Washington, DC. He was additionally scheduled to perform during the ABT 2022 summer season at the Metropolitan Opera House, where he was set to dance principal roles in *Don Quixote*, *Swan Lake*, and *Romeo and Juliet*, among other productions.

PERSONAL LIFE

Forster married Leann Underwood, a dancer affiliated with the ABT, in 2013. Their son, Benjamin, was born in 2016, and the couple later divorced. Forster lives in New Jersey.

SUGGESTED READING

"Brits Abroad—American Ballet Theatre's Thomas Forster." *Ballet News*, 15 Feb. 2011, www.balletnews.co.uk/ballet-news-brits-abroad-american-ballet-theatres-thomas-forster/. Accessed 7 Mar. 2022.

Deocariza, April. "Thomas Forster's New Children's Book 'My Daddy Can Fly!' Celebrates Men in Ballet." *Pointe*, 9 Nov. 2021, pointemagazine.com/thomas-forster-book/. Accessed 7 Mar. 2022.

Forster, Thomas. "Introducing . . . Thomas Forster." *OfficialLondonTheatre.com*, 20 Aug. 2013, officiallondontheatre.com/news/introducing-thomas-forster-113828/. Accessed 7 Mar. 2022.

___. "Principal Dancer Thomas Forster Shares His Favorite Books." *ALL ARTS*, 16 Sept. 2021, allarts.org/2021/09/ballerina-book-club-thomas-forster/. Accessed 7 Mar. 2022.

Giles, Jessica. "5 Workout Tips from an ABT Dancer Who's Also a Personal Trainer." *Dance Magazine*, 17 Feb. 2019, www.dancemagazine.com/ballet-personal-trainer/. Accessed 7 Mar. 2022.

Harss, Marina. "An Unassuming Prince Dons the Velvet Cloak at Ballet Theater." *The New York Times*, 20 Oct. 2021, www.nytimes.com/2021/10/20/arts/dance/thomas-forster-american-ballet-theater.html. Accessed 7 Mar. 2022.

York, Alice. "Sweet Success." *Sheridan Road*, 2 Apr. 2019, jwcdaily.com/sheridanroadmagazine/2019/04/02/sweet-success/. Accessed 7 Mar. 2022.

—Joy Crelin

Carolina Gaitán

Born: April 4, 1984
Occupation: Actor and singer

The 2021 animated film *Encanto* was a major hit both in theatrical release and on the streaming service Disney+, an outcome that was unsurprising considering the established popularity of the Disney brand. Less expected, however, was the popularity of the song "We Don't Talk about Bruno," an ensemble number from the film that went on to receive widespread radio play in the United States and in January 2022 reached the number-one position on the Billboard Hot 100 chart. Carolina Gaitán, one of the primary singers on the track as the voice of the character Pepa, was among those stunned but pleased by the song's major cultural impact. "None of us were expecting this phenomenon," she told Josh Smith in an interview for *Glamour UK* (10 Feb. 2022). "I also think that when you do things without expecting that much then the surprise is even more beautiful and that's exactly what happened here." The remarkable success of *Encanto* and, especially, "We Don't Talk about Bruno" also brought Gaitán a new level of international celebrity status as both an actor and singer.

Gaitán began her entertainment industry career in her native Colombia in 2002, when she was selected as a member of the pop group Escarcha during her appearance in the local edition of the reality series *Popstars*. After Escarcha disbanded, she established herself as a Colombian television star, with prominent roles in series such as *Gabriela, giros del destino* (2009–10), *Celia* (2015–16), and *Sin senos sí hay paraíso* (2016–18). While she occasionally appeared in projects geared toward the US market during that time, including episodes of the Netflix series *Narcos* in 2015, *Encanto* represented something of an international breakout role. Gaitán also appreciated how the animated film's Colombian setting and characters could help give international audiences a greater understanding of Colombia and its people. "Every scene, every song, every frame, even the dress and fashion of all of them represents different regions and parts of our country," she told Alexandra Whittaker in an interview for *Cosmopolitan* (2 Mar. 2022). "It's fantastic, being a Colombian and being a Latina, seeing that told in a different way."

EARLY LIFE AND CAREER

Carolina del Pilar Gaitán Lozano was born on April 4, 1984, in Villavicencio, Colombia. Her father worked as a pilot. Although drawn to performing from a young age, she initially planned to pursue a career in journalism. Her trajectory changed, however, after a friend encouraged her to enter a singing contest that was taking place.

The singing contest was, in fact, the 2002 season of the competitive reality show *Popstars*, and Gaitán was ultimately selected to appear in the program. Over the course of the show, she and four other female singers were assembled into the singing group Escarcha. The group's first album, also titled *Escarcha*, was released in 2002. Escarcha went on to release a second album, the 2003 record *Siempre hay algo más* (*There Is Always Something More*), before disbanding in 2004. Gaitán later spent time in the United States where she studied at the prestigious Lee Strasberg Theatre and Film Institute.

TELEVISION CAREER

Building on the fame she had earned with Escarcha, Gaitán—who also became known as La Gaita—found substantial success in Colombian television, especially on telenovelas. Her early credits included series such as *Vuelo 1503* [*Flight 1503*] (2005), *Zona rosa* (*Pink Zone*; 2007), and *Isa TKM* (2009–10). She took on her largest role to that point in 2009, when she debuted as the title character in the series *Gabriela, giros del destino* (Gabriela, Turns of Destiny). Encompassing more than two hundred episodes, the series aired in Colombia

Photo by Andrés Salgado, via Wikimedia Commons.

through 2010. She went on to appear in a variety of other television projects over the next several years, including the 2013 series *Alias el Mexicano*.

In 2015 Gaitán costarred in the series *Las hermanitas Calle* (*The Calle Sisters*), a fictionalization of the lives of the real-world Colombian singing duo of that name. Portraying Calle sister Nelly in the series, she also contributed vocals to the series' soundtrack album. Gaitán once again played a singer in the television series *Celia*, which aired between 2015 and 2016 and tells a story based on the life of the Cuban singer Celia Cruz. Gaitán portrayed Lola Calvo in that series, a fictional singer inspired by the Cuban singer La Lupe.

Also in 2015 Gaitán made her first significant appearance in a US project, with a multi-episode role in the hit Netflix series *Narcos*. She then went on to star in the Colombian television series *Sin senos sí hay paraíso* (*Without Breasts There Is Paradise*) from 2016 to 2018 and the follow-up *El final del paraíso* (*The End of Paradise*) in 2019. Those shows, both inspired by the work of Colombian writer Gustavo Bolívar, further cemented her status as a TV star within Colombia.

MUSIC CAREER

As her acting career progressed, Gaitán also gained attention as a singer. In addition to performing music as part of her roles in series such as *Las hermanitas Calle* and *Celia*, she recorded her own music from time to time. Perhaps most notably, in 2018 she released the six-song EP *La Gaita*.

Gaitán continued to release music digitally even while self-isolating during the early months of the COVID-19 pandemic in 2020, during which she released the single "Cerquita del mar [Close to the Sea]." Unlike her earlier work, "Cerquita del mar" enabled her to explore her interest in the bachata genre of music, to which she was introduced following the filming of *Celia*. "That got me into the tropical universe like bolero, salsa, and Cuban music which got me to bachata," she explained to Anthony Guivas in an interview for the *Young Folks* (3 Aug. 2020). "It's very fresh, you can dance to it, it's happy and romantic." In 2021 she released the EP *De Colombia*, a record featuring musical collaborations with fellow singers such as Mariana Gómez and Diana Ángel.

ENCANTO

Though already well known in Colombia, Gaitán reached a new level of fame in 2021 with the release of *Encanto*, the latest animated musical film created by Walt Disney Studios. Gaitán had initially auditioned for the film in person with the encouragement of a friend and, following the emergence of the COVID-19 pandemic, completed the remainder of her callback auditions through video calls. In addition to their unique format, the auditions surprised Gaitán by focusing on her experiences and personality more than her list of prior credits. "I thought that they were going to ask me about all my career and my achievements and what I have done but instead they said, 'Tell us about you. Who are you?'" she recalled to Smith. "I think that was the goal: they were hiring a human being behind a voice which was a really good lesson behind Disney, they are really looking for feelings behind the voices."

Following her auditions, Gaitán was cast as the character Pepa, the aunt of the film's protagonist, Mirabel Madrigal. *Encanto* follows the members of the Madrigal family, each of whom possesses a magical gift, with Pepa's being the ability to influence the weather with her emotions. Providing both the speaking voice and the singing voice for

the character was an enjoyable challenge for Gaitán, who sought to bring a great deal of expressiveness to the role. "With animation, it's about giving everything you've got and expressing using just your voice," she told Ana Escalante in an interview for *Glamour* (8 Feb. 2022). "It's a great experience."

Encanto premiered in November 2021 and opened in theaters worldwide over the next two months, becoming a box-office hit despite the lingering COVID-19 pandemic. In addition to proving popular among moviegoers, *Encanto* was received well by critics and went on to be nominated for numerous awards, including three Academy Awards. "Of course, we were not working to have [an award] or recognition of that kind because we are passionate about this and want to tell stories, but we want this as well!" Gaitán told Shirley Gómez in an interview for *Hola!* (16 Feb. 2022) about the nominations. The film ultimately won the Academy Award for best animated feature.

As a musical featuring songs written by the songwriter and performer Lin-Manuel Miranda, *Encanto* also received widespread recognition for its music, and particularly for the song "We Don't Talk about Bruno," an ensemble performance in which Gaitán is prominently featured. The song became a major hit in its own right following the release of the film, receiving extensive radio play and charting in several countries. In the United States, the song spent several months atop the Billboard Hot 100 chart after reaching the number-one position in January 2022. For Gaitán, the success of "We Don't Talk about Bruno" represented a crucial and exciting moment in her career, one further emphasized by the reception of *Encanto* overall. "This is opening a huge door to opportunities, so I have so much work to do and you'll hear a lot from me as an artist and as a person and as a human and as a singer," she told Whittaker. "I really want to work to make more dreams possible."

OTHER PROJECTS

Gaitán remained busy with Colombian television work in 2021 and 2022, appearing in series such as *MalaYerba* and *Juanpis González: La serie* (Juanpis González: The series). She also served as a judge on the Colombian edition of the competitive reality show *The X Factor*. In March 2022, the film-industry publication *Deadline* announced that Gaitán had been cast in a lead role in the thriller film *Quicksand*, which was set in Colombia and would be filmed there. In addition, she continued to record music, releasing the singles "I Am Bolero" and "Bailaito" in 2022. In May 2022, she was included in *Forbes Colombia*'s list of Colombia's fifty most powerful women.

Given the phenomenal success of *Encanto*, Gaitán also expressed interest in appearing in additional projects related to the film, such as a potential sequel or a stage musical version. "I think is not a crazy idea, and I also think that would be awesome," she told Gómez. "To not only do *Encanto 2* but also take it to Broadway."

PERSONAL LIFE

Gaitán married Nicolás Moreno, a DJ, in 2015. The couple had separated by mid-2021. Based in Colombia for much of her early career, Gaitán spent an increasing amount of time in the United States in the period leading up to and following the release of *Encanto*, although she maintained close ties with her home country.

SUGGESTED READING

Calvario, Liz. "'We Don't Talk about Bruno' Singer Carolina Gaitan on *Encanto*'s 'Surreal' Success and Oscar Noms (Exclusive)." *ET*, 9 Feb. 2022, www.etonline.com/we-dont-talk-about-bruno-singer-carolina-gaitan-on-encantos-surreal-success-and-oscar-noms. Accessed 9 May 2022.

Gaitán, Carolina. "Carolina Gaitán: The Multi-Hyphenate Colombian Superstar Shows the World the Magic of *Encanto*." Interview by Shirley Gómez. *Hola!*, 16 Feb. 2022, www.hola.com/us/entertainment/20220216309682/carolina-gaitan-reveals-if-encanto-will-have-second-part/. Accessed 9 May 2022.

___. "Carolina Gaitán on the Power of *Encanto*'s 'We Don't Talk about Bruno.'" Interview by Ana Escalante. *Glamour*, 8 Feb. 2022, www.glamour.com/story/carolina-gaitan-encanto-we-dont-talk-about-bruno. Accessed 9 May 2022.

___. "Carolina Gaitán Reveals Why We're All So Addicted to *Encanto*'s We Don't Talk about Bruno." Interview by Josh Smith. *Glamour UK*, 10 Feb. 2022, www.glamourmagazine.co.uk/article/encanto-carolina-gaitan-interview. Accessed 9 May 2022.

___. "Carolina Gaitán Talks about Her New Single 'Cerquita Del Mar.'" Interview by Anthony Guivas. *The Young Folks*, 3 Aug. 2020, www.theyoungfolks.com/music/145841/carolina-gaitan-talks-about-her-new-single-cerquita-del-mar/. Accessed 9 May 2022.

___. "*Encanto*'s Carolina Gaitán Is Ready to Talk about Bruno." Interview by Alexandra Whittaker. *Cosmopolitan*, 2 Mar. 2022, www.cosmopolitan.com/entertainment/movies/a39076542/encanto-carolina-gaitan-we-dont-talk-about-bruno-interview/. Accessed 9 May 2022.

Grater, Tom. "*Encanto* Actress Carolina Gaitán and *Jack Ryan*'s Allan Hawco Starring in Colombia-Set Thriller *Quicksand*." *Deadline*, 25 Mar. 2022, deadline.com/2022/03/encanto-actress-carolina-gaitan-jack-ryans-allan-hawco-starring-in-colombia-set-thriller-quicksand-1234986913/. Accessed 9 May 2022.

SELECTED WORKS

Zona rosa, 2007; *Gabriela, giros del destino* (2009–10); *Alias el Mexicano*, 2013; *Las hermanitas Calle*, 2015; *Narcos*, 2015; *Celia*, 2015–16; *Sin senos sí hay paraíso*, 2016–18; *Encanto*, 2021; *MalaYerba*, 2021– ; *Juanpis González: La serie*, 2022–

—*Joy Crelin*

Johnny Gandelsman

Born: March 27, 1978
Occupation: Violinist

Acclaimed violinist Johnny Gandelsman earned attention for his ability to seamlessly switch between the standard classical repertoire and crossover work blending elements of rock, jazz, and world music, among other genres. In 2005 he cofounded the group Brooklyn Rider, a string quartet that made a name for itself by merging longstanding classical-music traditions with contemporary compositions, a variety of international and folk styles, and a willingness to improvise. "I spend a lot of my time as a musician trying things I have not been officially trained to do," he told Corinna da Fonseca-Wollheim for *The New York Times* (30 Aug. 2013), noting that his experiments included forays into such disparate disciplines as fiddling and Baroque-style playing. "I do it because I love the music, and I want to understand how it works," he explained.

A highly collaborative musician, Gandelsman performed and recorded with other artists from around the world throughout his career, from fellow classical luminaries such as Yo-Yo Ma to rock icons such as David Byrne. In addition to Brooklyn Rider, he joined the acclaimed Silkroad Ensemble, with which he shared a Grammy Award for best world music album for *Sing Me Home* (2016). Gandelsman also became an in-demand producer, forming his own label, In a Circle Records, in 2008. He credited such extensive collaborations with informing his solo work, including his debut full-length album under his own name, *J. S. Bach Sonatas & Partitas for Violin* (2018), which topped the classical charts. He followed with *J. S. Bach: Complete Cello Suites* (2020), which drew praise for his distinctive adaptation of cello works to violin. "This music is something that every string player grows up with," Gandelsman told Vincent Harris for the *Greenville Journal* (12 Mar. 2020), while acknowledging the unusual nature of his approach. "It's very much part of our canon, and there's so much to learn there."

EARLY LIFE AND EDUCATION

Jonathan Gandelsman was born in Moscow, Russia—then part of the Soviet Union—in 1978. Music was an essential facet of life in his household: his parents, Yuri and Janna, played viola and piano, respectively, and both Gandelsman and his sister, Natasha, studied the violin. The family eventually moved to Israel after Yuri was hired by the Israel Philharmonic, and Gandelsman attended Thelma Yellin High School of the Arts in Israel during his teen years.

It was during that period that Gandelsman began his long relationship with the work of famed eighteenth-century German composer Johann Sebastian Bach, whose numerous compositions included a host of pieces for solo string musicians and string ensembles. "I was probably twelve or thirteen when I started working on my first solo Bach, which if I remember correctly was the D minor Partita," he recalled in an interview with Laurie Niles for *Violinist.com* (29 Mar. 2020). "I remember that even back then, the thing I was trying to understand and figure out was the feel of the

music." After leaving high school, Gandelsman moved to the United States in 1995 to study at the Curtis Institute of Music in Philadelphia, Pennsylvania. He remained at the institute into 1999 and subsequently relocated to New York City, where he supported himself by working at a local wine shop while building his reputation as a professional musician.

BROOKLYN RIDER

In 2005, Gandelsman joined fellow violinist Colin Jacobsen, viola player Nicholas Cords, and cellist Eric Jacobsen to form the string quartet Brooklyn Rider. This would be one of the primary ensembles with which Gandelsman performed over the next decades. The group established the Stillwater Music Festival in 2006, and released its debut album, *Passport*, on the independent record label In a Circle Records in 2008. Owned and operated by Gandelsman himself, In a Circle Records would go on to release works not only by Brooklyn Rider but also by artists such as the chamber orchestra The Knights and the singer and violinist Christina Courtin.

Brooklyn Rider soon began to earn a reputation as an innovative up-and-coming act on the classical music scene. Emphasizing collaboration and musical experimentation, the group worked with a diverse array of artists and drew from a wide range of influences, notably including international folk and popular musical styles that had at times been excluded from the world of classical music. "We are lucky that those distinctions are crumbling," Gandelsman told da Fonseca-Wollheim for another *New York Times* piece (30 Nov. 2014). "People can find connections that have always been there, but have long been forgotten. And people look at things with fresh eyes."

Gandelsman and his Brooklyn Rider bandmates went on to release further albums, including *Brooklyn Rider Plays Philip Glass* (2011), the first of several collaborations with the titular composer, and *The Brooklyn Rider Almanac* (2014). The group continued to record extensively following the 2016 departure of Eric Jacobsen, who left the group to focus on conducting and was replaced with cellist Michael Nicolas. Later releases included *Spontaneous Symbols* (2017) and *Dreamers* (2018), the latter a collaboration with vocalist Magos Herrera.

In addition to performing as a quartet and with featured soloists, Gandelsman and the other members of Brooklyn Rider at times served as members of the Silkroad Ensemble, an award-winning music collective founded by the acclaimed cellist Yo-Yo Ma. With the Silkroad Ensemble, Gandelsman won a Grammy Award for best world music album for the 2016 record *Sing Me Home* and also performed portions of the original score for the 2017 documentary series *The Vietnam War*, created by filmmakers Ken Burns and Lynn Novick.

SOLO WORK

Branching beyond his work with Brooklyn Rider and the Silkroad Ensemble, Gandelsman debuted his first solo record in 2018. "After years of playing in collaborative groups, I was looking for a project to do on my own, to see what my musical voice is," he told Katy Henriksen in an interview for *KUAF* (17 Jan. 2018) about the genesis of the project. Released under the In a Circle Records label, *J. S. Bach Sonatas & Partitas for Violin* features Bach compositions that Gandelsman had long appreciated. Returning to those works, he told Niles, was akin to "re-reading a great book—I notice things I haven't before, I make different voice-leading choices, I find new meaning in the musical phrases."

In addition to exploring compositions that were particularly meaningful to him, Gandelsman's performances as a soloist granted him further opportunities to experiment with varied musical styles. "Having had about twenty years of working with master musicians outside of the classical music tradition, I'm more drawn to direct and very honest expression from the folk tradition—very little, if any vibrato, small amounts of bow, but a lot of variation in articulation, staying rooted in the feel of the dance," he explained to Niles. However, Gandelsman acknowledges that his musical tastes and preferences as a performer could certainly shift again over time. "Who knows what will happen in another twenty years," he added.

In 2019, Gandelsman launched a Kickstarter fundraiser to fund a new solo recording project: a recording of Bach's cello suites, reinterpreted and performed with a violin. The project was inspired in part by Gandelsman's association with the cellist Anner Bylsma, through whom he was introduced to a violin transcription of

one of the cello suites. "The cello has a gravitas to it," he told Harris about the project. "It's a lower sound and a different kind of resonance that adds to the music. But what I love about these works on the violin is how light and nimble they sound. I've listened to the cello suites all of my life, but I've been enjoying discovering that music in a different light on the violin."

In a Circle Records released *J. S. Bach: Complete Cello Suites* in February 2020. Gandelsman also set out on a series of concerts performing the suites for live audiences. He told Harris how this process helped him gain a fuller understanding of the works themselves: "I've spent a lot of time in my practice room or in hotel rooms on the road working on my own, but then you come out and play for an audience, and things change. When I perform live, they feel completely different from the recordings." Although his touring schedule was interrupted due to the onset of the COVID-19 pandemic that March, he resumed giving Bach performances the following year.

SOCIALLY CONSCIOUS MUSIC

Although the COVID-19 pandemic forced Gandelsman to cut back on live performances throughout much of 2020 and early 2021, he continued to work on an array of projects during that period. In 2020, Brooklyn Rider released the double album *Healing Modes*, which featured both a performance of German composer Ludwig van Beethoven's Opus 132 and a selection of new compositions. Gandelsman also worked on a Silkroad Ensemble recording of the piece *Falling Out of Time* by composer Osvaldo Golijov, produced by In a Circle Records. "I started working on the album in February or March [of 2020]," Gandelsman told Anastasia Tsioulcas for *NPR* (18 Jan. 2021). "So it was right in the middle of the pandemic. Having something to do and something of this meaning and quality was just something that really gave my life some meaning during these really bleak and empty months, creatively speaking."

In addition to *Falling Out of Time*, Gandelsman dedicated a portion of the pandemic era to a project called *This Is America*. That work brought together twenty new solo violin pieces that were created by a diverse array of US composers and reflected life in the United States amid the pandemic and the social and political unrest of the period. As more concert opportunities reemerged in 2021, Gandelsman performed works from the project at various venues. He also resumed touring with Brooklyn Rider, and the group planned a concert program called *The Four Elements*, highlighting a combination of preexisting works and new commissions inspired by or representing the traditional four elements of water, earth, fire, and air.

PERSONAL LIFE

Gandelsman and his longtime partner, dancer, and educator Amber Star Merkens, have two children together. When not touring elsewhere, he lives in Brooklyn, New York.

SUGGESTED READING

da Fonseca-Wollheim, Corinna. "Crossovers Add Flavor to Classics." *The New York Times*, 30 Nov. 2014, nytimes.com/2014/12/01/arts/music/brooklyn-rider-joins-string-quartets-exploring-the-nonclassical.html. Accessed 12 Nov. 2021.

___. "Unleashing the Potential of the Strings." *The New York Times*, 30 Aug. 2013, www.nytimes.com/2013/09/01/arts/music/more-musicians-are-trying-period-instruments.html. Accessed 12 Nov. 2021.

Gandelsman, Johnny. "Collaboration across Genres Informs Violinist Johnny Gandelsman's Fresh Take on Solo Bach." Interview by Katy Henriksen. *KUAF*, 17 Jan. 2018, www.kuaf.com/post/collaboration-across-genres-informs-violinist-johnny-gandelsmans-fresh-take-solo-bach#stream/0. Accessed 12 Nov. 2021.

___. "Interview: Violinist Johnny Gandelsman on Bach and on FB Live." Interview by Laurie Niles. *Violinist.com*, 29 Mar. 2020, www.violinist.com/blog/laurie/20203/28170/. Accessed 12 Nov. 2021.

Harris, Vincent. "Virtuoso Violinist: Johnny Gandelsman Lightens Up Bach's Cello Concertos." *Greenville Journal*, 12 Mar. 2020, greenvillejournal.com/arts-culture/grammy-award-winning-virtuoso-violinist-johnny-gandelsman-transcribes-bach-to-violin/. Accessed 12 Nov. 2021.

Tsioulcas, Anastasia. "What Is the Sound of Grief? Osvaldo Golijov Puts It to Music." *All Things Considered*, NPR, 18 Jan. 2021, www.npr.org/2021/01/18/946288532/what-is-the-sound-of-grief. Accessed 12 Nov. 2021.

Weininger, David. "Violinist Johnny Gandelsman Finds 'Infinite Possibilities' in Bach's Cello Suites." *Boston Globe*, 24 Jan. 2020, www.bostonglobe.com/2020/01/24/arts/violinist-johnny-gandelsman-finds-infinite-possibilities-bachs-cello-suites/. Accessed 12 Nov. 2021.

SELECTED WORKS

Passport (with Brooklyn Rider), 2008; *Brooklyn Rider Plays Philip Glass* (with Brooklyn Rider), 2011; *The Brooklyn Rider Almanac* (with Brooklyn Rider), 2014; *Sing Me Home* (with Yo-Yo Ma and the Silkroad Ensemble), 2016; *Spontaneous Symbols* (with Brooklyn Rider), 2017; *JS Bach Sonatas & Partitas for Violin*, 2018; *Dreamers* (with Brooklyn Rider and Magos Herrera), 2018; *Healing Modes* (with Brooklyn Rider), 2020; *JS Bach: Complete Cello Suites*, 2020

—*Joy Crelin*

George F. Gao

Born: November 15, 1961
Occupation: Virologist and immunologist

"Outbreaks, epidemics, and chronic diseases have repeatedly shown to permeate every layer of human society and transcend national borders without discretion," Virologist and immunologist George F. Gao wrote in 2019, in his foreword to the debut issue of *China CDC Weekly*. "Furthermore, occupational, nutritional, environmental, radiation safety, and many other types of public health issues represent enormous challenges for the world. Thus, public health should be our top priority for our increasingly integrated global community." Indeed, Gao's prescient perspective on the global approach to public health would become particularly relevant over the course of the next year, as the coronavirus disease 2019 (COVID-19) pandemic emerged and spread throughout the world, straining public health systems worldwide and necessitating extensive cooperation among researchers and policymakers.

A prominent researcher specializing in infectious diseases, including those spread from animals to humans, Gao joined the Chinese

Center for Disease Control and Prevention (China CDC) in 2011. Over the next decade, he played a substantial role in that body's efforts to combat disease outbreaks, including an outbreak of Ebola that began in western Africa in 2013. He became director-general of the China CDC in 2017, and by early 2020 was tasked with managing China's response to the emerging COVID-19 pandemic. During that early period, his work focused on attempts to determine the origin of the SARS-CoV-2 virus and its means of transmission as well as efforts to contain and monitor its spread. Although Gao and other Chinese health authorities later faced some international criticism over their handling of the early pandemic, including allegations that they did not investigate the possibility of human-to-human transmission quickly enough, Gao continued to emphasize the importance of working together to combat the pandemic and develop means of preventing and treating COVID-19. "The virus is our common enemy," he told Jon Cohen in an interview for *Science* (27 Mar. 2020), "not the enemy of any person or country."

EARLY LIFE AND EDUCATION

Known in China as Gao Fu and in English-speaking countries as George Fu Gao, Gao was born in Shanxi Province, China, on November 15, 1961. After completing his secondary education, he enrolled in Shanxi Agricultural University, where he studied to become a veterinarian. That field of study was not his choice, however, as it had been selected for him through China's bureaucratic education system. He earned his bachelor's degree from the university in 1983 and went on to pursue graduate studies at Beijing Agricultural University. During that period, Gao developed an interest in virology and shifted his academic focus toward that field. "This changed my whole life," he recalled to Geoff Watts for the *Lancet* (28 July 2018). "I transformed myself from a vet into an infectious disease researcher." He completed a master's degree in 1986 and began teaching virology. In 1988, he received the Young Scientist Award from the China Association for Science and Technology. Pursuing formal studies in his desired field, Gao left China for the United Kingdom, where he enrolled in a doctoral program at the University of Oxford in 1991. He earned a doctorate in molecular virology in 1994.

Photo by J Marchn,
via Wikimedia Commons.

After completing his doctoral studies, Gao remained at Oxford as a postdoctoral researcher within the university's Nuffield Department of Clinical Medicine and Weatherall Institute of Molecular Medicine. He went on to join the university's Human Immunology Unit as a research associate following its establishment in 1998. After leaving Oxford, Gao relocated to the United States for a research fellowship at Harvard University. Working within the departments of molecular and cellular biology and molecular pharmacology, he was also affiliated with the Howard Hughes Medical Institute (HHMI) and the Boston Children's Hospital during that period. Gao remained in the United States into 2001 before returning to Oxford for a few more years.

ACADEMIC CAREER

As China's economy and research facilities began to improve in the early twenty-first century, Gao made the decision to return to his home country. In 2004, he joined the faculty of the Chinese Academy of Sciences (CAS), later known as the University of the Chinese Academy of Sciences (UCAS). There, he served as director-general of the Institute of Microbiology between 2004 and 2008, while also starting a professorship at the University of Science and Technology of China in 2006. In 2008, Gao took on the role of director of the CAS Key Laboratory of Pathogenic Microbiology and Immunology as well as the title of vice-president of the CAS Beijing Institutes of Life Science.

As a researcher and teacher, Gao was particularly interested in areas of virology and immunology related to emerging virus, interspecies transmission of viruses, and the treatment of relevant diseases. His research was initially based primarily on laboratory work, and he became known for his use of X-ray crystallography in studying the structure of viruses. As Gao's career progressed, however, he became increasingly interested in field research, including work in regions experiencing outbreaks of infectious diseases. "I've moved from basic research, though not completely, into more public health-oriented research," he explained to Watts. "I now combine my virology and immunology with more practical field work." Gao published widely throughout the first decades of his career and was also involved for a time with the editorial operations of a number of publications, including the *Chinese Journal of Biotechnology*, for which he served as a deputy editor-in-chief, and *Emerging Microbes and Infections*, for which he served on the editorial board. He held memberships in organizations such as the American Association of Immunologists, the Chinese Academy of Sciences, and the African Academy of Sciences, among others, and was the recipient of several major awards and honors, including the 2014 Nikkei Asia Prize in science, technology, and environment.

CHINA CDC

Gao took on a new role in 2011, joining the Chinese Center for Disease Control and Prevention, or the China CDC, in the position of deputy director general. In that role, he was heavily involved in the China CDC's response to the outbreak of Ebola in western Africa between 2013 and 2014. He traveled to Sierra Leone with a Chinese medical team in 2014. "We had many young scientists and public health workers," he told Watts of that experience. "But they needed someone in authority who was also experienced in lab work to go with them." Gao spent two months in Sierra Leone with the team, which worked to establish a mobile Ebola testing program there.

For Gao, the Ebola epidemic reinforced his beliefs about the importance of strong international responses to issues of public health. "This epidemic testifies to the fact that infectious diseases are a global issue that requires collaborative efforts from many countries," he told Mu-ming Poo and Ling Wang in an interview for *National Science Review* (22 Feb. 2015). "Given the absence of adequate public health systems in many developing countries, affecting their ability to deal with acute infectious diseases, more developed countries must provide rapid and effective responses when such an epidemic occurs again in the future." In 2016, Gao and a group of researchers and policymakers from around the world cofounded the Global Virome Project, an organization dedicated to preventing future epidemics.

Promoted to director-general of the China CDC in 2017, Gao continued to lead that body throughout the next several years and, in 2019, expanded its public health outreach through the creation of the publication *China CDC Weekly*. "*China CDC Weekly* represents a major step forward for global health," he wrote in the foreword to the first issue, further noting that the publication was intended to "act as a model for other developing countries to disseminate their public health experiences, findings, and progress." Gao also served as editor-in-chief of the weekly publication.

COVID-19 PANDEMIC

In late 2019, a novel coronavirus was detected in Wuhan, China. Later identified as SARS-CoV-2, the virus caused a disease that became known as COVID-19. Following the virus's emergence, Gao led the China CDC's response to the new virus, which included efforts to determine the virus's place of origin, which many believed was a local seafood market. "You are working like a detective," he later told Cohen about that process. "From the very beginning, everybody thought the origin was the market. Now, I think the market could be the initial place, or it could be a place where the virus was amplified. So that's a scientific question. There are two possibilities." Gao and his colleagues likewise worked to determine that the virus was zoonotic in nature, meaning that it was capable of being transmitted from animals to humans, and subsequently sought to determine whether human-to-human transmission of the virus was possible.

Among other researchers, Gao himself was involved in the process of sequencing the virus, a vital step in studying it. He and his colleagues were also responsible for sharing data about their findings with public health officials and international leaders, particularly as the virus began to spread extensively throughout the world in early 2020, though some critics felt Gao and his colleagues did not report their findings quickly enough. "We shared the information with scientific colleagues promptly, but this involved public health and we had to wait for policymakers to announce it publicly. You don't want the public to panic, right?" he explained to Cohen. "And no one in any country could have predicted that the virus would cause a pandemic. This is the first noninfluenza pandemic ever." Despite efforts to contain its spread through isolation and quarantine measures as well as other public health protocols, the virus spread rapidly, and on March 11, the World Health Organization (WHO) officially categorized the COVID-19 outbreak as a pandemic.

MOVING FORWARD

As the COVID-19 pandemic progressed through 2021 and into 2022, China's medical leadership and Gao himself continued to face criticism for their handling of the early pandemic, some of which focused on reports that Gao had claimed early in 2020 that the SARS-CoV-2 virus was not being transmitted between humans. Gao, however, refuted such criticism. "I never said [there was] no human-to-human transmission in the public—never, ever," he emphasized in a Chinese television interview, as reported by Holly Chik for the *South China Morning Post* (21 Apr. 2022).

In addition to defending the China CDC's handling of the pandemic, Gao spoke out in support of Chinese-produced vaccines, which medical personnel in some countries had characterized as ineffective. "The protection rates of all vaccines in the world are sometimes high, and sometimes low. How to improve their efficacy is a question that needs to be considered by scientists around the world," he told Siqi Cao for *Global Times* (11 Apr. 2021). "In this regard, I suggest that we can consider adjusting the vaccination process, such as the number of doses and intervals and adopting sequential vaccination with different types of vaccines." Gao published research on COVID-

related topics throughout that period, placing coauthored papers in journals such as *Biosafety and Health* and the *New England Journal of Medicine*. He likewise continued his research into a number of other threats to public health, including seasonal influenzas and zoonotic diseases beyond COVID-19.

PERSONAL LIFE

Gao lives in China.

SUGGESTED READING

Cao, Siqi. "Exclusive: Chinese CDC Director Refutes Interpretation of 'Low Protection Rate of Chinese Vaccines,' Says It Confuses Scientific Vision He Proposes to Improve Efficacy." *Global Times*, 11 Apr. 2021, www.globaltimes.cn/page/202104/1220774.shtml. Accessed 9 May 2022.

Chik, Holly. "China CDC Chief Defends Early Outbreak Action: 'I Never Said There Was No Human-to-Human Transmission.'" *South China Morning Post*, 21 Apr. 2020, www.scmp.com/news/china/society/article/3080838/china-cdc-director-defends-early-outbreak-action-i-never-said. Accessed 9 May 2022.

Gao, George F. "Foreword from Editor-in-Chief George F. Gao—China's Outreach to the World: Public Health Goes Global." *China CDC Weekly*, 2019, weekly.chinacdc.cn/en/article/doi/10.46234/ccdcw2019.001. Accessed 9 May 2022.

___. "George Fu Gao: The Past and Future of Ebola." Interview by Mu-ming Poo and Ling Wang. *National Science Review*, 22 Feb. 2015, academic.oup.com/nsr/article/2/1/117/2606164. Accessed 9 May 2022.

___. "Global Public Health with George F. Gao." Interview by Julie Wolf. *Meet the Microbiologist*, American Society for Microbiology, 15 Aug. 2019, asm.org/Podcasts/MTM/Episodes/Global-Public-Health-with-George-F-Gao-MTM-114. Accessed 9 May 2022.

___. "Not Wearing Masks to Protect against Coronavirus Is a 'Big Mistake,' Top Chinese Scientist Says." Interview by Jon Cohen. *Science*, 27 Mar. 2020, www.science.org/content/article/not-wearing-masks-protect-against-coronavirus-big-mistake-top-chinese-scientist-says. Accessed 9 May 2022.

Watts, Geoff. "George F Gao: Head of China CDC Signals a More Global Outlook." *The Lancet*, 28 July 2018, www.thelancet.com/journals/lancet/article/PIIS0140-6736(18)31658-1/fulltext. Accessed 9 May 2022.

—Joy Crelin

Michael John Garcés

Born: 1967
Occupation: Playwright

Michael John Garcés, a veteran theater-maker, has been the artistic director of the community-based ensemble theater company Cornerstone Theater since 2005. Garcés, whose father emigrated from Cuba in the 1950s, was born in Miami and raised in Colombia. He returned to Miami for college where, to his father's dismay, he studied theater. Moving to New York City in 1989, he fell into the orbit of Max Ferrá, the celebrated artistic director of INTAR Theatre, a long-running Off-Broadway theater company focused on the work of Latinx artists. Garcés was a writer and performer, but in the 1990s, made his name primarily as a director of new plays, collaborating with up-and-coming playwrights. His experience as a playwright, actor, and director lent a deeper perspective to his work. "Michael is a force of nature in rehearsal," a fellow playwright remarked about Garcés to Steven Leigh Morris for *American Theatre* magazine (1 Nov. 2010). "He feels each moment of the play in his body. The stakes of each scene pulse through his circulatory system."

Moved to create authentic, ensemble-driven political theater, Garcés eventually landed in Los Angeles as the head of Cornerstone Theater. There, Garcés wrote and premiered a play called *Los Illegals* (2007), which explored immigration through the lens of day laborers in Los Angeles. In keeping with Cornerstone's mission, the production featured a cast partially comprised of real-life day laborers. "I learned a tremendous amount about the world that I didn't know," Garcés told Sean Mitchell for the *Los Angeles Times* (27 May 2007), explaining that the diversity and range of education levels in the community of undocumented immigrants especially surprised him. Garcés went on to direct numerous plays with Cornerstone, including Larissa FastHorse's *Urban Rez* in 2016, and he wrote a sprawling ensemble piece called *Magic Fruit* in 2017. Garcés has twice received awards from the Princess Grace Foundation, and in 2020 he won the $275,000 Doris Duke Artist Award.

EARLY LIFE IN COLOMBIA

Michael John Garcés was born in Miami, Florida, in 1967. His father, Sergio, was an accountant from Cuba who emigrated to the United States for work in the 1950s, where he met Garcés's American-born mother, Lee, in Miami. Early in Garcés's childhood, the family moved to Medellín, Colombia, for a job opportunity. "It's a beautiful city—it's spring all the time, there's always flowers and fruit," Garcés told Morris, though he also conceded that "there was a lot going on politically then." His family lived a few miles away from a house that belonged to Pablo Escobar, the most notorious drug lord of the era. For the most part, Garcés was "in my kid world," though he recalls being aware of the profound chasm between the rich and the poor in Medellín.

As a young boy, Garcés's mother took him to the philharmonic and other music events, and he started performing in theater when he was in the fifth grade. "My parents were remarkably supportive of my fascination with the theatre—perhaps to my dad's later regret," Garcés recalled to Morris. At thirteen years old, Garcés moved with his parents and younger brother, Chris, to Bogotá, Colombia's capital, where Garcés won a role as an apostle in a production of *Godspell*—ironic, Garcés later said, because his family was not particularly religious. The production, the first American musical to be performed in Colombia, made national news.

EDUCATION AND EARLY CAREER

A few years later, Garcés's family moved back to Miami. His father pushed him to pursue business, but at nineteen Garcés enrolled at the University of Miami to study theater. Upon graduating in 1989, he landed a role in a Coconut Grove Playhouse production of Neil Simon's *The Gingerbread Lady* in Miami. The same year, Garcés moved to New York City, where he got an internship with INTAR (an acronym for International Arts Relations), a storied Off-Broadway Hispanic theater company. As Garcés recalled to Morris, he was sitting in on a rehearsal for Eduardo Machado's

Cabaret Bambu (1989) and laughed at a joke spoken in Spanish. Newly aware that Garcés was a fluent Spanish speaker, artistic director Max Ferrá offered him an audition. Thus began a rigorous mentorship that would shape Garcés's career. When Ferrá, who was also Cuban, died in 2017, Garcés wrote a moving tribute to him for *American Theatre* (14 Feb. 2017). "Max saw something in me, probably nothing more than a propensity for hard work, and, as he had for many others, he made a space for me at INTAR," he wrote. At Ferrá's directive, Garcés worked several odd jobs around the theater, eventually earning his bona fides to act, direct, and curate productions. "He was hard on me, pushing, sometimes to the point of being mean," Garcés continued in his tribute, "but at the same time consistently offering that next opportunity, the subsequent challenge."

For the next decade, Garcés enjoyed a fruitful career acting, writing, and directing in New York. In addition to working with INTAR, he contributed to the Puerto Rican Traveling Theater, the American Place Theater, and others. He also worked as a freelance director at regional theaters like the Hartford Stage Company, the Yale Repertory Theatre, and the Wooly Mammoth Theatre Company in Washington, DC. Garcés built his career as a director collaborating with new playwrights, including Adam Rapp (Garcés directed Rapp's *Finer Noble Gases* for the Humana Festival of New Plays in Louisville, Kentucky, in 2002); Kia Corthron; and Craig Wright. He first received the prestigious Princess Grace Award for his work with INTAR in 1995 and won a Drama League Fellowship for directing in 1998. In 1999, Garcés was invited to direct a play, based on Mayan creation myths, in Chiapas, Mexico, as a part of an eight-week residency. He described the experience as an important turning point in his career. "The impact, the quality of the aesthetic experience people were having watching the play, was so profound, so electric . . . all this made a huge impact I hadn't anticipated," he told Morris. "This was something I started looking for in my other work."

THE JUSTICE CYCLE

In 2005, Garcés was hired as the artistic director of the Cornerstone Theater Company, a community-based ensemble in Los Angeles.

For his first project with the company, Garcés commissioned an ambitious three-year cycle of plays, called the Justice Cycle, examining how laws impact US society. Cornerstone, which was founded in 1986, produces work differently than most American theaters. Historically, it operates according to consensus and collaborates with local communities to create work that explores the political issues most relevant to those communities, often incorporating community members alongside professional actors in its shows. But Garcés's play cycle took a slightly different approach. "For the first time we're looking at community through the prism of issues as opposed to looking at issues through the prism of community," Garcés told Mitchell. "It's a little different, deciding what we want to grapple with and then finding communities that are at the front lines of this issue."

Garcés wrote the first play in Cornerstone's Justice Cycle. Called *Los Illegals*, it premiered at the Armory Center for the Arts in Pasadena in June 2007. Garcés wrote the play about illegal immigration but emphasized that it was not documentary theater—text taken verbatim from a source—nor was it a collaboratively written piece. Using stories culled from interviews with real-life day laborers, Garcés created his own fictional work about a community of undocumented laborers who wait daily outside a home improvement store, hoping to find temporary work in construction or landscaping. Garcés based the main conflict in the play—when the day laborers come together to take responsibility after one of them is accused of a crime—on *Fuente Ovejuna*, a seventeenth-century play by Spanish playwright Lope de Vega. The first bilingual play to be produced at Cornerstone, it was performed in both English and Spanish, and neither language was translated to evoke, for monolingual viewers, the isolating experience of arriving in a new country without knowing the language. The cast was split between actual day laborers and professional actors. Reflecting on his experience working with both groups at once, Garcés told Mitchell that the "nonpros" brought "a kind of unpolished visceral connection to the material and to the sense of place and time that forces the [professional] actors to let go of some of their tricks and get real."

THE HUNGER CYCLE AND THE CHANGE SERIES

The Justice Cycle, which included five plays in total, ended in 2010. Garcés directed two of those plays: *Someday* (2008), by Julie Marie Myatt, and *3 Truths* (2010), by Naomi Iizuka. In 2011, Cornerstone launched the six-year Hunger Cycle, a series of nine plays about hunger and food inequity and their impact on various groups in California. Garcés directed the first play, *Cafe Vida* (2012), by Lisa Loomer, about gang rehabilitation. He also directed *California: The Tempest* (2015), by Alison Carey, an adaptation of Shakespeare's *The Tempest* that explores contemporary politics in California, and *Urban Rez* (2016), by award-winning playwright FastHorse about the experiences of American Indians living in Los Angeles. Garcés wrote the culminating play of the cycle, *Magic Fruit* (2017), based on Mozart's opera *The Magic Flute*. The play focused on climate change, incorporating communities featured in previous plays in the cycle, including gang members, homeless people, and farmers. Fantastical, surreal, and in the tradition of Cornerstone, performed with an enormous cast of varied ability, Margaret Gray, writing for the *Los Angeles Times* (6 Dec. 2017), described it as "such a quirky bag of fun that every odd piece fits right in."

In 2018, Cornerstone announced that, due to rising rent prices, it would leave its permanent space in Los Angeles and would seek to make work on-site with communities in New York City, Los Angeles, and Arizona. "Embracing our nomadic history and thinking forward to a more flexible and nimble future, this feels like the right moment for us to focus on what's most important," Garcés explained in a joint statement released with Cornerstone managing director Megan Wanlass, as reported in *American Theatre* (12 June 2018). Amidst the coronavirus disease 2019 (COVID-19) pandemic, the theater began a series of plays, mostly online, called the Change Series. In 2020, Garcés directed an online production of *Highland Park Is Here* as part of that series.

OTHER WORKS

While at Cornerstone, Garcés continued to write and direct plays in other parts of the country as well. His play *Acts of Mercy: passion-play* premiered at the Rattlestick Playwrights Theater in New York City in 2006. A loose allegory, the play follows the story of two brothers seeking to reconcile with their dying father. Another play, titled *points of departure*, premiered at INTAR the same year. Reviews for both works suggested that Garcés's own work was more abstract than his work with Cornerstone. Brad Bradley, who reviewed *Points of Departure* for *CurtainUp*, an online theater magazine (2006), wrote that the play was a "bold and worthy work," although it requires "heavy duty engagement on the part of the audience" and can be "overwhelming in its obliqueness." Garcés's play *The Web* premiered in Los Angeles with a theater troupe called Needtheater in 2010. That play was loosely adapted from Fyodor Dostoyevsky's 1846 novella *The Double* and has been described as a science-fiction story about identity theft.

PERSONAL LIFE

Garcés has a daughter, Christina, and a son, Louis.

SUGGESTED READING

Bradley, Brad. "A *CurtainUp* Review: *Points of Departure*." Review of *Points of Departure*, written by Michael John Garcés, and directed by Ron Daniels. *CurtainUp*, 2006, www.curtainup.com/pointsofdeparture.html. Accessed 8 Jan. 2022.

"Cornerstone Theater Company to Leave Los Angeles Home." *American Theatre*, 12 June 2018, www.americantheatre.org/2018/06/12/cornerstone-theater-company-to-leave-los-angeles-home/. Accessed 20 Jan. 2022.

Garcés, Michael John. "Crossing Over." Interview by Sonja Arsham Kuftinec. *Theater*, vol. 41, no. 2, 2011, pp. 63–67. *MLA International Bibliography with Full Text*, search.ebscohost.com/login.aspx?direct=true&db=mlf&AN=2011444191. Accessed 19 Jan. 2022.

___. "Remembering the Joy and Fierceness of INTAR's Max Ferrá." *American Theatre*, 14 Feb. 2017, www.americantheatre.org/2017/02/14/remembering-the-joy-and-fierceness-of-intars-max-ferra/. Accessed 8 Jan. 2022.

Gray, Margaret. "Review: Cornerstone Theater's Nine-Play Cycle on Hunger in America Finds Its Inspiration in Mozart." Review of *Magic Fruit*, written by Michael John Garcés, and directed by Shishir Kurup.

Los Angeles Times, 6 Dec. 2017, www. latimes.com/entertainment/arts/la-et-cm-magic-fruit-review-20171206-story.html. Accessed 9 Jan. 2022.

Mitchell, Sean. "Cornerstone Puts the Immigration Issue Center Stage." Review of "Los Illegals", directed by Michael John Garcés. *Los Angeles Times*, 27 May 2007, www.latimes.com/archives/la-xpm-2007-may-27-ca-cornerstone27-story.html. Accessed 8 Jan. 2022.

Morris, Steven Leigh. "The Garcés Ultimatum." *American Theatre*, 1 Nov. 2010, www. americantheatre.org/2010/11/01/the-garces-ultimatum/. Accessed 8 Jan. 2022.

SELECTED WORKS

Acts of Mercy: passion-play, 2006; *Points of Departure*, 2006; *Los Illegals*, 2007; *Magic Fruit*, 2017

—Molly Hagan

Ross Gay

Born: August 1, 1974
Occupation: Poet and educator

In many ways, Ross Gay's talent for poetry emerged in his life unexpectedly. As a child and even into college, his singular dream was to play professional football. However, when an English professor introduced him to the work of writer and political activist Amiri Baraka, Gay discovered the raw power of poetry. It made him want to write poems too. He immersed himself in literary studies and began reading, writing, and performing poetry extensively. He published several collections and by the 2020s had developed a reputation as one of the most important voices in contemporary American literature. Gay's work is celebrated by critics and readers alike for its clever wordplay, natural imagery, and ability to capture the beauty and brutality of humanity.

Gay earned particular attention for his decision to write about the emotion of joy and all its complexities. He established himself as perhaps the foremost explorer of this particular theme with the release of both his award-winning poetry collection *Catalog of Unabashed Gratitude* (2015) and the best seller *The Book of Delights: Essays* (2019). When asked by Caitlin Dicus for Butler University's magazine

Booth (2 Feb. 2018) why he writes poems about joy, he replied, "For me, what feels important is to truly attend to and meditate on the things that we love. So that we can preserve them, you know? So that we can care for them and tend them."

EARLY LIFE

Ross Gay was born in Youngstown, Ohio, on August 1, 1974. The eldest of two sons, he grew up outside of Philadelphia, Pennsylvania, in an interracial working-class family. His mother, a White woman, had a job at a bank. His father, who was Black, worked sixty to seventy hours a week at various restaurant chains. Gay watched his parents struggle with exhausting, unfulfilling careers and, at a young age, realized that he did not want a typical working-class job.

Gay was not especially interested in reading or writing during his formative years. Instead, he loved skateboarding, video games, and sports. One of his most beloved activities as a child was watching Philadelphia 76ers games with his father, during an era in the 1970s and 1980s when the basketball team was defined by their star player Julius Erving. A natural athlete, Gay enjoyed playing basketball but decided that he ultimately wanted to be a professional football player.

Gay had good friends growing up and spent a lot of time playing with the other kids in the apartment complex where his family lived. However, he still struggled with melancholy feelings. "If you ask my mom, I was a gloomy, sullen sucker," he said in an interview with Crystal Powell for New York University's *Washington Square Review* (1 Sept. 2017). "I think it probably came out of me needing to figure out how to get up some days. I had to work on that."

EDUCATION AND EARLY CAREER

After graduating from high school, Gay was accepted into Lafayette College in Pennsylvania. By his own recollection, he was admitted for his football skills rather than for his grades. He was serious about football, playing tight end and defensive end and hoping to earn enough attention to keep playing professionally. However, after a year of college he began to realize that a successful athletic career was unrealistic. Gay also often felt frustrated and alienated in the socioeconomic environment at Lafayette; he noticed, for example, that many teenage White students drove cars that were far more expensive than his hardworking father's. Increasingly, Gay was sharply aware of issues like income disparity, race, and power.

Everything began to change for Gay when he took a survey of American literature class in his sophomore year. Sensing the complex feelings that Gay was grappling with at the time, his professor, David Johnson, asked him to give a presentation on the poem "An Agony. As Now," (1964) by Amiri Baraka. Gay described this transformative moment in an interview with Loré Yusseff for the *Creative Independent* (16 Feb. 2021): "I read it and it changed my life. I read that poem and then I started reading poems. I got [Baraka's] collection *Translucency* out of the library and was just deeply reading his work, but also reading all the writers around him." Gay subsequently began expressing himself through writing and painting.

After graduating from Lafayette in 1996 with a BA in English and art, Gay enrolled at Sarah Lawrence College and earned an MFA in poetry in 1998. He later completed a PhD in English at Temple University in 2006. Meanwhile, Gay began his career as an educator when he returned to Lafayette on a humanities fellowship and taught several courses from 2001 to 2003. He then went on to teach poetry workshops at the University of Pittsburgh and Montclair State University as a visiting or assistant professor. He also worked as a faculty member at New England College's low-residency MFA poetry program from 2005 into 2008. Gay then settled into a more permanent position as an associate English professor at Indiana University-Bloomington in 2007.

BECOMING A PUBLISHED POET

As he studied and also taught literature, Gay wrote steadily and began getting poems published in various magazines and journals. He quickly attracted attention, including finalist spots for the James Hearst Poetry Prize in 2000 and the St. Louis Poetry Prize in 2001 as well as an honorable mention at the New Millennium Poetry Awards in 2002. He also earned a Cave Canem Literary Fellowship that ran from 2003 to 2009, and he was nominated for a Pushcart Prize every year from 2004 through 2009. His first book-length poetry collection, *Against Which*, was published in 2006.

Photo by Slowking4 via Wikimedia Commons

In an interview with Callie Siskel for the *Los Angeles Review of Books* (11 Nov. 2016), Gay explained the draw of poetry as his primary art form: "One of the pleasures of writing poems for me is that it's this real sort of intimate communication. Reading poems aloud is a way to let my body in time and space be the thing that's communicating the poem, and that feels important. So that in itself is really moving, the opportunity to carry the poem with one's body to people." Gay described his writing process as coming in waves, with moments of deep focus—even approaching obsession—and intense, furious writing interspersed with more relaxed periods of thinking or slower work. He noted he typically would go through many drafts of a poem, a process that could take months.

From early on in his career, Gay's work was wide-ranging, examining themes including nature, beauty, hope, gratitude, racism, love, loss, violence, power, and destruction. However, he acknowledged that his perspectives on such ideas evolved over time. Both *Against Which* (2006) and his second collection, *Bringing the Shovel Down* (2011), tend to present hope and despair, as well as life's beauty and destruction, as starkly divided—oppositional even. Conversely, his later work began to explore the ways in which the various forces of life are actually intertwined.

CATALOG OF UNABASHED GRATITUDE

Perhaps the most prominent example of Gay's shift in perspective was how he came to depict joy as being inseparable from sorrow in several acclaimed works. "Sometimes I think there's a conception of joy as meaning something easy," he explained to Krista Tippett for *On Being* (25 July 2019). "To me, joy has nothing to do with ease. And joy has everything to do with the fact that we're all going to die. When I'm thinking about joy, I'm thinking about—that at the same time as something wonderful is happening, some connection is being made in my life, we are also in the process of dying." Despite the underlying sense of morbidity, Gay's use of joy in his poetry has been described by critics as "celebratory." Furthermore, his decision to focus on the emotion made him something of an anomaly in the canon of contemporary poetry.

That unique focus is apparent in Gay's third collection of poetry, *Catalogue of Unabashed Gratitude* (2015), which he wrote over the course of four years. Anchored by the setting of his garden, the book explores life's ephemeral forces primarily through the lens of plants, fruit trees, seasons, and insects. It describes many personal moments in Gay's life, from hangovers to spreading his father's ashes, giving it a vibrant energy. "I think of *Catalog* [sic] as a meditation on gratitude and meditation on joy," he told Siskel.

Catalogue of Unabashed Gratitude proved to be a major breakthrough for Gay. Critics extolled his verse and use of natural imagery as well as the ideas his poems explored. The collection went on to win the 2015 National Book Critics Circle Award and the 2016 Kingsley Tufts Poetry Prize. It was also a finalist for the National Book Award and a nominee for the NAACP Image Award, among other honors.

THE BOOK OF DELIGHTS

For his next book, Gay veered into prose. Beginning on his forty-second birthday, he attempted to produce one handwritten essay about something that had delighted him every day for a year. The project lasted from August 1, 2016, through August 1, 2017—a period of heightened social tensions in the United States due in large part to the 2016 presidential election—and the resulting essays were released as *The Book of Delights* in 2019.

Despite the turbulent times, Gay found the exercise to be enlightening and heartening. He found himself surprised at how much delight he got from small things like air quotes and nicknames and realized how much pleasure comes from interactions with others. "One of the projects of the book is allowing oneself to be moved," he told Christina Cala for the NPR program *Code Switch* (19 Aug. 2021). "And I think one of the studies in the book is that to be moved is to be connected."

Reception of *The Book of Delights* was overwhelmingly positive. Many critics praised Gay's beautiful, clever prose as well as his ability to bring intelligent insight into the human experience and the guises that joy can take in life. The essay collection made *The New York Times* Best Sellers list and was featured as a best book of the year by several outlets.

BE HOLDING

Gay returned to poetry in a big way in 2020 with *Be Holding*, a book-length poem centered around basketball player Julius "Dr. J" Erving. At first glance, the work is a clear homage to Erving and especially the gravity-defying layup known as "The Move" that he performed late in the 1980 NBA playoffs. However, as the poem continues with its stream-of-consciousness couplets, Gay begins to connect to and explore various aspects of culture and history, with a focus on the Black American experience. He goes on to examine the different thematic meanings of the book's title, including the act of "beholding" something and the people whom he feels beloved by and "beholden" to, like his parents and sharecropper ancestors. In an interview with David Naimon for *Tin House* (16 Feb. 2021), Gay commented on these nuances, noting that he was "trying to reimagine the hold in a way, to be held, to behold, to be a hold, what does it mean?"

Continuing Gay's run of acclaim, *Be Holding* was met with highly positive reviews from critics. In 2021, the book won the prestigious Jean Stein Award at the PEN America Literary Awards. By that time Gay was widely acknowledged as a preeminent voice in American poetry.

PERSONAL LIFE

Gay settled in Bloomington, Indiana, while teaching at Indiana University. An avid gardener, he became actively involved with the

Bloomington Community Orchard, a nonprofit, free-fruit-for-all food justice and joy project. He also maintained a passion for sports and cofounded the online sports magazine *Some Call It Ballin'*. Among his other side projects, he worked with Shayla Lawson and Essence London to create the Tenderness Project, a collaborative art piece that explores radical empathy.

SUGGESTED READING

Gay, Ross. "Between the Covers, Ross Gay Interview." Interview by David Naimon. *Between the Covers*, 16 Feb. 2021. *Tin House*, tinhouse.com/transcript/between-the-covers-ross-gay-interview/. Accessed 2 Nov. 2021.

___. "A Conversation with Ross Gay." Interview by Caitlin Dicus. *Booth*, Butler University, 2 Feb. 2018, booth.butler.edu/2018/02/02/a-conversation-with-ross-gay. Accessed 27 Oct. 2021.

___. "How Ross Gay Finds Joy in the Smallest of 'Delights.'" Interview by Christina Cala. *Code Switch*, NPR, 19 Aug. 2021, www.npr.org/sections/codeswitch/2021/08/19/1029287927/how-ross-gay-finds-joy-in-the-smallest-of-delights. Accessed 28 Oct. 2021.

___. "An Interview with Ross Gay." Interview by Crystal Powell. *Washington Square Review*, 2017, www.washingtonsquarereview.com/crystal-powell-an-interview-with-ross-gay. Accessed 27 Oct. 2021.

___. "On Abandoning Capitalistic Achievement to Seek the Freedom to Play." Interview by Loré Yusseff. *The Creative Independent*, 17 Aug. 2021, thecreativeindependent.com/people/poet-and-professor-ross-gay-on-abandoning-capitalistic-achievement-to-seek-the-freedom-of-play/. Accessed 27 Oct. 2021.

___. "Tending Joy and Practicing Delight." Interview by Kristen Tippett. *On Being*, WNYC Studios, 26 Mar. 2020, onbeing.org/programs/ross-gay-tending-joy-and-practicing-delight/. Accessed 2 Nov. 2021.

___. "The Terrible and the Possible: An Interview with Ross Gay." Interview by Callie Siskel. *Los Angeles Review of Books*, 11 Nov. 2016, www.lareviewofbooks.org/article/the-terrible-and-the-possible-an-interview-with-ross-gay/. Accessed 27 Oct. 2021.

SELECTED WORKS

Against Which, 2006; *Bringing the Shovel Down*, 2011; *Catalogue of Unabashed Gratitude*, 2015; *The Book of Delights*, 2019; *Be Holding*, 2020

—*Emily E. Turner*

Timnit Gebru

Born: May 13, 1983
Occupation: Computer scientist

Computer research scientist Timnit Gebru loves working in science, technology, engineering, and mathematics (STEM). "I look forward to reading papers, thinking, discussing ideas, writing code. Anytime I get to do that I feel like I'm on vacation," she said in a profile for Million STEM, a network for women in STEM. Gebru has accumulated an impressive resume that includes working for US tech giants Apple, Microsoft, and Google. With three electrical engineering degrees from Stanford University under her belt, she is behind some of the most groundbreaking research on the ethics and social impacts of artificial intelligence (AI). She has studied how AI can perpetuate biases, spread racism and sexism, and cause harm to marginalized communities. Much of her work explores ways that computer scientists can avoid and mitigate this damage as AI and machine learning are used in applications such as facial recognition and data mining algorithms.

Gebru has become a staunch champion for equity and inclusivity in a field that has been strongly criticized for its sexism and racism. She cofounded a nonprofit, Black in AI, which aims to increase the diversity of people working in artificial intelligence and to counter algorithmic bias. "There's a lot of gatekeeping in the tech industry, but the industry needs people from all backgrounds," Gebru told Graham Hacia for *Wired* (9 Sept. 2020). "So don't let that gatekeeping make you feel like this is a thing you cannot do. It's important to find your support systems, find your advocates."

EARLY LIFE AND EDUCATION

Timnit Gebru was born on May 13, 1983, in Addis Ababa, Ethiopia, into a family of Eritrean descent. Gebru's early life was shaped by loss, war, and struggle. Her father, an electrical engineer, died when she was five years old, leaving her mother, an economist, to raise Gebru and her two older sisters in one of the most politically stifled countries in Africa.

Although Ethiopia was marred by violence and conflict, Gebru's household environment as she grew up did not reflect the instability outside. Her mother cultivated confidence in young Gebru, telling her she could accomplish her goals by working hard. As Gebru said to Million STEM, "When I was little, I was told I could do anything, and I believed it. If I wasn't among the top in my class, no one in my family was impressed!"

Gebru's mother's model of strength and determination, however, was mostly shown in her actions. When Gebru was in high school, her mother, who had a visa to come to the United States, relocated there to seek job opportunities and better support her family. "She came to the United States at the age of 55 and completely changed her profession," she told Ava Chisling for *ROSS Intelligence* (24 July 2017) before continuing to say, "My mom solves problems in life without complaining. That's something I try to take inspiration from."

When Gebru was a teenager, she sought to join her mother in the United States. Initially the United States denied her entry visa, forcing her to travel to Ireland for a brief period and stay with a sister who was there for work. After Gebru subsequently applied for and was granted political asylum, she moved to Massachusetts at the age of sixteen.

A NEW LIFE IN THE UNITED STATES

Living with her mother in the city of Somerville, a suburb of Boston, Gebru enrolled at a local public high school there. While culture shock and the blatant racism she experienced at school made it difficult for her to settle into her new life, Gebru turned to her family and piano lessons for solace, remaining dedicated to her classes—particularly math and physics, the ones she enjoyed the most. "What I had under my control was that I could go to class and focus on the work," she said to Tom Simonite for *Wired* (8 June 2021).

As her high school time drew to a close, Gebru set her sights on a STEM career, much to the disbelief of some of her teachers, who did not think she could thrive in such a field. It gave her a glimpse of the unfair treatment she would encounter throughout her future

Photo by TechCrunch via Wikimedia Commons

profession, propelled by the dated gender views that women are unfit for STEM careers. "Women are very much interested in STEM. They start out interested and drop off as time goes by," she told Chisling. "To stay in this field, you almost have to be like a warrior."

Following her high school graduation in 2001, Gebru commenced her studies in electrical engineering—following in the footsteps of her late father and older sisters—at Stanford University. She flourished during this time, building an experimental electronic piano key for one of her classes during her junior year in 2004 and landing a hardware internship at Apple, working on projects related to the audio quality of Apple computers. As her internship grew into a job as an audio systems engineer the following year, she took on the challenge of balancing full-time work while continuing her studies.

THRIVING AT APPLE

As an audio systems engineer at Apple, Gebru's work involved designing audio circuitry for a wide array of devices, including iPads and MacBooks, and researching innovative technologies that could enhance the audio quality of future generations of products. For instance, she was among the first to delve into delta-sigma modulators—a class of oversampling analog-to-digital converters—as a potentially usable technology for the iPhone. Neil Warren, Gebru's manager at Apple, was not shy in his praise and admiration for her. "As an electrical engineer, she was fearless," he told Simonite.

In 2007, Gebru worked as an audio software and hardware engineer at the company, a position that allowed her to work in audio-related projects that entailed digital signal processing. However, as committed as she was to her work and academic studies, Gebru also devoted her time championing diversity and inclusion. The following year, in 2008, she withdrew from one of her classes at Stanford to canvass for then senator Barack Obama's presidential campaign, traveling to Colorado and Nevada. "The positive impacts that you bring to the world don't have to necessarily be connected to your work," she said to Lisa Lahde for *Forbes* (10 July 2018). "For me, there was also a separate side of me where I was always involved in social justice. I always organized events, or I was always part of something towards that goal."

After graduating from Stanford with her bachelor's degree in 2008, Gebru continued her studies in electrical engineering, obtaining her master's degree from the same institution in 2010. She stayed at Stanford University, where, that same year, she started a PhD in electrical engineering, leaving her position at Apple after six years with the company. Although she had chosen to focus her research on device physics, she soon changed it to optics, having become interested in image processing—a transformative technology she thought could change the world. Still, by the end of her first year, she found herself lost, and, concerned about the direction her research was taking, decided to take a break from school. During this time, she cofounded the startup MotionThink in 2011, and then enrolled at Hacker School in New York City, in 2012, before making her way back to her doctoral studies.

MICROSOFT AND GOOGLE

Upon returning to Stanford, Gebru's doctoral studies focused on computer vision, which she described to Million STEM as "helping machines understand visual data." She studied under Professor Fei-Fei Li, then director of the Stanford Artificial Intelligence Laboratory, and completed her PhD in 2015. When she took a position with Microsoft Research in 2017, she joined the company's Fairness, Accountability, Transparency, and Ethics in AI team. That same year, she and some friends cofounded Black in AI during the Neural Information Processing Systems (NIPS) conference. She also collaborated with Massachusetts Institute of Technology graduate student Joy Buolamwini, with whom she coauthored a seminal 2018 study about how commercially available facial recognition programs such as those sold by IBM and Microsoft were more accurate in identifying White men than Black women.

Google recruited Gebru in 2018. At first, she was not sure if the culture and values of the organization aligned with her own, however, after the company offered her complete academic freedom, she accepted a position as a research scientist and one of two leaders of Google's Ethical AI team; the other being researcher Margaret Mitchell, whom she had met at Microsoft. While their team had the task of chiefly conducting research, they also wanted to make an impact on the products. For instance, when they noticed that Gmail's Smart Reply automatically used masculine pronouns when the email talked about an engineer, they set out to adjust the system to no longer have gendered pronouns.

Gebru and Mitchell took pride in their department—which, compared to others in the company, was more diverse in gender and race—but problems started to magnify as they clashed with the overall culture of Google. The company was led mostly by White men and was intensely hierarchical. Its 2021 Diversity Annual Report showed that only 1.6 percent of Googlers, as employees are called, were Black women in 2020. Both Gebru and Mitchell noticed that colleagues and managers were excluding them in different ways, such as not crediting them for their accomplishments and leaving them off of emails and out of meetings. "What is the likelihood that I will not be invited to a meeting that I should be at? What is the likelihood that my male colleague will be invited? You start to see the trends," Gebru said to Simonite.

Ultimately, it was a paper written by Gebru and her team, entitled "On the Dangers of Stochastic Parrots: Can Language Models Be Too Big?"—about large language models (LLMs) and their in-depth examination of who benefits from them and who gets harmed by them—that played a significant role in her departure from the company at the end of 2020. According to Gebru, Google had approved her paper for publication but then asked her to withdraw it or take her name off of it. When she asked them to explain why, they declined to do so and fired her on a pretext. The company maintained that she was not fired but had tendered her resignation, which they accepted. Gebru's apparent ouster made headlines. In early December 2020, 2,695 Googlers and 4,302 supporters signed a petition on Medium's Google Walkout for Real Change declaring that they were standing with Gebru against Google's "unprecedented research censorship."

In 2021 Gebru announced she was raising money to launch an independent institute of research, which she planned to model on the work she did while she headed the Ethical AI team at Google. As she continues to fight for more diversity, equity, and inclusivity in STEM careers, her advice for women in the field is to "find your network of other women and allies who will support you. I think it's impossible to survive in STEM as a woman (especially as a Black woman) without this network," she said to Million STEM. "The field is setup to push you out, and you constantly feel that force. Amplify your voice, this is very important."

SUGGESTED READING

Gebru, Timnit. "AI Innovators: How One Woman Followed Her Passion and Brought Diversity to AI." Interview by Lisa Lahde. *Forbes*, 10 July 2018, www.forbes.com/sites/nvidia/2018/07/10/ai-innovators-how-one-woman-followed-her-passion-and-brought-diversity-to-ai/?sh=2f5fd9c0286d. Accessed 10 Nov. 2021.

___. "Excuse Me, Sir, but Where Are All the Women?" Interview by Ava Chisling. *ROSS Intelligence*, 24 July 2017, blog.rossintelligence.com/post/where-are-the-women. Accessed 10 Nov. 2021.

___. "Timnit Gebru." *Million STEM*, www.1mwis.com/profiles/Timnit-Gebru. Accessed 10 Nov. 2021.

Hacia, Graham. "Meet This Year's WIRED25: People Who Are Making Things Better." *Wired*, 9 Sept. 2020, www.wired.com/story/wired25-2020-people-making-things-better. Accessed 10 Nov. 2021.

Metz, Cade, and Daisuke Wakabayashi. "Google Researcher Says She Was Fired over Paper Highlighting Bias in AI." *The New York Times*, 3 Dec. 2020, www.nytimes.com/2020/12/03/technology/google-researcher-timnit-gebru.html. Accessed 10 Nov. 2021.

Simonite, Tom. "What Really Happened When Google Ousted Timnit Gebru." *Wired*, 8 June 2021, www.wired.com/story/google-timnit-gebru-ai-what-really-happened. Accessed 10 Nov. 2021.

—*Maria del Pilar Guzman*

Natalie Geisenberger

Born: February 5, 1988
Occupation: Luger

For German luger Natalie Geisenberger, few things are more motivating than the experience of winning. "I motivate myself through my achievements," she told the magazine of the International Luge Federation (FIL). "I know the feeling of standing at the top of the steps and hearing the German national anthem. And I want to experience this feeling as often as possible." A competitive luger since childhood, Geisenberger experienced that feeling on quite a few occasions as an adult, claiming two gold medals at both the 2014 and 2018 Olympic Games and winning seven FIL Luge World Cup overall titles between 2012 and 2019. She was likewise a perennial contender at the FIL World Championships, competing in both the women's singles and team relay categories. After taking the 2019–20 FIL season off, Geisenberger returned to competition with a newly relaxed mindset. "I've achieved everything I wanted to achieve," she said, as reported by Andrew Binner for the website of the Olympic Games (9 Nov. 2021). "It's a lot easier for me because everything that's coming now is an encore." By the end of 2021, Geisenberger's so-called encore encompassed a silver-medal World Championships performance as well as yet another World Cup overall title.

EARLY LIFE AND EDUCATION

Natalie Geisenberger was born on February 5, 1988, in Munich, then part of West Germany. Along with her parents, Helmut and Birgit, she moved to the town of Miesbach as a young child. Geisenberger initially entered the world of winter sports as a skier but developed an interest in luge in fourth grade, while attending a trial event held by her school. In the sport of luge, an athlete navigates an open sled down a twisting downhill track, often reaching a high speed. Drawn to the fast-paced and thrilling sport, Geisenberger began competing in luge while attending primary school in Miesbach.

Geisenberger pursued her secondary education at the Gymnasium Miesbach but was eventually required to leave that institution, as her luge training and competitions were causing her to be absent from school frequently. Geisenberger and her father, who came to serve as her manager, subsequently relocated to Berchtesgaden, a city known for its winter-sports facilities. Geisenberger studied and trained in Berchtesgaden on weekdays during that period and returned to Miesbach on the weekends to spend time with her mother.

Luge had long been a popular sport in Germany and following the sport's addition to the Winter Olympic Games in 1964, German lugers proved particularly successful: between 1964 and 2006, lugers representing West Germany, East Germany, or a united Germany amassed a total of sixty-five Olympic medals. As such, the luge world into which Geisenberger entered as a child was highly competitive, with athletes struggling to earn the right to compete at the highest levels. "For us the competition starts in the juniors and goes all the way up to the seniors," she later explained to Karolos Grohmann for *Reuters* (14 Jan. 2010). "It also lasts the whole year not just the winter. Some very good athletes from our country, who would have easily qualified for other countries, do not make the cut." In addition to competing in luge as a teenager and adult, Geisenberger studied at a sports academy run by Germany's Federal Police, which offers training in winter sports in addition to helping athletes prepare for an eventual career outside of the sporting world.

EARLY CAREER

Active in both singles and group luge events, Geisenberger found significant success on the junior level, winning her first FIL Junior World Championships in 2004. She went on to win a total of six events at the Junior World Championships in addition to more than a dozen Junior World Cup events. After moving up to the senior level of competition,

Photo by Sandro Halank, via Wikimedia Commons

Geisenberger won her first senior title in 2008, at the FIL European Luge Championships in Italy. Her win there would become the first of twelve women's singles victories at the European Luge Championships between 2008 and 2021. She also won several team relay events during that period. Also a participant in FIL Luge World Cup events, she ranked second in the women's singles competition for three consecutive seasons beginning with the 2009–10 season.

INTERNATIONAL CONTENDER

Geisenberger made her Olympic debut in 2010, at the Winter Olympic Games held in and around Vancouver, Canada. In light of the popularity of luge in Germany, the tournament required her to compete not only against lugers from other countries but also against fellow members of Team Germany. While that competition could have sparked interpersonal conflicts within the German Olympic team, Geisenberger found that the atmosphere within the team was "very good," she told Grohmann. "Everyone understands that it is the fastest athlete who wins and not the most annoying athlete so we have a great time, in the evenings we all do something together," she added. In the Winter Olympics, the women's singles luge competition consists of four timed runs on the designated track. The times to complete each run are added together, and a competitor's final ranking is determined by that athlete's overall time. Geisenberger's total time of 2 minutes and 47.101 seconds at the 2010 Games resulted in a third-place finish, earning her the bronze medal.

The 2012–13 luge season was a particularly noteworthy one for Geisenberger, as she earned her first World Cup overall title. She would go on to claim that overall title on six more occasions between 2013 and 2019. Geisenberger likewise competed regularly in the BMW Sprint World Cup, winning the women's singles competitions for 2016–17, 2017–18, and 2018–19. She was also active in team relay competitions. She finished in first place in both the women's singles and team relay categories at the 2013 FIL World Championships and, by the end of 2019, had claimed an additional seven World Championships gold medals.

OLYMPIC GOLD MEDALIST

Geisenberger returned to Olympic competition at the 2014 Winter Games in Sochi, Russia. Competing in the women's singles competition, held outside of Sochi in Krasnaya Polyana, she faced off against both international competitors and rivals from her own country and worked to meet her own exacting standards. "Runs one, two and three were nearly perfect," she told *Sports Illustrated* (12 Feb. 2014) after the competition. "The last one was a little bit . . . wasn't perfect, but it was good enough." Although Geisenberger was dissatisfied with elements of her own performance, her total time of 3 minutes and 19.768 seconds was 1.139 seconds ahead of second place, a gap that was later reported to be the second-largest distance between first and second place in the five decades of Olympic luge competition.

Geisenberger's impressive performance put her ahead of defending medalist Tatjana Hüfner, earning the athlete her first Olympic gold medal. "It was a childhood dream that came true, and when I looked at the scoreboard after the fourth run and saw that I am now actually an Olympic champion, it was an indescribable feeling," she told the German magazine *Sport Bild*, as reported by Binner. "As an athlete, to finally achieve my lifelong dream could hardly be put into words. All of the hard work and hardship of the years before have been worth it. You can't beat that." Geisenberger also competed in the team relay luge event, the first such competition held at the Olympics. Competing in collaboration with teammates Felix Loch, a competitor in the men's event, and doubles lugers Tobias Arlt and Tobias Wendl, she defeated the Latvian and Russian relay teams to claim her second gold medal of the 2014 Games.

In light of her success in 2014, Geisenberger went into the 2018 Winter Olympics in South Korea with a degree of confidence but acknowledged that anything could happen in such a competition. "I know the feeling of being at the top, and I know what I've had to do for it," she told Simon Evans for *Reuters* (7 Jan. 2018). "You can do anything for it, but, in the end, whether it is going to be enough for a medal cannot be predicted." Geisenberger went on to successfully defend her Olympic title, beating Canadian bronze medalist Alex Gough and German silver medalist Dajana Eitberger to claim the women's singles gold. In the team relay, Geisenberger, Wendl, and Arlt partnered with men's singles luger Johannes Ludwig to beat teams from Canada and Austria, claiming Germany's second consecutive relay gold.

RETURN TO COMPETITION

Geisenberger took a break from competing during the 2019–20 season, as she was pregnant with her first child at that time but returned to international luge competition the following season. "It's a big challenge," she told journalists following her return, as reported by Binner. "But of course the other years before were also not so easy. I can't compare [to past years] because the situation is completely different now."

Following her return, Geisenberger claimed the Eberspächer World Cup overall title for the 2020–21 season, having won two events during the season and placed second in nine others, and placed second in the World Championships women's singles competition. "If someone had told me in the summer that I would win the overall World Cup as well as a silver medal at the World Championships, I would have taken it immediately," she later said, as reported by Binner. "I can be very proud of how it all went." Geisenberger also finished fourth in the women's sprint category at the World Championships and claimed second place in the BMW Sprint World Cup women's singles competition.

Due to Geisenberger's continued impressive performance following her return to competition, the winter-sports media widely projected that she would again join the German Olympic team and attempt to defend her gold medals at the 2022 Olympic Games in Beijing, China. She traveled to China in late 2021 to train and race but was displeased with her experience there. After an individual who traveled on a charter flight with Geisenberger tested positive for COVID-19, Geisenberger was required to participate in a strict quarantine process during which she was confined to her room for extended periods and provided with inadequate food. She subsequently spoke out about her experiences, noting that she was beginning to reconsider participating in the Olympics. "The conditions that we experienced there speak in favor of not necessarily going back there again," she told the German broadcaster BR, as quoted by *NBC Sports* (8 Dec. 2021). "It would be a very, very hard step because the Olympic Games are the biggest thing for an athlete."

PERSONAL LIFE

Geisenberger married Markus Scheer in 2018. Their first child, a son named Leo, was born in 2020. In addition to competing in luge events, Geisenberger enjoyed photography and skiing.

SUGGESTED READING

Binner, Andrew. "Four-Time Luge Olympic Champion Natalie Geisenberger: My Life as a Mother and History-Maker." *Olympics*, 9 Nov. 2021, olympics.com/en/news/luge-natalie-geisenberger-mother-history-maker. Accessed 10 Dec. 2021.

Evans, Simon. "Queen of the Luge, Geisenberger Eyes More Olympics Gold." *Reuters*, 7 Jan. 2018, www.reuters.com/article/csports-us-olympics-2018-luge-geisenberg-idCAKBN1EW0HY-OCASP. Accessed 10 Dec. 2021.

Geisenberger, Natalie. "INTERVIEW-Olympics-German Geisenberger Eyes Medal in First Games." Interview by Karolos Grohmann. *Reuters*, 14 Jan. 2010, www.reuters.com/article/olympics-luge-geisenberger/interview-olympics-german-geisenberger-eyes-medal-in-first-games-idUSLDE60D0L620100114. Accessed 10 Dec. 2021.

Gillen, Nancy. "Geisenberger Clinches Eighth Overall Women's Luge World Cup Title." *Inside the Games*, 7 Feb. 2021, www.insidethegames.biz/articles/1103963/geisenberger-wins-eighth-world-cup-title. Accessed 10 Dec. 2021.

"Natalie Geisenberger, Olympic Luge Champion, Mulls Skipping Beijing Games." *NBC Sports*, 8 Dec. 2021, olympics.nbcsports.com/2021/12/08/natalie-geisenberger-luge-olympics/. Accessed 10 Dec. 2021.

"Natalie Geisenberger Wins Olympic Luge Title." *Sports Illustrated*, 12 Feb. 2014, www.si.com/olympics/2014/02/12/ap-oly-lug-womens-luge. Accessed 10 Dec. 2021.

"News." *International Luge Federation*, www.fil-luge.org/en/news/natalie-geisenberger-in-fil-magazine-i-motivate-myself-through-my-achievements. Accessed 10 Dec. 2021.

—*Joy Crelin*

Aaron Gilbert

Born: 1979
Occupation: Artist

Painter Aaron Gilbert established himself as a force on the international art scene, with his work not only exhibited in galleries across the globe but also added to the permanent collections of prestigious institutions such as the Brooklyn Museum and the Whitney Museum of American Art, among others. Considering subjects covering multilayered emotional ground—domestic scenes in which sensuality and yearning abound between lovers and depictions of figures experiencing common societal predicaments—his visual narratives are noted for brimming with spirituality, symbolism, and intimacy while balancing human realism with a sense of possibilities.

Often drawing inspiration from sacred, religious art, including Byzantine iconography and Mexican retablos, and capturing figures that have personally been part of his life or that he has observed, Gilbert made art his most dedicated pursuit, viewing it as a resource in his quest to be an agent of change. As he related to Gavin Brown in an interview for *i-D* (1 Dec. 2021), "I would say that I operate on the idea that none of us know how powerful we are. None of us know what we're capable of doing or why we're here and, to me, the most interesting thing in being alive is trying to decipher that and unlock it and be a transformative force in the world."

EARLY LIFE AND EDUCATION

Aaron J. Gilbert's artistic trajectory commenced in Altoona, Pennsylvania, where he was born in 1979. While not much is known about his early life, he stated in interviews that he developed a keen interest in painting at an early age. That passion later extended to the appreciation of the visual language of Mexican retablos, traditional folk-art images often depicting Jesus, the Virgin Mary, or saints. "I am really interested in retablos, Mexican devotional paintings, because they combine that impulse for making a spiritual or metaphysical object with very personal narratives," he said to Emily Steer in an interview for the art magazine *Elephant* (20 July 2020).

Following his high school years, Gilbert enrolled at Pennsylvania State University, where he earned an Associate of Science (AS) degree in mechanical engineering technology in 2000. He later enrolled at the Rhode Island School of Design in Providence, Rhode Island, where he completed a Bachelor of Fine Arts (BFA) degree in painting in 2005. Not done with his formal education, he continued his academic journey at Yale University in New Haven, Connecticut, where he further learned about and experimented with art, graduating with a Master of Fine Arts (MFA) degree in painting in 2008. As a source of some income to support himself and his family, he worked a variety of jobs throughout this time, including in the areas of security and the fabrication of components and structures in workshops.

PAINTING BEGINNINGS

In 2010 Gilbert received the Rosenthal Family Foundation Award in Painting and was selected for the Art Purchase Program, both of which fall within the jurisdiction of the American Academy of Arts and Letters. This both helped sustain his painting career that had been slowly but surely taking off in the previous few years and brought him a new degree of recognition in the art world. Inspired, in part, by Byzantine icons and Mexican retablos, Gilbert's paintings were exhibited at various art galleries in his homebase, the New York City borough of Brooklyn, in 2011 and 2012, including North

Henry Annex, NURTUREart, and AMO Studios.

Although Gilbert's later work would evolve to typically feature more personal and vulnerable moments—with human subjects, including Gilbert himself, at the center of the visual narrative—his earlier paintings sometimes presented more mundane objects. His 2010 oil-on-aluminum painting *Carton*, for instance, illustrates a pinkish-red empty egg carton set against a greenish background. While to the untrained eye this may look random and meaningless, the seemingly mundane imagery of an egg carton evokes elements of existence for the artist. "There's something so synthetic about them," he said to Mary Jones in an interview for *BOMB* magazine (9 Mar. 2011). "It's the in-between space where the chicken's life force is held in suspension, like a synthetic womb."

The early 2010s additionally saw Gilbert's art—more precisely, his 2007 oil-on-canvas painting titled *The New One*—included in the *American Identities: A New Look* exhibition curated at the Brooklyn Museum. Described by Gilbert in interviews as an exploration of the concept of birth and the movement from one realm of existence to another, more conscious one, the subtle *The New One* appears to depict a woman kneeling by a bathtub as she bathes a young child whose fragile body floats in the water. The implicit but powerful narrative found in *The New One* would become a defining characteristic of his work.

In 2013 Gilbert joined the Fountainhead artistic community in Miami, Florida, as an artist in residence. He had previously been awarded residencies at Yaddo (2012) in Saratoga Springs, New York, and at the American Academy in Rome (2008) in Rome, Italy. Such appointments help provide artists with valuable resources to support their creative process.

CRAFTING DOMESTIC SCENES

Gilbert's artistic pieces were shown at prominent locations all over the world in 2014 and 2015, including the Mottahedan Projects Art Gallery in Dubai, United Arab Emirates, and the Amberwood House in London, England. With such exposure, the artist started gaining traction internationally. A large part of his national and international success was attributed to the meticulously crafted domestic scenes increasingly featured in his work. His painting *Phantom Limb*, completed around the mid-2010s, for instance, depicts an intimate moment of two lovers looking at each other while lying in bed. Even though the male figure is missing a limb, one can see a ghost limb caressing the woman's face, implying a yearning for an emotional connection no longer existing between the lovers. "I like domestic scenes because they can display the messiness of conflicting impulses that are inside of us," Gilbert explained to Julia Phillips in an interview for *Mousse* magazine (2 July 2018). "A painting of a love scene can lay bare these truths of what happens when two people become entangled in each other's lives."

In 2015, Gilbert was the recipient of the prestigious Louis Comfort Tiffany Foundation grant. The following year his work was exhibited at the Brooklyn-based arts organization BRIC. As he continued refining his style, he pushed the envelope with his domestic scenes. Notably, his depictions of physical closeness between lovers grant many of his paintings from this period a quality of surreal sensuality and a dreamlike mood. Examples of this intimacy can be seen in paintings such as *Quiet Storm* (2019), *Lincoln Town Car* (2019), and *Lupe, Aries* (2021).

Whereas some of Gilbert's artistic pieces evoked intimacy and privacy because of their focus on familial and romantic relationships, in other works he captured equally private interactions without the subjects clearly sharing such bonds. His 2016 painting *CitiBank*, for instance, features a bank teller and a patron engaged in a private conversation that does not seem to be bank-related, per se. As the client holds a note for the teller, the viewer is left wondering about the true nature of the exchange. "I leave the specifics of the interaction open to multiple interpretations (a flirtation or a heist), but what is clear is that the power and agency of both figures is not owned by any institution," Gilbert revealed to Phillips.

DELVING INTO SOCIAL ISSUES

Gilbert continued to make an impression on the art scene worldwide through both group exhibitions and solo shows. In 2019 his works were presented and largely well received at the Nicodim Gallery in Bucharest, Romania; New York City's Lyles and King gallery; and Lulu in Mexico City, Mexico, among others. As the 2020s began, the crises of an increasingly

socio-politically divided United States found their way into Gilbert's paintings. Incorporating pressing social issues into his artistic practice, including immigration, homelessness, the effects of incarceration, and the COVID-19 pandemic, added another layer to his already profound work. For example, the 2020 oil-on-linen painting *Ready Willing and Able* depicts three men drinking at a bar. Two of them don the uniforms of participants in Ready, Willing and Able, a New York program for people who have committed to rebuilding their lives as well as those of their family members following experiences with unemployment, incarceration, and homelessness.

In 2021, Gilbert's oil-on-linen piece *Empire State of Mind/ Flaco 730 Broadway* (2020) became a permanent part of the Whitney Museum of American Art collection in New York City. That same year, several of his visual narratives centering upon representations of people living through treacherous societal conditions, including the abovementioned *Ready Willing and Able*, were part of the *1981–2021* exhibition at PPOW gallery in New York City. The two-person show—deemed by *The New York Times* one of four art gallery shows people should see—combined Gilbert's artistic work with the work of the late Martin Wong, an artist of the late twentieth century whose work, like Gilbert's, delves deep into social crises. Other works by Gilbert, recognized by critics as displaying humans' potential for transformation, included in this exhibition were the oil-on-linen *Nightshift B15* (2020), the oil-on-canvas *Goddess Walks among Us Now* (2020), and the oil-on-canvas *Song to the Siren* (2020).

Gilbert continued to be an in-demand exhibitor. From December 2021 into early 2022 he was featured at the Chris Sharp Gallery in Los Angeles. He also continued to discuss the themes represented in his art and the social forces influencing it. Talking to Brown about how the scenarios presented in his paintings are a product of capitalism, Gilbert said, "I want that force to be very present. I want it to be as dominant in the work as it is in our lives. You have the presence of these forces but then I'm interested in finding where we can access the power that can circumvent the rules of the game, you know?"

PERSONAL LIFE

Gilbert based himself in Brooklyn, New York. He was married to artist and photographer Deana Lawson, whom he met in Pennsylvania in the early 2000s and with whom he went on to have two children: son, Judah, and daughter, Grace. Lawson. Gilbert remained close to both children after separating, and they have been regular subjects in his paintings. As he said to Jones, "If the work doesn't reflect my experience, it can't be coming from the right place. I can speak about my life with the most specificity and the most nuance, and I think that's how we live experience."

SUGGESTED READING

Gilbert, Aaron. "Aaron Gilbert's Paintings Convey the Profound Potential of Human Life." Interview by Emily Steer. *Elephant*, 20 July 2020, elephant.art/ aaron-gilbert-painting-interview-devotional-transformation-20072020. Accessed 30 Apr. 2022.

___. "Artist Aaron Gilbert on Circumventing the Rules of Capitalism." Interview by Gavin Brown. *i-D*, 1 Dec. 2021, i-d.vice.com/en_ uk/article/pkppb9/aaron-gilbert-interview. Accessed 30 Apr. 2022.

___. "Post Impressions: The Enlightenment by Mary Jones." Interview by Mary Jones. *BOMB*, 9 Mar. 2011, bombmagazine. org/articles/post-impressions-the-enlightenment. Accessed 30 Apr. 2022.

___. "Do You Believe in Evil? Julia Phillips and Aaron Gilbert in Conversation." Interview by Julia Phillips. *Mousse*, 2 July 2018, www. moussemagazine.it/magazine/julia-phillips-aaron-gilbert-2018. Accessed 30 Apr. 2022.

Wu, Simon. "Social Scales: Aaron Gilbert and Martin Wong at PPOW." *Art in America*, Art Media, 20 May 2021, www.artnews.com/ art-in-america/aia-reviews/martin-wong-aaron-gilbert-social-realism-1234593567. Accessed 30 Apr. 2022.

SELECTED WORKS

The New One, 2007; *Carton*, 2010; *CitiBank*, 2016; *Quiet Storm*, 2019; *Empire State of Mind/ Flaco 730 Broadway*, 2020; *Song to the Siren*, 2020

—*Maria del Pilar Guzman*

Leela Gilday

Born: 1974
Occupation: Singer-songwriter

Leela Gilday, a Dene singer-songwriter, has enjoyed a long and fruitful career since releasing her award-winning debut folk album, *Spirit World, Solid Wood*, in 2002. She has claimed multiple Juno Awards, Canada's most prestigious music award, and in 2021 was also named Indigenous Songwriter of the Year at the Canadian Folk Music Awards. Gilday, who was born in the Dene Nation located in Canada's Northwest Territories, has described her sound as Indigenous folk roots music. A classically trained vocalist who began performing at an early age, she studied opera at the University of Alberta. Although she has drawn inspiration from contemporary soul, jazz, and blues artists, her passion has continued to lie in the music and peoples of the North. When discussing her musical style, she has said that it is "rooted in traditional elements such as the drum, the heartbeat, and our Dene songs," as she told Jenna Melanson in an interview for *Canadian Beats Media* (4 Sept. 2019). Though many of her earlier songs incorporated Dene words and phrases, she began a serious study and reclaiming of her Dene language during the COVID-19 pandemic in 2020. That same year, she appeared in a pan-national interpretation of George Frideric Handel's *Messiah*, performing one of the opera's movements in her home community's Dene language.

Gilday's 2019 album *North Star Calling*, which earned her a Juno Award for Indigenous Artist of the Year, includes the song "K'eintah Natse Ju," which explores the painful legacy of Canada's residential school system and the need for healing. "The power and resilience for a people to survive legislated policies, genocidal policies to wipe out our families is remarkable and it's a story that needs to be told in different ways and celebrated. I think in my songs it's apparent that I'm inspired by that strength and resilience," she explained to Janet Smith for *Stir* (20 July 2021). Continuing to work on a collection of songs written entirely in her Dene language in 2022, she also relished a return to live touring performances.

EARLY LIFE AND EDUCATION

Leela Gilday was born in 1974, and raised largely in the area of Yellowknife in the Northwest Territories of Canada. Her father, Bill, was a White jazz musician who taught music. Her mother, Cindy, a Sahtu Dene survivor of Canada's brutal residential school system, came from the Great Bear Lake community of Déline. Jay, Gilday's brother, also went on to become an Indigenous folk musician.

With vocal talents that were obvious to her family from an early age, Gilday was often a part of local choirs. As a musician himself, her father nurtured and encouraged his children's talents as he introduced them to a wide variety of sound. "I began singing before I could walk and started performing solo when I was 8," she told Melanson. A highlight of that formative time was taking the stage at the established Northwest Territories festival Folk on the Rocks. For several years, her home was in Rae-Edzo (later Behchokǫ̀), a small Tłı̨chǫ community near Yellowknife. Occasionally, she had the chance to experience performing outside of her home province. At the age of thirteen, she and her brother were able to display their abilities at a Toronto venue alongside one of the city's prestigious children's choirs. "It was such an amazing opportunity," Gilday's mother told the journalist Jasmine Budak for Budak's blog (15 Dec. 2007). "A chance for the kids to do music—proper music."

To further her formal music education and training, Gilday enrolled at the University of Alberta in Edmonton, where she indulged her love of opera with a focus on the form. She told Budak that she had dreams of singing at the Metropolitan Opera in New York City, but several years into the program realized that the operatic format did not fit her true musical aspirations, especially writing her own pieces and telling her own stories. Instead, she found herself gravitating to folk music. "I just wanted to write songs about who I was and my home," she related to Budak. "In a sense I already knew how to write a folk song from growing up around it. It's a craft, but it's not rocket science."

SPIRIT WORLD, SOLID WOOD

Following her 1997 college graduation, Gilday relocated to Toronto, where she taught herself to play guitar. She wrote songs while holding

Photo by Vancouver 125 - The City of Vancouver, via Wikimedia Commons

various employment gigs to make ends meet, one of which eventually entailed working in the office of an Indigenous-owned production company called Big Soul Productions.

Self-managing her attempted music career at the same time, Gilday worked the open-mic circuit, test-driving her new songs in local bars. "I really put my whole effort into it," she recalled to Budak. "I did all my own postering, carried all my own gear. I certainly paid my dues." In 2001, she cold-called John Switzer, a producer, and asked him if she could play him a song. When he demurred, telling her to just send a demo, she maintained her position on playing for him live. It was a wise, if risky, gamble. "She knew her songs would come across better live," Switzer told Budak years later. "There's a personality to what she does that has to be seen."

With Switzer's guidance, Gilday released her debut album, *Spirit World, Solid Wood*, in 2002. The soft-rock songs that made up the track list drew on her memories of growing up in the North. *Spirit World* provided a powerful launching pad for her career, beginning prominently with the acclaim associated with her dominance at the 2002 Canadian Aboriginal Music Awards, where she secured wins in the categories of Best Female Artist, Best Folk Album, and Best Songwriter. In

2003, the album received a Juno nomination for Aboriginal Recording of the Year.

SUBSEQUENT ALBUMS

Later, Gilday would criticize her first album as "all over the place." "There's a country tune, and other stuff," she told Jim Barber for *Music Life Magazine* (22 Aug. 2019). With each subsequent recording, she said, "I have strived to move towards a consistent sound, but still be able to express myself in all the ways that I want to." However, success, with all the demands that come with it, particularly for someone managing themself, was so swift for Gilday that she felt burned out by 2004 and even considered quitting the music business altogether. Instead, she took some time off, traveling for herself instead of performing, before putting out her second album, *Sedzé*, in 2006. Commonly noted as her commercial breakthrough, it won the 2007 Juno Award for Aboriginal Recording of the Year and finally enabled her to hire an agent.

Gilday released *Calling All Warriors*, her third album, in 2010, and *Heart of the People* in 2014. The latter album earned her another Juno nod. Her music often explored the horror and indignity of Canada's colonial past and its lingering effects on the present. In 2021, she stated that Canada had reached "a time of reckoning." While preferring to write songs about resilience, she said, as quoted by Smith, that Canadians needed to confront their "dark history" as well as the "current realities that Indigenous people face."

GHO-BAH AND OTHER PROJECTS

In 2017, Gilday gathered a group of Indigenous musicians, as well as other allied artists outside of Indigenous communities, for a project titled Gho-Bah/Gombaa, which translates to "first light of dawn." She said the project, which debuted as a performance on National Indigenous Peoples Day before being captured on CD, was aimed at reconciliation. "Reconciliation is a big buzzword right now," she told Juanita Taylor for *CBC News* (21 June 2017). She was referring to a period that had begun largely in 2008 with the formation of a commission to work with the Canadian government to uncover and attempt to repair the impact from atrocities inflicted upon Indigenous groups. This Truth and Reconciliation Commission was particularly focused on survivors of Canada's residential schools. The goal of the project, Gilday said, was to allow artists to consider what reconciliation meant to them. "What we came to as a collective is what we wanted to focus on is the resilience of our people, as Indigenous people making it through culturally legislated genocide," she told Taylor. For the project, she performed a piece called "Give What Our Hearts Can't Take."

Further displaying her versatility and passion, in 2019 Gilday appeared as an actor in a film called *Red Snow*, made by the Métis writer and director Marie Clements. *Red Snow*, a film about grief and place, stars veteran Indigenous actor Tantoo Cardinal and follows the story of Dylan, a Gwich'in soldier in the Canadian Army who has been taken hostage by the Taliban during the war in Afghanistan.

NORTH STAR CALLING AND BEYOND

The year 2019 also saw Gilday release the product of her labor with Toronto-based producer Hill Kourkoutis, a creation she later described to *CBC News* (5 June 2021) as her "most vulnerable" album up to that point. *North Star Calling*, her first album in nearly five years, mines the singer's turbulent past and highlights her connection to the land. She told Barber that, like many Indigenous youth, she struggled with her mental health. "When I was 17 and heading off to study music and opera in university, my mom used to say to me, 'if you feel sad, my girl, you just go out onto the land and go and feel the wind in your hair, look up and see the stars, look at the trees, feel the earth, be by the water. It will help you to feel better,'" she recalled. "*North Star Calling* is about that exact connection. If you feel alone, if you feel sad, make sure you're going out and being reconnected to the land." Her work on the album ultimately brought home a Juno Award for Indigenous Artist of the Year in 2021. (The award ceremony had been postponed due to the COVID-19 pandemic.)

One song on *North Star Calling*, the folk rock, alt-country inflected "K'eintah Natse Ju," has a chorus written in Dene and explores the prolonged effects of colonization and residential schools. At the time, Gilday felt comfortable using Dene phrases in her songs, but as she was unable to speak the language, hesitated to engage with it further. During the COVID-19 pandemic, she committed to better acquainting herself with and reclaiming her Dene language. In 2020, the first year of the pandemic, she worked with the Toronto Theatre Company Against the Grain on a new interpretation of Handel's *Messiah*, called *Messiah/Complex*. It was the first time she had performed opera in decades, and she was happy to get the chance to return to the form. The piece, codirected by Inuvialuit, Dene, and Cree artist Reneltta Arluk, offers a pan-national, diverse take on the 1741 oratorio. Gilday sang the movement "I Know That My Redeemer Liveth" in the language of her Délı̨nę home community. Against the Grain, she told Blair McBride for *NNSL Media* (25 Nov. 2020), "invited me to make the piece my own." She then added, "I wasn't restricted to using the text or the language in the way it was originally used. So I rewrote the piece to reflect my spiritual connection to the land and water and the earth. And then I sat down with my mom and a few of my aunties, and we translated it into Dene K'e and I sang that piece."

This experience bolstered Gilday's confidence in incorporating the language in her writing and music, with the help of collaborators, on a larger scale. "I have always used phrases in the past, but being a Dene language learner, it wasn't within my power to embark on telling full stories," she told Brock Weir for the *Toronto Star* (31 Mar. 2022). "I have written and will be performing a selection of songs that are in my language." Returning to touring for the first time since the beginning of the pandemic, she debuted some of these songs on the road in 2022. At the same time, she joined with her brother to bring their act, Sechile Sedare, to public audiences as well.

PERSONAL LIFE

Gilday married Yellowknifer Darrel Mack. Together with Mack, she helped raise her stepson, Brandon. In 2021, Mack was diagnosed with esophageal cancer.

SUGGESTED READING

Barber, Jim. "*North Star Calling* Is Leela Gilday's Love Letter to the Healing Power of the Natural World." *Music Life Magazine*, 22 Aug. 2019, www.musiclifemagazine. net/north-star-calling-is-leela-gildays-love-letter-to-the-healing-power-of-the-natural-world/. Accessed 31 Aug. 2022.

Budak, Jasmine. "Folk (Rock) Hero." *Jasmine Budak*, 15 Dec. 2007, jasminebudak. com/2007/12/15/folk-rock-hero/. Accessed 31 Aug. 2022.

Gilday, Leela. "Five Questions with Leela Gilday." Interview by Jenna Melanson. *Canadian Beats Media*, 4 Sept. 2019, canadianbeats.ca/2019/09/04/five-questions-with-leela-gilday/. Accessed 31 Aug. 2022.

McBride, Blair. "Leela Gilday Brings Dene Language, Perspective to New Production of Handel's *Messiah*." *NNSL Media*, 25 Nov. 2020, www.nnsl.com/yellowknifer/leela-gilday-brings-dene-language-perspective-to-new-production-of-handels-messiah/. Accessed 1 Sept. 2022.

Smith, Janet. "Singer-Songwriter Leela Gilday Reconnects with the Land and Reflects on a Year of Reckoning." *Stir*, 20 July 2021, www. createastir.ca/articles/leela-gilday-mission-folk-festival. Accessed 31 Aug. 2022.

Taylor, Juanita. "Northern Musicians Explore Reconciliation through Song in Gho-Bah Project." *CBC News*, 21 June 2017, www.cbc.ca/news/canada/north/gho-bah-project-1.4170376. Accessed 1 Sept. 2022.

Weir, Brock. "Juno Winner Leela Gilday Brings Powerful, Personal Music to Aurora Cultural Centre." *Toronto Star*, 31 Mar. 2022, www. thestar.com/news/canada/2022/03/31/juno-winner-leela-gilday-brings-powerful-personal-music-to-aurora-cultural-centre. html. Accessed 1 Sept. 2022.

SELECTED WORKS

Spirit World, Solid Wood, 2002; *Sedzé*, 2006; *Calling All Warriors*, 2010; *Heart of the People*, 2014; *North Star Calling*, 2019

—*Molly Hagan*

Owl Goingback

Born: May 1, 1959
Occupation: Author

On February 5, 2020, the Horror Writers Association (HWA) announced that it was giving a Lifetime Achievement Award to Choctaw and Cherokee author Owl Goingback at that year's Bram Stoker Awards ceremony. One of the highest honors bestowed upon horror and dark fantasy writers, it was awarded to Goingback to acknowledge how his fiction, including award-winning novels like *Crota* (1996) and *Coyote Rage* (2019), had "substantially" influenced both genres in the thirty-three years that he had been a professional writer. Indeed, readers who become familiar with Goingback's prolific body of work can attest to why he is one of the most beloved and award-winning horror writers of his generation. In addition to being a deft storyteller with a dark, terrifying imagination, his fiction reflects his Indigenous heritage by revolving around Native American characters, folklore, and themes. For Goingback, writing horror stories has been both a way to give back to a genre that he has loved since childhood and to expand Native American representation in literature—both on the page and as author. "I also wanted to prove that Native Americans are much more than the cardboard stereotypes often portrayed in movies and on television," he explained to the Horror Writers Association (11 Oct. 2021). "We aren't heathens, or savages, and drunken Indian isn't one word. I felt that every accomplishment I achieved as a writer was being shared with other Indigenous people, and maybe even opening a few doors for others to follow in my footsteps."

EARLY LIFE

Owl Goingback was born on May 1, 1959, in St. Louis, Missouri, to Cherokee and Choctaw parents. He was named after an ancestor who, according to Cherokee legend, was separated from his family until an owl showed him the way back home. In his earliest years, Goingback's mother served in the military, leading the family to experience numerous moves. She remarried when he was five years old, and they moved to a town about seventy miles outside of St. Louis; it was so small that it only had one four-way stop sign.

It was in this small town that Goingback's family lived on five rural acres of land. An only child with no neighbors to play with, Goingback was often lonely but found comfort in fiction and was an avid reader. He would often check out books from the local library or purchase paperbacks from the drug store. In addition to being a science fiction fan, he also loved the horror genre. "I've always been in love with all things scary, even at a very early age," he stated in an interview with the HWA. "I remember watching horror movies with my family when I was only three or four years old,

my hands pressed tightly over my eyes during the scary parts, peeking through the cracks between my fingers, promising my parents that I wasn't scared."

For the young Goingback, films like *Jaws* (1975) and *The Exorcist* (1973) were especially formative. So was the magazine *Famous Monsters of Filmland*, which he loved for its pages full of images of Frankenstein and Dracula. Reflecting on his affinity for *Famous Monsters*, Goingback told Frances Susanna Nevill for the *Orlando Weekly* (23 Oct. 2019), "These magazines really captured the imagination of kids like me and I felt these monsters, like me, were lonely but also probably misunderstood."

It was not until middle school that Goingback discovered that he enjoyed writing fiction as much as he loved reading it. This revelation came about in the eighth grade when his teacher gave an assignment to write a one-page story. He turned in a comedic piece that was so good that the teacher read it out loud and even hung it on the classroom wall for the parents to see during an open house. At the time, Goingback was an outcast and so the experience of having his classmates laugh at the jokes he wrote bolstered his self-esteem. Later, while in high school, Goingback began charging his classmates money to write their papers for them.

JOINING THE MILITARY

In the mid-1970s, when Goingback turned seventeen, he graduated early from high school so that he could join the military. At the time, he was worried that he would be stuck in his small hometown forever. Thanks to the GI Bill, he was able to join the Air Force and receive training from Embry-Riddle Aeronautical University in Daytona Beach, Florida, where he learned to become a jet engine mechanic. While serving as a member of the Air Force, he was stationed in Europe and the Middle East and achieved the rank of sergeant. He left the military several years later, however, when they refused to allow him a say in where he would next be stationed.

Around the early 1980s, Goingback opened a restaurant and lounge in Georgia, with his wife, Nancy Santos Bello (a professional cook). Although he was not writing at the time, he still viewed the world through a writer's perspective. While running the restaurant, for example, he often found himself taking note of his customers and their stories. Then, one day in 1986, he and Nancy were watching a television interview with the horror writer Stephen King, and Nancy jokingly asked why her husband could not be as smart as King. Goingback took her hypothetical question as a challenge and decided to prove her wrong by publishing some of his own writing. He had heard that writers are supposed to write what they know, and so he decided to write a piece on one of his favorite hobbies: martial arts. To his surprise, the article was not only published in a magazine, but he got paid for it. When his next article was also a success, Goingback realized that he did, in fact, have the skills to become a professional writer.

FINDING SUCCESS AS AN AUTHOR

After gaining some experience as a freelance article writer, Goingback focused primarily on writing short horror and science fiction stories, most of which were led by Native American characters. During this time in the mid-1980s, there were almost no Native American writers working in those genres. Furthermore, the few books that did explore the Indigenous experience were not written by Native authors and subsequently got many aspects of their culture wrong.

In his interview with the HWA, Goingback explained why he was motivated to include his heritage into his work: "I've used Indigenous characters in most of my books and stories, because I wanted to share a culture rich in history, folklore, and ceremony, and often very misunderstood," he remarked. "Like the traditional oral storytellers of my people, I wanted to create stories that were enjoyable while weaving a bit of teaching into the narrative. That way I'm educating in addition to entertaining."

In the years that followed, Goingback began publishing short stories in various anthologies, including "Tacahale" (1992), "Spoils of War" (1993), "Animal Sounds" (1994), "Fang of the Wolf" (1994), and "Gator Bait" (1994). In 1995, his short story "Grass Dancer," about a Native American teenager drafted into the Vietnam War, earned a prestigious Nebula Award nomination for best short story of the year. Several of his stories were later compiled in a collection titled *Tribal Screams* (2018). He also published children's stories, screenplays, and comic books during this time. His children's picture book *Eagle Feathers* (1997) was a Storytelling World Awards Honor recipient.

WRITING NOVELS AND OTHER PURSUITS

In the mid-1990s, Goingback also began writing novels that were similar to his short stories in that they blended elements of the horror genre with Native American mythology. Thematically, Goingback's novels often depict the re-emergence of ancient, malevolent forces in more contemporary, suburban settings to communicate the idea that the evil that humankind must contend with never really dies. The conflict between nature and humankind is another recurring motif that can be found within his works.

Goingback's debut novel, *Crota* (1996), happened to be published exactly ten years after he and his wife had watched the Stephen King interview that inspired him to start writing. In an ironic twist, Goingback was up against King himself that year in the Bram Stoker Awards category for best novel of the year. Although King won best novel, Goingback did win the 1996 Bram Stoker Award for best first novel. A brilliant debut that was enthusiastically received, *Crota* follows a game warden who suspects the mutilated bodies being discovered are not from a bear as the police suspect but from a great beast known as a "Crota" that has awakened after centuries of being asleep. In an interview with Kelli Marchman McNeely for *Horror Fuel* (14 Apr. 2016), Goingback explained the origin of *Crota*, stating: "Back when I was a kid we weren't allowed to play outside after dark. There was something in the woods that would scream at night. People would say that they saw things. And one day I was out in the woods with friends and we found claw marks high in a tree. . . . That always stayed in my head."

Goingback achieved another Bram Stoker Award nomination for his novel *Darker Than Night* (1999), this time for best horror novel of the year. The story tells the tale of a family who faces supernatural forces inside their house. *Evil Whispers* (2001) continued his exploration of good versus evil in a novel that follows the events that take place when an ancient sorcerer murdered by Seminole people finds a way to rise again.

Set in the Cherokee spirit world of Galun'lati, *Coyote Rage* (2019) follows the bloodthirsty trickster and shapeshifter Coyote—a seminal figure in the folklore of various Native American cultures—as he attempts to eliminate the human race from Earth so that animals can again rise. The book won the 2019 Bram Stoker Award for best book of the year. In an interview with Cris Alvarez for the *Full Contact Nerd Podcast* (31 Jan. 2021), Goingback explained that he wanted this novel to include more traditional Native American folklore than his previous ones. "I was raised hearing these . . . trickster stories and a lot of people don't know them," he relayed on the podcast. "I just wanted to do something very traditional, something that almost seemed more like an oral story than a book."

In addition to writing, Goingback also lectures about Native American customs and folklore nationwide. His books have been included in the curriculum of schools around the country as well as in a youthful offender program at the Orange County Corrections Facility in Orlando.

PERSONAL LIFE

Goingback married Bello in 1978. The couple has two sons together. When Goingback's sons were young, he and his family moved to central Florida, where his mentor, the science fiction writer Andre Norton, lived. Goingback worked odd jobs while continuing to expand the breadth of his work. One of those jobs included being the caretaker of the Greenwood Cemetery in Orlando, Florida, where he participated in the burial of many of the victims of the Pulse Nightclub shooting, a massacre that occurred in 2016 in which a gunman killed forty-nine people, many of whom were part of the LGBTQ community. It was an experience that fortified Goingback's belief that the world was often scarier than anything the horror genre could produce. "I don't write about serial killers or shooters or stuff like that," he told Nevill. "Stories about werewolves, vampires and monsters are a place to escape all that is happening in the news and real life."

SUGGESTED READING

Goingback, Owl. "An Interview with Award Winning Horror Author Owl Goingback." Interview by Kelli Marchman McNeely. *Horror Fuel*, 14 Apr. 2016, horrorfuel.com/2016/04/14/interview-award-winning-horror-author-owl-goingback/. Accessed 5 Aug. 2022.
___. "Indigenous Heritage in Horror: Interview with Owl Goingback." *Horror Writers Association*, 11 Oct. 2021, horror.org/indigenous-heritage-in-horror-interview-with-owl-goingback/. Interview. Accessed 5 Aug. 2022.
___. "Secrets and Successes of an Award Winning [sic] Monster Writer with Owl Goingback." Interview by Cris Alvarez. *Full Contact Nerd Interviews*, 31 Jan. 2021, crisalvarez.com/2021/01/31/owl-goingback-interview-about-his-horror-novel-coyote-rage-independent-legions-publishing-2019/allthehorror/. Accessed 5 Aug. 2022.
Nevill, Frances Susanna. "Owl Goingback, Central Florida's Most Frightful Writer, Thinks Real Life Is Scarier Than Werewolves or Vampires." *Orlando Weekly*, 23 Oct. 2019, www.orlandoweekly.com/arts/owl-goingback-central-floridas-most-frightful-writer-thinks-real-life-is-scarier-than-werewolves-or-vampires-26184491. Accessed 5 Aug. 2022.

SELECTED WORKS

Crota, 1996; *Darker Than Night*, 1999; *Evil Whispers*, 2001; *Coyote Rage*, 2019

—*Emily Turner*

Dominique Gonçalves

Born: 1992
Occupation: Ecologist

Between the late 1970s and the early 1990s, a civil war killed about one million people in Mozambique, a country in southeastern Africa, and devastated the country's land infrastructure. In addition to its massive human cost, that period of warfare was highly detrimental to Mozambique's Gorongosa National Park and the animals living within it, many of which were killed for food or, in the case of the park's elephants, for their valuable ivory tusks. Efforts to revitalize the park in the early twenty-first century thus focused significantly on returning Gorongosa's animal populations to their prewar levels and improving interactions between local human communities and those animals, particularly the park's remaining elephants. "They're able to forgive, maybe forget," ecologist Dominique Gonçalves told *National Geographic* (25 Mar. 2021) about the Gorongosa elephants. "It might take time, but they're able to do that, even when humans have done so many bad things to them."

As manager of the park's Elephant Ecology Project, Gonçalves oversees work such as the tagging and tracking of the elephants, which enables her and her colleagues to understand the elephants' behavior and movements. It also helps prevent conflicts between humans and elephants, both within the park itself and in the buffer zone between the park and neighboring communities. Alongside a number of additional park initiatives, which include efforts to support local girls and women as well as to direct money into neighboring communities, Gorongosa's Elephant Ecology Project is part of an ongoing revitalization effort to which Gonçalves hopes to contribute for many years. "I plan to be alive in the year 2080 when the park celebrates its 120th birthday," she wrote in an article for the publication *Mongabay* (23 July 2020). "I hope to see Gorongosa as the hub of a green economy, functioning as an economic, education and human rights engine for prosperous families."

EARLY LIFE AND EDUCATION

Dominique D'Emille Correia Gonçalves was born in Beira, Mozambique, in 1992. She spent her childhood in that city, where she grew up learning about Mozambique's wildlife and ecosystems from her father. "My father used to tell me a lot of his adventures in the forest and also how to coexist with the animals," she explained in a video created for the *National Geographic Society*. Born around the end of a period of civil war in Mozambique, Gonçalves likewise learned about the hardships of that era at an early age. "My mother worked for the Red Cross during the war and she still tells me stories, even today, about the suffering of the people," she wrote for *Mongabay*. After completing her secondary education, Gonçalves moved to Maputo, Mozambique, to pursue studies in ecology and conservation.

While studying in Maputo, Gonçalves learned that a new research facility, the E. O. Wilson Laboratory, had opened at Gorongosa National Park in central Mozambique. "All I wanted was to get some experience and be an intern because of all the amazing scientists,"

she recalled to Bennett Krishock in a video interview for the Sun Valley Film Festival (7 May 2020). Gonçalves contacted the laboratory about internship possibilities, but as none were available at the time, she instead focused on other research projects after completing her undergraduate studies. Remembering her interest, Gorongosa later recruited Gonçalves to work for the park's recently established ornithology project. To gain further expertise in that area, Gonçalves spent several months in the United States, working at Boise State University's Intermountain Bird Observatory. After switching her focus to Gorongosa's elephant population, she relocated temporarily to the United Kingdom, where she completed a master's degree in conservation biology at the University of Kent's Durrell Institute of Conservation and Ecology (DICE). Gonçalves subsequently returned to Mozambique, where she pursued doctoral studies in biodiversity management remotely while working at Gorongosa.

GORONGOSA NATIONAL PARK

Located in central Mozambique, Gorongosa National Park originated in 1920 as a hunting reserve. The reserve expanded in size over the decades, eventually spanning some 1,540 square miles. In 1960, it was named a national park. During the 1960s and 1970s, the park became popular among tourists, welcoming numerous celebrity guests from countries such as the United States. As conflict arose in Mozambique, however, the park became both a combat zone and a hiding place for soldiers who hunted the animals there for food and harvested elephant ivory as a source of income. "The park lost 95 percent of its wildlife to soldiers and hunting opportunists," Gonçalves wrote for *Mongabay* about that period. While the park was home to approximately 2,500 elephants in 1972, fewer than 200 remained at the end of the war.

By the mid-1990s, conflict in the area around Gorongosa had largely ceased, and efforts to assess the extent of the damage and restore the park had begun. Restoration efforts increased beginning in 2008, when US businessman and philanthropist Greg Carr began funding efforts to restore the park through the Carr Foundation's Gorongosa Restoration Project. Working in partnership with Mozambique's government, Carr's project continued its work throughout the second decade of the twenty-first century and into the third. Among other initiatives, park employees worked to restore the park's animal populations, including by transporting wildlife from elsewhere in Africa to the park. By 2022, Gorongosa was home to a wide range of wildlife, including elephants, lions, crocodiles, pangolins, and a variety of birds and insects.

ELEPHANT ECOLOGY PROJECT

Initially part of the ornithology program at Gorongosa National Park, Gonçalves soon developed an interest in the elephants living in the park and was particularly intrigued by the concepts of human-elephant interaction and conflict mitigation. In 2015, she joined the elephant conservation project at Gorongosa as a research fellow, studying elephant behavior under researcher Joyce Poole. "That was an easy transition because I was trained in ecology and I always focused on large-medium mammals," Gonçalves told Krishock, adding that she was, by training, a mammologist rather than an ornithologist. After leaving Mozambique to pursue her master's degree, she returned to Gorongosa to work with elephants full time.

Taking on the role of manager of Gorongosa's Elephant Ecology Project, Gonçalves conducted a number of elephant-focused projects at the park, including placing Global Positioning System (GPS) trackers on lead female elephants as a means of tracking their movements; that initiative was completed with financial assistance from a National Geographic Fellowship. In 2018, Gonçalves was named a National Geographic Explorer, a title given to experts in various fields like science, conservation, and education, who receive funding, training, and other assistance from National Geographic in support of their work. In addition to tracking the elephants, Gonçalves sought to monitor their behavior and interactions with humans, which she noted had been shaped by lingering trauma among the elephant population that dated back to the Mozambican Civil War. "They remember," she told Claudine Spera and Irene Baqué for the *Guardian* (7 Sept. 2018). "Most of our elephants were killed for ivory. Some of them are becoming more tolerant of our presence. Now that the population is growing and they're

in a safer environment, we hope their behavior changes back to how it was before."

HUMAN-ELEPHANT COEXISTENCE

In her role as head of the Elephant Ecology Project, Gonçalves sought not only to ensure the well-being of the park's elephant population but also to promote coexistence between elephants and humans, a goal she considered to be challenging but achievable in the long term. "Coexistence takes time," she told *National Geographic* (25 Mar. 2021). "It takes people to understand and it also takes elephants to understand." One significant impediment to human-elephant coexistence at Gorongosa is the fact that the elephant habitats in the park and in the buffer zone surrounding it overlap with areas populated by humans, meaning that elephants at times pass through populated areas. When that occurs, elephants can destroy crops and buildings, devastating the livelihoods of local farmers and families. In turn, the individuals harmed by the roaming elephants sometimes might attempt to kill the elephants or become resistant to elephant-conservation efforts such as those conducted at Gorongosa.

To prevent such conflict, Gonçalves works to track and understand the movements of the park's elephant population. She implements methods to prevent the elephants from crossing into human-populated areas. One unusual means of doing so involves placing beehives along fences between the park and human-populated areas, a technique that works because the elephants fear being stung by bees. "Most things in the natural world are ruled by fear and risk aversion," Gonçalves explained to Alissa Greenberg for the PBS program *NOVA* (15 Oct. 2020). Another benefit of the beehives is that the local community sells the honey produced within them, providing much-needed alternative income to residents. Gonçalves and her colleagues work to forge other productive partnerships with the local community. In addition to honey, they also collaborate with local residents to grow and sell coffee. "The families make more money than ever before," Gonçalves wrote for *Mongabay*. "They help the Park restore the rainforest by replanting native trees in critical areas near streams and hillsides, thus protecting the catchment area of many rivers. It is a win-win for the people and for the rare and endemic species who live on Mt. Gorongosa."

HELPING GIRLS SUCCEED

In addition to dealing with the needs of Gorongosa's elephants, Gonçalves collaborates alongside her colleagues to ensure the future well-being of the park and the people living near it. One key initiative is the creation and operation of Gorongosa Girls' Clubs. Started in 2017, the clubs for local girls seek to promote education, reduce local rates of child marriage, and introduce the girls to the local wildlife through park visits and educational programs. In Mozambique, close to half of all girls get married before reaching the age of eighteen, and about half of girls have their first child by that age as well. Additionally, girls in particular are not encouraged to attend school. "Each year we help girls from forty primary schools go to high school, who would otherwise have ended their education at grade seven," Gonçalves wrote for *Mongabay* about the park's efforts, which also included the building of new primary schools to serve local communities.

Gonçalves and her colleagues have likewise sought to encourage women to take jobs within the park, including park ranger positions. "We're very strongly encouraging women to join to change perceptions about what women can and cannot do; to remind them what it means for all of us to have our natural heritage and this wildlife around us," she told Greenberg. Alongside such initiatives, Gonçalves has worked to draw greater international attention to Gorongosa, which she and her colleagues hope will result in an increase in financial contributions from international donors. She regularly conducts interviews and holds talks about her work around the world, and she narrated and was featured in the 2020 documentary film *Our Gorongosa: A Park for the People*. Gonçalves hoped the film would help the park attain further support as well as inspire the next generation of Gorongosa-based researchers and park employees.

SUGGESTED READING

"Dominique Gonçalves: Coexisting with the Elephants of Mozambique." *National Geographic*, 25 Mar. 2021, www.nationalgeographic.com/impact/article/dominique-goncalves-coexisting-with-the-elephants-of-mozambique. Accessed 11 Apr. 2022.

"Explorers at Work: Dominique Correia Gonçalves." *National Geographic Society*, www.nationalgeographic.org/video/explorers-work-dominique-correia-concalves/. Accessed 11 Apr. 2022.

Gonçalves, Dominique. "Mozambique's Trailblazing Gorongosa Park Celebrates 60th Anniversary, Announces 60 New Schools (Commentary)." *Mongabay*, 23 July 2020, news.mongabay.com/2020/07/mozambiques-trailblazing-gorongosa-park-celebrates-60th-anniversary-commentary/. Accessed 11 Apr. 2022.

___. "SVFF 2020 Exclusive Q&A with Dominique Gonçalves, Narrator of 'Our Gorongosa, A Park for the People.'" Interview by Bennett Krishock. *YouTube*, uploaded by Sun Valley Film Festival, 7 May 2020, www.youtube.com/watch?v=2VvGhJSWh9g. Accessed 11 Apr. 2022.

Greenberg, Alissa. "The Secret to Peace between Elephants and Farmers in Mozambique? Bees." *PBS*, 15 Oct. 2020, www.pbs.org/wgbh/nova/article/predators-fear-elephants-bees-gorongosa/. Accessed 11 Apr. 2022.

Quammen, David. "How One of Africa's Great Parks Is Rebounding from War." *National Geographic*, www.nationalgeographic.com/magazine/article/mozambique-gorongosa-national-park-wildlife-rebound. Accessed 11 Apr. 2022.

Spera, Claudine, and Irene Baqué. "Women Lead the Charge in Healing Scars of War in Mozambique Wildlife Park." *The Guardian*, 7 Sept. 2018, www.theguardian.com/global-development/ng-interactive/2018/sep/07/women-gorongosa-national-park-healing-scars-of-war-mozambique. Accessed 11 Apr. 2022.

—Joy Crelin

Patrick Gottsch

Born: June 3, 1953
Occupation: Business executive

Patrick Gottsch is the head of the Rural Media Group (RMG). According to RMG's corporate website, the group encompasses RFD-TV, which reaches fifty-two million homes; the

Cowboy Channel, seen in forty-two million homes; RURAL RADIO Channel 147 on SiriusXM Radio, with thirty-three million subscribers; and *RFD-TV The Magazine*, a magazine with a sizeable readership. "I've always felt confident that there was an audience in America for rural programming that was being ignored by urban broadcasters," Gottsch told Siri Stevens for *Rodeo News* (2 Dec. 2019). Many, however, did not share his belief that such shows as *American Farmer* and *Classic Tractor Fever* would prove profitable. "For nearly two decades, coastal financiers and TV honchos laughed at Gottsch for thinking he could make money by broadcasting shows aimed at America's heartland," Ryan Blitstein wrote for *Fast Company* (1 Nov. 2009). "They were wrong. . . . Gottsch's success demonstrates that while global media seems to be consolidating, consumer tastes are more diverse than ever."

Profit has never been the sole motive for Gottsch. "We have two goals," he explained to Charlene Weisler for *Media Village* (30 Nov. 2016). "They are, one, to serve the needs and interests of rural America, and two (which is just as important), to reconnect the city with the country. If there is one thing that unites rural America, whether they are in agriculture or not, it's that we have to do a better job of communicating with the folks in the city."

EARLY LIFE AND EDUCATION

Patrick Gottsch was born on June 3, 1953, in Elkhorn, Nebraska, to Gloria and Bernard G. "Pat" Gottsch. He had one brother, Mickey, and four sisters: Patricia, Toni, Tammy, and Terri. Gottsch's father had served in the military during World War II, and thanks to his prowess on the baseball diamond, he played in the first European World Series, in 1946. Upon his return to the United States, he was drafted by the St. Louis Cardinals. When his baseball career ended, he joined his brother Bob in founding Gottsch Brothers Transfer and Feed, which grew into a thriving business. Gottsch's father retained his love of baseball and regularly coached local youth teams, sometimes using his own money to buy needed uniforms and equipment. Batting practice was often held on the family farm and cattle feeding lot where Gottsch grew up.

Gottsch has credited his rural upbringing with giving him a solid sense of values and firsthand knowledge of how important professions such as farming and ranching are to the American way of life. After graduating from high school, Gottsch entered Sam Houston State University in Texas, but he dropped out after two and a half years and returned to Nebraska to farm with his father. That decision coincided with one of the longest and most severe droughts in state history, and his father encouraged him to pursue a different course of action.

EARLY CAREER

Gottsch moved to Chicago, Illinois, in 1977 to become a commodity broker on the Chicago Mercantile Exchange. He held that position, which involved trading assets such as grain, cattle, and cotton, until 1978. Missing Nebraska, he took a similar job based in Omaha; however, in early 1980, in response to the 1979 invasion of Afghanistan by the Soviet Union, President Jimmy Carter enacted a grain embargo, which sent the commodities market into a tailspin, causing Gottsch and many others to go broke.

Gottsch subsequently found a job installing satellite dishes, and he later launched his own company, E.T. Installations. In 1987, E.T. Installations became the largest privately owned home satellite retailer in the United States. He discovered that customers loved the product but often bemoaned the lack of programming for their demographic. As Blitstein wrote, "Westerns like *Gunsmoke* had become a rarity, overtaken by shows about urban cops or suburban housewives." That planted the idea for RFD-TV in Gottsch's mind. In 1988 he put together RFD as a small-scale venture focused on agricultural programming, but the enterprise went bankrupt within a year. In the early 1990s, he moved to Fort Worth, Texas, to take a job as sales director for Superior Livestock Auction, the largest such operation in the country and (thanks to him) the first to experiment with satellite video marketing.

RFD-TV AND ITS GROWTH

Through networking, Gottsch met others interested in channels focused on horses, country cooking, and other such topics. "I met up with Willie Nelson in 1993 and he had $4,000 of programming, classic country music from the old Porter Wagoner show, *Pop! Goes the Country*, things like that," Gottsch recalled to Joel Mathis for *Philadelphia Magazine* (26 Aug. 2014). "We were all trying to do the same thing, get financing, get launched on a cable or satellite to have a channel. We just kept going, why are we all doing this? Let's combine everything—a little music, a little lifestyle, and see how it works." The result was RFD-TV, a reference to Rural Free Delivery, the system instituted by the US Postal Service in 1896 to deliver mail directly to recipients in rural areas, eliminating the need for them to pick up their letters and packages from far-away post offices.

It took several years to find the necessary funding, but RFD-TV finally became viable in 2000as a nonprofit public-service concern. Although it initially was available only on DISH Network, with Gottsch loading a week's worth of programming at a time on a hard drive, within a few years other companies followed, including DIRECTV, Optimum, Comcast, AT&T/U-verse, Cox, and Time Warner Cable. The larger of these, including Comcast and Time Warner, joined after Gottsch arranged to simulcast a show featuring irreverent media personality Don Imus.

In 2007 the Federal Communications Commission (FCC) decreed that RFD-TV would no longer be considered a public-service channel, and it transitioned into a for-profit enterprise. Though Gottsch began producing more original content and hired several highly regarded industry executives to boost his company's profile, he struggled to find advertisers. Gottsch explained to Weisler that brands ignored rural audiences at their own peril. "Our viewers are heavy users of a variety of household items and enjoy a range of leisure activities," he said. "They also own an average of four pick-up trucks. There are advertisers like RAM and Chevy who do recognize and appreciate the rural consumer. But some advertisers think they are reaching this audience through other programming such as football. They are not. Don't take this audience for granted!" Asserting that RFD-TV reached more rural households than big-name stations like CNN, he declared, "RFD-TV is very important to rural America. So, we will stay the course whether advertisers come or not."

Although the network remained smaller than most, its mix of shows like *This Week in AgriBusiness*, *Big Joe Polka Show*, and *Best of America by Horseback*, along with reruns of old favorites like *The Lone Ranger* and *Hee-Haw*, attracted a receptive audience. Gottsch gradually expanded his empire, which he named the Rural Media Group, to include RURAL RADIO, airing on SiriusXM channel 147 since 2013, and the twenty-four-hour Cowboy Channel, which in 2017 began featuring Western lifestyle shows and live rodeo events. With a state-of-the-art television studio and headquarters in the Fort Worth Stockyards, the Cowboy Channel launched a streaming platform, Cowboy Channel+, in 2020. By early 2022, the channel was being viewed in some forty-two million homes—almost as many as RFD-TV, which reported fifty-two million households—and attracting major advertisers like Geico Insurance and General Mills.

PROVING ITS POPULARITY

In 2014, when Comcast and Time Warner were negotiating a merger, Comcast dropped RFD-TV from its lineup. In response, Gottsch encouraged viewers to bombard the FCC with pleas to force Comcast to reverse its decision. He told journalists that Comcast executives, headquartered in Philadelphia, were exhibiting total disregard for those outside their urban bubble. That seemed to be a reasonable assumption given that during one congressional hearing, David Cohen, a Comcast vice president, was asked about RFD-TV and replied, as quoted by Mathis, "We are primarily an urban-clustered cable company."

The merger failed due to antitrust issues raised by the federal government. Gottsch has speculated that his viewers may have had a hand in the reversal as well. During the hearings, the FCC published more than two hundred thousand messages decrying the lack of attention Comcast was paying to rural viewers. Gottsch himself has been the recipient of countless emails; he has said that he reads every one that reaches the Rural Media Group but that he stopped counting at five hundred thousand. He has also been approached often in public. "We go to state fairs. People just walk up and thank us for providing this kind of programming and we know what they need," he said to Mathis. "It all boils down to two things: (1.) It's about time somebody paid attention to rural America, and (2.) thank you for family-oriented programming because people can put it on their TV set and not worry about their kids or grandkids walking into the room."

POLITICAL INVOLVEMENT

In the run-up to the 2016 US presidential election, Gottsch attended both the Democratic National Convention and Republican National Convention, attempting to convince the parties to focus on rural issues, and he hosted a series of Rural Town Halls that won a CableFax Award for Public Affairs Programming. Hillary Clinton declined to advertise on RFD-TV, and Gottsch told interviewers that in speaking to women in rural regions during the days before the polls opened, he could not find a single one planning to cast a vote for the candidate many expected to become the first female president in US history. By contrast, he heard staunch support for Donald Trump, whose presumed independence and wealth was much admired and who did advertise on RFD-TV, spending $150,000 to buy every available spot on the network in the two weeks preceding the election.

Gottsch has decried the growing polarization in the country. "We cannot exist as the United States if there is a wall between urban and rural America," he said to Cynthia Littleton for *Variety* (19 Jan. 2017). "We think that our job is to do more to connect city and country again. If we just keep doing *Duck Dynasty* and that kind of thing, we are never going to get to a better understanding of who we are."

PERSONAL LIFE

Gottsch lives in Elkhorn. He and his wife, Angie Gottsch, were married in October 2017 and have a daughter, Rose Gottsch, together. He also has two older daughters: Raquel Gottsch Koehler, CEO of the Cowboy Channel, and Gatsby Gottsch Solheim, general counsel and chief financial officer for the Rural Media Group.

SUGGESTED READING

Blitstein, Ryan. "RFD-TV: How an Ex-Farmer Built a $25 Million Media Empire for Rural America." *Fast Company*, 1 Nov. 2009, www.fastcompany.com/1400900/rfd-tv-how-ex-farmer-built-25-million-media-empire-rural-america. Accessed 19 Jan. 2022.

Gottsch, Patrick. "The David to Comcast's Goliath." Interview by Joel Mathis. *Philadelphia Magazine*, 26 Aug. 2014, www.phillymag.com/news/2014/08/26/interview-david-comcasts-goliath/. Accessed 19 Jan. 2022.

___. "RFD-TV's Patrick Gottsch on How Rural Americans Became the Hot 'New' Demo." Interview by Charlene Weisler. *Media Village*, 30 Nov. 2016, www.mediavillage.com/article/how-rural-americans-became-the-hottest-new-demo-interview-with-patrick-gottsch/. Accessed 19 Jan. 2022.

Littleton, Cynthia. "Network Aimed at Rural America Speaks for Population That Feels Underserved by the Media." *Variety*, 19 Jan. 2017, variety.com/2017/tv/news/rfd-tv-rural-america-1201963217/. Accessed 19 Jan. 2022.

Stevens, Siri. "Patrick Gottsch." *Rodeo News*, 2 Dec. 2019, rodeonews.com/patrick-gottsch/. Accessed 19 Jan. 2022.

Yahr, Emily. "Inside RFD-TV, the Network That (Unlike the Others) Covets Rural and Older Viewers." *The Washington Post*, 20 Nov. 2017, www.washingtonpost.com/news/arts-and-entertainment/wp/2017/11/20/inside-rfd-tv-the-network-that-unlike-the-others-covets-rural-and-older-viewers/. Accessed 19 Jan. 2022.

—Mari Rich

Mikyla Grant-Mentis

Born: July 15, 1998
Occupation: Ice hockey player

In May 2022, the Buffalo Beauts of the Premier Hockey Federation (PHF)—a professional women's hockey league formerly known as the National Women's Hockey League (NWHL)—signed forward Mikyla Grant-Mentis to a one-year contract with an estimated value of $80,000. That salary was a significant milestone, as it not only represented a significant pay increase for the player herself but also was the highest-known salary paid to a woman in North American professional hockey. "It's crazy to think I'm making an actual living wage playing hockey. It hasn't sunk in yet," Grant-Mentis told Mark Zwolinski for the *Toronto Star* (13 May 2022). Indeed, her new salary was undoubtedly well deserved: following four well-regarded seasons at Merrimack College, Grant-Mentis had played briefly for the Beauts at the end of the 2019–20 NWHL season before joining the Toronto Six for her 2020–21 breakout season, during which she led the league in goals and earned Most

Valuable Player (MVP) and Newcomer of the Year honors.

Grant-Mentis's second season in Toronto further demonstrated her strong play at the professional level, establishing her as both a star in the league and a signing target for many teams, including the victorious Beauts, in the subsequent free agency period. While Grant-Mentis had long gone overlooked by Hockey Canada and had yet to represent her home country internationally, her accomplishments on the professional stage demonstrated the success of her positive and focused mindset. "Don't let anyone tell you what you are capable of doing," she related in an interview for *Six Magazine* (Dec. 2020). "Whatever your goals are, do what you need to do to complete them. And don't get discouraged if you don't make the best teams/school or even national team/ camps. Just focus on your goals."

EARLY LIFE AND EDUCATION

Mikyla Grant-Mentis was born on July 15, 1998, in Brampton, Ontario, Canada. One of three children born to parents Sandra and James, she has an older brother named Tre and a twin brother named Marquis. Hockey was a popular sport in the Grant-Mentis household: her father had represented Canada in international ball hockey competitions, and all three of the children began playing ice hockey before even starting school. Growing up, the young Grant-Mentis's greatest competitor was her twin brother, who would later play hockey professionally for the Federal Prospects Hockey League (FPHL). "You can't let your twin brother be better than you, it just doesn't work like that," she recalled to Sonny Sachdeva for *Sportsnet* about the competitive spirit that fueled her as a young player. "So I kept pushing and pushing to basically be at the same level as him."

After playing for various boys' youth teams alongside her twin, Grant-Mentis joined her first girls' league at age twelve. She joined the junior-level Provincial Women's Hockey League (PWHL) in the 2013–14 season, initially playing for the Oakville Jr. Hornets. She moved to the Toronto Jr. Aeros the following season. In 2015–16, her final season in the PWHL, Grant-Mentis played for the Mississauga Jr. Chiefs, accumulating twenty-one goals and twenty-eight assists for forty-nine total points in thirty-seven regular season

games. In addition to distinguishing herself during the regular season, she competed in the PWHL playoffs twice, helping the Jr. Chiefs claim second place in the Alumni Cup Playoffs in 2016. In addition to hockey, Grant-Mentis played several additional sports while in high school and particularly enjoyed playing basketball.

MERRIMACK COLLEGE

While playing in the PWHL, Grant-Mentis drew the attention of Merrimack College in North Andover, Massachusetts, which had recently established a Division I women's ice hockey program. The Merrimack College Warriors were set to compete within the Hockey East conference of National Collegiate Athletic Association (NCAA) women's hockey, and the college convinced Grant-Mentis to commit to attend the college and play for the new team while she was in just tenth grade. Despite other colleges urging her to break her commitment in her last year of high school, she remained dedicated to her choice. "The thought of, kind of, building a legacy there and building up a program from the bottom up, that really put me onto it," she later explained to Sachdeva.

Enrolling at Merrimack in 2016, Grant-Mentis had a strong freshman season, playing in thirty-five games and scoring nine goals and eighteen assists. For her performance, she was recognized as Hockey East Rookie of the Month for January 2017. Following her debut season, she played three more seasons at Merrimack, where she also majored in criminal justice and psychology. During her 2019–20 senior season with the Warriors, she amassed thirty-three points, the most of any player on the team, and achieved a point-per-game average over the thirty-three games in which she played. She was nominated for 2020 NCAA Woman of the Year. She ended her final year with the school as the Warriors' all-time leading scorer, with 117 points; having the all-time number of assists, with 61 assists; and having the second all-time number of goals, with 56 goals.

Grant-Mentis graduated with her bachelor's degree from Merrimack College in 2020.

PROFESSIONAL DEBUT

Grant-Mentis's play with Merrimack brought her to the attention of professional teams within the NWHL such as the Buffalo Beauts, which signed the young player in February 2020. "It was honestly a surreal experience—I literally felt like an NHL player," she recalled to Sachdeva about joining the team at the end of the 2019–20 professional season. "I had to leave school Thursday, fly out to Buffalo, we practiced in Buffalo on Friday, then drove to where we were playing for Saturday-Sunday, and then Sunday night we'd have to fly home to get back to school on Monday. It was a crazy three weeks that we did it for. But it was definitely fun and definitely showed me a lot—it showed me how much better I needed to be to compete in that league." Grant-Mentis played in two regular-season games with the Beauts and also played in the team's Isobel Cup Playoffs play-in game at the end of the season, although the Beauts did not progress beyond the first game.

TORONTO SIX

In May 2020, during the offseason, Grant-Mentis signed with the NWHL's new expansion team, the Toronto Six. "I am excited and proud to play the first full season of professional hockey career in my home and native land," she said at the time of her signing, as reported by Justin Levine for the *Puck Authority* (18 May 2020). Due to the coronavirus disease 2019 (COVID-19) pandemic, the 2020–21 season was shortened significantly and held in a so-called bubble in Lake Placid, New York. Grant-Mentis played in six games over the course of the season, during which she led the league in goals with five and also tallied four assists. The Six went on to compete in the Isobel Cup Playoffs but lost in the semifinals to the Boston Pride, the eventual champions. In recognition of her accomplishments over the course of the season, Grant-Mentis was named the NWHL's MVP and Newcomer of the Year for 2021 and was honored as one of the Three Stars of the Season, as determined by the league's fans.

Grant-Mentis remained with the Toronto Six for the 2021–22 season, the league's first season operating under its new name, the Premier Hockey Federation (PHF). She played in nineteen games over the course of the season, scoring thirteen goals and seventeen assists for thirty total points. She ranked second in the league in total points—falling only three points behind Connecticut Whale forward Kennedy Marchment—and led the league in game-winning goals with six. In addition to competing in regular season games, Grant-Mentis played in the PHF All-Star Showcase, the league's all-star game, in January 2022.

Toronto finished the 2021–22 season ranked second in the league standings and earned an automatic spot in the semifinal round of the Isobel Cup Playoffs. At the tournament, held at a neutral arena in Florida in March 2022, Grant-Mentis and her teammates again faced the Pride in the semifinal and once again lost to that team, which went on to become back-to-back champions. Though passed over for an MVP nomination, Grant-Mentis was again honored as one of the Three Stars of the Season at the PHF Awards.

LANDMARK CONTRACT

Following the 2021–22 season, the PHF implemented several major changes, including an increase to each team's annual salary cap that raised that cap from $300,000 to $750,000 and allowed team management to offer far greater salaries to players than in earlier years. In May 2022, it was announced that Grant-Mentis had left the Toronto Six to return to the Buffalo Beauts. "I really was torn between the two teams," she told Sachdeva for *Sportsnet* (12 May 2022) about her decision. "Toronto was an amazing spot to play. It was a dream of mine to play in my hometown again. . . . I accomplished so much here, the team accomplished so much. It's definitely an experience that I will never forget."

While Grant-Mentis's return to the team with which she had made her professional debut was certainly newsworthy, her new contract was even more notable. Although neither the Beauts nor Grant-Mentis released official information about the contract, hockey journalists reported that her salary for the 2022–23 season was an estimated $80,000, a portion of which was paid as a signing bonus. Though still significantly lower than salaries available in top-level men's hockey leagues, $80,000 was the highest known salary paid to a woman playing professional hockey in North America. It was likewise a substantial improvement over Grant-Mentis's earlier salaries. "I was with some teammates and they said, 'This is crazy,'" she told Zwolinski. "To think, two years ago I was making five grand." Notably, Grant-Mentis's new salary was high enough that the player, who had worked as a FedEx delivery driver during the previous season, would no longer need to balance her commitments to her team with a second job.

Grant-Mentis's strong performance during her seasons in the PHF and her groundbreaking contract made her the focus of extensive media attention, and she was featured on the 2022 *Forbes* magazine's 30 Under 30 list for sports. However, she received minimal acknowledgment from Hockey Canada—the national body governing ice hockey in that country—until August 2022, when she was invited to the National Women's Program Selection Camp in Calgary. The camp was intended to evaluate potential new additions to the women's national team, which competed in international tournaments such as the Winter Olympic Games and the International Ice Hockey Federation (IIHF) Women's World Championship. "It's a crazy experience, you know, something I hadn't experienced before, so it's pretty sweet," Grant-Mentis told Mark Masters in an interview for *TSN* (2022) about her time at the camp, adding, "It would mean a lot to put the maple leaf on."

Although Grant-Mentis was not selected to join the Canadian national team, she remained committed to her career in the PHF, which she found enabled her to serve as a valuable role model for younger athletes. "My aspirations are the same as they've always been: to win and be a role model for young black hockey players who look like me," she explained in a press release issued by the Beauts (9 May 2022). "On top of that, I want to be a part of Buffalo's great hockey community."

SUGGESTED READING

Grant-Mentis, Mikyla. "Mikyla Grant-Mentis." *The Six Magazine*, Dec. 2020. Interview. *Issuu*, issuu.com/torontosix/docs/the_six_magazine_issue01/s/11481713. Accessed 12 Sept. 2022.

___, and Marie-Philip Poulin. "Poulin on Grant-Mentis: 'She's Made a Name for Herself.'" Interview by Mark Masters. *TSN*, 2022, www.tsn.ca/video/poulin-on-grant-mentis-shes-made-a-name-for-herself~2497303. Accessed 12 Sept. 2022.

Levine, Justin. "Toronto Begins Busy Day with Signing of Forward Mikyla Grant-Mentis." *The Puck Authority*, 18 May 2020, thepuckauthority.com/toronto-begins-busy-day-with-signing-of-forward-mikyla-grant-mentis/. Accessed 12 Sept. 2022.

"Reigning League MVP Grant-Mentis Joins Beauts." *Buffalo Beauts*, 9 May 2022, beauts.premierhockeyfederation.com/news/reigning-league-mvp-grant-mentis-joins-beauts. Accessed 12 Sept. 2022.

Sachdeva, Sonny. "Hometown Hero." *Sportsnet*, www.sportsnet.ca/hockey/longform/how-mikyla-grant-mentis-quietly-became-one-of-hockeys-most-dynamic-talents/. Accessed 12 Sept. 2022.

___. "Mikyla Grant-Mentis Reflects on Becoming Highest-Paid Player in Women's Hockey." *Sportsnet*, 12 May 2022, www.sportsnet.ca/hockey/article/mikyla-grant-mentis-reflects-on-becoming-highest-paid-player-in-womens-hockey/. Accessed 12 Sept. 2022.

Zwolinski, Mark. "Brampton's Mikyla Grant-Mentis, Record Contract in Hand, Might Be the Future of Women's Hockey." *Toronto Star*, 13 May 2022, www.thestar.com/sports/hockey/2022/05/13/bramptons-mikyla-grant-mentis-record-contract-in-hand-might-be-the-future-of-womens-hockey.html. Accessed 12 Sept. 2022.

—Joy Crelin

Michael Greyeyes

Born: June 4, 1967
Occupation: Actor, choreographer, and director

Nêhiyaw (Plains Cree) actor Michael Greyeyes became a familiar face in film and television in the early 1990s, but it was his later performances in the critically acclaimed drama *Wild Indian* (2021) and the Peacock comedy series *Rutherford Falls* (2021) that earned him a new level of recognition and acclaim, as well as two Independent Spirit Award nominations. Those two starkly distinct roles exhibited Greyeyes's range and were hailed as part of a new era of complexity for Indigenous characters. Greyeyes, who trained as a ballet dancer, cut his teeth playing famed Native figures like Crazy Horse, Wandering Spirit, and, in the drama *Woman Walks Ahead* (2017), Sitting Bull. He was celebrated in these roles, but together they reinforced the notion that American Indian stories are all in the past. Opportunities for Greyeyes to portray contemporary Native characters in films such as *Dance Me Outside* (1994), *Smoke Signals* (1998), and even the zombie horror flick *Blood*

Quantum (2019) came few and far between until *Wild Indian* and *Rutherford Falls*, both made by Indigenous writers and producers.

Rutherford Falls showrunner and cocreator Sierra Teller Ornelas, argued that a "cultural shift" in Native representation was galvanized by the Standing Rock protest in 2017 against the Dakota Access oil pipeline. She told Stuart Miller for *The New York Times* (21 Apr. 2021) that it "was a watershed moment for Native visibility, where a lot of people became more aware of the issues we were experiencing." Greyeyes discussed in interviews what this cultural shift meant for his acting career. "I think one of the reasons why I'm achieving a certain kind of success at this moment is that I've been able to work with Indigenous creatives," he told Maureen Ryan for *Vanity Fair* (4 Jan. 2022). "When I have Indigenous creatives in decision-making roles around me, I know I can drill down on why I'm there when I'm there as an actor. I'm not there as a writer, I'm not there to fix the script or provide cultural understanding. . . . It's absolutely freeing. I've been happy to lay that down and just really enjoy the work and the trust that's inherent in the project."

EARLY LIFE AND DANCE CAREER

Michael Joseph Charles Greyeyes was born on June 4, 1967, in the Qu'Appelle Valley in Saskatoon, Saskatchewan, Canada, and raised as a member of the Muskeg Lake Cree Nation in Saskatchewan. As a child, he often visited the ancestral homes of his parents, both in Saskatchewan; his mother was raised on the Sweetgrass First Nation reserve, and his father was raised on the Muscade Lake Cree Nation reserve. When he was six years old, he snuck into his sister's dance class. The instructor overheard him saying that it looked easy and invited him to take the class. Greyeyes told Falen Johnson for the *CBC* (19 Feb. 2021) that he remembered little else, and reckoned he stuck with it because he was the only boy in the class. "I was the center of attention from all these little girls because I was an oddity," he said. But Greyeyes was also talented enough that his whole family moved to Toronto when he was nine, so that he could train at Canada's National Ballet School. As he explained to Paula Citron for the Canada *Globe and Mail* (20 Sept. 2011), his parents "had both gone through the residential school system, and

Photo by Gage Skidmore, via Wikimedia Commons

they were not going to have their son leave the family."

Greyeyes recalled the discipline of the school that made him a professional dancer. "I remember just sweating—like a little sweaty kid, dancing my butt off," he told Johnson. "I earned my stripes . . . at a very young age." He graduated in 1984, and then apprenticed with the National Ballet of Canada. Greyeyes officially joined the company in 1987. After three years, he moved to New York City and joined choreographer Eliot Feld's company, Feld Ballets/NY. However, a leg injury a few years after that made him reconsider his career path. "I'd come home at six, seven, absolutely exhausted. Too tired to make dinner. I'd sit there, I had five or six ice bags on various different parts of my body and I was throbbing with pain. I was like, 'This isn't living.'" he recalled in a conversation with Wolf Schneider for *Cowboys & Indians* magazine (1 Mar. 1998). Greyeyes retired from dancing in 1993.

EARLY ACTING CAREER

Performing as a dancer kindled his interest in acting, and Greyeyes set out to audition for film roles, gravitating toward Indigenous characters. "I got into Hollywood at a time when it was right to cast real Indian people in these roles. By virtue of that, I was auditioning for these parts against less competition," he told Schneider.

He appeared in the 1993 television movie *Geronimo*, and in 1994 played a character named Gooch in a film called *Dance Me Outside*, about a group of young men living on a First Nations reserve in Ontario. The latter film, based on a novel by W. P. Kinsella, won praise from critics and became a cult classic. "Indian Country just ate this film up," Greyeyes told Johnson. "To this day, when I meet people, some people go, 'Gooch!' Which to me is like, wow, what an honor."

Greyeyes played nineteenth-century Lakota leader Crazy Horse in a television movie of the same name in 1996. He also appeared in a number of television shows during this period, including *Rough Riders*; *Dr. Quinn, Medicine Woman*; *Promised Land*; and *Millennium*. After playing a romantic lead in the television movie *Stolen Women, Captured Hearts* (1997), Greyeyes' career really began to take off. "My agents started to complain, 'We're getting calls and letters every day,'" he recalled to Schneider. He appeared in *True Women* (1997), a miniseries starring Angelina Jolie, as well as a thriller called *Firestorm* (1998). That same year he played a small role in another Indian Country classic, *Smoke Signals*, and played the nineteenth-century Plains Cree war chief Wandering Spirit in a miniseries called *Big Bear*.

DIRECTOR, CHOREOGRAPHER, AND SCHOLAR

Greyeyes earned a Master of Fine Arts degree from the Kent State University School of Theatre and Dance in Ohio in 2003. The following year, he started teaching as an associate professor in the theater department of York University's School of Arts, Performance, Media and Design. In 2008, he collaborated on a Cree opera called *Pimooteewin: The Journey*.

Greyeyes founded a nonprofit musical performance company called Signal Theatre in 2010. As the company's artistic director, he went on to choreograph and direct numerous works, including *from thine eyes* (2011) by Yvette Nolan. That piece was in conversation with ideas Greyeyes had explored in a 2009 conference paper, *Notions of Indian-ness in Contemporary First Nations Dance*.

WOMAN WALKS AHEAD AND BLOOD QUANTUM

Along with his other pursuits, Greyeyes continued to act consistently, mostly appearing in guest roles on television through the early 2000s. In 2014 he appeared as a Tlingit leader in *Klondike*, a period miniseries about the 1890s gold rush in the Yukon territory. In 2017 he played Hunkpapa Lakota leader Sitting Bull in a film called *Woman Walks Ahead*. Based on a true story, the film follows the relationship between Sitting Bull and a painter named Catherine Weldon (played by Jessica Chastain) who travels to North Dakota to paint him in the 1880s. Greyeyes took the role, he told Amy Kaufman for the *Los Angeles Times* (21 June 2018), because of its nuanced portrayal of Sitting Bull. "Almost immediately, I recognized his humor—how funny he was on the page. And that, I think, is the most rare thing that I see in scripts not written by us about our communities and about our heroes," he said. Critics were less impressed. Jeannette Catsoulis for *The New York Times* (28 June 2018) called *Woman Walks Ahead* "ridiculously romanticized and self-serving." Still, she praised the actors' performances, writing, "Mr. Greyeyes, in particular, is a miracle of intelligence and dignity."

Also in 2017 Greyeyes guest starred as antagonist Qaletaqa Walker in the AMC television series, *Fear the Walking Dead*, a spin-off of the popular *Walking Dead*. Two years later he appeared in another zombie invasion story, a Canadian film called *Blood Quantum*, set in a First Nations Mi'kmaq community in the early 1980s. Greyeyes stars as Sherrif Traylor, the town's law enforcement officer. The film, written and directed by Indigenous director Jeff Barnaby, offers social commentary and a critique of colonialism; its title refers to "blood quantum," a controversial, racialized method of measuring Indigeneity. "We had a lot of fun making the movie," Greyeyes told Thom Ernst for the film blog *Original Cin* (28 Apr. 2020). "We were attacking serious subject matter, really complex kinds of stories." Greyeyes won a Canadian Screen Award for his role in 2021.

WILD INDIAN

In 2019, Greyeyes appeared in season three of the popular HBO anthology series *True Detective*. He played Brett "Trashman" Woodard, a Vietnam veteran who collects trash and lives on the outskirts of a small Arkansas town. In 2020, he appeared in the HBO miniseries *I Know This Much Is True*, starring Mark Ruffalo.

A particularly notable role came in 2021, when Greyeyes starred in a drama called *Wild Indian*. The film, which premiered at the Sundance Film Festival, tells the story of Ojibwe cousins Makwa (Greyeyes) and Teddo (Chaske Spencer), who grow up together on a reservation in Wisconsin. After Teddo witnesses Makwa committing a horrendous act of violence and helps him cover it up, the cousins' paths diverge. Teddo spends much of his young adult life in prison, while Makwa moves to California and pursues a successful corporate career. Some critics described the film as relentlessly bleak, but Greyeyes was universally praised for his chilling performance as a man haunted by trauma and generational violence. "Greyeyes is deeply unnerving as a horror movie in human form, his flat voice and sinewy frame layering serial-killer stereotypes into the fabric of a man who sustains himself through constant suffocation," David Ehrlich wrote for *IndieWire* (30 Jan. 2021). The performance earned the actor an Independent Spirit Award nomination.

RUTHERFORD FALLS

Greyeyes' other breakout role of 2021 presented him in a wholly different light. In the sitcom *Rutherford Falls*, he plays an ambitious casino owner whose reservation abuts the fictional small town of Rutherford Falls. Created by showrunner and writer Sierra Teller Ornelas, who is Navajo and Mexican American, and comedy veterans Michael Schur and Ed Helms, the show recalls Schur's beloved series *Parks and Recreation* in its style. When Greyeyes first received the script, he was excited but also "low-key terrified," he told Ryan. "I recognized quite quickly that Sierra and the writers had created a fully empowered Indigenous man," Greyeyes said. "I thought to myself, with Terry, I can't use some of the old ways of working. I've had a wonderful career. I've played a lot of broken men, and there are a lot of beautiful textures in those characters. But what was interesting about Terry is that he is not broken. He's actually whole. I had to work more quickly. And I couldn't use any of the previous roots that I knew—what is a character's dysfunction, where's that from, how does that manifest itself?"

Rutherford Falls won praise from audiences and critics and was picked up for a second season. Greyeyes' performance as Terry, who,

as Teller Ornelas told Miller, "says the things that our parents and our grandparents had to sort of mutter under their breaths," earned him another Independent Spirit Award nomination.

PERSONAL LIFE

Greyeyes met his wife, Nancy Latoszewski, when the two were dancers with Feld Ballets/NY. They had two children together, Eva and Lilia.

SUGGESTED READING

Citron, Paula. "Michael Greyeyes: 'I'm Not Interested in Staging Ethnicity.'" *The Globe and Mail*, 20 Sept. 2011, www.theglobeandmail.com/arts/theatre-and-performance/michael-greyeyes-im-not-interested-in-staging-ethnicity/article4256612/. Accessed 10 Feb. 2022.

Ehrlich, David. "*Wild Indian* Review: The Violence of a Severed Heritage Breeds a Serial Killer." *IndieWire*, 30 Jan. 2021, www.indiewire.com/2021/01/wild-indian-review-1234612729/. Accessed 10 Feb. 2022.

Greyeyes, Michael. "Original-Cin Q&A: An In-Depth Chat with Star Michael Greyeyes into Themes behind the Indigenous Zombie Horror *Blood Quantum*." Interview by Thom Ernst. *Original Cin*, 28 Apr. 2020, www.original-cin.ca/posts/2020/4/28/original-cin-qampa-a-deep-dive-with-star-michael-greyeyes-into-the-big-themes-behind-the-indigenous-zombie-horror-blood-quantum. Accessed 10 Feb. 2022.

___. "Why Michael Greyeyes Was 'Low-Key Terrified' to Do Something Brand New on *Rutherford Falls*." Interview by Maureen Ryan. *Vanity Fair*, 4 Jan. 2022, www.vanityfair.com/hollywood/2022/01/awards-insider-michael-greyeyes-rutherford-falls. Accessed 10 Feb. 2022.

Johnson, Falen. "From Ballet Dancer to Zombie Slayer: Cree Actor Michael Greyeyes on His Prolific Career." *CBC*, 20 May 2021, www.cbc.ca/radio/unreserved/from-ballet-dancer-to-zombie-slayer-cree-actor-michael-greyeyes-on-his-prolific-career-1.5919804. Accessed 10 Feb. 2022.

Kaufman, Amy. "As Sitting Bull in *Woman Walks Ahead*, Michael Greyeyes Continues to Educate through Native Roles." *Los Angeles Times*, 21 June 2018, www.latimes.com/entertainment/movies/la-ca-mn-michael-greyeyes-woman-walks-ahead-20180621-story.html. Accessed 10 Feb. 2022.

Miller, Stuart. "Sierra Teller Ornelas on the Roots of *Rutherford Falls*." *The New York Times*, 21 Apr. 2021, www.nytimes.com/2021/04/21/arts/television/rutherford-falls-sierra-teller-ornelas.html. Accessed 11 Feb. 2022.

Schneider, Wolf. "Michael Greyeyes: 1998 Cover Story." *Cowboys & Indians*, 1 Mar. 1998, www.cowboysindians.com/2021/08/michael-greyeyes-1998-cover-story/. Accessed 10 Feb. 2022.

SELECTED WORKS

Dance Me Outside, 1994; *Woman Walks Ahead*, 2017; *True Detective*, 2019; *Blood Quantum*, 2019; *Rutherford Falls*, 2021; *Wild Indian*, 2021

—Molly Hagan

Asmik Grigorian

Born: May 12, 1981
Occupation: Operatic soprano

"Every character that comes into my life changes me somehow," the Lithuanian operatic soprano Asmik Grigorian told Ona Jarmalavičiūtė for *OperaWire* (20 Oct. 2019). "I look at the roles I play as my teachers, both in vocal terms and in the art of living in general." Indeed, as a prolific performer since early in the twenty-first century, Grigorian has had the chance to learn from numerous roles to which she has returned repeatedly, including *Eugene Onegin*'s Tatyana, *The Flying Dutchman*'s Senta, and the title role in *Manon Lescaut*. Roles she came to later in her career likewise proved meaningful: performing the role of Salome in the 2018 Salzburg Festival production of the opera of the same name, for instance, brought Grigorian worldwide critical acclaim as well as the opportunity to reprise her role the following year, an uncommon practice at the festival. Her 2021 debut in the title role of the opera *Jenůfa* at the Royal Opera House in London earned similar recognition from critics and in many ways represented the start of a new era for Grigorian. She had contracted a symptomatic case of COVID-19 in early 2020 and, like many performers, had struggled to find purpose amid the pandemic's many theater closures. As theaters reopened, Grigorian began to look toward the future—and toward a busy schedule packed with high-profile engagements. "I realized there are so many beautiful things which I can do," she told Joshua Barone for *The New York Times* (17 Aug. 2021). "Now is my best age, and I must do it."

EARLY LIFE AND EDUCATION

Asmik Grigorian was born on May 12, 1981, in Vilnius, Lithuania, then part of the Soviet Union. Her parents were both opera singers; her father, Gegham Grigorian, was a tenor, while her mother, Irena Milkevičiūtė, was a soprano. Grigorian's parents separated when she was a child, and she spent the next years dividing her time between her mother's home in Lithuania and the locales to which she traveled with her father, who toured extensively in Lithuania and abroad. Raised within the world of music and performance, Grigorian studied piano as a child. She went on to pursue formal studies as a vocalist, although she initially hoped to work within genres such as jazz or pop rather than her parents' preferred genre of opera. "I was convinced in school that if I was already learning music, there was nothing else that I could be good in my life," she told Jarmalavičiūtė. "I had ambitions, but I felt neither confidence nor desire to sing opera."

Remaining in Vilnius as a student, Grigorian attended the National M. K. Čiurlionis School of Art but did not enjoy her time there. "It was an army approach—and the army isn't a good fit for the arts," she told Neil Fisher for the British newspaper the *Times* (28 Aug. 2021) about the style of instruction she observed. "You were always told you were nothing . . . and if you play or sing the wrong note you are the worst person. All my life I've tried to learn that my success or failure does not make me a better or worse person." Nevertheless, Grigorian successfully completed her studies at that institution and went on to enroll in the Lithuanian Academy of Music and Theatre. She completed her program there in 2006.

EARLY CAREER

Grigorian worked steadily in the years following her graduation from the Lithuanian Academy of Music and Theatre, performing at venues such as Russia's Mariinsky Theatre and with companies such as the Latvian National Opera

Photo by Augustas Didzgalvis,
via Wikimedia Commons

and the Lithuanian National Opera and Ballet Theatre. Operas performed during her early years as a professional soprano included Verdi's *La Traviata*, Bizet's *Carmen*, Dvořák's *Rusalka*, and Mozart's *Don Giovanni*. While Grigorian's full schedule enabled her to maintain a career in her field, her workload proved excessively demanding. "I was doing everything," she recalled to Barone. "And for many years I could not get out of this circle of doing too-hard roles, too much. It was never perfect, because it just can't be if you do so much. But I couldn't do less because my fee was too small and I needed to support my son." The vocal strain Grigorian experienced eventually forced her to undergo surgery and take a break from performing at the age of thirty, during which time she worked to improve her vocal technique. "I invested a lot in learning, and my singing became much better," she told Barone. "Then, step by step, my fee started to get bigger."

INTERNATIONAL BREAKTHROUGH

Over the next several years, Grigorian continued to perform in many of the operas she had appeared in previously but also added a host of new roles to her repertoire, each of which provided her with new opportunities to explore unique characters and their emotions. "Because I am not acting but expressing the character through myself, in each role I have

to find some personal story that is close to the character's experiences," she explained to Jarmalavičiūtė. "Otherwise, it will not work." Prominent roles Grigorian took on during the mid-2010s included Tatyana in Tchaikovsky's *Eugene Onegin*, Senta in Wagner's *The Flying Dutchman*, and the title role in Puccini's *Manon Lescaut*. She likewise delved into musical theater beyond the confines of opera, performing the role of Mrs. Lovett in a Vilnius City Opera production of the Stephen Sondheim musical *Sweeney Todd: The Demon Barber of Fleet Street* (2016).

While Grigorian earned critical recognition for her work throughout that period, winning the 2016 International Opera Award for young female singer, her most significant breakthrough to date came in 2018, when she sang the role of Salome in a staging of the Richard Strauss opera of the same name at Austria's Salzburg Festival. Although aspects of the staging drew mixed reviews, critics widely praised her performance, and a recorded version of the production garnered further praise following its release on Blu-ray. *Salome* was staged again at the Salzburg Festival the following year, and Grigorian reprised her role despite her initial worries that she would be unable to bring anything new to the role. "Over the year, this role has grown, I feel much more at ease, and vocally more mature performing it," she explained to Jarmalavičiūtė. "Now I know better where the main difficulties are and how to deal with it. As a result, the performance is quite different." Grigorian followed her turns in Salzburg with engagements in countries such as Lithuania and Italy and, in August 2019, returned to the role of Tatyana in a production of *Eugene Onegin* at the Edinburgh International Festival in Scotland. She was awarded the International Opera Award for Female Singer of the Year for 2019 and was also the recipient of the Lithuanian National Prize for Culture and Arts.

NEW ROLES AND UNFORESEEN SETBACKS

Grigorian began 2020 on a strong note, returning to the Lithuanian National Opera and Ballet Theatre for the first time in a decade to appear in a February production of the Prokofiev opera *The Gambler*. She was set to take on the new role of the title character of the Janáček opera *Jenůfa*, planned to be staged at the Royal Opera House in London in April of that year. That production was to be followed by a May engagement as the title character in the Bellini opera *Norma* at the Theater an der Wien in Vienna, Austria. "Jenůfa is a role debut, for which I feel a great responsibility," Grigorian told Jarmalavičiūtė. "*Norma* is something radically different from what I have [ever] done on a technical level. I know everyone is looking forward to this production because it is hard to imagine how I will interpret, perform, and whether I will be actually able to sing it. I feel the attention and it puts a lot of pressure on me."

In March 2020, however, Grigorian began to experience the symptoms of an unknown illness that hampered her throughout the rehearsal process for *Jenůfa*. "I was so weak, I couldn't understand it. I felt almost drunk," she later told Fisher. Grigorian's illness was eventually revealed to be COVID-19, and the spreading pandemic soon forced the postponement of *Jenůfa* and other upcoming productions. Grigorian eventually recovered (though she continued to experience long-term symptoms of COVID-19 for many months), while theaters in many countries remained closed throughout 2020 amid efforts to limit social gatherings and prevent the spread of the disease.

RETURN TO THE STAGE

As theaters finally began to reopen in 2021, Grigorian returned to the stage, appearing in productions of *The Gambler*, *Rusalka*, *Salome*, and other works. In June 2021, she performed in a concert dedicated to the works of Tchaikovsky that was held at the Opéra National de Paris. Grigorian made her debut at Germany's Bayreuth Festival in August of that year, again performing the role of Senta in *The Flying Dutchman*. Following a substantial delay, the Royal Opera House staging of *Jenůfa* finally opened in late September 2021 and earned Grigorian substantial critical acclaim throughout the production's run, which continued into mid-October. She closed out the year with performances in Italy, Germany, Sweden, and Austria.

Much in demand, Grigorian was scheduled to take on a challenging slate of performances throughout 2022, including a production of *Manon Lescaut* at the Wiener Staatsoper in Vienna in February and a German staging of *Jenůfa* later in the year. A recital dedicated to the songs of Rachmaninov is scheduled to be performed by Grigorian and pianist Lukas Geniušas at the Hamburg International Music Festival in May 24, 2022, as well as at other European locations later that year. While her performance schedule was set to be a strenuous one, Grigorian appreciated how much her career had changed since her overworked and underpaid early years in opera. "It's not scary," she told Fisher. "It's the opposite feeling, a feeling of stability."

PERSONAL LIFE

Grigorian married fellow performer Giedrius Žalys while attending the Lithuanian Academy of Music and Theatre. They had a son together in 2002, prior to their divorce. In 2015, Grigorian married Vasily Barkhatov, an opera director with whom she worked on projects such as the 2020 Lithuania production of *The Gambler*. "He knows very clearly what he wants, so I can just follow the instructions and not think too much," she told the website of the Lithuanian National Opera and Ballet Theatre (12 Feb. 2020) about the experience of working with her husband. "Such directors are rare." Grigorian and Barkhatov have a daughter together. When not performing elsewhere, Grigorian lives in Vilnius.

SUGGESTED READING

Ashley, Tim. "*Jenůfa* Review—Mattila Is Formidable in New Janaček Staging." *The Guardian*, 29 Sept. 2021, www.theguardian.com/music/2021/sep/29/jenufa-review-royal-opera-house-asmik-grigorian-karita-mattila. Accessed 10 Dec. 2021.

"Asmik Grigorian: 'This Theatre Is My Home.'" *Lithuanian National Opera and Ballet Theatre*, 12 Feb. 2020, www.opera.lt/en/news/asmik-grigorian-this-theatre-is-my-home/1023. Accessed 10 Dec. 2021.

"Asmik Grigorian (Soprano)." *Bach Cantatas Website*, 29 May 2017, www.bach-cantatas.com/Bio/Grigorian-Asmik.htm. Accessed 10 Dec. 2021.

Barone, Joshua. "A Soprano with a Bottomless Appetite for Risk." *The New York Times*, 17 Aug. 2021, www.nytimes.com/2021/08/17/arts/music/asmik-grigorian.html. Accessed 10 Dec. 2021.

Fisher, Neil. "Asmik Grigorian: Opera's Newest Star Heads for Covent Garden." *The Times*, 28 Aug. 2021, www.thetimes.co.uk/article/

jenufa-star-asmik-grigorian-at-my-academy-we-were-always-told-we-were-nothing-dvhfwsvxq. Accessed 10 Dec. 2021.

Grigorian, Asmik. "Q & A: Asmik Grigorian on 'Salome,' a New Chapter in Her Career & Letting Go of Her Father." Interview by Ona Jarmalavičiūtė. *OperaWire*, 20 Oct. 2019, operawire.com/q-a-asmik-grigorian-on-salome-a-new-chapter-in-her-career-letting-go-of-her-father/. Accessed 10 Dec. 2021.

—*Joy Crelin*

Luke Grimes

Born: January 21, 1984
Occupation: Actor

While most people know Luke Grimes for playing Kayce Dutton on the Western melodrama series *Yellowstone*, serving as a fixture of the main cast from the show's beginning in 2018, the actor had been making an impression on both the big and small screens long before then. From portraying a troubled teen in *War Eagle, Arkansas* (2007), to a young man adjusting to a family he only recently learned he was a relative of in the network drama *Brothers & Sisters* (2009–10), to a Navy SEAL serving in the Iraq War in *American Sniper* (2014), to a fatherless drifter in *El Camino Christmas* (2017), his wide spectrum of roles has become a true reflection of the span of his talent.

Despite having built his career from the ground up, like any other actor, Grimes's fierce determination to his craft—meshed with a stroke of luck—has allowed him to pursue roles that he wanted to take. As he said to fellow actor Bradley Cooper for *Interview* magazine (5 Oct. 2016), "For the most part, anything that I do is something that I'm passionate about and really believe in, no matter how it turns out. It's about the experience that you get, loving it." Landing the role of Dutton, arguably the actor's most celebrated character and also one that Grimes never envisaged getting to play, allowed him to further follow that philosophy. "Kayce Dutton, in *Yellowstone* is a dream. I couldn't have imagined it better myself than if I sat down and asked, what would be the perfect character to play? I'm literally playing it," Grimes revealed to Tatijana Shoan in an interview for *As If* magazine.

EARLY LIFE AND EDUCATION

Luke Timothy Grimes was born on January 21, 1984, in Dayton, a city in western Ohio. The last of four children born to Angie and Randy Grimes, he grew up in a close-knit, devoutly Christian household, with his father working as a pastor at the local Open Bible Christian Church. Though his views, at least on organized religion, would later change in his adulthood, religion was an important part of his upbringing. In addition to attending church camp over summers and playing the drums at church, he eventually attended Dayton Christian High School, from which he graduated in 2002. "Growing up the way I did and having a dad who's a pastor, it's just in you," he told Cooper before continuing to say, "And moving away, going to New York and then L.A., and doing what I do, you're trying your best to filter some of it out. No matter what I do in my life, though, it's there."

Having had a relative dearth of acting opportunities in his home state, Grimes made up his mind to pursue an acting career following high school and was intent on relocating to Los Angeles in search of opportunities. His parents, seeing how committed he was to this path, played an important role in kickstarting his career, paying his tuition to study acting at New York City's American Academy of Dramatic Arts. "My parents sacrificed a lot to send me there, and I think that changed my trajectory. . . . My training provided me with a good sense of the kind of actor I wanted to be and the kind of projects I wanted to do," he said to Shoan.

Armed with an acting degree and the experience of having lived in one of the nation's busiest cities, Grimes arrived in Los Angeles next, around 2005. As he searched for acting roles, he also got caught up in the hype of the alternative country music scene—a subgenre of country rock that had reached special acclaim and recognition by the mid-2000s. As a longtime music enthusiast, he became the drummer for Mitchells Folly, a band that would go on to record a 2008 full-length studio album titled *Whirlwind*. Eventually, he would also contribute lyrics and guitar playing.

ACTING BEGINNINGS

Just like many other actors, Grimes developed his career from the ground up, playing small roles at first. Commenting later on his rise in

Photo by Gordon Correll,
via Wikimedia Commons.

the industry in an interview for the magazine *At Large* (2014), he said, "It's been a slow burn, and I feel like pretty much every job I've ever had has been through the front door in a very traditional sense: I've auditioned for it, they haven't known who I was, and I've gotten the job." After getting his start in the slasher film *All the Boys Love Mandy Lane*, which initially earned praise on the film festival circuit in 2006 but was not theatrically released until 2013, he went on to portray troubled teen Enoch in *War Eagle* (2007), *Arkansas* before appearing alongside veteran actors such as Bruce Willis in *Assassination of a High School President*, a neo-noir comedy that was largely well received at its 2008 Sundance Film Festival premiere.

As Mitchells Folly reached its artistic zenith in 2008 with the release of its album, Grimes's acting career also started to take off. It would be in 2009 that he got his first major acting credit as Ryan Lafferty, a young man who becomes part of a complicated family upon learning the truth about his biological father, on the ABC drama *Brothers & Sisters*. Joining the critically acclaimed, hit ensemble series first as a guest star in season three, he was then a series regular in season four, which ran into 2010. Slowly but steadily, more prominent film roles began to come his way, including a part in the 2012 action-thriller *Taken 2*. A continuation of the popular film *Taken*

(2008)—in which ex-CIA agent Bryan Mills (played by Liam Neeson) goes to unbelievable lengths to save his daughter, Kim (Maggie Grace), when she is abducted by an Albanian sex-trafficking ring during her first European trip—this second film finds the father-daughter duo in action once more, with Grimes playing Kim's boyfriend, Jamie.

When the sixth season of the cultishly beloved HBO vampire show *True Blood* premiered in 2013, the young actor was seen portraying the character of James Kent. However, Grimes's presence on the show only lasted for six episodes, as he was replaced with actor Nathan Parsons. Although HBO said the reason behind recasting Grimes was that the actor was against the creative direction of his character—which, more precisely, included a gay story line—his publicist was quick to deny such allegations, citing that Grimes had left to pursue other opportunities. Other media sources also reported Grimes as asserting that his departure had been misunderstood.

AMERICAN SNIPER AND HIGH-PROFILE ROLES

The year 2014 saw Grimes play his most high-profile role until that point: US Navy SEAL Marc Lee in the dramatic, Academy Award–nominated war film *American Sniper*. Directed by Clint Eastwood and featuring Bradley Cooper in the lead role, the movie follows the life of Chris Kyle (Cooper), the deadliest sniper in US military history, across his four Iraq tours. Portraying Marc—a teammate of Kyle and the first Navy SEAL to die in combat in Iraq—proved to be an unforgettable role for the actor, as he learned a great deal. "I was able to experience first-hand how that war affected people. I will never truly understand what our military go through in battle, but I understand what the cost is," he told Shoan. "I see how necessary it is to stop war altogether. We should be way more evolved than resorting to war."

After Grimes's turn in *American Sniper*, another high-profile role followed in the 2015 erotic drama *Fifty Shades of Grey*, based on the 2011 best-selling novel of the same name by E. L. James. Starring Jamie Dornan as Christian Grey, a billionaire business executive, and Dakota Johnson as Anastasia Steele, a college student who falls for Grey, the film features Grimes portraying Elliot Grey, the brother of the male lead. While the film went on to generate generally negative reviews, it became a box-office hit, grossing over $569 million worldwide. When its sequels, *Fifty Shades Darker* and *Fifty Shades Freed*, premiered in 2017 and 2018, respectively—in which Grimes reprised his role as Elliot—they would meet the same fate as their predecessor: they were critical flops but box-office successes.

Meanwhile, it would be in 2016 that Grimes stopped playing solely supporting parts, landing a lead role in the crime-drama film *Shangri-La Suite*, opposite Emily Browning. In the film, which had a limited theatrical release, Jack Blueblood, portrayed by Grimes, begins a relationship with Karen Bird (Browning) while they are both residing at a facility for people with mental illness. Things take a turn for the worse, however, when Jack kills the resident doctor for mistreating Karen and the duo head toward Los Angeles with a murderous plan.

YELLOWSTONE AND RETURNING TO MUSIC

With the premiere of *The Magnificent 7* in 2016, Grimes added a Western-action film to his filmography repertoire. Featuring an all-star cast led by Denzel Washington and Chris Pratt, the film—about a small town named Rose Creek that resorts to the help of seven gunfighters to defend itself from a greedy mining magnate and his gang—has Grimes assuming the role of Teddy Q, a Rose Creek resident who aids in the recruitment of the Seven.

Grimes next portrayed a young drifter in search of his father who is wrongly accused of holding people hostage in a liquor store on Christmas Eve, in the 2017 Netflix-released *El Camino Christmas*. He then became part of the main cast of *Yellowstone*, a drama series that premiered in 2018 on the Paramount network. The highly acclaimed, modern-day Western series revolves around the Dutton family—owners of one of the largest ranches in Montana—as they navigate family drama and clashes with a neighboring national park, American Indian reservations, and power-hungry developers. In the series, Grimes breathes life into the character of Kayce Dutton, one of the four Dutton children and a former Navy SEAL. Of this role, he said to Shoan, "I love my character because he is caught in-between: he is a part of the Dutton family who own the cattle ranch, but he is married to a Native American woman, they have

a child together, and live on the reservation. Subsequently, he is not quite accepted by either side and, because of his need to take care of himself, he became a Navy SEAL. He served for America, and now he doesn't know where he belongs."

Yellowstone had its fourth-season, record-breaking premiere in late 2021 and was renewed for a fifth season in early 2022, which meant that Grimes, who was also seen as ex-criminal Nick Brenner in the 2019 action-drama *Into the Ashes*, would continue to be seen on the small screen as part of the Dutton family. The actor was also plotting a music comeback, penning songs and hoping to go solo on a new foray into the country genre.

PERSONAL LIFE

In November 2018, Grimes married Brazilian-born model Bianca Rodrigues.

SUGGESTED READING

Grimes, Luke. "*Into the Ashes* Star Luke Grimes on His New Film, Humility, and Why He Loves Horseback Riding." Interview by Tatijana Shoan. *As If*, www.asifmag.com/story/luke-grimes-into-the-ashes-as-if-magazine. Accessed 30 Mar. 2022.

———. "Luke Grimes." Interview by Bradley Cooper. *Interview*, 5 Oct. 2016, www.interviewmagazine.com/film/luke-grimes. Accessed 30 Mar. 2022.

———. "Luke Grimes on *Yellowstone*, Goodness, and Taking a Hot Springs Dip with Kevin Costner." Interview by Justin Kirkland. *Esquire*, 3 Dec. 2021, www.esquire.com/entertainment/tv/a38391065/luke-grimes-yellowstone-interview-season-four-kayce. Accessed 30 Mar. 2022.

———. "Luke Grimes." Interview by Michael Martin. *Interview*, 26 Nov. 2008, www.interviewmagazine.com/art/luke-grimes-1. Accessed 30 Mar. 2022.

Horn, John. "NY Noir: Luke Grimes." *At Large*, 2014, atlargemagazine.com/features/ny-noir/. Accessed 8 Apr. 2022.

Hudak, Joseph. "*Yellowstone* Truth-Seeker Luke Grimes Has a Vision: A Country Music Career." *Rolling Stone*, 5 Jan. 2022, www.rollingstone.com/music/music-country/yellowstone-kayce-luke-grimes-country-music-1278783. Accessed 30 Mar. 2022.

SELECTED WORKS

Brothers & Sisters, 2009–10; *American Sniper*, 2014; *Fifty Shades of Grey*, 2015; *Shangri-La Suite*, 2016; *The Magnificent 7*, 2016; *Fifty Shades Darker*, 2017; *El Camino Christmas*, 2017; *Fifty Shades Freed*, 2018; *Yellowstone*, 2018– ; *Into the Ashes*, 2019

—*Maria del Pilar Guzman*

Martine Gutierrez

Born: April 16, 1989
Occupation: Artist

Martine Gutierrez is a shape shifter. After her arrival to the New York City's art scene in 2013, the artist has used her photography, videography, makeup, costuming, and set design skills to produce more than a hundred images of herself embodying completely different personas. Her work has taken the form of everything from video installations to faux fashion magazines, and along the way has earned international acclaim for the way that it challenges society's perception of gender. This has always been important to Gutierrez, a nonbinary transgender woman who believes that gender roles are simply parts that people have learned to play. "The reality is we're all both. Our identities are fluid," Gutierrez explained to Lena Rawley in an interview for *The Cut* (9 Feb. 2017). "It's important to emphasize that outside of these artificial boundaries we're both inherently equal and profoundly, infinitely diverse."

EARLY LIFE

Martine Gutierrez was born in Berkeley, California, on April 16, 1989, to a Guatemalan father and an American mother. As her parents divorced shortly after she was born, she spent her formative years in two diverse cultural households. Through her father, Gutierrez was given a sense of how big the world was—a perspective that would continue to influence her as an adult. She commented on this fact in an interview with Marie Tomanova for *Ravelin Magazine* (15 May 2018), stating, "We traveled a lot growing up, back and forth visiting family in Guatemala while living in the States. All the cross-cultural mythology is instilled in my mind's eye."

When she was eleven years old, Gutierrez moved to rural Vermont with her mother. An architect, Gutierrez's mother recognized the young Gutierrez's creativity and signed her up for a wide range of activities, including dance, music, theater, and painting classes. Gutierrez would later incorporate many of these different mediums into her work. In addition to honing her skills, these classes gave Gutierrez the opportunity to explore her identity and express herself in ways that she could not in other areas of her life. "I've always navigated the world in a very gender fluid way," Gutierrez explained to Hilarie M. Sheets in an interview for *The New York Times* (13 Aug. 2021).

Gutierrez, who was assigned male at birth, grew up obsessed with fashion, Disney princesses, and Barbies. She started incorporating girls' clothes into her wardrobe when she was in the first grade and enjoyed playing dress up with costumes and wigs while dancing around the house. Her father's response to her interests was to get her to watch macho action movies with him in hopes that she would start to adopt more "masculine" behavior. Meanwhile, her mother was more supportive of her gender fluidity; when Gutierrez was in elementary school, she helped her build her own version of the popular three-foot-tall My Size Barbie toy, which they renamed "My Size Martine."

As a teenager, Gutierrez felt misunderstood and consequently her high school years were chaotic. Some days, after the school bus dropped her off, she would disappear into the woods to seek refuge in nature. Things start to click into place for her, however, one summer when she enrolled in a program that was intended to help young artists hone their craft. Surrounded by extremely talented, motivated peers, Gutierrez suddenly realized that creating art was what she wanted to do for the rest of her life and that art school was an option that she could pursue.

LAUNCHING HER CAREER

Gutierrez was accepted into the prestigious Rhode Island School of Design (RISD) in 2008. Much of the work she did during the four years that she studied there focused on themes of gender, identity, and self. Upon graduating with a BFA in printmaking in 2012, she was called in to the Ryan Lee gallery in New York City for what she believed was a job interview for the front desk position. As it turned out, one of her RISD professors had already introduced the gallery's owners to her work, and they wanted to represent her.

The following summer, Gutierrez's first show debuted at Ryan Lee. Entitled *Martín Gutierrez: Martin(e)*, it featured imagery of her through the mediums of photography and video. At that time in 2013, Gutierrez still identified as gender fluid and used male pronouns, however, the videos introduced her to audiences as a woman named Martine.

Out of all the show's pieces, the photography series *Real Dolls* garnered the most attention. Shot at Gutierrez's mother's house in Vermont, the photographs feature Gutierrez in domestic spaces like the kitchen, living room, and bedroom posed as four life-size female sex dolls named Ebony, Luxx, Mimi, and Raquel. Critics were quick to extol the series and compared her to other burgeoning artists like Kalup Linzy, Jacolby Satterwhite, and Ryan Trecartin for the way that she blended race, class, and gender. Several of the *Real Dolls* photographs were later included in the *Disturbing Innocence* exhibition at the FLAG art Foundation in 2014 as well as the *About Face* 2015 exhibition at Dartmouth's Hood Museum.

In 2014, Gutierrez exhibited two more photo series: *Girlfriends* and *Line Ups*. *Girlfriends* is shot in black-and-white and features Gutierrez and a mannequin dressed identically in different settings that are mostly outdoors. *Line Ups*, while similar in approach to *Girlfriends*, is almost the opposite series. Shot in color, the series depict Gutierrez in tight, indoor settings surrounded by a small group of mannequins who are all dressed in the same hyper-feminine outfits as her.

Both photo series had an enormous impact on Gutierrez's sense of identity because of the way that people reacted to them. "When I was in the gallery next to my work, viewers didn't recognize that I was the girl in the picture," she told Sheets. It was this fact that the public still saw a disconnect between how she presented herself and who she really was that made Gutierrez want to transition. In 2015, she began using female pronouns.

A RISING STAR IN THE NEW YORK ART SCENE

In the years that followed, Gutierrez quickly earned a reputation as one of the most important up-and-coming modern artists of

her generation. Through her photographs and videos, she began exploring a visual style that echoed fashion advertising while continuing to put her own image at the center of her work in different archetypes of glamorous women.

In 2014, she produced a large-scale video installation for the Ryan Lee gallery window, which was visible from the High Line Park in the neighborhood of Chelsea, Manhattan. Entitled *RedWoman91*, the video depicts Gutierrez wearing a red dress, laying on the ground and posing as she looked directly into a camera. In an interview with Houda Lazrak (3 Mar. 2017) for the International Studio and Curatorial Program (ISCP), she explained the purpose of the piece is to examine the "digital interrelationships of online personas related to social media and chatrooms, but also individuals' acts of curating their online presence."

From August 2016 to February 2017, Gutierrez was the Von Lier resident at ISCP. During that time, she produced a New York City billboard featuring a twenty-two-foot fake advertisement for #MartineJeans that featured her as the model. Gutierrez's trendy look and sexy pose is shot in black-and-white and surrounded by a bright pink background that is reminiscent of how many high-end brands typically present expensive products on cis-female super models. By mimicking this aesthetic, she was able to take control over how her body is used to represent transgender women of color. She explained this idea to Lazrak in their interview, stating, "I am fully versed in the confrontations that follow the spectacle of my gender. I therefore utilize large public installations such as *JEANS* as an opportunity to take back my power."

MARTINE PART I-IX AND *INDIGENOUS WOMAN*

In 2017, Gutierrez completed her semi-autobiographical film *Martine Part I–IX*, which she had been working on for six years. The nine-part film follows her as she traveled to distinct locations that had personal meaning to her including Providence, Rhode Island; New York City, New York; and various locations around Central America and the Caribbean. On each stop along the way on this journey of self-discovery, she navigates different perceptions of her identity, eventually dismantling the mainstream's myopic perception of gender.

"Subconsciously, I think the project has served to illustrate my rejection of societal binaries as I come to an understanding of my gender and identity as a trans woman," she told Rawley, "My work continues to inform how I see myself or want to be seen—it is the only way I have found to validate my beauty and my expression of gender without being manipulated by social constructs."

In 2018, Gutierrez published *Indigenous Woman*, a 124-page magazine that looks like a fashion magazine. Used to explore themes of gender and race, many of the magazine's photographs are of Gutierrez modeling different outfits that emphasize her Mayan heritage and are inspired by the textiles she had discovered at her grandparents' house in Guatemala. There are also satirical advertisements for fake products like a bar of soap called "white wash" that acknowledges the way that the mainstream media erases people of color from existence. In a different section of the magazine, Gutierrez imitates the #selfcare Instagram craze for facial masks with four photographs depicting her wearing food products on her face.

Indigenous Woman maintains the perspective that Gutierrez developed in *#MartineJeans* by continuing to use glossy, high-end fashion aesthetics to deliver commentary about the arbitrary social construct of identity. The project launched Gutierrez's notoriety to a new level, with several critics comparing her to Frida Kahlo. Many could not believe how multi-skilled she was as an artist. "Mine is a practice of full autonomy," she told John Paul Brammer in her *Them* (5 Sept. 2018) interview. "All photography, modeling, styling, makeup, hair, lighting, graphic design, and product design, I have executed myself."

BECOMING AN INTERNATIONAL PHENOMENON

In 2019, Gutierrez's work was featured in the 58th International Art Exhibition in Venice, a show that was put together by the renowned curator Ralph Rugoff. This proved to be a turning point in Gutierrez's career as it validated her talent while also introducing her to the international art scene. She has noted that the exhibition happened at a time when she felt physically beautiful; however, for Gutierrez beauty has often come with a price. She explained to Osman Can Yerebakan in an interview for *Art Net* (7 Sept. 2021), "Being a

beautiful woman cuts you through wealth and class—you can be broke but people will pay attention. Men think I am there for them, and to be made an object is a corrupting feeling."

Gutierrez's career momentum continued throughout 2019. That year her work was also featured in the exhibits *Kiss My Genders* at the Hayward Gallery in London and *Transamerica/n: Gender, Identity, Appearance Today* at the McNay Art Museum in San Antonio. Furthermore, her solo exhibition *Martine Gutierrez Body en Thrall* (2020) was featured at the Australian Centre for Photography.

ANTI-ICON

On August 25, 2021, Gutierrez's debuted her photo series *ANTI-ICON*. Commissioned by the Public Art Fund Project, *ANTI-ICON* comprises images of Gutierrez embodying different famous female figures including Helen of Troy, Cleopatra, Aphrodite, and Mulan. The photographs, which continued Gutierrez's glossy aesthetic, were placed in bus stops in New York City, New York; Boston, Massachusetts; and Chicago, Illinois, where perfume and fashion ads are typically placed.

The purpose of *ANTI-ICON* was to celebrate women who were not universally beloved but rather symbols of martyrdom. It was important to Gutierrez to remove pronouns and to challenge all of the pre-conceived ideas that people had about these historical and mythological figures. Ultimately, she wanted to explore whether she was "allowed" to represent these women who had been reproduced countless times throughout the years. "My first question was, 'Am I a woman?' What does being a woman mean?" she said to Sheets in her *New York Times* interview. "It's probably something I'll never stop asking myself."

SUGGESTED READING

Gutirrez, Martine. "A Trans Latinx Woman Takes Total Control of Her Narrative in New Magazine Art Project." Interview by John Paul Brammer. *Them*, 5 Sept. 2018, www. them.us/story/indigenous-woman. Accessed 26 Dec. 2021.

___. "Marie Tomanova's Conversation with Martine Gutierrez." Interview by Marie Tomanova. *Ravelin Magazine*, 15 May 2018, www.ravelinmagazine.com/posts/marie-

tomanovas-conversation-martine-gutierrez/.
Accessed 26 Dec. 2021.

———. "Martine Gutierrez: Jeans." Interview by
Houda Lazrak. *ISCP*, 3 Mar. 2017, iscp-nyc.
org/journal/martine-gutierrez-on-her-first-
billboard-jeans. Accessed 26 Dec. 2021.

Rawley, Lena. "This Artist Thinks Gender Is a
Drag." *The Cut*, 9 Feb. 2017, www.thecut.
com/2017/02/martine-gutierrez-thinks-
gender-is-a-drag-new-film.html. Accessed
26 Dec. 2021.

Sheets, Hilarie M. "A Shape-Shifting Woman
Plays All the Parts." *The New York Times*, 13
Aug. 2021, www.nytimes.com/2021/08/13/
arts/design/Martine-Gutierrez-bus-shelter-
photos.html. Accessed 26 Dec. 2021.

Yerebakan, Osman Can. "How Martine
Gutierrez Turned Herself into Cleopatra,
Mulan, and Other Historical Heroines for a
Public Art Project in Bus Shelters across the
U.S." *Art Net*, 7 Sept. 2021, news.artnet.
com/art-world/martine-gutierrez-public-art-
fund-2004044. Accessed 26 Dec. 2021.

SELECTED WORKS

Martin(e),   2013;   *RedWoman91*,   2014;
#MartineJeans, 2016; *Indigenous Woman*, 2018;
Body en Thrall, 2020; *ANTI-ICON*, 2021

—*Emily E. Turner*

Mickey Guyton

Born: June 17, 1983
Occupation: Country music artist

Around 2019, Mickey Guyton cowrote an
emotional ballad titled "Black Like Me." The
country musician felt as though it was the most
honest, important piece of music of her career.
Whenever she broached the topic of releasing
it, however, she was told by music executives
that it might not be country enough. She
was all too familiar with this coded language,
which she had been hearing since arriving in
Nashville in 2011: she was simply viewed as
"too Black" for country music.

By the end of May 2020, Guyton no longer
cared whether her songs fit the genre's myopic
format. As the horrific footage of George
Floyd's murder at the hands of Minneapolis,
Minnesota, police officer Derek Chauvin
circulated the Internet, she had become
increasingly upset about living in a world where

a person could be perceived as being a threat
just for the color of their skin. She told her
management team they had to do something.

On June 2, 2020, "Black Like Me" was
released on Spotify. What some feared would
be the end of Guyton's career ended up
launching it to an entirely new level. After
a decade of trying to break into a genre that
was dominated by White artists singing about
noninflammatory subjects like breakups and
beer, the singer had demonstrated that songs
about her experience living in America as a
Black woman also had a place on the radio.
"Black Like Me" skyrocketed to the fourth
position on the Billboard Country Digital
Song Sales chart. Later, it secured her a Best
Country Solo Performance Grammy Award
nod, making her widely recognized as the first
Black American woman to ever be nominated
in that category up to that point.

When reflecting on how she found the
courage to sing about racism to a musical
fandom comprised of predominantly White
listeners, Guyton told Kristin M. Hall in an
interview for the Associated Press (13 Aug.
2020), "Country music is three chords and the
truth. This is my truth."

EARLY LIFE

Candace Mycale Guyton was born on June 17,
1983, in Arlington, Texas. She was the second
child of four born into a family that had to
relocate within Texas, including to cities such
as Tyler, Crawford, and Mansfield, somewhat
often because her father, an engineer, was
employed by Oncor Electric Delivery. Although
regularly picking up and starting anew was
difficult, church was a steady presence in
her life, and it was there that she started
experimenting with her vocal range at around
the age of five. "My life centered around the
church," she explained to Amanda Petrusich for
The New Yorker (7 June 2021) while reflecting
on her childhood. "That's where I learned how
to sing and how to harmonize. It wasn't like I
had a love for music—our parents *made* us sing
in the choir, so we did."

It was not until Guyton was about nine years
old that her passion for music really began to
gel. While watching the Rangers play from high
up in the stadium seats with her church group,
she found herself completely enchanted by the
girl performing the national anthem: LeAnn
Rimes. Witnessing a person as young as her

perform so powerfully made Guyton want to do the same.

From that point on, Guyton listened to many different genres of music but found herself gravitating toward country music as it felt the most like her, and like the best way to convey her stories. In part, this was due to the influence of her grandmother, who was the first to introduce the young singer to the likes of Dolly Parton and Kenny Rogers. "At the time when everybody was playing Spice Girls, I was listening to Shania Twain," she told Taylor Weatherby in an interview for the Recording Academy website (24 Sept. 2021). "I think it was the diva facade of country singers that I loved. . . . I didn't think about it as a genre thing, I just liked it." To hone her vocal skills, she would use pretend microphones and mimic the vocal stylings of everyone from Faith Hill to Whitney Houston.

School proved to be a mixed experience for Guyton. After hearing racial slurs coming from a school bus for the local, mostly White public school, her parents decided to have her and her siblings go to a private Christian school. To cover their tuition, her mother worked as a substitute teacher at the school while their dad served as a basketball coach. Throughout these formative years, her love for singing and performing continued to gain momentum. While attending Mansfield High School, she became the go-to student to sing the national anthem before every basketball game.

EDUCATION AND EARLY CAREER

After earning her high school diploma, Guyton figured she did not yet have a chance of making it in Nashville, so she journeyed to Los Angeles to begin chasing her dream career as a musician. Once in California, she began attending Santa Monica College, where she focused on business management and took more than one job for some financial support, including at a cigar club. During this time, she worked hard to break into the entertainment industry, jumping at any opportunity, from singing backup for artists like Patti LaBelle and Babyface as well as appearing in the Nick Cannon film *Underclassman* (2005) to competing in the initial rounds of *American Idol* in 2008.

Years passed, however, and Guyton was not much closer to her dream than when she

Photo by Rob Ree,
via Wikimedia Commons

had first arrived in Los Angeles. In addition to still being a credit away from finishing her degree, she was struggling financially and sharing a small apartment. Feeling hopeless, she seriously entertained the idea of returning home.

However, a chance encounter turned Guyton's luck around. While at a mall, she bumped into DJ D-Wreck, whom she had befriended while working on different Cannon projects. D-Wreck mentioned to her that he had an industry connection who was looking for a Black country singer. Reflecting on this life-changing encounter, she told Petrusich, "He was, like, 'You do music, right? What kind of music do you sing?' And I was, like, 'I sing country.' It was the first time I'd said it. I was thinking I'd keep moving and that'd be it." She continued, "But a hip-hop guy got me in contact with a country guy."

D-Wreck got Guyton acquainted with the producer Julian Raymond, who in turn helped her land high-profile management and a record deal with Capitol Records Nashville. Now the summer of 2011, it seemed that Guyton's luck was changing. The sole Black woman signed to a prominent country label, she decided there was only one place she needed to be if she was going to make it in the industry: Nashville.

EARLY NASHVILLE CAREER

Despite having a record deal, being a tireless worker, joining the songwriter scene, and having the opportunity to perform at the White House in late 2011, success remained out of reach for Guyton in Nashville. For the first few years she lived there, she had to work a day job as her management team tried to determine what her sound and positioning would be in the market. Although the genre is rooted in Black music traditions and has had its share of Black singers, over the decades it had become dominated by White male artists singing about partying, pickup trucks, and girls. As a Black woman in country music, she found herself constantly facing biased criticisms about her authenticity and the music she wanted to make. "I was hearing trap beats in country songs, and here I was stressing out about whether I sounded country enough," she explained to Jewly Hight for the *Los Angeles Times* (9 Apr. 2020). "It was such a weird double standard."

In 2014, Guyton finally released her first EP, *Unbreakable*. The following year, she released her debut single, "Better Than You Left Me." A breakup song, it quickly made waves, climbing to thirty-four on the Billboard Country Airplay chart and earning her a spot on Brad Paisley's 2015 world tour as well as an Academy of Country Music (ACM) Award nomination for New Female Vocalist of the Year. Whatever popularity "Better Than You Left Me," which was included on her 2015 follow-up EP *Mickey Guyton*, enjoyed, however, was short-lived. In part, this was because she still, frustratingly, had not found herself as an artist and kept attempting different styles of songs to align with the genre's traditional mold. "I was trying to write everybody else's song and everybody else's story when I had a unique story of my own," she related to Hall. Some critics described the songs that she put out between 2016 and 2019 as lacking direction and being too heavily produced.

BREAKOUT

By 2019, Guyton, at a point of almost hopelessness, had decided to have honest conversations with family, friends, and supportive industry representatives about why she was not succeeding on the country music scene. Taking their words and advice to heart, she began a shift to writing songs about her own experiences as a Black American woman

trying to make it in country music. She was especially proud of a song titled "Black Like Me," cowritten with others while on a retreat and highlighting the persistence of racism in America with its chorus: "If you think we live in the land of the free / You should try to be Black like me." However, the idea of putting "Black Like Me" out as a single was not immediately embraced by music executives, who hesitated over its more provocative message. "In the country music industry, we're about peace, love and harmony, and we don't want to ruffle any feathers. We want everybody to feel comfortable," she detailed to Hall.

Guyton ended up selecting a different song to introduce her new, more honest music to the world. The song, titled "What Are You Gonna Tell Her?" dealt with the different types of gender discrimination and harassment that women endure throughout their lives. In February 2020, she performed "What Are You Gonna Tell Her?" at the Country Radio Seminar to a standing ovation—proof that she was on to something simply by being herself. "What Are You Gonna Tell Her?" was released in March 2020 and peaked at the eighteenth spot on the Billboard Country Digital Song Sales chart.

Following the death of Ahmaud Arbery, a young Black man chased and fatally shot by White men in a Georgia neighborhood in February, and days after footage of Floyd's murder in May was released, Guyton decided to act without executive authorization and released a snippet of "Black Like Me" on her social media. After it was clear that the song meant a lot to people at a difficult time in the nation's history, she released it in its entirety per Spotify's request on June 2, 2020. It quickly climbed to number four on the Billboard Country Digital Song Sales chart before going on to earn a Grammy nomination for Best Country Solo Performance, making her the first Black American woman to ever receive this honor. That same year, she released another, largely well-received EP, *Bridges*, and took the stage at the ACM Awards ceremony.

On September 24, 2021, after having delivered another praised high-profile performance, this time of "Black Like Me" in front of a Grammy audience and viewers, on top of cohosting that year's ACM Awards ceremony, Guyton released her debut album, *Remember Her Name*—in part an homage to the late Breonna Taylor, who was also a Black victim of police violence. In addition to mostly positive reviews, the album was nominated for a Grammy for Best Country Album, and the title song secured nods in two additional categories. When reflecting on her long-fought for success, which in early 2022 had additionally seen her presenting her rendition of the national anthem to millions of viewers of Super Bowl LVI, and what she hoped to achieve through her new, more honest country songs, Guyton told Weatherby, "I truly believe that this is giving people, not only hope for equality, but hope in the freedom that they can be themselves and still be accepted. That they can still push the envelope and still be accepted."

PERSONAL LIFE

Guyton married Grant Savoy, an attorney, in Hawaii in 2017. The couple had their first child, a son named Grayson, in 2021. By the early 2020s, she had returned to living in Los Angeles.

SUGGESTED READING

Christensen, Thor. "Country Singer Mickey Guyton's 'Overnight Success' Was Years in the Making." *The Dallas Morning News*, 16 Sept. 2021, www.dallasnews.com/arts-entertainment/music/2021/09/16/country-singer-mickey-guytons-overnight-success-was-years-in-the-making/. Accessed 14 June 2022.

Guyton, Mickey. "Mickey Guyton on Debut Country Album 'Remember Her Name.'" Interview by Lyndsey Parker. *Yahoo! Entertainment*, 17 Sept. 2021, www.yahoo.com/entertainment/mickey-guyton-debut-country-album-150000809.html. Accessed 10 June 2022.

___. "Mickey Guyton on Her 10-Year Journey to Debut Album 'Remember Her Name' and Paving the Way for Black Women in Country." Interview by Taylor Weatherby. *Grammy.com*, Recording Academy, 24 Sept. 2021, www.grammy.com/news/mickey-guyton-interview-10-year-journey-debut-album-remember-her-name-black-women-country. Accessed 10 June 2022.

Hall, Kristin M. "Mickey Guyton Is Speaking Her Truth after Years of Doubt." Associated Press, 13 Aug. 2020, apnews.com/article/virus-outbreak-entertainment-race-and-ethnicity-mickey-guyton-music-f6c3c0c2358f3ce641127e2a32cdfa9d. Accessed 14 June 2022.

Hight, Jewly. "Is Country Music Finally Ready for Mickey Guyton?" *Los Angeles Times*, 9 Apr. 2020, www.latimes.com/entertainment-arts/music/story/2020-04-09/mickey-guyton-country-singer. Accessed 14 June 2022.

Petrusich, Amanda. "Mickey Guyton Takes on the Overwhelming Whiteness of Country Music." *The New Yorker*, 7 June 2021, www.newyorker.com/magazine/2021/06/14/mickey-guyton-takes-on-the-overwhelming-whiteness-of-country-music. Accessed 10 June 2022.

SELECTED WORKS

Unbreakable, 2014; *Mickey Guyton*, 2015; *Bridges*, 2020; *Remember Her Name*, 2021

—*Emily E. Turner*

Kathryn Hahn

Born: July 23, 1973
Occupation: Actor

In March 2021, an unusual song titled "Agatha All Along" debuted on the Billboard Digital Song Sales chart. Originating in an episode of that year's popular Marvel Studios miniseries *WandaVision*, the short song is performed within the show to reveal the true identity and motives of a character previously known as Agnes, played by actor Kathryn Hahn. In some ways, the unexpected success of "Agatha All Along" could be said to encapsulate the twists and turns Hahn's career had taken to reach that point. "If someone were to have read my cards when I was in my twenties and they had been like, 'And I see you topping the Billboard charts because of this little ditty for a Marvel show,' like, that is something I never would've seen," she told Tierney Bricker in an interview for *E! News* (20 Mar. 2021). "The whole thing is just bananas."

In addition to making Hahn an unlikely hit singer, her fan-favorite role in the high-profile *WandaVision* earned her a nomination for the 2021 Emmy Award for Outstanding Supporting Actress in a Limited or Anthology Series or Movie. This success also brought further attention to the extensive body of work that had earned her critical acclaim and a dedicated following over the previous decades. Hahn first found steady work as a supporting actor in the crime drama *Crossing Jordan* (2001–07) and comedy films such as *How to Lose a Guy in 10 Days* (2003), and went on to appear in films such as *Afternoon Delight* (2013) and television projects such as *Transparent* (2014–16; 2019), *Mrs. Fletcher* (2019), and *I Know This Much Is True* (2020), each of which enabled her to demonstrate new facets of her skill as a performer. "I've been really lucky," she told Amy Wallace for *Vanity Fair* (21 May 2021) about her career. "I love actors so much, and I'm always in awe of performers. I constantly feel privileged."

EARLY LIFE AND EDUCATION

Kathryn Marie Hahn was born on July 23, 1973, in Westchester, Illinois. The first child born to Karen and Bill Hahn, she spent much of her childhood living, along with her two brothers, in the Cleveland Heights suburb of Cleveland, Ohio. Drawn to acting from early on—often preferring to slip for hours on end into pretend worlds such as that of the *Little House on the Prairie* books and television series—she began to take classes in acting while still a child. She was strongly shaped by her time studying at the Cleveland Play House, an influential local institution. "I loved the Play House," she told Clint O'Connor for *Cleveland.com* (12 Jan. 2019). "In my mind, there was nothing more beautiful than that little Drury Theatre. That's like my heaven. My happy place is a ghost light on that little stage. That's where I fell in love with acting." During this period she made her television debut, on the series *Hickory Hideout*, a children's program filmed and produced in Cleveland during the 1980s.

Hahn attended the Beaumont School, a private Catholic school in Cleveland from which she graduated in 1991. Going on to attend Northwestern University, she pursued theater studies and stood out as a highly creative and captivating talent. When not focused on her theater work, she earned money working at a local café.

EARLY CAREER

Following her graduation from Northwestern with a bachelor's degree in 1995, Hahn relocated to New York City, where she pursued

Photo by T'ruah, via Wikimedia Commons

acting while supporting herself with a job at a hair salon. She made her film debut in the independent film *Flushed* in 1997 and also worked extensively in theater, although the work was not always lucrative. "I got a lot of nonpaying, off-off-off-Broadway plays, or the plays you could only do if you brought 12 paying customers," she told Wallace. She also left New York on occasion to pursue more prestigious theater opportunities, participating in events such as the 1998 Williamstown Theatre Festival in Massachusetts. She moved to Connecticut for graduate studies at the Yale University School of Drama, which she completed in 2001.

A turning point in Hahn's career came in 2001, when she began to appear in the role of grief counselor Lily Lebowski on the NBC crime drama *Crossing Jordan*. "It was written as a one-episode or three-episode thing," she told Kyle Ryan in an interview for the *AV Club* (2 Sept. 2013) about the role. "They very sweetly made it a recurring after I did an episode, which was such a mixed blessing because I was so excited to work on that show and to maybe pay off my student loans, of which I had accrued so much." However, the show was based in Los Angeles rather than New York. "I was not ready to go," she recalled to Ryan. Despite her reluctance to relocate to Los Angeles, she did so and became a member of *Crossing Jordan*'s main cast, appearing in more than one hundred episodes of the show between 2001 and 2007.

WORKING ACTOR

In the years following her debut in *Crossing Jordan*, Hahn made a name for herself as a character actor and prolific supporting player in comedy films. She appeared in projects such as *How to Lose a Guy in 10 Days* (2003), *Win a Date with Tad Hamilton!* (2004), *Anchorman: The Legend of Ron Burgundy* (2004), and *Step Brothers* (2008). "Some of those could be like half a day's work. Blink, and you miss it," she told O'Connor about the many projects in which she appeared during that period. "But I know, it's like a body of work already. It's crazy. There's really no rhyme or reason. Right place, right time, right people."

In addition to working in film, Hahn gained a following among television audiences with guest roles in series such as *Girls* (2012) and *Parks and Recreation* (2012–15); her performance as sharp political strategist Jennifer Barkley in the latter proved especially memorable. She also costarred in the short-lived series *Free Agents*, which was canceled after the airing of four episodes but was hosted with its full eight filmed episodes on Hulu in 2012. Meanwhile, alongside her film and television work, Hahn returned to the stage occasionally as her career developed. In 2008, for example, she appeared in a revival of playwright Marc Camoletti's play *Boeing-Boeing* at Broadway's Longacre Theatre. "I felt like I had much more autonomy when I was onstage," she later told Katy Waldman in an interview for *The New Yorker* (4 Mar. 2021) about the differences between acting for the stage and for the screen. "I had much more control over the arc of my performance."

BREAKTHROUGH ROLES

Although Hahn appreciated the opportunity to explore complex characters in projects such as 2013's *Afternoon Delight*, which brought her first starring film role, she struggled at times with the overall trajectory of her career and grew dissatisfied with the types of roles she was often offered. "I just would show up and try to do the best that I could with the work that I was cast in—and had worked really hard to be cast in, and met lovely human beings. But creatively, I felt hollow," she told Wallace. As the years passed, however, her body of work became far more diverse, with several

intriguing new projects that allowed her to explore a range of nuanced characters. One such project was the Amazon television series *Transparent*, on which she portrayed Rabbi Raquel Fein between 2014 and 2016. She was nominated for the 2017 Emmy for Outstanding Supporting Actress in a Comedy Series for the role and returned to the part for the series' feature-length 2019 finale. Other projects of note included the films *Bad Moms* (2016) and *Private Life* (2018), one season as the main protagonist of the ultimately canceled Amazon comedy series *I Love Dick* (2016–17), the 2019 miniseries *Mrs. Fletcher*, and the 2020 miniseries *I Know This Much Is True*.

Hahn experienced a new burst of popularity beginning in January 2021, when the miniseries *WandaVision* debuted on the streaming service Disney+. A spin-off from the immensely popular superhero films of the Marvel Cinematic Universe, *WandaVision* stars Elizabeth Olsen as the titular Wanda, also known as the superhero Scarlet Witch, and features Hahn as Agnes, a nosy neighbor who is far more than she seems. "I felt a real surrender in just taking the big swing of it, which was so, so fun," she told Waldman about the project. "I mean, I'm kind of a newbie to this world. I don't know very much about Marvel. But, when I was pitched this story, I was so taken by the ambition of it. And the serialism and the sadness and the *all* of it." *WandaVision* was received well by both Marvel fans and critics, and Hahn herself earned a nomination for the 2021 Emmy for Outstanding Supporting Actress in a Limited or Anthology Series or Movie with her performance. She also found herself on the Billboard Digital Song Sales chart after the musical number "Agatha All Along," which features Hahn as one of its key performers, proved unexpectedly popular among viewers.

THE HAHNAISSANCE

Hahn's surge in popularity amid the airing of *WandaVision* led some within the media to proclaim that US popular culture was experiencing a so-called Hahnaissance, a concept that amused Hahn herself. "To hear it called the Hahnaissance and being on the inside of it and just feeling like I'm putting one step in front of the other as an actor, has been pretty trippy, for sure," she told Bricker. Coverage of her work at that time included rampant speculation that she might reprise her *WandaVision* role, praised and loved by fans and critics alike who saw Hahn's nuanced portrayal and versatile talent as a perfect fit for the character, in a later Marvel project, although Hahn herself was unable to confirm or deny any rumors. "It would be fun to see what universe she could pop up in," she told Erica Gonzales in an interview for *Harper's Bazaar* (5 Aug. 2021). "They are so tight-lipped, who knows?"

In November 2021, Marvel Studios announced that Hahn would indeed star in a new Marvel series on Disney+, called *Agatha: House of Harkness*. Meanwhile, the Hahnaissance also saw Hahn appear in the Apple TV+ miniseries *The Shrink Next Door* in late 2021 and lend her voice to a character in the animated film *Hotel Transylvania 4: Transformania* (2022).

PERSONAL LIFE

Hahn met her husband, actor and producer Ethan Sandler, while they were both attending Northwestern University. They married in 2002 and went on to have two children together. When not filming elsewhere, Hahn lives with her family in Los Angeles, California.

SUGGESTED READING

Hahn, Kathryn. "Kathryn Hahn and the Happily Ever After." Interview by James Ostime. *Interview*, 14 Aug. 2013, www.interviewmagazine.com/film/kathryn-hahn-afternoon-delight. Accessed 7 Feb. 2022.

___. "Kathryn Hahn on *Parks & Rec*, *Anchorman*, and Returning to Drama." Interview by Kyle Ryan. *AV Club*, 2 Sept. 2013, www.avclub.com/kathryn-hahn-on-parks-rec-anchorman-and-returning-t-1798240323. Accessed 7 Feb. 2022.

___. "Kathryn Hahn Steals the Show Again." Interview by Katy Waldman. *The New Yorker*, 4 Mar. 2021, www.newyorker.com/culture/the-new-yorker-interview/kathryn-hahn-steals-the-show-again. Accessed 7 Feb. 2022.

___. "Kathryn Hahn's Been Here All Along: A Conversation with *WandaVision*'s Secret Weapon." Interview by Tierney Bricker. *E! News*, 20 Mar. 2021, www.eonline.com/news/1250369/kathryn-hahns-been-here-all-along-a-conversation-with-wandavisions-secret-weapon. Accessed 7 Feb. 2022.

___. "*WandaVision*'s Agatha Harkness Taught Kathryn Hahn to Stand in Her Own Power." Interview by Erica Gonzales. *Harper's Bazaar*, 5 Aug. 2021, www.harpersbazaar.com/culture/film-tv/a37225611/kathryn-hahn-9-elements-wandavision-emmys-interview/. Accessed 7 Feb. 2022.

O'Connor, Clint. "From the Cleveland Play House to Hollywood: Kathryn Hahn Talks about Her Career and Latest Film, *This Is Where I Leave You*." *Cleveland.com*, 12 Jan. 2019, www.cleveland.com/moviebuff/2014/09/from_the_cleveland_play_house.html. Accessed 7 Feb. 2022.

Wallace, Amy. "Kathryn Hahn All Along." *Vanity Fair*, 21 May 2021, www.vanityfair.com/hollywood/2021/05/whats-so-enchanting-about-kathryn-hahn. Accessed 7 Feb. 2022.

SELECTED WORKS

Crossing Jordan, 2001–07; *Parks and Recreation*, 2012–15; *Afternoon Delight*, 2013; *Transparent*, 2014–19; *Mrs. Fletcher*, 2019; *I Know This Much Is True*, 2020; *WandaVision*, 2021; *The Shrink Next Door*, 2021

—Joy Crelin

Ryusuke Hamaguchi

Born: December 16, 1978
Occupation: Filmmaker

Filmmaker Ryusuke Hamaguchi's work became widely known in his native Japan after the release of *Passion*, a 2008 film he completed while still in graduate film school. He received increased global attention in 2021 following the release of two widely acclaimed films: *Wheel of Fortune and Fantasy* and the Academy Award–nominated *Drive My Car*. "It's not every day that an international filmmaker blows up overnight—but then again, Ryusuke Hamaguchi's got a knack for distinction," James Balmont wrote for *AnOther Magazine* (11 Feb. 2022). The critic went on to praise Hamaguchi's "delicate respect for the work of his actors," which Balmont said results in a " brand of limited-budget filmmaking that puts believable dialogue, naturalistic performances, and a phenomenal sense of realness at the forefront."

Other critics have also noted the director's relationship to his actors and the characters they embody. "What stands out the most is his ability to remain both somewhat firm and delicate towards the characters and their feelings," Lukasz Mankowski wrote for *Mubi Notebook* (15 Oct. 2021). "This is because Hamaguchi reaps wonders out of the emotional subsoil of his actors and manages to seize something of pure beauty in the wheel of repetition . . . Hamaguchi is able to establish a bridge between the audience and the substance of his film." Describing the emotional depth of Hamaguchi's work, Mankowski added, "No one has such tenderness towards the human component in modern Japanese cinema."

For his part, Hamaguchi has expressed a more straightforward view of his work. "Actors act. That's what they do, it's their job. They do it while imagining things; acting whilst using the fantasy of their own. They speak their lines, deliver the words, and move their bodies into motion," he told Mankowski. "And at some point, the things they do become truly real. [W]hy does it happen this way? Frankly speaking, that remains a mystery even for me."

EARLY YEARS AND EDUCATION

Ryusuke Hamaguchi was born on December 16, 1978, in Kawasaki, a large city in Japan's Kanagawa Prefecture, not far from Tokyo. His father was a civil servant and the family moved often throughout his childhood. He became a fan of film at an early age, with a particular fondness for big-budget Hollywood productions and directors such as Quentin Tarantino.

As a student at the University of Tokyo, Hamaguchi joined a cinema club. "The cinephile culture just poured right in," he recalled to Vadim Rizov for *Filmmaker* (22 May 2019). He noted how, during this period, he came to admire the work of Greek American actor and filmmaker John Cassavetes, whom Hamaguchi described as perhaps "the biggest inception for me to becoming a director." In 2003, Hamaguchi graduated from the University of Tokyo with a bachelor's degree in aesthetics, which the school describes as an integration of art theory and practice.

EARLY CAREER

Upon graduating, Hamaguchi realized that he had few industry connections and little idea of how to break into the type of filmmaking that truly interested him. He found work on a

Photo by Heiyinmatthewlo,
via Wikimedia Commons

handful of commercial films but struggled in that line of work. "I couldn't do the job well at all, and I couldn't communicate well with my senior assistant directors," he admitted to Rizov. "I didn't know any of the lingo or the production language that was used on sets—I just wasn't of use at all. I was on set for two films as assistant director, and after that, the director told me, 'Don't come to work.'" That director did, however, steer Hamaguchi to an employer who produced videos for television; while Hamaguchi accepted the job, he knew he could never find long-term satisfaction with it.

Fortunately, he discovered and enrolled in a new program at Tokyo University of the Arts that would allow him to study film and new media with acclaimed figures such as manga artist Hiroshi Takahashi and director Kiyoshi Kurosawa. In 2007, Kurosawa assigned Hamaguchi to write and direct a new version of the 1961 science-fiction novel *Solaris*, which had been adapted for the screen twice before. While Hamaguchi's ninety-minute film was well received, neither he nor Kurosawa had officially obtained the rights to the book, so it was screened only at the school rather than publicly.

Hamaguchi earned a master's degree in 2008 after directing his thesis film, *Passion*, which explores the tensions surrounding the engagement of a young couple. The film was screened at the 2008 Tokyo FILMex festival as an official selection.

GROWING REPUTATION IN JAPAN

Thanks to connections he had made while studying for his master's degree, Hamaguchi was hired to direct a film project cosponsored by Tokyo University of the Arts and a school in South Korea. Shot in Japan with a Korean cast, *The Depths*, which focuses on the relationship between a photographer and a gender fluid model, was released in 2010.

On March 11 of the following year, the strongest earthquake in Japan's recorded history up to that point, along with a tsunami triggered by the earthquake, devastated Tohoku, the northeastern region of Honshu, the largest island in Japan. More than 15,500 people died in the disaster, tens of thousands of homes were destroyed, and three nuclear reactors melted down at Fukushima Daichi Nuclear Power Plant, triggering a nuclear disaster. In the aftermath of this event, Hamaguchi and fellow director Ko Sakai traveled together to the region to shoot footage of the damage and interview survivors. Their work resulted in a trilogy of well-received documentaries: *The Sound of Waves* (2012); *Voices from the Waves: Kesennuma* and *Voices from the Waves: Shinchimachi* (2013), which are considered one installment; and *Storytellers* (2013).

Hamaguchi next gained attention for 2015's *Happy Hour*, which explores the lives and relationships of four female friends in their late thirties. Calling it "extraordinary both in its artistry and in its dimensions," Richard Brody, writing for the *New Yorker* (24 Aug. 2016), considered the film's five-hour, seventeen-minute runtime "entirely justified, indeed richly and deeply filled." Brody described Hamaguchi as "a genius of scene construction, turning the fierce poetry of painfully revealing and pugnaciously wounding dialogue into powerful drama that's sustained by a seemingly spontaneous yet analytically precise visual architecture." At the 2015 Locarno Film Festival, the four leads shared the Best Actress award, and Hamaguchi earned a special jury award at the 2016 Japan Movie Critic Awards.

Critics had similarly effusive praise for Hamaguchi's next film, *Asako I & II* (2018), about a young woman who falls in love with both a man and his doppelganger. "As in *Happy Hour* and *The Depths*," Rizov wrote, "the subject is not what happens when people lie to each other on purpose, but what happens when someone lies to themselves about who they are and what they want, creating unforeseen consequences for their relationships—a much more complicated and interesting proposition." *Asako I & II* contended for the prestigious Palme d'Or at the Cannes Film Festival in 2018.

DRIVE MY CAR AND INTERNATIONAL SUCCESS

Hamaguchi's international profile grew significantly in 2021 with the release of two critically acclaimed films. The first, released in Japan in August of that year, was *Drive My Car*, a three-hour adaption of a short story by Japanese author Haruki Murakami. The tale of a widowed stage director hired to work in Hiroshima on a multilingual production of the 1897 play *Uncle Vanya*, by Russian author Anton Chekhov, *Drive My Car* made history when it became the first Japanese film ever to be nominated for the Academy Award for Best Picture. Hamaguchi himself became only the third Japanese filmmaker to be nominated in the best director category, and *Drive My Car*'s total of four nominations, including Best International Feature Film and Best Writing (Adapted Screenplay), tied legendary director Akira Kurosawa's *Ran* (1985) for most-nominated Japanese film in Academy Award history up to that point.

Drive My Car won the Academy Award for Best International Feature Film and earned best picture of the year accolades from the New York Film Critics Circle, the Boston Society of Film Critics, and the Los Angeles Film Critics, as well as a Golden Globe in the category of Best Motion Picture—Non-English Language. The film also won the award for Best Screenplay at the Cannes Film Festival, where it was additionally nominated for the prestigious Palme D'Or.

Later that year, Hamaguchi released another film, *Wheel of Fortune and Fantasy*. The film takes the form of a triptych, with three seemingly unrelated but similarly evocative stories. In the first, a young woman grapples with the fact that her best friend is dating her ex; in another, a man coerces his girlfriend to try to seduce his hated former professor; and the final section involves two old high school acquaintances with faulty memories. "The world is abundant in coincidences," the director told Mankowski. "There is not a single person who hasn't experienced it. But to handle the randomness of our everyday life, to coin a narrative is extremely difficult. The question becomes: how much is there you can craft from the coincidences you have inside of yourself? For me, it gradually became a project about the circle of coincidences."

Wheel of Fortune and Fantasy was met with critical acclaim upon its release. Writing for the *New York Times* (14 Oct. 2021), Manohla Dargis called the film "a perfect entry point into Hamaguchi's work," and added that each time she viewed *Wheel of Fortune and Fantasy*, she "found something to admire, consider, argue with, and weep over." Like Hamaguchi's previous effort, *Wheel of Fortune and Fantasy* also amassed a long string of accolades, including the Silver Bear Grand Jury Prize at the Berlin Film Festival.

SUGGESTED READING

Balmont, James. "Five Transcendent Films to Watch by Oscar Nominee Ryusuke Hamaguchi." *AnOther Magazine*, 11 Feb. 2022, www.anothermag.com/design-living/13882/five-transcendent-films-to-watch-by-oscar-nominee-ryusuke-hamaguchi. Accessed 8 July 2022.

Brody, Richard. "A Five-Hour Japanese Film Captures the Agonizing Intimacies of Daily Life." *The New Yorker*, 24 Aug. 2016, www.newyorker.com/culture/richard-brody/a-five-hour-japanese-film-captures-the-agonizing-intimacies-of-daily-life. Accessed 8 July 2022.

Dargis, Manohla. "*Wheel of Fortune and Fantasy* Review: What We Talk About." Review of *Wheel of Fortune and Fantasy*, directed by Ryusuke Hamaguchi. *The New York Times*, 14 Oct. 2021, www.nytimes.com/2021/10/14/movies/wheel-of-fortune-and-fantasy.html. Accessed 8 July 2022.

Fu, Mike. "Ryusuke Hamaguchi's Cinema of Stillness." *Tokyo Weekender*, 28 Mar. 2022, www.tokyoweekender.com/2022/03/ryusuke-hamaguchis-cinema-of-stillness/. Accessed 8 July 2022.

Mankowski, Lukasz. "A Wonderful World of What-Ifs: A Conversation with Ryusuke Hamaguchi." *Mubi Notebook*, 15 Oct. 2021, mubi.com/notebook/posts/a-wonderful-world-of-what-ifs-a-conversation-with-ryusuke-hamaguchi. Accessed 8 July 2022.

Rizov, Vadim. "'My First Studio, Commercially Made Film': Ryūsuke Hamaguchi on *Solaris*, *Asako I & II* and Japanese Film School." *Filmmaker*, 22 May 2019, filmmakermagazine.com/107556-ryusuke-hamaguchi-solaris-asako-i-ii-japanese-film-school/. Accessed 8 July 2022.

Yamaguchi, Mari. "Director of *Drive My Car* Surprised by Oscar, Popularity." *KSAT*, 5 Apr. 2022, www.ksat.com/entertainment/2022/04/05/director-of-drive-my-car-surprised-by-oscar-popularity/. Accessed 8 July 2022.

SELECTED WORKS

Passion, 2008; *The Depths*, 2010; *The Sound of Waves*, 2012; *Happy Hour*, 2015; *Asako I & II*, 2018; *Wheel of Fortune and Fantasy*, 2021; *Drive My Car*, 2021

—*Mari Rich*

Emily Hampshire

Born: August 29, 1981
Occupation: Actor

When actor Emily Hampshire auditioned for the show *Schitt's Creek* in 2014, she had been out of work for a year and was going through a tumultuous time in her personal life, leaving her with only $800 to her name and no permanent address. Hampshire's fortunes changed dramatically, however, when she was cast as the acerbic, flannel-wearing motel clerk Stevie Budd in the quirky Canadian comedy. Although *Schitt's Creek* was not an immediate success when it premiered in 2015, the series gained traction after Netflix acquired the streaming rights two years later. Through strong word-of-mouth, it eventually became a domestic and international sleeper hit, with a particular boom in popularity as it aired its final season in 2020, when many people sought out comedy during the coronavirus disease 2019 (COVID-19) lockdowns. The series catapulted Hampshire from relative obscurity to mainstream recognition, though she had been acting professionally for more than two decades. "I think it's ironic that a show called *Schitt's Creek* is the show that really changed my life for the better," Hampshire told Victoria Messina for PopSugar (5 Feb. 2020). "I love that the show doesn't try to teach any lessons, it just shows by example," she added, explaining the feel-good appeal of the series. "It doesn't sacrifice humor for its heart."

EARLY LIFE AND EDUCATION

Emily Hampshire was born on August 29, 1981, in Montréal, Quebec, Canada. Her love for acting began at age eleven, when she first saw Andrew Lloyd Webber's musical *Les Misérables*, as a sixth-grade graduation present from her mother. "I really didn't want to go," she told Hannah Levin for *Master Chat* (26 May 2017), noting that there was a pool party she wanted to attend instead. "And then I went and it felt like I left the earth when I was seeing it. I instantly just wanted to be in musicals." Inspired, she began regularly acting in plays at her all-girls Catholic private school. However, she eventually steered away from musicals as she struggled with dancing and singing.

Encouraged by her school vice-principal, Hampshire began to seek out professional acting opportunities. Her earliest role was a small part in the children's horror anthology series *Are You Afraid of the Dark* in 1994. She also joined an acting troupe that performed for casting directors, one of whom suggested that Hampshire audition for a psychological thriller starring famed French Canadian actor Geneviève Bujold. Hampshire landed the role in *Dead Innocent* (1997), playing the kidnapped daughter of Bujold's character, and the older actor proved to be an important mentor.

EARLY ACTING CAREER

Following her big-screen debut, the sixteen-year-old Hampshire relocated to Toronto, Canada's film and television production capital, with the goal of attending the American Academy of Dramatic Arts (AADA). She auditioned for and was accepted to the school, but soon after was offered a film role, so she decided to jump into acting full-time rather than continue her education. After various minor television credits, a more prominent leading role came in director Jerry Ciccoritti's comedy film *Boy Meets Girl*, in which she starred with Sean Astin.

In 1998, Hampshire first appeared in the recurring role of Siobhan Roy, the spoiled daughter of a television network CEO on the dark comedy *Made in Canada* (broadcast in other markets as *The Industry*). That part

Photo by Canadian Film Centre, via Wikimedia Commons

provided some stability, as she appeared in fifteen episodes over the next few years. Meanwhile, she continued to find work on various series and made-for-television movies. Many of her roles were fairly small, and she was often typecast as "girl-next-door" characters. Still, thanks to the nature of the Canadian entertainment industry, she had many opportunities to develop her acting skills. "In Canada, I feel with the smaller pool and smaller community I had the chance to really hone my craft," she told Levin. "I'm so grateful for that now, but at the time when I was starting out, I really wanted instant success. I thought my career was over at like eighteen because I wasn't huge when I was sixteen."

Hampshire won a Gemini Award in 2001 for her portrayal of Siobhan in *Made in Canada*, helping her earn more mainstream attention. As she got older, she also found she was being offered a wider variety of parts. Although she later reflected that this was in part due to the industry's obsession with physical appearance, she nevertheless accepted this as an opportunity to expand her reach. "It taught me how to be more than the little 'box' I was being put into and it taught me comedy," she told Luaine Lee for the *Chicago Tribune* (12 Aug. 2021). "I always felt uncomfortable and had kind of an impostor syndrome in anything that would define me by my looks."

SUCCESSES AND STRUGGLES

Over the next few years Hampshire remained a steady presence on the small screen, with credits including voice work on the animated series *Anne of Green Gables* (2001–02) and *Braceface* (2001–05). Her big-screen performance as the loyal girlfriend of a neurotic, fatalistic store clerk in *A Problem with Fear* earned her a best supporting actress nod at the 2003 Genie Awards. She then reunited with Ciccoritti for the indie drama *Blood* (2004), which earned her another Genie Award nomination, this time in the leading actress category.

Hampshire earned her third consecutive Genie Award nomination for *Snow Cake* (2006), in which she played the vivacious, eccentric teenage daughter of an autistic woman played by Sigourney Weaver. She then landed voice acting parts on two more animated series: *Ruby Gloom* (2006–07), for which she earned a Gemini Award nomination in 2008, and *The Busytown Mysteries* (2007–10). Around this time, Hampshire moved to Los Angeles to further her career in Hollywood. However, she struggled to find a foothold and raise her profile. "I totally lost my confidence and was doing bad auditions," she told Violet Macleod for *FAJO* (16 Jan. 2017). "I was going in super nervous—breaking-out-in-hives nervous. I felt like I couldn't do this anymore, couldn't audition anymore. And I really wanted to do something else."

A string of appearances in 2012 helped Hampshire break out of her slump. These parts varied widely, from a supporting role in director David Cronenberg's dark drama *Cosmopolis* (2012) to a lead part in the Hallmark Channel original movie *Hitched for the Holidays* (2012). Most notably, she received strong reviews for her portrayal of an exotic dancer in the 2012 comedy *My Awkward Sexual Adventure*, which was named best female performance in a feature at the 2013 Canadian Comedy Awards. She further displayed her versatility with several roles in 2013, for example playing a cashier who becomes involved with her married boss in *All the Wrong Reasons* and a doctor desperately seeking a rare treatment for her zombie-infected husband in *The Returned*. A two-year stint on the Canadian procedural drama *Rookie Blue* (2013–15) followed. Yet Hampshire still struggled to make it in Hollywood, with only a few other minor credits through 2014, and she was dropped by her American agent.

BREAKING THROUGH WITH *SCHITT'S CREEK*

Hampshire's career experienced a major upswing when she was tapped to play sarcastic motel clerk Stevie Budd in the Canadian comedy series *Schitt's Creek*, about a wealthy family who relocate to the titular remote Ontario town after a business manager embezzles their fortune. Though she nearly backed out of the in-person audition due to her history of anxiety-induced hives, she showed up for the 2014 casting call and impressed series co-creator and star Dan Levy despite her own conviction that she had failed. "I really had no recollection of my audition," she told Messina. "I went in and I did the audition, and [Levy] says it was great, but then I proceeded to get on the couch where they were sitting, and lift my shirt over my head and hide my head in my shirt, and rock back and forth."

While filming the first season of *Schitt's Creek* in Toronto, Hampshire got another break when she landed the recurring part of Jennifer Goines, a mentally unstable math genius confined to a psych ward, in *12 Monkeys*, a television adaptation of the 1995 sci-fi thriller of the same name. Although her role was inspired by the character played by Brad Pitt in the original film, Hampshire made it her own. "It was such a lesson to never do what you think they want. You should always do what you create," she shared with Lauren Christensen for *Harper's Bazaar* (19 June 2017). *12 Monkeys* debuted on the Syfy network in January 2015, and *Schitt's Creek* premiered on the CBC and on Pop TV the following month. Both shows were mostly well received and quickly picked up for second seasons.

For her work on both series, Hampshire won newcomer of the year honors at the 2015 Golden Maple Awards, recognizing Canadian actors appearing in television programs broadcast in the United States. The following year she was nominated for the Golden Maple Award for best actress, as both *Schitt's Creek* and *12 Monkeys* continued to earn positive reviews. For the former, she also claimed the award for best supporting actress in a comedy series at the 2016 Canadian Screen Awards.

While *Schitt's Creek* was a moderate success upon its debut, it developed a devoted following and eventually became a sensation as more and more viewers around the world caught on over the years. This was especially the case after it became available on the streaming service Netflix in 2017, expanding its audience. Many of the core cast grew close and became deeply invested in the series and the community around it. Hampshire often expressed her appreciation for this positive atmosphere and the show's impact on her own life and career. She also noted that the part of Stevie Budd came very naturally to her, even if in real life she was not as laid-back as her character. "I always felt like I was very Stevie-ish, but I've realized that I'm definitely not as cool as Stevie," she told Christensen.

END OF *SCHITT'S CREEK* AND OTHER WORK

Hampshire went on to win the best supporting actress at the Canadian Screen Awards again in 2017 and would repeat that feat the next three years as well. The critical acclaim and growing media attention to *Schitt's Creek* helped raise her profile to a new level, and she appeared in some notable projects, such as Darren Aronofsky's controversial psychological thriller *Mother!* (2017). In 2018, the fourth and final season of *12 Monkeys* aired.

In 2019, Hampshire and the rest of the *Schitt's Creek* cast were nominated for best ensemble comedy performance at the Screen Actors Guild (SAG) Awards. Season five of the show aired that year, and included a particular highlight for Hampshire, as her character starred in a production of *Cabaret* and performed the song "Maybe This Time" in front of a live audience. That fall she attended the Primetime Emmys, where *Schitt's Creek* received four nominations. In January 2020, the *Schitt's Creek* cast earned another ensemble nomination at the SAG Awards, this time winning the honor.

Hampshire continued to earn accolades during the show's sixth season, which was purposefully written to conclude the series. After taking home the trophy for best supporting actress in a comedy at the 2020 Canadian Screen Awards in May, she returned to the Emmys after the series finale aired. *Schitt's Creek* made history at the awards show, sweeping all seven comedy categories to become the most awarded comedy in a single year. The series only increased in popularity amid the COVID-19 lockdowns of 2020, as the warmhearted comedy provided a welcome escape for many viewers. "I think everybody would like a place like Schitt's Creek to live," Hampshire told Messina about the show's

special appeal. "The DMs we get from people [about] how the show has affected them, it always ends up being 'love is love.' That is the takeaway, and I think it's done it better than anything I've ever seen."

In 2021, Hampshire debuted opposite Adrien Brody in the horror drama series *Chapelwaite*. That year she also launched the narrative fiction podcast series *The Beautiful Liar* with Sam Harris, lead singer of rock group X Ambassadors.

PERSONAL LIFE

Hampshire was married to soccer-player-turned-talent-agent Matthew Smith from 2006 to 2014. She announced an engagement to musician Teddy Geiger in 2018, but the relationship ended the following year. In September 2021, Hampshire officially announced that she identified as pansexual, noting that the characters on *Schitt's Creek* helped her recognize that. She also discussed her struggles with an eating disorder and depression.

SUGGESTED READING

Hampshire, Emily. "Emily Hampshire Balances Polar Opposites on *Schitt's Creek* and *12 Monkeys*." Interview by Lauren Christensen. *Harper's Bazaar*, 19 June 2017, www.harpersbazaar.com/culture/film-tv/a10042731/emily-hampshire-schitts-creek-12-monkeys-interview/. Accessed 7 Dec. 2021.

___. "Emily Hampshire Talks Character Building." Interview by Hannah Levin. *Master Chat*, 26 May 2017, masterchatmag.com/2017/05/26/emily-hampshire-talks-character-building/. Accessed 14 Dec. 2021.

___. "Play Back and Fast Forward with Emily Hampshire." *FAJO*, 16 Jan. 2017, www.fajomagazine.com/exclusives/emily-hampshire-cover. Accessed 14 Dec. 2021.

___. "Emily Hampshire on Her *Schitt's Creek* Audition, Breaking Character, and the Show's Legacy." Interview by Victoria Messina. *PopSugar*, 5 Feb. 2020, www.popsugar.com/entertainment/emily-hampshire-stevie-schitts-creek-interview-47164875. Accessed 7 Dec. 2021. Lee, Luaine. "Hampshire Goes from Front-Desk Clerk to Star Turn in *Chapelwaite*." *Chicago Tribune*, Aug. 2021, digitaledition.chicagotribune.com/

tribune/article_popover.aspx?guid =b0a96e31-5cdf-4605-a963-38d6184 d5bd4. Accessed 7 Dec. 2021.

Macke, Johnni. "Emily Hampshire: 25 Things You Don't Know About Me ('I Go to Sleep Listening to Murder Podcasts')." *Us Weekly News*, 28 Aug. 2021, www.usmagazine.com/ celebrity-news/news/emily-hampshire-25- things-you-dont-know-about-me/. Accessed 14 Dec. 2021.

White, Abbey. "Emily Hampshire Says the 'Schitt's Creek' Wine Label Scene Helped Her Identify as Pansexual." *The Hollywood Reporter*, 1 Sept. 2021, www. hollywoodreporter.com/tv/tv-news/ emily-hampshire-schitts-creek-sexuality- pansexual-1235007120/. Accessed 14 Dec. 2021.

SELECTED WORKS

Boy Meets Girl, 1998; *Made in Canada* (a.k.a. *The Industry*), 1998–2001; *Snow Cake*, 2006; *Ruby Gloom*, 2006–07; *My Awkward Sexual Adventure*, 2012; *The Returned*, 2013; *Rookie Blue*, 2013–15; *12 Monkeys*, 2015–18; *Schitt's Creek*, 2015–2020; *Mother!*, 2017; *Chapelwaite*, 2021

—Bertha Muteba

Yaya Han

Born: April 10, 1982
Occupation: Cosplayer

Yaya Han is one of the most famous cosplayers on the Internet, with millions of followers on social media, who have been wowed by her unique, handmade creations since 1999. Cosplay—a portmanteau meaning "costume play"—had its start when fans began to create costumes for themselves depicting characters from favorite TV series, movies, comic books, manga, anime, and video games, which they would wear to fan conventions. Initially, Han cosplayed for fun rather than profit, but her successful and imaginative costumes have enabled her to expand on her hobby, making a profitable enterprise out of it. In addition to creating more than four hundred costumes in a wide variety of genres, she has developed a popular cosplay accessory line and merchandising, which includes her own fabric line, intended for cosplayers.

Han has been featured on various television shows and has been a judge, host, and performer at more than two hundred conventions around the world. In 2020, she released a book about her experiences in the world of cosplay, *Yaya Han's World of Cosplay: A Guide to Fandom Costume Culture*. "It's a phenomenon that's very unique—it's fan expression and it's also a creative art form," Han told Patrick Williams in a feature for *ABC News Australia* (19 Sept. 2015). "It really has exploded in the last 15 to 20 years into an ingrained part of geek culture. As geek culture is growing, cosplay has become a staple not only at conventions, but for any sort of functions." Han appeared along with Stan Lee and World Cosplay Summit competitors in the feature documentary film, *Cosplay Universe* (2022), directed by Jonathan McHugh and Jordan Rennert.

EARLY LIFE

Yaya Han was born in China on April 10, 1982, and moved to Germany with her mother when she was still a student. She came to love Japanese anime and manga at an early age and loved to draw. "I was always the freaky Asian girl who drew these weird-looking Barbie dolls in class," she recalled to Liz Ohanesian for *LA Weekly* (5 July 2012).

Because few people in Germany at that time knew about the Japanese style of comic books known as manga, Han decided to create her own ninety-eight-page manga for a class project, which eventually was published in a German magazine. Around 1998 she moved to the United States, ending up in Arizona. About a year later, she traveled to Southern California with her local anime club to visit Anime Expo. She had planned to enter some of her artwork in the expo's competition, but soon became enamored with the cosplayers who were there. Inspired by the cosplayers' creativity and encouraged by a friend, she began producing costume after costume so they could enter cosplay competitions. Over the next eighteen months or so, they won every contest they entered—despite the fact that Han could not initially sew and used somewhat cheap materials for her first costume. Over time, however, she began to improve, even while working on a used sewing machine.

By the early 2000s, Han had developed a following in the cosplay community. She was asked to judge competitions and was a guest

Photo by Kyle Nishioka,
via Wikimedia Commons

cosplayer at various conventions—a rare honor at that time. She became respected for her expertise in designing and making costumes, as well as in creating professional photos. In the mid-2000s, she decided to quit her job as a systems technical analyst for a software company to set up her own small business, Yaya Han LLC. "It was the most boring job in the world," Han said of her tech job to Ohanesian. "I would just go home and work on costumes."

BUILDING HER BUSINESS

In the early days, prior to the rise of social media, cosplayers were a very niche group—a subgroup of ardent fans of "geek" devotions like comic books, manga, and old TV shows. Because it was such a small group, there was a lot of personal contact and interaction. She recalled to Charles Webb in an interview for *MTV.com* (14 Mar. 2013): "We'd look at [*Fansview.com*] pictures and go on the cosplayers' mailing list and literally be like, 'I saw this person, and the cosplay was really cool! Do you know who they are?'. . . The community was small enough that you could actually find each other. We'd just email each other [and] ask for techniques or tips that they had."

Han's initial business was designing accessories that other cosplayers could buy, both online and at conventions, and could use to augment or complete their own costumes.

The accessories, like her costumes, were ones she made by hand. Additionally, she continued to expand her own interests, by delving into areas of geek culture that she had not previously known. She recalled for Webb, "When I discovered that gaming had the same type of characters that's when I got into gaming."

Han traveled to between twenty and twenty-five conventions and expos each year as she built her business. In addition to making accessories, she also sold calendars and photos of herself in various costumes. Since the start of her career, she has made about four hundred costumes and has won numerous awards for her work. As she grew in popularity on the convention circuit and received recognition as a cosplayer and judge, she was asked to serve as a judge for two seasons of *King of the Nerds* (2013–15), a competition show on Turner Broadcasting System (TBS), and was featured in the documentaries *Cosplay! Crafting a Secret Identity* (2013) and *Heroes of Cosplay* (2013–14). She was also featured as the main character in *Wonderous 2: The Yaya Han Saga*, a 2014 comic that depicted her as gaining superpowers.

BIGGEST COSPLAY STAR ON THE INTERNET

Through all this exposure, she had gained a tremendous following, both at conventions and online. By August 2022, she had more than 1.94 million followers on *Facebook*, 252,200 on *Twitter*, 96,200 on *TikTok*, and 610,000 on *Instagram*. While much of her success was due to the great efforts she made with every costume, Webb attributed part of it to what he described as the "the undeniable cheesecake element to her outfits." For Han, making her costumes is a satisfying challenge, as she said to Webb: "I love challenging myself and learning new techniques. . . . I seek out costumes that get me frustrated and get me into the thick of it and those two are tied."

Though many of her fans have been respectful, Han, like many creators, has also had to contend with nasty online commentary. Often these comments are aimed at the fact that she is of Asian descent or that she might be too short or not the right build to portray a particular character. Han has learned to tune out the negativity. She discussed the negative criticism often heaped on cosplayers with Webb: "Hardcore fans have a vision in their head and if they look at your cosplay of it you may not fit their vision."

In 2015, Han collaborated with Cosplay Fabrics (formerly Wyla Fabrics) to develop the Yaya Han line of fabrics. The national fabric chain Jo-Ann launched the line in March 2016 with over seventy-five bolts of fabric that were based on cloth Han had kept from each costume she had made. She wanted to partner with Jo-Ann because traditional fabric stores outside of big cities would not normally carry the type of fabrics a cosplayer would need. The Yaya Han line began its pricing at $20 a yard. "I really approached this line with the mindset of 'What would I wear? What would I use?'" Han told Lauren Orsini for *Forbes* (17 Mar. 2016). "I want cosplayers to be able to get that kind of quality even at their local store."

THE COVID-19 PANDEMIC

The shutdown of in-person events during the global COVID-19 pandemic in 2020 and beyond devastated Han and other professional cosplayers whose income depended on appearances and contests. In an interview with Wendy Browne for *Women Write about Comics* (29 Sept. 2020) during the first year of the pandemic, Han noted: "My small business relies on conventions and tradeshows for sales but every event has been canceled. Instead, we pivoted to making face masks in April [2020] and that has primarily occupied my time since." Han noted that in addition to donating masks to hospitals and senior communities, her business sold masks to the public as a way to help support her employees and pay the rent and utilities for the warehouse. "It is a lot of work but I'm glad we have the sewing skills to make a useful product during these difficult times," she said to Browne.

In 2020, Han published *Yaya Han's World of Cosplay: A Guide to Fandom Costume Culture*, which sought to describe her experiences in the cosplay world since the late 1990s, how it has changed and what she believes the future holds for it. In it she notes that her good experiences have far outweighed her bad ones, and that cosplay itself allows individuals to be as creative and as original as they can possibly be. In her interview with Browne, she said of writing her book: "I had to overcome a lot of self-doubt and fear to put pen to paper. . . . Though the book is not perfect and I still have more to say, I am very proud of it." Han was also one of three contributors to *1,000 Incredible Costume and Cosplay Ideas: A Showcase of Creative Characters from Anime, Manga, Video Games, Movies, Comics, and More* (2013).

SUGGESTED READING

"About." *Yayahan.com*, www.yayahan.com/about. Accessed 4 Aug. 2022.

Han, Yaya. "Interview: The Secret Origins of Professional Cosplayer Yaya Han." Interview by Charles Webb. *MTV*, 14 Mar. 2013, www.mtv.com/news/aek928/cosplayer-yaya-han. Accessed 4 Aug. 2022.

___. "NYCC '15: An Interview with Yaya Han." Interview by Adam Wolfe. *Bleeding Cool*, 12 Oct. 2015, bleedingcool.com/comics/nycc-15-an-interview-with-yaya-han/. Accessed 4 Aug. 2022.

___. "Step into Yaya Han's World of Cosplay." Interview by Wendy Browne. *Women Write about Comics*, 29 Sept. 2020, womenwriteaboutcomics.com/2020/09/step-into-yaya-hans-world-of-cosplay/. Accessed 4 Aug. 2022.

Ohanesian, Liz. "Anime Expo 2012: Cosplayer Yaya Han on Turning Her Hobby into a Business." *LA Weekly*, 5 July 2013, www.laweekly.com/anime-expo-2012-cosplayer-yaya-han-on-turning-her-hobby-into-a-business/. Accessed 4 Aug. 2022.

Orsini, Lauren. "How the Internet's Most Famous Cosplayer Is Democratizing Costume Fabric.". *Forbes*, 17 Mar. 2016, www.forbes.com/sites/laurenorsini/2016/03/17/how-the-internets-most-famous-cosplayer-is-democratizing-costume-fabric/. Accessed 4 Aug. 2022.

Williams, Patrick. "Oz Comic Con: Cosplay Queen Yaya Han Talks about Her Unintentional Rise from Hobby to Career." *ABC News*, 19 Sept. 2015, www.abc.net.au/news/2015-09-19/oz-comic-con-cosplay-queen-yaya-han-talks-about-career-rise/6788900?nw=0&r=Gallery. Accessed 4 Aug. 2022.

—Christopher Mari

Nikole Hannah-Jones

Born: April 9, 1976
Occupation: Investigative journalist

"The only reason I ever wanted to become a journalist was to write about racial inequalities," Nikole Hannah-Jones revealed in an interview with Arnesa A. Howell for *Quill Magazine* (1 Dec. 2020). In 2015, Hannah-Jones joined *The New York Times Magazine*, covering civil rights and racial injustice as an investigative reporter. Four years later, she found herself thrust into the national spotlight following the launch of *The 1619 Project*, a collection of ten written essays, a photo essay, poems, and fiction that examine four centuries of US history through the lens of slavery. "Black people are largely treated as an asterisk in the American story," she explained to Arun Venugopal for NPR (17 Nov. 2021).

From its publication, *The 1619 Project* drew intense scrutiny from historians and scholars regarding its historical accuracy. The ambitious initiative also endured much pushback by conservatives determined to prevent it from being taught in classrooms. Despite the effort, more than 4,500 classrooms across the country had adopted *The 1619 Project* as part of their curriculum by July 2020. In 2020, the project's lead essay, written by Hannah-Jones, was awarded the Pulitzer Prize for Commentary. The award-winning initiative also inspired two books, a documentary series, and 1619 Freedom School, a free after-school literacy program in Hannah-Jones's hometown.

EARLY LIFE AND EDUCATION

The second of three children, Nikole Hannah-Jones was born Nikole Sheri Hannah to Cheryl (Novotny) and Milton Hannah on April 9, 1976, in the Black working-class town of Waterloo, Iowa. Her mother, of Czech and English descent, was a state probation officer while her African American father was a US Army veteran who worked as a Metropolitan Transit Authority (MET) bus driver. Growing up, Hannah-Jones was keenly aware of her racial identity. "I would say very young, my dad sat my sisters and myself down and told us that our mom might be white, but we were Black, and we were going to be treated in the world as if we were Black," she told Alexis Okeowo for *Vanity Fair* (Dec. 2021/Jan. 2022).

Hannah-Jones attended Longfellow Elementary in Waterloo until she was in the second grade, when her parents enrolled her at Kingsley Elementary School as part of a voluntary desegregation program. She would travel with her older sister to a White and affluent community, an hour each way by bus. Attending an all-White school proved to

Photo by Associacao Brasileira de Jornalism Investigativo, via Wikimedia Commons

be a struggle for Hannah-Jones. "It was very difficult. It was isolating," she shared with Chris Hayes for NBC News (31 July 2018). "And I remember . . . never really fitting in." Hannah-Jones found solace in the written word, bonding with her father through reading the state and local newspapers. By middle school, she was reading *Time* and *Newsweek* avidly. Hannah-Jones credited one of her teachers with nurturing her love of writing.

STUDENT JOURNALIST

Hannah-Jones first developed an interest in social-justice issues during her sophomore year at Waterloo West High School. While taking a Black studies elective course, she read historian Lerone Bennett Jr.'s *Before the Mayflower: A History of Black America* (1961), which designates the year 1619 as the start of slavery in the English colonies that became the United States. "It was powerful to me that Black people had been on this land that long, that we had that lineage, but the erasure was just as powerful," she recalled to Ben Kieffer in an interview for Iowa Public Radio (19 Nov. 2021). "I realized that we are taught a manipulated history. We are not taught everything that we should know." At her teacher's suggestion, Hannah-Jones joined her high school newspaper staff and penned a column, From the African

Perspective, highlighting her classmates' busing experiences. As a senior, she claimed her first-ever journalism prize from the Iowa High School Press Association.

Upon graduating in 1994, Hannah-Jones majored in African American studies and history at the University of Notre Dame. As a freshman, she struggled with feeling socially out of place and nearly flunked out of college. Eventually, she bonded with other students of color while protesting twelve controversial nineteenth-century murals on campus. The murals inaccurately depicted Christopher Columbus and romanticized the treatment of Native Americans. When a letter denouncing the student protests was published in the student-run newspaper, the *Observer*, she wrote a response letter to the editor that appeared in the issue for November 21, 1995. Hannah-Jones also experienced racism firsthand, being called the n-word for the first time by a group of football players driving past her, as she pushed her broken-down car back to campus. That incident prompted her to write another letter to the editor of the *Observer* in September 1996.

EARLY CAREER

After earning her BA in 1998, Hannah-Jones focused on becoming a journalist. From 2001 to 2003 she attended the Hussman School of Journalism and Media at the University of North Carolina (UNC) at Chapel Hill on a full-tuition, two-year Roy H. Park fellowship. Upon completing her master's degree in 2003, Hannah-Jones joined the reporting staff of the *Raleigh News and Observer*, where she spent nearly three years writing about Durham's Black public-school system and educational inequity. In August 2006, Hannah-Jones accepted a job at *The Oregonian*, the Pacific Northwest's largest daily newspaper. Along with covering the census and county government, she was assigned to the demographics beat.

Hannah-Jones also contributed to *The Kerner Plus 40 Report* (2008), commemorating the fortieth anniversary of the Kerner Commission, a panel appointed by President Lyndon Johnson to examine the causes of the Watts race riots and recommend solutions. Aided by a fellowship from the Institute for Advanced Journalism Studies, Hannah-Jones traveled with six other journalists to Cuba in 2008, to assess the country's universal health care and educational systems under leader Raúl Castro. While working at *The Oregonian*, she won the Society of Professional Journalists Pacific Northwest Excellence in Journalism Award three times, in 2007, 2008, and 2010.

INVESTIGATIVE REPORTER FOR *PROPUBLICA*

Hannah-Jones's stint at *The Oregonian* ended in December 2011, when she accepted an investigative reporting position at the New York City–based nonprofit news organization ProPublica. There, she wrote extensively on civil rights, particularly discrimination and segregation in housing and schools. "Living Apart: How the Government Betrayed a Landmark Civil Rights Law" (2012, updated 2015), Hannah-Jones's year-long report addressing the persistent failure by the federal government to actively enforce the 1968 Fair Housing Act, won the Columbia University Paul Tobenkin Memorial Award in 2013. While at ProPublica, she contributed another fair housing segment, "House Rules," with reporter Nancy Updike on the weekly public-radio show *This American Life* (*TAL*). The segment won the 2013 Sidney Award for socially conscious journalism.

The following year, Hannah-Jones visited Alabama to report for ProPublica on the resurgence of segregation in Southern public schools due to minimal judicial oversight. Her *Segregation Now* series followed three generations of the Dent family in Tuscaloosa, one of the country's fastest re-segregating school districts, and highlighted their experiences at the same public school. In a personal essay, "Ghosts of Greenwood" (2014), she chronicled her visit to her father's titular hometown while also exposing the history of racism in the Mississippi Delta region. After the fatal police shooting of unarmed Missouri teenager Michael Brown in August 2014, Hannah-Jones wrote an article, "School Segregation, the Continuing Tragedy of Ferguson," about the unaccredited, Black and low-income Normandy Schools Collaborative district from which Brown graduated, in an effort to highlight the achievement gap between Black and White students in St. Louis County. For her work, she was awarded the 2014 Fred M. Hechinger Grand Prize for Distinguished Education Reporting and Journalist of the Year honors (2015) from the National Association of Black Journalists.

THE NEW YORK TIMES

Hannah-Jones continued to focus on the inequities faced by people of color when she joined the staff of *The New York Times* in April 2015. "The Continuing Reality of Segregated Schools," her July 2015 follow-up report on the state of the troubled Normandy school district, inspired another *TAL* collaboration: the Peabody Award–winning "The Problem We All Live With," a two-part series on the advantages and consequences of school desegregation on students of color. The podcast episode also claimed the George Polk Award for radio reporting in 2016.

The topic of racial segregation in the New York City school system was at the heart of Hannah-Jones's cover story for *The New York Times Magazine*'s June 12, 2016, issue: "Choosing a School for My Daughter in a Segregated City," which earned her a 2017 National Magazine Award. For *The New York Times Magazine* education issue (10 Sept. 2017), she focused on the mostly White town of Gardendale, Alabama, and the attempted secession from its school district in "The Resegregation of Jefferson County." Hannah-Jones's work highlighting racial inequality in US schools won her a prestigious MacArthur Foundation Fellowship in October 2017.

THE 1619 PROJECT

To mark the four-hundredth anniversary of the arrival of the first enslaved Africans in Jamestown, Virginia, Hannah-Jones pitched the idea of documenting the modern-day legacy of slavery, as well as the sacrifices and contributions made by Black Americans. "I think it is critical for us to understand the black experience," she told Taryn Finley for *HuffPost* (19 Feb. 2019). "What's important is to say how and why it does happen, and that then helps us explain America to itself because the experience of black people is the experience of America."

The 1619 Project was published in the August 14, 2019, edition of *The New York Times Magazine*, and an interactive website and companion podcast series were also launched. Hannah-Jones sparked controversy with her lead essay, "The Idea of America," in which she questioned her military-veteran father's patriotism in the face of racial bigotry. She not only argued that the nation's vast wealth was due to slave labor but also claimed

that American colonies declared independence from British rule to preserve the institution of slavery for the sake of economic success and social order.

In an effort to engage students in important classroom discussions regarding the history and legacy of racism and slavery in the United States, *The New York Times* partnered with the Pulitzer Center to develop a free online curriculum for educators at all grade levels. The Center also provided copies of *The 1619 Project* and supplemental curricular resources to more than five hundred schools nationwide. However, the initiative sparked backlash regarding its historical accuracy. Shortly after its release, *The Times* asserted that the first enslaved Africans arrived in what is now present-day South Carolina in 1526. In December 2019, five prominent historians sent a jointly signed letter to *The New York Times*, disputing Hannah-Jones's claim that the Revolutionary War was fought in defense of slavery. Another December letter from a group of twelve Civil War historians and political scientists expressed a similar critique. (*The New York Times* would issue a clarification update regarding her claim about three months later.)

PULITZER PRIZE, CONSERVATIVE BACKLASH

Despite the criticism, Hannah-Jones's essay and project enjoyed solid support. By January 2020, school districts in five school systems—Buffalo, New York; Chicago, Illinois; Wilmington, Delaware; Washington, DC; and Winston-Salem, North Carolina—had adopted *The 1619 Project* as part of their curricula. In early May 2020, Hannah-Jones was bestowed one of journalism's most prestigious honors, the Pulitzer Prize, for her introductory essay.

Hannah-Jones made headlines again in June 2020, with her *New York Times Magazine* cover story, "What Is Owed," in which she attributed the wealth gap between Black and White Americans to four hundred years of slavery and called for reparations for descendants of the enslaved. A month later, she faced backlash with the introduction of legislation by Republican senator Tom Cotton of Arkansas to ban federal funds from public schools teaching *The 1619 Project*. Many conservatives conflated the project with critical race theory (CRT), an academic framework that examines the impact of systemic racism. That October, conservative columnist Bret Stephens, Hannah-Jones's *New York Times* colleague, questioned *The 1619 Project*'s transparency, objectivity, and accuracy in an opinion piece. As a rebuttal to the project, President Donald Trump signed an executive order in November to establish a 1776 presidential commission, which eventually released a January 2021 report downplaying the legacy of slavery and denouncing CRT as anti-patriotic. By February 2021 Republican lawmakers had started enacting legislation targeting public schools teaching CRT.

Despite attracting considerable controversy, Hannah-Jones also continued to earn honors. In April 2021 she was elected to the American Academy of Arts and Sciences. The following month she was appointed the Knight Chair in Race and Investigative Reporting at UNC, where she cofounded the Ida B. Wells Society for Investigative Reporting. Instead of tenure, however, she was offered a fixed, five-year contract amid ongoing conservative pressure, sparking protests from students and faculty. After Hannah-Jones decided against joining the UNC faculty without tenure, the trustees board reversed its decision in June. Hannah-Jones nevertheless rejected the tenured post in July, instead accepting a Knight Chair in Race and Journalism appointment at Howard University, where she founded the Center for Journalism and Democracy.

PERSONAL LIFE

Hannah-Jones is married to Faraji Hannah-Jones, an Information Technology (IT) specialist. They have a daughter, Najya, together and live in the Bedford-Stuyvesant neighborhood of Brooklyn, New York. Hannah-Jones's Twitter handle is Ida Bae Wells.

SUGGESTED READING

Hannah-Jones, Nikole. "Creator of *The 1619 Project* and Iowa Local Nikole Hannah-Jones on The Significance of 1619 and How Racism Is Taught in U.S. History." Interview by Ben Kieffer. *River to River*, produced by Matthew Alvarez, Iowa Public Radio, 19 Nov. 2021, www.iowapublicradio.org/racial-justice/2021-11-19/creator-of-the-1619-project-and-iowa-local-nikole-hannah-jones-on-the-significance-of-1619-and-how-racism-is-taught-in-u-s-history. Transcript.

___. "'1619 Project' Says Black People Shouldn't Be an Asterisk in U.S. History." Interview by Arun Venugopal. *Fresh Air*, produced by Sam Briger and Seth Kelley, NPR, 17 Nov. 2021, www.npr.org/2021/11/17/1056404654/nikole-hannah-jones-1619-project. Accessed 10 Dec. 2021.

___. "2020 Fellow Feature: Nikole Hannah-Jones." Interview by Arnesa A. Howell. *Quill*, 1 Dec. 2020, www.quillmag.com/2020/12/01/2020-fellow-feature-nikole-hannah-jones/. Accessed. 10 Dec. 2021.

Okeowo, Alexis. "Nikole Hannah-Jones Keeps Her Eyes on the Prize." *Vanity Fair*, 4 Nov. 2021, www.vanityfair.com/news/2021/11/nikole-hannah-jones-keeps-her-eyes-on-the-prize. Accessed. 10 Dec. 2021.

—*Bertha Muteba*

Tristan Harris

Born: ca. 1984
Occupation: Computer scientist and ethicist

Tristan Harris is the "closest thing Silicon Valley has to a conscience," Bianca Bosker wrote for *The Atlantic* (Nov. 2016). While working for the tech giant Google, Harris rose to attention for his talks about the addictive nature of technology, which gave rise to the Time Well Spent movement advocating for ethical software design. In 2018, he cofounded the Center for Humane Technology, a nonprofit organization aimed at bringing further attention to the ways in which tech companies manipulate human psychology to get people hooked on their platforms, in much the same way fast-food chains use peoples' physiologically based love of sugar, salt, and fat to attract and retain patrons. Harris also raised alarms about the ways in which social media functions as a polarizing hotbed of disinformation and mistrust. "This is really serious. We are not fooling around," he told Betsy Morris for the *Wall Street Journal* (23 Apr. 2019). "Technology is holding the pen of history right now."

Harris earned wide recognition as an important voice in an increasingly tech-dominated social landscape and was featured on lists such as *Rolling Stone*'s "25 People Shaping the World" in 2017 and *Time*'s "Next Leaders Shaping the Future" in 2021. He was a key contributor to the hit 2020 documentary film *The Social Dilemma*, which brought to light

Photo by Stephen McCarthy/Collision
via Sportsfile/Wikimedia Commons

the tactics large tech companies use to hijack the attention of unwitting users and the impact of constant connectivity on everyday life. And there were some indications of success in Harris's mission to encourage a major shift toward human-centered technology that serves the common good. For example, by the early 2020s both Google and Apple had added features making it easier for users to monitor their screen time and set self-imposed limits. "This is not about 'you're dumb if you're being manipulated,' or that you should be ashamed about it," Harris told Phil Barber for the Santa Rosa *Press Democrat* (15 Oct. 2020). "We're all caught in this system. The technology forces us to use systems that are contaminated and toxic."

EARLY YEARS AND EDUCATION

Tristan Harris grew up in the San Francisco Bay Area. He was raised by his mother, whose job working on behalf of injured workers helped instill a sense of social justice in her son. As a child, Harris enjoyed performing magic tricks, which he would later credit with giving him valuable insight into human nature. "You learn that there are things that work on all human minds," he told Nicholas Thompson for *Wired* (4 Oct. 2018). "It doesn't matter whether they have a PhD, whether they're a nuclear

physicist, what age they are. It's not like, Oh, if you speak Japanese I can't do this trick on you, it's not going to work. It works on everybody."

After living in San Francisco, Harris's family moved to Santa Rosa, California, where he attended junior high at the prestigious Sonoma Country Day School. He played piano in the school's jazz band and was fascinated by his teacher's use of music-arrangement software, which helped make him a computer enthusiast from an early age. "I was one of these Macintosh/Apple people as a kid. I was very passionate about that," he recalled to Barber. "I grew up on a Mac LC II. I thought since the age of 11 that I wanted to work for Apple, be on the next Macintosh team and change the world again."

After graduating from Sonoma Country Day School in 1998, Harris enrolled at Maria Carrillo High School. During this time, he furthered his interest in software, including through a computer programming class at Santa Rosa Junior College. He parlayed that experience into a job at a local computer store, where he proved to be an adept employee, capable of building and troubleshooting diagnostic software and other programs.

Harris graduated from high school in 2002 and entered Stanford University to study computer science. He had an internship at Apple before earning a bachelor's degree in 2006 and a Stanford Mayfield Fellowship that same year. Harris then enrolled in a Stanford master's program in human-computer interaction, taking a class with experimental psychologist B. J. Fogg, famous for formulating the principles of "behavior design"—in essence, teaching technologists to build software that facilitates behaviors a company hopes to encourage in consumers. However, Harris soon dropped out, eager to put what he was learning to use in an entrepreneurial venture of his own. "Stanford does an effective job of encouraging students to think creating a start-up is possible," he said in a profile for the Sonoma Country Day School website. "Start-ups recruit on campus, venture capitalists are welcome, and there are examples all around of people who have taken something from nothing in just a few years. It gives you a sense of what is possible, and that you are just as capable of doing the same thing."

APTURE AND GOOGLE

In 2007 Harris launched the start-up company Apture, based around a software program that provided internet users with additional layers of information and search capability directly in the page they were browsing rather than needing to open multiple windows. The technology sought to maximize engagement by catching users exactly when they became curious about something. "At that moment (literally a one-second opportunity) people are most open for furthering learning," he explained in the Sonoma Country Day School profile. The product was a success, incorporated on major websites such as that of *The New York Times.* This earned Harris attention as an up-and-coming figure in the booming world of tech, and in 2009 he appeared on *Inc.* magazine's list of the coolest entrepreneurs under age thirty.

In 2011, Apture was acquired by Google for a reported $20 million. Harris stayed on at Google and was assigned to work on the inbox function of the company's popular Gmail email service. Although the job was stimulating (and Google was known for lavishing benefits on its employees, like free meals and onsite massages), he gradually became distressed by the relentless and addictive nature of the app's user interface: few people were able to resist at least glancing at their devices when they received an email notification—a response seemingly elicited by design. In early 2013, a few months after returning from a mind-expanding trip to the Burning Man festival, Harris prepared a detailed slide presentation he titled "A Call to Minimize Distraction & Respect Users' Attention." Among other points, he stressed the fact that between the dominant tech companies Google, Apple, and Facebook, a small group of mostly young White men had an outsized "impact on how millions of people around the world spend their attention. . . . We should feel an enormous responsibility to get this right."

Although Harris initially sent the slides to only a handful of close colleagues, it rapidly created a stir within Google and beyond. Harris was subsequently given the title of design ethicist and product philosopher. In that capacity he worked at the intersection of technology and behavioral science to discover how Google's platforms were affecting users' thought patterns, relationships with others, and general well-being and to make recommendations for new interfaces that would promote healthier online interaction. However, he began to see his efforts as fruitless; despite paying lip service to his recommendations, the company remained focused on the bottom line rather than aiming for systemic change.

PROMOTING MINDFUL DIGITAL LIVES

Harris left Google in 2016 to focus on a social movement he dubbed Time Well Spent, with the mission of encouraging people to log off of their devices regularly and use them only in practical, intentional ways rather than allowing them to dominate daily life. He likened Time Well Spent to the movement for healthy organic foods but with healthy, better-developed software as a focus. Harris soon found himself attracting media attention, including a feature on the news program *60 Minutes* in 2017. That same year he gave a popular TED Talk expanding on his Google slide presentation, titled "How a Handful of Tech Companies Control Billions of Minds Every Day."

In early 2018, along with mathematician and physicist Aza Raskin, Harris founded the Center for Humane Technology, a San Francisco–based nonprofit with the stated mission "to drive a shift toward humane technology that supports our well-being, democracy, and shared information environment." The organization garnered funding from such major supporters as the Ford Foundation and the Knight Foundation. It also attracted the attention of government officials around the world as the sociopolitical impact of big tech generated increasing concern. For example, in advance of the 2020 US presidential election Harris testified at congressional hearings on social media's role in widening the country's partisan divide and spreading disinformation.

As his work garnered more and more mainstream attention, Harris remained steadfast in his basic approach. He advanced the idea that software developers should sign a sort of "Hippocratic oath," affirming that they would not exploit people's psychological vulnerabilities and would do their best to grant users agency. "There needs to be new ratings, new criteria, new design standards, new certification standards," Harris asserted to Bosker. "There is a way to design based not on addiction."

THE SOCIAL DILEMMA

Harris pointed to the growing public attention to the Center for Humane Technology as proof that the group was helping to spur positive change. In 2018 major tech companies and platforms including Google, Apple, Facebook, Instagram, and YouTube began introducing various features paying heed to the "time well spent" credo. Harris even noted that some of the exact language his group used to make its points often found its way into public statements by CEOs and other prominent figures. "We will often hear people in the tech industry, high-ranking executives, talk about what we've been talking about," he told Barber.

To further disseminate the Center for Humane Technology's mission, Harris launched the podcast *Your Undivided Attention* in 2019, which he cohosted with Raskin. The show explores the ways in which online platforms damage the social fabric as well as ways to work toward a better future. These issues were also at the heart of the documentary film *The Social Dilemma*, in which Harris appears as a key talking head and which the Center for Humane Technology touted, though it was not officially involved in the production. Debuting in September 2020, the film was made available on the streaming service Netflix and became a significant hit, seen in 190 countries by an estimated one hundred million people within weeks. It went on to win two Primetime Emmy Awards on seven nominations, as well as a Webby Award.

Following on such notable successes, Harris focused on keeping up momentum. "We're really trying to figure out how we harness this energy and not have it fizzle out, like it did with [Al Gore's climate change documentary] *An Inconvenient Truth* or my original Google presentation," he told Barber. "The world is experiencing a global awakening. The question is what we do with that."

Harris has spoken about trying to live up to his ideals about responsible technology use in his own life, for example noting that he kept a note taped to his laptop reminding him: "Do not open without intention." He also dedicated time to hobbies such as playing the accordion and piano, practicing the tango, and performing sleight-of-hand tricks.

SUGGESTED READING

Barber, Phil. "Santa Rosa Native Tristan Harris Takes on Big Tech in Netflix Documentary *The Social Dilemma.*" *The Press Democrat*, 15 Oct. 2020, www.pressdemocrat.com/article/news/santa-rosa-native-tristan-harris-takes-on-big-tech/. Accessed 23 Nov. 2021.

Bosker, Bianca. "The Binge Breaker." *The Atlantic*, Nov. 2016, www.theatlantic.com/magazine/archive/2016/11/the-binge-breaker/501122/. Accessed 23 Nov. 2021.

Harris, Tristan, and Yuval Noah Harari. "When Tech Knows You Better Than You Know Yourself." Interview by Nicholas Thompson. *Wired*, Condé Nast, 4 Oct. 2018, www.wired.com/story/artificial-intelligence-yuval-noah-harari-tristan-harris/. Accessed 23 Nov. 2021.

McNamee, Roger. "2021 Time100 Next: Tristan Harris." *Time*, 17 Feb. 2021, time.com/collection/time100-next-2021/5937599/tristan-harris/. Accessed 23 Nov. 2021.

Morris, Betsy. "A Silicon Valley Apostate Launches 'An Inconvenient Truth' for Tech." *The Wall Street Journal*, 23 Apr. 2019, www.wsj.com/articles/a-silicon-valley-apostate-launches-an-inconvenient-truth-for-tech-11556046000. Accessed 23 Nov. 2021.

Tiffany, Kaitlyn. "America Offline." *The Atlantic*, 20 May 2021, www.theatlantic.com/technology/archive/2021/05/life-returns-normal-great-offlining-may-begin/618936/. Accessed 23 Nov. 2021.

"Tristan Harris '98: Personifying the 'Pledge to Ourselves.'" *Sonoma Country Day School*, www.scds.org/news-detail?pk=859820. Accessed 23 Nov. 2021.

—*Mari Rich*

Kendra Harrison

Born: September 18, 1992
Occupation: Hurdler

Growing up, professional hurdler Kendra Harrison excelled at several sports, including gymnastics, cheerleading, and soccer. "Ever since I was a little girl, I have always been extremely competitive," she recalled for the website of World Athletics (30 Jan. 2017). "If I do something, I want to be the best at it and I won't stop working until I get there."

This ambitious commitment was displayed in her first foray into competitive track and field, when she took home the silver medal in the 300-meter hurdles at North Carolina's 2009 state championships. Quickly establishing herself as one of the nation's top scholastic hurdlers, she captured a pair of Junior Olympic golds in 2010 as well as consecutive state titles in both 2010 and 2011.

Harrison's dominance on the track continued throughout her college career, which included stints at Clemson University and the University of Kentucky. After earning back-to-back gold medals (2012–13) in the Atlantic Coast Conference (ACC), she claimed five Southeastern Conference (SEC) golds (2014–15) as well as the individual title in both the indoor and outdoor National Collegiate Athletic Association (NCAA) Division I Championships (2015). In 2016, her first full professional season, she had become the odds-on favorite to win Olympic gold, and though that hope was dashed by a shocking sixth-place finish at Trials, she rallied to clear the hurdles and cross the finish line in record-breaking time (12.20 seconds) in the 100-meter event of the Anniversary Games. She then went on to win her first senior international title in 2018 (IAAF World Indoor Championships) and silver at the 2019 IAAF World Championships before making a triumphant return to the Olympic Trials in 2021. Just weeks later, she finally made her debut at the Tokyo Games, where she claimed her very first Olympic medal.

EARLY LIFE AND BECOMING A STATE AND JUNIOR OLYMPICS CHAMP

Kendra "Keni" Harrison was born on September 18, 1992, in Tennessee. Not long after her premature birth and a brief stint in intensive care, she was adopted by Gary and Karon Harrison and raised alongside her ten siblings, eight of whom were also adopted. As the daughter of military parents, she had a peripatetic childhood, residing in several different states before her family made a more permanent home in Clayton, North Carolina, when she was still young. At the time, her father, a US Navy commander, had retired from service, while her mother continued to serve as a lieutenant commander in the Navy Reserve.

Although Harrison would ultimately hone skills ranging from strength and speed to

Photo by jenaragon94,
via Wikimedia Commons

agility from participation in several forms of athleticism, her introduction to sports came in the third grade, when her parents enrolled her in gymnastics. By the time she was attending Clayton High School, she had joined the cheerleading squad and soccer team. "Doing sports was my way of standing out and getting that light on me," she shared with Mark Story for the *Lexington Herald-Leader* (2 May 2015). Despite her belated entry into track and field, she notched an unlikely second-place finish in the girls' 300-meter hurdles at the North Carolina High School Athletic Association (NCHSAA) 4A State Championships in May 2009.

Following that surprising victory, and at the suggestion of her family, including older sister Casey, who offered to buy her a pair of track spikes to replace her tennis shoes, Harrison pursued the sport seriously. The decision proved eventful for her. After winning gold in the girls' 100- and 200-meter dashes and the 300-meter hurdles at the 2010 SSS Spartan Invitational, she found further success at the NCHSAA 4A State Championships, finishing first in the 100- and 300-meter hurdles. She then followed that up by advancing to the 2010 National Junior Olympics, where she proved victorious in both the 100- and 400-meter hurdles.

JOINING THE CLEMSON UNIVERSITY TIGERS

Harrison remained a formidable competitor during her senior year at Clayton, which saw her successfully defend her NCHSAA 4A State Championships titles in the 100- and 300-meter hurdles. Upon graduating in 2011, she was recruited on a full scholarship to play for South Carolina's Clemson University Tigers. At December's Clemson Orange and Purple Classic, the team's first indoor event in 2011, she triumphed in the 60-meter hurdles and the 4×400 relay.

Continuing to live up to the attention drawn to her as a promising star athlete, she secured 4×400 titles at three more events before contributing to her team's crowning in the women's 4×400 relay at the 2012 ACC Indoor Championships. Next dominating the competition at the ACC Outdoor Championships, placing first alongside her team in the 4×400 relay and claiming the 400-meter hurdles title for Clemson for the first time in eleven years, she capped off the 2011–12 season with two first-place finishes (4×100 relay and 100-meter hurdles) at the Clemson Tiger Qualifier. During the 2012 Olympic Trials, she finished twenty-second in the 100-meter hurdles, falling just shy of qualifying for the event. In 2013, after coming out on top once again at the ACC Outdoor Championships, where she finished first in both relays (4×100 and 4×400) and the 400-meter hurdles, she earned bronze in the 4×100 relay at the NCAA Division I Outdoor Championships while also posting top-five finishes in the 100- and 400-meter hurdles.

TRANSFERRING TO KENTUCKY AND DOMINATING THE SEC

Tim Hall's departure from Clemson for the University of Kentucky in 2013 led to a change in schools for Harrison, as she followed her sprint and hurdles coach to the SEC powerhouse. In her Wildcats debut, she won the 60- and 300-meter dashes at December's Hoosier Open before making history at the 2014 SEC Indoor Track and Field Championships, clinching the 60-meter hurdles crown in meet-record time (7.94 seconds) and becoming the first-ever Wildcat to win the event. She swept both the 100- and 400-meter hurdles events at the SEC Outdoor Championship, a feat a female athlete in the conference had last achieved in 1999. Her 2013–14 season ended with a second-

place finish in the 400-meter hurdles at the NCAA Division I Outdoor Championships.

In her final season (2014–15) at Kentucky, Harrison successfully defended her 60-meter hurdles title at the 2015 SEC Indoor Championships while setting a meet record (7.92 seconds) and helping the women's 4×400 relay squad place second. Over the next two months, she secured a first-place finish in the 60-meter hurdles at the NCAA Indoor Championships (with a personal best of 7.87 seconds) and collected additional gold medals at subsequent meets. She posted another personal best (12.50) en route to 100-meter hurdles gold at the 2015 SEC Outdoor Championships, where she was the 400-meter hurdles silver medalist, before recording similar results at the NCAA Division I Outdoor Championships. Later, she would explain to the World Athletics website that, regardless of her abilities, she had to work to build her confidence during this period: "My toughest point in my college journey was believing I could actually compete at the highest level. Being around such amazing athletes, I wanted to be just like them."

TURNING PROFESSIONAL AND BREAKING THE WORLD RECORD

In August 2015, Harrison reached the IAAF World Championships semifinals before being disqualified for a false start. Having graduated from the University of Kentucky that year with a bachelor's degree in community and leadership development, she began competing professionally in 2016. Still trained by Wildcats coach Edrick Floréal, she overcame her disqualification disappointment, amassing victories in the 60-meter hurdles as well as a second-place finish in that event at the USATF Indoor Championships.

Such success, which included chipping away at long-standing records, only made Harrison's setback experience at that year's Olympic Trials all the more heartbreaking. As the Olympic gold-medal favorite, she struggled under pressure, finishing sixth in the 100-meter hurdles finals. However, it was not long before she rebounded in a major way, shattering the 100-meter hurdles world record only weeks later with her time of 12.20 seconds at the Müller Anniversary Games. "I don't think I would want to change the past because not making that Olympic team made me hungrier for the next race," she told Stuart Weir in an interview for *Athletics Weekly* (30 Aug. 2018). Proving nearly unbeatable, she claimed 100-meter hurdle wins at several meets before hoisting the IAAF Diamond League trophy and earning a wild-card entry to the subsequent world championships.

FIRST WORLD TITLE AND AN OLYMPIC MEDAL

Harrison opened the 2017 season with a trio of 60-meter hurdles wins before winning the 100-meter hurdles at the Doha Diamond League meet, despite having broken a finger on her left hand. Though she narrowly missed the podium at the IAAF World Championships, her first international senior title came with her triumphant performance in the 60-meter hurdles at the 2018 IAAF World Indoor Championships. The following year she won a silver medal at the Müller Grand Prix and the IAAF World Championships—her first world outdoor medal.

Though Harrison's 2020 season and the upcoming Tokyo Olympics were abruptly sidelined by the COVID-19 pandemic that began in March 2020, she refocused her training efforts and overcame the delay to be the fastest to clear the hurdles at the 100-meter event at the 2021 Olympic Trials, thereby qualifying for her first Olympics. Widely considered a strong contender for a gold medal, she proved adept at managing the pressure, eventually finishing second behind Puerto Rico's Jasmine Camacho-Quinn. "I don't feel like I have anything to prove," Harrison told Tim Adams for *Athletics Weekly* (26 July 2021) in the lead-up to the Games. "I've already run the fastest time ever and I think that speaks for itself." Honored once more in November 2021, Harrison was inducted into her alma mater's Athletics Hall of Fame. Continuing to impress into 2022, she once again came out on top at the Tokyo track, this time in the Seiko Golden Grand Prix's 100-meter hurdles event.

PERSONAL LIFE

In 2018, Harrison began living next door to her best friend and training partner Jenna Prandini in Austin, Texas, where Harrison serves as a volunteer assistant track and field coach at the University of Texas.

SUGGESTED READING

Adams, Tim. "Keni Harrison: 'I Haven't Run My Fastest Time Yet. I'm Ready to Challenge Myself.'" *Athletics Weekly*, 26 July 2021, athleticsweekly.com/tokyo2020/keni-harrison-i-havent-run-my-fastest-time-yet-im-ready-to-challenge-myself-1039947469/. Accessed 22 June 2022.

Clarey, Christopher. "Keni Harrison, a World-Record Holder, May Finally Win a Title." *The New York Times*, 9 Aug. 2017, www.nytimes.com/2017/08/09/sports/keni-harrison-100-meter-hurdles.html. Accessed 14 June 2022.

Harrison, Kendra. "Catching Up With Hurdles Queen Kendra Harrison." Interview by Stuart Weir. *Athletics Weekly*, 30 Aug. 2018, athleticsweekly.com/interviews/catching-up-with-hurdles-queen-kendra-harrison-104020/. Accessed 14 June 2022.

___. "Kendra Harrison on the Hard Work and Support System That Brought Her to the Games." Interview. *Adidas*, 21 Aug. 2021, news.adidas.com/running/kendra-harrison-on-the-hard-work-and-support-system-that-brought-her-to-the-games/s/61b17671-fdca-4fd0-ae2a-88b54f6ff034. Accessed 14 June 2022.

"My Greatest Challenge—Kendra Harrison." *World Athletics*, 30 Jan. 2017, worldathletics.org/news/series/kendra-harrison-usa-hurdles-challenges. Accessed 21 June 2022.

Pope IV, Jonas. "Keni Harrison's Journey to the Olympics Started in Clayton, NC. She Doesn't Forget Home." *The Charlotte Observer*, July 2021, www.newsobserver.com/sports/article253115158.html. Accessed 14 June 2022.

Story, Mark. "From a Superhero, UK Track Star Kendra Harrison Finds Her Winning Edge." *Lexington Herald-Leader* [Kentucky], 2 May 2015, www.kentucky.com/sports/spt-columns-blogs/mark-story/article44597358.html. Accessed 22 June 2022.

—*Bertha Muteba*

Shamsia Hassani

Born: April 9, 1988
Occupation: Graffiti artist and professor

Graffiti, a form of street art that is often spray-painted and almost always treated as a criminal act, can be as minimal as a line of text or as provocative as the protester throwing a bouquet of flowers painted by the famed but anonymous British graffitist Banksy. While some critics consider it vandalism, others view it as one of the highest forms of modern art.

After the series of political uprisings known as the Arab Spring began in Tunisia and Egypt in 2010 and 2011, revolutionary graffiti became more common in the Middle East; street artists have a great many themes to draw upon but take much higher risks to exhibit their work than in many Western countries. In Afghanistan's capital city of Kabul, for example, graffiti movement groups must usually remain inconspicuous to complete their work, often sneaking out to paint at night before returning to their more socially acceptable careers during the day. Like many Afghans, including artists, Shamsia Hassani went to live in that country, her parents' home, only after the Taliban had been removed from power in 2001. At one point, she received firsthand veteran instruction arranged by the graffiti group Combat Communications, an anonymous band of "art activists" whose goal, in their own words, was to "make people ask questions," as reported by Jason Burke for *The Guardian* (12 June 2011). Long affiliated with Kabul University since her days as a student, she had also begun teaching at the institution as a fine arts faculty member in the early 2010s.

The first widely recognized female graffitist in Afghanistan, Hassani has used her art to, in part, bring a little-seen identity to her fellow Afghan women, portraying them as ambitious individuals determined to live and create freely despite the limitations imposed by deep-rooted cultural traditions, the extremist Taliban rule of the late 1990s, and a long history of foreign conflict. "Her art gives Afghan women a different face, a face with power, ambitions, and willingness to achieve goals," reads a description on the graffitist's official website. Hassani has pointed out that female artists have faced particularly high stakes in what has remained a generally conservative society in terms of gender norms. The Taliban's recapture of the country in August 2021 heavily impacted Hassani's work, while also making such work even riskier. Though she had long found it safer to create most of her graffiti at or close to home, rather than venturing into the more public city center, she has found the potential danger worthwhile on many levels. In addition to striving to redefine Afghanistan's war-torn reputation, she told Anuradha Sengupta for *The Hindu* (25 Oct. 2014), "I realized that

Photo courtesy of Hassani, via Wikimedia Commons

graffiti could be a great tool for developing consciousness, not just about art but also about important issues in Afghanistan. We don't have many galleries here. Neither are people well-educated or well-off. Graffiti is public and accessible."

EARLY YEARS

Ommolbanin "Shamsia" Hassani was born on April 9, 1988, in Tehran, Iran, to Afghan parents who had left their country to escape the harsh conditions resulting from years of violent conflict between invading Soviet troops and Afghan insurgents opposed to the government. As a child, and later as a teenager, in Iran, she already harbored an interest in painting and drawing, and she showed skills in such art that went beyond a youthful hobby. However, due to discriminatory restrictions placed on Afghan refugees within the nation—amid an overall environment of prejudice against Afghans— that prevented her from pursuing that interest formally, she was obliged to study accounting instead.

Around 2005, Hassani relocated with her family to Afghanistan, where she pursued a bachelor's degree in painting and, eventually, a master's degree in visual arts at Kabul University. Though living in Afghanistan also came with hardships, she would later express having felt a greater sense of connectedness there than anywhere else: "We could proudly say we were Afghans. I felt the sky, the earth, the air, the birds were all mine. Even if it was ruins, it was my ruins," she explained to Sarvy Geranpayeh for the *National* (15 Apr. 2019). At the time, she did not think of herself as a graffitist, as she would go on to recall, and never expected that one day she would switch from canvases to walls.

In 2009, Hassani helped found the contemporary-arts organization Berang Arts, which promotes the work of young Afghan artists, many of them women. The following year, in an early foray into graffiti made possible by the arts activism group Combat Communications, Hassani, along with a small group of other Afghan artists associated with Berang, spent a week collaborating with the experienced British graffitist Chu, who led a workshop in one of Kabul's abandoned industrial spaces. Quickly embracing this form, she told Geranpayeh, "I was really excited. I thought we have so many wrecked walls and I could start painting on them." With her artistic talent already having drawn attention and acclaim, in a short time span, she began garnering recognition as Afghanistan's "first serious graffiti artist," in the words of Emma Graham-Harrison for *The Guardian* (24 Feb. 2012).

ART AND TEACHING CAREER

Beginning in the early 2010s, Hassani was employed at Kabul University, first as a fine arts lecturer and eventually as an associate professor. Meanwhile, her unique street art, in which she creatively worked with the limited resources such as paint available to her, was already gaining international fame. This was, in part, due to the distinct female character that was becoming a defining aspect of her work. Typically rendered with no mouth as well as closed eyes while wearing a blue burka and sometimes holding some kind of musical instrument, this woman has often been the only point of color against backdrops meant to represent the extreme oppression of Afghan women, especially as promoted by the fundamentalist Taliban movement. Notably, the figure does not defy Islam itself but rather religious extremism and war—she is both portrayed in conservative religious garb and painted with bold, geometric outlines to suggest a newfound empowerment. Hassani has stated

that she does not condemn the burka itself, but rather encourages viewers to look beyond the clothing to what else needs to be changed about women's place in Afghan society.

In many ways, Hassani has found image-based graffiti to be a fitting art form for Afghanistan, a society with few art galleries long known as having one of the lowest literacy rates worldwide. Furthermore, outdoor spray paintings have not been heavily policed to the same degree there as in the Western world. Even so, as a woman using art to communicate her views of polarizing political topics, she has acknowledged how much she has been risking. Many Afghans continued to view it as sinful or un-Islamic for a woman to create art, Hassani has explained to journalists, and her protective spray-paint mask has served the double function of concealing her identity from a disapproving public. It is for this same reason that she has aimed to complete most of her public works in a very short amount of time. "It is impossible to work on street art here. People say this is not a good job for a woman; this is not allowed in Islam. At a safe place like an abandoned building or a restaurant, I can take a couple of hours. In the street, I finish in 15 minutes and run," she related to Sengupta. Occasionally, she also created what has been called "fantasy graffiti," digital or hand-painted designs added to photographs of blank city walls in the safety of the indoors. In 2013, Hassani contributed to putting together Kabul's first National Graffiti Festival.

It is partially due to her own worldwide success that other female artists from her country have come to the attention of the global arts community. For example, Hassani's name has often been associated with that of Malina Suliman, a young graffitist and metalworker whose street art has tended to feature female skeletons in burkas. After studying in Pakistan, she would eventually return to Kabul and become a member of Hassani's association, Berang Arts. Another name gaining prominence was that of the photographer and painter Rada Akbar, who, like Hassani and Suliman, has used her work to inspire a fresh look at history and gender roles, though she does so through more traditional self-portraits and photographs that capture daily Afghan life, rather than graffiti.

Over the course of the 2010s and into the 2020s, Hassani's profile further increased, earning her exhibitions throughout Europe, the

United States, and Asia-Pacific. She received a vast variety of honors, most notably inclusion on *Foreign Policy*'s one hundred top global thinkers list in 2014, a 2016 residency at Los Angeles's Hammer Museum, and recognition as California's ArtWalk Ventura's Global Artist of Distinction in 2017. A section in the 2017 children's book *Good Night Stories for Rebel Girls 2*, by Elena Favilli and Francesca Cavallo, was additionally devoted to her.

WORK RELATED TO THE TALIBAN'S RETURN TO POWER IN 2021

On August 15, 2021, Kabul was captured by the Taliban, an event coinciding with the largely final withdrawal of US troops from Afghanistan following a twenty-year war. After first taking over the more rural Afghan provinces, the Taliban rapidly narrowed in on Kabul, leading many Afghans, especially women, to fear for their livelihoods and even survival. During the Taliban's previous ruling period in the late 1990s, women were forbidden to attend school or take employment, and they were often arrested, beaten, and sometimes executed for disobeying these and other laws. Following the 2021 takeover there were concerning reports of similarly oppressive restrictions put upon women, even as the Taliban claimed to be less extreme than it had been in the 1990s.

Urban female artists, students, and other professional women in Afghanistan were particularly fearful and discouraged after the events of August 2021, and many began deleting their social media accounts. Several women, including Akbar, left the country for fear that the Taliban would retaliate against any show of female independence.

When Hassani's own online presence disappeared for a time following the fall of Kabul, many worried for her safety; however, she soon returned, posting what would become one of her most famous pieces up to that point. Titled *Death to Darkness*, the work was part of a larger series, including the piece *Nightmare*, that Hassani had been working on as the Taliban recaptured Afghanistan, and Kabul found itself under increasing threat. The piece depicts Hassani's familiar female character crying at the feet of an armed figure, having dropped the hope-symbolizing flower that she holds in other installments. It was reported that as had happened to others, many of Hassani's pieces painted onto walls in Kabul were removed. In spite of the hopelessness she admitted to

feeling at times, Hassani continued to create art and post it on her social media into 2022 to "stay afloat and not sink in this darkness" and represent the turbulent times, as she explained to Ruchi Kumar for *The Guardian* (23 Oct. 2021).

PERSONAL LIFE

Hassani is married to filmmaker Haroon "Shah" Noori. Following the resurgence of the Taliban and the heightened danger it entailed, Hassani became more careful than ever before, keeping details about her personal life and home necessarily vague. There are conflicting reports regarding her whereabouts.

SUGGESTED READING

Burke, Jason. "Kabul's Graffiti Guerillas Put the Writing on the Walls." *The Guardian*, 12 June 2011, www.theguardian.com/world/2011/jun/12/kabul-grafitti-guerrillas-walls. Accessed 10 June 2022.

Geranpayeh, Sarvy. "Meet Afghanistan's First Female Graffiti Artist, Who Is Risking It All for Her Murals." *The National*, 15 Apr. 2019, www.thenationalnews.com/arts-culture/art/meet-afghanistan-s-first-female-graffiti-artist-who-is-risking-it-all-for-her-murals-1.848877. Accessed 11 Aug. 2022.

Graham-Harrison, Emma. "Art in the Streets of Kabul." *The Guardian*, 24 Feb. 2012, www.theguardian.com/world/2012/feb/24/graffiti-street-art-kabul. Accessed 14 June 2022.

Hassani, Shamsia. "See How Graffiti Artist Shamsia Hassani Is Giving Afghan Women a Voice Despite the Danger." Interview by Deborah Vankin. *Los Angeles Times*, 3 Mar. 2016, www.latimes.com/entertainment/arts/museums/la-et-cm-afghan-graffiti-artist-shamsia-hassani-20160301-html-snap-htmlstory.html. Accessed 10 June 2022.

Kumar, Ruchi. "'We Planted a Seed': The Afghan Artists Who Painted for Freedom." *The Guardian*, 23 Oct. 2021, www.theguardian.com/global-development/2021/oct/23/we-planted-a-seed-the-afghan-artists-who-painted-for-freedom. Accessed 15 June 2022.

Saleem, Tahmina, and Farzana Wahidy. "Trailblazing Women of Kabul, Afghanistan—a Photo Essay." *The Guardian*, 8 Apr. 2019, www.theguardian.com/world/2019/apr/08/trailblazing-women-of-kabul-afghanistan-a-photo-essay. Accessed 10 June 2022.

Sengupta, Anuradha. "Urbanscape: Writings on the Wall." *The Hindu*, 25 Oct. 2014, www.thehindu.com/features/magazine/urbanscape-writings-on-the-wall/article6532929.ece. Accessed 11 Aug. 2022.

—*Mari Rich*

Thomas Heatherwick

Born: February 17, 1970
Occupation: Designer

The British designer Thomas Heatherwick rose to fame for his innovative, inspiring, and sometimes controversial designs. As founder and director of Heatherwick Studio, a large firm involved in designing everything from small objects to large buildings and expansive urban plans, he pursued a core mission of creating memorable and beautiful works that are economical, imaginative, and sustainable. As described on the studio's website, "our motivation is to design soulful and interesting places which embrace and celebrate the complexities of the real world."

After building a reputation in his native Great Britain, which included redesigning the iconic red double-decker buses of London, Heatherwick branched out to create such noteworthy public spaces as Vessel and Little Island in New York City as well as the 1,000 Trees shopping center in Shanghai, China. In 2022, his group participated in Queen Elizabeth II's Platinum Jubilee by building the *Tree of Trees* sculpture outside Buckingham Palace to honor the queen's commitment to conservation. During the course of his career, he and his firm won numerous architecture awards for design excellence. Heatherwick's influence on the design world cannot be overstated; as his former mentor, Terence Conran, once remarked, as reported by Nicholas Wroe for the *Guardian* (18 May 2012), Heatherwick is the "Leonardo da Vinci of our times."

EARLY LIFE AND EDUCATION

Thomas Alexander Heatherwick was born on February 17, 1970 in London, England, into an artistic British family. One of his grandmothers was the founder of the Marks and Spencer textile studio and went on to be an art therapy pioneer. His grandfather's family were the founders of Jaeger, a luxury watch manufacturer based in Switzerland. His mother, Stefany Tomalin, was an enameller who owned a jewelry shop in London but who also kept a workshop at home. His father, Hugh Heatherwick, was a pianist and community worker, who passed a love of Victorian designers and builders onto his son. The younger Heatherwick would recall to Tom Cheshire for *Wired* (18 July 2013): "I was more drawn to the inventors and I still am. There had been incredible confidence and derring-do. And a lack of fear of failure for vanity."

During his childhood, Heatherwick's room at his house in Wood Green, north London, was cluttered with old electronics that he would take apart and rebuild in new and interesting ways. When he was ten years old, he turned a pile of discarded innertubes from a nearby bus depot into inflatable furniture, complete with hand-dyed canvas covers. "My bedroom was a workshop," he told Cheshire. "I was finding that you could make your ideas happen."

In the late 1980s, Heatherwick studied 3D design at Manchester Polytechnic and later attended the Royal College of Art in London as a postgraduate. During his educational years, he found himself frustrated by what he felt to be the artificial divisions between disciplines like architecture, fashion, sculpture, and product and furniture design. He told Wroe that he did not consider these disciplines to be separate. "It's just the way we categorise things and the way we chose to educate people," he remarked.

EARLY DESIGN CAREER

Heatherwick always wanted to be both a designer and a maker, desiring to build the objects he envisioned. He founded Heatherwick Studio in 1994. One of the studio's first notable projects came in 1997, when Heatherwick was asked to dress the British department store Harvey Nichols' window display for London Fashion Week. Instead of a traditional display, he built a ribbon of illuminated wood that wove in and out between the store's twelve windows and the street. "When I initially proposed the Harvey Nichols project I was told that the head of building services would never allow it," he explained to Wroe. "But he was actually excited to be offered something so different. People often complain that planners stop them from doing radical things. That's not my

Photo courtesy of
Strelka Institute for Media,
Architecture and Design,
via Wikimedia Commons

experience at all. . . . Planners, in general, do want something special to happen."

In 2000, Heatherwick gained additional notice when he created a bag for Longchamp, a French luxury goods company, which doubled in size because it was made almost completely out of a single zipper. In the same year he went to New York City, where he collaborated with his mentor, Conran, whom he first studied with at the Royal College of Art, to create a large-scale plywood ribbon installation inside an event venue. In 2002, he met with some controversy when he designed a sculpture, called *B of the Bang*, for the Commonwealth Games in Manchester. The 180-foot-tall structure featured a starburst of nearly two hundred metal spikes. Because of safety concerns and technical problems, it was dismantled by Heatherwick's studio at a considerable cost.

PUBLIC ART PROJECTS IN THE UNITED KINGDOM

Despite that controversy, Heatherwick continued to meet with continuing success in the United Kingdom, expanding his studio as he took on more projects. He explained how the studio's process was to confront a potential project by asking questions and peeling away

reasons for why something can or cannot be done, as if conducting an investigation. Workers would then start the process of making, beginning with building small-scale models or prototypes. "It's a way to do true practical analysis, because drawings can fool you," Heatherwick told Cheshire. Through this methodology, the studio created hundreds of innovative works, both in Britain and across the globe.

Notable projects included those ranging from small restaurants to massive structures for international events like the Olympic Games. In 2007, Heatherwick unveiled the East Beach Café in Littlehampton, which was shaped like a large seashell. Three years later, he designed the UK pavilion at the 2010 World Expo in Shanghai, China, which was covered inside and out with silvery "hair" made of acrylic rods. That same year, Boris Johnson, then the mayor of London, tapped Heatherwick to redesign the city's iconic red Routemaster double-decker buses. Heatherwick retooled everything from the bus benches to the lighting, which was changed to softer, non-fluorescent bulbs; six hundred redesigned buses eventually made it to the streets of London. Two years later, in 2012, his studio built the Olympic Cauldron, for the London Games. The Cauldron was made up of more than two hundred flaming copper "petals" placed on mechanical tubes that rose into a cluster. The cluster was meant to symbolize the international athletes coming together from across the globe. He also proposed a "Garden Bridge" that would allow people to cross the Thames River in London by foot, though it was never built due to cost overruns. In each of his public projects, Heatherwick sought to bring a unique beauty and experience to people. In an interview with Anna Fixsen for *Architectural Digest* (15 Feb. 2020), he noted: "With my team, we're trying to always be very mindful of public experience, because I think that's been neglected a lot."

In 2018, Heatherwick and his studio completed the Coal Drops Yard in London, a project that took two rail buildings from the 1850s in the King's Cross neighborhood and converted them to a new shopping center and public space in the heart of the city. He also completed work on a new center for Maggie's, a charity providing free support to cancer patients, on the campus of St. James's University Hospital in Leeds in 2019.

The center included an expansive rooftop garden that patients could help tend. In 2022, Heatherwick studio completed work on a temporary structure designed for Queen Elizabeth's Platinum Jubilee called *Tree of Trees*, which was made up of 350 small potted trees placed on steel-tube branches. Although a number of notable critics berated Heatherwick for his design, including calling his use of trees a passing fad, he defended his studio's work. "Trees aren't a novelty," he explained to Tom Ravenscroft in an interview for *Dezeen* (7 June 2022). "They're essential in life. And so I think the architectural world can like to think things are fads but we need water, we need air, we need trees."

INTERNATIONAL WORK

While heavily involved in British design, Heatherwick's work also took him to various locations around the world, including New York City. Heatherwick first visited New York City as a teenager in the 1980s and was immediately enamored. Although he worked on many projects in the city over the years, his work there became bolder and more ambitious by the mid-2010s. In 2019, he unveiled Vessel, a privately funded structure that took six years to complete. The visitor attraction was the centerpiece of the Hudson Yards project, a sixteen-building complex designed to reinvigorate Manhattan's West Side. Shaped like a honeycomb, Vessel was made of 154 flights of stairs and rose to a height of about sixteen stories. Reviews of the project were mixed, but visitors flocked to it, with more than three million people visiting by early 2020. "Private development can allow some extraordinary things to happen," Heatherwick told Fixsen, defending Vessel against its detractors who often criticized the structure's lack of purpose. "And things that are different—surprise, surprise—attract comment. Of course they do." He went on to describe how impressions of public art often change over time, noting: "Everyone hated the Eiffel Tower. People thought that St. Paul's Cathedral was terrible. I'm not saying that our project is as good as St. Paul's Cathedral—I am just saying there's always controversy while things are being made. I think the real judge of projects is time." However, Vessel came under further scrutiny after several people committed suicide by jumping from it, and the structure was closed indefinitely in 2021.

Another project completed by Heatherwick in New York City was Little Island, a park and theater built on pilings in the Hudson River. As with Vessel, professional critical reception was mixed, but New Yorkers and tourists visited the public park in great numbers to enjoy its nature and art after its opening in the spring of 2021. In 2020, Heatherwick's team began work on Lantern House, an apartment building that was constructed around the High Line, a public park built on a former train trestle on Manhattan's West Side. Heatherwick's studio also contributed to a new Silicon Valley campus of the technology company Google, opened in May 2022, that spanned over forty acres and made headlines for its innovative, sustainable design.

Heatherwick's international reputation also allowed him to work in other countries around the world. In late 2021, his studio completed 1,000 Trees in Shanghai, China, a multi-use building and shopping center that featured one thousand trees placed atop concrete columns as well as a quarter-million plants. "The integration of plants was in response to the scale," Heatherwick said of 1,000 Trees, as reported by Nat Barker of *Dezeen* (9 June 2022). "To me, integrating nature is a very affordable way to get complexity and movement into the facade."

HONORS AND AWARDS

Over the years, Heatherwick and his studio received numerous awards and accolades for their innovative work. Some of the studio's honors include the Prix Versailles 2019 and the RIBA National Award 2019 for the Coal Drops Yard in London; the 2019 World Architecture Festival Award for the Coal Drops Yard and Vessel in New York City; the Stephen R. Kellert Biophilic Design Award 2021 and the 2021 Civic Trust Award for the center at Maggie's in Leeds; and the 2021 SARA NY Award for Innovation in Civic Work for Little Island in New York City. Heatherwick was appointed Commander of the Order of the British Empire (CBE) in 2013. That year he was also elected a Royal Academician by the Royal Academy of Art in London, a distinction reserved for world-leading artists and architects working in the United Kingdom.

SUGGESTED READING

"About." *Heatherwick Studio*, www.heatherwick.com/studio/about/. Accessed 22 Aug. 2022.

Barker, Nat. "Eight of Thomas Heatherwick's Most Controversial Projects." *Dezeen*, 9 June 2022, www.dezeen.com/2022/06/09/Thomas-heatherwick-controversial-projects-roundups/. Accessed 22 Aug. 2022.

Cheshire, Tom. "Thomas Heatherwick: Master Builder." *Wired*, Condé Nast, 10 July 2013, www.wired.co.uk/article/master-builder. Accessed 22 Aug. 2022.

Heatherwick, Thomas. "Thomas Heatherwick's New York State of Mind." Interview by Anna Fixsen. *Architectural Digest*, 15 Feb. 2020, www.architecturaldigest.com/story/thomas-heatherwick-new-york-state-of-mind. Accessed 22 Aug. 2022.

___. "'Trees Aren't a Novelty' Says Thomas Heatherwick." Interview by Tom Ravenscroft. *Dezeen*, 7 June 2022, www.dezeen.com/2022/06/07/trees-buildings-novelty-thomas-heatherwick-interview/. Accessed 9 Sept. 2022.

"Hudson Yards' Vessel: Like a Park, but Vertical." *CBS News*, 17 Mar. 2019, www.cbsnews.com/news/thomas-heatherwick-vessel-hudson-yards/. Accessed 22 Aug. 2022.

Wroe, Nicholas. "Thomas Heatherwick: The New Leonardo of Design." *The Guardian*, 18 May 2012, www.theguardian.com/artanddesign/2012/may/18/thomas-heatherwick-da-vinci-design. Accessed 22 Aug. 2022.

SELECTED WORKS

B of the Bang, 2002; UK Pavilion, Shanghai World Expo, 2010; Olympic Cauldron, 2012; Coal Drops Yard, 2018; Vessel, 2019; Little Island, 2021; 1,000 Trees, 2021; *Tree of Trees*, 2022

—*Christopher Mari*

Siân Heder

Born: June 23, 1977
Occupation: Filmmaker

Throughout her career as a writer and director, Siân Heder has gravitated toward characters who rarely get the spotlight. As a result, her work in both television and film has highlighted everyone from transgender people to incarcerated women to well-intentioned kidnappers. She continued this tradition of putting marginalized people at the center of narratives in her Oscar-nominated film, *CODA* (2021). An adaptation of the French film *La famille Bélier* [*The Bélier Family*] (2014), *CODA* follows the story of a seventeen-year-old hearing girl whose dreams of leaving home to become a singer conflict with her deaf family's need for her help as a translator and advocate. *CODA* demonstrates how, as a filmmaker, Heder is interested in examining the world through different people's unique perspectives to better understand the collective human experience. "The deaf and disabled community has seen a lot of harmful representation. So there's a lot of fear when someone is coming in as an outsider who's not a part of the community," Heder explained to actress Laverne Cox in a piece for *Interview Magazine* (19 Aug. 2021). "My favorite thing about writing is putting myself in someone else's shoes, especially someone different from me."

EARLY LIFE

Siân Heder was born in Cambridge, Massachusetts, on June 23, 1977, to Welsh sculptor Mags Harries and Hungarian environmental artist Lajos Héder. They raised her and her sister Thyra in Cambridge, where they formed the Harries/Héder Collaborative in 1990. Through the collaborative, the couple went on to complete over thirty public art projects together. In many ways, Heder's perspective as a filmmaker was shaped early on by her parents. Beyond learning about the power of visual art through their work, their experiences as immigrants taught her what it meant to be an outsider looking in on American society. Furthermore, they provided her with a unique perspective on the meaning of family. "My dad was a refugee and came here with nothing," she explained to Cox. "Family is everything to him. If it were up to him, we would all be in a room together. No one would ever leave. We'd be sleeping like dogs in a pile on the ground. So that is something that definitely shaped me. I'm always circling that as a storyteller."

Although she was not allowed to watch more than two hours of television a week, the young

Heder would sneak as much as she could when her parents were not around. In part, she found herself drawn to television because she loved the art of storytelling. "For my 6th birthday party, I wrote everybody a character description—who their character was, what their backstory was, what their relationship was with everyone else at the party," she told Ed Symkus for *The Patriot Ledger* (10 Aug. 2021). "Everybody had to stay in character the whole time." Despite the fact that she loved writing from a young age, Heder decided that the best way to pursue her creative tendencies was through acting. After graduating from Cambridge Rindge and Latin School, a public high school, she was accepted at Carnegie Mellon University in Pittsburgh.

EDUCATION AND EARLY CAREER

While studying film and drama at Carnegie Mellon, Heder was often told by her classmates and professors that she should become a director because she had an eye for evaluating other people's performances. However, she was too determined to make it as an actor to even consider their advice. After graduating from Carnegie Mellon in 1999, Heder moved to New York City, where she landed a few small roles in off-Broadway productions and on television shows. She eventually made her way to Hollywood to continue pursuing her dream of acting. There, she worked both as a nanny for wealthy families and as a bartender—two jobs that would unexpectedly launch her filmmaking career.

One day, while working as a bartender, Heder ended up serving a producer who asked her what her professional aspirations were. Tired of telling people she was another struggling actor, Heder lied and said that she was a screenwriter who was working on a story. Intrigued, the producer asked if he could help her try to sell her script. She agreed and went home to quickly write something up. Although no one bought the project, there was still enough interest in it that Heder realized she might have the talent necessary to make it as a writer. Soon afterwards, Heder was accepted into the 2005–06 American Film Institute (AFI) Directing Workshop for Women. The program not only helped her learn how to improve her writing but also made her realize how much she loved directing.

Photo by Lyn Fairly Media, via Wikimedia Commons

While at AFI, Heder wrote and directed a short film called *Mother* that was loosely inspired by her experiences as a nanny in Los Angeles. The seventeen-minute film followed the story of a wealthy Beverly Hills woman who hires a babysitter to take care of her toddler so that she can have an affair. "I don't think I envisioned myself as a filmmaker," she explained to Symkus. "It was the experience of making [*Mother*] when I just felt like I was at home on the set as a director. It's what made me understand what I was supposed to be doing." The film was rejected by eleven festivals before being accepted at the 2006 Cannes Film Festival. Although Heder had plans to transform *Mother* into a feature-length film, she was repeatedly told by producers that the film's three leading female roles would make that impossible. Ultimately, it would take Heder another nine years to get the film made.

WRITING FOR TELEVISION

The acclaim Heder earned for *Mother* legitimized her in the world of filmmaking, and she began to pursue her aspirations to write for television. It was not until she went against her agent's advice and submitted a script that was "too dark" to the showrunner of *Men of a Certain Age*, a TNT comedy about three middle-aged friends, that she ended up landing her first professional writing job in

2010. At first, the experience was terrifying for Heder, and she worried in the early days of the writers' room that she was not good enough. "There I was, sitting next to [actor and comic] Ray Romano, wondering how to pitch jokes and how this whole thing worked," she admitted to Kate Erbland in an interview for *IndieWire* (28 July 2016). "I thought my career was moving faster than my skill level. I had to frantically keep pace by giving myself a film school education along the way." Despite her fears, however, her time on the show proved to be a boon for her career as she and the rest of the writers won a Peabody Award for their work on it in 2011.

From 2013 to 2016, Heder was hired to write for the Netflix series *Orange Is the New Black*. She was in the writers' room from the show's first season, playing an integral part in helping it evolve from a project that Netflix was willing to take a risk on to an international sensation. The first episode that Heder wrote, "Lesbian Request Denied," introduced a transgender character played by Laverne Cox to audiences. She was one of the first transgender characters to ever be on television—let alone as part of the main cast. In turn, Heder played an important role in changing the culture's awareness of gender. "We were on the forefront of this movement of launching an awareness of transgender characters on TV. I was very nervous writing that episode," she told Anna Leszkiewicz for *The New Statesman* (1 June 2016). "It wasn't like that conversation was happening." Heder's next television project was as a director and producer of *Little America* (2020), a series that is inspired by the true stories of American immigrants.

TALLULAH

In 2015, Heder finally secured the opportunity to turn her short film *Mother* into a full-length feature film. Renamed *Tallulah*, the feature had a slightly more sympathetic perspective on its subject matter than the original film. Heder had written *Mother* in her twenties, at a time when she was a nanny and was feeling especially judgmental of older, wealthy women with children. By the time she shot *Tallulah*, she had given birth to her daughter and was pregnant with another child. As such, she came to realize the true challenges of motherhood. This did not stop her from revisiting the original narrative spine, however, about a young woman

kidnapping the daughter of an irresponsible trophy wife.

Tallulah was shot in New York City and included acclaimed actors Elliot Page and Allison Janney in its cast. It received predominantly positive reviews from both audiences and critics. In interviews, Heder stated that she felt the film was well-received because it depicted flawed mothers as multifaceted humans rather than one-dimensional villains. "I think when women see themselves reflected in a real way there's such a profound feeling of relief—because so often I think there's a disconnect between what it feels like to be a woman and what we see in movies and on TV," she told Charline Jao in an interview for the *Mary Sue* (19 July 2016). *Tallulah* debuted at the Sundance Film Festival in January 2016, where it was nominated for the Grand Jury Prize, before being released on Netflix later that year.

CODA

While at the Sundance premiere of *Tallulah*, Heder was approached by producers about writing an adaptation of the French film *La famille Bélier* (2014) for American audiences. After she turned in the script, the producers were so impressed with her take on the story that they agreed to let her direct it as well. The subsequent film became *CODA* (2021), a coming-of-age story about a teenager named Ruby who wants to study music in Boston but feels as though she cannot leave her mother, father, and brother, who are all deaf, because they depend on her to communicate with the outside world.

Heder borrowed heavily from her own life while making the film. In addition to centering the story around the fishing community of Gloucester, Massachusetts, a town where she spent her summers as a child, she also based Ruby's parents on her own. Played by deaf actors Marlee Matlin and Tony Kotsur, the parents in *CODA*—an acronym for "child of deaf adults"—are similar to Heder's in that they are madly in love and talk about sex in an embarrassingly open way. Heder gave them these qualities because she wanted to portray deaf people as real, multifaceted people with strengths and flaws.

To ensure the film was authentic and respectful to the deaf community, Heder cast all deaf actors in the deaf roles and ensured there were as many deaf crew members on set as possible. "I was really an outsider to the community," she told Tim Molloy for *MovieMaker* (13 Aug. 2021). "And it was really important to me that I find collaborators early on who were deaf and inside the community who could work with me from the script stage all the way through production." She also immersed herself in learning American Sign Language (ASL). Her attention to such details paid off. After winning the Grand Jury Prize at Sundance in 2021, Apple paid $25 million for the rights to the film—setting a new festival record—and *CODA* went on to earn overwhelmingly positive critical acclaim and three Oscar nominations, including for best picture and best adapted screenplay. In 2021, Heder signed a deal with Apple to develop series exclusively for the Apple TV Plus streaming platform.

PERSONAL LIFE

Heder has two children with her husband, photographer and producer David Newsom. They live in Los Angeles.

SUGGESTED READING

Heder, Siân. "How 'Tallulah' Director Sian Heder Overcame Rejection to Make Her Sundance Hit—Springboard." Interview by Kate Erbland. *Indiewire*, 28 July 2016, www.indiewire.com/2016/07/tallulah-director-sian-heder-sundance-hit-1201709613/. Accessed 1 Mar. 2022.

___. "Interview: Sian Heder, Director of *Tallulah* on Honest Portrayals of Motherhood." Interview by Charline Jao. *The Mary Sue*, 29 July 2016, www.themarysue.com/interview-sian-heder-director-of-tallulah/. Accessed 1 Mar. 2022.

___. "Siân Heder Tells Laverne Cox How She Made the Year's Biggest Crowd-Pleaser." Interview by Laverne Cox. *Interview Magazine*, 19 Aug. 2021, www.interviewmagazine.com/film/sian-heder-tells-laverne-cox-how-she-made-the-years-biggest-crowd-pleaser. Accessed 1 Mar. 2021.

Huver, Scott. "Deaf Collaborators Helped Shape and Specify 'CODA' Director Siân Heder's Vision—Contenders New York." *Deadline*, 4 Dec. 2021, deadline.com/2021/12/coda-sian-heder-interview-diane-lederman-contenders-new-york-1234883986/. Accessed 1 Mar. 2022.

Leszkiewicz, Anna. "'You Spend a Lot of Time Yelling at Each Other': Sian Heder on the Orange Is the New Black Writers' Room and Her New Film *Tallulah*." *The New Statesman*, 3 June 2016, www.newstatesman.com/culture/film/2016/06/you-spend-lot-time-yelling-each-other-sian-heder-orange-new-black-writers-room. Accessed 1 Mar. 2022.

Molloy, Tim. "How CODA Writer-Director Siân Heder Tells Stories of Cultures She Doesn't Belong to." *MovieMaker*, 13 Aug. 2021, www.moviemaker.com/coda-sian-heder/. Accessed 1 Mar. 2022.

Symkus, Ed. "Massachusetts Director of CODA Says Film Is 'Very Gloucester-Specific.'" *The Patriot Ledger*, 10 Aug. 2021. www.patriotledger.com/story/entertainment/2021/08/10/director-sian-heder-steps-outside-comfort-zone-gloucester-set-coda/5545827001. Accessed 1 Mar. 2022.

SELECTED WORKS

Men of a Certain Age, 2010–11; *Orange Is the New Black*, 2013–15; *Tallulah*, 2016; *Little America*, 2020; *CODA*, 2021

—*Emily E. Turner*

Matthew Heineman

Born: November 30, 1983
Occupation: Filmmaker

In the earliest days of the COVID-19 pandemic, the award-winning documentary filmmaker Matthew Heineman set out to humanize the mysterious and terrifying virus sweeping through New York City. "I remember waking up like everyone did in early March of 2020 and feeling terrified by the sense of a tsunami coming towards us," Heineman, who made his first film in 2009, recalled to Erik Luers in an interview for *Filmmaker Magazine* (13 Dec. 2021). "We were inundated with countless stats and headlines and misinformation about the pandemic, and I felt a huge obligation to try to put a human face to it." The resulting Academy Award–nominated film, *The First Wave* (2021), follows healthcare workers struggling to care for the sick and dying at the Long Island Jewish Medical Center in the New

York City borough of Queens between March and June 2020. The film also received seven Emmy nominations.

Before his pandemic film, Heineman was best known for gritty, gut-wrenching documentaries about war, including the Academy Award–nominated *Cartel Land* (2015) about drug cartels in Mexico. His film *City of Ghosts* (2017) follows a group of citizen journalists in Syria, while *A Private War* (2018), Heineman's only narrative film to date, explores the life of the late Marie Colvin, a renowned war correspondent who died on the job in 2012. Yet Heineman did not see the COVID-19 pandemic, or his role in it, in significantly different terms than his war subjects. "People kept talking about the pandemic as this 'war' we were fighting," he told Luers. "Science and truth really were under attack and that was a big part of why we felt an obligation to tell this story."

EARLY LIFE AND EDUCATION

Matthew Heineman was born to a prominent family in Washington, DC. Although his family may not have inspired him to pursue a career in film, they did encourage his intellectual curiosity and interest in social justice. His grandfather Ben W. Heineman was a railroad executive who later served as an advisor to President Lyndon B. Johnson and as chair of the White House Conference on Civil Rights. His father, Ben Heineman Jr., is an attorney who clerked for Supreme Court Justice Potter Stewart. The elder Heineman is also an author who has written books on law, public policy, and international affairs. Heineman's mother, Cristine Russell, is a pioneering environmental journalist who teaches at the Harvard Kennedy School. He also has one older brother, Zachary, who is an architect.

Heineman grew up in Darien and New Canaan, neighboring towns on the Connecticut shore. He graduated from the Brunswick School, a private high school in nearby Greenwich in 2001 and enrolled as a student at Dartmouth College in New Hampshire. "At Dartmouth, I studied history, and really had no idea what I wanted to do with my life," he recalled to Veronica Winham for the *Dartmouth* (3 Feb. 2022), the college's student newspaper. After graduating in 2005, he applied for a job with the nonprofit Teach for America. When he was rejected, Heineman "decided to go on this

Photo by Our Time Projects,
via Wikimedia Commons

sort of cross-country journey with three of my best friends to understand what our generation was about," he told Winham. He brought his camera to document the experience. "Through that sort of kaleidoscopic journey, I fell in love with filmmaking," he said.

EARLY FILMS

Over the course of the three-month trip, Heineman conducted interviews with people he met, including a man whose New Orleans home had been destroyed by Hurricane Katrina in 2005. The city had just reopened the devastated Ninth Ward during Heineman's visit, and the novice filmmaker followed the man as he went to view his home for the first time since the storm. "I'll never forget the power of this very intimate, emotional moment for this man, and being able to capture it through my lens," Heineman told Timothy Dumas for *Greenwich Magazine* (2018). "I look back at that moment as when I knew that this was something I wanted to do forever."

That experience yielded the documentary short, *Overcoming the Storm* (2006), while footage and interviews—including one with Facebook founder Mark Zuckerberg—from the larger trip were used to create the hour-long documentary *Our Time* (2011). Subsequently, Heineman worked with veteran documentary filmmaker Susan Froemke to make *Escape*

Fire: The Fight to Rescue American Healthcare in 2012. The Emmy-nominated film exposes profound flaws in the US healthcare system, demonstrating how it prioritizes profitable remedies over preventative care.

CARTEL LAND

Heineman began filming his first feature-length documentary, *Cartel Land*, in 2013. He had been focused on a citizen militia in Arizona when his father sent him an article about the Autodefensas, a similar group in Mexico. *Cartel Land*, which premiered at the Sundance Film Festival in 2015, follows the two vigilante groups, who are both at war with drug cartels along the US–Mexico border. "I wanted to know what happens when government institutions fail and citizens feel like they have to take the law into their own hands," Heineman told Dan Slater for *The New Yorker* (17 Sept. 2015). Slater praised the film for identifying vigilante groups as the "missing story" of the drug war.

Heineman, who served as director and primary cinematographer, shot the film using a hand-held digital camera that allowed him to utilize a technique known as cinéma vérité with his subjects; the style allows the filmmaker to focus on subjects in a realistic manner, through observation rather than narration. Shooting was grueling, dangerous, and confusing. "Over time, the line between good and evil blurred," Heineman told Slater. *Cartel Land* earned Heineman awards for directing and cinematography at Sundance. It also won three Emmy Awards and was nominated for an Academy Award for best documentary.

Critics, however, were divided in their reaction to the film. Although Manohla Dargis praised Heineman's "terrific eye" and "nerves of steel" in a 2015 review, she also posed serious questions about his intent. Dargis and others noted that the film, much of which rests on images of brutal violence, lacks the rigor that such a complex story requires. "The film moves so quickly and fluidly and with such unnerving violence that it doesn't give you much time or space to think through the serious, urgent issues it raises," Dargis wrote in *The New York Times* (2 July 2015).

COVERING EVENTS IN SYRIA

Heineman's next film, *City of Ghosts* (2017), covered a group of anonymous activists in Syria during the civil war that broke out after

Syrian citizens protested the totalitarian Bashar al-Assad regime. After the terrorist group the Islamic State of Iraq and Syria, or ISIS, seized a major Syrian city in 2014, a group of citizen-journalists called "Raqqa Is Being Slaughtered Silently" (RBSS) came together to record the atrocities that were being secretly inflicted on Syrian people. Heineman focuses on the actions of RBSS, again serving as director and primary cinematographer of the film. *City of Ghosts* was nominated for an Emmy Award for best documentary. It also received the Courage Under Fire Award from the International Documentary Association.

Heineman continued his investigation of events in Syria when he released his first narrative feature film, *A Private War*, starring award-winning actress Rosamund Pike, in 2018. The film is based on the career of war reporter Marie Colvin, who covered conflicts in Beirut, Chechnya, and Kosovo, among other war-torn locations. The veteran correspondent was advised against reporting in Syria in the early days of the war, but the warnings only fueled her determination to go. She perished in a bombing attack in Homs in 2012. Heineman said he was drawn to Colvin's story as a fellow documentarian. "I felt an enormous kinship to her being a documentary filmmaker," he told Bridget Arsenault in an interview for *Forbes* (31 Jan. 2019). "[I] admired how she approached storytelling: focusing on the human side of reporting on conflicts." Heineman researched Colvin's life as if he were making a documentary, but said he was most interested in showing Colvin's experiences on the ground, doing the work that defined her. Many reviewers agreed that Heineman succeeded in this endeavor, as the film jumps from one war zone to the next, giving a sometimes painfully realistic look at Colvin's work in some of the most dangerous places in the world.

OTHER DOCUMENTARY SUBJECTS

The year 2018 proved to be a prolific year for Heineman as he also premiered a documentary series for Showtime called *The Trade*. The series title refers to the illicit drug and human trafficking trades that the series explores. The first season of the show follows multiple narratives involving the opioid crisis, taking viewers from the poppy fields of Mexico to a US home where a young man struggles to get clean. The second season, which aired in

2020, is about the harrowing experiences of Central American migrants. Combining the efforts of multiple teams of journalists, one team is embedded with Border Patrol officers in Texas, while another follows a Honduran family's grueling journey to the US border. "I think the first priority with this show, as with anything I've ever done, is to try to take an issue that people think they understand, that's often plastered across the headlines, and to try to humanize it," Heineman told Austin Considine in an interview for *The New York Times* (6 Mar. 2020). *The Trade*'s second season won two Emmy Awards, including best director for documentary.

In 2020, Heineman also released a documentary called *The Boy from Medellín*, about Colombian reggaeton singer J Balvin. The film explores politics and the cost of fame. In it, Balvin prepares for a concert in his hometown amidst massive protests that erupt against the Colombian government. It was released the following year on Amazon Prime Video.

Heineman soon released another celebrity documentary, codirected with his longtime producer, Matthew Hamachek: a two-part feature about legendary golfer Tiger Woods that was released on HBO in January 2021. *Tiger* follows the turbulent life and career of the sports prodigy, from his complicated relationship with his father to the eagerness with which the media sought information about his sex life. The film was praised for its nuance and insights into Woods's life and career, though it did encounter controversy for its portrayal of a Black man created by two White men.

THE FIRST WAVE

In March 2020, the epicenter of the COVID-19 pandemic in the United States was New York City, where Heineman lives. The filmmaker was disturbed by the misinformation that was already beginning to spread about the virus, and sought to capture the stark reality of the pandemic from the front lines. After securing consent to shoot inside the Long Island Jewish Medical Center in Queens, Heineman gathered a small crew and set to work. They early identified the doctors, nurses, and patients who would anchor the film's narrative. Shooting through this unfolding traumatic event, in the middle of a statewide lockdown, was exhausting. "There was burnout and fatigue

and a loss of sanity," he explained to Luers. "Every aspect of making this film, especially the things we sometimes take for granted as filmmakers"—from placing microphones on subjects, to setting the camera on a hospital countertop—"were all potential weapons for transmitting the disease."

The First Wave premiered in select theaters in late 2021 and was later released on the Hulu streaming network. Tomris Laffly of *Variety* (8 Oct. 2021), described the film as "soul-piercing" and "undeniably moving." Though the reviewer wondered whether it might be "too much too soon," she concluded that it was "both a vital piece of historical record that bravely captures the unseen horrors of the pandemic and a generous celebration of human dignity whose existence feels miraculous."

PERSONAL LIFE

Heineman is based out of New York City.

SUGGESTED READING

Dargis, Manohla. "Review: In 'Cartel Land' Documentary, Vigilantes Wage Drug Wars." Review of *Cartel Land*, directed by Matthew Heineman. *The New York Times*, 2 July 2015, www.nytimes.com/2015/07/03/movies/review-in-cartel-land-documentary-vigilantes-wage-drug-wars.html. Accessed 3 Aug. 2022.

Dumas, Timothy. "Extreme Truth." *Greenwich Magazine*, 2018, greenwichmag.com/features/extreme-truth/. Accessed 3 Aug. 2022.

Heineman, Matthew. "'Burnout and Fatigue and a Loss of Sanity': Matthew Heineman on Making COVID-19 Documentary *The First Wave*." Interview by Erik Luers. *Filmmaker Magazine*, 13 Dec. 2021, filmmakermagazine.com/112666-matthew-heineman-covid-19-documentary-first-wave/. Accessed 4 Aug. 2022.

___. "How Oscar-Nominated Director Matthew Heineman Helped Rosamund Pike Transform into Marie Colvin." Interview by Bridget Arsenault. *Forbes*, 31 Jan. 2019, www.forbes.com/sites/bridgetarsenault/2019/01/31/how-oscar-nominated-director-matt-heineman-helped-rosamund-pike-transform-into-marie-colvin/. Accessed 3 Aug. 2022.

___. "With 'The Trade,' Matthew Heineman Puts a Human Face on a Divisive Issue."

Interview by Austin Considine. *The New York Times*, 6 Mar. 2020, www.nytimes.com/2020/03/06/arts/television/trade-matthew-heineman-showtime.html. Accessed 3 Aug. 2022.

Slater, Dan. "The Missing Story of the Drug War." *The New Yorker*, 17 Sept. 2015, www.newyorker.com/culture/culture-desk/how-to-tell-a-cartel-story. Accessed 3 Aug. 2022.

Winham, Veronica. "Alum Spotlight: Matthew Heineman '05 Discusses His New Film 'The First Wave.'" *The Dartmouth*, 3 Feb. 2022, www.thedartmouth.com/article/2022/02/alum-spotlight-matthew-heineman-05-discusses-his-new-film-the-first-wave. Accessed 3 Aug. 2022.

SELECTED WORKS

Our Time, 2011; *Cartel Land*, 2015; *City of Ghosts*, 2017; *A Private War*, 2018; *The Trade*, 2018–20; *Tiger*, 2021; *The First Wave*, 2021

—Molly Hagan

Anna Heringer

Born: October 13, 1977
Occupation: Architect

"Mud is not just dirt," German architect Anna Heringer told the website of the Obel Award (2020). "It is a real building material of high quality that you can use to build very exact structures—not only small huts but also large engineering structures and even public buildings." Heringer herself was introduced to the use of mud, or earth, as a sustainable building material in her late teens, when she spent a year in Bangladesh volunteering with the organization Dipshikha (Non-Formal Education, Training and Research Society for Village Development). She went on to study at the Kunstuniversität Linz (University of Art and Design Linz) in Austria, and the Technische Universität München (Technical University of Munich) in Germany, where she pursued her interest in sustainable architecture further and developed designs for facilities such as the Modern Education and Training Institute (METI) School and Dipshikha Electrical Skill Improvement (DESI) in Rudrapur, Bangladesh. Heringer followed those projects with numerous other designs that made use of materials such as earth and bamboo, which

she identified as low cost, environmentally friendly, and appropriate for many of the communities in which her structures are built. She also spoke against the widespread use of building materials such as concrete and metal, arguing that such materials are inefficient, inappropriate for many buildings, and detrimental to the environment. "It's not enough to make nice projects, you also have to speak up politically," she told Katinka Corts in an interview for *World Architects* (10 Mar. 2022) about her outreach efforts and activism. "That's why we also do exhibitions and make more and more public appearances—it's not about our ego." In recognition of her work, Heringer was awarded the Obel Award in 2020 and in 2021 shared the New European Bauhaus Prize with colleague Martin Rauch.

EARLY LIFE AND EDUCATION

Anna Heringer was born on October 13, 1977, in Rosenheim, Germany. She grew up in Laufen, a town in southeastern Germany, near the border with Austria. As a child, she was active in scouting, which taught her the importance of self-sufficiency. "I realized that I could create all the things we needed together with my group," she recalled to Corts. "We played music ourselves, we built furniture and tents, we thought up games. The added value of 'doing it yourself' was something I experienced directly in those days."

In 1997, after completing her secondary education, Heringer traveled to Bangladesh to spend a year volunteering with a local nongovernmental organization (NGO). While there, she observed the use of local building materials such as earth and bamboo and also took note of the particular needs of rural Bangladeshi communities. "I was nineteen and a volunteer at Dipshikha, a Bangladeshi NGO for rural development. And what I had learned from them was that the most sustainable strategy for sustainable development is to cherish and to use your very own resources and potential, and not get dependent on external factors," she explained in a 2017 TED Talk. Heringer's experiences during her year in Bangladesh would go on to shape the development of her architectural point of view as well as her dedication to using local materials, labor, and knowledge when developing projects.

After returning to Europe, Heringer pursued studies in architecture at Kunstuniversität

Linz. She traveled to Bangladesh to perform field research into local building materials and techniques during that period and in 2004 completed her diploma project, the design for a school in Bangladesh. In 2006 she began doctoral studies at the Technische Universität München, during which she completed her dissertation work focusing on sustainable architecture in Bangladesh.

SUSTAINABLE BUILDING MATERIALS

Inspired by the building materials and construction techniques she had seen while volunteering in Bangladesh, Heringer devoted much of her career to promoting the use of mud as a sustainable and appropriate material for construction. Her own education in that area included a workshop with architect Martin Rauch of the Austrian firm Lehm Ton Erde (Loam Clay Earth). It was Rauch who taught her about the practice of rammed earth construction. "When, for the first time, I had mud in my hands, I realized that mud was the missing link between my two passions, development—in terms of justice and ecology—and design, creativity and beauty," she recalled in an interview with the Architects' Council of Europe (ACE). "With mud I felt I would be able to design beautiful structures that were also healthy for the planet, for the people and society."

As Heringer increasingly identified mud as an environmentally friendly material worth promoting, she likewise grew concerned about the widespread use of materials such as cement and metal and argued that their use should be severely limited. "We need to have carbon tags on materials such as steel, aluminum and concrete. These not only have a lot of carbon dioxide in them but also need immense energy for production," she explained to Megha Balooni in an interview for *World Architecture* (28 Sept. 2020). "I believe these are precious materials and one should not necessarily label them as 'bad.' The only thing is that they should be used in small doses."

Heringer's diploma project, the Modern Education and Training Institute (METI) School in Rudrapur, Bangladesh, was her first major architectural work. Designed in collaboration with Eike Roswag, the two-story building, constructed largely from mud and bamboo, encompassed a total of five classrooms as well as cave-like areas on the

ground floor that children could explore and spend time in when engaging in independent work. Created on behalf of Dipshikha, the METI School was constructed over two three-month periods in 2005 and 2006 and went on to win an Aga Khan Award for Architecture in 2007. Heringer followed that project with the Dipshikha Electrical Skill Improvement (DESI) Training Center, also in Rudrapur, which she designed as part of her doctoral work. Constructed from materials similar to those used for the METI School, the DESI vocational center was completed in 2008 and included classrooms as well as restrooms, offices, and apartments for teachers. She went on to supervise the design of three residential buildings constructed in Bangladesh, designed by a group of university students from both Bangladesh and Austria.

DIVERSE PROJECTS

As founder and principal architect of the Laufen-based Studio Anna Heringer, Heringer collaborated with a small team of architects and interns, as well as with colleagues such as Rauch and her cousin, basket weaver Emmanuel Heringer, to design a wide range of structures that are both visually pleasing and environmentally conscious. "I'm not aiming for an eternal architecture, for buildings that are standing forever; this reality does not exist and we should admit it," she explained to ACE. "I try to generate buildings that, one day, can go back into their natural site, if they are no longer needed. A house built of earth can last for a long time, if maintained and it can be turned into a garden."

Though perhaps best known for her work in Bangladesh, Heringer also created designs intended for construction in a number of other countries. In 2012 she began work on a kindergarten for the PORET permaculture community in Zimbabwe, and in 2016 construction was completed on three Heringer-designed hostels in Baoxi, China, which made extensive use of bamboo. Heringer created installations for the Venice Biennale in both 2016 and 2018 and in the latter year collaborated with Rauch to design a new altar for St. Peter's Cathedral in Worms, Germany.

SOCIALLY CONSCIOUS ARCHITECTURE

In January 2020 construction was completed on the Anandaloy Building in Rudrapur, which was set to house a therapy center for people with disabilities as well as a textile-production workshop designed to improve the livelihoods of local women. Though designed by Heringer's studio, the building was constructed by a diverse array of local laborers out of clay and other local, sustainable materials. "Clay is a material that truly enables inclusion. We had everyone working on site: young and old, healthy and with disabilities, men and women," she told the website of the Obel Award. "It was wonderful to me that the workers did the structure on their own. Normally, they would wait to be told what to do, but with the construction of Anandaloy, they were completely engaged in it, finding their own solutions." Another socially conscious structure designed by Heringer, a prototype birthing space named the Room for Birth and Senses, was completed near the Women's Museum in Hittisau, Austria, later that year.

March of 2021 saw the beginning of construction of a new campus for a sustainable training center in Tatale, Ghana, which Heringer conceptualized and designed. Another major project underway during that period was the design and construction of a guesthouse for RoSana, an Ayurvedic center located in Germany. Created in collaboration with Rauch, the guesthouse was designed to incorporate earth, wood, and other environmentally friendly materials while limiting the use of concrete, metal, and other conventional building products.

TEACHING AND RECOGNITION

Heringer taught at various institutions throughout her career, leading courses and workshops at institutions such as Harvard University's Graduate School of Design in the United States, ETH Zürich in Switzerland, and the Technical University of Munich. She also held the title of honorary professor of the United Nations Educational, Scientific, and Cultural Organization (UNESCO) Chair of Earthen Architecture, Building Cultures, and Sustainable Development. For Heringer, teaching represented a vital opportunity to pass her architectural and environmental point of view on to a new generation of architects. "When I talk to my students, they say: 'How can I make a living making ethically sound and sustainable architecture?'" she told the website of the Obel Award. "I always tell them: 'Just follow your heart. If you do something that is in

favour of life, of social justice, a healthy planet, just trust that life will also support you on your way.'" In addition to teaching in university settings, Heringer delivered the informational TED Talk "The Warmth and Wisdom of Mud Buildings" at the TED conference in Vancouver, Canada, in 2017.

In addition to the Aga Khan Award received for her work on the METI School, Heringer received a number of significant awards and honors throughout her career, many of them specifically recognizing her contributions to the field of sustainable architecture. A recipient of the Architecture Review (AR) Emerging Architecture Award in both 2006 and 2008, she won the Global Award for Sustainable Architecture in 2011 and later received the International Award Biennale di Pisa. In 2020 the Henrik Frode Obel Foundation awarded her the Obel Award for her work on Anandaloy, an honor that was accompanied by a prize of €100,000. The following year, she and Rauch received the 2021 New European Bauhaus Prize in the category of Solutions for the Coevolution of Built Environment and Nature for their work on the RoSana guesthouse in Rosenheim, Germany.

PERSONAL LIFE

Heringer married geoinformatics researcher Stefan Lang, and the couple have a daughter. The Heringers purchased a building known as the Blauen Haus, or Blue House, in Laufen in 2019, and two years later opened a small shop dedicated to selling sustainable and handcrafted goods—Laden im Blauen Haus, or the Shop in the Blue House..

SUGGESTED READING

Heringer, Anna. "Architecture in Favour of Life." *Obel Award*, 2020, obelaward.org/architecture-in-favour-of-life-anna-heringer-interview/. Accessed 13 June 2022.

___. "' . . . Realise That in the End We Are All the Same'—Interview with Anna Heringer." Interview by Megha Balooni. *World Architecture*, 28 Sept. 2020, worldarchitecture.org/architecture-news/efnnh/-realise-that-in-the-end-we-are-all-the-same--interview-with-anna-heringer.html. Accessed 13 June 2022.

___. "A Talk with Anna Heringer." Interview. *Architects' Council of Europe*, www.ace-cae.eu/activities/publications/interviews-with-european-architects/a-talk-with-anna-heringer/. Accessed 13 June 2022.

___. "Talking Practice: Anna Heringer." Interview by Grace La. *Harvard Graduate School of Design*, 30 Oct. 2018, www.gsd. harvard.edu/2018/10/talking-practice-anna-heringer/. Accessed 13 June 2022.

___. "The Warmth and Wisdom of Mud Buildings." *TED*, Apr. 2017, www.ted.com/talks/anna_heringer_the_warmth_and_wisdom_of_mud_buildings. Accessed 13 June 2022.

___. "'We Must Arrive at a Happy Contentment.'" Interview by Katinka Corts. *World Architects*, 10 Mar. 2022, www.world-architects.com/en/architecture-news/insight/we-must-arrive-at-a-happy-contentment. Accessed 13 June 2022.

Maganga, Matthew. "'Sustainability Is a Synonym of Beauty': In Conversation with Anna Heringer." *Arch Daily*, 3 Apr. 2021, www.archdaily.com/959398/sustainability-is-a-synonym-of-beauty-in-conversation-with-anna-heringer. Accessed 13 June 2022.

SELECTED WORKS

Modern Education and Training Institute (METI) School (with Eike Roswag), 2006; Dipshikha Electrical Skill Improvement (DESI) Training Center, 2008; Bamboo Hostels, Baoxi, China, 2016; Anandaloy, 2020; Room for Birth and Senses, 2020

—*Joy Crelin*

Alfonso Herrera

Born: August 28, 1983
Occupation: Actor and singer

From the start of his career, Mexican actor Alfonso Herrera prioritized taking roles that doubled as learning experiences. "When I choose a story, when I choose a character, it has to be something that has to communicate a message," he told Liz Calvario for *ET* (12 Sept. 2018). "I am very much attracted to roles and stories that make me grow and that make me learn." After beginning to work as an actor early in the first decade of the twenty-first century, Herrera first developed a large following as a cast member of the soap opera *Rebelde* and the associated music group RBD, with which

he recorded several albums before the group's dissolution in 2009. Throughout the following years he starred in television and film projects that spanned a wide range of genres, from historical war drama to comedy to horror. Though best known in Mexico early on, he gained increasing recognition in the United States midway through the second decade of his career, making his debut in the science-fiction series *Sense8* in 2015 and costarring in the horror series *The Exorcist* beginning the following year. Herrera gained further critical recognition for his role in the historical drama *El baile de los 41* (2020; *Dance of the 41*) and in 2022 joined the cast of *Ozark*, an acclaimed crime drama series, for the show's fourth season. While working within such a wide range of genres and portraying such varied characters presented a challenge, it was a challenge he thoroughly enjoyed. "It's incredible to navigate in these different types of roles—it's fun," he told Justin Mastine-Frost in an interview for *Sharp* (19 May 2022). "Otherwise, what's the point? It's good to receive a story, to roll up your sleeves and say 'OK, now I'm going to try and do something completely different.'"

EARLY LIFE AND CAREER

Alfonso Herrera Rodríguez was born on August 28, 1983, in Mexico City, Mexico. An aspiring pilot as a teenager, he applied to study aviation at a school in San Antonio, Texas, and planned to attend that institution after completing his secondary education. Fatefully, however, the young Herrera was also working on an acting project at the time, and his career trajectory would soon change dramatically. "One of the people in the project was a very famous artist and singer, and her dad was a very famous movie director in Mexico City. And he was going to direct a movie, and she said, 'Hey, do you want to do a reading for a part?'" he recalled to Josef Rodriguez for *Latina* (2022).

Herrera decided to forgo his aviation studies and instead pursue a career in acting, initially within his home country. He made his film debut in the 2002 film *Amar te duele* (Loving You Hurts), for which he earned a 2003 Mexican MTV Movie Award for favorite villain. Herrera also appeared in more than fifty episodes of the television series *Clase 406* (Class 406) between 2002 and 2003.

REBELDE AND RBD

In 2004, Herrera's career took a new turn when he began to star in the high school soap opera *Rebelde* (Rebel). As part of the project, six members of the series' cast formed the music group RBD. "It was a massive project, specifically to Latin American cultures and in parts of Europe," Herrera told Rodriguez about his time with RBD. "I mean, we went to Romania, to Croatia, to Spain. It was great." Throughout *Rebelde*'s years on television, Herrera and fellow bandmembers Anahí, Christian Chávez, Christopher von Uckermann, Dulce María, and Maite Perroni performed music for the series in addition to recording albums such as *Rebelde* (2004) and *Nuestro amor* (2005; Our Love).

While *Rebelde* finished its run in 2006, RBD continued to record new music over the next several years, releasing further records such as *Celestial* (2006), the English-language album *Rebels* (2006), *Empezar dezde cero* (2007; Starting Over), and *Para olvidarte de mi* (2009; To Forget Me). The group was twice nominated for the Latin Grammy Award for best pop album by a duo or group and also performed live, touring in Mexico and abroad. Following the conclusion of *Rebelde*, Herrera and the other members of the group also starred as fictionalized versions of themselves in the comedy series *RBD: La familia* (RBD: The Family), which aired for a single season in 2007. RBD disbanded in 2009, and while several of the members reunited in 2020, Herrera was not among them.

NEW OPPORTUNITIES

Following *Rebelde*, Herrera found work in numerous television series, including *Terminales* (2008; Terminals), *Camaleones* (2009; Chameleons), *El equipo* (2011; The Team), and *El diez* (2011; The Ten). In 2015 he began to star as the title character, Daniel "El Dandy" Brach, in the series *El Dandy*, a crime drama loosely based on the 1997 US film *Donnie Brasco*. He also appeared in a number of films during that period, including the World War II period piece *Venezzia* (2009), the comedy *Así es la suerte* (2011; This Is Luck), and the horror film *Espectro* (2013; released under the title *Demon Inside* in the United States).

Although Herrera was a prolific actor and took on a wide range of roles, not every new

Photo courtesy
Secretaría de Cultura de la Ciudad de México,
via Wikimedia Commons

opportunity came to fruition. One such project was the pilot episode for the new series *Urban Cowboy*, produced for the US television channel Fox and based loosely on the 1980 film of the same name. A pilot starring Herrera was filmed, but in late 2015 Fox announced that it would not be moving forward with the series. Such near misses would be disappointing setbacks for many actors, but Herrera took these moments in stride. "Sometimes you see a role, and you're like 'hey, this could be a good opportunity for me' and sometimes it happens and sometimes it doesn't happen," he explained to Mastine-Frost. "That's normal, that's our life. We need to live with hearing 'no' constantly and that's OK." Yet, while he had grown accustomed to professional rejection, he nevertheless continued to find steady work. In 2016, Herrera starred in the historical drama *El elegido* (The Chosen), in which he portrays a fictionalized version of the man tasked with assassinating the Bolshevik leader Leon Trotsky in 1940.

SUCCESS IN THE UNITED STATES

Herrera was a prolific actor in Mexico by the second decade of the twenty-first century, and he increasingly pursued opportunities in the US film and television industries as well. "It doesn't matter the geographical area where you're working," he told Calvario. "The important thing is to generate a passionate team that believes in the project and believes in the story." In 2015 he debuted in a supporting role in the Netflix series *Sense8*, a science fiction series with a sizable ensemble cast. Canceled in 2017 after two seasons, the show returned for a feature-length series finale in 2018, in which Herrera also appeared.

In addition to working on *Sense8*, in 2016 Herrera debuted as one of the stars of the horror series *The Exorcist*, based on the 1973 film of the same name. "Touching the Holy Grail of horror, touching an important and an epic movie and connecting that to a TV show—there was a huge responsibility. Huge, huge, huge responsibility," he told Dominic Patten in an interview for *Deadline* (20 July 2017). "But at the same time, there was also a huge opportunity, and I think that we took that, and we tried to do our very best." Herrera portrays priest and exorcist Father Tomas Ortega in the series, which was canceled in 2017 following its second season.

In 2018 and 2019 Herrera appeared as Javier Jimenez in the third and fourth seasons of *Queen of the South*, an English-language crime series based on the US–produced Spanish-language series *La reina del sur*. He likewise remained active in Mexican film and television during this period and in 2019 starred in the miniseries *Sitiados: México* (Besieged: Mexico), a period piece set in the seventeenth century. The following year, Herrera starred as Ignacio de la Torre, the son-in-law of Mexican president Porfirio Díaz, in the historical drama *El baile de los 41* (Dance of the 41), for which he earned Mexico's Silver Ariel Award for best actor.

OZARK

In January 2022 Herrera made his debut in the fourth season of the award-winning Netflix crime drama *Ozark*, which follows a couple, played by Jason Bateman and Laura Linney, who have become involved in a money-laundering operation on behalf of a cartel. Herrera portrays Javi Elizonndro, the nephew of cartel leader Omar Navarro (Felix Solis) and a new arrival in the Missouri community in which the show takes place. The role of Javi presented a new challenge for the actor, who found the character to be far more violent than those he usually played. "I don't like violence.

I hate it actually," Herrera told Mastine-Frost. "Javi, from *Ozark*, he embraces violence, and it's part of his nature—and it would be unfair for the story, unfair for the character to judge that situation. So I had to find an organic point where I could connect that inner violence that he has and try to incorporate something that I have." Season four of Ozark met with critical acclaim following its release, and Herrera himself earned considerable recognition for his portrayal of Javi. Herrera followed his tenure on *Ozark* with work on a number of new projects, including the science fiction film *Rebel Moon*, which began filming in Los Angeles, California, in April 2022.

In addition to acting, Herrera served as a Goodwill Ambassador for the United Nations High Commissioner for Refugees (UNHCR), having been named to that role in September 2020. "We are witnessing an unprecedent refugee crisis around the world, and Latin America is not an exception," he explained about his work with that organization for the UNHCR's website. "UNHCR's role, together with civil society, is instrumental in protecting the dignity, integrity and security of refugees. It's painful to listen to the stories of forced displacement, you can only imagine what they must have been through in order to survive. Above all I want them to know that I admire their courage and strength."

PERSONAL LIFE

Though based in Mexico, Herrera lived in the United States when filming his US projects. He was previously married to Diana Vázquez, with whom he had two sons. Herrera announced his divorce from Vázquez in December 2021.

SUGGESTED READING

"Alfonso Herrera." UNHCR, www.unhcr.org/alfonso-herrera.html. Accessed 13 June 2022.

"Calvario, Liz. "Alfonso Herrera on the Importance of Telling Latinx Stories in Hollywood (Exclusive)." *ET*, 12 Sept. 2018, www.etonline.com/alfonso-herrera-on-the-importance-of-telling-latinx-stories-in-hollywood-exclusive-109461. Accessed 13 June 2022.

___. "'Rebelde': Where the Cast of the Fan-Favorite Mexican Telenovela Is Now." *ET*, 11 Jan. 2022, www.etonline.com/rebelde-where-the-cast-of-the-fan-favorite-mexican-telenovela-is-now-133632. Accessed 13 June 2022.

Herrera, Alfonso. "Alfonso Herrera on Avoiding Being Typecast, Violence, and His Love of Sneakers." Interview by Justin Mastine-Frost. *Sharp*, 19 May 2022, sharpmagazine.com/2022/05/19/alfonso-herrera-interview/. Accessed 13 June 2022.

___. "Comic-Con: 'Exorcist' Star Alfonso Herrera on Season 2 and 'Sense8' Finale." Interview by Dominic Patten. *Deadline*, 20 July 2017, deadline.com/2017/07/comic-con-exorcist-sense8-alfonso-herrera-interview-ben-daniels-1202132049/. Accessed 13 June 2022.

Ramírez, Alicia. "Alfonso Herrera, 'Javi' on 'Ozark,' Reflects as Final Season Debuts." *NBC News*, 29 Apr. 2022, www.nbcnews.com/news/latino/alfonso-herrera-javi-ozark-final-season-rcna26027. Accessed 13 June 2022.

Rodriguez, Josef. "Alfonso Herrera Stays Grounded." *Latina*, 2022, latina.com/alfonso-herrera-stays-grounded/. Accessed 13 June 2022.

SELECTED WORKS

Clase 406, 2002–3; *Rebelde*, 2004–06; *RBD: La familia*, 2007; *El Dandy*, 2015; *Sense8*, 2015–18; *The Exorcist*, 2016–17; *El baile de los 41*, 2020; *Ozark*, 2022

—Joy Crelin

Kathleen Hicks

Born: September 25, 1970
Occupation: Government official

Kathleen Hicks was sworn in as the US deputy secretary of defense, the second-highest ranking civilian job at the Pentagon, on February 9, 2021, under President Joe Biden. Hicks, whose father served in the Navy, began her career at the Department of Defense (DoD) as an intern in 1993. Nominated by President Barack Obama, she was confirmed as the principal deputy undersecretary for policy in 2012. She has also worked for the think tank Center for Strategic and International Studies (CSIS), where she published articles analyzing national security and other political issues.

Upon becoming deputy secretary of defense, Hicks was tasked with overseeing day-to-day operations at the DoD, as well as managing the department's gargantuan $700 billion annual budget. In terms of policy and vision, though, Hicks remained interested in developing the Pentagon's technological capabilities. In 2022, she announced the creation of the Chief Digital and Artificial Intelligence Office (CDAO). Within the larger culture of the Pentagon, this dramatic shift in focus—placing more emphasis on operating computers than building fighter jets—was considered quite bold. Accordingly, Hicks has placed significant pressure on the office to yield actionable results. "We have to be able to deliver. We have to advance and advance quickly on the challenge set that the warfighter faces," Hicks said at the DoD's digital and artificial intelligence symposium, as quoted by Jon Harper for *FedScoop* (8 June 2022). Furthermore, she emphasized the need for new, largely civilian, blood, suggesting that the Pentagon take cues from start-ups in Silicon Valley. "The CDAO has to be seen . . . [as] the go-to place for talent and technical expertise to get after that problem," she said, as reported by Harper.

EARLY LIFE AND EDUCATION

Kathleen Anne (Holland) Hicks was born on September 25, 1970, in Fairfield, California. Her father, Rear Admiral William Holland Jr., worked in the office of the Chief of Naval Operations (CNO) in various positions, including as director of nuclear weapons. Perhaps because of this, Hicks has said that she knew she wanted to work for the DoD from an early age. Her mother, Anne Holland, raised Hicks and her six siblings. Hicks began her high school career at Point Loma High School in San Diego but graduated from Lake Braddock Secondary School in Burke, Virginia, in 1988. She earned a bachelor's degree from Mount Holyoke College in 1991 and a Master of Public Administration degree at the University of Maryland in 1993. In addition to knowing she wanted to work at the DoD, she has also stated her strong desire to earn her PhD. Thus, in 2010, she earned a PhD in political science from the Massachusetts Institute of Technology. "I didn't do it for reasons of believing that it would help me in my career progression," she explained in an interview for *New Perspectives in Foreign Policy* (10 Oct. 2014), a publication of the CSIS. "I did it for my own intellectual growth."

Photo via Wikimedia Commons
[Public domain]

EARLY CAREER

Hicks began her career with the DoD as an intern in the Office of the Secretary of Defense in 1993. Later, she offered advice for other civilians seeking policy roles at the DoD. "If you're going to work here you have to have a basic appreciation for the military," she told *New Perspectives.* "In other words, don't come work in the Department of Defense if you don't actually like the idea that we have a military that helps to protect our interests."

Hicks was working at her desk in the Pentagon's Office of the Secretary of Defense when American Airlines Flight 77 crashed into the opposite side of the sprawling building on September 11, 2001; her oldest child was at the facility's daycare center. Both were unharmed, but the experience had a lasting impact on Hicks. The event also caused a seismic shift in the DoD's political goals, altering the course of her career as well. Hicks eventually became a senior executive in the Office of the Secretary of Defense, serving as director of strategy and chief of staff in 2005.

Then, taking a break from the DoD, Hicks served as a senior fellow at the Center for Strategic and International Studies (CSIS), a bipartisan think tank focused on national security, from 2006 until 2009, when she returned to the Pentagon to serve as the deputy undersecretary for strategy, plans, and

forces during the Obama administration. At the time, she noted a significant increase in the number of women working there. "When I entered the Department in 1993, it would have been extremely unusual to have another woman in any meeting I was ever in," she told *New Perspectives.* "When I went back to the Department in 2009, we had a meeting . . . and we all paused for a moment and looked around the table and every person in the room was a woman." In this role, Hicks led the creation of major military reports, including the 2010 *Quadrennial Defense Review* and the 2012 *Defense Strategic Guidance.* In 2012, Hicks was nominated and confirmed to serve as the principal deputy undersecretary for policy. In that position, she advised the secretary of defense on policy and strategy pertaining to regions including the Asia-Pacific, the Persian Gulf, Syria, and Europe.

CENTER FOR STRATEGIC AND INTERNATIONAL STUDIES

Hicks returned to the CSIS in 2014, when she was named senior vice president, Henry A. Kissinger chair, and director of the International Security Program at the research organization. During this period, she wrote numerous articles about the military and foreign policy under President Donald Trump, who was elected in 2016. She expressed particular concern about Trump's decision to afford the military more decision-making power at the expense of the State Department. "As former policymakers," Hicks wrote with Alice Hunt Friend for *Defense One* (7 July 2017), "we believe that delegating some operational decisions to the Defense Department could be helpful in demonstrating appropriate respect for military professionalism and meeting the operational challenges of the current environment. But there is a danger in overcorrection." Put simply, Hicks and Friend argued that ceding national security concerns entirely to the military—"while allowing the diplomacy, development, and trade elements of our toolkit to atrophy"—was a poor and alarming misuse of power.

In 2020, writing for the same publication with Michèle Flournoy, who served as the deputy assistant secretary of defense in the Bill Clinton administration, Hicks offered a more pointed critique of Trump's policies. "America is in crisis, and our national security is becoming a casualty," they wrote for *Defense*

One (9 June 2020). Endorsing presidential candidate Biden, they offered three imperatives for course correction: investments in education as well as public health and more welcoming immigration policies to sustain the United States as a competitive global power.

During this period, Hicks also held an academic position at the Johns Hopkins School of Advanced International Studies and served as a member of two congressionally mandated commissions dedicated to defense issues—the National Defense Strategy Commission and the National Commission on the Future of the Army. For the former, she contributed to a 2018 report on US defenses that won the praise of both Republican and Democratic members of Congress.

DEPUTY DEFENSE SECRETARY

After Biden won the presidency and took office in January 2021, he nominated Hicks to serve as deputy secretary of defense. Testifying before the Senate Armed Services Committee, she was straightforward about her vision for the DoD during her confirmation hearing. On the whole, she told committee members that her goal was to "have a qualitative advantage over adversaries" by focusing more on soft power and less on brute force. She also, surprisingly, expressed concerns that further inflating the defense budget offered a false sense of security. "A budget is about priorities, and we continue to overinvest in defense while underinvesting in public health and so much more that would keep us safe and that would save lives," she said, as quoted by Bryan Bender for *Politico* (3 Feb. 2021). Hicks was officially sworn into office on February 9, 2021, becoming the first woman to hold the position of a Senate-confirmed deputy secretary.

Once installed, Hicks was immediately tasked with planning the withdrawal of troops from Afghanistan—a monumental undertaking as US forces had occupied the country since 2001. It was a politically delicate endeavor, as Biden ordered a complete exit against the concerns of military generals. Hicks promised an orderly withdrawal and an "over-the-horizon" approach (the term used by the Biden administration) to counterterrorism, meaning that the United States would fight extremist groups from home rather than on the ground. In April 2021, Hicks told the Aspen Institute, as quoted by Stephen Losey for *Military.com*

(30 Apr. 2021), that she did not expect the exit to look like the "fall of Saigon," referring to the catastrophically botched evacuation of US troops and personnel from Vietnam in 1975. Hicks met criticism, however, following the withdrawal, when some commentators, in fact, later compared the event to the end of the Vietnam War.

The authoritarian Taliban took control of Afghanistan within days of the US troops' evacuation. Some expressed concern that the speed of the Taliban's takeover gave the group access to data and equipment that US troops were forced to leave behind. Hicks dismissed these fears but also said the withdrawal heightened her interest in developing the Pentagon's data and artificial intelligence (AI) capabilities. In early 2022, Hicks announced the creation of a new government office, named the Chief Digital and Artificial Intelligence Office (CDAO). The principal goal of the CDAO was to create faster and better-connected systems within the US military by employing digital tools such as AI. It also aimed to keep competitive with other countries such as China that were seen as technological threats. "What we want to be able to do is make sure we are leveraging the state of the art in order to increase accuracy, increase speed of decision-making, increase the quality of our ability to deliver effects," Hicks explained, as quoted by Harper. The newly formed office quickly proved enormously useful when Russia invaded Ukraine in February 2022. The DoD relied on the CDAO's experts to analyze data about the conflict, creating code and algorithms that were used to interpret Russian radio chatter and identify certain individuals in social media posts by using facial recognition technology.

PERSONAL LIFE

Hicks is married to Thomas Hicks, who served as acting undersecretary of the Navy during the mid-2010s. He is also the director of a defense consulting firm called the Mabus Group. The Hicks family lives in Washington, DC, with their three children.

SUGGESTED READING

Bender, Bryan. "Hicks Raises Prospect of Defense Cuts." *Politico*, 3 Feb. 2021, www.politico.com/newsletters/morning-defense/2021/02/03/hicks-raises-prospect-of-defense-cuts-793143. Accessed 27 July 2022.

Friend, Alice Hunt, and Kathleen Hicks. "Trump Gave the Military More Power, But Here's What Really Concerns Us." *Defense One*, 7 July 2017, www.defenseone.com/ideas/2017/07/trump-gave-military-more-power-heres-what-really-concerns-us/139259/. Accessed 5 Aug. 2022.

Harper, Jon. "Pentagon's Hicks Puts Pressure on New AI Office to Deliver Results." *FedScoop*, 8 June 2022, www.fedscoop.com/pentagons-hicks-puts-pressure-on-new-ai-office-to-deliver-results/. Accessed 28 July 2022.

Hicks, Kathleen. "Interview with Dr. Kathleen Hicks." *New Perspectives in Foreign Policy*, Center for Strategic and International Studies, 10 Oct. 2014, csis-website-prod.s3.amazonaws.com/s3fs-public/legacy_files/files/publication/150127_new_perspectives_issue8.pdf. Interview. Accessed 27 July 2022.

___, and Michèle Flournoy. "We Need Joe Biden." *Defense One*, 9 June 2020, www.defenseone.com/ideas/2020/06/we-need-joe-biden/166033/. Accessed 5 Aug. 2022.

Knight, Will. "To Win the Next War, the Pentagon Needs Nerds." *Wired*, Condé Nast, 2 May 2022, www.wired.com/story/to-win-the-next-war-the-pentagon-needs-nerds/. Accessed 28 July 2022.

Losey, Stephen. "Afghanistan Withdrawal Won't Be Like 'Fall of Saigon,' Deputy SecDef Says." *Military.com*, 30 Apr. 2021, www.military.com/daily-news/2021/04/30/afghanistan-withdrawal-wont-be-fall-of-saigon-deputy-secdef-says.html. Accessed 28 July 2022.

—*Molly Hagan*

Lina Hidalgo

Born: February 19, 1991
Occupation: Politician and judge

In November 2018, at the age of twenty-seven, Democratic politician Lina Hidalgo became the first Latina and the first woman to be elected county judge of Harris County, the largest county in Texas and the third-most populous county in the United States. A newcomer in the political arena, she unexpectedly defeated seasoned Republican politician Edward M. Emmett with 49.7 percent of the vote; Emmett obtained 48.2 percent.

By running a campaign focused on health care expansion, immigration, criminal justice reforms, flood control funding, and increased transparency and accountability in the local government, Hidalgo presented the community with a clear vision of her progressive agenda. However, her personal history—combined with an earnest desire to improve the lives of county members—convinced voters to cast a ballot for her. Hidalgo, a Colombian immigrant who arrived in Houston when she was fifteen years old, wanted to give back to the county that had welcomed her family by providing families in the community with an equitable life and caring for the most vulnerable members. As she told Blake Paterson for the *Texas Observer* (3 Apr. 2019), "If there's an issue facing our residents, we'll go over and around a wall to address it. I won't say it's not my problem. I'll figure out what we can do to help it."

EARLY LIFE AND EDUCATION

Lina Marie Hidalgo's life began in Bogotá, Colombia, where she was born on February 19, 1991. The eldest child of a stay-at-home mother and a mechanical engineer father, her early years coincided with the height of the Colombian drug wars, which only brought violence, unrest, and corruption to the South American nation. "You couldn't go to the grocery store without worrying about a bomb," Hidalgo told Mihir Zaveri for *The New York Times* (8 Nov. 2008). "Everyone knew somebody who had been kidnapped," she continued to say.

After a bomb went off close to her home, her parents decided to keep Hidalgo and her younger brother out of harm's way by fleeing to the neighboring nation of Peru; at the time, Hidalgo was just five years old. While the subsequent years saw her receive an education at private schools, where she learned English, she also developed an early interest in politics, realizing Peru was dealing with its own version of political corruption and mishandling at the hands of President Alberto Fujimori.

In 2000, Hidalgo and her family relocated to Mexico. They eventually moved once more, settling in Houston, Texas, where her father had secured a position at an industrial recycling company, in 2005. Fifteen years old at the time, Hidalgo was impressed by the city's grandeur, as it possessed towering oil refineries and an extensive port. When the family settled in a two-story house in Katy, a city west of Houston, she commenced attending Seven Lakes High School, where she excelled in the classroom. When not at school, Hidalgo could be found at the University of St. Thomas in Montrose, working on her college applications and learning about the National Hispanic Institute, an international nonprofit organization that trains future leaders, which she joined as a member.

STANFORD, CALIFORNIA, AND BEYOND

Following her graduation from Seven Lakes High School in 2009, Hidalgo left Texas for California, where she enrolled at Stanford University. Majoring in political science, she learned about failed states and oppressive regimes, and became engrossed in answering the question of why some governments succeed while others fail. While her undergraduate courses helped her lay a solid foundation for her eventual career in the political sphere, her drive to research different types of government led her to Egypt—where she witnessed the 2011 Tahir Square protests in Cairo that ended with the resignation of President Hosni Mubarak—and Beijing, China. "From the whole time I've known Lina, if there's been one motivating factor for her, it's been public service," Valentin Bolotnyy, one of Hidalgo's friends at Stanford, revealed to Paterson.

After crafting an honors thesis entitled "Tiananmen or Tahrir? A Comparative Study of Military Intervention Against Popular Protest," Hidalgo completed her bachelor's degree in 2013, the same year she obtained her US citizenship. Fresh out of college, Hidalgo next traveled to Bangkok, Thailand, where, for the next year, she would work alongside bloggers and artists for Internews Network, a nonprofit organization that trains journalists and advocates for freedom of press.

When she returned to Houston in 2015, she devoted her time and talents to serving the underserved communities of Harris County, the third-largest county in the United States, as a volunteer of the Texas Civil Rights Project. "I hope to learn more about civil rights work domestically and contribute to the current momentum and awareness around key civil rights issues," Hidalgo wrote in her application, as quoted by Ciara O'Rourke for *Politico* (2

Photo via Wikimedia Commons.
[Public domain.]

Sept. 2020). While at the legal nonprofit, she worked to identify the remains of immigrants who had attempted to cross the Mexico–US border but died in the desert. Her impactful work with vulnerable populations did not stop there, however. She also worked at the Texas Medical Center, where she employed her bilingual abilities as a Spanish-English interpreter.

GOING INTO POLITICS

Hidalgo's work with immigrants inspired her to continue her education, which led her to enroll in two master's programs by the fall of 2015: law at New York University and public policy at Harvard University. With no intention of getting involved in politics, Hidalgo envisioned a future as a civil rights lawyer or perhaps public policy researcher—as she profoundly desired to effect change, especially on issues like health care access and criminal justice reform.

Hidalgo's plans were upended, however, when Donald Trump was elected president of the United States in 2016. Having heard Trump make controversial statements about women, immigrants, and people of color, she began to think that, to effect change, she would have to do it from within the political sphere. "I'd worked on criminal justice issues and health care issues in Harris County and seen how broken things were there," she said to O'Rourke. "I have to go do something about this," she recalled thinking at the time.

Hidalgo had initially intended to run for a seat on the Texas House of Representatives, but after putting her studies on pause and moving back to Houston, she announced her bid for county judge of Harris County in the 2018 general elections. The news was initially rejected and even ridiculed, especially because she was a newcomer and would be challenging Emmett, a Republican politician several years her senior who had held the position for a decade. Not one to become deterred by this, she launched her campaign, prioritizing criminal justice reform, flood control funding, and increased transparency and accountability in the local government. With the support of groups like Black Lives Matter and Run for Something—a progressive political organization that recruits young, diverse Democrats to run for political office—Hidalgo was unopposed in the March 2018 Democratic Party primary election and expected to take on Emmett in the November elections.

In this two-person race, Hidalgo was the one who showed the community of Harris County, which is 40 percent Hispanic, that she could relate to them. As an immigrant, she continuously emphasized her desire to give back to the county that welcomed her family by providing families in the community with an equitable life and caring for the most vulnerable members. "There's an earnestness to her," Morales Rocketto, cofounder of Run for Something, told Stephania Taladrid for *The New Yorker* (28 June 2021). "People mistake that for being naïve—and they make that mistake at their own peril."

BECOMING A COUNTY JUDGE

On November 8, 2018, twenty-seven-year-old Hidalgo became the first woman and the first Latina elected as Harris County Commissioners Court Judge after she unexpectedly defeated Emmett by less than 2 percentage points. She was also the first Democrat to win the position in nearly three decades. Regarding the support she received throughout her campaign that led to her victory, she said to Zaveri, "I really hope that folks remember this year as the year in which people saw and stepped up and volunteered for the first time and got involved in campaigns for the first time."

When Hidalgo took office in January 2019, she began to make progress on the promises of health care expansion and immigration and criminal justice reforms. Regarding her pledge to increase transparency and accountability in the Harris County government, she refused to take contributions from county contractors. While her environmentalist outlook allowed her to commence planning on how to address climate change—as a way to minimize its considerable influence on flood risk—her tenure has been characterized by disaster responses.

During the beginning of the coronavirus disease 2019 (COVID-19) pandemic in early 2020, Hidalgo imposed public health orders early on to assuage its spread. Aside from asking the community of Harris County to shut down public venues in March and wear masks in public indoor places in April, she canceled the February 2021 Houston Livestock Show and Rodeo, which usually draws crowds of thousands from throughout the country.

Not everything has been good for Hidalgo, however. In 2019, her leadership came under scrutiny when a massive chemical fire in Deer Park raged for several days, causing school closures and shelter-in-place orders. Hidalgo's detractors heavily criticized the way she briefed the public, emphasizing her lack of experience in public speaking as she spoke in English and Spanish. Regardless of what her critics may say, however, Hidalgo's election also evoked admiration. As Latosha Lewis Payne, one of seventeen Black women voted in as judges in Harris County that year, said to Zaveri, "The effect of having that many African-American women, but also women in general in the judiciary, is amazing. It's one of those things that you dream it, but you don't believe that is actually going to happen."

SUGGESTED READING

Garcia, Samuel. "27-Year-Old Immigrant Lina Hidalgo's Election Marks a Change in Texas Politics." *Forbes*, 6 Dec. 2018, www.forbes.com/sites/samuelgarcia/2018/12/06/27-year-old-immigrant-lina-hidalgos-election-marks-a-change-in-texas-politics. Accessed 10 June 2022.

O'Rourke, Ciara. "The Latina Progressive Who Faced Down Texas Republicans." *Politico*, 2 Sept. 2020, www.politico.com/news/magazine/2020/09/02/latina-progressive-texas-lina-hidalgo-407001. Accessed 10 June 2022.

Paterson, Blake. "She's 28. She's an Immigrant. She's in Charge of Texas' Most Populus County. Get Used to It." *The Texas Observer*, 3 Apr. 2019, www.texasobserver.org/lina-hidalgo-harris-county-judge. Accessed 10 June 2022.

Taladrid, Stephania. "Lina Hidalgo's Political Rise." *The New Yorker*, 28 June 2021, www.newyorker.com/news/us-journal/lina-hidalgos-political-rise. Accessed 10 June 2022.

Zaveri, Mihir. "Lina Hidalgo, a 27-Year-Old Latina Will Lead Harris County, Texas' Biggest." *The New York Times*, 8 Nov. 2018, www.nytimes.com/2018/11/08/us/politics/lina-hidalgo-harris-county.html. Accessed 10 June 2022.

—*Maria del Pilar Guzman*

Jonathan Huberdeau

Born: June 4, 1993
Occupation: Ice hockey player

When then-teenage hockey player Jonathan Huberdeau began playing major junior hockey, no one predicted that he would go on to become one of the highest-ranked prospects of his draft class. "I wasn't even on the list, I think, when I started my 17-year-old season," he later told Jameson Olive in an interview for *FloridaPanthers.com* (10 June 2019). "I didn't think about it all that much. I was just focused on playing." Following a breakout second season with the Saint John Sea Dogs, however, he earned recognition as a promising prospect, and he went on to be selected third overall in the 2011 National Hockey League (NHL) Draft by the Florida Panthers. His first season in Florida confirmed that the Panthers had chosen well, as his performance earned him the Calder Memorial Trophy, awarded to the NHL rookie of the year.

Huberdeau remained a core member of the Panthers' roster throughout the next years, helping improve the franchise's performance and transform the team from one that repeatedly missed the playoffs to a legitimate postseason contender. A second-round defeat in the 2022 playoffs, however, led to a series of shakeups for the Panthers, including a highly publicized trade that sent Huberdeau to the Calgary Flames. Though reportedly displeased with the circumstances of his trade, he expressed optimism about his future career in Calgary. "They're the ones that traded for me. That means they want me," he explained after the trade, as reported by Tracey Myers for *NHL.com* (25 July 2022). "You want to play for a team that wants you, and that's all I want." He signed an eight-year, $84 million contract extension with the Flames the following month.

EARLY LIFE AND CAREER

Jonathan Huberdeau was born on June 4, 1993, in Laval, Québec, Canada. One of three children born to Alain Huberdeau and Josée Blondin, he spent much of his childhood in Saint-Jérôme, Québec, but also spent time in Florida, when his family regularly vacationed in the United States. His older brother, Sébastien, played hockey as a child and went on to play professionally in France, while his younger sister, Josiane, would later perform the national anthem at some of Huberdeau's hockey games.

Throughout his childhood, Huberdeau was a multisport athlete who not only played hockey but also competed in sports such as basketball. "I'm the type of guy who enjoys variety and it's always good to learn and play other sports," he later told Dave Stubbs for *NHL.com* (28 Mar. 2022). "They give you other tools, and things you learn in other sports can help you in hockey. A lot of kids play hockey all the time, but for me, playing other sports taught me many things." Eventually, though, he began to focus primarily on hockey, playing for teams such as the Saint-Eustache Vikings.

JUNIOR HOCKEY AND NHL DRAFT

In 2009, Huberdeau was selected eighteenth overall in the Québec Major Junior Hockey League (QMJHL) Draft by the New Brunswick–based Saint John Sea Dogs. Leaving home to live in Saint John, he attended St. Malachy's Memorial High School and began playing with the Sea Dogs during the 2009–10 Canadian Hockey League (CHL) season. Although he received little attention from scouts and professional teams during his first season in Saint John, he gained far more notice during his second season of junior hockey, throughout which he amassed a total of 105 points in sixty-seven games. He went on to lead the team to

Photo by Hugh Lee
from Edmonton Alberta, Canada,
via Wikimedia Commons

the QMJHL championship, leaving with the Guy Lafleur Trophy for most valuable player (MVP), and subsequently with the Memorial Cup, in which the Sea Dogs defeated the winners of the CHL's other major junior regional leagues to claim the championship. Huberdeau was again recognized as MVP for his contributions during the Memorial Cup tournament, receiving the Stafford Smythe Trophy after its conclusion.

In June 2011, the Florida Panthers selected Huberdeau as the third overall pick in that year's NHL Draft. "When I heard my name, that was one of the best moments in my life," he recalled to George Richards for *The Athletic* (7 June 2019) about his draft day. "I kind of knew I would go third, but I'm just glad I didn't have to wait too long because my parents were so nervous. I was really happy. I had a good feeling I was going to end up with the Panthers. It was probably 70–30. I was a little nervous because you never know. They could have gone with another guy." He played for the Panthers in the 2011 preseason and subsequently returned to the Sea Dogs, ultimately going on to win a second QMJHL championship. He also joined the Canadian under-twenty men's team for the International Ice Hockey Federation (IIHF) World Junior Championships, winning a bronze medal in that competition.

FLORIDA PANTHERS

Huberdeau began the 2012–13 hockey season with the Sea Dogs, serving as the team's captain, but was called up to the Panthers in January 2013, following the conclusion of a labor dispute that had delayed the start of the NHL season. He remained with the Panthers for the rest of the season, during which he worked to establish himself as a valuable member of the roster. "When you're coming in, you're just focusing on yourself and wanting to prove you can play in the NHL," he told Olive. "That's what I did. You don't want to be selfish, but you want to get there and work on yourself and prove to the team that you can play." He played in forty-eight games over the course of his debut NHL season, scoring fourteen goals and seventeen assists for a total of thirty-one points. His strong performance earned him the 2012–13 Calder Memorial Trophy, awarded to the league's rookie of the year.

The next several seasons were challenging ones for the Panthers, who qualified for the playoffs only once between the 2013–14 and 2018–19 seasons. "You'd like to win right away but there are some things you don't control," Huberdeau told Stubbs about such difficult periods. "We've had some adversity through the years but we've learned along the way. We're lucky that we have the same core group. Many of us have been through this forever. You take your team to heart and you want to win for this organization." He signed a two-year extension with the Panthers in September 2015 and the following year signed a six-year extension that would keep him under contract through the end of the 2022–23 season. While the Panthers repeatedly struggled to qualify for the playoffs, Huberdeau and his teammates were successful in doing so in 2016, having ended the season with the best record in the Atlantic Division. However, the Panthers lost to the New York Islanders in the first round of the 2016 Stanley Cup Playoffs.

PLAYOFF CONTENDERS

Huberdeau was well aware of the Panthers' struggles during his first several years with the team; however, he remained confident that he and his teammates were capable not only of qualifying for the playoffs on a regular basis but also of winning the Stanley Cup. "We have the group to win. It is coming. You never know what a team is going to do, but hopefully I get to stay and continue to be part of it," he told Richards. "It just feels like next year is really going to be something." Indeed, he put forth a strong performance during the 2019–20 season and, in January 2020, scored his 420th total point with the Panthers, becoming the highest-scoring Panthers player to date. He was also selected to appear in the 2020 All-Star Game.

The 2019–20 NHL season ended in March 2020 due to the emerging COVID-19 pandemic, and teams did not return to play until August, when they reconvened to compete in what came to be called the "bubble" playoffs. The Panthers were selected to compete in the qualifying round of the unusual playoff tournament, but the team was once again eliminated by the Islanders. Following another strong season for Huberdeau, who scored his first NHL hat trick during that period, the Panthers again clinched a spot in the playoffs in 2021 but fell in the first round to the Tampa Bay Lightning, the eventual champions.

2021–22 SEASON

Over the course of the 2021–22 season, Huberdeau accumulated a total of 115 points in eighty games and led the league in assists with eighty-five, earning his second All-Star Game selection. He reached a particularly important milestone on April 5, 2022, in a game against the Toronto Maple Leafs. He recorded three assists and two goals during the game, including the overtime game winner, to help the Panthers claim a comeback victory over the Leafs. In doing so, he reached a total of 102 points, becoming the first Panthers player ever to accumulate 100 or more points in a single season. "It is incredible. The atmosphere was awesome," he told reporters afterward, as reported by *ESPN* (5 Apr. 2022). "We've got to stop getting down by four goals, but just with the character of the team, we came back again tonight. A good win."

By the end of the season, the Panthers had recorded fifty-eight wins, eighteen losses, and six overtime losses, the best record in the NHL. That achievement won the team the Presidents' Trophy, and the Panthers qualified for the playoffs for the third year in a row. Facing the Washington Capitals in the first round of competition, the Panthers beat their opponents in a six-game series and advanced to the second round for the first time in Huberdeau's tenure with the team. However,

the Panthers were unable to win a single game against their second-round opponents, the Lightning, and were ultimately eliminated in a four-game sweep.

TRADE TO CALGARY

Following the 2022 playoffs, Huberdeau had one season left on his contract with the Panthers, and he spent the early weeks of the off-season hoping to sign another contract extension with his longtime team. Panthers leadership, however, opted to make several staffing and player changes following the team's elimination from the playoffs, and on July 22, 2022, traded Huberdeau, fellow players MacKenzie Weegar and Cole Schwindt, and a 2025 first-round draft pick to the Calgary Flames in exchange for forward Matthew Tkachuk and a 2025 fourth-round draft pick. Huberdeau was unsure of his next steps following the trade, as he did not know whether the Flames planned to keep him on the roster past the sole season remaining on his contract. "I'm open to staying with the Flames, but at the end of the day, it's not my decision," he said following the trade, as reported by Myers.

Huberdeau's uncertainty did not last long. On August 4, the Flames announced that they had signed the forward to an eight-year, $84 million contract extension that would go into effect following the 2022–23 season. "I'm thrilled to be part of the Calgary Flames organization long-term," he said in a statement released following his signing, as reported by *ESPN* (4 Aug. 2022). "I'm excited for this new chapter and I am committed to this team. I'll give everything I have, on and off the ice and I can't wait to play in front of the passionate Flames fans."

PERSONAL LIFE

In addition to playing ice hockey professionally, Huberdeau long enjoyed playing the off-ice sport of ball hockey and often expressed his approval of leagues and other organizations that sought to increase participation in that sport. "It's good, they're growing the game in Québec, and I just feel a lot more younger people should play that game," he told Jackie Spiegel in an interview for *NHL.com* (26 June 2022). "I think it's more accessible, too. There's less equipment, and then most people can run." Alongside promoting ball hockey in interviews, he served as a brand ambassador for the company Knapper, which manufactured equipment for the sport.

SUGGESTED READING

"Calgary Flames Sign Jonathan Huberdeau to 8-Year, $84 Million Extension." *ESPN*, 4 Aug. 2022, www.espn.com/nhl/story/_/id/34349352/calgary-flames-jonathan-huberdeau-putting-final-touches-8-year-84-million-extension. Accessed 8 Aug. 2022.

Huberdeau, Jonathan. "Huberdeau Talks New Panthers Coach Maurice, Career Season with NHL.com." Interview by Jackie Spiegel. *NHL*, 26 June 2022, www.nhl.com/news/sitting-down-with-florida-panthers-jonathan-huberdeau/c-334735096. Accessed 8 Aug. 2022.

___. "My Draft Day: Jonathan Huberdeau." Interview by Jameson Olive. *FloridaPanthers. com*, *NHL*, 10 June 2019, www.nhl.com/panthers/news/my-draft-day-jonathan-huberdeau/c-307791826. Accessed 8 Aug. 2022.

"Jonathan Huberdeau Becomes First Player in Franchise History to Top 100 Points during 'Incredible' Comeback Win by Florida Panthers." *ESPN*, 5 Apr. 2022, www.espn.com/nhl/story/_/id/33680185/jonathan-huberdeau-becomes-first-player-franchise-history-top-100-points-incredible-comeback-win-florida-panthers. Accessed 8 Aug. 2022.

Myers, Tracey. "Huberdeau 'Open' to Signing Long-Term Contract with Flames." *NHL*, 25 July 2022, www.nhl.com/news/flames-huberdeau-open-long-term-contract/c-335088508. Accessed 8 Aug. 2022.

Richards, George. "NHL Draft Memories: Jonathan Huberdeau Hoped to Go to Panthers, Wants to Stay with Them Now." *The Athletic*, 7 June 2019, theathletic.com/1010768/2019/06/07/nhl-draft-memories-jonathan-huberdeau-hoped-to-go-to-panthers-wants-to-stay-with-them-now/. Accessed 8 Aug. 2022.

Stubbs, Dave. "'Savour Every Moment': Huberdeau Reflects on First NHL Goal with Panthers." *NHL*, 28 Mar. 2022, www.nhl.com/news/panthers-jonathan-huberdeau-savour-every-moment/c-332322634. Accessed 8 Aug. 2022.

—*Joy Crelin*

Moses Ingram

Born: February 6, 1994
Occupation: Actor

For actor Moses Ingram, a key moment in her development as a performer came during high school, when she attended a production of the play *A Raisin in the Sun* and was deeply affected by the performance of one of the lead actors. "I believed everything she did," she told Dara McBride for the *Chautauquan Daily* (21 July 2017). "And I was like, 'Oh my gosh, she's not even acting.' I think I was like sixteen. I was like, 'Yeah, if I can do it like that, then that's what I want to do.'" Inspired by that actor's example, as well as by teachers who encouraged her to act throughout her early life, she went on to attend the Yale School of Drama, where she honed her skills and made a name for herself as a promising up-and-coming actor.

Ingram's professional breakthrough came in 2020, with the premiere of the Netflix miniseries *The Queen's Gambit*. Portraying the supporting character of Jolene in that series, she earned critical acclaim for her performance as well as a nomination for the Emmy Award for Outstanding Supporting Actress in a Limited or Anthology Series or Movie. She gained further notice in 2022, when she appeared in the Disney+ *Star Wars* miniseries *Obi-Wan Kenobi* in the role of Reva, also known as Third Sister, a villain with a complex agenda. "I remember reading about my character before we started and thinking, 'Wow, she is just so bad,'" she told fellow actor Regina Hall about the role in an interview for *Interview* magazine (2 June 2022). "Everything I've done before, I'm really grateful for, but it's only been a few scenes here and there. This is the first time that people will really see me do anything." Her work on *Obi-Wan Kenobi* garnered her further attention from both within and outside of the film and television industries, and she went on to impress additional producers like Apple TV+ and be cast in further projects.

EARLY LIFE AND EDUCATION

Ingram was born Monique Denise Ingram in Baltimore, Maryland, on February 6, 1994. Part of a large family that included her two sisters and two brothers, she began acting at an early age, with the encouragement of her family and teachers. "My teacher thought it would help with my behavior," she told Andria Moore for the website of the Motion Picture Association (30 Nov. 2020). "I was very blessed to have teachers who saw me early on. I had a teacher who would send me on errands around the school to get whatever and she would tell me what accent to do." Ingram participated in theater programs throughout her childhood and, as a teenager, attended the Baltimore School for the Arts, a public school devoted to both the visual arts and the performing arts.

Having assessed her options and considered her financial means, after graduating from high school in 2012, Ingram enrolled at Baltimore City Community College. Although that institution did not have a theater program, she founded a theater club at the college and honed her skills by appearing in local productions. She also remained active in theater after completing her associate degree, an achievement that had required her to earn money by juggling jobs in everything from overnight Amazon package processing and ushering at the city's symphony to teaching at the Boys and Girls Club. In 2015, not only did she earn an award for her work from the Washington, DC, chapter of the National Society of Arts and Letters, but her subsequent participation in the competition at the national level had led her to meet and receive career-shaping advice from a fellow aspiring actor and Yale School of Drama student.

YALE SCHOOL OF DRAMA

In 2016, with her confidence at succeeding boosted by her encounter at the competition, Ingram auditioned for the Yale School of Drama and was admitted into that prestigious institution, where she studied acting for the next three years. It was at Yale that she began using the first name Moses rather than her given first name, Monique. "They wanted us to register our names because this is the first time they would be publicized so people can see them," she told Moore. "And before I got to Yale I had, had such a time just trying to make things work that my name just didn't feel suited. So I prayed and asked God, 'What is it? I know it's not my name now, but it is something.' And a few days later, I just heard Moses in my head and that was it."

While at Yale, Ingram performed in multiple school productions, including stagings of the Shakespeare plays *Romeo and Juliet* and

Twelfth Night, as well as in Yale Cabaret productions. In 2018, she performed in the new work *Marty and the Hands That Could* as part of Yale's Carlotta Festival of New Plays. Also spending time performing elsewhere, in the summer of 2017 she participated in the summer conservatory program operated by the Chautauqua Theater Company, based in western New York. "I thought it would make me sharper," she told McBride during that summer. "It is keeping me on my toes every day." With the Chautauqua Theater Company, she performed in shows such as *Detroit '67* and *Building the Wall*. She was awarded the Princess Grace Award in theater in 2018.

Though primarily known for her stage performances during her years at Yale, Ingram also delved into screen acting during that time, appearing in the short film *Candace* (2018). The short went on to win the award for Best Short Film in the LGBTQ Showcase at the 2018 Cannes Film Festival's American Pavilion Emerging Filmmakers Showcase. She completed her studies at Yale the following year, earning a certificate in drama.

THE QUEEN'S GAMBIT

In short order, Ingram made her television debut in October 2020 in the Netflix miniseries *The Queen's Gambit*, based on a 1983 novel by Walter Tevis. A period piece set in the 1950s and 1960s, the series follows a young woman named Beth (Anya Taylor-Joy) who, following a stint in an orphanage, becomes an accomplished competitive chess player. Ingram portrayed the character Jolene, a friend Beth meets at the orphanage. "I think it's important to the story that we acknowledge that Jolene is not just some other girl in the orphanage," she told Ashley Ray-Harris in an interview for *Elle* (31 Dec. 2020) about the character. "She is very much a Black girl in this all-white orphanage, and that's definitely something I thought about going into it. That's what attracted me to Jolene. I didn't even have a script. I read the sides and said, 'Oh, this is a bad b———.'" As the story of *The Queen's Gambit* takes place over several years, Ingram played Jolene both as a young teenager and as an adult, and her performance made the character a fan favorite among many of the miniseries' viewers. Praised by both critics and those involved in making the series, she went on to be nominated for the Emmy for Outstanding Supporting Actress in a Limited or Anthology Series or Movie for her work on *The Queen's Gambit*, which drew in a particularly high number of viewers and ultimately won the Emmy for Outstanding Limited or Anthology Series.

Following the release of *The Queen's Gambit*, Ingram appeared in film projects such as the independent drama *The Same Storm*, which premiered at the Telluride Film Festival in September 2021. That month also saw the New York Film Festival premiere of *The Tragedy of Macbeth*, a Shakespeare adaptation directed by Joel Coen and featuring Denzel Washington in the title role and Ingram in the supporting role of Lady Macduff. "It really was an experience that when I look back on it it feels like something that I made up because it just sort of fell together in a way that was that organic," she told Moore about the project. She also played a supporting role in the action-crime film *Ambulance*, released in theaters in early 2022.

BECOMING THIRD SISTER

Although Ingram had found nearly immediate success in television and film after graduating from Yale, thanks to projects such as *The Queen's Gambit*, an even larger and higher-profile project was yet to come. "I thought to myself, 'Well, it can't get any bigger than this, can it?'" she told William Goodman in an interview for *Complex* (27 May 2022). "Then *Star Wars* comes and drops the mic and is like, 'Yeah, it can get bigger. This is the biggest that it gets.'" In March 2021, it was announced that she had been cast in the Disney+ miniseries *Obi-Wan Kenobi*, a television tie-in to the blockbuster *Star Wars* franchise—despite her general unfamiliarity with the *Star Wars* world. The series premiered on Disney+ in May of the following year.

Set a decade after the events of *Star Wars: Episode III—Revenge of the Sith* (2005), *Obi-Wan Kenobi* follows the titular Jedi in hiding (played by Ewan McGregor) as he works to retrieve a missing child, all the while pursued by the evil Empire and its lethal force of Inquisitors. Ingram portrayed Inquisitor Reva, also known as Third Sister, an apparent villain with a complex background and an agenda that does not completely align with that of the Empire. "I think a lot of times we get a villain who knows they're a villain," she told Olly Richards in an interview for *NME* (9 June

2022) about the character. "What's cool about her is that she doesn't think she's bad. She's just good at her job and she does it to the best of her ability. I think *that* is heart. . . . In her mind, she's the righteous one." While Ingram was subjected to racist backlash from a small subset of *Star Wars* fans following the show's premiere—a recurring issue for the franchise—her fellow cast members widely supported her, and critics generally praised her nuanced performance as Reva.

With her strengthened profile bringing her into consideration for even more opportunities, in June 2022, it was announced that Ingram had been cast to take over for Lupita Nyong'o in the Apple TV+ miniseries *Lady in the Lake*, adapted from a 2019 novel by Laura Lippman. Set in Baltimore, filming in the area had begun by April. By August, she was also revealed to have been cast in a recurring role in another Apple TV+ miniseries set to dramatize an eventful period in the life of Black Panther Party leader Huey P. Newton.

SUGGESTED READING

Alexander, Keith L. "'Queen's Gambit' Actor Moses Ingram's Unrelenting Journey from West Baltimore to Hollywood." *The Washington Post*, 25 Feb. 2021, www. washingtonpost.com/dc-md-va/2021/02/25/moses-ingram-baltimore-queens-gambit/. Accessed 11 Aug. 2022.

Ingram, Moses. "Inside Moses Ingram's Force Field." Interview by Regina Hall. *Interview*, 2 June 2022, www.interviewmagazine. com/film/inside-moses-ingrams-force-field. Accessed 8 Aug. 2022.

___. "Moses Ingram Has the Answers to Your *The Queen's Gambit* Questions." Interview by Ashley Ray-Harris. *Elle*, 31 Dec. 2020, www.elle.com/culture/movies-tv/a35099561/moses-ingram-queens-gambit-interview/. Accessed 8 Aug. 2022.

___. "Moses Ingram Shares How It Feels to Be the 'Vessel' That Brings Reva to Life in *Obi-Wan Kenobi*." Interview by William Goodman. *Complex*, 27 May 2022, www. complex.com/pop-culture/moses-ingram-obi-wan-kenobi-interview/. Accessed 8 Aug. 2022.

___. "*Obi-Wan Kenobi* Star Moses Ingram: 'Being in Star Wars Feels Too Big to Fathom.'" Interview by Olly Richards. *NME*, 9 June 2022, www.nme.com/features/tv-interviews/moses-ingram-star-wars-obi-wan-kenobi-interview-3242576. Accessed 8 Aug. 2022.

McBride, Dara. "Moses Ingram from CTC's 'Detroit '67' Talks about Community Engagement." *The Chautauquan Daily*, 21 July 2017, chqdaily.com/2017/07/moses-ingram-ctcs-detroit-67-talks-community-engagement/. Accessed 8 Aug. 2022.

Moore, Andria. "Moses Ingram on Her Debut Role as Jolene in *The Queen's Gambit*." *Motion Picture Association*, 30 Nov. 2020, www.motionpictures.org/2020/11/moses-ingram-on-her-debut-role-as-jolene-in-the-queens-gambit/. Accessed 8 Aug. 2022.

SELECTED WORKS

The Queen's Gambit, 2020; *The Tragedy of Macbeth*, 2021; *Ambulance*, 2022; *Obi-Wan Kenobi*, 2022

—Joy Crelin

Ketanji Brown Jackson

Born: September 14, 1970
Occupation: Supreme Court justice

From an early age, Ketanji Brown Jackson knew she wanted to be a judge. It was a goal she first announced to the world in her high school senior yearbook, when she wrote the simple yet prophetic words, "I want to go into law and eventually have a judicial appointment." Her peers at the time also recognized her potential, lauding her as the most likely to succeed of her graduating class of 1988. In the years that followed, Jackson worked tirelessly toward her judicial aspirations, excelling as an undergraduate and law student at Harvard University and building a diverse range of experience as an attorney, notably working as a public defender and serving on the US Sentencing Commission. Her dream then came true when President Barack Obama appointed her a district court judge, and she was confirmed to the post in 2013.

Jackson's rise did not stop there. In 2021, she was elevated to the District of Columbia Circuit Court of Appeals after being appointed by President Joe Biden. Then, in February 2022, Biden nominated her to succeed the retiring Justice Stephen Breyer on the US Supreme Court. Though Jackson faced some controversial opposition from Republicans, she was ultimately confirmed by the Senate in a history-making vote that April. In a speech following her confirmation she addressed the groundbreaking nature of the achievement: "It has taken 232 years and 115 prior appointments for a Black woman to be selected to serve on the Supreme Court of the United States. But we've made it. We've made it, all of us," she said, as transcribed by *CNN* (8 Apr. 2022) "And our children are telling me that they see now, more than ever, that here in America, anything is possible."

EARLY LIFE

Ketanji Brown Jackson was born Ketanji Onyika Brown on September 14, 1970, in Washington, DC. She was the first of two children of Johnny and Ellery Brown, who worked as public school educators. Both Jackson's parents had grown up amid the racial discrimination of the Jim Crow era and attended segregated schools as children. However, they had a deep sense of optimism about their young daughter's future in the wake of civil rights movement. "My parents taught me that, unlike the many barriers that they had had to face growing up, my path was clearer, such that if I worked hard and believed in myself, in America I could do anything or be anything I wanted to be," Jackson recalled in her opening remarks at her Supreme Court confirmation hearing, as quoted by Ed Pilkington for the *Guardian* (7 Apr. 2022).

When she was three years old, Jackson's family moved to Miami, Florida, so that her father could attend law school. This proved to be an influential decision for the young Jackson, as watching her father study became a fond early memory and laid the groundwork for her own interest in law. Eventually her father would become the chief attorney for the Miami-Dade County School Board. Her mother worked as a school principal, and Jackson was inspired by her dedication as the family's sole income earner for several years.

As a teenager Jackson attended Miami Palmetto Senior High School, where she not only excelled as a student but also became a leader among her peers. One of the most formative experiences of Jackson's early life was competing on the school's speech and debate team, which she first got involved with in junior high. Under the tutelage of deeply devoted coach Fran Berger, the Palmetto team earned

Photo by Rose Lincoln/Harvard University,
via Wikimedia Commons.

a reputation as one of the best in the country, and many alumni would go on to notable legal careers. Jackson, who won a national championship in the oratory category, would later attribute her time on the team to the self-confidence, sharp reasoning, and writing skills that helped her succeed as an attorney.

One of the debate team's many trips included an event at Harvard, and Jackson soon aspired to attend the prestigious Ivy League university. Yet despite her sparkling academic and extracurricular record, her guidance counselor suggested she aim lower. Jackson would later note how this was just one example of the systemic obstacles she often faced, especially as she was often the only person of color in her social circles. Still, she did not let such challenges slow her down. "I cannot recall a single time in my childhood in which I cared about the slights and misperceptions and underestimations that came my way," she said in a 2019 speech at the University of Chicago, as quoted by Erica L. Green for *The New York Times* (20 Mar. 2022). "What I do remember is often thinking, 'Hmm. Well, I'll show them.'" She applied to Harvard anyway and was accepted.

HIGHER EDUCATION

Initially Jackson did find her time at Harvard to be alienating. "I was really questioning: Do

I belong here? Can I, can I make it in this environment?" she recalled in her Supreme Court confirmation hearing, as quoted by Libby Cathey for *ABC News* (7 Apr. 2022). But a chance encounter helped restore her trademark self-confidence. "A Black woman I did not know was passing me on the sidewalk. And she looked at me. And I guess she knew how I was feeling. And she leaned over as we crossed and said, 'persevere.'"

Soon Jackson found her groove as a government major, and she quickly developed a reputation as a sharp thinker always able to see the big picture. When a White student hung a Confederate flag in their dorm window, for example, she helped lead the Black Students Association's response by ensuring that they did not allow their vigorous protesting to interfere with their studies. Her logic was that if Black students' grades suffered, it would only give fuel to racist arguments that they did not belong at Harvard. Jackson's levelheaded approach won her respect from many of her classmates.

In 1992, Jackson finished her senior honors thesis "The Hand of Oppression: Plea Bargaining Processes and the Coercion of Criminal Defendants." In it, she argued that there was too much incentive for defendants to take plea bargains to get lesser sentences. As such, some innocent people would agree to go to prison for crimes they did not commit, because if their case went to trial they might receive more severe punishment. The piece reflected Jackson's developing interest in criminal law, which would become an important focus of her career. She graduated with her bachelor's degree magna cum laude.

Jackson briefly worked for *TIME* magazine as a researcher and staff reporter. In 1993 she enrolled in Harvard Law School, where she won the coveted position of editor of the *Harvard Law Review*. She earned her Juris Doctor (JD) in 1996, graduating cum laude.

EARLY CAREER AS A LAWYER

After finishing law school Jackson clerked for a number of important judges, including Judge Patti B. Saris of the US District Court for the District of Massachusetts, Bruce M. Selya of the United States Court of Appeals for the First Circuit in Rhode Island, and Supreme Court Justice Stephen Breyer. In 2000, she entered private practice as an associate with the law firm Goodwin Proctor in Boston, Massachusetts. In 2002, she moved to the Feinberg Group in Washington, DC.

From 2003 to 2005 Jackson worked as an assistant special counsel to the US Sentencing Commission, an agency that oversees sentencing by federal courts. Her time there piqued her interest in public defense. Wanting to learn more about how the criminal justice system actually worked, she spent two years as an assistant federal public defender, handling cases before the US Court of Appeals for the DC Circuit. Although her role consisted mostly of researching and writing, she also won a number of victories against government prosecutors that either shortened or erased defendants' prison sentences. During this time, she also worked on the cases of several Guantanamo Bay detainees who were being held without formal charges. In 2007, she returned to private practice with the DC–based firm Morrison and Foerster.

In 2009, Jackson was nominated by President Obama for vice chair of the US Sentencing Commission and was unanimously confirmed by the Senate. As a commissioner she focused on sentencing disparities, and in particular supported amendments to reduce sentences for nonviolent drug offenses. For example, during this time the commission made sentencing guidelines for crack cocaine offenses more lenient.

EARLY JUDICIAL CAREER AND SUPREME COURT NOMINATION

In 2012, President Obama nominated Jackson to the federal judiciary on the US District Court for the District of Columbia. She was confirmed early the following year by the Senate with bipartisan support. During her career as a US District Court judge Jackson developed a reputation for being extremely thorough and writing long opinions on contentious cases. In 2019, for example, she wrote a 118-page ruling denying President Donald Trump's counsel Donald McGahn immunity from testifying in Trump's impeachment trial. The opinion earned significant attention for her statement that "presidents are not kings."

Jackson's growing profile as an experienced and respected judge brought her consideration for even more prominent positions. In 2021, President Joe Biden nominated her for the DC Circuit Court of Appeals. Although her appointment was opposed by many Republicans, she received Senate approval in a 53–44 vote. On the appeals court she again drew attention for ruling against executive privilege claims by the Trump administration. Then, after less than a year in that role, Jackson was nominated by President Biden for the Supreme Court in February 2022, after her former mentor Justice Breyer announced that he was retiring.

The Senate judiciary committee began confirmation hearings on March 21, 2022. Continuing the trend of contentious Supreme Court nominations in an age of deep political polarization, Jackson's confirmation hearing earned much media attention. Jackson's credentials were heavily scrutinized by Republican senators and pundits. Although many liberals celebrated her experience as a public defender, some conservatives claimed it was a liability and tried to argue that she was "soft on crime" by misrepresenting her past work, including her time defending Guantanamo Bay detainees. In response, she explained how the US Constitution guarantees everyone the right to legal representation—even war criminals—and that public defenders do not choose their clients. Her supporters pointed out her deep qualifications, including compared to other recent Supreme Court appointees. Polls also showed strong public support for her nomination.

The Senate Judiciary Committee split in an 11–11 vote on Jackson's nomination. After the matter was advanced to the full Senate, she earned three Republican votes along with unanimous Democratic support in a 53–47 vote on April 7, 2022. This made her the first Black woman in history to be confirmed to the nation's highest court. "In my family, it took just one generation to go from segregation to the Supreme Court of the United States," she noted in her speech after the confirmation. She also reiterated her commitment to serving the American people: "It is an honor—the honor of a lifetime—for me to have this chance to join the Court, to promote the rule of law at the highest level, and to do my part to carry our shared project of democracy and equal justice under law forward, into the future."

PERSONAL LIFE

Jackson married Patrick Jackson, a surgeon, whom she met as a fellow Harvard undergraduate. The couple has two daughters, Leila and Talia. A Protestant Christian, Jackson's faith was seen as notable given the fact that most of the other Supreme Court justices at the time of her appointment were Catholic.

SUGGESTED READING

Cathey, Libby. "Senate Confirms Judge Ketanji Brown Jackson to Supreme Court in Historic Vote." *ABC News*, 7 Apr. 2022, abcnews.go.com/Politics/senate-confirms-judge-ketanji-brown-jackson-supreme-court/story?id=83920099. Accessed 12 May 2022.

Green, Erica L. "At Harvard, a Confederate Flag Spurred Ketanji Brown Jackson to Act." *The New York Times*, 20 Mar. 2022, www.nytimes.com/2022/03/20/us/politics/ketanji-brown-jackson-harvard.html. Accessed 12 May 2022.

Jackson, Ketanji Brown. "United States Senate Committee on the Judiciary: Questionnaire for Judicial Nominees." *Senate Committee on the Judiciary*, www.judiciary.senate.gov/imo/media/doc/Jackson%20Senate%20Questionnaire%20Public%20Final.pdf. Accessed 5 May 2022.

McDaniel, Eric. "Jackson Notes the Progress She Represents in Her Journey to the Supreme Court." *NPR*, 8 Apr. 2022, www.npr.org/2022/04/08/1091459152/biden-harris-jackson-senate-historic-confirmation-vote. Accessed 5 May 2022.

Pilkington, Ed. "Ketanji Brown Jackson's Blazing Trail to Become the First Black Female Justice." *The Guardian*, 7 Apr. 2022, www.theguardian.com/law/2022/apr/07/ketanji-brown-jackson-us-supreme-court-profile. Accessed 12 May 2022.

"Read: Ketanji Brown Jackson's Remarks at the White House after Her Supreme Court Confirmation." *CNN*, 8 Apr. 2022, www.cnn.com/2022/04/08/politics/ketanji-brown-jackson-confirmation-speech/index.html. Accessed 5 Mar. 2022.

"The Senate Confirms Ketanji Brown Jackson." *The White House*, United States, 7 Apr. 2022, www.whitehouse.gov/kbj/. Accessed 5 May 2022.

—*Emily E. Turner*

Ashish Jha

Born: September 29, 1970
Occupation: Physician and public health expert

In March 2020, during the early stages of the coronavirus disease 2019 (COVID-19) outbreak, public health expert Ashish Jha garnered recognition for his criticism of the US federal government's delayed response to the pandemic. At the height of the pandemic, Jha quickly became a trusted voice for the American people on preparedness and response, with his background as an Ivy League physician, health policy researcher, and expert in disease research. Jha was tasked with an even bigger role in March 2022, when President Biden tapped him to serve as the administration's national COVID-19 response coordinator.

EARLY LIFE AND EDUCATION

Ashish Kumar Jha was born on September 29, 1970, in Pursaulia, a village located in the eastern Indian state of Bihar. In 1979, Jha immigrated, with his parents and older brother, to Canada, where his father had been accepted into a graduate teaching program at the University of Toronto. He first learned to speak English while attending an intensive summer class that taught English as a second language (ESL). In 1983, after four years in Canada, he moved with his family to the United States and settled in Morris County, New Jersey.

The following year, Jha attended Boonton High School, where he served as editor in chief of the student newspaper. Despite excelling in math and science, he briefly considered a career in journalism before giving in to familial pressure and deciding to become a medical doctor. After earning his high-school diploma in 1988, Jha, the valedictorian of his graduating class, gained admission to Columbia University in New York City, where he majored in economics while pursuing pre-medical studies. His passion for medicine grew considerably after spending summers in India visiting his uncle, a doctor who often made house calls in the village, usually for free or in exchange for rice or other food.

ATTENDING HARVARD AND JOINING ITS RANKS

Upon graduating magna cum laude in 1992 with a Bachelor of Arts degree, Jha was accepted into the five-year medical degree program at Harvard Medical School (HMS) in Boston, Massachusetts. After obtaining his MD in 1997, he was successfully matched into the internal medicine residency program at the University of California, San Francisco (UCSF). He followed up his first year of residency (1997–98), with a two-year stint (1998–2000) as a resident physician. In his final year (2000–01), he not only served as chief resident at UCSF but also as a staff physician (2000–02) at the San Francisco VA Medical Center. He subsequently returned to Boston, where he spent the next two years (2002–04) pursuing a master's degree at the Harvard T. H. Chan School of Public Health (HSPH) while also conducting postdoctoral research in general internal medicine at HMS, as well as Brigham and Women's Hospital.

In 2004, after receiving his MPH, Jha joined Harvard's faculty as an assistant professor of health policy and was named staff physician at the Boston VA Medical Center. A year later, he was also appointed assistant professor of medicine at HMS. During that period, his published research focused on the quality of care for Medicare patients in the nation's hospitals and disparities according to hospital type, geographic region, and clinical condition. From 2003 to 2005 he explored racial disparities in the use of high-cost surgical procedures among Medicare enrollees for a Robert Wood Johnson Foundation report. He spent the latter part of the decade (2005–08) evaluating the hospital quality and cost of care for minority populations, the benefits and barriers of electronic health records (EHRs) among physicians serving minority populations, the status of EHR systems in the United States, and EHR adoption and use across seven developed nations.

MAINTAINING FOCUS ON QUALITY OF CARE

In 2009, Jha was promoted from assistant to associate professor at Harvard's Medical School and School of Public Health. He was also appointed as special assistant to the secretary of the Department of Veterans Affairs in Washington, DC, after two years as special assistant to the undersecretary (2007–09). Jha's focus remained on improving patient safety. In a 2010 report, he and his coauthor, Arnold Epstein, assessed the level of quality management provided by one thousand US

Photo via Wikimedia Commons
[Public domain]

hospital board chairs and concluded most of those surveyed lacked familiarity and engagement with quality-of-care issues. A subsequent 2013 survey of 132 English hospital board chairs he and Epstein conducted found that English board chairs displayed more expertise and attention to quality of care when compared to their US counterparts.

Following the passage of the Health Information Technology for Economic and Clinical Health (HITECH) Act as part of the American Recovery and Reinvestment Act of 2009, Jha pushed for the creation of measurement programs allowing policymakers to track national progress on EHR adoption in US hospitals. His 2011 study addressed quality of care for older Medicare patients, concluding that most end-of-life surgeries performed on older patients may be ineffective and unnecessary. He later suggested focusing on end-of-life care, rather than end-of-life spending. To improve health care, he examined incentives such as Medicare's use of nonpayment for preventable complications, public reporting of medical harms, and pay-for-performance. He determined that Medicare's incentives yielded modest changes but failed to motivate hospitals to overhaul their health-care delivery methods. To appeal to a wider audience and interpret health-care policy, he founded the blog *An Ounce of Evidence* in 2012.

The following summer, Jha, who had been recently appointed as professor of health policy and management at Harvard, was confronted with his own patient safety issues, after dislocating his left shoulder in a rollerblading accident. He reported that the emergency room staff placed more focus and value on obtaining his insurance information than on providing treatment for his painful injury. His August 2013 blog post came four months after his published piece recalling his father's 2010 hospitalization from a suspected stroke, later diagnosed as transient ischemic attack (TIA). During his father's three-day stay, Jha observed several medical errors made by the staff, including administering the wrong medication, ordering the wrong type of MRI, and failing to provide his father with the right prescriptions upon his discharge from the hospital.

GAINING WIDER RECOGNITION

Jha continued to rise through Harvard's ranks. In 2014, he was promoted to professor of medicine at HMS, along with being named K. T. Li Professor of Global Health at HSPH. That July he was among the experts lobbying for better patient safety metrics at a Senate hearing on preventable medical errors. As the newly minted faculty director of the Harvard Global Health Institute (HGHI), he was tapped to cochair an independent panel of international experts that evaluated the global response to the Ebola virus outbreak (2015–16) and left a lasting impression. "He comes across as a caring, smart, listening person who also knows how to speak across political divides in language that's intelligible," fellow panel member J. Stephen Morrison told Sheryl Gay Stolberg for *The New York Times* (20 Mar. 2022). "There are not a lot of people that can do that." Along with being highly critical of the delayed reaction by the World Health Organization (WHO), Jha also cited pandemics as looming global health threats that could be prevented.

Jha remained a highly sought-after keynote speaker on infectious disease outbreaks while evaluating the US health-care system. When the incoming Donald Trump administration proposed replacing Obamacare with high-deductible plans, Jha enrolled his family in one of these plans as part of a personal experiment. After spending nearly $500 for his son's brief follow-up appointment with a specialist, Jha, who has supraventricular tachycardia, decided against an expensive emergency room visit, and concluded that high-deductible plans do not necessarily result in better health care.

SOUNDING ALARM ON COVID-19

Jha remained a fixture at Harvard. After spending a year (2017–18) as senior associate dean for research translation and global strategy at the HSPH, he was promoted to dean for global strategy in 2018. A year later, he addressed the economic and health consequences of climate change at a US House of Representatives Ways and Means Committee hearing. When the Centers for Disease Control and Prevention (CDC) confirmed its first case of the novel coronavirus causing the respiratory disease that would be named COVID-19 in late January 2020, Jha believed the US government was equipped to manage the outbreak via the National Security Council Directorate for Global Health Security and Biodefense, a pandemic response team previously established during the Obama administration. That changed a month later, when he realized that widespread testing had neither been developed nor deployed by the Trump administration, who had dismantled the pandemic-preparedness system while also politicizing the issue and fomenting distrust in US institutions.

Anticipating an onslaught of pressure on the US health-care system, Jha and his HGHI staff developed interactive models to pinpoint the communities whose hospital-care capacity would be hardest hit by COVID-19. After the data was published by *The New York Times* in March 2020, it attracted the attention of the Trump administration, whose COVID-19 response team started placing orders for ventilators. To reduce the virus spread, Jha also publicly expressed the urgent need for a nationwide shutdown and an increased production of ventilators and COVID-19 diagnostic testing. "I have sounded the alarm when I needed to, but I have tried to do it in a way that's both measured and gives people something to do," he explained to Julia M. Klein for the *Brown Alumni Magazine* (1 June 2022).

BECOMING A PUNDIT

Along with advising the White House, congressional members, governors, mayors, and health commissioners on the COVID-19 response, Jha became a trusted pandemic pundit, regularly appearing on liberal and conservative cable and network news outlets, including MSNBC, CNN, Fox News, and Newsmax. On the academic front, his stint as HGHI's faculty director ended in September 2020, when he was named dean of the Brown University School of Public Health. Two months later, he was appointed to the incoming Biden administration's COVID-19 advisory board.

Amid the vaccine rollout in early 2021, Jha testified virtually before Congress, calling for international collaboration, vaccination of the world's high-risk patients, as well as increased vaccine funding and production. With surging COVID-19 cases and variant outbreaks, he advocated for uniform, coherent messaging from the CDC; universal vaccinations and booster shots; vaccine passports and air travel mandates; widespread testing and social distancing; and a return to in-person learning.

To address the nation's ongoing COVID-19 response, President Biden tapped Jha to replace Jeffrey Zients as White House coronavirus response coordinator. After taking over in March 2022, Jha, who temporarily stepped down at Brown, pushed for increased funding for COVID-19 vaccines and new booster doses, as well as prioritized vaccination for high-risk patients, in anticipation of a stalled COVID-19 bill, waning immunity, and the projected resurgence of fall and winter cases.

PERSONAL LIFE

Jha lives in Newton, Massachusetts, with his wife, Deborah Stump, an environmental lawyer, and their three children.

SUGGESTED READING

Jha, Ashish K. "Pandemic Expert Dr. Ashish K. Jha '92: 'We Will Get through This.'" Interview by Jamie Katz. *Columbia College Today*, 2020, www.college.columbia.edu/cct/issue/spring20/article/pandemic-expert-dr-ashish-k-jha-92. Accessed 11 July 2022.

___. "Public Health: An Interview." *Leaders Magazine*, www.leadersmag.com/issues/2022.1_Jan/Purpose/LEADERS-Ashish-Jha-Brown-University.html. Accessed 11 July 2022.

___. "'We Have to Get Out of This Phase': Ashish Jha on the Future of the Pandemic." Interview by Dhruv Khullar. *The New Yorker*, 18 June 2022, www.newyorker.com/news/the-new-yorker-interview/we-have-to-get-out-of-this-phase-ashish-jha-on-the-future-of-the-pandemic. Accessed 20 July 2022.

Klein, Julia M. "The First Word in Public Health." *Brown Alumni Magazine*, Brown University, www.brownalumnimagazine.com/articles/2022-06-01/ashish-jha-COVID-czar-the-first-word-in-public-health. Accessed 11 July 2022.

Munjal Diksha. "Ashish Jha: Biden's COVID Response Chief." *The Hindu*, 22 Mar. 2022, www.thehindu.com/news/international/ashish-jha-bidens-covid-response-chief/article65240060.ece. Accessed 11 July 2022.

Stolberg, Sheryl Gay. "Can Ashish Jha, 'A Comforting Voice,' Tamp Down Covid's Political Divide?" *The New York Times*, 20 Mar. 2022, www.nytimes.com/2022/03/20/us/politics/ashish-jha-covid-biden.html. Accessed 11 July 2022.

—*Bertha Muteba*

Shelton Johnson

Born: 1958
Occupation: Park ranger

Shelton Johnson had been a park ranger at Yosemite National Park in California for some time when he found a photograph of several African American soldiers on horseback in the park's archives in the 1990s. Those men, he soon learned, were Buffalo Soldiers, members of African American cavalry regiments that had fought for the United States in several military conflicts during the late nineteenth century. Buffalo Soldiers were later stationed in western lands that would become national parks, including Yosemite, and effectively served as the first park rangers. Struck by this history, Johnson began to raise awareness of the history of early African American park rangers in the course of his work at Yosemite, including in his work as an interpretive ranger. "I basically was inheriting a history that had been expressed and communicated to the public but for whatever reason did not take root. The story was basically dead," he explained to Kurt Repanshek for *National Parks Traveler* (30 Sept. 2009). "What I realized was that the story has to live beyond the work, and the energy, and the efforts of the ranger telling the story. The story has to have a lifespan of its own, separate from that."

In addition to shedding light on the history of Buffalo Soldiers in the United States' national parks, Johnson focused much of his energy on addressing the dearth of African American visitors to wilderness parks and to Yosemite in particular, which he attributed to the "legacy of segregation" in the United States, as he told Chris Van Leuven for *Men's Journal*. "When people ask me why African Americans don't visit national parks, you have to remember something," he explained to Van Leuven. "We come out of a history of exclusion, rather than inclusion, segregation rather than integration." In recognition of his outreach work, Johnson was awarded the National Park Trust's American Park Experience Award for 2022.

EARLY LIFE AND EDUCATION

Shelton Johnson was born in 1958 in Detroit, Michigan. He was one of two sons born to Shirley Johnson and James O. Johnson Jr. His father served in the US military, and the family moved often when he was a young child, living in countries such as Germany and the United Kingdom as well as in states such as California. While residing in Germany, the family visited an alpine area that would later be designated Berchtesgaden National Park, where the young Johnson was awed by the natural beauty of the German Alps. "The mountains, the sky being so close—it affected me profoundly," he recalled to Mireya Navarro for *The New York Times* (2 Nov. 2010). The family returned to Detroit around 1968, and Johnson spent the remainder of his childhood there, often perusing magazine articles and viewing television documentaries about nature. An attendee of Cass Technical High School, he studied music and played clarinet in the school's musical ensembles before leaving with his high school diploma in 1976.

After high school, Johnson was a student at Wayne State University and, while there, worked as a research assistant in the Wayne State University Folklore Archive. In 1978, he transferred to the University of Michigan,

Photo courtesy the National Park Service, via Wikimedia Commons

where he studied English literature and poetry. He earned his bachelor's degree from the university in 1981. The following year, he traveled to Liberia with the Peace Corps to assume a position as a seventh-grade English teacher at the Booker Washington Institute in Kakata. While he had to leave Liberia earlier than expected after falling ill, he remained deeply influenced by the unfamiliar environment he had been able to explore. "It was hot, humid, equatorial, and everything was alive," he told Katherine LaGrave for *Outside* magazine (17 July 2019). Back in the United States, he enrolled in a graduate creative writing program at the University of Michigan. A poet, he earned several awards for his work while in college, including the 1984 Michael R. Gutterman Award in Poetry for his poem "Coaltar Road to Kakatah during Blackout."

PARK RANGER

Johnson began working for the US national parks system in 1984, when he traveled to Yellowstone National Park, which spans portions of Wyoming, Montana, and Idaho, to take on a summer job as a dishwasher at one of the landmark's historic lodges. Having submitted an application on somewhat of a whim, with the hope of getting to see more of America's natural, wild beauty while also potentially gaining writing tranquility and inspiration, he immensely enjoyed the experience of working in the park. Though initially doubting that his poetry-focused education would qualify him for such a role, he began to consider pursuing a career as a park ranger. He joined the National Park Service as a park ranger in 1987, beginning his ranger career at Yellowstone. "I can't think of anything better than what I am already doing, being a park ranger," he later told Rob Owen for the *Pittsburgh Post-Gazette* (27 Sept. 2009) about the role. "People that join the Park Service do it because it is a passion that unites what they feel internally with what they see and experience around them externally. So from my point of view, anything else would be going downhill, literally, from being a park ranger."

Over the next years, Johnson worked in several other national parks throughout the United States, including Grand Teton National Park in Wyoming and Great Basin National Park in Nevada, as well as in the more urban setting of the National Capital Parks–East in Washington, DC. However, he would become best known for his work at Yosemite National Park, which encompasses more than 750,000 acres of land in California. Joining Yosemite as a ranger in the mid-1990s, he would remain there throughout the next decades, establishing himself as perhaps the park's best-known interpretive ranger.

BUFFALO SOLDIERS

While working at Yosemite in the 1990s, Johnson developed an interest in the history of the Buffalo Soldiers after finding an antique photograph of African American cavalry soldiers in the park's archives. Buffalo Soldiers were African American men who served in a number of racially segregated cavalry regiments of the US Army that operated during the latter half of the nineteenth century and were involved in military campaigns against Indigenous nations as well as in conflicts such as the Spanish-American War. In the late nineteenth century and early twentieth century, some Buffalo Soldiers were stationed in lands in the western United States and tasked with caring for the land in a manner that, to Johnson, seemed very familiar. "As an African American who was a soldier 100 years ago, it was his job to arrest timber thieves, prevent poaching wildlife, extinguishing forest fires, and creating a sense of law and order in a lawless land," he told Van

Leuven about the responsibilities of a Buffalo Soldier working in a park such as Yosemite. "By any other name that job description is a wilderness or a backcountry ranger." That little-known history fascinated Johnson, who hoped to share his increasing knowledge about Buffalo Soldiers and historical African American park rangers with the public.

For Johnson, his role as an interpretive ranger represented an obvious opportunity to impart such information to visitors to Yosemite. "By the time I arrived in Yosemite, I was a fairly skilled interpreter and was doing what everyone else was doing: interpreting the geological history of the park, the cultural history of the park and so forth," he recalled to Repanshek. Having learned all he could about the park's earliest rangers, he began to develop presentations in which he assumed the character of a Buffalo Soldier as a means of educating visitors while working in the park. Later, he developed a podcast, *A Buffalo Soldier Speaks*, in which he took a similar approach, embodying Elizy Boman, a real-world Buffalo Soldier who served in Yosemite in the early twentieth century. In addition to such efforts, during the first years of the twenty-first century he ran a website dedicated to Buffalo Soldiers and wrote a novel titled *Gloryland*, which was published by the conservation-oriented publisher Sierra Club Books in 2009. *Gloryland* tells the story of Elijah Yancy, a man of African American and Indigenous descent who becomes a Buffalo Soldier and is later stationed at Yosemite.

OUTREACH

In addition to identifying the general public's lack of knowledge about Buffalo Soldiers and their contributions to the United States' national parks, which he sought to address through his interpretive programs and writing, Johnson became concerned about the relatively small number of African Americans who visited parks such as Yosemite during his time working there. As of 2009, only about 1 percent of the visitors to Yosemite each year were African American, and Johnson hoped to increase that number. To that end, he wrote a letter to African American television personality Oprah Winfrey, host of the popular talk show *The Oprah Winfrey Show*, in which he explained his concerns. "Every year, America is becoming increasingly diverse, but that diversity is not reflected in the national parks, even though

African-Americans and other groups played a vital role in the founding of national parks," he wrote in his letter, as quoted by Navarro. "If the national parks are America's playground, then why are we not playing in the most beautiful places in America?" In writing that letter, he hoped that Winfrey would help him raise awareness of the national parks, which could in turn encourage more members of her diverse television audience to visit parks such as Yosemite.

Johnson's attempt at outreach proved successful. As documented in an episode of *The Oprah Winfrey Show* that aired in October 2010, Winfrey and her friend Gayle King visited and camped in Yosemite, where they met with Johnson and received a tour from him. Johnson would later credit Winfrey with helping to increase the racial diversity of the park's visitors through her visit. "Many people first heard about my work to connect the disconnected by watching Oprah's talk show that year," he recalled in a press release from the National Park Trust (15 Feb. 2022). "I have had multiple African Americans come up to me in Yosemite Valley just to shake my hand, but Oprah convinced them to visit, and the beauty of Yosemite did the rest."

COMMUNITY ENGAGEMENT

Following many years of work as a park ranger, Johnson was promoted to community engagement specialist at Yosemite, a role in which he continued to highlight the stories of the park's early African American rangers and carry out his efforts to diversify the park's visitor base. "It's generating a sense of ownership and stewardship within populations that don't necessarily feel that national parks are there for them," he told Van Leuven of his approach. "But parks are part of their birthright not just as citizens of this country but also as human beings." In addition to working in the park and reaching out to influential figures such as Winfrey, he served as an adviser for and was featured prominently in the widely viewed 2009 PBS documentary *The National Parks: America's Best Idea*, created by the acclaimed documentary filmmaker Ken Burns; invited to a White House preview, he conversed with President Barack Obama about the experience of national parks. He was also featured in episodes of television documentary series such as *How the Earth Was Made* (2009) and *The*

Last Explorers (2011) as well as in the 2011 documentary film *High Sierra—A Journey on the John Muir Trail* and the 2022 documentary *Buffalo Soldiers: Fighting on Two Fronts*. For the 2014 documentary film *An American Ascent*, about a team of African American mountain climbers, he provided narration.

In recognition of his work, Johnson has been awarded several honors over the course of his career, including the 2015 Department of the Interior Superior Service Award. In early 2022, the National Park Trust announced that Johnson would receive that organization's 2022 American Park Experience Award. "I am humbled to be the recipient of National Park Trust's 2022 American Park Experience Award," he stated in the press release announcing the award. "This recognition reflects the work that I, and many others, have been engaged in for decades to make our public lands a welcoming environment for everyone." He received his award at a ceremony held in Yosemite in May 2022.

PERSONAL LIFE

Johnson met his wife, Roxann, at Discovery Park in Seattle, Washington. They have a son named Langston. Johnson lives in Mariposa, California, near Yosemite.

SUGGESTED READING

Johnson, Shelton. "John Muir, National Parks and Civil Rights: An Interview with Shelton Johnson." Interview by Jill Robinson. *The Statesider*, 1 Nov. 2020, statesider.us/shelton-johnson-john-muir-civil-rights/. Accessed 13 June 2022.

LaGrave, Katherine. "How Shelton Johnson Became a Yosemite Legend." *Outside*, 17 July 2019, www.outsideonline.com/culture/essays-culture/shelton-johnson-park-ranger-yosemite/. Accessed 13 June 2022.

"National Park Trust Honors National Park Service Ranger Shelton Johnson with American Park Experience Award." *National Park Trust*, 15 Feb. 2022, parktrust.org/news/national-park-trust-honors-national-park-service-ranger-shelton-johnson-with-american-park-experience-award/. Accessed 13 June 2022.

Navarro, Mireya. "National Parks Reach Out to Blacks Who Aren't Visiting." *The New York Times*, 2 Nov. 2010, www.nytimes.

com/2010/11/03/science/earth/03parks.
html. Accessed 13 June 2022.

Owen, Rob. "Yosemite Ranger Unexpected
Star of Burns' National Parks Series."
Pittsburgh Post-Gazette, 27 Sept. 2009,
www.post-gazette.com/ae/tv-radio/
2009/09/27/Yosemite-ranger-unexpected-
star-of-Burns-national-parks-series/
stories/200909270211. Accessed 13 June
2022.

Repanshek, Kurt. "Gloryland Brings Yosemite
National Park Ranger Shelton Johnson
Full Circle." *National Parks Traveler*, 30
Sept. 2009, www.nationalparkstraveler.
org/2009/09/gloryland-brings-yosemite-
national-park-ranger-shelton-johnson-full-
circle4649. Accessed 13 June 2022.

Van Leuven, Chris. "Neighborhood Heroes:
Shelton Johnson, Yosemite's Storyteller."
Men's Journal, n.d., www.mensjournal.com/
adventure/yosemite-ranger-tells-untold-
story-of-african-americans-in-national-
parks/. Accessed 13 June 2022.

—*Joy Crelin*

Gina Ortiz Jones

Born: February 1, 1981
Occupation: Intelligence officer and politician

On July 22, 2021, when the United States
Senate confirmed Gina Ortiz Jones as Under
Secretary of the Air Force, she viewed this as
a chance to make an impact on a larger scale.
She had previously had a promising career in
the Air Force as an intelligence officer, before
serving as director of investment at the Office
of the United States Trade Representative
(USTR) during President Barack Obama's
administration. She left the latter position
shortly after President Donald Trump took
office in January 2017. Although Jones then
tried to run twice for the Texas Twenty-Third
Congressional District seat⊠the Hispanic–
majority state district where she grew up⊠she
came up short both times, in 2018 and 2020.

Jones is the first out lesbian to be named
Under Secretary of the Air Force. For Jones,
who had begun her career by serving under
the draconian "Don't Ask, Don't Tell" military
policy, the role means having a voice on the
reform of discriminatory policies, fostering
more inclusion and diversity, and giving back.

"I have a small window of time to really serve in
the best way that I can," Jones said to Jennifer
Bendery for the *HuffPost* (29 Nov. 2021). "I'm
not here for any other reason than to . . . [give]
back to a country that has given me so much. .
. . So that's what this time is about."

EARLY LIFE AND EDUCATION

Born on February 1, 1981, in Arlington,
Virginia, Gina Maria Ortiz Jones was raised by
her mother Victorina Ortiz, who had emigrated
from the Philippines to the United States.
She grew up on the western outskirts of San
Antonio, Texas, alongside her younger sister,
Christi Jones. Jones recalls helping her mother
prepare for the US Citizenship Naturalization
Test as one of her earliest memories. A public-
school teacher, her mother embraced sacrifice
by working several jobs at a time to make ends
meet. Fortunately, subsidized housing and
reduced-price school lunch brought some
much-needed economic respite for Jones's
family.

Jones attended John Jay High School,
located in an area where gang violence and
drugs were part of everyday life. She was part
of the school student council and excelled in
her academics, graduating in the top ten of her
class in 1999. Talking with Daniel Malloy for
OZY (13 Feb. 2018) about Jones's years in high
school, a close friend of hers, Andrea Salazar,
said: "There were definitely a lot of influences
that could take you down the wrong path. And
she's always had tunnel vision and just saw
something at the end that she wanted, and she
didn't let anything distract her."

Having earned a four-year Air Force Reserve
Officer Training Corps (AFROTC) scholarship
to Boston University (BU), she completed a
bachelor's degree in East Asian Studies and a
master's degree in economics in 2003. While in
school, Jones—who had come out as a lesbian
to her family when she was fifteen years old—
lived with the fear that her scholarship could be
revoked if her sexual orientation became known
and so she resorted to keeping it a secret. That
secrecy continued after graduation when she
began serving with Air Force intelligence under
the "Don't Ask, Don't Tell" military policy,
which barred gay, lesbian, and bisexual service
members from openly serving. "It was actually
a very deep secret. I could not be as open
as I would have liked because I needed that
scholarship to stay at BU. I knew what I had to

do," she revealed to Joel Brown in an interview for *Bostonia* (18 June 2018) before continuing to say, "And when I served in the Air Force, that policy applied to me, too. If someone is ready and willing to serve their country, there shouldn't be any policies—especially policies rooted in bigotry—that would prevent that."

A CAREER IN THE INTELLIGENCE FIELD

Jones spent three years in active duty, during which time she was deployed to Iraq as an intelligence officer with the 18th Air Support Operations Group backing air operations and achieved the rank of captain. In 2006, she left the Air Force and briefly returned to Texas, before going back to work, this time as an intelligence analyst for the United States–Africa Command in Stuttgart, Germany. In 2008, she moved on to the Defense Intelligence Agency (DIA) as an advisor on military operations for Latin America, particularly Central and South Americas.

After Obama became president in 2009, Jones joined his executive office, serving as the intelligence community's senior advisor for trade endorsement before being named director of investment at the Office of the United States Trade Representative (USTR). Although she intended to remain in the post when Donald Trump became president in 2017, she left only five months after the new

administration had taken over. What caused her to step down from the role were her unyielding beliefs and values, which did not align with the Trump administration's political views. When Trump revealed that his proposed budget would slash housing aid and food assistance, it was a personal hit for Jones, whose childhood household had relied on these crucial programs for economic support.

Regarding immigration, Jones, the daughter of a Filipina immigrant, was against the Trump administration's "zero tolerance" immigration policy, which, during his four-year term, would separate thousands of families at the border. "It's egregious. The pictures we've seen!" she said to Brown, referring to the photographic images published in the media showing the detainment of children and the separation of families. "Frankly, as Americans, we all know that seeing a young child, a toddler, crying as they're being held in a cage like an animal— that's not the right thing to do."

In the center of all these disagreements, Jones thought that the public officers being recruited by Trump were not genuine in their interest in public service. "The type of people that were brought in to be public servants were interested in neither the public nor the service," Jones told Bendery for *HuffPost* (6 Jan. 2018). "That, to me, was a sign that I'm going to have to serve in a different way."

RUNNING FOR CONGRESS

After leaving her government position, Jones returned to San Antonio in 2017 with a goal of running for Congress. In the midterm elections of 2018, Jones, a Democrat, challenged Representative Will Hurd, a Republican, for the Texas Twenty-Third Congressional District seat, which he had held since 2015. Because her hometown district had never been represented by a woman, if elected, she would have made history not only as the first woman to fill a US House seat in Texas but also as the first Filipina, lesbian, and Iraq war veteran. For Jones, it was all about creating opportunities for people, however. "Talent is universal. Opportunity is not," she said to Bendery. "Folks in Congress, they do three things. They create opportunities, they protect opportunities, and they erase opportunities. That's how we have to be thinking about this very plainly."

Although Jones lost to Hurd by just 926 votes in what was called the most competitive race in the state, this only added to her resolve to run for a seat in Congress. In May 2019, she announced that she would run again in the 2020 general election. With Hurd retiring from the House at the end of his term, Jones faced Republican Tony Gonzales, a Navy veteran.

As Jones traveled the district, she made access to healthcare a key priority of her congregational campaign. "There are twenty-nine counties in this district, and eighteen counties have three or less doctors," she told John L. Dorman in an interview for *Business Insider* (30 Oct. 2020), before continuing to say, "There are three counties that have no doctors. It's so important that we invest in the pipeline of talent into rural healthcare." She also had a plan regarding strategies to mitigate the spread of the coronavirus disease 2019 (COVID-19)—which had ravaged Texas, the country, and the world beginning in early 2020—including more testing, contact tracing, and the acquisition of protective personal equipment. "It's just critical that we get this pandemic under control so that we're not needlessly losing lives and needlessly losing small businesses and jobs," Jones told Dorman.

When the November general elections arrived, she lost once again, this time by four percentage points to Gonzales. Though she lost, President Joe Biden, a Democrat, nominated Jones for a role that would make her number two at the Air Force the following year.

LOOKING AHEAD

On July 22, 2021, the Senate confirmed Jones as the Under Secretary of the Air Force, a national security position for which President Biden nominated her in April of that year. The first lesbian to serve as Under Secretary of any military branch, she made inclusivity a key part of her mission, something she did not have while serving under the "Don't Ask, Don't Tell" military policy.

Regarding the retention of mid-career women, a problem that has bedeviled the Air Force for years, the Under Secretary vowed to make more opportunities available for women who think they cannot have both a military career and a family. "Folks made a decision just a couple of years before that they couldn't have both. But you can, actually," she said to Bendery. "We're cutting ourselves off from talent. . . . I mean, we talk about pilot retention. Well, let's talk about women retention at a certain level."

When the Air Force announced its commitment to vaccinate all its personnel against COVID-19 in an ambitious timeline, Jones did not hide her pride in the branch becoming a leader of such initiative. With more than 97 percent of active-duty members vaccinated with at least one dose of the vaccine by late November 2021, she viewed the high number as an accomplishment while recognizing that thousands of active-duty airmen and airwomen have yet to comply with the requirement. "There are some folks that are exercising their right to request a religious accommodation, a medical exemption," she told Bendery. "And they should do that if that's what they feel is necessary." However, other members who refuse to follow orders could be penalized by being separated from the Air Force, Jones has stated.

As Jones spends her days attending meetings with military leaders, she is always looking to advocate for policies that are going to improve the quality of life of Air Force members with whom she does not meet often: single parents, members of color, and members of the LGBTQ+ community, among others.

SUGGESTED READING

Bendery, Jennifer. "Gina Ortiz Jones Had to Hide during 'Don't Ask, Don't Tell.' Now She's No. 2 at the Air Force." *HuffPost*, 29 Nov. 2021, www.huffpost.com/entry/gina-ortiz-jones-dont-ask-dont-tell-air-force-under-secretary_n_619da2ede4b0451e5500d740. Accessed 5 Mar. 2022.

___. "She Quit Working for Trump. Now She's Running for Congress to Fight Him." *HuffPost*, 6 Jan. 2018, www.huffpost.com/entry/gina-ortiz-jones-will-hurd-texas-2018_n_5a4c069ce4b0b0e5a7a94c48. Accessed 5 Mar. 2022.

Malloy, Daniel. "This Lesbian Airforce Veteran Is Setting Her Eyes on Congress." *OZY*, 13 Feb. 2018, www.ozy.com/news-and-politics/this-lesbian-air-force-veteran-is-setting-her-eyes-on-congress/83179. Accessed 5 Mar. 2022.

Ortiz Jones, Gina. "A Different Kind of Texas Candidate." Interview by Joel Brown. *Bostonia*, 18 June 2018, www.bu.edu/articles/2018/gina-ortiz-jones-texas-office. Accessed 5 Mar. 2022.

___. "Gina Ortiz Jones Could Become the First Filipina American Elected to

Congress." Interview by John L. Dorman. *Business Insider*, 30 Oct. 2020, www.businessinsider.com/gina-ortiz-jones-texas-23rd-district-house-congressional-election-interview-2020-10. Accessed 5 Mar. 2022.

Sanchez, Sam. "President Biden Nominates Gina Ortiz Jones for Under Secretary of the Air Force." *San Antonio Current*, 28 Apr. 2021, www.sacurrent.com/sanantonio/president-biden-nominates-gina-ortiz-jones-for-under-secretary-of-the-air-force/Content?oid=26100938. Accessed 5 Mar. 2022.

—*Maria del Pilar Guzman*

Wissam Joubran

Born: February 19, 1983
Occupation: Composer and musician

Palestinian oud player, composer, and luthier Wissam Joubran drew on his deep roots in traditional Arab music to become a highly respected figure in the international music scene. Born into a family full of performers and artisans, he initially made his name as a fourth-generation instrument maker specializing in the oud, a member of the lute family with a long history in the Middle East. His skill as a luthier was accompanied by dedicated training as a musician. "It is like eating and drinking for me—both are essential!" he told Allston Mitchell in an interview for the *Global Dispatches* (2 Sept. 2018) of his dual identities as a craftsman and a performer. Joubran's career as a virtuoso oud player and recording artist took off in the 2000s, bringing him a new level of global attention. He has been celebrated for his compositions, his improvisations, and his ability to modernize oud playing while not losing track of its heritage.

Joubran is best known for his work as a member of the group Le Trio Joubran, which he formed in 2005 with his two brothers and fellow oud players Samir and Adnan. The trio released several critically acclaimed albums and also received awards for their contributions to film soundtracks. Anastasia Tsioulcas summed up the group's impact in a review of their 2011 album *AsFâr* for NPR (22 June 2011): "The Joubrans are seriously gifted players whose knowledge of *maqam*—the melodic, modal traditions of Arab classical music—is as obvious as their technical chops. . . . The effect is hypnotic and bliss-inducing."

EARLY LIFE

Wissam Hatem Joubran was born in Nazareth, Israel, on February 19, 1983, into a Palestinian Arab family. Music was deep in his family's DNA: his father, Hatem Joubran, was a highly respected stringed-instrument maker and his mother, Ibtisam Hanna, was a singer noted for her performances of Muwachahats—traditional poems that were written during the Muslim conquest of Spain. Jourdan's brothers, Samir and Adnan, would also go on to become professional oud players, and his sister, Suha, became a choir singer. During their childhoods, the Joubran children were exposed to many different musical traditions, including jazz, flamenco, and both Eastern and Western classical music, as well as various Arabic styles. They were especially influenced by prominent oud players such as Farid Al Atrach, Mohamed Al Kasabji, and Munir Bashir.

Ancestrally, the Joubran family's musical roots went even deeper. Joubran's great-grandfather, Dib Joubran, who was born in 1876 and died in 1951, began the family's tradition of crafting fine stringed instruments. He is credited with important innovations in oud design, including an entirely new body shape for the ancient instrument, which has a history that can be traced back as much as five thousand years to the Akkadian period in the area of modern-day Iraq. Joubran's grandfather, Basem, continued that legacy as a master luthier. He also earned a reputation as a skilled musician on both oud and violin, often performing in Nazareth with his brother Badi.

TRAINING AS A LUTHIER

From an early age Joubran followed in the footsteps of his father, grandfather, and great-grandfather. "I am the fourth generation in a family of oud makers," he told Mitchell. "In the Arab world [oud-making] knowledge is traditionally passed down from father to son. It is important work and a very precise job and it requires special training." He started working with his father on building stringed instruments at age five, beginning with the oud. By six he had made his first instrument on his own—a simplified model, but one that gave him the confidence to continue. All the while he learned playing technique as well, first on the violin but soon concentrating on the oud.

While firmly grounded in family tradition, Joubran eventually sought to expand his education as a luthier. In 2001, he enrolled at the Antonio Stradivari Conservatory in Cremona, Italy, becoming the first student of Arab descent to train at the famed institution. "You could say that it was the dream of my father to see one of his sons go to a school or a university to study oud-making," Joubran told Mitchell, though he also noted that his father warned him it was hard to make a living as a luthier. By attending a Western professional luthier school, Joubran gained valuable insight into the science of acoustics, which he incorporated into his craft alongside the more traditional techniques passed down in his family. The results soon earned him recognition as a notable up-and-coming artisan luthier. He officially earned his degree from the Antonio Stradivari Conservatory cum laude in 2005.

Joubran's studies gave him a great appreciation for the history of the oud, as well as a prominent place in shaping the future of the instrument. As one of the world's oldest string instruments, the oud is considered to be the progenitor of the lute and the guitar. It spread to different regions as Islam spread out from the Middle East across the world, evolving along the way. "Its history as well as its rich sonorities favored its assimilation of many musical cultures both Arab and non-Arab, which explains the multiplicity of 'languages' that the instrument can express," Joubran noted in an interview for the Institute of Palestine Studies (29 June 2015). "It is considered to be the father of all Arabic string instruments and has preeminent position in the traditional eastern orchestra ensemble or *takht*, often accompanying singers and musicians." As both an oud maker and player, Joubran would seek throughout his career to merge this heritage with modern improvisational techniques, continuing the development of the instrument in general and its role in Palestinian music specifically.

LE TRIO JOUBRAN

Meanwhile, as his training as a luthier progressed, Joubran also continued to grow as a performing musician. An important influence was his brother Samir, ten years his senior, who had already established himself

as a professional oud player. In 1996, Joubran appeared with Samir in a successful concert in Paris, beginning a long partnership. "The main attraction was this chemistry that few other musicians beside brothers have," Samir told the Institute of Palestine Studies. "The harmony in our music is the result of feelings of mutual respect plus the fact that we've grown up in a very special atmosphere, rich with musical education." The two began performing together regularly, and Joubran appeared on Samir's album *Tamaas* in 2002.

Meanwhile, their younger brother Adnan was studying to become an oud virtuoso himself. Eventually, the three Joubran brothers decided to experiment with playing as an oud trio, something that was considered uncharted territory for the instrument. "We were inspired by the Paco De Lucia, Al Di Meola, and John McLaughlin [guitar] trio with their famous live album, *Friday Night in San Francisco*," Joubran told Mitchell. "The oud is the father of the guitar so there is no reason why we could not do the same thing with the oud." As Le Trio Joubran, the brothers released their first album, *Randana*, in 2005. Around that same time they based themselves in France while touring internationally.

A breakthrough came in 2007, when the group released the album *Majâz* to widespread acclaim. In a review for NPR (29 Apr. 2008), Banning Eyre noted, "The album title *Majâz* translates as 'metaphor' or 'deep meaning.' It's a suggestion that, although they rarely resort to words, these brothers do have things to say. With mysterious, seductive eloquence, they communicate profound ideas about history, musical evolution, and the beautiful aesthetics of Arabic music, still far too little-known in Western societies." The group's next two albums, *À L'Ombre des mots* (In the shadow of words; 2009) and *AsFâr* (2011), also earned strong reviews. Many world music critics especially remarked on the way the trio wove the modal sounds of traditional Arabic music with modern improvisations. Tsioulcas wrote that the album "provides a primer in how to keep Arab classical tradition fresh, vital and relevant," while also speaking to the brothers' "personal voyage beyond their troubled homeland."

In 2018, Le Trio Joubran released *The Long March*, an album that sought to bring oud music to an even wider audience. It features vocals by the Iranian singer Mohammad Motamedi and collaborations with Roger Waters, known for his work with the rock band Pink Floyd, on two tracks. Experimental elements such as electronic sounds and nontraditional orchestration complement the focus on oud melodies. The lyrics, meanwhile, come from the work of Palestinian poet Mahmoud Darwish, grounding the album in a message of shared humanity.

FILM SOUNDTRACKS AND AWARDS

Along with their regular studio albums, Joubran and his brothers found considerable success contributing to film soundtracks. In 2009, Le Trio Joubran received the Best Music Award from the Dubai International Film Festival and the Grand Prix de la Semaine de la Critique from the Cannes Film Festival for their work on the French film *Adieu Gary* (2009), directed by Nassim Amaouche. They won the 2012 Best Music Award from the Dubai Film Festival for their effort on director Yahya Al Abdallah's movie *The Last Friday*. They also appeared on the soundtracks of *Le dernier vol* (*The Last Flight*, 2009), collaborating with the group Chkrrr; director Julian Schnabel's *Miral* (2010); the Oscar-nominated documentary *Five Broken Cameras* (2011); and Majid Majidi's *Muhammad: The Messenger of God* (2015), scored by Indian musician A. R. Rahman.

Additionally, Le Trio Joubran received other honors for their exemplary musicianship and role in promoting Palestinian culture. In 2013, they earned the Artistic Creativity Award from the Arab Thought Foundation in Beirut, Lebanon. That same year they also received the Order of Merit and Excellence from the Palestinian National Authority. In 2016, they were presented with the Ziryab Award of Virtuosos from the International Lute Festival—UNESCO.

Joubran and his brothers often credited their sibling bond for their ability to play together seemingly effortlessly. "The success we have had comes partly because we are brothers and we understand each other implicitly," Joubran told Mitchell. In an interview with Angel Romero for *World Music Central* (3 Mar. 2019), Adnan Joubran further elaborated on the trio's core values as a group: "Depth of emotions, is one of the essential elements of our music, Le Trio Joubran do their best to understand why they use a note better than another, how

a melody becomes a melody, an image first, a direction, a feeling, and a message."

SUGGESTED READING

Eyre, Banning. "Le Trio Joubran: Brothers of the Oud." Review of *Majâz*, by Le Trio Joubran. *NPR*, 29 Apr. 2008, www.npr.org/2008/04/29/90035747/le-trio-joubran-brothers-of-the-oud. Accessed 31 Aug. 2022.

Joubran, Adnan. "Interview with Oud Maestros Le Trio Joubran." Interview by Angel Romero. *World Music Central*, 3 Mar. 2019, worldmusiccentral.org/2019/03/03/interview-with-oud-maestros-le-trio-joubran/. Accessed 31 Aug. 2022.

___. "Interview with Trio Joubran, Performers at Rainforest World Music Festival 2012." Interview by Angel Romero. *World Music Central*, 9 June 2012, worldmusiccentral.org/2012/06/09/interview-with-trio-joubran-performers-at-rainforest-world-music-festival-2012/. Accessed 31 Aug. 2022.

Joubran, Wissam. "Le Trio Joubran." Interview by Allston Mitchell. *The Global Dispatches*, 2 Sept. 2018, www.theglobaldispatches.com/articles/le-trio-joubran. Accessed 31 Aug. 2022.

___. "Le Trio Joubran: Interview with Palestinian 'Oud Brothers." *Institute for Palestine Studies*, 29 June 2015, Interview. www.palestine-studies.org/en/node/232400. Accessed 31 Aug. 2022.

"The Joubran Family." *Wissam Joubran*, wissamjoubran.com/en/the-joubran-family. Accessed 31 Aug. 2022.

Tsioulcas, Anastasia. "Le Trio Joubran: Making the Oud Rock." Review of *AsFâr*, by Le Trio Joubran. *NPR*, 22 June 2011, www.npr.org/2011/06/22/137344584/le-trio-joubran-making-the-oud-rock. Accessed 31 Aug. 2022.

SELECTED WORKS

With Le Trio Joubran—*Randana*, 2005; *Majâz*, 2007; *À L'Ombre des mots*, 2009; *AsFâr*, 2011; *The Long March*, 2018

—*Christopher Mari*

Wiliame Katonivere

Born: April 20, 1964
Occupation: Chief and politician

On November 12, 2021, Wiliame Katonivere was sworn in as the president of Fiji, an island nation in the South Pacific. His nomination and election were seen as especially notable because of his background in environmentalism, at a time when Fiji faced serious threats from climate change. The ocean comprises 98 percent of Fiji's 1.3 million-square-mile territory, and much of the population relies on fishing and the seafood industry for its livelihood. Fiji's biodiverse forests, mountains, and coral reefs also make tourism a significant contributor to the national economy. "We need to protect our resources for our children and their children," Katonivere told Serafina Silaitoga for the *Fiji Times* (13 Nov. 2021). "This is the message I have always preached about because we all play a vital role."

Born into a prominent family, Katonivere earned experience in the military and in business before inheriting the position of *tui* (chieftain) of Fiji's Macuata Province in 2013. In that role he earned a reputation as a champion of his country's natural resources—particularly the Great Sea Reef (known to locals as Cakaulevu), which has been subject to overfishing and habitat loss. As a chief, Katonivere collaborated with federal authorities to implement more sustainable management practices and stronger environmental protections, and he announced his continued support for those causes once he became president. He sought to unite both iTaukei (Indigenous Fijians) and Indo-Fijians, who together make up most of Fiji's population, behind the vital goal of environmental stewardship. As he asserted to Eli Kintisch for a July 2019 *Fiji Profile* report published by the David and Lucile Packard Foundation, "We need to have conservation entrenched into the society."

EARLY LIFE AND EDUCATION

Ratu Wiliame Katonivere was born on April 20, 1964, at the Colonial War Memorial Hospital in Suva, the capital of Fiji, located on the island of Viti Levu. (Although Fiji consists of more than 330 islands, only 110 of them have permanent inhabitants, with almost 90 percent of the population living on the two

major islands of Viti Levu and Vanua Levu.) He was the youngest of his parents' seven children. His mother, the former Samanunu Boteiviwa, hailed from the province of Bua, on Vanua Levu. His father, businessperson and parliamentarian Ratu Sepesa Soso Katonivere, was from the village of Naduri, in Macuata Province. The honorific title "Ratu" signified Soso Katonivere's rank as tui, or chief, of the province, a position that would be passed down to his eldest son, Aisea, after his death.

Katonivere attended Draiba Fijian School, a primary school in Suva that had been established in 1947 as an alternative to British mission schools for Indigenous children. He later recalled those years fondly, telling Silaitoga that much of his time was spent outdoors with friends, swimming, riding horses, and roaming wooded areas. "Our class was always full of adventures and experiences with the teachers and even until today, we keep in touch on social media," he said. "Some of my classmates became pastors, some worked in different companies and some were even prisoners, but we remain close and we often share about all the fun days we had."

Katonivere was then sent to Bua College to receive his secondary education—as well as to experience his more rural roots. Upon graduating in 1981, Katonivere assumed

Photo courtesy of the
Office of the President of Fiji

his father would use his parliamentary connections to secure him a job, but his father refused, wanting his son to be self-sufficient. Katonivere thus set out for Naduri, where he worked alongside his cousins in the sugarcane fields. "I loved it because we woke up early in the morning to cut cane and our day was always filled with laughter and jokes," he recalled to Silaitoga.

MILITARY AND BUSINESS CAREER

In 1984, Katonivere joined the Royal Fiji Military. He served two missions in Lebanon as part of the United Nations Interim Force and became the commanding officer of the Seventh Fiji Infantry Regiment of the Territorial Forces Brigade before returning to civilian life. He later credited his time in the military with teaching him discipline and giving him direction. "You start to get serious with your goals in life and your purpose of being alive in this earth," he explained to Silaitoga.

Returning to Fiji after his tour of duty had ended, Katonivere was hired by the Fijian Affairs Board (later known as the iTaukei Affairs Board), an agency concerned with the governance and welfare of the iTaukei people. The job allowed him to learn the administrative aspects of the Fijian government, especially its work in rural areas. Fiji had remained a British colony until 1970 and became a parliamentary democracy in 1987, following a series of military coups. Chiefly families such as Katonivere's continued to play a major role in the republic.

In 1998 Katonivere moved to the United States, where he lived with his older sister Adi Asenaca Vuibau for three years. He then moved back to Naduri and became involved in the lumber industry, rising to the chairmanship of Fiji Pine Limited, a group of companies devoted to forest management and sustainable harvesting. Additionally, he eventually sat on the boards of companies such as Airports Fiji, Fiji Sugar Corporation, and Rewa Rice, and he maintained interests in the mining industry as well.

TUI MACUATA AND CONSERVATION WORK

In 2013 Katonivere's older brother, Aisea, who had assumed the title of Tui Macuata from their late father, drowned while fishing. Katonivere then became the chief of Macuata Province and head of the Macuata Provincial

Council, which works to ensure the rights and interests of the iTaukei people within Fiji. "I never had the slightest idea I would be here," he told Kintisch of his elevation to tui. The sudden change in leadership also drew close attention from environmentalists in Fiji and beyond. His brother had been extremely dedicated to environmental causes, especially the issue of overfishing, as Macuata's rich reef ecosystems provide the majority of Fiji's seafood supply. In Fiji, the federal government shares responsibility for overseeing natural resources with the local leaders of villages and provinces. Chieftains wield considerable influence because they control the use of traditional fishing areas called *qoliqoli*, issuing licenses, decreeing when fishing is allowed, and fighting poachers. So when Katonivere stepped into the role, as Kintisch noted, there was some concern over whether he would continue his brother's level of stewardship.

Such anxieties proved to be unfounded. Although his earliest efforts as tui focused on jobs and education, Katonivere was well aware that growing tourism, overfishing, and climate change were placing untenable stresses on Macuata's ecosystems—and that those issues needed to be addressed as soon and as efficiently as possible. Such issues resonated beyond the province as well. As Kintisch put it, these local challenges were "a microcosm of the larger issues at play in rapidly growing Fiji. So as the chief considered his stance, all eyes among Fiji's conservationists were on Macuata." Ultimately, like his late brother, Katonivere soon became viewed as a good steward of his province. He managed the qoliqoli firmly but fairly, worked with Fiji's federal government to set new data-informed sustainability policies, and collaborated with international nonprofits like the World Wildlife Fund for Nature that lent their support.

Katonivere placed special emphasis on protecting the Great Sea Reef, the third-longest continuous reef system in the Southern Hemisphere, which spans more than 200,000 square kilometers. "For every Fijian who was brought up by the ocean, the first thing we see when we grow up is the reef," he said, as quoted by *RNZ* (21 Oct. 2021). "It prompts us to ask, what is the importance of the reef? In my qoliqoli, the Great Sea Reef is not only a source of life, it is a sanctuary for us, for the fish, and all marine life. That is why it matters to me. I wish to see those old glory days, when we have enough food, enough fish to eat, we will still have our pristine forests, and cleaner water runs through our streams." In 2018, working with Fijian Prime Minister Josaia Voreqe "Frank" Bainimarama, Katonivere was instrumental in developing a sustainable management plan for the Great Sea Reef, which was identified as a site of international importance in that year's Ramsar Convention. His efforts helped make him one of the most prominent conservationist voices in Fiji, a country that as a whole was increasingly seen as a leader in climate change awareness and national environmental action.

PRESIDENCY

When Fijian President Jioji Konrote left office in 2021, Prime Minister Bainimarama, himself a committed environmentalist, nominated Katonivere for the post. Bainimarama cited Katonivere's advocacy for the Great Sea Reef as a major strength. In a widely quoted *Facebook* post, he called Katonivere "one of the fiercest defenders of the ocean and of the right of Fiji's future generations to live in a clean, safe and natural environment."

Katonivere accepted the nomination for the presidency, which is largely ceremonial but does involve emergency powers during a crisis and oversight of Fiji's military forces. He faced off against Social Democratic Liberal Party member of Parliament Ro Teimumu Vuikaba Kepa, a former deputy prime minister and chief of the Burebasaga Confederacy, one of the groups that make up Fiji's hierarchical House of Chiefs. Katonivere ultimately won the parliamentary vote, 28–23, on October 22, 2021. He became the youngest person ever to be elected to the Fijian presidency and the first from Macuata Province.

Katonivere was sworn in to office on November 12, 2021. Although his predecessor, Konrote, was not an iTaukei chief, he had been a rare exception; Katonivere thus represented something of a return to tradition. Celebrations were particularly joyful in his home village of Naduri. While Katonivere retained the title of tui, another chief was appointed to assume his day-to-day duties in Macuata. Katonivere did, however, resign his board positions before officially taking the presidency. Among his earliest actions as president were opening a new session of parliament and urging his fellow Fijians to be vaccinated against coronavirus disease 2019 (COVID-19). In early 2022 he announced several government appointments, including to the federal Electoral Commission.

PERSONAL LIFE

Katonivere and his wife, Filomena, have two children: Wiliame Jr. and Adi Vilivili. A deeply religious person, he often credited his faith for his successes. "Two things I believe helped see me through all the years of my life is to always stay humble and to be obedient to God," he told Silaitoga. "I believe if we have these two traits in life, we can take on any challenge that comes our way."

SUGGESTED READING

Anand, Sampras. "President Returns Home, Villagers Overwhelmed." *Fiji Sun*, 25 Oct. 2021, fijisun.com.fj/2021/10/25/president-returns-home-villagers-overwhelmed/. Accessed 24 Jan. 2022.

Chand, Shalveen. "Ratu Wiliame Admitted to Office as President, Takes Formal Oath." *Fiji Sun*, 14 Nov. 2021, fijisun.com.fj/2021/11/14/ratu-wiliame-admitted-to-office-as-president-takes-formal-oath-2/. Accessed 24 Jan. 2022.

Doviverata, Rosi. "Chief: Never Dreamt It." *Fiji Sun*, 22 Oct. 2021, fijisun.com.fj/2021/10/22/chief-never-dreamt-it/. Accessed 24 Jan. 2022.

Kintisch, Eli. "A Culture of Conservation in Fiji." *Fiji Profile*, David and Lucile Packard Foundation, July 2019, www.packard.org/wp-content/uploads/2019/08/FIji-Profile.pdf. Accessed 24 Jan. 2022.

"Ratu Wiliame Katonivere Set to Be Fiji's Next President." *RNZ*, 21 Oct. 2021, www.rnz.co.nz/international/pacific-news/453970/ratu-wiliame-katonivere-set-to-be-fiji-s-next-president. Accessed 24 Jan. 2022.

Silaitoga, Serafina. "From Canecutter to Fiji's President." *Fiji Times*, 13 Nov. 2021, www.fijitimes.com/from-canecutter-to-fijis-president/. Accessed 24 Jan. 2022.

Thomas, P. C. "Fijian Parliament Elects New President Ratu Wiliame Katonivere." *FastTrack*, 22 Oct. 2021, english.newstracklive.com/news/fijian-parliament-elects-new-president-ratu-wiliame-katonivere-sc57-nu318-ta318-1188642-1.html. Accessed 24 Jan. 2022.

—*Mari Rich*

Lina Khan

Born: March 3, 1989
Occupation: Legal scholar and government official

One of the nation's leading antitrust reformers, Lina Khan began to disrupt business as usual among the technology giants while still in law school, through her research and writing. Speaking of online giants like Amazon and the need to lessen their powerful control over the American economy, Khan told David Streitfeld for *The New York Times* (7 Sept. 2018), "As consumers, as users, we love these tech companies. But as citizens, as workers, and as entrepreneurs, we recognize that their power is troubling. We need a new framework, a new vocabulary for how to assess and address their dominance." From her early papers published as an unknown law student to her role as head of the Federal Trade Commission (FTC), Khan's meteoric rise has influenced leaders to completely rethink American antitrust law. In 2019, *Foreign Policy* magazine included her in their list of 100 Global Thinkers. In 2021, *TIME* magazine listed her among their 100 Next Generation Leaders, and *Fortune* magazine included her as one of the 40 Under 40 list. "It's rare to come across a legal prodigy like Lina Khan," Rohit Chopra, a former FTC commissioner who worked with Khan, told Streitfeld. "You don't see many law students publish groundbreaking legal research, or research that had such a deep impact so quickly."

EARLY LIFE AND EDUCATION

Lina M. Khan was born in London, England on March 3, 1989. Her parents are of Pakistani descent, and the family immigrated to the United States when Khan was eleven years old so her parents could accept better work opportunities. Her mother was an information services executive, while her father was a management consultant. Following the terrorist attacks of September 11, 2001, the family faced some discriminatory treatment.

When Khan was only fifteen years old, she wrote an article for her school newspaper, criticizing a suburban New York Starbucks for a policy that banned students from sitting in the coffee shop. Employees answered her questions, although management did not respond to her calls. *The New York Times*, however, picked up the article and her argument.

Khan attended Williams College in Massachusetts, where she studied political theory and also participated in journalism, which had been her original choice of a profession. She was editor of the college student newspaper, with a desire to work for the *Wall Street Journal*. Her research skills kept her in the library for long hours; fellow student Amanda Korman told Streitfeld, "We were routinely emailing each other on separate floors of the library as it was closing at 2 a.m."

EARLY CAREER

Following an internship in India, Khan graduated from Williams in 2010 and moved to Washington, DC, where she was hired the following year by Open Markets Institute, a think tank that was at that time part of the New America Foundation and backed by advocates of breaking up technology giants. There, Khan researched industry consolidation in a wide range of industries, including publishing and poultry farming. In 2014, Khan and Sandeep Vaheesan, a special counsel at the American Antitrust Institute, wrote an article in *The Washington Post* called "How America Became Uncompetitive and

Photo by Wikimedia Commons

Unequal" that cited historical approaches to monopolies and oligarchies. The article made specific recommendations to the Federal Trade Commission (FTC), the government agency whose work includes protecting data privacy, investigating antitrust activity, and eliminating deceptive advertising in corporate America. Khan and Vaheesan recommended the FTC block mergers that would hurt competitors by rewriting guidelines for mergers. They also recommended the FTC create stronger policies to prevent anticompetitive ploys, including predatory pricing and exclusive deals, and end anticompetitive mergers. Khan's work was hailed by government leaders, such as Senator Elizabeth Warren. The two met in 2016, and later that year, Warren gave a rousing speech at the National Press Club, which borrowed from Khan's antitrust language and arguments.

"AMAZON'S ANTITRUST PARADOX"

Khan's work at Open Markets inspired her to attend Yale Law School with the specific intention of taking on antitrust cases. In 2017, while still a law student, Khan published a 24,000-word article that shook up the technology industry. "Amazon's Antitrust Paradox," published in the *Yale Law Journal*, received the Antitrust Writing Award for Best Academic Unilateral Conduct Article in 2018. In the article, Khan accused Amazon of violating monopoly laws, thereby reframing the conversation around antitrust. Khan argued that the contemporary interpretation of antitrust laws, which focused on consumer impact, did not take into consideration an online giant like Amazon, comparing the retailer to the railroad industry during the nineteenth century's Progressive Era. In fact, during that era journalist Ida Tarbell raised the same argument against companies such as Standard Oil. As Khan wrote, "The thousands of retailers and independent businesses that must ride Amazon's rails to reach market are increasingly dependent on their biggest competitor." The policies that Khan promoted have been called the New Brandeis School, after Justice Louis D. Brandeis, another of the era's opponents of the unregulated growth of the railroad, steel, and oil companies. Although Amazon had previously escaped much in-depth scrutiny, Khan's article brought widespread attention to Amazon's overwhelming domination of the online commerce industry. When Khan graduated from law school in 2017, Open Markets Institute rehired her as their policy director. Meanwhile, she continued to publish influential papers. Her 2018 article "The Separation of Platforms and Commerce" won the Jerry S. Cohen Memorial Fund's Best Antitrust Article on Remedies.

INVESTIGATING THE BIG FOUR

During 2018 Khan worked at the FTC as an advisor to Rohit Chopra, a commissioner at the organization, which was then contemplating the expansion of antitrust laws for the first time in many years. The following year, she served as a senior aide to the US House judiciary committee, where she worked for sixteen months on a lawsuit against technology's Big Four—Amazon, Apple, Facebook, and Google. The suit requested information from more than eighty companies about how the Big Four had hurt their businesses. The result was a 451-page report, detailing the abuses that companies such as Amazon and Google used to maintain their power. The report concluded that all four tech companies were monopolies that needed to be restructured, and it had a major impact on the technology industry. As former FTC Chair William Kovacic told Shannon Bond for *National Public Radio* (1 July 2021), "My understanding from looking at the writings of Chair Khan and the community of those who demand transformation of the antitrust system is that it is better to litigate and lose than to watch from the sidelines. So there's a belief that just bringing the case has a deterrent effect."

During 2020 Khan was hired as an associate professor of law at Columbia Law School, where she taught classes on antimonopoly law. Also that year Khan became a member of the New York State Bar Association and co-authored "The Case for 'Unfair Methods of Competition' Rulemaking," which received that year's Antitrust Writing Award for Best General Antitrust Academic Article. Khan has argued that monopolies can affect even the workings of democracy at its most basic level. "This is a moment in time that invites a movement," Khan explained to Streitfeld. "It's bigger than antitrust, bigger than Big Tech. It's about whether the laws serve democratic ends."

FEDERAL TRADE COMMISSION CHAIR

On June 15, 2021, the Senate confirmed Khan to a seat on the FTC in a bipartisan vote of 69 to 28. President Joe Biden then broke with the longtime policy of placing people from the private sector into FTC leadership when he appointed Khan to the chair of the FTC only hours after the vote. Khan became the youngest person, at thirty-two years old, to take the position in the commission's history; some critics cited her age as an argument against her. Just weeks after her appointment, both Amazon and Facebook called for Khan to recuse herself on antitrust cases, claiming she would not be impartial. However, Khan's work did not violate any of the federal ethics rules, such as employment history or investments, which would demand a recusal.

Although Republicans were mainly silent about Khan's new role, it was hailed by many Democrats, including Senator Amy Klobuchar, who remarked, as reported by David McCabe and Cecilia Kang for *The New York Times* (15 June 2021), "Deep understanding of competition policy will be vital as we strengthen antitrust enforcement. We need all hands on deck as we take on some of the biggest monopolies in the world." Similarly, antitrust advocates praised her appointment. Stacy Mitchell, codirector of the Institute for Local Self-Reliance, called her appointment a "gamechanger," as reported by Kari Paul for *The Guardian* (15 Aug. 2021), explaining that Khan "understands how these companies are harming workers, innovation and ultimately democracy and is committed to taking them head on."

Khan's appointment to the FTC came at a time when there was growing concern among lawmakers about Big Tech. In her new role, one of her first actions was to bring a lawsuit against the technology giants Amazon and Facebook. A suit against Facebook had already begun in the spring of 2021, but it had been dismissed for lack of evidence that it operated as a monopoly. Soon after Khan took office, President Biden signed an executive order with seventy-two initiatives for breaking up corporate antitrust moves.

PERSONAL LIFE

In 2018, Khan married Shah Ali, a Pakistani-born cardiologist and assistant instructor working at the University of Texas Southwestern Medical Center. Speaking to Khan's dedication to her career, Ali told Streitfeld, "Amazon is a monopoly, and I worry that it monopolizes Lina. I learn about what she is doing from looking at her Twitter feed."

Khan enjoys photography and sometimes posts her photos on her website.

SUGGESTED READING

Bond, Shannon. "New FTC Chair Lina Khan Wants to Redefine Monopoly Power for the Age of Big Tech." *National Public Radio*, 1 July 2021, www.npr.org/2021/07/01/1011907383/new-ftc-chair-lina-khan-wants-to-redefine-monopoly-power-for-the-age-of-big-tech. Accessed 6 Nov. 2021.

Knox, Ron. "How Washington Got Back into Trustbusting." *The Washington Post*, 25 June 2021, www.washingtonpost.com/outlook/2021/06/25/ftc-antitrust-monopoly-silicon-valley/. Accessed 5 Oct. 2021.

McCabe, David, and Cecilia Kang. "Biden Names Lina Khan, a Big-Tech Critic, as F.T.C. Chair." *The New York Times*, 15 June 2021, www.nytimes.com/2021/06/15/technology/lina-khan-ftc.html. Accessed 18 October 2021.

Meyer, Robinson. "How to Fight Amazon (Before You Turn 29)." *The Atlantic*, July/Aug. 2018, www.theatlantic.com/magazine/archive/2018/07/lina-khan-antitrust/561743/. Accessed 1 Nov. 2021.

Paul, Kari. "'They Should Be Worried': Will Lina Khan Take Down Big Tech?" *The Guardian*, 15 Aug. 2021, www.theguardian.com/us-news/2021/aug/14/lina-khan-big-tech-ftc-antitrust. Accessed 4 Nov. 2021.

Streitfeld, David. "Amazon's Antitrust Antagonist Has a Breakthrough Idea." *The New York Times*, 7 Sept. 2018, www.nytimes.com/2018/09/07/technology/monopoly-antitrust-lina-khan-amazon.html. Accessed 20 Oct. 2021.

SELECTED WORKS

"How America Became Uncompetitive and Unequal," *The Washington Post*, 2014; "Amazon's Antitrust Paradox," *Yale Law Journal*, 2017; "The Separation of Platforms and Commerce," *Columbia Law Review*, 2019; "The Case for 'Unfair Methods of Competition' Rulemaking" (with Rohit Chopra), *The University of Chicago Law Review*, 2020

—*Judy Johnson*

Tony Khan

Born: October 10, 1982
Occupation: Sports executive and promoter

Tony Khan built his reputation as a savvy sports executive in roles with the Jacksonville Jaguars of the National Football League (NFL) and the British soccer club Fulham—both franchises owned by his father, the billionaire entrepreneur Shahid Khan. Yet while the younger Khan clearly benefited from his family's wealth, he also carved out a niche for himself with a passion for cutting-edge statistical analysis. His success eventually gave him the opportunity to branch out with his own ventures, including the sports analytics firm TruMedia Networks. Most notable, however, was his creation of the professional wrestling organization All Elite Wrestling (AEW), which became his primary focus and brought him a new level of media attention.

Khan launched AEW in 2019, despite his father's initial disapproval. A lifelong fan of wrestling, Khan, who Hank Tucker described in an interview for *Forbes* (15 June 2021) as "a skinny stats geek," nevertheless cut a somewhat unlikely figure in the flamboyantly combative world of pro wrestling. Furthermore, his new promotion faced a tall task in challenging the long-standing dominance of the rival World Wrestling Entertainment (WWE). Yet Khan welcomed the competition: "There's no reason why there only needs to be one wrestling company," he told Tucker. "The wrestling business is hotter now than it's been in a long time." Indeed, under his leadership AEW quickly found an audience, with its flagship cable television program, *Dynamite*, proving particularly popular.

EARLY LIFE AND EDUCATION

Anthony Rafiq Khan was born in Champaign-Urbana, Illinois, on October 10, 1982. His father, Shahid Khan, was born and raised in Lahore, Pakistan, and arrived in the United States as a teenager, eventually becoming a billionaire in the auto parts industry. Khan's mother, Ann Carlson Khan, was born in the United States. Kahn was raised with a sister named Shanna.

Growing up, Khan loved sports, particularly basketball, football, and pro wrestling. Though he was not an athlete himself, his mind for

Photo by All Elite Wrestling,
via Wikimedia Commons

sports analysis was evident from an early age. When he was in the eighth grade, he appeared on a local radio station to offer his analysis and prediction for the 1997 Super Bowl. His parents encouraged his interests. "We let him absorb everything he could," his mother told Ryan O'Halloran for the *Florida Times-Union* (12 Sept. 2015). "Eventually, he found basketball and he knew everything [there was] to know about basketball. And he would go everywhere talking about statistics."

Khan attended the exclusive University of Illinois Laboratory High School, where he served as the varsity basketball team's statistician at age thirteen. A few years later, while still a student, he became the team's assistant coach. During his senior year, he was even called upon to fill in as head coach for one game when the regular coach fell ill, providing an early taste of leadership. "It was amazing," his mother recalled to O'Halloran. "They could have forfeited the game, but the players rallied around him." Though Khan himself downplayed the episode, noting that his team was facing a much weaker opponent and would likely have won even without his coaching effort, those around him recognized it as a notable accomplishment. The school even found Khan's commitment impressive enough to make him the inaugural recipient of the Tony Khan Most Dedicated Award.

Khan graduated from high school in 2001. He went on to enroll at the University of Illinois, where he initially focused on pursuing a basketball coaching career. However, he soon decided to study finance instead, and earned his bachelor's degree in 2007.

EARLY BUSINESS CAREER

After graduating from college, Khan took a job at one of his father's ventures, the biodiesel company BioAlternative, based in Covington, Indiana. He stepped into the position of general manager, a role that required intense attention to detail, as he told O'Halloran. "We were doing something nobody had ever done—a lot of people had tried to make biodiesel from used cooking oils, but not in the volume we were trying to make it and especially using the process we were trying to use," he recalled. "It was experimental and we had to make changes to the process and improvise along the way."

Although he was learning valuable business skills with BioAlternative, Khan soon found himself eager to return to his old passion for sports. An opportunity presented itself when his father sought to buy the St. Louis Rams of the NFL. Khan was deeply involved in the negotiations, which led to a preliminary purchase agreement in 2010. Although the deal ultimately fell through, the process convinced Khan that he wanted to work in the NFL. "I was heavily focused on football and I never took my eye off that," he told O'Halloran. "I wanted to transition out of BioAlternative. . . . The last couple of years there, I was working on football stuff most of the day."

JACKSONVILLE JAGUARS AND FULHAM

Khan's father ended up buying another NFL franchise, the Jacksonville Jaguars, in 2012, and Khan promptly left BioAlternative to work for the team. Specifically, he became head of a new analytics group within the organization, with the official title of senior vice president of football administration and technology. At first, Khan's lack of experience working in football and his privileged status as part of the ownership group did not sit well with many of the team's existing employees. But he made inroads, winning over the coach and general manager with his eagerness to collaborate. "I've tried to build a relationship with them to gain their trust and every year, I think they've

bought in a little more and given me more responsibility," he told O'Halloran in 2015.

A central part of Khan's role with the Jaguars was creating detailed statistical reports about the team's players and prospects, analyzing their potential. He also dabbled in scouting. His work soon proved good enough to quell complaints of nepotism. Football teams were increasingly recognizing the value advanced analytics could bring in finding the slightest competitive edge, and Khan was among a wave of young executives leading the way. As the Jaguars had been struggling on the field, the organization bet heavily on analytics to improve their fortunes.

Meanwhile, in 2013 Khan's father also bought Fulham Football Club, a venerable professional soccer team based in London. In 2015, Khan established an analytics department at the club, mirroring his work with the Jaguars. The following year, he took on even greater responsibility with Fulham, working directly with the head coach and staff to build a new roster with the hope of returning the club to the top tier of English pro soccer. In 2017, he was officially named vice chair and director of football operations at Fulham FC. In the 2017–18 season his work paid off as the club was promoted to the Premier League.

As he found success working for his father's sports teams, Khan also branched into other ventures. Continuing his interest in sports analytics, he took ownership of TruMedia Networks, a firm providing athletic organizations and sports media with advanced analytical technology. However, it was his next project that would raise his public profile considerably.

ALL ELITE WRESTLING (AEW)

In 2019, Khan launched a professional wrestling organization called All Elite Wrestling (AEW). It was the dream of a lifetime for Khan, who had grown up watching WWE (then known as the WWF) in its heyday in the 1980s and 1990s. As a boy, he had scribbled ideas for wrestling shows in notebooks, and in his teens he had moderated internet wrestling message boards. Khan saw a business opportunity in 2018, when he realized that WWE stars Chris Jericho and Cody Rhodes would be free agents the following year—with their names on his roster, he could build a truly competitive organization. His father eventually offered significant, if begrudging, financial backing for the project. "I absolutely didn't think this was a good idea," the elder Khan told Tucker. "But I told Tony, 'Look, when I'm dead and gone, I'm going to be leaving you and your sister a lot of money. Why don't you blow some of that while I'm alive?'"

In addition to Jericho and Rhodes, Khan was able to score other familiar talent, like announcer Jim Ross. But Khan was cautious, having seen so many other wrestling promoters fail against the WWE juggernaut. "I don't want to be the next 'blank' wrestling company of the past—fill in the blank," he told Tucker, explaining his approach. "We love wrestling of the past, wrestling of the present and wrestling of the future . . . That's what gives us a great chance to retain and gain audience share."

AEW officially launched on New Year's Day 2019, and the organization's first television show, *Dynamite*, premiered that October on the cable channel TNT. In early 2020, Khan secured a deal to expand with WarnerMedia, and although the COVID-19 pandemic temporarily halted those plans, AEW soon continued to grow. In 2021, *Dynamite* was consistently the number-one rated cable show in the key eighteen through forty-nine demographic on Wednesday nights. By the time the show moved to TBS in 2022, it had bested the ratings of WWE's *Monday Night Raw* at least once. A second AEW show, *Rampage*, premiered on TNT in August 2021.

Along with AEW's success on cable, Khan turned an eye to pay-per-view with AEW's annual *All Out* event. In a discussion with Blake Oestriecher for *Forbes* (2 Sept. 2022), he used a football analogy to compare the two media platforms. "They're independent in some ways, but the actions of one impact the other," he said. "Pay-per-view and TV go together like the offense and defense, and you need them both."

Khan also noted some remarkable differences between AEW and its chief competitor, WWE. While Khan himself was an avid consumer of WWE's scripted, circus-like version of pro-wrestling, he said that he did not want to reproduce it. Unlike WWE mastermind Vince McMahon, Khan did not present himself as a character in the AEW universe. Others involved in the promotion also appreciated the company's focus on actual physical wrestling and unscripted interactions. "It's not written as if it's a soap opera," Rhodes told Tucker of AEW shows, making pointed reference to the character-driven sagas of the WWE. "Tony hired some of the best wrestlers in the world and he doesn't change who they are."

Still, the AEW had its fair share of drama as it grew. The news cycle following *All Out 2022* was dominated by wrestler CM Punk's press room tirade against fellow wrestler Colt Cabana, with whom he was in a real-life legal dispute. His speech was likely planned, but it followed news of a backstage altercation between two other AEW wrestlers. When asked about reports of animosity stewing in the organization, Khan took it in stride. "I don't think that's a bad thing, as long as people aren't crossing the line with each other," he told *Wrestling Observer Radio*, as quoted by Geno Mrosko for SB Nation's *Cageside Seats* (4 Sept. 2022). "I think it's not always detrimental to the box office of a wrestling company when people find out the wrestlers hate each other."

SUGGESTED READING

Khan, Tony. "Meet All Elite Wrestling's Tony Khan, The Next Lord of the Ring." Interview by Hank Tucker. *Forbes*, 15 June 2021, www.forbes.com/sites/hanktucker/2021/06/15/all-elite-wrestling-tony-khan-interview-aew-next-lord-of-the-ring-cody-rhodes-vince-mcmahon/?sh=76cc34c74170. Accessed 8 Sept. 2022.Mrosko, Geno. "Tony Khan on AEW's Backstage Drama: It Can be Good When Wrestlers Really Hate Each Other." *Cageside Seats*, SB Nation, 4 Sept. 2022, www.cagesideseats.com/aew/2022/9/4/23336827/tony-khan-aew-backstage-drama-wrestlers-hate-each-other-cm-punk-colt-cabana-eddie-kingston-guevara. Accessed 9 Sept. 2022.

Oestriecher, Blake. "Tony Khan Talks AEW All Out, CM Punk, ROH and More." *Forbes*, 2 Sept. 2022, www.forbes.com/sites/blakeoestriecher/2022/09/02/tony-khan-talks-aew-all-out-cm-punk-roh-more/?sh=14d448f43324. Accessed 9 Sept. 2022.

O'Halloran, Ryan. "Tony Khan, Shad's Son, Using Passion for Analytics, Football to Help Build Jaguars." *The Florida Times-Union*, 12 Sept. 2015, www.jacksonville.com/story/sports/nfl/2015/09/13/tony-khanshads-son-using-passion-analytics-football-help/15679887007/. Accessed 8 Sept. 2022.

Sulla-Heffinger, Anthony. "'I Really Love Wrestling': How Tony Khan Brought AEW to Life." *Yahoo!*, 18 Nov. 2020, www.yahoo.com/now/i-really-love-wrestling-how-tony-khan-brought-aew-to-life-132401335.html. Accessed 15 Sept. 2022.

—*Molly Hagan*

Bharti Kher

Born: 1969
Occupation: Artist

Bharti Kher, an acclaimed British artist of Indian ancestry, has impressed the art world since the early part of the twenty-first century with her unique use of found materials in a wide variety of artistic mediums, including paint, collage, photographs, sculpture, and installation. Her works, which include elements of magical realism and dystopia, seek to explore the way viewers relate with her art and with life itself. Much of her work is also metaphysical, asking the viewer to make connections between the material world around us and the nature of reality beyond our given senses. Her signature image that she includes in many of her works is that of the bindi, a traditional forehead adornment worn by married Indian women that has its origins in Hinduism. "The bindis now for me have become a material," she explained to Felicia Taylor and Sumnima Udas for *CNN* (17 Jan. 2013). "I took the material, I repeated it again and again and again. I made it mine. I can use them like an alchemist."

Kher believes that all art has a way of connecting individual human beings to questions much larger than themselves. She explored this idea in *Not All Who Wander Are Lost* (2015), an installation at the Isabella Stewart Gardner Museum in Boston. The work was meant to celebrate the explorations Gardner made in her lifetime, but also the journeys all people take as they make connections to new places, people, and ideas. In an interview with *GBH News* (7 Aug. 2015) conducted shortly after the completion of that installation, Kher noted: "We are sitting on a little ball spinning in an infinite universe of which we know still very little. Yet, people,

books, art, museums make us remember why that little ball is also very special. Everything at some level is temporary, and that's the magic, that you experience something that perhaps you may never know again."

EARLY LIFE AND EDUCATION

Kher was born in London, England, in 1969, to parents who had emigrated from India. She planned on becoming an artist from a very young age. "All my cousins, friends, the people that we knew growing up as Asians are all doctors, accountants, lawyers," Kher told Taylor and Udas. "This is what Asian children did. If you were first generation in the UK, you had to be a professional. I think people were very surprised when we said we're going to art school. I did and so did my sister."

After attending the Greenacre School for Girls in Surrey, England, Kher took courses in art and design at Middlesex Polytechnic (now Middlesex University) in London around 1987. From there, she earned her Bachelor of Fine Arts degree from Newcastle Polytechnic (now Northumbria University), in Newcastle, which she attended from 1988 to 1991.

MOVING TO INDIA

Upon graduating, Kher decided that she wanted to travel, but she was not sure if she wanted to return to her family's roots in India—a place she had visited only once, when she was four years old—or travel to New York City. After a coin toss, she decided on India and traveled to New Delhi in 1993. She had a certain amount of culture shock when she arrived at a train station in New Delhi; the country was unlike anything she had previously experienced, and she knew little Hindi.

Kher's short sojourn to India became a permanent relocation, and she settled into her life as a struggling artist. It was a challenging endeavor professionally, as India had almost no art scene at the time. Her first solo exhibition came in 1993 at the All India Fine Arts and Crafts Society (AIFACS) in New Delhi. She followed that with a second exhibition in 1995 at Art Heritage, also in New Delhi. In the late 1990s, she would also have a pair of solo shows at the Foundation for Indian Artists in Amsterdam, but it would be some years before her work began to receive widespread notice.

THE SKIN SPEAKS A LANGUAGE NOT ITS OWN

Much of Kher's early work was in sculpture, which often depicted fantastical creatures that appeared to be hybrids of other beings. From the start, her work made prominent use of the bindi, a colored dot worn on the forehead by married Indian women. Although the bindi has its origins in Hinduism, it has developed wider uses in recent years. "Many people believe it's a traditional symbol of marriage while others, in the West particularly, see it as a fashion accessory," Kher explained on her official website. "But actually the bindi is meant to represent a third eye—one that forges a link between the real and the spiritual-conceptual worlds."

Kher's breakout success came in 2006 when she completed work on a life-size sculpture of an elephant titled *The Skin Speaks a Language Not Its Own*, which was composed of fiberglass and decorated with bindis. She recalled in interviews that the work was the first time people began to take notice and publicly acknowledge her art. Other notable sculptures of this period explored the form of the human body—a theme Kher has returned to throughout her career and that she has often accomplished through the use of body casts. *Arione* (2004) and *Arione's Sister* (2006), for example, reference Greek mythology and feature part-human, part-animal pieces that are covered in sperm-shaped bindis. These works enabled Kher to have two major shows in India, in 2006 and 2007. Additionally, it opened the door for her first solo exhibition at a major international gallery—the Jack Shainman Gallery in New York City, in 2007.

INTERNATIONAL ACCLAIM

As the 2010s dawned, Kher's stature as an artist was growing internationally. By this time, her work had been seen in solo exhibitions in galleries around the world, including ones in Paris; Washington, DC; London; Seoul, South Korea; and Shanghai, China. She became increasingly known for her large-scale installations that explored themes ranging from political unrest in India to female empowerment. One of her most iconic pieces from this period was *Six Women* (2012–14), which featured body casts of six sex workers from Kolkata. Kher's exhibit, *The Hot Winds That Blow from the West*, met with

considerable praise when it was unveiled at the Hauser and Wirth Gallery in New York City in March 2012. The show examined the concept of home through her paintings, sculptures, and installations, and included a seventeen-foot-high staircase covered in sperm-shaped bindis, titled *A Line Through Time and Space*. Another piece consisted of twenty-seven shattered mirrors decorated with round black bindis. She described the latter work as symbolizing her belief that everything one needs to know in life is within oneself and that the bindis can heal any fracture. When asked about the darkness often depicted in her work, she noted to Shivani Vora in an interview for *The New York Times* (15 Mar. 2012): "I know my work has darkness, but for me, the dark element is sort of funny in that British humor way. But I also depict what I see around me, and there is darkness sometimes along with the light around us."

In 2015, Kher produced another commanding installation, *Not All Who Wander Are Lost*, which made its debut at the Isabella Stewart Gardner Museum in Boston, Massachusetts. The work takes its title from "All That Is Gold Does Not Glitter," a poem by acclaimed fantasy writer and linguist J. R. R. Tolkien and uses maps and her signature bindi motif to explore the ways in which travel shapes and reshapes people as they come into contact with one another. Above all, Kher wanted to highlight the idea of movement across the planet. As she noted to *GBH News* at the time of her work's installation, "I think this work invites people to see how history can reveal itself to be a powerful marker of memory and the extraordinary journey of mankind to excel and grow and learn."

SOLO EXHIBITIONS

From 2016 to 2021, Kher's artwork continued to be in high demand. She had four solo exhibitions in 2016 alone, in galleries in Perth, Australia; Vancouver, Canada; London; and Paris. Her show in London, called *This Breathing House*, took place at the Freud Museum and featured her work *Bloodline* (2000) consisting of thousands of glass bangles like those traditionally worn by Indian women stacked on top of one another to form a singular tower. In 2017, her sketchbooks and diaries were displayed at the Isabella Stewart Gardner Museum, and another show, *Dark Matter MM*, had its debut at a museum in Berlin, Germany. In 2019, her solo exhibition *A Wonderful Anarchy* made its debut in Somerset, England; in 2020, *A Consummate Joy* premiered at the Irish Museum of Modern Art in Dublin, and *The Unexpected Freedom of Chaos* debuted in New York. The former exhibition explored ideas of femininity, mythology, and storytelling, often by manipulating found objects into works of art. In 2021, her work returned to New Delhi in a solo exhibition titled *Strange Attractions*. She also participated in dozens of group exhibitions during this period.

Kher believes that her unique approach to art has helped her to find an appreciative audience after years of struggle in relative obscurity. "To make art, you have to smell with your tongue, you have to use all your senses in this really non-linear way," she said in an interview with Rosalyn D'Mello for *Open Magazine* (24 Aug. 2016). "As an artist, I'm interested in a lot of things, but the central part is the body . . . and how the things that we accumulate carry meaning for us."

Kher has received numerous accolades during her career. In 2003, she received the Sanskriti Award, which recognized significant cultural work taking place in India. In 2007, she won the Woman Achiever of the Year, which is awarded annually to Indian women under the age of forty-five by the Federation of Indian Chamber of Commerce and Industry. Kher was also presented with the prestigious Chevalier dans l'Ordre des Arts et des Lettres (Knight of the Order of Arts and Letters) from the French government in 2015.

PERSONAL LIFE

About two weeks into Kher's 1993 trip to New Delhi, she met a fellow up-and-coming artist named Subodh Gupta, whom she eventually married. Kher recalled to Taylor and Udas how she and Gupta relied on one another in those early years: "The first ten or fifteen years were . . . very hard like any practicing artist now. To decide to be an artist takes a lot of courage because there are years of rejection and a lot of loneliness. To be able to believe in your work when nobody's even looking at it takes real stubbornness. Because we had each other, [we] really would support each other."

The couple live in Gurgaon, a city outside of New Delhi. They have two children: a daughter, Lola, and a son, Omi.

SUGGESTED READING

"CV." *Bharti Kher*, bhartikher.com/curriculumvitae. Accessed 26 Apr. 2022.

D'Mello, Rosalyn. "Bharti Kher: The Body Memoirist." *Open Magazine*, 24 Aug. 2016, openthemagazine.com/art-culture/bharti-kher-the-body-memoirist/. Accessed 26 Apr. 2022.

___. "How Keeping a Diary Helps Bharti Kher Create Her Art." *Elle India*, Dec. 2016, elle.in/article/bharti-kher-artist-journaling/. Accessed 26 Apr. 2022.

Kakar, Bhavna. "From Body Casts to Bindis: In the Studio with Artist Bharti Kher." *Art Basel*, 2021, artbasel.com/stories/bharti-kher-artist-portrait. Accessed 9 May 2022.

Kher, Bharti. "Art Up Close: Bharti Kher's 'Not All Who Wander Are Lost.'" Interview. *GBH News*, 7 Aug. 2015, www.wgbh.org/news/post/art-close-bharti-khers-not-all-who-wander-are-lost. Accessed 26 Apr. 2022.

Taylor, Felicia, and Sumnima Udas. "The British-Born Artist Who Became One of India's Leading Talents." *CNN*, 17 Jan. 2013, edition.cnn.com/2013/01/17/world/asia/bharti-kher-indian-artist/index.html. Accessed 27 Apr. 2022.

Vora, Shivani. "Artist Bharti Kher Explores the Idea of Home." *The New York Times*, 15 Mar. 2012, india.blogs.nytimes.com/2012/03/15/artist-bharti-kher-explores-the-idea-of-home/. Accessed 27 Apr. 2022.

SELECTED WORKS

Arione, 2004; *Arione's Sister*, 2006; *The Skin Speaks A Language Not Its Own*, 2006; *Six Women*, 2012–14; *Not All Who Wander Are Lost*, 2015

—*Christopher Mari*

Lee Kiefer

Born: June 15, 1994
Occupation: Foil fencer

When Lee Kiefer first began competing in the sport of foil fencing as a child, she could not have anticipated the highly decorated career that lay ahead. "I had no idea at all what was going on," she told Renee Peggs for the University of Notre Dame website (5 May 2015) about her early competitions. "For a while I was that little kid who just kind of wandered around with no sense of what was happening, and then there was a period where I would get really upset and do a lot of crying because I hated to lose." By her late teens, however, Kiefer had made it abundantly clear that she was a force to be reckoned with in the fencing world. She competed on the cadet, junior, and senior levels, won her first senior-level medal in 2011 at the International Fencing Federation (FIE) World Fencing Championships, and in 2012 made her Olympic debut at the London Games. She went on to win four college championships during her years at the University of Notre Dame while continuing to distinguish herself in both individual and team competition at events such as the FIE World Cup, the Pan American Games, and the Pan American Championships.

Although Kiefer initially planned to retire from competition and focus on her education following her appearance at the 2016 Olympic Games in Rio de Janeiro, Brazil, she eventually switched course, choosing instead to balance her fencing career with her studies at the University of Kentucky College of Medicine. "I felt like I still had more to give and more to learn," she later told Kristen Henneman for *USA Fencing* (9 Feb. 2021) about her decision. That feeling very quickly proved true, as in 2017 she became the first American women's fencer to be ranked No. 1 in the world, and she continued to rack up medals in international competition over the next several years. Kiefer made her third Olympic appearance in the summer of 2021 and further solidified her position as one of the most dominant figures in her sport, becoming the first American to win Olympic gold in an individual foil event.

EARLY LIFE AND EDUCATION

Lee Kiefer was born on June 15, 1994, in Cleveland, Ohio. The second of three children, she grew up in Versailles, Kentucky, a suburb of Lexington. Her mother, Teresa, was a psychiatrist, and her father, Steve, was a neurosurgeon and former college fencer. Although her father had taken time away from the sport of fencing after college, he began training and competing again when his children were young, fascinating Kiefer and her siblings. "My siblings and I thought the sport was strange and interesting-appearing, so my dad started teaching us the basics in our empty dining room and taking us to a club twice a

Photo by Marie-Lan Nguyen, via Wikimedia Commons

week," she recalled to *NBC Olympics* (8 Oct. 2021). "It started as a family activity, which we enjoyed and dreaded based on the day, and developed into something that we were good at, gave us focus, helped us make friends and allowed us to see new places."

By the age of six, Kiefer had begun competing in foil, a form of fencing in which an athlete scores points by hitting an opponent in the torso with the tip of a lightweight sword known as a foil. Her two siblings likewise competed in the sport, and both would go on to fence in college. A strong student as well as a skilled fencer, Kiefer graduated from Paul Laurence Dunbar High School in 2012. She went on to attend the University of Notre Dame, from which she earned a bachelor's degree in science preprofessional studies in 2017. She subsequently enrolled at the University of Kentucky College of Medicine with the goal of becoming a medical doctor.

EARLY CAREER

Kiefer began competing in foil fencing on the national level by the age of eight and on the international stage by her early teens. She forged close friendships with other fencers her age, with whom she often traveled. "When you're young, you fence without any inhibitions," she told Peggs about that period of her life. "You're just there to compete, you're in a cool place and it's exciting, you're not even thinking about winning because it just seems so out of the question." Competing initially on the cadet and junior levels, Kiefer won her first FIE Cadet World Championship medal in 2008, claiming the bronze. She went on to win a gold Cadet World Championship in 2010 and claimed a Junior World Championship gold medal in the team foil category in 2009. Kiefer also made her debut at the senior-level FIE World Fencing Championships in 2009, competing in both the individual foil competition and the team foil event; however, she did not medal. She returned to that competition regularly over the next few years and in 2011 won her first senior-level World Championship medal, a bronze in the individual foil category.

In addition to fencing in the cadet, junior, and senior World Championships, Kiefer was a recurring participant in both the Pan American Championships and the Pan American Games throughout the early portion of her career. She won her first Pan American Championship medals in 2010, claiming gold in both the individual and team competitions, and repeated that feat in 2011. She also won gold in both categories at the 2011 Pan American Games. In 2012, she secured double gold medals at the Pan American Championships yet again.

Although Kiefer initially focused simply on enjoying the competitions and improving her skills, she soon realized that her success could lead her to the highest level of international competition. "It started being a way for me to qualify for the Olympics," she told Peggs. "I was earning points toward being ranked internationally." Kiefer's strong performance paid off, earning her the right to represent the United States at the 2012 Olympic Games in London. Though she did not medal at the Games, finishing in fifth place in the individual women's foil competition and sixth in the team event, she enjoyed the experience of competing in her first Olympics, a significant milestone for any athlete. As she recalled to Henneman, "I was young and everything was new and I just had fun existing."

NOTRE DAME AND RIO

Kiefer began her studies at the University of Notre Dame in 2012 and joined the university's strong fencing program, which competed in Division I of the National Collegiate Athletic Association (NCAA). She experienced great success at the collegiate level, winning the title of NCAA Women's Foil Champion in 2013, 2014, and 2015. She considered the collegiate fencing experience critical to her development as an athlete and on a more personal level. "Being part of the team at Notre Dame has helped me grow into more of a leader," she explained to Peggs. "The University as a whole really works together to support what its student-athletes are capable of doing and is very invested in our well-being. The way Notre Dame cares for us has made the difference in what I've been able to do and who I still hope to become."

Kiefer also continued to compete internationally during her years at Notre Dame, performing at an increasingly elite level. She won gold individual and team medals at the 2014 Junior World Championships as well as at both the 2014 and 2015 Pan American Championships. She also earned a gold individual medal at the 2015 Pan American Games and finished first in women's individual foil at the FIE World Cup in early 2015.

Kiefer took a leave of absence from Notre Dame during the 2015–16 academic year to focus her energy on preparing for the 2016 Olympic Games in Rio de Janeiro. As her second Olympic outing, the 2016 Olympics represented a new opportunity for Kiefer to challenge herself on the international stage and represent the United States abroad. "I put a lot [of] pressure on myself, but in other senses, having one Olympics under my belt, I did probably make more of Rio itself as an experience," she later told Henneman. "I appreciated it more." She ultimately finished the individual foil competition in tenth place, losing to Chinese competitor Liu Yongshi in the round of sixteen.

Kiefer initially planned to retire from competition after the Rio Olympics but decided to continue fencing while completing her final year at Notre Dame. She promptly won an FIE Grand Prix title in December 2016 and another in March 2017, becoming the first American women's fencer to reach the No. 1 FIE ranking. She claimed a fourth NCAA championship in 2017, and that same year she increased her own record with her eighth consecutive gold medals in both the individual and team events at the Pan American Championships. She continued to fence successfully at the international level after enrolling in medical school at the University of Kentucky, and in 2018 she claimed a gold medal in the team foil event at the World Championships. She also continued her Pan American Championships winning streak in 2018 and placed first in the individual and team foil events at the 2019 Pan American Games.

OLYMPIC GOLD MEDALIST

Kiefer's strong performance on the international stage by early 2020 qualified her to compete in the Olympic Games scheduled to take place in Tokyo, Japan, later that year. The coronavirus disease 2019 (COVID-19) pandemic, however, forced the Games to be postponed and many athletes had to reconfigure their training routines amid restrictions on business operations and social gatherings. Kiefer and her husband and fellow fencer, Gerek Meinhardt, ended up building their own fencing strip in her parents' house. "We were trying to train with each other without having to go to the club. Granted, the club was closed a lot of the time too, so that was our move," she told Henneman about that period. "We just tried to maintain a baseline, so we didn't forget how to lunge and our point control didn't get too terrible." The Tokyo Olympics was ultimately scheduled for the summer of 2021, with fencing events beginning in July.

Making her third Olympic appearance, Kiefer progressed through the initial rounds of individual foil competition and went on to beat Yuka Ueno of Japan in the quarterfinals and Larisa Korobeynikova of the Russian Olympic Committee (ROC) in the semifinals. In the final stage of competition, she faced ROC fencer Inna Deriglazova, the defending Olympic champion. Kiefer defeated Deriglazova, claiming her first Olympic gold medal and becoming the first US fencer ever to medal in an individual foil event. "It's such an incredible feeling that I share with my coach, I share with my husband, with my family, just everyone that's been a part of this," she said after receiving her medal, as reported by *ESPN* (25 July 2021). "I wish I could chop it up in little pieces and distribute it to everyone I love." Kiefer also competed in the women's team foil event, in which the US team finished in fourth place.

Following the Tokyo Olympics Kiefer continued to compete internationally. In December 2021, she claimed a silver medal at the FIE World Cup in France.

PERSONAL LIFE

Kiefer married Meinhardt, a fellow Notre Dame graduate and Olympic foil fencer, in 2019. Meinhardt won a bronze medal in the men's team foil event at the Tokyo Olympics. The couple continues to live in Lexington, Kentucky, where Kiefer also trained and studied. "We are five minutes away from the fencing club and ten minutes away from the airport, which fits our lifestyle perfectly," she told *NBC Olympics*.

SUGGESTED READING

"'Behind the Blue': Lee Kiefer Balances Medical School and Olympic Dreams." *University of Kentucky College of Medicine*, 20 May 2019, meded.med.uky.edu/news/behind-blue-lee-kiefer-balances-medical-school-and-olympic-dreams. Accessed 7 Feb. 2022.

Kiefer, Lee. "Meet the Athletes: Lee Kiefer." Interview. *NBC Olympics*, 8 Oct. 2021, www.nbcolympics.com/news/meet-athletes-lee-kiefer. Accessed 7 Feb. 2022.

___. "Road to Tokyo: 21 Questions with Lee Kiefer." Interview by Kristen Henneman. *USA Fencing*, 9 Feb. 2021, www.usafencing.org/news_article/show/1145362. Accessed 7 Feb. 2022.

Murphy, Bryan. "Lee Kiefer Becomes First American to Win Individual Foil." *NBC Sports*, 25 July 2021, www.nbcsports.com/philadelphia/tokyo-olympics/lee-kiefer-becomes-first-american-win-individual-foil. Accessed 7 Feb. 2022.

Peggs, Renee. "Lee Kiefer: Student, Athlete, World Traveler and Still So Much More." *UND*, 5 May 2015, und.com/lee-kiefer-student-athlete-world-traveler-and-still-so-much-more/. Accessed 7 Feb. 2022.

"USA's Lee Kiefer Earns Olympic Gold Medal in Women's Foil, Beats Defending Champion in Final." *ESPN*, 25 July 2021, www.espn.com/olympics/story/_/id/31881631/usa-lee-kiefer-earns-gold-medal-women-foil. Accessed 7 Feb. 2022.

Yap, Audrey Cleo. "For Olympian Lee Kiefer, Fencing Is a Family Affair." *NBC News*, 12 July 2016, www.nbcnews.com/news/asian-america/olympian-lee-kiefer-fencing-family-affair-n606056. Accessed 7 Feb. 2022.

—*Joy Crelin*

Mina Kimes

Born: September 8, 1985
Occupation: Journalist

Journalist Mina Kimes—a Seattle Seahawks football team aficionado since childhood—has developed a career out of her deep-seated fondness for sports, particularly everything football. "I [expletive] love football," she told Thuc Nhi Nguyen for the *Los Angeles Times* (8 Sept. 2020). "Mina Kimes loves football more than I love anything," her friend and ESPN colleague Pablo Torre told Nguyen. "Her love of football is genuinely terrifying."

Having started a successful career writing award-winning pieces for *Fortune* magazine and Bloomberg News as a business and investigative reporter, it was evident that her heart was in the sports realm after she posted a blog on the social media site *Tumblr* detailing her relationship with her father, which had long been strengthened by watching and discussing football—largely the Seahawks—together. When ESPN recruited her soon afterward, they did not know that Kimes would become a widely popular figure in the sports commentating and analysis industry, both in writing and on television, for her unique expertise, insight, humor, and overall captivating personality.

Regarding her roles at ESPN, Kimes has not only worked in the capacity of a writer, composing enthralling features and profiles for *ESPN The Magazine* as well as ESPN's website, but has also had a noted presence on popular sports shows like *Around the Horn* and *Highly Questionable* as a commentator, as well as a host of ESPN's daily morning podcast *ESPN Daily*. Having earned a place providing analysis for ESPN's audience-drawing *NFL Live* by 2020, she has built up confidence in her abilities while also remaining humble about the need to continue learning: "It's amazing how much you get used to giving your opinions loudly and in front of hundreds of thousands

of people," she explained to Emma Carmichael for the website of the retailer Ssense (30 June 2021).

EARLY LIFE AND EDUCATION

Mina Kimes was born on September 8, 1985, in Omaha, Nebraska, to an American father who served in the US Air Force and a Korean mother who, having immigrated after beginning a relationship with Kimes's father, had become a US citizen in the early 1980s. Growing up, her family—which also included her brother—moved often, following wherever her father's military career led, including Michigan and Washington State.

When her father retired from the military and secured employment at a Lockheed Martin facility in Arizona, Kimes's family relocated there from Virginia right before the start of her high school career. Though she had never lived in the Southwest before, she acclimated well to Mesquite High School in Gilbert, where she continued playing soccer. While being the daughter of a Seattle native had made her an ardent supporter of the Seattle Seahawks football team competing as part of the National Football League (NFL), as well as other Seattle-based sports franchises, Kimes would cheer on the Arizona Cardinals when they played, gaining valuable insights about the game. At the time, she considered football a hobby and did not have any concrete intentions of making a career out of it. It was also during her teenage years that she cultivated a passion for independent music, falling in love with the sounds of bands like Minor Threat, the Cure, and Built to Spill.

Following her graduation from Mesquite, Kimes journeyed to the East Coast, set on making her longtime dreams of being a writer come true at Yale University in New Haven, Connecticut. As she enjoyed finishing lengthy essay assignments, what led her to get more into journalism, specifically, was Michael Azerrad's 2001 book *Our Band Could Be Your Life*, which she had learned of from one of her courses. Its focus on the growth of several underground rock bands—some very familiar to Kimes, like Black Flag and Fugazi—throughout the last decades of the twenty-first century prompted her to find out if there were connections between these bands and her alma mater. "In the eighties and nineties, writers at Yale were making 'zines," she revealed to Brita

Belli for *Yale News* (29 Jan. 2020). "I went to the archives and found that great bands had gone through Yale—like Dinosaur Jr."

FORTUNE MAGAZINE AND BLOOMBERG NEWS

In 2007, Kimes completed her bachelor's degree in English, graduating summa cum laude. Having held an internship at the now-defunct *Fortune Small Business* during her later college years, she landed a full-time position at the publication soon after finishing her studies. The next several years proved to be fundamental in her professional journey as she, a business reporter who had moved on to *Fortune* magazine proper by the fall of 2008, wrote award-winning pieces that would launch her career into the limelight. Her 2012 article "Bad to the Bone," for instance—a chilling account of how doctors performing surgery had experimented, with detrimental results, with an unapproved bone cement produced by the medical device company Synthes—earned her Time Inc.'s 2013 Henry R. Luce Award for Outstanding Story.

When she joined Bloomberg News as an investigative reporter in 2013, Kimes was quick to make her mark there, too. Her articles on CEOs Eddie Lampert and Doug R. Oberhelman of the holding company Sears and the construction equipment company Caterpillar, respectively, collectively won her the 2013 Front Page Award for Business Reporting. Furthermore, in early 2014, the young reporter became the inaugural recipient of the Larry Birger Young Business Journalist Prize, which recognizes journalists under the age of thirty. Her experience with Bloomberg News allowed her to expand the geographical scope of her stories. "When I joined Bloomberg, I was especially eager to take advantage of the organization's size," she told Lauren Meller in an interview for *Bloomberg Media Distribution* (18 Mar. 2014) before continuing to say, "Because I work on a wide variety of stories, bouncing between industries and countries, it's immensely useful to work together with so many journalists with such a wide range of expertise."

However, while she spent her work hours penning investigative, award-winning pieces, Kimes would spend much of her free time visiting Seahawks message boards and posting her thoughts on her favorite team; over previous

Photo via Wikimedia Commons
[Public domain]

years, she had begun watching games more regularly again and having intricate analytical conversations with her father once more. When she added a blog post to her *Tumblr* page in 2014 describing the foundations of her love for football and the Seahawks, she could not have predicted that it would get reprinted as "Me, My Father, and Russell Wilson" in *Slate* magazine or that an editor at the ESPN network would see it.

WRITING FOR *ESPN THE MAGAZINE*

Recruited in 2014, Kimes transitioned from Bloomberg News to ESPN, where she took the position of columnist and features writer for the network's magazine. All of a sudden, immersed in a platform where sports reigned supreme, she found herself adjusting to a new writing style: sports writing. At the same time, as a huge sports fan and veteran reporter, she already had at least some knowledge and skills to stand on. As she said to Joanna Demkiewicz in an interview for *The Riveter* (8 Oct. 2014), "I completely changed my reading diet. . . . Instead of waking up and reading the *Wall Street Journal* and the *Times* business section every day, I started reading sports publications. If there's something I don't understand, then I take the time to understand it."

As she began to establish this new stage in her career, reveling in being able to continue indulging in football games while being paid to do so, one of Kimes's first feature pieces to appear in *ESPN The Magazine* was published in October 2014. Titled "Free to Go," the story revolved around basketball player Devonta Pollard of the University of Houston and his relationship with his imprisoned mother, Jessie Pollard. In June of the following year, her feature "The Unkillable Demon King" was published, about a nineteen-year-old Korean gamer known as Faker who had achieved a global presence as a League of Legends prodigy. With her feature stories being largely well received by readers, by the late 2010s she had also become noted as a writer of absorbing profiles, including of NFL players like Von Miller, Aaron Rodgers, and Baker Mayfield.

Though initially intimidated about taking on whole new mediums, the work that allowed Kimes to let her personality shine the most were radio and television programs in which she had to share her opinions with a national audience. Despite having begun expanding into podcasting to an extent already, in 2016, when she was asked to participate in a fantasy football show with talk-radio host Dave Rothenberg and sports journalist Eric Karabell, she was hesitant, fearful of being criticized. However, she did it anyway, and, after launching a radio show in 2017 named *The Morning Roast*, alongside cohosts former football player Dominique Foxworth and columnist Clinton Yates, she continued to acclimate and found herself on more high-profile opinion shows.

AROUND THE HORN, HIGHLY QUESTIONABLE, AND NFL LIVE

When, also in 2017, Kimes landed a role as a panelist on ESPN's sports roundtable series *Around the Horn*—a popular show that began airing on the network in 2002—her profound understanding of the complexities of football, and sports in general, was evident to many observers. Her experience growing up as a sports fanatic, combined with her job as a writer and her continuous motivation to learn about sports happenings around the globe, had equipped her with the skills needed to be an analyst as she transitioned increasingly to providing insightful televised commentary on sporting events. Moreover, her willingness to not take herself too seriously was regarded as a breath of fresh air by viewers, earning her a legion of fans along the way.

After joining *Around the Horn*, she could additionally be seen as a frequent guest host for ESPN's daily sports-talk television program *Highly Questionable* beginning in 2017, sharing the screen with prominent figures in the world of sports, such as sports commentators Torre, Katie Nolan, and Israel Gutierrez. Like every other endeavor she had pursued, she left her stamp on *Highly Questionable*, staying until the show reached its conclusion in 2021. "Mina is not only a very intelligent, creative, enterprising person, she is also somebody who wants to master things," Torre said to Nguyen. "What she has done in sports, it's astonishing, really."

Kimes, who had started her NFL-related podcast *The Mina Kimes Show featuring Lenny* in late 2018, the same year in which she inked a new multiyear contract with ESPN, became the host of the network's new daily morning podcast, *ESPN Daily*, which debuted in 2019. With each episode running around twenty minutes long, the writer-turned-sports-analyst covered some of the most talked-about stories in sports until she passed the role on to Torre in 2020 in favor of joining the regular analysts of the typically well-rated *NFL Live* show.

Having not only covered sports in writing but also as a commentator, including in the booth for the Los Angeles Rams preseason games starting in 2019, and as a podcast host, Kimes continued to be recognized as a true asset for ESPN and the sports realm into the early 2020s. While it was no longer news that her passion for football was the force behind her work, many, including her colleagues on *NFL Live*, praised her ability, through her skills, knowledge, and humor, to ignite a passion for sports in anyone who gave her a chance. As she said to Nguyen, "People don't want to watch television or listen to the radio or listen to podcasts for perfect. They want personality."

PERSONAL LIFE

In 2015, Kimes married music producer Nick Sylvester. They live in Los Angeles, California, alongside their dog, Lenny. A self-professed fan of indie rock, Kimes has given her take on indie-rock artists and albums on platforms such as *Twitter*.

SUGGESTED READING

Belli, Brita. "Who's at the Super Bowl? ESPN's Mina Kimes '07 BA, for One." *Yale News*, 29 Jan. 2020, news.yale.edu/2020/01/29/whos-super-bowl-espns-mina-kimes-07-ba-one. Accessed 5 Aug. 2022.

Carmichael, Emma. "So, Mina Kimes Walks into a Bar . . ." *Ssense*, 30 June 2021, www.ssense.com/en-ca/editorial/culture/so-mina-kimes-walks-into-a-bar. Accessed 8 Aug. 2022.

Kimes, Mina. "Q&A with Bloomberg Reporter Mina Kimes." Interview by Lauren Meller. *Bloomberg Media Distribution*, 18 Mar. 2014, www.bloomberg.com/distribution/blog/2014-03-18/qa-with-bloomberg-reporter-mina-kimes. Accessed 5 Aug. 2022.

___. "Q&A with Mina Kimes, Staff Writer for ESPN." Interview by Joanna Demkiewicz. *The Riveter*, 8 Oct. 2014, www.therivetermagazine.com/qa-with-mina-kimes-staff-writer-for-espn. Accessed 5 Aug. 2022.

Nguyen, Thuc Nhi. "How Mina Kimes Turned Her Passion for Football into a Profession." *Los Angeles Times*, 8 Sept. 2020, www.latimes.com/sports/story/2020-09-08/how-mina-kimes-turned-her-passion-for-football-into-a-profession. Accessed 5 Aug. 2022.

Strauss, Ben. "Mina Kimes Will Host ESPN's New Morning Podcast." *The Washington Post*, 10 Oct. 2019, www.washingtonpost.com/sports/2019/10/10/mina-kimes-will-host-espns-new-morning-podcast. Accessed 5 Aug. 2022.

Winkie, Luke. "How Mina Kimes Became ESPN's Best Talking Head—and Indie Rock's Biggest Fan." *The Daily Beast*, 13 July 2022, www.thedailybeast.com/how-mina-kimes-became-espns-best-talking-head-and-indie-rocks-biggest-fan. Accessed 5 Aug. 2022.

—*Maria del Pilar Guzman*

Robin Wall Kimmerer

Born: 1953
Occupation: Professor and author

Botanist Robin Wall Kimmerer's longtime immersion in the study of plants began during her childhood, but throughout her career she remained well aware of how easy it can be to disregard or underestimate certain aspects of the natural world. "I've always been engaged with plants, because I grew up in the countryside. That was my world. But mosses I'd set aside in my mind as not worthy of attention," she explained to Rachel Cooke for the *Observer* (19 June 2021). "I was studying to be a forest ecologist. That little green scum on the rocks: how interesting could it really be?" Yet Kimmerer, who began her career as a college professor in Kentucky in the 1980s before moving to teaching in New York in the 1990s, eventually discovered that mosses can, in fact, be highly interesting, displaying fascinating adaptability and resiliency. She detailed this perspective in the 2003 book *Gathering Moss: A Natural and Cultural History of Mosses*, highlighting her great skill as a communicator of environmental and forest biology concepts that might otherwise go overlooked to general audiences.

The reevaluation of mosses in *Gathering Moss* is in many ways consistent with Kimmerer's long-standing effort to promote a more nuanced understanding of the natural world, one that not only incorporates scientific knowledge gleaned through laboratory and field research but also draws upon the traditional knowledge of indigenous communities. Her second book, *Braiding Sweetgrass: Indigenous Wisdom, Scientific Knowledge, and the Teachings of Plants* (2013), delves further into that concept and took on newfound significance amid the upheaval of the early 2020s, a time in which she believed people were increasingly seeking to reconnect with the natural world. "We are in the midst of a great remembering," she told Lucy Jones for the website of Penguin Books (20 Apr. 2020). "We're remembering what it would be like to live in a world where there is ecological justice, where other species would look at us and say those are good people, we're glad that this species is among us. We're remembering that we want to be kinfolk with all the rest of the living world."

EARLY LIFE AND EDUCATION

Kimmerer was born Robin Wall in 1953. She spent her childhood in upstate New York, where parents Patricia and Robert Wall helped to nurture her curiosity about the natural world around her. "I cannot remember a time when I haven't been fascinated by plants," she recalled to Stephanie Muise for the website of Northland College (19 May 2015). "I was lucky enough to grow up in the woods and fields and my parents really encouraged us to know the trees and wildflowers and birds." After graduating from high school, she enrolled at the State University of New York College of Environmental Science and Forestry (SUNY-ESF) in Syracuse, New York, where she majored in forest botany and minored in forest entomology. She earned a bachelor's degree from SUNY-ESF in 1975.

While studying botany, Kimmerer increasingly came to view the scientific understanding of plants and nature prominent in academia as lacking in some respects. "I was made to realize pretty quickly that the strictly materialist, reductionist ways of scientific thinking left very little room for other ways of knowing," she told Muise. Specifically, she found that the predominate form of scientific thinking tended to ignore or disregard traditional ecological knowledge held by indigenous groups such as the Citizen Potawatomi Nation, of which she was an enrolled member. She continued to take note of that disparity over the next years, during which she earned a master's degree (1978) and doctorate (1983) in botany from the University of Wisconsin–Madison. Later, in 2015, she would receive an honorary doctorate from Northland College, Wisconsin.

TEACHING CAREER

After completing her doctoral studies, Kimmerer relocated to Kentucky, where she took an assistant professorship position in biology at Transylvania University in 1983. She remained at that institution until 1985, when she joined the faculty at Kentucky's Centre College. Subsequently promoted to associate professor in 1992, she received the college's Distinguished Teaching Award that same year. In 1993 she left Centre College to return to SUNY-ESF, this time as an assistant professor. After earning a promotion to associate professor in 1996, she became a full professor in 2003 and in 2010 was appointed SUNY Distinguished Teaching Professor.

Kimmerer taught a wide range of courses during her years at SUNY-ESF, including classes in botany, principles of ecology, field ethnobotany, and the ecology of mosses, and she often took an unconventional approach when introducing students to plants. "In my own teaching as a naturalist, as a botanist, as

an ethno-botanist, the first thing people want to know is 'What's the name of that thing?'" she told Janice Lee in an interview for *The Believer* (3 Nov. 2020). "What I do with a lot of my students is to say, 'I'm not going to tell you the name. Get down on your hands and knees. Smell it, touch it, watch who it interacts with: What's its story? And if you fully engage with that being, you will come up with a name after having gotten to know it a little bit.'" Her approach to teaching earned her several accolades, including a 2008 ESF Foundation Award for Excellence in Teaching. At the same time involved in hands-on engagement outside of her regular lectures, between 1991 and 1999 she served as the associate or full director of both the SUNY-ESF Cranberry Lake Biological Station and the Onondaga-Cortland-Madison Board of Cooperative Educational Services' Adirondack Field Studies Program.

INDIGENOUS KNOWLEDGE

In addition to teaching at SUNY-ESF, in 2007 Kimmerer also helped found the college's Center for Native Peoples and the Environment, for which she served as founding director. "Part of our work lies in the realm of bringing indigenous knowledge into the education of mainstream environmental science and natural resources students," she said of the center's mission in an interview with Kyle Powys Whyte for the website of the Citizen Potawatomi Nation (3 Nov. 2015). "We are trying to 'indigenize' the science curriculum by exposing them to indigenous environmental values, practices and philosophies as potential approaches for sustainability." She continued to serve as the center's director into the 2020s.

Kimmerer was likewise a cofounder of the Traditional Ecological Knowledge Section, established in 2002, of the Ecological Society of America (ESA). The first chair of that body, she went on to receive the organization's Distinguished Research Mentor Award in 2010. An expert on indigenous knowledge and sustainability issues, she delivered talks on those subjects for various audiences and in 2015 delivered the presentation "Indigenous Worldviews for Sustainable Development" at the United Nations General Assembly's International Mother Earth Day event. "As a university professor and a plant scientist I am all too well aware that indigenous knowledge is not often valued or included in environmental decision making," she told the website of the Citizen Potawatomi Nation about her work. "I wanted to change that, because the indigenous worldview of respect and reciprocity carries the values that we need to survive."

LANGUAGE PRESERVATION

As well as calling for greater understanding and recognition of indigenous knowledge, Kimmerer promoted the preservation of indigenous languages. These included the Potawatomi language that had been spoken by her family prior to her paternal grandfather's forced enrollment in the Carlisle Indian Industrial School, one of several boarding schools in the United States that prohibited the speaking of Indigenous languages and suppressed Indigenous culture and traditions. While the Carlisle School closed early in the twentieth century, the damage it caused to Indigenous language only worsened as those who still spoke those languages grew older. "Our language hovers at the edge of extinction, an endangered species of knowledge and wisdom dwindling away with the loss of every elder," she wrote for the publication *Orion* (12 June 2017). Kimmerer herself worked to learn the Potawatomi language and incorporated elements of the language into her work, including her writings on the animacy of plants and other features of the natural world. Objecting to the use of the word "it" to refer to living plants such as trees, for example, she instead proposed the use of the pronoun "ki," derived from the Potawatomi word *aaki*, meaning "land."

PUBLICATIONS

As a researcher, Kimmerer published papers in a variety of journals throughout her career, including publications such as the *Journal of Forestry*, *Ecological Restoration*, the *Journal of Ethnobiology*, and the *Journal of Environmental Studies and Sciences*. Perhaps most influential among readers, however, were her longer works, through which she sought to inform general, rather than scholarly, audiences about her research and her perspective on the natural world. Her first book, *Gathering Moss: A Natural and Cultural History of Mosses*, was published in 2003. As its title suggests, *Gathering Moss* deals with the plants known as mosses, which Kimmerer characterizes as often overlooked but nevertheless important due to their use in

traditional medicine as well as their resilience and ability to adapt to different environments. "We're busy looking for biological, ecological and cultural solutions to climate chaos," she told Cooke about the lessons researchers could potentially learn from such plants. "But mosses, which have been with us ever since they arose, 400 million years ago, have endured every climate change that has ever happened." *Gathering Moss* met with a positive critical response upon its publication, and Kimmerer went on to receive the 2005 John Burroughs Medal, which honors excellence in nature writing, in recognition of her work.

Written in part during her writing residencies at the Sitka Center for Art and Ecology and the H. J. Andrews Experimental Forest, among other venues, Kimmerer's second book, *Braiding Sweetgrass: Indigenous Wisdom, Scientific Knowledge, and the Teachings of Plants*, was published in 2013. Delving into the lessons that can be learned from plants, *Braiding Sweetgrass* incorporates influences from both Kimmerer's academic background and her long-standing interest in traditional and Indigenous knowledge. "Science is a powerful tool for environmental problem solving, but it's not the only one," she explained in her interview for the Citizen Potawatomi Nation's website. "Traditional ecological knowledge offers important insights as well, based on our people's long knowledge of how to live sustainably on the land."

Though well received at the time of its initial publication, *Braiding Sweetgrass* took on new life beginning in 2020, appearing on the New York Times Best Sellers list. Though surprised by the book's sudden success, Kimmerer believed that reader interest in *Braiding Sweetgrass* could be attributed in part to a cultural shift amid the upheaval of the early twenty-first century. "I also think that the times we're living in are creating a longing for a connection to land and nature: what I call a longing for belonging," she explained to Cooke. By mid-April 2022, *Braiding Sweetgrass* had spent more than one hundred weeks on the *New York Times*'s list of best-selling paperback nonfiction.

PERSONAL LIFE

Kimmerer married scientist and writer Tom Kimmerer, with whom she had two daughters. The couple later divorced. Kimmerer lives near Syracuse, New York.

SUGGESTED READING

Cooke, Rachel. "Robin Wall Kimmerer: 'Mosses Are a Model of How We Might Live.'" *The Observer*, Guardian News and Media Limited, 19 June 2021, www.theguardian.com/science/2021/jun/19/robin-wall-kimmerer-gathering-moss-climate-crisis-interview. Accessed 11 Apr. 2022.

Jones, Lucy. "'Every Breath We Take Was Given to Us by Plants': Robin Wall Kimmerer on Climate Change and Covid-19." *Penguin*, 20 Apr. 2020, www.penguin.co.uk/articles/2020/april/robin-wall-kimmerer-interview-braiding-sweetgrass.html. Accessed 11 Apr. 2022.

Kimmerer, Robin Wall. "An Interview with Robin Wall Kimmerer." Interview by Janice Lee. *The Believer*, 3 Nov. 2020, believermag.com/an-interview-with-robin-wall-kimmerer/. Accessed 11 Apr. 2022.

___. "Q&A with Robin Wall Kimmerer." Interview by Stephanie Muise. *Northland College*, 19 May 2015, www.northland.edu/news/student-commencement-speaker-stephanie-muise-and-keynote-commencement-speaker-robin-wall-kimmerer-have-a-conversation/. Accessed 11 Apr. 2022.

___. "Q&A with Robin Wall Kimmerer, Ph.D." Interview by Kyle Powys Whyte, Ph.D., *Citizen Potawatomi Nation*, 3 Nov. 2015, www.potawatomi.org/blog/2015/11/03/q-a-with-robin-wall-kimmerer-ph-d/. Accessed 11 Apr. 2022.

___. "Speaking of Nature." *Orion*, 12 June 2017, orionmagazine.org/article/speaking-of-nature/. Accessed 11 Apr. 2022.

Yeh, James. "Robin Wall Kimmerer: 'People Can't Understand the World as a Gift Unless Someone Shows Them How.'" *The Guardian*, 23 May 2020, www.theguardian.com/books/2020/may/23/robin-wall-kimmerer-people-cant-understand-the-world-as-a-gift-unless-someone-shows-them-how. Accessed 11 Apr. 2022.

—*Joy Crelin*

Mikaël Kingsbury

Born: July 24, 1992
Occupation: Freestyle skier

Though mogul skier Mikaël Kingsbury demonstrated a talent for his sport from an early age, it was not until he began skiing in high-level international competitions that he began to realize his true potential as a competitor. "I was fifteen and beating twenty-three-year-old people," he told Devin Heroux for *CBC* (3 Dec. 2021). "At that moment, I felt confident. I loved beating the older guys." Kingsbury's success in those early competitions were in many ways a sign of things to come: Between 2010 and late 2021, he competed in more than one hundred International Ski Federation (FIS) World Cup events, accumulating more than sixty first-place finishes and winning nine overall World Cup titles in the men's moguls category. Kingsbury likewise proved successful on the Olympic stage, winning a silver medal in the 2014 games and claiming his first Olympic gold in South Korea in 2018. Yet rather than rest on those laurels, he remained focused on adding new moves to his repertoire, improving his performance in competition, and solidifying his reputation as the best men's moguls skier in history. "You always want to improve season after season," Kingsbury told Gregory Strong for the *Montreal Gazette* (12 Nov. 2018) about his mindset. "Sometimes, especially when you've reached all of your goals, you still want to dominate the sport."

EARLY LIFE AND EDUCATION

Mikaël Kingsbury was born on July 24, 1992, in Sainte-Agathe-des-Monts, Quebec, Canada. One of three children born to parents Julie and Robert, he began skiing at the age of four and grew up visiting the family's ski cabin near Saint-Sauveur, Quebec, a mountain town that featured multiple ski areas. A fellow young skier, future Canadian ski champion Alexandre Bilodeau, also spent time in the area, and he went on to become a friend and mentor to the young Kingsbury. "We grew up on the same ski slope. Had the same coaches. I was eight, he was thirteen. To train with people like Alex, who went on to win the Olympics, was incredible," Kingsbury recalled to Heroux. In addition to skiing, Kingsbury grew up ice skating and also played baseball during the summer for part of his childhood.

Having joined a local freestyle skiing club, Kingsbury was drawn to the sport of mogul skiing, in which skiers race down bumpy courses while performing a variety of difficult maneuvers, including jumps, twists, and flips. His interest was spurred on by TV coverage of the 2002 Winter Olympic Games in Salt Lake

City, Utah. "I remember watching the best moguls skiers in the world, and I remember saying that I want to be as good as them and go as fast as they go," Kingsbury told the Olympic Channel, as reported by Ashlee Tulloch and Andrew Binner for the website of the Olympic Games (23 Dec. 2020). "So I printed the Olympic rings, no one told me to do that, but I did it and stuck it over my bed." In addition to the image of the Olympic rings, the new addition to Kingsbury's room included a written declaration that he would one day win an Olympic medal. Working toward that goal over the next several years, Kingsbury began competing extensively in mogul skiing events. He also worked for a time as a summer camp instructor at a local trampoline club, although skiing would soon become his primary occupation.

EARLY CAREER

As he worked his way through the youth levels of competitive freestyle skiing and into the senior level, Kingsbury made a name for himself as a talented mogul skier who was not afraid to challenge himself by facing increasingly difficult competition. "Every time they have gave me an opportunity I was jumping on it," he told Heroux. "I gave them no choice but to keep giving me chances." In 2005, he competed in his first International Ski Federation (FIS) event, a North American Cup (Nor-Am Cup) competition at Canada's Beaver Valley, finishing in thirtieth place. After competing in a number of additional FIS events over the next several years, Kingsbury won his first Nor-Am Cup event in January 2010. Named the FIS World Cup's rookie of the year for the 2009–10 season, he went on to win his first World Cup event at Beida Lake in China in December 2010.

Though both dedicated and deeply competitive, Kingsbury stressed the importance of enjoying his sport for its own sake and not focusing solely on winning. "The most important thing is not to become too serious too fast," Guillaume Vincent for the *Tremblant Express* (16 Jan. 2018). "I have always skied with my friends and have kept on having fun. We were a good group of friends and we challenged each other to go further. That's what contributed to my development." Kingsbury's mindset soon began to pay off. He reached the podium at every FIS freestyle event

Photo by Clement Bucco-Lechat, via Wikimedia Commons

in the 2011–12 season, en route to winning his first World Cup moguls and overall titles (known as Crystal Globes) at just age nineteen. He repeated those titles the following season, in the process setting a record with nineteen straight top-three finishes from late 2011 to early 2013. He also earned his first FIS World Ski Championships gold medal in men's moguls in 2013, along with a silver in dual moguls.

OLYMPIC MEDALIST

Kingsbury made his Olympic debut in 2014, competing in the men's moguls event at the Winter Olympic Games in Sochi, Russia. "I felt like I was accomplishing something huge. It was a crazy feeling to realize that I had finally become an Olympian," he told Vincent about the experience. "At the opening ceremonies march, when you realize it's now you waving to the crowd and you're not in front of the television anymore, that you are part of the show, it's quite a feeling." Kingsbury placed second behind Canadian skier and longtime friend Alexandre Bilodeau, winning a silver medal.

In 2018, Kingsbury returned to Olympic competition, entering the men's moguls event at the Games in South Korea. "The run is hard to remember," he later told Heroux about his performance there. "I remember some of it. The thing I remember most is crossing the line." The run was much more memorable for spectators and earned him another medal: this time the gold, ahead of Japanese bronze medalist Daichi Hara and Australian silver medalist Matt Graham. In recognition of this crowning achievement, along with other victories that made him unequivocally one of the top skiers in the world, Kingsbury was awarded the Lou Marsh Trophy by the *Toronto Star* as Canadian athlete of the year in 2018.

SUCCESSES AND SETBACKS

Along with his Olympics success, Kingsbury continued to dominate in World Cup competition, winning the men's moguls and overall titles year after year with remarkable consistency. He also remained a top contender at the World Championships, taking a silver medal in moguls and a gold in dual moguls in 2015. However, he was disappointed with his performance at the 2017 World Championships—he earned a bronze medal in men's moguls and did not medal in dual moguls—and pledged to do better at the 2019 edition of the event. "My last world championships didn't go as well as I wanted it to," he told Alex Azzi for *NBC Sports*. "This year, [the world championships] are my main goal. . . . I'm trying to be at my peak there." Kingsbury fulfilled his goal, winning a gold medal in both the men's moguls and the dual moguls categories at the World Championships in early 2019.

Another major milestone came later in 2019, as Kingsbury made his hundredth appearance in a World Cup event while competing in Finland that December. His victory in that event marked his fifty-seventh World Cup win, further solidifying his status as one of the most decorated mogul skiers of all time. He went on to win several additional World Cup events over the course of the 2019–20 season, securing an incredible ninth consecutive title in both moguls and overall competition.

Unfortunately for Kingsbury, his run of dominance experienced a significant setback in December 2020, when he landed poorly while practicing a jump in Finland and fractured two vertebrae. Though not career ending, the injury was a painful one and forced him to skip the first events of the 2020–21 FIS season. "I think the most painful part for me at the beginning was just knowing that I was going to miss the start of the season, especially since I've been able to ski for 107 starts in a row basically since the Vancouver Olympics," he told the media following the incident, as reported by Donna Spencer for *CBC* (3 Dec. 2020). The ongoing coronavirus disease 2019 (COVID-19) pandemic also delayed his ability to pursue treatment, and Kingsbury spent several weeks resting and recovering.

RETURN TO COMPETITION

After more than a month of rehabilitation, Kingsbury returned to competition in February 2021, appearing in a World Cup event held at the Deer Valley Resort in Utah. He competed in both the men's moguls and dual moguls categories and showed few signs that his injury had slowed him down, claiming first place in both. The following month, Kingsbury once again put forth a dominant performance at the World Championships, winning the men's moguls and dual moguls competitions in Almaty, Kazakhstan.

Kingsbury began the 2021–22 season in Finland, winning a World Cup event there in December 2021. He earned another win later that month at Idre Fjäll in Sweden. Much of the media attention surrounding him, however, concerned whether the former gold medalist planned to compete at the 2022 Winter Olympics in Beijing, China. Kingsbury expressed interest in doing so, though he noted in interviews that those games could be his last. As he told the Olympic Channel, as reported by Tulloch and Binner, "I'm excited just to get another opportunity to win a medal."

PERSONAL LIFE

Alongside his passion for freestyle skiing, Kingsbury is an avid fan of hockey and supports the National Hockey League team the Montreal Canadiens. He also plays recreational hockey himself from time to time. "Believe it or not, for a guy who never played hockey growing up, I can actually handle myself quite well on the ice," he told Hugo Fontaine in an interview for the Canadiens' website (29 Aug. 2014). While often out on the road for competitions, he continued to base himself in Quebec. Kingsbury had sponsorships with several major companies, including the automobile manufacturer Volvo and the sportswear company Under Armour.

SUGGESTED READING

Azzi, Alex. "One Year after Winning Olympic Gold, Mikael Kingsbury Is Still Striving for More." *NBC Sports*, 8 Feb. 2019, olympics.nbcsports.com/2019/02/08/one-year-after-winning-olympic-gold-mikael-kingsbury-is-still-striving-for-more/. Accessed 10 Dec. 2021.

Heroux, Devin. "Inside the Mind of Canada's Mikaël Kingsbury, the Greatest Moguls Skier in History." *CBC*, 3 Dec. 2021, www.cbc.ca/sports/olympics/winter/skiing/mikael-kingsbury-moguls-inside-mind-greatest-in-history-devin-heroux-1.6269376. Accessed 10 Dec. 2021.

Kingsbury, Mikaël. "Exclusive! Mogul King Mikael Kingsbury Excited to 'Be the Hunter' after Quick Recovery." Interview by Ashlee Tulloch and Andrew Binner. *Olympics*, 23 Dec. 2020, olympics.com/en/featured-news/interview-mogul-mikael-kingsbury-new-challenge. Accessed 10 Dec. 2021.

___. "Hab at Heart—Mikaël Kingsbury." Interview by Hugo Fontaine, translated by Steven Nechay. *Montreal Canadiens*, NHL, 29 Aug. 2014, www.nhl.com/canadiens/news/hab-at-heart-mikael-kingsbury/c-729320. Accessed 10 Dec. 2021.

___. "Interview with Mikaël Kingsbury." Interview by Guillaume Vincent. *Tremblant Express*, 16 Jan. 2018, tremblantexpress.com/en/entrevue-avec-mikael-kingsbury/. Accessed 10 Dec. 2021.

Spencer, Donna. "Canadian Moguls Star Mikael Kingsbury Out 4 to 6 Weeks with Back Injury." *CBC*, 3 Dec. 2020, www.cbc.ca/sports/olympics/winter/freestyle-skiing/mikael-kingsbury-back-injury-1.5826510. Accessed 10 Dec. 2021.

Strong, Gregory. "New Health Regimen, New Moves Give Moguls Ace Mikaël Kingsbury a Lift." *Montreal Gazette*, 12 Nov. 2018, montrealgazette.com/sports/olympics/new-health-regimen-new-moves-give-moguls-ace-mikael-kingsbury-a-lift. Accessed 10 Dec. 2021.

—Joy Crelin

Katie Kitamura

Born: 1979
Occupation: Novelist

Katie Kitamura's approach to creating fictional worlds and characters is so rooted in a need to observe and understand one's surroundings as well as one's cultural place, on the process of unconfidently interpreting people and events, that for a long time she had trouble accepting authorial control and referred to herself as a teacher instead of a writer in formal settings. Yet despite such discomfort with writing authority, or perhaps because of it, by the early 2020s she had become a highly acclaimed novelist best known for her books *A Separation* (2017) and *Intimacies* (2021); the latter was named one of the top ten best books of the year by *The New York Times* and was longlisted for the National Book Award for Fiction. Both novels feature unnamed translators as their protagonist. In *A Separation*, a literary translator travels to Greece to search for her estranged husband. In *Intimacies*, a young woman works as a court interpreter in The Hague for a case in which a former world leader is accused of war crimes. Also an art critic and journalist, Kitamura is captivated by how people relate to the world and one another through language. For the two translators, their seemingly detached, first-person prose illustrates their desire to put some distance between themselves and the roiling emotions of their own life (*A Separation*) and the atrocities of the world (*Intimacies*). "I think I'm drawn to characters where language passes through them in some way," she explained to Christopher Bollen for *Interview* (16 July 2021). "I think it's not entirely different to what we're trying to do as novelists. It's kind of being inside a world, finding a voice for somebody other than yourself, and then putting that on the page."

EARLY LIFE AND EDUCATION

Katie Kitamura was born in Sacramento, California in 1979. She grew up in Davis, where her father was a member of the civil engineering department's faculty at the University of California, Davis. An early and enthusiastic reader in general, she was especially a fan of speculative fiction writer

Ursula K. Le Guin and mystery novelist Agatha Christie. When not reading or attending to her formal education, much of her time was consumed by hours of regimented, daily ballet training. Following high school in California, she enrolled at Princeton University when she was seventeen and graduated with a degree in literature in three years, in 1999. "She's not somebody to toot her own horn too much, but she was kind of a prodigy," her eventual husband, the writer Hari Kunzru, later told Brandon Yu for *The New York Times* (11 July 2021).

At twenty, Kitamura uprooted to London to study for her postgraduate degree at the London Consortium. The program involved different institutions and incorporated multiple artistic disciplines. "Sometimes your classes would be at the Architectural Association with design students in the room next door," she told Leo Robson for the *New Statesman* (21 Oct. 2021). "Sometimes you'd be at the British Film Institute, watching a series of films."

Living in London for six years, Kitamura worked part-time at the Institute of Contemporary Arts as she eventually submitted her dissertation and earned her doctorate. Her time in London, she told Molly Young for *Vulture* (12 July 2021), helped shape her sense of self. It was "the first place where I was a grown-up," she said. "First job. First apartment. First serious friendships."

THE LONGSHOT

In London, Kitamura, who was working as a journalist and art critic, also began writing her debut novel. Inspired by her brother, she had become a fan of mixed martial arts, and she decided to set her first piece of fiction in the traditionally hyper-masculine world of ultimate fighting. Assuming the third-person perspective of male characters, she sought to learn more about the sport through writing about it. She additionally ended up gaining firsthand insight into the writing process and authorial influence. "That was a lot of fun, it was a little bit like dressing up in men's clothes before you sit down to work," she told Alan Bett for *The Skinny* (28 Feb. 2018). "But then after I finished writing it I realised that you can't keep yourself out of it, so much of that first book had to do with this dance training that I'd done."

The novel, titled *The Longshot*, was published in 2009. Taking place over the course of three days, it follows the story of two men: Cal, a prize fighter poised to return to the ring after a humbling defeat, and Riley, his trainer. Critics noted Kitamura's almost economical but rhythmic prose; her style capabilities, tailored to her narrative and characters; and her artistic commitment to exploring complicated, not necessarily likeable characters—all of which would continue to be recognized as strengths as she continued her career. *The Longshot* was a finalist for the New York Public Library's Young Lions Fiction Award, given to promising novelists under the age of thirty-five.

GONE TO THE FOREST AND A SEPARATION

Gone to the Forest, Kitamura's second novel, a parable about colonialist occupation, was published in 2012. Set in an unnamed country at an unspecified time, the novel centers upon a White farmer named Tom and his domineering father. A White woman named Carine enters, increasing the tension between father and son that is exacerbated by the prospect of an Indigenous rebellion. In an interview with Jonathan Lee for *Guernica* (3 Sept. 2013), Kitamura explained her deliberation in "writing something that didn't belong to a specific place" to convey a sense of alienation associated with colonialism, and detailed her fascination with exploring the concepts of lived history and hindsight: "I'm interested in what happens to people who find themselves cornered in a given situation as Tom does in the book, when it's too late for him to leave or come to another view. What kind of behaviors are unleashed in that moment?" While the book received reservedly positive reviews as some critics noted flaws, Rob Nixon wrote for *The New York Times* (9 Nov. 2012) that *Gone to the Forest* "confirms Kitamura's prodigious talent," and praised her "austere, psychologically adept voice." The novel was also a finalist for the Young Lions Fiction Award.

Kitamura published her third novel, *A Separation*, five years later in 2017. Taking place in Gerolimenas, a small fishing village in Greece, the book is narrated in first person by an unnamed literary translator who arrives in search of her faithless husband, Christopher, who has gone missing. In this work, Kitamura's foundational subject of interest lay in whether complete transparency can exist in any relationship or with oneself, as she told Hannah Beckerman in an interview for the *Guardian* (19 Mar. 2017): "I think more often than not, there is some kind of persistent unknowability, even in somebody you're very close to. And I suppose there's an unknowability in ourselves." On the surface, *A Separation* does not seem as overtly political as her previous work, but Kitamura said she relished the chance to flip literature's pervasive "dead girl" trope. "It's almost as if that's the trigger for the narrative, like you press go by killing off a woman," she explained to Bett. With *A Separation*, "I knew that an inversion I wanted to do here was that it would be a missing man and a woman looking for a man," she added. In this way, *A Separation*, which received enthusiastic praise from readers and critics, incorporates aspects of popular suspense novels while also subverting them.

INTIMACIES

Kitamura's highly anticipated next novel, *Intimacies*, was published in 2021. The idea for the book had begun to form in 2009, after she had listened to the testimony of Charles Taylor, the onetime leader of Liberia. On trial in The Hague, where the United Nations' International Criminal Court (ICC) is located, Taylor was implicated in human rights atrocities committed in a brutal conflict with Sierra Leone. In hearing his arguments, Kitamura told Yu, she was struck by the "pliability and mutability of language" in his attempt to refute the heinous charges. "I had such a clear sense of a performance taking place," she said.

Like *A Separation*, *Intimacies* features an unnamed female protagonist who works in translation. When the book begins, the narrator has moved to The Hague to work for the ICC and has been assigned as an interpreter for a case in which a former West African president is on trial for war crimes. As research for the book, Kitamura traveled and spent an observational week in The Hague in 2016 that included talking with interpreters. The interviewees talked about experiencing conflicted feelings about some of the people they were assigned to work with and subsequently had a rapport with. "Logically and by the evidence that you've observed, this person has done the worst things that a person can do," Kitamura, in her

interview with Yu, recalled them telling her. "And yet you can feel relieved when they are found not guilty." This uneasy intimacy, as well as the psychological and moral dimensions of such a position, are subjects of her book. The narrator's dilemma reflects what Kitamura described to Yu as the "cognitive dissonance" of existing "as a person in the world" when so many terrible things are happening.

Additionally, Kitamura described in interviews how she was able to grow further as a writer just between *A Separation* and *Intimacies*, as evident in her continued use of the first-person perspective. "I didn't write in it for a long time because I found the authoritative quality of a first person somehow didn't seem to suit me," she told Bollen. "But when I realized I could use the first person to express doubt and uncertainty, when it could be like holding up an object and looking at it from as many different angles as possible. Then I realized it could work for me."

Intimacies was widely embraced by critics and readers, including former president Barack Obama, who listed it among his 2021 recommendations. It was also named one of the top ten books of the year by editors of *The New York Times* and was longlisted for the National Book Award for Fiction. Meanwhile, Kitamura continued serving on the creative writing faculty at New York University, which included working with students taking part in the university's low-residency MFA writers workshop in Paris.

PERSONAL LIFE

Kitamura married British novelist Hari Kunzru in 2012. They had two children together and live in New York City's Brooklyn borough.

SUGGESTED READING

Bett, Alan. "Katie Kitamura on *A Separation*." *The Skinny*, Radge Media, 28 Feb. 2018, www.theskinny.co.uk/books/features/katie-kitamura-on-a-separation. Accessed 5 Mar. 2022.

Kitamura, Katie. "Bare-Knuckle Writing." Interview by Jonathan Lee. *Guernica*, 3 Sept. 2013, www.guernicamag.com/bare-knuckle-writing/. Accessed 10 Mar. 2022.

___. "Katie Kitamura: 'I Still Feel Incapable of Processing What's Happening.'" Interview by Hannah Beckerman. *The Guardian*, 19 Mar. 2017, www.theguardian.com/books/2017/

mar/19/katie-kitamura-meet-the-author-a-separation-fiction-hannah-beckerman. Accessed 10 Mar. 2022.

___. "Katie Kitamura on the Psychological Residue of Bearing Witness." Interview by Christopher Bollen. *Interview*, 16 July 2021, www.interviewmagazine.com/culture/katie-kitamura-psychological-residue-bearing-witness. Accessed 10 Mar. 2022.

Nixon, Rob. "Unsettled." Review of *Gone to the Forest*, by Katie Kitamura. *The New York Times*, 9 Nov. 2012, www.nytimes.com/2012/11/11/books/review/gone-to-the-forest-by-katie-kitamura.html. Accessed 5 Mar. 2022.

Robson, Leo. "'Our Sense of Who We Are Is Constantly Shifting': Novelist Katie Kitamura on Agatha Christie and Being a Reluctant Critic." *The New Statesman*, 21 Oct. 2021, www.newstatesman.com/the-culture-interview/2021/10/our-sense-of-who-we-are-is-constantly-shifting-novelist-katie-kitamura-on-agatha-christie-and-being-a-reluctant-critic. Accessed 5 Mar. 2022.

Young, Molly. "The Interpreter." *Vulture*, Vox Media, 12 July 2021, www.vulture.com/article/katie-kitamura-intimacies-profile.html. Accessed 5 Mar. 2022.

Yu, Brandon. "Katie Kitamura and the Cognitive Dissonance of Being Alive Right Now." *The New York Times*, 11 July 2021, www.nytimes.com/2021/07/11/books/katie-kitamura-intimacies.html. Accessed 5 Mar. 2022.

SELECTED WORKS

The Longshot, 2009; *Gone to the Forest*, 2012; *A Separation*, 2017; *Intimacies*, 2021

—Molly Hagan

Troy Kotsur

Born: July 24, 1968
Occupation: Actor and filmmaker

When Troy Kotsur claimed the best supporting actor award and a best cast performance award at the Twenty-Eighth Annual Screen Actors Guild (SAG) Awards in February 2022 he wondered how he would manage to hold both statuettes and still make himself understood, as he communicates using American Sign Language (ASL). Lauded for his portrayal of a deaf fisherman navigating familial dynamics as his hearing teenager comes of age in the 2021 film *CODA*, Kotsur became the first deaf actor to walk away from the ceremony with an individual SAG Award. Additionally, his performance in this role secured him the first solo British Academy Film Award and Critics Choice Award ever garnered by a deaf actor in a main category, and at 2022's Academy Awards, he became the second deaf performer to take home an Oscar, winning that coveted prize in the category of best supporting actor.

Although *CODA* was almost universally praised for casting deaf actors to play deaf characters, who have often been portrayed inauthentically by hearing actors, some critics—including some in the Deaf community—took exception to certain issues around the film's depiction of the condition. "*CODA* pushes back against certain lazy Hollywood tropes by giving its deaf characters layered interior lives. The production's extensive use of ASL and its casting of deaf actors in deaf roles are milestones worth celebrating," John Hendrickson wrote for *The Atlantic* (25 Mar. 2022). "But the deaf performers play supporting roles, and we're principally following the journey of a hearing protagonist."

For his part, Kotsur, who had already patiently spent decades pursuing opportunities to share his craft in the entertainment industry, both on stage and on screen as well as behind and in front of the camera, has expressed hope that the film's popularity might lead to more balanced storytelling and equitable hiring in Hollywood. "It's so important to not think of deaf actors from a perspective of limitations, because as a deaf person, I can drive, I can cook, I can have sex, I can do all of these things," he told Kyle in an interview for *The New York Times* (16 Feb. 2022). "The only thing where there's a barrier is a communication barrier, and that's it."

EARLY YEARS AND EDUCATION

Troy Michael Kotsur was born on July 24, 1968, in Mesa, Arizona. His father, Len, worked in law enforcement and, for a period, served as the city's chief of police. Kotsur grew up with three brothers, the youngest of whom died in the early 1990s. When Kotsur was about nine months old, his mother, Jodee, realized he had not reacted to loud sounds close to him. Even louder noises, including the clanging of pot lids together, did not get his attention.

Upon learning that Kotsur was deaf, his parents were dismayed to find out that there were few resources available at the time for deaf children; therefore, they became proactive. The entire family would learn ASL while also ensuring that Kotsur interacted with other people his age in their community who could hear. They additionally often took him camping, tried water-skiing, and played golf, among other activities. Sometimes, his father turned on the flashing lights of his patrol car just so his son could watch them.

Kotsur, who attended the Phoenix Day School for the Deaf, where he crucially learned ASL himself, loved *Tom and Jerry* cartoons when he was young and has credited them with inspiring him to perform. "Tom and Jerry didn't have spoken dialogue. I could really relate to them. They were chasing each other around, cat and mouse, and it was so visual," he recalled in an interview to Daniel Arkin for NBC News (22 Mar. 2022). "I'd watch the cartoons, and then the next day on the school bus—a lot of Deaf kids didn't have a TV back then—I would retell the plot of the episode from the night before. When I saw those kids' eyes light up, and they would laugh . . . I realized I loved storytelling, and I wanted to learn more about the craft of acting."

Star Wars also made a deep impression on young Kotsur, and, by his count, he saw the original film almost thirty times. "Keep in mind that this is back in the 1970s, so there wasn't much access. There was no closed captioning on TV, smartphones didn't exist. We just depended on everything visual," he told Arkin. "*Star Wars* blew my mind as a kid. . . . When I saw those laser beams and the spaceships and the costumes and the aliens and the monsters and all of the above, I was so shocked."

Later, as a student at Westwood High School, Kotsur began taking part in school productions such as variety shows and started to envision a career on the stage. Shortly before his graduation from Westwood, he gained yet more perspective from his father, who was in a serious car accident that left him paralyzed from the neck down and unable to sign. Kotsur has emphasized that he had long looked up to his father, and they continued to remain close while Kotsur came to admire him even more for his persistence, which would inspire him in forging his acting career.

Photo by Lyn Fairly Media,
via Wikimedia Commons

In 1987, Kotsur entered Gallaudet University, a school specifically for those who are deaf or hard of hearing, in Washington, DC. There, he studied performing arts but left before graduating, first touring with the Sunshine Too outreach performance troupe of the Rochester Institute of Technology's National Technical Institute for the Deaf for a season between 1990 and 1991 before taking on a professional gig with the Connecticut-based National Theatre of the Deaf (NTD).

BREAKING THROUGH WITH A STAGE CAREER

From 1991 to 1993, Kotsur was on tour with the NTD, appearing in such shows as a children's adaptation of Robert Louis Stevenson's *Treasure Island* and *Ophelia*, a reimagining of the Shakespearean tale in which he portrayed Hamlet. In 1994, he joined and became a regular figure with Deaf West Theatre in Los Angeles, California, taking the stage initially that year as Lenny in *Of Mice and Men*. He would go on to assume a variety of roles with the company over subsequent years, including those of the brutish Stanley Kowalski in *A Streetcar Named Desire* (2000), the titular main character in *Cyrano* (2012), and several adult characters in *Spring Awakening* (2014), among other productions. Meanwhile, one of his most celebrated stage works was the 2003 Broadway revival (originally produced in this version by

Deaf West in 2001) of *Big River*, a musical based on *The Adventures of Huckleberry Finn* (1884), by Mark Twain. The production was unusual in that both Kotsur and hearing actor Lyle Kanouse played Huck's drunken father, appearing at the same time onstage in identical costumes. Kotsur signed the dialogue while Kanouse spoke and sang, and when it opened at New York City's American Airlines Theater in the summer of that year, it marked the first time a Broadway show had featured a cast consisting of both hearing and deaf actors since *Children of a Lesser God* was mounted more than two decades before.

APPEARING ON SCREEN

Kotsur has recalled lean years in which he slept in places such as his dressing room or a parked car to save money. As he tried to expand his career into television and film, he found the audition process almost futile. "I was doing it the old-fashioned way back in the '90s: I had to buy $300 worth of envelopes and stamps and send these headshots to 300 different casting directors, and out of that, I may get one audition," he told Buchanan. "And then I wouldn't get cast from that one audition! It was extremely demanding and it required a lot of sacrifice. . . . I had to keep moving forward, just to prove it to myself."

This perseverance gradually paid off; he got small parts in such television series as *Strong Medicine* (2001), *Sue Thomas: F.B.Eye* (2002–05), *CSI: NY* (2006), *Scrubs* (2007), and *Criminal Minds* (2012), as well as roles in such movies as *The Number 23* (2007), *Universal Signs* (2008), and *Wild Prairie Rose*, a well-received 2016 picture in which he played the romantic lead. "I like to play villains, then have police officers chase after me, which I did in *Criminal Minds*," he told Mandalit del Barco for the National Public Radio (NPR) show *All Things Considered* (8 Aug. 2021). "It's nice to see just kind of the range of the characters I portray and the diversity—romantic, mean, heroes—you name it." It was the realization of a childhood dream when he was cast in the popular *Star Wars* television show *The Mandalorian* in 2019. In it, he played a nomadic Tusken raider from the planet Tatooine. Kotsur earned plaudits not just for his acting but for creating a fictitious sign language for the Tuskens.

Kotsur—who in 2013 had realized another youthful ambition by directing a feature film, *No Ordinary Hero: The SuperDeafy Movie*—told Stuart Miller for *Variety* (28 Jan. 2022) that there is a marked difference between acting for the stage and the screen. "[In the theater] you exaggerate a bit with signs for deaf people all the way in the back, similar to the way hearing actors speak on stage," he explained. "On camera your emotions are more easily captured, so I wanted to use my eyes more, because the eyes can say so much."

CODA AND NEW VISIBILITY

When filmmaker Siân Heder had the idea to remake the 2014 French picture *La famille Bélier*, setting it in a New England fishing town, studio backers thought that A-list actors should be cast. It was not until Marlee Matlin, who had been signed to portray the main character's mother, and Heder threatened to walk away from the picture if deaf actors were not hired to play Matlin's character's husband and son that Kotsur was seriously considered. (Heder had witnessed his performances in Thornton Wilder's *Our Town* (2017) and Edward Albee's *At Home at the Zoo* (2017), both staged, in part, by Deaf West.) The name of the film was based on the acronym for "child of deaf adults," and the CODA in this case is Ruby Rossi, a high school student whose deaf parents and brother depend on her to communicate for them to others who can hear. When she becomes intent on pursuing a career as a singer, the family, struggling to understand, must cope with the knowledge that they will soon have to navigate the hearing world themselves.

CODA caused a sensation when it premiered at Sundance in January 2021, prompting highly competitive bidding among distributors. In the end, Apple acquired it for $25 million (a festival record), and it went on to win numerous awards, including 2022 Oscars for best picture, for Kotsur as best supporting actor, and for Heder as the writer of the best adapted screenplay. "I was so tired of financially struggling for so many years," Kotsur responded when asked by Clayton Davis in an interview for *Variety* (30 Mar. 2022) what the accolades meant to him. "Now, receiving these awards—it's saved my life, my career, my family. I've taken so many risks, and without these nominations and awards, I don't know what would have happened."

PERSONAL LIFE

Having previously worked with her on stage, Kotsur married actor Deanne Bray, who is severely deaf and starred between 2002 and 2005 in *Sue Thomas: F.B.Eye*, in 2001. They have one daughter. The family has continued to reside in Mesa.

SUGGESTED READING

del Barco, Mandalit. "How Troy Kotsur of *CODA* Broke Barriers as a Deaf Actor, on Stage and on Screen." *All Things Considered*, NPR, 8 Aug. 2021, www.npr.org/2021/08/08/1025124051/troy-kotsur-coda-deaf-actor-mandalorian-criminal-minds. Accessed 22 June 2022.

Hendrickson, John. "The Tension at the Heart of *CODA*." *The Atlantic*, 25 Mar. 2022, www.theatlantic.com/ideas/archive/2022/03/coda-deaf-actors-supporting-roles/627609/. Accessed 22 June 2022.

Kotsur, Troy. "*CODA* Star Troy Kotsur on His Historic, Healing Oscar Nomination." Interview by Kyle Buchanan. *The New York Times*, 16 Feb. 2022, www.nytimes.com/2022/02/16/movies/troy-kotsur-coda-deaf-actor.html. Accessed 22 June 2022.

———. "Troy Kotsur on *CODA*, Making Hollywood History and the Movie that Blew His Mind." Interview by Daniel Arkin. *NBC News*, 22 Mar. 2022, www.nbcnews.com/pop-culture/awards/troy-kotsur-coda-making-hollywood-history-movie-blew-mind-rcna18615. Accessed 22 June 2022.

———. "Troy Kotsur's Historic Oscar Win for *CODA* Is Only the Beginning: 'It's Saved My Life, My Career.'" Interview by Clayton Davis. *Variety*, 30 Mar. 2022, variety.com/2022/awards/awards/troy-kotsur-oscar-win-coda-1235218078/. Accessed 22 June 2022.

Miller, Stuart. "Troy Kotsur on His Impactful Input for One *CODA* Scene." *Variety*, 28 Jan. 2022, variety.com/2022/film/spotlight/troy-kotsur-coda-sian-heder-1235164690/. Accessed 22 June 2022.

Potkonjak, Marija. "Sound, Fury and Success on Stage." *East Valley Tribune*, 14 Aug. 2003, www.eastvalleytribune.com/get_out/sound-fury-and-success-on-stage/article_b6527fd8-8065-505e-b052-7ddeb4714051.html. Accessed 22 June 2022.

SELECTED WORKS

Sue Thomas: F.B.Eye, 2002–05; *CSI: NY*, 2006; *The Number 23*, 2007; *Criminal Minds*, 2012; *No Ordinary Hero: The SuperDeafy Movie*, 2013; *The Mandalorian*, 2019; *CODA*, 2021

—*Mari Rich*

Hersey Kyota

Born: May 1, 1953
Occupation: Ambassador

Hersey Kyota first began serving as Palau's ambassador to the United States in 1997, when President Bill Clinton was in office. In 2015 Kyota, as the longest-tenured diplomat in Washington, DC, became the dean of the city's diplomatic corps. As dean, much of his work is ceremonial rather than influential. David Walter, who wrote a profile of Kyota for *The Washington Post* (16 Nov. 2017), has noted that Kyota is among those people in Washington "who ply their trades and plead their causes in the halls *next to* the halls of power." Yet as ambassador of one of the world's smallest countries, Kyota's advocacy is of great import to Palau's citizens.

The Republic of Palau, a nation comprising over two hundred islands in the Micronesia region of the Pacific Ocean, had an estimated population of 21,613 in July 2021. As Kyota described it in a 1998 statement before the United Nations General Assembly, "We are an island paradise, the foremost scuba diving destination in the world. Our rock islands are an international treasure, and our waters are pristine." Kyota also speaks proudly of his nation's reputation as a global leader in conversations about the climate change crisis. In 2009 Palau was the first country in the world to declare itself a national shark sanctuary, but rising tides threaten the archipelago's very existence. Speaking of his own experience growing up in Palau, Kyota told Tanya Joshua for the podcast *There's More to Islands . . . OIA Conversations* (26 Mar. 2021), "Back then it was only, like, two times a year" that Palau experienced a "big, high tide. But now, it's constant." A number of Palauans living in coastal areas have already been forced inland due to rising sea levels.

In addition to advocating for action on climate change, Kyota is also heavily involved in negotiating the renewal of Palau's Compact of Free Association (COFA) with the United States, an agreement that has defined relations between the two countries since Palau's independence in 1994 and is subject to renewal every fifteen years. COFA dictates a significant amount of the infrastructure in Palau. The United States provides military protection and budgetary support but also the use of important services and programs, like the US post office, Head Start, and the Federal Emergency Management Agency (FEMA), an especially crucial program given that Palau faces imminent threats due to climate change. Palau's COFA agreement last lapsed in 2009. Although the administration of President Barack Obama signed the COFA renewal in 2010, Congress still had not approved it by December 2021.

EARLY LIFE AND EDUCATION

Hersey Kyota was born on May 1, 1953, in Palau and grew up in a village on Palau's largest island, Babeldaob (also Babelthuap), without electricity or running water. He studied at several different high schools across Palau. His father, Shiro Kyota, served as house speaker in Palau's National Congress.

In the 1970s Kyota moved to the United States to study at Suomi College (now Finlandia University) in Hancock, Michigan, his older sister's alma mater. Before he moved to Michigan, a cousin in Los Angeles invited him to visit and bought him winter clothes. After two years at Suomi, Kyota transferred to the United States International University in San Diego where he completed his bachelor's degree in 1977 and his master's degree in 1979.

EARLY POLITICAL CAREER

Kyota returned to Palau after completing his graduate education and found work as a legal researcher for the Palau House of Delegates, where he served from 1981 until 1984. At around this time, he was also an antinuclear activist and played second and third base in the Palau Major League, where his brother, Felix Kyota, was a legendary player. He was chief clerk for the Palau House of Delegates from 1985 to 1989 before serving as director. His proximity to Palau's power structure inspired him to pursue politics. "I told myself

Photo via Wikimedia Commons

that someday I might try my luck" and run for Senate, he told Joshua. In 1990, he won a special election to replace a senator in the Palau National Congress. In 1992, he won a general election to keep his seat. He was in the midst of his second term in 1994, when Palau gained independence from the United States on October 4.

While Kyota was a senator, COFA was the subject of intense debate among Palauan lawmakers. Under COFA, the United States is responsible for Palau's defense through 2044, as it does not have its own military. One sticking point between the two countries concerned nuclear weapons. Palau's constitution bans nuclear substances and weapons from its territory. This stipulation came from memories of World War II when Palau was brutally attacked as a colony of Japan. Palauans were also well aware that the United States had tested nuclear weapons on other Pacific islands. The United States wanted the ban reversed. To appease this demand, the Palauan government, as stipulated by the constitution, was forced to take the issue to the Palauan people in a national vote. Only with 75 percent voter support could the government legally override the ban. Votes in 1983 and 1984 failed to reach the 75 percent threshold. After seven failed referendums, Palau amended its constitution to allow nuclear-powered ships and submarines to call at Palauan ports; the rest of the ban remained in place.

AMBASSADOR TO THE UNITED STATES

In 1996, Kyota ran to keep his Senate seat in the Palauan National Congress but lost. On November 12, 1997, President Kuniwo Nakamura appointed Kyota Palau's ambassador to the United States. As a new ambassador, he told Joshua, he learned "the ropes" of diplomacy from veteran ambassadors like the late Banny deBrum of the Marshall Islands.

In 2009, Palau and the United States negotiated a new financial assistance plan through 2023, and President Obama signed its renewal. As Walter reported, congressional ratification should have been a formality, as COFA found bipartisan support. But the 2010 midterms brought an influx of staunch conservatives who implemented a rule that new spending (including funding for COFA) must be balanced by budget cuts elsewhere. Worse, the funding for the compact would come from the Department of the Interior (DOI), a chronically underfunded agency. The renewal remained in congressional limbo through 2016. "That agreement was submitted to the US Congress for approval in 2010, and it's still there," Kyota told Roland Flamini for the magazine *Diplomatic Connections* (1 Mar. 2016).

One anonymous DOI official told Walter that Congress's failure to ratify COFA was "embarrassing." Oregon senator Ron Wyden praised Kyota's patience. "Ambassador Kyota has been the epitome of diplomacy throughout this process," he told Walter. "Despite the years of setbacks, the ambassador has been a calm voice of reason as we forged ahead to ensure this compact stays in place." Understandably, Kyota's patience is wearing thin. As he told a group of ambassadors from Micronesia, as quoted by Walter in 2017, "I've said that Palauans are patient people, but *you are trying our patience*." Meanwhile, the financial assistance plan approached its own lapse, originally set for 2023. US COFA agreements with the Marshall Islands and the Federated States of Micronesia were also set to expire.

In 2017, the Donald Trump administration's 2018 budget set aside funds to renew the compact, in which the United States agreed to provide $130 million in aid through 2023. No prior budget had contained such a commitment. Talks between the United States and Palau were cut short by the coronavirus disease 2019 (COVID-19) pandemic in 2020, however. By the time Trump left office in January 2021, no agreement had been reached. Negotiations remained stalled by November 2021, prompting ten members of Congress to urge President Joe Biden to appoint a lead negotiator for renegotiating COFAs with all three Pacific countries, noting their strategic locations in the Pacific and China's increasing global influence.

DEAN OF DIPLOMATIC CORPS

Kyota was named dean of Washington, DC's diplomatic corps in 2015, after the death of Ambassador Roble Olhaye of Djibouti. Kyota, the longest-tenured ambassador, assumed the ceremonial role by default. Walter speculates that the longevity of Kyota's career has something to do with the fact that Palau has caucuses rather than organized political parties and is, therefore, less likely to experience political upheaval when administrations change. Kyota is not so sure. "It's two things," he joked to Walter. "Either I'm doing a good job, or people in Palau don't care who's in Washington representing them."

Walter described the unpretentious Kyota as "very unlike" previous, more "patrician" deans, like Count Wilhelm Wachtmeister of Sweden, who served the role in the late 1980s, or Prince Bandar bin Sultan of Saudi Arabia (1993–2005). The latter held considerable sway and was granted direct access to presidents and cabinet members. Walter emphasized that Kyota does not enjoy such access. In interviews, Kyota has wistfully imagined playing golf with Presidents Obama and, later, Trump. "Imagine if I could play a whole round of golf, 18 holes, with the president of the United States?" he asked Walter. "There's so many things we could talk about! Like the compact! Increase the funding!" Kyota nonetheless still enjoys the privileges accorded to him as dean. He greets incoming diplomats and sometimes, heads of state; he even received the pope. He represents the DC diplomatic corps at state functions such as the State of the Union address and joint sessions of Congress.

STATEMENT ON JANUARY 6, 2021

On January 6, 2021, pro-Trump rioters staged an insurrection at the US Capitol to disrupt

Congress's certification of the 2020 presidential election, which Trump had lost to President-elect Joe Biden. One of the rioters was waving a Palauan flag. On the day of the attack, Kyota issued an official statement that confirmed that while Palauans and Americans of Palauan descent had the right to protest peacefully, the flag's appearance at the insurrection was "unacceptable." He also spoke directly to the flag-bearer, saying, "If you love the Republic of Palau, please do not embarrass her and her people. I hope I will never see our flag displayed in such an embarrassing way again."

PERSONAL LIFE

Kyota is married to Lydia S. Kyota, who works with him as an embassy assistant. The couple has five children; the two oldest serve in the US military. Palau cannot afford to rent an office for its embassy, so the Kyotas and the attaché, First Secretary Tester N. Yalap—work out of the Kyotas' home in Alexandria, Virginia.

SUGGESTED READING

Joshua, Tanya, host and Ambassador Hersey Kyota. "Palau's Ambassador to the United States Hersey Kyota Shares His Work and Background." *There's More to Islands . . . OIA Conversations*, season 1, episode 5, 26 Mar. 2021. *Buzzsprout*, www.buzzsprout.com/1715060/8211656-h-e-hersey-kyota-palau-ambassador-to-the-united-states. Accessed 13 Dec. 2021.

Kyota, Hersey. "Dean of Washington Diplomatic Corps, Longest-Serving Ambassador." Interview by Roland Flamini. *Diplomatic Connections*, 1 Mar. 2016, www.diplomaticconnections.com/r5/showkiosk.asp?listing_id=5249056. Accessed 13 Dec. 2021.

___. "A Perspective from Palau." *UN Chronicle*, vol. 35, no. 3, 1998, p. 69. *EBSCOhost*, discovery.ebsco.com/linkprocessor/plink?id=4d1e6649-2498-3602-ac0e-eaff733fc3ba. Accessed 16 Dec. 2021.

Walter, David. "Can D.C.'s Longest-Serving Ambassador Get the U.S. to Stop Snubbing His Tiny Nation?" *The Washington Post*, 16 Nov. 2017, www.washingtonpost.com/lifestyle/magazine/can-dcs-longest-serving-ambassador-finally-get-a-deal-for-his-tiny-country/2017/11/15/75609abe-bb36-11e7-be94-fabb0f1e9ffb_story.html. Accessed 13 Dec. 2021.

—Molly Hagan

Barbara Lagoa

Born: November 2, 1967
Occupation: Judge

Barbara Lagoa made multiple headlines in 2019, as she was appointed to the Florida Supreme Court in January of that year and then appointed to the US Court of Appeals for the Eleventh Circuit by President Donald Trump that September. She further rose in prominence when President Trump considered her as a potential Supreme Court pick after the death of Justice Ruth Bader Ginsburg, in September 2020. With Cuban American family roots and longstanding membership in the conservative Federalist Society, many Republicans thought nominating Lagoa as the second Latina on the nation's highest court would not only secure a 6–3 conservative majority on the court, but also motivate Latino voters in Florida, a key battleground state, and help President Trump win reelection that November. As Jesse Panuccio, a former acting US associate attorney general in the Trump administration, told Corinne Ramey and James V. Grimaldi for *The Wall Street Journal* (23 Sept. 2020), "Unlike every other justice on the court, her formative experience and networks are not based around New York and DC. She's comfortable in that world, but at the end of the day, she grew up in Hialeah and went back to Miami." Though President Trump ended up nominating Amy Coney Barrett to the Supreme Court instead—and losing the election— Lagoa remained an influential presence as a conservative federal judge.

Lagoa earned many honors throughout her career. These include the 2019 Judicial Leadership Award from the National Hispanic Bar Foundation (HNBA), the 2019 Rosemary Barkett Award for Judicial Excellence from the American Inns of Court and the 2010 Outstanding Women of Color award from the Justice Peggy A. Quince chapter of the Black Law Students Association and Caribbean Law Students Association at the University of St. Thomas School of Law. Also in 2010 she received the Florida International University Medallion of Honor Outstanding Alumna award.

EARLY LIFE AND EDUCATION

Barbara Lagoa was born on November 2, 1967, in Miami, Florida, to Cuban immigrants and grew up in a Cuban American, blue-collar neighborhood in Hialeah, Florida. Her parents had left Cuba the year before she was born because her father had refused to align with the Cuban Communist Party and was consequently not permitted to attend law school there. Their decision to move to the United States shaped her life, as she told Carmen Sesin for *NBC News* (21 Sept. 2020), "In the country my parents fled, the whim of a single individual could mean the difference between food or hunger, liberty or prison, life or death."

Lagoa graduated from Monsignor Edward Pace High School in 1985. She then attended Florida International University, graduating *cum laude* in 1989 with a bachelor's degree in English. In 1992 she earned her law degree from Columbia University, where she was an associate editor of the *Columbia Law Review*. In November of that same year, she was admitted to the Florida Bar.

EARLY LEGAL CAREER

Following commencement from law school, Lagoa returned to Florida, working in several private law firms in Miami. Over a span of eleven years, these firms included Morgan Lewis and Bockius (1992–93), Schulte Blum McMahon Joblove and Haft (1993–94), Cohen, Berke, Bernstein, Brodie, and Kondell (1994–98), and Greenberg Traurig (1998–2002). Lagoa's area of emphasis was commercial litigation, particularly focused on business torts, construction, employment discrimination, insurance coverage disputes, and securities cases.

One of Lagoa's high-profile court cases was a *pro bono* endeavor as part of the team working on the Elián González asylum case in 2000. González was only six years old at the time; he and his mother were on their way from Cuba to relatives in Florida when his mother died. Lagoa and her team fought for González to stay with his family in Florida as opposed to accepting the Immigration and Nationalization Service's decision to return him to his father in Cuba. As Lagoa told Noah Adams for NPR's *All Things Considered* (2000), "The issue here is that a child, Elián González, regardless of the fact that he is six years old, has the right

Photo via Wikimedia Commons
[Public domain]

to file a petition for asylum. That's it. That's the question." Lagoa's team was unsuccessful, however, and the boy was ultimately returned to his father.

Lagoa turned from private law practice to become a federal prosecutor in 2003. Working as assistant United States attorney in the US Attorney's Office for the Southern District of Florida, she focused on civil, major crime, and appellate cases. Three years later Florida governor Jeb Bush appointed her as a district judge to the state's Third Circuit Court of Appeal. She was the first woman of Cuban American descent to serve on the Third Circuit Court. She served from 2006 to 2019, during which time she processed more than 11,350 cases, wrote more than 350 majority opinions, and served for a short time as the Court's chief judge. In addition, in 2011 she became a member of the Florida Judicial Ethics Advisory Committee and served as its chair from 2015 to 2016.

FLORIDA SUPREME COURT

In her October 2018 application for a position on Florida's Supreme Court, Lagoa summed up a section on her experience and qualifications, writing, "Anyone who applies for this position can say that they are committed to the separation of powers, the ideal of judicial restraint when deciding cases properly before them, and following the law rather than personal preference. I do not know if another applicant will have such an extensive track record proving a commitment to these ideals."

Florida's newly elected governor, Republican Ron DeSantis, appointed Lagoa and two other conservatives to the Florida Supreme Court in 2019. Three liberal justices had retired due to the state's mandatory age limits, giving DeSantis the opportunity to move the Florida Supreme Court from a liberal to a conservative majority. Lagoa became the first Cuban American and first Latina to serve on Florida's highest court. However, her time on the Florida Supreme Court would prove brief, as her conservative credentials attracted attention at the federal level.

US COURT OF APPEALS FOR THE ELEVENTH CIRCUIT

In September 2019, President Donald Trump appointed Lagoa as a circuit judge on the US Court of Appeals for the Eleventh Circuit, which includes Alabama, Florida, and Georgia. The Senate confirmed Lagoa's appointment with a bipartisan vote of 80–15. Notably, however, she chose not to answer certain questions, such as how Supreme Court justices might prevent abuses of presidential power and if Congress could use war powers to reign in a president during war. Lagoa also disagreed with former president Barack Obama's comments that judges should be empathetic. As Nina Totenberg and Domenico Montanaro reported for *NPR* (25 Sept. 2020), in response to Democratic senators during her confirmation hearing, Lagoa said, "A judge's decision must be governed by the law and the facts and cannot be affected by sympathy for one party or another. That obligation is embodied in the judge's oath to 'administer justice without respect to persons.' . . . Empathy does not supersede a judge's obligation to follow the law."

Lagoa's confirmation to the Eleventh Circuit had demographic impacts on the court's composition. While the court was balanced in terms of gender for the first time in its history, it also included five Trump appointees, including Lagoa, on its bench. During her first eleven months on the Eleventh Circuit, Lagoa wrote only seven opinions, the fewest of any of the judges during that period.

In 2020 the Eleventh Circuit debated the constitutionality of Florida's Amendment Four, an issue with potential implications for the November 2020 elections. Two years prior, Florida voters had passed the amendment, which automatically restored voting rights to more than a million Floridians who had completed felony sentences (except for sexual offenses and murders) starting in January 2019. By mid-2019, however, DeSantis had signed a Republican-sponsored state bill that prohibited formerly incarcerated citizens from voting unless they had paid off all legal financial obligations associated with their felony convictions, even if they could not afford to do so. The bill effectively disenfranchised more than 770,000 citizens, a disproportionate number of whom were Black. Federal courts had already upheld Amendment Four and ruled against the "pay-to-vote" law three times before the case was heard by the Eleventh Circuit.

Because Lagoa had begun hearing the case when it came before the Florida Supreme Court four months earlier, she was asked to recuse herself from the Eleventh Circuit case, as she had indicated she would do during her Senate confirmation hearings. She did not agree to do so, however, arguing that she had not heard final arguments on the case while serving on the Florida Supreme Court. Though she did not speak while the case was before the Eleventh Circuit, she was allowed to join the 6–4 majority who voted to allow the provision requiring all court costs and fees to be paid before formerly incarcerated citizens could vote, effectively repealing Amendment Four. As Patricia Mazzei wrote for *The New York Times* (11 Sept. 2020), the Eleventh Circuit Court ruled that "If a State may decide that those who commit serious crimes are presumptively unfit for the franchise, it may also conclude that those who have completed their sentences are the best candidates for re-enfranchisement."

POTENTIAL SUPREME COURT NOMINATION

After the death of Justice Ruth Bader Ginsburg in September 2020, many observers noted that Trump seemed poised to nominate Lagoa to fill the vacancy. Lagoa checked many boxes for conservatives: a child of Cuban immigrants and a Catholic, she was a conservative judge serving in a state that was crucial for Trump's reelection that November, and her opinions generally sided with business interests. She was among the twenty possible candidates for the Supreme Court Trump had announced on September 9, 2020, even before Ginsburg's death. However, as Ariane deVogue, Kaitlan Collins, and Kevin Liptak reported for *CNN* (26 Sept. 2020), some conservatives "felt there were too many unknowns about Lagoa's record. The bulk of her career [had] been spent on state courts, and she had few big opinions on the constitutional issues that now circle the court, those people argued, concluding there was no time to flesh out her record, scour media accounts, speeches or early writings."

Still, Trump continued to mention Lagoa as a possible replacement for Ginsburg. When he learned about the ties Lagoa had to Jeb Bush, however, he pivoted. Trump regarded the Bushes as failed politicians; he had long resented George W. Bush, who had appointed David Souter to the Supreme Court, for squandering an opportunity to appoint a conservative justice. After Amy Coney Barrett interviewed at the White House, aides did not schedule any other interviews. While Lagoa was not nominated for the Supreme Court, she continued to serve on the Eleventh Circuit.

PERSONAL LIFE

Lagoa, a practicing Catholic, married fellow attorney Paul C. Huck Jr. The couple has three daughters together, including a set of twins. Lagoa's hobbies include gardening, hiking, and reading, as well as doing crafts and cooking with her daughters. Justin Sayfie, a Republican lobbyist, lawyer, and friend of twenty years, told Sesin, "I think the world of her. I have great admiration for her as a judge and personally."

SUGGESTED READING

Adams, Noah. "Analysis: Federal Judge Hears Case Brought by Relatives of Elián González." *All Things Considered*, NPR, 9 Mar. 2000. *EBSCOhost*, search.ebscohost.com/login.aspx?direct=true&db=nfh&AN=6XN200003092005&site=ehost-live. Accessed 8 Feb. 2022.

deVogue, Ariane, et al. "How Trump Picked Amy Coney Barrett over Barbara Lagoa for the Supreme Court." *CNN*, 26 Sept. 2020, www.cnn.com/2020/09/26/politics/trump-supreme-court-barrett-lagoa/index.html. Accessed 8 Feb. 2022.

Mazzei, Patricia. "Ex-Felons in Florida Must Pay Fines before Voting, Appeals Court Rules." *The New York Times*, 11 Sept. 2020, www.nytimes.com/2020/09/11/us/florida-felon-voting-rights.html Accessed 12 Feb. 2022.

Ramey, Corinne, and James V. Grimaldi. "Barbara Lagoa Would Bring an Atypical Background to the Supreme Court." *The Wall Street Journal*, 23 Sept. 2020, www.wsj.com/articles/barbara-lagoa-would-bring-an-atypical-background-to-the-supreme-court-11600863300. Accessed 12 Feb. 2022.

Sesin, Carmen. "In Miami, Buzz over Barbara Lagoa Cuban American Judge as Potential Trump Supreme Court Pick." *NBC News*, 21 Sept. 2020, www.nbcnews.com/news/latino/barbara-lagoa-cuban-american-federal-judge-potential-trump-supreme-court-n1240588. Accessed 14 Feb. 2022.

Totenberg, Nina, and Domenico Montanaro. "Who Is Barbara Lagoa, a Top Contender for Trump's Supreme Court Pick?" *NPR*, 25 Sept. 2020, www.npr.org/2020/09/25/916719588/who-is-barbara-lagoa-a-top-contender-for-trumps-supreme-court-pick. Accessed 21 Feb. 2022.

—*Judy Johnson*

Kieran Larwood
Occupation: Children's author

British author Kieran Larwood become widely popular in the United Kingdom in 2016, when he published the first novel, *The Legend of Podkin One-Ear*, in his *Five Realms* fantasy series about a rabbit named Podkin One-Ear, who must risk everything to save his world. The book earned Larwood critical acclaim and several awards. Larwood's original trilogy spawned a second trilogy featuring another character named Uki, who enabled the author to further explore the rabbit world he had created. In addition to this series, Larwood has written fantasy books that take place in a magical Victorian London, including *Freaks* (2012) and a rewritten version of that novel, *Carnival of the Lost* (2022).

A father and former teacher, Larwood has been greatly inspired by the fantasy literature he read as a child, most notably the worldbuilding of J. R. R. Tolkien. In an interview with the *Blair Partnership* (8 Nov. 2017), Larwood said of his work: "I have tried hard not to 'preach' too much in the books, as I think it's important for children to draw their own messages and ideas from stories, but I think the overall lesson is that anyone can do great things if they try. I would love it if children who read the stories felt empowered to tackle things they find difficult with more confidence, even if—like Podkin discovers—it isn't an easy thing to do."

EARLY LIFE AND EDUCATION

Little has been published about Kieran Larwood's early life and education. He was born in Kenya, then moved to the United Kingdom when he was still a baby. At different times during his early life, he lived in Norwich and London, England, and Wales. His family eventually settled on the Isle of Wight in England when he was eight.

Larwood's early interest in the fantasy genre was sparked when he was around the age of six after reading J. R. R. Tolkien's *The Hobbit* (1937). The novel introduced him to the author's fantasy world of Middle Earth, and through it, he quickly became a fan of fantasy literature and passionate about storytelling.

Larwood received his degree in English literature from Southampton University. He then did a foundation year at Falmouth College of Art. Following college, Larwood got a job as a Reception class teacher on the Isle of Wight. Teaching four- and five-year-olds, Larwood expressed in an interview with the *Reading Realm* (5 May 2019), "I did especially enjoy the child-led style of learning and their boundless enthusiasm for anything new." He served as a teacher for about fifteen years.

FREAKS

Larwood has stated that his great hope was that he would someday write the kind of fantasy stories he had enjoyed as a child. His job, however, left him little time to focus on creating such a story. Eventually, he came upon an idea about a group of Victorian sideshow freaks. Despite revising multiple drafts, it was rejected by numerous literary agents and publishing houses. He then entered the story into the annual *Times*/Chicken House Children's Fiction in 2011. The story won first prize, earning Larwood a £10,000 advance and representation by a literary agent.

The winning story was published in 2012 as *Freaks*. It described the lives of several members of a "freak show" called the Peculiars, which includes a wolf girl, a teenage ninja, a monkey boy, a strongman who loves to write romance, and a woman with the ability to communicate with mice. This group of outcasts, who are shunned by "normal" society, find themselves helping the poor and oppressed in London of the 1800s. The book met with solid praise upon its publication. In a review for *Publishers Weekly* (4 Feb. 2013), a critic declared, "Newcomer Larwood spins a whimsical yet touching story, injecting the unpleasant reality of Victorian-era poverty with a touch of humor and fantastical elements, making for an enjoyable and none-too-serious adventure."

Freaks was published in the United States in 2018 under the title *Peculiars*. When Larwood spoke to *The Reading Realm*, he was asked to compare it to his more famous Five Realms series and noted: "It's really very different, as it is a historical/mystery story, but I think some of the themes are similar, such as inclusion, respect, friendship and being able to accomplish great things if you try hard enough."

THE FIVE REALMS TRILOGY

Although *Freaks* helped Larwood establish his name in the publishing world, the novel did not enable him to quit his job to write full time. He instead continued to work on his next novel in the evenings after teaching. In 2016, he published his second novel, *The Legend of Podkin One-Ear*. Illustrated by David Wyatt, the novel is written from the point of view of a traveling bard, who tells the story of a time long ago when rabbits walked on their hind legs and built great civilizations underground. This world was called the Five Realms, and the tale follows a rabbit named Podkin, who began life as a lazy son of a chief but went on to become a mighty warrior. When the Gorm, a race of evil, red-eyed rabbits, invade Podkin's realm to steal a magical knife called Starclaw, they kill Podkin's father and cut off Podkin's ear. He must save his sister, Paz, and brother, Pook, while at the same time keeping Starclaw from his enemies.

The first of a planned trilogy, the book immediately earned acclaim, winning Larwood the 2017 Blue Peter Book Award for Best Book. The award, presented by BookTrust, the largest children's reading charity in the United Kingdom, enabled him to resign as a teacher and commit to writing fiction fulltime. The book also earned the Waterstones Children's

Book of the Month Award in June 2017 and was shortlisted for the Waterstones Children's Book Prize in 2018.

When *The Legend of Podkin One-Ear* was published in the United States in 2017, it was also met with favorable reviews. In *Kirkus Reviews* (19 June 2017), an anonymous reviewer called it, "An original fantasy with warrior rabbits, fierce foes, sibling loyalty, riveting adventure, and genuine storytelling." *The Legend of Podkin One-Ear* was nominated for the Carnegie Medal in 2018.

The second novel of the trilogy, *The Gift of Dark Hollow*, followed in 2017. In it, Podkin and his siblings go on a quest to find the sacred hammer of Applecross. Along the way they avoid the Gorm and come across a remarkable gift that allows the possessor to leap from shadow to shadow. The sequel received strong praise. Writing for *Kirkus Reviews* (14 May 2018), a critic wrote: "The narrative device of a story within a story perfectly fits this tale. . . . Inclusion of ancient rabbit lore and action-filled black-and-white illustrations adds depth and drama."

The final novel in the trilogy was *The Beasts of Grimheart* (2018). Here, Podkin, Paz, and Pook must use all their skills, talents, and courage to prevent the Gorm from destroying everyone in the Five Realms. Narrating the story is an elderly Pook, who must tell the true tale of the battle to a pack of assassins in order to save his life. A reviewer for *Kirkus Reviews* (28 Apr. 2019) declared: "The gripping plot toggles between Pook's precarious storytelling dilemma and his dynamic personal recollection of the climactic battle, enhanced by dramatic illustrations. A storytelling tour de force culminating in a rousing series finale."

THE FIVE REALMS CONTINUED

Although Larwood had brought the *Five Realms* trilogy to a close, he wanted to continue adventuring in the world he had created with a new cast of characters. He returned to the Five Realms in the first book in a new projected trilogy, called *Uki and the Outcasts* (2019). The book followed outcast Uki, who was cast out from his tribe due to his two-toned fur, as well as two other misfits as they go on a quest in search of four escaped spirits. About the book's connection to the *Five Realms*, Larwood explained to the *Reading Realm* (5 May 2019),

"The tale of Uki is connected to the overall story of Podkin, but I wanted to explore some of the other parts of the rabbit world that I had created. . . . There's lots of adventure and new characters, and the bard and Rue have some excitement and danger as well."

Uki and the Outcasts was quickly followed by *Uki and the Swamp Spirit* in 2020. The second book in the series furthers Uki and his companions' quest to find the spirits, while they evade enemies and assassins. Larwood ended his second trilogy with *Uki and the Ghostburrow*, published in 2021, which finished Uki's adventure on a grand scale. As both Podkin's and Uki's adventures take place in the Five Realms, their stories have been billed as both two separate trilogies as well as one continuous Five Realms series.

OTHER WORKS

In 2022, Larwood revisited his original ideas and characters from *Freaks* by publishing a complete rewrite of the novel with Faber Children's Books. Newly titled *Carnival of the Lost*, Sheba the wolf girl, who remains the protagonist, joins a troupe of traveling performers, only to find herself in the thick of a mystery: children are being sucked up into the River Thames in London, while at the same time a mechanical monster has been sighted. Sheba is determined along with her new friends to unravel the mystery and bring the children back from wherever they have been taken. In a review posted on Waterstones, a critic declared, "Thrillingly dark and utterly original, *Carnival of the Lost* is a gripping new fantasy adventure that features a cast of unforgettable performers, determined to solve the mystery of some vanished children."

Faber ordered two more books about Sheba and her troupe. By the time *Carnival of the Lost* was published, Larwood had announced the titles of the two subsequent novels: *The Hunted*, to be published in July 2022, and *The Spider*, to be published in July 2023. At the same time, Larwood announced the stand-alone novel *The Treekeepers*, to be released in late 2022.

PERSONAL LIFE

Larwood lives on the Isle of Wight with his children.

SUGGESTED READING

Review of *Carnival of the Lost*, by Kieran Larwood. *Waterstones*, 2022, www.waterstones.com/book/carnival-of-the-lost/kieran-larwood/sam-usher/9780571364503. Accessed 12 Apr. 2022.

Review of *Freaks*, by Kieran Larwood. *Publishers Weekly*, 4 Feb. 2013, www.publishersweekly.com/978-0-545-47424-5. Accessed 7 Mar. 2022.

Larwood, Kieran. "Interview with Kieran Larwood: 2018 Carnegie Medal Nominee." *The Blair Partnership*, 8 Nov. 2017, www.theblairpartnership.com/news/interview-with-kieran-larwood-2018-carnegie-medal-nominee. Accessed 7 Mar. 2022.

___. "*Uki and the Outcasts*: An Interview with Kieran Larwood." *The Reading Realm*, 5 May 2019, thereadingrealm.co.uk/2019/05/05/uki-and-the-outcasts-an-interview-with-kieran-larwood/. Accessed 7 Mar. 2022.

Review of *Podkin One-Ear: The Legend Begins*, by Kieran Larwood, illustrated by David Wyatt. *Kirkus Reviews*, 19 June 2017, www.kirkusreviews.com/book-reviews/kieran-larwood/podkin-one-ear/. Accessed 7 Mar. 2022.

Review of *The Beasts of Grimheart*, by Kieran Larwood. *Kirkus Reviews*, 28 Apr. 2019, www.kirkusreviews.com/book-reviews/kieran-larwood/the-beasts-of-grimheart/. Accessed 7 Mar. 2022.

Review of *The Gift of Dark Hollow*, by Kieran Larwood. *Kirkus Reviews*, 14 May 2018, www.kirkusreviews.com/book-reviews/kieran-larwood/gift-dark-hollow/. Accessed 7 Mar. 2022.

SELECTED WORKS

Freaks, 2012; *The Legend of Podkin One-Ear*, 2016; *The Gift of Dark Hollow*, 2017; *The Beasts of Grimheart*, 2018; *Uki and the Outcasts*, 2019; *Uki and the Swamp Spirit*, 2020; *Uki and the Ghostburrow*, 2021; *Carnival of the Lost*, 2022

—Christopher Mari

Cato T. Laurencin

Born: January 15, 1959
Occupation: Physician-scientist and educator

For University of Connecticut researcher Cato T. Laurencin, achieving success in the field of regenerative engineering—a field dedicated to regenerating damaged or missing human tissue for purposes such as healing injuries—relies on taking a multidisciplinary approach that incorporates contributions from scientists working in a wide range of fields, from materials science to developmental biology. "The future of regeneration we believe is in taking an 'un-siloed' approach to thinking about regeneration," he explained to Amro Tambal in an interview for the *RE Society Journal* (19 Apr. 2017). "It is with this open perspective toward fully integrating disparate technologies that we can achieve new science and new solutions." Indeed, Laurencin himself has embodied such an "un-siloed" approach throughout his career: educated first as a chemical engineer, he went on to pursue simultaneous doctoral studies in engineering and medicine and over the subsequent decades established himself both as an orthopedic surgeon and as a researcher developing innovative means of regenerating anterior cruciate ligament (ACL) tissue. Through such work, Laurencin hopes to offer a viable alternative to surgery for some patients, among other potential applications of tissue-regeneration technology. "We don't have to do what we've always done," he told Kimberly A. Macuare in an interview for *Technology and Innovation* (2020). "We can do better, and we can do more."

EARLY LIFE AND EDUCATION

Cato Thomas Laurencin was born in North Philadelphia, Pennsylvania, on January 15, 1959. One of three children, he spent his childhood in North Philadelphia. His father, Cyril Laurencin, was a carpenter, while his mother, Dr. Helen Moorehead Laurencin, was a physician who inspired all three of her children to pursue careers in medicine. "I always was going to be a doctor. I knew that from the start," Laurencin later told Stan Simpson for the *Hartford Courant* (25 July 2009). "The influence of my mother was extremely strong in terms of medicine." He was particularly struck by the way in which his mother "treated patients with lots of compassion," he told Simpson.

After graduating from Philadelphia's Central High School in 1976, Laurencin enrolled at Princeton University, where he pursued studies in chemical engineering. He earned a bachelor's degree from that university in 1980. Subsequently relocating to Massachusetts, he enrolled at the Massachusetts Institute of Technology (MIT) and Harvard Medical School (HMS) simultaneously, seeking to combine his passion for engineering with his longtime interest in medicine. He graduated with degrees from both institutions in 1987, earning a doctorate in biochemical engineering and biotechnology from MIT and a medical degree (magna cum laude) from Harvard. Following that period, he pursued clinical training, completing a residency in orthopedic surgery with Harvard's combined orthopedic surgery program and a fellowship in sports medicine at the Cornell University Medical College.

CAREER IN ACADEMIA AND ADMINISTRATIVE CAREER

In addition to working as a surgeon, Laurencin established himself as an educator beginning in the 1980s, teaching courses in biochemical engineering at MIT between 1988 and 1993. In 1994 he moved to Drexel University, where he held a professorship in chemical engineering and served as a clinical professor of orthopedic surgery at the university's college of medicine. After nearly a decade, he relocated to the University of Virginia, where he held the title of Lillian T. Pratt Distinguished Professor of Orthopedic Surgery, among others.

A key point in Laurencin's career in academia came in 2008, when he took a position at the University of Connecticut (UConn). He filled several different roles during his early years in Connecticut, including professorships in biomedical engineering and chemical and biomolecular engineering, and he served as dean of the UConn School of Medicine and vice president for health affairs. In the latter roles, he was responsible for overseeing a proposed merger between UConn Health Center and Hartford Hospital, which he believed would benefit both university researchers and the patients treated at UConn and Hartford Hospital facilities. "This is a very vibrant community and we'd be pursuing the

Photo by Mikeenr,
via Wikimedia Commons

highest level of clinical care, at the same time pursuing the highest level of research and the highest level of teaching," he explained to Simpson. The merger proved unsuccessful, and Laurencin stepped down from the positions of dean and vice president for health affairs in mid-2011. He continued to hold multiple titles at UConn over the next decade, including the titles of University Professor (one of two on campus) and of Albert and Wilda Van Dusen Distinguished Endowed Professor of Orthopaedic Surgery, and likewise served as director of UConn Health Center's Raymond and Beverly Sackler Center for Biomedical, Biological, Physical, and Engineering Sciences.

RESEARCH

Much of Laurencin's major research falls within the field of regenerative engineering, a field of study that involves developing methods and tools for regenerating damaged or missing human tissue. "Regenerative engineering was born from the need to create therapies to help people, to affect the lives of people, to bring hope, comfort, help, and eventually cures," he explained to Tambal. He was initially drawn to the field during his time working in sports medicine, in which he took note of the prevalence of injuries to the knee's ACL among athletes. ACL tears were typically repaired through surgery. However, Laurencin was intrigued by the idea of finding a means to stimulate and direct the growth of ACL tissue and thus enable the ACL to regenerate with limited surgical intervention.

Laurencin and his colleagues continued to investigate tissue regeneration and the biocompatible materials that could be used as scaffolds for tissue growth. One major invention was the patented Laurencin-Cooper Ligament (L-C Ligament), developed by Laurencin and student James Cooper, which serves as a matrix onto which new tissue is produced through the use of stem cells. "Our work showed that we can regenerate ACL tissue," he told the *Hartford Business Journal* (23 Feb. 2009). "While a surgical procedure will still be needed, if the technology is successful it will revolutionize the way we treat this problem." Laurencin continued his work on ACL regeneration during his time at UConn, and in November 2020, he and his colleagues published a paper on the strengths and promise of their new bioengineered ACL matrix in *Proceedings of the National Academy of Science* (PNAS).

Widely recognized as a researcher and educator, Laurencin received numerous awards and honors for his work, including the Walsh McDermott Medal of the National Academy of Medicine (NAM), the Philip Hauge Abelson Prize of the American Association for the Advancement of Science (AAAS), the Nicholas Andry Award from the Association of Bone and Joint Surgeons, the Kappa Delta Award from the American Academy of Orthopaedic Surgeons (AAOS), and the Springarn Medal of the National Association for the Advancement of Colored People (NAACP). He was honored by the Obama administration on two occasions, receiving the Presidential Award for Excellence in Science, Math, and Engineering Mentoring (PAESMEM) in 2009 and the National Medal of Technology and Innovation (NMTI) in 2016. In addition to receiving such recognition, he was the first orthopedic surgeon elected to both the NAM and the National Academy of Engineering (NAE). He is also an elected fellow of scientific bodies such as the American Chemical Society (ACS) (2014), the Materials Research Society (MRS) (2014), the American Academy of Arts and Sciences (AAA&S) (2019), and the American Orthopaedic Association (AOA). In February 2022, he received the Orthopaedic Research Society's

Marshall R. Urist Award for Excellence in Tissue Regeneration Research.

CONVERGENCE INSTITUTE

Throughout his career in research, Laurencin has promoted a multidisciplinary approach to scientific innovation, noting in interviews that the field of regenerative engineering could succeed only by contributions from scientists working in diverse fields. He continued to promote that approach through the work of the Connecticut Convergence Institute for Translation in Regenerative Engineering, which formed in 2018 upon the merger of two preexisting institutes at UConn and for which Laurencin served as chief executive officer. "When we think about convergence, we think about bringing together ideas and concepts from different viewpoints and different aspects that, on first glance, may not seem to fit together," he explained to Macuare. "We're hoping to deeply connect across areas with our science and have the scientists who train with us deeply connect in terms of these areas." Among other initiatives, the Convergence Institute was home to the Hartford Engineering a Limb (HEAL) Project, which set the ambitious goal of regenerating an entire human limb. The Convergence Institute also performed research into addressing the disparately high prevalence of diabetes among racialized communities.

PUBLICATIONS AND PUBLIC OUTREACH

Laurencin has published prolifically throughout his career as a researcher, placing papers in journals such as the *Journal of Biomedical Materials Research*, the *Journal of Orthopaedic Surgery and Research*, *Stem Cell Research*, and others. He has also edited or coedited several books relevant to his field, including *Nanoscale Materials Science in Biology and Medicine* (2005) and *Biomedical Nanostructures* (2007). In 2014, he launched the new scientific publication the *Journal of Racial and Ethnic Health Disparities*, a journal published by *Springer Nature* that "reports on the scholarly progress of work to understand, address, and ultimately eliminate health disparities based on race and ethnicity," according to the publisher's website. He also launched the journal *Regenerative Engineering and Translational Medicine*, the first issue of which was released the following year. For Laurencin, the topics covered by both journals represented key areas of study that would become even more essential over time. "In both cases I think that we are in a transformational period for both areas of scientific inquiry," he told Celia Carver in an interview for *Springer Nature* (3 Mar. 2016). "Health disparities I think will define medicine in the twenty-first century. For *Regenerative Engineering*, we feel we are at the dawn of a new field. We anticipate great things." Laurencin served as editor in chief for both publications following their debut and went on to expand the scientific community's awareness of regenerative engineering further in 2017, when he founded the Regenerative Engineering Society. He published his autobiography, *Success Is What You Leave Behind: Fostering Leadership and Innovation*, in 2021.

As a prominent Black scientist interested in racial and ethnic health disparities, Laurencin spoke out about that topic extensively during the coronavirus disease 2019 (COVID-19) pandemic declared in 2020, noting in interviews that Black Americans became sick with and died from COVID-19 at higher rates than other Americans. In addition to raising awareness of that phenomenon, he sought to build greater trust in the medical community among Black Americans, particularly in the state of Connecticut. Among other efforts, he served as a member of Connecticut's NAACP COVID-19 Advisory Committee and as president of the relaunched Imhotep Connecticut National Medical Association Society (CT NMA). "The CT NMA will serve as a networking platform for Black physicians and play a role in the dissemination of health information to the Black Community," he told Melanie Burnat in an interview for *UConn Today* (9 Feb. 2021) about the latter organization. "I'm gratified to see that all the major health systems of the State of Connecticut have supported this relaunch." Laurencin remained active with the CT NMA into 2022 and likewise worked to understand and address the factors underlying vaccine hesitancy among people of color in Connecticut and beyond.

PERSONAL LIFE

Laurencin and his wife, Cynthia Laurencin, have three children. They live in Avon, Connecticut. Laurencin and his wife are the creators of the Helen I. Moorehead-Laurencin, MD, Research Fellowship Fund, a fellowship for UConn medical students performing summer research projects founded and named in honor of Laurencin's mother.

SUGGESTED READING

Laurencin, Cato T. "Honoring a Biomedical Legacy | Dr. Cato T. Laurencin, Dean, UConn School of Medicine." *Hartford Business Journal*, 23 Feb. 2009, www.hartfordbusiness.com/article/honoring-a-biomedical-legacy-dr-cato-t-laurencin-dean-uconn-school-of-medicine. Accessed 7 Mar. 2022.

___. "Importance of COVID-19 Vaccination for Black Community Stressed by National Experts including Dr. Cato T. Laurencin." Interview by Melanie Burnat. *UConn Today*, University of Connecticut, 9 Feb. 2021, today.uconn.edu/2021/02/importance-of-covid-19-vaccination-for-black-community-stressed-by-national-experts-including-dr-cato-t-laurencin/. Accessed 7 Mar. 2022.

___. "Interview with Cato T. Laurencin about Regenerative Engineering." Interview by Amro Tambal. *RE Society Journal*, 19 Apr. 2017, www.aiche.org/chenected/2017/04/interview-cato-t-laurencin-about-regenerative-engineering. Accessed 7 Mar. 2022.

___. "The NAI Profile: An Interview with Dr. Cato T. Laurencin." Interview by Kimberly A. Macuare. *Technology and Innovation*, vol. 21, 2020, pp. 1–11, www.ingentaconnect.com/content/nai/ti/2020/00000021/00000004/art00015?crawler=true&mimetype=application/pdf. Accessed 7 Mar. 2022.

___. "What to Know When Launching a Journal: An Interview with Dr. Cato T. Laurencin." Interview by Celia Carver. *Springer Nature*, 3 Mar. 2016, www.springernature.com/gp/researchers/the-source/blog/blogposts-for-editors/what-to-know-when-launching-a-journal/16606148. Accessed 7 Mar. 2022.

Newsome, Melba. "Cato T. Laurencin Has Innovated Ways to Regrow Injured Tissues." *C&EN*, 22 Feb. 2021, cen.acs.org/materials/biomaterials/Cato-T-Laurencin-has-innovated-ways-to-regrow-injured-tissues/99/i6. Accessed 7 Mar. 2022.

Simpson, Stan. "A Can't Miss Prospect." *Hartford Courant*, 25 July 2009, www.courant.com/news/connecticut/hc-xpm-2009-07-25-uconn-laurencin-simpson-0725-story.html. Accessed 7 Mar. 2022.

—*Joy Crelin*

Rachel Levine

Born: October 28, 1957
Occupation: Politician and pediatrician

When President Joe Biden formally nominated Rachel Levine to serve as the seventeenth assistant secretary for health at the US Department of Health and Human Services (HHS) in February 2021, the choice was hailed as a triumph by LGBTQ groups across the country. There was even greater reason for celebration on March 24 of that year when Levine made history as the first openly transgender federal official ever to be confirmed by the US Senate. The vote was 52–48 in her favor, with Republican naysayers categorizing the appointment as an empty political gesture on Biden's part and a blatant bid to pander to the left. Levine was not deterred by those who opposed her nomination. "I have no room in my heart for hatred, and frankly I do not have time for intolerance," she told Dawn Ennis for *Forbes* (21 Apr. 2021) when discussing her detractors.

Levine's long and distinguished medical career more than qualified her for her role in the federal government. As both Pennsylvania's physician general and the state's secretary of health, Levine succeeded in improving the health of thousands of people. Among her most lauded measures were allowing ordinary citizens to purchase the anti-overdose drug Naloxone without a prescription, insisting on increased focus on maternal health and mortality and establishing a Health Equity Taskforce to address racial disparities in care. Levine, who in October 2021 also became the first-ever female four-star admiral in the US Public Health Service Commissioned Corps, ascended to her new roles in the midst of the global coronavirus disease 2019 (COVID-19) pandemic; while that remained a top priority, she also expressed her determination to fight health inequity, address substance abuse, and advocate for the LGBTQ community, among other goals. Referring to her broad experience and qualifications, she told Ennis, "I have a really very important and unique perspective that I bring to this federal role. . . . Everything I've learned in my clinical background, my educational background as a professor, in terms of my administrative experience, in terms of my research experience . . . I bring to this position now."

EARLY LIFE AND EDUCATION

Rachel Leland Levine was born on October 28, 1957, in Melrose, Massachusetts, to Melvin and Lillian Levine, both lawyers. Lillian had been the only woman in Boston University Law School's Class of 1946. It was at law school that she met Melvin, who had served in the Air Force during World War II before earning his degree. Levine, who was assigned male at birth, and her older sister, Bonnie, were raised in a Jewish household in Wakefield, Massachusetts. She attended public grade school, but after experiencing bullying, her mother enrolled her in the Pike School, a private day school in Andover, in seventh grade. Levine then went to high school at Belmont Hill, an all-boys private school near Boston, which she remembers fondly. At the time, she compartmentalized any gender issues she was feeling. "I had no way to really conceptualize it or think about it," Levine explained to Barry Loveland during an interview with the LGBT Center of Central PA (6 Feb. 2017). "We're talking about the late 60s [and] early 70s and there was no context for it."

Levine played on the Belmont Hill football and hockey teams, took part in the drama and glee clubs, and excelled academically. Upon graduating in 1975, she entered Harvard College on a premedical track. There, she continued to excel academically and be involved in various sports including crew and hockey. Questions regarding her gender remained, though. "[I] went to the library to research transgender issues and found dusty psychological and psychoanalytic textbooks that seemed to indicate how crazy I was, [so] that was not as helpful as it might have been," she recalled to Loveland. Levine graduated from Harvard in 1979 and then moved to New Orleans to attend the Tulane University School of Medicine, where she earned her MD in 1983. Around this time, she married fellow physician Martha Peaslee, whom she met at Tulane, before moving to New York City to complete her medical training in pediatrics at Mount Sinai Medical Center.

MEDICAL CAREER

Although she loved pediatrics, Levine found teenagers to be the most challenging and interesting patients, which led her to complete a fellowship in adolescent medicine at Mount Sinai. After completing her training in 1988,

Levine practiced at Mount Sinai and at Lenox Hill Hospital. During this period, she developed a specialty in treating young people with eating disorders such as anorexia nervosa and bulimia nervosa. She was also a faculty member at the Mount Sinai School of Medicine. In 1993, dismayed at the cost of living in New York City, she and Peaslee moved to central Pennsylvania, where she joined the faculty of Pennsylvania State College of Medicine and worked at the Polyclinic Medical Center in Harrisburg. There, Levine served as director of pediatric ambulatory services and director of adolescent medicine. In 1996, she began working in the same positions at the Penn State Hershey Medical Center, where she would remain for the next two decades. At Hershey, Levine spearheaded a new, multidisciplinary eating disorders program involving the departments of nutrition, psychiatry, and psychology. Additionally, she served as a member of the medical school admissions committee, the LGBTQ student group facilitator, and a sexual-harassment coordinator, among other roles. Beyond Hershey, Levine was also involved in advocacy work, including serving as secretary of Equality Pennsylvania, a statewide LGBTQ advocacy group, and as vice president of the Capital Region Stonewall Democrats, a political action committee (PAC) run by LGBTQ citizens.

During her time at Hershey, Levine gradually began to adopt a more feminine appearance, growing her hair and changing her way of dressing. As she explained to Loveland, when she reached forty years old, she "started to have [stronger] feelings that become more difficult to compartmentalize." She began hormone therapy and transitioned fully in 2011, while serving as head of adolescent medicine and professor of pediatrics and psychiatry. Her employers were fully supportive—Levine helped write Penn State a new antidiscrimination policy that included gender identity and expression—and she was subsequently promoted to vice chair of clinical affairs for the pediatrics department. Most of her adolescent patients and their parents took her transition in stride as well, appreciating the elevated level of care and empathy she provided.

Photo via Wikimedia Commons

POLITICAL APPOINTMENTS IN PENNSYLVANIA

In January 2015, Tom Wolf, Pennsylvania's newly elected Democratic governor, nominated Levine to serve as the state's physician general, a post in which she would be responsible for advising him and the secretary of health on medical and public health matters. The nomination was brought before the state senate, and after Levine met one-on-one with all the members—the majority of whom were conservative Republicans—she was confirmed unanimously, an achievement for which she remains extremely proud.

Levine served in that capacity until 2018, when she was again unanimously confirmed by the Pennsylvania state senate, this time as secretary of health. In that role, Levine was widely praised for her response to the opioid crisis, for launching Pennsylvania's medical marijuana program, and for bringing needed attention to the inequities facing people of color and the LGBTQ community. Public opinion of Levine's handling of the COVID-19 pandemic was not as favorable, however, especially after mid-March 2020, when, in an attempt to relieve the burden on critical-care facilities, she advised Pennsylvania nursing homes to admit new patients. Criticism mounted when journalists discovered that Levine had moved her own mother out of a nursing home as the pandemic raged. (She countered that the move was at her mother's request.) By that summer, countless COVID-19 deaths were occurring in nursing homes, and Levine, who was also accused of misrepresenting data, came in for a large share of the blame. Despite the criticism, Wolf steadfastly defended Levine throughout the controversy. Addressing continued attacks and derogatory comments against her, Wolf issued a public statement in July 2020, calling Levine "a highly skilled, valued, and capable member of my administration . . . [who] is committed to keeping Pennsylvanians safe and healthy, even those who direct hate-fueled attacks at her."

THE BIDEN ADMINISTRATION

On January 19, 2021, President-elect Joe Biden announced Levine's nomination for assistant secretary of health, describing her as someone who could "bring the steady leadership and essential expertise we need to get people through this pandemic . . . and meet the public health needs of our country in this critical moment and beyond." The confirmation process was contentious; during the hearing, some Republicans were openly hostile, and in one widely reported attack, Senator Rand Paul of Kentucky condemned her support of gender-affirming care, accusing Levine of encouraging "surgical destruction of a minor's genitalia." Levine responded by explaining that if she were confirmed she would be happy to collaborate with him on establishing standards of care for transgender patients, and Rand was later publicly rebuked by Democrats for his remarks.

On March 24, Levine was confirmed by a vote of 52 to 48, with two Republicans breaking ranks with their party to achieve the majority. She thus became the first openly transgender person in US history to hold an office requiring Senate confirmation. (Other federal officials, such as Amanda Simpson, were transgender, but they held posts that did not require confirmation.) As the highest-ranking transgender official in the United States, Levine acknowledged her historic position. "I do see myself as an advocate," Levine told Ivey DeJesus for *PennLive* (2 Aug. 2021). "Advocating for equality and fairness and health equity for LGBTQ+ people is part of my role."

Levine immediately set out an ambitious agenda that included helping the Biden administration contain the COVID-19 pandemic—an issue that had become deeply politicized during the Donald Trump presidency. She also made plans to effectively address the opioid crisis, treat climate change as a public-health menace, eliminate health-care inequities of all types, and support LGBTQ youth. The latter issue was a mission she believed was particularly important given the number of states introducing bills targeting LGBTQ youth. "These are vulnerable youth who have suffered bullying and harassment, and we need to protect them and advocate for them not to have discriminatory laws passed against them," she explained, as quoted by Julianne McShane for *NBC News* (1 June 2021). Among her early accomplishments were establishing an office devoted to marginalized communities suffering the effects of environmental stress, such as asthma caused by pollution, and reversing the narrow Trump-era interpretation of the Affordable Care Act's nondiscrimination protections to include sexual orientation and gender identity.

A FOUR-STAR ADMIRAL

On October 19, 2021, Levine was sworn in as a four-star admiral in the US Public Health Service Commissioned Corps—one of the nation's eight uniformed services. The appointment made her the first female and first openly transgender four-star admiral in that corps, which was established by Congress in 1889 and charged with responding to health crises on behalf of the federal government. In recent years, for instance, the six-thousand-member corps helped distribute coronavirus vaccines and administer care after natural disasters. Two Republican lawmakers, Jim Banks of Indiana and Marjorie Taylor Greene of Georgia, were censored by Twitter for posting transphobic assertions that Levine should not be referred to as the corps' first "female" admiral. In an interview with Jonathan Franklin for *NPR* (19 Oct. 2021), Levine commended the Biden administration for its commitment to diversity and inclusion, remarking that her appointment "is symbolic of that commitment and for transgender youth and other transgender individuals that there are no glass ceilings and no limitation to what we can achieve."

Levine is a Fellow of the American Academy of Pediatrics, the Academy for Eating Disorders, and the Society for Adolescent Health and Medicine.

PERSONAL LIFE

She and Peaslee, whom Levine divorced in 2013, have two children: David, born in 1994, and Dana, born in 1996.

SUGGESTED READING

DeJesus, Ivey. "At the National Level, Dr. Rachel Levine Adheres to the Focus to Mission That Marked Her Time in Pa." *PennLive*, 2 Aug. 2021, www.pennlive.com/news/2021/08/at-the-national-level-dr-rachel-levine-adheres-to-the-focus-to-mission-that-marked-her-time-in-pa.html. Accessed 20 Dec. 2021.

Ennis, Dawn. "'No Time for Intolerance:' Dr. Rachel Levine Has a Job to Do." *Forbes*, 21 Apr. 2021, www.forbes.com/sites/dawnstaceyennis/2021/04/21/no-time-for-intolerance-dr-rachel-levine-has-a-job-to-do/. Accessed 20 Dec. 2021.

Franklin, Jonathan. "Dr. Rachel Levine Is Sworn in as the Nation's First Transgender Four-Star Officer." *NPR*, , 21 Oct. 2021, www.npr.org/2021/10/19/1047423156/rachel-levine-first-transgender-four-star-officer. Accessed 20 Dec. 2021.

Loveland, Barry. *LGBT Oral History: Rachel Levine*. LGBT History Project of the LGBT Center of Central PA, Dickinson College, 6 Feb. 2017, archives.dickinson.edu/sites/all/files/files_lgbt/LGBT-interview-transcription-Levine-Rachel-064.pdf. Accessed 20 Dec. 2021.

McShane, Julianne. "Transgender Federal Official Rachel Levine Tells LGBTQ Youths: 'I Have Your Back.'" *NBC News*, 1 June 2021, www.nbcnews.com/feature/nbc-out/transgender-federal-official-rachel-levine-tells-lgbtq-youths-i-have-n1268795. Accessed 20 Dec. 2021.

Pilkington, Ed. "Trans Doctor Rachel Levine Faces Historic Senate Confirmation Hearing." *The Guardian*, 25 Feb. 2021, www.theguardian.com/us-news/2021/feb/25/rachel-levine-assistant-health-secretary-senate-confirmation-hearing-historic. Accessed 20 Dec. 2021.

Wamsley, Laurel. "Rachel Levine Makes History as 1st Openly Trans Federal Official Confirmed by Senate." *NPR*, 24 Mar. 2021, www.npr.org/2021/03/24/980788146/senate-confirms-rachel-levine-a-transgender-woman-as-assistant-health-secretary. Accessed 20 Dec. 2021.

—*Mari Rich*

Fei-Fei Li

Born: 1976
Occupation: Computer scientist

Professor and computer scientist Fei-Fei Li is best known for her work in the field of artificial intelligence (AI), particularly her invention of ImageNet, a large-scale image database that enables computers to identify and "see" images. Li's invention helped pave the way for successful applications of deep learning and significant advances in AI. Over the course of her career, Li has published hundreds of scientific articles in peer-reviewed journals about her work. She believes that the development of artificial intelligence will produce widespread benefits to human society—not only for its applications in emerging technologies such as self-driving cars, but also in the possible role AI can play in the automation of mundane clerical tasks in the medical field and in efforts to combat manmade climate change.

Li believes the only way for humans to fully reap the benefits of AI is through widespread and ethical cooperation in the scientific community. As she told Will Knight in an interview for *MIT Technology Review* (9 Oct. 2017), "We need to be more human-centered . . . We also want to make technology that makes humans' lives better, our world safer, our lives more productive and better. All this requires a layer of human-level communication and collaboration."

EARLY LIFE AND EDUCATION

Fei-Fei Li was born in 1976 in Beijing, China, and spent her childhood in the southern city of Chengdu. An intelligent child, she was encouraged to read by her mother, who particularly loved the writings of the Brontë sisters, nineteenth-century English poets and novelists famed for works such as the romance *Jane Eyre* (1847). Her father immigrated to the United States when she turned twelve and settled in Parsippany, New Jersey, where

Photo by ITU Pictures,
via Wikimedia Commons

he hoped to put down roots and bring the family along later. Li and her mother eventually moved to the United States and reunited with her father when Li was sixteen.

Li quickly became the family translator, as her English improved greatly while she attended school. "I had to become the mouth and ears of my parents," she recalled to Jessi Hempel for *Wired* (13 Nov. 2018).

Li came to enjoy her education in the United States, particularly in the sciences. While she recalled in an interview with *National Geographic* (6 Aug. 2019) that physics initially led her to consider "big questions" about the origins of the universe and other topics, the writings of physicists such as Albert Einstein and Erwin Schrödinger helped direct her towards what would become her true passion. "I noticed that towards the end of their academic or intellectual life, they also pondered questions about life itself," Li told *National Geographic.* "Like them, I became very interested in the question of life and the foundational questions like what is life, what is human life, what is intelligence."

Li's intellectual curiosity and burgeoning passion for the sciences helped her become a star pupil at Parsippany High School. There, her math teacher, Bob Sabella, provided her with an improvised advanced calculus class during their lunch breaks, as the school did not

offer such a course at that time. Sabella and his wife warmed to the entire Li family, each lending the family over $20,000 so that Li's parents could open a dry-cleaning business and take Li on a Disney vacation.

Li's familial and school support, as well as her dedication to her schoolwork, paid off. In 1995 she won a scholarship to Princeton, where she earned her Bachelor of Arts (BA) degree in physics four years later; while in school, she continued working at her parents' business on weekends. She also took courses in computer science and engineering as an undergraduate. She then earned her master's degree in electrical engineering from the California Institute of Technology (Caltech) in 2001, and later a PhD from the same school in 2005.

ACADEMIC CAREER AND IMAGENET

Upon completing her doctorate, Li held teaching positions at a number of universities; she taught at the University of Illinois Urbana-Champaign from 2005 to 2006, then joined the faculty at Princeton from 2007 to 2009. After leaving Princeton she began teaching at Stanford University. From 2013 to 2018, she served as the director of Stanford's AI Laboratory (SAIL).

As she began her academic career, Li developed the idea that would later become ImageNet, a database designed for visual object recognition software research. While many of her computer science colleagues were looking at ways for computers to decode images, she wanted to do something larger. She believed that by having computers recognize objects in a wide variety of images, in context with other objects and in different scenes, these computers could learn to identify these images anywhere, just as a human child learns to identify objects through repetitive exposure and experience. For her idea to work, Li realized that computers had to learn how to "see" objects as well as comprehend them. "Understanding vision and building visual systems is really understanding intelligence," Li said to Marguerite McNeal for *Wired* (Apr. 2015). "And by see, I mean to understand, not just to record pixels."

In 2006, Li began proposing to her colleagues that they build an enormous database, with every object in each picture tagged in very specific ways. For example, an image of a cat would need to be generally identified as both an animal and a mammal, but also be labeled by its breed, color, and size. With this idea in mind, Li began assembling a team to begin building this database. In 2007, while teaching at Princeton, Li was able to secure help from Kai Li, a professor of computer architecture. After trying to hire Princeton students to do the tedious tagging work, she instead decided to employ Amazon Mechanical Turk (MTurk) online workers; to ensure that the work was performed accurately and not just quickly, Li created control groups of images.

By 2009, Li and her team at Princeton had amassed a database of 3.2 million tagged images; by 2022, the database grew to contain more than 15 million images in over 22,000 categories. The early success of ImageNet allowed Li and her colleagues to pen an academic paper about their findings. To promote their database's utility, Li and her team also asked participants in the ImageNet Large Scale Visual Recognition Challenge (ILSVRC), a yearly computer-vision competition held in Europe, to use the ImageNet database to teach computers their algorithms. By 2017, the applications of most teams in the competition were able to identify images with over 95 percent accuracy, a significant improvement over the accuracy rate before the adoption of ImageNet. Since the development of ImageNet, the deep computer learning that Li's efforts helped make possible has been applied in a wide range of settings, including phone cameras that can identify objects for sale, self-driving cars, and facial recognition software.

STINT AT GOOGLE

In January 2017, Li took a sabbatical from Stanford to work at Google, where she served as a vice president and chief scientist of AI/ML at Google Cloud, which was the tech giant's enterprise computing business. While at Google, she collaborated with large corporations to demonstrate how Google's AI tools would allow anyone to build machine-learning algorithms without needing to know how to code. The position also enabled her to better understand how the industry worked and how major corporations like Google interacted with prominent individuals such as politicians and industry leaders.

Li also found herself embroiled in a controversy at Google, due to her division's involvement with Google's Project Maven. Maven was part of a contract with the US Department of Defense (DoD), which wanted to use AI to interpret low-resolution video images for military drone operations. Thousands of Google employees signed a petition complaining that they did not want their work to be part of any military actions. However, Li believed that the technology was not as ethically challenging as some other aspects of AI, namely facial recognition, which is prone to error, particularly when attempting to identify darker-skinned individuals. About the protests against Maven, Li shared with Hempel, "It wasn't exactly what the thing is. It's about the moment—the collective sense of urgency for our responsibility, the emerging power of AI, the dialog that Silicon Valley needs to be in. Maven just became kind of a convergence point."

Befitting her involvement in some of the ethical controversies surrounding AI technologies, Li testified before the US House Committee on Science, Space and Technology in June 2018 to discuss the potential downsides and possible benefits of AI. During her testimony, she made the case that the best way to produce ethically beneficial AI was to make sure that it was being created by the most diverse group of computer scientists possible, as whatever biases various individuals brought to machine learning would inevitably become part of whatever AI system they create. Li built on this assumption to argue that scientists must develop AI in the most ethical and responsible ways possible.

RETURN TO STANFORD

After her two-year sabbatical working for Google, Li returned to Stanford in September 2018. She has described academia to be the best place for her to make sure that artificial intelligence is used as a source for good. After returning to Stanford, Li continued her work in the field of AI, remaining convinced that the technology has great potential to benefit humanity by improving medical care and addressing environmental challenges. She has pointed out that AI could be used to aid sick and older people to maximize their care and personal well-being. As she told *National Geographic* in 2019, "No matter what kind of fancy gadget that AI might enable, it is so personally important to me that this technology benefits human lives—not just for convenience, but for well-being, for dignity, for community, for society."

Despite her optimism about the benefits of AI, Li also expressed concern that AI could be used for more ethically dubious purposes, such as widespread facial recognition for monitoring large swaths of the population. "Every technology can be an enabler of vices," she explained to McNeal, "but as a scientist you have to have that social awareness and be very aware of these potential risks."

By that time, Li had also become heavily involved in efforts to encourage more people from underrepresented backgrounds to join STEM programs and to contribute to the future of AI. To further this cause, in 2017, Li cofounded the national nonprofit AI4ALL, to increase diversity in her field. In an article she cowrote with Tess Posner for *Nature* (9 Dec. 2020), she observed: "We are at a turning point. AI's influence continues to grow, but representation and inclusion of a diversity of researchers in the field does not. It's critical that we seize this moment to create structures that will support long-term, positive changes."

In 2022, Li was appointed the inaugural Sequoia Professor in the Computer Science Department at Stanford.

PERSONAL LIFE AND AWARDS

Throughout her career, Li has received numerous honors for her contributions to AI, including a fellowship from the Alfred P. Sloan Foundation (2011), the W.M. Keck Foundation Faculty Scholarship from Stanford University (2012), and the IBM Faculty Fellowship Award (2014). In 2016, she received the J.K. Aggarwal Prize from the International Association for Pattern Recognition (IAPR), the Mark Everingham Prize from the IEEE PAMI, and the Pioneer in AI Research Award, NVidia, while also being named one of forty "great immigrants" of the year by the Carnegie Foundation.

In 2020, Li received membership in the National Academy of Medicine (NAM), National Academy of Engineering (NAE), and the Council on Foreign Relations (CFR). In 2021, she was named a member of the American Academy of Arts and Sciences (AAAS).

PERSONAL LIFE

Li is married to roboticist Silvio Savarese, with whom she has a son and a daughter.

SUGGESTED READING

Gershgorn, Dave. "The Data that Transformed AI Research—and Possibly the World." *Quartz*, 26 July 2016, qz.com/1034972/the-data-that-changed-the-direction-of-ai-research-and-possibly-the-world/. Accessed 6 June 2022.

Hempel, Jessi. "An AI Pioneer, and the Researcher Bringing Humanity to AI." *Wired*, Condé Nast, 18 Sept. 2018, www.wired.com/story/wired25-kai-fu-lee-fei-fei-li-artificial-intelligence/. Accessed 12 May 2022.

___. "Fei-Fei Li's Quest to Make AI Better for Humanity." *Wired*, Condé Nast, 23 Nov. 2018, www.wired.com/story/fei-fei-li-artificial-intelligence-humanity/. Accessed 13 May 2022.

Li, Fei-Fei. "Meet Fei-Fei Li, the Recipient of the National Geographic Further Award." Interview. *National Geographic*, 6 Aug. 2019, blog.nationalgeographic.org/2019/08/06/meet-fei-fei-li-the-recipient-of-the-national-geographic-further-award/. Accessed 12 May 2022.

___. "Put Humans at the Center of AI." Interview by Will Knight. *MIT Technology Review*, 9 Oct. 2017, www.technologyreview.com/2017/10/09/3988/put-humans-at-the-center-of-ai/. Accessed 12 May 2022.

McNeal, Marguerite. "Fei-Fei Li: If We Want Machines to Think, We Need to Teach Them to See." *Wired*, Condé Nast, Apr. 2015, www.wired.com/brandlab/2015/04/fei-fei-li-want-machines-think-need-teach-see/. Accessed 12 May 2022.

Posner, Tess, and Fei-Fei Li. "AI Will Change the World, so It's Time to Change AI." *Nature*, 9 Dec. 2020, www.nature.com/articles/d41586-020-03412-z. Accessed 13 May 2022.

—Christopher Mari

Liu Cixin

Born: June 23, 1963
Occupation: Writer

The Chinese author Liu Cixin is one of the most celebrated writers of speculative fiction. His most famous trilogy of novels, *Remembrance of Earth's Past*, have sold more than eight million copies around the world and have been translated into more than twenty languages. He has won China's most prestigious science fiction award, the Galaxy Award, nine times, as well as two of the most famous science fiction awards presented in America, the Hugo and the Locus awards. His work has been praised by aerospace engineers for its scientific accuracy and has been cheered by officials in the Chinese Communist Party as well as by former US President Barack Obama.

Part of his international success is due to his ability to create realistic worldbuilding through sharp characterizations and scientifically accurate plots. That said, he does not believe that science fiction writers like himself can predict the future, but merely provide entertaining extrapolations on current events or world history. In a discussion with *The Wall Street Journal* (5 Oct. 2021), he told Natasha Khan, "The events of the past few years have made me feel the uncertainty of the future, and made me realize that we cannot use straight-line thinking to predict what is to come. Sudden twists and turns that we haven't anticipated could happen at any time."

EARLY LIFE

Liu Cixin was born in Beijing, China, on June 23, 1963. His mother was a schoolteacher and his father, a former commander in the Communist Eighth Route Army, worked as a manager at the Coal Mine Design Institute. In 1966, when Liu was just three, China's Communist Chairman Mao Zedong began the Chinese Cultural Revolution, one of the worst political upheavals in history, in which young people humiliated, beat, and murdered their elders at Mao's behest because he believed that they were insufficiently devoted to radical Communist ideas. When the Cultural Revolution ended in 1976, millions of Chinese citizens had been killed and millions more had their lives ruined.

Photo by opacity from Chicago, via Wikimedia Commons

Liu's father lost his job due to the Revolution because Lui's uncle had previously fought for the Nationalists. The elder Liu was forced to work in the coal mines in Yangquan, in Shanxi Province. When Liu was four, he was sent to live with his grandparents in Henan for several years. At about age six, he became interested in space exploration when China launched its first artificial satellite. Around the same time, his father gave him a copy of Jules Verne's *Journey to the Center of the Earth* (1871), which sparked an interest in science fiction and speculative fiction. The nineteenth century novel about the imagined exploration of Earth's interior thrilled him. "Everything in it was described with such authority and scrupulous attention to detail that I thought it had to be real," Liu said in a conversation with Jiayang Fan for *The New Yorker* (17 June 2019). He became an eager reader, devouring everything from classic world literature like the works of George Orwell, Leo Tolstoy, and Thomas Pynchon, to the science fiction imaginings of masters of the genre like Arthur C. Clarke, Ray Bradbury, and Kurt Vonnegut. "Reading all those books made me what I am today," Liu said in *China Daily* (3 Dec. 2021).

EARLY CAREER

Although he began working on his own stories in high school, writing did not become his career until later in life. In 1981, Liu instead enrolled in the North China University of Water Resources and Electric Power, where he studied engineering. After graduation, he began working at the Niangziguan Power Plant, where he remained until 2012.

While working as an engineer, Liu wrote stories of speculative fiction on the side, publishing stories regularly in *Science Fiction World*, a magazine devoted to the genre that began publication in the People's Republic of China in 1979. In 1989, he published one of his earliest novels, *Zhōngguó 2185* (China 2185). In 1999, he won his first Galaxy Award, for the short story known as "With Her Eyes" in English, which was published the same year. He won the Galaxy Award every year for later works until 2003.

His next popular novels included *Chāoxīnxīng jìyuán* (2003; *The Supernova Era*) and the *Santi* trilogy, published between 2006 and 2010. His novels and short stories quickly made him one of China's most renowned science fiction writers. His stories were even included as prompts in various levels of school testing. When asked about his stories being used to prompt questions about themes and other literary devices, Liu told Fan "I'm a writer. I don't begin with some conceit in mind. I'm just trying to tell a good story."

WESTERN POPULARITY

Liu became well-known and respected among Western lovers of speculative fiction when his *Santi* trilogy was translated to English as the *Three-Body* trilogy or the *Remembrance of Earth's Past* trilogy. The first novel of the series, *Santi*, was published in English translation as *The Three-Body Problem* in 2014. The novel begins during the Cultural Revolution, when a military project makes first contact with an intelligent alien civilization deep in space. When it is discovered that this civilization plans to conquer the earth, humanity splits into two distinct factions. One faction wants to welcome the aliens with open arms because they believe the human race needs to be reformed; the other faction wants to resist at all costs.

In an interview with Okuma Yuichiro for the *MCLC Resource Center* (6 Mar. 2021), Liu recalled how he was inspired to write the novel: "I thought of the most tragic memories of modern Chinese history, when China was invaded by other civilizations. At that time western civilization was more advanced and it was impossible for the old Chinese civilization to get an edge when facing such a foreign invasion. This history is engrained in the memories of the Chinese people, so I thought the invasion of Earth by an alien civilization would have the same shocking effect on the Chinese people." *The Three-Body Problem* earned Liu the 2015 Hugo Award, making it the first translated novel to win the US science fiction award.

First published as *Hei'an senlin* around 2008, the second novel in the series was translated into English as *The Dark Forest* in 2015. It continues the story as the aliens' human allies have been defeated but the human race still faces a challenge from the aliens, who will be coming in about 400 years. They have sent subatomic particles, known as sophons, that allow them instantaneous access to every piece of human knowledge, but a faction of humans, knowing that the aliens do not have access to the human mind, have created a plan codenamed the Wallfacers Project that gives four men complete control over the planet's counterattack.

The final book in the series, *Sishen yongsheng* (2010), was published in English as *Death's End* in 2016. It takes place about a half century after the aliens, known as the Trisolarans, have been defeated. Earth is at peace and prosperous and has merged much of the alien technology with their own. Now that humanity is on equal footing with the aliens, peaceful coexistence appears to be at hand, with the human race poised to move out among the stars. Then a young aerospace engineer emerges from hibernation from the early twenty-first century with knowledge of a secret program that may unravel the peace. *Death's End* won the 2017 Locus Award for Best Science Fiction Novel.

In addition to their prominent wins, the trilogy was nominated for numerous awards both in the United States and abroad. It was widely praised in the English-language press. In the *Guardian* (14 Nov. 2019), Steven Poole called it "a mind-bending hard sci-fi epic peopled by vivid and lovable characters, in which the story just happens to explain why we have the laws of physics we observe." In 2018, Liu himself received the Arthur C. Clarke Award for Imagination in Service to Society.

RECENT TRANSLATED WORKS

As Liu's series gained popularity, more of his works were translated into English. In 2019, *Chāoxīnxīng jìyuán* was translated to English and published as *The Supernova Era*. The novel describes the aftermath of human civilization when a supernova explodes eight light years from Earth. The resulting radiation will kill everyone on the planet over the age of thirteen, leaving adolescents in charge. As the radiation races toward the planet, those in charge must teach the children how to keep society going—everything from agriculture to technology to governmental organizations. In the novel Liu contrasts the way the Chinese tackle the problem versus their American contemporaries. As much as the adults make their best efforts, kids, according to Liu, will be kids: the Chinese build a huge theme park and build a city made of sweets, while the Americans spend a lot of time shooting cars. In a review for the *Guardian*, Steven Poole wrote: "The author, in an afterword, invites us to read it allegorically: first, as a fable about how the younger generation now are growing up in a world frankly incomprehensible to their elders; and secondly, as a description of the state of humanity itself, alone and infantile in the universe, with no user manual to guide us." Poole conceded, "It's a credit to the power of his imagination that such interpretations do not overpower the vivid and sometimes horrifying imagery of the story."

In 2020, a collection of Liu's previously untranslated short fiction was published in English under the title *To Hold Up the Sky*. The assembled stories were originally published in Chinese publications like *Science Fiction World* between 1999 and 2017. Many of them have a retro feel, as they were written in the past and are often speculating about a future that has already happened. Regardless of their seemingly outdated ideas, they still resonated with many reviewers, who loved the imaginative aspects of Liu's writing. Jason Sheehan, writing for *NPR* (25 Oct. 2020), declared, "It is magic, this collection of short stories Liu wrote and published ten, 20, 30 years ago. It is a time machine; a split-vision tunnel that lets you go back in time while staring forward, to see what 2003's or 1985's version of 2010 or 2020 or 3000 looked like from China." Sheehan explained, "science fiction, when done well, when done thoughtfully, engages ideas of humanness beyond nationality or ethnicity."

Other works of Liu's that have been translated into English include the novel *Qiúzhuàng shǎndiàn* (2004; *Ball Lightning*, 2018) and the novella *Liúlàng dìqiú* (2000), which was translated to English as *The Wandering Earth* and published in a short fiction collection alongside of the same name together with nine other stories in 2021. The latter was adapted into a film also called *The Wandering Earth*, released in China in early 2019 and in the United States later that year. Several more of his works were also adapted for film and television.

PERSONAL LIFE

Liu has one daughter and is married.

SUGGESTED READING

"Cixin Liu." *Cixin Liu Official Website*, cixinliu.com/. Accessed 13 Jan. 2022.

Cixin, Liu. "Interview with Liu Cixin." Interview by Okuma Yuichiro. *MCLC Resource Center*, Ohio State U, 6 Mar. 2021, u.osu.edu/mclc/2021/03/06/interview-with-liu-cixin/. Accessed 13 Jan. 2022.

Fan, Jiayang. "Liu Cixin's War of the Worlds." *The New Yorker*, 17 Jan. 2019, www.newyorker.com/magazine/2019/06/24/liu-cixins-war-of-the-worlds. Accessed 13 Jan. 2022.

Khan, Natasha. "Writer Liu Cixin on How His Visions of the Future Collide with Reality." *The Wall Street Journal*, 5 Oct. 2021, www.wsj.com/articles/writer-liu-cixin-on-how-his-visions-of-the-future-collide-with-reality-11633446000. Accessed 13 Jan. 2022.

Poole, Steven. "*The Supernova Era* by Cixin Liu Review—a World without Adults." Review of *The Supernova Era*, by Liu Cixin. *The Guardian*, 14 Nov. 2019, www.theguardian.com/books/2019/nov/14/the-supernova-era-cixin-liu-review. Accessed 13 Jan. 2022.

"Science Fiction Makes People More Open-Minded: Chinese Writer Liu Cixin." *China Daily*, 3 Dec. 2019, global.chinadaily.com.cn/a/201903/12/WS5c8711baa3106c65c34ee195.html. Accessed 13 Jan. 2022.

Sheehan, Jason. "*To Hold Up the Sky* Asks a Simple Question: What If. . .?" Review of *To Hold Up the Sky*, by Liu Cixin. *NPR*, 25 Oct. 2020, www.npr.org/2020/10/25/927268317/

to-hold-up-the-sky-asks-a-simple-question-what-if. Accessed 13 Jan. 2020.

SELECTED WORKS

Zhōngguó 2185 (China 2185), 1989; Liúlàng dìqiú (The Wandering Earth), 2000; Chāoxīnxīng jìyuán (The Supernova Era), 2003; Qiúzhuàng shǎndiàn (Ball Lightning), 2004; Santi Trilogy (The Three-Body Problem), 2006–10; To Hold Up the Sky, 2020

—Christopher Mari

Simu Liu

Born: April 19, 1989
Occupation: Actor

In 2019, Simu Liu made headlines when it was announced he had been cast as the lead in a new entry in the Marvel Cinematic Universe (MCU), an immensely popular series of interconnected superhero films and shows. Playing the titular hero in *Shang-Chi and the Legend of the Ten Rings* (2021) was a major career breakthrough for Liu, who was previously best known for the sitcom *Kim's Convenience*. But the role also had wider cultural impact, as it was the first time an Asian actor had led an MCU film. *Shang-Chi* proved to be a smash success and was hailed by many critics as a positive step for diverse representation in Hollywood. For his part, Liu, who often spoke candidly about his own struggles with his cultural identity, embraced both movie stardom and an elevated platform as a social activist, speaking out against anti-Asian discrimination and emphasizing projects that celebrate the varied experiences of people of Asian descent. As he explained to Victoria Ahearn for *The Chronicle Journal* (25 July 2019), "I spent a good part of my life trying to run away from my Asianness, and so a big part of what I do now is trying to get people to embrace it and to stand tall and to feel like they do belong—because they do. We do."

EARLY LIFE AND EDUCATION

Simu Liu was born in Harbin, China, on April 19, 1989. It was a tumultuous time in Chinese society—just weeks after his birth, the Tiananmen Square protests erupted against communist leader Deng Xiaoping's regime and resulted in the further elimination of civil rights

and job opportunities. Consequently, when Liu's parents were given the rare opportunity to pursue graduate studies at Queen's University in Ontario, they accepted without hesitation. Liu was left to be raised by his grandparents for five years. When his parents finally came to pick him up and bring him to Canada in 1995, it had been so long that he did not recognize them.

Liu's earliest years in Ontario proved to be challenging. Because he did not speak English, there was no one to talk to at daycare, and he would spend hours crying alone. Although he eventually adapted to the new culture and language, he found himself struggling to gain approval from both his peers and his parents. He subsequently turned to sports and entertainment for solace. "I was raised as an only child," he told Guy Dixon for *The Globe and Mail* (27 June 2017), "My parents worked a lot. I was basically raised on TV and movies. They would drop me off at a movie theater on a Saturday morning and say, 'Here's $20, knock yourself out.'"

Liu's parents did push him to succeed academically and sent him to the University of Toronto Schools, a private secondary school connected to the university. Liu explained to Mary Green in an interview for *People* (25 Aug. 2021) how the pressure on him to become a doctor, lawyer, or high-level businessperson made for a challenging home dynamic. "My parents were academics, so it was the only path to success. But I wanted to play sports and chase girls, that's all I was really interested in. I wanted to be the high school quarterback. And it led to a lot of tension in our family." During high school Liu spent as much time at friends' houses as possible to avoid arguments with his parents. After graduating, however, he grudgingly acquiesced to their wishes by attending business school. He was accepted at the prestigious Richard Ivey School of Business at the University of Western Ontario, where he studied accounting.

FROM ACCOUNTANT TO ACTOR

Upon graduating in 2011, Liu landed a job as an accountant with the giant firm Deloitte. However, he found the work to be deeply unfulfilling and felt like a poor fit in the office environment. Then in 2012, just eight months after being hired, he was unceremoniously laid off. "It was just so disheartening," he told

Green, "I felt like my life was over and like I was at rock bottom." To combat an overwhelming sense of shame, he realized he would have to forge a path toward his own definition of success, rather than his parents' expectations.

Liu decided to take a chance and try to find work in the film and television industry. Soon he stumbled on a Craigslist ad seeking extras for the film *Pacific Rim* (2012). Although it only paid minimum wage, the job sparked something in him. "That was like the first time I had been exposed to an on-set environment, it was just gorgeous," he told Franceska Wolf Isaly for *The Shorthorn*, the newspaper of the University of Texas, Arlington (22 Oct. 2021). "There's such a kinetic work environment, you know, everyone's like, moving with such purpose. I just remember walking through and just being like 'Oh my god this is incredible, I want to do that.'"

In the months that followed, Liu applied to every performance opportunity he could find. These included modeling for stock photos and even dressing up as Spider Man for children's birthday parties. He also held various other side jobs to support himself. As he started earning parts of commercials aired across Canada, he had no choice but to tell his parents of his new career. Although they were not happy with his decision at first, Liu was enjoying his new path enough that he felt confident about continuing to act regardless of his family's approval.

From there, Liu's career slowly but steadily gained momentum. He moved from working as an extra to small roles in television and short films, taking night classes to improve his acting skills. He also worked as a stunt double, including in the band Fall Out Boy's 2014 music video "Centuries." A notable step came when he landed a reoccurring role on the Chinese Canadian television series *Blood and Water* (2015), a part that eventually brought him a nomination for a 2017 Canadian Screen Award for best supporting actor in a drama. He also earned a writing credit on one episode.

KIM'S CONVENIENCE

In 2016, Liu was cast in the part of Jung Kim on the CBC television series *Kim's Convenience*. Based on writer Ins Choi's play of the same name, the sitcom debuted in October 2016 to positive reviews and an enthusiastic Canadian audience. After the streaming platform Netflix purchased the rights to the show in 2018, it

Photo by Gage Skidmore, via Wikimedia Commons

won even more popularity at the international level. Many critics were quick to call the show revolutionary for the nuanced but heartfelt way that it depicted a Korean immigrant family.

For Liu, the part of Jung was not just his first main role, but also especially meaningful as the character's journey paralleled his own. In an open letter to his parents that he wrote for *Maclean's* (4 Dec. 2017) he commented on this fact, stating, "I am now playing myself on TV: a troubled kid, burdened by his relationship to his parents, trying to find his place in the world." Like Liu, the character of Jung also had rebellious tendencies that led him to defy his family and society's definition of success.

Kim's Convenience went on to win several honors, including the 2017 Association of Canadian Television and Radio Artists (ACTRA) Award for outstanding performance by an ensemble and the best comedy series at the 2018 Canadian Screen Awards. Its popularity also earned Liu attention from Hollywood, which in turn led to guest roles in shows like *Taken* (2017), *Orphan Black* (2017), *Bad Blood* (2017), *The Expanse* (2018), and *Fresh Off the Boat* (2019).

In early 2021 it was announced that *Kim's Convenience* was going to end after its fifth season, despite being renewed for a sixth, because the showrunner, Kevin White, and Ins Choi had decided to walk away from the project. The news was not well received by the cast, and Liu became the most prominent voice to express their collective frustration. In a scathing, somewhat controversial statement he posted on *Facebook*, he described how the tense cancellation reflected other issues he and other cast members struggled with, including poor pay, a primarily White writers' room that resisted any input from the actors, and culturally inaccurate storylines that occasionally bordered on racism. Liu clarified his feelings in an interview with Britt Hennemuth for *Vanity Fair* (10 June 2021), noting that despite the challenges he was deeply appreciative of the show. "The immigrant experience is rarely depicted in mainstream media in a positive light, and for that very reason, Kim's Convenience has a very special place in the hearts of countless fans globally—including mine," he said. "The show was integral in allowing me to find my voice and shape the perspective and platform that I now have."

SHANG-CHI AND THE LEGEND OF THE TEN RINGS

Meanwhile, by the time *Kim's Convenience* ended, Liu was taking his career to a new level with a major breakout film role. In fact, in some ways his transformation into a movie star was long foreshadowed. Back in 2014 he had posted on social media that it was time for Marvel, the comics company behind the hugely successful MCU, to greenlight a film led by an Asian American superhero. In December 2018, as it emerged that Marvel Studios was going to do just that with the comics character Shang-Chi, Liu followed up with another tweet: "OK @Marvel. Are we gonna talk or what #ShangChi." "I didn't seriously expect Marvel to call me back or anything," he later told Ahearn. "But I do think it's a really interesting case study in the power of giving yourself permission to want things and to set goals." He later submitted a taped audition for the project, which led to an intensive process of further tests, and he was finally offered the lead role just days before Marvel officially announced *Shang-Chi and the Legend of the Ten Rings*.

Shang-Chi proved to be a groundbreaking movie in several ways. Written by Dave Callaham and directed by Destin Daniel Cretton, both of Asian descent, the film's cultural perspective and celebration of Asian pride were unprecedented for an American blockbuster. The production did run into some snags, as principal photography began in February 2020—just weeks before the outbreak of the coronavirus disease 2019 (COVID-19) pandemic. However, it eventually was completed, and the film debuted in theaters in September 2021 to positive reviews and an impressive box office total of $432 million. Many critics praised Liu's performance, as well as the film's role in improving diversity in the film industry. In December 2021, it was announced that a sequel was officially in the works.

The international success of *Shang-Chi* had many important effects on Liu's life. In addition to launching him into stardom, the film helped Liu better understand his own role in the world and how he could use his fame as a platform to try to change society for the better. He became a vocal advocate for improving both the onscreen depiction of Asian people as well as equitable treatment in the real world. He often connected this to his own experiences as a child—he had rarely seen himself represented on television or in film while growing up, which, compounded by the racism his family experienced in their everyday lives, made him feel like he did not belong. "I think having an Asian superhero in the MCU, I don't think it solves everything all of a sudden in one movie, but I think it's a really critical step," he told Isaly.

PERSONAL LIFE

Connected to both his fame and his activism, Liu often spoke candidly about his personal life, including challenges and struggles. For example, in a guest column for *Variety* published in March 2021, he described the racism that his family had endured for decades while living in Canada because they were immigrants, and also condemned the spike in hate crimes against Asian Americans during the COVID-19 pandemic. Other experiences were more positive, however. Notably, he described how his acting success marked a new chapter in his relationship with his parents; the cultural impact of *Shang-Chi* in particular helped them understand what he had been striving for. "Now they're my best friends," he told Green. "I can't wait to experience whatever's next with them."

SUGGESTED READING

Ahearn, Victoria. "Simu Liu's 'Craziest Dream' a Reality with Groundbreaking Marvel Role, Shang-Chi." *The Chronicle Journal*, 25 July 2019, www.chroniclejournal.com/entertainment/entertainment_news/simu-liu-s-craziest-dream-a-reality-with-groundbreaking-marvel/article_9a3d73bd-0680-5634-8db2-5026e985ae36.html. Accessed 1 Mar. 2022.

Cai, Delia. "Simu Liu Is the Superhero We Need Now." *Vanity Fair*, 17 Feb. 2022, www.vanityfair.com/hollywood/2022/02/simu-liu-2022-hollywood-portfolio. Accessed 7 Mar. 2022.

Dixon, Guy. "Reluctant Accountant Changes Careers for a Better Role—As an Actor." *The Globe and Mail*, 27 June 2017, www.theglobeandmail.com/report-on-business/careers/business-education/accountant-changes-careers-for-a-better-role-as-an-actor/article35450687/. Accessed 1 Mar. 2022.

Isaly, Franceska Wolf. "Marvel Actor Simu Liu Shares Career Journey, Life Advice during Virtual Maverick Speakers Series." *The Shorthorn*, 22 Oct. 2021, www.theshorthorn.com/news/marvel-actor-simu-liu-shares-career-journey-life-advice-during-virtual-maverick-speakers-series/article_2de40eca-3399-11ec-a2d9-9b0b26bf7a2d.html. Accessed 1 Mar. 2022.

Liu, Simu. "A Chinese-Canadian to His Parents: 'Privately, I Yearned for Your Love.'" *Maclean's*, 4 Dec. 2017, www.macleans.ca/opinion/a-chinese-canadian-to-his-parents-privately-i-yearned-for-your-love/. Accessed 1 Mar. 2022.

___. "How *Shang-Chi*'s Simu Liu Went from Unemployed Accountant to Marvel's First Asian Superhero." Interview by Mary Green. *People*, 25 Aug. 2021, people.com/movies/how-shang-chis-simu-liu-went-from-unemployed-accountant-to-marvels-first-asian-superhero/. Accessed 1 Mar. 2022.

___. "*Shang-Chi* Star Simu Liu: 'Anti-Asian Racism Is Very Real.'" *Variety*, 11 Mar. 2021, variety.com/2021/film/news/shang-chi-simu-liu-anti-asian-racism-1234928348/. Accessed 1 Mar. 2022.

___. "Simu Liu Is Still Proud of *Kim's Convenience*—and Ready to Take on Marvel." Interview by Britt Hennemuth. *Vanity Fair*, 10 June 2021, www.vanityfair.com/hollywood/2021/06/simu-liu-proud-of-kims-convenience-ready-to-take-on-marvel. Accessed 28 Feb. 2022.

SELECTED WORKS
Blood and Water, 2015–16; *Kim's Convenience*, 2016–21; *Shang-Chi and the Legend of the Ten Rings*, 2021

—Emily Turner

Elisa Loncón

Born: January 23, 1963
Occupation: Linguist and activist

In July 2021, the 155 elected members of the Chilean constitutional convention convened to begin the process of writing a new constitution for the country and to elect a member of that body to serve as president of the convention. More than 60 percent of those delegates voted to elect Elisa Loncón, a linguist, professor, and activist known for her long advocacy for the rights of the Mapuche people, the Indigenous population to which she belongs. For Loncón, her election as president of the constitutional convention symbolized the Chilean people's willingness to work toward a more equitable society. "Today, a new Chile is created: one that is pluralistic, multilingual, with all its cultures, with all its peoples, with its women and with all its territories," she said following her election, as quoted by Verónica Figueroa Huencho for *Time* (15 Sept. 2021). "This is our dream for writing the new constitution."

Raised in the Mapuche community of Lefweluan, Loncón initially pursued a career as an English teacher but following a formative period of study at the International Institute of Social Studies in the Netherlands in the mid-1980s, rededicated herself to teaching the Mapuche language, Mapudungún. Indigenous languages had no governmental recognition in Chile at that time, and the Chilean government and education system had long worked to discourage young Mapuche people from learning and speaking their traditional language. Loncón remained a resolute advocate for Indigenous language rights over the next decades, and following her election to the constitutional convention, she hoped to codify those rights as well as address systemic inequity and growing environmental concerns.

Photo via Sinflitros.tv/Wikimedia Commons

"From my point of view, it's an opportunity for Chile and the world in general to adopt values from Indigenous thinking," she told Ciara Nugent for *Time* (28 Oct. 2021).

EARLY LIFE AND EDUCATION

Elisa del Carmen Loncón Antileo was born in Traiguén, Chile, on January 23, 1963. One of seven children born to parents Margareta and Juan, she spent her childhood in Lefweluan, a rural village near the central Chilean city of Traiguén. Like many of Lefweluan's residents, Loncón and her family belonged to the Mapuche people, the largest Indigenous group in Chile. By 2017, Mapuche people made up more than 82 percent of Chile's Indigenous population, which in turn constituted 12.8 percent of the country's total population. Despite their significant numbers, the Indigenous people of Chile faced significant economic and social disadvantages during Loncón's childhood and beyond, due to discriminatory government and economic policies. "Like all Mapuche families we faced hardship," she told the newspaper *El País* in Spanish, as quoted in English by Eva Ontiveros for *BBC News* (11 July 2021). Living as subsistence farmers, Loncón's family brought in extra income by selling surplus produce and eggs, and her father eventually began a furniture-making business.

Loncón was raised in a bilingual household, speaking both Spanish and the Mapuche language, Mapudungún. She was heavily influenced by the experiences of the older Mapuche people around her, many of whom had struggled to preserve their language and culture amid forceful attempts to subsume them into Spanish-speaking Chilean society. "The education system stripped the entire generation of their language," she explained in an interview for the Pontificia Universidad Católica de Chile (Pontifical Catholic University of Chile; UC Chile) magazine *Revista Universitaria* in 2016 (30 July 2021). "It denied it and created a precedent that being indigenous and having one's language was useless, foul, and had no value. Indigenous people must learn Spanish, to the point of washing out the mouth of children who spoke Mapudungun with soap. That's how hard it was." Although such experiences made some in Loncón's family skeptical of formal education, her parents encouraged their children to attend school, and Loncón made lengthy trips into town to attend the Liceo de Niñas de Traiguén (Traiguén Girls' High School).

ACADEMIC CAREER

Planning to become an English teacher, Loncón attended Chile's Universidad de la Frontera (University of the Frontier), from which she earned a teaching degree in 1986. That same year she received a scholarship from the International Institute of Social Studies in the Netherlands, where in 1987 she took postgraduate courses in development, law, and social justice. She later took courses in research, management, and administration at the University of Regina in Canada. Loncón went on to complete a master's degree in humanities with a concentration in linguistics at Mexico's Universidad Autónoma Metropolitana, Iztapalapa (UAM-I, Metropolitan Autonomous University) in 2006 and subsequently earned doctorates in linguistics and literature from Universiteit Leiden (Leiden University) in the Netherlands and UC Chile, respectively. She defended her thesis, *El poder creativo de la lengua Mapudungun y la formación de neologismos* (*The creative power of the Mapudungun language and the formation of neologisms*), in 2017.

Loncón began her professional career as an English teacher but began to rethink her career path after studying at the International Institute of Social Studies, where she met "other young human rights leaders of different nationalities," she told *Revista Universitaria*. "When I returned, I decided not to teach English anymore, but Mapudungún," she continued. "Anyone can teach English, but [there are] few Mapudungún speakers and even fewer know how to teach it." Loncón taught a variety of courses while pursuing graduate studies at UAM-I and by 2010 had joined the faculty of the Universidad de Santiago de Chile (University of Santiago, Chile), where she taught both at the undergraduate and graduate levels. Loncón has also taught courses at UC Chile. A prolific writer, she published papers on education, Mapudungún, and related topics in journals such as *Cadernos de Pesquisa*, *Psicología Escolar e Educacional*, and *Revista Literatura y Lingüística*.

ACTIVISM

Long dedicated to Indigenous rights, Loncón was a member of the activist group AdMapu while an undergraduate and in the 1990s was involved with the Council of All Lands activist initiative, which, in addition to staging protests, worked to design a Mapuche flag. She was later one of the founding members of an organization dedicated to the educational and linguistic rights of Chile's Indigenous populations and helped to develop and advocate for the proposed Ley General de Derechos Lingüísticos de los Pueblos Originarios de Chile (General Bill on the Linguistic Rights of Native Peoples), which would reshape Chile's governmental approach to Indigenous languages. "The bill proposes that they be recognized as pre-existing and become official," she told *Revista Universitaria*. "It also suggests creating an institute of Indigenous languages that would elaborate policies to coexist with Spanish. This coexistence would have to be at the level of public spaces, not only in schools but also in the institutional framework and the media."

In addition to calling for governmental recognition of Indigenous languages and identifying language rights as a form of human rights, Loncón stressed the importance of bilingual education. She criticized many educational-reform initiatives for failing to consider the needs of Indigenous students.

CONSTITUTIONAL CONVENTION

In October 2019, more than a million people held peaceful protests in the Chilean capital of Santiago against mass inequality, which led President Sebastián Piñera to agree to hold a referendum on the national constitution, which dated back to the dictatorship of General Augusto Pinochet. Loncón and others who supported the creation of a new constitution hoped that a revised constitution would help reduce systemic inequity in Chile and protect the rights of Indigenous populations, among other groups. When the referendum took place in October 2020, voters overwhelmingly voted in favor of both the writing of a new constitution and the creation of a constitutional convention, the elected members of which would collaborate to draft the document. A total of 155 convention seats were available, seventeen of which were required to be filled by members of Chile's Indigenous communities. Seven of those seats were designated for Mapuche delegates, while the remainder were divided among Chile's other Indigenous groups.

Elected to one of the Mapuche seats in May of 2021, Loncón was tasked with helping to reshape Chile's constitution. She took on further responsibilities two months later, when 96 of the 155 delegates voted to make Loncón the first president of the constitutional convention. "I would like to thank the different coalitions that joined their dreams in the call made by the Mapuche nation to vote for a Mapuche person, a woman, to change the history of this country," she said after the vote, as quoted by Soledad Quartucci for *Latina Republic* (22 July 2021). As president of the constitutional convention, Loncón was tasked with leading the body in drafting and approving the new constitution, which was set to be completed in 2022.

MOVING FORWARD

As a teacher and activist, Loncón was unswerving in her efforts to protect the right of Mapuche people and the other Indigenous peoples of Chile to speak their languages. "They need changes in the constitution so the demand for linguistic rights can advance because the non-indigenous decide for us," she told Bella Macdonald for *Critic* (5 Oct. 2014) more than half a decade before her election to the constitutional convention. "The Mapuche language does not hold the same status and social prestige of Castilian (Spanish)." Loncón hoped to make strides in that area through the constitutional convention and also promoted the establishment of a plurinational state in which Indigenous communities would have greater legal recognition and autonomy.

Loncón also expressed concerns about the environmental ramifications of the Chilean government's exploitation of natural resources, which has long been connected to the appropriation of Indigenous land and has at times prevented Mapuche and other Indigenous communities from maintaining their traditional lifestyles. "There's a development model that's based on seeing nature as a resource for humans—especially men—to exploit and dominate," she told Nugent. "But Indigenous people have always had the philosophy that humans are interdependent with nature and must conserve nature as a mother." As president of the constitutional convention, Loncón hoped to encourage the Chilean government to forge a more balanced relationship with nature and to ensure equitable access to resources such as water.

Loncón enjoyed a heightened international profile following her election as president of the constitutional convention. She was named to the BBC's list of the hundred most influential women of 2021 as well as *Time* magazine's list of the year's hundred most influential people. In December 2021, she was awarded the title of Hija Ilustre de Traiguén (Illustrious daughter of Traiguén).

SUGGESTED READING

Figueroa Huencho, Verónica. "Elisa Loncon Antileo." *Time*, 15 Sept. 2021, time.com/collection/100-most-influential-people-2021/6096000/elisa-loncon-antileo/. Accessed 10 Dec. 2021.

Laing, Aislinn. "Mapuche Woman Picked to Lead Architects of Chile's New Constitution." *Reuters*, 5 July 2021, www.reuters.com/world/americas/protests-delay-inauguration-chiles-new-constitutional-assembly-2021-07-04/. Accessed 10 Dec. 2021.

Loncón, Elisa. "Elisa Loncon: The Decolonization of Language." Interview. *Revista Universitaria*, no. 104, UC Chile, 30 July 2021, pp. 50–55, www.uc.cl/en/news/elisa-loncon-the-decolonization-of-language/. Accessed 10 Dec. 2021.

___. "An Indigenous Rights Leader Is Trying to Rewrite Chile's Constitution to Put Its Ecosystems First." Interview by Ciara Nugent. *Time*, 28 Oct. 2021, time.com/6109428/elisa-loncon-interview-cop26/. Accessed 10 Dec. 2021.

Macdonald, Bella. "The Mapuche: The People of the Land and Their Struggle to Retain It." *Critic*, 5 Oct. 2014, www.critic.co.nz/features/article/4504/the-mapuche-the-people-of-the-land-and-their-strug. Accessed 10 Dec. 2021.

Ontiveros, Eva. "Elisa Loncón: From Poverty to PhD to Writing Chile's Constitution." *BBC News*, 11 July 2021, www.bbc.com/news/world-latin-america-57733539. Accessed 10 Dec. 2021.

Quartucci, Soledad. "Elisa Loncón, Indigenous Mapuche Professor Is President of the Constituent Convention of Chile." *Latina Republic*, 22 July 2021, latinarepublic.com/2021/07/22/elisa-loncon-indigenous-mapuche-professor-is-president-of-the-constituent-convention-of-chile/. Accessed 10 Dec. 2021.

—Joy Crelin

Anthony Mackie

Born: September 23, 1978
Occupation: Actor

Born into a family of entrepreneurs, actor Anthony Mackie was never one to accept unnecessary limitations. "I grew up with the idea that you never want someone telling you what you can and cannot do," he told Crystal G. Martin for *Oprah.com* (2012). "I took that to heart." That mindset served him well throughout the first decades of his career; as a recent graduate of the Juilliard School's drama program, for instance, he worked with the director of his feature-film debut, 2002's *8 Mile*, to make changes to his character and ultimately succeeded in helping to develop the role into one far more substantial than the few lines in the original script suggested. That willingness to take chances likewise paid off in 2012 when he was cast as the Marvel superhero the Falcon—a milestone that came after he spent several years actively pursuing roles in the Marvel Cinematic Universe (MCU).

Although Mackie's debut as the Falcon—also known as Sam Wilson—in 2014's *Captain America: The Winter Soldier* and subsequent appearances in several additional MCU films made him a household name, superhero blockbusters made up only a portion of his repertoire. In addition to On- and Off-Broadway theatre, his body of work has included films in a wide range of genres, from the war drama *The Hurt Locker* (2008) to the comedy *The Night Before* (2015) to the period piece *The Banker* (2020), and he has portrayed real-world figures as iconic as Tupac Shakur and Martin Luther King Jr. Sam Wilson's debut as the new Captain America in the 2021 television series *The Falcon and the Winter Soldier*, however, was an entirely new milestone for Mackie. "I didn't go to Hollywood and say, 'Make me a star,'" he told Janelle Okwodu for *Vogue* (3 May 2021). "I worked for 21 years to get to where I am. [So] to have that moment of realizing that all of your hard work has paid off, it's very humbling."

Photo via Wikimedia Commons

EARLY LIFE AND EDUCATION

Anthony Dwane Mackie was born on September 23, 1978, in New Orleans, Louisiana. He was the sixth and last child born to Willie and Martha Mackie. His father and uncle were entrepreneurs who owned and operated the company Mackie Roofing, and the young Mackie began working in that business during the summers at the age of thirteen. In interviews, he would later credit his family's entrepreneurial mindset with shaping his work ethic and willingness to take professional risks.

Drawn to theater thanks in part to early encounters with the works of William Shakespeare, Mackie studied drama at the New Orleans Center for Creative Arts and found that he thrived within that institution's creative atmosphere. "The great thing about going to an art school [is] it's kind of like it's all the odd kids. It's all the kids that don't fit in at their regular schools, because you're into something and excited about something that other kids really aren't into," he told Emma Brown for *Interview* magazine (9 Nov. 2012). "When you go to art school, everybody's kind of on the same page." After graduating through the high school drama program of the University of North Carolina School of the Arts in 1997, Mackie considered following

an older brother into the field of engineering. However, he ultimately decided to study acting and relocated to New York City to attend the prestigious Juilliard School. Part of the Juilliard drama division's Group 30 class of students, he graduated from the institution in 2001. It was there that he became involved in the staging of a theatrical script, written by a friend also attending the school, that would result in kickstarting his screen career.

EARLY CAREER

Following the completion of his studies at Juilliard, Mackie focused initially on theater, a medium he particularly enjoyed. "Theatre has that tangible aspect that film does not have," he told Hermione Hoby for *The Observer* (26 Feb. 2011). "You see 'em, they're real people, right there!" He appeared in an Off-Broadway production of *Talk* in 2002 that garnered an ensemble Obie Award and, the following year, made his Broadway debut in a revival of *Ma Rainey's Black Bottom*. He participated in The 24 Hour Plays on Broadway in 2003 and would take part in further shows in the series over the ensuing years.

Mackie also sought on-screen roles, and his turn as real-life rapper Tupac Shakur in his Juilliard friend's play, *Up Against the Wind*, drew the attention of casting director Mali Finn after the show moved to the Off-Broadway venue at the New York Theatre Workshop in 2001. Encouraged by Finn to audition, he appeared in the film *8 Mile* in 2002 and, the following year, made an appearance in an episode of the television series *Law & Order Criminal Intent*, one of just a few television projects he would take on during the first two decades of his career. "Everyone says to be considered a real New York actor you have to do *Law & Order*," he told Stevie Wong in an interview for *Deadline* (14 Nov. 2019) about the experience. "That was my only TV experience and it was the hardest ten days of shooting in my entire career." Focusing primarily on securing film roles over the next years, he took on parts in projects such as *Brother to Brother* (2004), *Million Dollar Baby* (2004), and *We Are Marshall* (2006).

MAJOR ROLES

As Mackie took on larger film roles, he was increasingly involved in shaping both his performances and the characters themselves, a practice that he linked in interviews to his early experiences on the set of *8 Mile*. "When I showed up, I only had like six lines in that movie. Every day I would meet with [director Curtis Hanson] and we would develop stuff, so the character grew and grew and grew," he recalled to Wong. "I realized at that point you hire me because I'm good with character, I'm good with dialogue. If you want a person that's not good at character development and script work, you can go hire that person." He took a similar approach when filming the 2008 drama *The Hurt Locker*, developing his role further through his conversations with director Kathryn Bigelow. "I've always felt that filmmaking is collaboration. No one person can make a movie good," he told Wong. Along with his fellow cast members, he was nominated for the Screen Actors Guild (SAG) Award for Outstanding Performance by a Cast in a Motion Picture for his work in *The Hurt Locker*.

Mackie took on roles in a wide variety of projects over the next years, including the Broadway debut of the new Martin McDonagh play *A Behanding in Spokane* (2010) as well as the films *The Adjustment Bureau* (2011), *Pain & Gain* (2013), *The Fifth Estate* (2013), *Runner Runner* (2013), and *Shelter* (2014). He played real-world figures on several occasions, portraying Shakur again in *Notorious* (2009). Later, he played Martin Luther King Jr. in the

HBO television film *All the Way* (2016) before going on to portray civil rights activist Hakim Jamal in the film *Seberg* (2019). Alongside his work in film, in 2011 Mackie opened NoBar BKNY, a New Orleans–influenced restaurant and bar in Crown Heights, the New York neighborhood in the borough of Brooklyn in which he lived at the time. "When I'd walk past construction sites in the area, I'd just say, 'I wonder what's going there,'" he told Martin about the genesis of the project. "It suddenly dawned on me that there was something I ought to be saying instead: 'I know what's going there because I'm building it.'" NoBar BKNY remained in operation until mid-2015.

MARVEL CINEMATIC UNIVERSE

Amid his other projects, Mackie spent several years actively pursuing a role in the increasingly popular Marvel Cinematic Universe (MCU) of superhero films. His persistence paid off, bringing him to the attention of the filmmakers behind an upcoming MCU film, who offered him a role that, at the time, was still a secret. "They couldn't tell me about the character, or when or where they were shooting, but they wanted to know, 'If we had a movie, would you be interested?'" he told Kyle Buchanan for *Vulture* (2 Apr. 2014). He accepted the role, which was soon revealed to be that of Sam Wilson, an Air Force veteran and superhero known as the Falcon.

"One thing I'm excited about with Falcon is that he's so different from any other superhero from any other comic series," Mackie told Buchanan about his MCU character. "What Marvel has been able to do with constantly developing and evolving and changing the Falcon has just made him cooler and cooler for every generation that's had the privilege of experiencing him." Making his MCU debut in 2014's *Captain America: The Winter Soldier*, the character teams up with Captain America, also known as Steve Rogers (Chris Evans), in pursuit of the assassin known as the Winter Soldier (Sebastian Stan). Mackie went on to reprise the role in the MCU films *Avengers: Age of Ultron* (2015), *Ant-Man* (2015), *Captain America: Civil War* (2016), *Avengers: Infinity War* (2018), and *Avengers: Endgame* (2019), becoming a key member of the franchise's cast.

While Mackie's MCU commitments exhausted much of his time from his casting in 2012 on, he was nevertheless able to take on roles in a wide range of other projects over the years. His film credits included *The Night Before* (2015), *Detroit* (2017), *The Hate U Give* (2018), and *The Banker* (2020). Despite having taken on few television projects earlier in his career, he also appeared in a 2019 episode of the anthology series *Black Mirror* and in 2020 starred in the second season of the science-fiction series *Altered Carbon*.

BECOMING CAPTAIN AMERICA

Mackie's MCU role took a significant step in 2021. By the end of *Avengers: Endgame*, Rogers has stepped down as Captain America and given his iconic shield to Wilson, intending for him to assume the Captain America name. Throughout the 2021 television series *The Falcon and the Winter Soldier*, released on the streaming service Disney+, Wilson grapples with whether to take on that role despite the challenges facing Black people in American society, while also dealing with a host of new threats that have emerged in the aftermath of *Infinity War* and *Endgame*. He ultimately chooses to accept the title of Captain America, ushering in a new era for the character and for the MCU. "I think Sam Wilson is more so about unifying and equality," Mackie explained to Okwodu. "A Captain America for everyone instead of Captain America for a specific few." In August 2021, the media reported that Mackie had signed on to reprise the role of Sam as Captain America in a forthcoming Captain America film.

PERSONAL LIFE

Mackie married longtime girlfriend Sheletta Chapital, whom he first met while attending elementary school in New Orleans, in 2014. The couple had four sons together before divorcing in 2018. Although Mackie lived in New York during much of his early career, he later returned to New Orleans, which became his home base when he was not filming elsewhere. "I live in a very simple neighborhood. I do simple stuff with simple people," he told Wong. "I enjoy my anonymity, and I've always been that way since I was a kid." In addition to working on film and television projects, Mackie cofounded the I Am a Man voter-registration campaign, which sought to encourage Black American men to register to vote and take part in the 2020 general election.

SUGGESTED READING

Mackie, Anthony. "Anthony Mackie: 'There Are a Lot of Limitations Placed on Young Black Actors.'" Interview by Hermione Hoby. *The Observer*, Guardian News and Media, 26 Feb. 2011, www.theguardian.com/film/2011/feb/27/anthony-mackie-actor-interview. Accessed 10 Dec. 2021.

—. "Anthony Mackie's Aha! Moment: How I Learned to Take Action." Interview by Crystal G. Martin. *Oprah.com*, July 2012, www.oprah.com/spirit/anthony-mackie-interview-in-o-magazine. Accessed 10 Dec. 2021.

—. "Anthony Mackie on Bringing Truth to *Seberg* & *The Banker* & How He Felt 'Extremely Emotional' Taking on the Captain America Mantle." Interview by Stevie Wong. *Deadline*, 14 Nov. 2019, deadline.com/2019/11/anthony-mackie-the-banker-seberg-apple-tv-amazon-studios-interview-news-1202785392/. Accessed 10 Dec. 2021.

—. "Anthony Mackie on *Captain America*, Spandex, and Crashing the *Avengers* Sequel." Interview by Kyle Buchanan. *Vulture*, Vox Media, 2 Apr. 2014, www.vulture.com/2014/04/anthony-mackie-on-avengers.html. Accessed 10 Dec. 2021.

—. "What Anthony Mackie Can Do in a Day." Interview by Emma Brown. *Interview*, 9 Nov. 2012, www.interviewmagazine.com/culture/anthony-mackie-24-hour-plays-on-broadway. Accessed 10 Dec. 2021.

—. "Anthony Mackie on Representation, Role Models, and Becoming Captain America." Interview by Janelle Okwodu. *Vogue*, 3 May 2021, www.vogue.com/article/anthony-mackie-captain-america-falcon-winter-soldier-interview. Accessed 10 Dec. 2021.

SELECTED WORKS

8 Mile, 2002; *The Hurt Locker*, 2008; *The Adjustment Bureau*, 2011; *Captain America: The Winter Soldier*, 2014; *Avengers: Age of Ultron*, 2015; *Captain America: Civil War*, 2016; *Avengers: Infinity War*, 2018; *Avengers: Endgame*, 2019; *The Banker*, 2020; *The Falcon and the Winter Soldier*, 2021

—Joy Crelin

Emily St. John Mandel

Born: 1979
Occupation: Novelist and essayist

The author of six novels, including *Station Eleven* (2014), which earned the coveted 2015 Arthur C. Clarke Award, *The Glass Hotel* (2020), and *Sea of Tranquility* (2022), Emily St. John Mandel has become a literary star not only in her native Canada but in the United States and around the world. Widely regarded as an author within the crime genre because of her three first novels—*Last Night in Montreal* (2009), *The Singer's Gun* (2010), and *The Lola Quartet* (2012)—Mandel was tenacious in her efforts to get out of that particular box, reinventing herself in the literary fiction realm. The award-winning *Station Eleven* was a testament to this tenacity as it explored a post-apocalyptic world in which a traveling theater troupe finds hope in performing Shakespeare's best plays. *The Glass Hotel*, a best seller, followed, enmeshing a Ponzi scheme, ghosts, and a hotel on a remote Canadian island.

In 2022, Mandel's novel *Sea of Tranquility*, a product of the "creative recklessness" she experienced during the COVID-19 pandemic, was published. "It's a book I don't think I would've written, if not for this weird time that we've all just lived through," she said to Adrienne Westenfeld in an interview for *Esquire* (5 Apr. 2022). "That being said, it's not a bleak book. There's a lot of humor and joy in there, I hope." The release of *Sea of Tranquility* was followed by the news that HBO Max was going to adapt it, along with *The Glass Hotel*, with Mandel serving as a screenwriter.

EARLY LIFE AND EDUCATION

Emily St. John Mandel was born in 1979 in Comox, a town on the east coast of Vancouver Island, British Columbia. Her father, a plumber and gas fitter, and her mother, a social worker who helped victims of domestic violence and homelessness, had five children, of whom Mandel was the second.

Little about Mandel's early life was conventional. The family home in rural Merville was not quite finished after her birth, forcing the family to sleep in a tent in the backyard while her father completed the structure. When she was seven years old, she and her family moved briefly to Comox before settling on the remote Denman Island when she was ten. There, her parents created a home environment that fitted their peculiar lifestyle. "There was a pillar that supported part of the living room ceiling that was a massive tree, with the bark carved away. It was beautiful and interesting," she revealed in an interview to Emma Brockes for *The Guardian* (9 Apr. 2022).

Having been homeschooled through the age of fifteen, Mandel was a shy adolescent who channeled her imagination into writing that she mostly kept to herself. The piano was also a close companion to Mandel, as she would sit for hours in front of it, playing Frederic Chopin's nocturne compositions. But regardless of how much she enjoyed writing or studying the piano, she had her sights set on another type of art for a professional career: dancing. Thus, in the late 1990s when she was eighteen, she left Denman Island for Toronto, Ontario, to enroll at the School of Toronto Dance Theatre, where, for the next three years, she trained arduously to become a dancer.

When Mandel completed her degree, however, she found herself at a crossroads. "I remember wondering, like, what comes next?" she told Katy Waldman for *The New Yorker* (1 Apr. 2022). "And I thought, Well, maybe I could take the writing more seriously."

FORGING A WRITING CAREER

Serious about the idea of one day being able to call herself a writer, Mandel commenced working low-to-moderately paying jobs to make ends meet, while devoting her off-hours to writing fiction and personal essays. She also embraced an itinerant lifestyle, living in Toronto, Montreal, and eventually settling in New York City in 2002. As she later remarked to Claire Kirch for *Publishers Weekly* (9 Mar. 2012), "There have been times in my life when I've had to decide to pay the rent or buy groceries. I had a job in Montreal where I had to unload a truck at 7 a.m. in the winter."

It was after she decided to settle in the New York City borough of Brooklyn that her first novel, *Last Night in Montreal*, was published by Unbridled Books in 2009. Following the life of Lilia Albert, a compulsive traveler who leaves behind scores of lovers as she migrates from city to city, this first offering did more than earn respectable reviews: it marked Mandel's introduction to the literary scene. "It took a long time to get published," she said to Kirch.

"In 2006, 2007, there wasn't a big market for books that were more than one genre."

Unbridled Books was also the publisher of Mandel's 2010 sophomore novel, *The Singer's Gun*, a noir thriller in which the well-intentioned and honest protagonist, Anton Waker, tries to escape the shadow of his criminal family. But while Anton finds himself on the run from his past, Mandel crafted the main character of her third novel, *The Lola Quartet* (2012), to do the exact opposite. When journalist Gavin Sasaki finds out through his sister that he may have fathered a child in high school, he begins to dig into the past, unearthing dangerous truths that he may not be able to digest.

Much like her first book, *The Singer's Gun*, *The Lola Quartet* managed to garner good reviews, but with low book sales, meager royalty checks, and bookstore events drawing poor attendance, Mandel continued relying on other sources of income, including working as an administrator at Rockefeller University's Anderson Center for Cancer Research. She has explained in interviews that she was hesitant to leave that job even after gaining greater success as an author, having been raised in a working-class family and also finding the work rewarding. She finally quit in 2015.

During this period, Mandel also worked as a staff writer at *The Millions*, an online literary magazine, where she published numerous essays and book reviews between 2009 and 2018. Her essays have also been anthologized in essay collections and published in other periodicals, including *Humanities* and *The New Republic*.

STATION ELEVEN AND OTHER BEST SELLERS

When her fourth book was published in 2014, it did not have the signature mystery that had permeated her past works. Instead, *Station Eleven* was promoted as a post-apocalyptic novel, as it revolved around a Shakespearean troupe whose members—the remnants of a devastating world flu pandemic—travel the country, performing plays by the famous English playwright. As she explained to Waldman, "I wanted to write about our technology. And I thought an interesting way to do that would be to write about its absence, like delivering a eulogy."

While the dystopian genre had reached its zenith during the time of *Station Eleven's*

Photo by librairie mollat, via Wikimedia Commons

release, Mandel's book was like no other: it did not depict a depressive environment brought about by the (almost) end of the world but a post-apocalyptic scenario in which art could accomplish hope. As Mandel revealed to Westenfeld, "When I was writing *Station Eleven*, my philosophy was, 'If you're going to kill off 99 percent of the population, you've got to have the lightest possible touch.' It can't just be horror. . . . There's got to be joy. There has to be lightness and art and the things that make life worth living."

Indeed, the success of this fourth offering by Mandel earned the coveted 2015 Arthur C. Clarke Award and the 2015 Toronto Book Award. Mandel, however, struggled to produce her next novel, in part due to the pressure of producing an adequate follow-up to the hugely successful *Station Eleven*. Six years and many rounds of revisions later, her fifth novel, *The Glass Hotel*, was published. A tale that deals with a Ponzi scheme collapse and its aftermath, the 2008 financial crisis, and ghosts hunting their wrongdoers, *The Glass Hotel* presented a collection of characters who were all struggling to find meaning in their lives. As rave reviews poured in, the novel ended up on several "best books of the year" lists, including *Entertainment Weekly's* list, and was shortlisted for the 2020 Scotiabank Giller Prize.

FROM THE PAGE TO THE SCREEN

When the COVID-19 pandemic struck the United States and the world in early 2020, it sparked a renewed interest in Mandel's somewhat-prescient *Station Eleven*. HBO Max was quick to capitalize on this interest by adapting the award-winning novel into a ten-part series (2021–22) starring actor Mackenzie Davis in the lead role of Kirsten Raymonde, the star of the traveling acting troupe. With Mandel serving as a producer and featuring a talented cast of actors, it was no surprise that the small-screen adaptation went on to receive universal acclaim or that it was named one of the best series of 2021 by many critics.

That success did not stop Mandel from continuing to author new novels. She published her sixth work of fiction, *Sea of Tranquility*, in April 2022. Relating the lives of characters who exist in varied timelines, between the years 1912 and 2401, this ambitious novel explores the wonders of time travel and the physics involved in it, bringing back some of the beloved characters from *The Glass Hotel* to enrich the arcs of its protagonists. "If you've already developed some characters, it can be nice to bring them back rather than crafting a whole new set of characters from scratch," she explained to Westenfeld. The novel also drew on events from Mandel's own life, including her experience of becoming a best-selling author while continuing to work a nine-to-five job.

Soon after the release of *Sea of Tranquility*, it was announced that the novelist would be again partnering with television writer Patrick Somerville and HBO Max to bring her novels *The Glass Hotel* and *Sea of Tranquility* to the small screen. Unlike with *Station Eleven*, she told Westenfeld that she would serve as cowriter in both projects, an experience she looks forward to. "I think what's changed in my life is that I've discovered this deep love for collaboration. Also, it's just fun to learn a different form," she told Westenfeld. "Screenwriting is so different and that's so invigorating to me."

PERSONAL LIFE

Mandel lives with her husband, the playwright and executive recruiter Kevin Mandel, and their daughter in the Greenwood Heights neighborhood of Brooklyn.

SUGGESTED READING

Andreeva, Nellie. "Station Eleven's Emily St. John Mandel and Patrick Somerville Team for 'The Glass Hotel' and 'Sea of Tranquility' Series Adaptations in Work at HBO Max." *Deadline*, 1 Apr. 2022, deadline.com/2022/04/emily-st-john-mandel-patrick-somerville-the-glass-hotel-sea-of-tranquility-series-hbo-max-station-eleven-1234992609/. Accessed 10 July 2022.

Kirch, Claire. "Emily St. John Mandel: Once a Dancer, Now a Noir Phenom." *Publishers Weekly*, 9 Mar. 2012, www.publishersweekly.com/pw/by-topic/authors/profiles/article/50998-dark-and-literary-emily-st-john-mandel.html. Accessed 10 July 2022.

Mandel, Emily St. John. "Emily St. John Mandel: 'Readers Have Tattoos from Station Eleven. It Blows My Mind.'" Interview by Emma Brockes. *The Guardian*, 9 Apr. 2022, www.theguardian.com/books/2022/apr/09/emily-st-john-mandel-readers-have-tattoos-from-station-eleven-it-blows-my-mind. Accessed 10 July 2022.

___. "In Emily St. John Mandel's Future, We'll Still Be Chopping Vegetables." Interview by Adrienne Westenfeld. *Esquire*, 5 Apr. 2022, www.esquire.com/entertainment/books/a39630494/emily-st-john-mandel-sea-of-tranquility-interview. Accessed 10 July 2022.

Waldman, Katy. "The Rewriting of Emily St. John Mandel." *The New Yorker*, 1 Apr. 2022, www.newyorker.com/culture/persons-of-interest/the-rewriting-of-emily-st-john-mandel. Accessed 10 July 2022.

SELECTED WORKS

Last Night in Montreal, 2009; *The Singer's Gun*, 2010; *The Lola Quartet*, 2012; *Station Eleven*, 2014; *The Glass Hotel*; 2020; *Sea of Tranquility*, 2022

—*Maria del Pilar Guzman*

Anthony Marx

Born: February 28, 1959
Occupation: President and CEO of New York Public Library

In 2011, Anthony W. Marx became president and chief executive officer (CEO) of the New

York Public Library (NYPL), the iconic library founded in New York City in 1895. Marx came to NYPL, which by 2020 consisted of 214 public libraries, with a background in political science and having served eight years as the president of Amherst College in Massachusetts. During his tenure at Amherst, his achievements included increasing enrollment of low-income students three-fold. At NYPL, Marx tackled wide-ranging responsibilities. To support fundraising efforts for the library, which is funded half publicly and half privately, Marx regularly met with elected officials who represented poorer communities as well as wealthy New Yorkers who were potential private donors. Though he was met with a few controversies as CEO—some of which were of his own making and some, such as the global coronavirus disease 2019 (COVID-19) pandemic, of which were out of his control—he succeeded in leading the library through an unprecedented time, increasing access to digital services, and shifting education programs online while the pandemic forced branches to close. Of his leadership style, Marx explained in an interview with *LEADERS Magazine* (2020) that "leadership means being able to foresee the future as best as possible, which is clearly so much more difficult in our current uncertainty. . . . I embrace that challenge and have been fortunate to find myself first at the helm of a college and now at a library ready to rethink."

In 2012, Marx was elected to the American Academy of Arts and Sciences (AAA&S). As an academic, he received several fellowships, including those from the Harry Frank Guggenheim (HFG) Foundation, the Howard Foundation, the National Humanities Center (NHC), and the United States Institute of Peace (USIP).

EARLY LIFE AND EDUCATION
Anthony William "Tony" Marx was born on February 28, 1959, in New York City. Both of Marx's parents fled Germany in 1933, after Adolf Hitler rose to power. His father worked as a middle manager at a steel trading company. His mother, who graduated from the University of California, Berkeley, was a physical therapist who worked with cerebral palsy patients.

Marx was raised in upper Manhattan and grew up using the Inwood branch of the New

Photo via Wikimedia Commons

York Public Library. As he related in an interview with David Wallis for the *Observer* (24 Mar. 2016), "My mom used to park me there when she had errands to do . . . . and the librarians looked after us, and it was unbelievable. I could have any book I wanted and it was fabulous—much more fun than shopping." Marx went to P.S. School 98, followed by the Bronx High School of Science. After graduating from high school in 1977, Marx attended Wesleyan University but transferred after two years. He earned his undergraduate degree in 1981 from Yale University. His senior thesis discussed the role of education in society, using Plato's *Academy* as his basic text. He then earned a Master's Degree in Public Affairs (MPA) from the Woodrow Wilson School at Princeton University in 1986; his doctoral degree in international politics also came from Princeton in 1990.

EARLY CAREER IN EDUCATION
Following graduation from Yale, during the early 1980s, Marx worked for more than three years off and on in South Africa. He helped to establish Khanya College, a school that prepared Black students for college. Because of the apartheid system then in force, Black students faced significant roadblocks to further education. Of that experience, he told Angela Montefinise in a *New York Public Library*

press release (6 Oct. 2010), "I discovered the transformational power of education for those students who, against overwhelming odds, were able to get one. From that was born my intense desire to extend the possibilities of education and access to information to as many people as possible, and to achieve this through the power of community and institutional partnerships."

Marx became a political science professor at Columbia University in 1990, where he also served as director of undergraduate studies of political science. At the Woodrow Wilson National Fellowship Foundation, Marx directed the Early College High School Initiative, a program that linked public high school systems and universities. In addition, Marx founded the Columbia Urban Educators Program, which recruited and trained public school teachers. In 1992, Marx published *Lessons of Struggle: South African Internal Opposition, 1960–1990.* Six years later, he wrote *Making Race and Nation* (1998); that work received the American Political Science Association's (APSA) Ralph J. Bunche Award for the best book on ethnic and cultural pluralism in 1999, as well as the 2000 Barrington Moore Prize given by the American Sociological Association (ASA).

AMHERST COLLEGE

When a friend who was an Amherst graduate put Marx's name in the mix as a potential president at Amherst College, according to William C. Symonds in *BusinessWeek* (Feb. 2006), Marx said, "That is very nice. But I've never been a chairman, a dean, or a provost, and besides, I didn't go to Amherst." The search committee agreed, but after failing to be impressed with other candidates, they revisited Marx and decided he was the best choice for the presidency. The search committee was especially impressed by Marx's commitment to tackling inequalities in who could afford elite colleges like Amherst and his vow to increase enrollment of disadvantaged populations.

Marx became the eighteenth president of Amherst College in 2003. He was the youngest person ever to serve in that role. Despite his lack of experience, Marx made a significant impact on the college. While there, he tripled the number of low-income students enrolled at Amherst. In addition, in 2009 the college received a gift of $100 million, the largest unrestricted cash gift a liberal arts college had ever received. By the time Marx left, the college

had a higher percentage of its student body receiving financial aid than nearly any other liberal arts college in the country, fulfilling Marx's goal of increasing diversity in the student body. As Amherst's chair of the board of trustees, Jide Zeitlin, told Montefinise: "[Marx] understands instinctively that America's greatest institutions need to be more accessible to all Americans, based on merit rather than elitism based on wealth and connections. . . . He is successfully leading the largest campaign in the history of Amherst College, setting fundraising records and enabling the college's remarkable progress."

NEW YORK PUBLIC LIBRARY

In 2011, Marx was tapped to head the New York Public Library, the nation's largest library system and among the most respected. The system, which that year celebrated the centennial of its opening, included four research centers and eighty-eight branches. When Marx took the job, the library had suffered deep budget cuts during the previous four years, due in part to the 2008 economic crash. Things would need to change, and Marx seemed the best fit to head that change. As Joshua Steiner, a member of the board of trustees at NYPL, told Jacob Bernstein for *The New York Times* (11 Oct. 2012), "If you look at Tony's experience in a complex environment pushing through meaningful change, that to my mind was a clear and important indicator of his willingness to think deeply about issues and to believe strongly in the importance of change."

As president, Marx grappled with questions about the library that were both philosophical and practical. "How do we build and deploy our staff to meet the educational needs of this city?" he wondered, as reported by Bernstein. "How do we ensure that we are providing ideas and information to New Yorkers and to the world at a moment when that is all becoming digital while preserving our great book collection?" Within the first fiscal year, Marx won over some skeptical board members by raising contributions of $98 million, the result of more than three hundred meetings Marx had with potential donors. That amount set the record for the highest dollar amount raised in a single fiscal year. Marx also aimed to reopen parts of the library, which had been increasingly used to host elite events for fundraising purposes rather than for their intended educational purposes.

A CONTROVERSIAL PLAN

In addition to his successes, Marx also encountered his share of controversy, including a driving while intoxicated (DUI) charge shortly after he was hired in November 2011. Marx and his planning team ran into further opposition in 2012, after unveiling a plan—created in secret and without input from the public or the staff—to modernize the library's historic main branch, located on Fifth Avenue in midtown Manhattan. The plan included moving as many as three million research volumes to off-site storage in Princeton, New Jersey, with a possible five days wait before patrons could obtain them. It also included selling off other branches and building a glass atrium that would face Bryant Park. Public outcry was immediate and loud; Mayor Bill de Blasio was skeptical of the idea as well. Although the plan had originated earlier than his tenure, Marx received the brunt of criticism for the idea, known as the Central Library Plan (CLP).

Not only did patrons dislike many of the ideas, such as tearing down the smaller, mid-Manhattan library across the street from the main building, but economic reality also factored into the decision to downscale the original idea. (The renovations to the main building were purported to cost at least $300 million.) A further consideration was the need to support the underfunded eighty-eight branch libraries. Ultimately, only one library, instead of the three that the CLP initially proposed, was sold. The mid-Manhattan library, which was not sold, was upgraded to include more adult-education space and computer labs. Marx remarked on the input he and the trustees received from the public at an event for board members and scholars in 2012. "We're really grateful to everyone who contributed," Marx said, as reported by Bernstein. "That's how I think democracy should work. It's certainly how I think publicly supported institutions should work."

THE COVID-19 PANDEMIC

The COVID-19 pandemic caused major disruptions at the NYPL, as it did in most public institutions in the country. However, because the library system had added a chief digital officer, with a staff of fifty, a decade prior, it was prepared to pivot to more online offerings when the pandemic caused the library to shutter for a time in 2020. Under Marx's leadership, the library increased emphasis on digital access and Wi-Fi hot spots to help New Yorkers cope during the pandemic. It also shifted education programs online, including English-language programs, homework help, and pre-K literacy support. Marx was also able to avoid layoffs during the pandemic. Still, Marx acknowledged the challenges of the time. "We have to reopen physically while massively expanding digitally in uncharted waters," he explained to *LEADERS Magazine*, referring to the library's gradual reopening later in 2020. "[But] the basic mission of spreading learning and ideas for free to everyone has only gained in import. That has not changed."

Marx continued to make improvements and push the NYPL in new directions during his tenure. In the face of social movements such as Black Lives Matter, the library added new online resources to its collections, such as those from the Schomburg Center, located in Harlem. That center houses the world's largest collection of materials by and about African Americans and people of the African diaspora. In September 2021, NYPL's first permanent exhibit opened after a three-year effort to identify items to be included. The exhibit, entitled *Treasures*, contained about 250 items displayed in glass cases, including a handwritten copy of the Declaration of Independence and a fifteenth-century medieval book. By the end of the year, more than 75,000 people had visited the display.

PERSONAL LIFE

Marx met his wife, Karen Barkey, a sociology professor, at Columbia. They made history when both won tenure the same year, the first academic couple at Columbia to do so. As Marx told Laura Butchy for *Columbia College Today* (May 2000) about their academic careers, "The beauty of what we do for a living is the luxury to do new things and see new places." The couple has two children, Joshua and Anna-Claire, and the family often vacations in Turkey, his wife's native country. Marx serves on the board of trustees of Barnard College; in addition, he is also on the national board of directors of Teach for America.

SUGGESTED READING

Bernstein, Jacob. "The Education of Tony Marx." *The New York Times*, 11 Oct. 2012, www.nytimes.com/2012/10/11/fashion/tony-marxs-challenges-running-the-new-york-public-library.html. Accessed 20 Dec. 2021.

Butchy, Laura. "A Columbia Couple." *Columbia College Today*, Columbia College, May 2000, www.college.columbia.edu/cct_archive/may00/may00_cover_marriage.html. Accessed 3 Jan. 2022.

Marx, Anthony. "NYPL Head Tony Marx on Dealing with Both Billionaires and the Homeless." Interview by David Wallis. *Observer*, 24 Mar. 2016, observer.com/2016/03/new-york-public-library-head/. Accessed 3 Jan. 2022.

—. "The Power of Learning." Interview with Anthony Marx. *LEADERS Magazine*, vol. 43, no. 4, Oct.– Dec. 2020, www.leadersmag.com/issues/2020.4_Oct/PDFs/LEADERS-Anthony-Marx-New-York-Public-Library.pdf download. Accessed 11 Jan. 2021.

Montefinise, Angela. "New York Public Library Names Dr. Anthony Marx Next President." *New York Public Library*, 6 Oct. 2010, www.nypl.org/press/press-release/2010/10/06/new-york-public-library-names-dr-anthony-marx-next-president. Accessed 22 Dec. 2021.

Symonds, William C. "Campus Revolutionary." *BusinessWeek*, no. 3973, Feb. 2006, pp. 64–70. *EBSCOhost*, search.ebscohost.com/login.aspx?direct=true&db=bth&AN=19787137. Accessed 28 Dec. 2021.

—Judy Johnson

Fiamē Naomi Mata'afa

Born: 1957
Occupation: Politician

After a contested election and an unprecedented constitutional crisis, Fiamē Naomi Mata'afa was officially recognized as the democratically elected prime minister (PM) of Samoa in July 2021. Mata'afa is Samoa's first female prime minister. Her victory ended the reign of Tuila'epa Sa'ilele Malielegaoi, the world's second-longest-serving prime minister, who took office in 1998. Samoa—which was

called Western Samoa until 1997 to distinguish it from American Samoa—is a Pacific Island nation with a population of just 200,000 people. Samoa has no military, and a largely unarmed police force, but it has enjoyed a reputation of maintaining the most stable democracy in the region after declaring its independence from New Zealand in 1962. Mata'afa, a political veteran, is a present-day reminder of this triumph; her maternal grandfather helped draft Samoa's constitution, and her father served as the country's first prime minister.

Mata'afa was first elected to parliament in 1985. She joined the ascendent Human Rights Protection Party (HRPP), of which she was a faithful member until 2020. By that time, Mata'afa was serving as deputy prime minister under Malielegaoi, but expressed alarm at his proposals to dismantle Samoa's democracy. Mata'afa later said that HRPP's overwhelming popularity—it had had no significant opposition since its inception—contributed to Malielegaoi's sense that the party was invincible. The prime minister's authoritarian tendencies "became a lot more rampant," she told Natasha Frost for *The New York Times* (26 July 2021), continuing that "even the internal checks weren't there—I was getting to feel a bit like the lone voice." She resigned from her position and broke from the party to challenge her former ally, arguing, "If you can't do it from the inside, you have to step outside."

EARLY LIFE AND EDUCATION

Afioga Fiamē Naomi Mata'afa was born in Samoa in 1957. She comes from a royal and politically connected lineage. Her maternal grandfather helped draft Samoa's constitution in the 1950s, and her father, Fiamē Mata'afa Faumuina Mulinu'u II, was a village chief, who also served as Samoa's first prime minister from 1962 to 1970. He served again from 1973 until his sudden death in 1975. Mata'afa is the only child of her father and her mother, Masiofo La'ulu Fetauimalemau "Fetaui" Mata'afa, a teacher and politician. Fetaui Mata'afa served in the Samoan parliament in the 1970s, when she was elected to fill her late husband's seat. She bore the queenly honorific, Masiofo.

Mata'afa was just four years old when Samoa won its independence in 1962, and had only a vague sense that something historic, and something in which her father played an important part, was happening around her. These events and their influence over the course of her life did, however, convince Mata'afa from an early age that she wanted to enter politics.

As a child, Mata'afa began attending the local village school across the street from her house, but her mother was concerned that she was afforded too many special privileges. "My mother could see me walking around looking like I was one of the teachers," Mata'afa recalled to Ian Johnstone for *Radio New Zealand* (1 Nov. 2011). "Because I was the daughter of the chief of the village, the teachers thought they'd better just let me do what I wanted." Mata'afa's mother enrolled her in a school in a different village before settling on Ma'alefa, a larger government school.

In 1969 at age eleven, Mata'afa was enrolled by her mother—who had also studied in New Zealand—at Samuel Marsden Collegiate School, a boarding school in Wellington, New Zealand. Mata'afa and her cousin Pamela were the only two Samoan students at the school. Mata'afa and Pamela made clear that they would not stand to be bullied by their peers. "Being Pacific kids, we could hold our own so we knocked a few heads around and that sorted it out," she told Johnstone.

In fact, Mata'afa came to love the school, eagerly embracing most of its extracurricular activities, including sports, theater, and debate. She signaled her interest in running for public office in 1975, her last year of school, after her father died. She asked to claim one of his vacant titles: the chiefly ranking title Fiamē. "I understood that I needed to have that ticket to get into politics," she told Johnstone. She attributes her ease in making this decision to her mother and aunts. "My mother was a very big role model. And also her sisters," she told Johnstone. "They were all very strong women and they had been brought up that they could really do anything."

EARLY POLITICAL CAREER

Mata'afa enrolled as a student at Victoria University in Wellington in 1976 but left in 1977 because she was involved in court proceedings to secure her father's title in Samoa. She officially claimed the Fiamē title in 1978 and returned to university the following year. But her departure from Samoa did not sit well with her extended family members, some of whom had likely wanted the Fiamē

Photo by Penny Wong
via Wikimedia Commons

title themselves. As Mata'afa explained to Johnstone: "I was told, not formally, they didn't write it down on a piece of paper, but they said, 'Listen kiddo, if you want to keep your title, you better stay put and look like you're serious about it.'"

As Fiamē is a chiefly title, Mata'afa's family members were arguing that she was not fulfilling her chiefly duties. She was frustrated by this attitude, as other people in her position were afforded the freedom to study abroad—but as she noted, those people were usually men. Still, Mata'afa took their warning seriously, and returned to her village for seven years, becoming, as she told Johnstone, "the quintessential Samoan Matai" or chief.

Mata'afa's community-building efforts bolstered her bid for a Member of Parliament (MP) position in 1985. She won the parliamentary seat, representing the Lotofaga constituency, that had been held by her parents. In 1991, Samoan prime minister Tofilau Eti Alesana of the Human Rights Protection Party (HRPP) named Mata'afa Minister of Education. She was the first female cabinet member in Samoa's history.

HRPP AND FAST

Mata'afa continued to serve as a cabinet member, holding various portfolios, including those pertaining to women and the environment, under Tuila'epa Sa'ilele Malielegaoi, who was elected prime minister in 1998. In 2016, she was elected Samoa's first female deputy prime minister.

By then, Malielegaoi was one of the world's longest-serving PMs. While he maintained his seat through democratic election, his HRPP party had been the dominating party since it was founded in 1982. A series of crises in the 2010s revealed Malielegaoi's weaknesses as a leader and also his authoritarian ambitions. In 2019, a devastating measles outbreak swept the island, killing eighty-three people, most of them children. The epidemic was worsened by low vaccination rates, a product of anti-vaccine propaganda that Malielegaoi did little to dispel.

In 2020, Malielegaoi used the state of emergency created by another health crisis, the coronavirus disease 2019 (COVID-19) pandemic, to try to push through a spate of bills undermining the Samoan judiciary and the rule of law. Mata'afa and other lawmakers were appalled. "Once I understood the impact of these laws, it was very clear in my mind that I could not support it and I could not remain in the party. It was not a difficult decision for me to make," Mata'afa told Lagipoiva Cherelle Jackson for *The Guardian* (1 Nov. 2020). "Creating these kinds of legislations that are taking us away from the rule of law, is a classic example of the level of power that the HRPP now has: it feels like it can do anything."

Mata'afa abruptly resigned her position and relinquished her HRPP party membership in September 2020. The same month, opposition groups banded together to form a new political party, called Fa'atuatua i Le Atua Samoa ua Tasi, or FAST. In November, Mata'afa announced that she would run on the FAST ticket, challenging Malielegaoi's twenty-year reign as prime minister.

2021 ELECTION AND CONSTITUTIONAL CRISIS

Malielegaoi expressed fury that his former ally would run against him and accused Mata'afa of breaking away from his party for personal political gain. He was also dismissive of the FAST coalition, confident that his undeniable popularity would easily carry him to victory in the 2021 elections.

Elections on April 9, 2021, yielded a dead-heat between the two parties, with the HRPP and FAST winning an equal number of parliamentary seats, save one independent.

Complicated legal machinations and challenges followed; HRPP, through some questionable maneuvering, appeared to have an upper hand until the lone independent MP decided to back the FAST party in May. Although Malielegaoi refused to concede, Mata'afa was expected to be sworn in on May 24.

However, when Mata'afa arrived at the Parliament House that morning, its doors were locked. Later in the day, FAST held a makeshift swearing-in ceremony, but Malielegaoi called it illegitimate, insisting that he still held power. "I am appointed by God," Malielegaoi, a devout Christian, said, as quoted by the *Agence-France Presse* (25 May 2021). Referring to the crowd that had gathered to support Mata'afa and the peaceful transfer of power, he added, "If they want me to stand down, they should go to a church and pray instead of protesting in front of the courthouse. The judiciary has no authority over my appointment as prime minister."

The image of Mata'afa, a universally respected leader, standing outside the locked doors of parliament was emotional for many Samoans, even those who did not vote for her. "People were singing songs about our Mau [independence] movement," a Samoan journalist told Natasha Frost for *The New York Times* (24 May 2021). "One of the leaders of the Mau movement was Fiame's grandfather. No matter which side you're on, that is just a very, very emotional thing to witness."

The stand-off lasted about two months. In July, Samoa's Court of Appeals officially recognized the legitimacy of Mata'afa's swearing-in; Malielegaoi was forced to concede several days later. After taking office, Mata'afa's administration set to work navigating Samoa's relationship to China, the country's largest creditor, as China looked to expand its military operations to the Pacific islands. She is also concerned with the urgent threat of climate change, which threatens the very existence of the island nation. "Our land masses are such that we don't have the luxury of moving to a different part of the country," she said at a meeting of the Pacific Island Forum, as quoted by Lucy Craymer for Reuters (17 June 2022).

SUGGESTED READING

"'Appointed by God': Samoan Leader Defiant After Vote." *Agence-France Presse*, 25 May 2021, news.yahoo.com/appointed-god-samoan-leader-defiant-024041313.html. Accessed 14 July 2022.

Craymer, Lucy. "Samoa's Prime Minister Says Pacific Can Deal With Its Own Security Issues." *Reuters*, 17 June 2022, www.reuters.com/world/asia-pacific/samoa-pm-says-pacific-can-deal-with-own-security-issues-2022-06-17/. Accessed 14 July 2022.

Frost, Natasha. "After Weeks of Twists, Samoa Is Set to Have Its First Female Leader." *The New York Times*, 26 July 2021, www.nytimes.com/2021/05/21/world/australia/samoa-election-prime-minister.html. Accessed 14 July 2022.

___. "She Was Supposed to Become Prime Minister but Was Locked Out of Parliament." *The New York Times*, 24 May 2021, www.nytimes.com/2021/05/24/world/asia/samoa-election-parliament.html. Accessed 14 July 2022.

Jackson, Lagipoiva Cherelle. "Allies Turned Adversaries: Samoa's Former Deputy PM to Challenge Her Former Leader." *The Guardian*, 1 Nov. 2020, www.theguardian.com/world/2020/nov/02/allies-turned-adversaries-samoas-former-deputy-pm-to-challenge-her-former-leader. Accessed 14 July 2022.

Johnstone, Ian. "Hon. Fiamē Naomi Mataʻafa." *Radio New Zealand (RNZ)*, 1 Nov. 2011, www.rnz.co.nz/collections/nff-women/naomi-mataafa. Accessed 13 July 2022.

—*Molly Hagan*

Damodar Mauzo

Born: August 1, 1944
Occupation: Writer

The Konkani language has perhaps its greatest literary champion in the Indian author Damodar Mauzo, who has used the language to describe the lives and experiences of the everyday people of his native Goa, India, in short stories, novels, and nonfiction works since the early 1970s. Mauzo is the author of dozens of books, some of which have been translated into English. Titles available in English translation include the short story collections *Teresa's Man and Other Stories from Goa* (2014), *These Are My Children* (2019), and *The Wait and Other Stories* (2022), along with the nonfiction work *Ink of Dissent: Critical Writings on Language, Literature and Freedom* (2019).

For much of his literary career, Mauzo could only write sporadically while working at his family's general store. From his interactions with his customers and friends grew many of the seeds of his stories, which have garnered a host of awards, including the 2022 Jnanpith Award, the oldest and most prestigious literary award in India, presented each year to authors for their unique contributions to the country's literature.

In an interview with Arti Das for the *Firstpost* (5 June 2022), Mauzo discussed the reasons why he writes, saying, "For me, creative writing is also a tool for self-discovery. Many times when I write a particular character that has negative shades, at that time I think, do I also react in the same way in that particular situation? In that whole process, I also try to correct myself and my behavior. So, writing also helps me, to become a better person."

EARLY LIFE AND EDUCATION

Damodar Mauzo was born on August 1, 1944, in the village of Majorda in the Indian state of Goa. He enjoyed reading as a child and his love of writing came to him during his college years, when he began penning short stories; he wrote his first in 1963. He also acted in student productions and wrote plays, some of which were broadcast over the radio during this same period.

In 1966, after Mauzo earned his bachelor's degree in commerce and economics from R. A. Podar College of Commerce and Economics in Mumbai, he returned to his coastal hometown of Majorda, where his family owned a general store. To satisfy his family's expectations, Mauzo entered the family business and began working at the store.

Mauzo pursued other ventures during his early life. He was involved politically with a successful protest movement that sought to keep Goa from being merged into the neighboring state of Maharashtra. After a historic vote in 1967, Goans voted to retain their own state. Mauzo also served in the Indian military in his youth, moving up the ranks to serve as National Cadet Corps under-officer in command of a battalion.

EARLY WRITING CAREER

Although he very much enjoyed writing, Mauzo knew there was not enough money in it to support himself, let alone his family. Moreover,

Photo by Frederick Noronha,
via Wikimedia Commons

because his stories were written in the Konkani language, which is the state language of Goa but not widely known outside the region, his reach as a writer was somewhat limited.

Nevertheless, Mauzo continued to write at night and whenever he could find free time, typically writing about the people who entered his shop. Even though he is not Catholic, he was particularly enchanted by his shop's majority Catholic clientele. A social person, he enjoyed interacting with everyone he met and learning about their opinions, worries, similarities and differences. He noted an example of how stories came to him in an interview with Kankana Basu for the *New Indian Express* (10 July 2022), describing how he witnessed a farmer walk by the shop with two bulls, headed towards a local cattle market; later that day, the same farmer passed the shop once again, looking "disheartened" and leading his two bulls, which presumably had not been sold. Noting how this inspired his writing, Mauzo said, "The stark contrast of the situation fired my imagination and I wrote a short story that very night. Such stray incidents often fuel my fiction." In the same interview, Mauzo further explained his writing process. "I usually wait for a story to come to me," he said to Basu. "When the story comes, it comes with the style. Spontaneity is the right word."

Mauzo's first literary success came in 1971 when his debut collection of short fiction, *Gathon*, was published. Another collection, *Zagrannam*, was published in 1975, along with a novel, *Sood*. In 1976 he published a children's story book entitled *Kani Eka Khomsachi*, and a novel centered on young people, *Ek Ashil'lo Babulo*.

KARMELIN AND BREAKTHROUGH

Mauzo's major breakthrough came in 1983 with the publication of a short novel, *Karmelin*, which described the lives of Goan women who worked as babysitters. It was translated into English, among other languages, and earned the Sahitya Akademi Award. "Never before had this subject come into any language, not even in Kerala literature. For the first time in the history of Konkani literature, the Catholic community got reflected in *Karmelin*," Mauzo said, as quoted by Govind Kamat Maad for the *Times of India* (8 Dec. 2021).

More awards and accolades followed this initial success. These include two Konkani Bhasha Mandal (KBM) awards and two Goa Kala Academy Awards, as well as the Janaganga Award and the Goa State Cultural Award. In 1985, as his literary reputation grew beyond Goa, Mauzo was asked to preside over the All India Konkani Sahitya Sammelan literary conference. He also served as president of the Konkani Bhasha Mandal, an organization dedicated to promoting the language, literature, and culture of Goa.

Despite his growing reputation, Mauzo remained mostly unknown outside India into the early 2000s. However, his international exposure began to increase following the publication of an English translation of *Tsunami Simon* (2009), a novella about a thirteen-year-old named Simon who must try to survive the aftermath of a tsunami hitting his village. The book was translated into English by the author's good friend Xavier Cota, a retired bank employee. The pair's friendship began when Cota would visit Mauzo's shop. After they shared their love of reading with one another, Mauzo asked Cota to begin translating his works into English.

INTERNATIONAL ACCLAIM AND ACTIVISM

Mauzo and Cota continued their fruitful collaboration when Cota served as a translator for *Teresa's Man and Other Stories from Goa*

(2014), a collection of Mauzo's stories selected from the entire forty-year expanse of his career. Most of the stories describe the ordinary lives of people living in Goa, in both its urban and rural communities.

The collection expanded Mauzo's international reputation significantly. It received considerable acclaim upon its publication in India, and its English translation was nominated for the Frank O'Connor International Award, which honors excellence in short fiction. In his review for the *Hindu* (12 Nov. 2014), S. Ravi noted, "Time has not eroded the relevance of the tales. . . . The life of the poor, downtrodden, and economically backward are depicted vividly and the plight is heart-rending." Speaking with Ravi for this review, Cota explained why he felt Mauzo was such a successful writer: "He observes people and knows exactly what an individual is thinking. Even though he knows the what, why, and how of a human action, he is not judgmental nor does he condemn it." This collection was followed by another translated into English by Cota, *These Are My Children*, which was published in 2019.

That same year, Mauzo published *Ink of Dissent: Critical Writings on Language, Literature and Freedom*, a nonfiction work published shortly after he faced death threats from right-wing Hindu extremists in 2018. While Mauzo had been politically active for much of his adult life, during the 2010s he became an increasingly vocal critic of India's rising nationalism, growing hostility to multiculturalism, and increasing suppression of free speech. For example, in 2015, Mauzo participated in a march with fellow writers in the state of Gujarat to protest the actions of Sanatan Sanstha, a right-wing Hindu nationalist group.

Mauzo's support of India's multicultural identity has remained consistent throughout his life and career. In both his writings and his personal life, he has always sought to be open to the various cultures and people around him, believing that Goa has a distinct humanism that could be beneficial for India and the world at large. He also feels that, as a writer, he has an obligation to be politically and socially engaged. As Mauzo noted to Arti Das in an interview for *Firstpost*, "Literature is also a reflection of the times we live in. A writer must ask questions, and raise issues. . . . I hope that in times to come the people who are opposing such things will realise that [there] was nothing wrong with it."

Another one of Mauzo's short story collections, *The Wait and Other Stories*, was also translated by Cota and published in English in 2022. Like Mauzo's previous works, it garnered considerable praise and comparisons to earlier masters of short fiction. Reviewing the collection for *Firstpost* (1 June 2022), Karthik Keramalu compared some of the collection's stories to American short story author O. Henry's "whimsical narratives," and praised Mauzo's ability to depict a diverse cast of characters in a realistic way, "as they are—naïve, cunning, affable, playful, and even brave."

PERSONAL LIFE

Mauzo met his wife, Shaila Apte, while the two were acting together in a student production. They married in 1965 and have three daughters and multiple grandchildren. Mauzo has credited Shaila for giving him all the support he has needed to work as a writer, as she typically serves as the first reader and the editor of much of his work.

SUGGESTED READING

Cota, Xavier. "Damodar Mauzo, from Life Struggle to Jnanpith Award." *Herald of Goa*, 9 Jan. 2022, www.heraldgoa.in/Review/Damodar-Mauzo-from-life-struggle-to-Jnanpith-Award/185027. Accessed 29 July 2022.

Keramalu, Karthik. "Book Review: Damodar Mauzo's *The Wait and Other Stories* Feel Like an Oven Baked Snack." Review of *The Wait and Other Stories*, by Damodar Mauzo. *Firstpost*, 1 June 2022, www.firstpost.com/art-and-culture/book-review-damodar-mauzos-the-wait-and-other-stories-feel-like-an-oven-baked-snack-10743951.html. Accessed 29 July 2022.

Maad, Govind Kamat. "Damodar Mauzo Wins India's Highest Literary Prize." *Times of India*, 8 Dec. 2021, timesofindia.indiatimes.com/city/goa/damodar-mauzo-wins-indias-highest-literary-prize/articleshow/88152963.cms. Accessed 29 July 2022.

Mauzo, Damodar. "Damodar Mauzo on Winning the Jnanpith Award: It Is Not for Me but for the Konkani Language, in Which I Write." Interview by Arti Das.

Firstpost, 5 June 2022, www.firstpost.com/art-and-culture/damodar-mauzo-on-winning-the-jnanpith-award-it-is-not-for-me-but-for-the-konkani-language-in-which-i-write-10759401.html. Accessed 29 July 2022.

___. "I am a Sporadic, Spontaneous Writer: Jnanpith Award-Winning Writer Damodar Mauzo." Interview by Kankana Basu. *New Indian Express*, 10 July 2022, www.newindianexpress.com/lifestyle/books/2022/jul/10/i-am-a-sporadic-spontaneous-writerjnanpith-award-winning-writer-damodar-mauzo-2474027.html. Accessed 29 July 2022.

Menezes, Vivek. "Review: *Ink of Dissent* by Damodar Mauzo." *Hindustan Times*, 29 Mar. 2019, www.hindustantimes.com/books/review-ink-of-dissent-by-damodar-mauzo/story-9pxOg9iHtMNEBCcgDr4hXI.html. Accessed 1 Aug. 2022.

Ravi, S. "Timeless Tales." Review of *Teresa's Man and Other Stories from Goa*, by Damodar Mauzo, translated by Xavier Cota. *The Hindu*, 12 Nov. 2014, www.thehindu.com/features/metroplus/on-xavier-cotas-english-translation-of-damodar-mauzos-teresas-man-and-other-stories/article6590190.ece. Accessed 1 Aug. 2022.

SELECTED WORKS

Gathon, 1971; *Zagrannam*, 1975; *Karmelin*, 1983; *Mirage and Other Stories*, 1988; *Tsunami Simon*, 2009; *Teresa's Man and Other Stories from Goa*, 2014; *These Are My Children*, 2019; *Ink of Dissent: Critical Writings on Language, Literature and Freedom*, 2019; *The Wait and Other Stories*, 2022

—Christopher Mari

Mohamed Mbougar Sarr

Born: June 20, 1990
Occupation: Writer

In November 2021, writer Mohamed Mbougar Sarr was awarded the prestigious Prix Goncourt for his novel *La plus secrète mémoire des hommes* (The Most Secret Memory of Men), becoming the first sub-Saharan African author to win that award in its hundred-plus years of existence. For Sarr, this recognition was welcome but also emphasized the limited attention that most African and African-born writers who write in French tend to receive from the French literary establishment—or from international audiences overall. "Africa's writers have never stopped writing and producing important works," he told Georges Ibrahim Tounkara in an interview for *DW* (29 Nov. 2021). "One should not fall into the trap of thinking that just because it is suddenly recognized internationally, African literature has suddenly begun to exist and is experiencing a renaissance. Perhaps the [African] continent should also have international literary awards that recognize not only African writers, but writers from all over the world."

Born and raised in Senegal, Sarr moved to France to study as a young man and subsequently began a career in writing, publishing his first novel, the award-winning *Terre ceinte* (Encircled Earth; later retitled *Brotherhood*, 2021), in 2015. He followed that work with two additional novels before receiving worldwide notice for his Prix Goncourt–winning fourth novel in 2021. Although his work did not earn universal acclaim—the 2018 novel *De purs hommes* (Pure Men), for instance, proved controversial in Senegal—Sarr did not object to the varied reception of his writing. "I accept all opinions," he told *New African* magazine (2021). "All I ask is to read me. My job is nothing other than to write."

EARLY LIFE AND EDUCATION

Mohamed Mbougar Sarr was born in Dakar, Senegal, on June 20, 1990. The oldest of seven brothers, he grew up in Diourbel, in western Senegal. Sarr's father was a doctor, and his family valued learning as well as storytelling. "I was born in an environment that encouraged me from a very young age to seek words and books," he told Norimitsu Onishi for the *New York Times* (22 July 2022) about his early life. "But there was no library at home where I found an existing collection of books. Instead, there were books that were bought for me or given to me when I asked for them." He also spent time listening to stories told by his mother and grandmother, which would influence both his storytelling and the development of characters in his later work.

After attending a local Catholic school throughout his early childhood, Sarr enrolled in Prytanée Militaire, a military school located in

Saint-Louis, Senegal, where he completed his secondary education. He subsequently moved to France, where he studied at the Lycée Pierre d'Ailly in Compiègne before enrolling in the École des Hautes Études en Sciences Sociales (School for Advanced Studies in the Social Sciences) in Paris. Sarr left that institution without completing his studies and soon left Paris for the city of Beauvais, where he pursued a career as a writer.

WRITING CAREER

Though an avid reader during his early years in Senegal, Sarr did not pursue a career in writing until living in France. "I started to write because of solitude," he told Onishi, "and there was also the experience of immigration, and all the little problems that immigration exposes." In 2014, he published the short story "La cale (The Hold)," for which he won that year's Prix Stéphane Hessel. His first novel, *Terre ceinte*, was published in 2015. Set in a fictional town ruled by an Islamist regime called the Brotherhood, the novel follows the town's residents' resistance to the regime and efforts to survive there. *Terre ceinte* became the first of Sarr's novels to be fully translated into English and was published under the title *Brotherhood* by Europa Editions in 2021. Following its initial publication, *Terre ceinte* earned Sarr multiple awards, including the Grand Prix du Roman Métis and the Prix Ahmadou Kourouma.

While Sarr received recognition for his writing from early on in his career, he was acutely aware of the limited notice typically given to works by African writers, even when written in French. "A lot of African writers have been published since the early twentieth century in France—why aren't they more recognized? Because they come from the margins," he told Anne-Sylvaine Chassany for the *Financial Times* (7 Dec. 2021). "We could be a label, a niche, but there was a glass ceiling, that still exists in the media, commercially, editorially—which doesn't mean that once in a while there isn't a singular trajectory of an African author who gets an award." Still, Sarr noted, the situation appeared to be improving. "But it's changing. It has to change," he told Chassany. Following the success of *Terre ceinte*, Sarr published the novels *Silence du chœur* (2017; Silence of the Choir), which deals with immigration, and *De purs hommes* (2018; Pure Men), a fictionalized depiction of

Photo courtesy of librairie mollat, via Wikimedia Commons

contemporary homophobic violence in Senegal. A portion of the latter novel was translated into English by Anna Leader, who won the Harvill Secker Young Translators' Prize for that work, and published under the title "Real Men" in *Granta* in 2019. The following year, Sarr was a recipient of the Berlin Fellowship in Literature, which granted him a residency at Germany's Akademie der Künste (Academy of Arts).

LA PLUS SECRÈTE MÉMOIRE DES HOMMES

Sarr's fourth novel, *La plus secrète mémoire des hommes* (The Most Secret Memory of Men), was published in France and Senegal in 2021. Set within the world of writers and literature, the novel is dedicated to and was inspired in part by the case of the award-winning Malian writer Yambo Ouologuem, who was accused of plagiarism in the 1960s and subsequently left both France and the literary scene. *La plus secrète mémoire des hommes* follows a young writer from Senegal, Diégane Latyr Faye, who, while living in France, discovers mentions of a forgotten novel by an African author named T. C. Elimane, who in the past was referred to as the "Black Rimbaud"—a name referencing the nineteenth-century French poet Arthur Rimbaud. Intrigued by the mystery of Elimane's apparent disappearance from the literary world, Faye sets out to find the novel itself as well as to determine what happened to the author.

Through Faye's search for the truth about Elimane, Sarr takes the opportunity to explore connections between history, literature, and identity as well as to assess the impact of colonialism and racism on African writers and their work. "First of all, there is the question of writing, the mystery of writing," he told Tounkara about the novel. "Then, of course, there is the question of the silence of the writer and the question of the reception of African writers in the Western world." *La plus secrète mémoire des hommes* met with critical acclaim following its publication and was nominated for several major French literary prizes, including the Prix Renaudot and the Prix Femina.

PRIX GONCOURT
In November 2021, the Goncourt Literary Society (Société Littéraire des Goncourt, also called the Académie Goncourt) announced that Sarr had been awarded the Prix Goncourt for *La plus secrète mémoire des hommes*. A prestigious French literary award given annually since 1903, the award does not include a sizable monetary prize—the prize was only about ten euros, or about ten US dollars—but ensures that its recipient becomes the center of substantial media attention. That was very much the case for Sarr, who gained additional notice for being one of the youngest writers to win the prize and the first sub-Saharan African writer ever to do so. As *La plus secrète mémoire des hommes* included criticism of the French literary community, Sarr was somewhat suspicious of the Goncourt Literary Society's intentions and, when speaking to journalists such as Onishi, questioned whether that body had truly appreciated his work or whether its membership was merely seeking to "silence" him by granting him limited mainstream recognition. However, Sarr responded positively to the award, so long as it did not overshadow the work itself. "What I can say is that I am a writer first, an African writer who received the Goncourt, that I am very happy, that this forms a whole," he told Chassany. "But this whole is structured around literature first, not politics."

Following the awarding of the prize, interviews with Sarr were featured in numerous publications in France and beyond, and he was included in *NewAfrican* magazine's list of the 100 Most Influential Africans of 2021. Throughout that period, he continued to stress the importance of actually reading his work rather than simply focusing on his identity and the accolades he received. "People underline the fact that I am the first prize winner from sub-Saharan Africa and, on top of that, one of the youngest ever. There is a lot of talk about this being a signal for the Francophone region, which is true, they have a point—or will have a point in the years to come," he told Tounkara. "However, I think you have to ask literary questions first: that is, read the book, talk about it, and find out what the literary value of this book is." In addition to media coverage, efforts to translate his work into English and other languages were underway, and an Italian translation of *La plus secrète mémoire des hommes, La più recondita memoria degli uomini*, was published in September 2022. That year also saw Sarr travel to Senegal to promote his work, making his first public appearance there since winning the Prix Goncourt.

PERSONAL LIFE
Sarr moved to Beauvais, in northern France, after leaving the School for Advanced Studies in the Social Sciences. In addition to French, he speaks Serer, his first language, as well as Wolof. Sarr has expressed interest in writing in both of those languages and told Chassany that he hopes to "explore what they have to offer, what parts of me they carry."

SUGGESTED READING
Calhoun, Doyle. "Putting French Literary History on Trial." *Public Books*, 6 Apr. 2022, www.publicbooks.org/mohamed-mbougar-sarr-yambo-ouologuem-prix-goncourt/. Accessed 12 Sept. 2022.

Chassany, Anne-Sylvaine. "Goncourt Winner Mohamed Mbougar Sarr: 'French Is My Language Too.'" *Financial Times*, 7 Dec. 2021, www.ft.com/content/bb4e4e4a-11fa-4c33-b0ea-0c7b38191979. Accessed 12 Sept. 2022.

Henley, Jon. "Senegal's Mohamed Mbougar Sarr Wins Top French literary Prize." *The Guardian*, 3 Nov. 2021, www.theguardian.com/books/2021/nov/03/senegals-mohamed-mbougar-sarr-wins-french-literary-prize-prix-goncourt. Accessed 12 Sept. 2022.

Laurent, Caroline D. "Mohamed Mbougar Sarr: Senegalese Novelist's Win Is a Landmark for African Literature." *The Conversation*, 9 Nov. 2021, theconversation.

com/mohamed-mbougar-sarr-senegalese-novelists-win-is-a-landmark-for-african-literature-171416. Accessed 12 Sept. 2022.

"Mohamed Mbougar Sarr." *New African*, 2021, 100.newafricanmagazine.com/influencer/mohamed-mbougar-sarr. Accessed 12 Sept. 2022.

Onishi, Norimitsu. "After Mocking France's Literary Elite, a Fraught Invite into the Club." *The New York Times*, 22 July 2022, www.nytimes.com/2022/07/22/world/europe/france-goncourt-mohamed-mbougar-sarr.html. Accessed 12 Sept. 2022.

Sarr, Mohamed Mbougar. "Mohamed Mbougar Sarr: Reinventing Africa." Interview with Georges Ibrahim Tounkara. *DW*, 29 Nov. 2021, www.dw.com/en/mohamed-mbougar-sarr-reinventing-africa/a-59944951. Accessed 12 Sept. 2022.

SELECTED WORKS

Terre ceinte, 2015 (*Brotherhood*, 2021); *Silence du chœur*, 2017; *De purs hommes*, 2018; *La plus secrète mémoire des hommes*, 2021

—Joy Crelin

Sarah McBride

Born: August 9, 1990
Occupation: Politician and activist

In the 2020 national election, politician and activist Sarah McBride was one of six transgender candidates elected to state offices in the United States. Winning with seventy-three percent of the vote, McBride became Delaware's first transgender state senator, making her the highest-ranking transgender lawmaker in the nation. Her campaign focused on three major priorities: reform of the criminal justice system, an increase of the state's minimum wage, and greater access to health care and paid leave.

After her victory, as Mariana Brandman wrote for the website of the National Women's History Museum (June 2021), McBride said, "It is my hope that a young LGBTQ kid here in Delaware or really anywhere in this country can look at the results and know that our democracy is big enough for them, too."

EARLY LIFE AND EDUCATION

Sarah McBride was born on August 9, 1990, to David and Sally McBride. She and her two older brothers grew up in Wilmington, Delaware. From the age of ten, she had felt like a girl in a boy's body.

McBride attended Cab Calloway School of the Arts, a public magnet school for the arts for students in grades six through twelve, which her mother helped to found. McBride graduated in 2009; her major area of study was film. As McBride told Zach C. Cohen for American University's *Eagle Online* (28 Mar. 2011), "The arts are a fantastic resource, for not only creative expression obviously, but expanding our minds in ways that affect our academics, our intellectual capabilities and our empathy for others."

Even as a young person, McBride was interested in politics; at age fourteen, she volunteered for Wilmington mayoral candidate Sandy Poppiti's political campaign. Although Poppiti lost her run for mayor, McBride saw that volunteering could make a difference. Within three years, she cofounded and headed the Delaware chapter of Young Democrats.

McBride also worked on Jack Markell's successful 2008 campaign for governor, recruiting some fifty other high school students to volunteer. She made a friend in the process; after Markell's win, she sometimes assisted him with writing speeches. As McBride told Cohen, "[Markell has] been a really close mentor and someone whose opinion I really admire and respect and who is an honest, trustworthy, intelligent, compassionate person."

When Beau Biden, son of then senator and later vice president Joe Biden, ran for Delaware attorney general in both 2006 and 2010, McBride worked on both campaigns and served as his driver and aide, forming a lasting connection with the Biden family. Beau served as attorney general from 2007 until 2015, the year he died of brain cancer.

McBride was attending American University (AU) in Washington, DC, when she came out to her family as transgender when she was home for Christmas in 2011; the analogy that got through to their initial resistance was that of feeling perpetually homesick. In 2012, after completing a year as AU student body president, McBride wrote a coming-out letter, published in the college's newspaper. At the time, she was in a fraternity at the university.

Photo courtesy of McBride,
via Wikimedia Commons

Several of her fraternity brothers came to her room to offer their support, telling her she would always be their sister. Joe Biden, who was US vice president at the time, sent her congratulations. She graduated in 2013 with a Bachelor of Arts (BA) degree from AU's School of Public Affairs.

EARLY CAREER

McBride remained connected to Delaware politics while still a college student. Wanting to return to her home state after college, but aware that no laws protected her from housing or job discrimination, she contacted Delaware Governor Markell during her senior year, advocating for a law to protect the rights of LBGTQ citizens. She lobbied for the bill during her senior year; despite threats and harassment, she appeared at events to put a human face on the issue.

Governor Markell signed the Gender Identity Nondiscrimination Act, which passed by a narrow margin, into law in June 2013. He credited McBride for her work toward its successful passage, as he told *Delaware.gov* (19 June 2013), saying, "I especially want to thank my friend Sarah McBride, an intelligent and talented Delawarean who happens to be transgender. She courageously stood before the General Assembly to describe her personal struggles with gender identity

and communicate her desire to return home after her college graduation without fear. Her tireless advocacy for passage of this legislation has made a real difference for all transgender people in Delaware." Those who fought for the bill, including McBride, later were given the Order of the First State, which is the highest honor the state's governor can present.

White House Intern and Advocacy

McBride had applied to work at the Barack Obama White House in 2012, stating on her application that she was transgender. Hired as an intern in the Office of Public Engagement that August, she became the first openly transgender person to work at the White House. She viewed it as a strong win for other transgender people. As she told Juliet Eilperin for *The Washington Post* (28 July 2016), "There's no question that the best way to get people to care about an issue is to humanize it. It was easier to forget, or be dismissive about, transgender issues when there weren't transgender staffers or interns walking the halls of the White House."

In 2013, McBride joined the board of directors of Equality Delaware as a community representative. That same year, she joined the Center for American Progress (CAP) as campaign and communications manager with the center's LGBT Research and Communications Project. She worked with CAP for three years before leaving to become the national press secretary for the Human Rights Campaign (HRC), the nation's largest LGBTQ lobby. In April 2016, she gave a talk, "Gender Assigned to Us at Birth Should Not Dictate Who We Are," at TED×MidAtlanticSalon.

DEMOCRATIC NATIONAL CONVENTION 2016

While McBride was working for the HRC, the organization endorsed former First Lady, senator, and secretary of state Hillary Clinton, a Democrat, for president in January 2016. McBride was also invited by the Congressional LGBT Equality Caucus to speak at the July 2016 Democratic National Convention, held in Philadelphia. On the same night that Clinton accepted the party's nomination, McBride became the first openly transgender person to speak at a national party convention. As Chad Griffin, the HRC's president and another speaker at the convention, told Rebecca Savransky for *The Hill* (24 July 2016), "Sarah's inclusion in Thursday's program is a significant milestone for our community, and it sends a strong message that transgender people and their voices matter." Convention delegates gave McBride a standing ovation for her moving speech.

TOMORROW WILL BE DIFFERENT

McBride joined the University of Delaware's Biden Institute in 2018, where she taught courses on LGBTQ public policy during the 2018–19 academic year. As she told AU's *School of Public Affairs News* (16 Nov. 2020), "The students were brilliant, passionate, [and] pragmatic in all the right ways, sort of the perfect mix to deliver meaningful results and real change."

Also in 2018, McBride published her memoir, *Tomorrow Will Be Different: Love, Loss, and the Fight for Trans Equality*. Joe Biden, who remained connected to her after his son Beau's death, wrote the forward to the book. The memoir is deeply personal and honest, including McBride's difficult conversations with her parents as she came out and the immediate acceptance she received from her brothers. She also includes the story of her relationship with Andy Cray, another transgender advocate, whom she married and then lost just days after their wedding, when he died of cancer. She interviewed friends and family and referenced her *Facebook* posts in writing the memoir, which she was initially hesitant to publish. As she told Leigh Giangreco for *The Washington Post* (2 Mar. 2018), "I think for me [the memoir] has defined the way I approach advocacy . . . that at the core of this has to be personal stories. My job is not to necessarily articulate the most cogent case but rather the most compelling case, and that is done through people understanding the hopes, dreams and fears that transgender people have that are shared with really everyone."

DELAWARE STATE SENATOR

In 2019, McBride announced her candidacy for state senator representing Delaware's First District, a seat being vacated by Harris McDowell III, who was retiring after forty-four years. She did not focus her campaign on her status as a transgender person, telling Reid J. Epstein for *The New York Times* (15 Sept. 2020), "My identity and the symbolic ramifications of my elections, that doesn't come up. What comes up is that we need

creative and courageous leadership that will meet this moment with meaningful action for people's lives."

After her landslide victory in November 2020, McBride convened a series of roundtable discussions with constituents, other government officials, and businesspeople. Her first priority was passage of SB1, or Healthy Delaware Families Act, for which she was the primary sponsor. The bill was designed to address the need for paid family leave. Several other states had already moved ahead of any federal programs to address the pressures of families; SB1 was modeled on those state programs. After about a year of discussions and compromises, the bill was amended and passed by both houses of the state legislature in April 2022; the governor signed the bill into law that May. As Deanna Paul reported for *The Washington Post* (9 July 2019), McBride stated, "I've spent my life standing up so that people can have dignity, peace of mind, and a fair shot at staying afloat and getting ahead."

In May 2022 McBride filed to run for reelection. In her *Facebook* post announcing her reelection bid, she cited the accomplishments of her first term, including passage of SB1: "We've passed paid family and medical leave, a $15 minimum wage, historic investments in public education, legislation to combat climate change, bills expanding access to health care, and reforms to our criminal justice system."

PERSONAL LIFE

In 2014, McBride married her partner and fellow advocate Andrew Cray. As she recounted during her speech before the 2016 Democratic National Convention, "I met Andy, who was a transgender man, fighting for equality, and we fell in love. And yet even in the face of his terminal illness, this 28-year-old, he never wavered in his commitment to our cause and his belief that this country can change. We married in 2014, and just four days after our wedding, he passed away." McBride has said in interviews that Cray continued to inspire her as a politician and advocate.

SUGGESTED READING

Cohen, Zach C. "Meet McBride: AU's Next Student Gov Prez." *The Eagle Online*, 28 Mar. 2011, www.theeagleonline.com/article/2011/03/meet-mcbride-aus-next-student-government-prez. Accessed 19 July 2022.

Eilperin, Juliet. "Who Is Sarah McBride? A Transgender Activist Who Broke Barriers at the White House." *The Washington Post*, 28 July 2016, www.washingtonpost.com/news/the-fix/wp/2016/07/28/who-is-sarah-mcbride-a-transgender-activist-who-broke-barriers-at-the-white-house/. Accessed 10 Aug. 2022.

Epstein, Reid J. "Sarah McBride Is Set to Be the Nation's Highest-Ranking Transgender Official." *The New York Times*, 15 Sept. 2020, www.nytimes.com/2020/09/15/us/politics/sarah-mcbride-delaware-transgender.html. Accessed 25 July 2022.

Giangreco, Leigh. "Putting a Face on the Struggle for Transgender Rights." *The Washington Post*, 2 Mar. 2018, www.washingtonpost.com/outlook/putting-a-face-on-the-struggle-for-transgender-rights/2018/03/02/13d38068-1333-11e8-9065-e55346f6de81_story.html. Accessed 12 July 2022.

McBride, Sarah. "To the Husband I Lost at 24." *Human Parts*, Medium, 24 Aug. 2015, humanparts.medium.com/forever-and-ever-losing-my-husband-at-24-800af5a6c53d. Accessed 21 July 2022.

Paul, Deanna. "A Transgender Activist Made Waves When She Spoke at the DNC. Now She's Running for State Senate." *The Washington Post*, 9 July 2019, www.washingtonpost.com/politics/2019/07/09/transgender-activist-made-waves-when-she-spoke-dnc-now-shes-running-state-senate/. Accessed 12 July 2022.

Savransky, Rebecca. "Dems Add First Transgender Speaker to Convention Lineup." *The Hill*, 24 July 2016, thehill.com/blogs/blog-briefing-room/news/289020-hrc-press-secretary-to-be-first-openly-transgender-person-to/. Accessed 26 July 2022.

—*Judy Johnson*

Jonathan McReynolds

Born: September 17, 1989
Occupation: Gospel musician

The Chicago-born musician Jonathan McReynolds has been cheered as one of the best gospel singer-songwriters performing today. With his powerful singing voice and considerable range, as well as the gifts of a multi-instrumental musician with the ability to play acoustic guitar, piano, organ, and drums, he has developed a legion of fans for his uplifting and emotional gospel performances. His music has been influenced by both traditional gospel as well as modern pop and R&B sensibilities, enabling it to reach younger generations of listeners.

His successful music career began in 2012 with the release of a viral single, "I Love You," which he recorded in his dorm room, and then his first full-length LP, *Life Music*, later that year. From that time into the early 2020s, he produced two more full-length albums, *Life Music: Stage Two* (2015) and *Make Room* (2018), and an EP, *People* (2020), which have all shot up the Billboard pop and gospel charts. These records also won him praise from fans and music critics, as well as accolades that included a Grammy Award and five Grammy nominations, eight Stellar Award nominations, and two Gospel Music Association (GMA) Dove Awards. Additionally, he has had a fruitful recording and performing collaboration with singer-songwriter and musician Mali Music (Kortney Pollard).

Despite all of the challenges the world has faced during the COVID-19 pandemic, McReynolds's belief in God has not dimmed, though he believes it has made many people question their purpose and sense of what matters. "I think people are looking for that unchanging answer that has remained throughout centuries and I'm really excited about the new eyes and new attention and the new sense of gravity," McReynolds said to Cortney Wills in an interview for the *Grio* (16 Apr. 2020) regarding the response many people were having to the pandemic. "Particularly us in America. . . . We are all pretty spoiled and surface and we're just lonely skating around life with our first world problems. Situations like this humble us and remind us that we can't do it by ourselves."

EARLY LIFE AND EDUCATION

Jonathan Caleb McReynolds was born in Chicago, Illinois, on September 17, 1989. Raised by his mother on the city's South Side, McReynolds has said in interviews that he developed a powerful faith in God and believes that nothing occurs without purpose. He received considerable love and attention from his mother and from the members of their church, the New Original Church of God in Christ.

McReynolds's love of music began early. He learned to play drums at five and piano at eight. Later, he became skilled at acoustic guitar, an instrument not normally associated with gospel music. He often played these instruments during weekly church services but was never interested in singing. That began to change when he started to attend high school at Whitney Young Magnet High School. There, after joining the school's podcast program, he developed more confidence in his singing. While an undergraduate at Columbia College Chicago, he recorded his first single, "No Gray," in his dorm room with no expectations that it would amount to anything. When the single went viral, it made him reconsider his initial plan to become a meteorologist, but he maintained an active devotion to his Christianity. After completing his bachelor's degree in music in 2011, he earned his master's degree in biblical studies at Moody Theological Seminary in 2015.

Photo by Sister Circle TV, via Wikimedia Commons.

EARLY CAREER

Prior to embarking on a solo career, McReynolds was a member of the group Mind Over Matter for a brief time and recorded an EP with them. He followed this musical effort by recording an EP of solo work, later titled and released as *The Very Unofficial EP*, which he initially planned to present solely to family and friends. The record, however, found its way to a Chicago-based pastor named John Hannah, who was also a radio DJ. He played some of the songs on his station, WGRB in Chicago, where it received a very favorable response from listeners, prompting McReynolds to release it to a wider audience.

In May 2012, McReynolds decided to record an official single, "I Love You," which broke into Billboard's gospel charts. Feeling more confident, he took the plunge and recorded *Life Music*, his debut solo album, which was released in September 2012 on Light Records. It proved a considerable success on the Billboard's US gospel charts, reaching number three, and peaking on the US pop charts at number ninety-eight. A hit single from that album, "No Gray," provided him with the opportunity to appear on Black Entertainment Television's *Celebration of Gospel*. His relationship with BET would be

reaffirmed in 2019 and 2020, when he served as a judge on the channel's series *Sunday Best* for two seasons. In 2021, he was featured in a BET+ original movie titled *Favorite Son*.

McReynolds followed that successful debut album with *Life Music: Stage Two*, which was released in 2015. His sophomore effort proved even more successful. In addition to topping the Billboard gospel charts at number one for four weeks, it also reached number forty-four on the US pop charts. Additionally, it won the GMA Dove Award and was nominated for a Grammy Award. Featuring contributions by guest musical artists like Israel Houghton and India.Arie, the album also produced a top-five gospel hit single, "Gotta Have You." It was also critically acclaimed. "The Chicago-born McReynolds is one of the few gospel solo artists who plays acoustic guitar," Bob Marovich wrote in the *Journal of Gospel Music* (18 Sept. 2015). "His mellow blend of acoustic neo-soul with churchy conviction may be somewhat novel today, but it mirrors the intimacy of his lyrics, which feel like informal conversations with God."

In 2018 McReynolds produced his biggest hit record yet, *Make Room*. In addition to topping the Billboard charts, this LP also produced three hit singles, "Cycles," "Make Room" and "Not Lucky, I'm Loved," the latter two of which hit number one on the

Billboard gospel charts. The album found itself receiving lots of critical acclaim as well, including eight nominations for Stellar Awards and two nominations for Grammy Awards. "It's something you work for, you work toward, you hope that this is going to happen," McReynolds said to Marsha Jordan for ABC 7 Chicago (7 Feb. 2019). "Especially, the last album, it was mature, we felt good about it, we really want this one to have it."

In addition to releasing his album *Make Room* in 2018, McReynolds also published his first book that year with R. H. Boyd, a Christian publishing house founded by a Black Baptist leader, Rev. Dr. Richard Henry Boyd, in 1896. In *Make Room: Finding Where Faith Fits*, McReynolds draws on his knowledge of Scripture and personal experience to delve into what it means to make room in one's life for God.

WORKS OF THE EARLY 2020S

McReynolds was unable to perform live while the coronavirus disease 2019 (COVID-19) pandemic restrictions shuttered venues in 2020 and 2021. Instead of feeling bitter, however, he found the worldwide lockdown to be a humbling experience that brought him closer to God. He told Wills, "Right now, we're not artists and we're not celebrities; we are just artistic humans. Rich and poor, talented, not as talented, pretty, crazy-looking; everyone is on the same wavelength and in the same predicament and that's what gives us a sense of hope and eases this pain because we're all suffering from this great pause together."

While in lockdown, McReynolds recorded an EP, *People*, which was released in April 2020. Its single, "Grace," topped the Billboard gospel charts, as did a second single, "Movin' On," which he performed with Mali Music. "Movin' On" also secured his first Grammy Award for Best Gospel Performance/Song, which he received in 2021. The duo enjoyed recording so much together that they released a Grammy-nominated EP, *Jonny x Mali: Live in LA*, in September 2021, and then performed live for *NPR*'s long-running Tiny Desk concert series to perform traditional spiritual Christmas songs along with some of their own compositions. Writing of this concert, Mitra I. Arthur noted for *NPR* (20 Dec. 2021), "An unapologetic expression of faith and gratefulness is paired with festive lighting, poinsettias and ornaments in this holiday Tiny Desk (home) concert from Jonathan McReynolds and Mali Music. . . . Both musicians are prominent in the latest generation of contemporary gospel and inspirational artists, incorporating secular sounds and outreach as an entry point into the 'good news' of gospel music."

In addition to recording and performing his music, McReynolds has taught in the music department at his alma mater, Columbia College Chicago. He was also a contributor to *HuffPost*, penning three articles in 2016.

PERSONAL LIFE

McReynolds founded a nonprofit, Elihu Nation, in 2016. From that point, the nonprofit sought to aid young people in following the Christian faith and awarded scholarships of more than $40,000. He is also an honorary member of Alpha Nu Omega, Inc., an international Christian fraternity.

In 2018 McReynolds fulfilled a lifelong dream to become a member of Mensa, the largest and oldest high–intelligence quotient society on the planet. "This past summer, when I got in, was the realization of a real childhood dream," he said to Jordan. "This reminds me of who I am."

SUGGESTED READING

Arthur, Mitra I. "Tiny Desk (Home) Concert: Jonathan McReynolds and Mali Music." *Tiny Desk Concerts*, National Public Radio, 20 Dec. 2021, www.npr.org/2021/12/20/1064861832/tiny-desk-home-concert-jonathan-mcreynolds-and-mali-music. Accessed 9 Mar. 2022.

"Bio." *Jonathan McReynolds*, jonathanmcreynolds.com/. Accessed 8 Mar. 2022.

"Biography." *All Music Guide*, www.allmusic.com/artist/jonathan-mcreynolds-mn0002571020/biography. Accessed 9 Mar. 2022.

Jordan, Marsha. "South Side Gospel Artist Jonathan McReynolds Nominated for Grammy." *ABC 7 Chicago*, 7 Feb. 2019, abc7chicago.com/jonathan-mcreynolds-make-room-cycles-god-is-good/5126463/. Accessed 9 Mar. 2022.

Marovich, Bob. "Jonathan McReynolds: Life Music: Stage Two." *Journal of Gospel Music*, 18 Sept. 2015, journalofgospelmusic.com/reviews-2/jonathan-mcreynolds-life-music-stage-two/. Accessed 9 Mar. 2022.

McReynolds, Jonathan. "Jonathan McReynolds Looks on Bright Side of Quarantine: 'Situations Like This Humble Us.'" Interview by Cortney Wills. *The Grio*, 16 Apr. 2020, thegrio.com/2020/04/16/jonathan-mcreynolds-quarantine-interview/. Accessed 9 Mar. 2022.

SELECTED WORKS

Life Music, 2012; *Life Music: Stage Two*, 2015; *Make Room*, 2018; *People*, 2020; *Jonny x Mali: Live in LA*, 2021

—Christopher Mari

Angelbert Metoyer

Born: July 7, 1977
Occupation: Afrofuturist visual artist

Angelbert Metoyer is an American painter, sculptor, sound, and video artist who uses his work to explore everything from "the hidden language of religion" to ancestral memory and what it means to be human. In recent years, he has become a leading figure in Afrofuturism—a movement that blends African diasporic culture with ideas about science and technology to create a utopic vision of the future for Black people. When Afrofuturism first emerged in the 1980s and 1990s, it was helmed by figures like funk musician George Clinton and the novelist Octavia E. Butler, each of whom respectively used futuristic aesthetics and science-fiction storytelling to both capture and transcend the challenges of being Black in America.

As a contemporary Afrofuturist, however, Metoyer tends to focus on more metaphysical ideas than the movement's previous members. "Art is the way I engage with who I am through a human act," he told Rachel White for *Life and Letters* (18 Nov. 2016). It is because of this perspective that many of Metoyer's pieces reflect existential ideas as well as his fascination with quantum physics, outer space, and cosmology, or the study of the universe's origins.

Beyond his examination of the creation and meaning of life, Metoyer's work also focuses heavily on the nature of time. While some of his work does aim to create a mythology for African Americans' future existences, he also uses art to preserve his ancestors' past and document his own present. "An artist's body of work represents a journey," Metoyer told Maurice Bobb for the *Houston Chronicle* (6 June 2002). "It represents how he sees life and the world around him. And once he's gone, that's it. There will never be any more work from that artist. You have to realize that art is a recording of history. Art is filled with important lessons."

EARLY LIFE AND EDUCATION

Angelbert Metoyer was born on July 7, 1977, in Houston, Texas, into one of America's most historically significant Creole families. His great-great-great-grandmother was Marie Thérèse Coincoin, an enslaved Black woman who had descended from African medicine makers. She and her partner, the French nobleman Claude Metoyer, were one of the first interracial couples to live openly in Louisiana together. After Claude purchased Marie Thérèse's freedom in 1778, some of the couple's children went on to establish the Isle Brevelle Colony in Natchitoches, Louisiana—a place where Black and mixed-race people could be free and run their own businesses in the late eighteenth and nineteenth century.

While growing up, Metoyer's parents taught him about his Creole heritage, which greatly impacted how he saw himself. His father, a Vietnam veteran, taught him at an early age that there was power in having French and African blood, which he could use to overcome life's myriad obstacles. As Metoyer got older, the fascination and feeling of connectivity he had with his ancestors would not only grow but become a reoccurring theme throughout his work. Meanwhile, history books like *The Forgotten People: Cane River's Creoles of Color* (1977) by Gary B. Mills became like "bibles" to him—a way for him to better understand his ancestors who came before him and, in turn, himself.

As a child, Metoyer was an errant student prone to daydreaming and getting lost in drawing. He had his first art show when he was seven years old in his father's office so that he could earn money for a Mother's Day gift. The show was a success thanks to his father who had secretly given his colleagues $5 each to buy a piece of artwork. At the time, Metoyer did not know that all of his customers were being funded by his father, but the experience sparked something in him. He reflected on this formative life event to White, stating, "I don't know why he did it, but it changed everything for me. He taught me that I could live off my mind, my effort, and the things I feel and believe. He brought another layer to it."

In high school, Metoyer did not mind being different and standing out from his classmates. "I was ahead of my time," Metoyer told Bobb. "Usually, it takes years for people to appreciate an artist's work because he's so far ahead of everyone else in his journey. I'm not of this world. I know what I know, so I paint it and maybe people will get it, maybe not. I just paint truth in the purest sense."

Despite being ahead of his time, Metoyer's artistic talent was recognized while he was still in high school. In 1994, at just seventeen years old, he had his first solo exhibition at Project Row Houses, a nonprofit community arts center in Houston that had helped foster young Metoyer's art since he was in middle school. This led to his work being exhibited at the Contemporary Arts Museum Houston in the *Perspective* series the following year. Soon afterwards, his reputation was bolstered by a rave review from art critic Shaila Dewan.

With acclaim already under his belt, Metoyer went on to study drawing at the prestigious Atlanta College of Art (now part of the Savannah College of Art and Design). He stayed there for three years before deciding to return to Houston to take classes at Texas Southern University, a historically Black college.

RISE TO STARDOM

Returning to Houston in the late 1990s proved to be fortuitous for Metoyer as the city's art scene was in the midst of a particularly heady, exciting era. When he was not producing new work, Metoyer spent time with several other rising stars in the art world, including Shahzia Sikander, Julie Mehretu, and Trenton Doyle Hancock. It was not long before his sales were booming, and he became known as one of the city's most important up-and-coming artists.

In the years that followed, Metoyer became a self-proclaimed nomad, living in far-flung locations all over the world, but he continued to use his studio in Houston as his homebase. From 1994 to 2019, he had more than fifty solo exhibitions all around the world—from major cities in the United States to cities in India, Mexico, the Arab Emirates, and other countries in Europe and Asia. During this time, his work was also shown in more than sixty group exhibitions. Eventually, several of his pieces became part of permanent collections housed in the US Department of State; the Museum of Fine Arts in Leipzig, Germany; The Museum of Fine Arts, Houston; the African American Museum of Contemporary Art in Dallas; and the Charles H. Wright Museum of African American History in Detroit.

MAJOR THEMES AND MEDIUMS

Throughout his prolific career, Metoyer's work has explored a range of themes including global mythologies and the course of social changes throughout human history. He also often uses his pieces to examine scientific and philosophical questions about the universe and multi-dimensionality—including ideas he has learned by taking quantum mechanics and astrophysics classes at the National Aeronautics and Space Administration (NASA) and Yale University. Another reoccurring theme throughout Metoyer's body of work is that of ancestral memory, or the way that people's existences are a compilation of their ancestors. He spoke on this concept to Douglas Britt in an interview for the *Houston Chronicle* (11 Oct. 2008), stating, "My DNA is a receptor, but also a physical manifestation of time on Earth as a form that my blood generates, and other people who came before me."

Although Metoyer is best known for his paintings, he has also created album covers for award-winning hip-hop artists like Saul Williams and Mike Ladd, and is a sculptor, sound, and performance artist. When it comes to the production of his pieces, Metoyer uses a wide range of thoughtfully selected, symbolic materials. While exploring existential ideas like destruction and death, for example, he will use waste materials like coal, glass, mirrors, tar, and gold dust. Meanwhile, pieces about his connection to his ancestors have included personal tchotchkes, cultural totems, and indigo—a crop that his great-great-great-grandparents used to grow in Louisiana. On his decision to harness the blue color that indigo produces, Metoyer has explained that he likes to adapt "indigenous pigment" and give it his own meaning. "It's been an experiment making it my own, mixing a blend of materials. I find meaning in the formula," Metoyer explained to White.

LU-X (DREAMS) AND ICON EXECUTION

In October 2008, the New Gallery in Houston hosted a solo exhibition of Metoyer's work entitled *LU-X (Dreams)*. The collection was largely inspired by the artist's family heritage—specifically his ancestors who had descended from Marie Thérèse Coincoin and Claude Metoyer's ten children in Louisiana. For Metoyer, the exhibition's pieces proved to be an opportunity to try to understand what it meant to be "Creole." In this effort, he attempted to fuse French, Native American, and African spirituality, folklore, and culture together on the canvas.

When Britt asked Metoyer what the message of *LU-X (Dreams)*'s largest painting, entitled *House of Warriors*, was Metoyer replied, "It's almost like looking in the mirror and then seeing how many of your relatives you see in your face. When I stare in the mirror, I see my dad, I see my grandfathers, I see my brothers, then I see my mom, then I see my uncle."

Another notable exhibition in Metoyer's career was *Icon Execution*, which was held at the N'Namdi Center for Contemporary Art in Detroit, Michigan, in 2010. The show included a series of works depicting beheaded Confederate generals as well as a series entitled *M-Windows*, which featured images behind glass representing the "apparatus of collective memory." Several of the pieces comprised found objects and symbols of the African diaspora.

For Metoyer, the exhibition was about dismantling the haunting threat of racism in America. In an interview with John-Paul Pryor for *AnOther Magazine* (19 Aug. 2010), he shared his thoughts on the pieces, stating, "I think that race is something far more abstract than we can even understand. It's not about black or white, it's more about which archetypes you choose to align yourself with. Essentially, I'm dealing with alchemy, religion, ritual, and science. I mean, there is a scientific element to what I am doing in these works and yet they still create beauty. The whole process is actually alive."

WRESTLING HISTORY

In 2016, Metoyer had an exhibition at the John L. Warfield Center for African and African American Studies at the University of Texas at Austin. Entitled *Wrestling History: Points Along a Journey of Dis/covery Hidden in the Temple*, it explored the theme of individual and collective transformation within the context of identity, history, and race. Reflecting Metoyer's fascination with religion, philosophy, and astronomy, the pieces were eclectic in both their medium and the materials they used. Additionally, most of the pieces had been produced at completely different points in Metoyer's career and were loaned to the show by various art collectors in the region. He also created one new artwork for the show, *Untitled 123 and 4*, a three-dimensional piece that explored his feelings about creating work in a new environment. While explaining the complexity of the breadth of his work, Metoyer told White, "It's just like a human body. All of your interests are stored in a small space above your eyes, and the volume of electricity your brain produces is overwhelming. All of my thoughts and interests make up what I am and what I create."

In 2021, Metoyer began a residency at the Tripoli Gallery in Long Island, New York, where he also presented a solo exhibition titled *Magnificent Change*.

PERSONAL LIFE

Metoyer married Dutch photographer Charlie Koolhaas in 2008 while living in Hong Kong. They have one son named Zi, born in 2012. Metoyer works from his main studio at the Project Row Houses art center in Houston. He also periodically holds artist-in-resident positions throughout the country.

SUGGESTED READING

"Afrofuturist Painter Angelbert Metoyer Introduces New Exhibit 'Magnificent Change.'" *Highbrow Magazine*, 23 Apr. 2021, www.highbrowmagazine.com/12077-afrofuturist-painter-angelbert-metoyer-introduces-new-exhibit-magnificent-change. Accessed 14 July 2022.

Anspon, Catherine D. "Coming Home." *Paper City Magazine*, Jan. 2015, papercitymagazine.uberflip.com/i/439445-january-2015-houston/21. Accessed 6 July 2022.

Bobb, Maurice. "Young Artist Sees Himself as Prophet." *The Houston Chronicle*, 6 June 2002, www.chron.com/neighborhood/heights-news/article/Young-artist-sees-himself-as-prophet-2071179.php. Accessed 6 July 2022.

Metoyer, Angelbert. "Angelbert Metoyer, Artist." Interview by John-Paul Pryor. *AnOther Magazine*, 19 Aug. 2010, www.anothermag.com/art-photography/386/angelbert-metoyer-artist. Accessed 8 July 2022.

___. "For Artist Angelbert Metoyer, Paintings Are Family." Interview by Douglas Britt. *The Houston Chronicle*, 11 Oct. 2008, www.chron.com/culture/main/article/For-artist-Angelbert-Metoyer-paintings-are-family-1540547.php. Accessed 8 July 2022.

White, Rachel. "Living Off His Mind: Angelbert Metoyer's Patient Pursuit to Understand." *Life and Letters*, The University of Texas at Austin, 18 Nov. 2016, lifeandletters.la.utexas.edu/2016/11/living-off-his-mind-angelbert-metoyers-patient-pursuit-to-understand/. Accessed 8 July 2022.

SELECTED WORKS

LU-X (Dreams) exhibition, 2008; *House of Warriors*, 2008; *Icon Execution* exhibition, 2010; M-*Windows*, 2010; *Wrestling History* exhibition, 2016; *Untitled 123 and 4*, 2016; *Magnificent Change* exhibition, 2021

—*Emily E. Turner*

Leon Michels

Born: ca. 1982–83
Occupation: Musician and producer

Musician and record producer Leon Michels rose to attention with a signature style built on the warm, analog sounds of classic funk and soul but also embracing the experimentalism of jazz and hip-hop. He launched his music career early, getting a break at age sixteen to play saxophone with retro-soul singer Sharon Jones and touring for years with her band, the Dap-Kings, who also served as the house band for Daptone Records. Michels soon became heavily involved in record production, but also continued to hone his skills as a multi-instrumentalist, including with his own group, El Michels Affair, which released its debut album in 2005. "My whole approach to music—even my approach to engineering and recording music—it's all performance-based," he told Geoff Stanfield for *Tape Op* (1 May 2021). "Before I even started recording

music, it was always about a performance, or improvising and capturing a performance."

Michels's talents both as a player and a producer led to numerous collaborations with high-profile artists. The El Michels Affair gigged with members of the iconic hip-hop group the Wu-Tang Clan, leading to two albums of Wu-Tang covers, *Enter the 37th Chamber* (2009) and *Return to the 37th Chamber* (2017), that became cult favorites. Michels also collaborated closely with fellow musician and producer Dan Auerbach, touring with his band the Black Keys, cofounding the group the Arcs, and lending a hand on Auerbach-produced music by artists as varied as New Orleans legend Dr. John and pop star Lana del Rey. In 2016 Michels cofounded Big Crown Records, giving him a new outlet for genre-bending El Michels Affair albums such as *Adult Themes* (2020) and *Yeti Season* (2021) as well as releases by other artists.

EARLY LIFE AND THE MIGHTY IMPERIALS

Leon Marcus Michels was born into a creatively minded family. His mother, Francine Prose, was a successful novelist and essayist, and his father, Howard Michels, was an artist. The family moved often as Prose took various positions teaching writing, but Michels and his brother, Bruno, were raised mostly in upstate New York. Michels enjoyed music from an early age, and his school music teachers introduced him to jazz greats like Duke Ellington, Benny Goodman, and Benny Carter. "In fifth or sixth grade, I got pretty obsessed with jazz," Michels told Stanfield. He learned to play saxophone, and soon he was introduced to classic funk acts like James Brown and the Meters.

In high school Michels teamed up with classmates Homer Steinweiss, Nick Movshon, and Sean Solomon to form a funk band called the Mighty Imperials. In 1999, when Michels was sixteen, the band recorded an album called *Thunder Chicken* with Desco Records, a small label that was an early player in the resurgence of retro soul at the time. Michels played organ, and four of the album's tracks also featured vocals by guest artist Joseph Henry. Two singles were released, but when Desco Records folded in 2000, the album was shelved. However, one of the founders of Desco, Gabriel Roth, helped found Daptone Records in 2001, and officially released *Thunder Chicken* in 2004. The Mighty Imperials had parted ways by then, but the album garnered considerable critical praise in jazz and funk circles. "The Meters fully exploited the organ/guitar/bass/drums unit as a vehicle for funk in the '70s, and the Mighty Imperials continue in their early tradition with a bump and grind that seductively and irresistibly demands that you shake your booty," a reviewer for *All About Jazz* (7 Oct. 2004) wrote, noting that listeners would likely not imagine that the musicians were teenagers simply by listening.

SHARON JONES AND THE DAP-KINGS

Meanwhile, the teenage Michels landed a gig playing saxophone with the soul act Sharon Jones and The Soul Providers, who were affiliated with Desco Records. The band, which included Roth, strove to emulate and expand the deep funk sound of the 1960s and 1970s. In 1999 Michels began touring with the group, including an overseas trip with a leg in England. "I had convinced my parents to let me miss my finals and go on tour with a bunch of thirty-year-olds," he told the blog *Flea Market Funk* (30 July 2020).

After Desco Records folded the Soul Providers disbanded, but Michels continued to tour extensively with Jones as part of her new backing group, the Dap-Kings, who also served as the house band for Daptone Records. He played on the albums *Dap Dippin' with Sharon Jones and Dap-Kings* (2002) and *Naturally* (2005) with her. The Dap-Kings also supported various other artists, giving Michels a firm foothold in the burgeoning New York City soul and funk revival scene.

Michels was also involved with Soul Fire Records, a label founded by Phillip Lehman, who had been the other founder of Desco and played in the Soul Providers. Among the Soul Fire artists Michels worked with was Lee Fields, a soul singer who had debuted in 1969 but revitalized his career in the twenty-first century. After Lehman retired from music, he left Soul Fire to Michels and fellow musician Jeff Silverman. Together they relaunched the label as Truth & Soul Records in 2004 and continued the mission of putting out vintage-style soul and funk, working as producers and songwriters as well as musicians.

EL MICHELS AFFAIR AND THE WU-TANG CLAN

As his work with Truth & Soul Records ramped up, Michels left the Dap-Kings after the release of *Naturally*. He then formed his own band,

called the El Michels Affair, which released their first album, *Sounding Out the City*, in 2005. "This instrumental group has created a near-perfect simulacrum of late-'60s/early-'70s deep funk, jazz-funk, and soul-jazz, right down to the dub-like lo-fi quality of the sound," Stewart Mason wrote in a review of the record for *AllMusic*. "If that were all *Sounding Out the City* was, however, it would be an impressive technical achievement but not a particularly interesting album. As it happens, however, Michels and crew have created an album that has as much melodic content . . . and soul as any of the albums it's an homage to."

The album attracted the attention of promoters with the car company Scion/Toyota, who were putting on a series of concerts pairing hip-hop emcees with live bands. El Michels Affair was booked for a small club gig with rapper Raekwon, of the Wu-Tang Clan. "To this day it's probably the best concert I've ever played. It was so much fun," Michels told Stanfield. "The crowd was going crazy. It snowballed." El Michels Affair went on to record an instrumental version of Wu-Tang's 1993 hit "C.R.E.A.M.," which sold very well. Other Wu-Tang cover singles followed, and the El Michels Affair played more live shows with various Wu-Tang members. In 2009, the band released a full album of Wu-Tang Clan and Wu-Tang member solo songs called *Enter the 37th Chamber* (a tribute to the Wu-Tang Clan's 1993 debut album, *Enter the Wu-Tang (36 Chambers)*). Nate Patrin, who reviewed the album for *Pitchfork* (11 May 2009), called it "an instant rap-geek curio for anyone who likes hearing bands cross the bounds of sample-based and live hip-hop instrumentation," suggesting that the record "works best as a series of familiar touchstones sifted through a filter of hazy, almost psychedelic mud-fidelity gloom, getting at the sorrow and menace of classic Wu-Tang at a somewhat different angle." Ironically, the El Michels Affair covers proved popular for sampling by rappers, including Wu-Tang's Ghostface Killah.

El Michels Affair released a follow-up album called *Return to the 37th Chamber* in 2017. Patrin also reviewed that album, this time for *Bandcamp Daily* (20 Apr. 2017), and assured fans that it was not just "a more-of-the-same sequel." The album features several deep cuts from the broader Wu-Tang catalog, as well as guest vocals from artists like Lee Fields and Lady Wray. "It's not the homage to the gamut-running Murderer's Row of Wu-Tang classics that its predecessor was, but *Return*'s deep-dive strangeness is a complementary piece that Shaolin disciples and acid-funk enthusiasts should prize," Patrin wrote.

WORK WITH OTHERS

Alongside his El Michels Affair work, Michels collaborated with many other artists. He became part of the Menahan Street Band, a group that brought together various musicians from the Daptone Records community; their 2008 album *Make the Road by Walking* generated samples for many major hip-hop artists such as Jay-Z and Kendrick Lamar. Michels also helped propel Fields's career renaissance, backing the veteran singer with the Truth & Soul label house band, the Expressions, and releasing the album *My World* in 2009. Lee Fields and the Expressions went on to put out several further records on the label, including *Faithful Man* (2012) and *Emma Jean* (2014), with Michels as a producer.

By the late 2000s the neo-soul revival was in full swing, and Michels found himself in demand with artists seeking to achieve an authentic retro sound. The pop star Adele brought him in to work on her debut album *19* (2008), and he was credited as a songwriter on the track "Right as Rain." He also co-produced Aloe Blacc's album *Good Things* (2010). One of Michels's most productive collaborations was with Dan Auerbach of the blues-rock band the Black Keys. "Dan cold-called me, because I put out the first Lee Fields record, *My World*, which he liked," Michels told Stanfield. "They were looking for a bass player and a keyboard player for the Black Keys live. I started touring with them and we got on well. I started doing sessions with him in the studio." Michels worked with Auerbach to produce the albums *Locked Down* (2012) for pianist Dr. John and *Ultraviolence* (2014) for Lana Del Rey. In 2015, Michels and Auerbach teamed up with Steinweiss and Movshon to form a band called the Arcs. They released an album called *Yours, Dreamily* the same year.

In 2016, Michels closed Truth & Soul, replacing it with a new label called Big Crown Records. Many Truth & Soul artists moved to Big Crown, and Michels continued his steady stream of production work and other appearances. In 2018, an instrumental he created was used on "Summer," a song released by Beyoncé and Jay-Z as The Carters. In 2019, Michels played saxophone for a viral NPR "Tiny Desk" concert featuring rappers Freddie Gibbs and Madlib.

ADULT THEMES AND *YETI SEASON*

In 2020 El Michels Affair released their fourth album, though only their second of original work, called *Adult Themes*. The album was inspired by the 1960s and 1970s composer François de Roubaix, who "made really crazy soundtracks to slasher B-movies in France," as Michels told Phillip Mlynar in an interview for *Bandcamp Daily* (28 May 2020). Michels noted that approaching the project like a movie score was liberating in many ways. "It's not like standard song forms," he told Mlynar of the album. "I wanted to make each song have these little mood shifts halfway through. When I listened to all those soundtrack records, that's what they basically do. That's what I took from the soundtracks—to make mood pieces, rather than traditional songs." That intent was clear and successful for Austin Trunick, who reviewed *Adult Themes* for *Under the Radar* (25 May 2020): "Half the fun of it is closing your eyes and dreaming up the movies these pieces could have been pulled from."

Michels worked on the band's next album, *Yeti Season*, while he was quarantined with his family in upstate New York during the height of the COVID-19 pandemic. During the process of making the unusual album, influenced by Turkish psych-pop and folk rock, Michels embraced "complete freedom," he told T. M. Brown in an interview for *Rolling Stone* (26 Mar. 2021). The title evokes a moment from Michels's quarantine, when he donned a yeti costume and chased his kids around the yard. The album itself exudes a sense of comfort and play; it was even released in tandem with a children's book written by Michels's novelist mother. Michels noted that the eclectic approach would likely continue in his personal musical project. "I'll probably never make another record like this," he told Brown. "I like the idea of El Michels Affair becoming just an outlet to do different sh— and weird sh— and stuff that interests me."

PERSONAL LIFE

Although he was based out of New York City for much of his early career, Michels later relocated primarily to Rhinebeck, New York (though he continued to share a studio space in Queens). He told *Flea Market Funk* about the relative quietness of life upstate: "There is not much to do and very little distractions except for the occasional all-consuming house project." Michels and his partner have three children together.

SUGGESTED READING

Michels, Leon. "Big Ups with Leon Michels." *Flea Market Funk*, 30 July 2020, fleamarketfunk.com/2020/07/30/big-ups-with-leon-michels/. Accessed 10 Jan. 2022.

—. "El Michels Affair Finds a New Groove." Interview by T. M. Brown. *Rolling Stone*, 26 Mar. 2021, www.rollingstone.com/music/music-features/el-michels-affair-yeti-season-interview-1146483/. Accessed 11 Jan. 2022.

—. "El Michels Pays Homage to Classic Film Scores on *Adult Themes*." Interview by Phillip Mlynar, *Bandcamp Daily*, 28 May 2020, daily.bandcamp.com/features/el-michels-interview. Accessed 11 Jan. 2022.

—. "Leon Michels: No Options." Interview by Geoff Stanfield. *Tape Op*, May 2021, tapeop.com/interviews/143/leon-michels/. Accessed 10 Jan. 2022.

Patrin, Nate. "Album of the Day: El Michels Affair, *Return to the 37th Chamber*." *Bandcamp Daily*, 20 Apr. 2017, daily.bandcamp.com/album-of-the-day/el-michels-affair-return-to-the-37th-chamber-review. Accessed 11 Jan. 2022.

—. Review of *Enter the 37th Chamber*, by El Michels Affair. *Pitchfork*, 11 May 2009, pitchfork.com/reviews/albums/13011-enter-the-37th-chamber/. Accessed 11 Jan. 2022.

Trunick, Austin. Review of *Adult Themes*, by El Michels Affair. *Under the Radar*, 25 May 2020, www.undertheradarmag.com/reviews/el_michels_affair_adult_themes. Accessed 11 Jan. 2022.

SELECTED WORKS

Thunder Chicken (with The Mighty Imperials), 2004; *Enter the 37th Chamber* (with El Michels Affair), 2009; *Adult Themes* (with El Michels Affair), 2020; *Yeti Season* (with El Michels Affair), 2021

—Molly Hagan

Myron Mixon

Born: May 31, 1962
Occupation: Chef and businessperson

"There's no bad barbecue anymore," chef Myron Mixon told John Soltes in an interview for *Hollywood Soapbox* (13 June 2012). "You've just got the best and then you've got good. But the line that separates them is very, very small." Mixon's goal was to stay on the "best" side of that line, and as his performance in barbecue cooking competitions throughout the early twenty-first century demonstrated, he had long been successful in doing so. With his Jack's Old South barbecue team, he was a fixture at competitions such as the World Championship Barbecue Cooking Contest in Memphis, Tennessee, and first earned the title of grand champion there in 2001. He would go on to win a record four more grand championships at that competition over the next two decades, in addition to many other competitive titles, and was inducted into the Barbecue Hall of Fame in 2013.

The son of parents who operated a barbecue business throughout his childhood, Mixon has explored several business ventures in addition to his competitive cooking, including opening several locations of the restaurant Myron Mixon's Pitmaster Barbeque. He has also authored several cookbooks, taught barbecue classes at his home in Georgia, and starred in television programs, including five seasons of judging for the reality series *BBQ Pitmasters* in the 2010s. Although such ventures have kept him busy, Mixon remained devoted to the competition circuit and in 2021 won his fifth grand championship in Memphis, which he considered one of his most exciting achievements. "You'd think it would feel like old hat, but it doesn't," he told Rachel Kiser for *Alexandria Living* (6 July 2021). "Not many people can say they have won five world championships in anything."

EARLY LIFE

Myron Mixon was born on May 31, 1962. One of three sons born to Gaye and Jack Mixon, he spent his childhood in Vienna, Georgia. His father ran a barbecue business called Jack's Old South, and the young Mixon spent much of his childhood assisting his father with the manual labor crucial to the business. "My dad fired the pits. I'd get the wood up in the pits, too," he recalled to Ashok Selvam in an interview for *Eater Chicago* (17 June 2016). "That was our whole chore. Not only did we cook, we had to go get the wood that we burned. We actually carried, chain-sawed it, spread it through the wedges, it wasn't fun for somebody young." His parents later expanded their business, producing a locally popular line of barbecue sauce.

BARBECUE CHAMPION

Following his father's death in the late 1990s, Mixon began to consider entering barbecue-cooking competitions as a means of promoting his family's barbecue sauce, which was still in production. In 1996, he entered the Lock-&-Dam BBQ Contest, a competition located in Augusta, Georgia. Exhibiting the skills he had learned under his father's tutelage, he placed first in two categories, whole hog and pork ribs, and third in another. The experience was a formative one for Mixon, who over the next years entered many other competitions, including the Big Pig Jig in his childhood hometown of Vienna and the Safeway Barbecue Battle in Washington, DC, with success at the former contest securing him his first grand championship in 1997. "I got very good at it and started making a living off the prize money," he later told Pete Martin for the *Greenville News* (4 Oct. 2016). "I don't know if anybody else has ever done that, but I did it for about 10 years. That was my sole income. That puts a lot of pressure on you to be good or figure out a way to be good at whatever it is you are doing." Many of the competitions he entered were team competitions, and he named his team Jack's Old South in honor of his father's business.

As Mixon became a fixture on the competition circuit, he quickly found that his barbecue could hold its own against the other top contenders at the United States' most prestigious barbecue contests. One such contest was the World Championship Barbecue Cooking Contest (WCBCC), held in Memphis, Tennessee, as part of that city's annual Memphis in May festival. Mixon and Jack's Old South claimed their first victory at that competition in 2001, winning both the whole hog category and the title of grand champion. A recurring winner for the whole hog, Mixon went on to reclaim the grand

champion title in 2004 and 2007. He captured that title for a fourth time in 2016, leaving with more than $30,000 in prize money. In addition to his successes at the WCBCC, he claimed multiple titles at events such as the Jack Daniel's World Championship Invitational Barbecue competition and the Safeway Barbecue Battle. In recognition of his contributions to the field, he was inducted into the Barbecue Hall of Fame in 2013.

TELEVISION AND TEACHING

As a recurring competitor in high-profile barbecue contests, Mixon came to the attention of television producers working within the cooking and reality genres, who found him to be a good fit for television. In 2009, he appeared with the Jack's Old South barbecue team in the competition series *BBQ Pitmasters*, serving as a contestant. He returned to the series as a judge in 2010 and continued to appear in that role for several seasons through 2015. "People want to be entertained," he told Soltes about the series' appeal. "They want a little competition going on, but they want it to be very simple. And that's what we give them. They get to see some good recipes being done, some good BBQ techniques. And you get to see some drama—a little bit of drama, a little bit of action." He went on to take part as a competitor in *BBQ Pit Wars* (2014–15) and in 2015 began to appear alongside his son Michael in the series *BBQ Rules*. In addition to such projects as hosting the competition series *Smoked* in 2016, he maintained a television presence as a guest on many other programs, including talk shows such as *Conan* and *Today* as well as food-oriented programs such as *Good Eats* and *Chopped*.

While demonstrating his barbecue talents on television, Mixon also sought to share his knowledge with others, including through in-person cooking classes. In addition to teaching short-term classes in various cities, he taught classes at his Jack's Old South Cooking School, based out of his home in Georgia. "It's old school, it's for the person that's never lit a fire or never picked up a piece of meat because they don't want to do that," he told Selvam about his style of cooking class. "But it's also for the barbecue enthusiast or the competition cook who wonders what it takes to get to the next level. They get to do something they've never tried before." Continuing to juggle different media formats for his specialty, he further shared his recipes and techniques in several cookbooks, including *Smokin' with Myron Mixon* (2011), *Everyday Barbeque* (2013), *Myron Mixon's BBQ Rules* (2016), and *BBQ&A with Myron Mixon* (2019).

RESTAURANTS AND BUSINESS VENTURES

Mixon was active in the restaurant business throughout the first two decades of the twenty-first century, with mixed success. He licensed the Jack's Old South name for a restaurant in Georgia early in that period but was otherwise largely uninvolved in that establishment's operations, and he eventually commented in interviews that he would prefer not to take the licensing route again in the future. Later, he collaborated with several partners to establish the restaurant Pride and Joy BBQ, which opened in Miami, Florida, in 2012. While the group initially planned to open a Pride and Joy BBQ location in New York City as well, Mixon eventually cut ties with his partners and filed a lawsuit against them, thus ending their collaboration. Another venture, Myron Mixon Smokers, proved more successful. Founded in 2013, the business has produced a Mixon-branded line of barbecue smokers, including both pellet- and charcoal-fueled models.

A new restaurant, Myron Mixon's Smoke Show Barbecue, opened in Chicago in 2016; however, it closed not long afterward. Mixon followed that effort with the opening of Myron Mixon's Pitmaster Barbeque in 2017. The restaurant was located in Alexandria, Virginia, just outside of Washington, DC, and he hoped that his long-standing reputation in the Washington area would help ensure the eatery's success. "Washington barbecue fans have always been there, even before I was on TV," he told Jim Shahin for *The Washington Post* (7 July 2016). "They've always embraced me." A second Myron Mixon's Pitmaster Barbeque opened in Miami in 2020.

FIVE-TIME GRAND CHAMPION

Like many other areas of life, the competitive barbecue circuit was disrupted in 2020 by the emergence of the COVID-19 pandemic, which forced the cancellation of that year's WCBCC, among other barbecue competitions. In May 2021, however, Mixon and Jack's Old South returned to Memphis for the competition, once again hoping to demonstrate their mastery of barbecue. The team was successful in doing so, winning its fifth grand champion title. "I've been doing this game a long time and you figure sometimes your time has come and gone," Mixon told Katherine Burgess for *Commercial Appeal* (28 June 2021) following his team's victory, "but I've got some new teammates who've been with me a few years and have never got to experience this and I'm most happy for them to be able to get this world championship." Jack's Old South also claimed first place in the whole hog category at the championship.

In addition to resuming in-person competition, Mixon released a new barbecue cookbook in 2021 called *Keto BBQ*. The cookbook features recipes appropriate for a Keto diet—a popular diet involving the consumption of very low quantities of carbohydrates—heavy in barbecued meats, which Mixon himself credited with helping him lose more than one hundred pounds over the course of nine months. He also spent much of 2021 preparing for the launch of a new Myron Mixon's Pitmaster Barbeque restaurant, which opened in Hoboken, New Jersey, in December of that year. Remaining active in barbecue competition into 2022, in May he returned to Memphis for WCBCC, where Jack's Old South placed ninth in the whole hog category.

In addition to competing, teaching, and pursuing business ventures related to barbecue, Mixon has been active in local government and, in January 2016, was sworn in as mayor of Unadilla, Georgia, a small city of fewer than four thousand residents. "This is my hometown and I ought to be able to give something back and try to fix some things," he told Martin about that role. "I just didn't know how bad it was and how much time it was going to take to fix it. I work harder than I do at my other businesses." He was reelected mayor in 2019.

PERSONAL LIFE

Mixon lives in Unadilla with his wife, Faye. Together, they raised four children.

SUGGESTED READING

Burgess, Katherine. "Memphis in May: Meet the Winners of 2021 World Championship Barbecue Cooking Contest." *Commercial Appeal*, 28 June 2021, www.commercialappeal.com/story/

entertainment/2021/05/15/memphis-in-may-world-championship-barbecue-cooking-contest-winners-2021/4930288001/. Accessed 11 July 2022.

Kiser, Rachel. "Politics, a Whole Hog and the State of Barbecue." *Alexandria Living*, 6 July 2021, alexandrialivingmagazine.com/food-and-dining/politics-a-whole-hog-and-the-state-of-barbecue/. Accessed 11 July 2022.

Martin, Pete. "Barbecue Champion Myron Mixon Finds Passion in the Pit." *Greenville News*, 4 Oct. 2016, www.greenvilleonline.com/story/life/2016/09/30/barbecue-champion-myron-mixon-finds-passion-pit/91309250/. Accessed 11 July 2022.

Mixon, Myron. "BBQ Guru Myron Mixon on Why 'Barbecue Is the Backbone of America.'" Interview by Mariella Mosotho. *Mediaite*, 8 June 2012, www.mediaite.com/food/myron-mixon-bbq-backbone-america/. Accessed 11 July 2022.

___. "Celebrity Barbecuer Myron Mixon Reveals Details on Upcoming Chicago Restaurant." Interview by Ashok Selvam. *Eater Chicago*, 17 June 2016, chicago.eater.com/2016/6/17/11964744/myron-mixon-interview-chicago-wrigleyville-barbecue-restaurant. Accessed 11 July 2022.

___. "A Delicious Talk with Myron Mixon, Star of Destination America's 'BBQ Pitmasters.'" Interview by John Soltes. *Hollywood Soapbox*, 13 June 2012, www.hollywoodsoapbox.com/a-delicious-talk-with-myron-mixon-star-of-destination-americas-bbq-pitmasters/. Accessed 11 July 2022.

Shahin, Jim. "Celebrity Pitmaster Myron Mixon Is Opening a Restaurant in Old Town." *The Washington Post*, 7 July 2016, www.washingtonpost.com/news/going-out-guide/wp/2016/07/07/myron-mixon-of-bbq-pitmasters-is-opening-a-restaurant-in-old-town/. Accessed 11 July 2022.

SELECTED WORKS

Smokin' with Myron Mixon, 2011; *Everyday Barbeque*, 2013; *Myron Mixon's BBQ Rules*, 2016; *BBQ&A with Myron Mixon*, 2019; *Keto BBQ*, 2021

—Joy Crelin

Rozana Montiel

Born: 1972
Occupation: Architect

Architect Rozana Montiel joined the forefront of creating beautiful and sustainable public works of architecture across Mexico after founding her eponymous firm in 2009. She has revitalized all manner of public spaces, from playgrounds to wilderness trails, as well as more pertinent facilities such as emergency shelters, waste disposal units, and public restrooms. Her work has earned her a slew of accolades, both in her native Mexico and internationally, and has provided her the opportunity to lecture about her methods and vision in architectural colleges all over the world.

Montiel has expressed a belief that work such as hers will provide a fresh look at social participation in public spaces, as well as making such spaces sustainable over the long haul. She said to Thomas de Monchaux for *Hauser & Wirth* (28 Feb. 2020), "For me, the primary idea of architecture is building relations. . . . When you create place, you build relationships. Relationships activate a space. It's the people who make the place."

EARLY LIFE AND EDUCATION

While little has been published in English about her early life, it is known that Rozana Montiel was born in Mexico City, Mexico, in 1972. She was raised by parents with a great love of art. She came to realize she wanted to be an architect at age twelve, when she had a hand in designing her bedroom during a renovation project that added an art gallery to the family home. "My father was obsessed with Mexican paintings," she recalled to de Monchaux. "He had a small gallery added to the house. Downstairs was the art, and upstairs was my room. . . . My parents let me design the room. First I wanted gray and white lines. After I studied architecture, it became like a Japanese room—wood, nothing on the floors, very simple with few elements."

Montiel's love of design proved a constant as she got older, leading her to study architecture in college. She received her bachelor's degree in architecture and urban planning from the Universidad Iberoamericana in Mexico in 1998, and her master's degree in architecture theory and criticism from the Universitat Politéchnica de Catalunya in Spain in 2000.

EARLY CAREER

After graduating, Montiel worked for a short time with Diego Villaseñor Arquitecto y Asociados. She also taught at several different universities in Mexico City, as well as at Columbia University's Graduate School of Architecture, Planning and Preservation and Cornell University in the United States. In 2009, she founded her own firm, Rozana Montiel Estudio de Arquitectura. In an interview for *WHYTT Magazine* (18 May 2016), she explained what set her apart from other architects, stating, "I listen to space, to people, to chance and I care to understand what I hear. My work largely consists of finding ways in which design can speak for itself, in which public spaces make their voice heard."

During her first few years as an independent architect, Montiel worked primarily for private individuals, but before long her career began to move in a different direction. In an interview with Katherine Keane for *Architect Magazine* (30 July 2019), she described her biggest career leap: "When I began to receive commissions for public projects. It was then that I realized the urban responsibility that architects have when designing collective living spaces." Collective living spaces have been particularly important in Mexico, where upwards of a quarter of the population lives in housing projects, which are usually not adequate for all people's needs. Moreover, Mexico has some of the greatest income inequality in the world, with the top one percent of the country holding half of the country's wealth.

One of Montiel's first major public projects came in 2011, when she was tasked with creating an outdoor sculpture that came to be known as *Void Temple*. She designed a forty-meter circular concrete wall that was to be one of several modern sculptures built along the seventy-two-mile Ruta del Peregrino Catholic pilgrimage path in Jalisco, Mexico. Although it is a wall, it is not always imbedded in the ground, sometimes rising above it, sometimes beneath it, but always staying level. She told de Monchaux, "[Moving above and below] the horizon line of that circle, you feel contained. But you feel open. It's a way of changing barriers into open boundaries." Its success helped to pave the way for future public projects,

both in Mexico and beyond. In addition, that project, as well as other projects, helped her earn the National Art Creators System Grant (CONACULTA) from Mexico in both 2010 and 2013.

MAJOR COMMUNITY-BASED PROJECTS

In 2015, Montiel created a water supply project in the Mexico City neighborhood of Miravalle, located in the borough of Iztapalapa. Prior to her work, the neighborhood only had access to the city's water supply once a week. To provide more water, she took an existing domed canopy and repurposed it into a rainwater and condensation collector, then reengineered a bicycle to pump fresh water from a collection cistern. The design gave the entire neighborhood access to water through this low-cost system whenever they need it.

In 2016, she completed two ambitious community projects. In the first of these, called "Common Unity," she reworked a common area of an interior block of a San Pablo Xalpa housing complex in Azcapotzalco. She removed fences and barriers from this interior and developed a multipurpose common area of platforms, pergolas, and pavilions in an effort to make better use of the space. She then turned her attention to a project in the port city of Veracruz, which she called "Court." For this project, she converted a housing project's basketball court into a multipurpose area of small classrooms, balconies, overlooks, and nooks that are covered by a large, steel space-frame roof structure that also serves as a rainwater collection device.

Following a devastating earthquake in Mexico in September 2017, in which 350 people were killed across the nation, Montiel threw her firm into constructing a pro-bono home for a family in the town of Ouilan. In addition to serving all of the family's basic needs, it was also physically attractive and built from environmentally friendly bricks called ecoblocks. It was Montiel's hope that the home might serve as a prototype shelter for families in need. "The word 'sustainability' gets so misused, but there's a common sense of it, of sustaining different abilities. Very simple forms. Not many materials. Often with very few resources," she explained to de Monchaux before continuing, "But my question is always: What can we do with what we have? We try to be congruous with the environment of every project."

In recognition of these community-changing works, Montiel received a Schelling Architecture Prize nomination from Germany (2016) and won the 2016 Emerging Voices Award granted by the Architectural League of New York. In 2017, she earned a Rockefeller Foundation Fellowship as an arts and literary resident to the Bellagio Center in Italy and received first place in both the moving category and the overall award of the Miami Archmarathon Awards. The same year, she won the Moira Gemmill Award given by the *Architectural Review* in London. Winning the Moira Gemmill Award, she told Keane, was "an important turning point in my career not only because the prize validated my studio's approach to architecture, but also because it has funded my research."

MORE AWARD-WINNING DESIGNS

In 2018, Montiel and her team were tasked with redesigning a forty-year-old public-housing development in the city of Zacatecas, Mexico. Long a haven for criminal activities, it contained a canal area that was being used by children as a makeshift playground. She and her team decided to transform a section of it into a real playground by adding cement steps, latticework, and bridges across the canal area. The project transformed the location into a popular playground not just for the children who live there, but for children across the city.

That same year, her firm published a book titled *HU: Common Spaces in Housing Units* (2018), which collects a series of Post-It-style graphics to show their solutions for creating revitalized public spaces. "The book is one of my favorite projects because it involved a great deal of reflection about how we design and the role language plays in building," she recalled to Keane.

In addition to her public-space projects, Montiel has also improved more basic accommodations, including solid waste incineration and toilet facilities. For the former, her firm has built modules to house furnaces to burn solid waste at seventeen airports and ports across Mexico. These modules are easy to build, durable, and require little in the way of maintenance. Additionally, she has designed low-maintenance toilet facilities at highways across Mexico, which are attractive, well lit, and clean. These ventures earned her the Sustainable Global Award for Architecture in 2019, given by the Cité de l'Architecture et du Patrimoine museum in France. After receiving the award, Montiel remarked to Monica Arellano for *Arch Daily* (5 Apr. 2019), "Our projects propose spaces for a resilient social management; the occurrence of these spaces can be the result of 'being together' or not. . . . The activation of the public space makes it easier for a group to observe what they 'are together' and what is not, build community by providing forums for the open discussion of existing problems. The good of a community may or may not reside in 'being together,' but its starting point for dialogue is a space in common."

In 2020, Montiel was presented with the Most Outstanding Architectural Designs prize in the Design and Build Awards organized by *BUILD* magazine.

PERSONAL LIFE

Montiel married architect Mauricio Gómez de Tuddo. Their family resided in a neighborhood of Mexico City.

SUGGESTED READING

Arellano, Monica. "Rozana Montiel Wins the Global Award for Sustainable Architecture 2019." *Arch Daily*, 5 Apr. 2019, www.archdaily.com/914532/rozana-montiel-wins-the-global-award-for-sustainable-architecture-2019. Accessed 16 June 2022.

de Monchaux, Thomas. "From Space to Place: The In-Between Architecture of Rozana Montiel." *Hauser & Wirth*, 28 Feb. 2020, www.hauserwirth.com/ursula/27430-space-place-architecture-rozana-montiel/. Accessed 17 June 2022.

Lol, Leslie. "Rozana Montiel: Something from Nothing." *Cornell University*, 3 Mar. 2021, aap.cornell.edu/news-events/rozana-montiel-something-nothing. Accessed 16 June 2022.

Montiel, Rozana. "Interview with Rozana Montiel." *WHYTT Magazine*, 18 May 2016, whyttmagazine.com/all/interview-with-rozana-montiel. Interview. Accessed 16 June 2022.

—. "Rozana Montiel Estudio de Arquitectura." Interview by Katherine Keane. *Architect Magazine*, 30 July 2019, www.architectmagazine.com/practice/rozana-montiel-estudio-de-arquitectura_o. Accessed 17 June 2022.

"Rozana Montiel." *Cornell Architecture Art Planning*, Cornell University, aap.cornell.edu/people/rozana-montiel. Accessed 16 June 2022.

"Rozana Montiel." *Swiss Architectural Award, Sixth Edition 2017-2018*, swiss architecturalaward.com/en/editions/2017-2018/candidates/profiles/rozana-montiel/. Accessed 16 June 2022.

"Rozana Montiel: Sustainability through Social Participation." *Design Build Network*, 20 Oct. 2021, www.designbuild-network.com/analysis/rozana-montiel/. Accessed 21 June 2022.

—Christopher Mari

Carissa Moore

Born: August 27, 1992
Occupation: Professional surfer

Photo by CeeX,
via Wikimedia Commons.

Carissa Moore first made history when she was eleven years old at the 2004 National Scholastic Surfing Association (NSSA) Nationals, considered the Super Bowl of amateur surfing, where she captured titles in three divisions (Open, Explorer, and Interscholastics). With these victories, she would evoke comparisons to Kelly Slater, the most highly decorated surfer of all time. She also joined Nea Post as one of only two competitors to claim the NSSA Triple Crown up to that point—a feat that she duplicated over the next two years (2005–06). By 2009, she had not only amassed a record number of amateur national championship titles (eleven) but had also clinched her first elite tour event win. Having further exhibited her ability to compete at a high level regardless of the conditions, her name only grew on the sport's radar upon her official qualification for the 2010 Association of Surfing Professionals (ASP) Women's World Tour.

About a year after embarking on the professional circuit, Moore claimed her first ASP World Championship Tour title in 2011, becoming the youngest-ever winner at age eighteen. Over the next decade, she would be crowned world champion three more times (2013, 2015, and 2019), becoming the first Hawaiian surfer to secure four world titles. After taking home surfing's first-ever gold medal at Tokyo's pandemic-delayed Summer Olympic Games in 2021, she collected a fifth world title while also continuing to serve as a role model and ambassador for the sport. "She's not just a world champion," US Olympic teammate Caroline Marks told Christine Yu in an interview for *The Red Bulletin* (11 Nov. 2021). "She's the people's champion."

EARLY LIFE AND LAUNCHING AN AMATEUR CAREER

Honolulu, Hawaii, native Carissa Kainani Moore was born on August 27, 1992, to Carol Lum and Christopher Moore. The latter was a two-time Waikiki Roughwater Swim champion (1987 and 1990) who was the first to get his young daughter into riding a board on the waves at a local beach. Holding her own in the division for girls seven to nine years old of the Haleiwa Menehune Surfing Championships and even coming out on top, such as in 2000 and 2001, she quickly impressed spectators and announcers. Having turned her passion for the ocean and spending quality time surfing and bonding with her father (particularly as a ten-year-old following her parents' divorce) into a serious competitive commitment, she ultimately decided to embark on an amateur career with his support and guidance. "Carissa's technical ability at 10 was better than the best women in the world that were winning worlds," her father recalled to Christopher Kamrani for *The Athletic* (8 July 2021).

After placing third in the Open Mini Grom (age ten and under) division at the 2003 NSSA National Championships, Moore performed well at Hawaii's regional championships in 2004 before claiming three division titles (Open Women's, Explorer Women's, and Middle School Girls) at that year's NSSA Nationals. Pushing through the pressure of more and more heats, her winning streak continued at the 2005 NSSA Nationals, where she successfully defended her Open Women's and Middle School Girls titles while also taking home the Explorer Girls (age fourteen and under) crown. In October, she claimed individual bronze (women under-eighteen category) while competing on the gold medal–winning Hawaiian team at the 2005 Quiksilver International Surfing Association (ISA) World Juniors. The 2007 NSSA Nationals saw yet another extension of her victorious run, as she rode her way to two more titles (Open Women's and Explorer Women's), bringing her record-breaking total amateur collection to eleven. This came in addition to her wildcard run at the 2007 ASP Women's World Tour's Roxy Pro Gold Coast event that ended with her in the runner-up position as the youngest person to compete as a finalist in one of the elite tour's events as well as a first-place finish at the Quiksilver King of the Groms.

TURNING PROFESSIONAL AND BECOMING WORLD CHAMPION

Over the next two years, Moore and her coach-manager father focused on joining the pros as a ranking competitor on the ASP Women's World Tour. Shortly after capturing the 2008 Roxy Pro Junior title with impressive heat scores, the sixteen-year-old dominated successive heats to become the youngest competitor to win a Vans Triple Crown of Surfing event (Reef Hawaiian Pro) as she defeated the likes of longtime world champion Layne Beachley. She then followed this accomplishment with a wildcard victory, her first in an ASP World Tour event, at the 2009 Gidget Pro Sunset Beach. First competing as a qualifier on the 2010 ASP Women's World Tour during her senior year at Punahou School, she claimed her first win at the TSB Bank Women's Surf Festival in New Zealand. Proving herself a formidable competitor, upon graduation from high school, she pursued surfing full-time, quickly securing victories at the US Open of Surfing and the

Rip Curl Women's Pro Portugal. She closed out an impressive freshman season with a second-place finish at November's Rip Curl Search in Puerto Rico and sitting third overall in the rankings before receiving rookie-of-the-year honors at 2011's ASP World Surfing Awards.

Moore kicked off 2011 with a Roxy Pro Gold Coast victory in March and runner-up finishes at the Rip Curl Pro Bells Beach and the Subaru Pro TSB Bank Women's Surf Festival. After several more successful event outings, she earned the 2011 ASP World Championship title, becoming the youngest surfer ever to do so. In an interview with Casey Butler for *ESPN* (15 July 2011) shortly after her triumph, she indicated the high professional bar she set for herself and would continue to come up against as her career evolved: "I've had this goal written on my door and it's been waiting there for a long time to be checked. I can't wait to go home and cross it out." Upon returning to the ASP World Tour in 2012, she amassed top-five results at the Roxy Pro Gold Coast, Rip Curl Pro Bells Beach, Billabong Rio Pro, and Roxy Pro France before completing the tour season ranked at number three.

GAINING TWO MORE WORLD TITLES

In 2013, Moore's name was listed at the top of the scoreboard for her performances in half of the eight tour events she participated in. After so many triumphs, she ended the year with her second ASP World Championship Tour title. While she maintained momentum in 2014, successfully defending her Drug Aware Margaret River Pro and Rip Curl Pro titles before coming in second at the Rio Women's Pro, she struggled the rest of the season, finishing fifth or below in her remaining tournaments and ultimately placing third in the world title race.

With the ASP becoming the World Surf League (WSL), Moore started the 2015 season with a newly rebranded world tour and two victories under her belt: the Roxy Pro Gold Coast and Rip Curl Pro. After top-three finishes in the Margaret River Pro and Oi Rio Pro, she failed to make the podium at the Fiji Pro and the US Open of Surfing before largely rebounding to come away with her third world-champion title. At the same time, she made headlines personally when she discussed living with binge eating disorder and body-image issues as well as her road to self-acceptance.

"It's all about balance for me, and that's translated to every part of my life," she shared with Audrey Cleo Yap in an interview for *ESPN* (30 Dec. 2015). "I'm just really comfortable and happy in my own skin at this point."

FACING PROFESSIONAL STRUGGLES

After bringing Mitch Ross onto her team as her primary coach, Moore experienced modest success in 2016, managing only a lone victory in the Roxy Pro France. Continuing to struggle in 2017, she slipped to number five in the rankings despite successfully defending her Roxy Pro France title. During an equally disappointing 2018 season overall, she missed the podium at the Oi Rio Pro, the Corona Bali Protected, and the Corona Open J-Bay. The latter event, which took place in Jeffreys Bay, South Africa, became a turning point for Moore. "The waves were pumping, they were amazing," she told Josh Peter for *USA Today* (23 July 2021). "Usually when the swell provides, I feel like I step up and I perform well. And I just totally fell apart," she continued, adding, "I was overcome with anxiety." Subsequently, she enlisted the regular help of a mental coach and also reconnected with her father, who helped his daughter execute a more assertive strategy.

Both decisions had an immediate, positive impact on the rest of Moore's season, which culminated in a pair of third-place finishes and two victories. Scoring a perfect ten thousand points in the Beachwaver Maui Pro tournament proved life-changing for Moore, who felt more at peace with herself as both a competitor and a person; she returned to the third position in the rankings. "That was a big defining moment for me. I remember there was just this freedom within myself," she recalled to Aoife Glass in an interview for Red Bull's website (10 Feb. 2021).

COMPETING IN THE OLYMPICS

Moore had continued success while competing on the 2019 WSL Tour. She finished no lower than fifth, including second place finishes at the Boost Mobile Pro Gold Coast and Oi Rio Pro. She closed out the season with top-three finishes in her last four tournaments while notching her fourth world title—the first in four years. It was during the tour's last event, the lululemon Maui Pro, that she additionally cemented a spot on the US Olympic squad alongside Marks.

In March 2020, after Moore had previously announced a season-long hiatus to deal with professional burnout, the WSL imposed a suspension due to the coronavirus disease 2019 (COVID-19) pandemic, which also led to the yearlong postponement of the Summer Olympic Games in Tokyo. By July, the league had canceled the entire season. When the WSL tour resumed in December 2020, Moore quickly regained her form, coming in second at the Maui Pro and winning the first digital Vans Triple Crown of Surfing, for which competitors submitted footage that captured their two best waves from Haleiwa Ali'i Beach, Sunset Beach, and Banzai Pipeline.

In July 2021, after having finished second at the Jeep Surf Ranch Pro in June, Moore made her Olympic debut, winning the first-round qualifying heat and automatically advancing to the third round. In her third-round knockout heat, she edged out Peru's Sofía Mulánovich before handily defeating Brazil's Silvana Lima in the quarterfinals. After squeaking past Japan's Amuro Tsuzuki in the semifinals, Moore posted her highest scores in the women's shortboard finals, claiming gold over South Africa's Bianca Buitendag to become surfing's first female gold medalist. "I hope that it sparks someone else to take their own passion or to get on a surfboard for the first time. I hope it will encourage people to remain authentic to themselves," she told Don Wallace for *Honolulu* magazine (21 Dec. 2021). "I want them to know there isn't one specific mold and we aren't meant to fit it."

REJOINING THE TOUR

Moore rejoined the WSL tour in August 2021. After finishing third at the Corona Open Mexico, she was among the top five women who competed at the inaugural one-day, winner-take-all Rip Curl WSL Finals in September. As the world's top-ranked female surfer, she received an automatic bye into the finals, where she defeated Brazil's Tatiana Weston-Webb by being the first to win two out of three heats in the title match. Moore ended the season on a high note by claiming her fifth career world title and becoming the first Hawaiian woman to earn consecutive WSL championship tour crowns since 1981.

In January 2022, Moore captured her second consecutive Vans Triple Crown of Surfing title. Just weeks later, she was back on the WSL tour, eventually racking up top-three finishes at three out of her first five events.

PERSONAL LIFE

Moore, an Oahu resident, has also cofounded a nonprofit aimed at inspiring and empowering young women through surfing. In December 2017, she married Luke Untermann, the co-owner of a locally sourced banana smoothie business. They had met as students at Punahou School.

SUGGESTED READING

Butler, Casey. "Carissa Moore Wins First World Title." *ESPN*, 15 July 2011, www.espn.com/action/surfing/news/story?page=2011-roxy-pro-biarritz-carissa-moore-wins-asp-world-title. Accessed 18 May 2022.

Kamrani, Christopher. "From Hawaiian Surfing Prodigy to Olympic Medal Contender, Carissa Moore Keeps Living in the Moment." *The Athletic*, 8 July 2021, theathletic.com/2692257/2021/07/08/carissa-moore-olympics-surfing/. Accessed 12 May 2022.

Moore, Carissa. "Carissa Moore: 'I Don't Feel Imprisoned by Food Anymore.'" Interview by Audrey Cleo Yap. *ESPN*, 30 Dec. 2015, www.espn.com/espnw/athletes-life/story/_/id/14464723/feel-imprisoned-food-anymore. Accessed 12 May 2022.

___. "Carissa Moore, the Surfer Who Loves Lists—and Ticking the Boxes." Interview by Aoife Glass. *Red Bull*, 10 Feb. 2021, www.redbull.com/us-en/carissa-moore-discover-your-wings. Accessed 12 May 2022.

Peter, Josh. "10 to Watch: USA's Carissa Moore on Finding Balance before the Olympics." *USA Today*, 23 July 2021, www.usatoday.com/story/sports/olympics/2021/07/23/tokyo-olympics-us-surfer-carissa-moore-better-spot-mentally/7922905002/. Accessed 12 May 2022.

Wallace, Don. "Carissa's World: How a Self-Effacing Girl from Kaimuki Surfed Her Way to Olympic Gold." *Honolulu*, 21 Dec. 2021, www.honolulumagazine.com/carissas-world-how-a-self-effacing-girl-from-kaimuki-surfed-her-way-to-olympic-gold/. Accessed 12 May 2022.

Yu, Christine. "Crowning Achievement." *The Red Bulletin*, Red Bull, 11 Nov. 2021, www.redbull.com/us-en/theredbulletin/carissa-moore-heroes-2021. Accessed 12 May 2022.

—Bertha Muteba

Hannah Moscovitch

Born: June 5, 1978
Occupation: Playwright

In 2021, Canadian playwright Hannah Moscovitch added another honor to her long list of career achievements when she earned a Governor General's Literary Award, Canada's most prestigious literary prize, for her play *Sexual Misconduct of the Middle Classes* (2020). The award was a validation of sorts, as despite already being entrenched as one of the most acclaimed playwrights in Canada, Moscovitch was initially worried about how *Sexual Misconduct* would be received. The play explores the trope of an affair between a middle-aged college professor and a younger student but complicates it with questions of power dynamics and point of view. "I thought, the audience is going to be so shocked to hear that this young woman had mixed feelings about this affair with her professor," she told Ameeta Vohra for *Unravel* magazine (7 Jan. 2022). However, from the time she began writing the play in the mid-2010s to its official debut in 2020, the #MeToo movement against sexual misconduct took off, driving widespread attention to just the kind of issues Moscovitch sought to engage with, as well as increased demand for more complex stories about women.

While *Sexual Misconduct* proved well-timed, Moscovitch had been mining similar territory for years. From *In This World* (2008), a drama about teenage girls, to the Trillium Book Award-winning *This Is War* (2013), which features a female Canadian soldier in Afghanistan, she built a reputation for presenting challenging female characters. Her acclaimed plays *What A Young Wife Ought to Know* (2015) and *Secret Life of a Mother* (2018) further demonstrated her ability to craft gripping drama out of thorny social and political topics, including those related to sex and gender. "There's always a desire on my part to show a more nuanced version, to show an unusual voice, to hear something we haven't heard about what the world is," she told Vohra. "I always want to go into those places."

EARLY LIFE AND EDUCATION

Hannah Moscovitch was born in Ottawa, Ontario, on June 5, 1978. She later described her parents, who eventually divorced, to Rita Zekas for the *Toronto Star* (19 Jan. 2008) as "old left-wing, social activists, unionists and socialists." Her father was an economist who taught at Carleton University and her mother was a feminist writer who focused on labor issues. Moscovitch grew up in a communal house in the Glebe, one of Ottawa's oldest suburbs. She was immersed in her parents' intellectual circles from an early age and encouraged to express herself, including through writing and performance. "I was the weird academic kid who read too much," she told Zekas.

Moscovitch graduated from the Glebe Collegiate Institute in 1996, and on the advice of her drama teacher she auditioned for the prestigious National Theatre School (NTS) in Montreal. She was not accepted, however. Instead of applying elsewhere, she took a year off from school, traveling to Israel and working on a kibbutz in Golan Heights before spending time in Uxbridge, England. After landing back in Canada, she auditioned for NTS again, if only to prove that she could get in. "I was determined that no one turn me down for anything," she told Amanda Sage for *Kickass Canadians* (22 June 2012). Moscovitch won admittance to the school as an actor but described herself as a terrible student. "I was very hostile about the program itself, and that was reflected in how I behaved," she told Sage. Despite her behavior, she finished her degree in 2001.

ENTRY TO PLAYWRITING

Moscovitch took her first playwriting course while at NTS. She enjoyed it and earned praise from her instructors, but when they tried to get her to shift her major from acting to writing, she was insulted. "I think it was very clear, to everyone except me, that I was a writer," she told Sage. Reflecting on her acting background, later in her career Moscovitch would become known as an actor's writer, embracing the fact that it typically takes many different people to truly present a play. "If you write fiction, you're writing an object. If you write theater you're writing a temporal-spatial event," she told Hattie Klotz in an interview for *Ottawa Magazine* (18 Mar. 2016). "You're writing text

that will—in collaboration with designers, a director and performers—become a finished work."

After graduating from NTS, Moscovitch moved to Toronto, where she enrolled at the University of Toronto to study literature and supported herself as a waiter. She also frequently returned to Ottawa to act with the Salamander Theatre for Young Audiences. However, she increasingly shifted away from performance and toward writing. Two of her earliest notable plays, *Essay* (2005) and *The Russian Play* (2006), debuted at Toronto's SummerWorks Festival. *Essay*, which won the Contra Guys Award for Best New Play, is about an undergraduate student writing an essay about an obscure female historical figure. *The Russian Play*, which won the Jury Prize for Best New Production, is a satire about how the West views Slavic states.

INCREASING ACCLAIM

Over the next several years, Moscovitch won positive attention for her growing body of plays. Her full-length debut, *East of Berlin* (2007), would become one of her best-known works. It premiered at the Tarragon Theater in Toronto, which would serve as Moscovitch's longtime artistic home as playwright in residence and was produced there again in 2009 and 2010. The play follows a man named Rudi, who discovers his father's horrifying past life as a Nazi doctor who performed experiments on prisoners at the Auschwitz concentration camp during the Holocaust. Later, Rudi meets and forms a relationship with the daughter of a Holocaust survivor. "The astonishing thing about Moscovitch's play is how funny it is," Richard Ouzounian wrote in a review for *Variety* (31 Oct. 2007). "She's not afraid to plunge right through areas that others might consider poor taste in order to come out the other side in search of a deeper truth." *East of Berlin* was a finalist for the Governor General's Literary Award and the Susan Smith Blackburn Prize in 2010.

In 2008 Moscovitch premiered *In This World*, a play for young audiences. It is centered on a fight between two high school friends, but turns on issues of classism, racism, and sexism. The work earned a Dora Award, a significant honor in the Toronto theater community. Moscovitch's next play, *The Children's Republic* (2009), explores the same era as *East of Berlin*.

It is based on the story of a doctor who ran an orphanage in the Warsaw Ghetto during World War II.

Moscovitch's one-act play *Little One*, a psychological thriller in which two adopted siblings unpack their upbringing, premiered at SummerWorks in 2011. It ran again, alongside another one-act called *Other People's Children*, at the Tarragon Theater in 2013. Continuing Moscovitch's penchant for exploring delicate social situations and tensions, the latter play is about a Sri Lankan caregiver's relationship to a young, wealthy couple and their infant child.

Moscovitch's next full-length play, *This Is War*, also premiered at the Tarragon Theater in 2013. It explores Canada's involvement in the war in Afghanistan. In a series of fragmented scenes, four Canadian soldiers are interrogated about, and recall the events surrounding a possible atrocity on a mission. The play draws on research from Moscovitch's time as a contributing writer for the CBC Radio drama *Afghanada*, a role she held from 2007 until 2015. *This Is War* was nominated for the Governor General's Literary Award and won the Toronto Theatre Critics' Award as the best Canadian play of the year. In 2014 it won the Trillium Book Award, making Moscovitch the first playwright to ever receive that honor.

EXPLORING NEW FORMS

As her reputation grew, Moscovitch branched into other areas, including working on several opera librettos. For example, she worked with composer Lembit Beecher on *I Have No Stories to Tell You* (2014), *Sophia's Forest* (2017), and *Sky on Swings* (2018). Another musical collaboration was with violinist Njo Kong Kie, who composed a score for her 2015 play *Infinity*. That work also represented a departure from her usual themes in that it is based around the theories of Lee Smolin, a Canadian physicist who has challenged Einstein's conception of time. Moscovitch joked that, fittingly for a play about time, the work took her many years to write after originally being commissioned.

Moscovitch returned to a historical setting for her play *What A Young Wife Ought to Know*, which premiered in 2015. Set in rural Ottawa in the 1920s, the play follows a young woman named Sophie who marries young, and is thrown, bewildered, into motherhood. She desperately seeks guidance about birth control, while her sister dies from a botched abortion. *Young Wife* was well received, with many critics appreciating Moscovitch's complex take on such universal but often somewhat taboo subjects as sex and childbirth. For example, Karen Fricker of the *Toronto Star* (23 Mar. 2018), reviewing a production of the play at Crow's Theatre in Toronto directed by Christian Barry, wrote that "What makes it important, but also challenging to watch, is that the subject matter feels uncomfortable." Fricker also praised the "searing intelligence of Moscovitch's writing" and the multilayered inner lives of the characters.

By the mid-2010s Moscovitch was not only widely regarded as a major figure in Canadian theater but also attracted increasing international attention. In 2016, she won the prestigious Windham-Campbell Prize, worth $150,000, from Yale University. The same year she premiered a play called *Bunny*, about a professor of Victorian literature grappling with her relationship to sex, which earned much acclaim. Her next play, *Old Stock: A Refugee Story* (2017), was a musical, written with Barry and singer-songwriter Ben Caplan. The story was inspired by her great-grandparents, Romanian Jews who arrived in Canada in the early twentieth century, but it is also a commentary on the mass migrations happening around the world in the twenty-first century. *Old Stock* played Off-Broadway in New York City in 2018, where it was named a Critic's Pick by *The New York Times* and was nominated for three Drama Desk Awards, including Outstanding Musical.

STAR PLAYWRIGHT

Firmly established as one of Canada's top playwrights, in 2018 Moscovitch premiered a play called *Secret Life of a Mother* at the Theatre Center in Toronto. In a review for the *Toronto Star* (27 Oct. 2018), Fricker described it as "a typical" Moscovitch work, with one key difference: Moscovitch "tends to tell stories about people—increasingly, women—in extreme emotional states," Fricker wrote. "What's different here is that the masks are off and Moscovitch is writing about her own experience." Focusing on the often-difficult realities of pregnancy and childbirth, it focuses on Moscovitch as the main character, played by her close friend Maev Beaty, who was closely involved in the production along with director Ann-Marie Kerr and producer Marinda de

Beer. Elements of Beaty's own experience of motherhood are also woven into the play, which takes a meta approach by using pages of script as props. Fricker praised *Secret Life* as "honest and risky."

Moscovitch had yet another critical success with *Sexual Misconduct of the Middle Classes*, which premiered at the Tarragon Theater in January 2020, just before the COVID-19 pandemic shut down performing arts venues around the world. Reviewers praised the way Moscovitch takes on the all-too-familiar setup of an affair between a male professor and a younger female student, crafting a subtle commentary on issues of power and perspective. "The intrigue in Moscovitch's script is in discovering why she's playing with such traditional tropes, so out of character for the playwright who has written so frankly about female sexuality and taboos," Carly Maga wrote in a review for the *Toronto Star* (9 Jan. 2020). The play won the prestigious Governor General's Literary Award, for which Moscovitch had previously been a finalist, in 2021.

Moscovitch premiered a play called *Post-Democracy* in 2021. Critics compared it to the HBO drama *Succession*, as it tells the story of a family-owned corporation embroiled in a sexual harassment scandal.

PERSONAL LIFE

Moscovitch married theater director Christian Barry. The couple have a child, named Elijah, and have settled in Halifax, Nova Scotia. Over time, Moscovitch increasingly identified with her home country as an artist. "I don't think I really thought about Canada much at the beginning of my career," she told Sage. "Now, I think about what it means to be a Canadian playwright in particular, and to want to write about Canada for Canadian audiences."

SUGGESTED READING

Fricker, Karen. "Secret Life of a Mother Is Honest and Risky." Review of *Secret Life of a Mother*, by Hannah Moscovitch. *Toronto Star*, 29 Oct. 2018, www.thestar.com/entertainment/stage/review/2018/10/26/secret-life-of-a-mother-is-honest-and-risky.html. Accessed 2 June 2022.

Maga, Carly. "'Sexual Misconduct of the Middle Classes' Is a Familiar Story of Seduction—Until It Isn't." Review of *Sexual Misconduct of the Middle Classes*, by Hannah Moscovitch. *Toronto Star*, 9 Jan. 2020, www.thestar.com/entertainment/stage/review/2020/01/09/sexual-misconduct-of-the-middle-classes-is-a-familiar-story-of-seduction-until-it-isnt.html. Accessed 3 June 2022.

Moscovitch, Hannah. "Q&A with Hannah Moscovitch." Interview by Hattie Klotz. *Ottawa Magazine*, 18 Mar. 2016, ottawamagazine.com/arts-and-culture/award-winning-playwright-speaks-about-life-changing-prize-plus-an-excerpt-from-her-play-what-a-young-wife-ought-to-know/. Accessed 2 June 2022.

Ouzounian, Richard. "East of Berlin." Review of *East of Berlin*, by Hannah Moscovitch. *Variety*, 31 Oct. 2007, variety.com/2007/legit/reviews/east-of-berlin-1200554903/. Accessed 1 June 2022.

Sage, Amanda. "Hannah Moscovitch, Playwright-Sensation." *Kickass Canadians*, 22 June 2012, kickasscanadians.ca/hannah-moscovitch/. Accessed 1 June 2022.

Vohra, Ameeta. "The Conversation: Hannah Moscovitch." *Unravel*, 7 Jan. 2022, unravelhalifax.ca/the-conversation-hannah-moscovitch/. Accessed 7 June 2022.

Zekas, Rita. "Play's the Thing with Hannah Moscovitch." *Toronto Star*, 19 Jan. 2008, www.thestar.com/news/2008/01/19/plays_the_thing_with_hannah_moscovitch.html. Accessed 1 June 2022.

SELECTED WORKS

East of Berlin, 2007; *This Is War*, 2013; *What a Young Wife Ought to Know*, 2015; *Old Stock: A Refugee Love Story*, 2017; *Secret Life of a Mother*, 2018; *Sexual Misconduct of the Middle Classes*, 2020

Molly Hagan

Mia Mottley

Born: October 1, 1965
Occupation: Politician and attorney

After brandishing her formidable political skills for decades, including holding national government ministerial positions across administrations beginning in the early 1990s, spending approximately five years as deputy prime minister between 2003 and 2008, and twice serving as the leader of the opposition party, Mia Mottley was elected prime minister of Barbados, a small island nation in the eastern Caribbean, in 2018. Coming from a political family, with her grandfather serving as the first mayor of Bridgetown, the country's capital, and her father representing Barbados at the consulate in New York, she pursued legal studies at the London School of Economics and Political Science and first became involved in the parliamentary political arena as a senator in 1991.

However, there was little time to celebrate Mottley's overwhelming 2018 victory. That year, Barbados faced a growing debt crisis and endured punishing floods. Like other Caribbean nations, Barbados has struggled with the interlocking challenges of climate change and debt. Mottley has become a strong advocate of clauses in debt agreements that protect countries like Barbados from financial collapse in the event of natural disasters. For Mottley, climate change and financial instability in the Caribbean are two issues that grow from the same root and must be addressed through sound, prioritized policy.

Meanwhile, Barbados, a British colony prior to its independence in 1966, had kept Queen Elizabeth II as its official head of state through a representative governor general. In 2020, Mottley, who had been quickly recognized as a leader with a progressive agenda aimed at moving the country forward, declared that Barbados would officially replace the Queen and finally become a republic with its own appointed president. Though largely a symbolic gesture, she emphasized that it was a key step in Barbados's efforts to break from its painful colonial history. In addition to expressing her support upon the election of Sandra Mason as president in 2021, Mottley continued to serve as Barbados's voice for greater global action against climate change, especially from larger developed nations, and carried on with other initiatives for positive change. "The one luxury I don't have is to remain static," she told Gary Younge for British *Vogue* (13 Aug. 2021). "I know that when you have power, when you have access to make a difference in people's lives, you need to do it."

EARLY LIFE AND EDUCATION

Mia Amor Mottley was born in Barbados to a politically well-connected, experienced, and committed family on October 1, 1965. Her grandfather, Ernest Deighton Mottley, became

Photo by Timothy Sullivan (UNCTAD)
via Wikimedia Commons

the city of Bridgetown's inaugural mayor in 1959, while Elliott Deighton Mottley, her father, fulfilled the duties of Barbados' consular general at the country's New York consulate. In the 1990s he secured the post of Bermuda's attorney general; later, he served for nearly two decades on the Court of Appeal of the Turks and Caicos Islands. As a child growing up with her two brothers and sister, Mottley attended Barbados' Merrivale Private School and, briefly, the United Nations (UN) International School in New York during her father's work at the consulate. Having finished her high school education at Queen's College in Barbados, she went on to receive a legal degree from the London School of Economics and Political Science in 1986. The following year, with her admittance to the bar, she began practicing law on her home island.

ADVANCING POLITICAL CAREER

Mottley's political career was launched in 1991 with her effort to represent the North East constituency of the parish of St. Michael in the national legislature's House of Assembly. Though she missed winning the election by a narrow margin, she received an appointment to the Senate, the upper house of the Barbados Parliament, and served as the minister of culture and community development in the opposition's shadow cabinet. Once the party of which she was a member, the Barbados Labour Party (BLP), proved victorious in the 1994 general election and she won the House of Assembly seat for St. Michael North East, her parliamentary experience and political status only grew as she was appointed to serve as Prime Minister Owen Arthur's minister of education, youth affairs, and culture. Noted as one of the youngest Barbadians to ever hold a ministerial post, during her tenure, she pushed for major reforms to the education system, with an emphasis on technology. She oversaw the ministry's largest-ever investment project, the Education Sector Enhancement Program, commonly referred to as "EduTech." According to her conversation with Younge, Mottley saw the sweeping changes to the country's educational infrastructure as part of a larger assertion of national and regional identity. "We are moving into a second generation of those who were born after independence," she told him in 1999. "We now know what it is to determine our own fate, and there is a new confidence that is reflected in everything from our music to our school curriculums."

In addition to gaining influence in the ranks of the BLP by the end of the 1990s, in 2001 Mottley was made attorney general of Barbados, marking the first time in the country's history that a woman had assumed the role; meanwhile, she was also given the responsibilities of the minister of home affairs. The following year, she was chosen to join the governmental advisory Privy Council. With her strong, effective style of leadership already acknowledged, in 2003 she was appointed to serve as the country's deputy prime minister, a role that also made her chairperson of the Social Council of Barbados. Some of the work that would prove particularly useful in her future career at the top level of government, expanding her understanding of the nation's economic sector, came during her time as the minister of economic affairs and development beginning in 2006.

PRIME MINISTER OF BARBADOS

Continuing a successful ascent of the political ladder, Mottley, whose reputation within the BLP had only strengthened, was given the opportunity to helm the party as leader of the opposition for two tenures, between 2008 and 2010 as well as between 2013 and 2018, while further serving in Parliament. At the same time,

practicing law for her father's Barbadian firm helped her to maintain her legal skills. In 2018, she challenged incumbent prime minister Freundel Stuart of the Democratic Labour Party (DLP), which had been in power for ten years. Mottley campaigned on restructuring the country's massive debt linked to the impact, particularly in the tourism industry, of the global recession of the late 2000s, and in doing so, finding money for tax cuts, higher pensions, garbage trucks, school buses, and university fees. She also focused on frustrations with the poor economy and the country's sewage system on the tourist-heavy southern coast. The government had installed a new sewage system in the region in 2003, but the pumps had since been clogged with waste and refuse. Unable to fix it, the Barbados Water Authority (BWA) described the situation as an acute "crisis." In 2016, there were reports of raw sewage spewing from manholes, forcing businesses to close and residents to vacate their homes. The waste system's collapse also dealt a massive blow to tourism, the country's primary source of income. Pointing out that she had explicitly cautioned the government in 2015 about such a collapse being imminent, Mottley criticized the government for ignoring the problem.

Members of the DLP, on the other hand, attempted to turn the discussion from an inadequate sewage system to the subject of sexual orientation because Mottley and her party favored a more tolerant approach to sexual orientation and gender identity (SOGI) policy. This remained a charged topic in Barbados, where sexual activity between people of the same sex has long been criminalized and carries a sentence of lifetime imprisonment. (Although such laws, considered draconian, against LGBTQ people are rarely enforced, activists argue that the laws existence contributes to a dangerous atmosphere of discrimination and acts or speech of hate.) Mottley was already massively popular, however. Younge described her as the "'rock star' of the Caribbean political scene." On May 24, 2018, she and the BLP swept the general election with an overwhelmingly decisive majority of the vote and each of the House of Assembly's thirty seats. Not long after the results, Rihanna, arguably the world's best-loved Barbadian, posted on Instagram to offer congratulations and remark that Mottley's victory was deserved.

TACKLING DEBT AND CLIMATE CHANGE THREATS

After winning the historic election on May 24, 2018, Mottley was sworn into office the next day. She was the country's first female prime minister, but there was little time for celebration. In June, Mottley announced that her government would begin restructuring the country's BBD$15 billion public debt. In September, many areas of Barbados experienced tropical storm flooding, underscoring the island's dire position—both geographically and financially—as climate change continues to accelerate. The same month, Mottley made her inaugural address to the UN, passionately pleading for global climate action. "This is a matter of life or death for us," she said in her speech, as quoted by Ezra Fieser for *Bloomberg* (4 Apr. 2020). "We cannot plan our affairs or that of our people on the basis of luck," Fieser quoted her as adding. "It must be on the basis of policy and decisive action, but above all else on the basis of caring and empathy. I ask the world to pause, pause, and just get this one right."

Despite her heartfelt words, Mottley understood that for the foreseeable future, Barbados was on its own. In 2019, she convinced Barbados's creditors to include natural-disaster clauses in their sovereign debt contracts, meaning that Barbados could have a period of payment deferment upon the occurrence of natural disasters. Refusing to waver and assisted by a bailout from the International Monetary Fund (IMF), she was able to hold up negotiations long enough that creditors buckled. Her expansion of the use of such clauses was considered by many experts as providing a template for fiscally responsible rebuilding for other Caribbean nations that risk financial ruin sitting on the front lines of climate change.

BREAKING TIES WITH BARBADOS' COLONIAL PAST

In 2020, Mottley's government agreed to recognize same-sex civil unions—a major step forward for SOGI rights, and a referendum on same-sex marriage was promised. The decision to embrace same-sex civil unions was presented as a step in the country's long process of ending discrimination and breaking ties to its colonial history. In the same spirit and spurred by the global racial justice uprisings following the police killing of George Floyd in the United States, Mottley announced that Barbados would no longer have Queen Elizabeth II as its head of state but would instead become a republic. "The time has come to fully leave our colonial past behind. Barbadians want a Barbadian head of state," Mottley wrote as part of a September 2020 speech given by Sandra Mason, who was then the governor general but would become the first president-elect of Barbados following an October 2021 election. The quote was reproduced by Mark Landler and Azam Ahmed, writing for *The New York Times* (18 Sept. 2020).

The move, while historic and perceived as a defining policy of Mottley's administration, was largely symbolic but was emphasized as a crucial step forward for the nation and its people. That year was also marked, in part, by Mottley's demand for reparations. She argued that upon Barbados' independence, it had been left economically hindered by the United Kingdom and other European countries that had extracted wealth through colonialism and enslavement. Therefore, Barbados and other nations in the Caribbean deserved financial aid as well as an acknowledgment of injustice to achieve economic and sociological rehabilitation, particularly amid the coronavirus disease 2019 (COVID-19) pandemic. In July 2020, Mottley addressed this issue as part of a Caribbean Community (CARICOM) Reparations Commission virtual session. As quoted by the *CARICOM* website (14 July 2020), she stated, "We need the assistance of the global community to right the injustices of the past, and to give us the appropriate platform, not just money, but space to ensure that we too can deliver for our people." In 2021, she made further efforts toward moving the country forward that included celebrating Mason's election as president and assertively declaring at the UN's conference for climate change that global efforts to combat climate change were still not enough.

SUGGESTED READING

"Barbados Prime Minister Calls for a Reparations 'Caribbean Marshall Plan.'" *CARICOM Caribbean Community*, 14 July 2020, caricom.org/barbados-prime-minister-calls-for-a-reparations-caribbean-marshall-plan/. Accessed 8 Nov. 2021.

Fieser, Ezra. "A Prime Minister Tries to Storm-Proof Her Island's Finances." *Bloomberg*, 4 Apr. 2020, www.bloomberg.com/news/features/2020-04-04/barbados-prime-minister-mottley-tries-to-storm-proof-her-budget. Accessed 8 Nov. 2021.

Landler, Mark, and Azam Ahmed. "'The Time Has Come': Barbados Casts Off the Queen as Head of State, and Others May Follow." *The New York Times*, 18 Sept. 2020, www.nytimes.com/2020/09/18/world/europe/britain-barbados-queen-elizabeth-commonwealth.html?searchResultPosition=2. Accessed 8 Nov. 2021.

Younge, Gary. "'It Didn't Stop Rihanna . . .': History-Making Prime Minister Mia Mottley Has Monumental Plans for Barbados." *Vogue*, 13 Aug. 2021, www.vogue.co.uk/arts-and-lifestyle/article/mia-mottley. Accessed 5 Nov. 2021.

—*Molly Hagan*

Photo by Unus32, via Wikimedia Commons

Ronaldo Mouchawar

Born: January 1, 1966
Occupation: Entrepreneur

When Ronaldo Mouchawar launched *Souq.com* in 2005, he helped introduce e-commerce to the Middle East. Initially an auction site similar to eBay, Souq had, by 2011, morphed into a business-to-consumer (B2C) platform on which merchants could offer their products directly to potential customers, a model similar to that of commerce giant Amazon. The site became so popular that by early 2016, some financial experts deemed it the Arab world's first "unicorn," as companies projected to be worth $1 billion are known. In 2017, Amazon itself acquired the company for $580 million.

Souq's success, in many ways, mirrors the trajectory of web development and tech adoption in the Middle East. Mouchawar founded his venture in the United Arab Emirates (UAE) at a time when the number of people gaining access to the Internet there was rapidly growing. Additionally, the site quickly attracted the attention of the UAE's youthful population, which had both disposable income and the desire to spend it on the electronic devices that made up the bulk of Souq's wares. Mouchawar's decision to launch a smartphone app for Souq as smartphones grew in popularity helped Souq further expand its reach, and within years of its launch, the company was undeniably the largest and most important e-commerce platform in the region.

As of 2022, the enterprise—operating under the Amazon umbrella, with Mouchawar as a vice president of Amazon Middle East North Africa (MENA)—consistently attracts more than 45 million monthly customers drawn in by its almost 10 million listed products in categories ranging from consumer electronics to household goods, clothing, jewelry, toys, and more.

While Mouchawar is grateful for the growth Souq has experienced over the years, he has told interviewers he is particularly proud of the many jobs the company provides in the Middle East, both directly and indirectly, through its selling partners and suppliers. "Right now, people in India are choosing to come and work for us rather than a big US firm—and that's flattering," he told Ed Attwood in an interview for *Arabian Business* (5 Apr. 2014). "We're committed to the region. We're from the Arab world and we love the Arab world."

EARLY YEARS AND EDUCATION

Ronaldo Mouchawar was born on January 1, 1966, in Aleppo, Syria, a city considered by historians to be one of the world's oldest active trading hubs. It is also the location of several renowned open-air marketplaces, known as *souqs* or *souks* in Arabic, which inspired the name of his venture.

Mouchawar hails from a family of engineers and merchants. His father was an entrepreneur or trader in Aleppo's agricultural sector. As a youth, Mouchawar often accompanied him on his travels around the city, which was a bustling commercial center prior to its destruction during the Syrian civil war, which began in 2011. "Seeing what is happening to a place you love and grew up in is hard," Mouchawar told Elizabeth MacBride in an interview for *Forbes* (26 Mar. 2016). "At the same [time], building positive stories and opportunities out of the region has been a big motivation."

After finishing secondary school, Mouchawar moved to the United States to study at Northeastern University in Boston, Massachusetts; he was interested in the school's engineering programs as well as its diversity. There, he earned a bachelor's degree in electrical and computer engineering in 1988 and a master's degree in digital communications in 1990.

FORGING A CAREER IN TECH

Mouchawar began his professional life in the United States at a series of engineering and IT firms, including Electronic Data Systems (EDS), founded by Ross Perot, who would later make an unsuccessful run for the US presidency during the 1992 presidential election. At EDS, Mouchawar focused on video scanning and image processing (then cutting-edge technologies) for clients in a wide variety of industries, including automobile manufacturing and healthcare.

As the Internet grew in popularity in the United States during the late 1990s, Mouchawar recognized that the Middle East presented a new frontier for this emerging industry. In 2000, he settled in the UAE and joined the web services startup Maktoob, which had been founded in the late 1990s. "There was a calling," he explained to MacBride. "You could do so much more here."

Maktoob's founders, Samih Toukan and Hussam Khoury, were pioneering online services in the Middle East at a time when the Internet mostly lacked Arabic-language content and services. They built the first Arabic-language email service, set up chat rooms and instant-messaging (IM) services,

and offered tools that allowed users to write in Arabic regardless of what operating system they were using. "We immediately saw traction with young people. It was all about self-expression," Mouchawar recalled to George Charles Darley for *Arab News* (17 Jan. 2022). "We would get energizing emails from customers who were using our platform to communicate, post blogs, and create forums."

The partners next turned their attention to e-commerce, seeking to better monetize their platform. However, early efforts to introduce e-commerce to Maktoob's existing platform, such as *Shop@Maktoob*, proved unpopular with young users, who typically came to the site to interact and express themselves, not to buy merchandise. With Mouchawar's help, the employees of Maktoob hit upon the idea to develop an entirely separate site—*Souq.com*—with its own identity and brand.

SOUQ'S INITIAL STAGES

Mouchawar launched Souq in 2005 with funding from Toukan. Far from the independent web giant it would later become, the new startup remained part of Maktoob and operated in just three countries—Saudi Arabia, Egypt, and the UAE. Initially an auction site modeled on eBay that offered B2C and peer-to-peer selling, Souq gradually grew to include real estate and automotive markets. Within a few years, Souq was recording monthly transactions of close to $1 million. "It was a bit of chaos theory at work, in terms of learning, trying many new things, and building trust," Mouchawar told Attwood of Souq's early stages.

In 2009, after US–based internet giant Yahoo acquired Maktoob in a deal worth more than $160 million, Toukan and Khoury cofounded a venture capital firm, Jabbar Internet Group, which helped Souq spin off as an independent entity that same year. By 2010–11, Mouchawar and his partners had decided to shift Souq's focus, transforming it from primarily an auction site into a platform dedicated to B2C sales. They had decided that future growth would depend primarily on connecting customers to a plethora of retail options. Although the volume of transactions initially dropped, within six months of the transition, revenue began skyrocketing.

At the time, Jabbar was one of the few venture funds in the region willing to seek investment opportunities outside of such traditional sectors as petroleum and construction; as a result, Mouchawar and his partners often struggled to secure investment from other companies in the Middle East. Mouchawar also found it difficult to get larger brands to sign on to sell via Souq. "Hundreds of times we would meet the same people, and explain, this is the way your brand can work online," he told MacBride. "If the answer is no . . . we'll go back to the office and work with the smaller merchants." Mouchawar was keenly aware of his responsibility to those smaller entities, many of whom were staking their livelihood on Souq's success. "It [was] humbling to be so directly confronted by the human consequences of your business decisions," he wrote in a piece for the *Harvard Business Review* (Sept./Oct. 2013).

Still, he had confidence in the potential of e-commerce to transform the Middle Eastern economy. "If you see where the jobs are, it's got to come from small and medium businesses," he asserted to Deborah Amos for *Morning Edition* of National Public Radio (4 Dec. 2014.), explaining that the company could complete deliveries even in areas without an established postal system, thus tapping into new markets across the region. "Imagine the access [a] merchant can have from a street in Cairo to a customer base in Saudi Arabia, to the UAE. If we can connect all these dots, you will have an incredible customer base."

Some challenges Mouchawar faced were specific to the Arab world. At one time, for example, some governments, including Saudi Arabia, considered credit cards that charged interest to not be compliant with Islamic Sharia law, forcing Souq to establish other forms of payment for consumers in certain countries. Additionally, the concept of "Black Friday" sales had to be modified because, in Islam, Friday is traditionally devoted to prayer. Mouchawar decided to rebrand the day as "White Friday," putting what consumers considered a positive spin on the name. Souq successfully debuted this sale in 2014 and doubled its sales figures the following year.

Mouchawar has explained to interviewers that the ability to customize product descriptions, services, and other aspects of e-commerce for different countries in the Middle East helped him find ways to give Souq an edge, and that he relished meeting the challenges that came his way. "The feeling of going to work to solve problems is in my DNA,"

he told Fida Chaaban for *Entrepreneur* (21 Sept. 2015).

A GROWING COMPANY

As smartphone use proliferated in the Middle East in the early 2010s, Mouchawar realized that customers were going online to make purchases using their phones, rather than on desktop computers. He decided that Souq would have to make an additional pivot, and in 2012 he launched Souq's first mobile app. By 2017, more than 70 percent of user visits and transactions occurred via smartphone, confirming Mouchawar's prediction.

During this period, Mouchawar explored acquiring or launching related enterprises, and in 2013 he introduced Payfort, an online payment service that eventually became the Middle East's leading online payment provider. His own courier service, Q Express, which used smartphone geolocation technology, soon followed.

In early 2016, Souq attracted about $275 million in venture capital, at that time the biggest funding round ever recorded by a Middle Eastern e-commerce business. The news raised Souq's profile significantly, and big-name firms, including the Dubai-based mall operator Emaar, began expressing interest in acquisition. In November 2016, Mouchawar met with Amazon CEO Jeff Bezos in Dubai, sparking rumors that Amazon was planning to buy Souq. Many industry insiders felt this would be a perfect fit: Souq could provide Amazon with access to a burgeoning market, and Amazon could help the smaller company scale up in important ways.

"I thought that with Amazon, we could build a large business with exciting innovations in a region with high mobile adoption, a young user base and a huge opportunity for commerce, cloud content and devices," Mouchawar told Darley. "Also, with more than 420 million Arabic-speaking people in the world, there are still many services that we could develop for them."

In March 2017, Amazon acquired Souq for $580 million, and Mouchawar agreed to remain as vice president for the Middle East and North Africa (MENA). Amazon's retention of Souq's existing site and branding was seen as a mark of respect on Amazon's part, as the company's usual practice upon entering a new geographic market was to immediately deploy its own existing platform.

In 2019, Amazon began rebranding Souq as a series of country-specific versions of *Amazon.com*. For example, by the start of 2022, consumers in the UAE could visit *Amazon.ae*, those in Saudi Arabia could use *Amazon.sa*, and those in Egypt, *Amazon.eg*. The sites collectively draw more than 45 million customers each month as of 2022. Amid this rebranding and expansion, Mouchawar remained vice president of Amazon MENA.

AWARDS AND PERSONAL GROWTH

Mouchawar has garnered numerous honors for his work, including the Gulf Business Industry Awards' IT/Technology CEO of the Year award in 2013 and the Entrepreneur of the Year award in 2015. He says joining Amazon has provided him with opportunities for continued growth as a businessperson. "For me, it's always about working with smart, bright people, both locally and globally," he told Darley. "As long as I'm learning how to bring new things to the region, I still feel excited about the role I play."

SUGGESTED READING

Amos, Deborah. "A Syrian Entrepreneur Looks to Build the Amazon of the Arab World." *Morning Edition*, National Public Radio, 4 Dec. 2014, www.npr.org/sections/parallels/2014/12/04/368242510/a-syrian-entrepreneur-looks-to-build-the-amazon-of-the-arab-world. Accessed 1 Feb. 2022.

Chaaban, Fida. "Follow the Leader: Ronaldo Mouchawar, Founder and CEO, Souq." *Entrepreneur*, 21 Sept. 2015, www.entrepreneur.com/article/250860. Accessed 1 Feb. 2022.

Coletti, Claudine. "Inspirational: Amazon's Ronaldo Mouchawar on Expansion in MENA, and Selling Souq.com." *Forbes*, 13 Dec. 2020, www.forbesmiddleeast.com/leadership/leaders/amazons-ronaldo-mouchawar-on-expansion-in-mena-and-selling-souqcom. Accessed 1 Feb. 2022.

Darley, George Charles. "Souq Founder Ronaldo Mouchawar Remains MENA's Online Guru at Amazon." *Arab News*, 17 Jan. 2022, www.arabnews.com/node/2005206/business-economy. Accessed 1 Feb. 2022.

Mouchawar, Ronaldo. "The Middle East's First Unicorn: Souq.com's CEO on Leadership, Timing and Coping with Rejection." Interview by Elizabeth MacBride. *Forbes*, 26 Mar. 2016, www.forbes.com/sites/elizabethmacbride/2016/03/25/e-commerce-gold-in-the-middle-east-behind-souqs-success-story/?sh=743463b71ee0. Accessed 1 Feb. 2022.

—. "Ronaldo Mouchawar: How I Created Souq.com." Interview by Ed Attwood. *Arabian Business*, 5 Apr. 2014, www.arabianbusiness.com/gcc/ronaldo-mouchawar-how-i-created-souq-com-545057. Accessed 1 Feb. 2022.

—. "Souq.com's CEO on Building an E-Commerce Powerhouse in the Middle East." *Harvard Business Review*, Sept./Oct. 2013, hbr.org/2017/09/souq-coms-ceo-on-building-an-e-commerce-powerhouse-in-the-middle-east. Accessed 1 Feb. 2022.

—Mari Rich

Vivek Murthy

Born: July 10, 1977
Occupation: United States Surgeon general

In March 2021, the US Senate confirmed Vivek Murthy as the twenty-first surgeon general of the United States, following Murthy's nomination for the role by recently inaugurated president Joe Biden. That confirmation came as somewhat of a surprise for Murthy, who had previously served as surgeon general under President Barack Obama but was dismissed following the election of Donald Trump. "I didn't think I was going to come back to government, certainly not that quickly," he told Clay Skipper for *GQ* (11 Mar. 2022). "But it felt like an opportunity to be a part of a process of healing for our country." An established physician long affiliated with Boston's Brigham and Women's Hospital and a founder of the advocacy group Doctors for America, Murthy brought a great deal of public-health experience to the surgeon general position. During his second stint in the role, one of his main priorities was addressing the ongoing COVID-19 pandemic. At the same time, however, he recognized the importance of continuing to confront other public-health issues, many of which were worsened by the social impact of COVID-19 but also overshadowed by the viral disease. Murthy made a balanced approach to public health a priority. "We cannot neglect the other public health crises that have been exacerbated by this pandemic, particularly the opioid epidemic, mental illness and racial and geographic health inequities," he told the Senate, as quoted by Ricardo Alonso-Zaldivar for the Associated Press (23 Mar. 2021).

EARLY LIFE AND EDUCATION

Vivek Hallegere Murthy was born in Huddersfield, England, on July 10, 1977. He was one of two children born to Hallegere and Myetriae Murthy (his sister, Rashmi, would also go on to become a doctor). The family left England when Murthy was still a young child and, after living in Canada for a short time, settled in Miami, Florida. There, his parents operated a medical clinic, offering a level of patient care that would strongly influence Murthy and inspire him to pursue a career in medicine himself. "As a child, I watched them make house calls in the middle of the night and wake up early to visit patients in the hospital before heading to their office," he told the Senate, as reported by Alonso-Zaldivar.

After graduating from Miami Palmetto Senior High School in 1994 as valedictorian, Murthy enrolled at Harvard University. He earned a bachelor's degree in biochemical sciences after just three years, in 1997. He went on to attend Yale University's School of Medicine, earning his medical degree in 2003. Murthy also studied health-care management at Yale's School of Management, completing that degree in 2003 as well.

Following his time at Yale, Murthy returned to Massachusetts for a residency in internal medicine at Brigham and Women's Hospital and Harvard Medical School. Although he appreciated the experience he gained through the residency, he soon grew concerned about the highly stressful and all-consuming nature of the work. "I came to the realization that even though I also deeply valued family and friends, I was not living a people-centered life," he explained to Skipper. "I was living a work-centered life. During my residency training, where I was faced with life and death every day, I saw patients, including young patients who were my age—I was in my twenties at the time—who had advanced gastric cancer and other terminal illnesses. I was thinking, 'That could be me. Am I living my life the way I want to live it right now?'" Murthy's concerns from that period would continue to inform his thinking during the next decades of his career, shaping his perspective on issues such as stress

Photo by United States Department of Health and Human Services, via Wikimedia Commons [Public domain.]

and burnout among medical professionals. He completed his residency in 2006.

PHYSICIAN AND ADVOCATE

Immersed in the medical field throughout his schooling, Murthy cofounded VISIONS Worldwide, a nonprofit organization dedicated to the prevention of acquired immunodeficiency syndrome (AIDS) in India, with his sister while attending Harvard. Following his medical residency, he remained at Brigham and Women's Hospital, where he worked as an attending physician. Murthy also served as an instructor in medicine at Harvard Medical School (HMS) during that period and in 2010 cofounded the business TrialNetworks, a company dedicated to optimizing clinical trials. He remained affiliated with Brigham and Women's Hospital and Harvard Medical School into 2014.

Intrigued by the intersections between medicine and politics, in 2008 Murthy cofounded the organization Doctors for Obama, which supported the candidacy of Senator Barack Obama for president. Following Obama's election, the organization evolved into Doctors for America, a group made up of medical professionals who advocated for health-care reform. "I was struck by how few physicians were organizing and gathering their ideas to actually make an impact on the candidates' platforms and, ultimately, on a health reform bill," Murthy told *Hospitalist News* in 2012, as reported by Sabrina Tavernise for *The New York Times* (16 Dec. 2014). "A few colleagues and I began Doctors for America with a simple belief that physicians should play a leadership role in designing and running our nation's health care system." In addition to advocating for health care reform through Doctors for America, Murthy went on to advise President Obama on several health issues beginning in 2011, when he was appointed to the Presidential Advisory Council on Prevention, Health Promotion, and Integrative and Public Health.

SURGEON GENERAL

Continuing his close association with the Obama administration, Murthy was nominated to succeed Regina Benjamin as US surgeon general in November 2013. His confirmation process was lengthy, in part due to opposition from many conservatives over his support for gun control as a public health measure. Nevertheless, he officially assumed the role in December 2014.

As the nineteenth United States surgeon general, part of the US Department of Health and Human Services (HHS) and vice admiral of the Commissioned Corps. of the US Public Health Service (USPHS), Murthy was tasked with providing essential medical information to the American public and issuing reports and guidance on a variety of public health concerns. Some of the prominent subjects he focused on included addiction, especially the opioid epidemic; the US response to an Ebola outbreak occurring in Africa; and the rise of electronic cigarette use among young people. Notably, he also worked to call attention to the broad health ramifications of poverty, which he characterized as a serious problem that often goes overlooked. "Being poor, which affects one in five children, is too great a factor in determining who is healthy and who is not," he explained after his confirmation as surgeon general, as reported by *Yale Medicine Magazine* (2014). "These realities hurt all of us. They threaten our economy, our educational system, the productivity of our workers, and even our national security. They bend the arc of the moral universe away from justice. To put it simply, health equity is a civil rights issue."

Murthy served as surgeon general throughout the remainder of the Obama presidency and, as the position is set at a four-year term, he continued to serve following the 2017 inauguration of President Donald Trump. In April 2017, however, the Trump administration dismissed Murthy from his position. Murthy later reported that he had been asked to resign from the post but refused to do so. "I have been truly humbled and honored to serve as your Surgeon General," he wrote in a statement posted to Facebook following his dismissal, as reported by *Yale Medicine Magazine* (2017). "I look forward to working alongside you in new ways in the years to come. Our journey for a stronger, healthier America continues." Murthy was succeeded as surgeon general by Jerome M. Adams.

NEW PROJECTS

Murthy took on a number of new projects over the next several years, including a venture into the private sector as a cofounder of SVN Med, a medical device company seeking to develop innovative means of treating cancer. He also delved into the world of sports, serving on the board of governors for the National Collegiate Athletic Association (NCAA) as well as the board of directors for the US Olympic and Paralympic Committee. In 2018 he began writing his first book, seeking to explore the phenomenon of loneliness and the importance of interpersonal connections. The resulting work, *Together: The Healing Power of Human Connection in a Sometimes Lonely World*, debuted in April 2020.

Murthy also increasingly began to speak out about the dangers of stress and burnout among the general population as well as among medical professionals specifically. The latter became an issue of increasing concern amid the highly stressful COVID-19 pandemic that began in 2020. As he explained in interviews, stress and burnout in the medical field harm both medical practitioners and their patients, and he advocated for substantial reform to reduce contributing factors. "We can't endure more and more years of doctors burning out at the rates that they are," Murthy told Bridget Balch for the website of the Association of American Medical Colleges (18 Nov. 2020) about the problem. "We have an opportunity to reflect, reevaluate, and change direction—to build the kind of culture in medicine that we need and that our trainees, in particular, truly deserve." In May 2020, the Vilcek Foundation and the Arnold P. Gold Foundation awarded Murthy that year's Vilcek-Gold Award for Humanism in Healthcare in recognition of his prior work in areas such as addiction as well as his overall focus on human-centered health care.

RETURN TO WASHINGTON

Following the election of former vice president Joe Biden to the presidency in November 2020, Murthy joined Biden's COVID-19 Advisory Board, serving as cochair of that body during the transitional period between the election and Biden's inauguration in January 2021. Biden subsequently nominated Murthy to take the role of surgeon general once again. Following his confirmation in the Senate in March 2021, Murthy took on the title of the twenty-first surgeon general of the United States.

In returning to the HHS, Murthy faced a host of new challenges, including the ongoing struggle against the COVID-19 pandemic. He was particularly concerned about the mental health of the US population, noting that he found loneliness, lack of human connection, and social and political polarization to be increasingly prevalent in US society. "That question of 'How do we rebuild connection and community at a time where we have seen that fundamental underpinning of society deteriorate over the last several decades?'— that's a question I wanted to grapple with," he told Skipper. "Because I see human connection as a powerful and essential source of healing for all of us."

At the start of the second year of his term in 2022, Murthy's priorities included raising awareness of mental health issues among teenagers, a population he identified as particularly at risk. He likewise continued to address the public about the continuing pandemic, cautioning that periodic surges in positive cases could occur as further variants of COVID-19 emerged.

PERSONAL LIFE

Murthy married physician and professor Alice Chen in 2015. They had two children. Murthy lives in Washington, DC.

SUGGESTED READING

Alonso-Zaldivar, Ricardo. "Newly Confirmed Surgeon General to Focus on COVID, Opioids." Associated Press, 23 Mar. 2021, apnews.com/article/joe-biden-opioids-coronavirus-pandemic-vivek-murthy-barack-obama-2e1643c5f69e2f64ef04a46d b60e95d7. Accessed 11 Apr. 2022.

Balch, Bridget. "Former Surgeon General Vivek Murthy, MD, Reflects on the Power of Our Shared Humanity." *AAMC*, 18 Nov. 2020, www.aamc.org/news-insights/former-surgeon-general-vivek-murthy-md-reflects-power-our-shared-humanity. Accessed 11 Apr. 2022.

"Building the Great American Community." *Yale Medicine Magazine*, 2014, medicine. yale.edu/news/yale-medicine-magazine/article/building-the-great-american-community/. Accessed 11 Apr. 2022.

Murthy, Vivek. "Surgeon General Dr. Vivek Murthy Sees Polarization as a Public Health Issue." Interview by Clay Skipper. *GQ*, 11 Mar. 2022, www.gq.com/story/surgeon-general-vivek-murthy-interview. Accessed 11 Apr. 2022.

Tavernise, Sabrina. "Vivek Murthy, the New Surgeon General, Isn't Afraid to Take a Stand." *The New York Times*, 16 Dec. 2014, www.nytimes.com/2014/12/17/science/a-new-surgeon-general-unafraid-of-taking-a-stand-on-a-divisive-issue.html. Accessed 11 Apr. 2022.

"Vivek Murthy Dismissed as US Surgeon." *Yale Medicine Magazine*, 2017, medicine.yale. edu/news/yale-medicine-magazine/article/vivek-murthy-dismissed-as-us-surgeon/. Accessed 11 Apr. 2022.

Wen, Patricia, and Noah Bierman. "High Praise at Home for Surgeon General Nominee." *Boston Globe*, 15 Nov. 2013, www.bostonglobe.com/metro/2013/11/15/murthy-obama-choice-for-surgeon-general-who-likes-practice-outside-hospital-walls/KwrWaarq2lkrDMy1vXLNEP/story.html. Accessed 11 Apr. 2022.

—*Joy Crelin*

Jonathan Nez

Born: May 26, 1975
Occupation: Politician

Jonathan Nez knew that he wanted to make a difference in the world from an early age. While growing up in rural Arizona his family had limited resources, but this did not stop them from doing what they could to improve the lives of others in the Navajo community. "I was taught well," Nez told Arelis Hernández in a discussion with *The Washington Post* (19 Oct. 2021). "My parents would always say you help others before you help your own."

Nez continued to heed his parents' advice when he became the president of the Navajo Nation—the largest Native American reservation in the United States—in 2019. Rather than prioritize what was best for him and his inner circle, like many Washington politicians, Nez has put the needs of the Nation's most vulnerable citizens first. His altruistic leadership style came into the spotlight in 2020 when the Navajo Nation was hit harder by the coronavirus disease 2019 (COVID-19) than anywhere else in America. In a call to President Donald Trump in late March 2020, New Mexico's governor Michelle Lujan Grisham reflected on the Navajo Nation's alarmingly high infection rates and warned that they could be "wiped out." Despite challenging circumstances, Nez succeeded in getting the virus's spread under control and demonstrated that he was the kind of leader who would put his people's well-being above all else.

EARLY LIFE

Jonathan Nez was born in Tuba City, Arizona, on May 26, 1975, to parents John and Mabel Nez. He was raised in Shonto, Arizona, a small, rural Navajo community with fewer than six hundred residents. Nez is of the Áshįįhí, or Salt Clan, his mother's clan, and he was born for his father's clan, the Ta'neeszahnii, or Tangle Clan. His maternal grandfather's clan is the Tódích'íi'nii, or Bitter Water Clan, and his paternal grandfather's clan is Táchii'nii, or Red Running into the Water Clan. Because Navajo society is matrilineal, children identify as members of their mother's clans first.

Nez became interested in Navajo politics at an early age. His grandfather H. T. Donald was a Navajo Nation Council delegate who represented his district in the tribal government's legislative branch. During his formative years, Nez was inspired by how much his grandfather had impacted others. In a conversation with the *Navajo-Hopi Observer* (1 May 2012), Nez reflected on his grandfather. "[He] was known for his generosity and compassion," Nez recalled. "I grew up with stories and people sharing with me how he helped the people. I felt I wanted to help out my community and, with guidance from my grandma, started from the bottom."

It was because of his grandfather that as a high school student Nez started attending Shonto chapter meetings. Chapters are the most local form of government in the Navajo Nation. Across the entire territory, which comprises 17.8 million acres of land in New Mexico, Utah, and Arizona, there are 110 chapters.

EDUCATION AND EARLY POLITICAL CAREER

After graduating from Monument Valley High School in 1993, Nez began earning college credits at nearby schools. He continued working as an active member of his hometown's tribal government, eventually becoming the Shonto Chapter vice president. In 1999, Nez's political career began to take off when he followed in his grandfather's footsteps and was elected as a Navajo Nation Council delegate. He was only twenty-four years old at the time—the youngest person to ever become an elected official in the history of the Navajo Nation.

While in his position as a delegate, Nez enrolled at Northland Pioneer College in 2001 where he completed the five courses that he needed for his associate degree. After graduating with high honors, he immediately enrolled in Northern Arizona University (NAU), graduating in 2002 with a BA degree in political science. He then went on to earn a master's degree in public administration from NAU. When asked by the NAU alumni magazine, *Pine* (20 May 2020), why he decided to continue pursuing higher education despite already being an elected official, Nez replied, "I wanted to be the most effective leader I could become."

During his three terms as a Navajo Nation Council delegate, Nez represented the chapters of Shonto, Oljato, Tsah Bi Kin, and Navajo Mountain in the central government's legislative branch. He also served two terms

Photo by Wikiuser159597 via Wikimedia Commons

on the Navajo County Board of Supervisors, where his responsibilities included overseeing department budgets and tax rates.

In 2015, Nez was elected vice president of the Navajo Nation under President Russell Begaye's administration. During his inaugural speech on May 12, 2015, Nez announced that his focus as vice president would be to help the Navajo people fight the "monsters" of depression, suicide, obesity, poverty, and post-traumatic stress disorder (PTSD) that had long haunted them, while also working to have people's fundamental needs met, including affordable housing, safe drinking water, healthy food, and quality education.

PRESIDENTIAL CAMPAIGN

When Begaye proved to be an unpopular leader, Nez decided to run against him in the 2018 presidential election. There were many hopefuls in the primary that summer, but Nez and former President Joseph Shirley Jr. garnered the most votes and subsequently became the two official candidates. This angered Begaye, who performed poorly in the primary and caused him to endorse Shirley instead of his own vice president.

Nez's campaign hit a roadblock in September 2018 when a former presidential candidate named Vincent H. Yazzie claimed

that Nez was not eligible to run because he had failed to disclose on his candidate application a misdemeanor for driving under the influence (DUI) that he received in 2002. The courts dismissed Yazzie's complaint, citing that the DUI had not happened within the previous five years and, therefore, Nez was not legally required to report it.

Ultimately, the Yazzie controversy did not hurt Nez's impression among voters, in part because he had been open in discussing his previous struggles with alcohol. Nez reflected on how overcoming his substance abuse problem as a young man had affected him as a leader, as quoted by Noel Lyn Smith for the *Farmington Daily Times* (26 Sept. 2018). "We all make mistakes," he explained. "We learn from those mistakes, [sic] and we utilize it as a teaching tool."

On November 6, 2018, Nez won the presidential election in a landslide, finishing with 39,783 votes to Shirley's 20,146. At the age of forty-three, he became the youngest president in the Navajo Nation's history.

EARLY PRESIDENCY

Nez and his vice president, Myron Lizer, were sworn into office on January 15, 2019. While addressing the thousands of people who had gathered for the event, Nez promised that he would both prioritize Navajo-owned businesses and work with tribal lawmakers. Additionally, he emphasized his desire to tackle issues like physical wellness and the high rates of depression, bullying, and suicide among Navajo teens. "Change presents opportunity— the opportunity to work together to strengthen and empower ourselves as individuals and as communities," he told the crowd in his inaugural speech.

One of the biggest challenges that Nez faced in his first year as president was the closure of the coal-burning Navajo Generating Station (NGS) and its supply mine on November 18, 2019. Up until then, the power plant, which was located on Navajo lands, brought in an annual revenue of $40 million in addition to providing hundreds of Navajo people with well-paying jobs. After the NGS shut down, Nez supported the cleanup of the site as well as efforts from Navajo grassroots groups to move away from coal to the clean energy industry.

THE COVID-19 CRISIS

Progress on how to replace the lost revenue from the NGS's closure was derailed, however, by a greater challenge. By March 2020, the COVID-19 pandemic had hit the United States and erupted across the Navajo Nation. Many factors made the Navajo people more susceptible to the virus and its spread; in addition to living in large, intergenerational households, many Navajo families are without basic infrastructure such as running water and electricity. Combined with common pre-existing comorbidities like diabetes and hypertension, the Navajo people were at a much higher risk for death or serious complications from COVID-19. Consequently, it was not long into the pandemic that the Navajo Nation had surpassed New York state for having the highest infection rate in the country.

Nez quickly stepped into action and began taking measures to keep his community safe, including some of the strictest measures in the country. In addition to aggressive testing, he established a mask mandate in public places, contact tracing, daily curfews, and weekend lockdowns. To overcome any resistance to these rules, Nez regularly communicated with citizens through the media and speeches. He framed the virus as a "monster," comparing it to the monsters in traditional Navajo stories. Furthermore, he emphasized how much more vulnerable older individuals were to the virus. As elders are a highly valued part of the Navajo community and culture, people took the threat very seriously.

Nez also advocated for the Navajo Nation and other Native Americans in the US Congress, pushing President Joe Biden's administration to allocate funds to Native Americans in the $2.2 trillion Coronavirus Aid, Relief, and Economic Security (CARES) Act. After the bill was signed into law on March 27, 2020, and funds to the Navajo Nation were delayed, Nez's administration took the federal government to court to get the $714 million that it was owed. The court case was successful, and Nez began working with Navajo lawmakers to use the funds for economic relief and to hire more first responders. Additionally, the money was used for expenditure plans that prioritized water, electricity, and broadband. By planning to invest in infrastructure across the Navajo Nation, Nez hoped to provide the community with the fundamental amenities that could both improve their lives and better prepare them for future disasters.

Nez's leadership proved effective. By the summer of 2021, 70 percent of people living on the reservation had been fully vaccinated against COVID-19—a higher rate than the rest of the country. Furthermore, by maintaining aggressive testing, social distancing, contact tracing, and mask mandates, the Navajo Nation had succeeded in getting its infection rate under control. When asked by *Arizona Central* (31 Aug. 2021) what made the Navajo so successful at battling COVID-19, Nez replied, "T'áá hwó' ajít'éego, self-reliance or self-determination, is a very important teaching that serves to tell our people that we have the power within us to do anything and overcome anything. True sovereignty is the ability to take care of our own people and then being able to help others." While virus rates surged again unexpectedly in the fall of 2021, Nez attributed this to looser COVID-19 regulations in surrounding counties and continued to work to bring case numbers down.

PERSONAL LIFE

While earning his master's degree at NAU, Nez met Phefelia Herbert, a Navajo political science and criminal justice student. The two bonded over their shared desire to help the Navajo community and got married in the summer of 2005. They have two children together, Christopher and Alexander.

An avid runner, Nez has dreams of completing a marathon in every state across the country. In late 2021, he was working on his PhD in political science, collecting research on the potential benefits of increasing the sovereignty of the Navajo Nation's local chapters and decreasing its reliance on the central tribal government.

SUGGESTED READING

"County Supervisor Jonathan Nez Named Outstanding NPC Alumnus." *The Navajo-Hopi Observer*, 1 May 2012, www.nhonews.com/news/2012/may/01/county-supervisor-jonathan-nez-named-outstanding-/. Accessed 26 Oct. 2021.

Fonseca, Felicia. "New Leader of Navajo Nation Delivers Message of Hope, Change." *The Salt Lake Tribune*, 15 Jan. 2019, www.sltrib.com/news/nation-world/2019/01/16/

new-leader-navajo-nation/AP%202019/
AP%202019/. Accessed 28 Oct. 2021.

"Leading a Nation with Passion and Purpose."
Northern Arizona University, 20 May 2021,
nau.edu/boundless/navajo-nation-president-
takes-action. Accessed 26 Oct. 2021.

"Next Generation: Water with Sarah Diringer,
PhD, Jonathan Nez & Emma Robbins."
The Washington Post, 19 Oct. 2021, www.
washingtonpost.com/washington-post-
live/2021/10/19/next-generation-water-
with-jonathan-nez/. Accessed 26 Oct. 2021.

Nez, Jonathan. "Jonathan Nez Leads Navajo
Nation Members During COVID-19
Pandemic." Interview. *Arizona Central*,
31 Aug. 2020, www.azcentral.com/
in-depth/opinion/op-ed/2020/08/30/
leaders-of-change-jonathan-nez-covid-
pandemic/3347995001/. Accessed 26 Oct.
2021.

Smith, Noel Lyn. "Navajo Nation VP Cleared
for Run for Tribal Presidency." *Farmington
Daily Times*, 27 Sept. 2018, www.daily-
times.com/story/news/local/navajo-
nation/2018/09/26/jonathan-nez-eligible-
navajo-presidency/1437949002/. Accessed
26 Oct. 2021.

—*Emily E. Turner*

Francis Ngannou

Born: September 5, 1986
Occupation: Mixed martial artist

Known to fans as the Predator, mixed martial
artist Francis Ngannou took a long and
dangerous path to success as a heavyweight
fighter in the Ultimate Fighting Championship
(UFC) Octagon. Born into a poor family in
Cameroon, Ngannou worked in a local quarry
throughout his childhood but dreamed of
becoming a professional boxer. The chance
to pursue his dream came in 2013, when he
arrived in Paris, France, after completing an
arduous journey from Africa to Europe via the
Strait of Gibraltar. In Paris, Ngannou switched
from boxing to mixed martial arts (MMA), a
sport that combines techniques from a variety
of combat sports, and began competing in his
new sport after only several months of training.
His strong performances in these early fights
motivated the UFC, the largest and most

lucrative MMA promotion company in the
world, to sign Ngannou.

Ngannou made his UFC debut in late 2015
and went on to become a prominent competitor
in that promotion, winning twelve of his first
fourteen UFC bouts. "When you get to the
point where you're not afraid of losing, that's
when you become a winner," he told Josh Ellis
for the *Success* magazine *Achievers Exclusive*
interview series, as reported by Spencer
Cappelli (4 Nov. 2021).

In 2021, Ngannou defeated heavyweight
champion Stipe Miocic to claim the UFC
heavyweight title, his highest-profile victory up
to that point. Although he came into conflict
with UFC leadership over a potential contract
extension during 2021 and 2022, Ngannou
remained confident in both his skills in the
Octagon and his willingness to take professional
risks. "They may think I have no options, but I
am a free man," he told Tim Keown for *ESPN*
(21 Jan. 2022). "I might be UFC champion,
but I have no problem going back to Africa and
doing my thing. This is not what defines me. It
is not the title of UFC champion that makes
Francis Ngannou. Francis Ngannou makes the
UFC champion."

EARLY LIFE AND MOVE TO EUROPE

Francis Zavier Ngannou was born in Cameroon
on September 5, 1986, and grew up in the
town of Batié. His parents divorced when he
was six years old, and Ngannou lived with
relatives for a time before rejoining his mother's
household. He and his four siblings struggled
during their childhoods, often lacking food and
school supplies. To help support the family,
Ngannou began working in a local sand quarry
at the age of nine and continued to work in the
quarry throughout his childhood. Although that
period was challenging for Ngannou, he later
credited his difficult childhood with helping to
shape his future. "I now believe without that
childhood, the life that I had, I wouldn't be
here," he told Ellis, as reported by Cappelli.
"Everything came together to bring me where
I am."

Drawn to the sport of boxing from at an
early age, Ngannou dreamed of becoming a
professional boxing champion and worked
toward that goal as a young adult. Hoping to
train at a real boxing gym, he moved to Douala,
the largest city in Cameroon, to work and
practice his chosen sport. "I was just surviving,"

Photo by X2o, via Wikimedia Commons

he told Emmanuel Morgan for *The New York Times* (21 Jan. 2022). "Everyone thought I was crazy, but I wanted to do something and have a purpose." However, Ngannou soon determined that he could not pursue his dream further in Cameroon and would have to make his way to Europe, where he could train and enter boxing competitions.

In April 2012 Ngannou left Cameroon and began a lengthy journey to Morocco, where he stayed for an entire year. From there, Ngannou made repeated attempts to reach Spain by crossing the Strait of Gibraltar. Although he was caught by the Moroccan authorities during his first six attempts, Ngannou persisted, and in March 2013 succeeded in captaining a raft with eight other passengers out of Moroccan waters. The group was rescued by an American Red Cross ship and transported to Spain, where Ngannou spent two months in a detention facility before being granted asylum.

MIXED MARTIAL ARTS

After being granted asylum and released from detention in Spain, Ngannou traveled to Paris, France, where he experienced homelessness and lived in the stairwell of a parking garage for a time. Immediately after arriving in Paris, Ngannou found a local boxing gym and resumed his training as a boxer. Ngannou's living situation improved after he befriended

a gym employee, Didier Carmont, who helped him find housing and encouraged him to pursue a career in mixed martial arts (MMA) rather than boxing; this helped Ngannou realize that MMA could potentially be more lucrative for an up-and-coming athlete. On Carmont's suggestion, Ngannou began training at a local gym, the MMA Factory, run by coach Fernand Lopez. Though initially reluctant to switch sports due to his longtime love of boxing, Ngannou soon found that MMA represented a valuable chance to build a new life for himself in Europe. "At the end of the day, all I needed was an opportunity," he later told Morgan.

Ngannou's athletic prowess and size quickly earned the respect of Lopez, who pushed Ngannou to begin competing in MMA events only four months after he began training. Ngannou initially participated in events put on by 100% Fight, a French MMA promotion, and made his professional MMA debut in November 2013 at the 100% Fight: Contenders 20 event. In his first professional bout, Ngannou defeated Rachid Benzina by submission and won a prize of €2,000 (about $2,084 US). The following month, he faced Zoumana Cisse but lost by unanimous decision.

Ngannou would not lose again in the next four years, during which he beat Bilal Tahtahi and Nikolas Specq in 100% Fight events. He also defeated Luc Ngeleka at the Strength and Honor Championship 10 event in Switzerland. Ngannou's strong performance in European MMA soon caught the attention of the Ultimate Fighting Championship (UFC), a major MMA promotion based in the United States. He signed a contract with that promotion and went on to make his UFC debut on December 19, 2015, beating Luis Henrique via knockout (KO).

UFC

Following his UFC debut, Ngannou remained affiliated with the promotion; by the start of 2017, he had amassed four consecutive UFC wins. That January, he faced a challenging new opponent in the form of UFC veteran Andrei Arlovski, an accomplished competitor who had held the UFC heavyweight title more than a decade before. "I've had four fights, but I have never fought a legend like Arlovski," Ngannou told Peter Carroll for *Vice* (22 Dec. 2016) prior to the bout. "If you want to be a legend you have to fight a legend." Ultimately, Ngannou finished the fight in less than two minutes, defeating his opponent by KO in the first round.

By May 2017, Ngannou had left France and relocated to Las Vegas, Nevada, where he began training with coach Eric Nicksick at the Xtreme Couture MMA gym. He went on to finish the year with a December KO victory over Alistair Overeem.

In January of 2018, Ngannou suffered his first UFC loss at UFC 220 in Boston, Massachusetts, losing by unanimous decision to UFC heavyweight champion Stipe Miocic in five rounds. He followed that disappointing loss with a second consecutive loss in July of that year, this time losing by unanimous decision to Derrick Lewis. Ngannou later told journalists that he had not been mentally focused on the Lewis fight and had instead still been struggling to cope with his loss to Miocic. "I was fighting against the weaknesses I showed against Stipe," he explained to Gareth A. Davies in an interview for the *Telegraph* (28 June 2019). "I was five months behind the fight." Still, Ngannou considered his back-to-back losses to have been valuable learning experiences. "I'm new blood in this sport, I'm very new to it," he told Davies. "My ride was too fast. I went so high so quickly, I didn't have time to get my experience. I was in need of experience and that's what happened."

Ngannou began turning his record around in November 2018, when he faced and quickly defeated Curtis Blaydes. This set off a new winning streak; Ngannou went on to beat Cain Velasquez and Junior Dos Santos in 2019 and Jairzinho Rozenstruik in 2020.

UFC CHAMPION

On March 27, 2021, Ngannou faced Miocic for a second time, this time in Las Vegas, once again hoping to claim the UFC heavyweight title from his opponent. The fight, which lasted two rounds, ended when Ngannou defeated Miocic by KO to become the UFC heavyweight champion. In addition to winning that title, he won the Performance of the Night award and received a $50,000 bonus.

While the UFC asked him to defend his title after only a few months, Ngannou opted not to fight again until January 2022, when he defeated Ciryl Gane by unanimous decision after five rounds. Gane held the interim heavyweight title at that time; therefore, by claiming that title and defending his own, Ngannou was considered to have unified the heavyweight and interim heavyweight titles with his victory. For Ngannou, this victory represented something of a pushback against UFC leadership, which he believed had attempted to rush him into defending his title. He also felt that the UFC had disrespected him by creating the interim heavyweight title, a controversial move among UFC fighters and fans, after he declined to face a second opponent in 2021.

The UFC's payment structure contributed to further conflict with Ngannou. He expressed reluctance to sign a new contract with the organization, as he believed the existing compensation structure for UFC athletes to be unfair; the organization typically classifies fighters as independent contractors and keeps 85 percent of all revenue. "I signed a contract before, and it didn't play out very well on my end," he explained to Tyler R. Tynes in an interview for *GQ* (18 Aug. 2021). "So, in order to sign another contract I think it's my right to at least look out for myself and get what is right for me to fix whatever was the mistake in the previous one. And if someone doesn't believe they should fix their mistake, then that means that person is not looking for anything good for you." The two parties remained at an impasse by mid-2022.

OTHER VENTURES

In addition to training and participating in MMA competitions, Ngannou has been involved in charity work. He founded the Francis Ngannou Foundation, a nonprofit organization intended to benefit children in Cameroon. "The idea is just to make them feel worth it—to feel like somebody cares about them. And from there on, they can pick up their own dream, and believe in their dreams," he explained to Ellis, as reported by Cappelli. Among other initiatives, Ngannou worked to open a gym in Cameroon focused on combat sports where local youth could learn new skills as well as the ideals of sportsmanship.

Ngannou lived in France between 2013 and 2017, when he moved to Las Vegas. He also returned to Cameroon at times to visit family, including after winning the UFC heavyweight title.

PERSONAL LIFE

Ngannou currently resides in Las Vegas.

SUGGESTED READING

Cappelli, Spencer. "UFC's Francis Ngannou's Keys to Overcoming Obstacles and Visualizing Success." *Success*, 4 Nov. 2021, www.success.com/ufcs-francis-ngannous-keys-to-overcoming-obstacles-and-visualizing-success/. Accessed 13 July 2022.

Carroll, Peter. "Francis Ngannou Talks about Learning English ahead of Joining the Title Fray." *Vice*, 22 Dec. 2016, www.vice.com/en/article/ezebjz/francis-ngannou-talks-about-learning-english-ahead-of-joining-the-title-fray. Accessed 13 July 2022.

Keown, Tim. "Francis Ngannou's Miraculous Journey." *ESPN*, 21 Jan. 2022, www.espn.com/espn/feature/story?id=33100543&_slug_=francis-ngannou-miraculous-journey-ufc-stardom. Accessed 13 July 2022.

Morgan, Emmanuel. "The Fearsome, Quiet Champion." *The New York Times*, 21 Jan. 2022, www.nytimes.com/2022/01/21/sports/francis-ngannou-ufc-fight.html. Accessed 13 June 2022.

Ngannou, Francis. "Exclusive Interview: UFC Heavyweight Francis Ngannou Bringing Hope to Homeless Children in Cameroon—and Eyes Future Heavyweight Boxing Fight." Interview by Gareth A. Davies. *The Telegraph*, 28 June 2019, www.telegraph.co.uk/mma/2019/06/28/exclusive-interview-ufc-heavyweight-francis-ngannou-bringing/. Accessed 13 June 2022.

___. "Francis Ngannou Is Still the UFC's Baddest Man." Interview by Tyler R. Tynes. *GQ*, 18 Aug. 2021, www.gq.com/story/francis-ngannou-interview. Accessed 13 June 2022.

___. "Interview: Francis Ngannou." Interview. *Fight Disciples*, 25 June 2019, www.fightdisciples.com/2019/06/25/interview-francis-ngannou/. Accessed 13 June 2022.

—*Joy Crelin*

Sigrid Nunez

Born: 1951
Occupation: Writer

While Sigrid Nunez held various college teaching positions to afford modest living expenses, she devoted the majority of her adult life to what she considered the profession she was meant for: writing solely for the sake of the art. She began publishing longer works consistently in 1995 with her first novel, *A Feather on the Breath of God*, and consistently prioritized her craft over fame and prominence. "I wanted to do one thing well, and that was the thing," she told Alexandra Alter for *The New York Times* (13 Dec. 2018). For more than two decades Nunez found minimal renown and a limited readership, despite critical praise. However, she saw her literary talents receive widespread, mainstream recognition and attention in 2018 when her seventh novel and eighth book overall, *The Friend*—which delves deep into love, loss, and the human-canine bond—won the 2018 National Book Award for Fiction.

Nunez readily accepted the warm embrace given by the literary community and a more expansive range of readers. Still, she told the audience while accepting the National Book Award, as quoted by Alter, "I became a writer not because I was seeking community but rather because I thought it was something I could do alone. How lucky to have discovered that writing books made the miraculous possible, to be removed from the world, and to be a part of the world at the same time." Unintimidated by any commercial pressure to repeat her success, Nunez stayed true to her dedication and finished her next novel, 2020's *What Are You Going Through*, in the same way as she had all of her previous manuscripts. That book earned largely positive reviews as another thought-provoking and affecting effort and also went on to become a best seller.

EARLY LIFE AND EDUCATION

Sigrid Nunez was born in New York City, New York, in 1951. Raised in a Staten Island housing project, she later recalled in interviews that she was very aware of her parents' experience as immigrants from different cultures in America. Her mother had grown up in Germany, and homesickness shaped her sense of identity. Her father had been born in Panama and raised mostly in Shanghai, China, before he moved to the United States as an adolescent. Her father worked nonstop—in a hospital kitchen during weekdays and as a waiter on the weekends—while her mother had the most influence over the household; Nunez's youth as part of this complex family and her desire for a greater understanding of it would inspire the foundation for her first novel. For her part,

Nunez, an avid reader from an early age, let her imagination run unrestrained as she devoured the stories in book after book.

Wanting to create her own stories, potentially as a children's book author, and receiving encouragement from teachers, Nunez began to write as a child. She often centered her tales on children and animals, the latter of which she had a particular fondness for despite never having pets of her own. When she was around twelve years old, however, she steered her attention toward another form of art: ballet. "I didn't actually start until I was in high school though it was in my mind before that," she told Robert Birnbaum for the *Morning News* (29 Mar. 2007).

As she immersed herself in the study of ballet as a high schooler, Nunez realized how physically arduous it was, and, having started late compared to her peers, her fantasy of dancing professionally began to weaken. Nonetheless, following her high school graduation in 1968, she enrolled at Barnard College, where she planned to continue taking dance classes. Her plans did not work out as expected, however.

Nunez's first year of college was affected by the realization that she was not going to fulfill her dancing dream. Feeling at a loss, she no longer went to her dance or academic classes. "What I feel is probably close to other kinds of loss," she said to Birnbaum about mourning the loss of her dream. "Say you're young and you fall in love with someone, and then you lose that person. Though you move on, you don't ever completely get over it. That loss is part of your life and who you are forever."

A WAY BACK TO WRITING

After navigating a challenging freshman year, Nunez took the lessons she had learned from dance about discipline and coping with feelings of failure—as well as the natural fit of being involved in art in general—to continue her college journey. As she majored in English, she returned to her writing roots, formed well before stepping onto the college campus.

After receiving her bachelor's degree in 1972, Nunez embarked on a stint as an assistant to Robert Silvers during his tenure as editor of the *New York Review of Books*. She also continued her education in the writing program at Columbia University, where she earned an MFA in 1975. Through her *New York Review of*

Photo via Wikimedia Commons

Books connections, she then worked as a typist for famed writer Susan Sontag. Nunez began a romantic relationship with Sontag's son, David Rieff, and even lived in Sontag's apartment for a time; this close association gave her a detailed view of Sontag's legendary persona, lifestyle, and serious philosophy on the vocation of writing. In particular, Sontag further stoked Nunez's affinity for "hybrid" writing, which blends elements from more than one genre, such as autobiography and fiction. However, Nunez also realized she was not at all drawn to the trappings of fame.

Nunez began publishing her writing, including short stories, in various outlets over the years. However, her first published long-form work, titled *A Feather on the Breath of God*, did not appear until 1995. Evoking intimate memories from her childhood and fusing fiction with biographical accounts, that novel has as its central character a nameless young woman, born to a Chinese Panamanian father and a German mother, whose young life spent in a housing project in New York is enriched by the power of reading and the graceful art of ballet. In describing her approach to her debut novel, Nunez explained to Kimiko Hahn for *BOMB* (1 Jan. 1995) that she wanted the less-imagination-restricting format of fiction to enable her to freely go beyond historical facts to imagined experiences: "I found myself moving between these two forms, the essay and the story. And it was very comfortable. It came quite naturally, to move back and forth."

AWAY FROM THE MAINSTREAM LITERARY SCENE

While her first work was met with critical acclaim, Nunez decided that, as she moved onward, she was going to build stories that were not as overtly parallel to her life experiences. "Once I finished, it was so memoir-like and it was so obvious that the distance between the narrator and the author was thin, I very much wanted to do the opposite with my next novels," she told Seija Rankin for *Entertainment Weekly* (2 Sept. 2020).

Nunez continued to publish more books in the succeeding years, including the novels *Naked Sleeper* (1996) and *Mitz: The Marmoset of Bloomsbury* (1998). These met with further critical praise and industry awards but remained on the periphery of the popular literary scene, as was her preference. Nonetheless, her work opened doors to more opportunities, including creative writing teaching and fellowships. Between 2000 to 2001 she was the Rome Prize Fellow in Literature at the American Academy in Rome, and the American Academy of Arts and Sciences accepted her as an elected member in 2003.

Nunez released her fourth novel, *For Rouenna*, in 2001. It revolves around the relationship forged between a writer and a woman who served during the war in Vietnam as a combat nurse. She followed this with *The Last of Her Kind* (2005), which was inspired when she was teaching writing at Smith College in Massachusetts and read her students' essays on hippie culture. "I felt that the late '60s and early '70s were so interesting and confusing, and I realized I hadn't read a novel about it that seemed to work for me," she told Rankin. *The Last of Her Kind*, seen by many critics as a unique take on this counterculture period, centers around Georgette and Ann, who share a room during their freshman year at Barnard College in 1968. Over time, however, Ann's determination to turn away from her privileged background in favor of social justice causes puts a strain on their friendship.

MORE WIDESPREAD RECOGNITION AND READERSHIP

With five published novels under her belt—each exploring a unique topic and showcasing engaging writing—Nunez published her sixth offering, titled *Salvation City*, in 2010. Unlike her other novels centered on female protagonists, this work, features a teenage boy named Cole at the heart of the story. When a fictitious global flu pandemic leaves the secularly raised Cole an orphan, he is taken in by a small-town Indiana evangelical pastor and his wife, leading to an exploration of belief. The book was mostly well received by readers and critics; in a review for *The New York Times* (1 Oct. 2010) Abraham Verghese described *Salvation City* as a "satisfying, provocative and very plausible novel" full of "powerful insights." Notably, many commentators revisited the book in the context of the coronavirus disease 2019 (COVID-19) pandemic that gripped the world in early 2020, noting the real-life parallels in the plot.

Nunez veered into nonfiction with her next publication *Sempre Susan* (2011), a memoir of her onetime mentor Sontag. Yet despite her consistent and highly regarded output since 1995, it would be her seventh novel, *The Friend* (2018), that represented a true breakthrough, expanding her readership and ushering her onto the main stage of popular literature. The book is an account of an unnamed woman who is in mourning after her best friend killed himself. Soon, her grief is compounded by the responsibility of caring for and forming a connection with the grief-stricken Apollo, a Great Dane she inherited from her late friend. Though much of the resounding praise for *The Friend* was aimed at Nunez's exploration of themes such as memory and loss through an intimate examination of the human-canine connection, she revealed to Rankin that this element of the story was not planned. "It came from nowhere except for the fact that I'd always wanted to write a book where an animal, particularly a dog, played a major role."

The Friend won Nunez the prestigious 2018 National Book Award for Fiction and put her in the spotlight as never before. Her much-anticipated eighth novel, *What Are You Going Through* (2020)—which, like its predecessor, deals with the concept of death—was released to mostly positive reviews and good sales. Meanwhile, she continued to hold teaching positions and writing residencies at various institutions, including Columbia, Princeton, the New School, and Boston University. In 2021, she became an elected member of the American Academy of Arts and Letters.

SUGGESTED READING

Alter, Alexandra. "With *The Friend*, Sigrid Nunez Becomes an Overnight Literary Sensation, 23 Years and Eight Books Later." *The New York Times*, 13 Dec. 2018, www.nytimes.com/2018/12/13/books/the-friend-sigrid-nunez.html. Accessed 25 Oct. 2021.

Nunez, Sigrid. "Sigrid Nunez." Interview by Kimiko Hahn. *BOMB*, 1 Jan. 1995, bombmagazine.org/articles/sigrid-nunez/. Accessed 2 Nov. 2021

—. "Sigrid Nunez." Interview by Robert Birnbaum. *The Morning News*, 29 Mar. 2007, themorningnews.org/article/sigrid-nunez. Accessed 25 Oct. 2021.

Rankin, Seija. "Sigrid Nunez on Dogs, Death, and Her Best Books." *Entertainment Weekly*, 2 Sept. 2020, ew.com/books/sigrid-nunez-best-books. Accessed 25 Oct. 2021.

Shea, Renée H. "The Secret Facts of Fiction: A Profile of Sigrid Nunez." *Poets & Writers*, 1 Jan. 2006, www.pw.org/content/the_secret_facts_of_fiction_a_profile_of_sigrid_nunez. Accessed 25 Oct. 2021.

Verghese, Abraham. "Alien Nation." Review of *Salvation City*, by Sigrid Nunez. *The New York Times*, 1 Oct. 2010, www.nytimes.com/2010/10/03/books/review/Verghese-t.html. Accessed 2 Nov. 2021.

SELECTED WORKS

A Feather on the Breath of God, 1995; *Naked Sleeper*, 1996; *Mitz: The Marmoset of Bloomsbury*, 1998; *For Rouenna*, 2001; *The Last of Her Kind*, 2005; *Salvation City*, 2010; *The Friend*, 2018; *What Are You Going Through*, 2020

—Maria del Pilar Guzman

Joe Ollmann
Born: March 25, 1966
Occupation: Cartoonist

Though Joe Ollmann's authentic work as a comic artist had been available to the public in some form since the 1980s, whether through self-publication or in the pages of local newspapers in his home country of Canada, his profile remained relatively low until he began reaching more expansive audiences and garnering critical acclaim through the professional release of his books. These included *Fictional Father*, his 2021 graphic novel, which was short-listed in the fiction category for a Governor General's Literary Award.

Born and raised in Hamilton, Ontario, Ollmann developed an early love of comics. In the 1990s, he drew comic strips for the local *Hamilton Spectator* and the alternative magazine *Exclaim!*, but it was *Wag!*, his eclectic, self-published zine, that caught the attention of publishers around 2000. He went on to publish two collections of graphic short stories, *Chewing on Tinfoil* (2002) and the 2007 Doug Wright Award–winning *This Will All End in Tears* (2006). His work has been described as bleak, but also life-affirming and humorous, and is depicted in his distinct, largely black-and-white style typically presented in a nine-panel grid framework. Subsequent graphic works, including *Mid-Life* (2011) and *The Abominable Mr. Seabrook* (2017), with the latter about the real-life writer William Seabrook, to whom he devoted years of research, have emphasized his guiding interest as an artist. Ollmann, Brad Mackay wrote for the *Comics Journal* (7 July 2021), "can't shake his affinity for the messy struggles of real people."

EARLY LIFE AND EDUCATION

Joe Ollmann was born in Hamilton, Ontario, Canada, on March 25, 1966. In his own telling—in an interview with Mackay for the *Comics Journal* (30 Mar. 2017)—he was "a rural child." His family owned and operated a Christmas tree farm, but his father was also a manager at Stelco, a major steel manufacturer in Hamilton. His mother stayed at home to raise Ollmann and his five siblings, of which he was the youngest. Inherently creative and often spending his free time drawing and storytelling, he purchased his first comic, an issue of *Spider-Man*, when he was around nine. "It was one of those lightning bolt moments y'know. From that moment on I was addicted to comics," he told Mackay.

Ollmann was also inspired by a local comic artist named Doug Wright, whose work appeared in the *Hamilton Spectator*. Being young and brought up in a society that typically viewed American productions as the standard, Ollmann assumed that all quality work came from the United States. Therefore, seeing a Canadian's strip published in a large newspaper was foundationally significant, as it shaped his perspective on the potentials of professional drawing pursuits. "Finding out that Doug Wright was from around here was very influential. It made me think 'Oh, I could actually do that.' It made it real for me," he explained to Mackay.

Ollmann attended St. Mary's High School, entering drawing contests and honing his skills copying existing comic strips whenever he had a chance. Following his high school graduation, he held a night-shift job at a box factory to support his family, which had come to include a wife and child, but he continued to find time to draw. Several years passed, and he took a job in a machine shop. He was half-heartedly laboring as a machinist apprentice to continue paying the bills while thinking up story ideas and drawing diligently at night when a government work program offered him the opportunity to go to college. He thus took part in a short graphic design program at Mohawk College in Hamilton in the late 1980s.

EARLY CAREER

With this more formal training, Ollmann was able to work for printers and draw ads as a career. Around that same period, he independently put out three issues of a black-and-white, science-fiction comic titled *Dirty Nails Comics*. In the 1990s, he drew a comic strip, called *Job's Palace*, featured each week in the *Hamilton Spectator* for five years. "They gave me complete freedom to do whatever I wanted," he related to Mackay. "So sometimes it was politics. . . . Sometimes it would be . . . like the kind of stuff I do now, just stories about people." Though he lost this regular gig when the *Spectator* changed editors, he was then hired to draw a monthly comic for

the Canadian alternative newspaper *Exclaim!*, a job he also held for about five years.

Meanwhile, by the early 1990s, Ollmann had also taken advantage of his access to a press through his employment with a printer to begin making and selling issues of a small, bound zine titled *Wag!*. The books were charming oddities, full not only of comics but also drawings from his children and poetry. (He published a collection of these early works, titled *The Big Book of Wag!*, in 2005.) His first opportunity for industry publication and reaching an even wider audience came around 2000, when, amid a growing market for graphic novels, Toronto's Insomniac Press reached out to him. Impressed by his work with *Wag!*, they offered him a book contract. Within seven months, he produced a collection of illustrated stories titled *Chewing on Tinfoil* (2002).

Chewing on Tinfoil, Ollmann joked to Mackay, "set the tone of all my books: mildly depressing stories that have the relief of humor throughout to make them not unbearable." Though this first book, which received largely critical praise, consists of a larger number of short stories and was completed in a shorter time span, his second effort saw him experiment with a smaller number of longer stories. The resulting second short-story collection, *This Will All End in Tears*, came out in 2006 and won the Doug Wright Award for Best Book in 2007. Drawn in black and white, the book demonstrated that Ollmann was honing his artistic voice. His signature elements— complex characters with disproportionate bodies and tightly gridded panels—began to coalesce into something unique. In interviews, he would discuss his noted preference for working within the nine-panel grid format considered more traditional. "I see the panels as a movie screen or a TV screen. No one changes the size or shape of a movie screen in the middle of a movie. . . . I just pan and scan, close-up and longshot, within that framework," he explained to Tom Spurgeon in an interview for the *Comics Reporter* (6 June 2011). "It also is a technical necessity, as that nine-panel grid gives me tall, narrow panels that better accommodate my voluminous narrations."

MID-LIFE AND SCIENCE FICTION

In 2011, Ollmann published his first, overall well-reviewed graphic novel, *Mid-Life*. In interviews, he has described the book as half-autobiography and half-fiction. In it, John, similarly to the artist, is a middle-aged man with two adult daughters navigating a second marriage and a new young son. He also develops an infatuation with a woman on a children's television show, with part of the book told from her perspective. Ollmann, becoming increasingly recognized for the honesty characterizing his stories, told Chris Mautner in an interview for *CBR.com* (12 Feb. 2011) that the story line with the woman was fictional. "I guess it's a strange mix," he admitted. Citing narrative forebears like the film *Being John Malkovich* (1999) and *The Larry Sanders Show* (1992–98), he said, "I kind of like messing around with, blurring the truth and fiction. . . . It's kind of wonderfully disconcerting."

Another graphic novel, titled *Science Fiction*, followed in 2013, focusing on a sober-minded science teacher who suddenly remembers being abducted by aliens as a child. His obsession with uncovering the truth sours his relationship with his wife. A reviewer for *Publishers Weekly* (1 July 2013) wrote that Ollmann impressively demonstrated an "uncanny ability to expose the reality of contemporary relationships." The next year, he released a volume of mostly previously published stories titled *Happy Stories about Well-Adjusted People* (2014).

THE ABOMINABLE MR. SEABROOK

Since the mid-2000s, Ollmann had been carefully collecting information, which involved a large amount of reading, scouring library archives, and other out-of-state research trips, about the obscure writer William Seabrook, whose name he had stumbled upon in an anthology of zombie stories. Seabrook, historically considered eccentric, was a travel writer in the early twentieth century who was deeply interested in bondage and the occult; he is best remembered for having cooked and eaten human flesh in a quest to understand ritual cannibalism. However, Ollmann saw Seabrook as a more complex figure than these attention-grabbing details might suggest, comparing Seabrook to Hunter S. Thompson, a similarly eccentric writer whose career was curtailed by his own demons.

Committing to a shift to nonfiction, he published *The Abominable Mr. Seabrook*, a graphic biography with dialogue, in 2017. Mautner, who reviewed the book for the *Comics Journal* (19 Apr. 2017), observed that Seabrook aligns with Ollmann's fictional characters, like the protagonists of *Science Fiction* and *Mid-Life*: "Smart, sensitive folks who become consumed by their own obsessions, predilections or just plain bad luck," Mautner wrote. "To rehash an old cliché, if Seabrook didn't exist, Ollmann might have had to invent him."

FICTIONAL FATHER

Returning next to graphic fiction, this time working fully in color, Ollmann published the well-received graphic novel *Fictional Father* in 2021. The book is structured as a faux memoir written by a man named Caleb, who is the long-suffering son of a (fictional) famous cartoonist named Jimmi Wyatt. Jimmi is the beloved creator of a saccharine comic strip titled *Sonny Side Up*, about a father and son who share a relationship markedly different from that of Jimmi and Caleb. Ollmann expressed in interviews that he was inspired to write a premise revolving around a cartoonist not only because of his own experience with and passion for the medium but because of his overall respect for the craft, deepened by a 2019 museum show on the history of Canadian indie comics that he helped curate. "I guess I was so immersed in comics, I started thinking about cartoonists," he told Graham Rockingham for the *Hamilton Spectator* (2 June 2021). "It made sense to write about the world that I know, which is old school newspaper cartoonists."

Fictional Father was a finalist for the Governor General's Literary Award, Canada's highest literary honor, in 2021. It was reported that up to that point, no other graphic novel had been included for consideration in the adult fiction category in the history of the awards.

PERSONAL LIFE

Ollmann has lived in and around Hamilton his entire life. After his divorce from his first wife, with whom he had two daughters, he moved to Montreal in 2001. Having remarried and had another child, he returned in 2013 to Hamilton, which was then experiencing an artistic renaissance, to care for his ailing father. In interviews, he has described heavily drinking for much of his adult life, including when working on many of his comic publications.

When asked about his use of color in *Fictional Father*, Ollmann revealed that he is severely color-blind, a trait he said he had worked for many years to conceal. When working, he has applied color using color theory as well as a software that identifies colors when they appear on a screen.

SUGGESTED READING

Mackay, Brad. Review of *Fictional Father*, by Joe Ollmann. *The Comics Journal*, 7 July 2021, www.tcj.com/reviews/fictional-father/. Accessed 12 July 2022.

Mautner, Chris. Review of *The Abominable Mr. Seabrook*, by Joe Ollmann. *The Comics Journal*, 19 Apr. 2017, www.tcj.com/reviews/the-abominable-mr-seabrook/. Accessed 12 July 2022.

Ollmann, Joe. "CR Sunday Interview: Joe Ollmann." Interview by Tom Spurgeon. *The Comics Reporter*, 6 June 2011, www.comicsreporter.com/index.php/resources/interviews/33166. Accessed 18 July 2022.

—. "Creator Q&A: Joe Ollmann Confronts His 'Mid-Life.'" Interview by Chris Mautner. *CBR.com*, 12 Feb. 2011, www.cbr.com/creator-qa-joe-ollmann-confronts-his-mid-life/. Accessed 18 July 2022.

—. "An Interview with Joe Ollmann." Interview by Brad Mackay. *The Comics Journal*, 30 Mar. 2017, www.tcj.com/an-interview-with-joe-ollmann/. Accessed 11 July 2022.

Rockingham, Graham. "Joe Ollmann's Latest Graphic Novel, 'Fictional Father,' Explores the Relationship between a Comic Strip Artist and His Son." *The Hamilton Spectator*, 2 June 2021, www.thespec.com/entertainment/opinion/2021/06/02/joe-ollmanns-latest-graphic-novel-fictional-father-explores-the-relationship-between-a-comic-strip-artist-and-his-son.html. Accessed 18 July 2022.

Review of *Science Fiction*, by Joe Ollmann. *Publishers Weekly*, 1 July 2013, www.publishersweekly.com/9781894994750. Accessed 12 July 2022.

SELECTED WORKS

Chewing on Tinfoil, 2002; *This Will All End in Tears*, 2006; *Mid-Life*, 2011; *The Abominable Mr. Seabrook*, 2017; *Fictional Father*, 2021

—*Molly Hagan*

Kunle Olukotun

Occupation: Computer   scientist   and entrepreneur

In the 1990s the British-born computer scientist Kunle Olukotun became known as the "father of multicore processors" when he led the Hydra chip multiprocessor research program at Stanford University. At the time computer scientists had sought to improve upon existing computer hardware that used superscalar designs. Olukotun responded to this effort by pioneering one of the first chips with support for thread-level speculation (TLS). Although Hydra was a controversial design initially, its multicore processor design has since found applications in every manner of electronic devices, including in all modern cellular phone microprocessors.

Olukotun went on to develop the Niagara multicore processor, which would go through multiple generations, and made important contributions to the fields of parallel programming, scalable parallel systems, and high-level compilers, among other computer architecture projects. He authored more than 150 peer-reviewed scientific papers and filed a dozen patents. In 2017, he helped to cofound SambaNova Systems, a startup company targeting the potentially lucrative field of artificial intelligence (AI). The company focused on using AI processors to build high-performance machine learning and big-data analysis platforms and received a $150 million investment from the chipmaker Intel and Alphabet, the parent company of Google, in 2019. By April 2021, SambaNova Systems had raised $1 billion in funding and was valued at $5.1 billion.

EARLY LIFE AND EDUCATION

Oyekunle Ayinde "Kunle" Olukotun was born in London, England, to a lawyer and a secretary who had immigrated to the United Kingdom from Nigeria. At an early age he became interested in science and mathematics, primarily through school. When Olukotun turned twelve, his parents moved the family back to Nigeria. There he continued to explore his scientific interests, which included computers and engineering.

Olukotun would later credit his early life experiences with helping to shape his outlook in computer design. He noted in an discussion with the Duquesne Light Company, "In the first twenty years of my life I lived on three continents, and that gave me broad exposure to different people, cultures and ideas. It made the idea of trying new things and expanding into new areas seem kind of natural, and gave me a pioneering spirit."

When it came time for Olukotun to consider what to study for his bachelor's degree, he believed he should go to the United States and study engineering. He studied electrical engineering at Calvin College in Grand Rapids, Michigan, and graduated with a Bachelor of Science (BS) degree. In 1985, he enrolled at the University of Michigan, where he completed his doctoral program in computer science and engineering in 1991. His doctoral thesis, written under the guidance of Trevor Mudge, was on high-speed gallium arsenide microprocessors.

STANFORD UNIVERSITY

In November 1991, Olukotun joined the faculty of Stanford University as a professor of electrical engineering and computer science. During his early years at Stanford, Olukotun began to look at ways to make microprocessors more complex. He led the research team that developed the Hydra chip, the first general-purpose multicore central processing unit (CPU). Instead of constructing a single, complex CPU for the Hydra chip, the team put four copies of a simpler CPU on it, which allowed for more scalability. It was the first chip multiprocessor with support for thread-level speculation (TLS), which is a technique important to the goal of automatic parallel computing.

Although Hydra had considerable benefits from its inception, it was controversial when it was first unveiled in the 1990s because computer programmers had to write parallel programs that needed to be executed simultaneously. Despite the controversy, Olukotun's design would remain the standard approach for a wide variety of devices, including cellular telephone microprocessors.

During his time at Stanford University, Olukotun held numerous positions. He began as an assistant professor, but by 2021 he had become the Cadence Design Systems Professor in the School of Engineering and Professor of Electrical Engineering and Computer Science at Stanford. He also served as a faculty affiliate

at the Institute for Human-Centered Artificial Intelligence (HAI) and a member of the Wu Tsai Neurosciences Institute. Additionally, according to a report on the University of Michigan's website (17 Dec. 2020), "Olukotun now leads the Stanford Pervasive Parallelism Lab, which focuses on making heterogeneous parallel computing easy to use, and he is a member of the Data Analytics for What's Next (DAWN) Lab, which is developing infrastructure for usable machine learning."

COFOUNDER AND CHIEF SCIENTIST

While at Stanford, Olukotun cofounded several companies for which he led research and development as chief scientist. In September 2000, he formed Afara Websystems, aimed at finding commercial applications for the Hydra multiprocessor, specifically in the area of designing and building low power server systems with multiprocessor chips. He thought Hydra chips would be particularly beneficial to data centers, which could employ multiprocessors. He called the commercial version of his technology Niagara, and Afara found an interested buyer in Sun Microsystems, a company that was well known for its computers and software. Sun purchased Afara in August 2002 and began to implement Niagara in its products. In 2010, Sun was bought out by Oracle, which continued to use the Niagara multiprocessor in various devices.

In April 2014, Olukotun became the cofounder and chief scientist of Migo, a tech company in the San Francisco Bay Area. This company focused on the financial services of emerging markets. It used predictive analytics to generate instant credit scores for people without bank accounts who have access to cellular phones, to aid them in getting loans. These analytics also provided banks with ways to offer lines of credit and other financial products to this previously untapped group of consumers. According to Olukotun's LinkedIn profile, he continued to work for the company into the 2020s.

SAMBANOVA SYSTEMS

In November 2017, Olukotun cofounded SambaNova Systems with his fellow University of Michigan alumni Rodrigo Liang and Christopher Ré. Olukotun served as chief technologist for the company. Liang, SambaNova's CEO, had previously worked with Olukotun at Afara as its director of engineering and went on to work at Sun and then Oracle where he became a senior vice president for Oracle. Ré, a Macarthur Fellow in 2015, was an assistant professor of computer science at Stanford. Located in Palo Alto, California, SambaNova focused on creating a new platform for chips meant specifically for AI operations. Improved AI was widely seen as a next step for computing technology, due to its vast potential in predicting customer needs and optimizing processes to meet them.

One of the company's first products was DataScale, a rack-based system intended for high-performance computing and data centers running advanced AI programs. The proprietary chip system was designed to optimize dataflow and allow cutting-edge speeds, which would help users bring new AI-driven products and services to consumers. DataScale was touted for the potential to create improvements in everything from self-driving automobiles to image processing to developing training models for treating complex health issues. The company also offered DataScale as part of a monthly "dataflow-as-a-service" subscription product.

One of SambaNova Systems' first customers was the Argonne National Laboratory, the first national laboratory in the United States. Based in Chicago, Argonne was chartered by the US Atomic Energy Commission in the 1940s to work on the Manhattan Project. Since then, it has pioneered research in nuclear energy, computing, and energy storage. Rick Stevens, an associate laboratory director at Argonne, told the University of Michigan, "We're working on important research efforts including those focused on cancer, COVID-19, and many others, and using AI to automate parts of the development process is key to our success. The SambaNova DataScale architecture offers us the ability to train and infer from multiple large and small models concurrently and deliver orders of magnitude performance improvements over GPUs." Other customers included the Lawrence Livermore National Laboratory (LLNL), the Los Alamos National Laboratory (LANL), and the National Nuclear Security Administration (NNSA) at the US Department of Energy.

Olukotun's startup also received the attention of Silicon Valley giants like Intel and Alphabet, who liked the idea of AI applications that could build new hardware and software platforms from the ground up. By 2019, those two companies had already invested $150 million in SambaNova Systems, which allowed it to expand its number of employees from fifty to one hundred.

In October 2021, SambaNova launched its Generative Pre-trained Transformer (GPT) language model as part of its dataflow-as-a-service product. The company said that GPT would allow subscribers to develop AI and machine learning (ML) language applications quickly and easily, which they expected would further increase the market for AI and ML.

AWARDS, ACCOLADES, AND PUBLICATIONS

Over the course of his decades-long career Olukotun received numerous honors and recognitions for his pioneering work. In 2006, he became a fellow of the Association for Computing Machinery (ACM), which recognizes professional and technical excellence by professionals in the computing field. In 2008, he was named a fellow of the Institute of Electrical and Electronics Engineers (IEEE), which similarly honors individuals who have produced an extraordinary accomplishment in the realm of electrical and electronics engineering.

In 2017, the University of Michigan presented Olukotun with the Michigan Engineering Alumni Merit Award. The following year he received the IEEE Computer Society Harry H. Goode Award. In 2021, he was inducted into the National Academy of Engineering (NAE), a nonprofit entity that seeks to promote engineering and research as well as honor the accomplishments of preeminent engineers across the United States.

Olukotun also cowrote the book *Chip Multiprocessor Architecture: Techniques to Improve Throughput and Latency (Synthesis Lectures on Computer Architecture)*, published in 2007. He served as coeditor, with Stephen W. Keckler and H. Peter Hofstee, of another book, *Multicore Processors and Systems (Integrated Circuits and Systems)*, published in 2009.

SUGGESTED READING

"Bio." *Stanford University*, 2012, arsenalfc. stanford.edu/kunle/. Accessed 18 Oct. 2021.

D'Onofrio, Jillian. "SambaNova Systems, a Startup in the Hot AI Hardware Space, Scores $150 Million Investment from Intel and Alphabet." *Forbes*, 1 Apr. 2019, www.forbes.com/sites/jilliandonfro/2019/04/01/sambanova-systems-a-startup-in-the-hot-ai-hardware-space-scores-150-million-investment-from-intel-and-alphabet/. Accessed 18 Oct. 2021.

"For Black History Month, CSE Spotlights Faculty and Alumni in Academia." *Electrical Engineering and Computer Science Department*, University of Michigan, 1 Feb. 2017, cse.engin.umich.edu/stories/for-black-history-month-cse-spotlights-faculty-and-alumni-in-academia. Accessed 20 Oct. 2021.

"Kunle Olukotun." *Stanford Profiles*, Stanford University, profiles.stanford.edu/kunle-olukotun?releaseVersion=9.4.0. Accessed 18 Oct. 2021.

"SambaNova, Founded by Alumnus Kunle Olukotun, Emerges from Stealth Mode with AI-Accelerated HPC System." *Electrical Engineering and Computer Science Department*, University of Michigan, 17 Dec. 2020, cse.engin.umich.edu/stories/sambanova-founded-by-alumnus-kunle-olukotun-emerges-from-stealth-mode-with-ai-accelerated-hpc-system. Accessed 20 Oct. 2021.

"Spotlight on Kunle Olukotun." *Duquesne Light Company*, newsroom.duquesnelight.com/black-history-month-spotlight-on-kunle-olukotun#. Accessed 27 Oct. 2021.

—*Christopher Mari*

Burgess Owens

Born: August 2, 1951
Occupation: Politician

On November 2020, business executive, entrepreneur, and former professional football safety Burgess Owens was elected to represent Utah's Fourth Congressional District in the US House of Representatives, narrowly edging out Democratic incumbent Ben McAdams, a onetime Salt Lake County mayor and state senator. Although his victory had initially seemed improbable due in part to McAdams's established political career, Owens, a Black Republican, noted that his desire to preserve conservative values in the country and foster unification had prompted him to officially enter the political world. His unlikely new role as congressman came after ten seasons in the National Football League (NFL) and nearly forty years after his Super Bowl championship with the Oakland Raiders. "It's amazing to look back and see the things that influence our lives," he told Lee Benson for *Deseret News* (5 Feb. 2021). "I never thought I'd be in this position after my career in football."

EARLY LIFE, EDUCATION, AND LAUNCHING A FOOTBALL CAREER

Clarence Burgess Owens was born on August 2, 1951, in Columbus, Ohio, where his Texas-raised father, a World War II veteran, could pursue postgraduate studies in agronomy at Ohio State University (OSU). During the era of Jim Crow laws, education and learning opportunities were inequitable in the racially segregated South. By the 1960s, Owens had relocated with his family to Tallahassee, Florida, as his father had joined the faculty of Florida A&M University (FAMU); his mother taught at the middle/secondary school level. Later, he would often credit his parents with instilling in him the conservative values, such as family, education, and patriotism as well as work ethic that he became so enthusiastic about. "I had a very good mom and dad, and they asked us always to think outside the box, to ask questions, and to be involved," he told Henri Mattila for *Merion West* (26 Feb. 2018). As a teen, he received his education at James S. Rickards High School, which became fully desegregated in the 1967–68 school year. Serving as a running back for the school's Raiders, he was one of the first Black players on the newly integrated team. During his final two years at Rickards, he made an impression in the sport as he amassed over 1,550 rushing yards and nineteen touchdowns.

After graduating high school in 1969, Owens accepted a scholarship to play for the University of Miami, where he wanted to study marine biology. From 1970 to 1972, he amassed 160 tackles, three recovered fumbles, and eight interceptions as a defensive back for the Hurricanes. In 1972, he earned first team, All-American honors from *Time* and the *Sporting News*, along with being named to the first team, All-South independent team. A year later, he was invited to play for the South team

Photo via Wikimedia Commons

in the Senior Bowl, an annual showcase for elite senior college players. His performance earned him defensive Most Valuable Player (MVP) honors and a first-round selection in the 1973 NFL Draft.

JOINING THE NFL AND WINNING THE SUPER BOWL

Upon receiving his Bachelor of Science degree in biology with a minor in chemistry, Owens embarked on a professional playing career with the New York Jets, who picked him first and thirteenth overall in 1973. His rookie year as a safety was particularly marked by two kickoff returns totaling 103 yards, including an 82-yard touchdown against the Denver Broncos in the home opener. For his effort, he was named the Jets' Rookie of the Year and voted to the NFL's All-Rookie Team. After taking part in a consecutive fourteen-game season beginning in 1974, the following year's season saw him register three interceptions in eleven games. Starting in fourteen games once more in the 1976–77 season, he set the team up for a 14-yard rushing touchdown after recovering a fumble in the Jets' 34–0 shutout of the Tampa Bay Buccaneers. Over the next three seasons, he intercepted the ball fourteen times.

Following his 1980 trade to the Oakland Raiders for a sixth-round Draft pick, he started all sixteen regular-season games and made three interceptions. With a regular-season finish in second in the AFC West with an 11–5 record that clinched a wild card berth, the Raiders went on to defeat the Houston Oilers and eke out a surprising 14–12 divisional playoff victory against the Cleveland Browns, amid below-freezing temperatures. Also beating the San Diego Chargers, the AFC's top seed, 34–27 before defeating the Philadelphia Eagles 27–10, they were the first to claim the Super Bowl trophy after having gone into the playoffs as a wild card team. "We had a good time being the underdogs. There is nothing more rewarding than winning when you're looked at as not being capable of doing so," Owens told Trent Toone for the *Deseret News* (30 May 2013).

Owens followed that achievement with a disappointing 1981 season, however, managing only two interceptions in sixteen regular-season starts and watching his Super Bowl championship team miss the playoffs. In his final 1982 NFL season, he had eight starts and four interceptions for the Raiders, newly relocated to Los Angeles. After amassing an 8–1 record during the strike-shortened season, LA claimed the AFC's top seed and a first-round playoff victory (27–10) against the Browns before suffering a second-round loss to the Jets (14–17) in the AFC divisional playoffs.

A POST-NFL CAREER IN BUSINESS

Prior to retiring in January 1983, Owens experienced another life-changing event: his conversion to the Church of Jesus Christ of Latter-day Saints, which became official on December 31, 1982. Owens, who grew up practicing the Baptist faith, learned more about the Church of Jesus Christ of Latter-day Saints from Raiders teammates who were members. "We had won a Super Bowl, I was starting (on the defense) and having success, and we were doing pretty well financially," he told Toone. "But there was still a void that needed to be filled. . . . We knew something else was out there that had some answers for us."

Once his football career ended, Owens, inspired to explore the opportunities of free enterprise, moved his family back to New York City and launched an electronic technology venture with his brother focused on sales of expense-tracking devices. After seven years, he had filed for bankruptcy and was forced to relocate his family to a small apartment in the borough of Brooklyn. He took on odd jobs, sweeping chimneys during the day and working as a security guard for overnight shifts, to support his family. "That was a very humbling moment," he admitted to Thomas Burr for *The Salt Lake Tribune* (6 July 2020). "It was also a very key moment in my life that at the end of the long day, standing in the basement apartment, looking outside and just thinking that I knew this was not the way it was going to end because I believe in the American promise of second chances."

Owens's fortunes turned around in January 1989, when he accepted a position in Philadelphia, working as a sales manager for the software firm WordPerfect. During his five years (1989–94) with the company, he marketed their products to area companies while also offering seminars and collaborating with clients to get any problems with the software resolved. In January 1995, he began serving as senior vice president of the sports division at Summit Financial, where he offered educational, support, and financial resources tailored toward professional athlete clients. After six years, he went on to work as an account executive for Sprint/Nextel (2001–08) before taking on a similar role at Motorola (2008–09).

MOVING TO UTAH AND RUNNING FOR CONGRESS

From 2009 to 2013, Owens returned to entrepreneurship, operating his own business, Pure and Simple Systems, which provided residential and commercial clients with environmentally sensitive products. During that four-year period, he not only relocated to the Salt Lake City, Utah, suburb of Draper but also wrote the e-book *It's All about Team: Exposing the Black Talented Tenth* (2012). Continuing to write, he followed with two more books: *Liberalism: Or How to Turn Good Men into Whiners, Weenies and Wimps* (2016), in which he blames liberal and Democratic policies for the decline of the Black community, and *Why I Stand: From Freedom to the Killing Fields of Socialism* (2018), in which he identifies Marxism and socialism as dangerous to American culture, particularly for the Black community.

Meanwhile, Owens also garnered attention as a conservative commentator on several Fox News channel shows, including *Hannity* and *Trish Regan Primetime*. During a September 2018 appearance on the Fox Business Network's *Varney & Co.*, he described a Nike campaign featuring professional football quarterback Colin Kaepernick, who had instigated NFL protests by kneeling during the national anthem, a move previously publicly condemned by Owens, as a leftist assault comparable to the September 11, 2001, attacks and Pearl Harbor. After penning a May 2019 opinion piece in *The Wall Street Journal* opposing reparations, he testified at a House Judiciary subcommittee hearing on the subject.

In November 2019, after stepping down as CEO of the nonprofit aimed at providing services to combat generational incarceration that he had recently founded, Second Chance 4 Youth (SC4Y), Owens announced his bid to represent Utah's primarily White Fourth Congressional district in the House. Despite his lack of political experience, he campaigned as a pro-Donald Trump Republican, adopting a platform opposing socialist ideologies that he viewed as divisive in favor of conservative policies and a strong work ethic. "I happen to be drawn to a party that believes in freedom . . . and believes that each and every one of us can succeed if we pay the price to do so," he told Burr.

WINNING THE CONGRESSIONAL RACE

At the virtual state party convention in April 2020, Owens was nominated to appear on the primary ballot. His next major appearance was the June 2020 Republican primary debate, during which he faced off against state representative Kim Coleman, nonprofit CEO Trent Christensen, and former KSL NewsRadio host Jay McFarland. During the televised event, Owens positioned himself as a patriotic candidate who denounced Black Lives Matter (BLM) protests and mask-wearing requirements to combat the coronavirus disease 2019 (COVID-19) pandemic as tools being used by the left to divide the entire country.

On June 30, Owens claimed the Republican primary, after earning over 43 percent of the vote. Within days, he had received President Trump's endorsement, and in August he was invited to speak at the Republican National Convention (RNC), which he regarded as a huge accomplishment in his political run. "I'm a part of a much bigger team in Congress that can turn things around," he told Kristian Dyer for *Sports Illustrated*'s Jets Country channel (26 Aug. 2020). "In the perspective of my life, this is much bigger than the Super Bowl." Facing Democratic incumbent Ben McAdams at October's general election debate, Owens again criticized BLM protests and mask mandates as well as COVID-19 relief for Democratic states while also backing health-care protections for people with pre-existing conditions. He additionally downplayed appearances on QAnon-linked programs. In the November election, he defeated McAdams by a small margin (47.7 percent to 46.7 percent).

Shortly after taking office in January 2021, following the January 6 riot at the US Capitol, Owens objected, alongside fellow Republican lawmakers, to the certification of some of the Electoral College votes from the 2020 presidential election that had indicated Democrat Joe Biden's victory. At the end of January, he was assigned to the Committee on the Judiciary and the Committee on Education and Labor. Citing his childhood experiences of segregation, he denounced comparisons of Georgia's voter ID law signed in March to Jim Crow, arguing that such comparisons were offensive and perpetuated what he viewed as leftist stereotypes regarding the capabilities of the Black community. By the beginning of 2022, he had opposed several pieces of legislation, including the pandemic relief package The American Rescue Plan, the sweeping police reform bill The George Floyd Justice in Policing Act, and a voting rights bill. Meanwhile, he also introduced legislation to restrict the teaching in federal institutions of critical race theory.

PERSONAL LIFE

Owens and his wife, Josie, had six children together before divorcing. He is also a prostate cancer survivor.

SUGGESTED READING

Benson, Lee. "From the Super Bowl to Congress, with a BYU Assist." *Deseret News*, 5 Feb. 2021, www.deseret.com/utah/2021/2/5/22261712/burgess-owens-nfl-player-from-the-super-bowl-to-congress-with-a-byu-assist. Accessed 10 Jan. 2022.

Burr, Thomas. "Meet Burgess Owens, the Utah Republican Who Seeks to Replace Rep. Ben McAdams." *The Salt Lake Tribune*, 6 July 2020, www.sltrib.com/news/politics/2020/07/06/meet-burgess-owens-utah/. Accessed 10 Jan. 2022.

Dyer, Kristian. "For Burgess Owens, Speaking at the Republican National Convention Is Bigger Than the Super Bowl." *Jets Country*, Sports Illustrated, 26 Aug. 2020, www.si.com/nfl/jets/news/ny-jets-burgess-owens-says-republican-convention-bigger-than-super-bowl. Accessed 10 Jan. 2022.

Owens, Burgess. "From Super Bowl Champion to Conservative Thinker: An Interview with Burgess Owens." Interview by Henri Mattila. *Merion West*, 26 Feb. 2018, merionwest.com/2018/02/26/from-super-bowl-champion-to-conservative-thinker-an-interview-with-burgess-owens/. Accessed 14 Jan. 2022.

Toone, Trent. "Former Oakland Raider Recounts LDS Conversion." *Deseret News*, 30 May 2013, www.deseret.com/2013/5/30/20520441/former-oakland-raider-recounts-lds-conversion#the-burgess-and-josie-owens-family. Accessed 10 Jan. 2022.

—*Bertha Muteba*

Oyèrónké Oyěwùmí

Born: November 10, 1957
Occupation: Sociologist

Oyèrónké Oyěwùmí is a Nigerian sociologist who studies gender and familial relationships in precolonial Yoruba culture as well as race and Western perceptions of Africa. She won the Distinguished Africanist Award from the US–based African Studies Association in 2021, becoming the first African woman to receive the award. In her acceptance speech, she described her work in broader terms. "The focus of my research is on gender, hierarchy, and the construction of knowledge," she said, as quoted by the *Black Agenda Review* (9 Feb. 2022). "My work exposes gender as a colonial category calling into question the Eurocentric idea that gender categories are natural, universal, and inherent in the way in which human communities have organized and thought about themselves."

The cornerstone of Oyěwùmí's work is a book called *The Invention of Women: Making an African Sense of Western Gender Discourses*, which was first published in 1997. In it,

Oyěwùmí, who comes from the Yoruba people in West Africa, writes that precolonial Yoruba culture was organized according to age and seniority, not gender. As evidenced by its genderless language, gender was simply not a way in which the Yoruba made distinctions among people. The concept of gender, and with it the subjugation of those who were gendered as female, came to Yoruba through Western contact during the slave trade. *The Invention of Women*, which won a Distinguished Book Award from the American Sociological Association, among other honors, changed the way scholars across the globe thought about gender.

EARLY LIFE

Oyèrónké Oyěwùmí was born in Jos, Nigeria, on November 10, 1957. As a Yoruba—a member of a West African ethnic group whose people live mostly in the southwestern part of Nigeria—she described herself as an immigrant in the city of Jos. "Spending my early years in a space that was not Yoruba-dominant attuned me to the fact that there are different ways of being and ingrained in me a profound understanding of the Yoruba saying, 'Ona kan ko w'oja' (There is not one road to the market)," she explained when she received the Distinguished Africanist Award in 2021. She came to appreciate the diversity of cultures and languages in Jos, which would later aid her academic life.

Her father, Oba Oladunni, became the Soun, or ruler, of Ògbómòṣó, a city in Nigeria's Oyo State, in 1973. Her mother, Igbayilola, was the olori, or senior royal wife among several others. Oyěwùmí is the eighth of twenty-six siblings, all of whom lived at the royal palace. In the introduction to her book *The Invention of Women*, Oyěwùmí wrote that the palace was "the center of daily rituals and of a constant stream of townspeople coming to pay homage and bringing their various stories to my father and mother." In Ògbómòṣó, Yoruba tradition, and the viscerally immediate presence of her ancestors buried in the palace courtyard, shaped her daily life.

EDUCATION IN NIGERIA AND THE UNITED STATES

Oyěwùmí earned her bachelor's degree from the prestigious University of Ibadan in western Nigeria in the early 1980s. One of her professors was Peter Ekeh, a scholar who

Photo courtesy of Oyeronke Oyewumi, via Wikimedia Commons

was best known for his theories about how the legacy of colonialism has shaped modern Africa. His thinking, Oyěwùmí said in her speech, "influenced my own research, particularly as I was thinking of how gender is implicated in the operation of publics in the post-colonial state."

With Ekeh's encouragement, Oyěwùmí pursued her graduate studies at the University of California, Berkeley. Intrigued by burgeoning scholarship in women and gender, she enrolled as a student in the sociology department in 1983. The unexpected notions she encountered as a student at Berkeley—about Africa, women, and race—profoundly influenced her scholarship. For instance, professors and peers wondered why Oyěwùmí was studying sociology, and not anthropology. She was confused by the question. "When I asked why I must study anthropology, several of my peers informed me that sociologists studied their own societies, but anthropologists studied other societies. I said, 'Voilà, that is why I am a sociologist! I am African, studying African societies,'" she said in her speech. "But what they were alluding to is the deeply ingrained racial and racist idea that sociology was founded to study modern societies, and Africa was not a part of the modern world."

In many ways, Oyěwùmí's graduate school experience was a crash course in Western notions about other cultures. She worked as a teaching assistant in the African American Studies department, where she learned about race as a social category and as an aspect of her identity. "It was my involvement with the emerging interdiscipline of Black Studies that taught me about American society and provided me with practical knowledge that I needed in order to survive graduate school, and indeed life," she said in her speech. She was also introduced to Black Feminism, studying with the groundbreaking scholar Barbara Christian, who provided her with the language to describe intersections of race, gender, and nationalism.

Other classes in gender left her frustrated and puzzled. Descriptions of the supposedly universal concept of womanhood, rooted in subservience to men, did not ring true to her. She was told that physical differences between men and women were exaggerated in every culture, and always to the detriment of women. Oyěwùmí struggled with this assertion because the Yoruba language, as with many African languages, does not distinguish among genders. English words like "sister" and "husband" are not gender-specific in Yoruba, and many African social institutions are non-gendered. This observation provided the cornerstone of her scholarship.

THE INTERSECTION OF AFRICAN AND WESTERN CULTURES

The first chapter of Oyěwùmí's doctoral dissertation was called "White Woman's Burden: African Women in Western Feminist Discourse." Inspired by African American feminist discourse, the chapter signaled her interest in how Western cultural thought smothers people's ability to describe their own experiences. "I was looking at the way African women were represented [in the West] as victims, as beasts of burden, as prostitutes, as coming from a violent culture, as coming from a culture in which men had impunity," Oyěwùmí said on a podcast for Radio Web MACBA (10 Jan. 2020). These "historical colonial stereotypes of Africans" overwhelm the actual experiences of African women and dominate transnational feminist discourse, she argued.

Naming this confluence of anti-Black racism, colonialism, and feminism, Oyěwùmí said on the podcast, felt radical at the time, particularly coming from an African woman. It was certainly too radical for some; the chapter

lost Oyěwùmí the chair of her dissertation committee, a White woman, who described it as "a slap in the face."

Oyěwùmí was surprised by the reaction of her professor and others who accused her of undercutting their own studies and the discipline of women's studies itself, which depends on the existence of women and gender. But Oyěwùmí says that this is a misinterpretation of her work, which actually gives credence to one of the foundational assertions of feminist thought: that gender is a social construct. "Part of what I'm doing is to historicize how gender became important in the colonies as a result of colonizers [bringing] their ideas of gender" to cultures like the Yoruba, she explained on the podcast.

Oyěwùmí wanted to investigate how gender was differently constructed in Yoruba society, and returned to Nigeria for field work. She set out with the intention of interviewing families about how gender informed their relationships with one another. She wrote out a questionnaire, realizing belatedly that she had written it in English. The mistake proved to be prophetic. Translating the questions to Yoruba presented the same conflict she had encountered at Berkeley. She could not ask: how many sons do you have, and how many daughters? There were no words to distinguish between the two. "It became clear that my questionnaire was imposing gender on the discourse through language," she said on the podcast. Oyěwùmí was forced to approach her questions about gender epistemologically. "Much of the evidence that I needed, I already knew," she shared. "It was *how* those things constitute evidence, and how these things were understood in the culture that was the issue."

THE INVENTION OF WOMEN

Oyěwùmí explores these quandaries in her best-known book, *The Invention of Women: Making an African Sense of Western Gender Discourses*, published in 1997. The book challenges the assumption she had encountered in her classes at Berkeley: that gender is "a fundamental organizing principle in all societies," as Nupur Chaudhuri stated in a review for the *NWSA Journal* (Spring 2001). In the book, Oyěwùmí writes that "woman" was not a social category in Yoruba culture in precolonial times. She argues that Western culture is body-oriented, while Yoruba was a hierarchical culture, but status was organized by seniority or age. Contact with Western ideas through the slave trade not only changed the Yorubas' ideas about gender, but their social and political structures. When Yorubas recognized distinct genders, people gendered as women became ostracized. They lost property rights and political power as they were pushed from their previous positions in favor of people who Westerners deemed to be men.

The Invention of Women won the Distinguished Book Award from the Sex and Gender Section of the American Sociological Association in 1998 and that year was also a finalist for the prestigious Herskovits Award of the African Studies Association. Moreover, the work had a huge influence on other scholars. As she explained in her own words in her speech, "My research caused a paradigm shift in the academic study of gender."

OTHER WORKS

Oyěwùmí's subsequent work rested on the foundation of the ideas presented in *The Invention of Women*. Influential articles include "Alice in Motherland: Reading Alice Walker on Africa and Screening the Color Black" (2001), which philosopher Lewis Gordon wrote in an online article for the American Philosophical Association (23 Mar. 2018), "offers a courageous critique of the famed novelist Alice Walker's portrayal of female circumcision/genital mutilation in Africa as ultimately not about its purported subject matter." Oyěwùmí's critique argues that Walker's writings play into harmful stereotypes about African women.

In the articles "Ties that (Un)Bind: Feminism, Sisterhood and Other Foreign Relations" (2001) and "Abiyamo: Theorizing African Motherhood" (2003), Oyěwùmí examines familial relationships, one of her animating sociological interests. In the latter article, she writes about the Yoruba concept of motherhood as a community project—motherhood being distinct from the individual concept of a mother. Oyěwùmí returns to these ideas in her 2015 book, *What Gender Is Motherhood?: Changing Yorùbá Ideals of Power, Procreation, and Identity in the Age of Modernity*.

Other notable articles and book chapters include: "Conceptualizing Gender: The Eurocentric Foundations of Feminist Concepts and the Challenge of African Epistemologies" (2002); "Multiculturalism or Multibodism: On the Impossible Intersections of Race and Gender in White Feminist and Black Nationalist Discourses" (2001); and "Conceptualizing Gender in African Studies," (2006). Oyěwùmí has also edited several collections, including *African Women and Feminism: Reflecting on the Politics of Sisterhood* (2003); *African Gender Studies: A Reader* (2005); and *Gender Epistemologies in Africa: Gendering Traditions, Spaces, Social Institutions, and Identities* (2011).

Oyěwùmí is a professor in the Department of Sociology at Stony Brook University in New York state.

SUGGESTED READING

Chaudhuri, Nupur. Review of *The Invention of Women: Making an African Sense of Western Gender Discourse*, by Oyèrónké Oyěwùmí. *NWSA Journal*, vol. 13, no. 1, 2001, pp. 172–76.

Gordon, Lewis. "Black Issues in Philosophy: The African Decolonial Thought of Oyèrónké Oyěwùmí." *American Philosophical Association*, 23. Mar. 2018, blog.apaonline.org/2018/03/23/black-issues-in-philosophy-the-african-decolonial-thought-of-oyeronke-oyewumi/. Accessed 11 July 2022.

"Son[i]a #303: Oyèrónké Oyěwùmí." *Soni[i]a* from Radio Web MACBA, 10 Jan. 2020, rwm.macba.cat/en/sonia/sonia-303-oyeronke-oyewumi. Accessed 6 July 2022.

"SPEECH: (Re)Centering African Epistemologies: An Intellectual Journey, Oyèrónké Oyěwùmí, 2021." *Black Agenda Report*, 9 Feb. 2022, blackagendareport.com/speech-recentring-african-epistemologies-intellectual-journey-oyeronke-oyewumi-2021. Accessed 6 July 2022.

SELECTED WORKS

The Invention of Women, 1997; *African Gender Studies*, 2005; *Gender Epistemologies in Africa*, 2011; *What Gender Is Motherhood?*, 2015

—Molly Hagan

Regé-Jean Page

Born: April 27, 1988
Occupation: Actor

Initially, the news that unknown actor Regé-Jean Page had been cast as the Duke of Hastings in producer Shonda Rhimes's television series *Bridgerton* was met with backlash. Some people argued that the casting was wrong because the duke character, Simon Bassett, was originally described as being a blue-eyed White man in the series' source material, Julia Quinn's best-selling novel *The Duke and I* (2000). Despite such objections, however, Page stayed on to play the leading man. And after *Bridgerton* debuted on Netflix in late 2020 and proved a smash hit, the casting was widely seen as an enormous success. Page quickly became an international sensation, deemed the next Brad Pitt by both friends and fans. It was a somewhat ironic twist then, that the next outcry surrounding his role in *Bridgerton* would be over his decision to leave the series to pursue other film and television projects.

Although his departure from *Bridgerton* was mourned by fans, Page's performance in the series was not only a career breakthrough for him but had significant cultural resonance. For one of the first times in Hollywood's history, a Black man was playing a Regency-era Duke. While reflecting on the impact of his presence in *Bridgerton*, Page told Angelique Jackson for *Variety* (26 May 2021), "It's so simple. I can get on a horse and I can put it on the screen; that's step one. I can be royalty, and [other people of color] can see the possibility of being royalty. Standing there, wearing the boots and the jacket, doing the dances, inhabiting a space that is perfectly possible for me to inhabit, changes how you see the world."

EARLY LIFE AND EDUCATION

Regé-Jean Page was born in London, England, on April 27, 1988, to a Zimbabwean nurse and an English preacher. The third of four children, his family moved to his mother's home of Harare, Zimbabwe, when he was a toddler, and it was there that he attended elementary school. While growing up in the city, Page developed a love of storytelling and would put on plays with his toys. He also often found himself marveling at the natural beauty of his surroundings.

Life in Zimbabwe was not always easy, however. The country did not gain its independence until 1980 and subsequently vestiges of European imperialism were still everywhere—especially when it came to racial tensions. As such, Page was especially young when he became aware of just how contentious his parents' relationship was. "In America, you can still feel the echoes of slavery, and Zimbabwe is *very much* feeling the echoes of British colonial rule," he told Emma Brown for *Interview Magazine* (1 June 2016). "It's very hard to craft an identity in that environment as a young, mixed-race man. I learned from the age of three that I was a walking political statement."

When he was fourteen, Page's family returned to the United Kingdom, where they settled in North London. As a teenager Page found himself angry at the world's injustices and decided to channel his frustrations into punk rock music after starting a band with his brother. In addition to performing and building a community with other artistic people, he loved how punk let him challenge societal norms and break down walls. He explained this to Max Williams in an interview for *Square Mile* magazine (8 Dec. 2020), "What else are you going to do as a teenager? You're going to scream at people one way or another. You might as well do it in a productive way." It was around this time that his parents decided to enroll Page into a Saturday school program where he spent three hours every week dancing, singing, and acting. The school recognized his natural talent and helped him land small, paid roles. At first, acting was a hobby for him—a way to make a little extra money to buy himself a Gameboy.

Page began studying sound engineering at university as a compromise with his mother, as it was a technical degree, which made her happy, but still allowed him to be in the arts. However, after taking part in the National Youth Theatre program, something shifted in him, and he realized that he wanted to be an actor. Over the next two years he auditioned until he was accepted at the Drama Centre—a London-based university that had produced famous alumni including Tom Hardy, Michael Fassbender, and Pierce Brosnan. He would go on to graduate from the renowned institution in 2013 with a Bachelor of Arts (BA) degree in acting.

EARLY CAREER

During his last year at the Drama Centre, Page was cast in the role of Crowther in a production of *The History Boys* at the Crucible theater in Sheffield, England. Reflecting on the experience in *Interview* magazine, the actor stated, "It was a perfect first job. There were some great senior cast members for us to look up to and learn from, but enough young cast members that we were always messing about with each other. We had a great young director, Michael Longhurst. I owe him a huge amount for giving me that first break. You don't forget that."

In 2015 Page landed a supporting role in the BBC's *Waterloo Road*, in which he played a down-on-his-luck young gay teacher named Guy Braxton. Soon afterwards, he was cast as Solanio in the Shakespeare's Globe Theatre production of *The Merchant of Venice*.

Page was introduced to US audiences in 2016 when he was cast to play the character of Chicken George in the History Channel's reboot of the television miniseries *Roots*. It was not until he gave his mother a copy of the script pages that he realized how important and meaningful the project really was. Up until then, Page's mother had not been particularly interested in the productions in which he had acted. However, with *Roots* she suddenly became concerned that he would not give a good enough performance. Fortunately, however, that was not the case, and Page stood out as a highlight on the series. Reflecting on dynamic among the largely Black cast of *Roots* for *Interview* magazine, he stated, "There's something that happens when someone walks on set and they're carrying something personal to them, you feel it as another actor and you become very careful and caring with them. The thing that you're throwing back and forth at each other in the scene is electric, and also incredibly precious."

It was thanks to his performance in *Roots* that Hollywood's doors began to open for Page. In 2016 he found himself awestruck in a conversation with actor Sterling K. Brown, whom he admired greatly for his performance as prosecutor Christopher Darden in *American Crime Story: The People v. O. J. Simpson* (2016). Brown was equally impressed with Page's clear interest in illuminating the human condition rather than making millions of dollars. Over time, Brown became a mentor to Page.

In 2017, Page was cast in the legal series *For the People* in the role of US attorney Leonard Knox. Famed television producer Shonda Rhimes backed the series, and while it was not considered a success and only ran for two seasons, it put Page on Rhimes's radar. This would lead to what would become his breakout role.

BRIDGERTON

On July 20, 2018, Netflix released a statement that Rhimes was producing an adaptation of the *Bridgerton* historical romance novels by Julia Quinn. The novels, which Quinn began writing in 2000, were already international best sellers that had been translated into more than forty languages worldwide. When it was announced in 2019 that the series would reinvent Regency London by having a racially diverse cast—with Page playing the romantic lead of the Duke of Hastings, Simon Bassett—the news was met with a significant negative response. Some fans of the books claimed to be disappointed that Page did not have Simon's trademark "icy blue eyes," seemingly a coded way to say that he was not White.

Despite these pointed complaints, *Bridgerton* proved to be a smash success. After debuting in December 2020 it became the most-watched Netflix program in dozens of countries worldwide and broke numerous records for the streaming platform. A large part of its overwhelming reception was due to Page's performance and newfound status as a heartthrob. He was quickly deemed the breakout star of the series, and earned an Emmy nomination for his role. He also won the 2021 NAACP Image Award for Outstanding Actor in a Drama, among other honors.

The series also generated significant cultural attention for its once-controversial racially diverse casting, Many critics and commentators noted the groundbreaking nature of having people of color play European nobility. Page himself discussed the significance of his career's trajectory from *Roots* to *Bridgerton*, telling Jackson, "The last time, and only other time, I had sat in a nineteenth-century carriage I was being dragged away from my family [and sold to a new master] in the UK. Next time I sat in that carriage, I own the carriage as royalty. That is the progress in storytelling to fill out that picture. What gave me the greatest satisfaction was balancing that scale."

Despite the fact that it had skyrocketed his career to a new level, Page decided to leave the *Bridgerton* series after the first season. He felt comfortable doing so because Quinn's book series follows a different member of the Bridgerton family in each novel and the second season would no longer focus on his character's relationship with Lady Daphne. Furthermore, Page believed that it would allow the show to leave their happy ending intact instead of trying to find a way to inject more drama into it.

FURTHER WORK

As a rising international star, Page was quickly offered numerous exciting film and television projects. However, the actor still had to navigate the rocky terrain of racial representation in Hollywood. For example, according to the *Hollywood Reporter* in 2021, DC Entertainment's chief creative officer, Geoff Johns, allegedly rejected Page for the role of Superman's grandfather Seg-El on the Syfy network's series *Krypton* because he was Black.

Page did not let that rejection stop his career's momentum, however. As a result of his performance in *Bridgerton*, he was invited to host *Saturday Night Live* in February 2021 and was cast in the Russo brothers' action movie *The Gray Man* (2022). He was also announced to have a role in *Dungeons and Dragons: Thieves Honor*, a film based around the iconic role-playing game. The significance of landing high-profile roles as a Black man was not lost on Page, who saw his work as a way to bring change to the societal problems that he raged against as a punk rock teen. "As Black people, we're very used to empathizing with the world through white people's eyes, because they're the protagonists," he told *Variety* magazine. "I know what it's like to look at the world and empathize with Superman because I spent my whole life doing that. What's revolutionary, in its own way, is getting folks to see the world through my eyes, because then they are in my skin and looking at the world through me."

SUGGESTED READING

Jackson, Angelique. "From Dashing Duke to Hollywood Heartthrob: Regé-Jean Page Reflects on Life beyond *Bridgerton*." *Variety*, 26 May 2021, variety.com/2021/film/features/rege-jean-page-bridgerton-dungeons-and-dragons-james-bond-1234980721/. Accessed 5 May 2022.

Page, Regé-Jean. "Discovery: Regé-Jean Page." Interview by Emma Brown. *Interview Magazine*, 1 June 2016, www.interviewmagazine.com/culture/rege-jean-page. Accessed 5 May 2022.

____. "'Everything's Fuel.' The Wonderful Mind of Regé-Jean Page." Interview by Max Williams. *Square Mile Magazine*, 8 Dec. 2020, squaremile.com/features/rege-jean-page-bridgerton-interview/. Accessed 5 May 2020.

____. "Regé-Jean Page: 'The Reason You Think History Is White Is Because You've Been Lied To.'" Interview by Stuart McGurk. *GQ*, 1 Sept. 2021, www.gq-magazine.co.uk/culture/article/rege-jean-page-interview. Accessed 5 May 2020.

SELECTED WORKS

Waterloo Road, 2015; *Roots*, 2016; *For the People*, 2017; *Bridgerton*, 2020

—*Emily E. Turner*

Pidgeon Pagonis

Born: March 15, 1986
Occupation: Activist

Pidgeon Pagonis is a Chicago-born activist and filmmaker. Though they have been honored by the White House and received a host of other accolades during their life, Pagonis had many hurdles before beginning their activism career. Growing up in Chicago, Pagonis was told that they were born with cancer in their ovaries, but this was an obfuscation of the truth. Pagonis was actually born intersex. Though it is common to be born intersex—some estimates report it as common as being born with red hair, in fact—the term itself is often poorly understood. Intersex people are born with sexual characteristics that thwart attempts to categorize them into strictly binary understandings of sex. These characteristics can include one's genitalia, chromosomes, or sex organs. Intersex people can be any gender, and they may or may not identify as nonbinary, as Pagonis does.

Pagonis, who was raised as a girl, endured a host of painful surgeries as a child, but did not know the real reason for them until they were eighteen years old and gained access to their medical records. The information in these documents drove Pagonis, who was still struggling with their intersex identity, to activism; they did not want others to suffer as they had. In 2020, Pagonis and their organization, Intersex Justice Project, successfully lobbied the Chicago children's hospital where Pagonis had been treated to address the harm its policies had caused intersex people. But for Pagonis, the work is far from over. "While I embrace being intersex, I also mourn what the medical industrial complex did to me to prevent me from ever knowing what it would be like to experience this world, especially intimate relationships, with the beautiful intersex body I was born with," Pagonis told the anti-bullying charity *Ditch the Label* (26 Oct. 2016).

EARLY LIFE AND AIS DIAGNOSIS

Pidgeon Pagonis, who is of Mexican and Greek ancestry, was born on the northwest side of Chicago on March 15, 1986. When they were a few months old, they were diagnosed with a condition called androgen insensitivity syndrome (AIS). People with AIS have XY chromosomes but are resistant to androgens, or male hormones such as testosterone. As they grow up, they develop an outwardly feminine appearance, while remaining genetically male. When Pagonis was one year old, they underwent a gonadectomy, meaning, in Pagonis's case, that doctors removed their internal testes. Doctors told Pagonis's parents that their internal testes were underdeveloped ovaries and needed to be removed or else they would become cancerous during puberty—but this risk may have been overstated. In an explainer video called "Hi I'm Intersex" for their YouTube channel, *Pidgeon* (14 Oct. 2016), Pagonis considered their young parents' alarm and confusion. (Their mother, Laurie Garcia, was only twenty-three years old at the time.) "Imagine being a parent, getting all this information on your firstborn child," they said. "Everything you kind of took for granted is just kind of thrown out the window, and now all these doctors are throwing all these terms at you."

SUBSEQUENT SURGERIES AND GENDER CONFUSION

Pagonis and many other intersex people argue that the medical establishment has been more

Photo courtesy of Pidgeon Pagonis, via Wikimedia Commons

invested in preserving notions of "normal" sex categorization than serving intersex people as they are. Our society, Pagonis says in another video on their YouTube channel (21 Nov. 2016), has "rigid, outdated definitions of gender as two, and only two, opposing, opposite, black-and-white categories that literally never overlap." Driven by these outdated ideas—and the work of controversial psychologist John Money, who advocated that the gender of intersex children should be decided early in life and be supported by genital surgeries—doctors worked to make Pagonis's sex organs and genitalia "match" their assigned gender. After recovering from their gonadectomy, Pagonis's doctors recommended a clitoridectomy, a cosmetic procedure to reduce the size of their clitoris. At eighteen years old, when Pagonis read their medical records, they found that when they were four years old, doctors removed their clitoris entirely.

Pagonis underwent a vaginoplasty when they were eleven years old, though at the time, they did not realize it. Doctors performed the procedure under the auspices of bladder surgery. The surgery left lasting physical and emotional scars. "No matter what they say, or how they sugarcoat it, it's medically sanctioned violence and torture," they told Nara Schoenberg for the *Chicago Tribune* (1 Nov. 2018).

By the time they were in early adolescence, Pagonis knew they would never menstruate, or be able to give birth, but wholeheartedly embraced other aspects of being a girl. They had a cisgender boyfriend, read fashion magazines, played on a travel softball team, and worked for the exclusive retailer Abercrombie & Fitch. Neither Pagonis nor their parents were ever explicitly told that Pagonis was intersex. "My diagnosis was a secret, and I believed the lies they told me about the surgeries and even thought of myself as a cancer survivor," they wrote in their master's thesis, which was titled "The Son They Never Had" and later published in the journal *Narrative Inquiry in Bioethics* (Nov. 2015). "Sparked by the feminizing hormones I began taking in fifth grade, my sexual identity seemed 'normal,' that is, heterosexual female, which satisfied my endocrinologists and family." Pagonis excelled as a student at Trinity High School in River Forest, an all-girls Catholic school, but they felt out of place. "I was so angry about everything: about my body, and about those doctor's appointments, and just knowing that something was horribly wrong," they recalled to Schoenberg.

COLLEGE AND PERSONAL DISCOVERY

In 2004, Pagonis began attending DePaul University in Chicago, becoming the first person in their family to attend college. They first saw their medical records as a first-year student. In a women's studies class, Pagonis learned about AIS for the first time. The description sounded a lot like their own experience, and the medical records proved it. "To say my world fell apart in that instant would be an understatement," Pagonis told *Ditch the Label*. "Everything I thought I knew about myself, and the world around me, became jolted." Pagonis shared the discovery with their professor Laila Farah, who offered emotional support and introduced them to the intersex activist Lynell Stephani Long. With Long's encouragement, Pagonis delved deeper, learning the full breadth of their medical history. "The first thing I read in my medical records was 46, XY male pseudo–hermaphrodite," they wrote in their thesis. "My ears burned. I wanted to beat those words until they admitted they weren't true." Pagonis spoke publicly about their experience for the first time several years later, in 2008, when they presented their undergraduate thesis, an

ethnography about their intersex surgeries. They went on to earn a bachelor's degree that year and a master's degree in 2014 in women and gender studies, both from DePaul.

INTER/ACT AND EARLY ACTIVISM

After coming out to friends and family, Pagonis became an ardent activist on behalf of intersex people. They were angry about the lies they were told and the traumatic procedures they were forced to endure; they did not want other intersex children to suffer the same fate. They began working with an intersex civil rights group as an intern while in college, and later became the communications manager and coordinator of the organization's intersex youth group—the world's first—called Inter/Act. During their time with Inter/Act, Pagonis managed all of the social media accounts and consulted on the MTV comedy series *Faking It*, which featured an intersex character played by actor Bailey de Young. Pagonis's involvement with Inter/Act also launched their career as a public speaker.

In 2012, Pagonis was featured in the documentary film *Intersexion*, directed by New Zealand activist Mani Bruce Mitchell. Mitchell became a mentor to Pagonis, who was also interested in making films. Pagonis participated in the 2012 International Intersex Forum in Stockholm, Sweden, and in 2013, they testified before the Inter-American Commission on Human Rights in Washington, DC. The same year, they were named one of Chicago's "30 Under 30" by the *Windy City Times*. In 2015, the Obama White House honored Pagonis as an LGBT Champion of Change. Recalling the event, Pagonis told Carrie Maxwell for the *Windy City Times* (26 Oct. 2016), "It was a beautiful moment to be able to speak my truth about being intersex in front of everyone there, but most importantly my dad who told me how proud he was of me." At the event, Pagonis also met Joey Soloway, the Emmy Award–winning creator of the television show *Transparent*, about a parent who transitions late in life, who invited Pagonis to play an intersex character on an episode of the show.

THE SON I NEVER HAD AND THE INTERSEX JUSTICE PROJECT

Pagonis adapted their college thesis into a short film called *The Son I Never Had: Growing Up Intersex* in 2014. "I was inspired by Audre

Lord's autobiography which she called a 'biomythography,'" Pagonis told Maxwell. "I string together two different voices—one is myself and my family's subjective voice and the other is the objective voice of science and reason which is me reading my medical records." Pagonis received a grant from the Astraea Lesbian Foundation for Justice's Intersex Fund to complete the film. It screened at venues across the United States. Several years later, in 2019, Pagonis was the subject of another short documentary called *A Normal Girl*, directed by Aubree Bernier-Clarke.

In 2017, Pagonis helped found an organization called the Intersex Justice Project, with activists Long and Sean Saifa Wall, which called for an end to nonconsensual surgeries on intersex children. "Nobody should make a decision about someone else's genitalia and future gender identity." Pagonis told Lauren Williamson for *Chicago Magazine* (21 Sept. 2020). "They need to allow that person to have a role in the decision with meaningful consent." The group had the backing of prominent figures and organizations, including the United Nations High Commissioner for Human Rights, three former US surgeons general, and the Human Rights Watch, all of which have supported the global movement to stop intersex surgeries.

In 2020, the Intersex Justice Project successfully pressured the Ann & Robert H. Lurie Children's Hospital in Chicago—the same hospital where Pagonis had been treated as a child—to issue a public apology for the harm it caused intersex people. Lurie was the first hospital in the United States to issue such a statement. The hospital further pledged to end surgeries that modified the genitals of intersex children—but Pagonis was hesitant to celebrate the victory too soon, believing aspects of the pledge were too vague and left the door open for other intersex surgeries. Pagonis continues to demand a legislative ban on intersex surgeries, as well as reparations for intersex patients. "They took out my testes and performed a clitorectomy and a vaginoplasty. I'm going to need therapy for the rest of my life," Pagonis explained to Williamson. "It's the humane thing to do to offer a medical fund."

In 2020, Pagonis received a startling diagnosis. A new doctor, combing through their medical history and running more tests, told Pagonis that they did not have AIS, but rather a different condition known as NR-5A1. This misdiagnosis has had far-reaching consequences. Pagonis, who wrote about the discovery on Twitter, said that they have suffered from dangerously low levels of estrogen, resulting in osteopenia (low bone density) since their mid-twenties.

PERSONAL LIFE

Pagonis enjoys exercising, painting, photography, and seeing live music in their spare time. They also make T-shirts with gender-affirming slogans, which they sell through their Too Cute to Be Binary clothing line. Pagonis lives in Chicago.

SUGGESTED READING

Maxwell, Carrie. "Pidgeon Pagonis: On Their Film, White House Visit, Being on 'Transparent.'" *Windy City Times*, 26 Oct. 2016, windycitytimes.com/m/APPredirect.php?AID=56934. Accessed 13 Dec. 2021.

Pagonis, Pidgeon. "'Female Genital Mutilation and Intersex Genital Mutilation Are Similar Procedures': Pidgeon Pagonis on Their Journey of Discovering They Were Born Intersex." *Ditch the Label*, 26 Oct. 2016, mx.ditchthelabel.org/pidgeon-pagonis-interview/. Accessed 13 Dec. 2021.

—. "Hi I'm Intersex." *YouTube*, uploaded by *Pidgeon*, 14 Oct. 2016, www.youtube.com/watch?v=W9q7ic533Vk. Accessed 15 Dec. 2021.

—. "Hi, I'm Intersex—Part 3 (Clitorectomy)." *YouTube*, uploaded by *Pidgeon*, 21 Nov. 2016, www.youtube.com/watch?v=dUmmPftumnU. Accessed 15 Dec. 2021.

—. "How Pidgeon Pagonis Helped End Intersex Surgeries at Lurie." Interview by Lauren Williamson. *Chicago Magazine*, 21 Sept. 2020, www.chicagomag.com/chicago-magazine/october-2020/pidgeon-pagonis/. Accessed 13 Dec. 2021.

—. "The Son They Never Had." *Narrative Inquiry in Bioethics*, vol. 5, no. 2, 2015, pp. 103–06, doi:10.1353/nib.2015.0053. Accessed 15 Dec. 2021.

Schoenberg, Nara. "'It's Medically Sanctioned Violence and Torture': Intersex Patients Call for End to Genital Surgeries on Children." *Chicago Tribune*, 1 Nov. 2018, www.chicagotribune.com/lifestyles/ct-life-intersex-surgeries-20181018-story.html. Accessed 12 Dec. 2021.

—Molly Hagan

Chamath Palihapitiya

Born: September 3, 1976
Occupation: Venture capitalist

Chamath Palihapitiya is a venture capitalist and financial guru, best known as an evangelist for a once-obscure financial instrument called a special-purpose acquisition company, or SPAC. A SPAC is a shell company founded for the sole purpose of merging with a private company and taking it public. Few people are better at selling this risky venture than the charismatic Palihapitiya, who has been dubbed "the SPAC King" by Bloomberg.

Palihapitiya was born in Sri Lanka and raised in Ottawa, Ontario. He studied electrical engineering but pursued a career in tech. He was put in charge of AIM, the popular instant messaging feature at AOL, and joined the staff of Facebook in 2007, just as the company was looking to expand its reach; he convinced the company to put him in charge of its growth. Credited with introducing Facebook's controversial People You May Know feature, which pushed the site to nearly one billion users, he left Facebook in 2011 to found the venture capital firm Social Capital. The firm won respect for its early investment in Slack, but by 2018, Palihapitiya's erratic behavior and open disdain for the financial elite had scared away most of the firm's investors. By late 2021, Palihapitiya had become known as a financial influencer, appearing on CNBC and ruffling feathers on Twitter with his unorthodox financial advice.

EARLY LIFE AND EDUCATION

Chamath Palihapitiya was born on September 3, 1976, in Sri Lanka. His father, Gamage, a Sri Lankan government official, took a post in Ottawa, Ontario, Canada, in 1982. Due to the civil war that started the following year between the Sri Lankan government and the Tamil Tigers, the family applied for and was granted refugee status to remain in Canada in 1986. The Palihapitiya family, which included Chamath's sisters Hasini and Kithmini, lived in a modest apartment above a laundromat. His mother, Srima, worked as a housekeeper, while his father was intermittently employed and developed an alcohol use disorder. Palihapitiya has put their difficulties in stark terms. "My parents were deeply dysfunctional," he told

Kara Swisher and Teddy Schleifer for the Vox podcast *Recode Decode* (4 Mar. 2019). "Alcoholism, psychological issues, depression, abuse, all of that stuff. They didn't have time to unpack. Job to job. Housekeeper, photocopy store clerk, unemployed, vacuum salesman, encyclopedia salesperson. That's what they did." From an early age, Palihapitiya felt he had to fend for himself. In high school, he worked at Burger King and dealt blackjack games in the school cafeteria for extra cash. He earned a degree in electrical engineering from the University of Waterloo in Ontario in 1999.

AOL AND FACEBOOK

After brief stints in banking and product and business development, AOL's Josh Felser hired Palihapitiya as a director of product and premium services. Felser, who later became an angel investor, told Zeke Faux for *Bloomberg Businessweek* (13 May 2021), "[Palihapitiya] knew little about tech, yet he had chutzpah and was an in-your-face negotiator, which we needed." Felser added that Palihapitiya also regularly had the chutzpah to steal his parking spot. Palihapitiya rose through the ranks quickly, eventually becoming the youngest vice president in the company's history, helming AIM, the company's ubiquitous instant messaging service. He left the company in 2005 and took a job with Mayfield Fund, a venture capital firm, in 2006.

Palihapitiya had met Facebook CEO Mark Zuckerberg while he was still at AOL, when he had arranged a deal in which AIM was linked to Facebook's website. In 2007, Zuckerberg hired Palihapitiya to help the social network grow its user base. "Growth had plateaued around 90 million people," Zuckerberg told Steven Levy for his book *Facebook: The Inside Story* (2020), excerpted on *Medium* (25 Feb. 2020). "I remember people saying it's not clear if it was ever going to get past a 100 million at that time. We basically hit a wall, and we needed to focus on that."

After a rocky start, Palihapitiya convinced Zuckerberg to let him form a team—he dubbed it the Growth Circle—focused on identifying and producing monthly active users (MAUs). Most companies measure how many people were using a site each day; Palihapitiya argued that figuring out who was using the site each day for an entire month was a more useful metric. He wanted to make all users MAUs, but first he had to figure out how. In 2008, the Growth Circle, borrowing from the business networking site LinkedIn, introduced a feature called People You May Know (PYMK). The tool, which identifies the profiles of people a user might know in real life, was eerily effective, though not all of its suggested connections were welcome. One man, a sperm donor, was connected with his unknown biological child; in another instance, a psychiatrist found that the feature identified her patients as potential Facebook friends even though she had not friended her patients herself. When asked, repeatedly, Facebook refused to say how the feature worked. Later, Palihapitiya would suggest—contradicting Zuckerberg's congressional testimony—that PYMK made use of "shadow profiles," or data that Facebook collected about people who were not on the site. During Palihapitiya's tenure, Facebook grew from fifty million users to about seven hundred million.

Photo by Cmichel67 via Wikimedia Commons

SOCIAL CAPITAL

Palihapitiya left Facebook in 2011, just as the company was about to go public. "I left an enormous amount of equity on the table," he told Ainsley Harris, years later, for *Fast Company* (26 Feb. 2018). "I thought, I don't want to be a slave to money. I want to be a slave to something bigger: an ambition, a goal." The audacious move was in keeping with the persona Palihapitiya had created for himself: brash, independent, and against the grain. He spent a month living at the Mandarin Oriental in Las Vegas and won over $2 million playing poker. He had also bought a 10 percent stake in the Golden State Warriors for $25 million, an underdog team that would go on to win the National Basketball Association (NBA) Championship in 2015, 2017, and 2018 and accrue a 2021 value of $5.21 billion.

That same year, 2011, Palihapitiya and a few partners, including his wife at the time, Brigette Lau, founded an investment firm called Social Capital. The firm raised more than a billion dollars and made a few successful early investments in companies like Slack. But as Charles Duhigg, in his extensive profile of Palihapitiya for *The New Yorker* (31 May 2021), wrote, Palihapitiya began to seem less interested in the fund and more interested in himself as a public figure. "Chamath wanted to optimize for what served *him* best, instead of

the companies we invested in or the team we built," a former Social Capital executive told Duhigg.

In 2017, Palihapitiya gave "quite a humdinger of a speech," as Swisher put it, at the Stanford Business School. Palihapitiya characterizes the speech as a turning point in his career. In it, he revealed deep misgivings about the technological infrastructure he helped to build. "I feel tremendous guilt," he said in the speech, as transcribed by Michael David Murphy for *Medium* (11 Dec. 2017). Referring to social media, he said, "I think we've created tools that are ripping apart the social fabric of how society works." He further talked about how "bad actors" could manipulate algorithms to stoke violence and that he personally has rarely ever used Facebook. He added, "I guess I kind of innately didn't want to get programmed, so I just tuned it out, but I didn't confront it."

Palihapitiya later walked back some of his harshest words, particularly his criticisms of Facebook, but stood by his larger statement. Things were bad, and he wanted to fix them through strategic investment. Palihapitiya called it activist capitalism. He sent out stinging tweets and went on television to voice his displeasure with the status quo. A venture capitalist and hedge fund manager, Palihapitiya called VCs and hedge-fund managers, as quoted by Duhigg, "soulless cowards." He criticized the greed and racism of the financial elite, pledging to "f—— some sh—— up."

Some see Palihapitiya as a rebel who speaks truth to power; others note that Palihapitiya, a billionaire, is himself a part of the power structure he rages against. Still others see the blatant contradiction as the point. "People either love Chamath or they hate him, and that's fantastic, because polarization gets attention," one investor told Duhigg. "Polarization gets you on CNBC, it gets you Twitter followers, it gets you a megaphone. . . . Attention *is* money."

KING OF SPACS

By 2018, Palihapitiya's public antics—grandiose pronouncements and rumors of an extramarital affair—were hurting Social Capital. Two of the firm's founding partners resigned, and investors indicated that they would not be giving Palihapitiya more money. In September, Palihapitiya announced that he was changing the structure of the firm; going forward it would be a "technology holding company" investing off of its "balance sheet," meaning, essentially, that the firm would be focused on investing his own money. Dan Primack, writing for *Axios* (21 Sept. 2018), described the pivot differently. In an article headlined "Chamath Palihapitiya Burns Down What He Built," Primack wrote that Social Capital suffered "an ego-fueled collapse." Palihapitiya was defensive about the bad publicity the firm's demise had received and did not shy away from saying so. "It's my company, and I had the right to make that choice," he told Duhigg.

In the wake of this tumultuous year, Palihapitiya became an evangelist for an obscure financial instrument called a special purpose acquisition company, or SPAC. A SPAC is a publicly listed shell corporation whose purpose is to acquire a private company and take it public. A private company that merges with a SPAC is able to bypass the traditional regulatory process of an initial public offering (IPO). SPACs were invented in 1993 but were rarely used until the late 2010s. Palihapitiya argues that the SPAC model is more democratic, favoring start-ups and common investors over bankers and hedge-fund managers, who usually have a lock on most of an IPO's profits. "I fundamentally believe we've *robbed* most people of returns," he told Duhigg.

SPACs are sometimes called "blank check" companies because they are founded and funded before they merge with an existing company—meaning that investors choose SPACs based on trust in the SPAC's founder. Palihapitiya and Social Capital launched their first SPAC, Social Capital Hedosophia, known by the ticker symbol IPOA, in 2017. Palihapitiya suggested that the SPAC would sponsor a technology company, but instead, it merged with Virgin Galactic, a private space exploration company founded by Virgin CEO Richard Branson in 2004. The merger formed a new company, Virgin Galactic Holdings (VGH), and the audacious $1.4 billion deal inspired a SPAC renaissance. Soon, the tool was spoken of alongside non-fungible tokens (NFTs) and meme-stocks as a hot new financial trend.

By 2021, six hundred SPACs had raised more than $186 billion. Palihapitiya "created a template that all SPACers could follow," billionaire Mark Cuban told Faux. "He knew what made them work and created a narrative that new investors could understand." He went on to raise more than $4 billion and sponsor five more SPACs for companies including Opendoor Technologies and Clover Health, though in March of that year he sold his personal stake in VGH, worth around $213 million.

PERSONAL LIFE

Palihapitiya met Lau at the University of Waterloo, where they were members of the class of 1999. The couple married and had three children, Braeden, Sloane, and Cole. The couple divorced in 2018, after Palihapitiya was spotted with Nathalie Dompé, CEO of the Italian pharmaceutical company established by her family in 1940. The couple have one child.

SUGGESTED READING

Duhigg, Charles. "The Pied Piper of SPACs." *The New Yorker*, 31 May 2021, www. newyorker.com/magazine/2021/06/07/the-pied-piper-of-spacs. Accessed 9 Nov. 2021.

Faux, Zeke. "The SPAC King Is Doing Just Fine Even as the Bubble Starts to Burst." *Bloomberg Businessweek*, 13 May 2021, www. bloomberg.com/news/features/2021-05-13/spac-king-chamath-palihapitiya-hopes-his-hype-will-keep-mesmerizing-you. Accessed 9 Nov. 2021.

Harris, Ainsley. "Social Capital's Chamath Palihapitiya Wants to Fix Capitalism." *Fast Company*, 26 Feb. 2018, www.fastcompany.com/40525495/social-capitals-chamath-palihapitiya-wants-to-fix-capitalism. Accessed 9 Nov. 2021.

Levy, Steven. "The Untold History of Facebook's Most Controversial Growth Tool." *Medium*, 25 Feb. 2020, marker.medium.com/the-untold-history-of-facebooks-most-controversial-growth-tool-2ea3bfeaaa66. Accessed 9 Nov. 2021.

Palihapitiya, Chamath. "Transcript of Excerpt from Chamath Palihapitiya's Stanford Biz School Talk." *Medium*, transcribed by Michael David Murphy, 11 Dec. 2017, whileseated.medium.com/transcript-of-excerpt-from-chamath-palihapitiyas-stanford-biz-school-talk-9856ed0beba9. Accessed 10 Nov. 2021.

Primack, Dan. "Chamath Palihapitiya Burns Down What He Built." *Axios*, 21 Sept. 2018, www.axios.com/social-capital-chamath-burns-down-6bf0f8de-854f-4ad9-86da-2eb9ec520871.html. Accessed 11 Nov. 2021.

Schleifer, Theodore, and Eric Johnson. "After an 'Identity Crisis,' Social Capital CEO Chamath Palihapitiya Says He's Taught Himself How to Be Happy Again." *Recode Decode*, 4 Mar. 2019. *Vox*, www.vox.com/podcasts/2019/3/4/18247010/chamath-palihapitiya-social-capital-happiness-identity-crisis-kara-swisher-teddy-schleifer-podcast. Accessed 11 Nov. 2021.

—*Molly Hagan*

Artemi Panarin

Born: October 30, 1991
Occupation: Ice hockey player

When Artemi Panarin was growing up in Korkino, Russia, the grandparents who raised him did everything they could to give their grandchild, a talented young ice hockey player, the chance to pursue a career outside of the mining industry that employed many within their hometown. "I was pretty young at the time. I was a child. So I didn't understand all of this, all of what they did for me," he recalled to Aaron Portzline for *The Athletic* (11 Apr. 2018). "Now I understand how difficult it was, and, of course, I owe them so much. Everything." Having once competed in hand-me-down and homemade equipment, the young Panarin eventually made his way into the highest levels of Russian hockey, helping the under-twenty national team claim a gold medal at the World Junior Championship in 2011 and competing with several professional teams in the domestic Kontinental Hockey League (KHL).

Panarin's move to the United States in 2015 marked the beginning of a new chapter in his life, which saw him play two seasons each with the National Hockey League's (NHL) Chicago Blackhawks and Columbus Blue Jackets before signing with the New York Rangers in 2019. With the Rangers, Panarin further established himself as a dominant forward, ranking third in the league in points per game for both the 2019–20 and 2020–21 seasons. A key member of the Rangers' roster and one of the team's alternate captains for the 2021–22 season, Panarin has publicly proclaimed his disinterest in the vacant role of captain, preferring to exert his influence on the ice rather than off of it. "I can only influence with my own game," he explained, as quoted by *NHL.com* (19 Sept. 2021).

EARLY LIFE AND HOCKEY CAREER

Artemi Sergeyevich Panarin was born on October 30, 1991, in Korkino, a mining town in Russia that was then part of the Soviet Union. "It is my home," he later told Portzline about his birthplace. "But there is not much opportunity there outside of the mine." Panarin's parents, Elena and Sergey, separated when he was three months old, and his maternal grandparents, Vladimir and Nina Levin, subsequently took custody of him.

Panarin's grandfather had played ice hockey earlier in life and encouraged Panarin to play the sport as well, teaching him the basics at an early age. As new hockey equipment was too expensive, the young athlete often made do with used or improvised equipment that at times hindered his play and made him the subject of ridicule by other young players. "It was not really comfortable to skate in my equipment," he recalled to Portzline. "The other kids, they had the stuff. I used things that were left by the older guys. Some of the things, my grandma was making herself." Despite such challenges, Panarin showed promise as a player and, while still a child, began to commute to

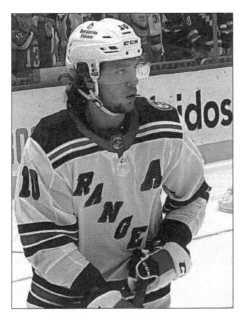

Photo by Tiop2000 via Wikimedia Commons

the city of Chelyabinsk in order to train and compete. In his early teens, he moved to Moscow to attend the Podolsk boarding school, which was affiliated with a strong hockey program. The experience was a formative one for Panarin, who distinguished himself as a skilled player and, having obtained new and improved equipment, was able to achieve a level of puck control that had previously been out of reach.

Eligible to play hockey professionally in the KHL by his late teens, Panarin entered the league in 2008, joining the Vityaz Chekhov team. He played for that team, as well as the KHL team Ak Bars Kazan, on and off over the next several years. He also spent time with the developmental-level Russkie Vityazi. During the 2012–13 season, he was traded to the KHL team SKA St. Petersburg. Panarin found his greatest KHL success with SKA St. Petersburg, winning the Gagarin Cup in the playoffs following the 2014–15 season.

In addition to playing professionally, Panarin represented Russia in international competition and became especially known for scoring both the first Russian goal and the game-winning goal in the under-twenty national team's gold-medal game against Canada at the 2011 International Ice Hockey Federation (IIHF) World Junior Championship. "That is something, a memory, that I will always think about," he told Portzline. "It is a proud moment for Russia, right?" Panarin continued to represent Russia during his senior career and in 2015 was a member of the Russian team that claimed second place at the IIHF World Championship.

NHL CAREER

In 2015, Panarin left Russia for the United States, having signed as a free agent with the NHL's Chicago Blackhawks. "I wasn't thinking about it before, I didn't consider myself ready to the NHL," he explained about the timing of the move in a Russian interview with Leonid Varshavsky, as reported in translation by Alessandro Seren Rosso for *The Hockey Writers* (18 Nov. 2015). "But I was twenty-three, twenty-four now. We also won the Gagarin Cup. I understood that it was the right time to go to the NHL. It was the right time to make a step forward."

Panarin made his debut with the Blackhawks on October 7, 2015, and played in eighty games over the course of the season, scoring a total of seventy-seven points. In recognition of his impressive performance during his rookie NHL season, he was awarded that season's Calder Memorial Trophy in addition to being named to the NHL All-Rookie Team. Panarin likewise competed in the first round of the 2016 NHL playoffs, during which the Blackhawks lost to the St. Louis Blues. Remaining with the Blackhawks for the 2016–17 season, he scored a total of seventy-four points in eighty-two regular-season games and went on to compete in the playoffs for the second consecutive year, although the Blackhawks were once again eliminated in the first round.

Following two seasons in Chicago, Panarin was traded to the Columbus Blue Jackets in June 2017, during the league's off-season. "I didn't expect it," he later told journalists, as reported by Chris Hine for the *Chicago Tribune* (19 Sept. 2017). "But I'm glad I'm here." Panarin put forth a powerful performance during his first season with the Blue Jackets, reaching a one point per game average for the first time in his NHL career. Competing with the Blue Jackets in the playoffs for the first time, he notably scored the game-winning overtime goal in a first-round game against the Washington Capitals, although the team was eliminated by the end of the series. The 2018–19 season saw Panarin score eighty-seven points in seventy-nine games and played on the NHL All-Star first team for the second time. The postseason also brought a milestone for Panarin, who progressed past the first round of competition for the first time with the Blue Jackets' victory over the Tampa Bay Lightning. The team lost to the Boston Bruins in the second round of the playoffs.

NEW YORK RANGERS

Entering free agency following the 2018–19 season, Panarin faced the arduous task of choosing which team to sign with, having received offers from several organizations. He signed a seven-year, $81.5 million deal with the New York Rangers on July 1, 2019. "I just sat down for ten minutes and really thought about it, and my heart told me that New York would be the better place for me," he explained, as reported by Allan Kreda for *The New York Times* (1 Dec. 2019). "I dreamed of playing for the Rangers. I like the people here. I feel the energy."

Joining the Rangers for the start of the 2019–20 season, Panarin played in sixty-nine games over his first outing with the team. In addition to scoring thirty-two goals during the season, he tallied the second-most assists in the league with sixty-three, had the third-highest points total in the NHL with a career high of ninety-five points, and ranked third in points per game with 1.38. While games proceeded as planned throughout late 2019 and early 2020, the NHL suspended the season in mid-March in response to the coronavirus disease 2019 (COVID-19) pandemic. Play resumed in August 2020, when the NHL held a reformatted playoff series in Canada. The Rangers competed in the qualifying round of the so-called bubble playoffs but lost to the Carolina Hurricanes.

A CHALLENGING SEASON

Delayed due to the ongoing pandemic, the 2020–21 NHL season introduced a number of safety restrictions for players and fans and shortened the season to fifty-six games. NHL leadership also reorganized the league's divisions to minimize travel, eliminating the Rangers' usual Metropolitan Division and instead placing the Rangers and seven other teams from Metropolitan and Atlantic divisions into the temporary East Division. Panarin played in forty-two games during the shortened season, scoring seventeen goals and forty-one assists over the course of that period and ranking third in the league in points per game for the second season in a row.

In February 2021, Panarin took a leave of absence from the Rangers after a Russian periodical published coach Andrei Nazarov's allegations that Panarin had physically assaulted a woman in Europe a decade before. Hockey commentators widely theorized that Nazarov, a supporter of Russian leader Vladimir Putin, had attempted to conduct a smear campaign against Panarin in retaliation for Panarin's public criticism of Putin and support for one of his political opponents. The allegations were never substantiated, and Panarin returned to the Rangers in March. He missed additional games late in the season after he was injured in an on-ice altercation with Capitals forward Tom Wilson. The incident sparked controversy within the league, as Rangers leadership believed that Wilson had violated the unwritten rules of hockey fights by slamming Panarin onto the ice after Panarin had already lost his helmet. "Any player will get emotional," Panarin later told the media, as reported by the website *Forever Blueshirts* (25 Sept. 2021). "You're not thinking about if you have a helmet on or not. All you want to do is get out from under him and start fighting back. That's when I got hurt." Panarin missed the final three games of the season.

MOVING FORWARD

Having recovered from his injury over the off-season, which also saw a coaching change for the Rangers, Panarin was optimistic going into 2021–22 NHL season. "We have a good team—well organized. Now the team is even stronger with a new coach," he told journalists, as reported by *Forever Blueshirts*. "Going forward, there's just a positive outlook on everything." He played in thirty-one of the team's first thirty-five games, accumulating ten goals and twenty-six assists during that period. In January 2022, however, Panarin was required to miss several games after entering the NHL's COVID-19 quarantine protocol.

PERSONAL LIFE

When not traveling with the Rangers, Panarin lives in Greenwich, Connecticut. He announced his engagement to longtime girlfriend Alisa Znarok in 2020. Panarin is known for his love of dogs, and he and Znarok run a dedicated Instagram account for their dog, Riziy.

SUGGESTED READING

Hine, Chris. "Artemi Panarin on Trade to Blue Jackets: 'This Is Business, Baby.'" *Chicago Tribune*, 19 Sept. 2017, www.chicagotribune.com/sports/blackhawks/ct-artemi-panarin-on-trade-to-blue-jackets-20170919-story.html. Accessed 7 Jan. 2022.

Kreda, Allan. "Artemi Panarin Has Been the Player the Rangers Wanted and Needed." *The New York Times*, 1 Dec. 2019, www.nytimes.com/2019/12/01/sports/hockey/artemi-panarin-rangers.html. Accessed 7 Jan. 2022.

Panarin, Artemi. "Interview with Young Gun Artemi Panarin." Interview by Leonid Varshavsky. Translated by Alessandro Seren Rosso. *The Hockey Writers*, 18 Nov. 2015, thehockeywriters.com/interview-with-artemi-panarin/. Accessed 7 Jan. 2022.

Portzline, Aaron. "An Incredible Journey: Artemi Panarin's Path from Poverty to NHL Stardom." *The Athletic*, 11 Apr. 2018, theathletic.com/308056/2018/04/11/an-incredible-journey-artemi-panarins-path-from-poverty-to-nhl-stardom/?redirected=1. Accessed 7 Jan. 2022.

"Rangers' Artemi Panarin Opens Up on Tom Wilson Incident; Leave of Absence; and Upcoming Season." *Forever Blueshirts*, 25 Sept. 2021, www.foreverblueshirts.com/rangers-artemi-panarin-opens-up-on-tom-wilson-incident-leave-of-absence-and-upcoming-season/. Accessed 7 Jan. 2022.

Rosen, Dan. "Panarin Out Rest of Season for Rangers with Lower-Body Injury." *NHL.com*, 4 May 2021, www.nhl.com/news/new-york-rangers-artemi-panarin-injury-status-out-for-season/c-324342372. Accessed 7 Jan. 2022.

—. "Panarin Takes Leave from Rangers, Denies Russia Altercation Report." *NHL.com*, 22 Feb. 2021, www.nhl.com/news/new-york-rangers-artemi-panarin-leave-of-absence/c-321676832. Accessed 7 Jan. 2022.

—Joy Crelin

Fiann Paul

Born: August 15, 1980
Occupation: Adventurer

"I like challenges and I like physical training," the Iceland-based adventurer Fiann Paul wrote for *Oceanographic* magazine. Indeed, that assertion is a bit of an understatement. A dedicated rower known for traveling some of the most daunting sea routes on Earth, Paul accumulated more than thirty Guinness World Records over the first two decades of his career and endured wet and cold conditions, sleep deprivation, dangerous waves, and numerous other discomforts in the name of challenging himself. He is the first person to have completed the so-called Ocean Explorers Grand Slam, which requires participants to row open-water routes on five different oceans. He gained particular notice for expeditions such as the 2017 Polar Row, which saw Paul and a group of teammates set the Guinness World Record for fastest row on the Arctic Ocean Open Waters but ultimately left Paul dissatisfied after equipment problems and flight restrictions in the Norwegian Arctic forced the expedition to end earlier than planned.

Paul's next major expedition required extensive planning and preparation, including the recruitment of a team of adventurers up for the challenge. "When you filter the whole world's population and you find people who have courage, skills, time, fitness and money then you have maybe ten individuals on the planet," he told Mark Agnew for the *South China Morning Post* (25 Nov. 2019). "That's a big deal." Despite such logistical challenges, Paul succeeded in completing his greatest challenge to date in December 2019, when he and five others set out to row across the dangerous Drake Passage that separates Chile and Antarctica. Known as the Impossible Row, the journey took twelve days, covered more than five hundred nautical miles, and was the subject of a 2020 Discovery Channel documentary.

EARLY LIFE AND EDUCATION

Fiann Paul was born in Poland on August 15, 1980. Though not active in rowing early in life, he was drawn to the outdoors from a young age. "I somehow always trusted nature as a close friend. As a child I connected with it more than with people," he later wrote for *Oceanographic* magazine. Paul studied architecture and teaching during his young adulthood in Poland. He later developed an interest in the psychiatric and psychoanalytical theories of the Swiss thinker Carl Jung and in 2021 defended a thesis in psychology at the C. G. Jung Institute in Zürich, Switzerland.

In 2006, Paul relocated to Iceland, which would become his home for the next decades. He focused his energies primarily on the visual arts during his early years in Iceland and was particularly active in photography. In 2008, he and fellow artist Anna Leoniak debuted their *Dialogue* (sometimes written as *Dialog*) project, for which the artists had traveled throughout Iceland and taken photographs of children from different communities. Intended to be a commentary on the phenomenon of movement from rural to urban communities, the photographs were affixed to the exterior of a ruined building in the Icelandic capital of Reykjavík and displayed there as part of the 2008 Reykjavík Arts Festival. In addition to working on the *Dialogue* project, Paul remained active in photography over the next years and in 2011 debuted the photography installation *See It!*, for which he displayed images of breastfeeding mothers on the side of a building in Reykjavík.

ROWING EXPEDITIONS

By 2010, Paul had developed an interest in the sport of ocean rowing, in which teams of rowers work together to propel human-powered boats through the open ocean, often for long distances. The journeys themselves can be dangerous due to the ocean's waves and the presence of hazardous weather or other obstacles, and the rowers often endure a host of physical and psychological hardships in the process. "What would often make me hold on was knowing that it could be worse," Paul told Ryan Stuart in an interview for *Men's Journal* about the mindset that helped him overcome such challenges. "The levels of comfort that we are used to are not enjoyed by the vast majority of the world. When I feel hopeless on expeditions, I always remind myself how people endure similar or worse deprivations of comfort in their daily lives, sometimes every day, yet manage to remain impressively joyful." Paul completed his first ocean crossing in 2011, serving as a member of a six-person crew that

Photo courtesy Fiann Paul, via Wikimedia Commons

rowed across the Atlantic Ocean from Tarfaya, Morocco, to Port St. Charles, Barbados, between June and August of that year.

Accompanied by five other rowers, Paul next set out to cross the Indian Ocean in June 2014, rowing from Geraldton, Australia, to Mahé, Seychelles. The journey was a strenuous one and proved particularly difficult due to the sleep deprivation the rowers experienced. "When you are very tired and on the edge of your bodily abilities, your brain also stops functioning or flips out a bit, and you see things that don't exist, and experience all sorts of weird things," Paul told the Icelandic publication *Vísir*, as reported by the *Iceland Review* (14 Aug. 2014). "Sometimes it was scary, sometimes it was funny. Once in the middle of the night I saw a hand come out of the sea, wanting to shake my hand and I almost did it, almost going out of the boat." In June 2016, Paul became the youngest person to date to have rowed three different oceans, when he completed a mid-Pacific row from Monterey, California, to Waikiki, Hawaii.

THE POLAR ROW

In July and August 2017, Paul set out to row a fourth ocean, tackling the Arctic Ocean Open Waters in an expedition known as the Polar Row. Along with rowers Carlo Facchino, Tathagata Roy, Jeff Willis, and Tor Wigum, Paul rowed from Tromsø to Hornsund and subsequently from Hornsund to Longyearbyen, all locations in northern Norway. The team completed the row from Tromsø to Hornsund at an average speed of 2.557 knots, thus setting a Guinness World Record for fastest row on the Arctic Ocean Open Waters by average speed. The expedition also made Paul the first known person to have rowed on four different oceans and the person to complete the first known row of the Barents Sea, a portion of the Arctic Ocean that borders northern Norway and Russia.

Several members of the crew departed after reaching Longyearbyen, and Paul and Facchino were joined by Alex Gregory, Sam Vye, Tyler Carnevale, and Danny Longman for the next phase of the expedition. After setting out, the group was forced to stop on the island of Jan Mayen on August 21 due to problems with their navigational equipment. Although Paul hoped to continue the Polar Row from there, the group was unable to bring in any new crew members due to restrictions on flights to the island, which was inhabited only by a small group of scientists and military personnel and was ultimately required to end the expedition and travel to the mainland by a nonhuman-powered boat. Though disappointed with that outcome, Paul pledged to seek out even greater challenges in the future. "We will row again," he told Megan Specia for *The New York Times* (28 Aug. 2017), "maybe an even bigger route than this one."

THE IMPOSSIBLE ROW

In the years following the Polar Row, Paul worked to plan his most audacious expedition yet: the Impossible Row, a journey across the dangerous Drake Passage between Chile and Antarctica. The process of planning for such a voyage was a tricky one due in large part to the logistics involved. "I needed to irreversibly prepay substantial sums of money 18 months in advance of the expedition to secure the assisting vessel, which is a requirement of the Antarctic Treaty in order to receive a departure permit," Paul wrote for *Oceanographic* magazine. "Maritime law requires that small human-powered boats and primitive sailboats be accompanied by an assisting vessel during open-water journeys. At the time, it was all the money I had." Paul was likewise required to assemble a team of adventurers who were both qualified to row the Southern Ocean and

inclined to take on such a task, which would involve significant hazards.

On December 13, 2019, Paul and fellow rowers Colin O'Brady, Cameron Bellamy, Jamie Douglas-Hamilton, Andrew Towne, and John Petersen left Cape Horn, Chile, aboard the twenty-nine-foot rowboat the *Ohana*. The team was followed by a support boat, the passengers of which included Discovery Channel personnel tasked with filming a documentary about the Impossible Row. Traversing the Drake Passage, Paul and his teammates rowed for twelve days, one hour, and forty-five minutes—split into ninety-minute shifts—and covered a distance of 529 nautical miles before reaching Antarctica's Charles Point on December 25. "When we finally saw Antarctica after our arduous journey, it was significant," Paul wrote for *Oceanographic* magazine about the experience. "Many of us had tears in our eyes upon first sighting of the land. We looked at each other and we didn't talk." In addition to completing the journey from Chile to Antarctica, Paul had rowed on his fifth ocean in the course of the Impossible Row, thus becoming the first person to complete the rowing challenge known as the Ocean Explorers Grand Slam. Documented in the DiscoveryGo video series *The Impossible Row*, the expedition became the subject of a long-form documentary broadcast on the Discovery Channel in 2020.

LIFE ON LAND

In addition to leading his rowing expeditions, Paul remained active in the field of photography and also worked as a motivational speaker, addressing corporations as well as groups interested in endurance sports. In December 2019, the cruise company Abercrombie & Kent announced that Paul was set to fill the role of explorer in residence for the company's Arctic cruises scheduled for the summer of 2020. The emergence of the coronavirus disease 2019 (COVID-19) pandemic, however, interfered with those plans, forcing the adventure-oriented Paul to find new pastimes at home. "For explorers, difficulty is the native environment and therefore it is very difficult to outperform them in difficult conditions. In contrast, daily life and leisure are often hardships for us," he told Stuart. "For me, what was especially challenging was working out at home. When sport is your profession, working out is not fun. You're always pushing really hard." Paul turned his attention to hiking and photography during the pandemic, taking the opportunity to explore nature in Iceland rather than abroad.

In addition to such activities, Paul led the Ocean Rowing Society International's effort during that period to develop a detailed database of expeditions and statistics that would be accessible online. "Until today, there has been no real database for adventure or exploration expeditions. At least, none that filters, sorts and systematizes data without human processing," he told Craig Glenday in an interview for the Guinness World Records website (7 Apr. 2021). "It seems stranger still, considering the increasing interest and participation in various forms of expeditions and adventures. That and the competitive spirit of many adventurers and explorers!" The new database launched in early 2021 and provided ready access to information about a variety of prior expeditions, including Paul's Impossible Row.

PERSONAL LIFE

Paul is based in Reykjavík, Iceland. He gained Icelandic citizenship around 2011. In July 2021, he was recognized as a chartered geographer of the Royal Geographical Society.

SUGGESTED READING

Agnew, Mark. "The Impossible Row: Who Are the Men Joe Rogan Labelled 'Crazy' for Attempting to Row Across the Drake Passage?" *South China Morning Post*, 25 Nov. 2019, www.scmp.com/sport/outdoor/extreme-sports/article/3039258/impossible-row-who-are-men-joe-rogan-labelled-crazy. Accessed 7 Feb. 2022.

Myers, Amanda Lee. "6 Men Become 1st to Cross Perilous Drake Passage Unassisted." Associated Press, 28 Dec. 2019, apnews.com/article/us-news-ap-top-news-south-america-az-state-wire-nd-state-wire-733e3e da7d1f318cc8beabd961c424d3. Accessed 7 Feb. 2022.

"Ocean Rower Sets Four World Records for Iceland." *Iceland Review*, 14 Aug. 2014, www.icelandreview.com/news/ocean-rower-sets-four-world-records-iceland/. Accessed 7 Feb. 2022.

Paul, Fiann. "Across the Drake." *Oceanographic*, www.oceanographicmagazine.com/features/impossible-row/. Accessed 7 Feb. 2022.

___. "Frustration as Fuel: Fiann Paul, 'The World's Most Record-Breaking Explorer,' on How the Pandemic Can Make You Stronger." Interview by Ryan Stuart. *Men's Journal*, www.mensjournal.com/adventure/record-smashing-ocean-rower-fiann-paul-on-using-frustration-as-fuel/. Accessed 7 Feb. 2022.

___. "Ocean Rowing Society International Launches the First Real Adventure Database." Interview by Craig Glenday. *Guinness World Records*, 7 Apr. 2021, www.guinnessworldrecords.com/news/2021/4/ocean-rowing-society-international-launches-the-first-real-adventure-database-653509. Accessed 7 Feb. 2022.

Specia, Megan. "Stranded on Norwegian Island, Rowers End Their Arctic Mission." *The New York Times*, 28 Aug. 2017, www.nytimes.com/2017/08/28/world/arctic-polar-row-norway-rowers.html. Accessed 7 Feb. 2022.

—Joy Crelin

Lincoln Peirce

Born: October 23, 1963
Occupation: Cartoonist

Middle-schooler Nate Wright, Lincoln Peirce's most celebrated cartoon character, has become a long-standing favorite among young readers since the *Big Nate* novels first appeared in 2010. With eye-catching covers showcasing Nate sporting jeans, a yellow T-shirt, and a blue towel fastened around his neck, posing as a cape, young readers realize, as they devour the novels, that the outfit is only a speck of Nate's adventurous, larger-than-life personality.

Though the character only reached a wider audience in the 2010s, Big Nate has been the protagonist of an ongoing cartoon strip whose first appearance in newspapers dates back to 1991. The idea of adapting the strip to a novel format did not come to Peirce until the 2000s when children's books that combined text and cartoons gained special attention from publishing houses. When the first of eight *Big Nate* novels, *Big Nate: In a Class by Himself*, was released, the beloved cape-wearing Nate, who until then had found only a moderate readership, earned a global following. "I think it's really an unlikely story that after the strip

Photo by GeorgeJK61,
via Wikimedia Commons.

years old. By the time he reached fifth grade, Peirce was scripting and drawing his own comic book featuring a main character named Super Jimmy. After attending Oyster River High School, the future cartoonist continued his education at Colby College in Waterville, Maine, where, aside from focusing his studies on art and history, Peirce created a comic strip for the school newspaper. Entitled *Third Floor*, the weekly publication related the lives of two Colby College roommates. Peirce graduated from Colby College with a Bachelor of Fine Arts (BA) degree in 1985

He then moved to New York City, where he attended Brooklyn College, earning a master's degree in studio art. He also spent time studying at the Skowhegan School of Painting and Sculpture. While his rich knowledge of art allowed Peirce to spend three years teaching art at Xaverian High School—an all-boys institution in New York City where he dabbled as a baseball coach—he continued working on his strips.

had been around for almost twenty years, it gained this second life," Peirce told Alex Dueben in an interview for *The Beat* (26 Oct. 2016).

While 2016 marked the end of the novels, the *Big Nate* animated series debuted on the streaming service Paramount Plus in 2022, giving fans of Peirce's work new adventures of Nate to look forward to. At the same time, he also began penning new children's stories.

EARLY LIFE AND EDUCATION

Born on October 23, 1963, in Ames, Iowa, Lincoln Peirce grew up in Durham, New Hampshire, where his family moved shortly after his birth. As a young boy, he was captivated by the animated *Popeye* cartoons featured in a local television show and learned to appreciate the ingenuity, surrealism, and absurdity fostered in such stories from a young age. "You notice things that your friends don't notice," Peirce told Tom Heintjes in an interview for *Hogan's Alley* (8 Feb. 2022). "They're just watching a cartoon while you're watching it with the eyes of someone who, even at a young age, this is sort of in your DNA."

His fascination for animated television shows soon blossomed into a love for reading four-panel cartoon strips—including *Peanuts* by Charles M. Schulz and *Doonesbury* by Garry Trudeau—when he was around seven

HOW BIG NATE CAME TO BE

Realizing that scripting and drawing comic books were where he saw his future, Peirce commenced sending his story ideas to cartoon syndicates in the late 1980s, receiving many rejections from them in return. "I had a comic strip set in a nursing home, set in a hotel," Peirce told Steven H. Foskett, Jr. for *Telegram and Gazette* (3 Oct. 2010) before continuing to say, "Finally I did something called *Neighborhood Comics*, which was based on the neighborhood where I grew up, and it was sort of a precursor to *Big Nate*."

Among the cast of characters in *Neighborhood Comics* were brothers Nate and Marty: the former, a quiet, serious older brother as opposed to the latter, a jokester younger brother. After sending the strip to many syndicates, Peirce received valuable feedback from Sarah Gillespie, the comics editor at United Media, who told him to pick one of the characters to be the focal point. Peirce chose Nate and, infusing this character with the energetic, clever personality of Marty, the cartoonist created what would become his most celebrated cartoon protagonist.

In January 1991, the first *Big Nate* comic made its debut in about 135 newspapers. In 1992, Peirce left New York City and moved to Portland, Maine, where he began a full-time writing career. With Gillespie as his editor, Peirce devoted his time to concocting stories revolving around sixth-grader Nate, whose adventures and misadventures transpired at home—at least at first. "When I started it, it was more of a domestic humor strip with the family unit," the cartoonist revealed to Foskett. "Because he's got a single father and an older sister, I thought I'd write a lot of jokes about that dynamic, but in fact, probably because I taught school myself, I started writing jokes about school life, and that just took over." With this important shift in the narrative, Peirce established a loyal readership of children and adults alike.

FROM COMIC BOOKS TO NOVELS

The appearance of the *Big Nate* strip on newspapers would continue uninterrupted for the coming decades, increasing its reach to 200 newspapers in the 2000s. Still, Peirce wanted more publications to enlist his work and began developing ideas to make this happen.

Before Jeff Kinney published the children's book series *Diary of a Wimpy Kid*—the first released in 2007—it had not crossed Peirce's mind to pen novels. However, with the ingenious structure of Kinney's books, an amalgamation of text and comics, bringing commercial success to the author, Peirce realized the overwhelming interest to publish these kinds of stories had prompted publishing houses to look for potential authors. After receiving some advice and connections from Kinney—whom Peirce had previously advised and grown a friendship with while Kinney was still in college—Peirce was confident that he could be one of these authors. "I'd never written a novel, but since I'd been doing the comic strip for almost twenty years at that point, I felt confident that I could create longer stories for those same characters. I just had to get used to the pacing," he said to Tiziano Thomas Dossena in an interview for *L'Idea Magazine* (1 Aug. 2014).

After submitting proposals to eight publishing houses, Peirce ended up signing a book deal with HarperCollins and commenced penning what would be the first of eight novels soon afterward. Although it took him some time to adjust to this new platform, which was not only longer than a comic strip but also differed in rhythm and style—a style that required actual text instead of speech bubbles—he eventually got the hang of it. As he said to Dossena, "It took a lot of getting used to, but I was pleasantly surprised by how much I enjoyed writing novels."

In March 2010, his first book, entitled *Big Nate: In a Class by Himself*, was released to commercial and critical acclaim, earning a place on the New York Times Best Sellers list and a 2011 nomination for a Children's Choice Book Award, given by the Children's Book Council. Having adapted the strip skillfully into a full-length story, though using the art and storytelling of comic books, *Big Nate: In a Class by Himself* introduced Nate and his friends, Teddy and Francis, to a much wider audience.

FROM NOVELS TO TELEVISION

After releasing the second installment of the *Big Nate* series, *Big Nate Strikes Again*, in October 2010, Peirce put out a book every year until 2016: *Big Nate on a Roll* (2011), *Big Nate Goes for Broke* (2012), *Big Nate Flips Out* (2013), *Big Nate in the Zone* (2014), *Big Nate Lives It Up* (2015); and *Big Nate Blasts Off* (2016). Just like the first novel had accomplished, each of the seven books that followed found a spot on the New York Times Best Sellers list.

Aside from marking the end of the *Big Nate* novels, 2016 saw the *Big Nate* cartoon strip celebrate twenty-five years of publication in newspapers. For the occasion, hundreds of cartoons chosen by Peirce were published in a compendium called *Epic Big Nate*. The cartoons were not the sole feature in the book, however, as the cartoonist dedicated a section to the background and history of how *Big Nate* had come to be. The book also featured a question-and-answer between Peirce and Kinney.

In early 2022, the children's television channel Nickelodeon adapted *Big Nate* into an animated series, which debuted on the streaming service Paramount Plus. (*Big Nate* had previously been adapted into a musical by Adventure Theatre-MTC in 2013.) Making the transition from solitary work as a writer to working as part of a team for the television project was an adjustment for Peirce, though one that came accompanied by the promise of endless possibilities. "I am thrilled with how faithful an adaptation this is of *Big Nate*. And at the same time, there's a lot of sort of room for it to become more and different from *Big Nate*, too, because you can do so many things in animation that you can't do in four panels in the morning newspaper," he said to Heintjes.

Having become more comfortable writing novels, Peirce shifted his narrative skills to a new story in the late 2010s. He released the first installment of a predicted three-book series set in the Middle Ages in 2019. The story, titled *Max and the Midknights*, chronicles the adventures of Max, the niece of a bard, whose heart yearns to be a knight. The New York Times Best Seller, which combines comic and prose, was followed by *Max and the Midknights: Battle of the Bodkins* (2020) and *Max and the Midknights: The Tower of Time* (2022).

PERSONAL LIFE

Peirce is married to painter Jessica Gandolf, with whom he has two children: son Elias and daughter Dana. The *Big Nate* cartoon creator and his family reside in Portland, Maine.

SUGGESTED READING

Foskett, Steven H. Jr. "*Big Nate*'s World Keeps Getting Bigger." *Telegram and Gazette*, 3 Oct. 2010, www.telegram.com/story/lifestyle/2010/10/03/big-nate-s-world-keeps/51451045007. Accessed 10 May 2022.

Kennedy, Elizabeth. "10 Things You Should Know about *Big Nate* Creator Lincoln Peirce." *ThoughtCo*, Dotdash-Meredith, 3 July 2019, www.thoughtco.com/big-nates-creator-lincoln-peirce-627149. Accessed 10 May 2022.

McLeod, Susanna. "Review of *Big Nate from the Top* and *Big Nate Out Loud* Comics Collections by Creator Lincoln Peirce." *The Cartoonists*, 21 May 2011, www.thecartoonists.ca/Index_files/2011Pages/TC-ReviewLincolnPeirceBigNate.htm. Accessed 10 May 2022.

Peirce, Lincoln. "*Big Nate*, Small Screen: An Interview with Lincoln Peirce." Interview by Tom Heintjes. *Hogan's Alley*, 8 Feb. 2022, www.hoganmag.com/blog/2022/2/8/big-nate-small-screen-an-interview-with-lincoln-peirce. Accessed 10 May 2022.

___. "The Evolution of *Big Nate* from Comic Strips to Novels to Musical: An Interview with Lincoln Peirce." Interview by Tiziano Thomas Dossena. *L'Idea Magazine*, 1 Aug. 2014, lideamagazine.com/evolution-big-nate-comic-strips-novels-musical-interview-lincoln-peirce. Accessed 10 May 2022

___. "Interview: Looking Back, the Epic *Big Nate*'s Lincoln Peirce Gives Advice to His Younger Self." Interview by Alex Dueben. *The Beat*, 26 Oct. 2016, www.comicsbeat.com/interview-looking-back-the-epic-big-nates-lincoln-peirce-gives-advice-to-his-younger-self. Accessed 10 May 2022.

—*Maria del Pilar Guzman*

Viktor Pelevin

Born: November 22, 1962
Occupation: Fiction writer

Although Viktor Pelevin owes much of his writing style to such noted Russian authors as Nikolay Gogol, Maxim Gorky, and Mikhail Bulgakov, his life—as much as the public knows of it—is modeled on reclusive American authors like Thomas Pynchon and J. D. Salinger. During his early career in 1990s post-Soviet Russia, Pelevin rarely gave interviews, and he has not given one since about the turn of the century. Despite the fact that the last time he was verifiably photographed was in 2001, he is one of the most popular authors in Russia in 2022, with books coming out in an almost annual stream. While his work pulls from the genres of fantasy and science fiction, it is often written in a surreal, philosophical way as it reflects on the more absurd aspects of modern Russia.

Although Pelevin critiques modern Russian society, his work is not particularly political, and he has avoided any notion that he is some kind of revolutionary. He believes his work should speak for itself and avoids any personal or political entanglements. "In the Soviet era, being a writer meant being a real scoundrel. People like [Aleksandr] Solzhenitsyn were actually fighting the system," Pelevin remarked in a rare interview published in *The Guardian* (29 Apr. 2000). "I never was a hero. I would never be able to do that. So I'm not really sure that I would have been writing if the Soviet Union had not collapsed. Perhaps I would be writing something, but I would never try to publish it."

EARLY LIFE AND EDUCATION

Viktor Olegovich Pelevin was born in Moscow, Russia, in the former Soviet Union, on November 22, 1962. His parents, Oleg and Zina Pelevin, were a Soviet military officer and a school teacher, respectively. Little has been published in English about his early life and education, and Pelevin has been reluctant to discuss his personal life even when he was still giving interviews. It has been reported that he studied electrical engineering in college. After graduation he worked for a time as a journalist and as an advertising copywriter in the late 1980s, just prior to the collapse of the Soviet Union, which was formally disbanded in December 1991.

After the various Soviet states began forming their own governments, Russia found itself attempting to establish a democracy under President Boris Yeltsin, one of the leaders who had sought to disband the oppressive communist regime. But widespread corruption hampered Yeltsin's efforts at forging a true democracy. Much of Pelevin's writing comes from attempting to understand the society in which he came of age. Although his writing has become wildly popular among the people of his own generation, Generation X, as well as with younger generations, he has sought to largely avoid the trappings of celebrity. He told *The Guardian*: "I do my best to avoid the limelight. . . . I'm not a public person. I never appear on television and never give interviews. Well, sometimes I do, but it's not a normal thing. I really don't know. I'm just trying to write good books."

Unlike many writers who enjoy the company of other literati, Pelevin believes that it would be detrimental to his writing. In *The Guardian*, he noted that he has little interest in the literary scene: "A literary scene is something that never produces literature. It only produces the so-called literary life, which has nothing to do with books. If you want to write books, you've got to keep as far from it as you can. So I never mix in literary circles. I don't spend my time talking with other writers."

EARLY CAREER

Pelevin began writing fiction in his late twenties and was soon publishing regularly in his native Russia. One of his first publications was a collection of short stories titled *Siny fonar* in 1991. The work earned him the Russian Booker Prize, as well as several other awards, and set the tone for many of his following works. In *Publishers Weekly* (29 Sept. 1997), a critic wrote of the collection: "Although the eight stories in this collection sometimes suffer from plots that develop too quickly or epiphanies that overwhelm their fictional context, Pelevin's raw, bold voice makes a welcome addition to the literature of a soul-searching Russia." The novel *Omon Ra*—an absurdist look at the Soviet way of life as seen through the eyes of a boy who wants to become a cosmonaut like the first man in space—quickly followed in 1992.

In 1993, two of Pelevin's novels were released: *Zhizn nasekomykh*, which described the lives of characters who could be both bugs and human beings, and *Zhyoltaya strela*, a slim novel about a Russian train with no beginning or end that is speeding along toward a collapsed bridge. The collection of characters aboard the train represents a listless and drifting Russia in the post-Soviet era, with no idea of where they are going or what they should be doing. In addition to receiving critical acclaim, *Zhyoltaya strela* became his first novel to be translated into English. Translated from Russian by Andrew Bromfield—who later translated the majority of his other works—the novel was published as *The Yellow Arrow* in 1994. More English translations of Pelevin's works soon followed, including *Omon Ra* under the same name in 1994, *Zhizn nasekomykh* as *The Life of Insects* in 1995, and *Siny fonar* as *The Blue Lantern and Other Stories* in 1996.

Pelevin followed the critical and commercial success of these works with another short story collection with *Problema vervolka v sredney polose* (1994; *A Werewolf Problem in Central Russia and Other Stories*, 1998). Again, the author uses satire to mock the ways in which communism corrupted Russia during its decades-long reign. Reviewing *A Werewolf Problem in Central Russia and Other Stories*, a critic for *Publishers Weekly* (29 Apr. 2003) wrote that the "short fiction collection brilliantly and poignantly satirizes the economic, cultural and spiritual decay of Mother Russia under Communism." The collection also earned Pelevin his second Russian Booker Prize.

MORE ENGLISH WORKS

Although not all of Pelevin's novels have been translated to English, many of his most popular works have. Pelevin's next novel, *Chapayev i pustota* [1996; *Buddha's Little Finger*, 2000]—also known as *Chapayev and Pustota* in Russia or *The Clay Machine Gun* in the United Kingdom—was one of his most celebrated, winning acclaim both inside Russia and in the international community. Most notably, it was nominated for the 2001 Dublin Literary Award. The novel depicts two periods in Russia history, the Russian Civil War (1917–23), which resulted in the establishment of the Soviet Union, and Russia of the mid-1990s, when it became clear that the political reforms hoped for after the collapse of the Soviet Union had not materialized. The novel was adapted into an English language film titled *Buddha's Little Finger* in 2015.

Pelevin's next novel, *Generation "P"*—which was released in Russian under the English title—became a cult classic in Russia after its publication in 1999. In it, he describes a budding writer who has just graduated from the Institute of Literature in Moscow, who has little success after graduation. Eventually he gets a job in the world of advertising, where he is exposed to the seedy underbelly of Russian life, which includes gangsters, drugs, and sex. The novel was published in English as *Babylon* in 2000. In 2011, the Russian novel was adapted for the screen by Victor Ginzburg.

In 2001, Pelevin published another collection of short stories translated to English under the title *4 By Pelevin*. (The collection has previously been published in Russian in 1994). The quartet of stories explores very unusual situations: a refugee named Six-Toes awaits a transformation; a disembodied life force struggles to free itself from a utility shed; a public toilet attendant faces both commercial success and a septic mess; and people confront the entanglements of the corrupt Russian and Chinese communist bureaucracies. Writing about the collection for *Publishers Weekly* (20 Aug. 2001), a critic noted, "Pelevin's allegories are reminiscent of children's fairy tales in their fantastic depictions of worlds within worlds, solitary souls tossed helplessly among them. But the dark undercurrent—the saga of a people lost between a doomed ideology and its floundering replacement—is anything but simple."

RECENT WORKS

As the turn of the century dawned, Pelevin continued to produce new fiction at an almost yearly pace. Some of these works have been translated into English. His 2004 science fiction novel was translated into English as *The Sacred Book of the Werewolf* in 2008. The novel is written from the point of view of a 2,000-year-old werefox who has the ability to turn herself into a very young and beautiful woman so she can steal the lifeforce from men. She eventually begins a romance with a werewolf named Alexander, who is also a Russian intelligence officer. The pair's affair is intertwined with philosophical debates. The book met with mixed reviews in the United States. In a review for *Publishers Weekly* (7 July 2008), a critic wrote, "Pelevin creates interesting enough characters, but the unexplainable plot twists and the author's preoccupation with philosophical ramblings are nearly as perilous as a silver bullet."

Pelevin's next novel, *Ampur V* (2006; *Empire V: The Prince of Hamlet*, 2016), also explores folklore, this time from the point of view of a young man named Roman who turns into a vampire named Rama, but has difficulty being one. Again, the main character debates larger than life questions about God, life after death, and truth throughout the novel. Like its predecessor, the book received mixed reviews in America.

Many of Pelevin's works have yet to be brought into English translation. Some of these novels include *Betman Apollo* (2013); *Smotritel'* [*Caretaker*] (2015); *Lampa Mafusaila, ili Kraynyaya bitva chekistov s masonami* [*Lamp of Methuselah, or the Ultimate Battle of the Chekists with the Freemasons*] (2016); *Taynyye vidy na goru Fudzi* [*Secret Views of Mount Fuji*] (2018); *Iskusstvo lyogkikh kasanii* [*The Art of Light Touch*] (2019); *Sol Invictus* (2020); and *Transhumanism Inc* (2021).

PERSONAL LIFE

Pelevin is a student of Buddhism and has gone on numerous Zen retreats across Asia. He did a three-month long retreat in South Korea in 2000, in which he ate rice and seaweed the entire time, except for when he was allowed to have a slice of pizza and a can of Coke for New Year's.

SUGGESTED READING

Paikova, Valeria. "Victor Pelevin, Russia's Most Mysterious Modern Writer." *Russia Beyond*, 29 Sept. 2021, www.rbth.com/arts/334247-victor-pelevin-modern-writer. Accessed 2 Mar. 2022.

Pelevin, Viktor. "I Never Was a Hero." *The Guardian*, 29 Apr. 2000, www.theguardian.com/books/2000/apr/30/fiction. Accessed 2 Mar. 2022.

—."Viktor Pelevin." Interview by Leo Kropywiansky. *BOMB*, 1 Apr. 2002, bombmagazine.org/articles/victor-pelevin/. Accessed 11 Mar. 2022.

Review of *4 By Pelevin*, by Victor Pelevin, translated by Andrew Bromfield. *Publishers Weekly*, 20 Aug. 2001, www.publishersweekly.com/9780811214919. Accessed 2 Mar. 2022.

Review of *The Blue Lantern and Other Stories*, by Victor Pelevin, translated by Andrew Bromfield. *Publishers Weekly*, 29 Sept. 1997, www.publishersweekly.com/9780811213707. Accessed 2 Mar. 2022.

Review of *The Sacred Book of the Werewolf*, by Victor Pelevin, translated by Andrew Bromfield. *Publishers Weekly*, 7 July 2008, www.publishersweekly.com/9780670019885. Accessed 2 Mar. 2022.

Review of *A Werewolf Problem in Central Russia and Other Stories*, by Andrew Bromfield and Viktor Pelevin. *Publishers Weekly*, 28 Apr. 2003, www.publishersweekly.com/9780811215435. Accessed 2 Mar. 2022.

SELECTED WORKS

Siny fonar (Blue Lantern and Other Stories) 1991; *Omon Ra*, 1992; *Zhyoltaya strela (The Yellow Arrow)*, 1993; *Zhizn nasekomykh (The Life of Insects)*, 1993; *Problema vervolka v sredney polose (A Werewolf Problem in Central Russia and Other Stories)*, 1994; *Chapayev i pustota (Buddha's Little Finger)*, 1996; *Generation "P" (Babylon)*, 1999; *4 by Pelevin*, 2001; *The Sacred Book of the Werewolf*, 2004; *Ampur V (Empire V)*, 2006; *Betman Apollo*, 2013; *Smotritel' (Caretaker)*, 2015; *Lampa Mafusaila, ili Kraynyaya bitva chekistov s masonami (Lamp of Methuselah, or the Ultimate Battle of the Chekists with the Freemasons)*, 2016; *Taynyye vidy na goru Fudzi (Secret Views of Mount Fuji)*, 2018; *Iskusstvo lyogkikh kasanii (The Art of Light Touch)*, 2019; *Sol Invictus*, 2020; and *Transhumanism Inc*, 2021

—*Christopher Mari*

Gay Jane Perez

Born: ca. 1981–82
Occupation: Scientist and educator

In 2010, physicist Gay Jane Perez changed the trajectory of her career forever when she traveled from the Philippines to the United States to take a postdoctoral position at the National Aeronautics and Space Administration (NASA) Goddard Space Flight Center. While Perez's earlier research concerned the dynamics of collective behavior, her work at Goddard focused on the processing and analysis of data gleaned from satellites. After returning to the Philippines and taking a position at the University of the Philippines Diliman, her newfound expertise in satellite data began to intersect with a different field, that of agriculture. "My background is in physics, far from agriculture. I didn't know a lot about agriculture except for the rice that's on my plate," she later joked, as reported by Jose Santino Bunachita for *Inquirer.net* (21 Oct. 2018). Working with data collected by satellites, Perez developed a means of analyzing environmental data to predict phenomena such as droughts and advise farmers accordingly.

In addition to working with data collected by satellites, Perez was heavily involved in the Philippines' efforts to develop the country's own satellites, which resulted in the 2016 launch of debut microsatellite Diwata-1. Subsequent efforts increased the number of domestically produced satellites in use, and in late 2019, the government of the Philippines authorized the creation of the Philippine Space Agency (PhilSA). Appointed PhilSA's deputy director general for space science and technology in January 2021, Perez was tasked with overseeing the country's efforts to develop space technology such as additional satellites and to use such technology to promote food security, mitigate the effects of climate change, and otherwise improve the lives of the nation's populace.

EARLY LIFE AND EDUCATION

Gay Jane P. Perez was born in the Philippines in the early 1980s. She spent her early years in Naga City, where she attended a Catholic girls' school. After completing her secondary education, Perez enrolled in the University of the Philippines (UP) Diliman, located in Quezon City. Studying within UP Diliman's National Institute of Physics (NIP), she earned a bachelor's degree in applied physics in 2003 and went on to pursue graduate studies in physics at that institution, completing a master's degree in 2005.

As both an undergraduate and a graduate student, Perez focused her research primarily on the dynamics of collective behavior. Her doctoral dissertation, "Understanding the Dynamics of Unassisted Group Egress," won an Outstanding Thesis Award from the Philippine Council for Advanced Science and Technology Research and Development, an award that granted Perez both academic recognition and a cash prize. She likewise earned a Dean's Medallion for excellence in PhD studies from UP Diliman for her work. Perez completed her doctorate in physics in 2009.

CAREER IN ACADEMIA

Perez began teaching at UP Diliman in 2003, while completing her graduate studies there. In 2010, after earning her doctorate, she traveled to the United States to take a postdoctoral position at the NASA Goddard Space Flight Center in Maryland. "Guided by my mentor Josefino Comiso, a leading physical scientist at the Goddard Space Flight Center and NASA, and interacting with scientists and programmers, I learned how to process, analyze, and interpret satellite data," she told Paul Icamina for *SciDev.Net* (19 Nov. 2018) about her time there. In addition to teaching Perez valuable practical skills in the use of satellite data, her work with NASA taught her further lessons that, though not immediately applicable to her career, would prove particularly useful a decade later in the Philippines. "I was exposed to some of the best practices of a national space agency, which I think can serve as a benchmark as we work towards the establishment of our own space agency," she told Icamina.

Following her return to the Philippines, Perez held an assistant professorship in the Institute of Environmental Science and

Meteorology at UP Diliman, from January 2012 through December 2013. She was promoted to associate professor in 2014. In those roles, Perez taught courses on a range of topics related to environmental science and meteorology, in addition to conducting her own research and supervising a number of research projects. She also served for a time as secretary general of the Physics Society of the Philippines and in 2012 became president of the Philippine Geosciences and Remote Sensing Society (GRSS).

SATELLITES AND ENVIRONMENTAL RESEARCH

Much of Perez's research concerns the analysis of satellite data for the purpose of gaining a better understanding of climate and environmental issues, particularly those that affect the cultivation of crops within the Philippines' agriculture industry. "I was always looking at the Philippines through satellite images [and] saw that there really is a relationship between temperature and vegetation," she explained, as reported by Bunachita. Perez has focused significantly on droughts, environmental events that can have a devastating effect on agriculture, and through the Drought and Crop Assessment Forecasting (DCAF) research initiative has worked to develop means of identifying droughts and projecting their effects on crops in the region. Such projections can, in turn, be used to provide practical guidance for the agriculture industry. "Farmers can be advised early on where to plant and what to plant, and if there's drought, when to irrigate," Perez said, as reported by Bunachita. "We can also advise them to harvest or plant earlier." As Perez and her colleagues have noted, such initiatives could lead to improved food security in the Philippines and elsewhere.

In addition to studying the data collected by satellites originating in other countries, Perez played a key role in the Philippine Scientific Earth Observation Microsatellite (PHL-Microsat) and Sustained Support for Local Space Technology and Applications Mastery, Innovation and Advancement (STAMINA4Space) programs, which worked to develop small satellites known as microsatellites between 2014 and 2018. As small, lightweight, and relatively inexpensive to manufacture devices capable of collecting a variety of data, microsatellites were particularly appropriate for use by a nation such as the Philippines, which did not have a space program or the means of launching satellites into orbit domestically at that time. The first such satellite from the Philippines, Diwata-1, entered orbit in 2016 after being transported first to the United States and subsequently to the International Space Station. Perez's involvement in the Philippines' burgeoning satellite program included her role as head of the STAMINA4Space initiative's Project 5, which focused on remote-sensing data.

RECOGNITION AND PUBLICATIONS

A significant contributor to her field and to the broader scientific community in the Philippines, Perez has received a variety of honors for her work, including several awards and prizes. In October 2018, she was named the recipient of the ASEAN-U.S. Science Prize for Women, a $20,000 prize awarded by Association of Southeast Asian Nations (ASEAN), the United States Agency for International Development (USAID), and Underwriters Laboratories (UL). In addition to offering a monetary award, the ASEAN-U.S. Science Prize for Women drew further attention to Perez's work and to Perez herself as a researcher. "Since getting the award, I have received several invitations to discuss my research and share my journey

in becoming a scientist," she told Icamina. "I hope that through these platforms I can inspire the younger generation." Perez went on to receive the 2019 Outstanding Women in the Nation's Service Award, and in 2021, the National Academy of Science and Technology (NAST), Philippines named her a 2021 Outstanding Young Scientist for her work in satellite technology.

In addition to receiving such recognition, Perez has publicized her research at a number of conferences and events both within and outside of the Philippines. In 2018, she delivered a talk titled "Why We Should Think about the Beyond" at the event TEDxXavierSchool in San Juan, Philippines. Perez has also published papers on her research in a variety of publications, including the *Proceedings of the National Academy of Science (PNAS)*, *Physica A: Statistical Mechanics and its Applications*, *Philippine Journal of Science*, *Journal of the Philippine Geosciences and Remote Sensing Society*, *Journal of Climate*, and *Scientific Reports*.

PHILIPPINE SPACE AGENCY

While scientists in the Philippines had worked to launch microsatellites in partnership with researchers and agencies based in other countries, the Philippines did not operate its own space agency during the twentieth century or beginning of the twenty-first. In 2019, however, the Congress of the Philippines voted in favor of the 2019 Philippine Space Act, which was signed into law by President Rodrigo Duterte that August and went into effect the following month. The act established the Philippine Space Agency (PhilSA), an agency dedicated to overseeing research, educational efforts, and national security initiatives related to space. PhilSA was likewise responsible for managing the use of space technology to respond to issues such as climate change and natural disasters, an area for which Perez's work on satellites and agriculture was particularly relevant.

In January 2021, Perez was appointed PhilSA's deputy director general for space science and technology, a role in which she was tasked with overseeing PhilSA's range of space science and technology initiatives, including its satellite programs. Perez was likewise tasked with communicating the agency's goals to the public as well as to international bodies such as the United Nations Committee on the Peaceful Uses of Outer Space (COPUOS). "The enactment of the Philippine Space Act marks the Philippines' formal recognition of the increasing strategic importance of space and its peaceful uses for the benefit of Filipinos and all humanity," she said in a statement before COPUOS's Legal Subcommittee (2 June 2021). "The law provides a framework for the Philippine Space Policy that will enable the country to become a truly space-capable and space-faring nation." Perez further confirmed PhilSA's "unwavering commitment to international cooperation and collaboration in the peaceful uses of outer space." In both national and international communications, Perez stressed the importance of PhilSA's efforts to use satellite data to deal with climate change, as the Philippines is particularly vulnerable to climate-related phenomena such as rising sea levels, floods, and droughts, all of which can be monitored through satellite and other remote-sensing data.

MULA

In addition to working with microsatellites such as the Diwata satellites and the Maya series of CubeSats, PhilSA leaders such as Perez plan to expand the agency's body of satellites over the next several years to include new satellites that are significantly larger than earlier technologies. One such satellite in development is the Multispectral Unit for Land Assessment (MULA), a collaborative project of PhilSA, UP Diliman, and the Department of Science and Technology–Advanced Science and Technology Institute. Scheduled for launch in 2023, MULA is intended to be an improvement upon earlier satellites created in the Philippines and a particularly useful tool for researchers focusing on the environment and agriculture. "We will be able to better monitor terrestrial ecosystems, as well as our land and marine resources to ensure both agricultural productivity and environmental integrity," Perez explained in a televised interview, as reported by the *Manila Standard* (15 June 2021). MULA's planned features include a camera capable of capturing higher resolution images than the cameras used in predecessors such as Diwata-1.

SUGGESTED READING

Bunachita, Jose Santino. "Award-Winning Pinay Scientist Gives Farmers Crucial Tool: Satellite Data." *Inquirer.net*, 21 Oct. 2018, newsinfo.inquirer.net/1045202/award-winning-pinay-scientist-gives-farmers-crucial-tool-satellite-data. Accessed 7 Jan. 2022.

"Filipina Wins Asean Science Prize." *SunStar*, 19 Oct. 2018, www.sunstar.com.ph/ampArticle/1769955. Accessed 7 Jan. 2022.

Icamina, Paul. "More Role Models Needed to Inspire Women to Pursue Science." *SciDev.Net*, 19 Nov. 2018, www.scidev.net/asia-pacific/role-models/more-role-models-needed-to-inspire-women-to-pursue-science/. Accessed 7 Jan. 2022.

Perez, Gay Jane. "Philippine National Statement: Agenda Item No. 3 'General Exchange of Views.'" *UNOOSA*, 2 June 2021, www.unoosa.org/documents/pdf/copuos/lsc/2021/statements/item_3_Philippines_ver.1_2_June_AM.pdf. Accessed 7 Jan. 2022.

"PH to Launch Its Largest Satellite in 2023." *Manila Standard*, 15 June 2021, manilastandard.net/tech/tech-news/357204/ph-to-launch-its-largest-satellite-in-2021.html. Accessed 7 Jan. 2022.

"Pinay Scientist Sees Great Potential in 'Precision Agriculture.'" *ABS-CBN News*, 14 Nov. 2018, news.abs-cbn.com/video/business/11/14/18/pinay-scientist-sees-great-potential-in-precision-agriculture. Accessed 7 Jan. 2022.

Uy, Jocelyn R. "Images Captured by Diwata-1 a Click Away at No Cost." *Inquirer.net*, 1 May 2017, technology.inquirer.net/61954/images-captured-diwata-1-click-away-no-cost. Accessed 7 Jan. 2022.

—*Joy Crelin*

Imani Perry

Born: September 5, 1972
Occupation: Scholar and author

Princeton University professor Imani Perry is a noted scholar of law, literature, and cultural studies as well as an award-winning author of creative nonfiction. From her first books, *Prophets of the Hood: Politics and Poetics in*

Hip Hop (2004) and *More Beautiful and More Terrible: The Embrace and Transcendence of Racial Inequality in the United States* (2011), to *The New York Times* Best Seller *South to America: A Journey Below the Mason-Dixon to Understand the Soul of a Nation* (2022), her work "primarily focuses on the history of Black thought, art, and imagination crafted in response to, and resistance against, social, political and legal realities of domination in the West," according to her Princeton faculty page. In 2018, she published three award-winning books: *Looking for Lorraine: The Radiant and Radical Life of Lorraine Hansberry*, the first full biography of the playwright; *May We Forever Stand: A History of the Black National Anthem*; and *Vexy Thing: On Gender and Liberation*, her critical study of patriarchy, capitalism, the transatlantic slave trade, and the age of conquest. Asked in an interview by Jamie Saxon for *Princeton University News* (24 Aug. 2018) how she managed such productivity, she responded, "I'm a person who likes to work on multiple projects at once and so they all sort of just emerged around the same time, after years of working on each." She has also written for *The Atlantic* and its newsletter, *Unsettled Territory*.

EARLY LIFE

Imani Perry was born on September 5, 1972, in Birmingham, Alabama, to a Black Catholic family involved in the civil rights movement. Her mother was Black, and her adoptive father was a White Jewish man from Brooklyn, New York. By the time she was three, Perry was accompanying her parents to protests.

Perry's early years were filled with family and happiness, as she wrote in an essay for *The Atlantic* (15 June 2020): "I cannot remember a time in my life when I wasn't earnestly happy about the fact of my blackness. When my cousins and I were small, we would crowd in front of the mirrors in my grandmother's house, admiring our shining brown faces, the puffiness of our hair."

Perry's family moved to Cambridge, Massachusetts, when she was five years old so that her mother could attend Harvard University for her doctorate. Perry attended the Cambridge Friends School from kindergarten through middle school, which she has said her mother chose for her because it was small and progressive. As Perry wrote for *The*

Photo by HowlRound Theatre Commons, via Wikimedia Commons

Prep School Negro (13 Sept. 2010), "She was preparing me for a life of meaning, but also for an integrated life, one that from early on would be a realization of the beloved community she and others had fought so hard for in the Movement." She graduated from Cambridge Friends in 1986.

An avid reader, Perry's favorite books during childhood included the Logan Family series, a nine-volume fictional saga by Mildred D. Taylor. The Logan Family novels, which include the Newbery Medal–winning *Roll of Thunder, Hear My Cry* (1976), taught her both political and social history along with the tales. As she told Saxon for *Princeton University News* (15 Jan. 2015), "When I was young, books provided comfort and security and also a space for imagination. When my mother was busy writing her doctoral dissertation, I always had a book with me. I read all day long."

EDUCATION AND CAREER

Perry was not always comfortable, however, in the largely White, northern community, so different from her life in Alabama. "I was in the second generation of Black children in elite white schools. But knowledge of how to navigate such places wasn't passed along to us. So it was like we were beginning again," she wrote for *The Prep School Negro*. "I have a trinitarian tradition, just as I lived in three regions by age five, I went to three different high schools, and later earned three graduate degrees trying to find a place where I didn't feel like a square peg." She eventually ended up at Concord Academy (CA), in nearby Concord, Massachusetts, for high school. Students at the academy were politically aware, demanding class rings with no ties to the diamonds that came from South Africa, for example. President of her senior class, she graduated from CA in 1990.

Although she began college at Yale University as a math major, Perry switched to American studies and literature, including Latin American literature, earning a bachelor's degree in 1994. She went on to earn a doctorate in the history of American civilization from Harvard University in 2000, while at the same time earning a JD from Harvard Law School, where she studied from 1996 until graduating in 2000.

Perry was a professor at Rutgers University School of Law in Camden, New Jersey, from 2002 until 2009, when she left Rutgers to join the faculty of Princeton University. As Princeton's Hughes-Rogers Professor of African American Studies in the Center for African American Studies, she has taught American history and culture, along with literature and law. She has also been a faculty associate with programs in law and public affairs, gender and sexuality studies, and jazz studies.

TRAFFIC STOP

In February 2016, two police officers, a man and a woman, stopped Perry in Princeton, New Jersey, for speeding, and, upon finding out that she had unpaid parking violations dating back to 2013, arrested her. (The police said she had two violations; Perry said she had just one). Perry alleged that the police had treated her "inappropriately and disproportionately" due to her race, she said, as quoted by Susan Svrluga for *The Washington Post* (10 Feb. 2016). According to her, she was handcuffed and placed in a squad car. At the station, she was handcuffed to a workstation. After she paid the outstanding fine, she was released. The event shook her, as she commented on both *Facebook* and *Twitter*. She noted that although a woman police officer was present, the male officer had performed her body search. In addition, she had not been allowed to make a phone call or text before being taken into custody. Although

Perry acknowledged that other Black women have experienced harsher treatment in custody, the incident left her feeling frightened and humiliated as well as motivated her to push for greater police accountability and reform. As Christine Hauser reported for *The New York Times* (10 Feb. 2016), Perry wrote on *Facebook*, "I hope that this circle of attention will be part of a deeper reckoning with how and why police officers behave the way they do, especially towards those of us whose flesh is dark."

MAY WE FOREVER STAND

In 2018, Perry published *May We Forever Stand: A History of the Black National Anthem*, based on her research on "Lift Every Voice and Sing." The book's title comes from one of the final lines of that song. With lyrics composed in 1900 by noted Black poet James Weldon Johnson and music by his brother John Rosamond Johnson, the piece was designed to celebrate Abraham Lincoln's birthday. After that initial performance, it became rooted in Black culture before "The Star-Spangled Banner" became the official national anthem in 1929.

Perry used her skills as a researcher to create an archive of references to the song and its performances, tracing the history of its importance to the Black community. She discovered that the music has also inspired visual artists as well as other writers. In addition, it cut across ideologies, as she related to Saxon (2018), saying, "I am really moved by how, on the one hand, Martin Luther King Jr. would cite passages of it in his sermons, but also members of the Black Panther Party and other Black nationalist organizations would sing it at gatherings. It was a touchpoint, and a way of communicating fellow feeling, notwithstanding different perspectives."

The book's several awards have included the 2019 American Studies Association John Hope Franklin Book Award for the best book in American Studies, as well as the Hurston Wright Award for Nonfiction. It was also a finalist for an NAACP Image Award in Nonfiction.

LOOKING FOR LORRAINE AND BREATHE

Perry published her biographical study of the playwright Lorraine Hansberry (1930–65) in 2018. It was the first full biography of Hansberry, who is best known for becoming the first Black playwright and the youngest to win a New York Critics' Circle Award for her 1959 Broadway play *A Raisin in the Sun*. Before beginning work on the book, Perry wrote for *New York Review* (1 July 2021), "I often worried that it was too late to fill the gap of decades when her work was neglected, although even now much of her writing is out of print or has never been published." Perry argued that the neglect was due not only to Hansberry being Black but also because she married a Jewish radical, was a member of the Communist Party, and was bisexual. Hansberry served as a role model for Perry, as she told an interviewer for the Graduate School of Arts and Sciences at Harvard University (20 Nov. 2018): "Ultimately, understanding her life made me less critical of my own because I thought, oh, it's OK: Here is someone who created beautiful things who was also going in a thousand directions at once."

Looking for Lorraine won several awards, including the Pen Bograd-Weld Award for Biography, the Phi Beta Kappa Christian Gauss Award for outstanding work in literary scholarship, and the Lambda Literary Award for LGBTQ Nonfiction. *The New York Times* designated it a 2018 notable book, and the Black Caucus of the American Library Association named it an honor book. In addition, it was a finalist for the African American Intellectual History Society Pauli Murray Book Prize.

The following year, Perry released *Breathe: A Letter to My Sons*, a public letter to her two sons. A reviewer for *Kirkus Reviews* wrote (1 July 2019), "Perry emphasizes the critical life discipline of making choices—not in the shallow sense of choosing success or achievement but rather within the depths of the long, historic freedom struggle to answer important questions—e.g., 'How will you treat your word? How will you hold your heart? How will you hold others?'" *Breathe* was honored as a finalist for the NAACP Image Award in Nonfiction and also was a finalist for the 2020 Chautauqua Prize.

SOUTH TO AMERICA

In January 2022, Perry published *South to America: A Journey Below the Mason-Dixon to Understand the Soul of a Nation*, a blend of memoir, travelogue, and historical inquiry written from the perspective of a returning exile. She began her research for the book with the assumption that race was central to the South, and her travels to states south of the Mason-Dixon line, where slavery had been legal before the Civil War, bore out that idea. As Carlos Lozada quoted from the book for *The Washington Post* (20 Jan. 2022), Perry believed that the South was key in understanding the nation, writing, "To be an American is to be infused with the plantation South, with its Black vernacular, its insurgency, and also its brutal masculinity, its worship of Whiteness, its expulsion and its massacres, its self-defeating stinginess and unapologetic pride."

PERSONAL LIFE

Perry still loves to read. Asked what her perfect reading experience would be, Perry wrote for *The New York Times* (12 Sept. 2019), "I love to read in a comfortable chair, sitting in front of an open window while it is raining, preferably torrential rain. The scent, the breeze and a book: a perfect combination." Perry has two sons, Freeman and Issa, and lives near Philadelphia.

SUGGESTED READING

Hauser, Christine. "Princeton Professor's Arrest Reignites Debate about Racial Profiling." *The New York Times*, 10 Feb. 2016, www.nytimes.com/2016/02/10/nyregion/black-princeton-professor-protests-her-parking-ticket-arrest.html. Accessed 21 July 2022.

Perry, Imani. "Imani Perry." *The Prep School Negro*, 13 Sept. 2010, www.theprepschoolnegro.org/imani-perry. Accessed 5 July 2022.

___. "In Her Own Voice." *The New York Review*, 1 July 2021, www.nybooks.com/articles/2021/07/01/lorraine-hansberry-in-her-own-voice/. Accessed 7 July 2022.

___. "Perry Explores History of the Black National Anthem in 'May We Forever Stand.'" Interview by Jamie Saxon. *Princeton University News*, 24 Aug. 2018, www.princeton.edu/news/2018/08/24/perry-explores-history-black-national-anthem-may-we-forever-stand. Accessed 5 July 2022.

___. "Racism Is Terrible. Blackness Is Not." *The Atlantic*, 15 June 2020, www.theatlantic.com/ideas/archive/2020/06/racism-terrible-blackness-not/613039/. Accessed 7 July 2022.

___. "The Way Home." *TIME Magazine*, 14 Feb. 2022, pp. 46–50. *EBSCOhost*, search.

ebscohost.com/login.aspx?direct=true&db=edb&AN=155039280&site=eds-live. Accessed 27 June 2022.

___. "What I Think: Princeton Professor Imani Perry." Interview by Jamie Saxon. *Princeton University News*, 15 Jan. 2015, www.princeton.edu/news/2015/01/15/what-i-think-princeton-professor-imani-perry-0. Accessed 22 July 2022.

___. "Why Imani Perry Doesn't Like Jane Austen's Novels." Interview. *The New York Times*, 12 Sept. 2019, www.nytimes.com/2019/09/12/books/review/imani-perry-by-the-book-interview.html. Accessed 2 July 2022.

SELECTED WORKS

Prophets of the Hood: Politics and Poetics in Hip Hop, 2004; *More Beautiful and More Terrible*, 2011; *May We Forever Stand*, 2018; *Vexy Thing: On Gender and Liberation*, 2018; *Looking for Lorraine*, 2018; *Breathe: A Letter to My Sons*, 2019; *South to America: A Journey Below the Mason-Dixon to Understand the Soul of a Nation*, 2022

—Judy Johnson

Evan Peters

Born: January 20, 1987
Occupation: Actor and producer

Following his acclaimed debut in the independent drama *Clipping Adam* (2004), Evan Peters became known for his ability to embody a wide variety of characters on the big and small screens. He first honed his acting skills through supporting roles in the critically acclaimed ABC series *The Days* and *Invasion* between 2004 and 2006, as well as a string of guest appearances on several popular shows throughout 2009. After appearances in films such as *An American Crime* (2007) and *Gardens of the Night* (2008), he achieved a career breakthrough in 2011 when he landed a starring role in *American Horror Story*. Over the next decade he continued making a name for himself on the FX anthology series, embodying a wide range of roles that included a mass-murdering teen, a serial killer, a modern-day alt-right cult leader, and several historical cult figures.

In addition to taking on dark and villainous characters, Peters proved adept at lighter fare, as evidenced by his witty, scene-stealing turns as the superhero Quicksilver in three of the X-Men franchise films (2014's *Days of Future Past*, 2016's *Apocalypse*, and 2019's *Dark Phoenix*) and several episodes of the Disney+ series *WandaVision* (2021). He also showed himself to be equally comfortable playing relatable, more common characters, like the young, eager Pennsylvania detective in HBO's *Mare of Easttown*—a portrayal that earned him a 2021 Emmy Award. Peters credited this diversity of parts with helping him to further develop as an actor. "All the roles were challenges and different sides of people that I can sort of try on when I need them," he shared with Alisha Brophy for *Esquire Singapore* (30 June 2019). "I feel like there was a certain maturity that came along with having the responsibility to play all those different roles. That helped me grow a lot."

EARLY LIFE AND LAUNCHING AN ACTING CAREER

Evan Thomas Peters was born to Julie and Phil Peters on January 20, 1987, in St. Louis, Missouri. He grew up alongside his older brother, Andrew (he also has an older sister,

Photo by Vogue Taiwan via Wikimedia Commons

Michelle), in the suburb of Ballwin. By 2001 he had been uprooted, resettling with his father, mother, and brother in Grand Blanc, Michigan, where his father worked as an administrative executive at Flint's Charles Stewart Mott Foundation.

As Peters began high school, he also made a foray into acting at the age of fifteen, signing with the talent agency Avante and studying acting at the Flint Youth Theatre. His initial interest in performing had been sparked while indulging in his favorite after-school activity: watching TV, including the Disney Channel series *Even Stevens*, which starred Shia LaBeouf. With the help of a local photographer whose attention he had drawn, he recorded himself reciting a monologue and submitted the tape to a California talent agent. Subsequently, around 2002 he relocated with his mother from Michigan to an apartment complex in Burbank, California. He continued to attend high school there and attempted to balance his schoolwork with auditioning and taking dedicated acting classes.

After landing commercials for Kellogg's, Sour Patch Kids, PlayStation, and Progressive, Peters successfully auditioned for the title role in the film *Clipping Adam* (2004), portraying a teen still grieving two years after his mother and younger sister were involved in a fatal car accident. The performance earned him the special jury breakthrough performance award at the 2004 Phoenix Film Festival. "I had no idea what I was doing. I was just trying to be truthful in the role, basically," he told James Franco in an interview for *Hero* (19 May 2016). Still working up his confidence in his ability to act professionally, he later added, "That was a huge pat on the back, getting out there and getting a lead on a movie."

EARLY ROLES

Peters followed uphis acting debut by playing a goofy skateboarder in the teen comedy *Sleepover* (2004). Meanwhile, by the time he was a junior, he had transitioned to the homeschooling program Options for Youth, through which he would receive his diploma. The year 2004 also saw him make a leap to television with the six-episode ABC drama *The Days* (2004), in which he costarred as the middle child of the titular suburban family. Quickly becoming a small-screen fixture, he had a recurring stint as Seth Wosmer, the

title character's friend in five first-season episodes (2004–05) of *Phil of the Future*, a sitcom running on the Disney Channel. Peters returned to ABC in the short-lived sci-fi drama *Invasion* (2005–06), portraying the teenage son of a park ranger investigating the alien takeover of a small Florida town. Later, he would explain to Franco that as he was still young and relatively inexperienced at that point, he had still not entirely figured out how to be an actor: "I was taking things for granted and just wanted things to happen and be what I wanted them to be, in terms of performances, without really knowing what to do or the amount of work that was needed to put into it."

Next came a string of big-screen appearances in the dramas *An American Crime*, which premiered at the 2007 Sundance Film Festival, and *Gardens of the Night* (2008), winner of the jury's Critics Award at the Deauville American Film Festival. After costarring in the martial arts flick *Never Back Down* (2008), Peters guested on several high-profile television shows, including the procedurals *Without a Trace* (2008) and *Monk* (2008), as well as the Fox medical drama *House* (2008) and the CBS supernatural series *Ghost Whisperer* (2009). He also played recurring character Jack Daniels in season six (2008–09) of the CW teen drama *One Tree Hill*.

From 2010 to 2011, Peters remained a presence on the small screen. In addition to guest-starring roles on the psychological dramas *The Mentalist* and *Criminal Minds* in 2010, he appeared in several critically acclaimed series, including the NBC sitcom *The Office* (2010), the NBC ensemble drama *Parenthood* (2011), and the ABC medical drama *The Good Doctor* (2011). At the same time, he made his return to the big screen in the superhero black comedy *Kick-Ass* (2010).

BREAKING THROUGH WITH *AMERICAN HORROR STORY*

Peters's acting career reached another level in 2011, when he was cast on *American Horror Story (AHS): Murder House*. In the inaugural installment of what would prove to be FX's immensely popular supernatural anthology series, he played Tate Langdon, a teen who had carried out a school shooting and whose ghost haunts his former home. After many years and characters later, Peters often still cited portraying Langdon as one of his most memorable roles for the series: "We didn't know what the show was, it was exciting, and it was crazy. He was such a complex character, like the dualism involved with that guy was just a real challenge to play," he related to Brophy. Front and center once again in *American Horror Story: Asylum* (2012–13), Peters portrayed Kit Walker, who is held at a mental-health facility for people deemed criminally insane during the 1960s following accusations that he had committed several murders. For *Coven*, the third *AHS* installment (2013–14), he had a supporting role, costarring opposite Emma Roberts as a fraternity student killed and resurrected.

Beginning in 2014, Peters rose to further fame as part of the ensemble cast of director Bryan Singer's *X-Men: Days of Future Past* (2014), playing a witty mutant with super speed. The X-Men franchise blockbuster went on to gross nearly $750 million worldwide, with his part as Quicksilver widely acknowledged as a highlight. Now increasingly in demand and often juggling projects, Peters then returned for the fourth part of *AHS* (2014–15) in the role of Jimmy Darling, a traveling carnival performer born with fused fingers resembling lobster claws. He subsequently made big-screen appearances in the low-budget horror flick *The Lazarus Effect* (2015) and the coming-of-age drama *Safelight* (2015) before playing yet another intense character in *AHS*'s fifth installment (2015–16): James Patrick March, the serial-killing owner/architect of a hotel built in the 1920s that is inhabited by his specter—and those of his victims.

BRANCHING OUT

Following a supporting role in the comedy biopic *Elvis and Nixon* (2016), Peters was back as Quicksilver in *X-Men: Apocalypse* (2016), which also had a successful box-office showing and featured another memorable sequence highlighting his character. During *AHS*'s sixth season (2016), Peters further impressed by performing double duty, portraying pompous actor Rory Monahan and Edward Philippe Mott, an eighteenth-century nobleman.

For *American Horror Story: Cult* (2017), Peters was tasked with playing fictional, power-hungry, 2010s cult leader Kai Anderson as well as real-life historical figures including David Koresh, Jim Jones, and Charles Manson. Having prepared by watching several documentaries and reading books like Steven Hassan's *Combating Cult Mind Control* (first published in 1988), his performance in the series' seventh season earned him a nod for the 2018 Critics' Choice Award for Best Actor in a Movie Made for Television or Limited Series.

Peters continued to challenge himself as an actor. During the first season of *Pose* (2018), a groundbreaking drama focusing on 1980s New York City's LGBTQ ballroom culture, he took on the role of Stan Bowes, a cisgender, married businessman who embarks on a doomed affair with Angel Evangelista, a transgender sex worker. When the FX series premiered in early June, it was largely well received by critics and television audiences. Peters went on to appear in *AHS: Apocalypse* (2018), the show's eighth season, once again portraying multiple characters. In discussing his lengthy tenure with the series, he told Lynn Hirschberg for *W* magazine (23 July 2018) that he always found it difficult to turn down creator Ryan Murphy's complex but ever-intriguing characters: "He just makes it so, I don't know, so appealing, and makes it sound so fun and interesting to do— and always, always a challenge. Then you can't resist." However, the show's intense shooting schedule and threat of burnout prompted him to announce in April 2019 that he would not participate in the following season.

In 2019, Peter costarred as Jeff Wald, singer Helen Reddy's husband, in the biopic *I Am Woman*. He also reprised his Quicksilver role on the big screen in *X-Men: Dark Phoenix* (2019). Then in 2021 he made a surprise appearance with a different take on the superhero character for the Marvel Studios television miniseries *WandaVision*.

EMMY WINNER

While shooting *WandaVision*, Peters was also filming the HBO limited series *Mare of Easttown* (2021), which went on to receive considerable acclaim. In it he plays Colin Zabel, a young detective brought in to assist the titular character, a troubled veteran detective, with a murder investigation in a small Pennsylvania town. In preparation for the role, he participated in a ride-along while also working with a dialect coach. His at-points vulnerable performance helped him nab his first-ever Emmy Award, in the category of Outstanding Supporting Actor in a Limited or Anthology Series or Movie.

That same year, Peters made his return to *AHS*, playing writer Austin Sommers in *Red Tide*, the first half of the series' double feature. Stepping behind the camera for the first time, he additionally served as a producer on six episodes. Meanwhile, in March 2021 it had been announced that he would assume the role of another sinister real-life figure, this time having been cast as serial killer Jeffrey Dahmer for Netflix drama. Regardless of the role, the ability to entertain audiences was something that Peters consistently valued. "You go to the movies to have a great time and to be blown away," he told Anthony Rotunno for *Teen Vogue* (10 Sept. 2013). "It's kind of amazing to be a part of the other side of that."

PERSONAL LIFE

Peters had a tumultuous on-and-off relationship beginning around 2012 with costar Emma Roberts. Though they were engaged to marry, they separated by 2019. Peters then began dating the singer Halsey, though that relationship ended in 2020. Over the years, he continued living in the Los Angeles area.

SUGGESTED READING

Brophy, Alisha. "Evan Peters: On Playing Jeff Wald in *I Am Woman*, Being Quicksilver in *X-Men*, and Staying Loyal to Tate Langdon of *American Horror Story*." *Esquire Singapore*, 30 June 2019, www.esquiresg.com/features/evan-peters-on-playing-jeff-wald-in-i-am-woman-being-quicksilver-and-staying-loyal-to-tate-langdon-of-american-horror-story/. Accessed 15 Nov. 2021.

Peters, Evan. "Evan Peters Came to Hollywood Because He Wanted to Meet the Olsen Twins." Interview by Lynn Hirschberg. *W*, 23 July 2018, www.wmagazine.com/story/evan-peters-ryan-murphy-pose-ahs-american-animals. Accessed 15 Nov. 2021.

—. "James Franco Offers Evan Peters Career Guidance ahead of His Starring Role in X-Men Apocalypse." Interview by James Franco. *Hero*, 19 May 2016, hero-magazine.com/article/61183/james-franco-offers-evan-peters-career-guidance-ahead-of-his-starring-role-in-x-men-apocalypse. Accessed 17 Nov. 2021.

Rotunno, Anthony. "Breakout Star Evan Peters Takes on *American Horror Story*." *Teen Vogue*, 10 Sept. 2013, www.teenvogue.com/story/evan-peters-american-horror-story. Accessed 15 Nov. 2021.

SELECTED WORKS

Clipping Adam, 2004; *One Tree Hill*, 2008–09; *American Horror Story*, 2011– ; *X-Men: Days of Future Past*, 2014; *X-Men: Apocalypse*, 2016; *Pose*, 2018; *X-Men: Dark Phoenix*, 2019; *Mare of Easttown*, 2021

—Bertha Muteba

Kim Petras

Born: August 27, 1992
Occupation: Singer-songwriter

Kim Petras's rise to fame took years of sacrifice and tenacity as she pursued her passion: music. In 2011, when she relocated to Los Angeles from Cologne, Germany, she did so with only $500 to her name and nowhere to stay. When Petras first started out, her hopes for getting a life-changing opportunity within the music industry abounded, though she was more known for being transgender than for her music. As she began to create opportunities for herself, she found allies in the industry, including English singer Charli XCX, and media personality Paris Hilton. Petras's career took off from there, propelled by the bold, bright pop anthems compiled in her two first studio albums: *Clarity* and *Turn Off the Light*, both released in 2019.

In 2021, ten years after she arrived in Los Angeles, Petras landed a major label contract with Republic Records, and while she knows that her transgender journey is a big part of who she is, she is adamant in letting her audience know that there is more to her than her gender identity. As she told Jim Farber for *The New York Times* (17 Mar. 2018), "I don't care about being the first transgender teen idol at all. I just want to be known as a great musician. On the other hand, that would be totally sick."

EARLY LIFE AND EDUCATION

The third child of Lutz Petras, an architect, and Kornelia Petras, a dance teacher, Kim Petras was born on August 27, 1992, in Cologne, Germany. Theirs was a household where music was always playing, and Petras, a child growing up in the 1990s and early 2000s, wholeheartedly embraced the icons of the

Photo by Ted Eytan from Washington, DC, USA, via Wikimedia Commons

era, including the Spice Girls, Kylie Minogue, and Gwen Stefani. Disney movies were also popular among her and her two older sisters, so much so that she yearned to be a Disney kid. "We used to lip-synch Disney songs," she told Alessa Dominguez for *BuzzFeed News* (3 Dec. 2021).

Music played a significant role during her school years, bringing solace to Petras, a shy and bullied middle schooler. As she told Jeff Nelson in an interview for *People* (2 Oct. 2019), "It means everything to me. When I was a kid, I used to not really have friends in school. I hated going to school—I got bullied pretty bad. I used to run home from school and watch Gwen Stefani music videos, and I felt like I could escape my problems with that." This was exacerbated by an intense feeling of grief, as Petras, who was assigned male at birth, could not identify with her body.

With the support of her parents, when Petras was twelve years old, she was among the first children to undergo hormone therapy, covered by German healthcare. Although the rule in Germany is that an individual must be eighteen years or older to undergo gender reassignment surgery, she petitioned for the surgery at age sixteen, to which doctors agreed after a psychiatric evaluation. At the time, Petras was the youngest person to undergo gender reassignment surgery, and with her transition journey documented by the media, she received national and international attention.

MOVE TO LOS ANGELES

Petras had begun writing music at the age of thirteen. Using the GarageBand software on her MacBook computer, she drew from her experiences at school for her songs. "I was just writing about boys that didn't like me back. Really cheesy, but I eventually got much better, and kind of wouldn't stop," she revealed to Dan Wootton for *The Sun* (25 Nov. 2021). After turning those songs into demos using a friend's small, attic studio, Petras reached out to local recording labels to introduce them to her music. Her unwavering efforts soon earned her a publishing deal with Universal Germany when she was still in her teens, but the deal was unsuccessful except for producing a jingle for a detergent brand and a string of little-known singles. The jingle did, however, help Petras afford a trip to Los Angeles, California, a city that thrummed with energy and musical opportunities.

Arriving in Los Angeles in 2011 at age nineteen with a three-month tourist visa and just $500, Petras slept on the couches of studios, where she sequestered herself to write songs. She was unrelenting in her efforts to network with people in the music industry, hoping to get a life-changing opportunity. However, finding the right people to help her with her career proved challenging, especially at first. "All the labels were just talking about me being transgender constantly and didn't even listen to the music. All the meetings I had with them were just like, 'How do we promote it? How do we not promote it? Can you be a pop star and be transgender?'" Petras said to Wootton before continuing, "All these old men would talk about my gender, and I was like, 'Ugh.'" She instead continued performing at local gay clubs to build a supportive following.

Her breakthrough came when a songwriting partner introduced her to the Stereotypes—a production team that would later achieve major success thanks to their work on Bruno Mars's 2016 album *24K Magic*. Through them, Petras became a writer for pop star JoJo's 2013 album *Jumping Trains*, which was shelved, and wrote a song that singer Fergie recorded, though did not end up using. Nonetheless, her collaborations generated enough hype for her to appear on several other artists' singles, including German DJ Klaas's "Flight to Paris" (2013) and Isaac Phase's "You" (2015).

WRITING MUSIC FOR HERSELF

Around 2016, Petras began partnering with producer Dr. Luke—who was facing legal issues after being accused by singer-songwriter Kesha of psychological and sexual abuse—the collaboration was frowned upon by many in the industry. At the same time, she collaborated with English singer Charli XCX, who featured Petras in her 2017 tune "Unlock It." She also became close friends and music partners with Aaron Joseph, a Los Angeles–based songwriter. "There wasn't a plan," she said to Dominguez. "It was just kind of like, OK, use studios with Aaron, make more songs, make more demos, write songs for other people, maybe." She eventually turned her focus to writing music for herself, instead of writing music to sell to others.

After finding it difficult to garner interest from record labels, she decided to create her own, named BunHead, through which she began releasing her original music. The first song she released was the dance-pop single "I Don't Want It at All" in August 2017. The song was later accompanied by a music video, released in October, which features a cameo by media personality Paris Hilton. With the single reaching the number one spot on Spotify's Global Viral Chart, the fan following that she had been slowly building during the past few years increased.

Petras followed "I Don't Want It at All" with the 2018 track "Heart to Break," a breakup-inspired song written and produced by Dr. Luke that had its premiere on BBC Radio 1 on February 19. Still, with few radio stations playing her music, Petras was not getting the exposure she needed. "All the radio stations were weirded out," Petras said to Dominguez. "And it was like a lot of them had probably never met a trans person, also it was like, 'This is, like, loud, and you sing really loud, and it's not what's happening right now.' They were like, 'Sorry.'"

Taking matters into her own hands, she capitalized on her social media presence to promote *Turn Off the Light, Vol 1*, a Halloween-themed extended play (EP) composed of eight songs, which was released in October 2018. Drawing from her long-time interest in horror films, Petras relied on theatrics and drama for this work, whose title track featured singer and actor Elvira, Mistress of the Dark. Moreover, the song "There Will Be Blood" was among the most streamed songs on Spotify. The same year, she joined the Bloom Tour as the opening act for singer Troye Sivan.

CLARITY AND TURN OFF THE LIGHT

Petras released her first full-length album, *Clarity*, in June 2019. The twelve songs—including "Icy," "All I Do Is Cry," and "Sweet Spot"—delved deep into the matters of the heart, though they were slower, a clear difference from her past creations that were more upbeat. As she said to Dominguez, "It was like everyone was like, 'You need to do midtempos, you need to not sing, that's how we're going to play you on the radio.'"

In support of the album, Petras embarked on a worldwide tour, called the Broken Tour, of US cities and European countries, starting in Nashville, Tennessee, and concluding in her native Cologne. Soon after she finished touring in September 2019, Petras released her second album, a full-length version of her previous EP now titled *Turn Off the Light*, that October. Comprising seventeen songs—including the eight songs of *Turn Off the Light, Vol 1*, and nine new songs—the album was positively received by critics and peaked at number fourteen on Billboard's Top Heatseekers chart. Furthermore, one of the new songs featured in the album, "Party Till I Die," was selected as one of the best twenty-five LGBTQ songs of 2020 by Billboard.

Although the coronavirus disease 2019 (COVID-19) pandemic halted Petras's plans to release more albums and tour as an opening act for singer Camila Cabello, Petras was still continually active in the music sphere. After being featured on Norwegian-born superstar Kygo's tune "Broken Glass" from his album *Golden Hour* (2020), Petras went on to sign a label contract with Republic Records in 2021. She released her first single with the label, the neo-disc "Future Starts Now," which was also the lead single of her future third studio album in August.

Also in 2021, Petras performed "Future Starts Now" at the MTV Video Music Awards. She later performed at the MTV Europe Music Awards, regaling the audience with extravagant performances of the singles "Coconuts" and

"Hit It from the Back," showing that she is at her best doing what she loves the most. "I'm a shy person until I get onstage," Petras told Dominguez before adding, "I get to be this person I wish I was in real life. That's when I feel like I don't think about what I do. I just am and I feel powerful, and I feel like I can do anything." She was the first openly trans artist to perform at each award show.

PERSONAL LIFE

Petras, a dog lover, adopted three dogs during the COVID-19 pandemic: a Chihuahua mix, a pug, and a Pomeranian. She lives in Los Angeles.

SUGGESTED READING

Aswad, Jem. "Pop Singer-Songwriter Kim Petras Signs with Republic Records." *Variety*, 26 Aug. 2021, variety.com/2021/music/news/kim-petras-republic-records-1235049989/. Accessed 5 Aug. 2021.

Dominguez, Alessa. "Kim Petras Wants to Be the Next Big Pop Star." *BuzzFeed News*, 3 Dec. 2021, www.buzzfeednews.com/article/alessadominguez/kim-petras-coconuts-met-gala-vmas. Accessed 5 Feb. 2022.

Farber, Jim. "Kim Petras Just Wants to Be a Pop Star." *The New York Times*, 17 Mar. 2018, www.nytimes.com/2018/03/17/style/kim-petras-is-fire.html. Accessed 5 Feb. 2022.

Petras, Kim. "Kim Petras on Designer Clothes and (Not) Dating." Interview by Ernesto Macias. *Interview Magazine*, 15 Oct. 2021, www.interviewmagazine.com/music/kim-petras-on-designer-clothes-and-not-dating. Accessed 5 Feb. 2022.

___. "Kim Petras Opens Up about How Bullies—and Childhood Idols—Prepared Her for Pop Stardom." Interview by Jeff Nelson. *People*, 2 Oct. 2019, people.com/music/kim-petras-rise-to-pop-stardom. Accessed 5 Feb. 2022.

Wootton, Dan. "'I Feel Blessed': Transgender Pop Star Kim Petras Says Transitioning at Sixteen Allowed Her to Chase Stardom." *The Sun*, 30 Aug. 2019, www.thesun.co.uk/tvandshowbiz/9832006/kim-petras-transition-clarity-fame. Accessed 5 Feb. 2022.

SELECTED WORKS

Turn Off the Light, Vol 1, 2018; *Clarity*, 2019; *Turn Off the Light*, 2019

—*Maria del Pilar Guzman*

Marie-Philip Poulin

Born: March 28, 1991
Occupation: Ice hockey player

Considered one of the best women's ice hockey players ever, Canadian Marie-Philip Poulin became especially known for her clutch scoring. She helped Team Canada clinch the gold medal in the 2010 Olympic Games, scoring both goals in a 2–0 win over the United States. She repeated that success in even more dramatic fashion at the 2014 Olympics, scoring a pivotal goal to tie the final tournament game (again against the United States) with less than a minute to go in the third period and then, in overtime, shooting another game-clinching "golden goal." The win added to Poulin's already impressive collection of trophies, which included several World Championship medals, and cemented her superstar status. Yet, she was perhaps most excited about the public attention the competitive game between the North American rivals brought to the sport of women's hockey. "Knowing there were 13 million Canadians watching that game, it is really something that I am so proud to be a part of," she later told Mark Zwolinski for the *Toronto Star* (17 Nov. 2017).

A hockey player since early childhood, Poulin began playing on senior-level teams as a teenager, competing with the Montréal Stars (later Les Canadiennes de Montréal) of the Canadian Women's Hockey League (CWHL) and joining the senior Canadian national team in 2009. Following four seasons with the Boston University Terriers, she returned to the CWHL until that league disbanded in 2019. She then joined several other prominent women's hockey players as an early member of the Professional Women's Hockey Players Association (PWHPA), an organization with the goal of establishing a truly professional women's league that would pay its players a living wage. "We believe in what we are doing.

We want to create that viable league and we're united," Poulin told CBC Sports reporter Andi Petrillo about the project, as quoted by John Wawrow for the CBC (22 Apr. 2020). "We're going to keep working together and that's something that's going to happen." Poulin also remained active in international competition, becoming Team Canada's captain in 2015. She earned a silver medal at the 2018 Olympics before once again proving herself as a key crunch-time player with a winning overtime goal to secure a World Championship gold medal for Canada 2021.

EARLY LIFE AND CAREER

Marie-Philip Poulin was born on March 28, 1991, in Québec City, Canada. She was the second of two children born to parents Robert and Danye, along with her older brother, Pier-Alexandre. As a young child living in the small town of Beauceville, Québec, she began her skating career as a figure skater but switched her focus to hockey when she was around five years old, joining her brother in that sport. "My parents did everything for me and my brother to be able to play hockey. They knew how passionate we were about playing," she recalled to Zwolinski. "They worked two jobs to be able to pay for hockey. I don't come from a wealthy family and they did everything they could do for us to play and it's something I'll never be able to put into words, how grateful I am to them." A talented young athlete, Poulin aspired to join the Canadian women's national hockey team one day, particularly after watching the Canadian team win a gold medal at the 2002 Winter Olympics.

As a teenager, the French-speaking Poulin moved to Montréal to attend Kuper Academy, where she worked to improve her English in the hope that doing so would help her secure a spot on the roster of the predominantly English-speaking Canadian national team. Her talent landed her a spot in the CWHL for the 2007–08 season with the Montréal Stars, and she was named league rookie of the year after leading her team in scoring. While attending Montréal's Dawson College between 2008 and 2009, she also competed with the Dawson College Blues.

Meanwhile, Poulin represented the province of Québec in national championships as well as in the 2007 Canada Winter Games. She went on to compete with the Canadian under-

Photo by hockeyMedia via Wikimedia Commons

eighteen (U18) national team, helping Canada claim silver medals at the International Ice Hockey Federation (IIHF) U18 Women's World Championship in both 2008 and 2009. Hockey authorities were already noting her talent, as she was crowned the top forward in the 2008 tournament. In 2009 Poulin made her debut at the senior-level IIHF Women's World Championship, contributing to the Canadian team's second-place finish.

OLYMPIC HERO

Poulin made her Olympic debut in 2010, at the Winter Games in Vancouver, Canada. Team Canada performed well throughout the women's hockey tournament, proceeding through the group stage and beating Finland in the semifinal round before facing the United States in the final game. "I didn't expect much ice time," she recalled to Kristina Rutherford for *Sportsnet* (22 Jan. 2018). "It was my first year and I was on the fourth line. I was young, I was learning a lot." Nevertheless, she soon demonstrated the extent of her hockey skills in front of an international audience. "I had two shifts in the first [period] and all of the sudden I scored," she told Rutherford. "I remember going back to the dressing room and I was like, 'Did that just happen right now?'" Remarkably, the young athlete scored again, accounting for Team Canada's entire output in a 2–0 victory.

With her first Olympic gold medal, Poulin was a hero for many Canadians and a rising hockey star.

Poulin remained a fixture of Team Canada's roster, helping to win silver medals at the World Championships in 2011 and 2013 and a gold medal in that tournament in 2012. She then returned to the Olympics for the 2014 Games in Sochi, Russia, and once again played a decisive role in Canada's victory. With less than a minute left in the final period, she scored a goal against the United States, tying the score and forcing the game into overtime. After about eight minutes of overtime play, she scored again, ending the game and securing her second consecutive Olympic gold medal. Poulin's clutch performance at two straight Olympics solidified her folk hero status in Canada. Yet, as she typically did, she reflected upon the game with an emphasis on it being a team effort overall. "I couldn't believe it," she told Rutherford. "I don't know if it's the right moment or the right place, but they gave me the pass. [Teammates] Laura Fortino and Rebecca Johnston made amazing plays in the overtime and I was there and I shot it."

COLLEGE CAREER

Meanwhile, in 2010 Poulin had relocated to the United States to enroll at Boston University (BU), an institution with a strong women's hockey program. While studying psychology, she joined the BU Terriers as a freshman and quickly distinguished herself as a player, setting new school records for both goals and points scored during a single season and earning the title of Hockey East Rookie of the Year. Following two more successful seasons, she took a leave of absence from the team to prepare for the 2014 Olympic Games, before returning to the Terriers for the 2014–15 season, during which she served as team captain.

While Poulin was proud of her achievements as a college athlete, having amassed a total of 181 points over the course of her BU career, she was even more pleased to have earned a bachelor's degree from the institution. "That's one of my proudest moments," she told Eric Duhatschek for *The Athletic* (23 Jan. 2018). "To be able to say, I graduated from Boston University, in my second language. Having that diploma." She went on to add, "I know we talk a lot about the Olympics, but being able to receive that diploma was something special

as well." Having successfully balanced her education with her playing, she graduated from BU in 2015.

CWHL AND TEAM CANADA CAPTAIN

As Poulin's college hockey career came to an end, she faced a situation familiar to many new college graduates: the challenge of finding a job. "I don't know what I'm going to do—if I'll go back to Canada. I want to coach, eventually. I'm debating," she told Avery Stone for *USA Today* (6 Mar. 2015) prior to graduating. "But, hopefully, I'll be playing hockey." She indeed opted to return to Canada after leaving BU, and returned to the CWHL to play for Les Canadiennes de Montréal (the renamed Montréal Stars) via their first pick in the draft, beginning in the 2015–16 season. Although joining the CWHL enabled her to continue playing hockey on a regular basis, it did not help her make a living—the league did not begin paying its players until the 2017–18 season, and even then, the maximum annual salary possible was only C$10,000 (about US$8,000). Supplementing her income with work as a coach throughout that period, Poulin was part of the team staff for institutions such as Dawson College and McGill University. She also benefited from sponsorships, including a deal with the cleaning-product brand Tide.

While playing the CWHL Poulin also remained active in international competition and was made captain of Team Canada in 2015 (which, together with her knack for timely scoring, would give rise to the nickname "Captain Clutch"). She helped the national team claim additional World Championship silver medals in 2015, 2016, and 2017. Returning to the Olympics in 2018, she and her teammates once again reached the gold medal game. This time, however, they lost to the United States in a shootout, leaving with the silver medal.

Although the national team's loss to the United States in the 2018 Olympics broke Canada's longstanding gold-medal streak, Poulin was not overly discouraged by that loss and focused instead on continuing to improve both individually and as a team. "We train so hard every year, not just in the Olympic year, to try to get better," she told Duhatschek about her mindset. However, Poulin missed most of the 2019 IIHF Women's World Championship due to an injury, and Canada earned only the bronze medal after falling to Finland in the semifinals.

INTERNATIONAL ROLE MODEL

The CWHL ceased operations in mid-2019, highlighting the struggles professional women's hockey faced as an industry. Poulin and several other former CWHL players opted not to join the US–based National Women's Hockey League (NWHL, later renamed the Premier Hockey Federation) and instead joined the newly founded Professional Women's Hockey Players Association (PWHPA), an organization that called for the creation of a true professional hockey league for women that would pay adequately and operate at a high standard of professionalism. "We're not asking for millions like the NHL guys, just something [where] we can wake up every day and go to work," she told Petrillo, as quoted by Wawrow. Poulin was affiliated with the Montréal branch of the PWHPA and competed against other regional PWHPA teams in events such as the 2021 Secret Dream Gap Tour.

As a member of both the Canadian women's national team and the PWHPA, Poulin worked steadily to promote the sport of ice hockey within Canada and to serve as a role model for younger players and children just joining the sport. "It was special for me coming up as a kid to have those role models for my career," she explained to Zwolinski. "[Former national team and CWHL teammate] Caroline Ouellette helped me for all those years, and being able to be that role model for younger girls is something I really cherish and something I strive for. Coming out onto the ice and having those girls with big eyes and being able to spark their dreams, it's really important to me." In addition to serving as role models by example, she and Ouellette collaborated to establish the Ouellette Poulin Hockey organization in 2018, and over the next years they held an array of hockey camps for players of multiple ages and levels.

Meanwhile, Poulin and her Team Canada teammates were unable to strive for a better World Championship result in 2020, as that year's tournament was canceled because of the coronavirus disease 2019 (COVID-19) pandemic. However, they returned to the World Championship in 2021, defeating the United States to claim Canada's first gold medal in the tournament since 2012. Poulin sealed that victory with yet another overtime golden goal, adding to her legacy as an all-time great. The Canadian national team went on to play a Rivalry Series of games against the US national team to prepare for the 2022 Winter Olympic Games.

SUGGESTED READING

Duhatschek, Eric. "Marie-Philip Poulin, 'the Sidney Crosby of Women's Hockey,' Becomes Canada's Leader on and off the Ice." *The Athletic*, 23 Jan. 2018, theathletic.com/218947/2018/01/23/marie-philip-poulin-the-sidney-crosby-of-womens-hockey-becomes-canadas-leader-on-and-off-the-ice/. Accessed 12 Nov. 2021.

Khatchaturian, Andre. "Women's Ice Hockey Team's Unstoppable Marie-Philip Poulin." *BU Today*, Boston University, 23 Jan. 2015, www.bu.edu/articles/2015/womens-ice-hockey-teams-unstoppable-marie-philip-poulin/. Accessed 12 Nov. 2021.

"Marie-Philip Poulin's Power-Play Goal in OT Gives Gold to Canada." *ABC News*, 20 Feb. 2014, abcnews.go.com/Sports/marie-philip-poulins-power-play-goal-ot-gold/story?id=22608450. Accessed 12 Nov. 2021.

Poulin, Marie-Philip. "Q&A: Canadian Captain Poulin Sets Bar on and off Ice." Interview by Mark Zwolinski. *Toronto Star*, 17 Nov. 2017, www.thestar.com/sports/hockey/2017/11/17/qa-canadian-captain-poulin-sets-bar-on-and-off-ice.html. Accessed 12 Nov. 2021.

Rutherford, Kristina. "'Captain Clutch' Marie-Philip Poulin Ready to Lead Canada to Gold Again." *Sportsnet*, 22 Jan. 2018, www.sportsnet.ca/olympics/captain-clutch-marie-philip-poulin-ready-lead-canada-gold/. Accessed 12 Nov. 2021.

Stone, Avery. "The Greatest Women's Hockey Player in the World Needs to Find a Job." *For the Win*, USA Today Sports, 6 Mar. 2015, ftw.usatoday.com/2015/03/marie-philip-poulin-canada-womens-ice-hockey-boston-university. Accessed 12 Nov. 2021.

Wawrow, John. "NWHL's Expansion to Toronto Gets Mixed Reviews from Women Players." *CBC*, 22 Apr. 2020, www.cbc.ca/sports/hockey/nwhl-toronto-expansion-team-official-1.5540780. Accessed 12 Nov. 2021.

—*Joy Crelin*

Thalappil Pradeep

Born: July 8, 1963
Occupation: Clean water advocate and chemist

For researcher Thalappil Pradeep, successful initiatives to provide the world's population with clean water must not only incorporate new scientific innovations but also take socioeconomic factors into account. "If you have money, of course, you get clean water," he told Akira Hayakawa for the *Nikkei* (30 Apr. 2020). "So, I was only interested in clean water technologies for the poor." As head of the Pradeep Research Group at the Indian Institute of Technology (IIT), Madras, Pradeep has long focused his research on making "clean water . . . available to the bottom of the pyramid," as he told Hayakawa, developing innovative means of removing a variety of pollutants from water through the use of materials such as metallic nanoparticles. His laboratory's creations, including the Arsenic and Metal Removal through Indian Technology (AMRIT) water-purification system, were geared particularly toward use in rural India. In rural regions, several problems contribute to poor water quality, including contaminants in the groundwater such as arsenic that render well water dangerous for human consumption and existing water-purification technologies that are too expensive and energy intensive for sustained use. Although Pradeep himself has been a key force in water-purification research since joining the faculty of IIT Madras in 1993, he has long credited the success of much of his work to the researchers, students, and scientific environment around him. "My work is because of the intense devotion of my students, the environment we have at IIT Madras, my funding agencies and my country," he told Dia Rekhi for the *Economic Times* (1 May 2020). "It has been my dream to do something for my country."

EARLY LIFE AND EDUCATION

Thalappil Pradeep was born in India on July 8, 1963. His parents were both educators, and his father was also a writer who published under the name N. N. Thalappil. Pradeep aspired to become a poet early in life, having not yet developed the passion for scientific research that would come to shape his career. "When I was a student I didn't really know what the excitement of science was," he later explained to Nithyanand Rao for *Immerse, the IIT Madras Magazine on Research in Science and Engineering* (2014). "Today, science possesses me. You get engulfed into it, you become so passionate about it."

After completing his secondary education, Pradeep enrolled in Calicut University in southern India, where he earned a bachelor's degree and master's degree between 1980 and 1985. He went on to pursue doctoral studies at the Indian Institute of Science in Bangalore, earning his PhD in chemical physics from that institution in 1991. The Indian Institute of Science would go on to award Pradeep its Distinguished Alumni Award for 2021.

ACADEMIC CAREER

Following his departure from the Indian Institute of Science, Pradeep traveled abroad to pursue postdoctoral work in the United States, completing fellowships at the University of California, Berkeley, and at Purdue University. He returned to India afterward and in 1993 joined the Indian Institute of Technology (IIT), Madras, as a visiting faculty member. A member of the IIT Madras faculty for the next several decades, Pradeep was promoted to assistant professor in 1995 and to associate professor in 2000. He was granted a full professorship in 2004 and six years later rose to the rank of senior professor. In 2016, Pradeep was named the Deepak Parekh Institute Chair Professor— one of the first people in university history to receive such a designation. In addition to teaching and conducting research at IIT Madras, Pradeep served as a visiting scientist at many institutions throughout his career, including Pohang University of Science and Technology in South Korea, Leiden University in the Netherlands, and the University of Hyogo in Japan.

WATER PURIFICATION

In addition to teaching at IIT Madras, Pradeep served as head of the Pradeep Research Group, a laboratory that specializes in research related to nanoscience and nanomaterials. Though the lab did not attract much attention or financial support in its early years, by 2006 it was a busy center of activity and innovation. Much of Pradeep's research concerns the use of nanomaterials in water-filtration systems, an area of research that stemmed from

Photo by Pradeep Office via Wikimedia Commons

Pradeep's realization that certain exceedingly small particles—or nanoparticles—have the ability to capture or break down pollutants commonly found in water and could thus be used to remove those substances from the water. "I found that nanoparticles of metals (such as silver) break the common pesticides molecules—by science, which we call reductive dehalogenation," he told Hayakawa about one form of that process. Pradeep's work was particularly significant due to the common reliance on well water in rural communities, which could face significant health risks when the local groundwater was contaminated with pollutants such as pesticides or naturally occurring arsenic.

Building upon their early findings, Pradeep and his colleagues developed the first water-purification system to use nanotechnology in the world. Their work included inventing filters that used nanoparticles to remove contaminants from water and creating relevant technologies that could be used by governments, nonprofit organizations, or for-profit companies. The research was necessarily complex, as different regions dealt with vastly different pollutants and faced varied infrastructural challenges. "There is no solution which is a complete solution," Pradeep explained to Rao. "The problem of water is so vast, so big, every solution has a role. Moreover, water itself is so diverse.

That is, your well water is different from your neighbor's well water. There is a lot of diversity in this, the chemistry is different. So therefore, there is a need for diverse products."

One of the most common toxins that naturally occurs in much of rural India's well water is arsenic. Arsenic poisoning can cause a host of problems, including cognitive deficiencies, skin lesions, and cancer. Water-filtration technologies developed within Pradeep's laboratory included the Arsenic and Metal Removal through Indian Technology (AMRIT) system, which used a nanomaterial based on iron oxyhydroxide to remove arsenic from water. The Pradeep Research Group was issued a patent for the AMRIT technology in 2014 and went on to be issued forty-three further patents between December 2014 and November 2021, many of them related to water-purification technology.

MAKING CLEAN WATER AFFORDABLE

Although Pradeep was abundantly concerned with the effectiveness of his water-purification technologies in removing dangerous contaminants from water, he was similarly concerned with ensuring that the technologies would be suitable for use in the communities most in need of them, which were often rural and poor. The technologies developed in Pradeep's laboratory, including AMRIT and later inventions, were particularly well suited for use in such communities because of their low operating costs, which Pradeep asserted would render clean water widely affordable. "We defined affordability as 5 paise [about US$0.06] per liter of clean water delivered at home," he told Rao. "Can you give arsenic-free water at 5 paise per liter delivered at home on your kitchen table? That's what these materials can do." In the end, Pradeep was able to surpass his goal, providing pure water at just 2 paise (US$0.03) per liter.

Pradeep and his colleagues also worked to ensure that their filtering technology was not reliant on electricity, which would not necessarily be available in all communities, and needed little maintenance to remain operational. The AMRIT technology was likewise highly customizable, as different nanomaterials could be used to filter out the pollutants of greatest concern in a given area. By 2020, dozens of water-purification units had been installed in Punjab, Uttar Pradesh, West

Bengal, and other Indian states, bringing clean drinking water to more than 7.5 million people. "He truly aims to provide an environment in which Indians can drink clean water without anxiety," Tatsuya Tsukuda, a University of Tokyo professor, told Hayakawa. "It is his life's work, which he is doing not for profit but from love for humanity."

In light of the continued need for clean water in regions throughout the world, Pradeep and his colleagues in 2018 founded the International Centre for Clean Water (ICCW), an initiative of IIT Madras. As head of the ICCW, Pradeep sought to encourage further research and collaboration, with the goal of ensuring the availability of clean water to all in need of it. Based in a facility at the IIT Madras Research Park in Chennai, the ICCW operated seven laboratories as of late 2021 and also offered consultancy services to governments, organizations, or corporations working within the water sector.

PUBLICATIONS AND OTHER RESEARCH

A prolific researcher, Pradeep published extensively on his work throughout his career, contributing more than 450 papers to journals such as the *Journal of Physical Chemistry*, *Industrial and Engineering Chemistry Research*, and *ACS Sustainable Chemistry and Engineering*. He likewise contributed chapters to a number of books, including *Catalysis: Principles and Applications* (2002), the *Springer Handbook of Nanomaterials* (2013), and *Advances in Water Purification Techniques* (2019). The author of the 1999 volume *Advances in Physical Chemistry*, Pradeep went on to author or coauthor several books dedicated to nanoscience, including *Nanofluids: Science and Technology* (2007), *A Textbook of Nanoscience and Nanotechnology* (2012), and *Aquananotechnology* (2014).

In addition to water-purification projects, Pradeep and the Pradeep Research Group performed research into numerous areas related to nanomaterials, nanotechnology, and chemistry over the years. Among other projects, scientists affiliated with the laboratory worked to replicate space-like conditions for the purpose of analyzing the forms that certain chemicals might take in space. "What we have found is that molecules like methane and ammonia in space could exist in a completely different form than what is known to us,"

Pradeep explained to the *Hindu BusinessLine* (9 Jan. 2019). Scientists affiliated with the research group suggested that crystalline solids known as clathrate hydrates, potentially produced in interstellar conditions, could possibly be used as fuels in the future.

INTERNATIONAL RECOGNITION

Widely celebrated for his work throughout his career, Pradeep was the recipient of numerous honors during the first decades of the twenty-first century. He received medals from the Materials Research Society of India in 2002 and the Chemical Research Society of India (CRSI) in 2004, and in 2008, the Indian government awarded him the National Research Award in nanoscience and technology as well as the Council of Scientific and Industrial Research's Shanti Swarup Bhatnagar Prize. An elected fellow of organizations such as the Royal Society of Chemistry, the Indian National Science Academy (INSA), and the National Academy of Sciences (NAS), Pradeep was a 2020 recipient of the prestigious Padma Shri, one of India's highest civilian honors. He likewise earned recognition outside of India and in 2018 received The World Academy of Science (TWAS) award in chemistry, and in 2020 was awarded the Japan-based Nikkei Asia Prize, which recognizes contributions to sustainable development in Asia. In addition to international publicity, the latter prize granted him a monetary award of three million yen (about US$26,000). Although Pradeep noted that his research would proceed as planned regardless of whether he earned such honors, he told the website of the ICCW in 2020 that awards such as the Padma Shri served as "recognition for the years of dedication" and "provide[d] energy for continued dedication."

PERSONAL LIFE

Pradeep lives in Chennai, India.

SUGGESTED READING

Hayakawa, Akira. "Indian Researcher Opens Taps on Cheap Drinking Water." *Nikkei Asia*, 30 Apr. 2020, asia.nikkei.com/Spotlight/Nikkei-Asia-Prizes/Indian-researcher-opens-taps-on-cheap-drinking-water. Accessed 12 Nov. 2021.

"IIT-Madras Scientists Create 'Space Fuel' in Lab." *The Hindu BusinessLine*, 9 Jan. 2019, www.thehindubusinessline.com/news/

science/iit-m-create-space-fuel-in-lab/
article25947889.ece. Accessed 12 Nov.
2021.

Rao, Nithyanand. "Walking on Water." *Immerse*,
Indian Institute of Technology Madras,
2014, pp. 6–11. *Issuu*, 7 Feb. 2021, issuu.
com/t5eiitm/docs/immerse_2014. Accessed
12 Nov. 2021.

"Recognition Provides Energy for Continued
Dedication, Says Professor Thalappil
Pradeep." *International Centre for Clean
Water*, IIT Madras Initiative, 2020, iccw.
world/news/recognition-provides-energy-
for-continued-dedication-says-professor-
thalappil-pradeep-recepient-of-padma-shri-
award-2020/. Accessed 12 Nov. 2021.

Rekhi, Dia. "IIT-Madras Professor T Pradeep
Chosen for Nikkei Asia Prizes 2020."
The Economic Times, 1 May 2020,
economictimes.indiatimes.com/news/
politics-and-nation/iit-madras-professor-t-
pradeep-chosen-for-nikkei-asia-prizes-2020/
articleshow/75493743.cms. Accessed 12
Nov. 2021.

SELECTED WORKS

Advances in Physical Chemistry, 1999;
Nanofluids: Science and Technology (with Sarit
K. Das, Stephen U. S. Choi, and Wenhua
Yu), 2007; *Nano: The Essentials*, 2007;
Aquananotechnology (with David E. Reisner),
2014

—Joy Crelin

Azim Premji

Born: July 24, 1945
Occupation: Business executive and
philanthropist

Business executive Azim Premji rose to become
one of the richest people not only in his native
India but in the world, with a personal wealth
of more than $9 billion in the early 2020s.
The vast majority of his wealth came from
developing his family's cooking-oil business into
Wipro Limited, a highly diversified company
best known as one of India's largest software
service providers. An international powerhouse
with customers around the world, the
company's areas of expertise came to include
artificial intelligence, cloud computing, cyber
security, data analytics, and robotics, among

other technology consulting services. Wipro
continued to expand even as Premji himself
began to move out of the active management
of the firm in 2019.

After building his fortune, Premji also
became well known for his philanthropic efforts,
earning a reputation as a modest and ethical
billionaire. Focusing heavily on educational
efforts, he formed the Azim Premji Foundation
nonprofit in 2001 to focus on primary schooling
in India and established Azim Premji University
in his hometown of Bengaluru (formerly known
as Bangalore) in 2010. Premji became the first
Indian billionaire to sign the Giving Pledge, a
campaign developed by fellow billionaires Bill
Gates and Warren Buffett that asks the world's
richest people to give the majority of their
wealth to charity. "If anyone personifies India's
economic transformation, it is Azim Premji,"
Gates himself wrote in a profile of Premji for
Time magazine's 2011 list of the hundred most
influential people in the world (21 Apr. 2011).
"But it may be his pioneering leadership in
India's nascent field of philanthropy that will
be Premji's lasting legacy. . . . He is setting
a remarkable example for those who have
benefited so enormously from India's economic
expansion and are looking for ways to give
back."

EARLY LIFE AND EDUCATION

Azim Hashim Premji was born on July 24,
1945, in Bombay (now Mumbai), India, two
years before India received its independence
from the British Empire. Around the time of
Premji's birth, his father established Western
Indian Vegetable Products, later known as
Wipro, a company that focused on making
a popular hydrogenated shortening called
vanaspati. When India became independent
in 1947, Pakistan was created as a separate
Muslim state. Although Premji's family was
Muslim and was invited to move to Pakistan,
his father decided to remain in India because
of his successful business dealings.

In his youth, Premji developed an
appreciation for capitalism through his father
and for philanthropy through his mother.
In an article he wrote for the *Indian Express*
(11 Oct. 2019), he discussed his mother's
influence: "My mother was one of the founder
members of a charitable orthopaedic hospital
for disabled children—one of the first in the
country after Independence—which she ran

Photo courtesy
the World Economic Forum,
via Wikimedia Commons

for 50 years as the executive chairperson. I observed, through my childhood, what it took to do that, and the difference it made in the lives of people." Premji also became a great admirer of Mahatma Gandhi, the famed activist who used nonviolent methods to push for Indian independence and civil rights until his assassination in 1948. Gandhi's belief that the wealthy held great social responsibility resonated with Premji from a young age.

In the early 1960s Premji enrolled at Stanford University in the United States, where he studied engineering. He did not initially complete his degree, however, as his father died suddenly in 1966, and so he returned to India to sort out the family business. He recalled for the BBC News (14 July 2003) how one shareholder emphatically told him he was too young and inexperienced to lead a company. "That really made me more and more determined to make a success of Wipro," he noted. Returning to his studies years later, Premji finally earned his degree from Stanford in 1999.

BUILDING WIPRO

At just age twenty-one, Premji decided that he would take up his father's mantle as chair of the family company. The first thing he began to

do was to diversify the business's investments beyond cooking oil. Under his direction the company became involved with a wide range of products, including home goods such as lightbulbs and toiletries as well as industrial components such as hydraulics. In 1977, he officially changed the company's name to Wipro.

In 1979, the Indian government forced technology giant IBM to leave the country over charges that it was selling the government obsolete equipment. Sensing an opportunity, Premji started to shift his company into the computer and information technology market. Through international partnerships with more established tech companies, Wipro began producing computer hardware for the Indian government and then the public. Premji then turned to developing software, relying on the wide supply of Indian software developers to do the work at a fraction of the cost compared to programmers in the United States. Wipro became known for heavily investing in training, and attracted many of the most skilled tech workers in India. Before long, the company was exporting software around the world, including to the key US market.

By the 1990s Wipro's stock value was taking off, aided in large part by the boom in mobile telephones as well as economic deregulation in India. Some of Wipro's major clients in this period included Nokia and NEC. The internet boom of the late 1990s and early 2000s further benefited the company, which expanded into information technology (IT) services. As a result, Premji's net worth increased to the point that he became one of the richest people in India. He was also among the first in the country to earn a fortune in the IT field with an international focus. When asked how Wipro had managed its spectacular rise, Premji told David Smith for The Guardian (26 Aug. 2006), "I don't think there's any secret. I think we've built a strong culture in the organisation through mentoring, through leadership, through sensitivity to the customer in terms of being able to service every day, sensitivity to employees and a strong spirit of winning without compromising at any stage the highest standard of integrity. These combinations make us successful."

Although often praised for its corporate culture, Wipro did occasionally attract criticism for its role in the "offshoring" phenomenon, in which business activity shifts to places with lower labor costs, like India. Some observers contend that this contributes to economic inequalities of globalization. However, Premji took a more optimistic view on the realities of globalization. "I don't think it's a question of who's going to win and who's going to lose," he told Smith. "I think what you're going to see is a significantly higher degree of partnering. . . . There's no alternative but to go on developing parts of the world."

Like many companies, Wipro faced challenges with the global financial crisis in 2008, but it soon recovered and continued to grow. By 2014, the diversified company had revenues of approximately $7 billion. In 2019, Premji began transitioning away from company operations, passing on the role of executive chair to his son Rishad. Wipro continued to prosper, with revenues of over $8 billion in the early 2020s. Premji also held many investments in other companies, many through his management organization Premji Invest.

PHILANTHROPY

Although famed for his great wealth, Premji earned a reputation for being humble and modest compared to many other billionaires. Part of this stemmed from his longtime admiration of Gandhi, who believed that the wealthy must, of their own accord, use their resources to benefit others. "The people saw in him a beacon, an ideal, and a leader whom they were inspired to follow," Premji wrote for the *Indian Express*. "Those of us who are privileged to be in leadership roles will realise that the power of position diminishes with time, whereas moral leadership endures."

Building on those beliefs, after earning his fortune Premji began thinking of ways that he could use his money to benefit others. Improving Indian society through education and economic development became a major focus. Ultimately, he decided that he would guide his philanthropic investments the same way he had guided his company to success. "I became convinced that markets, public systems and philanthropic initiatives all had a significant role to play if the country was to have inclusive development, and that we needed to work purposefully towards establishing a more humane, equitable and ethical society for all our citizens," Premji said, as quoted by *India Today* (23 Feb. 2013).

To this end, he founded Azim Premji Foundation in 2001. The nonprofit organization began with the primary aim of improving educational opportunities for children in India's rural regions. Within a decade, it had provided computer systems to thousands of schools and supported various programs benefiting over 2.5 million children. In December 2010, Premji announced that he would donate an additional $2 billion for improving education across India—then the largest charitable contribution in India's history. His efforts were not limited to primary education, however. Also in 2010 his foundation created Azim Premji University in Bengaluru, with the express goal of training social sector workers including teachers and public administrators. The university would also grow to offer both undergraduate and postgraduate studies in a wide variety of fields.

In 2013, Premji announced he would join the Giving Pledge campaign to give most of his wealth to charity. Over the next several years he made several further major donations, much of it from his Wipro stock. In early 2019, for example, he earmarked another $7.5 billion to his foundation. That put his total charitable contributions at about $21 billion, making him the biggest giver in India and among the top philanthropists in the world. After the global COVID-19 pandemic emerged in 2020, Premji authorized his foundation to aid in response efforts, and it worked with the Indian National Centre for Biological Sciences (NCBS) and the Institute for Stem Cell Science and Regenerative Medicine to build out testing infrastructure. The foundation also continued its core mission of improving education throughout India.

Premji characterized his philanthropic work as a necessary outgrowth of his success in business. He said, as quoted by *TimesDrop* (21 Jan. 2021), "I strongly believe that those of us, who are privileged to have wealth, should contribute significantly to try and create a better world for the millions who are far less privileged."

AWARDS

Throughout his long career Azim Premji earned many accolades for both his business acumen and his philanthropic efforts. He was often named to various lists of the most influential or powerful people in the world or in the business community, including by *Fortune* and *Forbes* in

2003, the *Financial Times* in 2005, and *Time* in 2004 and 2011. In 2007, *BusinessWeek* placed him among the top thirty entrepreneurs in world history, and the *Journal of Foreign Policy* ranked him among the top global thinkers in 2011. The *Economic Times* gave him its Lifetime Achievement Award in 2013.

In addition to receiving numerous honorary doctorates from various universities, Premji was awarded the Faraday Medal by the Institution of Engineering and Technology (IET) in the United Kingdom, becoming the first Indian to receive that award. He was inducted into France's Legion of Honor and in 2011 he was given one of India's highest civilian awards, the Padma Vibhushan. In 2017, he was honored with the Carnegie Medal of Philanthropy.

PERSONAL LIFE

Azim Premji and his wife, Yasmin, have two sons, Rishad and Tariq. Despite his great wealth, Premji became known for living a quiet life, for example flying economy class on business trips, driving an old car, and maintaining a modest home in Bengaluru. He enjoys simple pleasures such as reading, hiking, jogging, and golf.

SUGGESTED READING

"Azim Premji." *Forbes*, www.forbes.com/profile/azim-premji/?sh=ac5ab7f79247. Accessed 10 May 2022.

"Azim Premji." *TimesDrop*, 21 Jan. 2022, www.timesdrop.com/azim-premji. Accessed 10 May 2022.

"Defining Moments: Azim Premji." *BBC News*, 14 July 2003, news.bbc.co.uk/2/hi/south_asia/3064335.stm. Accessed 10 May 2022.

Gates, Bill. "The 2011 Time 100: Azim Premji." *Time*, 21 Apr. 2011, content.time.com/time/specials/packages/article/0,28804,2066367_2066369_2066101,00.html. Accessed 10 May 2022.

"I Believe Those of Us Who Are Privileged Should Contribute Significantly to Try and Create a Better World: Noble Words and Noble Deeds of Azim Premji." *India Today*, 23 Feb. 2013, www.indiatoday.in/mail-today/story/azim-premji-wipro-chairman-donates-millions-154693-2013-02-23. Accessed 10 May 2022.

Premji, Azim. "Mahatma Gandhi's Idea of the Rich as Trustees Can Make an Effective, Sustainable Difference." *The Indian Express*, 11 Oct. 2019, indianexpress.com/article/opinion/columns/mahatma-gandhi-wealth-6063201/. Accessed 10 May 2022.

Smith, David. "The Story of Bangalore Bill." *The Guardian*, 26 Aug. 2006, www.theguardian.com/business/2006/aug/27/theobserver.observerbusiness3. Accessed 10 May 2022.

—*Christopher Mari*

Christian Pulisic

Born: September 18, 1998
Occupation: Soccer player

In May 2021, soccer player Christian Pulisic became the first American player to compete in the Union of European Football Associations (UEFA) Champions League finals. His achievement in that final round of competition, which he and the Chelsea Football Club ultimately won, was truly just one in a string of impressive accomplishments for the athlete, who had previously been the youngest foreign player to score in Germany's Bundesliga as well as the youngest player ever to score for the US men's national soccer team. Pulisic, however, tended to downplay such milestones. "It's one of those things I don't really listen to," he explained to Matt Welty in an interview for *Complex* (9 Aug. 2021). "I mean I try to accomplish these things for myself, for my team, not to be the first American to do something." Regardless of his motivations, Pulisic successfully made a name for himself as a strong player throughout his professional career, first with the German team Borussia Dortmund and later with Chelsea, which competed within England's Premier League.

He was also a core member and one of the faces of the US men's national team, earning US Soccer male player of the year three times between 2017 and 2021 and helping the United States to qualify for the 2022 *International Federation of Association Football* (FIFA) World Cup. Although Pulisic faced some setbacks, including the loss of his starting position with Chelsea during a team management change, he remained focused on competing at the highest possible level. "I want to be on the pitch," he told Jonathan Liew in an interview for *The Guardian* (13 May 2022). "I'm hoping that I can get more opportunities."

EARLY LIFE

Christian Mate Pulisic was born in Hershey, Pennsylvania, on September 18, 1998. The son of Kelley and Mark Pulisic, he grew up alongside his two older siblings. The sport of soccer played a significant role in the Pulisic family: both of Pulisic's parents had played soccer while attending George Mason University, and his father later played for a professional indoor soccer team and also coached the sport. Although he additionally played sports such as baseball as a child, Pulisic was drawn to soccer from a young age and aspired to play professionally. A fan of the Argentine player Lionel Messi, he also drew particular inspiration from the members of the US men's national soccer team (USMNT). "I think there was just always that feeling . . . that somehow they would come away with a result," he later told Welty. "They had that fight to them. They had that American spirit."

In 2005, the Pulisic family moved to England for a year. There, Pulisic played for the Brackley Town under-eight soccer team and became more familiar with the Premier League, the highest professional soccer league in England. Following his return to the United States, he played for various youth teams, including teams affiliated with the Pennsylvania Classics soccer program. Pulisic began to represent the United States on the youth level in 2012 and went on to play in nearly thirty international matches as an under-fifteen player.

MOVE TO GERMANY

In 2015, at the age of sixteen, Pulisic left the United States for Germany, where he joined the academy of the professional soccer club Borussia Dortmund. Although accompanied by his father, he initially struggled with moving to a new country and team. "The first two years in Germany were very tough for me: a foreign country, a new language, being away from my family and friends," he recalled to Dominic Fifield in an interview for *The Guardian* (21 May 2019). "I thought people were looking at me, asking: 'Who is this American trying to take my spot?'" Nevertheless, Pulisic was determined to let his play speak for itself. "If they see you can play, they respect you," he told Fifield.

Pulisic began his Borussia Dortmund career with the club's under-seventeen team but moved up to the senior team when he turned

Photo by Erik Drost,
via Wikimedia Commons

seventeen, making his debut appearance in Germany's Bundesliga in January 2016. He played in nine matches with the senior club during the 2015–16 season and scored his first goal with the club in April 2016, becoming the youngest foreign player to score a Bundesliga goal. He remained a key member of the club throughout Borussia Dortmund's next two seasons. During the 2017–18 season, he started twenty-seven of the thirty-two matches in which he played.

USMNT

In addition to playing for Borussia Dortmund, Pulisic continued to represent the United States in international competition during that period. In May 2016, he became the youngest player ever to score for the senior-level national team. In addition to competing in various friendly matches, he appeared in events such as the 2016 Copa América Centenario, in which his team finished in fourth place. He was voted US Soccer male player of the year for the first time in 2017. The following year, he became the youngest player to captain the USMNT, serving as captain for a game against Italy.

Although Pulisic and his teammates hoped to qualify for the 2018 FIFA World Cup, they were unsuccessful in doing so, much to Pulisic's disappointment. "The worst stuff to hear is 'They just didn't care. They didn't give enough effort,'" he told Oliver Franklin-Wallis for *GQ* (19 Jan. 2021). "Because I felt like I gave everything I had, and it wasn't enough." Despite that setback, the USMNT went on to win the Confederation of North, Central America and Caribbean Association Football (CONCACAF) Gold Cup the following year.

CHELSEA

In January 2019, Pulisic signed with the soccer club Chelsea, which competed within England's Premier League. His transfer fee reportedly exceeded $73 million and was the highest ever paid for a player from the United States. Although he signed in January, he finished the 2018–19 season in Dortmund before leaving Germany for England. "I'm still trying to take it all in," he said to Fifield following his arrival. "It's been a huge dream of mine, to play here in England. So to be here is incredible." He made his first appearance with the team in a preseason game in Japan in July 2019 and made his Premier League debut with Chelsea the following month. He scored his first Premier League hat trick in October of that year.

Pulisic played in twenty-five Premier League matches during his first season with Chelsea, starting in nineteen of them. He struggled with injuries throughout the season, including a torn muscle that forced him to miss matches in early 2020. Pulisic had few opportunities to play during the first half of that year, as Premier League play was suspended in March 2020 due to the coronavirus disease 2019 (COVID-19) pandemic. "It's been tough," he told Franklin-Wallis about his experiences during quarantine. "I haven't seen my family in a long time. I don't really go out besides being at the training ground. That's really all I do." The Premier League resumed operations in June 2020, although spectators were not permitted to attend games in keeping with social-distancing protocols.

SETBACKS AND ACHIEVEMENTS

The start of the 2020–21 Premier League was delayed by over a month due to the ongoing pandemic, ultimately taking place in September 2020. The season was a difficult one for Pulisic, who missed several matches in November following a muscle injury. In January 2021, team manager Frank Lampard

was fired and replaced by Thomas Tuchel. While Pulisic had played under Tuchel in Germany, he struggled to retain his starting position following Tuchel's arrival and lost that position for a time. "Obviously, I wasn't playing right from the start when he came in," he commented on that situation, as reported by John Muller for *The Athletic* (14 June 2022). "That doesn't mean we have a bad relationship in any way, but I had to earn a spot—just like I always do." By the end of April, Pulisic had once again become a starter.

In addition to playing in the Premier League, Chelsea competed in the 2020–21 UEFA Champions League during that period and beat Spanish club Real Madrid in the semifinals before defeating fellow English club Manchester City in the final round of the tournament. "I don't know if it's totally sunk in yet, it was such an incredible achievement," Pulisic told Jack Rosser in an interview for the *Evening Standard* (29 July 2021). "It's starting to hit us—it gives us a lot of confidence." Chelsea went on to win the UEFA Super Cup, beating the Spanish club Villarreal in August 2021.

Having injured his ankle while playing for the USMNT, Pulisic was forced to sit out a dozen matches in the early months of the 2021–22 Premier League season. He subsequently returned to play and in February 2022 made his hundredth overall appearance with Chelsea. The club finished third in the Premier League standings at the end of the season, its best finish thus far during Pulisic's tenure.

AN UNCERTAIN FUTURE

As a prominent member of the USMNT, Pulisic felt a great deal of pressure in the leadup to the 2022 FIFA World Cup, particularly in light of the United States' failure to qualify for the World Cup in 2018. However, the team's performance in events such as the June 2021 final match of the CONCACAF Nations League, which saw Pulisic score the game-winning goal against Mexico, strengthened his belief that the team would qualify for the upcoming tournament. "I'd say we have a lot of confidence just from recent games and different tournaments we've played in. And just how much this team has grown," he told Welty. "I think we should definitely be confident in going in, but we know that we have to go in there and get a job done." In March 2022, the USMNT officially qualified to compete in the upcoming World Cup, which was scheduled to be held in Qatar in November and December of that year. March was also a milestone month for Pulisic personally, as he scored his first USMNT hat trick in a match against Panama.

While the future of the USMNT seemed promising, the direction of Pulisic's professional career was less certain. His contract with Chelsea was set to end in 2024, but rumors spread within the soccer media that he might depart the club earlier than that and join a new professional club elsewhere. Chelsea leadership was likewise reportedly open to receiving transfer offers for Pulisic, with clubs such as Juventus rumored to be interested in adding Pulisic to their rosters. Despite such rumors, Pulisic remained with Chelsea for the 2022–23 preseason.

PERSONAL LIFE

In addition to playing soccer, Pulisic enjoys the game of chess, having learned to play as a child thanks to his paternal grandfather. Pulisic played online chess extensively in 2020 and 2021 and later credited the game with helping him navigate a psychologically challenging period in his life.

In June 2022, it was announced that Pulisic's first book, *Pulisic: My Journey So Far*, was scheduled for publication in October of that year. The book was set to feature numerous photographs, personal recollections, and other material that he hoped would help inspire the next generation of soccer players. "I like to lead by example," Pulisic explained about the project, as reported by SherShah Atif for *ESPN* (21 June 2022). "I hope guys can see my mentality going into games and the way that I compete. I hope that they can see that and want to do the same."

SUGGESTED READING

Atif, SherShah. "U.S., Chelsea Star Christian Pulisic Shares His Story in New Book 'My Journey So Far.'" *ESPN*, 21 June 2022, www.espn.com/soccer/blog-the-toe-poke/story/4689093/uschelsea-star-christian-pulisic-shares-his-story-in-new-book-my-journey-so-far. Accessed 11 July 2022.

Franklin-Wallis, Oliver. "America Finally Has a Global Soccer Star." *GQ*, 19 Jan. 2021, www.gq.com/story/americas-global-soccer-star-christian-pulisic. Accessed 11 July 2022.

Muller, John. "How Chess (So Much Chess) Explains Christian Mate Pulisic." *The Athletic*, 14 June 2022, theathletic.com/3362188/2022/06/14/pulisic-chess-usmnt-kante/. Accessed 11 July 2022.

Pulisic, Christian. "Chelsea's Christian Pulisic: 'I Want to Be on the Pitch. I Enjoy This Club a Lot.'" Interview by Jonathan Liew. *The Guardian*, 13 May 2022, www.theguardian.com/football/2022/may/13/chelsea-christian-pulisic-enjoy-this-club-a-lot-fa-cup-final. Accessed 11 July 2022.

___. "Christian Pulisic Interview: Confident Chelsea FC Can Win Premier League and FA Cup Double after Ruling Europe." Interview by Jack Rosser. *Evening Standard*, 29 July 2021, www.standard.co.uk/sport/football/christian-pulisic-interview-chelsea-fc-champions-league-premier-fa-cup-b948202.html. Accessed 11 July 2022.

___. "Christian Pulisic Talks Signing to Puma and Qualifying for the 2022 World Cup." Interview by Matt Welty. *Complex*, 9 Aug. 2021, www.complex.com/sneakers/christian-pulisic-signing-to-puma-interview. Accessed 11 July 2022.

___. "Christian Pulisic: 'There's a Champion Mentality at Chelsea.'" Interview by Dominic Fifield. *The Guardian*, 21 May 2019, www.theguardian.com/football/2019/may/21/christian-pulisic-champion-mentality-at-chlesea. Accessed 11 July 2022.

—*Joy Crelin*

Rudi Putra

Born: February 7, 1977
Occupation: Biologist

For Indonesian biologist Rudi Putra, saving threatened species and habitats requires a great deal of both time and patience. "Conservation isn't a two or a five-year program," he told Ellen Lomonico for the website of the Goldman Environmental Prize (15 Apr. 2021). "We are planning for the long-term." Beginning in the late 1990s, Putra dedicated himself to protecting the Leuser Ecosystem, a large area of rainforest, mountains, and wetlands in the north of the Indonesian island of Sumatra. To that end, in 2013 he founded the Leuser Conservation Forum, a nongovernmental organization working in partnership with the provincial government to protect the Leuser Ecosystem from a variety of threats, including deforestation and the encroachment of illegal palm oil plantations. Of particular concern for Putra and other conservationists was the welfare of the many animals living within the region, which included critically endangered species such as the Sumatran rhino. Threatened by both habitat loss and poachers, only about fifty Sumatran rhinos were living in the wild by the early 1990s, but Putra and his colleagues steadily worked to increase that number, including by implementing antipoaching patrols and beginning construction on a rhinoceros sanctuary within Leuser. "I am very optimistic we can still save Sumatran rhinos and thousands of other endangered species with the right interventions and with enough unity and energy," he told *National Geographic* (2 Feb. 2022). "I feel that this hope is not just a fantasy—in fifty years when this question is asked again I believe it is possible that the Sumatran rhino is no longer critically endangered." Widely recognized for his work, Putra was the recipient of the 2014 Goldman Environmental Prize and in 2019 was named a fellow of the National Geographic Society.

EARLY LIFE AND EDUCATION
Rudi Putra was born on February 7, 1977, in Aceh, a province of Indonesia located in the northern portion of the island of Sumatra. Interested in nature from an early age, Putra pursued studies in conservation biology at Syiah Kuala University in Banda Aceh, during which he developed a greater appreciation for the natural features of his home province, particularly the region known as the Leuser Ecosystem. "I remember reading an article in my undergraduate biology days about the magnificence and global significance of the Leuser Ecosystem and realizing this important landscape is in my home," he later recalled in -a discussion with *National Geographic*.

Putra visited the Leuser Ecosystem for the first time in 1998. Increasingly drawn to the region, he took a research position in 2000 with the primatologist Carel van Schaik, who was studying Indonesia's orangutan population at the time. To Putra's disappointment, however, the job was short-lived. "I really wanted to continue the research in 2000, but it was cancelled due to the heated security situation

in Aceh at the time," he told Junaidi Hanafiah in an interview for *Mongabay* (17 June 2021). "In fact, our research station where we did our research was burned down." Putra later studied tropical biodiversity conservation at Bogor Agricultural University (later known as IPB University), from which he earned a master's degree in 2014.

LEUSER ECOSYSTEM
Putra continued to dedicate his career to the welfare of the Leuser Ecosystem, an area spanning more than 6.5 million acres in northern Sumatra, much of it within Aceh. The ecosystem is one of the most biodiverse regions in Southeast Asia, encompassing tropical rainforests, wetlands, and the mountains of the Leuser Range. It is also home to about two hundred species of animals, including critically endangered species such as Sumatran elephants and orangutans.

Of particular concern to Putra was the critically endangered Sumatran rhino population, which had dwindled to as few as fifty individual rhinoceroses by the mid-1990s. "I love Sumatran rhinos because they are very unique, needing the safest place in the world," he told *National Geographic*. "They choose to live far from human activities, and even from other animals. They don't like noise. They are shy yet they are so strong." Over the course of more than two decades, Putra steadily worked to protect and increase the Sumatran rhino population. His main focus at first was to combat poaching by establishing anti-poaching patrols and to conserve the rhinoceroses' habitat.

LEUSER CONSERVATION FORUM
In 2013, Putra founded the Forum Konservasi Leuser (FKL; Leuser Conservation Forum), an organization dedicated to protecting the Leuser Ecosystem while working in partnership with bodies such as the Aceh provincial government. The organization was a small one at first, with a staff of only about ten members. "We were the little guy," Putra told Lomonico. "It's a huge forest, but no one knew about it. No one knew about us." By the start of the next decade, however, the FKL had expanded significantly, employing more than three hundred staff members. Putra and his colleagues were responsible for conducting a number of key initiatives in the ecosystem,

including patrolling the region and dismantling snares left by would-be poachers. They also collected data on local wildlife populations and operated research stations for use by visiting scientists.

Putra received international recognition for his work in the Leuser Ecosystem and in 2013 was awarded the Future for Nature Award. The following year he won the Goldman Environmental Prize, an award that recognizes achievement among environmentalists and is accompanied by a monetary award. "Receiving this award exceeded all my expectations," Putra told Tommaso Perrone in an interview for *Lifegate* (28 Apr. 2015) about the Goldman Prize. "I feel stronger and more motivated in continuing in my fight to protect the environment in Indonesia." The recognition Putra received also drew further attention to the work of the FKL, which would forge partnerships with international organizations such as Global Forest Watch and the International Rhino Foundation.

COMBATING DEFORESTATION

One major area of environmental concern in the Leuser Ecosystem throughout the early years of the FKL was deforestation, a phenomenon in which wide areas of trees are cut down and which has severe ramifications for the animal species living there. "We have already lost a lowland forest habitat that was home to elephants, tigers, rhinos and orangutans, due to the expansion of oil palm plantations, mining concessions and infrastructural development," Putra explained to Perrone. "These animals will become extinct in the near future if Indonesia doesn't halt deforestation in lowland forests." In Indonesia, approximately two million acres of rainforest are lost to deforestation each year. While the Indonesian government placed a two-year moratorium on forest-clearing in certain types of forest in 2011 and later extended that moratorium several times, deforestation remained a major threat due to both illegal forest-clearing and the limited scope of the moratorium itself.

A major cause of deforestation and habitat destruction in the Leuser Ecosystem has come from palm oil plantations. Palm oil is a resource that is in high demand globally as it is used in soaps and in many packaged foods like cereal, potato chips, and other snack foods. Much of the world's palm oil is grown in Indonesia, often illegally through a corrupt system of government bribing. Putra and his colleagues worked to restore areas that had been converted to palm oil plantations to their natural forested state. While Putra focused in large part on removing palm oil trees that had been illegally planted in the Leuser Ecosystem, he also criticized many of the legally operated plantations throughout Indonesia for their effects on the local environment. "Some companies I know manage their estates well. They have to maintain plantations in the long term, without damaging forests, protecting those areas that are important to biodiversity and without interfering with water sources," he told Perrone. "But many other plantations are destroying forests, killing animals and creating conflicts with surrounding communities. There are more 'bad' companies than 'good' ones." In addition to removing palm oil trees, Putra negotiated with plantation owners, reminding them of their illegal actions and alerting them to conservation boundaries. As a result, more than 1,200 acres of illegal plantations had been shut down by 2014, many of them voluntarily, allowing Putra's team to better restore those areas. Furthermore, Putra and his colleagues worked to rid the forest of illegally planted rubber trees, which were also present in some areas.

AGROFORESTRY AND COMMUNITY EMPOWERMENT

Aware of the socioeconomic factors underlying practices such as poaching and the illegal planting of oil palms, Putra encouraged local communities to adopt the practice of agroforestry. This included planting forest-based crops, such as bamboo and fruiting plants like durian, that benefit the local human population but are less harmful to the forest than oil palms. "This agroforestry system is admittedly not comparable with the natural forest, but it is much better than conventional farming," he told Hanafiah. "There are usually two to three types of plants on farms, but with this system, 20–30 types can be planted, including some types of forest plants." Putra and his colleagues also supported the introduction of honeybees into the area, which could provide local beekeepers with honey for consumption or sale.

In 2019, the FKL began a community empowerment program, through which Putra and his colleagues sought to build much-needed connections with nearby villages. "For me, Leuser's natural beauty and its wildlife are not the most interesting aspects that drive me to work here," he explained to Hanafiah. "Leuser's function as the vital part of the community's life is the main reason, such as providing water, clear air and preventing ecological disasters." FKL staff also worked to prevent conflicts between the animals of the Leuser Ecosystem and human villages by constructing barriers to prevent animals such as elephants from entering villages, which can cause widespread destruction and result in the animals being killed in response. Such projects became even more important during the COVID-19 pandemic that began in 2020, as increasing numbers of people moved from cities to rural areas where they were more likely to plant crops that encroached on nearby forests like those in the Leuser Ecosystem. Despite setbacks during the pandemic, Putra's work proved successful; by 2021, encroachment had decreased by about 95 percent, and six hundred communities were helping the FKL achieve its reforestation goals.

THINKING LONG-TERM

A 2019 fellow of the National Geographic Society, Putra continually stressed the environmental significance of the Leuser Ecosystem throughout his career, not only to the island of Sumatra but also to the world. In particular, he worked to call attention to the Leuser rainforest's role as a carbon sink—an area, such as a forest, that takes in carbon dioxide and thus prevents that gas from becoming trapped in the atmosphere. The Leuser Ecosystem, for example, is capable of absorbing 1,700 gigatons of carbon per year. This, in turn, prevents that carbon dioxide from contributing to the greenhouse effect, the phenomenon that causes global warming.

In addition to educating the world about the benefits of restoring and protecting the Leuser Ecosystem's trees and other plant life, Putra and the FKL worked to assure the long-term viability of the region's species as well, focusing in particular on the Sumatran rhino. In late 2021, conservationists broke ground on a new Sumatran Rhino Sanctuary in Leuser, which would be overseen by the FKL. The sanctuary was designed to protect the rhinoceroses living within it as well as facilitate the breeding of Sumatran rhinos that could later be introduced into the wild, thus helping to grow the population and promote genetic diversity.

PERSONAL LIFE

Putra lives in Aceh, Indonesia.

SUGGESTED READING

Lomonico, Ellen. "Prize Winners Today: Rudi Putra on Conserving Indonesia's Leuser Ecosystem." *The Goldman Environmental Prize*, 15 Apr. 2021, www.goldmanprize.org/blog/prize-winners-today-rudi-putra-on-conserving-indonesias-leuser-ecosystem/. Accessed 13 June 2022.

Putra, Rudi. "Never Too Late to Save Earth: Q&A with Leuser Forest Guardian Rudi Putra." Interview by Junaidi Hanafiah. Translated by Intan Iskandar. *Mongabay*, 17 June 2021, news.mongabay.com/2021/06/never-too-late-to-save-earth-qa-with-leuser-forest-guardian-rudi-putra/. Accessed 13 June 2022.

___. "Rudi Putra: 'What Use Is It to Be Rich If We Can't Enjoy Nature?'" Interview by Tommaso Perrone. *Lifegate*, 28 Apr. 2015, www.lifegate.com/rudi-putra-environment-forests-indonesia. Accessed 13 June 2022.

"Rudi Putra." *Future for Nature*, futurefornature.org/ffn_winner/rudi-putra/. Accessed 13 June 2022.

"Rudi Putra." *The Goldman Environmental Prize*, www.goldmanprize.org/recipient/rudi-putra/. Accessed 13 June 2022.

"Rudi Putra." *National Geographic*, www.nationalgeographic.org/find-explorers/rudi-putra. Accessed 13 June 2022.

"Rudi Putra: Restoring the Sumatran Rhino Population." *National Geographic*, 2 Feb. 2022, www.nationalgeographic.com/impact/article/rudi-putra-protecting-the-critically-endangered-sumatran-rhino. Accessed 13 June 2022.

—*Joy Crelin*

Quinn

Born: August 11, 1995
Occupation: Football (soccer) player

At the 2020 Summer Olympic Games held in Tokyo in 2021, soccer player Quinn made history as part of Canada's gold medal-winning women's team. The Toronto-born midfielder became the first openly transgender, nonbinary person to compete in the Olympics, as well as the first to win a medal. The victory came after a decade spent playing for the youth national team that finished second at the 2012 Confederation of North, Central, America and Caribbean Association Football Under-17 (CONCACAF U-17) Championship and the senior national squads that claimed bronze at the 2016 Rio Olympics and three additional CONCACAF silver medals (2016–20).

Quinn also achieved success at the collegiate level, helping Duke University reach the quarterfinals in 2013 and the national title game in 2015 before she became the highest-drafted Canadian player in the National Women's Soccer League (NWSL) in 2018. Quinn's accomplishments come as no surprise to their first-ever soccer coach, Breagha Carr-Harris. "[Quinn] is relentless and unapologetic when it comes to . . . preparation, resilient in the face of crushing setbacks, the epitome of what a true teammate is and humble almost to a fault," Carr-Harris wrote for *Streets of Toronto* (6 Dec. 2018).

EARLY YEARS AS AN ATHLETE

Quinn (formally born Rebecca Quinn) and their twin sister, Jillian, were born on August 11, 1995, in Toronto, Ontario, where they grew up alongside two other sisters, Lauren and Erin, in an athletic family. In the early to mid-1980s, Quinn's mother, Linda Quinn, played basketball for the University of Waterloo and their father, Bill Quinn, played rugby for the University of Western Ontario. At age six, Quinn joined the youth team of the North Toronto Soccer Club (NTSC); they also grew up swimming, skiing, and playing hockey. While attending high school at Havergal College (2009–13), Quinn helped the varsity basketball team win two Conference of Independent Schools of Ontario Athletic Association (CISAA) championships (2009, 2012) and was named most valuable player (MVP) of 2010–11. They also helped

Photo by Jamie Smed,
via Wikimedia Commons

Havergal claim another CISAA title (2011), in volleyball.

As a member of the Erin Mills Mighty Eagles, Quinn won two consecutive Ontario Cup outdoor titles (2010–11) in the under-15 and under-16 divisions, respectively. (The Ontario Cup is the provincial soccer championship and one of Canada's most prestigious amateur sports tournaments.) Quinn captured back-to-back gold medals, while representing their province at the 2010 and 2011 under-sixteen (U-16) National All-Star Championships, an event where players are scouted for the Canadian national team. In May 2012 Quinn was part of the Canadian youth squad that finished second to the United States at the CONCACAF Women's U-17 Championship in Guatemala. The silver-medal finish qualified Quinn and teammates for the Fédération Internationale de Football Association (FIFA) U-17 Women's World Cup, where they were narrowly eliminated in the quarterfinals by North Korea (2–1). Quinn closed out the year as a finalist for the Canadian U-17 female player of the year award, eventually won by Ashley Lawrence.

PLAYING FOR DUKE AND TEAM CANADA

Soccer, basketball, and volleyball were not the only sports at which Quinn excelled. During their final year of high school (2013), they competed against the province's top high school track and field athletes and recorded top-five finishes in three 1,500-meter steeplechase competitions. After placing fifth at the Durham Track and Field Champions, Quinn was runner-up at the CISAA Senior Track and Field Championships. Quinn had their best showing at Ontario Federation of School Athletic Associations' (OFSAA) Metro Regional Track Championships, where they finished first. For their achievements, Quinn was named senior Athlete of the Year in May 2013.

Upon graduating from Havergal College, Quinn was recruited by Duke University's soccer program. At the time, Quinn was also participating in soccer training camps organized by the Canadian Women's National Team (WNT) designed to identify promising youth players in the under-17 to under-19 group. As a freshman, Quinn made four starts in seven appearances in 2013, notching an assist for Duke, seventh-place finishers in the Atlantic Coast Conference (ACC) with a 5–5–3 record. After reaching the ACC quarterfinals, the team earned a National Collegiate Athletic Association (NCAA) Championship berth. Quinn appeared in two games as a substitute during the team's quarterfinal loss to Virginia Tech.

Quinn's senior international debut came in March 2014, during Canada's 3–1 victory against Italy at the Cyprus Women's Cup, where Quinn was an injury replacement call-up for the eventual fifth-place finishers. After being promoted to starter for an international exhibition match against the United States in early May, Quinn represented host country Canada at the 2014 FIFA U-20 Women's World Cup, advancing to the tournament quarterfinals in late August. In their second season (2014) at Duke, they started twelve of fourteen games, recording two assists along with their first two goals—one during a 4–3 loss to Penn State and the other against North Carolina State (1–0). After notching an 8–9–1 overall record and a 4–5–1 conference record, Duke failed to advance to the postseason.

MAKING WAVES ON NATIONAL AND COLLEGIATE LEVELS

In January 2015 Quinn and the Canadian national team claimed their first win of the year at the Four Nations Cup, followed by a second-place finish at the Cyprus Women's Cup in March. Despite being left off the roster for the upcoming FIFA Women's World Cup, Quinn, who took the spring semester off to train with the senior women's squad, was selected to represent their country at the Toronto 2015 Pan American Games in July. They appeared in five matches and played all ninety minutes during the team's run, which culminated in a fourth-place finish.

Returning to Duke in August 2015, Quinn made twenty starts in twenty-two appearances for a defensive powerhouse that led the ACC with fourteen shutouts and earned an invite to the 2015 NCAA Division I Women's Soccer Tournament. Their game-tying goal during a Sweet 16 victory over Florida helped the Blue Devils reach the quarterfinals, where they defeated Stanford in a double-overtime penalty shootout. After a semifinal win (2–0) against Florida State in early December, Duke lost the finals to Penn State (1–0) in their third NCAA championship appearance. Quinn's performance earned them All-ACC Third Team and NSCAA All-South Region Third Team honors.

Upon being named to the roster for the 2016 CONCACAF Women's Olympic Qualifying Championship, Quinn took a leave from Duke during the spring semester to prepare for the February tournament, in which the top two teams automatically earn Olympic berths. The Canadian women were successful, going undefeated until their final match, a 2–0 loss against the United States. Quinn was also part of the national squad that won gold at the 2016 Algarve Cup in early March. Following a string of exhibition matches, known as friendlies, against the Netherlands, Brazil, China, and France, Quinn made their Olympic debut in late August at the Summer Games in Rio de Janeiro, Brazil, where Canada narrowly defeated Brazil 2–1 in the bronze medal game. Quinn subsequently returned to Duke and recorded two assists in three starts for the third-best team in the ACC (7–2–1). The Blue Devils reached the quarterfinals of both the 2016 ACC and NCAA tournaments before losing to Florida State and West Virginia, respectively.

Quinn's next international appearance came in March at the 2017 Algarve Cup, where the Canadian team claimed a silver medal before taking on Sweden, Germany, and Costa Rica in a series of friendlies. By August, Quinn had returned to Duke for their final season, during which the Blue Devils claimed the regular-season title with a perfect 10–0–0 record in conference play. After advancing to the ACC Tournament finals, they also earned an automatic berth to the 2017 NCAA Tournament and held opponents scoreless until a 4–3 penalty kick shootout loss to UCLA in the semifinals.

Along with being named a Mac Hermann Trophy semifinalist, Quinn was honored as All-ACC First Team, All-ACC Academic Team, United Soccer Coaches First Team All-American and United Soccer Coaches All-East Region First Team.

NWSL AND BEYOND

In January 2018, Quinn entered the National Women's Soccer League (NWSL) College Draft. The NWSL was created to be the top women's professional league in the United States, with players drafted from around the world. Quinn was selected third overall by the Washington Spirit, making them the highest-drafted Canadian player in league history. After graduating in the spring with a biology degree, Quinn made sixteen starts for Washington, who finished eighth with a disappointing 2–17–5 record and failed to qualify for the NWSL Playoffs. In October, Quinn and the national squad competed at the 2018 CONCACAF Women's Championship, giving up just one goal before losing 2–0 to the US in the finals.

With the second-place finish, Canada qualified for the 2019 FIFA Women's World Cup. To prepare for the upcoming tournament, Quinn signed with the elite European club Paris Saint-Germain (PSG) in February 2019 and appeared in two games prior to competing at the Algarve Cup. After finishing third, the Canadian women took part in international friendlies against Mexico and Spain before the World Cup, where they reached the summer tournament's Round of 16. Quinn rejoined the NWSL in mid-July 2019, after signing with Reign FC. The club's fourth-place finish that season earned them a berth in the playoffs, where they suffered a semifinal loss to the North Carolina Courage.

By late January 2020, Quinn had been added to Canada's roster for the 2020 CONCACAF Olympic Qualifying Championship, where they finished second to the United States and earned a spot in the upcoming Tokyo Olympics. Amid the coronavirus pandemic outbreak in early March, Quinn helped Canada win the bronze at the inaugural Tournoi de France while competing in an empty stadium. The pandemic led to the yearlong postponement of the Tokyo Olympics and the abrupt resignation of Kenneth Heiner-Møller, Quinn's national team coach, in early June.

Quinn returned to the field in late June for the 2020 NWSL Challenge Cup. Their club, now known as the OL Reign, reached the quarterfinals before losing to the Chicago Red Stars in a 4–3 penalty shootout. In August, Quinn headed to Sweden as part of a loan deal with Vittsjö GIK, a team in Sweden's first-tier women's soccer division (Damallsvenskan). Quinn made eight appearances for Vittsjö, whose regular season ended with a fifth-place finish and an overall 9–4–9 record. (Only the top three teams qualify for the Union of European Football Association (UEFA) Women's Champions League.)

While playing abroad that year, Quinn made off-the-field headlines for coming out as nonbinary in an Instagram post. "I really didn't like feeling like I had a disconnect between different parts of my life, being a public figure, and so I wanted to live authentically," they told Katie Gornall and Kate Falkingham for *BBC Sports* (23 Sept. 2020). "I wanted to live my authentic self, dress the way I wanted to, present the way I wanted."

TOKYO GAMES

In February 2021, Quinn represented Canada at the SheBelieves Cup, the national team's first competition under coach Bev Priestman. After placing third behind the United States and Brazil, Quinn and their teammates prepared for the Tokyo Olympics by competing in a series of international friendlies. In late July Quinn made their second Olympic appearance in Tokyo, where Canada finished second in the group stage to advance to the knockout stage. Following penalty shootout victories in the quarterfinals and semifinals, they outscored Sweden 3–2 on penalty kicks to claim the gold medal. With the victory, Quinn became the first openly transgender athlete to compete in an Olympics, as well as the first to ever win a medal. They closed out the year as part of the roster that faced New Zealand and Mexico in a series of exhibition games.

PERSONAL LIFE

Quinn split time living in Toronto and Seattle. They also served as an advocate for the LGBTQ+ community. "If I can allow kids to play the sports they love, that's my legacy and that's what I'm here for," they told Andrea Janus for *CBC Sports* (2 Aug. 2021).

SUGGESTED READING

Carr-Harris, Breagha. "T.O.'s Most Inspirational Women: Rebecca Quinn." *Streets of Toronto*, 6 Dec. 2018, streetsoftoronto.com/t-o-s-most-inspirational-women-rebecca-quinn/. 16 Feb. 2022.

Gornall, Katie, and Katie Falkingham. "Quinn: Canada's Transgender Footballer on Being 'Visible' and Playing at the Olympics." *BBC Sport*, 4 Aug. 2021, www.bbc.co.uk/sport/olympics/58061475. Accessed 11 Feb. 2022.

Grossman, David. "North York Soccer Player Heads to North Carolina's Duke." *Toronto. com*, 22 June 2013, www.toronto.com/community-story/3850680-north-york-soccer-player-heads-to-north-carolina-s-duke/. Accessed 11 Feb. 2022.

Hart, Robert. "Canada's Quinn Makes History as First Openly Transgender and Nonbinary Athlete to Win Olympic Medal." *Forbes*, 6 Aug. 2021, www.forbes.com/sites/roberthart/2021/08/06/canadas-quinn-makes-history-as-first-openly-transgender-and-nonbinary-athlete-to-win-olympic-medal/?sh=3064f077d61e. Accessed 11 Feb. 2022.

Janus, Andrea. "Canada's Quinn to Become First Openly Transgender, Nonbinary Athlete to Win Olympic Medal." *CBC Sports*, 3 Aug. 2021, www.cbc.ca/sports/olympics/summer/soccer/quinn-first-openly-transgender-nonbinary-athlete-medallist-1.6126845. Accessed 11 Feb. 2022.

—*Bertha Muteba*

Zahid Quraishi

Born: 1975
Occupation: Judge

On June 10, 2021, Zahid Quraishi was confirmed by the US Senate as a United States district judge for the District of New Jersey. It was a historic moment—he was the first Muslim to become a federal district court judge in the history of the American court system. The achievement had been a long time coming for Quraishi, whose ambition and shrewd litigation skills had helped him excel in both the public and private spheres of the law for more than twenty years. He began his career with a prestigious law firm before joining the US Army and serving in the Judge Advocate General's Corps from 2003 to 2007, including two tours in the Iraq War. He then had stints with the US Department of Homeland Security and the US Attorney's Office in New Jersey, after which he returned to private practice for several years. He was appointed a United States magistrate judge for the District of New Jersey in 2019, setting up his historic nomination by President Joe Biden two years later. Reflecting on his experience, Quraishi told a class at Rutgers Law School, "A legal career is a marathon, not a sprint," as quoted in a piece for the school's website (11 June 2021). "I was fortunate to find what interested me early in my career. Loving the work I have done and currently do positively impacts every other facet of my life."

EARLY LIFE AND EDUCATION

Zahid Nisar Quraishi was born in 1975 in New York City. His parents, Shahida and Nisar Quraishi, were Pakistani immigrants who raised him and his brother Abid in the town of Fanwood, New Jersey. As a boy, Quraishi's father played an especially formative role in his life. A doctor, Nisar Quraishi set up a practice in the Manhattan neighborhood of Tribeca in 1976 at a time when its residents were lacking local health-care services. He would practice medicine there for the next thirty-seven years. In an interview with Carl Glassman for the *Tribeca Tribune* (19 Apr. 2021), Quraishi stated that his father "was very selfless in what he gave to family and neighbors and the community, whether it was somebody in the Muslim community or just a neighbor who was a different religion, different race." These values would go on to shape Quraishi's worldview.

As a teenager, Quraishi felt enormous pressure to follow in his father's footsteps, but eventually he realized that he had no real interest in becoming a doctor. Still, he wanted to make his parents proud, so after graduating from Scotch Plains-Fanwood High School in 1993, he enrolled at John Jay College of Criminal Justice. He explained the logic behind this decision in a podcast interview with Myra Din for the *Muslim Bar Association of New York* (28 Jan. 2021), stating, "Without any real goal in mind, I thought why not go to law school? I like to argue, I talk all the time." Quraishi went on to complete his undergraduate degree at John Jay in 1997 before enrolling at Rutgers Law School, where he earned a JD in 2000. Although he still did not know exactly what he wanted to do with his life, he felt confident that he was headed in the right general direction.

EARLY CAREER AND MILITARY SERVICE

After finishing his graduate studies, Quraishi clerked for Judge Edwin Stern of the New Jersey Superior Court from 2000 to 2001. He then accepted a job at the law firm LeBoeuf, Lamb, Greene & McRae. "I took a job at the biggest law firm I could get a job at with the biggest salary," he told Din. "I thought that would make my parents proud." However, he started work just as the September 11, 2001, terrorist attacks shook American society. A wave of Islamophobia swept through the nation, but for Quraishi there was an even more direct impact on his life and career. In 2002, he decided that he would apply to join the US Army.

The following year he was accepted into the Judge Advocate General's (JAG) Corps, a legal branch of the US military that oversees both the defense and prosecution of military law. Quraishi served in the JAG Corps for four years, a time during which he was deployed to Iraq twice and rose to the rank of captain. The experience provided him with what he had been searching for: an understanding of what he wanted to do with his life. "That's really where my career turned for the better. It was for me a calling," he told Din. "I knew at that point that I wanted to continue to serve in some capacity in public service."

PRACTICING LAW IN THE PUBLIC AND PRIVATE SECTORS

After being honorably discharged from the military in 2007, Quraishi worked for the US Department of Homeland Security for eight months as an assistant chief counsel. His job there required him to represent US Immigration and Customs Enforcement (ICE) in myriad immigration and political asylum cases.

In 2008 Quraishi landed a job at the US Attorney's Office for the District of New Jersey, where he worked as a federal prosecutor for the next five years. The experience proved to be formative; for the first time in his career, he felt connected to the federal judiciary and realized he wanted to join its ranks. However, part of him believed that he would never be given such an opportunity. He told Din, "I looked at that as almost this unreachable goal—that one day I might dream of being a judge."

Quraishi subsequently returned to private practice in 2013 after accepting a job at the large New Jersey law firm Riker Danzig Scherer Hyland & Perretti. During his six years there, he became a partner, chair of the white-collar criminal defense and investigations group, and the firm's first chief diversity officer. He especially enjoyed this last role as it allowed him to recruit, train, and promote attorneys within the firm that were of diverse backgrounds—something that he had come to believe was extremely important. Along the way he earned many professional recognitions, including honors from organizations such as the *New Jersey Law Journal*, the Asian Pacific American Lawyers Association, and the South Asian Bar Association.

US MAGISTRATE JUDGE

In 2019, two US magistrate judge vacancies opened up in the District of New Jersey. Suddenly, Quraishi's dream of joining the federal judiciary seemed more possible. Knowing the odds were still likely against him, he developed a plan to apply early and often so that those in charge of reviewing candidates would become familiar with his name. In his interview with Din, Quraishi remarked that this strategy was one he had implemented repeatedly throughout his career: "If you keep knocking down the door, eventually somebody's going to open it up for you."

However, Quraishi did not have to keep knocking long. He was selected for the magistrate judgeship upon his first application. The appointment, which was announced on June 3, 2019, earned local media attention, especially in the Asian American community, as Quraishi became the first Asian American to hold a place on the federal bench in the state of New Jersey. As quoted in an announcement on the Rutgers Law School website (30 July 2019), he described how much being in this position of public service meant to him: "Serving as a United States Magistrate Judge is the greatest honor of my career."

As a magistrate judge, Quraishi's duties included conducting settlement conferences for civil cases, appointing counsel for defendants, determining bail, and approving search warrants for criminal investigations. He was also able to conduct trials in certain misdemeanor cases. In addition to his judicial work, in 2020 he began teaching as an adjunct professor at Rutgers Law School.

US DISTRICT JUDGE

In early 2021, President Joe Biden announced that his administration would seek to bolster diversity in the federal judiciary in an attempt to better reflect the diversity of the American people and began nominating a slate of federal circuit and district court judges. Quraishi was included in Biden's initial group of selections that March, as a nominee for the New Jersey District Court. According to reports, Quraishi was recommended by New Jersey senators Cory Booker and Bob Menendez, both of whom went on to publicly extol his legal mind, experience, and commitment to impartiality.

As the first Muslim to ever be nominated as a potential federal district judge, Quraishi was suddenly thrust into the national spotlight. In interviews, he remarked on how his nomination felt bittersweet because it reflected just how underrepresented Muslims had been in the legal system throughout history. Noting that if confirmed he would make history, he said, "Candidly, I would prefer to be the hundredth, if not the thousandth" rather than the first, as quoted by Carl Hulse for *The New York Times* (28 Apr. 2021). However, he also added, "I understand what it means to the community."

Quraishi's nomination did attract some controversy, including within the Muslim American community. Although some advocacy groups were excited by his candidacy, others expressed concern that not enough was known about his legal views, especially given his connections to ICE and the US military. In particular, critics pointed out there were no public records about what Quraishi did during his time as a "detention adviser" in Iraq. As such, it was not clear whether the legal advice he provided JAG Corps facilitated the torture of the Muslim prisoners at the notorious Abu Ghraib prison. Some Muslim American and progressive activists also suggested Quraishi was simply less experienced than many other potential candidates, especially in key areas such as civil rights.

Some controversy also arose during the Senate Judiciary Committee hearing on Quraishi's nomination on April 28, 2021, when Senator Dick Durbin asked Quraishi what he knew about "sharia law." Though the question was, in fact, intended to head off any Islamophobic stereotypes and misconceptions, some observers criticized it as inappropriate. Some also took issue with Quraishi's response that he knew nothing about sharia, which they argued itself perpetuated stereotypes of "good" Muslims who distanced themselves from principles of Islam. To many observers, the exchange was demonstrative that Muslim Americans have still been viewed as "dangerous" and, therefore, more heavily scrutinized than their peers.

Despite these hurdles, on June 10, 2021, Quraishi's nomination was confirmed by the Senate in an 81–16 vote. He officially took office later that month. As quoted by Azi Paybarah for *The New York Times* (11 June 2021), Senator Menendez was among those who hailed Quraishi's achievement: "We should all draw inspiration from his story, because it is a story that could only take place in the United States of America."

PERSONAL LIFE

Quraishi and his wife, Amanda, have two children together, Zoe and Aiden. On April 11, 2020, Quraishi's father died from complications from coronavirus disease 2019 (COVID-19), which he had contracted while assisting patients during the pandemic that broke out that year.

SUGGESTED READING

Din, Myra, and Gregory A. Phillips, moderators. "Pathways to Becoming a Federal Magistrate Judge." *Muslim Bar Association of New York*, 28 Jan. 2021. *Apple Podcasts*, podcasts.apple.com/my/podcast/ pathways-to-becoming-a-federal-magistrate-judge/id1549560548?i=1000506930754. Accessed 2 Dec. 2021.

Glassman, Carl. "Nisar Quraishi, 73, Longtime Tribeca MD, 'Gave His Life to What He

Loved.'" *Tribeca Tribune*, 19 Apr. 2021, www.tribecatrib.com/content/nisar-quraishi-73-longtime-tribeca-md-gave-his-life-what-he-loved. Accessed 2 Dec. 2021.

Hulse, Carl. "Senate Begins Considering Diverse Slate of Biden Judicial Nominees." *The New York Times*, 28 Apr. 2021, www.nytimes.com/2021/04/28/us/politics/biden-judicial-nominees.html. Accessed 2 Dec. 2021.

Ismail, Aymann. "A Biden Judge Would Be the First-Ever Muslim on the Federal Bench. Some Muslims Are Furious." *Slate*, 27 Apr. 2021, slate.com/news-and-politics/2021/04/zahid-quraishi-muslim-federal-judge-criticism.html. Accessed 2 Dec. 2021.

Paybarah, Azi. "US Confirms First Muslim Federal Judge." *The New York Times*, 11 June 2021, www.nytimes.com/2021/06/11/nyregion/zahid-quraishi-first-muslim-federal-district-judge.html. Accessed 2 Dec. 2021.

"Rutgers Alumnus Zahid Quraishi RLAW'00 Becomes Nation's First Article III Muslim Federal Judge." *Rutgers Law School*, 11 June 2021, law.rutgers.edu/news/rutgers-alumnus-zahid-quraishi-rlaw00-becomes-nation%E2%80%99s-first-article-iii-muslim-federal-judge. Accessed 2 Dec. 2021.

"Rutgers Law Grad Becomes First Asian American Federal Judge in New Jersey." *Rutgers Law School*, 30 July 2019, law.rutgers.edu/news/rutgers-law-grad-becomes-first-asian-american-federal-judge-new-jersey. Accessed 2 Dec. 2021.

—Emily E. Turner

Shahrzad Rafati

Born: 1979
Occupation: Business executive

Shahrzad Rafati founded BroadbandTV (BBTV) Corp. in 2005, beginning what would become a global media and technological empire with offices in Canada, the United States, Brazil, Mexico, India, France, and Japan. By the 2020s BBTV was the third-biggest digital video company in terms of unique monthly viewers, after only the tech titans Facebook and Google, with tens of billions of interactions each month. The company's massive success was built around its software for tracking uploaded audio and video content, such as clips from TV, movies, sports events, and video games, and then placing advertisements with the content. BBTV then receives a percentage of the advertising revenues going to the owners of that content. Rafati's company also developed technology tools to help its more than thirty thousand content providers promote their work and gain additional followers. Clients of BBTV included major names such as the National Basketball Association (NBA), Viacom, and Sony Pictures, as well as thousands of smaller ones.

Rafati's success brought her repeated recognition as an important business leader, including numerous awards and appearances on media lists of influential entrepreneurs. She became especially well known in her adopted home country of Canada and brought her expertise to several government and private-sector advisory roles. Friends and observers often remarked at the work ethic and determination that aided her rise. "She has the strength and energy of six grown men," Hamed Shahbazi, CEO of TIO Networks, a longtime mentor of Rafati's and BroadbandTV's first investor, told Eric Blattberg for *Digiday* (26 May 2015). "Her charisma really bowls you over."

EARLY LIFE

Shahrzad Rafati was born in Tehran, Iran, in 1979, the same year as the Iranian Revolution, which overthrew the shah and established a fundamentalist Islamic state. Shortly thereafter, the new Iranian regime went to war after neighboring Iraq invaded. The Iran-Iraq War lasted from 1980 to 1988, claiming the lives of at least a half million people. The upheaval greatly impacted Rafati's family, who previously had a comfortable life due to her parents' entrepreneurship. Her father, Iraj Rafati, owned a real estate company, while her mother, Hourah Moslehi, was the owner of a textile company. "Iran was at war for eight years, and a lot of my family's success had been taken from them," she told Andreane Williams for *BBC News* (24 Aug. 2020). "I knew that I needed a different future, and a life where I could make a difference, and where equal was equal."

Rafati was a strong student, and her formative experiences stoked her desire to forge her own path—ideally in a democratic,

Photo courtesy Shahrzad Rafati,
via Wikimedia Commons.

practiced typing, and I could just get the rest of it later? He laughed at me." Nevertheless, she eventually procured a computer and brought herself up to speed.

Rafati went on to excel at computer programming and earned her bachelor's degree in 2000. During this period she did database work for the humanitarian agency UNICEF (United Nations International Children's Emergency Fund). She also founded her own nonprofit, an organization known as Make Change that aimed to create internet channels connecting donors to non-governmental organizations (NGOs) and similar groups. However, although she found some high-profile partners, the venture soon folded. Still, Rafati would credit the experience with affirming her desire to work on projects that would positively impact society.

Rafati also attended the Université Paris-Sorbonne in France, where she studied French. Later she took leadership courses at the Saïd Business School at the University of Oxford in the United Kingdom.

BREAKING INTO BUSINESS

As she began her business career, Rafati was mindful of how technology was disrupting economic revenue streams. She took particular note of how the technology company Apple had changed the way people consumed music, moving them from physical formats like LPs and CDs to digital distribution of audio files. She predicted that a similar change was coming for video, which at the time was primarily distributed by traditional television channels or on DVDs. "The shift in the music consumption trend was a clear indication of where video content was heading," she told Williams. "Audio was at the start of the evolution, and it was clear to me that video was going to be next."

In 2005, at the age of twenty-five, Rafati founded Broadband TV, also known as BBTV, to capitalize on that technological sea change. She initially established it as a hardware company that developed and sold cable-TV-like boxes that would allow people to watch online videos on their televisions. Within a few months, however, she realized that such an approach was not viable as most people were content to watch such videos on their computer screens. Meanwhile, the online video platform YouTube was also launched in

capitalist country that provided opportunities. She explained to Blattberg how Iranian "society does not provide you real choice. If you want to start your own business tomorrow, or go learn something new, it's so challenging to study what you're passionate about and be in charge of your life." She resolved to complete her high school education as soon as she could and move somewhere where she could thrive. Although her parents were reluctant to have her study and live abroad, she was undaunted, and at age seventeen she officially decided to leave Iran.

MOVE TO CANADA

In 1996 Rafati moved to Vancouver, British Columbia, because an old school friend had invited her there and also because the United Nations (UN) had ranked it among the world's best cities. Because her English-language skills were poor, she decided to take English classes while she supported herself as a math tutor for Persian students. The next year she enrolled at the University of British Columbia, where she planned to major in computer science. There was one problem, however. "At the time, I actually couldn't afford to buy a computer," she shared with Blattberg, and she was also not exactly computer savvy. "I was having this conversation with my boyfriend at the time—what if I just got the keyboard and

2005 and quickly grew in popularity. Rafati noticed how fans of television shows, movies, and sports teams would upload pirated clips to *YouTube* and similar video services, and media companies would quickly force people to take the content down for copyright infringement. Rafati realized she could offer copyright holders a different approach: by using software that could recognize audio and video, she could help them identify uploads of their content but rather than remove it, monetize it by attaching advertisements. Her company would profit by taking a cut of the advertising revenue.

To make her vision a reality, Rafati needed a big-name client willing to take a risk on the idea. She found it in the National Basketball League (NBA), which agreed to have a meeting with her. "I was in my 20s and I was very nervous, but I really believed in our solutions," she recalled to Williams. The NBA agreed to a trial run after their meeting in 2007, which led to a deal that would prove increasingly lucrative as the years passed. Perhaps even more importantly, the NBA deal helped BBTV to secure additional high-profile clients, such as Sony Pictures and A&E. The company also began making deals with smaller organizations and individuals who wanted to make money from the videos they posted online. Initially this was a smaller part of BBTV's business, but that began to change as online video continued to gain popularity and some independent content creators began racking up views in the millions.

TAKING BROADBANDTV TO THE TOP

Rafati soon sought investors to grow her business. A major boost came through the European entertainment group RTL (Radio Television Luxembourg), which bought a 51 percent stake in 2013 and later increased its share to more than 57 percent. The deal gave Rafati's company access to many television channels in Europe and Asia, and expanded its video ad platforms.

By 2015 BBTV had grown considerably, with over two hundred direct employees and a broad network of consultants and talent representatives. Its core business continued to be connecting video owners with advertisers, while taking in a portion of the profit generated by the content. In addition, the company began to build video networks similar to traditional television channels, focused on themes such as gaming, hip-hop, or children's programming.

BBTV also developed other tools for its tens of thousands of content creators. For example, it launched the VISO Catalyst platform to help clients build their audience and better monetize their content with features such as additional language support, marketplace integration, and collaboration tools. The company also branched into systems helping its customers actually create their content.

In 2020, Rafati negotiated a deal for RTL Group to sell its majority stake in BBTV for $120 million. As the deal was finalized in October of that year, BBTV went public on the Toronto Stock Exchange (TSX). Through the process Rafati increased her ownership stake to about 34 percent of the company's total equity shares and a significant majority of the voting power on the BBTV board. She continued to stand behind her company's mission to provide a unique level of support to a wide range of clients. "In a world where new platforms continuously emerge and supply and demand for video are rising, content owners need a comprehensive solution to help them navigate the complex and expansive digital video landscape," Rafati said in a statement, as quoted by Todd Spangler for *Variety* (28 Oct. 2020). "That's exactly what we solve for. BBTV is the only provider of end-to-end solutions for content owners of any size to help them build, engage and monetize their audiences."

ACCOLADES AND ADDITIONAL ACTIVITIES

Rafati's success as the founder and CEO of BBTV brought her much attention in the business community, both in Canada and internationally. She wrote about her entrepreneurial experiences for such periodicals as *Fortune*, the *Wall Street Journal*, and *Wired*, and was frequently featured as a speaker at business events and conferences. Her business acumen was honored by various outlets: *Fast Company* named her as one of the 100 Most Creative People in Business; the *Hollywood Reporter* selected her as one of the Most Powerful Women in Global Television; the British Columbia Technology Association awarded her its Person of the Year Award; and *TheWrap* named her to its Innovators List. In 2014, the Vancouver Economic Commission appointed Rafati to its board of directors and the World Economic Forum welcomed her as a Young Global Leader. The next year she was presented with the Woman of the Year Award by the Business Intelligence Group, recognized as an influential young businessperson by *Adweek*, and included on *Variety*'s Power of Women list. She was also named one of Canada's Top 40 under 40 business leaders in 2017. In 2022, she was named one of Business in Vancouver's Most Influential Women in Business.

Rafati's status as a widely respected business leader also led to her involvement in government initiatives. In 2019 she was appointed vice-chair of Invest in Canada, a federal agency aimed at generating foreign investment in the country. "Having been on both sides of the table as an investor and an entrepreneur in Canada and abroad, I've seen first-hand the amazing potential for Canada to draw powerful international appeal," Rafati noted, as quoted by *Business Wire* (20 May 2019). "I'm excited to increase foreign investment in Canada that drives our economy, creates more Canadian jobs, and inspires leadership in innovation nationwide."

SUGGESTED READING

Blattberg, Eric. "From War Zone to Boardroom: The Improbable Rise of BroadbandTV's Shahrzad Rafati." *Digiday*, 26 May 2015, digiday.com/media/broadbandtvs-shahrzad-rafati/. Accessed 22 Apr. 2022.

"Shahrzad Rafati." *World Economic Forum*, www.weforum.org/people/shahrzad-rafati. Accessed 22 Apr. 2022.

"Shahrzad Rafati Appointed as Vice-Chairperson of Invest in Canada." *Business Wire*, 20 May 2019, www.businesswire.com/news/home/20190520005177/en/Shahrzad-Rafati-Appointed-Vice-Chairperson-Invest-Canada. Accessed 22 Apr. 2022.

Silcoff, Sean. "Vancouver's BroadbandTV Moves toward IPO as Founder Seeks to Buy Out Bertelsmann Unit's Controlling Stake." *The Globe and Mail*, 2 Oct. 2020, www.theglobeandmail.com/business/article-shahrzad-rafatis-broadbandtv-pursuing-ipo-on-tsx-sources/. Accessed 22 Apr. 2022.

Spangler, Todd. "RTL Group Sells Stake in BroadbandTV for $120 Million as BBTV Launches IPO." *Variety*, 28 Oct. 2020, variety.com/2020/digital/news/rtl-group-sells-broadbandtv-stake-ipo-1234817663/#!. Accessed 22 Apr. 2022.

Williams, Andreane. "The Iranian Immigrant Who Conquered Online Video Tech." *BBC News*, 24 Aug. 2020, www.bbc.com/news/business-53833035. Accessed 22 Apr. 2022.

—*Christopher Mari*

Catherine Raîche

Born: 1989
Occupation: Sports executive

In 2015, after serving as an unpaid intern in the Canadian Football League (CFL), Catherine Raîche made the surprise decision to leave her full-time job as a corporate and tax lawyer in order to pursue a career in professional sports. Less than a year later, she was appointed football coordinator for the Montreal Alouettes. With her 2017 promotion to assistant GM, Raîche made history as the first female executive in nearly three decades to land a front office position in the CFL.

Following brief stints with the CFL's Toronto Argonauts and XFL's Tampa Bay Vipers, she joined the National Football League (NFL) in 2019, serving as the Philadelphia Eagles' football operations coordinator. Raîche achieved another career milestone two years later when she was promoted to vice president of football operations and became the highest-ranking female executive up to that point in the NFL's history. She moved further up the ladder after she was named assistant general manager and vice president of football operations for the Cleveland Browns in June 2022.

For Raîche, working in three of North America's most prominent football leagues has proven to be a satisfying experience. "I feel so lucky to be able to work in this field," she shared with Guillaume Gervais for *Le Reflet* (17 Dec. 2021). "When you're passionate like I am, you don't consider it a job anymore."

EARLY LIFE AND EDUCATION

Catherine Raîche was born in 1989 in Montreal, Quebec. She first developed an interest in sports while watching football games with her father, an accountant who supported the Montreal Alouettes, a professional club that competed in the eastern division of the Canadian Football League (CFL).

Growing up, Raîche became equally passionate about the team, becoming a fan of one player in particular: running back Mike

Pringle, whose jersey was the first she ever owned. Raîche also credited her love of sports to her mother, a nurse who volunteered weekends managing logistics for her brother's football team: the Diablos of La Prairie, an amateur youth club in the Ligue de Football Montréal-Métro (Montreal Metro Football League). She would often accompany her mother to the games, watching from the sidelines while also helping refill the players' water bottles.

Upon completing her secondary education at Collège Jean de la Mennais, a private school in Montreal, Raîche attended a pre-university program (CEGEP) at another private institution, Montreal's Collège André-Grasset, a French language college preparatory school. In 2007, Raîche began attending the University of Sherbrooke, a public university in Quebec, and graduated in 2011 with a bachelor's degree in law.

While a student at Sherbrooke, Raîche often attended football games and spent time cheering for the Sherbrooke Vert et Or (Green and Gold) team, ultimately reaching an important conclusion. "When I was studying law, I realized that I wanted to work in sports. Initially, I thought I would go into a career as an agent, because that's often what lawyers do," she recalled to Miguel Bujold in a French language article for *La Presse Canadienne* (26 January 2017).

GROWING INTEREST IN FOOTBALL

In 2012, a year after obtaining her degree, Raîche gained admission to the Quebec Bar Association (QBA). She subsequently served as a law intern with the Société de l'assurance automobile du Quebec (SAAQ), which provides licensing and auto insurance for drivers and vehicles in Quebec and also issues driver's licenses and vehicle license plates.

In January 2013 Raîche joined the Montreal-based firm Gascon and Associates, specializing in corporate and tax law during the day while pursuing a master's degree in taxation in the evening. However, Raîche quickly realized that something was missing in her career. "I was not really passionate on a daily basis," she confided to Ariane Lacoursière for *La Presse Canadienne* (20 December 2020). "I always wondered what excites me. The only thing that came to mind was football."

In 2014, Raîche made the fateful decision to attend a weekend networking conference in Indianapolis, Indiana, to explore career opportunities in the football industry. "I saw all the possibilities there were. That's when I knew that's what I wanted to do," she recalled to Lacoursière. After reaching out to numerous teams in the CFL, Raîche eventually landed an unpaid weekend internship, working as a consultant with her favorite childhood team—the Alouettes—during the spring of 2014.

At the conclusion of training camp, Joey Abrams, the Alouettes' assistant general manager, allowed Raîche to remain with the club. "It was obvious she was extraordinarily smart and motivated," Abrams shared with Herb Zurkowsky for the *Montreal Gazette* (30 Sept. 2016). "The thing I noticed right away was her work ethic." Raîche continued to work at the law firm during the day while attending classes at night and spending weekends with the Alouettes organization.

For the remainder of the season, she worked across various departments and helped with a variety of tasks, including administrative duties, legal advising, and travel logistics. "I had no life during those six months outside of those three things, but I loved it," she shared with Rachel Brady for the *Globe and Mail* (16 Mar. 2017).

CFL CAREER

In December 2015 Raîche's hard work paid off when Jim Popp, the Alouettes' general manager and head coach, offered her a full-time job in the operations department as the team's coordinator of football administration. Raîche's appointment was notable, as she was the first woman in the CFL to hold a front office position since Ottawa Rough Riders general manager Jo-Anne Polak in the late 1980s. The job offer allowed Raîche to leave the legal profession and devote herself entirely to the Alouettes.

In her new role, Raîche served as an intermediary between the operations and administration departments, overseeing daily logistics and activities for the team's players and coaches. Her other duties included negotiating and structuring team and individual player contracts, tracking the team's salary cap, and assisting with the team's travel arrangements, logistics, and sponsorship deals. During Raîche's first season (2016) in the CFL, the Alouettes finished third in the Eastern Division with a 7–11 record.

In January 2017, Raîche was named the Alouettes' assistant general manager (AGM) of football operations. With this promotion she made history, becoming the first woman to hold that executive position in the CFL. As AGM of football operations, Raîche helped oversee daily operations and player scouting, subsequently attending three regional showcases and the league's annual three-day player evaluation camp: the CFL Combine, which is used to assess the physical skills (strength, speed, and agility) of draft-eligible prospects from Canadian universities and Canadian-born National College Athletic Association (NCAA) players.

In addition to being tasked with drafting, negotiating, and renewing the contracts of players and other team personnel, Raîche was responsible for evaluating the market value of the team players, reviewing the team's annual football operations budgets, managing the team's salary cap, and ensuring the team's compliance with the league's collective bargaining agreement. Her first season as AGM would end on a disappointing note, however, as the Alouettes finished last in the Eastern Division with a 3–15 record and missed the playoffs for the second straight year.

In late December 2017 Raîche made the surprising announcement that she was stepping down from the Alouettes to explore other opportunities. While this move came amid some team restructuring and Kavis Reed's decision to not involve Raîche in the team's search for a new head coach, Raîche said she made the move for personal reasons.

MOVING UP THE EXECUTIVE LADDER

Raîche returned to the league a month later when Popp, her former boss and the general manager for the CFL's Toronto Argonauts, tapped her to work as the team's director of football administration. In her new front office position, Raîche managed a number of duties, including the negotiation and drafting of player contracts, management of the team's salary cap, and the administration of the operations department's budgets. She also worked with Popp and Argonauts head coach Marc Trestman to hone her recruitment and player evaluation skills. Raîche's first season (2018) with her new team proved disappointing, as the injury-plagued Argonauts, winners of the 2017 Grey Cup, the CFL's championship trophy, failed to

qualify for the playoffs, finishing last in their division with a 4–14 regular-season record.

In early 2019, after Trestman was named head coach and general manager for the Tampa Bay Vipers in the newly rebooted XFL football league, Raîche accepted his offer to join the Florida-based team as director of football operations. Her responsibilities included hiring coaching and operations personnel, supervising various departments such as equipment, video technology, and operations, and reviewing the practice facility's architectural layout.

NFL CAREER

Raîche's brief stint with the XFL franchise came to an end in late July 2019, however, when she achieved her longstanding dream of joining the NFL after the Eagles chose her to serve as football operations and player personnel coordinator. Raîche's new role involved managing player and personnel contracts; overseeing the team's player development program; analyzing college prospects' skills and compiling background information from team scouts and scouting tools; and assessing professional players for free agent acquisitions and possible trades.

Raîche's first season in Philadelphia ended on a favorable note for the team. The Eagles posted a 9–7 record during the regular season and finished first in the National Football Conference (NFC) East before a loss to the Seattle Seahawks led to the Eagles' elimination from the playoffs. The following season marked the first time since 2016 that the Eagles failed to advance to the playoffs, and they closed out the 2020 season with a 4–11–1 regular-season record.

Despite the team's mixed performance on the field, Raîche continued to move up in the Eagles organization. In May 2021, she succeeded Andrew Berry as vice president of football operations for the franchise. She remained involved in player development, player evaluation, and contract management while also collaborating with the executive vice president of football operations and the general manager regarding football operations. The Eagles returned to the postseason in 2021 after posting a 9–8 record and placing second in the NFC East division, securing one of the wild card spots in that year's NFL playoffs. However, the team failed to advance any further, losing to the Tampa Bay Buccaneers, that season's eventual Super Bowl champions, in the wild-card playoff game.

By this point, Raîche had begun exploring new opportunities outside the Eagles organization. In January 2022, shortly after the regular NFL season ended, the Minnesota Vikings interviewed Raîche for the vacant general manager post, which ultimately went to Kwesi Adofo-Mensah.

Raîche's disappointment proved to be short-lived. In late June, Berry, who had become the general manager of the Cleveland Browns after leaving the Eagles, hired Raîche as the Browns' assistant general manager and vice president of football operations. Along with helping oversee the team's daily operations, Raîche became involved with making strategic roster decisions regarding player personnel and football operations.

PERSONAL LIFE

According to her personal Twitter account, Raîche is a self-described foodie and the cofounder of the organization Women in Football Ops. She is also fluent in three languages.

SUGGESTED READING

Brady, Rachel. "How Catherine Raîche Rose from Unpaid Intern to Assistant GM of the Montreal Alouettes." *The Globe and Mail*, 16 Mar. 2017, www.theglobeandmail.com/sports/football/raiche-alouettes-montreal-cfl-football-women-sports-assistant-general-manager/article34318714/. Accessed 11 July 2022.

Bujold, Miguel. "Passionate and Pioneer." *La Presse Canadienne*, 26 Jan. 2017, plus-lapresse-ca.translate.goog/screens/bca04db5-5026-47a1-8994-d426511ded1f__7C___0.html?_x_tr_sl=fr&_x_tr_tl=en&_x_tr_hl=en&_x_tr_pto=sc. Accessed 11 July 2022.

Epstein, Jori. "Philadelphia Eagles Make History, Promoting Catherine Raiche to Vice President of Football Operations." *USA Today*, 28 May 2021, www.usatoday.com/story/sports/nfl/eagles/2021/05/27/nfl-history-eagles-catherine-raiche-vp-football-operations-philadelphia/7466805002/. Accessed 11 July 2022.

Gervais, Guillaume. "A Laprairiane Shatters a Glass Ceiling in the NFL." *Le Reflet*, 17 Dec. 2021, www-lereflet-qc-ca.translate. goog/une-laprairienne-brise-un-plafond-de-verre-dans-la-nfl/?_x_tr_sl=fr&_x_tr_tl=en&_x_tr_hl=en&_x_tr_pto=sc. Accessed 11 July 2022.

Lacoursière, Ariane. "The Quebecer to Conquer the NFL." *La Presse Canadienne*, 20 Dec. 2020, www-lapresse-ca.translate.goog/sports/football/2020-12-20/catherine-raiche/la-quebecoise-a-la-conquete-de-la-nfl.php?_x_tr_sl=fr&_x_tr_tl=en&_x_tr_hl=en&_x_tr_pto=sc. Accessed 11 July 2022.

Zurkowsky, Herb. "Alouettes Assistant GM Catherine Raîche Says Her Resignation Is Personal." *Montreal Gazette*, 18 Dec. 2017, montrealgazette.com/sports/football/cfl/montreal-alouettes/alouettes-assistant-gm-catherine-raiche-says-her-resignation-is-personal. Accessed 11 July 2022.

—. "Inside the CFL: Lawyer Parlays Her Love for Football into Position with Alouettes." *Montreal Gazette*, 30 Sept. 2016, montrealgazette.com/sports/football/cfl/montreal-alouettes/inside-the-cfl-lawyer-parlays-her-love-for-football-into-position-with-alouettes. Accessed 11 July 2022.

—Bertha Muteba

Toshi Reagon

Born: January 27, 1964
Occupation: Musician and curator

In an article for *Herizons Magazine* (22 June 2008), Karen X. Tulchinsky described Toshi Reagon as "a strong woman with a big voice, a big heart and big dreams for our world and the people in it." Reagon is known for both her solo efforts and her work with the band BIGLovely, as well as for collaborations with her mother, Bernice Johnson Reagon, the highly respected founder of the a cappella group Sweet Honey in the Rock.

Like her mother, Reagon performs socially conscious, politically progressive songs. As Mikki Halpin wrote for *Spin* (8 Mar. 2017), "Reagon's onstage banter is likely to be about prison reform, voting, slavery, or sexism, and the concerts themselves are likely to be benefits for incarcerated women, LGBTQ centers, or other causes." As listeners regularly do, Halpin struggled to classify Reagon's music, which contains elements of gospel, rock, soul, blues, and folk, among other genres, and wrote, "Having an uncategorizable sound is itself a form of resistance in her mind." Reagon finds the attempt to pigeonhole her style unhelpful. "People are very obsessed with trying to say what my music is because they're trying to sell records and think that's the best way to sell it," she explained to Halpin.

In addition to releasing music, Reagon is the creator of the WordRock&Sword festival—which was founded in 2011 to celebrate the lives of women—and has written and produced several theater productions. Her rock opera *Parable of the Sower* (2018), which she created with her mother, is a musical adaptation of the 1993 science-fiction novel of the same name by Octavia E. Butler and earned Reagon critical praise.

EARLY YEARS AND EDUCATION

Toshi Reagon was born on January 27, 1964, in Atlanta, Georgia. Her father, Cordell Hull Reagon, and mother, Bernice Johnson Reagon, were members of the Student Non-Violent Coordinating Committee, which had emerged in the wake of the student-led protests at segregated lunch counters of the 1960s to become an important arm of the civil rights movement. In 1962, Cordell founded, and Bernice performed in, the Freedom Singers, a quartet singing group whose music, often gospel-based, served to rouse people to their cause. Their version of "We Shall Overcome" is considered an important civil rights anthem.

Reagon's godparents were iconic folk singer Pete Seeger and his wife, Toshi Seeger, after whom she was named. She was deeply influenced by his music, as well as that of her parents. After her mother founded Sweet Honey in the Rock in the early 1970s, that all-female group provided yet another source of inspiration. "I can feel that she's picked up some of the sounds from the culture I was reared in," Bernice told Judith Evans for *The Washington Post* (31 Oct. 1997), speaking about how she might have influenced her daughter. "But it is very affirming to look at the next generation speaking in their own voice, on their own terms, and still finding a connection to where it comes from. She was not going to be Bernice Reagon. She staked her own territory." Reagon's musical tastes also included rockers like Kiss and Led Zeppelin and blues masters like Howlin' Wolf and Big Mama Thornton;

Photo by Vera de Kok via Wikimedia Commons

one family story relates that when she was a preschooler, she insisted on purchasing a Jimi Hendrix recording.

When Reagon was two years old, her parents separated. She and her brother, Kwan, moved with their mother to a house on Ashby Street in Atlanta, where neighbors included renowned Black American historian Vincent Harding, and the campuses of historically Black colleges Morehouse and Spelman were close by. "I loved that house," she told Sharon Pendana for *The Trove* (2019). "It felt like the center of the universe. There was so much activism happening. It was the edge of us—black people—starting to take up space." In Atlanta, Reagon attended the Martin Luther King Jr. Community School, which her mother helped to found.

When Bernice got a job as the musical director of the DC Black Repertory Company and began earning her doctorate at Howard University, the three moved to a relatively rough neighborhood in southeast Washington, DC. Reagon unhappily attended a succession of public schools before being enrolled in the Burgundy Farm Country Day School, a progressive private school in Fairfax County, Virginia. She later boarded at Sandy Spring Friends School, in Maryland, angering the administration by mounting protests on policies she felt unfair.

Reagon loved sports, particularly football, but an injury at age thirteen made it difficult to run. She instead began focusing her considerable energies on playing music. She had taught herself drums and guitar at an early age, and in high school formed a band that played covers of Neil Young and the Beatles. Twice a month, she and Kwan took the bus to New York to visit their father, and while Kwan eventually opted to move to the city, Reagon remained in Washington with Bernice, regularly attending the Smithsonian's American Folklife Festival, and sitting in on sessions with Sweet Honey in the Rock.

ALBUMS

Reagon saved her own money for studio time, and, in 1985, she recorded *Demonstrations*, a cassette that featured her mother on backing vocals and credited them both as producers. In 1990, Flying Fish Records released *Justice*, which is counted by most as her first album. *Justice* got the attention of singer Lenny Kravitz, who invited her to open for him during his first world tour in 1991. By the time she returned from Europe, Reagon had received contract offers from both sides of the Atlantic Ocean; she opted to sign with major label Elektra in 1993.

When the company neglected to release any of her music—a common occurrence in that era—she walked away. Although she has described that as the start of a low period, she used the next few years to hone her producing skills. She also cultivated a new attitude: "I didn't care if I was on a label or not," she recalled to Pendana. "I knew I was gonna be relentless about it and I was not gonna stop until I either sucked or I was dead."

Her relentlessness paid off. In 1997, Smithsonian Folkways Recordings released Reagon's album *Kindness*, which the company's catalog describes as "the sound of Reagon's roots—gospel, folk, and blues—merged with her brand of urban acoustic." Reagon—whose backing band, BIGLovely, takes its name from an endearment she once received in a letter from a paramour—followed that with her fourth official studio album, *The Righteous Ones*, in 1999, which was released on the independent Razor and Tie label. Although neither album attracted much mainstream attention, the track "Darling" from *The Righteous Ones* was

used on the soundtrack to the hit television drama *Felicity*.

In 2002, Reagon released the eponymous *Toshi*, also on Razor and Tie. The album won praise for its spirited cover of the Cars' hit "Just What I Needed." The album *Have You Heard* followed in 2005. "*Have You Heard* is a title likely meant to echo a fan's pitch to a friend. *Have you heard Toshi Reagon?*" Will Layman wrote for *PopMatters* (22 Nov. 2005). "Reagon is a classic 'talent deserving wider recognition'—not just a hipster's oddball taste. It's a safe bet that she'll never be a superstar as she shows zero interest in bending herself to fashion, glamour or trend, but her talent is as accessible as it is huge."

Reagon self-released her next four albums on services such as Bandcamp, including 2008's *Until We're Done* and 2010's *There and Back Again*. In 2018, she released the album *SpiritLand*, an homage to her mother and grandmother. Throughout, Reagon also spent an expansive amount of time touring with her band and playing at festivals and benefit concerts.

OTHER MUSIC PROJECTS

Between recording albums with BIGLovely, Reagon has taken on a wide array of projects, including producing several of Sweet Honey in the Rock's works. In 2011, she founded the ongoing women's music festival WordRock&Sword, which includes musical acts, art installations, and film presentations. As Reagon explained to Miles Marshall Lewis for *AfroPunk* (21 Sept. 2018), "WordRock&Sword is not just a music festival. Literally anything can happen that anyone is willing create." In 2013, she collaborated with the dancer and choreographer Michelle Dorrance on *The Blues Project*, an award-winning multimedia performance. She has also partnered with Alexis Paulin Gumbs on a pair of meditative albums featuring sounds from nature and has served as an Andrew W. Mellon Foundation Creative Futures Artist-in-Residence.

Long a fan of the Black science-fiction writer and Afro-futurist Octavia E. Butler, Reagon taught a Princeton seminar on Butler's 1993 novel *Parable of the Sower* and spent a decade creating an opera based on the book, a prescient look at a world beset by climate change, political upheaval, and economic inequality. Created, in part, during Reagon's

Doris Duke Foundation Building Demand for the Arts Fellowship, the show, also titled *Parable of the Sower*, opened to great acclaim in 2017, at the Arts Center at NYU Abu Dhabi, and became the breakout hit of the following year's Under the Radar festival at the Public Theater. Pointing out that the dystopian novel even features a brash politician who promises to "make America great again," a cornerstone of Donald Trump's presidential campaign, Reagon told Jeremy D. Goodwin for *The New York Times* (1 Jan. 2018), "It's not that Octavia predicted him. It's that she knew us so well and knew we would allow it to happen. That's chilling. It gives me bumps on my arms."

Reagon also hosts a podcast, *Octavia's Parables*, on which she discusses Butler's oeuvre one chapter at a time. In recognition of her accomplishments in music and the arts, Reagon has been awarded the Black Lily Award (2007), Foundation's Art of Change Fellowship (2015), the Herb Alpert Award in the Arts (2021), and the Association of Performing Arts Professionals (APAP) Award of Merit for Achievement in the Performing Arts (2021).

PERSONAL LIFE

Reagon lives in the New York City borough of Brooklyn with her partner of several years, J. Bob Alotta, a filmmaker and former director of the powerful nonprofit Astraea Lesbian Foundation for Justice, which supports and funds groups led by lesbians and queer women, transgender and gender nonconforming people, intersex people, and people of color.

The two adopted Kwan's daughter, Tashawn, when she was a baby. Now grown, Tashawn holds a doctoral degree in criminology and sociology from Howard University and is an activist for justice reform.

SUGGESTED READING

Evans, Judith. "A Hint of Sweet Honey and a Touch of Rock." *The Washington Post*, 31 Oct. 1997, www.washingtonpost.com/archive/lifestyle/1997/10/31/a-hint-of-sweet-honey-and-a-touch-of-rock/e2edeeb2-61a8-4bdb-a68c-09c7e2a463c9/. Accessed 24 Oct. 2021.

Goodwin, Jeremy D. "A Prescient Sci-Fi 'Parable' Gets Set to Music." Review of *Parable of the Sower*, directed by Eric Ting. *The New York Times*, 1 Jan. 2018, www.nytimes.com/2018/01/01/theater/parable-of-the-sower-octavia-butler-toshi-reagon.html. Accessed 24 Oct. 2021.

Layman, Will. "Toshi Reagon: Have You Heard." Review of *Have You Heard*, by Toshi Reagon. *PopMatters*, 22 Nov. 2005, www.popmatters.com/reagontoshi-haveyouheard-2496056445.html. Accessed 24 Oct. 2021.

Pendana, Sharon. "Toshi Reagon." *The Trove*, 2019, inthetrove.com/toshi-reagon-interview. Accessed 24 Oct. 2021.

Reagon, Toshi. "*AfroPunk* Interview: Toshi Reagon." Interview by Miles Marshall Lewis. *Afropunk*, 21 Sept. 2018, afropunk.com/2018/09/afropunk-interview-toshi-reagon/. Accessed 24 Oct. 2021.

—. "Toshi Reagon: 'We Have to Put Women at the Center of the Universe.'" Interview by Mikki Halpin. *Spin*, 8 Mar. 2017, www.spin.com/2017/03/toshi-reagon-we-have-to-put-women-at-the-center-of-the-universe/. Accessed 24 Oct. 2021.

Tulchinsky, Karen X. "Finding the Good: It Has Been 18 Years since Toshi Reagon Broke onto the New York Music Scene with Her Debut Album and Her New Projects Are Proof That Her Star Is Still Rising." *Herizons Magazine*, 22 June 2008. *The Free Library*, www.thefreelibrary.com/Finding+the+good%3A+it+has+been+18+years+since+Toshi+Reagon+broke+onto...-a0180317111. Accessed 24 Oct. 2021.

SELECTED WORKS

Demonstrations, 1985; *Justice*, 1990; *Kindness*, 1997; *The Righteous Ones*, 1999; *Toshi*, 2002; *Have You Heard*, 2005; *There and Back Again*, 2010; *SpiritLand*, 2018

—*Mari Rich*

Hannah Reyes Morales

Born: 1990
Occupation: Photojournalist

With a single camera click, photojournalist Hannah Reyes Morales has frozen in time powerful moments of lives affected by poverty, violence, and injustice. Coming from a humble beginning in the Philippines—which one can credit for the palpable empathy with which she photographs her subjects and seeks new projects—Reyes Morales has established herself as a leading photojournalist whose work has been featured in publications worldwide. For *The New York Times*, she reported on human, labor, and environmental abuses happening at sea in 2015; for *Al Jazeera America*, on war crimes committed against women in Cambodia the same year.

Regardless of the assignment she is working on, for Reyes Morales, photography is about capturing people's authenticity, beauty amid adversity, and finding connection, even in the aftermath of tragedy. As she told Pauline De Leon in an interview for *Hypebae* (16 June 2021), "I've always been drawn to images. I loved that I could stay with a moment for as long as I wanted and that it felt like I was looking through someone else's eyes. At the same time, it also made me feel connected to others, and it allowed me to see into different worlds."

With these as the central pillars of her work, Reyes Morales has covered the drug war in the Philippines and worked for *National Geographic* magazine on a project called Redefining Beauty before earning the coveted 2020 Infinity Award for Documentary Practice and Visual Journalism, given by the International Center of Photography.

EARLY LIFE AND EDUCATION

Born in 1990 in Manila, Philippines, Hannah Reyes Morales was raised by her mother in a humble home inhabited by twelve additional relatives. As a child, she spent most of her time indoors, discovering old copies of *Life* and *National Geographic* magazines, which ignited the spark of a life-long passion. For Reyes Morales, it was the lively photographs enclosed in those magazines that captured her attention, as they had the power to transport her to places she had never seen before. "I felt very connected to the people and the animals and the nature that I was seeing . . . and that connection hasn't left me since," she -told *National Geographic* (2 Feb. 2022).

Seeing those images not only fueled Reyes Morales's desire to search for more—which she did by using the sole computer at home when everyone else was asleep—but also gifted her with a profound understanding and empathy for the different realities lived around the world. As a student at an all-girls Catholic school run by activist nuns, the curriculum encouraged students to travel to poor neighborhoods to assist people in need. Later on, while attending high school, she would return to these disadvantaged communities as a reading and writing tutor. "I was always very much aware and curious about their lives, and I was already interested in photography, but I didn't have a camera yet," she expressed to James Estrin for *The New York Times* (6 Mar. 2018). "I wanted to photograph them, but I just didn't have the means."

Following her high school graduation in 2007, Reyes Morales enrolled at the University of the Philippines, where she majored in speech communication. During this time, she took a class in photography for one of her modules and landed an internship with the European Pressphoto Agency, an international news photo agency where she covered the daily news in the Philippines.

TELLING STORIES THROUGH PHOTOGRAPHY

After graduating cum laude from the University of the Philippines in 2011, Reyes Morales ventured out to start her career in photography, however, breaking into the profession proved difficult. To support her career, she resorted to sleeping at a dental clinic for months, selling clothes at a market, and living off noodles. Exacerbating her already-dire circumstances was the struggle to claim a space in the male-dominated photography industry. As she wrote for *BRIGHT Magazine*, "Entering the industry was not easy—I was constantly dismissed and discouraged, both by colleagues and people I met when photographing. But this made me see things from a different angle. The hardship I faced growing up and starting out became instrumental in my ability to tell stories with nuance."

Despite these early setbacks, Reyes Morales, showing an impressive commitment to her craft, earned a National Geographic Young Explorer grant in 2013. The grant allowed her to create a platform where she documents, through powerful visuals, the changing Indigenous cultures in her native Philippines. She soon after moved to Phnom Penh, Cambodia, for work. Phnom Penh became the setting where Reyes Morales would not only commence to establish a strong journalistic portfolio but, more importantly, tell important stories through the visual art of photography.

In 2015, the photographer reported for *The New York Times*'s The Outlaw Ocean Project, a nonprofit investigative journalism platform detailing human, labor, and environmental abuses transpiring at sea. That same year, for *Al Jazeera America*, she reported on war crimes committed against women in Cambodia.

As an arsenal of Reyes Morales's impactful visuals shone a light on people affected by poverty, injustice, and violence, broader recognition of her work began to take shape. Emily Anne Epstein from the monthly periodical the *Atlantic* (14 Aug. 2016), for instance, wrote about Reyes Morales's unique journey that followed two years of photographing young fighters, aged six to twelve, as they trained to enter the circuit of child boxing in Cambodia. Alternating between photos that depict children at play as they take a break from their training sessions and images that place them in the ring staring fiercely at their rivals, Reyes Morales captured her subjects' lived experiences as they tried to forge their way out of poverty.

THE PHILIPPINES AND THE DRUG WAR

Even though Reyes Morales had been building her career away from home, this changed after seeing the atrocities generated by the drug war happening in the Philippines. After three years of living in Cambodia, she made the decision to move back home in 2016, where she joined the ranks of the photographers covering the war. "Initially, I really wanted to use photography as a tool and as a passport to leave this country," she revealed to *National Geographic* (2 Feb. 2022) before continuing to say, "But as I went deeper into my practice, I realized that it was really important for me to understand home."

After Philippine President Rodrigo Duterte took office in mid-2016, his violent antidrug campaign resulted in the killings of thousands of people. With the nation grappling with more pressing issues, such as devastating poverty, his government was heavily criticized nationally and internationally. Documenting the horrors wrought by the drug war were photojournalists, including Reyes Morales, who, aware they were putting their lives at risk, knew that it was up to them to expose such a harsh reality. "I look up to the Filipino reporters and photographers who were there night after night, from the very first month. Their commitment to the story taught me a lot," she wrote for *BRIGHT Magazine*. "The local media connected victims with people who were able to support them.

Storytelling from local outlets was instrumental in many discussions, even as reporters received accusations and threats. This was a story where the photographs played a major role in the mass discourse."

As Reyes Morales began to document the effects of the war, most of her photos featured grieving families, police officers, and more than twenty dead bodies. However, with her colleagues also photographing the murder scenes, she felt like she had little more to contribute to the coverage; thus, her focus soon shifted to the people and communities where these violent acts were taking place. Walking through the streets that had seen so much bloodshed, she commenced to knock on doors and ask about the daily life in those shanty communities, camera in hand. As she heard from neighbors of the deceased and, occasionally, from the families themselves, she took photos, with the ensuing pictures revealing moments of tenderness between family and community members set against a backdrop of poverty and crime.

WORKING FOR *NATIONAL GEOGRAPHIC*

As the killings continued—with estimates reporting as many as 30,000 between mid-2016 and March 2019—Reyes Morales continued to photograph these communities, even when foreign journalists started to leave the Philippines and other projects began to occupy her time. In 2017, encouraged by *National Geographic* photo editor Jennifer Samuel, Reyes Morales pitched to the magazine she had grown up reading, a move that led her to get her first assignment from them. "I never imagined that I could be a photographer, let alone a photographer for a magazine I grew up reading as a child," she said to De Leon. In 2019, she won her second grant from *National Geographic*, which funded a project titled *Living Lullabies* based in Liberia. In addition to those grants, Reyes Morales has won worldwide accolades for her work, including the 2019 Tim Hetherington Visionary Award and the coveted 2020 Infinity Award for Documentary Practice and Visual Journalism, given by the International Center of Photography.

As Reyes Morales continues her work as a photographer, she is always on the lookout for meaningful projects, such as *Redefining Beauty*, which was published by *National Geographic*. Through the project, she connects with her subjects as she asks what beauty means to them. "For some, beauty is armor. For others, it means transformation. A lot of folks I met gathered together through beauty rituals to create safe spaces that allowed them to come as they are, to heal, and to celebrate their bodies," she told De Leon. With *Redefining Beauty*, Reyes Morales challenges the preconceived notions about beauty, something that has been a recurrent subject in her work, as her photos have captured beauty even in the most adverse situations.

PERSONAL LIFE

Reyes Morales is married to Jon Morales, who works in economic reform.

SUGGESTED READING

Epstein, Emily Anne. "Cambodia's Child Boxers." *The Atlantic*, 14 Aug. 2016, www.theatlantic.com/photo/2016/08/Cambodias-Child-Boxers/495083. Accessed 10 Apr. 2022.

Estrin, James. "Finding Tenderness in Communities Affected by Manila's Anti-Drug Killings." *The New York Times*, 6 Mar. 2018, www.nytimes.com/2018/03/06/lens/finding-tenderness-in-communities-affected-by-manilas-anti-drug-killings.html. Accessed 10 Apr. 2022.

"Hannah Reyes Morales: Using Photography to Inspire Empathy." *National Geographic*, 2 Feb. 2022, www.nationalgeographic.com/impact/article/hannah-reyes-morales-explorer-story. Accessed 10 Apr. 2022.

Jaucian, Don. "Filipino Photographer Hannah Reyes Morales Wins Prestigious Photojournalism Prize." *CNN Philippines Life*, 20 May 2020, www.cnnphilippines.com/life/culture/2020/5/20/hannah-reyes-morales-icp-prize.html. Accessed 10 Apr. 2022.

Reyes Morales, Hannah. "Coming Home to Cover the Philippines' Deadly War." *BRIGHT Magazine*, 30 Nov. 2017, brightthemag.com/health-photography-philippines-duterte-drug-war-c48147e3222c. Accessed 10 Apr. 2022.

___. "Filipino Photographer Hannah Reyes Morales Has an Eye for Capturing Warmth Amidst Adversity." Interview by Pauline De Leon. *Hypebae*, 16 June 2021, hypebae.com/2021/6/hannah-reyes-morales-filipino-photographer-photojournalist-national-geographic-explorer-interview. Accessed 10 Apr. 2022.

—*Maria del Pilar Guzman*

Roddy Ricch

Born: October 22, 1998
Occupation: Rapper

Arriving on the music scene with the 2017 mixtape *Feed Tha Streets*, rapper Roddy Ricch earned a reputation for music that defies categorization and avoids predictability. "I have a progressive sound: It changes with my experiences, and the music changes with it," he explained to Andrew Barker for *Variety* (2020). "So I never like to put myself in any category. I take my life experiences and put it on a different beat. I'm not an overthinker when it comes to music." Ricch's approach proved successful: after gaining a dedicated following with *Feed Tha Streets* and 2018's *Feed Tha Streets II* as well as several high-profile collaborations, he experienced a full-fledged breakthrough with his debut studio album, *Please Excuse Me for Being Antisocial* (2019), which reached the top of the Billboard 200 album chart and earned him several Grammy Award nominations.

Even the coronavirus disease 2019 (COVID-19) pandemic that began in 2020 and prevented many musical artists from touring and promoting their work could not slow Ricch's rise. Indeed, the self-described antisocial rapper thrived during that period, garnering more industry honors and recording material for his second studio album, *Live Life Fast*, which debuted in December 2021. Ricch also announced a third *Feed Tha Streets* mixtape, a collection of songs that would harken back to his musical roots. "Coming off one of the biggest albums I could've done, I feel like taking [fans] back to the basics with me," he told Eric Skelton for *Complex* (2021).

EARLY LIFE

Roddy Ricch was born Rodrick Wayne Moore Jr. in Compton, California in 1998. While he grew up mainly in the greater Los Angeles area, including Compton, where he attended local schools, he spent a brief period in San Diego as a teenager. His family also had Southern roots, and he developed a particular connection to the city of Atlanta, Georgia. Interested in rap music from an early age, Ricch drew inspiration from the hip-hop styles of both the West Coast and the South. As a young teen, he had an unexpected yet meaningful encounter with then up-and-coming Compton-based rapper Kendrick Lamar, who he met at the church Ricch's mother attended. "Just randomly, I went one day, and he was there with his peoples. This was before [Lamar's 2012 single] 'Swimming Pools' had came out," he recalled to Charles Holmes for *RollingStone* (23 Dec. 2019). "I had rapped for him and he told me, 'You going to be somebody in the world.'"

Despite such encouragement, Ricch did not pursue music seriously over the next several years. He became involved with the Crips gang network and got into trouble on the streets, at one point spending a week in jail. His brief time behind bars was a key moment for Ricch, who decided that he did not want to waste the rest of his life. "I had nothing to show for that," he explained to Carl Lamarre for *Billboard* (5 Dec. 2019). "I just wanted to do something positive. I feel like music was the talent that I had, I just had to tap into it." Around age sixteen, he began dedicating himself to music, a calling that took on even greater importance for him following the death of a close friend who had recently been released from prison.

FEED THA STREETS

As an independent artist, Ricch benefited significantly from some early exposure to the process of music production. "My uncle used to try to rap. I learned how to use Pro Tools watching him," he explained to fellow rapper Future in an interview for *RollingStone* (1 Dec. 2020). "But I didn't really know what was going on until I took it into my own hands. That's why I understand sound—how music is supposed to sit behind vocals—and arranging." Putting that knowledge to effective use, Ricch began recording songs and posting his work to music-sharing websites such as *Soundcloud* by 2016. He almost immediately began to build an online following, with some of his early singles earning hundreds of thousands of streams.

In 2017, Ricch released his first mixtape, *Feed Tha Streets*, which he noted included all seventeen songs he had written to that point. Inspired in part by the signature rap styles of cities like Atlanta and Chicago, his music

was heavily influenced by his experiences of life in Compton. Ricch quickly succeeded in building a dedicated fan base in his home city and the surrounding areas. "That first project connected with who it was supposed to connect with, which was the streets," he told Barker. "I campaigned a lot for that and did a lot of legwork in my surrounding areas: Compton, Watts, South Central, all the projects that started supporting me. And I feel like once the world caught wind, it just spread and spread." Ricch's music also continued to spread online, gaining popularity on streaming music and video services and attracting praise from several established hip-hop figures.

BREAKTHROUGH

Ricch quickly followed his early success with a second mixtape, *Feed Tha Streets II*, in 2018. "I did it with the motivation of having more songs to work with," he told Will Schube for *GQ* (24 Jan. 2020) about the process of making his follow-up release. "If I had more songs to work through, there would be a higher percentage chance of making more good ones. I didn't really know how rappers did it. I just made the music." One single from *Feed Tha Streets II*, "Die Young," proved particularly popular and performed well enough to appear on the Billboard Hot 100 music chart. That track eventually earned platinum certification, helping break Ricch into the mainstream.

As Ricch grew increasingly well known, he collaborated with a number of other artists, including the rappers Nipsey Hussle and Meek Mill and the producer Mustard. Hussle—who also hailed from the Los Angeles area—in particular became an important mentor, bringing Ricch on as a guest in live performances and teaching him lessons about the music industry that Ricch would credit with helping him sign a major-label deal in 2019 with Atlantic Records. Ricch was featured on Hussle's single "Racks in the Middle," released in February 2019, which became a notable chart hit. However, Hussle was shot and killed that March, an event that resonated throughout the hip-hop community.

"Racks in the Middle" went on to be nominated for a Grammy Award for Best Rap Song and won the Grammy Award for Best Rap Performance, giving Ricch his first major industry honor. He also earned a nomination for Best Rap/Sung Performance for the song

"Ballin'," a collaboration with Mustard. At the Grammy Awards ceremony in January 2020, Ricch performed in a tribute to Hussle, alongside notable artists such as rapper YG and singer John Legend. He also spoke out about his intention to follow Hussle's example as a philanthropist and community leader following his friend's death. "Being from my city and being a part of Nipsey's legacy just go hand in hand," he told Schube. "The groundwork that he started, we now get the chance to carry it forward."

PLEASE EXCUSE ME FOR BEING ANTISOCIAL

Meanwhile, Ricch released his first full-length studio album in December 2019. Titled *Please Excuse Me for Being Antisocial*, the album peaked at the number-one position on the Billboard 200 album chart and produced several charting singles, including the number-one hit "The Box," which gained viral popularity among users of the app TikTok. "It hasn't really registered yet. I don't know how I'm supposed to feel," he told Schube about having a number-one album and number-one single at the same time. "I just wanna keep doing music for my people and explaining how we live. That's it."

Along with commercial success, Ricch continued to earn industry acclaim, including eight nominations at the 2020 American Music Awards. At the 63rd Grammy Awards "The Box" earned nominations for Best Rap Song, Best Melodic Rap Performance, and Song of the Year. Ricch was also nominated for three Grammys, including Record of the Year for "Rockstar," a 2020 collaboration with fellow rapper DaBaby. He was named breakthrough artist of 2020 by *Variety*.

This success came even as the COVID-19 pandemic put much of the music world on pause in 2020, forcing the cancellation of tours and other promotional events. Rather than let this disrupt him, Ricch appreciated the opportunity to step away from the public eye. "It really ain't been bad for me," he told Barker. "It's definitely been a time of reflection, a time to plan little trips to where I can go and get peace of mind. We train ourselves to think on the go, and this time has given us a chance to have a really clear thought process." Ricch continued to work on music throughout 2020 and 2021, connecting with fans by releasing snippets of new projects online through social media services such as Instagram. He likewise collaborated with a number of artists during this period, notably featuring on the song "Pure Souls" from rapper Kanye West's 2021 album *Donda*.

LIVE LIFE FAST

In June 2021, Ricch released "Late at Night," the first single from his upcoming second studio album. The track performed well, peaking at number twenty on the Billboard Hot 100 chart and number six on the Hot R&B/Hip-Hop Songs chart. The full album, *Live Life Fast*, followed in December 2021 and found similar success, entering the Billboard 200 chart in the number-four spot on January 1, 2022. Ricch was set to promote the album with a musical guest appearance on the television sketch show *Saturday Night Live* later that January.

In addition to promoting *Live Life Fast*, Ricch repeatedly hinted in interviews that he planned to release a third mixtape, presumed to be titled *Feed Tha Streets III*, at some date in the near future. "I want to bridge the gap between my old fans and my new fans," he explained to Skelton. "That's what I'm on a mission to do with this next situation that I'm working on."

PERSONAL LIFE

In addition to making music, Ricch became active in real estate investment and other business ventures, with a long-term goal "to create generational wealth for everybody in my family," as he told Skelton. "I've been putting my money in the right areas," he explained. "Even just making the right decisions, as far as my family is concerned. Just making sure everybody's got health insurance, and things we weren't taught about when we grew up." He purchased a home in the Beverly Hills area of Los Angeles in late 2021. Ricch had a son in 2020 with his partner, Allie Minati.

SUGGESTED READING

Barker, Andrew. "Roddy Ricch Is *Variety*'s Breakthrough Artist of 2020." *Variety*, 2020, variety.com/2020/music/news/roddy-ricch-variety-breakthrough-artist-hitmakers-please-excuse-me-for-being-antisocial-1234843745/. Accessed 7 Jan. 2022.

Holmes, Charles. "Roddy Ricch Is a Star, But Has No One to Celebrate With." *RollingStone*,

23 Dec. 2019, www.rollingstone.com/music/
music-features/roddy-ricch-please-excuse-
me-for-being-antisocial-profile-923361/.
Accessed 7 Jan. 2022.

Lang, Cady. "Going Viral Helped Catapult
Roddy Ricch and 'The Box' to No. 1—but
There's More to the Story." *Time*, 14 Feb.
2020, time.com/5784337/roddy-ricch-the-
box-interview/. Accessed 7 Jan. 2022.

Ricch, Roddy. "How Roddy Ricch Went from
Compton 'War Baby' to Grammy-Nominated
Star." Interview by Carl Lamarre. *Billboard*,
5 Dec. 2019, www.billboard.com/music/
rb-hip-hop/roddy-ricch-please-excuse-me-
for-being-antisocial-interview-8545512/.
Accessed 7 Jan. 2022.

—. "Roddy Ricch Won't Let Superstardom
Change Him." Interview by Will Schube.
GQ, 24 Jan. 2020, www.gq.com/story/roddy-
ricch-the-box-interview-2020. Accessed 7
Jan. 2022.

Skelton, Eric. "Break the System: The Rise and
Rebellion of Roddy Ricch." *Complex*, 2021,
stories.complex.com/roddy-ricch-2021-
cover-story/. Accessed 7 Jan. 2022.

Thompson, Paul, et al. "Musicians on Musicians:
Roddy Ricch & Future." *RollingStone*, 1 Dec.
2020, www.rollingstone.com/music/music-
features/roddy-ricch-future-musicians-on-
musicians-1096222/. Accessed 7 Jan. 2022.

SELECTED WORKS

Feed Tha Streets, 2017; *Feed Tha Streets II*,
2018; *Please Excuse Me for Being Antisocial*,
2019; *Live Life Fast*, 2021

—*Joy Crelin*

Fatima Robinson

Born: August 29, 1971
Occupation: Dancer and choreographer

Fatima Robinson emerged from relative
obscurity in the early 1990s, after being tapped
to choreograph her first music video: Michael
Jackson's "Remember the Time." Despite
having no formal training, Robinson, who
honed her skills in Los Angeles hip-hop clubs,
quickly made her mark within the industry,
developing iconic dance sequences that
merged her unique blend of modern hip-hop,
classical dance-styles and technical elements.
In addition to featuring the tango in Dr. Dre's

"Been There, Done That" (1997), Robinson was
responsible for the Backstreet Boys' "Thriller"-
inspired moves in "Everybody" (1997), as well
as the flamenco dance in Aaliyah's "Are You
That Somebody?" (1998).

Robinson has parlayed her fame as a music-
video choreographer into a big-screen career.
After achieving success with the sleeper hit
Save the Last Dance (2001), which merged
hip-hop and ballet, Robinson handled more
mainstream fare, including the ballroom dance
film *Shall We Dance* (2004); the musical
remakes of *Dreamgirls* (2006) and *Sparkle*
(2012), for which she incorporated gospel,
blues, and rock dance styles into Motown's
synchronized gestures; as well as the sequel
Coming 2 America (2021), in which she blended
hip-hop with African dance. Throughout her
career, Robinson also choreographed several
high-profile television specials, most notably
the Academy Awards and the Super Bowl. In
addition to being the second African American
woman to choreograph the Oscars (Debbie
Allen was the first), Robinson was responsible
for overseeing the Super Bowl's first-ever hip-
hop halftime show, in 2022.

EARLY LIFE AND CAREER

The eldest of three girls, Fatima Robinson
was born on August 29, 1971, in Little Rock,
Arkansas. When she was five, Robinson
relocated to Los Angeles, California, with
her mother, Kadijah Furqan, and two sisters.
Robinson, who grew up watching the 1980s
television shows *Solid Gold* and *Fame*,
inherited her passion for performing from her
mother, a college marching-band majorette and
salon owner, and her father, a lead guitarist.
"I loved dancing," she recalled to Kayla A.
Greaves for *Upscale* (9 June 2015). "So I
would always make up dance routines with my
sisters whenever my mom had friends or guests
over." After graduating early from San Pedro
High School, the sixteen-year-old followed
in her mother's footsteps and obtained her
cosmetology license. Dance provided an outlet
for Robinson, who frequented the local clubs,
eventually joining a hip-hop dance crew that
competed in club talent-show contests. During
one such competition, Robinson caught the
attention of recent University of Southern
California film graduate John Singleton, who
cast the eighteen-year-old hairdresser as an
extra (she appeared briefly during a backyard

barbecue scene) in his directorial debut, *Boyz n the Hood* (1991), which earned two Academy Award nominations.

Singleton next recruited Robinson to work on another high-profile project: Jackson's "Remember the Time" music video. By this time, Robinson was marketing herself as a choreographer, after running into fellow dancer Rosie Perez at a nightclub. She collaborated with co-choreographer Buddha Stretch on the nine-minute, Egyptian-themed short film, drawing heavily from her freestyle hip-hop background for the dance sequences while incorporating technical aspects of the dance favored by Jackson. Robinson was also among the twenty-five backup dancers featured in the video, which premiered in February 1992 and featured cameos from actor-comedian Eddie Murphy, basketball legend Magic Johnson, and supermodel Iman.

In the wake of Robinson's newfound success, she left her job as a certified cosmetologist to pursue dancing full time and was hired by Classic Concept Productions, co-owned by Lionel C. Martin. At around the same time she choreographed former New Edition singer Bobby Brown's videos for "Humping Around" (1992) and "Get Away" (1993), her first directing credit, Robinson collaborated with Brown's then-wife, pop superstar Whitney Houston, on "I'm Every Woman" (1993) video. From the early-to-mid 1990s, Robinson's choreography skills were increasingly sought after by some of R&B and hip-hop's biggest names including Mary J. Blige ("You Bring Me Joy," 1995) and Brandy ("Baby," 1995), whose video earned Robinson her first MTV Video Music Award (VMA) nomination. Robinson received subsequent VMAs nods in the best choreography category for collaborations with Dr. Dre ("Been There, Done That," 1996), Busta Rhymes ("Put Your Hands Where My Eyes Could See," 1997) and Will Smith ("Wild Wild West" music video short, 1999).

MUSIC VIDEO COLLABORATIONS

During the late 1990s, Robinson was the resident choreographer to one of pop music's biggest boy bands, the Backstreet Boys. Along with creating the folding chair routine featured in the Florida quintet's "As Long as You Love Me" (1997) music video, Robinson came up with opening and closing dance sequences in their horror themed "Everybody (Backstreet's

Back)" (1997), inspired by her previous work with Jackson. "The moves . . . came from my love for Michael, and particularly his 'Thriller' video, " she revealed to Leena Tailor for *ET* (20 Apr. 2018). She also choreographed the Backstreet's Back tour (1997–98), as well as their fourth worldwide concert tour, Into the Millennium (1999–2000).

R&B singer Aaliyah became another of Robinson's regular collaborators. After providing choreography for "Hot Like Fire" (1997), Robinson performed alongside the singer in "Are You That Somebody?" (1997), highlighting hip-hop dance moves and a surprising flamenco dance sequence during which Aaliyah, a self-proclaimed tomboy, donned a high-slit dress and heels. In 2000, the pair reunited for "Try Again," the lead single for the soundtrack to Aaliyah's film debut: the Jet Li action-thriller *Romeo Must Die*. Robinson, whose routines incorporated hip-hop and martial arts-inspired dance moves, received a fifth MTV VMA best choreography nod.

Aaliyah and Robinson's subsequent music video collaborations included the experimental R&B single "We Need a Resolution" (2001), which featured Middle Eastern dance; and the electronic dance-pop track "More Than A Woman" (2001), which incorporated contemporary R&B. "Rock the Boat" (2001) would be the pair's final collaboration, following Aaliyah's untimely death in a twin-engine plane crash shortly after filming ended in the Bahamas. Robinson's choreography for the sexy, tropical-themed music video combined African dance, Jamaican dancehall, and freestyle. She then collaborated with electro-pop group the Black Eyed Peas, capturing her first best choreography VMA for "Hey Mama" (2004) and directing the group's "My Humps" (2005) and "Fergalicious" (2006), a solo effort from Peas' front woman Fergie.

FILM AND TELEVISION

Robinson made her foray into film with the interracial teen romance *Save the Last Dance* (2001), about two seventeen-year-olds—an aspiring ballet dancer (Julia Stiles) and a talented hip-hop dancer (Sean Patrick Thomas)—who bond over their shared passion for dance while attending an inner-city Chicago high school. Robinson worked closely with Thomas to make his dance movements appear natural and oversaw the film's climactic audition scene, incorporating hip-hop and ballet, along with a chair routine. Robinson was subsequently tapped by renowned director Michael Mann to oversee choreography for the Will Smith biopic *Ali* (2001), the Tom Cruise action thriller *Collateral* (2004), and the film adaptation of the 1980s police procedural *Miami Vice* (2006). Other credits included the big-screen comedies *Shall We Dance* (2004), *Fat Albert* (2004), *Be Cool* (2005), and *Miss Congeniality 2: Armed and Fabulous* (2005). On the small screen, Robinson choreographed the *Essence Awards* (2002–03), the *NAACP Image Awards* (2003–04), the *Victoria's Secret Fashion Show* (2003, 2005) and the *VH1 Hip-Hop Honors* (2005–06), as well as the television adaptation of *Their Eyes Were Watching God* (2005).

Robinson was selected to oversee choreography for the 2006 film adaptation of Michael Bennett's 1981 Broadway musical, *Dreamgirls*, loosely based on 1960s vocal trio The Supremes. To prepare, she pored over vintage tapes of Dick Clark's *American Bandstand* and *Soul Train*, melding Motown's synchronized dance moves with her signature street-dance style. *Dreamgirls* received the most nominations (eight) at the 2007 Academy Awards, which Robinson also choreographed.

After her second *Hip-Hop Honors* (2007–08) stint, Robinson managed President Barack Obama's inaugural Lincoln Memorial concert (2009) before overseeing her second Oscars ceremony (2009). For her next high-profile event, Robinson choreographed the 2011 Super Bowl halftime show featuring the Black Eyed Peas and also assumed creative-director duties for the group's interactive Wii and Xbox 360 video game, *The Black Eyed Peas Experience*, released in November 2011. The following year, Robinson choreographed the late rapper Tupac Shakur's hologram performance at the Coachella Festival and the late-summer release *Sparkle*, Whitney Houston's final performance. Then came another VMA nod (2013) for the Will.i.am and Justin Bieber collaboration "#thatpower" and co-choreographer duties (with Kathryn Burns) on the Pharrell Williams tune "Happy," featured on *Despicable Me 2* (2013) soundtrack. Throughout the guerrilla-style video, which was shot throughout LA over a twenty-four-hour period, she oversaw semi-choreographed and freestyle dance segments by Williams, various Hollywood celebrities,

and others. She played a similar role during the song's live performance at the 2014 Oscar telecast, produced by Craig Zadan and Neil Meron.

In 2014, Robinson directed music videos for the group Fifth Harmony ("Sledgehammer" and "Bo$$") and singer-songwriter Meghan Trainor ("Dear Future Husband") before being recruited by Zadan and Meron to bring a modern take to NBC's live-adaptation of the 1978 musical *The Wiz*. "[Robinson] comes from hip hop and a lot of her point of view on dance is very gritty and authentic and raw," Zadan told Lesley Goldberg for *The Hollywood Reporter* (4 Dec. 2015). Robinson incorporated the latest dance moves for *The Wiz Live!*, which aired in December 2015 and drew over 11 million viewers. After reuniting with Bieber on Major Lazer's "Cold Water" (2016) music video, she choreographed performances for the 2016 Grammys (Kendrick Lamar's "The Blacker the Berry") and the 2018 Oscars (Blige's "Mighty River").

FIRST EMMY NOD, SECOND SUPER BOWL

Robinson then joined forces with Adrian Wiltshire on the first season of BET's *American Soul*, a 1970s drama about *Soul Train* creator Don Cornelius that debuted in February 2019. The following year, Houston's estate tapped Robinson as tour director and choreographer for the singer's posthumous hologram tour, *An Evening with Whitney*, which kicked off a month-long European leg in late February, followed by a Las Vegas residency from 2021 to 2022.

The year 2021 was a banner year for Robinson. She achieved a career milestone, earning her first-ever Emmy Award nomination in the outstanding variety special (live) category, as one of the creative directors for that year's Grammy Awards. For Eddie Murphy's *Coming 2 America*, released in March 2021 on Amazon Prime Video, Robinson created numbers inspired by dance styles that have significantly influenced her work. "I'm a hip-hop choreographer 'til I die, and African dance is really just the mother of hip-hop dance," she told Rebecca Milzoff for *Billboard* (12 Mar. 2021). "So it's always been the foundation for me, and I revisit it often." Robinson also worked on movement techniques with the cast, including Wesley Snipes, whose military character often made choreographed entrances with his soldiers. Robinson's next film was another with a largely Black cast: the Western *The Harder They Fall*, which debuted in late October 2021. That same month, she reunited with Brandy for ABC's musical drama *Queens*, about a former 1990s hip-hop quartet that launches a comeback.

Robinson returned to familiar territory in February 2022, overseeing Super Bowl LVI's halftime show, an homage to 1990s West Coast rap featuring previous collaborators Dr. Dre, Snoop Dogg, Blige, and Lamar as well as Eminem and 50 Cent. As choreographer and stage director, Robinson managed performances on an elaborately designed two-story set highlighting Compton's landmark buildings. She personally enlisted more than a hundred paid professional dancers for the nostalgic fourteen-minute show, which was watched by about 103 million viewers. After returning to produce the Grammy Awards in April 2022, Robinson was scheduled to choreograph the musical remake of *The Color Purple*, slated for release in late 2023.

PERSONAL LIFE

Robinson lives in Ojai, California, and has a son, Xuly Williams, from her previous relationship with poet Saul Williams.

SUGGESTED READING

Bloom, Julie. "Supreme Commander." *The New York Times*, 26 Nov. 2006, www.nytimes.com/2006/11/26/arts/dance/26bloo.html. Accessed 6 Apr. 2022.

Goldberg, Lesley. "*The Wiz* Producers on How the Oscars Turned NBC's Live Musical into a Hit—and Why *Peter Pan* Was a 'Mistake.'" *The Hollywood Reporter*, 4 Dec. 2015, www.hollywoodreporter.com/tv/tv-news/wiz-producers-how-oscars-turned-845893/. Accessed 6 Apr. 2022.

Greaves, Kayla A. "Person of Interest: Choreographer, Fatima Robinson." *Upscale*, 9 June 2015, upscalemagazine.com/person-of-interest-choreographer-fatima-robinson/. Accessed 6 Apr. 2022.

Milzoff, Rebecca. "Choreographer Fatima Robinson on 'Coming 2 America' and Surprises to Expect at the Grammys." *Billboard*, 12 Mar. 2021, www.billboard.com/music/awards/fatima-robinson-coming-2-america-grammys-9539211/. Accessed 13 Apr. 2022.

Sangweni, Yolanda. "Closet Envy: Choreographer Fatima Robinson." *Essence*, 29 Oct. 2020, www.essence.com/news/closet-we-envy-fatima-robinson/. Accessed 10 Apr. 2022.

Tailor, Leena. "Backstreet Boys Turn 25: Untold Stories About the World's Best-Selling Boy Band (Exclusive)." *ET*, 20 Apr. 2018, www.etonline.com/backstreet-boys-turn-25-untold-stories-about-the-worlds-best-selling-boy-band-exclusive-100728. Accessed 6 Apr. 2022.

SELECTED WORKS

Michael Jackson: "Remember the Time" (with Buddha Stretch), 1992; Brandy: "Baby," 1995; Aaliyah: "Try Again," 2000; *Save the Last Dance*, 2001; *Ali*, 2001; Mary J. Blige: "Family Affair," 2001; The Black Eyed Peas: "Hey Mama," 2004; *Dreamgirls*, 2006; Will.i.am feat. Justin Bieber: "#thatpower," 2013; *The Wiz Live!*, 2015; *An Evening with Whitney*, 2020–22; *The Coming 2 America*, 2021; *Super Bowl LVI Halftime Show*, 2022

—*Bertha Muteba*

Olivia Rodrigo

Born: February 20, 2003
Occupation: Actor and singer

After making a name for herself on the teen sitcom *Bizaardvark*, Olivia Rodrigo rose to fame in 2019, with a costarring role in the Disney series *High School Musical: The Musical—The Series*, a spinoff of the 2006 hit Disney Channel Original film *High School Musical*. In 2021, the teenage actor was catapulted to musical superstardom, thanks to the surprise breakout hit "Drivers License," about a heartbroken teenage girl whose ex-boyfriend has moved on with someone else.

Fueled by deeply personal and relatable lyrics, as well as considerable buzz surrounding the song's theorized subject, "Drivers License" debuted atop the Billboard Hot 100, where it spent eight consecutive weeks before going on to become the most-streamed song of 2021 with more than one billion global streams. After its January release, the song achieved quadruple-platinum status. In addition, Rodrigo's double-platinum debut disc, *Sour*, holds the distinction of being 2021's most-streamed album. She capped off an incredible breakout year with seven Grammy Award nominations. Despite her quick entrance into the spotlight, Rodrigo has stated that acting and singing stardom is not her end goal. "Songwriting is the thing I take most seriously in my life," she told Lucy Feldman for the *Time* (9 Dec. 2021). "It's the most personally gratifying too."

EARLY LIFE AND CAREER

Olivia Isabel Rodrigo was born in Temecula, California, to Sophia and Ronald Rodrigo on February 20, 2003. Her mother is an elementary school teacher, while her father is a therapist. An only child, she was influenced by her parents' musical interests growing up, listening to bands like the Clash, Smashing Pumpkins, and No Doubt. Her personal music journey began at age five, when she started taking voice lessons with local vocal coach Jennifer Dustman. Rodrigo's parents took notice of her early interest in music and encouraged her to also learn the piano. "I hated it," she recalled to Lizzie Widdicombe for *Elle* (19 May 2021). "I'd literally cry before every piano lesson." Her new abilities with the piano, however, encouraged Rodrigo to begin dabbling in songwriting. She wrote her first song on piano, which she titled "Superman," around the age of nine. She later learned how to play guitar.

Rodrigo honed her music and performing skills while appearing in musicals at Lisa J. Mails Elementary School and Dorothy McElhinny Middle School. She also competed in local talent contests, including Temecula Live and an annual *American Idol*–inspired vocal competition sponsored by the Boys and Girls Club (BGC) of Southwest County. In 2011, she reached the finals of BGC Idol and advanced to the semifinals two years later. She also began taking acting classes and auditioning professionally.

Around age twelve, Rodrigo appeared in her first major commercial for clothing brand Old Navy. She then landed her first starring role, as the title character in the direct-to-video movie *An American Girl: Grace Stirs Up Success* (2015). Her transition into professional acting led the family to move to Los Angeles, and Rodrigo began homeschooling or attending school on set.

Photo via Wikimedia Commons

DISNEY CHANNEL STAR

Shortly after appearing in her first film, Rodrigo earned a costarring role in the new Disney comedy series *Bizaardvark*. Premiering in 2016, the thirteen-year-old Rodrigo costarred as Paige Olivera alongside Madison Hu as Frankie Wong in the series about two teenage best friends who produce quirky songs and music videos for their titular vlogging channel. The show lasted three seasons before its conclusion in 2019. During the show's run, Rodrigo was featured on the first two seasons' soundtracks and reprised her role on *Bizaardvark Shorts*, a series of webisodes that aired separately on YouTube. She also guested on the Fox sitcom *New Girl* in 2017.

In February 2019, Rodrigo joined the cast of Disney's *High School Musical: The Musical—The Series* (HSMTMTS), a mockumentary centered around a group of drama students who stage a production of the 2006 Disney Channel classic *High School Musical* at East High School, where the original movie was filmed. Rodrigo plays shy, determined Nini, a perennial understudy who lands the female lead role, opposite her ex-boyfriend Ricky, played by actor and singer Joshua Bassett. In October 2019, a month before the show premiered on streaming platform Disney Plus, HSMTMTS earned a second-season renewal. The second season premiered in May 2021.

Rodrigo also made her songwriting debut during the first season, when series creator Tim Federle suggested she write a song for her character after listening to music Rodrigo had written and shared on her Instagram page. Three days later, Rodrigo had written the piano-driven power ballad "All I Want," which the homeschooled sophomore penned during finals week. "All I Want" debuted in episode four and went viral on the social-media platform Tik Tok, cracked the *Billboard* Hot 100 in January 2020, and eventually achieved platinum status. The accompanying video, featuring Rodrigo performing the tune on the piano while clad in a pink tulle gown, was released in March 2020. Her other *HSMTMTS* songwriting credit was "Just A Moment," a collaboration with Bassett.

CHART-TOPPING SINGLE

The success "All I Want" earned outside of *HSMTMTS* led to Rodrigo meeting with record label executives in 2020 regarding a solo deal. She eventually signed with Interscope and Geffen Records, with a stipulation in her contract that gave her future control of her master recordings. "You definitely have to be a businesswoman to be a musician," she shared with Rachel DeSantis for *People* (9 Dec. 2021). "There's a path for me to have a stake in the music and art I create, which is only fair."

On January 8, 2021, Rodrigo released "Drivers License," the lead single from her debut album. The song was an immediate hit. In its first week, "Drivers License" debuted atop three *Billboard* categories: the Hot 100, the Digital Song Sales, and the Streaming Songs charts. By mid-January, it had become the fastest song to surpass 100 million streams on Spotify, where it also amassed the most streams in a single week—65.8 million—and the most streams in a single day for a non-holiday song—15.7 million streams on January 11 and 17.01 million streams on January 12. The song simultaneously occupied the top of the US iTunes Chart and the US Apple Music singles chart.

Much of the song's popularity was due to Rodrigo's relatable emotions, however, it also received buzz from the public's deep dive into the lyrics. Rumors surrounded the song's perceived subject, which many believed was the failed relationship between Rodrigo and costar Bassett, as well as his new alleged relationship with fellow Disney actor and singer Sabrina Carpenter. Some critics accused both Rodrigo and Bassett of using the drama as a publicity stunt to promote their music. Rodrigo, however, was not discouraged by such public scrutiny and criticism. As she told Laura Snapes for the *Guardian* (7 May 2021), "I'm a teenage girl, I write about stuff that I feel really intensely—and I feel heartbreak and longing really intensely—and I think that's authentic and natural."

SOUR

In early February 2021 Rodrigo made her late-night television debut on *The Tonight Show Starring Jimmy Fallon*, performing a stripped-down, acoustic version of "Drivers License." She also appeared on February's *Time100 Next* 2021 list, which highlights emerging leaders. On April 1, 2021, Rodrigo released her long-awaited follow-up single, "Deja Vu," which sampled Taylor Swift's song "Cruel Summer." (Swift later earned cowriter credits on the song.) The psychedelic pop, post-breakup anthem evoked comparisons to "Drivers License" for its lyrics, alluding to an old flame who has moved on with a new girlfriend. Like her previous song, "Deja Vu" debuted in the top ten of the *Billboard* Hot 100.

In mid-May, following her debut performance at the BRIT Awards, Rodrigo unveiled her third single, the angry emo/pop-punk track "Good 4 U," while making her *Saturday Night Live* debut as musical guest. "Good 4 U" became Rodrigo's second number-one debut on *Billboard* Hot 100 chart. Later that month, Rodrigo released *Sour*, her full-length debut album, which she recorded during the coronavirus disease 2019 (COVID-19) pandemic. *Sour* debuted atop the *Billboard* 200 chart.

By June, Rodrigo had four of her songs, including the non-single "Traitor," simultaneously reach the top ten of the *Billboard* Global 200 chart, which ranks the world's most popular songs. Her *Sour Prom* concert film also premiered on YouTube that same month. Following a White House visit in July, as part of a COVID-19 youth vaccination campaign, Rodrigo found herself under scrutiny again in August 2021, when she gave Paramore songwriting credit on "Good 4 U" after the song drew comparisons to Paramore's "Misery Business." "Every single artist is inspired by artists who have come before them. It's sort of a fun, beautiful sharing process," she told P. Claire Dodson for *Teen Vogue* (5 Oct. 2021) in defense. "Nothing is ever new. There's four chords in every song. That's the fun part—trying to make that your own."

GARNERS ACCOLADES

On September 12, 2021, Rodrigo attended her first MTV Video Music Awards (VMA), where she won three statues, including Best New Artist and Song of the Year for "Drivers License." The next day she made her debut at the 2021 Met Gala. Nearly a week later, Rodrigo was among the performers at the iHeart Radio Music Festival in Las Vegas. After unveiling the official music video for "Traitor," Rodrigo performed the song during her appearance on *Jimmy Kimmel Live* in late October and at November's American Music Awards (2021), where she claimed the New Artist of the Year prize. She followed with three Apple Music Awards: Song of the Year ("Drivers License"); Album of the Year (*Sour*); and Breakthrough Artist of the Year.

Rodrigo's whirlwind year culminated in late November, with seven nominations for the 2022 Grammy Award. In addition to being the second-youngest artist nominated in the general field categories (Album of the Year, Record of the Year, Song of the Year, and Best New Artist), Rodrigo was also the first Filipina American to receive all four nods. In December, she was named *Time* Entertainer of the Year (2021); *Variety* tapped her for Songwriter of the Year (2021). Rodrigo also announced plans to return for a third season of *HSMTMTS* and to embark on her sold out, headlining tour, playing small venues across North America and Europe in 2022.

PERSONAL LIFE

After graduating from high school in June 2021, Rodrigo moved out of her parents' home and into her own apartment in California.

SUGGESTED READING

DeSantis, Rachel. "Olivia Rodrigo Says It Was 'Frustrating to See People Discredit' Her Songwriting amid Credit Adds." *People*, 9 Dec. 2021, people.com/music/olivia-rodrigo-frustrating-people-discredit-her-songwriting-amid-credit-adds/. Accessed 10 Dec. 2021.

Feldman, Lucy. "Time 2021 Entertainer of the Year: Olivia Rodrigo." *Time*, 9 Dec. 2021, time.com/entertainer-of-the-year-2021-olivia-rodrigo/. Accessed 20 Dec. 2021.

Rodrigo, Olivia. "Olivia Rodrigo at the Crossroads." Interview by Claire P. Dodson. *Teen Vogue*, 5 Oct. 2021, www.teenvogue.com/story/olivia-rodrigo-october-2021-cover-interview. Accessed 10 Dec. 2021.

Snapes, Laura. "Olivia Rodrigo: 'I'm a Teenage Girl. I Feel Heartbreak and Longing Really Intensely.'" *The Guardian*, 7 May 2021, www.theguardian.com/music/2021/may/07/olivia-rodrigo-im-a-teenage-girl-i-feel-heartbreak-and-longing-really-intensely. Accessed 10 Dec. 2021.

Widdicombe, Lizzie. "Olivia Rodrigo Is in the Driver's Seat." *Elle*, 26 Apr. 2021, www.elle.com/culture/celebrities/a36133166/olivia-rodrigo-drivers-license-profile/. Accessed 10 Dec. 2021.

—*Bertha Muteba*

Michaela Jaé Rodriguez

Born: January 7, 1991
Occupation: Actor and singer

When Michaela Jaé Rodriguez, previously known as Mj Rodriguez, made her Off-Broadway debut in a 2011 revival of the 1996 musical *Rent*, veteran actor Billy Porter, the musical's associate director, was immediately struck by her talent. "From the minute she walked into the room, it was like, 'This person is a star,'" he recalled to Pari Dukovic for *nj.com* (23 Feb. 2022). The industry also took notice of the promising young performer, awarding Rodriguez the prestigious Clive Barnes Award in 2011. Seven years later, Porter had a front-row seat to her meteoric rise to fame when he starred alongside Rodriguez in *Pose* (2018–21), a groundbreaking television drama set in the 1980s and 1990s that explored New York City's iconic drag ball culture.

When *Pose* premiered in 2018, Rodriguez made history as one of five transgender actors cast as series regulars, the highest number up to that point on a scripted television show. Rodriguez starred in the breakout role of Blanca Rodriguez-Evangelista, an HIV-positive Afro-Latina transgender woman who serves as the mother figure to a group of homeless LGBTQ youths. This role helped catapult Rodriguez from relative obscurity to national

Photo courtesy the Peabody Awards, via Wikimedia Commons

Upon completing elementary school, Rodriguez honed her vocal skills at Newark Arts High School, the United States' first public high school for the visual and performing arts.

In 2005, Rodriguez experienced a life-changing event when her father took her to see the film adaptation of the Tony Award-winning play *Rent* (1996). She was immediately drawn to one of the movie's main characters, originally written as an HIV-positive drag queen. "When I saw Angel's character, I saw a female," she recalled to Jed Gottlieb for *BerkleeNow* (20 Nov. 2019). "But they didn't have the vernacular; they didn't have words back in the 1990s . . . for us." Another major influence for the fourteen-year-old was Timotheus "Timothy" J. Smart, a runway and print model who introduced Rodriguez to New York City's LGBTQ+ underground ballroom culture. Starting in 2005, Rodriguez spent the next three years immersing herself within the ballroom community, first as a spectator and then as a competitor.

OFF-BROADWAY DEBUT

During her senior year of high school, the aspiring performer was among the finalists for the 2009 *Star-Ledger* Scholarship for the Performing Arts. Following graduation, Rodriguez attended an exhaustive summer program (Aspire: Five-Week Music Performance Intensive) at the prestigious Berklee College of Music in Boston, Massachusetts, where she subsequently took music business and songwriting courses. She left the school after two semesters.

By 2010, Rodriguez had seized her dream role, playing Angel in New Jersey Youth Theatre's (NJYT) summer production of *Rent*, staged by NJPAC.

Impressed by Rodriguez, Fredi Walker-Browne, an original *Rent* cast member, helped her land an audition to play the same role in an Off-Broadway revival of the musical. After four callbacks, Rodriguez was cast in the production, which opened in August 2011 at New World Stages. For her critically acclaimed performance, Rodriguez earned the prestigious Clive Barnes Award in December 2011.

BRANCHING OUT INTO TELEVISION

In May 2012, Rodriguez made her television debut, portraying a transgender woman in the Showtime drama *Nurse Jackie*, which ran from 2009 to 2015.

fame, During the show's three-season run, Rodriguez proved to be a trailblazer, becoming the first transgender actress to receive an Emmy nomination in a leading acting category, as well as the first to win a Golden Globe.

Rodriguez has also emerged as a style icon and role model in the LGBTQ community through her modeling work. Along with becoming *Latina Magazine*'s first-ever transgender cover model in November 2021, she appeared in *Elle*, *Vanity Fair*, and *Harper's Bazaar*. She was also featured on *Time*'s Next 100 list in 2019 and its annual Women of the Year list in 2022.

EARLY LIFE AND ARTISTIC AWAKENING

Michaela Antonia Jaé Rodriguez was born Michael Anthony Rodriguez Jr. to Audrey and Michael Rodriguez on January 7, 1991, in Newark, New Jersey, where she also grew up.

By age seven, Rodriguez had fallen in love with performing while attending Queen of Angels School, a private Catholic K–8 school. "When I was little all I could think about was just being on some kind of stage," she recalled to Marc Malkin for *Variety* (19 June 2019).

Four years later, Rodriguez decided to pursue acting with the support of her mother, who enrolled her in an immersive musical theater summer program at the New Jersey Performing Arts Center (NJPAC) in Newark.

When the Off-Broadway revival of *Rent* closed in September 2012, Rodriguez put her career on hold to pursue gender-affirming surgery; she had identified as female since the age of seven. "There was never really any change," she told Michael Gioia for *Playbill* (7 June 2016). "There was an enhancing that had to take place—mental enhancing, physical enhancing . . . but that was specifically for me, and I needed time for myself."

In the meantime, Rodriguez continued working, branching out into television and briefly appearing in *The Carrie Diaries* (2013), the CW's teen-drama and *Sex and the City* prequel, as well as some web comedy series.

By April 2016, Rodriguez had fully resumed her acting career, hoping to break away from being typecast as a transgender character. After unsuccessfully auditioning for the dual roles of Peggy Schuyler/Maria Reynolds in Lin-Manuel Miranda's Broadway musical *Hamilton*, she appeared in a July revival of the 1978 Off-Broadway musical *Runaways*, which staged all five performances at the New York City Center, and continued to pursue other theater work. With her guest appearance in a 2016 episode of the Netflix series *Luke Cage*, Rodriguez played the first-ever transgender character to appear onscreen in the Marvel Cinematic Universe (MCU).

Then came a starring role in the coming-of-age musical drama *Saturday Church* (2017), which debuted at the Tribeca Film Festival. Rodriguez's performance as Ebony, a transgender woman who befriends a Bronx, New York, teen grappling with his sexuality and gender identity, earned her a best-actress nomination from the festival.

Subsequent big-screen appearances included the short films *Bun in the Oven* (2017) and *Gema* (2018), in which she played the title character, who is faced with the nerve-wracking prospect of meeting her fiancé's parents. She also continued to work on the stage during this time.

POSE AND BREAKTHROUGH

Rodriguez experienced a career breakthrough when she was cast in the drama *Pose*, which explores New York City's underground ballroom scene during the height of the AIDS epidemic in the 1980s and early 1990s. In her first regular series role, Rodriguez was tapped to play Blanca Rodriguez-Evangelista, a transgender and HIV-positive nail technician who serves as the matriarch of a fledgling ballroom community of younger African American and Afro Latino transgender, queer, and gay performers known as House of Evangelista.

Rodriguez quickly realized that the part would change her life dramatically. "I was still extremely happy knowing that the world was going not only [to] see my story as Mj Rodriguez, and the many stories of women like me out there," she told Jocelyn Silver for *Paper Magazine* (19 July 2018). When *Pose* debuted on FX in early June 2018, the series was well-received by both critics and audiences, earning a second-season renewal in July.

That summer, Rodriguez collaborated with costar Porter on a rendition of "Home" from *The Wiz* (1978), which was also featured on episode six of *Pose*, as well as the accompanying soundtrack. She also graced the August 2018 cover of *Out* Magazine, alongside her other *Pose* costars Indya Adrianna Moore and Dominique Jackson.

Pose made history in December 2018. With its two Golden Globe nominations (best actor and best television drama), it became the first television series with a mostly transgender cast to achieve this feat. Meanwhile, Rodriguez's next film, the-coming-of-age comedy *Adam*, premiered at the 2019 Sundance Film Festival, where she also cohosted the Gay & Lesbian Alliance Against Defamation (GLAAD) Media Awards nominations ceremony. She also shared grand marshal duties with Moore and Jackson at the NYC Pride March in June.

When *Pose* returned in the summer, its premiere became the show's most-watched episode up to that point, leading to the show's renewal for a third season. During season two, which took place between the late 1980s and early 1990s, Rodriguez's character found herself wrestling with an AIDS diagnosis, a transphobic landlord, and the loss of her nail-care business. After the season finished airing in August, Rodriguez starred as Audrey in Pasadena Playhouse's Fall production of *Little Shop of Horrors*, becoming the first transgender actress to play the role. In September she attended the 2019 Primetime Emmys; *Pose* was nominated for six awards; Porter became the first openly gay man to win the lead drama actor prize, helping elevate the show's profile.

FIRST EMMY NOMINATION

While starring in *Pose*, Rodriguez also started earning industry recognition. In November 2019, Olay Body tapped her as its first transgender Latina spokesperson. The following January, she received a best actress nomination at the 2020 Critics' Choice Awards. Production on the third and final season of *Pose* was suspended in March 2020 due to the onset of the coronavirus disease 2019 (COVID-19) pandemic, which claimed the lives of Rodriguez's grandmother and aunt. Amid the outbreak, Rodriguez remained visible, virtually reuniting with Porter for a GLAAD fundraising event in April of that year and *Pose-A-Thon*, a Disney/FX Pride Month special in June.

By October 2020, two months after being overlooked for an Emmy nomination, Rodriguez had resumed filming for *Pose*, which officially wrapped in March 2021 and premiered two months later. During the final season, her character, Blanca, finds a new job as a nurse, a new love, and closure with her ballroom family amid the growing AIDS crisis in the mid-1990s. For her performance, Rodriguez received an Emmy nomination for Outstanding Lead Actress in a Drama Series, becoming the first transgender nominee in the category. "Seeing a woman like myself strive and get the things that I feel like I've always wanted . . . It feels so good. I feel seen," she told Ryan Fleming for *Deadline* (18 Aug. 2021).

Rodriguez also launched her recording career that summer, releasing the debut dance single, "Something to Say," and accompanying music video, under her full name Michaela Jaé, instead of the nickname "Mj," a moniker based on her initials. "I need people to see the person that is behind Mj . . . that there's more to me than just the characters I play," Rodriguez explained to Chris Gardner for *Hollywood Reporter* (17 Nov. 2021). "I want people to see who I truly am."

FIRST GOLDEN GLOBE WIN

Although she did not win the Emmy for Outstanding Lead Actress at September's Emmy ceremony, Rodriguez claimed the best-actress prize at the inaugural Hollywood Critics Association (HCA) and an individual achievement in drama nod from the Television Critics Association (TCA). After costarring in Lin-Manuel Miranda's feature directorial debut, *tick, tick . . . Boom!* (2021), Rodriguez achieved another career milestone in December 2021, earning her first Golden Globe nomination for her work on *Pose*. At the January 2022 ceremony, Rodriguez made history once again by being the first openly transgender performer to win a Golden Globe. She followed that with her second Critics Choice Award nomination.

For her next project, Rodriguez made the transition to comedy, starring opposite Maya Rudolph in the Apple Plus ensemble comedy series *Loot* (2022), about a billionaire (Rudolph) who turns to philanthropy following a high-profile, scandal-plagued divorce. "I want to constantly break that mold," Rodriguez told Danielle Turchiano for *Variety* (12 Aug. 2021). "I want to constantly show people that we as people of LGBTQIA community, especially the trans community . . . it's important to know that we're multifaceted."

In addition to her acting, Rodriguez is a comic-book enthusiast who has worked on writing her own graphic novel.

SUGGESTED READING

Fleming, Ryan. "Ballroom Hits: Pose Star MJ Rodriguez on Being the First Trans Woman to Be Nominated for a Lead Acting Emmy." *Deadline*, 18 Aug. 2021, deadline.com/2021/08/pose-mj-rodriguez-fx-emmy-nominated-actress-1234817247/. Accessed 15 Nov. 2021.

Gardner, Chris. "Why Mj Rodriguez Now Goes by Full Name Michaela Jae Rodriguez." *Hollywood Reporter*, 17 Nov. 2021, www.hollywoodreporter.com/news/general-news/mj-rodriguez-pose-full-name-michaela-jae-rodriguez-1235048589/. Accessed 15 Nov. 2021.

Gioia, Michael. "Mj Rodriguez Talks Her Transition and Hamilton Audition." *Playbill*, 7 June 2016, www.playbill.com/article/mj-rodriguez-talks-her-transition-and-hamilton-audition. Accessed 15 Nov. 2021.

Gottlieb, Jed. "Mj Rodriguez Finds Roles That Reflect Her True Identity." *BerkleeNow*, 20 Nov. 2019, www.berklee.edu/news/berklee-now/mj-rodriguez-finds-roles-reflect-her-true-identity. Accessed 15 Nov. 2021.

Malkin, Marc. "Pose Star Mj Rodriguez Says Simply Being Trans Is Activism." *Variety*, 19 June 2019, variety.com/2019/tv/news/mj-rodriguez-pose-activism-1203246568/. Accessed 15 Nov. 2021.

Silver, Jocelyn. "Talking *Pose* with Mother Mj Rodriguez." *Paper Magazine*, 19 July 2018, www.papermag.com/pose-mj-rodriguez-2588190874.html?rebelltitem=2#rebelltitem2. Accessed 15 Nov. 2021.

SELECTED WORKS

Nurse Jackie, 2012; *The Carrie Diaries*, 2013; *Luke Cage*, 2016; *Pose*, 2018–21; *Loot*, 2022–

—Bertha Muteba

Tamara Rojo

Born: May 17, 1974
Occupation: Ballet dancer and artistic director

Ballet star Tamara Rojo is known both for her exhilarating performances on stage and her innovative work behind the scenes. She rose to fame with the Scottish Ballet and the English National Ballet (ENB) in the 1990s and was named a lead principal dancer with the United Kingdom's Royal Ballet in 2000, achieving international acclaim for her power and grace in all of the major' classical ballet roles as well as in more modern works. In 2012 she returned to the ENB, continuing to dance while also taking over as the company's artistic director. In her leadership role she revitalized the company through an ambitious slate of progressive moves, such as highlighting female choreographers and expanding the group's reach by adding more modern ballets to the repertoire. In an interview with Rosa Alvares for Iberia airline's *Talento a bordo* website (8 Oct. 2019), Rojo discussed her dual roles as performer and artistic director: "Dancing is my first love, and directing, my second. I feel very privileged to have the opportunity to feel what one feels on stage. At this point in my career, every performance is a gift. As a dancer, I've already done everything: I performed in the most important venues in the world, I've shared the stage with the greatest artists, I've worked with splendid companies."

Throughout her career Rojo received many prestigious honors in recognition of her talent and passionate advocacy for the performing arts. She led the ENB to the 2014 National Dance Award for outstanding company, was made a Commander of the British Empire (CBE) in 2016, and received the Gold Medal of the Academy of Performing Arts of Spain in 2021.

EARLY LIFE AND EDUCATION

Tamara Rojo was born in Montreal, Quebec, on May 17, 1974. Her parents were from Spain, and the family moved back there when she was an infant. She grew up in Madrid, where both her mother and father were active opponents of Spanish dictator Francisco Franco.

Rojo first discovered ballet at age five. She recalled to Anna Tyzack for the *Telegraph* (25 Oct. 2012): "My parents weren't into dancing but one day when I was waiting in the rain for my mother to pick me up from school, the ballet teacher suggested I should come into the gym where it was dry and warm. I walked inside and instantly fell in love with ballet. It was many years before I saw a proper performance but by the time I was nine, ballet was part of my daily routine."

Rojo enrolled at the Victor Ullate School, where she enjoyed an open-minded and supportive atmosphere. As she progressed, she began dancing with the Ballet de la Comunidad de Madrid and the company of her teacher Victor Ullate, performing both classical repertoire and other works. She also pursued a more traditional education, studying theatrical arts and dance at the Universidad Rey Juan Carlos de Madrid, where she received both a bachelor's degree and a master's degree.

In 1994, at age nineteen, Rojo first received notice in the wider dance world when she earned a gold medal and a special jury award at the Paris International Dance Competition. In 1996 she received an offer to join the Scottish National Ballet as a dancer, which she accepted even though she knew no English at the time. In order to advance in her profession, she knew she had to leave Spain. "There is no major classical ballet company in Spain," she wrote in the *Observer* in 2009, as quoted by Ruaridh Nicoll in *The Guardian* (14 Apr. 2012). "Many ballet companies around the world have excellent Spaniards in their ranks, dancers who have been nurtured and trained in Spain, but who are then orphaned by their mother country and forced to emigrate to pursue their careers."

SUCCESS IN THE UNITED KINGDOM

Working with the Scottish National Ballet, Rojo found herself dancing in principal roles in such ballets as *Swan Lake*, *Romeo and Juliet*, and *La Sylphide*, among others. Although her performances met with rave reviews, Rojo's time in Scotland proved brief. In 1997 she was specially invited by artistic director Derek Deane to join the English National Ballet (ENB), another of the major ballet companies in the United Kingdom and one of the most prestigious European touring companies.

Rojo moved to London to join the ENB as a principal soloist. "My flat seemed to have been carved out of a gap under the stairs," she recalled of her first apartment in the city, as quoted by Nicoll. "The place was crawling with cockroaches. I was a bit lonely. I found I was talking to myself and would spend hours walking from one end of town to the other." Loneliness aside, Rojo found she blossomed professionally in London. She was promoted to principal dancer about a half a year after joining the ENB, and in her first year she was hailed as "Dancer Revelation of the Year" by the *Times*. Rojo was particularly acclaimed for her leading performances in *Romeo and Juliet*, as Juliet, and *The Nutcracker*, as Clara, which Deane developed specially for her. She also had the opportunity to perform in such famed ballets as *Alice in Wonderland*, *La Bayadere*, *Cinderella*, *Rite of Spring*, *The Sleeping Beauty*, *Swan Lake*, and *Who Cares?*, among others.

After dancing in an ENB production of Kenneth MacMillan's *Rite of Spring* in 1999, Rojo was intrigued by the prospect of performing in more works by the famed choreographer. Therefore, she inquired about moving to the Royal Ballet, with which MacMillan was long associated. In 2000, while waiting on contract negotiations, Rojo was asked to fill in on short notice as an injury replacement in a Royal Ballet production of *Giselle*. Following her success as a guest artist, she joined the Royal Ballet full-time as a principal dancer. With that company she continued to perform a full range of classical and other roles, including many developed specifically for her. She also toured internationally as a guest artist with many other companies.

Despite facing a few health challenges over the years, Rojo established herself as one of the brightest stars in ballet. She earned numerous awards and accolades, including a 2005 Prince of Asturias Award—one of Spain's highest honors, which reflected her great popularity in her home country. In 2010, she and choreographer Kim Brandstrup won the Laurence Olivier Award for Best New Dance Production with *Goldberg—The Brandstrup-*

Photo by Erik Doble via Wikimedia Commons

Rojo Project. She was awarded a Kennedy Center Gold Medal in the Arts in 2012.

ARTISTIC DIRECTOR

In 2012 Rojo departed the Royal Ballet when she was offered the opportunity to return to the ENB as its artistic director, in addition to continuing to dance as its principal ballet dancer. Some of her close colleagues warned her against accepting the position because it appeared that government funding to the ENB would be cut. However, she had been open about her desire to take on directorial work, and her application to lead the Royal Ballet when its search for a new director in 2011 had been unsuccessful. Industry observers also speculated about how she would fare with the ENB, which has a significantly different programming style than the Royal Ballet and is smaller than other major companies. Far from seeing that as a disadvantage, Rojo argued the ENB's more intimate size allows greater opportunities to up-and-coming performers. "If you're a young, talented dancer and you want to be principal in five years, would you go to somewhere with 200 dancers, like Paris, or one with 68, like here?" she asked Judith Mackrell in a conversation for *The Guardian* (17 Feb. 2015).

As artistic director of the ENB, Rojo quickly earned a reputation for strong leadership and ambitious thinking. Notably, she sought to bring ballet to more people by expanding the types of works the company produced beyond the classical repertoire. She also made it a point to feature more women behind the scenes. "There are so many talented female choreographers out there, but they're much less quick than men to accept work," she told Mackrell. "Some felt they were not ready for a big London commission. I find it's the same with the choreographic workshops in the company. There's no shortage of men who want to experiment and put themselves forward, but we have to go out to find the women."

Rojo's initiatives helped the ENB move beyond its financial struggles and revitalize its reputation as a hotbed of artistic creativity. Under her leadership the organization won the 2014 National Dance Award for outstanding company, a major honor in the British ballet community. Rojo herself also continued to garner many awards as both a director and dancer, and in 2016 she was granted the rank of Commander in the Order of the British Empire for her services to the arts. The following year the ENB won the Olivier Award for Outstanding Achievement in Dance for their repertoire expansion.

PERFORMING ARTS ADVOCATE

Rojo and the ENB faced a serious challenge with the onset of the coronavirus disease 2019 (COVID-19) global pandemic in early 2020. Health and safety protocols aimed at slowing the spread of the viral disease meant that large gatherings, including performances like ballets, were largely canceled. The economic impact was severe: about 85 percent of the ENB workforce was furloughed, while Rojo and many others who remained took significant pay cuts. In order to drum up some interest in the company during lockdown, Rojo instituted innovative programming such as virtual ballet classes conducted from her kitchen and online watch parties of recorded performances, attracting millions of viewers. She also served as a vocal advocate for public funding of the arts in Great Britain. "We in the cultural and arts sector have for some time been making the financial case for our existence: how every pound of public money invested in the arts turns into £5 returned to the economy; how we

support and sustain other industries, such as hospitality and tourism," she wrote in a piece for the *Economist* (17 Nov. 2020). "In Britain, the sector provides more than 350,000 jobs. But there are more profound spiritual, cultural and emotional reasons that are often forgotten, because they are less measurable."

In late 2020, as lockdown restrictions began to ease, the ENB, along with other cultural institutions, began putting on performances again, albeit socially distanced ones with audiences at less-than-full capacity. Rojo noted the ongoing importance of creative expression. "The performing arts and dance have survived millennia," she said in an interview with Lindsay Winship for *The Guardian* (12 Oct. 2020). "They've survived pandemics and hundred-year wars and all kind of disasters. Getting together to share stories is intrinsic to humanity. People will gather, live performance will continue to exist."

PERSONAL LIFE

While typically guarded about her private life, Rojo often told interviewers that she was a demanding perfectionist and used her personal experiences, including negative ones, to propel her artistry. "I abuse my emotions and manipulate my past," she said, as quoted by Nicoll. "Things like anger and the desire for revenge, you can do a lot with that." Rojo's relationship with Isaac Hernández, a dancer at the ENB, generated media attention, especially amid reports in 2018 that it was among the causes of tensions within the company. The couple had a child together in 2021.

SUGGESTED READING

Mackrell, Judith. "The Tamara Rojo Revolution: Bringing Ballet into the 21st Century." *The Guardian*, 17 Feb. 2015, www.theguardian. com/stage/2015/feb/17/the-tamara-rojo-revolution-english-national-ballet. Accessed 27 Oct. 2021.

Nicoll, Ruaridh. "Tamara Rojo: Born under a Dancing Star." *The Guardian*, 14 Apr. 2012, www.theguardian.com/theobserver/2012/apr/15/observer-profile-tamara-rojo-english-national-ballet. Accessed 29 Oct. 2021.

Rojo, Tamara. "Tamara Rojo: Commitment on Points." Interview by Rosa Alvares. *Talento a bordo*, Iberia, 8 Oct. 2019, www. talentoabordo.com/en/cinema-and-theatre/tamara-rojo. Accessed 29 Oct. 2021.

—. "The Show Must Go On, Argues Tamara Rojo of the English National Ballet." *The Economist*, 17 Nov. 2020, www.economist.com/the-world-ahead/2020/11/17/the-show-must-go-on-argues-tamara-rojo-of-the-english-national-ballet. Accessed 27 Oct. 2021.

"Tamara Rojo: Biography." *Royal Opera House*, www.roh.org.uk/people/tamara-rojo. Accessed 27 Oct. 2021.

Tyzack, Anna. "My Perfect Weekend: Tamara Rojo, Artistic Director and Principal Dancer, English National Ballet." *The Telegraph*, 25 Oct. 2012, www.telegraph.co.uk/lifestyle/9631882/My-perfect-weekend-Tamara-Rojo-artistic-director-and-principal-dancer-English-National-Ballet.html. Accessed 27 Oct. 2021.

Winship, Lyndsey. "Tamara Rojo: 'Despite Everything, It's a Very Creative Moment.'" *The Guardian*, 12 Oct. 2020, amp.theguardian.com/stage/2020/oct/12/tamara-rojo-interview-english-national-ballet-despite-everything-its-a-very-creative-moment. Accessed 27 Oct. 2021.

—*Christopher Mari*

Alison Roman

Born: September 1, 1985
Occupation: Chef and internet personality

For American chef and internet personality Alison Roman, developing the perfect recipe requires a lengthy period of hands-on research and a truly personal touch—key elements that rendered her unable to hand recipe-testing duties off to an assistant. "I could never do that. I will always struggle as a result," she told Emily Gould in an interview for *Elle* (23 May 2019). "I will always be behind, and I will always miss my deadlines and always be stressed out because of my inability to let someone else do the work." Though perhaps inefficient, Roman's approach has proven highly successful, as she built a substantial following with the published cookbooks *Dining In* (2017) and *Nothing Fancy: Unfussy Food for Having People Over* (2019), columns in publications such as the *New York Times*, and posts on social media platforms such as *Instagram*, which helped her highly photogenic creations repeatedly go viral.

As her work focused primarily on cooking and dining at home, Roman's recipes and Roman herself gained further popularity during the early months of the COVID-19 pandemic in 2020, as quarantined foodies sought new inspiration for meals at home. That period was also a turbulent one for Roman, who lost her *New York Times* column after making controversial comments in an ill-advised interview. However, she largely rebounded from the controversy, launching a successful subscription-based newsletter, recording a new video series, and pursuing a number of additional projects that would expand the Alison Roman brand. "I'm doing all these different things, and I'm not sure I would have taken any of those leaps had last year not happened," she told Lauren Collins for the *New Yorker* (13 Dec. 2021). "I'm trying to create things that will outlive this moment, and that will be able to exist without me."

EARLY LIFE AND EDUCATION

Alison Elisabeth Roman was born in Los Angeles, California, on September 1, 1985. Her parents divorced when she was a young child. Growing up in Los Angeles, Roman developed an interest in cooking at an early age but initially had a very limited repertoire. "I knew how to do like, two things," she told Sophie Missing in an interview for the *Gannet* (10 Aug. 2017). "One was make pasta sauce and I remember I became really obsessed with learning how to make scones. Which is weird because I never had a scone, it just became a thing I wanted to learn how to make."

By her teen years, Roman discovered that cooking was both a useful distraction from schoolwork and a valuable avenue for creative expression. "I wasn't bad at school, it just didn't excite me," she revealed in an interview for the magazine *Gossamer*. "Cooking did." Initially aspiring to become a writer, Roman briefly attended college in Santa Cruz, California, after graduating from high school in the early 2000s. She left school before completing her degree, instead opting to pursue a career in the restaurant industry.

EARLY CAREER

Although Roman initially considered attending culinary school, a chef she met encouraged her to begin working in restaurant kitchens immediately. She began her cooking career with a position at the Los Angeles restaurant Sona, working for the pastry shop associated with the restaurant. "I loved the energy of the kitchen, and how fast people were moving, and how gruff and short with each other they were," she recalled to Collins. After working in the Los Angeles area for several years, Roman relocated to San Francisco, where she worked as a pastry chef at restaurants such as Frisson and Quince. In 2009, Roman moved to New York City, where she eventually took a position at the recently established bakery Milk Bar, run by chef Christina Tosi. She also worked for a time at the New York restaurants Momofuku and Pies 'n' Thighs.

By 2011 Roman had decided that she no longer wanted to work in restaurants and began to move into the food media industry, working as a recipe tester for the magazine *Bon Appétit*. She was later hired on as an assistant food editor and senior food editor at the publication, positions that included appearing in online videos. In the Sweet Spots video series, for instance, she visited various dessert restaurants in New York. During that period, she also published her first cookbook, *Lemons*, a short collection of recipes devoted to the titular fruit. Roman left *Bon Appétit* in September 2015, moving on to a position at BuzzFeed, which she held for less than a year.

FREELANCE CAREER

In April 2016 Roman left BuzzFeed to focus on her freelance work, which included developing recipes for publication in cookbooks. "It was definitely much harder at the beginning," she told *Gossamer* about the transition to freelance. "It really took a toll on me—and my friendships—because I became really needy. The people in my life were spending all day with other people and would be drained or done, and I was like, 'Hey guys! Want to hang out?'" Roman's first full-length cookbook, *Dining In*, was published in 2017 and highlighted her simple, vegetable-heavy style of cooking. The following year she began writing a column for the *New York Times*, and in 2019 she published the cookbook *Nothing Fancy: Unfussy Food for Having People Over*. In addition to publishing recipes in books and traditional venues like her *New York Times* column, Roman became known for her use of social media platforms such as *Instagram*, which enabled her to share

enticing photographs of her creations and further develop her personal brand.

As Roman became more widely known as a food and cooking influencer, a number of her recipes gained fame, including one for a pasta dish that prominently featured shallots. Another popular recipe, this one for chocolate shortbread cookies, gained popularity online but also sparked debate as it spread across the Internet in 2017. "There was some contention around the cookies," she recalled in 2019, as reported by Alex Abad-Santos for *Vox* (22 Apr. 2020). "People were like, is this better [than regular chocolate chip cookies]? Is it worth it? People were kind of mad about the cookies! So I think a lot of people made it because it was a social conversation: People wanted to weigh in on whether or not they thought it was better, and try it for themselves, go up against other cookies—it was a whole thing." Alongside promoting her recipes online, Roman appeared on a variety of major television programs to discuss food and cooking, including the talk shows *The Kitchen*, *Good Morning America*, and *Today*.

COVID-19 AND CONTROVERSY

As a cookbook author who emphasized dining at home, Roman gained further popularity throughout the first months of the COVID-19 pandemic in early 2020, during which restaurants closed or shifted to takeout-only models and home cooking became increasingly popular as both a hobby and a matter of necessity. "I really like doing nice things for people, and there's so much I can't do right now," she told Abad-Santos during that period. "So I think that just being able to help people [cook], as a thing I *can* do, it makes me feel useful. It makes me feel like I still have something to provide."

While the attention paid to Roman and her recipes during the early pandemic was largely positive, her increasing prominence also made her the subject of greater public scrutiny and contributed to a perhaps inevitable backlash. In May 2020, the *New Consumer* published an interview with Roman in which she criticized two public figures—decluttering expert Marie Kondo and model and cookbook author Chrissy Teigen—for what she considered the excessive commercialization of their brands. Although she apologized for her assertions after Teigen objected to them, Roman's comments proved controversial, in part because both Kondo and Teigen had large fan followings on *Twitter* who disagreed with Roman's assessment. More concerning for some members of the public, however, was that both of the women Roman mentioned were of Asian descent, which led to allegations of racism on Roman's part. The controversy was fueled further by earlier complaints in 2018 that a popular chickpea stew recipe published by Roman was similar to the Indian dish chana masala but did not acknowledge the dish's Indian origins. Also of concern was Roman's prior association with *Bon Appétit*, which was itself mired in controversy that included allegations of racism and exploitation of staff members of color. In response to the controversy, the *New York Times* suspended Roman's column later that month.

A NEWSLETTER

In the aftermath of the controversy in mid-2020, Roman launched a newsletter, simply called *A Newsletter*, through which she would connect with dedicated readers and share recipes and advice. She likewise sought to take a more thoughtful approach to expressing herself and to be more transparent about the international inspirations of some of her recipes. "I'm not trying to pivot to being, like, 'All right, buckle up, this is my new food blog, and I'm going to teach you about racism,'" she explained to Collins. "It's about continuing to be myself, a more sensitive version of myself." The newsletter effectively replaced the *New York Times* as the primary venue for Roman's writing, and in December 2020, she announced that her affiliation with the newspaper had officially ended. "I'm proud of the work we made together but excited for this new chapter," she wrote in an *Instagram* post about her departure, as quoted by Jenny G. Zhang for *Eater* (17 Dec. 2020).

In addition to writing for *A Newsletter*, Roman focused on a number of new projects during 2021 and 2022, including creating content for her YouTube channel. While she had previously posted videos as tie-ins to *Dining In*, in January 2021 she officially launched a new series of videos titled *Home Movies with Alison Roman*. Early the following year it was announced that Roman would star in a cooking show for the subscription-based streaming service CNN+. However, CNN+

shut down in April of that year, only about a month after the service launched and before Roman's show was ever completed or aired. In September 2022, Roman announced that her unaired show, called *(More Than) a Cooking Show with Alison Roman*, would instead begin airing on the CNN cable channel later that fall.

PERSONAL LIFE

After many years in California, Roman moved to New York City in 2009. She lived in several locations throughout the city and eventually settled in the borough of Brooklyn. Roman later purchased a house in upstate New York, where she hopes one day to open a retail establishment.

SUGGESTED READING

Abad-Santos, Alex. "How Alison Roman Became the Reluctant, Pasta-Loving 'Prom Queen of the Pandemic.'" *Vox*, 22 Apr. 2020, www.vox.com/2020/4/22/21222868/alison-roman-shallot-pasta-pandemic-cooking. Accessed 12 Sept. 2022.

Collins, Lauren. "Alison Roman Just Can't Help Herself." *The New Yorker*, 13 Dec. 2021, www.newyorker.com/magazine/2021/12/20/alison-roman-just-cant-help-herself. Accessed 12 Sept. 2022.

Roman, Alison. "Alison Roman." *Gossamer*, vol. 4, Interview. www.gossamer.co/articles/alison-roman. Accessed 12 Sept. 2022.

___. "Alison Roman." Interview by Sophie Missing. *The Gannet*, 10 Aug. 2017, thegannet.co/interviews/alison-roman/. Accessed 12 Sept. 2022.

___. "Alison Roman Gives Instagram Food Trends a Good Name." Interview by Emily Gould. *Elle*, 23 May 2019, www.elle.com/culture/travel-food/a27561224/alison-roman-interview-dining-in/. Accessed 12 Sept. 2022.

___. "Alison Roman on Loving Carly Simon, Killer Playlists and Music as a Secret Ingredient of Her New Cookbook." Interview by Hilary Hughes. *Billboard*, 17 Oct. 2019, www.billboard.com/music/music-news/alison-roman-nothing-fancy-music-interview-8533078/. Accessed 12 Sept. 2022.

Zhang, Jenny G. "After Months-Long Hiatus, Cookbook Author Alison Roman Officially Departs from the New York Times." *Eater*, 17 Dec. 2020, www.eater.com/22180425/

alison-roman-officially-departs-from-the-new-york-times. Accessed 12 Sept. 2022.

SELECTED WORKS

Lemons, 2015; *Dining In*, 2017; *Nothing Fancy: Unfussy Food for Having People Over*, 2019

—*Joy Crelin*

Francesca Rossi

Born: December 7, 1962
Occupation: Computer scientist

For Italian computer scientist and artificial intelligence (AI) researcher Francesca Rossi, characterizing AI technology as ethical or unethical is a misguided approach. "Technology is not ethical or unethical, it's the whole ecosystem around it," she explained to Marcus Baram for *Fortune* (13 Dec. 2021). "The goal is obvious—to take the best out of AI, to make it as beneficial as possible, and to avoid the negative impacts."

As AI ethics global leader at the technology company International Business Machines Corporation (IBM), Rossi has worked to do just that, providing guidance to ensure that the company's AI-based products are developed and used in an ethical manner and are able to gain the trust of the user for which the products are intended.

Rossi's work in her position at IBM, which she assumed in 2015, builds upon her previous decades of AI research at the Università degli Studi di Padova (University of Padua) in Padua, Italy, where she became an expert in areas such as constraint programming, a multidisciplinary approach to solving combinatorial problems. As concerns about the ethical implications of AI became more prevalent in the twenty-first century, Rossi became increasingly interested in the field of AI ethics, and her interest was stoked further during a year spent at Harvard University's Radcliffe Institute for Advanced Study.

As a leading expert in her field, Rossi has expressed her hope to encourage AI-focused companies worldwide to develop and adhere to appropriate ethics guidelines, which she has identified as essential to making the most of such technology while remaining mindful of its effects on human society. "If we focus on our humanity as we create our technologies, our potential is unlimited," she explained in a profile for IBM's website (2020), "because the ultimate goal is not to improve AI, but to improve us as human beings through the advancement of AI."

EARLY LIFE AND EDUCATION

Francesca Rossi was born on December 7, 1962, in the small coastal city of Ancona, Italy. As a child, she developed an interest in science and, after watching the 1969 moon landing, became particularly fascinated by astronomy.

However, by the 1980s, her focus had shifted to computer science. After completing her secondary education, she left her hometown and enrolled at the Università di Pisa (University of Pisa) to pursue studies in that field. "At that time, there were very few universities in Italy that had a computer science curriculum," she told Brent Venable and Ken Ford in an interview for the Institute for Human and Machine Cognition (IHMC) podcast *STEM-Talk* (15 Oct. 2019) about her decision. "Pisa was one of them, and actually the first one to have a computer science curriculum." She earned her Laurea degree, similar to a bachelor's degree in the United States, in information sciences from the University of Pisa in 1986.

Photo courtesy of Rossi, via Wikimedia Commons

Following her time at Pisa, Rossi moved to the United States and took a position as a visiting scholar at the Microelectronics and Computer Technology Corporation (MCC), a research center in Austin, Texas. "This research center had been built in response to the Japanese so-called Fifth Generation computer project, because at that time—1986, 87—the Japanese were really very, very advanced in AI," she explained to Venable and Ford. "They were building very powerful machines . . . they were defining new programming languages to do things with AI. So in response to that, the United States decided to build this research center that was hosting researchers from many different companies." She spent nearly two full years at MCC, working there throughout much of 1987 and 1988. She also took courses at the University of Texas at Austin during that period.

Upon returning to Italy, Rossi pursued doctoral studies at the University of Pisa, completing the thesis "Constraints and Concurrency" under the supervision of advisor Ugo Montanari. She went on to earn her doctorate in computer science in 1993.

CAREER IN ACADEMIA

After completing her doctorate, Rossi remained at Pisa as an assistant professor of computer science. She left the university in 1998 when she took a job as an associate professor of computer science at the University of Padua. Teaching courses across a range of relevant topics during her years in Padua, including AI and constraint programming, she became a tenured full professor at the university in 2001. In addition to working in Padua, she took on visiting positions at various institutions throughout her career, including the Massachusetts Institute of Technology (MIT) in Cambridge, Massachusetts, the Weizmann Institute in Rehovot, Israel, and University College Cork in Cork, Ireland.

In September 2014, Rossi went on sabbatical to take a fellowship at the Radcliffe Institute for Advanced Study at Harvard University in Cambridge, Massachusetts. "I was the only computer scientist and then there were people covering all the other sciences, all the arts, and all the humanities," she told Mia Dand in an interview for *Women in AI Ethics* (15 Feb. 2022) about the fellowship. "So it's really a very multidisciplinary environment." She remained at the Radcliffe Institute until mid-2015.

In addition to teaching, Rossi was active in multiple organizations related to her areas of research, including the Association for Constraint Programming, for which she served as president between 2003 and 2007. She was also a trustee of the International Joint Conferences on Artificial Intelligence Organization (IJCAI) between 2009 and 2016 and served as president of the board of trustees between 2013 and 2015. In addition to leading such bodies, she edited or advised several journals over the course of her career, including the *Journal of AI Research* and *Annals of Mathematics and Artificial Intelligence*.

AI RESEARCH

As an AI researcher, Rossi explored numerous areas of study throughout her academic career, including decision making, constraint programming, and preferences. When considering the practical use of AI, she was primarily interested in "AI systems that augment human intelligence instead of replacing human intelligence," as she explained in an interview with Ariel Conn for the Future of Life Institute (26 Jan. 2017). "I think that in that space of augmenting human intelligence there really is a huge potential for AI in making the personal and professional lives of everybody much better," she added. "I don't think that there are upper limits of the future AI capabilities in that respect."

Rossi published widely on her research throughout her career, placing papers in journals such as the *Artificial Intelligence Journal* and the *Journal of Logic and Computation*. She cowrote the volume *A Short Introduction to Preferences* (2011) and coedited several publications, including *Handbook of Constraint Programming* (2006) as well as special issues of *Constraints* and the *Journal of Heuristics and Computational Intelligence*.

As her career progressed, Rossi became increasingly interested in the area of AI ethics, particularly following her time at Radcliffe. "My interactions at the Radcliffe Institute motivated my thinking about ethical questions in artificial intelligence, my area of research," she told IBM's website. "Collaborating with experts from outside of my core discipline helped me recognize the need to consider both the humanistic and technological perspectives when designing AI systems." Indeed, AI ethics had become a hot-button issue by the 2010s, particularly as law enforcement agencies and surveillance programs began to make greater use of AI-based technology.

That trend became particularly concerning for privacy advocates as well as experts concerned about the phenomenon of algorithmic bias, in which the algorithms used in such technology are shaped by the implicit biases of the companies and individuals designing them. To confront these challenges and others, Rossi shifted much of her focus to determining whether AI technology could be developed and used in an ethical manner, and if so, how.

IBM

In 2015, Rossi left the University of Padua to take a research scientist position at IBM's Thomas J. Watson Research Center in Yorktown Heights, New York. Holding the official title of AI ethics global leader, she was responsible for "ensuring that AI systems complement humanity in beneficial ways," as she explained in a profile for the IBM website. In that role, she founded the AI Ethics Board, for which she served as co-chair, and worked to provide ethical guidance to IBM's many internal departments. She was named an IBM Fellow in 2020.

For Rossi, an important element of her work at IBM was the promotion of trust and transparency, which she has identified as essential to consumer adoption of AI technology. "AI needs to be trusted by those who adopt it, use it, or are affected by it," she told the Association for Computing Machinery newsletter *People of ACM* (15 Jan. 2019). "This means AI that is fair and explainable, and AI producers that are transparent on the design choices to develop AI systems." In addition to working within IBM, she represented that company as a member of the board of directors for the nonprofit Partnership on AI, which was founded by several companies working within the AI field.

PROMOTING AI ETHICS

In addition to advising IBM on the ethical development and use of its AI technology, Rossi remained active within AI research, often through her involvement with conferences and industry bodies. In 2017, she attended the Beneficial AI conference and signed the Asilomar AI Principles, a list of twenty-three

principles governing the goals, development, and use of AI that focused especially on ethical issues, such as protecting personal privacy. In February 2020, Rossi chaired the Association for the Advancement of Artificial Intelligence (AAAI) Conference on Artificial Intelligence, and in June of that year, she was elected as the AAAI's next president. She was set to spend two years as president-elect following her election; she will serve as the two-year term president from 2022–2024.

Alongside her work with organizations such as the AAAI, Rossi sought to promote ethical practices at companies beyond IBM. In April 2022, she published an opinion piece about the importance of AI ethics in *Inc.* magazine. Cowritten with Christina Montgomery, the chief privacy officer at IBM, the article listed several steps that organizations should take to promote AI ethics, urging those businesses to "establish a governance approach to implement AI ethics" and "integrate ethics into the AI lifecycle," among other tips. "The playbook for AI ethics is becoming clearer, more practical, and more tangible," Rossi and Montgomery wrote. "But, it's on all of us—across industry, government, research and academia, and the whole of society—to champion it."

PERSONAL LIFE

Rossi's work has led her to live in multiple places in Italy and the United States. Upon joining IBM in 2015, she moved to the state of New York to live near the Thomas J. Watson Research Center. In addition to researching AI and advocating for its ethical and development and use, she spent a portion of her time painting, a creative activity she particularly enjoyed for its mental component. "I feel that when I paint I really completely concentrate and am focused on that activity," she explained to Venable and Ford.

SUGGESTED READING

Baram, Marcus. "How IBM Is Preparing for a New Era of A.I. Ethics." *Fortune*, 13 Dec. 2021, fortune.com/2021/12/13/ibm-artificial-intelligence-ethics-regulation-francesca-rossi/. Accessed 11 July 2022.

Rossi, Francesca. "Episode 97: Francesca Rossi Talks about AI Ethics and the Development of New AI Systems." Interview by Brent Venable and Ken Ford. *IHMC*, 15 Oct.

2019, www.ihmc.us/stemtalk/episode-97/. Accessed 11 July 2022.

___. "Ethics of AI Surveillance Tech— Conversation with Francesca Rossi." Interview by Mia Dand. *Women in AI Ethics*, 15 Feb. 2022, medium.com/women-in-ai-ethics/ethics-of-ai-surveillance-tech-conversation-with-francesca-rossi-3252f9bdf9e. Accessed 11 July 2022.

___. "Francesca Rossi Interview." Interview by Ariel Conn. *Future of Life Institute*, 26 Jan. 2017, futureoflife.org/2017/01/26/francesca-rossi-interview/?cn-reloaded=1. Accessed 11 July 2022.

___. "People of ACM—Francesca Rossi." *People of ACM*, 15 Jan. 2019, www.acm.org/articles/people-of-acm/2019/francesca-rossi. Accessed 11 July 2022.

___, and Christina Montgomery. "How to Put AI Ethics into Practice at Your Company." *Inc.*, 30 Apr. 2022, www.inc.com/francesca-rossi-christina-montgomery/artificial-intelligence-ethics-strategy-ai-innovation.html. Accessed 11 July 2022.

"2020 IBM Fellows: Meet IBM's Best and Brightest; Francesca Rossi." *IBM*, 2020, newsroom.ibm.com/francesca-rossi. Accessed 11 July 2022.

—Joy Crelin

Rainbow Rowell

Born: February 24, 1973
Occupation: Writer

After years of deadlines and assignment-based writing as part of a local newspaper staff, Rainbow Rowell shifted to exploring creative writing for herself, eventually making that her full-time career and becoming one of the most popular and successful authors of young adult fiction of the twenty-first century. Her rise to literary stardom, propelled by the publication of her first novel—marketed for adults—*Attachments* (2011), was thanks to her masterful storytelling as well as her ability to bring new depths to worn-out genres. Many readers gravitate toward Rowell's books because the type of characters she puts in the spotlight are ones who have traditionally been ignored by mainstream literature. In the worlds she creates, it is these socially marginalized characters who get to be the fearless heroes and romantic leads. Although this approach has proved to be a best-selling one, it has not always been a conscious one. Rowell began writing young adult fiction by plumbing the depths of her own painful past. "All my characters feel like they're on the outside looking in, struggling to fit in and accept love and being loved," she told Shreeja Ravindranathan for *Friday* magazine (24 June 2014). "I definitely felt that when I was younger." Continuing to find fulfillment in the possibilities of fictionally probing teenage life and connecting with enthusiastic younger readers, she made her mark in the fantasy genre with the hit *Simon Snow* series, the third of which, *Any Way the Wind Blows*, was published in 2021.

EARLY LIFE AND EDUCATION

Rainbow Rowell was born in Nebraska on February 24, 1973 and raised largely in the area of Omaha. Her early childhood was spent in a rural part of the state that lacked both electricity and a municipal water system. She later emphasized that it was a tough time in her life; her father, who struggled with alcohol and drug addiction, was often absent and unfamiliar. One of the few good memories she has mentioned of him is when he read *The Lion, The Witch, and The Wardrobe* (1950) to her. In the years that followed, reading remained one of her most cherished activities.

When she was in the second grade Rowell's parents separated, and she moved with her mother to Omaha. Though her mother did everything she could to provide for her family, which included Rowell's four siblings, money continued to be tight. Furthermore, Rowell experienced social anxiety, felt like an outcast at school, and had an unhealthy relationship with her stepfather. She coped by reading prolifically—so much so that she would sneak books to read in her desk during class. "Reading and then fantasising was my source of escape," she told Ravindranathan. "My rich fantasy life helped me stay true to who I was, sane and not get lost in the pain." This love for reading had, meanwhile, helped give rise to a talent for writing that drew praise and encouragement from her teachers, solidifying her belief that her future lay in writing. However, she would also later state that she did not originally aspire to write creatively, as the trying financial and social conditions of her youth had made her hesitant to pursue such a risky livelihood. "It's

Photo by Larry D. Moore via Wikimedia Commons

not like I was miserable all the time, but when you are that poor, it's present in your every moment and interaction," she told Ashley C. Ford for *BuzzFeed* (7 Aug. 2014). "That poverty is a huge part of who you are in every moment."

Rowell finally found a community in the seventh grade when she became part of a group enthusiastic about games like Dungeons and Dragons and reading comic books. At the time, she was a big fan of anything that had to do with *Star Wars* and the X-Men but often had trouble finding others with similar interests. At Omaha's North High School, from which she would go on to graduate in the early 1990s, she nurtured her writing by becoming editor of the school newspaper and launching a column titled Of Cabbages and Kings.

HIGHER EDUCATION AND EARLY CAREER

While studying at the University of Nebraska-Lincoln, Rowell had a focus in news-editorial, advertising, and English. After graduating in the mid-1990s, she landed a job at the *Omaha World-Herald* and earned the opportunity to author an individual column shortly after. The job proved to be an excellent bootcamp for her subsequent career as a novelist. In an interview with Jen Doll for *Mental Floss* (11 Sept. 2014), Rowell described how the experience benefited her as a writer: "A good thing about working at a newspaper is you're on deadline constantly.

You turn in one thing and start working on the next. There's no room for writer's block. Having done that for 10 years, I'd trained my brain."

Eventually, Rowell grew tired of writing her restrictive column according to assignment. Upon reflection, she thought that after several years perhaps it was time to commit to writing something purely for herself for a change. To foster more faith in her ability to take on this new endeavor, around 2006 she shifted her day job from the newspaper to a position copywriting for a nearby advertising agency. She later became a creative director at the agency while carving out time for drafting fiction. The subsequent manuscript would become *Attachments* (2011), a romantic comedy novel about an IT professional at a newspaper who falls in love with a female coworker through her flagged emails. Although it did not become a best seller, *Attachments* earned enough critical acclaim and reader connection to provide the self-assurance she needed to write another novel.

ELEANOR & PARK

Rowell decided to write her follow-up effort, focusing on a first love and titled *Eleanor & Park*, on her own and worry about selling it to a publisher later. Her initial but unintentional foray into the young adult genre, *Eleanor & Park*, published first in the United Kingdom in 2012 and in the United States in 2013, follows two high schoolers living in Omaha from 1986–87. Eleanor, who is bullied at school, comes from an extremely poor family and is often afraid to go home because of her abusive stepfather, Richie. Meanwhile, Park is her classmate who feels insecure about his maternal Korean heritage because he lives in a predominantly White area. After initially bonding over music and comic books, the two fall in love as Park helps Eleanor try to escape her increasingly dangerous homelife.

Rowell noted that she wrote *Eleanor & Park* to capture the intensity of young love between two teenagers—something that she felt most mainstream romantic comedies did not do well. She explained this to Martha Schulman in an interview for *Publishers Weekly* (29 Jan. 2013), stating, "My motivation was to make people actually feel love, to give them a realistic view of it. If they're young and never been in love, for them to know—yes, this [is] how it feels. And if they're older and they have, to feel it as a sense memory."

Reception of *Eleanor & Park* was mostly enthusiastic. Within a few months of its publication, the novel had generated extensive online fan art and readership, making it Rowell's breakout work. It also went on to earn rave reviews and several awards, including being named by the American Library Association (ALA) as a Michael L. Printz Honor Book for 2014. However, some critics felt that Rowell's depiction of Park and other aspects of the book perpetuate stereotypes about Asian Americans and biracial identities. In 2013, another controversy arose when the Anoka-Hennepin School District in Minnesota tried to ban *Eleanor & Park* from libraries because of its instances of coarse language and sexuality. Ultimately, the book was kept on the shelves. Although Rowell defended her work, challenges continued in ensuing years, with the book making the ALA's list of the top ten challenged books of 2016.

FANGIRL

Rowell continued writing feverishly, mostly using a local Starbucks as an office. She cemented her reputation as a noted young adult novelist with the publication of *Fangirl* (2013). The book tells the story of Cath, a freshman at the University of Nebraska-Lincoln (UNL) who struggles to enjoy her college experience because of her deep social anxiety. While her twin sister and fellow UNL student Wren are always going out with friends, Cath stays in to write fan fiction of the *Simon Snow* book series about a British boy with magical powers. Rowell includes excerpts of Cath's fan fiction throughout the novel.

Fangirl was well received by readers, many of whom enjoyed its realistic portrayal of the world of online fandom. Several critics praised the book, including for the way that it depicts common but seldom-discussed adolescent issues. A reviewer for the *Guardian* (26 July 2014) declared that "*Fangirl* is a must–read for any teenage girl going through any kind of change, as it explores many themes, from the fear of making new friends, to the change of relationships with people, as you move on in life." By that point, Rowell had given up any other regular work to devote herself full-time to writing. In 2014, she released her fourth book, the adult novel *Landline*. That same year the studio DreamWorks obtained film rights for *Eleanor & Park*; while DreamWorks did not go through with adapting the film, Rowell embraced a new medium by working on a screenplay draft. (The rights were later picked up in 2020 by a different production company.)

THE *SIMON SNOW* SERIES AND WORK OUTSIDE OF NOVELS

Rowell surprised her readers in 2015 when she published *Carry On*, a full-on fantasy book that follows the Simon Snow character in the world that Cath had been obsessed with in *Fangirl*. In interviews, Rowell explained that she grew up reading a lot of fantasy but had never tried to write a whole work in the genre before. When she realized that one of her favorite parts of *Fangirl* was creating Cath's fan fiction, she thought that it might be worth exploring the Snow character further. Snow has been noted as an obvious homage to Harry Potter in that he is a teenage orphan with magical powers who attends a boarding school and is known as "the Chosen One." Ultimately, however, Rowell subverts the cliché "Chosen One" story line by making Simon somewhat inept at executing his magic powers, and takes a different track by exploring sexual orientation. In *Carry On*, Snow and other characters must defeat an evil force that is threatening to kill magic forever. Due to the first installment's popularity, Rowell further explored what happens to "the Chosen One" in the sequels *Wayward Son* (2019) and *Any Way the Wind Blows* (2021).

All three *Simon Snow* books were largely well received and sold well. Readers and critics alike were delighted by the way Rowell breathed new life into many tired young adult fantasy genre tropes and put an LGBTQ relationship at their center. For Rowell, a former outsider, telling the stories of characters from marginalized communities was always extremely important. Still, she came to realize that while she tried to contribute to the diversification of the literary landscape through realistic writing, her stories only represent a fraction of the human experience. She told Joanna Robinson for *Vanity Fair* (5 July 2021), "The conversation and the reality of queer characters in fiction is radically different now from when I started *Carry On*. It isn't that there weren't [other queer] books then, but there's better representation everywhere. . . . I don't think that any character I write can bear the weight of the world."

A longtime fan of Marvel Comics, in the mid-2010s Rowell also successfully pitched a return of her favorite *Runaways* comic series. The first volume of a new series featuring her writing was released in 2017, and by the end of 2021 five additional volumes had been published. Meanwhile, she wrote and published the largely well-received graphic novel *Pumpkinheads* in 2019, demonstrating her willingness to try her hand at many different writing formats.

PERSONAL LIFE

After college, Rowell began dating her friend Kai, whom she had originally met as a junior high schooler. They went on to marry and have two sons together. Around 2015 Rowell was forced to take a break from writing novels for health reasons; doctors discovered that she had a parathyroid disorder that was causing a dangerous calcium imbalance. After they removed a contributing tumor, she made a full recovery.

SUGGESTED READING

Ford, Ashley C. "How Rainbow Rowell Turned a Bomb into a Best-Selling Novel." *BuzzFeed*, 7 Aug. 2014, www.buzzfeed.com/ashleyford/how-rainbow-rowell-turned-a-bomb-into-a-best-selling-novel. Accessed 26 Dec. 2021.

Ravindranathan, Shreeja. "Rainbow Rowell: I'm a Better Reader Than a Writer." *Friday*, 24 June 2014, fridaymagazine.ae/life-culture/people-profiles/rainbow-rowell-i-m-a-better-reader-than-a-writer-1.1351567. Accessed 26 Dec. 2021.

Rowell, Rainbow. "How Rainbow Rowell Went from Newspaper Reporter to Superstar Novelist." Interview by Jen Doll. *Mental Floss*, 11 Sept. 2014, www.mentalfloss.com/article/58469/how-rainbow-rowell-went-newspaper-reporter-superstar-novelist. Accessed 26 Dec. 2021.

—. "Q&A with Rainbow Rowell." Interview by Martha Schulman. *Publishers Weekly*, 29 Jan. 2013, www.publishersweekly.com/pw/by-topic/authors/interviews/article/55711-q-a-with-rainbow-rowell.html. Accessed 26 Dec. 2021.

—. "Rainbow Rowell on Tapping into Her Own Demons for *Any Way the Wind Blows*." Interview by Joanna Robinson. *Vanity Fair*, 5 July 2021, www.vanityfair.com/style/2021/07/any-way-the-wind-blows-rainbow-rowell-simon-snow-baz-ending-trilogy-future-plans. Accessed 26 Dec. 2021.

ShazzSharingan. "*Fangirl* by Rainbow Rowell—Review." Review of *Fangirl* by Rainbow Rowell. *The Guardian*, 26 July 2014, www.theguardian.com/childrens-books-site/2014/jul/26/review-rainbow-rowell-fangirl. Accessed 26 Dec. 2021.

SELECTED WORKS

Eleanor & Park, 2012; *Fangirl*, 2013; *Carry On*, 2015; *Wayward Son*, 2019; *Any Way the Wind Blows*, 2021

—*Emily E. Turner*

Shahrbanoo Sadat

Born: 1990
Occupation: Filmmaker

Afghan filmmaker Shahrbanoo Sadat earned international attention with her debut feature-length work, *Wolf and Sheep* (2016), which won top honors in the Directors' Fortnight segment at the prestigious Cannes Film Festival. She received further acclaim for her second feature, *The Orphanage* (2019), which also premiered at Cannes, marking her as a notable up-and-coming figure in world cinema. Sadat's first two feature films are fictional but shot in the cinema verité style, with largely unscripted dialogue and nonprofessional actors. With these artistic choices, she sought to present Afghan life in all of its vibrant variability.

Born to Afghan refugees in Iran, Sadat spent much of her childhood in a remote mountain village in Afghanistan—an isolated setting similar to the one in *Wolf and Sheep*. She then attended Kabul University, where, through a twist of fate, she was introduced to the world of filmmaking. After studying documentary filmmaking and creating several shorts, she set out to make her own features that tell vastly different stories from typical Hollywood films about Afghanistan, despite the challenges in taking such an independent path. "One of the biggest problems we have in financing a film like *The Orphanage*, which I consider an important story to tell, is the fact that there's no one who shares my point of view," Sadat told Karin Schiefer for *Eurimages* (June 2019) of her film about a young boy living in a Soviet orphanage in Kabul in the 1980s. "It's a story about Afghanistan that doesn't refer to the violation of women's rights, extremists, war or terrorism—which means my stories disappoint people's expectations about a film from Afghanistan."

EARLY LIFE AND EDUCATION

Sadat was born to an Afghan refugee family in Tehran, Iran, in 1990. Her parents had escaped Afghanistan after the Soviet invasion in 1979. Sadat excelled in school, and although she was at times conflicted about her cultural identity, she embraced her experience. "We lived in a special situation, and you get your character from the society you live in," she told Judith Kelly for *Pax Christi USA*, the website for the national Catholic peace movement (12 Sept. 2021). But after Iran's policies toward Afghan refugees became more restrictive and her education was cut off, her family returned to Afghanistan when she was eleven years old. They settled in the remote mountain village near the city of Bamiyan where her parents had previously lived. There was no school for Sadat to attend, so she spent two years teaching herself English from books in her house. "I was completely disconnected from the rest of the world," she told Schiefer.

As a teenager, Sadat won permission to attend a school in another village, and her drive to learn was strong enough that she walked for hours each day to attend. Once again excelling at her studies, she advanced quickly. After high school, she moved to the Afghan capital of Kabul to attend Kabul University. Arriving in the city was a pleasing cultural shock, she recalled to Schiefer: "It was the first moment of my life when I had time to think about other things," she said. Sadat had intended to study physics but took the wrong exam and was not able to join the program. Then, by chance, she was recruited to play a role on a local television series, an experience that helped introduce her to the world of TV and film. When she heard about a three-month course on documentary filmmaking run by the globally minded French filmmaking association Ateliers Varan, she jumped at the opportunity.

During the Ateliers Varan workshop, Sadat was particularly inspired after viewing *Les glaneurs et la glaneuse* (2000), by the French filmmaker AgnèsVarda. "The film made a deep impression on me," she told Schiefer. "I started to dream about making films." Sadat eventually

Photo by Vera de Kok via Wikimedia Commons

left Kabul University and went on to study in Europe. She began to make short films of her own with essentially no budget, and in 2010 was among several young international filmmakers chosen for a residency with the Cinéfondation at Cannes Film Festival. Thanks in part to the connections she made in that program, she was able to promote her first official film, the fiction short *Vice Versa One*, about a little girl collecting votes in Afghanistan, which was then chosen for Directors' Fortnight at Cannes in 2011.

WOLF AND SHEEP

Sadat took another step in her career when she met Katja Adomeit, a Danish producer, at the Copenhagen International Documentary Film Festival in 2012. Through a program at the festival encouraging international collaboration, the two codirected the film *Not at Home* (2013). They then began working together to produce Sadat's first feature-length work, titled *Wolf and Sheep*. Sadat developed a script about a group of children living in a remote village like the one where she grew up, basing the story loosely on parts of an unpublished memoir by her friend Anwar Hashimi. Financing the project proved difficult, which led Sadat to launch her own production company, Wolf Films, in 2013.

Sadat had hoped to shoot the film in Afghanistan, but political turmoil and safety issues made that impossible. Instead, she chose a location in neighboring Tajikistan, meticulously recreating an Afghan village set from scratch. But there were other complications that threatened the entire production. It took Sadat months to secure visas for her Afghan cast. Equipment arrived late and the entire crew became sick from drinking the water in the remote valley. Much of the process, Sadat conceded to Laura Berger for *Women and Hollywood* (6 Oct. 2016), "was a true hell." Still, she said, "What I learned from *Wolf and Sheep* is that I should never give up on the things I've always wished to do. There is always a way—always—and you just need to concentrate and find it."

Wolf and Sheep is a fictional film shot in the cinema verité style using a nonprofessional cast. In it, village children bring goats and sheep into the mountains to graze. Sediqa (Sediqa Rasuli), an eleven-year-old girl with poor eyesight, is ostracized from the group because they believe her glasses suggest that she is cursed. Sediqa finds a friend in a young boy named Quodrat (Quodratollah Qadiri), a fellow outsider. The story offers a unique view of life in the village and incorporates elements of magical realism inspired by village fables and lore. Sadat did not rely on her young cast memorizing a script. Instead, she explained each scene to them just before shooting. "They put so much of themselves into it," Sadat told Wendy Mitchell for *Screen Daily* (15 May 2016). "They take it as a game. The rules are that they shouldn't talk to me, they shouldn't say anything they don't say in real life and they shouldn't look at the camera."

Wolf and Sheep premiered in 2016 at Cannes' Directors' Fortnight, where it won the top award. It went on to receive much acclaim from critics. In a review for *Screen Daily* (22 May 2016), Allan Hunter offered a typical assessment: "*Wolf and Sheep* is simple but sincere, respectful and heartfelt and marks the arrival of a promising new talent."

THE ORPHANAGE

In 2017 Sadat won a three-month residency through the Nipkow Programm in Berlin, Germany, where she completed the script for her second feature film, *The Orphanage*. Again based on Hashimi's memoir, the film is a sequel to *Wolf and Sheep* in that it features the character Quodrat, again played by Qadiri.

The film is set in Kabul during the Soviet occupation in the late 1980s. Its plot focuses on Quodrat's life in a Soviet orphanage, where he is sent after being arrested for selling tickets to Bollywood movies on the underground market. Hashimi himself appears in the film as the orphanage supervisor, the only major adult role.

Sadat was again forced to shoot in Tajikistan, and she cut the size of her cast because of ongoing visa and security issues. She again worked with nonprofessional actors, in this case mainly boys she had found visiting schools in Kabul. "I invest a lot of time in casting the right person," she told Schiefer. "I look for someone who looks and talks exactly as I imagine the character." Instead of auditioning her actors, Sadat preferred to interview them and record their conversations. "I can see very quickly if they are able to open their heart," she said.

The Orphanage premiered at Directors' Fortnight at Cannes in 2019. Like *Wolf and Sheep*, it earned a strong critical response. "*The Orphanage* is a terrific child's-eye movie, bustling with freshness and old-fashioned storytelling gusto," Peter Bradshaw wrote in an enthusiastic review for *The Guardian* (13 May 2020), adding that "Sadat is a filmmaker to watch."

THWARTED PLANS

With the success of her first two films, Sadat was increasingly seen as an important new voice in world cinema. She used her elevated platform to often speak critically about typical depictions of her home country. "I'm so sick of the way the media portrays Afghanistan—it's all about scary and bad things happening there. At the same time, I'm so sick of very optimistic points of view that show good and bright sides of Afghanistan that only an idiot can believe," she told Berger. She noted how the focus on universal stories in her work was part of a direct effort to bring more nuance to Afghan film.

After *The Orphanage*, Sadat began work on her third feature, a romantic comedy about a woman who works at a television station. She continued her socially conscious filmmaking approach, especially given the increasingly unstable political situation in Afghanistan at the time. "It's not a cheap comedy, in fact it's a very political film," Sadat said of the project at the San Sebastian Film Festival, as quoted by Anna Marie de la Fuente for *Variety* (21 Sept.

2021). "It shows Afghanistan in a rosy pink light because we need hope, we need to laugh, we need color."

However, geopolitics interrupted Sadat's plans. In August 2021 the US military, which had invaded and occupied Afghanistan since 2001, began a final withdrawal from the country. Within weeks the Afghan government collapsed, and the Taliban, the militant Islamist group that had ruled Afghanistan from 1996 to 2001, returned to power. Hundreds of thousands of Afghans sought to flee the country to escape the repressive regime, which was known for its oppression of artistic and cultural figures and especially women. Sadat noted that, like many others, she was shocked at how quickly things progressed. "Living in Afghanistan, your ears get used to hearing about how the Taliban are on the way, the Taliban are in this part of the country and that part of the country," she told Alex Ritman for the *Hollywood Reporter* (17 Aug. 2021). "So you don't really differentiate the danger anymore, because you hear these sentences all the time."

Sadat in fact declined an initial opportunity to leave Afghanistan, as she did not want to abandon her family. She then endured a tense waiting period, hoping to get a flight out even as the Taliban took full control of Kabul all around her. "I feel like I'm observing, I'm watching injustice and something really horrible, and I just need to save it in my body, remember it and put it in films later, to share it with the world," she told Ritman. "If I survive this, I will make films about what happened." With support from Adomeit and the French government, Sadat and several members of her family finally escaped Afghanistan weeks later, initially relocating to Paris.

SUGGESTED READING

Bradshaw, Peter. "*The Orphanage* Review—Terrific Tale of an Afghan Teen in Trouble." Review of *The Orphanage*, directed by Shahrbanoo Sadat. *The Guardian*, 13 May 2020, www.theguardian.com/film/2020/may/13/the-orphanage-review-shahrbanoo-sadat. Accessed 12 Nov. 2021.

De la Fuente, Anna Marie. "Afghan Filmmaker Shahrbanoo Sadat on her Hopes for a New Wave of Afghan Cinema." *Variety*, 21 Sept. 2021, variety.com/2021/film/festivals/shahrbanoo-sadat-afghan-cinema-new-wave-1235070319/. Accessed 13 Nov. 2021.

Kelly, Judith. "Shahrbanoo Sadat in Kabul: Forever Young and Ardent." *Pax Christi USA*, 12 Sept. 2021, paxchristiusa.org/2021/09/12/shahrbanoo-sadat-in-kabul-forever-young-and-ardent/. Accessed 12 Nov. 2021.

Mitchell, Wendy. "Cannes: Shahrbanoo Sadat, Katya Adomeit Talk 'Wolf and Sheep.'" *Screen Daily*, 15 May 2016, www.screendaily.com/cannes/cannes-shahrbanoo-sadat-katja-adomeit-talk-wolf-and-sheep-/5103958.article. Accessed 12 Nov. 2021.

Ritman, Alex. "Cannes-Winning Afghan Director Trying to Escape Kabul: 'If I Survive This, I Will Make Films about What Happened.'" *The Hollywood Reporter*, 17 Aug. 2021, www.hollywoodreporter.com/movies/movie-news/afghan-director-shahrbanoo-sadat-trying-to-escape-afghanistan-1234998538/. Accessed 13 Nov. 2021.

Sadat, Shahrbanoo. "Interview with Shahrbanoo Sadat." Interview by Karin Schiefer. *Eurimages*, Council of Europe, June 2019, rm.coe.int/interview-with-shahrbanoo-sadat/1680971c7f. Accessed 12 Nov. 2021.

—. "LFF 2016 Women Directors: Meet Shahrbanoo Sadat—'*Wolf and Sheep*.'" Interview by Laura Berger. *Women and Hollywood*, 6 Oct. 2016, womenandhollywood.com/lff-2016-women-directors-meet-shahrbanoo-sadat-wolf-and-sheep-f46db9e8970c/#.dxiwfhc7g. Accessed 12 Nov. 2021.

SELECTED WORKS

Not at Home, 2013 (with Katja Adomeit); *Wolf and Sheep*, 2016; *The Orphanage*, 2019

—Molly Hagan

Hiroyuki Sanada

Born: October 12, 1960
Occupation: Actor

Prolific actor Hiroyuki Sanada began making films in 1965, when he was just five years old. For many years he was highly regarded in his native Japan, but little known outside of it. However, roles in the hit 1998 Japanese horror film *Ring* (released in the United States as *Ringu*), the acclaimed Japanese historical drama *The Twilight Samurai* (2002), and the Hollywood blockbuster *The Last Samurai* (2003) began to bring him recognition internationally as well. Maintaining his status as one of the best-known actors in Japan, he further widened his exposure to American audiences in such big-budget films as *Rush Hour 3* (2007), *The Wolverine* (2013), *47 Ronin* (2013), *Minions* (2015), *Life* (2017), *Avengers: Endgame* (2019), *Mortal Kombat* (2021), and *Army of the Dead* (2021).

In interviews Sanada has described himself as having diverse interests as an actor, while also being especially dedicated to ensuring that Japanese culture and traditions are accurately depicted on film. Moreover, he became a student of the technical aspects of filmmaking, always eager to see how the industry evolves. In an interview with Steve Weintraub for *Collider* (4 Nov. 2013), he indicated how the long span of his career let him witness all kinds of changes: "When I started filming when I was five years old, it was a long time ago. It was a black and white film. And then it changed to colour film, and I was surprised and culture shocked when I was six or seven years old. And then HD, then 3D now. So what's going? What's coming next? It's so exciting."

EARLY LIFE AND CAREER

Hiroyuki Sanada was born in Shinagawa City, Tokyo, Japan, on October 12, 1960. Little has been published in English about his home life or education, but he began his acting career as a child. At age five he made his film debut in a Japanese crime drama, *Rokyoku komori-uta* (*Game of Chance*, 1965), in which he starred alongside legendary actor and martial artist Sonny Chiba. He had a few other credits through the 1960s, but then temporarily stepped away from acting at age ten to avoid burnout. "My manager and my parents said to me that if I want to be an actor in the future that I should spend more time as a normal kid," he told Saleah Blancaflor for *NBC News* (22 Mar. 2017). "It gave me a good chance to watch movies as the audience. Before that, my experience watching movies was always in studio so I'd never actually been in a theater before."

During his acting hiatus Sanada sought to broaden his talents, practicing skills like dancing, singing, and horseback riding. When he was eleven years old his father died, and

Photo by Keith McDuffee via Wikimedia Commons

he soon turned to Chiba as a mentor. At age twelve Sanada joined Japan Action Club, an organization led by Chiba, in which he honed his martial arts abilities. In the late 1970s he began acting again, first taking minor television roles.

FILM CAREER IN JAPAN

Sanada's first breakthrough as an actor came in 1978, when he appeared as the clan fighter Nayate in the film *Yagyû ichizoku no inbô* (*Yagyu Clan Conspiracy*). Over the next two decades he built a reputation as a prominent action star in the Japanese film industry. In many roles he made extensive use of his martial arts training, often doing his own stunts. Through the 1980s and 1990s he typically appeared in two or three films a year, and he also made television appearances. Although his work was often popular domestically, , it received little international attention.

In the late 1990s Sanada began to break out beyond typecasting in action flicks. In 1998, he starred in the horror film *Ring* (1998; also known as *Ringu*), playing a university professor capable of detecting supernatural auras who investigates a cursed videotape that brings death to anyone who watches it. He also appeared in a sequel released at the same time, *Spiral* (also known as *Rasen*), as well as a better-received alternate sequel,

Ring 2, released in 1999. The first film was a major critical and commercial success, earning worldwide attention and eventually spawning American remakes.

Sanada also branched into theater, joining a Japanese production of *Hamlet* held in London in 1998. This led to an offer to play the Fool in *King Lear* for the Royal Shakespeare Company. "I had never done anything in English before so I was scared," Sanada told Blancaflor. "I had to think about it for a while. But the producers said to me 'You are an actor first before you are Japanese or Asian.'" He appeared in *King Lear* to great acclaim from 1999 to 2000 and was named an honorary Member of the British Empire for his work in 2002.

Another notable success for Sanada during this period was the Japanese drama film *The Twilight Samurai* (2002). In it, he portrayed Seibei Iguchi, a low-ranked samurai living during the tail end of the feudal Japanese period who struggles to provide for his family and fulfill his clan duties. The film garnered much critical praise internationally, with many critics highlighting Sanada's performance. He was named best actor at the Japan Academy Film Prize awards ceremony, often called the Japanese Academy Awards, while the film overall won a record twelve awards at the event. *Twilight Samurai* also earned an Academy Award nomination for best foreign language film, among other honors.

TAKING ON HOLLYWOOD

Encouraged by his success on the English stage, Sanada resolved to pursue one of his longtime dreams: breaking into the American film industry. He quickly landed a supporting role in *The Last Samurai* (2003), a big-budget production featuring Tom Cruise as Captain Nathan Algren, a US Army officer, sent to help modernize the Japanese military as they face a samurai rebellion. Sanada's character is a master swordsman who teaches Cruise's character how to swordfight. The film was critically and commercially successful, which helped convince Sanada to move to the United States and become more actively involved in Hollywood. He was especially interested in increasing Asian representation in American films, as he told Blancaflor: "There is no wall between East and West or if there is a wall, I should break the wall and make a bridge to the future in our generation."

Sanada went on to become a Hollywood staple over the next decade or so, often as a supporting character in action-oriented films. In 2007 he appeared in the high-profile, if poorly reviewed, action-comedy sequel *Rush Hour 3* alongside Jackie Chan and Chris Tucker, and in 2008 he had a role in *Speed Racer*, an adaptation of the classic anime series. Sanada also occasionally took parts in quieter dramas, such as the literary adaptation *The City of Your Final Destination* (2009), which starred Anthony Hopkins, Laura Linney, and Charlotte Gainsbourg. He made television appearances as well, notably including on the popular series *Lost* in 2010.

In 2013, Sanada had a prominent role in *The Wolverine*, a spin-off of the X-Men superhero franchise, opposite star Hugh Jackman. Another high-profile credit came that same year in *47 Ronin*, starring American actor Keanu Reeves. The film is loosely based on a real-life historical event that occurred in eighteenth-century Japan, in which forty-seven rōnin—a name for samurai without a leader—avenged their master's death. "This is almost the most famous story—Samurai story—in Japan," Sanada explained to Weintraub. "But we have a lot of original stuff in the script so we changed a lot, taking it in a fantasy way. It's a very special movie for me. . . . It has a very special mixture between Japanese traditional culture and Western culture for the costume, set, story. Everything." Although *47 Ronin* ultimately received mixed to negative reviews and was a box-office bomb, it furthered Sanada's reputation as a dependable supporting actor with vivid action skills.

VERSATILE SIDEMAN

Sanada continued to take on a wide variety of roles through the 2010s and into the 2020s. His range was demonstrated by two different film credits in 2015, for example. In the drama *Mr. Holmes*, his character helps an aged Sherlock Holmes (Ian McKellen) with a final case before the great detective's memory fails him. In the hugely successful animated film *Minions*, he lent his voice talents to the character of Dumo, a sumo fighter villain.

In 2017, Sanada was featured in the sci-fi thriller *Life*, about a crew aboard the International Space Station struggling to contain a malevolent extraterrestrial. In 2018, he debuted in another sci-fi project, the television series *Westworld*. The following year he returned to the world of Marvel Comics, after his role in *The Wolverine*, with a brief appearance in the mega-blockbuster *Avengers: Endgame* (2019) as a Yakuza crime lord. In 2020, Sanada switched directions to costar in *Minamata*, a film based on real-life American photojournalist Eugene Smith (played by Johnny Depp), who documented how extreme mercury poisoning was affecting the people of Minamata, Kumamoto, Japan.

Sanada was again involved in a high-profile action blockbuster in 2021, when he took on the role of Hazo Hasashi, a.k.a. Scorpion, in a reboot of the *Mortal Kombat* film series, based on the tremendously popular video game franchise of the same name. In the film Sanada shows off his continuing skills with action choreography—including his character's trademark attack of harpooning opponents and pulling them closer while calling out "Come here!" "When I performed that signature move with the words in the rehearsal on set for the first time, I had a great reaction from the cast and crew," Sanada recalled in an interview with Nick Romano for *Entertainment Weekly* (18 Feb. 2021). "They said, 'Yeah! I've waited for this moment.' Then I realized how popular this move is." Though the much-anticipated film earned mixed reviews, it was a financial success.

Sanada was next featured in *Army of the Dead* (2021), a zombie heist film directed by Zack Snyder. In late 2021 it was announced that he would again costar with Keanu Reeves, this time in *John Wick 4*, a sequel in the long-running action series about a former hitman who comes out of retirement. Sanada was also cast in a key role in *Shogun*, a limited television series based on the best-selling novel of the same name by James Clavell.

PERSONAL LIFE

Sanada was married from 1990 to 1997 to Satomi Tezuka. The couple had two sons together before divorcing.

In interviews, Sanada often spoke of his efforts to improve Asian representation in Hollywood, including acknowledgement of the diversity among Asians. "If somebody has an Asian face they're offered parts for every

nationality," he told Ned Ehrbar for *CBS News* (24 Mar. 2017). "Every Asian country has its own, different culture. So sometimes it can be insulting to other cultures or countries. I want to make sure that people understand that."

SUGGESTED READING

Blancaflor, Saleah. "After Half a Century, Actor Hiroyuki Sanada Is Still Renewing His Craft." *NBC News*, 22 Mar. 2017, www.nbcnews.com/news/asian-america/after-half-century-actor-hiroyuki-sanada-still-renewing-his-craft-n736111. Accessed 7 Jan. 2021.

"Hiroyuki Sanada." *IMDb*, www.imdb.com/name/nm0760796/. Accessed 23 Dec. 2021.

Ormond, Steph. "Actor Spotlight: Hiroyuki Sanada." *Palatinate*, 4 Aug. 2021, www.palatinate.org.uk/actor-spotlight-hiroyuki-sanada/. Accessed 23 Dec. 2021.

Sanada, Hiroyuki. "'The Birth of Scorpion': Mortal Kombat Star Goes behind Iconic Character's Vengeful Origins." Interview by Nick Romano. *Entertainment Weekly*, 18 Feb. 2021, ew.com/movies/mortal-kombat-scorpion-hiroyuki-sanada-interview/. Accessed 23 Dec. 2021.

—. "Hiroyuki Sanada Talks Telling a Classic Japanese Samurai Story, Working with Keanu Reeves, the Fantasy Element, and More on the Set of 47 RONIN." Interview by Steve Weintraub. *Collider*, 4 Nov. 2013, collider.com/hiroyuki-sanada-47-ronin-interview/. Accessed 30 Dec. 2021.

—. "'Life' Star Hiroyuki Sanada Doesn't Like Being Offered Chinese Roles." Interview by Ned Ehrbar. *CBS News*, 24 Mar. 2017, www.cbsnews.com/news/life-hiroyuki-sanada-interview-asians-hollywood/. Accessed 7 Jan. 2021.

SELECTED WORKS

Yagyû ichizoku no inbô (*Yagyu Clan Conspiracy*), 1978; *Ring* (*Ringu*), 1998; *The Twilight Samurai*, 2002; *The Last Samurai*, 2003; *Rush Hour 3*, 2007; *The Wolverine*, 2013; *47 Ronin*, 2013; *Life*, 2017; *Westworld*, (2018–20); *Mortal Kombat*, 2021

—*Christopher Mari*

Claudia Sheinbaum

Born: June 24, 1962
Occupation: Politician

Claudia Sheinbaum, whose full name is Claudia Sheinbaum Pardo, was elected mayor of Mexico City in 2018, becoming the first woman and the first Jewish person to be elected to that position. With over nine million residents, the capital of Mexico City was the world's fifth-largest city at the time. The role of mayor is considered to be a stepping-stone for Mexico's presidency, and indeed, Mexican president Andrés Manuel López Obrador (popularly known as AMLO) hinted that he might tap Sheinbaum as his successor in 2024. But political conflict around the coronavirus disease 2019 (COVID-19) pandemic and controversial new energy policies also demonstrated a growing ideological gulf between Sheinbaum, a climate scientist, and López Obrador.

Trained as an engineer, Sheinbaum served with scientists from around the world on the United Nations' Intergovernmental Panel on Climate Change (IPCC), which won the Nobel Peace Prize in 2007. When López Obrador was elected mayor of Mexico City in 2000, he appointed Sheinbaum minister of the environment. She subsequently was elected mayor of Tlalpan, Mexico's City's largest district, in 2015. A devastating earthquake in 2017 colored her tenure and emphasized the urgent need to address the city's structural problems and history of corruption. Sheinbaum was celebrated as a problem solver and pragmatist willing to tackle these myriad challenges, but her staunch support for the populist López Obrador, as well as her unconventional background, did raise concerns from some observers. Sheinbaum, however, dismissed the idea that she might not be suited to take on some of the toughest tasks. As she told supporters during her mayoral campaign, as reported by Carrie Kahn for *NPR* (25 July 2018): "Don't think because you see this skinny scientist up here that we won't be strong enough to take on the subject of crime fighting."

EARLY LIFE AND EDUCATION

Claudia Sheinbaum Pardo was born in Mexico City on June 24, 1962. Her father, Carlos Sheinbaum, was a chemical engineer whose

Photo by EneasMx,
via Wikimedia Commons

family emigrated from Lithuania in the 1920s. Her mother, Annie Pardo, an award-winning chemist and professor at the Universidad Nacional Autónoma de México (UNAM) in Mexico City, came from a family that emigrated from Bulgaria in 1942, narrowly escaping the Holocaust. Both of Sheinbaum's parents participated in the leftist movements of the 1960s, which influenced Sheinbaum's own politics. Though her parents were both Jewish, she was raised in a secular household.

Sheinbaum studied physics at UNAM in the 1980s and went on to earn her master's and doctorate degrees in energy engineering. This background, she told Lizzie Wade for *Science Magazine* (2 July 2018), helped prepare her for a career in politics. "Training in physics makes you always look for the root causes. Why is something happening? That's fundamental for politics," she said. "And then engineering is much more focused on the 'how.' How can I solve it?"

As a doctoral student, Sheinbaum received a grant to work at the Lawrence Berkeley National Laboratory in Berkeley, California, where she researched the differences in energy use between Mexico and other industrialized countries. Her doctoral thesis examined the effect of energy policies on marginalized communities. She joined UNAM's faculty as a professor of engineering in 1995.

EARLY POLITICAL CAREER

As her engineering career progressed, Sheinbaum concurrently pursued political activism. She participated in an influential student strike over tuition increases at UNAM in 1986 and 1987. Veterans of this movement would go on to found the Party of Democratic Revolution (PRD) in 1989, and the PRD would become one of Mexico's three major political parties. Sheinbaum met Andrés Manuel López Obrador, then a rising star in the party, in the 1990s, when he came to her house to meet with her husband and other activists.

In 2000, López Obrador was elected mayor of Mexico City, ending the seventy-year reign of the Industrial Revolutionary Party (PRI), which was widely criticized as corrupt. He appointed Sheinbaum as his environment minister. In this role she led the construction of the Metrobus, Mexico's first Rapid Transit Bus line, and developed the city's first climate change program. Meanwhile, Sheinbaum's husband, Carlos Ímaz Gispert, became an influential political figure in Mexico City during this period. In 2004, however, he was caught on camera accepting what appeared to be a bribe. He resigned from politics, and though he was sentenced to serve a short prison sentence, he was later exonerated. Sheinbaum offered to resign her post as well but was refused.

MAYOR OF TLALPAN

López Obrador was an enormously popular mayor, and when he ran for president in 2006, Sheinbaum served as his spokesperson. When he lost by a small margin, he refused to accept the results of the election and led several weeks of protests. Still, Sheinbaum remained a loyal acolyte. While she returned to her research work, including joining the UN Intergovernmental Panel on Climate Change (IPCC) that won the 2007 Nobel Peace Prize, she also continued working with López Obrador. In 2008, when President Felipe Calderón proposed privatizing the oil industry, López Obrador launched the Movement to Defend Mexico's Oil. As part of this movement, Sheinbaum led female brigades dressed as Las Adelitas, the women soldiers of the Mexican Revolution. The Adelitas, as they also called themselves, staged several major street protests, once throwing themselves in front of politicians' cars to prevent them from a secret vote to push the privatization proposal through congress.

López Obrador lost another presidential bid in 2012. He again refused to accept the results of the election, though he eschewed protests like the ones he had led in 2006. Instead, he left the PRD to found his own progressive, left-wing party called the National Regeneration Movement (MORENA) in 2014, and Sheinbaum followed. In 2015, she ran on the MORENA ticket and was elected to lead Tlalpan, the largest of Mexico City's sixteen boroughs.

Mexico City had long suffered from a water crisis, exacerbated by climate change. Effects were felt most acutely in Tlalpan, a fact of which Sheinbaum was keenly aware upon taking the job. But Sheinbaum's term was unexpectedly defined by the 7.1-magnitude earthquake that struck Mexico City on September 19, 2017. The devastating quake killed hundreds and rendered thousands more homeless. In Tlalpan, the hardest hit district in the city, a school collapsed killing more than twenty children and adults. The building's shoddy construction laid bare a long history of bribery and corruption, and many placed culpability on Sheinbaum.

MAYOR OF MEXICO CITY

In 2018 Sheinbaum ran for mayor of Mexico City, while López Obrador ran, once again, for president. Their MORENA party adopted the campaign slogan that translated as "We are not them," referring to Mexico's three major political parties. Yet there was ongoing widespread anger with politicians, including Sheinbaum, in the aftermath of the earthquake. Frustration with Sheinbaum centered on the collapse of the school and a Tlalpan public housing complex. Referring to the latter, one constituent said to Kahn: "She couldn't even take care of this one simple building, how is she going to deal with the district or an entire city?"

Sheinbaum made the city's water crisis and public transportation problems the central issues of her campaign. Mexico City is built on what used to be a lake and pumps most of its water from the aquifer that lies beneath it. "We've overexploited the aquifer, and as a result, the city is sinking," Sheinbaum told Wade. The sinkage makes the ground unstable, which in turn makes earthquakes more dangerous.

To address these interlocking challenges, Sheinbaum offered a series of proposals to fix leaks, build treatment plants for recycling water, and subsidize rainwater collection. She also proposed investments in public transportation, as 70 percent of the city's greenhouse gas emissions come from cars. These proposals were concrete expressions of López Obrador and the MORENA party's promises to end corruption and focus on improving the lives of poor and struggling Mexicans. Emphasizing this point, she told Wade: "I'm not particularly attracted to a political career. I just want to make a difference for the city I live in."

Sheinbaum enjoyed a twenty-point lead in the polls in the months before the election. On July 1, 2018, she bested six other candidates to be elected mayor of Mexico City with nearly 50 percent of the vote. López Obrador, meanwhile, won the presidency in a landslide. Both politicians took office in December 2018.

COVID-19 RESPONSE AND SUBWAY COLLAPSE

Sheinbaum faced her first major crisis as mayor in early 2020, when the COVID-19 pandemic hit Mexico. Sheinbaum began imposing lockdowns in Mexico City in late March. Her actions were in stark contrast to López Obrador, who minimized the threat of the virus and refused to take any action at all. While Sheinbaum pushed for free testing and aggressive contact tracing, her mentor, Natalie Kitroeff for *The New York Times* (5 Sept. 2020) wrote, "was still kissing babies at rallies and comparing the virus to the flu." This dissonance, strikingly displayed in an April 2020 photo-op in which Sheinbaum was the only government official masked and social distancing, put the mayor in an uncomfortable political position. Even as she pursued measures to stop the spread of the virus, including requiring masks on public transportation, she refused to criticize the president. "I will not allow this to become a political conflict," she told Kitroeff. "But I also believe I have a role here in the city, and I'm going to abide by what I believe in."

Despite Sheinbaum's efforts, Mexico became a world hotspot for the virus and Mexico City its epicenter. By early 2021, the city's hospitals were overwhelmed. Sheinbaum also came under fire later that year for distributing medical kits containing tablets of ivermectin, an antiparasitic drug widely discredited as a treatment for COVID-19.

In May 2021 Sheinbaum was forced to confront another crisis when a section of the subway in Mexico City collapsed, killing twenty-six people. Mexican citizens again placed much of the blame on Sheinbaum, as critics faulted her administration for failing to detect cracks that led to the disaster. In response, Sheinbaum hired a company to perform a thorough analysis of the accident. "We are in agreement to get to the bottom of this and work together to find the truth and know what caused this incident," she told reporters, as published by Maria Abi-Habib and Oscar Lopez for *The New York Times* (4 May 2021).

CONTROVERSIAL REFORMS

As mayor, Sheinbaum followed through on her campaign promises to expand rainwater collection programs and invest in modernizing the city's waste management. However, she also encountered more controversy. One of her social programs introduced in 2019 that provided so-called "scholarship cards" to schoolchildren to buy food and supplies was deemed unethical by critics who believed she was using the cards as a bribe to gain support. While Sheinbaum denied the allegations, opponents maintained that the cards were presented at assemblies that celebrated Sheinbaum and her accomplishments, accusing her of using public funds for the purpose of self-promotion.

Sheinbaum also offered her support for López Obrador's controversial proposal to reform Mexico's energy sector, which climate experts warned would delay the country's transition to clean energy. López Obrador wanted to prioritize contracts with government-owned energy companies that were heavily reliant on fossil fuels—at the expense of Mexico's private companies, including those that were working to expand renewable energies like wind and solar. The policy sought to unravel reforms introduced in 2013 that prioritized renewable energies, and thus private companies over public ones.

Despite the potential environmental consequences, Sheinbaum lobbied for the reforms. As quoted by Benjamin Russell for *Americas Quarterly* (2 Dec. 2021), she argued that they would strengthen Mexican sovereignty and "reduce environmental impact including, yes, mitigating climate change." Her support for López Obrador's energy policy left many people confused, particularly as many expected her to run for president in 2024. "Sheinbaum is close to the president . . . to the point where perhaps she has been pushing more his agenda than her own," Eugene Zapata, a director at the Resilient Cities Network, told Russell. "It would be great to hear more about her own vision of the country."

PERSONAL LIFE

Sheinbaum met fellow activist Carlos Ímaz Gispert during the 1980s UNAM student strike, and they married in 1987. They had a daughter together, Mariana Ímaz Sheinbaum, before divorcing in 2017.

SUGGESTED READING

Abi-Habib, Maria, and Oscar Lopez. "Vowing Inquiry into Mexico City Train Crash, Officials Struggle to Identify Victims." *The New York Times*, 4 May 2021, www.nytimes. com/2021/05/04/world/americas/mexico-city-train-crash-claudia-sheinbaum-mayors. html. Accessed 15 Feb. 2022.

Kahn, Carrie. "Meet Mexico City's First Elected Female Mayor." *Morning Edition*, NPR, 25 July 2018, www.npr. org/2018/07/25/631465464/meet-mexico-citys-first-elected-woman-mayor. Accessed 9 Feb. 2022.

Kitroeff, Natalie. "Between the Pandemic and the President: Mexico City Mayor's Balancing Act." *The New York Times*, 5 Sept. 2020, www.nytimes.com/2020/09/05/world/americas/mexico-mayor-amlo-sheinbaum. html. Accessed 8 Feb. 2022.

Russell, Benjamin. "Claudia Sheinbaum: Technocrat or True Believer?" *Americas Quarterly*, 2 Dec. 2021, www. americasquarterly.org/article/claudia-sheinbaum-technocrat-or-true-believer/. Accessed 10 Feb. 2022.

Wade, Lizzie. "Can This Environmental Engineer—Now Elected Mayor—Fix Mexico City?" *Science Magazine*, 2 July 2018, www.science.org/content/article/can-environmental-engineer-poised-become-mayor-fix-mexico-city. Accessed 8 Feb. 2022.

—*Molly Hagan*

Jay Shetty

Born: September 6, 1987
Occupation: Author and podcaster

While Jay Shetty began earning a large following in the late 2010s, his career as a wellness podcaster, author, and influencer was inspired almost a decade earlier. After a Hindu monk gave a speech at Shetty's university about his commitment to a minimalist life and the genuine contentment it led to, Shetty moved to Mumbai, India, and spent the next three years training as a monk himself at an ashram. There, he cultivated mindfulness through meditation and service to others. As he explained to Erin Donnelly and Kat Vasquez for *Yahoo! Life* (7 Feb. 2022), "the morning hours were dedicated to understanding yourself: understanding your own mind, training your own habits, training your own ego and character and your own resilience." Shetty further expanded, "And then the rest of the day was about: 'Can we take that out to the world? Can we go out there and share it?'"

While Shetty initially found himself without job prospects and in debt following his departure from the ashram in 2013, the lessons learned and skills acquired during his time there soon propelled him to success. Wanting to spread this knowledge in a world increasingly looking for wellness support, he proved adept at using social media as well as more traditional platforms to bring his message to the public. Known for his hit health and wellness podcast *On Purpose* and his best-selling book *Think Like A Monk* (2020), he established himself as a prominent voice in the lucrative self-help mediascape.

EARLY LIFE AND EDUCATION

Jay Shetty was born on September 6, 1987, in north London, England. His mother and father raised him and his younger sister with the expectation that they would pursue careers as lawyers or doctors. While his parents were non-practicing Hindus, when Shetty was around ten years of age, he witnessed his father embark on a search for a richer understanding of spirituality—planting a seed in his mind about creating a lifestyle that could enhance one's own flourishing.

Shetty attended the all-boys Queen Elizabeth's School, and his time there was marked by confusion and a sense of not fitting in. "I was a really well-behaved, obedient kid. I was raised that way," he told Megan Agnew for the *Sunday Times* (6 Mar. 2022). "But I was bullied about being overweight, and I had racist experiences because I was one of the few Indian people in my school." This led him to go through a rebellious phase, spending his teenage years experimenting with drugs and alcohol and getting in trouble at school, which often resulted in suspensions.

After graduating from Queen Elizabeth's School in 2006, Shetty enrolled at Cass Business School (later known as Bayes Business School) at City, University of London. During this time, he became captivated by the stories of self-made entrepreneurs and chief executive officers, claiming a seat in the university auditorium every time one of them gave a lecture. However, it was a different kind of talk that would change his life forever. At first he did not even plan to attend that lecture, apathetic about the idea of hearing about the life of a monk named Gauranga Das. Lured to it by a friend with the promise of getting drinks afterward, Shetty went and was struck by the sense that Das possessed something invaluable. "I'd met people who were rich. I'd met people who were famous. I'd met people who were beautiful and attractive and strong and powerful. But I don't think I'd ever met anyone who was truly happy, who was truly content. And this monk had that," he explained to Donnelly and Vasquez.

MONASTIC LIFE

Following that fateful talk, Shetty continued to study in London for his business degree and earned several corporate internships, but spent his summers in Mumbai, India, at a monastic community (ashram) overseen by Das. After graduating in 2010, twenty-two-year-old Shetty made the decision to move full-time to the ashram in Mumbai, committing to growing in spirituality as he practiced mindfulness, meditation, and service to others during his quest to become a monk. With a monastic life also came a vow of celibacy and the transition to a minimalist lifestyle, exchanging clothes for monk robes and a comfortable bed for the floor in a dormitory room.

After three years in the monastery, Shetty decided to leave this secluded life to share the knowledge he had acquired with the outside

Photo by Steven Erle,
via Wikimedia Commons

world. As he said to Danielle Cohen in an interview for *GQ* (9 Oct. 2020), "One of the biggest factors was, I had gained the self-awareness through the practices that I didn't think I should be a monk for the rest of my life. There were parts of the practices I wanted to share and give back to the world I came from." But when the time to reintegrate into society came, it proved difficult for Shetty to do so. He had $25,000 worth of debt and received more than forty rejections to job applications because of the three-year gap in his career resume.

However, the self-improvement movement had grown in popularity by 2013. With Shetty's recent experience leading a calm, stress-free life through mindfulness at the monastery, his skills and knowledge were suddenly in considerable demand. "That gave me a huge boost of confidence because it made me realize that people needed these tools. So that's where I started to see that there was a need for this," he told Cohen.

THE BIRTH OF AN INFLUENCER

Shetty soon began accepting invitations to speak at corporate events about the lessons learned throughout his journey to monkhood. Noticing the world was undergoing a digital adaptation with the rising popularity of social media platforms, he began work for the information technology and consulting company Accenture in late 2013, taking the role of a social media strategy and innovation coach for executives.

Aside from managing a plethora of social media channels, including Facebook, Twitter, and LinkedIn, Shetty advised on digital marketing solutions and developed audience engagement strategies, eventually becoming the number one media influencer in Accenture globally. His digital savvy caught the attention of media mogul Arianna Huffington, who in 2016 hired him to produce videos for the *Huffington Post* as a senior host and producer. During the year he spent in New York City at the *Huffington Post*, Shetty created a hugely popular mindfulness video series whose topics ranged from career success to entrepreneurship to technology habits, amassing millions of views along the way. His daily show, *HuffPost Live #FollowtheReader*, also became a hit. It featured interviews with influencers such as basketball star Kobe Bryant, alternative medicine proponent Deepak Chopra, and entrepreneur Russell Simmons, among others.

In 2017, *Forbes* included Shetty on the 30 Under 30 Europe List of influential young figures. That same year he left his position at the *Huffington Post* and moved to Los Angeles to open his own company, Jay Shetty Media and Coaching. When asked by Dan Schawbel in an interview for *Business Insider* (30 July 2019) about how, throughout his successful career, he determined where to transition next, Shetty said, "The biggest thing for me in a transition is research. I get so lost in other people's journeys and other people's trajectories. I wonder 'what did this person do; how did they do it differently?' and 'how did they think about it?' Because when you research the lives of people you admire, you realize there's no pattern, formula, or step-by-step format."

ON PURPOSE AND THINK LIKE A MONK

Having started a YouTube channel that soon boasted subscribers in the millions, and a popular Facebook page, Shetty next launched a podcast called *On Purpose with Jay Shetty* in early 2019. Keeping self-care at the heart of the show, he sat down with insightful guests from around the globe—including tennis star Novak Djokovic, singer-songwriter Alicia Keys, and reality television personality Khloe Kardashian—to have conversations about wellness. When the coronavirus disease 2019

(COVID-19) pandemic began in 2020, Shetty's *On Purpose* became even more popular as an outlet to address mental health struggles, which reached crisis levels as much of the world was forced into isolation. By March 2022, *On Purpose* was the number-one health and wellness podcast worldwide, racking up more than 300 million downloads.

To further his reach, in January 2020 Shetty founded the Jay Shetty Certification School, a program offering industry accredited life and success coach training. Later that year he published his first book, *Think Like a Monk: How to Train Your Mind for Peace and Purpose Everyday* (2020), based on his experience in the Mumbai ashram. The book conquered several best-seller lists, including *The New York Times*, *The Wall Street Journal*, and Amazon.

In early 2022 Shetty became the first chief purpose officer of the relaxation and meditation company Calm, founded in 2012 by Michael Acton Smith and Alex Tew. Regarding this new role and how it fit his skill set, Shetty said to Agnew, "The 'chief purpose officer' title feels the most aligned with me because purpose is what I'm invested in." With the national and international communities paying increasing attention to mental health issues and how to address them, Shetty's skills and expertise were widely seen as highly relevant, boosting his rise to prominence. Throughout his rapid ascent, he continued to emphasize his commitment to the well-being of others. As he said to Agnew, "My genuine intention and purpose is to help train people to find peace and purpose in every day. I really believe that my purpose is to help other people find their purpose."

PERSONAL LIFE

In 2016, Shetty married nutritionist Radhi Devlukia-Shetty, whom he met during a meditation class. The couple live in Los Angeles. Shetty has stated that he abstains from eating meat and drinking.

SUGGESTED READING

Agnew, Megan. "Jay Shetty: The Monk Who Became a Self-Help Sensation." *The Sunday Times*, 6 Mar. 2022, www.thetimes.co.uk/ article/jay-shetty-the-monk-who-became-a-self-help-sensation-v7hgd7592. Accessed 5 June 2021.

Donnelly, Erin, and Kat Vasquez. "Former Monk Jay Shetty Shares His 'Equation' for

Finding Purpose: 'Passion Plus Expertise Plus Service.'" *Yahoo! Life*, 7 Feb. 2022, www.yahoo.com/lifestyle/jay-shetty-purpose-calm-monk-150055602.html. Accessed 5 June 2021.

Shetty, Jay. "How to Live with More Intention, According to Former Monk Jay Shetty." Interview by Danielle Cohen. *GQ*, 9 Oct. 2020, www.gq.com/story/how-to-live-with-more-intention-according-to-jay-shetty. Accessed 5 June 2021.

___. "Social Media Phenomenon Jay Shetty on His Wild Journey from Monk to Entrepreneur—and Why He Says Being Disappointed Is a Normal Part of a Meaningful Life." Interview by Dan Schawbel. *Business Insider*, 30 July 2019, www.businessinsider.com/social-media-phenomenon-jay-shetty-on-going-from-monk-entrepreneur-2019-7. Accessed 5 June 2021.

Wolfson, Sam. "'I'm Living My Highest Purpose': Mogul Monk Jay Shetty on Free Market Teachings." *The Guardian*, 12 Sept. 2020, www.theguardian.com/lifeandstyle/2020/sep/12/im-living-my-highest-purpose-mogul-monk-jay-shetty-on-free-market-teachings. Accessed 5 June 2021.

—*Maria del Pilar Guzman*

Mary Simon

Born: August 21, 1947
Occupation: Politician

By the time Canadian Prime Minister Justin Trudeau appointed Mary Simon to serve as the country's thirtieth governor general, a largely ceremonial but prominent role representing Canada's official head of state approved by Queen Elizabeth II, in 2021, Simon, an Inuk who had devoted years to public service and both Arctic and Indigenous advocacy, was more than prepared to take on the position. Speaking to her qualifications and ambitions upon her installation, she said that she had the ability to serve as "a bridge between the different lived realities that together make up the tapestry of Canada," as quoted by Paula Newton for *CNN* (26 July 2021). "I can relate to all people no matter where they live, what they hope for or what they need to overcome."

While her early professional life involved employment with the Canadian Broadcasting Corporation (CBC), Simon soon became involved in Indigenous rights groups in the 1970s. A skilled diplomat, she took part in the negotiations for a milestone land claim settlement between provincial communities of Cree and Inuit and the Québec government in 1975 and served as a representative of Inuit communities during Canadian Constitution patriation and amendment efforts in the early 1980s. She also chaired the Inuit Circumpolar Conference (ICC) from the late 1980s and into the early 1990s, bringing together Inuit from several Arctic nations, and, as Canada's first ambassador for circumpolar affairs, she helped create the international Arctic Council.

In 2008, while serving as president of Inuit Tapiriit Kanatami, Canada's national Inuit organization, Simon spoke on behalf of the country's Inuit communities in response to Prime Minister Stephen Harper's official apology for the detrimental impact of residential schools. The brutal history of these schools, a system of assimilation and abuse that operated for over one hundred years, would figure into Simon's appointment as governor general as well. Her appointment came amidst a national outcry after the remains of nearly one thousand people were discovered at the sites of two residential schools. Her nephew, Dennis Lock, told Omar Sachedina and Jackie Dunham for *CTV News* (26 July 2021) that Simon's appointment as Canada's first Indigenous governor general was a major step toward reconciliation. "It's what the country needs right now," he said. Referencing the discovery of the remains, he added, "With everything that's been going on with all the kids they've been finding. . . . I'm getting emotional."

EARLY LIFE AND EDUCATION

Mary Jeannie May Simon was born on August 21, 1947, in Kangiqsualujjuaq, a village in the Canadian area of Arctic Québec that became known as Nunavik. She was raised, along with her seven siblings, by her father, Bob Mardon May, a White man with English heritage who had moved to the region due to his employment with the Hudson Bay Company, and her mother, Nancy, an Inuk who did not speak English. The family relocated to the bigger village of Kuujjuaq, then called Fort Chimo, in the Nunavik region while she was still a small

Photo by Justin Trudeau via Wikimedia Commons

child. They lived, as Simon has detailed, in accordance with Inuit traditions, traveling by dog team, hunting and harvesting the land, and sleeping in log cabins or tents. "We used to take all the spruce boughs from the trees, all of the lower branches, put it all on the floor in the tent so there was no snow, and it was warm because we had a wood stove. It was beautiful," she recalled to Gloria Galloway for *The Globe and Mail* (1 May 2012).

Between grades one and six, Simon was educated, due to the limited opportunities for Indigenous peoples, at the local federal day school, where one of her sisters has recalled teachers shooting BB guns at their brother's legs as punishment. In addition to a policy prohibiting her from speaking her Inuit language of Inuktitut, she received instruction only in English and did not get the opportunity to learn French. Her education after sixth grade was piecemeal. As her paternal grandparents had gone to live in Colorado, she completed some schooling in the United States. Otherwise, she was homeschooled by her father. Other young people in her community were forcibly sent away to residential schools, and she has stated in interviews that as she remained, she could sense the sorrow experienced by community families of those missed children when she would visit. After earning her high school diploma via correspondence, around 1969 she

assumed a position announcing and producing for the CBC's Northern Service.

DIPLOMATIC CAREER

Simon became involved with Indigenous rights organizations in the 1970s. Through an affiliation with the Northern Quebec Inuit Association, she contributed to the negotiation of the James Bay and Northern Quebec Agreement between the Cree and Inuit communities living in northern Québec and the Québec government in 1975. It is considered to have been the first comprehensive land claims agreement in Canada. In 1977, she played a key role in the first Inuit Circumpolar Conference (ICC)—later becoming the Inuit Circumpolar Council—which first gathered Inuit in Alaska, Canada, and Greenland together to coordinate advocation for Inuit involvement in Arctic conservation as well as any policies that would affect their communities. For Simon, the historic gathering was the realization of one of her grandmother's dreams. When she was growing up, her Inuit grandmother, Jeannie, often used the family's short-wave radio to hear bits of transmitted speech or sound from the Inuit of Greenland. "We would be playing outside and she'd call us and she'd say: 'Come, come and listen to your faraway relatives! Listen to their singing!'" she recalled to Bill Curry for *The Globe and Mail* (31 Aug. 2007).

Maintaining a commitment to the 1975 treaty, she additionally held the position of vice president (1978–80) and president (1983–85) of the Makivik Corporation, which had been established to oversee the agreement's proper implementation. Having solidified her leadership abilities, she was next elected president of the ICC in 1986, serving two terms that ended in 1992. During her tenure, she led lobbies of the Soviet government to allow the Inuit of Siberia to be a part of the ICC. The Soviet government relented in 1989, allowing Inuit of Siberia to attend the assembly.

Meanwhile, beginning in 1982, Simon served as an Inuit rights representative during the patriation process of the Canadian Constitution.

CREATION OF THE ARCTIC COUNCIL

In 1994, Canadian Prime Minister Jean Chrétien appointed Simon Canada's first ambassador for circumpolar affairs. In this role, she was tasked with defending Canada's interests in the Arctic. Another responsibility of her position involved the ongoing effort to evolve the Arctic Environmental Protection Strategy (AEPS), an existing organization, into a council representing the eight Arctic nations, which include Canada, Denmark (administrator of Greenland), Finland, Iceland, Norway, Sweden, Russia, and the United States. "We needed something more than the AEPS, something more than the environment focus," Simon told Stig Brøndbo for *Shared Voices* magazine of the University of the Arctic (2016). She vowed to make Indigenous participation an important part of the new council, noting that AEPS had managed such relations poorly. Though, due to her ICC position, she had been brought in to present at a planning meeting for the AEPS in 1990, she recalled to Brøndbo, "I soon realized that I was not a participant in this meeting—I was more of an observer that was invited to give a talk." She added, "When international forums talk about sustainability in the Arctic, they are dealing with the core issue for indigenous communities. To me it is obvious that we need to be at the table as participants." With Indigenous organizations ultimately designated as merely observers in the AEPS establishment declaration and left out of closed negotiations despite her activism, she was all the more determined to have the new council be different.

Negotiations to create the Arctic Council were long and arduous, but after two years, the 1996 Ottawa Declaration made its founding official, and Indigenous peoples were part of a permanent participant category that ensured seats at the table and involvement in dialogue. Still, Simon and others concede that the council was slow to get off the ground, as it took several more years for the body to define its various groups and mandates. She stepped down as ambassador for circumpolar affairs, thus ending her role in the council, in 2003. This period also saw her hold the position, from 1999 to 2001, of Canada's ambassador to Denmark.

CANADA'S GOVERNOR GENERAL

Striving to represent Inuit communities further politically, she prioritized the issues of education and health upon the start of her tenure in 2006 as president of Canada's national Inuit organization, Inuit Tapiriit Kanatami. In 2008, she provided remarks as a representative of Inuit communities upon the Canadian government officially apologizing for residential schools, with approximately 150,000 Indigenous children having been forced to attend. By that point, Canada had increasingly been forced to grapple with the history of these schools, which, run for several decades, were aimed at erasing cultural memory and assimilating Indigenous children and had employed rampant abuse. Seven years later, the National Truth and Reconciliation Commission would deem the residential school system "cultural genocide." Though Simon stepped down as Inuit Tapiriit Kanatami president in 2012, she continued to chair a national committee to improve education and culturally informed learning in Inuit communities. Due to her widely recognized expertise on Arctic issues, in 2016 she received a new appointment from the minister of Indigenous and northern affairs that involved consulting with a range of Arctic leaders and organizations and advising the national government on sustainable development goals as well as the economic and social priorities of Arctic communities; she produced her report, *A New Shared Arctic Leadership Model*, in 2017.

While some had speculated in 2010 that Prime Minister Harper would appoint Simon Canada's governor general, this never happened. Her name was raised again more than ten years later, after Governor General Julie Payette resigned in 2021. "Today after 154 years, our country takes a historic step," Trudeau said when he announced in July that Simon would be Canada's next, and first Indigenous, governor general, as quoted by Dan Bilefsky for *The New York Times* (6 July 2021). "I cannot think of a better person to meet the moment." Trudeau's remarks were an oblique reference to the discovery of hundreds of unmarked graves at the sites of former residential schools in Saskatchewan and British Columbia. The remains, nearly one thousand in total, were mostly Indigenous children. The discovery renewed public outrage at the Canadian government and demands that it be held accountable for its treatment of Indigenous people. "I can confidently say that my appointment is a historic and inspirational moment for Canada and an important step forward," Simon said, as quoted by Bilefsky, upon accepting her new role, noting that it "comes at an especially reflective and dynamic time in our shared history."

In October 2021, Simon traveled to Germany, her first international visit as governor general. Doug Saunders, who wrote about the visit for *The Globe and Mail* (22 Oct. 2021), described it as "symbolic" but illustrative of how she would actively use her ceremonial role. She said she spoke with German president Frank-Walter Steinmeier about how a country's leader might atone for the atrocities of the past; for decades, Germany has grappled with this in respect to the Holocaust. The question of how to atone is "a common theme that he and I both share," she told Saunders. "We need to tell the truth about the past . . . the hard truth and the hard things that we have to overcome as part of reconciliation. . . . I as a Governor General have decided that I'll be devoting a lot of time to it during my term." The following month, she addressed issues such as reconciliation and the pandemic in her agenda speech launching the new Parliament's first session.

PERSONAL LIFE

After two marriages and three children, in 1994 Simon married journalist Whit Fraser, who had previously worked for the CBC. She has detailed that when she was around forty years old, she experienced an intense episode of depression that inspired her to address the lack of resources for those with mental illnesses in Inuit communities and otherwise work to destigmatize mental illness.

SUGGESTED READING

Bilefsky, Dan. "Trudeau Appoints Canada's First Indigenous Governor General." *The New York Times*, 6 July 2021, www.nytimes.com/2021/07/06/world/canada/indigenous-governor-general-mary-simon.html. Accessed 7 Jan. 2022.

Curry, Bill. "Inuit Leader Tackles Mental-Health 'Crisis.'" *The Globe and Mail*, 31 Aug. 2007, www.theglobeandmail.com/news/national/inuit-leader-tackles-mental-health-crisis/article4092716/. Accessed 6 Jan. 2022.

Galloway, Gloria. "After Four Decades Leading the Inuit People, Mary Simon Steps Down." *The Globe and Mail*, 1 May 2012, www.theglobeandmail.com/news/politics/after-four-decades-leading-the-inuit-people-mary-simon-steps-down/article4104061/. Accessed 6 Jan. 2022.

Newton, Paula. "Canada's First Indigenous Governor General Is Installed." *CNN*, 26 July 2021, www.cnn.com/2021/07/26/americas/mary-simon-governor-general-canada/index.html. Accessed 14 Jan. 2022.

Sachedina, Omar, and Jackie Dunham. "From Nunavik to Rideau Hall: How Mary Simon's Home Will Shape Her Future as Governor General." *CTV News*, 26 July 2021, www.ctvnews.ca/politics/from-nunavik-to-rideau-hall-how-mary-simon-s-home-will-shape-her-future-as-governor-general-1.5523460. Accessed 7 Jan. 2022.

Saunders, Doug. "For Mary Simon, a Visit to Germany Is Symbolic—but Her New Job Is Not." *The Globe and Mail*, 22 Oct. 2021, www.theglobeandmail.com/opinion/article-for-mary-simon-a-visit-to-germany-is-symbolic-but-her-new-job-is-not/. Accessed 7 Jan. 2022.

Simon, Mary. "Interview with Mary Simon." *Interview by* Stig Brøndbo. *Shared Voices*, University of the Arctic, 2016, www.uarctic.org/shared-voices/shared-voices-magazine-2016-special-issue/interview-with-mary-simon/. Accessed 6 Jan. 2022.

—*Molly Hagan*

Sinach

Born: March 30, 1973
Occupation: Singer-songwriter

Amid the global coronavirus pandemic in 2020, the anthem "Way Maker" (sometimes styled as "Waymaker") was adopted as a go-to song to serenade and uplift frontline medical workers and first responders battling COVID-19. "Way Maker" gained worldwide popularity after Christian contemporary superstar Michael W. Smith released his recording of the song in February 2020. Unbeknown to most, however, "Way Maker" was written and originally recorded in 2015 by the Nigerian singer-songwriter Sinach. As senior worship leader for the megachurch Christ Embassy, Sinach released many albums and wrote hundreds of songs over the years, including the hits "The Name of Jesus" and "I Know Who I Am." Though she became one of the most successful gospel artists in Nigeria and across Africa, she long received little mainstream attention in the United States. Nevertheless, Sinach was fine with the progression of her career and her art. "The joy of a writer is that when you write a song, the whole world will sing it, because the song is really not about you," she told Megan Fowler for *Christianity Today* (12 June 2020). "If the song goes ahead of you to announce you before you even show up, that means the song is successful."

The success of "Way Maker," which was covered by more than sixty recording artists, proved a turning point for Sinach's intercontinental profile. In 2020 Smith's version and another band's version were simultaneous hits on Billboard's Hot Christian Songs top-ten, a first for the chart. Sinach also received recognition from the recording industry, becoming the first African artist to top the Billboard Christian Songwriters chart. At the Fifty-First Dove Awards, "Way Maker" earned song of the year honors, making Sinach the first gospel artist from Nigeria to claim the award. She reached another milestone in August 2021 when "Way Maker" won song of the year at the BMI Christian Awards—a victory that made Sinach the first African artist to achieve this historic feat. Yet, mainstream recognition was not Sinach's primary goal. "I am uninterested in hit records that give me short-term relevance even though that can be sweet," she told Motolani Alake for *Pulse* (30 Jan. 2021). "I want impactful records that can stand the test of time."

EARLY LIFE AND EDUCATION

Sinach was born Osinachi Kalu Okoro Egbu on March 30, 1973, in Afikpo South, situated in the southern region of Ebonyi State, Nigeria. The second daughter of seven children, she would cite her mother, a schoolteacher, and her father, a civil servant, as early creative influences. "When I was a child, my mum found my poetic desire of being a writer; my dad had a vast music catalogue that I always listened to," she shared with Funke Babs-Kufeji for the Nigerian publication *ThisDay* (27 June 2021). Growing up, Sinach developed a passion for performing, often entertaining her parents with singing and dancing. She also honed her voice while singing in her school's drama and music group. Despite her love of music, she was encouraged by her father to study medicine, and eventually majored in physics at the University of Port Harcourt in Rivers State.

Photo by Psegs via Wikimedia Commons

FINDING HER VOICE

Sinach's life changed in November 1989, when she was invited by friends to attend service at Christ Embassy, a global music-driven ministry then known as Believers' LoveWorld International, located in Lagos, Nigeria. "When I got to the church, it was filled with young people and the music was so good, not the usual boring church songs and I was so drawn to that," she recalled to Alake. The visit made a strong impression on her, and she subsequently joined the church. As a member of the choir, she tried her hand at songwriting, penning her first song at age nineteen, following an uplifting sermon.

After graduating from Port Harcourt, Sinach accepted an administrative position at Christ Embassy, as part of Nigeria's National Youth Service Corps (NYSC), a yearlong, government-mandated work program for under-thirty college graduates. She eventually pursued a career in music ministry, after being inspired by an encounter with Christ Embassy founder Pastor Chris Oyakhilome, who recognized her potential. "I didn't even realize, but he told me that when I sang, it was like 'BOOM!'" Sinach revealed to Alake. "For some reason, I felt like God was speaking to me." Following her administrative stint, she became more actively involved in the ministry, joining the LoveWorld

Music team. As a worship leader and music minister, she produced praise and worship music performed during church services led by Oyakhilome.

EARLY SINGING CAREER

Sinach launched her recording career in 2008, with the release of her debut studio album, *Chapter One*, which included the single "This Is Your Season." Sinach's sophomore effort, *I'm Blessed*, was released in 2011. That same year she was nominated for the Nigeria Entertainment Awards (NEA) Gospel Artist of the Year award, though she lost out to Lara George. Then came a pair of live albums: 2012's *Shout It Loud* and *From Glory to Glory*, released in 2013. The former, which was recorded during a concert at the Lyric Theatre in Johannesburg, South Africa, featured the upbeat, feel-good anthem "I Know Who I Am," while the latter boasted the rousing hymn "Great Are You Lord."

In September 2013 Sinach performed a major worship concert in Houston, Texas. Later that year came the release of the seasonal EP *Sinach at Christmas*. In 2014 she not only released *The Name of Jesus*, a live recording of her Texas concert, but also performed at Africa's largest annual gospel music gathering, The Experience, held in Lagos. The following year she headlined an Easter weekend worship concert at the Miracle Centre Cathedral in Kampala, Uganda.

By 2015, Sinach had already achieved a certain level of success but was struggling with being called to step out of her comfort zone and advance in her career. That struggle inspired her to write "Way Maker," which she released as a single and video in late December 2015. Her ode to a higher power became the centerpiece of her next album, *Way Maker—Live* (2016), which she recorded at the Mosaic Theatre in Johannesburg, South Africa. She also headlined the 2016 Festival of Life London—her second consecutive appearance at the event—and the Christian music festival Praise Fest 2016, held in Nairobi, Kenya.

Sinach's contributions to gospel music earned her several accolades in 2016 and 2017. Along with being named winner of the LoveWorld International Music and Arts (LIMA) Songwriter of the Decade Award for 2016, she was honored as Western Africa Artist of the Year at the Groove Awards in Kenya. The following year she captured the prize for global excellence at the African Achievers Awards and inspirational artist at the Nigerian Entertainment Awards while also earning a nod in the best gospel category at the African Music Magazine Awards (AFRIMMA).

REACHING A WIDER AUDIENCE

With steadily growing critical acclaim, Sinach began to earn increasing international attention. She embarked on her first major tour of the United Kingdom in January 2018, performing at Central Hall Westminster in London, the SEC Armadillo in Glasgow and Birmingham's O2 Institute. Two months later, she was crowned best international artist of the year at the Sterling Gospel Music Awards, held in Jamaica.

Sinach's song "Way Maker" was also starting to reach a wider audience. When the British worship compilation disc *Everlasting Arms* was released in May 2018, the song appeared as one of the tracks, after having been licensed by UK music publisher Integrity Music. That July, *Way Maker—Live* received gold certification from the Recording Industry of South Africa (RISA). Sinach followed that with two more live albums, *There's an Overflow* and *Great God (Live in London)*, released in December 2018 and March 2019, respectively. By the latter disc's release, Sinach found herself back in the headlines when her video for "Way Maker" amassed 100 million YouTube views, making her the third Nigerian musical artist, behind singer-songwriter Davido and Afropop singer Yemi Alade, to achieve that feat.

By August 2019, Sinach had formally entered into partnership with Integrity Music to promote her songs globally. She collaborated with the Christian rock band Leeland, also signed to Integrity, on a live rendition of "Way Maker," along with an accompanying music video. The track was also featured on Leeland's first full-live album, *Better Word*, which hit record shelves in September 2019. However, they were not the only artists to record a cover of "Way Maker." The Redding, California–based Christian worship and praise collective Bethel Music recorded a live worship video for the song, also released that September. As "Way Maker" started to garner mainstream attention, Sinach found herself increasingly in demand. She made history that fall as the first African gospel artist to visit India, where she headlined September concerts in New Delhi and Pune.

In October 2019 Sinach traveled to Houston, Texas, to visit Joel Osteen's Lakewood Church, where she took the stage to perform "Way Maker," which continued to gain traction. Christian reggae band Christafari released a gospel version of the song featuring Avion Blackman, in November 2019—the same month Sinach claimed the song of the year prize for "Overflow" at the LIMA Awards. The following January, Grammy Award–winning gospel and contemporary Christian artist Mandisa recorded a cover of "Way Maker," which reached the Top Forty of the Billboard Hot Christian Songs and Christian Airplay charts.

WORLDWIDE PHENOMENON

"Way Maker" would take on a deeper meaning in February 2020, when contemporary Christian superstar Michael W. Smith released his own version of the song. (He also recorded an Italian cover, "Aprirai una via." [You Will Open a Way]) By March 2020, following the outbreak of the COVID-19 pandemic, Smith's rendition had already cracked the Top Ten of Billboard's Hot Christian Songs. "'Waymaker' is a very special song that moves people," Smith told Jim Asker for *Billboard* (12 Mar. 2020). "From the first time I played it at Nashville's Bridgestone Arena in 2018 to now, it just brings the audience to a very special place." Sinach's song continued to strike a chord with audiences in other versions as well. Leeland's rendition reached number nine on Billboard's Hot Christian Songs in early April 2020, marking the first time in the chart's history that two versions of the same song occupied the Top Ten at the same time. Meanwhile, Mandisa's cover had also reached the chart's top forty, along with another version by contemporary worship band Passion.

Fueled by the "Way Maker's" immense popularity, Sinach topped Billboard's Christian Songwriters chart. In May 2020, a month after releasing two acoustic EPs, Sinach took to social media to announce that she had made history as the first Black person and the first African to sit atop that chart for more than seven weeks. She maintained the top spot for another five weeks, becoming the first female singer-songwriter to achieve this feat.

In August 2020 "Way Maker" received nominations for the Fifty-First Dove Awards in three categories: song of the year, worship recorded song of the year, and Spanish language recorded Song of the Year. That October Sinach attended the Nashville-based Dove Awards ceremony, where she performed "Way Maker" alongside Leeland and Mandisa. She also became the first Nigerian gospel artist to claim the coveted Song of the Year prize. In April 2021 Sinach released the studio album *Greatest Lord*, featuring Leeland, Grammy-nominated gospel singer Jekalyn Carr, and world-renowned Australian worship leader Darlene Zschech. Increasingly recognized as a major figure in worship music around the world, she continued touring widely, including another performance at Lakewood Church in the fall of 2021 and an appearance at a September 11 tribute concert in New York City.

PERSONAL LIFE

Sinach married Christ Embassy pastor Joseph Egbu in 2014. The couple had a daughter in 2019.

SUGGESTED READING

Asker, Jim. "Michael W. Smith Hits Hot Christian Songs Top 10 with 'Waymaker': 'It Brings the Audience to a Special Place.'" *Billboard*, 12 Mar. 2020, www.billboard.com/pro/michael-w-smith-waymaker-hot-christian-songs-top-10/. Accessed 15 Nov. 2021.

—. "There's a Second Version of 'Waymaker' in the Hot Christian Songs Top 10 and That's a First for the Chart." *Billboard*, 9 Apr. 2020, www.billboard.com/pro/leeland-michael-w-smith-waymaker-hot-christian-songs-chart/. Accessed 15 Nov. 2021.

Fowler, Megan. "How 'Waymaker' Topped the US Worship Charts from Nigeria." *Christianity Today*, 12 June 2020, www.christianitytoday.com/ct/2020/june-web-only/way-maker-worship-song-sinach-leeland-michael-w-smith.html. Accessed 15 Nov. 2021.

Sinach. "Interview with Popular Gospel Artist 'Sinach.'" *GospelLover*, 25 Jan. 2020, gospellover.com/interview-with-popular-gospel-artist-sinach/. 19 Nov. 2021.

Sinach. "Sinach: Global Voice." Interview by Funke Babs-Kufeji. *ThisDay Style*, 27 June 2021, www.thisdaystyle.ng/sinach/. 19 Nov. 2021.

Sinach. "Sinach: The Makings of an African Superstar." Interview by Motolani Alake. *Pulse.ng*, 30 Jan. 2021, www.pulse.ng/

entertainment/music/sinach-tells-pulse-about-christ-embassy-chris-oyakhilome-way-maker-her-upcoming-album/w67c6my. 19 Nov. 2021.

SELECTED WORKS

Chapter One, 2008; *I'm Blessed*, 2011; *Name of Jesus*, 2014; *Way Maker—Live*, 2018; *There's An Overflow*, 2018; *Great God (Live in London)*, 2018; *Greatest Lord*, 2021

—Bertha Muteba

Hayat Sindi

Born: November 6, 1967
Occupation: Biotechnology scientist and entrepreneur

Hayat Sindi is a biotechnologist, inventor, and entrepreneur. Growing up in Saudi Arabia, Sindi saw no Middle Eastern female scientists. The lack was profoundly discouraging, making her own path to becoming a scientist all the more difficult. Now, as the chief executive officer of a company called i2 institute (i2), the Institute for Imagination and Ingenuity, Sindi hopes to support aspiring scientists, and encourage young people in Arab countries, particularly young women, to pursue careers in science technology. This was one of her major goals when she was appointed one of the first female members of the Shura Council, the Saudi Arabian advisory council that advises the king, in 2013. "I want to concentrate on innovating education and scientific research, and inspire the youth to take an interest in science," she told Ifran Muhammad and Afshan Aziz for the *Arab News* (17 Jan. 2013). "The idea is to make them motivated, creative and most importantly to unlock their own potential and move ahead using their talent for the benefit of our country."

Sindi, who was named a science ambassador for the United Nations Educational, Scientific and Cultural Organization in 2012, studied pharmacology at Kings College in London, but her research eventually led her to the field of biotechnology. As a doctoral student at Cambridge, she invented a device called a magnetic acoustic resonance sensor (MARS) that can detect early-stage cancers. Later, as a visiting scholar at Harvard University and the Massachusetts Institute of Technology (MIT),

Sindi worked on a team that developed a radically simple diagnostic tool. They designed a patterned paper the size of a postage stamp that can assess liver function using only a drop of blood or urine. In 2007, Sindi cofounded the nonprofit company Diagnostics for All to distribute the tests in impoverished rural areas.

EARLY LIFE AND EDUCATION

Hayat bint Sulaiman bin Hassan Sindi, the oldest of eight siblings, was born in Makkah, Saudi Arabia, on November 6, 1967. Her father supported her early interest in science and encouraged her to pursue her education. Sindi was lucky to enjoy such support within her family as a young girl in Saudi Arabia at that time. Still, she struggled to find her place in a field dominated by men and longed for a role model. "Scientists were always thought of as old, bald men," she told a journalist for *National Geographic* (10 Sept. 2011). "And I was a young, Arabic woman!"

After completing her secondary education in Makkah, Sindi enrolled at a medical college in Saudi Arabia. She wanted to study abroad, and to that end, she told her father a lie. She said that she had been accepted to a prestigious university in London. Her father, a traditional Muslim, was appalled by the thought of his young, single daughter living alone in a foreign country. "He told me, 'Over my dead body,'" she recalled to Abigail Pesta for the *Daily Beast* (13 July 2017). Remarkably, Sindi eventually won his permission, but obstacles remained: she had not been accepted to any university in London. She did not even speak English.

Sindi arrived in London in 1991, terrified. "My first night there, I went to a youth hostel," she recalled to Pesta. "I was in an attic room. I panicked. I looked at my plane tickets—my father had bought a return ticket. I thought, I'll go home tomorrow." Instead, Sindi sought assistance at an Islamic cultural center. With the help of a translator, she met with university administrators. "I was naive," she told Pesta. "I thought they would just let me in."

Sindi spent a year in London studying English and working to pass her A-levels, courses required for college admittance in the United Kingdom. She was accepted to King's College London and graduated with a degree in pharmacology in 1995. She studied for her doctorate at the University of Cambridge, where she faced discrimination and harassment. "When I first started at Cambridge a well-known scientist told me that I'd fail unless I let go of my cover 'hijab' and changed my ways," she told Maali Al-Ghamry for the *Arab News* (31 July 2004), referring to her traditional Muslim head covering. "He gave me three months to fail." Sindi earned a doctorate in biotechnology in 2001, becoming the first woman from the Persian Gulf to earn that degree from Cambridge. Her family did not find out about the lie that launched her career until many years later, when Sindi mentioned it in a speech.

MARS INVENTION

After earning her undergraduate degree, Sindi began medical research. She was inspired to develop a machine to further her research, placing her on the path that led her to biotechnology. While working on her doctorate at Cambridge, Sindi developed and patented an invention called the magnetic acoustic resonance sensor (MARS). The device utilizes light and ultrasound for the early detection of various cancers. The aviation industry and NASA expressed interest in the machine, but Sindi was adamant that her invention be made available to help people in Saudi Arabia. "I want Arab countries to benefit from this new machine and my research," she told Al-Ghamry. "I'm committed to my principles and I believe that a person must leave a mark that benefits the human race, however I want to begin this benefit in the lands where my roots are."

DIAGNOSTICS FOR ALL

Sindi moved to the United States during the 2000s, where she was a visiting scholar at Harvard University and MIT for five years. There, collaborating with a team of scientists, Sindi helped develop a novel paper-based diagnostic tool to evaluate liver function in people with acquired immunodeficiency syndrome (AIDS), tuberculosis, and hepatitis. The drugs that treat these conditions can cause liver failure if not properly monitored. As *The New York Times* reported in 2011, AIDS patients in African countries were twelve times more likely to die of liver failure than American AIDS patients because many lacked access to liver tests that were expensive, took weeks to process, and required tubes of blood.

The paper tests Sindi and the team developed are the size of a postage stamp and

Photo by PopTech, via Wikimedia Commons.

cost less than a penny to make. They require only a drop of blood or urine, and are designed to be used in rural, hard to reach places that lack clean water or electricity. "Health care workers will be able to visit as many as 200 homes each day, perform tests, and take action immediately," Sindi told *National Geographic*, when she was named an Emerging Explorer by the magazine in 2011. Layered with tiny channels lined with dried proteins, chemically triggered dyes embedded in the paper indicate a diagnosis that can be read within fifteen minutes.

In 2007, Sindi and other scientists cofounded a nonprofit company called Diagnostics for All to commercialize and distribute the liver function tests, with plans to develop more tests. In 2008, she and the Diagnostics for All Business Plan Team, won both the Harvard Business School's annual business plan contest and MIT's $100,000 Entrepreneurship Competition. They were the first team to win both coveted prizes in the same year. In 2009 and 2010, Sindi was named a PopTech Social Innovation Fellow. She was the first person to receive the fellowship in two consecutive years.

I2 AND THE ISDB

Sindi won the Mekkah Al-Mukarramah prize for scientific innovation in 2010. The following year she founded a company called i2, the

Institute for Imagination and Ingenuity, with the goal of encouraging young people to pursue careers in science technology. Sindi sees the field as an opportunity to use science to solve problems. "It is crucial . . . to have a passion and set a goal in this field," she told Muhammad and Aziz. "A target helps us when we aren't sure how to tackle hardships. . . . I want to see meaningful scientific technology become a part of the curriculum of our universities so our people can make this world a better place."

In 2012, *Newsweek* magazine included Sindi on their 150 Women Who Shake the World list. That same year, *Forbes* magazine named her the second most powerful woman in Saudi Arabia, and in 2014 she received the Clinton Global Citizen Award for Leadership in Civil Society. In 2017, Sindi was appointed the chief scientific advisor of the Islamic Development Bank (IsDB), which finances infrastructure and social development in Muslim countries. There, she was integral in launching the $500 million Transform Fund and Engage Platform digital hub in 2018. The multimillion-dollar fund finances the work of science and technology innovators. Engage, the digital hub, connects participants—scientists, non-governmental organizations (NGOs) and private sector companies among others—across the Muslim world. She also led the bank, in a joint initiative with the International Atomic Energy Agency (IAEA), to help save the lives of women with breast and cervical cancer in poor countries.

In 2021, Sindi was awarded the World Academy of Sciences (TWAS) Medal Lecture for her achievements in biotechnology. The honor was exceptional in that Sindi was not, as is traditionally the case, a TWAS fellow. In her lecture, she spoke of her passion for science technology, and the opportunities the field offers. She emphasized innovations in medical technology, and the ability of scientists to grow artificial human organs. She also spoke of hyperbaric therapy, an oxygen therapy that might prove helpful in treating Alzheimer's and cancer. "Hyperbaric therapy reveals how little we know of the human body," she said, as quoted by Cristina Serra for the TWAS website (9 Nov. 2021). Sindi noted the role of mRNA technology in the treatment of COVID-19 and suggested that gene-editing techniques could offer a host of possibilities for treating other diseases. She even referenced research toward extending human life beyond 200 years. "This is biotechnology at its best," Sindi concluded. "We can target potentially any disease, give a better quality of life to people, and help them to be more productive. Achievements that are given for granted in developed countries, gradually move to the developing countries. Future goals will certainly be achieved, with hope for all human beings."

SUGGESTED READING

Al-Ghamry, Maali. "The Scientist Way." *Arab News*, 31 July 2004, www.arabnews.com/node/253130. Accessed 8 Apr. 2022.

"Biotechnologist and Entrepreneur: Dr. Hayat Sindi." *National Geographic*, 10 Sept. 2011, www.nationalgeographic.org/article/real-world-geography-dr-hayat-sindi/. Accessed 7 Apr. 2022.

"Hayat Sindi." *National Geographic*, 2011, www.nationalgeographic.org/find-explorers/hayat-sindi. Accessed 8 Apr. 2022.

Muhammad, Ifran, and Afshan Aziz. "Hayat Sindi to Women: Opt for a Career in Science." *Arab News*, 17 Jan. 2013, www.arabnews.com/saudi-arabia/hayat-sindi-women-opt-career-science. Accessed 8 Apr. 2022.

Pesta, Abigail. "Women in the World: Saudi Innovator Hayat Sindi's Science Breakthrough." *Daily Beast*, 13 July 2017, www.thedailybeast.com/women-in-the-world-saudi-innovator-hayat-sindis-science-breakthrough. Accessed 7 Apr. 2022.

Serra, Cristina. "Biotech Will Lead Us to a Better Path." *World Academy of Sciences (TWAS)*, 9 Nov. 2021, twas.org/article/biotech-will-lead-us-better-path. Accessed 9 Apr. 2022.

—*Molly Hagan*

Leni Sorensen

Born: July 20, 1942
Occupation: Culinary historian

Although some might wonder what it was like to cook an elaborate meal in an eighteenth- or nineteenth-century Virginia kitchen, Leni Sorensen knows for sure. "It's exhausting," she told *C-VILLE* (21 Oct. 2020). "You're in the smoke, constantly in the smoke. Your clothes smell of smoke, and your hair smells of smoke.

You burn the hell out of yourself. And all the pans are heavy, except the copper pots on the stew stove. And you're bending over all the time." As a culinary historian and teacher, Sorensen devoted her career to exploring the recipes and techniques of that earlier era. She has also worked to introduce the foods of that time, as well as valuable related skills such as home canning, to contemporary audiences.

A former folk singer and farmer, Sorensen moved to Virginia in the 1980s and began her career in historical education as a costumed reenactor at museums and historic sites in the region. She was particularly drawn to the culinary history of the area and to the work of the enslaved African Americans tasked with harvesting produce, slaughtering livestock, and preparing the elaborate meals for the wealthy owners of the local plantations. "I thought, 'Here we are in this place, and no one knows how to talk about slaves,'" she recalled to Lorraine Eaton for *The Virginian-Pilot* (1 Dec. 2013). "Shouldn't we be talking about the very people who made it happen?" Over the years Sorenson dedicated herself to doing just that, putting her knowledge and research findings to use as a research historian at Monticello, the home of US President Thomas Jefferson, and as a teacher and lecturer. Her guest appearances on television programs such as the 2021 documentary series *High on the Hog* introduced her to a broad new audience and drew further attention to the role of enslaved African Americans in developing the cuisine of the antebellum South.

EARLY LIFE

Leni Ashmore Sorensen was born Len Isabel Bedney in Los Angeles, California on July 20, 1942. Her mother, Lisa, was White and worked in a factory during Sorensen's early childhood, while her father, Billy, was a Black ranch worker who served in the US military during World War II. Her parents divorced when she was a young child, and her mother later remarried. Influenced by her mother, who was a skilled gardener, Sorensen began gardening herself as a child, gaining experience in the agricultural work that would shape her career and personal philosophy. "I was gardening since I was nine or ten years old," she told Melissa V. Pinard Rossow for the College of William & Mary website (13 Aug. 2011) about that period. "I always felt connected to rural people . . . people who are making their economy from the land. They have an element of self-reliance."

In addition to gardening, the young Sorensen developed an interest in food and cooking. She was particularly influenced by her stepfather, who was originally from New Orleans, Louisiana, and taught her about Southern foods. Those early experiences with cooking impressed upon her the importance of teaching children to cook and the connections between cooking and contributing to one's household. "You want to have as many people [as possible] in your household able to cook, which is why you want to teach kids to cook so that you get to be sick once in awhile," she explained to Margaret Leef for the *Charleston Gazette-Mail* (12 Feb. 2022). "There is nothing that kids can do but by God they can make a sandwich and they can make a bowl of soup, and they can feed someone in the family and that is how we help them give to the family." Also an avid dancer and musician during her early life, as a teenager Sorenson opted out of finishing her education at high school to pursue a career as a folk singer.

EARLY CAREER

Initially a solo singer and guitarist, Sorensen cofounded the folk ensemble the Womenfolk in 1963. The group released five albums between 1963 and 1966, and also toured widely, appearing in live shows and on television programs such as *The Ed Sullivan Show*. Sorensen and her bandmates primarily performed traditional songs or covers of existing tracks, and one such cover song, "Little Boxes," became a minor hit following its release in 1964. After the group disbanded, Sorensen returned to California and transitioned to musical theater for a time, appearing in a production of the musical *Hair*. She was drawn to food and cooking during the late 1960s and, for a time, operated a tamale-making business with a friend.

By the early 1970s Sorensen's career aspirations had evolved once again, and she left California to work on a farm in Canada. She subsequently moved to South Dakota, where she married and spent the next years working on her husband's family farm, milking cows and tending to other livestock as well as acres of vegetable plants. Soon, however, an economic crisis forced Sorensen and her family to leave their home. "In spring 1982, when we went in to re-up on our loan with the Farm Home Administration, we were informed that all agricultural loans below $120,000 were being unilaterally foreclosed," she recalled to Kendra Hamilton for *Virginia Living* (20 July 2010). "We had to get out."

EDUCATION AND HISTORICAL REENACTING

After departing their farm, Sorensen and her family, hopeful about her husband's prospects for finding more house construction and remodeling gigs, relocated to Virginia. There Sorensen found work as a costumed reenactor or interpreter, initially at President James Monroe's estate Ash Lawn-Highland and then at several different museums and historic sites. Often tasked with demonstrating household skills such as cooking and soapmaking in the course of her work as a reenactor, she became increasingly interested in the lives of the people who had worked in Virginia's historic houses during the eighteenth and nineteenth centuries, many of whom were enslaved African Americans. "My focus is always 'who were the people?'" she told Eaton. "If a text says 'the food was carried,' it becomes 'the food was carried by whom?'"

Sorensen's growing interest in history led her to enroll as an adult undergraduate in history at Mary Baldwin College (which later became a university) in 1988. "I always tell my children I lived my life backwards," she told Rossow about her decision, "because I didn't start college until I was 46." With a bachelor's degree in history in hand in 1992, she went on to enroll at the College of William & Mary, where she completed a master's degree in American studies in 1997. Following her submission of the dissertation "Absconded: Fugitive Slaves in the 'Daybook of the Richmond Police Guard, 1834–1844,'" she earned a doctorate in the same discipline from William & Mary in 2005.

CULINARY AND AFRICAN AMERICAN HISTORY

As a culinary historian, Sorensen performed a great deal of her research at Monticello, where she had put on presentations since 1993. In 2006, she was given the title of African American research historian and was able to search the historic home's library for references to the meals once prepared and served there. During the lifetime of the home's most prominent owner, US President Thomas Jefferson, the kitchen was staffed by highly skilled enslaved

African Americans such as James Hemings, who had trained in French cooking during his time with Jefferson in France. "They were not house cooks; they were indeed chefs by any standard," Sorensen told Eaton about Hemings and those like him. "To call them anything but chefs is to do a disservice." In her role at Monticello she contributed to major historical projects such as an exhibition on slavery at the estate, held at the Smithsonian Institution's National Museum of American History in 2012.

Sorensen worked regularly in museums and historic sites until mid-2012, when she retired to focus on her independent work. One major independent project involved cooking all of the recipes included in *The Virginia House-Wife*, a cookbook published by plantation owner and later boarding house owner Mary Randolph in 1824. Sorensen was interested not only in the recipes themselves but also in the essential yet minimally documented enslaved people who would have been responsible for following them. As part of her Cooking Mary Randolph project, in the 2010s Sorensen published the short books *Through the Seasons: A Baker's Dozen of Breads and Sweets from* The Virginia House-Wife and *Through the Seasons: A Garden of Recipes from* The Virginia House-Wife, each of which presents recipes from the original cookbook alongside Sorensen's commentary. Though primarily engaged in independent research and educational initiatives after 2012, at times she took on projects at museums and historic houses. During the coronavirus disease 2019 (COVID-19) pandemic declared in 2020, for instance, she appeared in online videos for Monticello in which she demonstrated how cooking was historically performed there during Jefferson's lifetime. She also gained notice from a far wider audience in 2021, when she appeared in the Netflix documentary series *High on the Hog: How African American Cuisine Transformed America*.

PUBLIC OUTREACH

In addition to working for several museums and educational institutions, Sorensen long considered her own farmstead, Indigo House, a venue in which to tutor small groups of visitors about food and history. Among other projects, she became known for hosting dinner events in which attendees would eat meals based on historical recipes and learn about the circumstances in which the dishes were originally made and the people who made them. For Sorensen, the dinner party format was particularly well suited for that kind of education. "I like making connections," she explained to Leef. "For years I've done food presentations out in public settings over open fires and in historic kitchens and I've found when people are in the smell and anticipating the taste, they are more open and responsive to the information because all their sensory receptors are open." While opportunities to host in-person events were limited during the early months of the COVID-19 pandemic, she eventually resumed hosting dinners.

Alongside teaching about intertwined histories of Southern food and African American life, Sorensen remained particularly dedicated to practicing and teaching what she termed "rural life skills," which include skills such as gardening, raising livestock, and canning. She taught classes in canning at her home in Virginia and in 2014 published the book *The Gen-Xers, Millennials & Hipster Guide: 6 Basic Things to Know about Sharing a Kitchen with Housemates—with Recipes*, a work emphasizing the importance of key kitchen and household food-management skills. In addition to granting her a larger platform as a culinary historian, the media attention resulting from her 2021 appearance in *High on the Hog* provided her with further opportunities to highlight the ways in which knowing such skills can combat food insecurity and allow practitioners to help others. "Being prepared helps those in need," she told Leef. "It is an essential kind of helping. Having our own bounty means we really can give a half a cup of sugar to our neighbor . . . and being able to share food I think is one of the great graces."

PERSONAL LIFE

Sorensen married twice while living in California and had two children during that period. Later, in the 1970s, she married carpenter Kip Sorensen, whom she met after publishing a personal ad in the periodical *Mother Earth News*. She and Kip had two children together and remained married until Kip's death in 2017. She lives in Crozet, Virginia, at her farmstead, Indigo House.

SUGGESTED READING

"Carving Out History: Leni Sorensen Bridges the Gap between Kitchen and Table at Monticello." *C-VILLE*, 21 Oct. 2020, www.c-ville.com/carving-out-history-leni-sorensen-bridges-the-gap-between-kitchen-and-table-at-monticello/. Accessed 7 Mar. 2022.

Eaton, Lorraine. "Virginia Woman Works Her Way through 1824 Cookbook." *The Virginian-Pilot*, 1 Dec. 2013, www.pilotonline.com/food-drink/article_1badcdcd-e293-561a-9c20-466c8b22bf70.html. Accessed 7 Mar. 2022.

Hamilton, Kendra. "Living by Hand." *Virginia Living*, 20 July 2010, www.virginialiving.com/house-and-garden/living-by-hand/. Accessed 7 Mar. 2022.

Leef, Margaret. "A Taste of the Past: A Food Historian Discovers Hidden Cooks." *Charleston Gazette-Mail*, 12 Feb. 2022, www.wvgazettemail.com/life/a-taste-of-the-past-a-food-historian-discovers-hidden-cooks/article_8fd12fb9-7f94-599f-b047-095dd7d67d46.html. Accessed 7 Mar. 2022.

McNeill, Brian. "At VCU, a Culinary Historian Describes the Human Costs of Serving Meals to Early Virginia Elites." *VCU News*, 7 Feb. 2020, news.vcu.edu/article/At_VCU_a_culinary_historian_describes_the_human_costs_of_serving. Accessed 7 Mar. 2022.

Rossow, Melissa V. Pinard. "Cultivating Life." *William & Mary*, 13 Aug. 2011, www.wm.edu/as/news/as-news-archive/2011-12/cultivating-life.php. Accessed 7 Mar. 2022.

Severson, Kim. "Food Scholar, Folk Singer, Blunt Speaker: The Many Lives of Leni Sorensen." *The New York Times*, 21 Sept. 2021, www.nytimes.com/2021/09/21/dining/leni-sorensen-food-scholar-historian.html. Accessed 7 Mar. 2022.

—*Joy Crelin*

Katrina Spade

Born: September 9, 1977
Occupation: Entrepreneur and death care advocate

Katrina Spade was a graduate student in her thirties when she suddenly realized that around the time her two young children would be middle-aged people, she was likely to die. Though she had no reason to think her death was imminent, she continued to reflect on her own mortality in the days that followed and began researching what her family would do with her body once she died. She learned that despite a $20 billion death industry in the United States, there were really only two options for her future corpse: burial or cremation. While finishing her master's degree in architecture, Spade decided to make it her mission to find a more economic and environmentally friendly death ceremony. She subsequently launched the Urban Death Project, a techno-biological initiative that enabled people to recompose into Earth, and in the process became one of the leading voices in the burgeoning "alt-death" movement rethinking American death-care and funerary culture.

In addition to improving the options that people have for their bodies once they have passed, Spade also sought to change the way that she and many other Americans think about life in relation to death. She reflected on how her work has impacted her perspective in an interview with Vanessa Quirk for *Metropolis* (24 Feb. 2017), stating, "Overall it's given me more appreciation for being alive, honestly. I think about death and death care all day every day. There was an adjustment period. But overall, it's been really positive. It's not only increased my appreciation of life, but imparted the realization that life is short."

EARLY LIFE

Katrina Mogielnicki Spade was born on September 9, 1977. Her formative years were spent in a small, rural community in New Hampshire where neighbors shared an old tractor and made their own maple syrup. The belief that death was simply a natural part of life's cycle was something that Spade accepted at a young age as her family raised animals for slaughter. Her parents' careers further amplified this perspective—her father worked as a physician and her mother as a physician's assistant, which meant that the human body and death were regular topics at home.
Spade developed a deep respect for the natural world from her mother, who also worked as an environmental activist. "We weren't religious," Spade told Brendan Kiley for *The Stranger* (3 Mar. 2015), "but we saw nature as somehow

Photo by Katrinaspade,
via Wikimedia Commons.

spiritual." When developers planned to build a dam in a nearby river that would flood the island home of the rare cobblestone tiger beetle, Spade's mother campaigned to make the beetle their town's official insect and later also made the dwarf wedge mussel the town mollusk. After journalists started reporting on her efforts, the developers became so afraid of bad publicity that they decided to walk away from the dam altogether. The experience helped Spade recognize just how significant the impact of human life on the environment could be.

STUDYING ECOLOGY AND ARCHITECTURE

After graduating from high school, Spade went on to earn a BA in anthropology at Haverford College, a small liberal arts college in Pennsylvania. She then followed her girlfriend to San Francisco, where she worked on a study at the Stanford School of Medicine that examined the impact of long-distance running on people's bones. After her grandfather's dementia diagnosis, she and her girlfriend moved in with her grandmother in rural Vermont, where she enrolled at the nearby Yestermorrow Design/Build School in Waitsfield. There she studied ecological thinking, whole-systems design, permaculture, and other environmental ideas. As part of her program she built a bioenergy system, known as a Pain Mound, that was capable of generating energy for an entire farm while it turned waste into nutrient-rich compost.

In 2011 Spade was accepted into the Master of Architecture program at the University of Massachusetts, Amherst, with the intention of integrating the sustainable practices that she learned at Yestermorrow into urban designs. It was around this time that she had the epiphany that she would not always be there for her children. "When you have babies, you can see them age physically," she revealed in her interview with Kiley. "I thought, 'If they're growing up, I'm going down. Holy cr——, I'm going to die!' Mundane, I know. But I wondered, 'What would my family do with me when I die?'"

After conducting research on what options were available for her corpse, Spade quickly discovered how limited, monopolized, and environmentally unsafe the death-care industry really was. In addition to taking up valuable plots of land, burials result in large amounts of toxic embalming fluid being dumped into the ground every year, along with sizable quantities of metal and concrete. Meanwhile, cremation produces a significant amount of carbon emissions and strips the human body of all the potential nutrients that it could reintroduce back into the earth. Spade decided to brainstorm a solution that better aligned to her own values as someone who not only sought to preserve nature but wanted her body to be returned to it.

When she learned of a practice called livestock mortality composting, used by some farmers to turn their dead animals into compost, Spade wondered if the same could be done with human remains. She decided to tap into the power of microbes as she had done with the Pain Mounds at Yestermorrow and integrate bacteria into her solution to America's death-care problem. She was also inspired by "natural burials," which use simple materials like pine and biodegradable cloth and were becoming more popular in rural areas; Spade wanted to find a similar solution that she could implement in urban areas where space did not exist for natural burials. In 2013, she completed her thesis paper, titled "Of Dirt and Decomposition: Proposing a Place for the Urban Dead." It included the ecological design for a core composting system to turn people into soil.

URBAN DEATH PROJECT

After graduating from UMass Amherst in 2013, Spade took jobs as an architect while working on her "human composting project" on nights and weekends. In 2014, she submitted her proposal to the Echoing Green Fellowship and was one of thirty people selected from thousands of applicants to become a two-year fellow. This enabled her to create the nonprofit Urban Death Project (UDP) and work on it full time by assembling a team of soil scientists and engineers to experiment with the idea of a human composting system. In 2015, Spade conducted a feasibility study with Western Carolina University's department of forensic anthropology. After the process proved to be a success, she drummed up publicity and support by launching a UDP Kickstarter campaign.

For Spade, garnering support for her project was no easy feat, as many people found the concept of human composting to be alien and even disturbing. From her research, however, Spade learned that such reactions were relatively new when considered in the context of history. For tens of thousands of years, people would wash their dead and lay them directly in the ground on a family burial site. In the United States, however, that tradition changed during the Civil War when there was a huge demand to bring dead soldiers' bodies back to their families so they could be given proper funerals. The practice of embalming was subsequently developed, which enabled undertakers capable of the practice to monopolize the death-care industry. Because most Americans do not want to think about death, they continue to rely on undertakers' costly suggestions instead of exploring other options.

Spade felt that people would ultimately be receptive to her idea if she provided them with a beautiful space where they could perform personal goodbye rituals—something UDP aimed to do. She also sought to help people get over their hesitations and fears by educating them on why human composting was a superior option to casket burials and cremation. Her 2016 TED Talk on the subject, entitled "When I Die, Recompose Me," proved popular and the video of the presentation would go on to earn over 1 million views. Spade explained one of the core ideas behind her TED Talk with Brendan Kiley for the *Seattle Times* (28 Oct. 2016): "Our bodies are full of potential. We have nutrients in us and there's no way we should be packed into a box that doesn't let us go into the earth. Decay and decomposition are amazing processes we are terrified of because they might seem icky and scary—your body aging, your food rotting—but without those processes, we would not be alive."

Ultimately, this became one of Spade's primary selling points for the UDP. While topsoil takes centuries to develop, industrial farming practices can use it up in less than two years. A 200-pound person, meanwhile, can produce the same amount of nitrogen, phosphorous, and potassium as a cubic yard of cottonseed fertilizer and in turn can help ameliorate the global erosion of nutrient-rich soil. In this way, people's last gesture could be, as Spade explained to Kiley, "at the very least benign, or even beneficial."

RECOMPOSE

In 2017, Spade decided to relaunch her project as a public-benefit corporation known as Recompose. It proved to be a turning point in her venture, as the rebranding helped raise the funding necessary for building infrastructure, hiring experts, and increasing publicity. Instead of placing bodies in a collective, multistory "core," as she had proposed in the UDP, Recompose planned to put each body in an individual vessel—a change that seemed to make the idea of human composting more palatable to outsiders.

Spade continued to fundraise, eventually raising about $6.75 million. This allowed Recompose to launch a pilot study on natural organic reduction (NOR)—another, less harsh term used to describe human composting—in 2018 with the Washington State University soil science department. Using six donor bodies, they were able to prove that the NOR process removes any pathogens and metals from human remains that could be harmful to the environment. That same year, Spade received the Ashoka Fellowship for spearheading a "dramatically new approach that reconnects death to natural cycles of life and reengages people through meaningful participation."

In order for Recompose to launch, however, it had one more hurdle to face: the legalization of human composting. Spade won the support of many researchers, professors, and funeral directors, as well as Washington State senator Jamie Pedersen. Consequently, "Senate Bill 5001: Concerning Human Remains" was passed in both Washington state's House of Representatives and Senate in 2019. That spring, Governor Jay Inslee signed the bill into law, making Washington the first state to legalize NOR. Colorado and Oregon followed suit in 2021, and legislators introduced bills concerning NOR legalization in several other states as well.

After close to a decade of work, Spade opened Recompose's headquarters outside of Seattle in late 2020 and started accepting human bodies for composting. Just as she had always envisioned, its funerary services combined science, beautiful design, and human emotion. Families could perform their desired rituals and ceremonies before the Recompose staff laid the body of their loved one in a stainless-steel vessel where it is covered with organic material. (During the COVID-19 pandemic, families participated in that process via video.) Over the next six to eight weeks, the body would be transformed into nutrient-rich soil. Family members could then pick up their loved one's remains or donate them to the nearby Bells Mountain conservation forest.

In an interview with Manoush Zomorodi for *NPR* (11 Mar. 2022), Spade described the beauty she and many other people saw in the handling of death at Recompose, remarking, "What happens during the composting process is our molecules are rearranged, and we cease to be human. And that is pretty powerful, I think, to just think about truly going back to the earth and then kind of dissipating."

SUGGESTED READING

Kiley, Brendan. "The Architect Who Wants to Redesign Being Dead." *The Stranger*, 3 Mar. 2015, www.thestranger.com/features/feature/2015/03/03/21792773/the-architect-who-wants-to-redesign-being-dead. Accessed 8 Apr. 2022.

___. "Recompose, the First Human-Composting Funeral Home in the U.S., Is Now Open for Business." *The Seattle Times*, 22 Jan. 2021, www.seattletimes.com/life/recompose-the-first-human-compositing-funeral-home-in-the-u-s-is-now-open-for-business/. Accessed 12 Apr. 2022.

___. "Seattle Could Get an Urban Death Project Human Composter in Just 7 Years." *The Seattle Times*, 28 Oct. 2016, www.seattletimes.com/life/from-corpse-to-compost-the-urban-death-projects-modest-proposal/. Accessed 8 Apr. 2022.

Ross, Robyn. "Inside the Machine That Will Turn Your Corpse into Compost."*WIRED,* Condé Nast, 25 Oct. 2016, www.wired. com/2016/10/inside-machine-will-turn-corpse-compost/. Accessed 8 Apr. 2022.

Spade, Katrina. "Katrina Spade: Could Our Bodies Help New Life Grow after We Die?" Interview by Manoush Zomorodi. *TED Radio Hour,* National Public Radio, 11 Mar. 2022, www.npr.org/transcripts/1085814515. Accessed 9 Apr. 2022.

—. "The Urban Death Project: Bringing Death Back into the Urban Realm." Interview by Vanessa Quirk. *Metropolis,* 24 Feb. 2017, metropolismag.com/viewpoints/the-urban-death-project-bringing-death-back-into-the-urban-realm. Accessed 8 Apr. 2022.

—*Emily Turner*

Isabella Springmühl Tejada

Born: October 23, 1996
Occupation: Fashion designer

When models wearing Isabella Springmühl Tejada's creations strut down the runway, her pieces—blouses covered with floral embroidery, skirts made of colorful Guatemalan textiles, and artfully crafted ponchos, among others—are a vibrant celebration of her Central American heritage. Since 2016, Springmühl Tejada has been taking the fashion world by storm, becoming the first designer with Down syndrome to exhibit her creations at the high-profile London Fashion Week. That same year, her emerging clothing line, Down to Xjabelle, which aims to make fashion more inclusive of people with disabilities, earned her a spot on the BBC's list of the one hundred most influential and inspirational women of the year.

With her designs shown on runways all over the world, including Panama, Mexico, Italy, and England, the young fashion designer has found success, even though it seemed improbable initially. "The truth is, people were critical and didn't believe I could do things. I was discriminated against," she told Ahmen Khawaja for *BBC News* (29 Nov. 2016). However, every rejection only fueled her desire to continue her journey within the fashion industry, which has led her ever-expanding clothing line to become a reference for inclusive fashion. As she said to Khawaja, "I had the love of my family and my friends and that helped me to make my dream come true."

EARLY LIFE AND EDUCATION

Isabella Springmühl Tejada was born on October 23, 1996, in Guatemala City, Guatemala. The fourth and youngest child in her family, she was born with Down syndrome, a genetic condition caused by the presence of an extra chromosome that causes developmental and intellectual delays.

When Springmühl Tejada was three years old, her parents enrolled her at Centro de Enseñanza Educare in the neighboring town of San Lucas Sacatepéquez, where she would spend the next fifteen years getting a personalized, adaptive education. As she relayed in her 2018 TED Talk, it was not always easy for her to keep up with her classmates; nonetheless, she looks back at this time fondly, feeling always included in school activities and supported by receiving the help of a supplementary teacher.

At home, Springmühl Tejada exhibited a creative streak from an early age, spending her time flipping through the glossy pages of fashion magazines, mesmerized. Soon, she began drawing designs on paper and creating outfits for her dolls, utilizing colorful fabrics and pins. Following in the footsteps of her grandmother, Blanca de Tejada—a fashion designer who once had her own clothing brand called Xjabelle—she was also influenced by watching her mother tailor her clothes to fit her body shape. "It was difficult for me to get clothes," she told Khawaja. "[People with Down syndrome] have a different body constitution; we are shorter, wider, or very thin. My mother always had to fix the clothes she bought for me."

As she grew up, she became more aware of the lack of clothing available for people with Down syndrome, which became a catalyst for creating her future clothing line, Down to Xjabelle. "I decided to design clothes that fit people with Down's syndrome," she revealed to Khawaja. "Plus I really love Guatemalan textiles and the diversity of colors and textures they represent."

PROVING PEOPLE WRONG

By the time Springmühl Tejada graduated from Centro de Enseñanza Educare in 2014, her mind was made up about pursuing a career in the fashion industry. However, when she tried to enroll at two different universities, both institutions denied her admission, citing that coursework would be too challenging because of her condition. "I was furious that these institutions did not give Isabella a chance to learn," Springmühl Tejada's mother, Isabel Tejada, said to Khawaja. "It was so sad, but it made her change everything."

Proving that her desire to learn was far greater than any rejection, Springmühl Tejada began attending Las Tijeras, a sewing academy for women, where she not only learned how to use a sewing machine but also how to cut and creatively assemble pieces of clothing. She soon supplemented this hands-on learning experience with knowledge on the use of fashion design computer programs such as Virtual Fashion. With her newly acquired skills, Springmühl Tejada commenced sewing outfits for worry dolls, tiny dolls traditionally used by children who tell them their fears and place them under their pillows at night. Soon, she graduated to larger dolls she made herself. "She created life-sized dolls and dressed them in the colorful embroidered jackets and ponchos that she's now famous for," Tejada told Khawaja.

As her skills developed, so did her sense of style, and her fashion vision came to life through the Guatemalan vintage textiles, colorful floral embroidery, and playful pompoms and fringe featured in her work. When the Museo Ixchel de Traje Indígena in Guatemala City gave her the opportunity to display her designs in a 2015 event called *Guate Extraordinaria*, she worked in concert with Guatemalan Indigenous artists to create a collection of vibrant accessories, bags, ponchos, and dresses—a homage to her Central American roots. The exhibition was an enormous success for Springmühl Tejada: not only was every single piece of her collection sold, but the platform gave her the exposure she needed to kickstart her career as a fashion designer.

LONDON FASHION WEEK

Though the Museo Ixchel de Traje Indígena brought local attention to Springmühl Tejada, the February 2016 London Fashion Week, a fashion show featuring the industry's top designers, made her a globally recognized personality. As her designs made their way down the runway, emanating Guatemalan folklore, she became the first person with Down syndrome to exhibit a clothing collection at such a high-profile event. Moreover, at only nineteen years of age, she was among the youngest emergent designers of the show.

After gaining success with her collection at London Fashion Week—where, as she later revealed in her 2018 TED Talk, she felt deeply loved, supported, and respected by event organizers and the public—Springmühl Tejada endeavored to start her own clothing line. A combination of the words "Down," a reference to her genetic condition, and "Xjabelle," in honor of her late grandmother's brand of clothing, Down to Xjabelle became a project guided by the young fashion designer's passion and history. Aside from seeking to represent Guatemalan colors and traditions through her designs, Springmühl Tejada's mission was to make more clothing available for people with Down syndrome, which, as she knew from experience, was difficult to find.

Another highlight of 2016 came in October when the BBC television network named Springmühl Tejada to its 100 Women list—a list celebrating the most influential and inspirational women of the year. According to the BBC website, the women who are chosen for the list are "those who are leading change and making a difference during these turbulent times," qualities that the young fashion designer firmly demonstrated through her Down to Xjabelle brand. The only woman with Down syndrome to make the list and one of eight Latinas—including Mexican journalist Carmen Aristegui and Brazilian soccer player Marta Vieira da Silva—she told Khawaja about her big dreams for her clothing line and how she hoped to use this opportunity to inspire people like her: "I want to export my brand Down to Xjabelle all over the world. I want people to know my designs and to know that people with Down's syndrome can do what they set out to do. I want to be able to live on my own and be 100 percent self-sufficient. I want people to know me for my work and what is inside my heart."

INCLUSIVE FASHION AND TED TALK

A year later, in 2017, Springmühl Tejada continued to gain recognition on an international scale when she participated in a fashion event in Guadalajara, Mexico. On this occasion, her collection, which she called *Volar* (Fly), featured twenty-five pieces—a mix of blouses, skirts, belts, and vests—drawing from the rich Mayan tradition of Guatemala, as had become the signature look of her brand. Demonstrating that her line is inclusive of people with different body types, including individuals with disabilities, her colorful pieces were worn on the runway by models with disabilities, creating more awareness for the inclusive fashion movement. When Springmühl Tejada showed the same collection in her home country later that year, it was the first time an inclusive runway was used in Guatemala.

In February 2018, Springmühl Tejada delivered an inspiring TED Talk entitled "Moda sin Obstáculos" [Fashion without Obstacles], which has amassed thousands of views. Her talk focused on her life story, particularly the adversities and setbacks she encountered early on in her career as she tried to enroll at universities to learn about fashion design and how her attempts were met with rejection. "They said 'no' to me," Springmühl Tejada said to the audience. "Why? All because I had Down syndrome, imagine how it felt. Because of the discrimination I faced, I thought my dream would not be realized. But I overcame it." By the end of her talk, when she told the audience that if she possessed the ability to be a fighter, so too could anybody else, she received a standing ovation.

More fashion shows featuring Springmühl Tejada's clothing line followed in 2019, including in Panama, Miami, and Chicago, where audiences continued to be receptive of her designs. Her ability to overcome so many adversities and discrimination to become a globally known fashion designer, whose creations have become a reference for inclusive fashion, is something to be admired. Furthermore, Springmühl Tejada has provided jobs to more than one hundred Indigenous Guatemalan women, who have helped her to bring her creative designs to life through her brand. Indeed, there is no stopping Springmühl Tejada in her rise in the fashion industry; after all, as she emphasized in her TED Talk, fashion design changed her life.

PERSONAL LIFE

When Springmühl Tejada is not busy designing clothing, she likes to sing opera, dance Zumba, and practice horseback riding.

SUGGESTED READING

Arevalo, Rita. "Isabella Springmuhl." *Look Magazine*, 27 Oct. 2015, www.lookmagazine.com/2015/10/27/isabella-springmuhl/. Accessed 23 Feb. 2022.

Fragoso, Yahir. "Isabella Springmühl, la Diseñadora Que le Dio Espacio a los Modelos con Discapacidad." ["Isabella Springmühl, the Designer Who Gave Space to Models with Disabilities."] *El Sol de México*, 3 Aug. 2021. *Google Translate*, www.elsoldemexico-com-mx.translate.goog/circulos/moda/down-to-xjabelle-la-linea-de-isabella-springmuhl-que-lucha-contra-los-prejuicios-en-la-moda-7041422.html?_x_tr_sl=auto&_x_tr_tl=en&_x_tr_hl=en-US&_x_tr_pto=wapp. Accessed 9 Feb. 2022.

"Isabella Springmuhl: La Primera Diseñadora de Moda con Síndrome de Down." ["Isabella Springmuhl: The First Fashion Designer with Down Syndrome."] *Diario de Finanzas*, 6 Jan. 2020. *Google Translate*, eldiariodefinanzas-com.translate.goog/isabella-springmuhl-la-primera-disenadora-de-moda-con-sindrome-de-down/?_x_tr_sl=auto&_x_tr_tl=en&_x_tr_hl=en-US&_x_tr_pto=wapp. Accessed 9 Feb. 2022.

Khawaja, Ahmen. "100 Women 2016: Designing Clothes for People with Down's Syndrome." *BBC News*, 29 Nov. 2016, www.bbc.com/news/world-latin-america-38132503. Accessed 30 Jan. 2022.

Ola, Ana Lucía. "La Diseñadora Guatemalteca Isabella Springmuhl Crea un Arcoíris." ["Guatemalan Designer Isabella Springmuhl Creates a Rainbow."] *Prensa Libre*, 23 Nov. 2016. *Google Translate*, www-prensalibre-com.translate.goog/vida/moda-y-estilo/la-diseadora-guatemalteca-isabella-springmuhl-crea-un-arcoiris/?_x_tr_sl=auto&_x_tr_tl=en&_x_tr_hl=en-US&_x_tr_pto=wapp. Accessed 30 Jan. 2022.

Springmuhl Tejada, Isabella. "Moda sin Obstáculos." ["Fashion without Obstacles."]

TED, Feb. 2018, www.ted.com/talks/isabella_springmuhl_tejada_moda_sin_obstaculos. Accessed 30 Jan. 2022.

—*Maria del Pilar Guzman*

Hailee Steinfeld

Born: December 11, 1996
Occupation: Actor and singer

At the tender age of thirteen, despite a sparse résumé, Hailee Steinfeld was selected out of a reported fifteen thousand other young hopefuls to play the part of Mattie Ross in the 2010 remake of the classic 1969 Western *True Grit*. Her star-making performance as a spunky teen who recruits an alcoholic gunslinger to avenge her father's death earned her audience praise as well as an Academy Award nod for best supporting actress. Subsequently, she made a career out of playing angst-ridden teenagers in several films, including *Romeo and Juliet* (2013), *Pitch Perfect 2* (2015), *Term Life* (2016), *The Edge of Seventeen* (2016), and *Bumblebee* (2018). Beginning in 2019, she graduated to more mature roles, playing the title role in *Dickinson* (2019–21), Apple TV+'s three-season comedy series about the real-life nineteenth-century poet Emily Dickinson, and costarring in the Disney+ Marvel superhero miniseries *Hawkeye* (2021). Meanwhile, having always been passionate about music as well, she juggled a parallel career in the music industry following her cinematic display of her vocal talents in *Pitch Perfect 2*. With a foot firmly in both creative worlds after the release of her second EP, *Half Written Story* (2020), she noted that she felt particularly fortunate regarding the shape that her professional career had taken. "I feel so lucky that I get to do what I love," she told Jeff Nelson for *People* (Jan. 2021). "Everything that comes along with it is just a bonus for me."

EARLY LIFE AND LAUNCHING AN ACTING CAREER

Hailee Steinfeld was born on December 11, 1996, to parents Cheri, who worked in interior design, and Peter, employed as a personal fitness trainer, in the Los Angeles, California, neighborhood of Tarzana. She was raised in Agoura Hills before relocating to Thousand Oaks with her parents and older brother,

Griffin. Her interest in acting was first sparked at eight years old, in part through a cousin who had landed gigs on television commercials. A childhood friend was also involved in school theater, and she witnessed one of her performances. "I was sitting a few rows back from the stage," Steinfeld recalled to Karen Lindell for the *Ventura County Star* (24 Dec. 2010). "To watch somebody I knew and grew up with do that, it was just so cool to me. It made me believe it was possible to do it." At the same time, she dabbled noncommittally in activities such as sports and dancing and also found herself drawn to performing as a singer, often belting out lyrics on a microphone and amplifier gifted by her parents.

After a year of studying at Cynthia Bain's Young Actor Studio (CBYAS) in Studio City, the nine-year-old Steinfeld secured an agent, subsequently landing a 2006 Soda Pop Girls commercial and a 2007 episode of the Fox comedy *Back to You*. Around 2008, she transitioned to homeschooling, after having gone to local elementary and middle schools. Next came roles in the award-winning student short *She's a Fox* (2009) as well as the Young Artists Ensemble's 2009 production of *The Witch Academy*, and an appearance in a Kmart back-to-school "blingitude" television commercial.

Photo by Gage Skidmore, via Wikimedia Commons

MAKING HISTORY WITH *TRUE GRIT*

In 2010 Steinfeld continued to hone her skills in front of the camera, appearing in more short films as well as the short-lived Fox sitcom *Sons of Tucson*. Her big break came when the thirteen-year-old submitted a self-taped audition for a new film adaptation of Charles Portis's 1968 novel *True Grit*, about a teenage girl who enlists an alcoholic bounty hunter to track down her father's killer. Though she had missed a nationwide casting call involving thousands of hopefuls, her tape submission led to auditioning twice in person within a five-week span while donning nineteenth-century frontier garb. At a subsequent meeting with the film's directors, Joel and Ethan Coen, she read lines with the male lead, Jeff Bridges, as part of a chemistry test. Following an impressive audition, she was officially cast as Mattie Ross in February 2010. To prepare for the Western drama, Steinfeld, who had already readied herself for the audition process by viewing the 1969 big-screen version, spent time refining her horseback-riding abilities, accompanying her father to a shooting range, and reading Portis's novel. Her acting coach also guided her in mastering a Texas dialect.

The fourteen-year-old Steinfeld made history in January 2011, becoming one of the youngest ever to receive an Oscar nomination for best supporting actress. Despite losing out on that award to Melissa Leo for *The Fighter* (2010), Steinfeld claimed best supporting actress honors from several regional film critics associations. Her performance also earned nominations from the likes of the British Academy of Film and Television Arts (BAFTA) and the Screen Actors Guild (SAG), among others. Amid her meteoric rise to fame, she decided to take a yearlong hiatus. "It took me that long to kind of come off that experience and sort of really figure out what it was that I wanted to do next and what I wanted it to be about," she shared with Nicholas Bostick for the *Dallas Observer* (1 Nov. 2016). "But making the right decision and working on something that was going to challenge me, that's really been my goal with any decision I feel I made since then; finding something that will challenge and will better me as a person and as an artist."

Steinfeld returned to the big screen in 2013, appearing in the films *Hateship Loveship* and *Romeo & Juliet* as well as the blockbuster adaptation of Orson Scott Card's 1985 sci-fi novel *Ender's Game*. Then came a string of largely forgettable films: Kevin Costner's spy thriller *3 Days to Kill* (2014), the Western ensembles *The Homesman* (2014) and *The Keeping Room* (2014), and the coming-of-age drama *Ten Thousand Saints*, which premiered at the 2015 Sundance Film Festival.

HITTING THE RIGHT NOTE ON- AND OFF-SCREEN

In 2015 Steinfeld appeared opposite Anna Kendrick in *Pitch Perfect 2*, the sequel to the 2012 sleeper hit, and headlined the teen spy caper *Barely Lethal* (2015). In the former film, Steinfeld played legacy college student Emily Junk, who joins her mother's former a cappella group, the Barden Bellas. The role gave her the opportunity to exhibit her vocal skills, most notably her on-screen version of the Jessie J. ballad "Flashlight." *Pitch Perfect 2* was a major commercial success and boosted her path to mainstream stardom.

Also in 2015, Steinfeld started to establish herself in the music industry. After appearing in the star-studded, action-packed music video for Taylor Swift's single "Bad Blood," she performed alongside Shawn Mendes in the acoustic music video duet for "Stitches." Having recently signed with Republic Records, in early August she released the pop ballad "Love Myself," originally regarded as an empowerment anthem and later also viewed as an ode to self-pleasure. "I've always been incredibly moved and inspired by music, so I was excited by the idea of being part of a song that can make people feel something," she told Nick Levine in an interview for *Vice* (5 Oct. 2015).

By November 2015, Steinfeld had released the four-track EP *Haiz*, which eventually spawned another hit in 2016: "Rock Bottom," a revamped duet with the Joe Jonas–fronted funk-pop band DNCE. "Starving," a popular collaboration with Zedd and electronic music duo Grey, also came out that year. To promote her debut album, she served as the opening act for Meghan Trainor's 2016 US tour.

GARNERING ACCLAIM FOR *THE EDGE OF SEVENTEEN*

Meanwhile, Steinfeld continued to land high-profile roles alongside some of Hollywood's biggest stars. After playing the estranged daughter of a fugitive in Vince Vaughn's crime-thriller *Term Life* (2016), she appeared opposite Woody Harrelson in the coming-of-age drama *The Edge of Seventeen* (2016), earning critical raves for her portrayal of a snarky, socially awkward high school student grappling with the onset of puberty and loss of her only close friendship. "Ever since her big-screen debut . . . Hailee Steinfeld has gathered confidence as a performer, and *The Edge of Seventeen* is her breakthrough," Owen Gleiberman wrote for *Variety* (17 Sept. 2016). For her effort, Steinfeld earned Critics Choice Award and Golden Globe Award nominations.

In April 2017 Steinfeld resumed her musical career with the release of the electropop track "Most Girls," which eventually became a top-thirty hit on the *Billboard Adult Pop Airplay chart*. That fall, she collaborated with country music duo Florida Georgia Line and Swedish DJ Alesso on the tropical house-pop tune "Let Me Go," which topped the *Billboard* Dance/Electronic Digital Song Sales chart. After closing out the year by reprising her role as Emily in *Pitch Perfect 3*, her next hit single, "Capital Letters," cowritten with singer Ellie Goulding and producer BloodPop, was featured on the 2018 *Fifty Shades Freed* soundtrack and reached the twelfth spot on the *Billboard* Bubbling Under Hot 100. Returning to the road that year as well, she was the opener for Katy Perry in the United Kingdom and Charlie Puth in North America.

CEMENTING HER STAR STATUS

Steinfeld's next big-screen appearance came in a spin-off of the live-action *Transformers* series: the sci-fi adventure flick *Bumblebee* (2018), in which she played an eighteen-year-old who befriends the title character, a shape-shifting intergalactic robot disguised as a yellow Volkswagen Beetle, while grieving the loss of her father. Along with her starring role, she contributed the soundtrack tune "Back to Life." In another blockbuster role, she lent her voice to the character of Gwen Stacy in *Spider-Man: Into the Spider-Verse*, a Marvel animated film (2018) that received best animated feature honors at the Academy Awards, Golden Globes, and Critics Choice Awards.

By March 2019 Steinfeld had wrapped filming on the first season of *Dickinson*, a historical comedy-drama series for streaming service Apple TV+ chronicling the early life of renowned nineteenth-century poet Emily Dickinson, including her professional writing ambitions, defiance of social and gender norms, and fascination with mortality. "Overall, after playing this character, fully embodying her and learning to appreciate her and her work, I have a more fearless approach to my art in all aspects," she told Hilary Lewis in an interview for *The Hollywood Reporter* (20 Nov. 2019). When *Dickinson* premiered that November, it focused on the aspiring poet's quest for recognition, the contentious relationship with her traditional father, and the love triangle involving her brother and childhood best friend. The series earned critical raves, taking home a prestigious Peabody Award in June 2020, a month after Steinfeld's second EP, *Half Written Story*, was released. By year's end, she had been tapped to play the female lead in a miniseries inspired by Marvel Comics superhero archer Hawkeye, part of the hugely popular Marvel Cinematic Universe (MCU).

In early January 2021, Steinfeld reprised her role for the sophomore season of *Dickinson*, during which Emily grapples with impending literary fame before finally getting published. That fall, Steinfeld returned for the show's third and final season, in which Emily's poetry serves as the backdrop for the Civil War and the conflicts within the Dickinson family. Steinfeld made her MCU debut in late November 2021, costarring opposite Jeremy Renner in the Disney+ live-action series *Hawkeye*. As Kate Bishop, a socialite and gifted archer who becomes a superhero sidekick, Steinfeld quickly became a fan favorite for her witty banter with Hawkeye (Renner) and rival Yelena Belova (Florence Pugh).

PERSONAL LIFE

For many years, despite her career success from an early age, Steinfeld's home base remained her parents' Thousand Oaks house. During the coronavirus disease 2019 (COVID-19) pandemic declared in 2020, she noted that she found it especially comforting to spend time with her family. However, in late 2021, it was reported that the actor had purchased a multimillion-dollar house in Encino, California.

SUGGESTED READING

Bostick, Nicholas. "Hailee Steinfeld on Her New Movie, Music Career and Fame Since *True Grit*." *Dallas Observer*, 1 Nov.

2016, www.dallasobserver.com/arts/hailee-steinfeld-on-her-new-movie-music-career-and-fame-since-true-grit-8861718. Accessed 11 Apr. 2022.

Gleiberman, Owen. "Film Review: The Edge of Seventeen." Review of *The Edge of Seventeen*, directed by Kelly Fremon Craig. *Variety*, 17 Sept. 2016, variety.com/2016/film/reviews/the-edge-of-seventeen-review-toronto-film-festival-hailee-steinfeld-1201862910/. Accessed 11 Apr. 2022.

Lindell, Karen. "Hailee Steinfeld Is Still in a Daze over the Accolades She's Receiving for *True Grit*." *Ventura County Star*, 24 Dec. 2010. *Internet Archive: Wayback Machine*, web.archive.org/web/20101231042026/http://www.vcstar.com/news/2010/dec/24/really-me-hailee-steinfeld-of-thousand-oaks-is-a/. Accessed 11 Apr. 2022.

Nelson, Jeff. "Hailee Steinfeld on Child Stardom 10 Years after True Grit: Family Is 'Keeping Me Grounded.'" *People*, Jan. 2021, people.com/movies/hailee-steinfeld-on-child-stardom-10-years-after-true-grit/. Accessed 11 Apr. 2022.

Steinfeld, Hailee. "From *True Grit* to Pitch Perfect Pop: An Interview with Hailee Steinfeld." Interview by Nick Levine. *Noisey*, Vice, 5 Oct. 2015, www.vice.com/en/article/rmjp4x/hailee-steinfeld-interview. Accessed 11 Apr. 2022.

___. "How Emily Dickinson Helped Hailee Steinfeld Find 'A More Fearless Approach to My Art.'" Interview by Hilary Lewis. *The Hollywood Reporter*, 20 Nov. 2019, www.hollywoodreporter.com/tv/tv-news/hailee-steinfeld-emily-dickinson-interview-1254489/. Accessed 11 Apr. 2022.

SELECTED WORKS

True Grit, 2010; *Ender's Game*, 2013; *Pitch Perfect 2*, 2015; *The Edge of Seventeen*, 2016; *Pitch Perfect 3*, 2017; *Bumblebee*, 2018; *Spider-Man: Into the Spider-Verse*, 2018; *Dickinson*, 2019–21; *Hawkeye*, 2021

—Bertha Muteba

Susanne Sundfør

Born: March 19, 1986
Occupation: Singer-songwriter and producer

Singer-songwriter and producer Susanne Sundfør has long been considered a superstar in her native Norway. Her folk-inspired first record, *Susanne Sundfør* (2007), reached number three on the Norwegian albums chart, introducing her dreamy, impeccable voice and catapulting her to national fame. Although every record after her initial release would chart at the top position in her homeland, Sundfør boldly changed her musical formula to fit the nature of the songs and their message. "I guess I'm old fashioned and see an album as a chapter in a person's life," she told Laura Copley in an interview for *Clash* (17 Aug. 2017). "I just make what I feel like. What feels right at the time in order to convey what I wanna say." From folk to an electronic-driven sound with *The Brothel* (2010) and *The Silicone Veil* (2012) to a more pop-forward sound with *Ten Love Songs* (2015), her unique work elicited critical praise repeatedly, as she proved herself more than capable of performing across various styles and sounds.

By the time Sundfør went back to her folk roots with *Music for People in Trouble*, released in 2017, her musical talents had drawn more international audiences and regard as well. Despite the various stages of her career, including a point of near burnout that led to a period of explorative international journeys that proved both physical and emotional, she has asserted that a genuine passion for musical expression is what drives her. In an interview with Laura Studarus for *Nylon* (8 Sept. 2017), musician and collaborator John Grant admiringly noted her commitment to artistic authenticity. "She is simply an individual. . . . She does her own thing and isn't interested in adhering to any pre-prescribed norms."

EARLY LIFE AND EDUCATION

Susanne Aartun Sundfør was born on March 19, 1986, in Haugesund, a small Norwegian city built on herring fishing in the nineteenth century. Growing up there, she was exposed to instruments and sounds throughout her childhood, forming a love for music early on.

Photo by Jarvin - Jarle Vines,
via Wikimedia Commons

Her musical trajectory began casually with classes at age six, during which the students' voices were complemented by the cheerful sounds of the tambourines they played. Violin lessons followed when she was eight years old, and, a year later, she began to study the piano. By the time she commenced attending a music high school, she was a skilled instrumentalist whose taste in music included the folk songs featured on the records and tapes her father loved and would be played at home or on frequent car trips to the family's mountain cottage.

While Sundfør had ventured into the world of music from an early age, she had no plans at that time to turn this interest into a career in adulthood. "I didn't really decide for it to be my profession until I was 23. So I started it more as a hobby," she said to Andy Malt in an interview for *Complete Music Update* (26 Mar. 2013), before continuing to say, "I didn't really see that I could live off making songs." Even so, Sundfør continued receiving music education, adding opera into her litany of activities; between ages twelve and eighteen she focused her formal vocal training on opera through the singing of arias such as those by Mozart. "We would learn coloratura, where you stretch one word, one syllable, over many notes," she explained to Tim Jonze for *The Guardian* (15 Oct. 2015). "It's good for training your vocal control . . . but

restrictive also." Her ultimate dissatisfaction with operatic limitations contributed to her first venturing into making her own music in her late teens.

Soon after graduating from high school, Sundfør started putting to good use all the eclectic musical knowledge and experience she had gained during her upbringing. After playing several gigs in her hometown and Oslo, she supported British singer-songwriter Tom McRae as his opening act while he toured Norway in 2005. She continued touring her country in 2006, this time with Norwegian band Madrugada, performing the track "Lift Me" with them; at the same time, she appeared solo, along with her guitar, at different venues.

SUSANNE SUNDFØR AND BECOMING A REGIONAL STAR

Toward the end of 2006, at twenty-one years old, Sundfør digitally released "Walls," the lead single of her debut studio album, *Susanne Sundfør*. "Walls," which received radio airtime, eventually claimed the third spot on the Norwegian singles chart, just as her folksy first record would rise to the number-three spot on the albums chart following its 2007 release. As Sundfør launched her music career to critical praise, she achieved a growing fanbase and recognition in her home region, which she was quick to capitalize on. When she released her 2008 live album, *Take One*, she granted fans a stripped-down edition of her debut effort, consisting of eleven tracks featuring her dreamy vocals solely accompanied by two instruments: the piano or guitar.

It would also be in 2008, at the Spellemannprisen, a Norwegian music awards ceremony viewed at the same level as the Grammy Awards in the United States, that her album, *Susanne Sundfør*, won her a trophy for best female artist. However, her acceptance speech sparked some disagreement when she criticized the award for being categorized first according to gender, a dig at the gender discrimination that she has viewed as pervasive in the music industry and society as a whole. Although she was chastised by some in the media for her remarks, she was also seen as a pioneer for starting a tough but crucial discussion, something she viewed as empowering. "A lot of the old guys, music journalists, hated me," she related to Jonze. "I got a lot of bad reviews and comments in the papers. But I felt confident. It was more: 'Yes! The fight is on!' So I will never regret it."

Having left folk and the serene sounds of the guitar and piano behind since the writing of her first track list in favor of electronica, Sundfør embraced a more electronic-driven sound with her second original album, *The Brothel*, which she put out in 2010. This offering, spawning the singles "It's All Gone Tomorrow" and "Turkish Delight" in addition to its title song, proved to be both a commercial and critical triumph on its release, securing the number-one spot on the Norwegian albums chart. Her success with *The Brothel* did not end there, however, as it earned her the best composer award at the 2011 Spellemannprisen ceremony. Despite the plaudits received, for the young singer, the album represented more than that—it allowed her to realize that music was the art to which she wanted to devote her life. As she said to Malt, "Actually, I think I only decided that this is something that I wanted to spend my entire life doing after I released *The Brothel*, cos that was the first time I really felt like I had 'found' a sound."

THE SILICONE VEIL, TEN LOVE SONGS, AND INTERNATIONAL REACH

Invited to perform as part of the lineup at the 2011 Oslo Jazz Festival, Sundfør took to the stage at the city's Sentrum Scene venue and presented, alongside other selected keyboard players, an instrumental composition broken into six movements. This performance was captured for the album *A Night at Salle Pleyel*, released that year. In February 2012, "White Foxes," the single that preceded her third full-length album of new songs, was released and proved immensely popular. "White Foxes" was an ideal example of Sundfør's musical direction on the album *The Silicone Veil*, released the following month, which, critics agreed, was an ambitious, bold offering of ten songs not only because of her powerful vocals but for its effective mash of synthesizers and heavy electronics.

Having established herself as one of Norway's best musical talents, it was no surprise that *The Silicone Veil* reached number one on the Norwegian albums chart—nor that other bands wanted to collaborate with her, and her music was garnering more interest overseas. Also in 2012, she was featured on the song "Away," by emerging Norwegian singer

Morten Myklebust, and contributed vocals for electronica duo Röyksopp's "Running to the Sea." Around that same time, she saw her first UK album release when *The Silicone Veil* came out in that country in October. Moreover, the singer worked alongside the French electronic band M83, with whom she had performed on European tour stops the previous year, on a piece included on the soundtrack of the post-apocalyptic film *Oblivion* (2013).

Production work for Sundfør's next studio album, which she titled *Ten Love Songs*, finished in 2014. The tunes charged with promoting the album, "Fade Away" and "Delirious," were released in October 2014 and January 2015, respectively. The overall more pop-sounding but still unique *Ten Love Songs*, featuring the widely impressive ten-minute track "Memorial," came out in February 2015 and spawned two more singles: "Kamikaze" and "Accelerate." Drawing from personal experience, Sundfør explored the concept of love, and its connection to hate, as a theme, bringing together an honest, vulnerable collection of songs that led to the album's number-one success on the Norwegian albums chart. "To write the perfect love song, you have to be heartbroken," she related to Jonze. "It needs to be naked. That's how you write the best."

While the record proved to be yet another commercial and critical triumph for the singer, allowing her music to spread even more outside of Norway and even Europe, it was also Sundfør's most arduous project until that point, as she was not only the singer but writer and producer, exhaustively working up to twelve hours per day. Feeling physically and mentally drained by the process and the preceding years of work, she told Studarus, "I think I had just gone through so many hard things that my body and mind wasn't coping with it anymore." Still, *Ten Love Songs* also claimed awards in three categories, including best album of the year, at the 2016 Spellemannprisen ceremony.

TRAVELING THE WORLD AND MUSIC FOR PEOPLE IN TROUBLE

Upon the completion of touring around *Ten Love Songs*, Sundfør decided that before working on what would end up being her mostly acoustic follow-up project, she would take a break to recharge by traveling solo, visiting countries from Iceland to Nepal, North Korea, Guatemala, and Brazil over the course of approximately one year. Although her camera—packed with photos of the various places and people she wanted to capture forever—became the new means of satisfying her artistic inclinations during this time, she did not intend to make a travelogue album. She would, however, sit down and write after every trip, composing songs informed by her encounters and experiences. "The visual part is an extension of the album. It's not like 'this song is about this tower in North Korea,'" she explained to Kieron Tyler in an interview for the *Arts Desk* (25 Aug. 2017). "There isn't a direct link between the photos and the songs, but there is a connection which makes it interesting."

In 2017, Sundfør released *Music for People in Trouble*, which again sat at the top of the Norwegian chart. Switching back to her foundations in sparer, more intimate acoustic arrangements in which she accompanies her voice with piano and guitar, this ten-track record includes the lead single "Undercover" and the song "Mountaineers," featuring Grant. Talking about the process of writing the lyrics for this latest offering and creating the melodies, she told Tyler that she did both at the same time. "With this album, a lot of it came simultaneously. For me, that always creates the best songs because the words fit the music," she told him. In November 2019, she put out *Music for People in Trouble: Live from the Barbican*, a staged concert production of the album recorded in 2018 in London. Having been invited to contribute, she then composed the soundtrack for *Self Portrait* (2020), a documentary whose subject is Norwegian photographer Lene Marie Fossen.

PERSONAL LIFE

In 2020, it was reported by some sources that Sundfør had given birth to her first child.

SUGGESTED READING

Hann, Michael. "Singer-Songwriter Susanne Sundfør: 'I'm Tired of the Apocalypse.'" *Financial Times*, 17 Aug. 2018, www.ft.com/content/f5172fa6-a06f-11e8-b196-da9d6c239ca8. Accessed 25 Feb. 2022.
Jeffries, David. "Biography—Susanne Sundfør." *AllMusic*, www.allmusic.com/artist/susanne-sundfør-mn0001953486/biography. Accessed 25 Feb. 2022.

Jonze, Tim. "Susanne Sundfør: 'Making *Ten Love Songs* Made Me Feel Naked, without Skin.'" *The Guardian*, 15 Oct. 2015, www.theguardian.com/music/2015/oct/15/susanne-sundfor-ten-love-songs-made-me-feel-naked. Accessed 25 Feb. 2022.
Sundfør, Susanne. "The Arts Desk Q&A: Musician Susanne Sundfør." Interview by Kieron Tyler. *The Arts Desk*, 25 Aug. 2017, theartsdesk.com/new-music/theartsdesk-qa-musician-susanne-sundfør. Accessed 25 Feb. 2022.
—. "The Curious Life of Norwegian Pop Musician Susanne Sundfør." Interview by Laura Studarus. *Nylon*, 8 Sept. 2017, www.nylon.com/articles/susanne-sundfor-interview. Accessed 11 Mar. 2022
—. "In Conversation: Susanne Sundfør." Interview by Laura Copley. *Clash*, 17 Aug. 2017, www.clashmusic.com/features/in-conversation-susanne-sundf%C3%B8r. Accessed 11 Mar. 2022.
—. "Q&A: Susanne Sundfør." Interview by Andy Malt. *Complete Music Update*, 26 Mar. 2013, completemusicupdate.com/article/qa-susanne-sundfor. Accessed 25 Feb. 2022.

SELECTED WORKS

Susanne Sundfør, 2007; *The Brothel*, 2010; *The Silicone Veil*, 2012; *Ten Love Songs*, 2015; *Music for People in Trouble*, 2017; *Music for People in Trouble: Live from the Barbican*, 2019

—*Maria del Pilar Guzman*

Dhivya Suryadevara

Born: April 14, 1979
Occupation: Business executive

When Dhivya Suryadevara assumed the role of chief financial officer (CFO) at General Motors (GM) in September 2018, she became the first woman ever to hold this office. The appointment also made the Detroit-based automobile manufacturing company one of only two Fortune 500 companies at the time to boast a female chief executive officer (CEO) and CFO at the helm, as Suryadevara reported to Mary Barra, GM's first female CEO. Suryadevara herself preferred not to focus on gender, however. As she shared with Julia Hanna on Harvard Business School's alumni website (4 Sept. 2019), "To me, it's less about gender or where I'm from; it's about bringing in diverse perspectives to make better decisions that add value to the company and to our shareholders."

Throughout her nearly two decades in the male-dominated auto industry, Suryadevara, who held various financial positions at GM between 2004 and 2020, garnered many accolades for her achievements. These included *Automotive News'* Rising Star (2016), World Economic Forum's Young Global Leaders (2016), *Fortune'*s 40 Under 40 (2018), and *Finance Monthly'*s CFO Awards (2019). In 2020, she began a new chapter in her already robust career, joining the online-payments company Stripe as its CFO. "I really enjoy leading complex, large-scale businesses and I hope to use my skills to help accelerate Stripe's already steep growth trajectory," she explained upon the announcement of her hire, as reported in a press release on Stripe's website (11 Aug. 2020).

Photo by Steve Fecht,
via Wikimedia Commons

EARLY LIFE AND EDUCATION

Dhivya Suryadevara was born on April 14, 1979, in Chennai (previously Madras), the capital city of Tamil Nadu, India's tenth-largest state. After losing her father at an early age, Suryadevara, who grew up alongside her two sisters, learned the value of hard work from her mother. She was an employee at the local branch of the Syndicate Bank, formerly one of India's oldest commercial banks. "My mom had to raise three children on her own, which is difficult to do anywhere, let alone in India," Suryadevara recalled to Jane Porter in an interview for *Real Simple* (19 July 2016). "She wanted to make sure there were no corners cut when it came to our education and to prove that we could have the same resources as a two-parent household."

Upon completing primary and middle school, Suryadevara studied at St. John's Senior Secondary School in Mandaveli, India, eventually passing her Class 12 exams in 1996. Over the next four years, Suryadevara attended the University of Madras in Chennai, where she pursued bachelor's and master's degrees in commerce. While there, Suryadevara worked at PricewaterhouseCoopers' assurance and business advisory group and completed a three-year professional course (1997–2000) at the Institute of Chartered Accountants of India

to become qualified as an associate chartered accountant.

In 2001, the twenty-two-year-old Suryadevara traveled to the United States for the first time to attend Harvard Business School in Boston, Massachusetts. "At that time, Harvard Business School took people with a certain amount of work experience, and I had worked through undergrad but had come straight out of college," she shared with Porter. The following year, Suryadevara interned for four months at the World Bank. She received her MBA degree in 2003 and accepted an associate director position at UBS Investment Bank, where she worked for just over a year.

FORGING A CAREER IN THE AUTO INDUSTRY

In 2004 Suryadevara began working at the GM Treasurer's Office, where she served as a senior financial analyst in foreign exchange and commodities trading. In 2006, she transferred to GM's Asset Management (GMAM) unit. As a fixed income investment analyst, she conducted research to assess the value and the risks involved with fixed income securities. She spent nearly three years in this role before being promoted to fixed income portfolio manager in late 2008. By June 2009, however, GM was on the brink of financial collapse, due to slowing car sales and mounting debt ($81 billion in losses over four years) amid a severe global recession in 2008–09. As part of the Obama administration's effort to rescue the struggling US auto manufacturing industry, GM subsequently declared Chapter 11 bankruptcy—the largest-ever for an industrial company—and received nearly $20 billion in US taxpayer loans, a $30 billion bailout from the Treasury Department, and nearly $11 billion in aid from Canada's federal and provincial governments.

Despite GM's tumultuous year, Suryadevara continued to rise through the company's ranks. In 2010 she was tapped to supervise GMAM's multi-asset investment strategies team, which is tasked with achieving balanced, diversified investment portfolios by allocating various asset types that are aimed at maximizing return and minimizing risk. By that October, she had been promoted to director of the investment strategy division, where she remained for nearly five years (2011–15), monitoring investments and allocation of assets made on behalf of GMs' various pension plans. In 2012, Suryadevara played a key role in completing a risk-transfer deal that reduced her company's pension liability by offloading $29 billion to Prudential Financial. Part of the solution involved providing lump-sum payouts to some of the retired salaried employees receiving monthly group annuities. "That was one of the most interesting things I've worked on in my career," Suryadevara told Dustin Walsh for *Crain's Detroit Business* (29 Sept. 2017). "It was unprecedented. Nobody had done anything of that size before and we're grateful we did it. It was a good deal for everyone."

CLIMBING THE RANKS AT GENERAL MOTORS

In 2013, Suryadevara, then managing director of investment strategy and fixed income at GMAM, was selected as the subsidiary's chief investment officer (CIO) and CEO. In her additional roles, she was tasked with overseeing investment of the automotive manufacturer's pension operations, worth more than $80 billion in assets.

Meanwhile, Suryadevara was not the only groundbreaking executive to climb the ranks at the major global automaker. In January 2014 Barra was appointed the chair and CEO of GM. Barra was motivated to foster the careers of other women at GM, promoting several women to high-profile management positions, and Suryadevara thrived under her leadership.

In 2015, Suryadevara took on yet another role as vice president of finance and treasurer. In this position she was placed in charge of managing GM's financial affairs, including capital planning, risk management, investor relations, and worldwide banking, and reported directly to Chuck Stevens, GM's CFO. During her two-year tenure in that role from 2015 to 2017, Suryadevara helped upgrade the company's corporate credit ratings. She also oversaw a $2 billion offering of twenty- and thirty-year senior unsecured notes to pay down the debt for the company's US hourly pension plan. (Senior notes are high-priority bonds that must be repaid first, in the event that a company files for bankruptcy.)

CFO AT GM AND STRIPE

In July 2017 Suryadevara was named GM's vice president of corporate finance, in charge of financial planning, investor relations, and other special projects. Prior to her appointment, she stepped down from her previous roles as CIO and CEO at GMAM, as well as vice president of finance and treasurer. While serving in this new role, Suryadevara presided over the $2.2 billion sale of the German-based Opel division to French automaker PSA Group; the billion-dollar purchase of the self-driving vehicle start-up company Cruise; GM's $500 million investment in ride-sharing service Lyft; and Japanese tech investor Softbank's $2.25 billion stake in Cruise. "We want to think about how we are reinvesting in our core business, but also invest in future technology," Suryadevara told Walsh. Discussing the effects of how such technology as autonomous vehicles, electrification, and ride-sharing would impact the automobile industry, she continued: "[Automakers] are going to be disrupted; we don't want to be the one that's disrupted. We want to be the disruptor, but with a strong balance sheet."

Suryadevara continued to serve in this capacity until June 2018, when she was tapped to succeed Stevens as CFO. Suryadevara officially stepped into the role in September 2018, becoming the first woman at GM to ever hold this position. Later that year she focused on cutting costs, which included the closure of five North American manufacturing facilities and reduction of the company's salaried workforce by 15 percent. Suryadevara also oversaw the company's transition toward self-driving and electric vehicles. "The auto industry has a reputation for being stodgy and bureaucratic, but that perception is outdated," she told Hanna. "I think the professional opportunities are unmatched when it comes to working on large, complicated issues in an industry that is changing incredibly fast and is at the forefront of technology." Amid the global coronavirus pandemic that began in early 2020, which led to government-mandated shutdowns of auto manufacturing plants, Suryadevara implemented another cost-cutting measure: zero-based budgeting, which involved making significant cuts in advertising and travel, deferring compensation, and furloughing employees.

Suryadevara's tenure with GM ended in August 2020, when she was recruited to join the San Francisco-based firm Stripe. The online payments-processing company was experiencing tremendous growth as a result of increased demand for its services during the COVID-19 pandemic. "Dhivya is a rare leader who has run an industry-leading leviathan but also gets excited about enabling the brand-new products and the yet-to-be invented products, too," Stripe cofounder John Collison commented on Stripe's website. After taking over as Stripe's new finance chief, Suryadevara oversaw a multi-pronged growth strategy. It included an expanding roster of products, such as Stripe Treasury, Stripe Payment Links, and Stripe Identity; a series of strategic partnerships, including with audio-streaming subscription service Spotify; and high-profile startup acquisitions, such as the Nigerian-based payment startup Paystack and the Indian-based payment software company Recko.

PERSONAL LIFE

Suryadevara and her husband, Raj, a senior portfolio manager at an investment-banking firm, had a daughter. A fitness enthusiast, she enjoys boxing. She served on the board of directors for the Girl Scouts of Greater New York.

SUGGESTED READING

Colias, Mike, and Nina Trentmann. "GM Financial Chief Dhivya Suryadevara Steps Down in Surprise Departure." *The Wall Street Journal*, 11 Aug. 2020, www.wsj.com/articles/gm-names-john-stapleton-acting-finance-chief-as-cfo-leaves-11597153015. Accessed 15 Feb. 2022.

DeBord, Matthew. "Dhivya Suryadevara Is Leaving GM, Where She Was Part of the Only Female CEO-CFO Team in the Auto Industry." *Business Insider*, 11 Aug. 2020, www.businessinsider.in/thelife/news/dhivya-suryadevara-is-leaving-gm-where-she-was-part-of-the-only-female-ceo-cfo-team-in-the-auto-industry/articleshow/77487860.cms. Accessed 15 Feb. 2022.

"Dhivya Suryadevara to Join Stripe as Chief Financial Officer." *Stripe*, 11 Aug. 2020, stripe.com/newsroom/news/dhivya-suryadevara. Accessed 16 Feb. 2022.

Muller, Joann. "Another Woman at the Top of GM: 39-Year-Old Finance Whiz Dhivya Suryadevara Is New CFO." *Forbes*, 13 June 2018, www.forbes.com/sites/joannmuller/2018/06/13/another-woman-at-the-top-of-gm-39-year-old-finance-whiz-dhivya-suryadevara-is-new-cfo. Accessed 15 Feb. 2022.

Suryadevara, Dhivya. "How 1 Woman Balances a Job in 1 City and a Family in Another." Interview by Jane Porter. *Real Simple*, 19 July 2016, www.realsimple.com/work-life/general-motors-dhivya-suryadevara. Accessed 15 Feb. 2022.

___. "3-Minute Briefing: Dhivya Suryadevara (MBA 2003)." Interview by Julia Hanna. *Harvard Business School*, 4 Sept. 2019, www.alumni.hbs.edu/stories/Pages/story-impact.aspx?num=7089. Accessed 15 Feb. 2022.

Walsh, Dustin. "Dhivya Suryadevara, 38." *Crain's Detroit Business*, 29 Sept. 2017, www.crainsdetroit.com/awards/dhivya-suryadevara. Accessed 15 Feb. 2022.

—*Bertha Muteba*

Seiya Suzuki

Born: August 18, 1994
Occupation: Baseball player

On April 7, 2022, baseball player Seiya Suzuki made his first appearance with the Chicago Cubs during the team's season opener against the Milwaukee Brewers. Playing in his first US major-league game represented a significant milestone for the athlete, who had previously played in Japan and had signed with the Cubs as

Photo by STB-1, via Wikimedia Commons

a free agent less than a month prior. "Obviously, this is just my first year in the majors, and I feel like it's a learning experience," Suzuki, who typically delivered interviews through an English-language interpreter, later said of his fledgling US career, as reported by Gordon Wittenmyer for NBC Sports Chicago (12 June 2022). "I'm trying to get acclimated to the atmosphere here." Though perhaps a daunting experience for Suzuki, his debut game was a memorable one: the Cubs beat the Brewers, and Suzuki himself scored one of the runs that proved key to the team's success.

A 2012 selection in the Nippon Professional Baseball (NPB) Draft, Suzuki began his professional baseball career with the Hiroshima Toyo Carp organization, which he debuted with the following year. Over the course of nine seasons with the organization, many of them with the top-level Carp team, he established himself as a valuable member of the roster and helped lead the team to multiple Central League championships. "I can't really praise myself that much because I feel I can get even better as a player," he told Andrew Baggarly for *The Athletic* (13 Jan. 2022) about his skill level. "But I feel I'm good at being disciplined at the plate, and not just hitting home runs but also getting on base and being a contact hitter as well." He demonstrated those skills on the international level as well, winning a gold medal

in baseball with Team Japan at the Olympic Games in 2021. In signing with the Cubs in March 2022, Suzuki entered a new stage of his career, bringing his extensive professional and international experience to the major leagues.

EARLY LIFE AND EDUCATION

Seiya Suzuki was born on August 18, 1994, in Arakawa, a ward of metropolitan Tokyo, Japan. He spent his childhood in Arakawa, where he was raised by parents who encouraged his athletic aspirations. The young Suzuki proved himself to be a skilled baseball player, and he competed in that sport while attending Nishōgakusha High School. He planned to pursue a career in professional baseball after completing his schooling and in October 2012 was selected by the Hiroshima Toyo Carp in the second round of that year's Nippon Professional Baseball (NPB) Draft at age nineteen.

HIROSHIMA TOYO CARP

Suzuki made his debut with the Hiroshima Toyo Carp organization in 2013, initially playing for the Carp's minor-league affiliate, also called the Carp, which competed within Japan's Western League. He joined the major-level Carp team, which competed in NPB's Central League, in September of that year and continued to play in the majors into early October. After splitting his second professional season between the Western and Central leagues, Suzuki played primarily in the Central during the 2015 season, establishing himself as a recurring member of the Carp's roster. He remained a major-league player throughout the subsequent six seasons.

While Suzuki played in multiple positions during his early career, including shortstop and first base, he became primarily known as an outfielder during his later seasons with the Carp and developed a reputation as a skilled position player and strong batter. His success was fueled in part by his desire to play in the United States one day, a goal he set during his early years with the Carp. "I was fascinated with how many better players there are in the States," he told Baggarly. "That motivated me to play harder and get better so I could play with them someday." With the Carp, Suzuki helped the team become Central League champions three times and was selected as an NPB all-star on five occasions beginning in 2016. By the end of his tenure with the Carp, he had played in more than nine hundred games and accumulated a .315 batting average with 182 home runs and 562 runs batted in (RBI). He also earned a host of honors, including five Central League Gold Glove Awards. He led the Central League in batting in both 2019 and 2021.

INTERNATIONAL COMPETITION

In addition to playing with the Carp, Suzuki represented Japan in international baseball competition. In 2014, he competed in the World Baseball Softball Confederation (WBSC) Under-Twenty-One (U-21) Baseball World Cup, helping his country claim second place. In November 2019, he competed in the WBSC Premier12 tournament, during which he led the tournament in runs scored, RBIs, and batting average. Suzuki and his teammates placed first in that tournament, and Suzuki was honored with the title of most valuable player (MVP).

As host nation for the 2020 Olympic Games in Tokyo, Japan automatically qualified to compete in baseball at the Games and was set to field a roster that included Suzuki and other prominent players. However, the Olympics were postponed to 2021 following the emergence of the coronavirus disease 2019 (COVID-19) pandemic, and the fate of the event remained uncertain by the beginning of that year. "The players don't have control over the decision, but I do hope the Olympics take their regular place this summer," Suzuki said at the time, as reported by the WBSC (29 Jan. 2021). "Competing for Japan in the Games is something I really want to do." The postponed 2020 Olympics ultimately took place in July and August of 2021, during which Suzuki and his teammates progressed steadily through the rounds of competition until defeating the United States in the final game to claim the gold medal.

FREE AGENCY

In late 2021, baseball journalists began to report that Suzuki was considering leaving the Carp to sign as a free agent with a major-league team in the United States. In light of his demonstrated skills and success in both domestic and international competitions, a number of major-league organizations were rumored to be interested in signing Suzuki, including the New York Yankees, Boston Red Sox, Toronto Blue Jays, and Chicago Cubs. "I

can't stop thinking about which team to pick," he told Baggarly in early 2022. "I'm going to be honest with you: I'm still very confused. I can't sleep every night because a lot of the teams hit my heart. I still have to give it a lot of thought."

Suzuki was ultimately able to take his time making a decision, as Major League Baseball (MLB) was in the midst of a lockout—a work stoppage that occurred following the expiration of the league and the players association's collective-bargaining agreement (CBA). "In Japan, you don't experience a lockout so it's a first for me," he told Baggarly. "At first, I was a little worried about it. But when you think about it, it's going to end sometime soon. Just having that positive mindset that it will end sometime has allowed me to keep my head up." As the lockout did not end until mid-March, the start of the baseball season was shifted from late March to early April. Having made his decision, Suzuki signed with the Chicago Cubs on March 18. In addition to signing a five-year contract worth $85 million, he opted to wear the number twenty-seven based on his admiration for Los Angeles Angels centerfielder Mike Trout, who also wore that number.

CHICAGO CUBS

Suzuki made his debut with the Cubs on April 7, 2022, in the team's season opener against the Milwaukee Brewers. He scored one of the Cubs' five runs scored during the game, which his new team ultimately won. Suzuki's performance during his debut game signaled a strong start to his MLB career, and he continued to perform well over the next several weeks, breaking several franchise and league records by the end of his fifth game. A setback arose, however, on May 26, when Suzuki injured his hand while sliding into second base and had to leave mid-game. The injury was later revealed to be a finger sprain, and Suzuki was placed on the Cubs' injured list four days after the incident. Dealing with significant swelling in his hand, he worked to recover from the injury over the next month, and by the end of June was prepared to take a rehabilitation assignment with the Cubs' triple-A minor-league affiliate, the Iowa Cubs. "Obviously with all this time off and all these at-bats I haven't been able to take at this level, I feel that could be necessary, some rehab at-bats to get to be playing here again," Suzuki said, as reported by Wittenmyer. He ultimately played three games with the Iowa Cubs between late June and early July.

On July 4, Suzuki returned to major-league play and hit an inside-the-park home run during a game against the Brewers. Although the Cubs lost the game, he was pleased with his performance and level of recovery. "The fact that I was able to display what I did today was something that I'm very satisfied with," he said after the game, as reported by Jordan Bastian for *MLB.com* (4 July 2022). Suzuki also commented in a postgame interview that he had made a concerted effort to avoid incurring another injury during the game, including when sliding into home base. "After I rounded third, I saw the catcher kind of coming towards me," he explained, as reported by Bastian. "That's when I thought, like, 'I don't want to get injured again.' I just did my best to [slide] where it prevented me from getting another injury." The attempt to avoid injury proved successful, and he remained an active member of the Cubs' roster. By mid-July, Suzuki had played in fifty of the Cubs' first eighty-eight games of the 2022 season and had scored twenty-six RBIs and hit 6 home runs in 168 at-bats during that period.

PERSONAL LIFE

Suzuki married retired Olympic gymnast and television personality Airi Hatakeyama in 2019. He moved to the Chicago area in 2022, following his signing with the Cubs.

SUGGESTED READING

Baggarly, Andrew. "'A Lot of Teams Hit My Heart': A Superstar in Japan, Seiya Suzuki Craves a New Challenge in MLB." *The Athletic*, 13 Jan. 2022, theathletic.com/3065621/2022/01/13/japanese-superstar-seiya-suzuki-is-determined-to-be-an-impact-player-in-the-major-leagues-now-he-just-has-to-pick-a-team/. Accessed 11 July 2022.

Bastian, Jordan. "Suzuki Makes Return with Electric Inside-the-Parker." *MLB*, 4 July 2022, www.mlb.com/news/seiya-suzuki-hits-go-ahead-inside-the-park-home-run. Accessed 11 July 2022.

"Premier12 2019 MVP Seiya Suzuki Expresses Strong Desire to Play in the Olympics." *WBSC*, 29 Jan. 2021, www.wbsc.org/en/news/premier12-2019-mvp-seiya-suzuki-expresses-strong-desire-to-play-in-the-olympics. Accessed 11 July 2022.

"Seiya Suzuki." *Cubs*, MLB, 2022, www.mlb.com/player/seiya-suzuki-673548. Accessed 14 July 2022.

Wittenmyer, Gordon. "Cubs Reactions: Another Seiya Suzuki Historic Milestone, Big Day for Willson Contreras in Loss." *NBC Chicago*, 13 Apr. 2022, www.nbcchicago.com/news/sports/nbcsports/cubs-another-seiya-suzuki-rarity-big-day-for-contreras-in-loss/2806308/. Accessed 11 July 2022.

___. "Why Weeklong Shutdown of Suzuki Could Push Return to July." *NBC Sports Chicago*, 12 June 2022, www.nbcsports.com/chicago/cubs/why-cubs-shutdown-seiya-suzuki-could-push-his-return-july. Accessed 11 July 2022.

—*Joy Crelin*

Tai Tzu-ying

Born: June 20, 1994
Occupation: Badminton player

While Taiwanese badminton player Tai Tzu-ying had competed in the Olympic Games twice before joining the competition in Japan in 2021, she had a true breakthrough on her third Olympic outing. Having progressed successfully through the early-stage competition that had stymied her in previous Games, she proceeded on to the final round of competition and claimed a silver medal in the women's singles event. Although Tai would have preferred a gold medal, she considered her second-place finish to be both a powerful motivator and a significant milestone in its own right. "There is always a little regret, but imperfection always [exists], only to be motivated to pursue better results," she wrote on Instagram following the competition, as quoted by *ESPN* (1 Aug. 2021). "Maybe I won't have another chance to participate in the Olympics, but I've achieved this goal." Indeed, Tai's response to her Olympic result was in many ways characteristic of her overall approach to her sport, which emphasized continual improvement. "This is a game where one has to work continuously and work hard," she told K. Keerthivasan in an interview for *Sportstar* (19 Jan. 2020). "I train with my coaches and team and every match needs to be looked [at] as a fresh challenge. You have to always give your 100 per cent and not take any match lightly." In addition to earning her an Olympic medal, Tai's successful approach made her the first Taiwanese athlete to win a gold medal in badminton at the Asian Games and one of the top women's badminton players in the world.

EARLY LIFE AND CAREER

Tai Tzu-ying was born on June 20, 1994, in Kaohsiung City, Taiwan. Her parents, Tai Nan-kai and Hu Jung, were both avid badminton players, and her father worked as a police officer and later as a firefighter. As a child, Tai was especially close with her parents as well as with a grandmother with whom she enjoyed watching televised sports. "I spent a lot of time with my parents and we would play lot of games as a family which was great fun," she told Shivani Naik for *Indian Express* (12 Feb. 2020) about her childhood. "We'd play for hours on holidays and after my father came back from work." Following her parents' example, Tai learned to play badminton as a child and soon began to pursue the sport competitively, participating in badminton tournaments held in Taiwan (referred to by some international sporting bodies as Chinese Taipei).

As a young teenager, Tai began to compete regularly outside of Taiwan, traveling to international competitions in countries such as Vietnam and Indonesia. In 2009, she claimed third place in the women's singles badminton competition at the East Asian Games in Hong Kong and progressed to the final round of the women's singles competition at the Yonex-Sunrise Vietnam Open (Yonex is a Tokyo-based sports equipment manufacturer). Other memorable tournaments of Tai's early career included the 2010 Li-Ning Singapore Open Super Series, during which she progressed to the final round, held in June of that year. "It was my first Super Series final and it was my birthday," she later recalled, as reported by ZK Goh for the website of the Olympic Games (9 Dec. 2019). "The audience collectively gave me their well wishes when I entered the court. That is the most memorable experience I have in the sport so far." The following year saw Tai win her first major competition, the 2011 Yonex OCBS US Open Grand Prix Gold, in addition to claiming third place in several tournaments.

OLYMPIC DEBUT

Tai made her Olympic debut in 2012, competing in the women's singles badminton event at that year's Games in London, England.

Photo by Chartlin, via Wikimedia Commons.

She succeeded in progressing through the group stage of competition, but she was eliminated in the subsequent round, finishing the Games tied for ninth place. "I was very young back then and playing the Olympics for the first time was way more exciting for me while representing my country," she later told Naik about the experience. "So more than the performance, my excitement took over me." Tai found greater success in Badminton World Federation (BWF) events that year, winning the 2012 Yonex Open Japan and Yonex Chinese Taipei Open.

Over the next several years, Tai continued to establish herself as a promising up-and-coming player, winning tournaments such as the 2013 Maybank Malaysia Open and the 2014 BWF Destination Dubai World Superseries Finals and earning second-place finishes at tournaments such as the 2015 OUE Singapore Open. At the Rio de Janeiro Olympic Games in 2016, she beat her competition in the group stage before losing to Indian athlete P. V. Sindhu, the eventual silver medalist, for another ninth-place finish. "I put a lot of pressure on myself," Tai later told Dev Sukumar about the 2016 Games in an interview for the BWF's website (12 July 2021). "Plus, I was injured so my performance wasn't ideal." Though disappointed with her performance in Brazil, Tai had an otherwise-strong year, during which she won tournaments in Indonesia, Taiwan, Hong Kong, and Dubai. In December 2016, Tai claimed the number-one spot in the BWF's world ranking, becoming the first Taiwanese athlete to do so.

NUMBER-ONE PLAYER

Ranked number one in the world throughout the year, Tai had a particularly productive 2017, winning BWF events such as the Yonex All England Open, Badminton Asia Championships, Yonex French Open, and Yonex-Sunrise Hong Kong Open. She proved similarly successful the following year, winning the Daihatsu Indonesia Masters, the Yonex All England Open, the Badminton Asia Championships, and the Danisa Denmark Open, among other tournaments. A particularly satisfying victory came in August, when Tai competed in the 2018 Asian Games, held in Jakarta, Indonesia. After progressing through the early rounds of competition, she defeated Japanese player Nozomi Okuhara in the quarterfinals and Indian player Saina Nehwal before facing Sindhu in the final round of the tournament. While Tai had long considered Sindhu to be a particularly difficult opponent, Tai proved victorious in the final, beating Sindhu to claim Taiwan's first Asian Games gold medal for badminton. "I did nothing different, just played my usual game," she told Naik about the experience. "But I had to be at the top of my game as Sindhu was very tough to beat. One mistake and the match was gone. I am happy that I could win the first badminton gold for my country."

In the midst of maintaining her top ranking, Tai studied sports science at the University of Taipei and earned a degree from the university's Graduate Institute of Sports Training in 2018. She remained a strong contender in 2019, winning the women's singles competition at the Celcom Axiata Malaysia Open and Singapore Open in April and the Danisa Denmark Open in October of that year.

A CHALLENGING YEAR

For Tai, like many other athletes, 2020 was a challenging year, as the COVID-19 pandemic prompted changes to training schedules and necessitated the cancellation of some sporting events and the postponement of others, including the 2020 Olympic Games. Tai played in only two BWF competitions that

year, placing second at the Perodua Malaysia Masters in January and winning the Yonex All England Open in March. Over the next months, she trained when possible and also occupied herself by taking online English lessons, hoping to improve her English so that she could communicate better with English-speaking fans. "Sometimes when I'm translated, some of the key meanings of my message to fans were not fully interpreted," she explained to Sukumar for the BWF World Tour website (21 Nov. 2020). "At the moment, I'm still able to engage with fans using basic English, but when it comes to more complex thoughts, it's been challenging for me and I'm still trying to learn."

While Tai kept busy throughout 2020, she missed competing and hoped to resume doing so as soon as possible. "I'm looking forward to be back at international competitions again and getting back my competition rhythm," she told Sukumar (21 Nov. 2020). "Missing out competition for a long duration like this, it is normal for me to lose some motivation in training and rhythm in competition too." Tai returned to competition in January 2021, claiming second place at the Yonex Thailand Open. She went on to win the HSBC (an international bank) BWF World Tour Finals, an event that had been postponed from the previous year.

TOKYO OLYMPICS

Postponed to 2021, the 2020 Olympic Games began in Tokyo, Japan, in July of that year. For Tai, the Games represented a new opportunity—and potentially Tai's final opportunity—to compete on that international stage. "This Olympics will be my last major tournament before I hang up my racket," she told Sukumar (12 July 2021) prior to the event. "I have yet to decide if I will continue to play after the Olympics. I have not made a firm decision." Following the group stage of the women's singles competition, Tai defeated Thai athlete Ratchanok Intanon in the quarterfinals and Sindhu in the semifinals before progressing to the final round. Tai lost to Chinese athlete Chen Yufei, claiming a silver medal.

In recognition of Tai's strong performance over the year, including at the Olympics, the BWF awarded her its Female Player of the Year honors in early December 2021. Although she had previously indicated that she would likely retire from play following the Tokyo Olympics, she returned to competition later that month and placed second in the women's singles event at the TotalEnergies BWF World Championships. Tai recorded her two-hundredth week atop the BWF women's singles rankings in January 2022, becoming the first player to do so. She continues to compete and in March 2022 placed third at the Yonex All England Open Badminton Championships.

PERSONAL LIFE

When not competing elsewhere, Tai lives in Taiwan. In addition to playing badminton, she enjoys spending time outdoors and participating in several outdoor sports, which she found particularly beneficial to her training process after the COVID-19 pandemic put her competition schedule on hold. "I would always look for outdoor activities such as hiking and cycling which are higher intensity," she told Sukumar (21 Nov. 2020). "It makes me sweat a lot and train my cardio."

SUGGESTED READING

Goh, ZK. "Meet Tai Tzu-ying, Chinese Taipei's Badminton Star." *Olympics*, 9 Dec. 2019, olympics.com/en/featured-news/tai-tzu-ying-chinese-taipei-badminton-star. Accessed 11 Apr. 2022.

Naik, Shivani. "The Private World of a World-Beater, Tai Tzu-Ying." *Indian Express*, 12 Feb. 2020, indianexpress.com/article/sports/badminton/tai-tzu-ying-chinese-taipei-private-world-6258202/. Accessed 11 Apr. 2022.

"'PV Sindhu's Sincere Encouragement Made Me Cry'—Tai Tzu Ying." *ESPN*, 1 Aug. 2021, www.espn.com/olympics/badminton/story/_/id/31938178/pv-sindhu-sincere-encouragement-made-cry-tai-tzu-ying-losing-tokyo-olympics-final. Accessed 11 Apr. 2022.

Sukumar, Dev. "Road to Tokyo: Tai Aware Errors Could Prove Costly." *BWF*, 12 July 2021, olympics.bwfbadminton.com/news-single/2021/07/12/road-to-tokyo-tai-aware-errors-could-prove-costly/. Accessed 11 Apr. 2022.

Tai, Tzu-ying. "Tai Tzu Ying: 'I Love the Outdoors.'" Interview by Dev Sukumar. *HSBC BWF World Tour*, 21 Nov. 2020, bwfworldtour.bwfbadminton.com/news-single/2020/11/21/tai-tzu-ying-i-love-the-outdoors/. Accessed 11 Apr. 2022.

———. "Tai Tzu Ying: I Want to Win in Tokyo Olympics." Interview by K. Keerthivasan. *Sportstar*, 19 Jan. 2020, sportstar.thehindu.com/badminton/tai-tzu-ying-interview-tokyo-2020-olympics-pbl-badminton-sindhu-saina/article30600625.ece. Accessed 11 Apr. 2022.

———. "Tai Tzu Ying: 'This Break Is Good for Me.'" Interview by Dev Sukumar. *HSBC BWF World Tour*, 22 Nov. 2020, bwfworldtour.bwfbadminton.com/news-single/2020/11/22/tai-tzu-ying-this-break-is-good-for-me. Accessed 11 Apr. 2022.

—*Joy Crelin*

Adi Tatarko

Born: ca. 1972
Occupation: Business executive

Adi Tatarko is the cofounder and chief executive officer (CEO) of Houzz, a home design and décor website launched in 2009 meant to serve as a central, convenient, and inspirational space to bring together homeowners, contractors, architects, designers, and other industry professionals interested in collaborating on design and renovation projects. While the concept started as a project worked on between regular jobs spun out of the dissatisfaction Tatarko and her husband, Alon Cohen, felt while trying to find the right contractor and resources to express their imagined concepts to remodel their home, the business has since evolved into a massively successful and versatile platform.

Beginning in the Silicon Valley area, Houzz quickly expanded nationally and then internationally, with offices in major cities around the world. Houzz's user-friendly, visual platform allows homeowners to view the works and services of local professionals to give them a better understanding of their experience and skills and enables professionals to easily find and acquire clients. Valued at approximately $4 billion by the late 2010s and reporting millions of monthly users exploring designs, making connections, or purchasing products as of 2021, the company's employees continued actively finding new ways to forge home design connections. These have included creating mobile applications, expanding further into commerce and marketing endeavors, and allowing the sharing of 3D representations of products, designs, and renovations. Though Tatarko and the company initially struggled under lockdowns that prevented contractors from working on home projects during the first months of the coronavirus disease 2019 (COVID-19) pandemic in 2020, she managed adjustments and adaptations that included a rise in renovations desired by homeowners to accommodate increased, altered time spent living and working at home. Articulating her passion behind establishing and overseeing Houzz, she told Tay Suan Chiang for *The Business Times* (27 May 2017), "It is fulfilling, being able to touch people's lives, seeing how Houzz has improved the quality of life for users, by letting them create a place that is uniquely theirs."

EARLY LIFE AND EDUCATION

Adi Tatarko was born in Tel Aviv, Israel, around 1972, and grew up there. Throughout her early life, she was influenced by the women of her family and their entrepreneurial spirits. While her mother operated a real-estate company, her grandmother, who survived the Holocaust during World War II, built a career as a fashion designer. Tatarko recalled to Lori Fradkin for *HuffPost* (6 Dec. 2017), "My grandmother was a fashion designer in the '40s and '50s, when it was absolutely not the norm for a mother of two kids to travel the world and go to fashion shows. My grandfather supported her, but people really looked at her and said, 'What is she doing?' I think that we are fortunate that today women can actually choose." In 1996, Tatarko received her bachelor's degree from the Hebrew University of Jerusalem.

EARLY CAREER

After having met her future husband, Alon Cohen, on a trip to Thailand, she and Cohen started a small technology services company in their native Israel. They then decided to move to the United States around 1998, settling first in New York City and securing start-up tech work before relocating to the Silicon Valley area of California around 2001. At that point, they agreed that she would move into a different field so that their time could be more flexible. Cohen became a senior director of engineering at eBay, while Tatarko went into

financial advisement. "I started working in a small boutique investment firm," she said to Fradkin. "I felt that working 10 hours a day and raising two kids is fun and great. You don't have to work 16 in order to be happy."

SETTING UP HOUZZ

The seeds for Houzz were planted in Palo Alto in 2006, when the couple bought a fixer-upper mid-twentieth-century ranch house and wanted to hire a designer and architect to remodel it. Despite trying over the next couple of years to consult different periodicals and books as well as other sources for representative pictures and conducting a wide-ranging search for likeminded professionals who could understand and realize their conceived ideas, they were unable to find anyone suitable. While attempts at plans were made, they were left unsatisfied. "It became miserable," Tatarko recalled to Jason Coles for the website of the business plan advisory firm JDC Consultancy (19 Mar. 2019). "After a long process and a lot of time and money that we couldn't afford, we ended up with plans that we didn't like, and we had to throw it away and start all over again."

Without an existing organizational tool to serve their purpose, they then decided to try something different. While still keeping their day jobs, they set up a website from home with an initially small group of users, most of whom were people they were connected to or were otherwise local, to find the best people for the job. The website allowed users to establish contacts with architects, contractors, and designers from around the area of San Francisco Bay who could upload selections of their work to the aggregative platform.

Houzz was officially launched, with Tatarko serving as CEO, on a small budget in 2009, featuring both product information and images as well as articles from professionals eager to show off their experience and aesthetic in addition to discussion forums for advice and conversations between homeowners and professionals. Before long, their site, transformed into an online community, had gained a reputation, and was growing in demand as recommendations were coming in from far and wide. "After about six months we got requests from New York and Chicago, asking if we could open a section for them on the website," Tatarko said to Sarah Finley for *BBC News* (3 June 2019). "Before we knew it this little community website had 350,000 users."

EXPANDING AND MONETIZING

As the website took off and they had evidence that there was a widespread need for others in similar renovation situations to have such a resource available, Tatarko and Cohen decided to take what had been a side project and give it their full attention, including securing investors to finance further expansion. Their first outside investment came in 2010, when venture capitalist Oren Zeev orchestrated a round of financing involving several investors, raising a total of $2 million. This enabled them to secure onboard employees for the first time, and by 2012, the site was already attracting millions of monthly unique users. Over the ensuing years, the company's valuation increased as they would receive millions more through additional funding rounds, including one in 2014 that secured $165 million and one in 2017 that raised another $400 million, from prominent venture capital firms like Sequoia. Explaining the website's immediate appeal to Tay, Tatarko said, "It used to be that you would rely on word of mouth to find a professional, but that didn't necessarily result in you finding the right person. But with Houzz, we give people an easy overview of everything and everyone, which then narrows their search for the right person."

From its initial local success, the company had also begun geographic expansion, first across the United States into other metropolitan areas and then internationally. To better serve their increasing number of users who were living beyond the United States' borders, they decided to branch out to other countries. By 2014, they had launched tailored versions of the website in Europe and Australia, opening offices in cities like Berlin, Germany; London, England; and Sydney, Australia. Tatarko felt that these developments would help cue users from various locations into an even wider range of trends. Beginning in 2015, she oversaw the setup of localized platforms in more of Europe as well as parts of Asia such as Japan. By 2017, locally adapted versions of Houzz had been launched in a total of fifteen countries. From the beginning, Tatarko indicated in interviews that evolution of the site to meet users' needs remained paramount: "If Alon and I take a step back, it's always to think about what's next, where we're going and how we can make it an even better tool for everyone," she told Anh-Minh Le in an interview for *SFGate* (10 June 2012).

Meanwhile, the founders also began creating mobile applications, including for the iPad, and eventually established the ways Houzz would make money, such as by offering paid marketing services for professionals. Another way this was accomplished was by opening a consumer marketplace feature in 2014, which housed industry product listings that eliminated the need for Houzz to maintain inventory stock by sending users' orders on to the associated merchant or manufacturing vendors directly; Houzz then received a 15 percent commission on products sold.

FURTHER DEVELOPMENTS AND WEATHERING A PANDEMIC

Tatarko continued to helm the company as it further built up its consistently growing and popular site and apps with new features, technology, services, and even acquisitions. The year 2015 saw the kickoff of Houzz TV, an online channel that shows video series of home improvement projects, including some by celebrities like supporter Ashton Kutcher. "Ashton was really keen on not just investing in the brand but also being as involved as possible," Tatarko recalled to Finley. "We did the pilot and it worked really well, so decided to launch it as a show and have had celebrities such as Gordon Ramsey and Olivia Munn take part." While, like other prominent companies, Houzz received criticism, including from professionals such as designers who disliked its incorporation of e-commerce, its CEO has remained impassioned about its progress. Her ambitions have also included the 2017 technological innovation of adding 3D modeling to the Houzz' apps previously introduced two-dimensional View in My Room tool, allowing users to preview how potential purchases like new fixtures, accessories, or styles might look in their actual homes; this update added to the tool's already established popularity. Into the end of the 2010s, Tatarko led Houzz through additional developments, such as the 2018 acquisition of the interior design business management platform IvyMark.

During the COVID-19 pandemic, which began in early 2020 and forced workplaces, schools, and other public venues to close and people to isolate to control the spread of the virus, Tatarko instinctively worried about Houzz's future. Indeed, lockdown effects, causing a collapse of the home remodeling market, prompted a difficult layoff of 155 employees. However, as needs for renovations increased once more upon changed home living and working dynamics, she remained in control and adaptive, overseeing company moves such as enhancing its marketing and business management services for professionals with virtual communication and collaboration tools to aid in remote client relations. "Home is a much more prominent thing, not just [a place] to get up in the morning and to go to sleep at night," she said to Jen Rogers for Yahoo! Finance (18 Mar. 2021). "But also for work, for study, for many different things that before you didn't think about your house this way." As of late 2021 her company had continued to grow, despite the economic downturn that resulted from the onset of the pandemic.

PERSONAL LIFE

Adi Tatarko married Alon Cohen, also an Israeli, in 1998 after having met him on a trip to Thailand. They have three sons together. In interviews, Tatarko has spoken often about the dedication to and strategies for balancing work and parenthood that she and Cohen share. The family has continued living in the remodeled house in Palo Alto that originally inspired Houzz.

SUGGESTED READING

Anders, George. "Houzz's Founders Have Become Tech's Newest Power Couple." *Forbes*, 15 Oct. 2014, www.forbes.com/sites/georgeanders/2014/10/15/houzzs-founders-have-become-techs-newest-power-couple/?sh=1d1e845218f2. Accessed 8 Dec. 2021.

Coles, Jason. "Houzz's Adi Tatarko: How an Israeli Immigrant Couple's Home Improvement Platform Revolutionized an Industry." *JDC Consultancy*, 19 Mar. 2019, jdcconsultancy.com/houzz-israeli-immigrant-success-story/. Accessed 3 Nov. 2021.

Finley, Sarah. "'Before We Knew It This Little Website Had 350,000 Users.'" *BBC News*, 3 June 2019, www.bbc.com/news/business-48395181. Accessed 4 Nov. 2021.

Rogers, Jen. "How Houzz Is Benefiting from the Housing Boom." *Yahoo! Finance*, 18 Mar. 2021, www.yahoo.com/now/how-houzz-is-benefiting-from-the-housing-boom-185736600.html. Accessed 8 Dec. 2021.

Tatarko, Adi. "Adi Tatarko: CEO and Co-founder of Houzz." Interview by Tay Suan Chiang. *The Business Times*, 27 May 2017, www.businesstimes.com.sg/lifestyle/weekend-interview/adi-tatarko. Accessed 4 Nov. 2021.

—. "Couple Shares Wisdom of Remodeling with Houzz Site." Interview by Anh-Minh Le. *SFGate*, 10 June 2012, www.sfgate.com/homeandgarden/stylemakerspotlight/article/Couple-shares-wisdom-of-remodeling-with-Houzz-site-3620922.php. Accessed 8 Dec. 2021.

—. "Houzz CEO Adi Tatarko: 'You Can't Have It All and You Have to Live Peacefully with That Knowledge.'" Interview by Lori Fradkin. *HuffPost*, 6 Dec. 2017, www.huffpost.com/entry/houzz-adi-tatarko_n_3976882. Accessed 3 Nov. 2021.

—Christopher Mari

Shakuntala Haraksingh Thilsted

Born: October 29, 1949
Occupation: Scientist

When Trinidad and Tobago–born Shakuntala Haraksingh Thilsted was announced as the recipient of the 2021 World Food Prize, the long-overlooked role of fish and its profound impact on human development was at last recognized. Thilsted—the global lead for nutrition and public health at WorldFish and the first woman of Asian heritage to win the prestigious award—has dedicated her life's work to developing pond polyculture systems, farming small and large fish as a way to combat malnourishment, hunger, and poverty in developing countries.

Inspired by her grandmother, who instilled in young Thilsted the importance of eating nutritious food, including fish, she has helped scientists around the globe understand the benefits of a fish-rich diet: from its essential micronutrients and fatty acids to its crucial role in the cognitive development of infants and children. Having helped millions of people achieve nutrition security and healthier diets,

Thilsted says that, as the world continues its quest to produce sustainable food, aquatic food solutions are key. "Governments interested in boosting both health and economic growth, and doing so sustainably, should find ways to redesign supply chains to deliver fish to poor, malnourished people," Thilsted wrote in *Scientific American* (8 Jan. 2020). "With the right policies in place, ensuring local populations have better access to more fish could cut public health costs, help meet climate goals and foster the rise of lucrative, domestic fish industries."

EARLY LIFE AND EDUCATION

Shakuntala Haraksingh Thilsted was born Shakuntala Haraksingh on October 29, 1949, in Reform Village near the Caribbean town of San Fernando, Trinidad and Tobago, where most of the inhabitants, including Thilsted's family, were descendants of Indigenous labor migrants. She grew up in a multigenerational household, spending endless hours watching her grandmother cook the family meals. These moments in the kitchen would become pivotal in her future career, as it was her grandmother who taught her the benefits of eating good, nutritious food. "My grandmother instilled in us the value of healthy food for good brain—[including] fish—and for being strong," she said in an interview with Janine Mendes-Franco for *Global Voices* (5 June 2021).

Thilsted learned the meaning of demanding work at an early age, as she helped her mother run the postal office and her grandfather attend to his grocery shop, where she was often tasked with balancing the ledger. In 1960, when she was ten years of age, Thilsted began studies at Naparima Girls' High School in San Fernando—cultivating interest in a wide array of subjects, including math, science, and history.

Following her graduation from high school in 1967, Thilsted set out to the St. Augustine campus of the University of the West Indies, one of the world's most globalized institutions of higher learning. As she focused her studies in tropical agriculture, she learned about the production of nutritious food through animal production and how the body absorbs nutrients derived from food. She earned her Bachelor of Science degree in 1971.

Photo via Wikimedia Commons

FIGHTING MALNOURISHMENT

When Thilsted commenced work as an agricultural officer at the Ministry of Agriculture, Lands, and Fisheries in Tobago in 1971, she became the first and only woman to work in that institution until that point. After spending two years in this role and a year as a research assistant at the Faculty of Natural Sciences of the University of the West Indies (1973–74), she migrated to Denmark, where between 1977 and 1980, she pursued her PhD at the Royal Veterinary and Agricultural University (now part of the University of Copenhagen). Thilsted focused her postgraduate studies in the field of the physiology of nutrition, performing research under the mentorship of Dr. Poul Martin Riis. After obtaining her degree, she stayed at the Royal Veterinary and Agricultural University in the capacity of assistant professor (1981–82) and then of associate professor (1982–87) while cementing her long-lasting commitment to research on food security and nutrition in the developing countries within the continents of Asia and Africa.

In the late 1980s, when she began work as a coordinator at the International Centre for Diarrhoeal Disease Research in Dhaka, Bangladesh, Thilsted was able to witness firsthand an elevated level of malnourishment among children and women. As she saw over six thousand children suffering severe cases of malnourishment brought to the center each year, she turned to various disciplines, including the provisioning of food through farming and gardening, to improve their nutrition and health. "Working with severely malnourished children and their mothers [in Bangladesh], I witnessed firsthand the power of diverse, nutritious foods in keeping people well-nourished and healthy," she said to Mendes-Franco. "This can be done sustainably, through employing very many pathways . . . producing diverse foods; paying attention to quantity as well as quality, nutritional quality, and food safety; consuming sufficient [food], not excess; greatly reducing food waste and loss." Her job, however, did not end once the children she had helped were discharged from the center. Thilsted would send field workers to their homes to educate mothers on how to maintain the child's nourishment.

FISH ARE THE ANSWER

While her tireless work in Bangladesh reaped rewards by significantly improving the nutrition outcomes of the children she had treated, Thilsted worried about those who came too late to the center or who never sought help at all. When she voiced her concerns to her supervisor, he suggested that Thilsted work on a strategy that would incorporate small fish into the diet of families within the community, as a way to improve the children's nutrition. Knowing that fish were filled with essential nutrients, including proteins, Thilsted became a woman with a mission. "Working in Bangladesh, the most nutritious food in the diet, small fish, comes from water," she told Mendes-Franco before continuing: "The sea is not the only source of aquatic foods. Inland waters—lakes, rivers, seasonal water bodies, floodplains—are extremely important sources of diverse aquatic foods [like] animals, plants, seaweed."

In 1991, she returned to teach at the Royal Veterinary and Agricultural University, though with many stays in Bangladesh, Egypt, Kenya, and Nepal to continue her fight against malnourishment. During most of the 1990s, she and a group of Danish students partnered with the Bangladesh Agricultural University to develop pond polyculture systems, where they farmed small and large fish together. As

she said to Mendes-Franco, "Two-thirds of the planet is covered by water, so we must make use of this potential for harvesting and growing diverse, nutritious foods, sustainably." She also advocated for an end to the widespread practice by fish farmers of using pesticides to "clean" ponds—a practice that killed native small fish considered less desirable than larger species—leading the government of Bangladesh to ban the use of pesticides in cleaning ponds in 2004.

Additionally, Thilsted's group conducted groundbreaking research into the nutritional value of small fish, which revealed that small fish species, once considered to be low in nutrients, were in fact packed with fatty acids and essential micronutrients. As the development of her project gained traction, consumption of fish in households increased when Thilsted introduced Bangladeshi women to harvesting mola, a small fish abundant in the region, for cooking purposes. This strategy was successful in keeping families more nourished, as it was proved that a small amount of daily consumption of mola provided them with vitamin A, vitamin B, calcium, and iron. Furthermore, Thilsted began producing products such as fish chutney and fish powder that contained four times the nutritional value of fresh fish and were especially designed to meet the needs of mothers and young children. Realizing that these techniques could be adaptable to the needs and conditions of each region, she initiated them in other countries, including Malawi, India, Cambodia, and Myanmar. Her research also inspired dozens of other organizations to employ her fish-based methods, including a program for Rohingya refugees developed by the World Food Programme.

2021 WORLD FOOD PRIZE RECIPIENT

Thilsted remained at the Royal Veterinary and Agricultural University until 2011, at which time she left to fully assume the position of senior nutrition scientist at WorldFish, a global research center based in Bangladesh. There, Thilsted continued promoting nutrient-rich small fish and their potential to combat malnourishment and prevent mineral and vitamin deficiencies, sharing her knowledge and speaking at large conferences, such as the Borlaug Dialogue International Symposium in Des Moines, Iowa, in 2015. As Thilsted rose through the ranks at WorldFish, she assumed the position of research program leader for value chains and nutrition from 2016 to 2018, which was based in Cambodia. In 2018, she became the global lead for nutrition and public health of the research institution, with the post headquartered in Penang, Malaysia. As part of her role, she was tasked with guiding not only WorldFish but also governmental agencies, other research institutions, and major funders around the globe in reshaping food systems to achieve the United Nations' (UN) Sustainable Development Goals, which include advocacy for more native small fish-based foods for women and children and the implementation of more women-driven aquaculture. "Policies, investments and programs from governments are key," Thilsted said to Mendes-Franco. "However, in many low- and middle-income countries, policymakers and government officials need to have knowledge of the multiple benefits of aquatic foods—for people, planet and national development. Global funding agencies can play a role in influencing governments and assisting with aid."

In May 2021, the World Food Prize Foundation announced Thilsted as the recipient of the World Food Prize—often referred to as the Nobel Prize for Food and Agriculture—a prestigious global award given to an individual who has worked to enhance human development through the improvement of food quality and quantity. The first woman of Asian heritage to win the esteemed award, Thilsted was recognized for helping millions of people in developing countries achieve nutrition security and healthier diets; nonetheless, she admits there is still a long way to go. With the coronavirus disease 2019 (COVID-19) pandemic shedding light on the glaring disparities that exist in developing countries, she has stressed the need to produce fish-based products that are safe, accessible, and affordable. "We understand that food systems are broken—and the COVID-19 pandemic has exposed the fragility of the system—with the poor, marginalized and vulnerable suffering most in terms of their ability to sustain sufficient and healthy diets," she stated in an interview with Nigel Brett for the *International Fund for Agricultural Development* (31 May 2021).

PERSONAL LIFE

Thilsted met husband Finn Thilsted, a Danish diplomat, while working as an agricultural officer at the Ministry of Agriculture, Lands, and Fisheries in Tobago. After marrying in 1974, Thilsted migrated to Denmark with her husband; she holds dual citizenship: Trinidad and Tobago and Denmark.

SUGGESTED READING

Haraksingh Thilsted, Shakuntala. "Diversity Is Key: Speaking with Dr. Shakuntala Haraksingh Thilsted, Winner of the 2021 World Food Prize. Part 2 of 2" Interview by Janine Mendes-Franco. *Global Voices*, 5 June 2021, globalvoices.org/2021/06/05/diversity-is-key-speaking-with-dr-shakuntala-haraksingh-thilsted-winner-of-the-2021-world-food-prize. Accessed 10 Dec. 2021.

—. "Reflections on Improving Rural People's Nutrition: A Conversation with 2021 World Food Prize Winner Dr. Shakuntala Thilsted." Interview by Nigel Brett. *International Fund for Agricultural Development*, 31 May 2021, www.ifad.org/en/web/latest/-/2021-world-food-prize-qa. Accessed 10 Dec. 2021.

—. "Sustainable Nutrition: Speaking with Dr. Shakuntala Haraksingh Thilsted, Winner of the 2021 World Food Prize. Part 1 of 2" Interview by Janine Mendes-Franco. *Global Voices*, 5 June 2021, globalvoices.org/2021/06/05/sustainable-nutrition-speaking-with-dr-shakuntala-haraksingh-thilsted-winner-of-the-2021-world-food-prize. Accessed 10 Dec. 2021.

"Shakuntala Haraksingh Thilsted." *World Food Prize Foundation*, 2021, www.worldfoodprize.org/documents/filelibrary/images/laureates/2021_thilsted/EMBAROGED_2021_Laureate_Story_3C68129698A74.pdf. Accessed 10 Dec. 2021.

Thilsted, Shakuntala. "Fishing Can Be Profitable for Emerging Economies, But . . . ." *Scientific American*, 8 Jan. 2020, blogs.scientificamerican.com/observations/fishing-can-be-profitable-for-emerging-economies-but/. Accessed 13 Dec. 2021.

"Trinidad-Born Scientist Cops 2021 World Food Prize Award." *Daily Express*, 11 May 2021, trinidadexpress.com/newsextra/trinidad-born-scientist-cops-2021-world-food-prize-award/article_81094412-b266-11eb-8111-a7fd2cfd45f1.html. Accessed 10 Dec. 2021.

—*Maria del Pilar Guzman*

Elaine Thompson-Herah

Born: June 28, 1992
Occupation: Sprinter

Leading up to the qualification trials for the Tokyo Olympic Games, Jamaican sprinter Elaine Thompson-Herah shaped her mindset by repeating a mantra of sorts. "I will be the fastest woman alive," she told herself following training sessions, as reported by Mike Henson for *BBC Sport* (20 Oct. 2021). "Say it, believe it, work for it and pray for it. I will be the double Olympic champion. Today is my day. I am the greatest." Thompson-Herah's strategy and extensive training paid off: having qualified to compete in her second Olympic Games, she went on to win three gold medals in Tokyo, officially establishing herself as the world's fastest living woman.

An avid runner since childhood, Thompson-Herah found limited success in track and field during her early years of competition but improved her times dramatically in her early twenties. She won her first national championship title in 2015. The following year she made her Olympic debut in Rio de Janeiro, Brazil, where she overcame tough competition to win gold medals in the 100- and 200-metre sprints. Though pleased with such accomplishments, Thompson-Herah remained focused on continuing to challenge herself and push the boundaries of her sport. "I just want to continue to have my starting journey to be as good as the ending journey. And I think my journey hasn't fully started as yet," she told Evelyn Watta in an interview for the official website of the Olympic Games (15 Sept. 2020). In successfully defending her Olympic medals in 2021, Thompson-Herah made history with her impressive times, sparking widespread speculation that she might one day break the women's world record for fastest 100-metre sprint.

EARLY LIFE AND EDUCATION

Elaine Thompson-Herah was born Elaine Sandra-LeeThompson in Manchester Parish, Jamaica, on June 28, 1992. The only child of Rose Richards and Keith Thompson, she spent her childhood in the Banana Ground neighborhood of Manchester Parish, Jamaica, where she was raised largely by her grandmother, Hycenth "Gloria" Thompson. Thompson-Herah developed an interest in running at a young age, initially as a means of completing household tasks quickly so she could spend more time watching cartoons. As she grew older, she also drew inspiration from Jamaica's prominent track and field athletes, including the Jamaican-born sprinter and Olympic medalist Merlene Ottey.

As a teenager attending Christiana High School and later Manchester High School, Thompson-Herah competed as a sprinter in a variety of high school and youth track and field events. She finished in second place in the 200-metre race at a girls' under-seventeen (U17) competition in 2009 and placed fourth in the 100-metre and sixth in the 200-metre races at the under-eighteen (U18) level that year. Though at times dissatisfied with the

Photo by Editor4wikip,
via Wikimedia Commons

results of her track meets, Thompson-Herah remained dedicated to her sport and focused on improving her sprint times. "I didn't win much when I was smaller, I wasn't going to international competitions, but I stood by the sport because the love I have for it," she explained to Henson. "The love takes me to higher places. I wasn't the champion in high school, other girls were faster than me. But I'm competitive, hard working and motivated because of where I'm coming from."

After completing high school in 2011, Thompson-Herah enrolled in the University of Technology, Jamaica. She would go on to earn a bachelor's degree in food service management and culinary arts.

EARLY CAREER

A turning point in Thompson-Herah's track career came when she began training with coach Stephen Francis of the Maximising Velocity and Power (MVP) Track and Field Club, a Kingston-based club that had produced a number of successful Jamaican athletes. "I saw so many stars there," she told Watta (2020). "They were already running Diamond League [a high-level series of World Athletics competitions], going into Championships, and I always wanted to be like them. So I aimed to work hard and be like them." Running in a number of different sprint events during her early years with MVP, including 100-metre, 200-metre, and relay events, Thompson-Herah competed primarily in Jamaica during that period. However, by 2014 she had begun to travel abroad as well, appearing in competitions in countries such as the United States and Italy.

Thompson-Herah won her first Intercollegiate Championships title in 2014, placing first in the women's 100-metre sprint, and went on to defend her title successfully the following year. Her first major success on the international stage also came in 2015, during which she competed in the International Association of Athletics Federations (IAAF) World Championships (later known as the World Athletics Championships) in Beijing, China, and claimed a silver medal in the 200-metre sprint and a team gold medal for the 4×100-metre relay. She won her first Jamaican National Championships title in 2015, placing first in the 200-metre race. She would go on to win the women's 100-metre title at the National Championships the following year.

RIO OLYMPICS

In 2016 Thompson-Herah traveled to Rio de Janeiro, Brazil, to compete in the Summer Olympic Games, having qualified to compete in the 100-metre, 200-metre, and 4×100-metre relay events. She began the Games on a strong note, running 100 metres in 10.71 seconds during the final round of that event and claiming her first Olympic gold medal. She went on to compete in the 200-metre race, finishing in second place in her heat and semifinal race but securing first place in the final round of competition with a time of 21.78 seconds. The first woman since 1988 to win Olympic gold medals in both the 100- and 200-metre events, Thompson-Herah found the experience of winning two gold medals to be somewhat overwhelming. "I didn't quite know how to celebrate," she later told the media, as reported by Andrew Keh and Doug Mills for *The New York Times* (13 Aug. 2016). In addition to her solo events, Thompson-Herah competed for Jamaica in the final round of the 4×100-metre relay, ultimately claiming a silver medal alongside her teammates.

Thompson-Herah remained a prolific and successful competitor in the years following the Rio Olympics, repeatedly claiming the 100-metre title at her National Championships and racing in many Diamond League meets. She was likewise active in international competition, finishing fourth in the 200-metre sprint and second in the 4×100-metre relay at the 2018 Commonwealth Games. Although she won the 100-metre title at the Pan American Games in August of 2019, Thompson-Herah struggled to compete at the World Championships in Doha, Qatar, the following month due to a lingering Achilles tendon injury that had bothered her for several years. Although she was able to run the 100-metre sprint, placing fourth, she withdrew from the remainder of the competition. "I didn't go to a championship to lose. It was beyond my control," she told Watta (2020) about the disappointing experience. "When you have pain, you think you can still do your best. I always tell myself that even if I am having pain, I am going to give my 100 percent. Even if it's not going to be 100 percent, I know I am going to do my best." Despite such setbacks, Thompson-Herah succeeded in qualifying for the upcoming Olympic Games in Tokyo, Japan, placing third in the 100-metre event at the Jamaican Olympic trials.

TOKYO OLYMPICS

Though initially scheduled for mid-2020, the Tokyo Olympic Games were postponed to July and August of 2021 due to the COVID-19 pandemic, a decision that had significant ramifications for athletes' training schedules. "We were training and preparing our mind for the Olympics this year and it hasn't happened," Thompson-Herah told Watta in 2020. "So whatever goals that we had set, we had to push them back because you must set your goals no matter what. We still have to keep training because we have to keep fit." Thompson-Herah had limited opportunities to participate in meets during 2020 but was able to compete more extensively in 2021, placing third in both the 100- and 200-metre races at that year's National Championships.

In July 2021, Thompson-Herah traveled to Japan to compete in the rescheduled Olympics and, she hoped, to defend her medals. "I was super nervous, more than normal," she later told Henson. "I felt like I was going to explode. I could not wait to get into my blocks and just run." With a final time of 10.61 seconds, Thompson-Herah beat fellow Jamaican sprinters Shelly-Ann Fraser-Pryce and Shericka Jackson to win the 100-metre sprint, claiming her second consecutive gold medal in that event. She went on to run the 200-metre final in 21.53 seconds, winning gold once again. "I am so, so happy. Oh my God, it's amazing that I have ever seen this day. That I could complete another double. I can't believe it," Thompson-Herah said after the event, as reported by Joe Hernandez for *NPR* (3 Aug. 2021). In addition to winning her medals, Thompson-Herah's sprint times made her the fastest living woman—and the second-fastest woman in recorded history, after US sprinter Florence Griffith Joyner. She and her teammates also won the 4×100-metre relay with a final time of 41.02, bringing Thompson-Herah her fifth Olympic gold medal.

NEW CHALLENGES

Following the Tokyo Olympics, in August 2021 Thompson-Herah went on to compete in the Prefontaine Classic in Eugene, Oregon, where she won the 100-metre event with a personal-best final time of 10.54. Having set new personal records in the 100-metre sprint at the Olympics and again at the Prefontaine Classic,

she became the center of widespread attention within the track and field community by late 2021, with some commentators speculating that she might beat Griffith Joyner's 100-metre world record of 10.49 seconds. Though she noted in interviews that breaking Griffith Joyner's record was not an immediate priority, Thompson-Herah admitted that she could see herself doing so. "A few years ago I was asked whether I could break that record and I said it was not possible, but for me to run a 10.54 means it is definitely within reach," she told Watta for the website of the Olympic Games (8 Sept. 2021). "It's good to be able to challenge a record that women thought for a long time was impossible to break, and it speaks to the evolution of sprinting." In recognition of her accomplishments during 2021, Thompson-Herah was also named one of two World Athletics athletes of the year.

Thompson-Herah began 2022 with an appearance at the January Queens/Grace Jackson Meet in Jamaica, during which she placed first in the sixty-metre sprint with a time of 7.19 seconds. Thompson-Herah went on to compete in the Müller Indoor Grand Prix in Birmingham, England, and claimed first place in the sixty-metre sprint with an even faster time of 7.08 seconds. A trip to Poland's Copernicus Cup followed, during which she ran sixty metres in 7.04 seconds but finished in second place behind Polish sprinter Ewa Swoboda.

PERSONAL LIFE

Thompson-Herah married coach and former track and field athlete Derron Herah in 2019. When not competing elsewhere, she lives in Jamaica.

SUGGESTED READING

Graham, Raymond. "Elaine Thompson's Preparation Geared towards 200m—Francis." *Gleaner*, 27 June 2015, jamaica-gleaner.com/article/sports/20150628/elaine-thompsons-preparation-geared-towards-200m-francis. Accessed 7 Mar. 2022.

Henson, Mike. "Elaine Thompson-Herah on Taming the Demons En Route to Tokyo Gold." *BBC Sport*, 20 Oct. 2021, www.bbc.com/sport/athletics/58920272. Accessed 7 Mar. 2022.

Hernandez, Joe. "Jamaican Sprinter Elaine Thompson-Herah Wins Historic 'Double-Double' in Track." *NPR*, 3 Aug. 2021, www.npr.org/sections/tokyo-olympics-live-updates/2021/08/03/1024188791/jamaican-sprinter-elaine-thompson-herah-wins-historic-double-double-in-track. Accessed 7 Mar. 2022.

Keh, Andrew, and Doug Mills. "Jamaica's Elaine Thompson Is the Fastest Woman in the World." *The New York Times*, 13 Aug. 2016, www.nytimes.com/2016/08/14/sports/olympics/elaine-thompson-jamaica-100-meter-dash.html. Accessed 7 Mar. 2022.

"Olympic Champion Thompson-Herah Headlines Birmingham 60m." *World Athletics*, 27 Jan. 2022, www.worldathletics.org/news/news/thompson-herah-60m-birmingham-muller-grand-prix. Accessed 7 Mar. 2022.

Thompson-Herah, Elaine. "Exclusive! Elaine Thompson-Herah: 'Disappointment Makes You Better and Stronger.'" Interview by Evelyn Watta. *Olympics*, 15 Sept. 2020, olympics.com/en/featured-news/exclusive-elaine-thompson-herah-disappointment-makes-you-better-and-stronger. Accessed 7 Mar. 2022.

Watta, Evelyn. "Elusive World Record Now within Reach for Elaine Thompson-Herah." *Olympics*, 8 Sept. 2021, olympics.com/en/featured-news/elusive-world-record-within-reach-elaine-thompson-herah. Accessed 7 Mar. 2022.

—*Joy Crelin*

David Thomson

Born: June 12, 1957
Occupation: Media magnate

In 2006 David Thomson took over the reins of his family's eponymous media empire, which was launched by his grandfather Roy in the 1930s and made the Thomsons the richest family in Canada. Thomson inherited control of a company worth $29.3 billion and British peerage as Baron Thomson of Fleet but did not rest on his laurels. Indeed, he quickly oversaw a major business expansion, kicking off a merger of the family-owned company with the British conglomerate Reuters to form the global media juggernaut Thomson Reuters in 2008. Like his grandfather and father before him, Thomson would be perennially featured in compilations of the world's wealthiest people. He appeared on the 2022 *Forbes* global list of billionaires at number twenty-six, with an estimated worth of more than $50 billion in April of that year.

David Thomson earned a reputation as a highly private person, rarely giving interviews and operating mostly under the radar despite occasional tabloid attention to his personal life. Many profiles focus on his personal art collection, renowned for both its quality and its scope encompassing everything from antiquities to modern photography. (He is often said to have among the world's most comprehensive collections of the works of nineteenth-century British landscape painter John Constable.) Reporters also often note his unusual, instinctual approach to both business and life in general. "In the end, judgment and instinct are still the elements of great success," Thomson told Peter C. Newman in a rare, in-depth interview for *Maclean's* (6 May 2002). "One can have all of the numbers prepared, all the logistics, all the statistics run, but until one faces a human being or a corporate entity, one really has no sense of its service, let alone its potential. . . . I am absolutely compelled to follow my feelings, or I forfeit the right to live."

EARLY YEARS AND FAMILY BACKGROUND

David Kenneth Roy Thomson was born in Toronto, Ontario, Canada, on June 12, 1957, into a prominent family. His paternal grandfather, Roy Thomson, began a radio station in Ontario in 1931 despite having little money and no broadcasting license. Sinking the revenue from that single station back into the business, he soon purchased three more, along with four small newspapers, beginning what would become a major international media empire by the late 1950s. Investments in the oil industry and other sectors also proved successful. Roy Thomson was granted the British hereditary title Baron Thomson of Fleet in 1964, further signaling the family's rise.

David Thomson's father, Kenneth, worked in the family's media business. His mother, Marilyn Lavis, was a gifted classical musician. The daughter of a railway employee, she was said to remain relatively frugal throughout her life because of her modest background, even after becoming very wealthy. Thomson was raised with his two siblings: Taylor, born in 1959, and Peter, born in 1965. They had an affluent upbringing in Toronto's upscale Rosedale neighborhood. Thomson was particularly close to his grandfather. "He was very lonely and we conversed for hours about business and people," Thomson told Newman. "He was an optimist with an uncanny ability to seize opportunities that others couldn't see. This approach was in complete parallel to my own nature."

EDUCATION

Thomson attended the Hall School, in England, and Upper Canada College, a prestigious private high school to which he was chauffeured each day from the family's Georgian mansion. Although those schools stressed sports and military service, Thomson had little interest in either. Classmates later remembered him as a shy and sensitive person.

In 1976 Thomson's grandfather died, and his father inherited both the peerage and control of the family company—which by then included a wide array of newspapers and magazines as well as lucrative interests in radio, television, and publishing. The future seemed set in stone for Thomson, as he was already marked as the next heir in the family business. Many journalists attempting to examine Thomson's life have pointed to a passage in Roy Thomson's 1975 autobiography that reads, "David, my grandson, will have to take his part in the running of the organization, and David's son, too." With the business tied up in trusts to avoid estate taxes, Roy explained, "These Thomson boys that come after Ken are not going to be able, even if they want to, to shrug off these responsibilities."

Despite that looming obligation, Thomson chose to study not business but history, at the University of Cambridge's Selwyn College. There, he focused on the civil service in India from the late eighteenth to mid-nineteenth centuries. He graduated in 1978.

LAUNCHING A BUSINESS CAREER

After graduating from college, Thomson began his career as an associate at McLeod Young Weir, a venerable Canadian financial firm; however, he left after a brief time to join the Hudson Bay Company (HBC), which had then recently come under the control of his family. HBC had been established in 1670 as a fur-trading enterprise and is acknowledged to be the oldest incorporated joint-stock merchandising company in the English-speaking world. In 1979, in a heated contest among Canadian billionaires, Kenneth Thomson acquired a 75 percent stake in HBC, which by then encompassed several department store chains, real estate holdings, and other assets. Learning the business from the ground up, David Thomson did stints selling socks at one of the Toronto department stores and worked for a time at a fur-trading post in Saskatchewan. He later moved up the corporate ladder to head Simpsons and Zellers, two retail chains that fell under the HBC umbrella.

In the early 1990s Thomson founded Osmington Incorporated, a commercial real estate company that was his own venture, independent of his family. Osmington would go on to develop a key partnership with True North Sports and Entertainment, which purchased the Atlanta Thrashers National Hockey League (NHL) franchise in 2011 and moved them to Manitoba as the Winnipeg Jets, leading many sources to refer to Thomson as an owner of the team. Meanwhile, Thomson continued to rise in the hierarchy of the family business. In the mid-1990s he became deputy chair of Woodbridge, the private company under which the Thomsons manage their holdings. (Woodbridge also held some 10 percent of Bell Globemedia, giving the family a stake in the *Globe and Mail* newspaper and CTV as well as many other high-profile assets, such as a minority share of the Montreal Canadiens NHL franchise.)

THOMSON REUTERS

In June 2006 Thomson's father died, so control of the business empire fell to Thomson as the eldest son. The hereditary peerage was also passed down to him, and he became known as the 3rd Baron Thomson of Fleet. The following year the Thomson Corporation announced a plan to acquire Reuters Group—a news and business information company serving the financial, legal, science, health-care, and media sectors—for a reported $17 billion. The merger was completed in April 2008, with the new publicly traded entity dubbed Thomson Reuters and boasting operations in more than ninety countries. Thomson served as chair of the newly structured company.

Over the following years Thomson Reuters's valuation would fluctuate along with the global markets. Yet after a rocky debut amid the global financial crisis, it stabilized as a profitable enterprise with revenues in the billions. The success considerably heightened the net worth of Thomson and his family. The company did see its share of controversy, however. In 2009, the European Commission launched an antitrust investigation against Thomson Reuters for possible anticompetitive practices involving data feeds; in 2012, an agreement was reached in which the company agreed to make changes. In 2019 there was an outcry among human rights activists over the fact that one of Thomson Reuters's subsidiaries, Westlaw, was providing information to US Immigration and Customs Enforcement (ICE) that enabled mass deportations. Nevertheless, the company remained a large and influential player in the data and media sectors. Reports noted that the Thomson family's net worth increased sharply even amid the COVID-19 pandemic that broke out in 2020.

ART COLLECTION

By the early 2020s, Thomson was considered by far the richest person in Canada and one of the wealthiest billionaires in the world. Yet he continued to lead a low-profile life, almost never granting interviews or releasing direct statements. Still, despite taking pains to stay out of the media spotlight, he did occasionally attract attention. Perhaps most notably, he developed a reputation as a serious and prolific art collector, earning mentions in various art-related publications. Following in his father's footsteps, Thomson became avidly interested in art as a teen. Early on he began collecting the paintings of John Constable (1776–1837), who is known primarily for landscapes depicting the English countryside. "[Constable's] sensibility has had a strong influence on my personal philosophy, which I carry forward in all walks of life, including business," Thomson told Newman. "So few people openly see and question scenes and events as he did. All too often subjects are viewed from a narrow perspective. Being possessed by imagination, curiosity and such dreamlike qualities doesn't mean one is incapable of pragmatism and tough decision-making."

Thomson's extensive collection also grew to include medieval artifacts; indigenous Inuit items; fifteenth-century Flemish and German paintings; nineteenth-century Scandinavian works; numerous drawings by Victorian-era polymath John Ruskin; pieces by famed artist Pablo Picasso; twentieth-century Canadian paintings; photography from the nineteenth and twentieth centuries; and animation cels. In his *Maclean's* profile, Newman referred to Thomson's Rosedale mansion as "an art gallery with kitchen, bathrooms and bedrooms attached."

Thomson at times lent his privately owned pieces to public exhibitions and also made several notable donations to museums. For example, in 2002 he paid $117 million at auction for *The Massacre of the Innocents*, a seventeenth-century painting by Peter Paul Rubens, and later gave it to the Art Museum of Toronto. He also donated over $275 million toward the Art Museum of Toronto's renovation and created a permanent $20 million endowment. "I take art so seriously because it's one of the few pursuits in which I can totally unravel my soul," he told Newman. "For me, the act of creation comes through in a better appreciation of business."

PERSONAL LIFE

Thomson's intensely private nature has meant there is limited information about his personal life. Yet while the Thomson family long sought to cultivate an image of being down-to-earth despite their great wealth, the few details that emerged over the years often cast them as an eccentric, sometimes troubled group behind the scenes. Thomson's romantic relationships, in particular, generated a fair amount of tabloid coverage.

His first marriage, to Mary Lou La Prairie, who worked for the Simpsons department store, lasted from 1988 until an acrimonious divorce in 1997 that resulted in a $6.3 million settlement and shared custody of their two daughters, Thyra Nicole and Tessa Lys. In 2000 Thomson married Laurie Ludwick, a reporter and public relations executive. The relationship was tumultuous from the beginning, and Thomson filed for divorce on their one-year anniversary. The two reconciled briefly, separated again, and then reunited. They split for good in 2005, after which their son, Benjamin, was born. Once again the divorce was acrimonious, with the tabloids detailing various allegations of ill conduct by both sides.

In 2007, Thomson became engaged to actor Kelly Rowan. The two had a daughter in 2008 but split up around the same time, before the marriage took place. Thomson next dated Séverine Nackers, an art expert with the auction house Sotheby's, and together they had two children.

SUGGESTED READING

Austin, Ian. "In Canada, the Torch Is Passed on a Quiet but Profitable Legacy." *The New York Times*, 3 July 2006, www.nytimes.com/2006/07/03/business/media/03thomson.html. Accessed 18 Mar. 2022.

Casey, Quentin. "Who's David Thomson? A Peek into the Mysterious, 'Reluctant' Head of Canada's Richest Family." *Financial Post*, 19 Aug. 2021, financialpost.com/personal-finance/high-net-worth/whos-david-thomson-a-peek-into-the-mysterious-reluctant-head-of-canadas-richest-family. Accessed 18 Mar. 2022.

Kingston, Anne, and Nicholas Kohler. "Canada's Richest Family, the Thomsons, Are Worth $23.8 Billion . . . and They're Just a Little Bit Strange." *Maclean's*, vol. 119, no. 19, 8 May 2006, pp. 22–32. *EBSCOhost*, search.ebscohost.com/login.aspx?direct=true&db=edb&AN=20756566&site=eds-live. Accessed 18 Mar. 2022.

Thomas, David. "Fortune's Child." Interview by Peter C. Newman. *Maclean's*, 6 May 2002. *EBSCOhost*, search.ebscohost.com/login.aspx?direct=true&db=f6h&AN=6581717&site=eds-live. Accessed 18 Mar. 2022.

Soliven, Ernesto. "David Thomson Net Worth: Media Mogul's Family Owns 320 Million Thomson Reuters Shares." *International Business Times*, 17 July 2020, www.ibtimes.com/david-thomson-net-worth-media-moguls-family-owns-320-million-thomson-reuters-shares-3012729. Accessed 18 Mar. 2022.

"Top 200 Collectors: David Thomson." *ARTNews*, www.artnews.com/art-collectors/top-200-profiles/david-thomson/. Accessed 18 Mar. 2022.

—*Mari Rich*

David Treuer

Born: October 21, 1970
Occupation: Writer

Throughout his career, award-winning Ojibwe writer David Treuer has made it his mission to create a new story for American Indians. This aspiration is evident in every piece in his body of work, which includes books, essays, and articles spanning the genres of fiction, memoir, lexicography, and history. For Treuer, writing is a way to make Indigenous Americans and their traditions truly known for the first time in history. This is because for centuries outsiders controlled the narrative, typically depicting American Indians as either brutal savages or ethereal beings with the power to teach White people how to connect with nature. Treuer commented on this problematic phenomenon in a conversation with Dinitia Smith for *The New York Times* (16 Aug. 2006), stating, "The stories America tells itself about itself involve us, but most people will never meet or talk to one of us."

Treuer began his literary career as a novelist but earned growing recognition with *Native American Fiction: A User's Manual* (2006), a work of criticism. That book drew attention—and some controversy—for not only condemning stereotypical White portrayals of American Indians but also critiquing the work of the few American Indian writers of the previous generation who had achieved mainstream literary fame. Centrally, Treuer sought to counter what he saw as a narrative of tragedy and identity loss surrounding American Indian experience, and he continued this effort with later works. For example, in his acclaimed nonfiction book *The Heartbeat of Wounded Knee: Native America from 1890 to the Present* (2019), he emphasized his "simple, fierce conviction that our cultures are not dead and our civilizations have not been destroyed."

EARLY LIFE AND EDUCATION

David Treuer was born on October 21, 1970, in Washington, DC, to Margaret Seelye Treuer and Robert Treuer. He was the couple's second child, born in between his older brother, Anton, and his younger siblings, Micah and Megan.

Both of Treuer's parents had a significant impact on him as a child. His mother was an

Ojibwe woman who grew up in an impoverished family in Minnesota. She worked to improve healthcare on Minnesota reservations and went on to become the first female American Indian lawyer in the state and later the nation's first female American Indian judge. She also taught Treuer and his siblings about Ojibwe traditions, instilling a deep sense of pride in their heritage and a resistance to cultural assimilation.

While Treuer's mother helped him connect with his American Indian roots, his interest in writing was fostered by his father. A Jewish Holocaust survivor, Robert Treuer moved from Austria to the United States as a child and went on to have a celebrated career as an educator, a union organizer, an Indian rights activist, and a government worker. He was also a prolific author of books and articles and would often awaken the young Treuer with the sound of his typewriter.

Treuer was seven years old when his family relocated from Washington, DC, to the Leech Lake Indian Reservation in Minnesota. The rest of his formative years were spent on the edge of the reservation in a small house and trailer. Although his parents were not able to afford niceties like luxurious vacations, they did not struggle as much as many other Leech Lake families. "By reservation standards we were very comfortable," Treuer told Smith. As a teenager, Treuer attended Bemidji High School, which had a mix of both Native and White students. Around this time he became a dedicated player of the game Dungeons and Dragons, drawn to its fantasy worlds and storytelling.

COLLEGE AND EARLY CAREER

Treuer followed his older brother Anton to Princeton University—a school that both boys decided to apply to after watching the film *Risky Business* (1983). Although he had grown up believing that reservations were something to escape, Treuer felt lonely at Princeton without other Native people around. He spent the first two years there studying music with the intention of becoming a composer. He switched to anthropology and began taking creative writing classes with professor and acclaimed author Toni Morrison. She encouraged him to write his own story as a Native person instead of letting other people define it for him. Treuer reflected on the connection he felt with Morrison in an interview with Hannah

Photo by Larry D. Moore, via Wikimedia Commons

Gordon for *Midwestern Gothic* (1 Sept. 2015): "Our work together (when I was a student) and our relationship (still one of mentor and mentee) subsequently remains one of the most profound relationships of my life. Not because of what she is but who she is. We are, I think, similar in that we demand writing to be more than simply pretty or moving. The writing has to do some kind of work." Upon Morrison's encouragement, Treuer wrote two senior theses at Princeton, one in anthropology and the other in creative writing.

Treuer began writing his first novel while he was still a student in Morrison's class. Although he landed a literary agent immediately after graduating from Princeton in 1992, most publishers were not receptive to his debut. *Little* (1995) follows the story of seven people living in extreme poverty on an Indian reservation in Minnesota. According to Treuer, *Little* was rejected dozens of times while his agent shopped it around. "It needed work; what book doesn't?" He explained to Shannon Gibney in an interview for *Mn Artists* (23 Aug. 2006). "But I think it was also because I didn't perform, culturally, the way that they wanted me to. There are no feathers, there's no ceremony, there's no reclaiming of Indian-ness, there's no Indian pride. It's just living. So it confused a lot of people, and they rejected it." Even after the novel was finally published by

Graywolf, it received mixed reviews from critics who, like publishers, were often unsure of what to do with a story about American Indians that did not align with mainstream stereotypes.

Despite these challenges, Treuer did begin to earn attention as a rising literary voice. He won a Pushcart Prize in 1996 and earned a Fulbright fellowship that same year. *Little* was also a finalist for the Minnesota Book Award.

NATIVE AMERICAN FICTION: A USER'S GUIDE

Treuer's second novel, *The Hiawatha* (1999), similarly struggled to find an audience, though it received several strong reviews. Also in 1999 Treuer earned a PhD in anthropology from the University of Michigan. He began work as a professor soon afterwards, teaching English at the University of Minnesota for several years before accepting a job at the University of Southern California (USC) in 2010.

Meanwhile, Treuer had a breakout year in 2006 with the publication of two books. His novel *The Translation of Dr. Apelles* was more critically successful than his previous efforts and was named a best book of the year by *The Washington Post* and other outlets. But drawing even more attention was *Native American Fiction: A User's Guide*, a collection of nonfiction essays providing a novel approach to assessing some of the most historically popular works of American Indian fiction. In it, Treuer argues that too often Native American fiction is regarded as actual history or "cultural artifacts" instead of works of literature. "They're fantasies, they're fairytales that seduce us, but they're not *true*. And they shouldn't be judged on their truth value, they should be judged on their literary value," Treuer explained to Gibney. "And frankly, a lot of Native American fiction is really bad." The book caused a particular stir in the literary community for its sharp critiques of established American Indian authors such as Sherman Alexie and Louise Erdrich.

Although it was seen as controversial, *Native American Fiction: A User's Guide* received mostly positive reviews and raised Treuer's profile. In 2007, he was awarded a prestigious Guggenheim Fellowship for his nonfiction work.

REZ LIFE: AN INDIAN'S JOURNEY THROUGH RESERVATION LIFE

Although he never aspired to becoming a nonfiction writer, Treuer continued to write

in the genre. In 2005, he learned of a deadly school shooting at Minnesota's Red Lake Reservation—the place where his parents had met. Frustrated by the negative way the media was depicting reservations while reporting on the event, Treuer decided to write a full-length nonfiction work that demonstrated that they were not just places of suffering. This resulted in *Rez Life: An Indian's Journey Through Reservation Life* (2012), a blend of investigative journalism and memoir that examines the history, politics, and laws of American Indian reservations in America. In an interview with Neal Conan for *NPR* (20 Feb. 2012), Treuer explained how his own experience growing up at Leech Lake as well as his time spent researching other reservations led to the book's thesis: "The truth to me seems to be that reservations are places of surplus. There's more of everything. There might be more hardship, but there's more joy. There might be more pain, but there's more opportunity."

Rez Life was enthusiastically received by critics and readers alike, further establishing Treuer as an important voice in American literature and specifically American Indian writing. He followed up with his fourth novel, *Prudence* (2015), a story set in Minnesota during World War II.

THE HEARTBEAT OF WOUNDED KNEE

Treuer continued his mission of challenging the mainstream perception of American Indians with another nonfiction work, *The Heartbeat of Wounded Knee: Native America from 1890 to the Present* (2019). He wrote it as a counternarrative to *Bury My Heart at Wounded Knee* (1970), a bestselling history book by author Dee Brown. Treuer explained to Lily Rothman in an interview for *Time* (27 Jan. 2019) why he felt compelled to challenge Brown's text: "It tries to draw attention to a legacy of injustice, but on the other hand it says the massacre at Wounded Knee in 1890 was the point at which Indian culture and civilization died, period. I remember reading that as a student at Princeton, far from home, missing my tribe and thinking how preposterous it was."

Through a combination of styles including investigative journalism, history, and memoir, *The Heartbeat of Wounded Knee* posits that Native people today should stop being viewed as "victims" who have endured nothing but suffering for the past two centuries. Treuer argues that this is not only untrue, but it also negatively impacts how Native people perceive themselves. Instead, American Indians must be viewed as tenacious survivors who continue to find ways to thrive despite the challenges they face. The book was well-received, earning extensive acclaim from critics and becoming a best seller. It went on to be a finalist for the 2019 National Book Award and was longlisted for the Carnegie Medal for Excellence.

In 2021, Pantheon Books announced it had hired Treuer as an editor at large. He would cover both fiction and nonfiction, focusing on books from Indigenous and emerging writers.

PERSONAL LIFE

Treuer has three children with writer and educator Gretchen Potter, a member of the Tonawanda Seneca tribe. He divides his time between Southern California and the Leech Lake Reservation in Minnesota. In addition to his writing career, Treuer has worked extensively to record and revitalize the Ojibwe language, including projects with his brother Anton, a professor at Bemidji State University and expert on the language.

SUGGESTED READING

Smith, Dinitia. "American Indian Writing, Seen Through a New Lens." *The New York Times*, 19 Aug. 2006, www.nytimes.com/2006/08/19/books/19indi.html. Accessed 8 Feb. 2021.

Treuer, David. "Author David Treuer Mentored a Generation of Native Authors. Now, He'll Publish Them." Interview by Dorothy Pineda. *Los Angeles Times*, 14 Dec. 2021, www.latimes.com/entertainment-arts/books/story/2021-12-14/david-treuer-joins-pantheon-to-acquire-and-edit-native-authors-and-books. Accessed 9 Feb. 2021.

___. *"The Heartbeat of Wounded Knee* Author David Treuer on Why We Need to Change the Way Indian Stories Are Told." Interview by Lily Rothman. *Time*, 14 Jan. 2019, time.com/5511505/david-treuer-interview/. Accessed 29 Jan. 2022.

___. "Interview: David Treuer." Interview by Hannah Gordon. *Midwestern Gothic*, 1 Sept. 2015, midwestgothic.com/2015/09/interview-david-treuer/. Accessed 4 Feb. 2022.

___. "Ojibwe Writer Celebrates the Beauty of *Rez Life*." Interview by Neal Conan. *NPR*, 20 Feb. 2012, www.npr.org/2012/02/20/147156103/ojibwe-writer-seeks-out-the-beauty-of-rez-life. Accessed 3 Feb. 2022.

___. "Portrait of the Coyote as a Young Man." *Harper's Magazine*, 1 Nov. 2021, harpers.org/archive/2021/11/portrait-of-the-coyote-as-a-young-man-david-treuer/. Accessed 1 Feb. 2022.

___. Treuer, David. "Thinking Souls: An Interview with David Treuer." Interview by Shannon Gibney. *Mn Artists*, 23 Aug. 2006, mnartists.walkerart.org/thinking-souls-an-interview-with-david-treuer. Accessed 3 Feb. 2022.

SELECTED WORKS

Little, 1995; *The Hiawatha*, 1999; *The Translation of Dr. Apelles*, 2006; *Native American Fiction: A User's Manual*, 2006; *Rez Life: An Indian's Journey Through Reservation Life*, 2012; *Prudence*, 2015; *The Heartbeat of Wounded Knee: Native America from 1890 to the Present*, 2019

—*Emily E. Turner*

Kyle Troup

Born: June 11, 1991
Occupation: Professional bowler

In the weeks prior to the 2021 Professional Bowlers Association (PBA) Tour Finals, professional bowler Kyle Troup was ready to take on any competitor. "I feel that my game is top level right now and I am going to be the guy that they are gunning for," he told Jill Winters for *FloBowling* (17 June 2021). Indeed, Troup's success over the previous seasons aptly established him as a strong contender for the championship. The winner of three national PBA titles in 2020, including the 2020 Tour Finals title, Troup won both the PBA Players Championship and the PBA Playoffs during the 2021 bowling season and in so doing set a new PBA record for tournament earnings in a single season.

Troup began bowling as a young child, competing in his native North Carolina, and neighboring states throughout his teen years. After establishing himself as a strong competitor on the PBA Regional Tour, he won his first National Tour title in 2015. He went on to win five additional national titles before entering his record-breaking 2021 season. Although Troup lost the championship match of the 2021 PBA Tour Finals, he remained pleased with both the progression of his career and the increasing public awareness of his sport. "I'm just blessed to be a bowler," he told Sonny Fulks for *Press Pros Magazine* (13 Aug. 2021). "It's what I do. I travel the world and do what I love for a living. Yes, the golfers make more money, but as far as publicity, I think it'll come. We just need to get more eyes on bowling."

EARLY LIFE AND EDUCATION

Kyle Troup was born on June 11, 1991. One of two sons born to Sherri and John "Guppy" Troup, he spent his early life in Taylorsville, North Carolina. His father was a professional bowler who competed in regional and national events overseen by the Professional Bowlers Association (PBA), while his mother worked a variety of jobs, including in corrections and in social services. Troup enjoyed watching his father compete and was strongly influenced by the elder Troup, who won eight PBA national titles over the course of his career in addition to numerous regional titles. "His style and his actions on the lanes, I think I just bleed him with that," he told Winters (17 June 2021). "I have always wanted to be a showman like him because he always had a lot of fun it seemed like when I was a kid watching him."

Troup himself began bowling as a toddler and grew increasingly dedicated to the sport as he aged. "I was one of those kids that didn't fit the profile for other sports," he explained to Fulks. In addition to traveling with his father and spending a great deal of time in bowling alleys throughout his childhood, he attended local schools in the Taylorsville area, including Alexander Central High School. He graduated from high school in 2009. The following year, he attended Catawba Valley Community College, where he studied accountancy.

EARLY CAREER

A competitive bowler from childhood, Troup began his career competing in youth bowling leagues in North Carolina, before entering competitions both in North Carolina and in neighboring states. He demonstrated a signature style of play early on, holding his

Photo by RCraig09 via Wikimedia Commons.

bowling ball in two hands rather than the more traditional single hand. "I wanted to throw my dad's ball, but wasn't strong enough," he told Fulks about the origin of his play style. "So I had to throw it with two hands and I just stuck with it as I got older. Really, I'm not very good as a one-handed bowler." Having demonstrated his talents at the youth level, he moved up to the adult level of competition while still in his teens, competing against bowlers with far more years of experience.

Hoping to establish himself as a professional bowler, Troup began competing in events overseen by the PBA, initially participating in PBA Regional Tour competitions. He won his first regional title in 2010 and competed in his first PBA National Tour event in 2010. He became a regular competitor on the National Tour over the next years and also found success at the regional level, earning his region's Player of the Year honors on two separate occasions. The year 2015 saw his best National Tour performance to that point. In addition to competing in a total of seventeen events, he won his first national title in May of that year, at the PBA Wolf Open in Oklahoma. "It's a dream come true and it makes it all that much better that my family was able to be here to be a part of it," he told *BowlingDigital.com* (17 May 2015) after the competition.

PROFESSIONAL SUCCESS

Troup was a recurring participant in PBA National Tour events throughout 2016 and 2017, competing in twenty such events in the former year and thirty-two in the latter. He won his first National Tour doubles title in 2017, partnering with Swedish bowler Jesper Svensson to win the Mark Roth/Marshall Holman Doubles Championship in Maine. The following year, he competed in twenty-eight national events and won the Storm Luck Larsen Masters, held in Malmo, Sweden. He then competed in the 2018 Weber Cup—a tournament contested by a team representing the United States and a team representing Europe—where he was named most valuable player (MVP) of the tournament. Amid such successes, Troup sought to remain focused on improving his game and avoid becoming overconfident. "You can't hit the cruise button bowling against the best bowlers in the world who are always working on their game," he later told Winters for *FloBowling* (19 July 2021) about his mindset.

In addition to competing in events such as the Weber Cup, Troup became an official member of the United States' national bowling team in 2018, following a successful performance during the 2018 Team Trials. He competed with the United States in the 2018 World Bowling Men's Championships, winning a bronze medal in the singles competition, silver medals in the team and masters categories, and a gold medal in trios. That year he also ranked second in the 2018 QubicaAMF Bowling World Cup, behind Australian Sam Cooley. After a 2019 season in which he claimed no additional national titles, Troup bowled a career-best season in 2020, claiming three national titles through victories at events such as the PBA Jonesboro Open in Jonesboro, Arkansas. That year, he also partnered with Svensson once again to win the Mark Roth/Marshall Holman Doubles Championship, held in Indianapolis, Indiana. In July 2020, he beat bowler Anthony Simonsen in the championship match to win his first PBA Tour Finals title.

MAJOR TITLEHOLDER

The year 2021 proved to be another breakthrough year for Troup, who reached a major milestone in February when he won the PBA Players Championship. That win was particularly significant because the PBA Players Championship is one of the five PBA events considered a major championship, and so became Troup's first major title win. He also competed outside of his usual slate of tournaments in February 2021, bowling in the doubles competition of the inaugural PBA Junior National Tournament alongside seventeen-year-old Nate Purches. Troup and Purches defeated the competition decisively to win the event, which paired each junior player with a seasoned professional bowler.

In May 2021, Troup faced off against Cooley in the PBA Playoffs, an event in which the player who won three games would be crowned champion. Troup won the first match against Cooley but lost the second; he did not view that loss as a setback. "I felt really confident," he told Jef Goodger for *BowlersJournal.com* (16 May 2021). "I knew I pretty much lost that game by the seventh or eighth frame, so I switched my focus to rooting Sam on. I wanted to see him bowl 300 and get the extra $10,000. It's one to one, all right, I just need to win a game. I really wanted to win game three to put the pressure on him to make him feel like it was a must-win situation." He went on to beat Cooley in the third and fourth games, claiming his second national title of the year as well as the competition's grand prize.

Troup's success in the PBA Playoffs increased his total winnings for 2021 to $469,200, the most ever accumulated in a single season by a PBA bowler. "I never thought I would be a PBA record holder so that was something that caught me off guard," he told Winters for *FloBowling* (17 June 2021). "I want to stretch this record out a little bit but hopefully it gets beat which means we will be bowling for even more money." He went on to compete in the PBA Tour Finals in June 2021 and progressed to the championship match but ultimately lost to Simonsen, whom he had defeated the previous year. Despite that loss, he remained focused on achieving further success on the PBA National Tour. "The goal was to become a professional bowler, and now the goal is to win more titles than my father," he told Mel Busler for 7 *News WWNYTV* (29 Oct. 2021).

PERSONAL LIFE

In addition to his skill as a bowler, Troup is well known within the bowling community for his distinctive physical appearance, which includes his signature curly hair and eye-catching clothing reminiscent of the fashions once worn by his father. "My dad wore the wild pants when he bowled. That was a tradition that I just carried on," he explained to Fulks. "I didn't like my curly hair as a kid and kept it short for a lot of times, but now that I'm older it's a way to being recognized, and definitely a brand." In addition to serving as a form of promotion for Troup himself, his attention-grabbing appearance could ultimately benefit the sport of bowling as a whole. "If people can recognize me and tune into bowling, that's the ultimate goal," he told Fulks.

Troup lives in Hickory, North Carolina.

SUGGESTED READING

Busler, Mel. "Kyle Troup Brings His Flamboyant Bowling Style to the North Country." *7 News WWNYTV*, 29 Oct. 2021, www.wwnytv.com/2021/10/29/kyle-troup-brings-his-flamboyant-style-north-country/. Accessed 12 Nov. 2021.

Curtis, Bryan. "Can Bowling Win over the 'Lebowski' Generation?" *The Ringer*, 25 July 2019, www.theringer.com/sports/2019/7/25/20726901/bowling-pba-tv-kyle-troup-big-lebowski-rob-stone-fox-sports. Accessed 12 Nov. 2021.

Fulks, Sonny. "PBA Bowling: What You'd Like to Know about Kyle Troup." *Press Pros Magazine*, 13 Aug. 2021, pressprosmagazine.com/pba-coldwater-what-you-might-like-to-know-about-kyle-troup/. Accessed 12 Nov. 2021.

Goodger, Jef. "Kyle Troup Wins 2021 PBA Playoffs for $100K, Eight Career PBA Tour Title." *BowlersJournal.com*, 16 May 2021, www.bowlersjournal.com/kyle-troup-wins-2021-pba-playoffs-for-100k-eight-career-pba-tour-title/. Accessed 12 Nov. 2021.

"Kyle Troup Wins PBA Wolf Open for First PBA Tour Title." *BowlingDigital.com*, 17 May 2015, www.bowlingdigital.com/bowl/node/14389. Accessed 12 Nov. 2021.

Winters, Jill. "Kyle Troup Frontrunner for Player of the Year Heading into PBA Summer Tour." *FloBowling*, 19 July 2021, www.flobowling.com/articles/7114925-kyle-troup-frontrunner-for-player-of-the-year-heading-into-pba-summer-tour. Accessed 12 Nov. 2021.

—. "Like Father, Like Son: Guppy and Kyle Troup Are Showmen Through and Through." *FloBowling*, 17 June 2021, www.flobowling.com/articles/7084969-like-father-like-son-guppy-and-kyle-troup-are-showmen-through-and-through. Accessed 12 Nov. 2021.

—Joy Crelin

Stefanos Tsitsipas

Born: August 12, 1998
Occupation: Tennis player

In June 2021, Greek tennis player Stefanos Tsitsipas progressed to the final round of the French Open, becoming the first Greek athlete to reach the final not only at that competition but also at any of professional tennis's Grand Slam tournaments. Although he ultimately fell to Novak Djokovic in the final, reaching that point remained a significant and meaningful milestone for Tsitsipas. "All I can think of is my roots, where I came from, a really small place outside Athens," he told the media, as reported by Andrew Reid for *Yahoo!Sport Australia* (11 June 2021). "My dream was to play in a big stadium at the French Open one day, but I never thought I could." As Tsitsipas aptly demonstrated in 2021, he was capable not only of playing in the French Open but also of putting forth an impressive performance in that tournament, one of professional tennis's most prestigious events.

A skilled tennis player since childhood, Tsitsipas found substantial success on the junior level and went on to make a name for himself as a senior player, progressing through the developmental Futures tournaments and Association of Tennis Professionals (ATP) Challenger Tour before becoming a fixture in top-level ATP Tour events. He won his first ATP Tour title in 2018 and the following year became one of the top-ten men's singles players in the ATP Tour rankings. Although his career has been not without its challenges, Tsitsipas remained both dedicated to and passionate about his chosen sport. "At the end of the day," he told Christopher Bollen for *Interview* magazine (5 June 2019), "tennis has made my life and fulfilled my dreams."

EARLY LIFE AND EDUCATION

Stefanos Tsitsipas was born in Athens, Greece, on August 12, 1998. He was the first of four children born to parents Apostolos Tsitsipas and Julia Apostoli-Salnikova, both of whom were former tennis players and coached the sport as well. His father was native to Greece, while his mother was Russian. Growing up in the coastal Greek town of Vouliagmeni, Tsitsipas began playing tennis at the age of three, initially under his parents' instruction, and started taking formal lessons at the age of six. He also enjoyed playing soccer, but tennis soon became his primary athletic focus.

As Tsitsipas grew older, he began competing in youth tennis tournaments in Greece as well as in competitions outside of his home country, to which he would travel with his father. "I saw it as something fun for me, something entertaining," he told Ben Rothenberg for *The New York Times* (28 May 2018) about those experiences. "I tried to be professional and disciplined, but it was nice traveling with my dad." Tsitsipas's father ultimately quit his job to accompany Tsitsipas to tournaments, a decision for which he would later express deep appreciation. "Now, I understand the importance of it, and what a big role it played in my career," he told Rothenberg.

EARLY CAREER

Tsitsipas began competing in International Tennis Federation (ITF) Futures tournaments by the age of fifteen, competing in several singles and doubles Futures competitions held in Greece over the course of 2013. He continued to compete on the ITF Futures circuit over the next several years and in 2015 claimed his first ITF Futures title at an event held in Nicosia, Cyprus. Tsitsipas also made his debut on the Association of Tennis Professionals (ATP) Challenger Tour that year, competing in seven tour events. He went on to split much of 2016 between Futures and Challenger Tour events but also made his debut top-level ATP Tour appearance that year, competing in the qualifying round of a tournament in Basel, Switzerland.

In January 2017, Tsitsipas reached a new milestone, making his first appearance in the Australian Open. As one of tennis's Grand Slam tournaments, the Australian Open—alongside the French Open (or Roland-Garros), Wimbledon, and the US Open—is one of the most prestigious and most lucrative tournaments in professional tennis. Although Tsitsipas was eliminated in the qualifying

Photo by JC, via Wikimedia Commons.

round of that tournament, he went on to play in all three remaining Grand Slam tournaments over the course of the year, progressing as far as the Round of 128 at both the French Open and Wimbledon. Tsitsipas also competed in numerous other ATP Tour events in 2017 and in October achieved his best ATP Tour singles finish of 2017, progressing to the semifinals at a tournament in Antwerp, Belgium.

ATP TITLEHOLDER

The year 2018 was a noteworthy one for Tsitsipas, who in October of that year won his first ATP Tour singles title upon beating Latvian player Ernests Gulbis in the final round of the Stockholm Open. That year also saw Tsitsipas progress to the Round of Sixteen at Wimbledon, his best Grand Slam performance to date, as well as to the final round of the Barcelona Open and the ATP Masters 1000 Canada. Ranked fifteenth in the ATP Tour singles rankings by the end of the year, he was named the ATP Most Improved Player of the Year for 2018.

The following year started off strong for Tsitsipas, who progressed to the semifinal round at the Australian Open in January. He went on to claim three ATP Tour titles over the course of the season, winning the Open 13 Provence in February and the Estoril Open in May. In November, he claimed his third

ATP Tour title of the year at the Nitto ATP Finals, beating Austrian player Dominic Thiem while cheered on by an enthusiastic crowd of supporters. "It's been a rollercoaster," he said afterward, as reported by the ATP Tour (17 Nov. 2019). "Holding this trophy right now feels amazing. . . . I have never received so much support in a stage like that, ever." In addition to those victories, Tsitsipas competed in the final rounds of several other tournaments during the year and in September participated in the Laver Cup team competition as a member of the tournament-winning Team Europe. By the end of the 2019 tennis season, Tsitsipas became the first Greek men's singles player to attain a top-ten ranking in the ATP Tour.

MILESTONE TOURNAMENTS

Like many athletes, Tsitsipas had comparatively few opportunities to compete in 2020, as the COVID-19 pandemic forced the cancellation or postponement of many sporting events. He claimed one ATP Tour title during that year, winning the Open 13 Provence in February, and went on to reach the semifinal round of the postponed French Open in October. Tsitsipas returned to regular competition in 2021 and in January of that year reached the semifinal round of the Australian Open, a result that was no longer as satisfying for Tsitsipas as it once was. "It's nice to get to the semi-finals of the Australian Open and it's a valuable thing, but to be honest I aim higher," he later told the Greek magazine *DownTown*, as reported in English translation by Vicky Georgatou for *Tennis Majors* (19 Apr. 2021). "This semi-final did not bring me as many emotions as the previous ones, but it is an excellent result. I'm getting close, in any case! I am happy that I can reach two consecutive Grand Slam semi-finals, it also helps me in terms of adding ranking points. There are many advantages to it."

After winning the ATP Masters 1000 Monte Carlo in April and the Open Parc Auvergne-Rhone-Alpes Lyon in May, Tsitsipas had yet another opportunity to put forth a strong Grand Slam performance, competing in the French Open in May and June of 2021. Surpassing his previous efforts in that tournament, Tsitsipas progressed all the way to the final round, becoming the first Greek player to reach the final of a Grand Slam tournament. Although he ultimately lost the final to Serbian player Djokovic, he was pleased to have reached that

point and to have done so while representing his birthplace. "A lot of people today were raising flags, cheering me on in Greece," he said afterward, as reported by Reid. "It was very important for me to do my job well enough." Tsitsipas also competed in the Olympic Games in Tokyo, Japan, finishing tied for ninth place in men's singles and fifth in mixed doubles. In September, he competed in his second Laver Cup, again contributing to a Team Europe victory.

2022 ATP TOUR

Tsitsipas began his 2022 ATP Tour season in early January, participating in the ATP Cup team competition held in Sydney, Australia. He remained in that country for the Australian Open, an event that represented a daunting early-year challenge. "You don't know what to expect," Tsitsipas told Richard Osborn for the ATP Tour website (15 Jan. 2022). "Everyone has trained for almost two months prior to the Australian Open. They've done pre-season training, fitness training. There has been a lot of change." Tsitsipas ultimately progressed to the semifinal round of the tournament, during which he lost to Russian player Daniil Medvedev.

Over the next several months, Tsitsipas put forth several strong performances, including a second-place finish at the ABN AMRO World Tennis Tournament in Rotterdam, Netherlands, in February. That month Tsitsipas also claimed his first ATP Tour doubles title, winning at the Abierto Mexicano Telcel presentado por HSBC alongside Spanish doubles partner Feliciano López. He went on to play in tournaments in Mexico and the United States over the next month, competing in both singles and doubles events. In April 2022, he was ranked fifth in the ATP Tour in singles. Tsitsipas's performance during the first months of 2022 called attention both to his prior successes and to his future potential, something of which Tsitsipas himself took note. "I feel like I had few good years on the Tour, but I'm kind of in the beginning of it," he told Osborn.

PERSONAL LIFE

In addition to his success in competitive tennis, Tsitsipas has become known for his love of travel and dedication to sharing his experiences with the public, including through a series of travel videos posted to YouTube.

"I want to inspire other people that want to do the same, to give them an idea how the tour works and how tennis is, and how good traveling can be, sometimes," he explained to Rothenberg. Tsitsipas has also delved into the realm of podcasting, creating the podcast *A Greek Abroad*.

SUGGESTED READING

Mesic, Dzevad. "Stefanos Tsitsipas: I'm in the Zone, I Have No Plans of Getting Out of It." *Tennis World*, 26 Jan. 2022, www.tennisworldusa.org/tennis/news/Tennis_Interviews/108344/stefanos-tsitsipas-i-m-in-the-zone-i-have-no-plans-of-getting-out-of-it/. Accessed 11 Apr. 2022.

Osborn, Richard. "Tsitsipas: It's Only the Beginning." *ATP Tour*, 15 Jan. 2022, www.atptour.com/en/news/tsitsipas-australian-open-2022-preview. Accessed 11 Apr. 2022.

Reid, Andrew. "Stefanos Tsitsipas Breaks Down in Emotional French Open Scenes." *Yahoo!Sport Australia*, 11 June 2021, au.sports.yahoo.com/french-open-2021-stefanos-tsitsipas-emotional-speech-after-beating-zverev-022214073.html. Accessed 11 Apr. 2022.

Rothenberg, Ben. "Stefanos Tsitsipas Balances His Greek and Russian Sides to Rise in Tennis." *The New York Times*, 28 May 2018, www.nytimes.com/2018/05/28/sports/tennis/stefanos-tsitsipas-french-open.html. Accessed 11 Apr. 2022.

Tsitsipas, Stefanos. "For Stefanos Tsitsipas, Tennis Greatness Is Only a Matter of Time." Interview by Christopher Bollen. *Interview*, 5 June 2019, www.interviewmagazine.com/culture/stefanos-tsitsipas-tennis-greatness-only-a-matter-of-time. Accessed 11 Apr. 2022.

___. "Stefanos Tsitsipas: 'My Goal Is to Create the Best Possible Memories, on and off the Court.'" Interview by Vicky Georgatou, *Tennis Majors*, 19 Apr. 2021, www.tennismajors.com/atp/stefanos-tsitsipas-my-goal-is-to-create-the-best-possible-memories-on-and-off-the-court-325569.html. Accessed 11 Apr. 2022.

"Tsitsipas Completes Successful Transition, Lands Nitto ATP Finals Crown." *ATP Tour*, 17 Nov. 2019, www.atptour.com/en/news/thiem-tsitsipas-nitto-atp-finals-2019-sunday-final. Accessed 11 Apr. 2022.

—*Joy Crelin*

Nsé Ufot

Occupation: Political organizer and activist

In 2014, Nseabasi "Nsé" Ufot began serving as the chief executive officer of the New Georgia Project, a nonpartisan voter registration and civic engagement organization founded by politician Stacey Abrams in 2013. Ufot has said that organizing is about power, as in determining who has it, and who does not. A former labor lawyer, Ufot has spent her career building successful coalitions of working people and voters to challenge the status quo. For decades, Georgia has been considered a Republican stronghold, but where other progressive groups (and the national Democratic Party) saw a lost cause, Ufot and Abrams saw opportunity, particularly in efforts to reverse the historic disenfranchisement of Georgians of color.

With the New Georgia Project, Ufot helped register hundreds of thousands of voters, most of them young people of color. In 2020 and 2021, that hard work paid off. In 2020, Black Georgia voters helped flip the state and deliver the presidency to Joe Biden, the Democratic former vice-president and senator. In run-off elections in 2021, voters turned out in record numbers to elect two Democrats to the US Senate, shifting the balance of power on a national level. Since then, laws restricting voting rights in Georgia and other states—have forced the New Georgia Project to evolve yet again, mobilizing to target disinformation about voting and voters' rights while also seeking to register new voters. In 2021, Ufot was named one of *Glamour* magazine's Women of the Year and appeared on the TIME100 Next list.

EARLY LIFE AND EDUCATION

Nseabasi Ufot was born in Akwa Ibom, a state in southeastern Nigeria. Her family moved to Atlanta when she was in elementary school. There, her mother got involved in organizing African immigrants. Ufot grew up attending meetings and protests, and in an interview with Katie Schank for the *Two-Party Georgia Oral History Project* through the University of Georgia Special Collections Libraries (20 Dec. 2018), described herself as a "movement baby." While her parents, a poet and a pastor, inspired and encouraged her to pursue political organizing, her individual political perspective was forged by her conservative upbringing. "I am the only daughter of some really conservative, lower-case 'c,' Christian African immigrants," Ufot told Amy Farley for *Fast Company* (10 Aug. 2021). "I would be playing trash can basketball with my brothers and the boys from the neighborhood, and then would get yelled at by my mom to come in and make dinner for the family. Bringing my family along with my politics—because they weren't going to change me—meant shifting their gender politics."

At fourteen, Ufot served as a page in the Georgia House of Representatives. She graduated from Georgia Tech—her father's alma mater—with a degree in psychology in 2002. Ufot went on to study law at the University of Dayton in Dayton, Ohio. There Midwest has a strong history of labor organizing, and Ufot, who received a "master's level education in the Civil Rights movement" growing up in Atlanta, as she told Schank, added this history to her developing analysis of power.

WORK IN LABOR LAW

After graduating from law school, Ufot felt compelled to take a well-paying job in corporate law while pursuing activism on nights and weekends. "I made tons of money," she recalled to Schank, "but I was also miserable." Ufot began meeting with local labor leaders and Democratic party officials, trying to figure out a way that she could get paid to organize full time. Eventually, Ufot got a job working in the legal department for the American Federation of State, County and Municipal Employees (AFSME), a public employees union in Ohio. There, she negotiated labor contracts for workers in Cincinnati, Cleveland, and Columbus. The experience, she told Schank, taught her the importance of institutions in helping working people build power. Ufot went on to work as a senior lobbyist and government relations official for the American Association of University Professors (AAUP), and also served as the assistant executive director of the Canadian Association of Teachers. All told, Ufot helped negotiate some fifty labor contracts over the course of her law career.

THE NEW GEORGIA PROJECT

Ufot met Abrams, then the minority leader in Georgia's House of Representatives, at a New Year's Day brunch in Georgia in 2014. The two women discussed Georgia politics, noting that the margins separating losing

Photo by Nate Steiner, via Wikimedia Commons.

candidates from winning ones were curiously consistent throughout the state. Many races were decided by about 200,000 votes—not insignificant, but a small number compared to another one. "[Abrams] told me that there were over a million Georgians of color, mostly Black Georgians, who were eligible to vote and completely unregistered," Ufot told Audra D. S. Burch for *The New York Times* (29 Dec. 2020). "And that made me sit up and stop eating my eggs." Ufot and Abrams wondered what would happen if those people did vote—would their voices shift the balance of political power in Georgia? As Ufot recalled to Schank, she and Abrams came to the same conclusion: "Why not find out?"

By 2014, the New Georgia Project and its allied groups had registered about 100,000 voters in the state. The accomplishment, as Ray Levy Uyeda wrote for *Mic* (4 Jan. 2021), "proved that [voter] engagement wasn't a matter of interest, but rather of systemic and long-standing disenfranchisement." The success of the project drew the attention of Brian Kemp, then Georgia's Secretary of State. Kemp issued a subpoena to the New Georgia Project, warning, as quoted by Burch, that a "preliminary investigation has revealed significant illegal activities" by the group. The investigation never revealed any evidence of wrongdoing, however.

2018 MIDTERMS

Ufot points out that the New Georgia Project is not interested in merely electing Democrats, but rather changing the political priorities in the state to reflect the concerns of Black Georgians, and other groups who have been cut out of the state's power structure. Democrats ran the state government until the 1990s, but they were conservative Dixiecrats, she told Schank, uninterested in issues like reproductive justice or civil rights. In Ufot's description, the New Georgia Project brings together disparate groups within the "progressive ecosystem," she told Schank, "so we can move beyond looking good losing, and actually [start] winning."

By the 2018 midterms, the New Georgia Project had helped register about 200,000 voters. It was a big year for Georgia politics. Abrams ran for governor against Kemp, but despite widespread support, she lost by a slim margin of about 55,000 votes out of almost 4 million. The narrowness of Kemp's victory suggested how far the New Georgia Project and other groups had come in their efforts to build a "new" Georgia. There is also strong evidence that voter suppression played an important role in the election, as Kemp, then secretary of state, was in charge of how the election was run. Through a number of dictates restricting ballot boxes and polling stations, he limited voting access in areas with large numbers of Black voters. He also put more than 50,000 voter registration forms on hold before the election, claiming various minor discrepancies. Abrams sued the state for suppressing the vote after the election; the case went to trial in April 2022.

Ufot saw Kemp's voter suppression tactics as both ominous and encouraging. "Georgia, like many states across the country, is becoming more and more racially and ethnically diverse. There are legislators who are terrified by this reality and are actively trying to defend the status quo," she told Tanya Christian for *Ebony* (9 Mar. 2022). "Voter suppression has always been an active player in Georgia, but Republicans know that the only way for them to hold on to their power is by cheating."

2020 PRESIDENTIAL ELECTION

After the blow of Abrams's loss to Kemp, the New Georgia Project—alongside her new organization, Fair Fight—doubled down, registering hundreds of thousands of voters across the state. (In one interview, Ufot claimed that the organization helped register 600,000 voters between 2018 and 2020, but in other interviews, she suggests that this number might include voters registered prior to 2018.) The 2020 election year was historic for a number of reasons. Voters went to the polls during a global pandemic, amidst mass uprisings over racial oppression. They were charged with selecting the next president of the United States, and in Georgia, both of the state's US senators in a run-off election on January 5, 2021. In the lead-up to the elections, Ufot put her coalition-building skills to good use, bringing together disparate groups, like White suburban women motivated by their aversion to incumbent president Donald Trump, a Republican, and young Black people pushing for a more progressive political agenda.

In November 2020, new and infrequent voters flipped Georgia, helping to deliver the presidency to Democrat Joe Biden by a margin of 11,799 votes. It was the first time the state had voted for a Democratic presidential candidate since Bill Clinton in 1992. It was a huge victory, but Ufot's work was far from over. The New Georgia Project set a goal of registering 10,000 voters before the December 7 cut-off date for the January run-offs.

In late November, Georgia secretary of state Brad Raffensperger launched an investigation into the New Georgia Project, as well as three other voter-registration organizations. Raffensperger accused the New Georgia Project of violating election laws when volunteers, including some in other states, sent postcards to eligible Georgia voters encouraging them to vote. "When you look at what we are being accused of, it also makes you realize just how sad and desperate it is," she told Jewel Wicker for *Teen Vogue* (3 Dec. 2020). "The way that we do our work, at the core of the New Georgia Project, is direct voter contact. We need to have high-quality—face-to-face, if we can—direct communication with the people that we register to vote."

Ufot argued that the charges had more to do with the fact that Raffensperger was facing heat from his own party about the historic electoral outcome in Georgia. President Trump, pushing voter fraud conspiracy theories, retweeted calls for Raffensperger and Kemp to be jailed. Raffensperger was certainly being bullied by his fellow Republicans, Ufot told Burch, "but what you can't do is bully our civil rights organizations and voting rights organizations to re-establish your Republican bona fides."

2021 RUN-OFF ELECTIONS

By December 7, 2020, the New Georgia Project managed to register about 7,000 voters for the Senate run-offs—a bit shy of their goal, but Ufot told Burch that the organization had other tactics at hand. "We will have knocked on two million doors by the end of this year," Ufot said in 2020. "We will have had five million phone calls with Georgia voters by the end of this year and the same number of text messages by the end of this year. . . . It is a full-on campaign to make sure that people know that there's another election and that they show up." Indeed, Georgians did show up, and in record numbers. About 4.5 million people cast a ballot in the Georgia run-offs, doubling the previous record for run-off voting in the state. Black Georgians helped deliver victories to both Democratic candidates, John Ossoff, the state's first Jewish senator, and Reverend Raphael Warnock, the state's first Black senator.

In the wake of these victories, the Republican-led Georgia legislature passed a ninety-eight-page voting law in 2021. The law created myriad restrictions and made it harder to vote by absentee ballot. Nick Corasaniti and Reid J. Epstein of *The New York Times* (2 Apr. 2021) called it a "breathtaking assertion of partisan power in elections." Among the restrictions are possible misdemeanor charges for offering food or water to people waiting in line to vote. The law went into effect in time for the 2022 midterm elections, in which Abrams will again challenge Kemp for the governor's seat.

Ufot told Brakkton Booker for *Politico* (7 Jan. 2022) that local elections in 2021 had already demonstrated the profound power of the Georgia law. "We're starting to see glimpses of the powers that state GOP legislators have given themselves to overturn elections, to unilaterally remove county election officials," she said. "There is also a clarity in their communications, that they are coming for elections, that they are going to hold on to power by hook or by crook, and in this instance, it is all by crook. And they are daring us to say something about it." To help voters in 2022, Ufot and the New Georgia Project are focused on combating deliberate misinformation about how to vote, and what rights voters have in casting a ballot.

PERSONAL LIFE
Ufot lives in Atlanta.

SUGGESTED READING
Booker, Brakkton. "Georgia: Ground Zero for the Voting Rights Battle." *Politico*, 7 Jan. 2022, www.politico.com/newsletters/the-recast/2022/01/07/georgia-voting-rights-swing-state-politics-495643. Accessed 14 Apr. 2022.

Burch, Audra D. S. "Turning Out the Vote in Georgia." *The New York Times*, 29 Dec. 2020, www.nytimes.com/2020/12/29/magazine/georgia-senate-runoff-election.html. Accessed 12 Apr. 2022.

Christian, Tanya. "Nsé Ufot Is Charged Up and Ready to Make Change Happen in Georgia." *Ebony*, 9 Mar. 2022, www.ebony.com/news/nse-ufot-is-charged-up-and-ready-to-make-change-happen-in-georgia/. Accessed 14 Apr. 2022.

Farley, Amy. "How This Top Voting Rights Activist Uses Business and Data to Protect the Vote." *Fast Company*, 10 Aug. 2021, www.fastcompany.com/90651384/most-creative-people-2021-nse-ufot. Accessed 9 Apr. 2022.

Ufot, Nsé. "Interview with Nsé Ufot, December 20, 2018." Interview by Katie Schank. *UGA Special Collections Libraries Oral History Collections: Two-Party Georgia Oral History Project*, 20 Dec. 2018, georgiaoralhistory.libs.uga.edu/RBRL425TPGA/RBRL425TPGA-073. Accessed 12 Apr. 2022.

Uyeda, Ray Levy. "Inside the New Georgia Project, the Stacey Abrams Org That's Trying to Register Every POC in the State." *Mic*, 4 Jan. 2021, www.mic.com/impact/inside-the-new-georgia-project-the-stacey-abrams-org-thats-trying-to-register-every-poc-in-the-state-53983970. Accessed 13 Apr. 2022.

Wicker, Jewel. "Nsé Ufot: New Georgia Project Being Investigated Is a 'Sad and Desperate' Republican Effort." *Teen Vogue*, 3 Dec. 2020, www.teenvogue.com/story/nse-ufot-new-georgia-project-investigated-sad-desperate-republican. Accessed 14 Apr. 2022.

—*Molly Hagan*

Kevin VanDam

Born: October 14, 1967
Occupation: Professional angler

For professional angler Kevin VanDam, the key to success in bass fishing is understanding the true nature of the sport. "Non-fisherman, especially, think there is a lot of luck involved. That you got out there on the water and you just sit back and cast out and wait for the fish to come and bite," he explained to Ed Godfrey in an interview for *The Oklahoman* (14 June 2013). According to VanDam, nothing could be further from the truth. "I don't believe in luck at all," he told Godfrey. "Getting them to bite in the first place is not luck. There's a lot to it. It's a science that is far from exact." Over the course of his extensive career in bass fishing, VanDam's understanding of that inexact science certainly paid off. KVD, as he became known to fans, established himself as one of the highest-earning professional anglers in the United States and earned numerous honors beginning in the early 1990s, including multiple Angler of the Year titles and a spot in the Bass Fishing Hall of Fame.

A regular contender in competitions such as the Bass Anglers Sportsman Society (BASS) Bassmaster events, VanDam found further success after moving to the Major League Fishing Bass Pro Tour (BPT) in 2019, winning his first BPT title at Tennessee's Lake Chickamauga two years later. VanDam's impressive record earned him major accolades as an angler, including many assertions that he was the greatest of all time in his sport. Yet he often asserted that he could never simply coast on his reputation, as variations in water conditions, fish populations, and fishing technology mean that every competition is a unique challenge that must be approached on an individual basis. "It's hard not to get into a mind-set of thinking you know what you are doing, based on what happened before," he told Lydia Lohrer for the *Detroit Free Press* (26 Aug. 2017). "I pretty much have to relearn to go in open minded, every time."

EARLY LIFE AND CAREER

Kevin VanDam was born in Kalamazoo, Michigan, on October 14, 1967, to Nadine and Dick VanDam. He grew up in Otsego, Michigan, where he attended local schools.

VanDam began fishing as a young child and quickly developed a passion for the sport, which soon consumed much of his free time. "My grandparents had a place on the lake and I would go out there in the summer and stay a week at a time and that's all I did, all day long, every day, was fish," he recalled to Godfrey. "My grandmother had a bell that she would ring, so that no matter where I was, walking the bank around the lake, that I could hear it to know to come in for lunch or dinner." Particularly drawn to bass fishing, VanDam joined the Kal-Valley Bass Club while still a child and completed in his first tournament at the age of fourteen. After graduating from high school, VanDam completed two years of college before leaving school to enter the workforce.

Following his departure from college, VanDam took a job at D&R Sports Center, a hunting and fishing store owned by his older brother, Randy. In addition to being a source of income, the job enabled him to meet a number of accomplished anglers when they visited the store—or at least to watch them from afar. "I remember one time Larry Nixon and Tommy Martin came to our store and I was too embarrassed to go up and even talk to them," VanDam told Godfrey, referring to two prominent members of the bass fishing community. In addition to working at D&R Sports Center, VanDam continued to compete in bass fishing events himself and in 1987 participated in the New York Invitational, his first BASS event, finishing in 110th place.

CHAMPION ANGLER

By the early 1990s VanDam had left his job at D&S Sports Center to pursue a full-time career as a competitive bass fisherman. He competed in his first complete Bassmaster Invitationals season in 1990 and in 1992 was named BASS Angler of the Year for the first time. He continued to make a name for himself over the course of the 1990s, competing in a range of major competitions, including the prestigious annual Bassmaster Classic. Following numerous attempts, he won his first Bassmaster Classic title in 2001, overcoming all competition—and an oncoming hurricane—at that year's event in New Orleans, Louisiana. That year also saw VanDam win the Fishing League Worldwide (FLW) Angler of the Year title.

Photo by Lance Cpl. Jonathan G. Wright,
via Wikimedia Commons [Public domain.]

Establishing himself as a fixture of bass fishing competitions, VanDam had numerous opportunities to master his skills and hone all elements of his fishing practice, from his rod and bait selection to his strategies for dealing with adverse weather conditions or the disruptive presence of spectators. "I want to control all the variables that I possibly can," he explained to Bill Heavey in an interview for *Field & Stream* (21 Apr. 2014). "Look, the competition out there is so tough, so tight, that losing one fish can mean the difference between winning and losing. Or it can knock you down twenty places in the standings. So you have to eliminate as many mistakes as you can. . . . My mindset, you know, is why wouldn't you do everything possible to put yourself in a position to succeed?" VanDam's approach brought him a great deal of success indeed during the early twenty-first century, including Bassmaster Classic wins in 2005, 2010, and 2011 and four consecutive BASS Angler of the Year titles between 2008 and 2011.

SLUMP AND REBOUND
Although he had already cemented his place in the uppermost ranks of professional angling, following the 2011 bass fishing season VanDam experienced what many within the bass fishing community would come to describe as a significant multiyear slump. While he had

accomplished a significant feat when he won the Bassmaster Classic in 2011, becoming only the second angler to win two Bassmaster Classics in a row, that victory ushered in a lengthy period in which VanDam not only failed to win a Bassmaster Classic but also did not win a single other Bassmaster event. He did not break the slump until May 2016, when he finished in first place in the A.R.E. Truck Caps Bassmaster Elite at Toledo Bend in Louisiana. He went on to win another Bassmaster Elite event at Cayuga Lake in June of that year, once again demonstrating his mastery of his sport.

Although VanDam succeeded in breaking his winless streak on the Bassmaster Elite circuit, further Bassmaster Classic titles continued to elude him. "It's just one of those things," he told Heavey. "The way the Classic is, it's an all or nothing event. Second place means nothing." Despite his struggles at the Bassmaster Classic, though, VanDam remained a strong contender in many Bassmaster Elite competitions. For example, he claimed first place at St. Lawrence River in New York in 2017 and at Oklahoma's Grand Lake in 2018, the latter of which marked his twenty-fifth Bassmaster win. He likewise tallied several other top-twenty finishes in 2017 and 2018, including a second-place finish at Mississippi's Ross Barnett Reservoir in 2017 and a third-place result at Lake Dardanelle in Arkansas later that year. VanDam was inducted into the Bass Fishing Hall of Fame in 2018, reflecting his reputation as one of the best competitors of all time. By that time he had won more money in professional bass fishing tournaments than any other angler, with over $6 million in career earnings.

BASS PRO TOUR
After competing for many years mainly in BASS events such as the Bassmaster Elite Series, VanDam helped found a new competitive circuit, the Major League Fishing (MLF) Bass Pro Tour (BPT), which launched in 2019. In his BPT debut in January 2019 he placed seventieth at the BPT Kissimmee Chain of Lakes event in Florida. Over the next few years he remained a prominent BPT competitor, earning several top-twenty finishes, though it took a while to record an overall win. In June 2021, he entered the BPT B&W Trailer Hitches Stage Four at Tennessee's Lake Chickamauga and began the tournament on a strong note.

"The first competition day in the elimination round, I started off, caught a few, and really just kind of worked through the day, learned a lot and really had a solid day," he told Patrick Nothaft for *MLive* (15 June 2021). "I think I ended up at the end of the day in second place overall, and at that point, I knew I was going to have a chance to have a really good week." His hunch proved to be correct, as he finished the final round of the tournament with eighty points and claimed his first BPT title, which came with $100,000 in prize money.

For VanDam, winning at Lake Chickamauga represented an important career milestone, as BPT tournaments featured what he described to Nothaft as "a little bit different format" in comparison to his previous events. "It's really special because over the years, under every format, every style and different type of event, I've been able to win," he explained to Nothaft. "It's something you definitely want to use to measure yourself against the competition, and I've had a lot of success in my career, so it was just another milestone-type tournament that I really wanted to have." Following his victory in Tennessee, VanDam continued to compete on the BPT circuit throughout the remainder of 2021 and into 2022. By then his career earnings exceeded $7 million, maintaining his place as the all-time bass-fishing money leader.

PERSONAL LIFE

VanDam lives in Kalamazoo, Michigan, with his wife, Sherry. They had twin sons together, both of whom grew up fishing alongside their father. "We're having fun with it," VanDam told Lohrer about fishing with his children. "They're definitely much younger in the overall career aspect of it, learning all kinds of things all the time. Every new place they go they're figuring out new things and new techniques and new lures and learning more about electronics." His nephew Jonathon VanDam also became a noted professional angler.

Over the years VanDam earned a reputation as a popular and friendly figure in the fishing community, often working to promote outdoor education and sharing fishing tips. He also contributed to many college scholarships and charitable efforts. In 2015, he and his wife launched the KVD Foundation to support causes including children's hospitals and children's health organizations such as the March of Dimes.

SUGGESTED READING

"Kevin VanDam Makes Big Sponsorship Change." *Wired2Fish*, 18 Jan. 2022, www.wired2fish.com/news/kevin-vandam-makes-big-sponsorship-change. Accessed 11 Apr. 2022.

Lohrer, Lydia. "Outdoors: Fishing's First Family? It's the VanDams by Mile." *Detroit Free Press*, 26 Aug. 2017, www.freep.com/story/sports/outdoors/2017/08/26/outdoors-fishings-first-family-its-vandams-mile/605114001/. Accessed 11 Apr. 2022.

McGuckin, Alan. "Kevin VanDam at REDCREST: A Good Day for the Ducks." *Major League Fishing*, 22 Mar. 2022, majorleaguefishing.com/bass-pro-tour/kevin-vandam-at-redcrest-a-good-day-for-the-ducks/. Accessed 11 Apr. 2022.

Nothaft, Patrick. "Fishing Legend, Michigan Native Kevin VanDam Savoring the Moment after First Bass Pro Tour Win." *MLive*, 15 June 2021, www.mlive.com/sports/2021/06/fishing-legend-michigan-native-kevin-vandam-savoring-the-moment-after-first-bass-pro-tour-win.html. Accessed 11 Apr. 2022.

VanDam, Kevin. "More from the Kevin VanDam Interview." Interview by Ed Godfrey. *The Oklahoman*, 14 June 2013, www.oklahoman.com/story/sports/columns/2009/11/08/more-from-the-kevin-vandam-interview/60911727007/. Accessed 11 Apr. 2022.

___. "Q&A: Bill Heavey Takes on Kevin VanDam." Interview by Bill Heavey. *Field & Stream*, 21 Apr. 2014, www.fieldandstream.com/articles/fishing/bass-fishing/2014/04/bill-heavey-takes-kevin-vandam/. Accessed 11 Apr. 2022.

___. "VanDam Turns 50: 'It's Just a Number.'" Interview by Todd Ceisner. *BassFan*, 12 Oct. 2017, www.bassfan.com/news_article/9032/vandam-turns-50:-%E2%80%98it%E2%80%99s-just-a-number%E2%80%99. Accessed 11 Apr. 2022.

—Joy Crelin

John R. Velazquez

Born: November 24, 1971
Occupation: Jockey

Over his long and decorated career, John R. Velazquez, affectionately known as Johnny V., established himself as the most dominant jockey in North American Thoroughbred horseracing. He made his professional debut in 1990, and by the early 2000s was a top competitor, winning the Eclipse Award for Outstanding Jockey in both 2004 and 2005, after finishing first in purse earnings each year. Inducted into the National Museum of Racing and Hall of Fame in 2012, he continued to excel over the next decade, including further wins in the prestigious Breeder's Cup and Triple Crown series. In 2013, Velazquez became the all-time leader in purse earnings in North America, and by early 2022, he had accrued more than $450 million across more than 35,000 races, placing first in more than 6,300, second in more than 5,100 and third in more than 4,600.

In addition to his undisputed success on the track, Velazquez became well known for his general dedication to his sport and community. For example, he served as chair of the Jockeys' Guild Board of Directors and on the board of the Permanently Disabled Jockeys Fund (PDJF), earning respect from fellow jockeys and beyond. "He's one of the greatest guys ever," his agent, Ron Anderson, said in a press release for the Santa Anita Park website (1 Dec. 2021). "He's really, really a special person at the end of the day. He's positive, he's classy, he's considerate, he's kind to everybody. As a rider, his numbers and his records speak for themselves. He's the number one leading rider of all-time."

EARLY LIFE AND CAREER

John R. Velazquez was born on November 24, 1971, in Carolina, Puerto Rico. He attended jockey school in his native Puerto Rico beginning in 1988, a move that was not initially well received by his family, particularly his mother, Margarita. "Like a typical parent, she did not want this for my career," Velazquez said in his National Museum of Racing and Hall of Fame induction speech, as quoted by Jerry Bossert of the *New York Daily News* (11 Aug. 2012). However, after he decided to take a chance on horseracing anyway, his mother eventually became highly supportive.

Velazquez participated in his first professional race in early 1990 and that March he moved to New York City to better pursue his career. There he began to be mentored by veteran jockey Ángel Cordero Jr., a major star in the New York horseracing scene. During his early days in New York, Velazquez lived with Cordero and his wife. He learned to speak English after two and a half months by watching the Disney film *The Little Mermaid* (1989) over and over with the Corderos' daughter.

Although Cordero and others quickly recognized Velazquez's enormous potential, things were not always easy for the young rider. He won a few races early on, but also saw plenty of struggles on the racetrack and even at times questioned his decision to become a jockey. All of his worries came to a head in 1992, when it appeared nothing was going right. "It was probably one of the worst years that I had," Velazquez said in his Hall of Fame speech. "I was thinking of going back home." However, in part due to encouragement from agent Ralph Theroux Sr., he persevered and by the mid-1990s was on an upward trajectory in the racing world.

MAKING HIS MARK ON HORSERACING

Velazquez won his first Grade I stakes race in 1995, while riding Turk Passer at the Turf

Photo by Maryland GovPics, via Wikimedia Commons

Classic at Belmont Park. But his career really began to take off in 1998, after Cordero retired from racing and became his full-time agent. That year Velazquez won the riding championship at Saratoga Race Course, the first of several he would accumulate over the years. Riding for noted trainer Todd Pletcher, among others, he soon ensconced himself in the New York racing scene as a top jockey.

In the early twenty-first century Velazquez was a frequent contender in the Breeders' Cup series of races. For example, he won the juvenile fillies category in 2000 and 2002, also taking the filly and mare turf category the latter year. He excelled in other competitions as well, and some of his achievements began to make history. On September 3, 2001, Velazquez won six races at Saratoga, setting a track record for a single day. In 2004, he set another Saratoga record with sixty-five wins that year. He also hit the 3,000 career wins mark that year. He finished 2004 as the leading North American rider in earnings and won his first Eclipse Award. He repeated both those feats in 2005—when his earnings set a single-season record—solidifying his place as one of the best jockeys of the era.

Velazquez also occasionally raced internationally, winning the Dubai World Cup riding Roses in May 2005. However, despite so much success, for years he struggled to win any of the three events in horseracing's illustrious Triple Crown of Thoroughbred Racing: the Kentucky Derby, the Preakness Stakes, and the Belmont Stakes. This seemed unlikely to change in 2007, as his horse at the Belmont Stakes, Rags to Riches, stumbled badly out of the gate. "My heart stopped," Velazquez recalled to Steve Haskin for *Blood Horse* (18 Mar. 2016). "The first thing I thought of was, hopefully, she doesn't pull a shoe and get hurt." However, not only did Rags to Riches avoid injury, she and Velazquez went on to win the race in what was widely considered one of the most memorable finishes in years.

After finally breaking through in Triple Crown competition, Velazquez continued to win. On September 28, 2008, he clocked his 4,000th career victory, riding Rogue Agent at Belmont Park. In 2009, he was presented with the George Woolf Memorial Jockey Award, a top honor recognizing illustrious riding careers as voted on by fellow jockeys.

HALL OF FAME JOCKEY

Velazquez entered the 2010s already widely seen as one of the best riders in horseracing, and he only further added to his impressive résumé throughout the decade. In 2011, he won his first Kentucky Derby—arguably the most famous Triple Crown event. This was a particularly sweet victory for the veteran jockey, as he had previously competed in the famed horserace eleven times without success. It was also the third time that the odds-on favorite horses he was to ride were sidelined with injuries. That year, after his original horse, Uncle Mo, was scratched, Velazquez ended up riding Animal Kingdom for the first time ever and securing the win. He also rode Animal Kingdom at that year's Preakness Stakes but lost the chance for a Triple Crown title with a second-place finish.

In 2012, Velazquez won his second Belmont Stakes, riding Union Rags to a neck victory over Paynter. He sustained a broken collarbone in a fall later that year, but also won the Breeder's Cup Mile riding Wise Dan, who he would regularly jockey for two years and who won back-to-back American Horse of the Year titles. Also in 2012, Velazquez was inducted into the Racing Hall of Fame. At the ceremony, the normally cool-under-pressure jockey choked back tears as he thanked his family and important figures in his career such as Cordero, Theroux, and Pletcher.

On June 14, 2013, Velazquez earned career win number 5,000 riding Galloping Giraffe at Belmont. The next month he secured his 694th victory at Saratoga specifically, setting a rider record for that racetrack. Then, on October 13 of the same year, he became North America's all-time leading money-earning jockey after completing his races at Belmont Park. "It's something that happened to happen," he modestly told *USA Today* (13 Oct. 2013) about the feat. "I'm happy it happened." Continuing his consistent performance, in 2014 he became the first jockey ever to surpass $300 million in career purse earnings.

MORE KENTUCKY DERBY WINS

In 2017, Velazquez captured another Kentucky Derby victory, riding Always Dreaming. Notably, the horse was trained by Velazquez's frequent collaborator Pletcher, marking a milestone for both men. Also in 2017, Velazquez won two Breeders' Cup races. He added another the following year. He earned his 6,000th career win in 2018 as well—once again on a Pletcher-trained horse, Singapore Trader—becoming just the eighteenth jockey to reach that mark. "Everybody kept asking me when it was going to happen, but for me it was just another number," Velazquez said about that achievement, as quoted by *Blood Horse* (30 Nov. 2018). "One day I'll look back and know I accomplished something great, but my job is to come here and win races. That's what I care about."

Velazquez won the Kentucky Derby again in 2020 on Authentic, trained by Bob Baffert. At the Preakness Stakes Velazquez rode Authentic again but finished second. He jockeyed Authentic once more at the 2020 Breeders' Cup Classic and won that race for the first time in his career. Overall, the win was Velazquez's eighteenth at the Breeders' Cup. Meanwhile, Velazquez also became the first jockey to win 2,000 races at Belmont Park in October 2020.

In 2021, Velazquez rode the Baffert-trained Medina Spirit to another Kentucky Derby victory. "You couldn't ask more of a horse. When you ride a horse like this who is competitive, you can't ask for anything else," he said after the race, as quoted by Mark Story for the *Lexington Herald-Leader* (2 May 2021). However, Medina Spirit was later stripped of the title when the Kentucky Horse Racing Commission concluded that the horse had the steroid betamethasone in its system. Baffert was also suspended and fined, though he appealed the decision, claiming that the drug came from an ointment used to treat a skin condition rather than an injected attempt to enhance performance. Velazquez himself did not face consequences aside from officially losing his third Derby title.

Velazquez continued to race and perform at a high level into his fifties. His career did begin to evolve, however, after hiring Ron Anderson, a celebrated agent in the field, to represent him in 2019. In late 2021 Anderson secured Velazquez a deal to ride fulltime at Santa Anita Park in California for the winter, a notable change of scenery for the jockey after being based on the East Coast his whole career. "We're kind of looking forward to a change," Anderson told John Cherwa for the *Los Angeles Times* (1 Dec. 2021). "We've already gotten a lot of interest."

PERSONAL LIFE

Like most jockeys, Velazquez is small and slight, weighing just 112 pounds and standing five feet six inches tall. In 1994, he married Leona O'Brien, daughter of noted horse trainer Leo O'Brien. They have two children together, daughter Lerina and son Michael Patrick.

SUGGESTED READING

Bossert, Jerry. "Jockey John Velazquez Fights Back Tears, Enters Racing Hall of Fame Friday." *New York Daily News*, 11 Aug. 2012, www.nydailynews.com/sports/more-sports/jockey-john-velazquez-fights-back-tears-enters-racing-hall-fame-speech-friday-article-1.1134235. Accessed 28 Feb. 2022.

Cherwa, John. "Hall of Fame Jockey John Velazquez to Ride Fulltime at Santa Anita This Winter." *Los Angeles Times*, 1 Dec. 2021. *MSN*, www.msn.com/en-us/sports/more-sports/hall-of-fame-jockey-john-velazquez-to-ride-fulltime-at-santa-anita-this-winter/ar-AARmgG9. Accessed 25 Feb. 2022.

"Hall of Fame Jockey John Velazquez to Ride Full-Time at Santa Anita This Winter with Superstar Agent Ron Anderson." *Santa Anita Park*, 1 Dec. 2021, www.santaanita.com/press-releases/hall-of-fame-jockey-john-velazquez-to-ride-full-time-at-santa-anita-this-winter-with-superstar-agent-ron-anderson/. Accessed 25 Feb. 2022.

Haskin, Steve. "Rags to Riches: Greatest Victory for Pletcher." *Blood Horse*, 18 Mar. 2016, cs.bloodhorse.com/blogs/horse-racing-steve-haskin/archive/2016/03/18/rags-to-riches-pletcher-s-greatest-victory.aspx. Accessed 14 Mar. 2022.

"John Velazquez Gets Win No. 6,000." Blood Horse, 30 Nov. 2018, www.bloodhorse.com/horse-racing/articles/230957/john-velazquez-gets-win-no-6-000. Accessed 14 Mar. 2022.

"John R. Velazquez." *National Museum of Racing and Hall of Fame*, www.racingmuseum.org/hall-of-fame/jockey/john-r-velazquez. Accessed 25 Feb. 2022.

Story, Mark. "Winning Jockey Velazquez Completes Trip from Kentucky Derby Also-Ran to Derby Legend." *Lexington Herald-Leader*, 2 May 2021. *MSN*, www.msn.com/en-us/sports/motorsports/mark-story-winning-jockey-velazquez-completes-trip-from-kentucky-derby-also-ran-to-derby-legend/ar-BB1ggLOe. Accessed 25 Feb. 2022.

Suckow, Alex. "Medina Spirit Disqualified from 2021 Kentucky Derby, Bob Baffert Fined." *WBAL News Radio*, 21 Feb. 2022, www.wbal.com/article/555158/3/medina-spirit-disqualified-from-2021-kentucky-derby-bob-baffert-fined. Accessed 28 Feb. 2022.

"Velazquez Becomes All-Time Money-Earning Jockey." *USA Today*, 13 Oct. 2013, www.usatoday.com/story/sports/horseracing/2013/10/13/john-velazquez-jockey-leading-money-earner/2977177/. Accessed 14 Mar. 2021.

—*Christopher Mari*

Iman Vellani

Born: September 3, 2002
Occupation: Actor

In 2020 Iman Vellani, an unknown Pakistani Canadian high school student and Marvel Cinematic Universe (MCU) superfan, was cast as the MCU superhero Kamala Khan in the Disney+ television series *Ms. Marvel*, which premiered in June 2022. Observers were quick to note the apparent similarities between actor and character, as both were Pakistani Muslim teenagers obsessed with Marvel comics. And while Khan is imbued with superpowers that allow her to fight alongside her heroes, it could be said that Vellani herself underwent an exceptional transformation when she was cast in her dream role. "My entire world, everything I talked about was Marvel," Vellani told Dave Itzkoff for *The New York Times* (6 June 2022). "And now people actually have to listen when I talk about it." These "people" included Kevin Feige, the president of Marvel Studios, who Vellani openly admired. "I've pitched Kevin Feige so many movies," she told a journalist for *Esquire Middle East* (18 May 2022), also describing how she often peppered him with questions about future MCU storylines. "I think he really likes how nerdy I am about the Marvel stuff," she said. "Because when I visited his office, he said, 'God, it's so nice to show people stuff who actually care!'"

EARLY LIFE AND EDUCATION

Iman Vellani was born in Karachi, Pakistan, on September 3, 2002. Her family moved to Canada, settling in Markham, Ontario, outside of Toronto, when she was a year old. She was a Marvel fan from an early age. "I have a brother who's six years older than me and we only ever watched stuff that he wanted to watch—*Lord of the Rings*, *Pirates of the Caribbean* and the MCU," she told Coco Khan for *The Guardian* (6 June 2022). Vellani saw her first MCU movie, *Iron Man* (2008), when she was five. The experience made her a lifelong devotee of the title character and the actor that played him in the MCU, Robert Downey Jr. "I just had the fattest crush on Iron Man," the gregarious Vellani told Clement Goh for *CBC News* (7 June 2022).

Vellani auditioned for the Unionville High School drama club as a teen, and said at the time that her dream role would be a character in the MCU. Vellani's school sat across the street from a comic bookstore, where she first encountered the character of Kamala Khan on the cover of an *Ironheart* comic. "I was like, 'Who's this brown girl?'" she recalled to Soraya Roberts for *Toronto Life* (7 June 2022). She was so taken with Khan that she dressed as her for Halloween. She wore a costume her grandmother had made but found that few people recognized her inspiration. "No one knew who I was," Vellani told Itzkoff. "Everyone thought I was the Flash. So I had to buy a comic book and hold it with me."

AUDITIONING FOR *MS. MARVEL*

Vellani heard about the casting call for *Ms. Marvel* through her aunt, who had seen it on a group chat on WhatsApp. Vellani was skeptical, but sent an audition tape in early 2020. A few days later, casting agents called to set up an in-person audition in Los Angeles. In February 2020, Vellani traveled with her father, taking full advantage of being in a room full of people as immersed in the MCU as she was. "I just wanted to use that experience as much as I could, because I didn't know if I'd ever be in the same room with Marvel employees again, or if I was going to get the part or not," she told *Esquire Middle East*. "I think they saw that outside of the acting I was so in love with this world. That definitely gave me a bit of an upper hand."

The audition process was stalled by the COVID-19 pandemic and subsequent shutdowns. Though casting agents assured Vellani that she was still in the running for the part, she was nervous. She was accepted to her first-choice university, but the achievement was overshadowed by her earlier brush with Hollywood. "I got this little taste of what life could be like," she told Itzkoff. "I was like, I can't possibly go to university after this. I can't think of anything else I would want to do."

On Vellani's last day of high school, she got a call from Feige. He told her she had won the part. Vellani had been riding in a car with friends who did not know that she had auditioned, and she did her best to keep her cool. After she got off the phone, she told Itzkoff, "I got back into the car and my friends were like, 'Did you win the lottery?' I was like, 'Basically.'"

BECOMING KAMALA KHAN

Created by G. Willow Wilson, Adrian Alphona, Sana Amanat, and Stephen Wacker, Kamala Khan made her Marvel Comics debut in 2013, and was given her own series in 2014. The character, whose family is from Pakistan, is a Muslim teenager growing up in New Jersey. She idolizes the superheroes Captain Marvel (also known as Carol Danvers) and, notably, Iron Man. One night, she comes into contact with a substance that gives her the power to control the size and shape of her body. She can grow larger and smaller, and stretch her limbs to incredible lengths. To honor her favorite superhero, she adopts the name Ms. Marvel (which Danvers had previously used before becoming Captain Marvel). But Khan struggles to balance being a teen and a superhero with the tenets of her Muslim faith and the views of her more conservative older brother. Comic editor Amanat, a Pakistani American Muslim who grew up in New Jersey, wanted to embrace these aspects of Khan's character and incorporate some of her own culturally dissonant experiences, like fasting while playing basketball, into Khan's story.

Khan's struggle with her identity is only one aspect of her story, but it gave Vellani an opportunity to think about her own heritage. "Being Pakistani was a part of my life I was very dismissive about, and I felt disconnected from my culture prior to this show," she told *Esquire Middle East*. "I think it's so cool that the parallels between Kamala and I, that we both went on the same journey of self-discovery, learning about our family and our heritage as the show progressed. And now I could not be prouder to be Pakistani. It's cheesy, but it's true."

Ms. Marvel's creators also incorporated aspects of Vellani's life in their on-screen portrayal of Khan. As Vellani told *Esquire Middle East*, Amanat became "like a big sister" to her during the filming process. On one of their early video calls, Amanat noticed a bottle of Iron Man branded–cologne in the actor's room. This quirky talisman, speaking to the depth of Vellani's fandom, went on to appear in Khan's bedroom in the show.

MS. MARVEL

Vellani also found a mentor in Academy Award–winning actor Brie Larson, who played Carol Danvers/Captain Marvel in the MCU. Two days after Vellani got the role, she got a call from Larson, who told Vellani that appearing in a Marvel movie utterly changed her career. Vellani recalled the conversation to Angelique Jackson in an interview for *Variety* (8 June 2022). "The sheer amount of attention you get being a Marvel actor is completely unmatched to anything else in this industry, and she wanted to prep me for that mentally and hold my hand throughout it," Vellani said.

In playing Khan, Vellani drew inspiration from acclaimed depictions of awkward teen characters, like those in the films *Ladybird* (2017), *Eighth Grade* (2018) and *Scott Pilgrim vs. the World* (2010). Indeed, Sarah Shaffi, who reviewed *Ms. Marvel*'s first two episodes for the *AV Club* (8 June 2022), described moments in which Khan interacts with other kids at school as authentically "cringe." Those episodes center the conflict between Khan's desire to do typical teen things and her obligations to her family, as her parents plan for her older brother's wedding and Khan longs to attend AvengerCon. Her father (played by Mohan Kapur) finally agrees to take her, but insists that they wear matching Incredible Hulk costumes, each fashioned from a shalwar kameez. Khan balks at the outfits, hurting her dad's feelings. "This scene . . . is the most powerful in this episode, because it feels so true," Shaffi, a British Pakistani Muslim, wrote. "It's a rare brown child living in a white world who hasn't at some point, however momentarily, rejected their heritage and then regretted it instantly."

Shaffi went on to praise the show for how easily it presents Khan's cultural background and Muslim religion. "This is a representation of Islam we rarely see onscreen: subtle but not hidden, and one that feels realistic to me," she wrote. "Islam is woven into the fabric of my life, not something that lives separately to me."

Shaffi also noted that the television show makes some changes to its source material, including Khan's origin story. In the comic, Khan develops powers after a run-in with a mutant substance. In the television series, her powers seem to derive from a family heirloom, suggesting that they are in some way related to her heritage. The show also reimagines Khan's powers. Her body itself does not stretch and shrink; colorful beams of light shaped like limbs do, instead.

While filming the series, Vellani was told that she would be a featured character, alongside Larson, in a new film called *The Marvels*. Vellani described her positive experience on the set of that film to Angelique Jackson in an interview for *Variety* (8 June 2022), calling director Nia DaCosta her "favorite human ever." *The Marvels* is slated for release in 2023.

Despite Vellani's enthusiasm for playing Khan, she noted she had not planned to pursue a career as an actor. "I never wanted to be an actor, even though I went to school for theater in high school," she told *Esquire Middle East*, and went on to say that it was the "behind-the-scenes stuff" that really grabbed her attention. Expressing some interest in directing, she added that her early experiences in the industry had given her "the greatest crash course on how to make a movie."

SUGGESTED READING

Goh, Clement. "How Ms. Marvel Channeled Her Hometown of Markham, Ont. In a Coming-of-Age Superhero Story." *CBC News*, 7 June 2022, www.cbc.ca/news/canada/toronto/ms-marvel-markham-iman-vellani-1.6476947. Accessed 7 June 2022.

Itzkoff, Dave. "'Ms. Marvel' Introduces a New Hero (And a New Actress)." *The New York Times*, 6 June 2022, www.nytimes.com/2022/06/06/arts/television/ms-marvel-iman-vellani.html. Accessed 7 June 2022.

Khan, Coco. "'This Show Is So Monumental!' Iman Vellani on Playing Marvel's First Muslim Superhero." *The Guardian*, 6 June 2022, www.theguardian.com/tv-and-radio/2022/jun/06/iman-vellani-playing-marvels-first-muslim-superhero-ms-marvel. Accessed 7 June 2022.

Roberts, Soraya. "'I Spent All My Allowance Money on Comic Books': Iman Vellani on Her Transformation from Superhero Fangirl to the Star of *Ms. Marvel*." *Toronto Life*, 7 June 2022, torontolife.com/culture/q-a-iman-vellani-miss-marvel-disney-plus-series/. Accessed 7 June2022.

Shaffi, Sarah. "Ms. Marvel Starts on a Bright, Fun, Authentic Note." *AV Club*, 8 June 2022, www.avclub.com/ms-marvel-review-season-1-episode-1-1849031519. Accessed 8 June 2022.

Villani, Iman. "Ms. Marvel: How Iman Vellani Became Marvel's First Muslim Superhero." Interview. *Esquire Middle East*, 18 May 2022, www.esquireme.com/culture/interviews/ms-marvel-how-iman-vellani-became-marvels-first-muslim-superhero. Accessed 7 June 2022.

___. "'Ms. Marvel' Star Iman Vellani Shares Superhero Advice from Brie Larson, Previews Her Role in 'The Marvels.'" Interview by Angelique Jackson, *Variety*, 8 June 2022, variety.com/2022/tv/features/ms-marvel-iman-vellani-interview-1235287742/. Accessed 8 June 2022.

—*Molly Hagan*

Rochelle Walensky

Born: April 5, 1969
Occupation: Physician-scientist

As a physician, researcher, and public-health advocate, Rochelle Walensky sought to focus on the big picture. "I've always sort of fashioned myself as someone who takes care of the whole patient, not the heart, not the GI tract," she explained in an interview for the Massachusetts General Hospital (MGH) podcast *Charged* (23 Jan. 2019). "I take care of an infection wherever it is. And then the sort of root causes of those infections in social justice sorts of ways." Immersed in the field of infectious diseases, especially HIV/AIDS research, since a formative residency at the Johns Hopkins Hospital in the mid-1990s, she continued in that vein as a researcher affiliated with both Harvard Medical School (HMS) and MGH, working to assess the viability of screening and prevention approaches and speaking out against the excessive costs of potentially lifesaving pharmaceuticals. After gaining notice for her work in the field of infectious diseases, in 2017 she was named chief of MGH's Infectious Diseases Division.

An in-demand adviser to politicians and other policymakers concerned about issues of public health, Walensky became the center of widespread media attention in December 2020, when incoming president Joe Biden selected her as the new director of the Centers for Disease Control and Prevention (CDC). That role was particularly important as the ongoing coronavirus disease 2019 (COVID-19) pandemic that had been declared in early 2020 continued to threaten the US population, and efforts to vaccinate the public and reduce transmission remained underway. While the responsibility may have been daunting for some, Walensky was well suited to take on that challenge starting in early 2021. "I began my medical career at the height of the HIV/AIDS crisis, and I've spent my life ever since working to research, treat, and combat infectious diseases," she wrote on Twitter following her selection, as quoted by Scottie Andrew for *CNN Health* (8 Dec. 2020). "I'm honored to be called to lead the brilliant team at the CDC. We are ready to combat this virus with science and facts."

EARLY LIFE AND EDUCATION

Rochelle Walensky was born Rochelle Paula Bersoff on April 5, 1969, in Peabody, Massachusetts. She was one of two daughters born to Carol Bersoff-Bernstein, a human resources worker, and mathematician Edward Bersoff, a National Aeronautics and Space Administration (NASA) engineer. Because her father took a job in the Washington, DC, area with a computer engineering company, eventually becoming a business executive and founder of his own company, she grew up in Potomac, Maryland, where she attended Winston Churchill High School. Although she had not yet dedicated her life to combating infectious diseases, she knew as a teenager that she wanted to pursue a career in medicine. "I came from sort of a pedigree where my father was really good in quantitative methods and my mother had a really high EQ and worked in human resources," she told Judy Monroe for the CDC Foundation podcast *Contagious*

Photo by CDC/Centers for Disease Control, via Wikimedia Commons

Conversations (Apr. 2021). "I really wanted to combine the skillsets that I had in math and sciences with being a people person. I like to socialize; I like to be with people. And that led me to the field of being a physician." After graduating from high school in 1987, she studied biochemistry and molecular biology at Missouri's Washington University in St. Louis, earning her bachelor's degree in 1991.

Following her graduation from Washington University, Walensky relocated to Baltimore, Maryland, to attend the Johns Hopkins School of Medicine, where she studied internal medicine. In 1995, she earned her Doctor of Medicine (MD) degree. Subsequently, she completed a residency at the Johns Hopkins Hospital in Baltimore, where she gained firsthand experience caring for patients struggling with the human immunodeficiency virus (HIV) and acquired immunodeficiency syndrome (AIDS). Her time in Baltimore came at a key turning point in the HIV/AIDS crisis. Although AIDS had been considered inevitably fatal since its emergence in the 1980s, a new, US Food and Drug Administration (FDA)–approved combination of medications—referred to as a "cocktail"—was now prolonging patients' lives and giving new hope to both those patients and the doctors and researchers seeking to help them. "We had nothing to help these people, and then suddenly, we did,"

Walensky recalled to Paul Goldsmith for the MGH website (3 Sept. 2019). "The cocktail was literally the difference between life and death for these patients. That was a pretty formative time." Her experiences during that three-year period contributed to her interest in HIV/AIDS research as well as her broader dedication to the study and treatment of infectious diseases and to the field of public health. She would go on to earn a Master of Public Health (MPH) degree from the Harvard School of Public Health in 2001.

MEDICAL CAREER

Upon joining the faculty of HMS in 2001, Walensky dedicated much of her energy to performing research to inform infectious disease policy. "I knew I wanted to do something quantitative with regard to science," she recalled in her interview for *Charged*. "I met Ken [Freedberg], a wonderful research mentor of mine, and he was doing cost effectiveness analysis in HIV policy." Joining Freedberg in his work, she collaborated with him on several research papers. "Every time there's a new intervention, we try and model it to demonstrate what are the costs that'll be associated with it, what are the clinical outcomes that might be associated with it, and can we demonstrate the cost and the outcomes in a cost effectiveness analysis?" she added.

Although much of Walensky's research focused on strategies for the treatment and detection of HIV, she also dealt with other infectious diseases, including tuberculosis. Papers she authored or coauthored appeared in journals such as the *New England Journal of Medicine*, *Clinical Infectious Diseases*, the *Journal of Acquired Immune Deficiency Syndromes*, and *Annals of Internal Medicine*. She became a full professor of medicine at HMS in 2012.

Alongside her work at HMS, Walensky practiced medicine at MGH and Brigham and Women's Hospital. She held the position of Steve and Deborah Gorlin MGH Research Scholar between 2015 and 2020, and in 2017 she became chief of MGH's Infectious Diseases Division. In addition to working in the discipline herself, she stressed the continuing need for infectious-disease specialists and expressed the hope that younger researchers would continue to enter the field. "Infectious diseases aren't going away," she told Goldsmith.

"I like to say if it's medicine and it's in the news, it's probably infectious diseases. The field needs you. The world needs you."

PUBLIC HEALTH EXPERT

As an expert on infectious diseases with a strong interest in public health, Walensky was well suited to advise lawmakers on issues related to public health and health policy, and she was called upon to do so on several occasions. "I'm not a picketer, I'm not an economist, I'm a physician scientist," she told Goldsmith. "My role is to convey my findings to the policy makers in plain English so they can make the most informed decisions." Among other projects, she advised bodies such as the World Health Organization (WHO) and served for a time as chair of the National Institutes of Health's Office of AIDS Research Advisory Council.

Widely known for her research dealing with the costs and outcomes of HIV/AIDS interventions, Walensky often expressed concerns about the soaring prices of the drugs used to treat such illnesses. She made headlines in 2019 when she testified before Congress about the prohibitive cost of pre-exposure prophylaxis (PrEP), medication that can be used to prevent individuals who are exposed to HIV from becoming infected with the virus. "Rep. Elijah Cummings' office called me with some questions about the cost of PrEP. They asked if I'd be open to being part of a hearing on the subject," she told Goldsmith about the events leading up to her testimony. "Previously, I'd briefed congressional staffers, and participated in some advocacy on Capitol Hill—but never anything like that. The setting was high stress, but it was something I felt I could uniquely speak to." She additionally advised state and local politicians on health matters at times, and in 2020 she offered guidance to Massachusetts governor Charlie Baker during the initial stages of the COVID-19 pandemic.

CDC DIRECTOR

In December 2020, incoming president Joe Biden chose Walensky as his preferred candidate to replace Robert Redfield as director of the Centers for Disease Control and Prevention (CDC). Walensky accepted the position, a role that was well in line with her long-standing dedication to public health.

"You can do so much good in the world by addressing public health," she told Monroe. "There is nothing more fulfilling than laying your head on the pillow at night and knowing that your actions of that day improve the health of somebody else or improve the health of tomorrow." Following Biden's inauguration, she assumed the role of CDC director in January 2021.

Overseeing the CDC's response to the COVID-19 pandemic, Walensky had the difficult responsibility of communicating and explaining the organization's recommendations to the public, a tricky task considering the ever-evolving nature of those recommendations. Another major challenge was overseeing the ongoing vaccination initiative, which the CDC and other health experts considered crucial to reducing the pandemic's strain on the health care system. "We still have 70 million Americans who are unvaccinated in this country, and these are people who are 10 times the risk of being hospitalized and 11 times more likely to die," she explained to Margaret Brennan for the CBS News program *Face the Nation* (26 Sept. 2021). "So, we have hard work in making sure we get those people vaccinated."

By late 2021, Walensky and the CDC were tasked with encouraging eligible individuals to get booster shots and facilitating the vaccination of children between the ages of five and eleven, as well as adults. They also monitored the spread of new virus variants such as the Omicron variant, which arose late in the year. In addition to combating COVID-19, Walensky also sought to address other areas of public-health concern during her tenure with the CDC, including HIV treatment, mental health, and opioid addiction.

PERSONAL LIFE

Walensky met her husband, pediatric oncologist Loren Walensky, while they were both pursuing medical studies at the Johns Hopkins Medical School. They married in 1995 and had three sons together. Walensky lived in Newton, Massachusetts, prior to taking her position with the CDC. She subsequently relocated to Atlanta, Georgia, where the CDC headquarters is located, but continued to spend many of her weekends in Massachusetts.

SUGGESTED READING

Andrew, Scottie. "Get to Know Dr. Rochelle Walensky, Biden's CDC Director Pick." *CNN Health*, 8 Dec. 2020, www.cnn.com/2020/12/08/health/rochelle-walensky-cdc-trnd/index.html. Accessed 10 Dec. 2021.

Brennan, Margaret, host. "Transcript: CDC Director Rochelle Walensky on *Face the Nation*, September 26, 2021." *Face the Nation*, CBS News, 26 Sept. 2021, www.cbsnews.com/news/transcript-cdc-director-rochelle-walensky-face-the-nation-09-26-2021/. Accessed 14 Dec. 2021.

Damrad, Kelsey, host. "Rochelle P. Walensky, MD, MPH: HIV—Treating a Changing Epidemic." *Charged*, episode 42, Massachusetts General Hospital, 23 Jan. 2019, www.massgeneral.org/charged/episodes/rochelle-walensky. Accessed 10 Dec. 2021.

Goldberg, Carey. "Biden's Straight-Talking CDC Director Has Long Used Data to Save Lives." *Morning Edition*, NPR, 24 Feb. 2021, www.npr.org/sections/health-shots/2021/02/24/970529519/bidens-straight-talking-cdc-director-has-long-used-data-to-save-lives. Accessed 10 Dec. 2021.

Mandavilli, Apoorva. "The CDC's New Leader Follows the Science. Is That Enough?" *The New York Times*, 10 June 2021, www.nytimes.com/2021/06/10/health/walensky-cdc-covid.html. Accessed 10 Dec. 2021.

Monroe, Judy, host. "A Conversation with CDC Director Dr. Rochelle P. Walensky: A Pivotal Time for Public Health." *Contagious Conversations*, CDC Foundation, Apr. 2021, www.cdcfoundation.org/conversations/rochelle-walensky#transcript. Transcript. Accessed 10 Dec. 2021.

Walensky, Rochelle. "MGH Research Scholar Is Determined Policy Advocate." Interview by Paul Goldsmith. *Massachusetts General Hospital*, 3 Sept. 2019, giving.massgeneral.org/stories/mgh-research-scholar-advocate/. Accessed 10 Dec. 2021.

—*Joy Crelin*

James Wan

Born: February 26, 1977
Occupation: Filmmaker

Director James Wan rose to prominence with his first widely released feature, the 2004 horror film *Saw*, which became a surprise hit and eventually came to be regarded as highly influential. However, the further success of *Saw*'s sequels—which he did not direct and with which he had little creative involvement—earned Wan an inaccurate reputation for being more interested in brutal scenes of torture than quality storytelling. His next two directorial efforts, *Dead Silence* (2007) and *Death Sentence* (2007), diverged significantly from *Saw* in terms of genre and style, but were commercially unsuccessful. "That was two strikes against my name and I'm thinking, am I in director's jail?" he later told Dave Itzkoff in an interview for *The New York Times* (14 Dec. 2018) about that period. In 2010, however, Wan succeeded in revitalizing his career with *Insidious*, a work of supernatural horror that showcased his strengths as a director and set the tone for much of his creative output during the next decade. He further established himself as a major figure in the horror scene with *The Conjuring* (2013), which like *Insidious* spawned a successful franchise.

Although famed for his horror movies, Wan also demonstrated his versatility with other types of projects. Most notably, he directed the 2015 action film *Furious 7* and the superhero blockbuster *Aquaman* (2018) both of which crossed the $1 billion box office mark. Such success made Wan one of the most commercially successful directors ever, which in turn offered him further opportunity to explore a wide range of cinematic genres and styles. "I don't want to be just stuck just doing, you know, the one thing that I've become known for right now," he explained to Steve Weintraub in an interview for *Collider* (17 Sept. 2021). "I don't like to repeat myself."

EARLY LIFE AND EDUCATION

James Wan was born on February 26, 1977, in Kuching, Sarawak, Malaysia. His family immigrated to Australia when he was a young child, and he spent much of his early life in Perth. A fan of comic books as well as the medium of film, the young Wan was drawn

Photo by Gage Skidmore, via Wikimedia Commons.

to the horror genre early in life and was particularly influenced by the 1982 horror film *Poltergeist* and other horror films of the 1980s. "It's one movie—because I saw it at a very young age—which had a huge impact on me," he told Rob Frappier in an interview for *ScreenRant* (13 Mar. 2011) about his first encounter with *Poltergeist*, when his mother took him to see it in the theater. "Ever since then I've had this really freakish obsession with creepy clown dolls."

Long nurturing a passion for telling stories through cinema, after completing his secondary education, Wan enrolled at the Royal Melbourne Institute of Technology (RMIT) to study media, with the goal of becoming a filmmaker. While at RMIT, he befriended actor and screenwriter Leigh Whannell, with whom he would forge a productive creative partnership. In an interview the two had with Scott Tobias for *A.V. Club* (29 Oct. 2010), Whannell described to Tobias how the institution's culture shaped their learning as well as the direction of their craft: "RMIT was a very art-based film school. It wasn't a school where they were trying to pump out the next Steven Spielberg or Guy Ritchie." Wan earned a bachelor's degree in media from RMIT in 1998.

EARLY CAREER

After graduating from RMIT, Wan worked to establish himself as a filmmaker in Australia, often in collaboration with Whannell. "We spent a few years after film school doing jobs we were not passionate about, like everybody else," he told Tobias. "In the meantime, we were saving up money and hoping to come up with a really simple concept we could shoot ourselves, in our backyards, with our mates." He made his feature-length directorial debut with the independent horror film *Stygian*, codirected with Shannon Young, which received an extremely limited release in Australia around the year 2000.

A turning point in Wan's career came when he and Whannell developed the story for a film they called *Saw*, for which Whannell wrote the screenplay. Unable to secure funding to make the film in Australia, they began pursuing leads within the US film industry and made a short film based on their concept, which they hoped to use as a sample when pitching the film to studios. The pair eventually secured a modest budget, and the feature-length *Saw* premiered at the Sundance Film Festival in 2004. The film proved popular among its early viewers and was subsequently released in US theaters later in the year.

Featuring memorable scenes and an iconic villain, *Saw* quickly earned a strong following despite mixed reviews from professional critics. It also proved a considerable commercial hit, especially given its relatively low production budget. This success helped spawn a host of sequels and spin-offs, many of which contained increasingly brutal scenes of torture and dismemberment and were thus classified as belonging to the so-called "torture porn" subgenre of horror films. Wan, however, objected to the original *Saw*'s inclusion in that category and to those who often identified him as a progenitor of the subgenre. "We didn't set out to make a torture movie," he told Tobias. "We had a really short segment that focused on that. But even then, it was shot in such a way where the focus wasn't really on torture, but it was more focused on the overall mystery. The first movie played out like a mystery thriller." Although Wan served as an executive producer for many of the later films in the *Saw* series and also received a story credit for 2006's *Saw III*,

he did not return to the franchise as a director, instead pursuing new projects in the hope of distancing himself from his early work's not-entirely-accurate reputation.

NEW PROJECTS

In the years following the release of *Saw*, Wan took on several new projects that differed substantially from that earlier work. As a director, he first helmed the films *Dead Silence* (2007), another collaboration with Whannell, and *Death Sentence* (2007), a crime thriller based on a 1975 novel by Brian Garfield. Although those two films performed poorly, he found greater success with his 2010 effort *Insidious*, a supernatural horror film written by Whannell. "With *Insidious*, we set out to prove that we're genuine horror fans who know how to make scary films in the PG-13 realm," he told Matt Barone in an interview for *Complex* (6 Aug. 2013). "Making a scary PG-13 movie is a badge of honor. We wanted people to take us seriously outside of these gory films we got pigeonholed for." *Insidious* succeeded in establishing Wan as a director of gore-free horror, and he subsequently returned to the world of that film for a sequel, 2013's *Insidious: Chapter 2*. While Whannell would remain with the series following the second installment, writing and directing *Insidious: Chapter 3* (2015), Wan served only as a producer for the later films, including *Insidious: The Last Key* (2018).

Continuing to work within the supernatural horror subgenre, Wan launched a new series in 2013 with the release of *The Conjuring*, which follows a pair of paranormal investigators as they look into a supernatural presence that is terrorizing a family. He also directed the 2016 sequel *The Conjuring 2*, though he stepped aside for *The Conjuring: The Devil Made Me Do It* (2021), receiving only story and producer credits. Meanwhile, in 2014 Wan founded the production company Atomic Monster, through which he produced several other supernatural horror films, including works in the *Annabelle* series, a spinoff from the *Conjuring* universe. He also served as an executive producer for a variety of television series over the next several years, including the shows *MacGyver* (2016–21), *Swamp Thing* (2019), *Archive 81* (2022), and *Samurai Rabbit: The Usagi Chronicles* (2022).

MAINSTREAM BLOCKBUSTERS

Another milestone for Wan came in 2013, when he was hired to direct the seventh installment in the long-running *Fast and Furious* action series, ultimately titled *Furious 7*. Though it was a daunting challenge to work outside his comfort zone and on a long-running, well-established franchise, the film represented a valuable opportunity to demonstrate his versatility as a director. "*Furious 7* was difficult to make, if not the toughest of my career," he told Itzkoff. "But that movie really allowed people to look at me as a more complete filmmaker." *Furious 7* premiered in 2015 and became a huge commercial success, grossing more than $1.5 billion worldwide.

Wan's next opportunity to direct a blockbuster film came soon after *Furious 7* hit theaters, as the entertainment company Warner Brothers announced that he had been brought on to direct a stand-alone film about the DC Comics superhero Aquaman, the film incarnation of whom was set to be introduced to audiences in 2016's *Batman v Superman: Dawn of Justice*. "Having made 'The Conjuring,' I was part of the Warner Bros. family, and I knew they were doing their DC thing," Wan told Itzkoff about the events leading to his hiring. "I spoke with Kevin Tsujihara [the Warner Bros. chairman and chief executive] at a premiere and I said, 'I'm interested in the properties that you have at DC.' A few months later, I was in a general meeting with DC and they floated two properties that didn't have filmmakers on board: the Flash and Aquaman." Of those two options, Wan was drawn more to the character of Aquaman, in part because he believed an Aquaman film could be presented as "a horror monster movie," he told Itzkoff. Starring actor Jason Momoa in the title role, Wan's *Aquaman* premiered in 2018 and went on to become his second film to gross more than $1 billion worldwide.

BACK TO BASICS

The year 2021 saw the release of the film *Malignant*, directed by Wan and based on a story he developed in collaboration with his wife, Ingrid Bisu, and screenwriter Akela Cooper. For Wan, the project represented an opportunity to return to a style of filmmaking that he associated with the early portion of his career. "I've had the aspiration to go back to the early kind of films that I started my career

with—like *Saw*, *Dead Silence*, *Death Sentence* days—where I was allowed to make these films that were a lot more gritty and more visceral," he explained to Weintraub. "I just felt naturally this particular concept and story really lend itself to that." Much like his breakthrough *Saw*, *Malignant* combines the genres of horror and mystery as well as medical and psychological elements. Some critics suggested it also showed traces of self-parody in its over-the-top approach to horror tropes.

In addition to the release of *Malignant*, 2021 marked the beginning of the production process for *Aquaman* sequel *Aquaman and the Lost Kingdom*, which Wan returned to direct. Filming was completed in January 2022. In April of that year, it was announced that Atomic Monster was launching a partnership with the production company Truly Original, with the goal of producing unscripted television content.

PERSONAL LIFE

Wan married actor and producer Ingrid Bisu in 2019. When not filming elsewhere, he bases himself in California.

SUGGESTED READING

Wan, James. "The Director James Wan: If 'Aquaman' Doesn't Work, Blame Me." Interview by Dave Itzkoff. *The New York Times*, 14 Dec. 2018, www.nytimes.com/2018/12/14/movies/james-wan-aquaman.html. Accessed 9 May 2022.

___. "Interview: James Wan Is the Man Who Made Horror Personal Again." Interview by Hayley Williams. *Kotaku*, Pedestrian Group, 18 June 2016, www.kotaku.com.au/2016/06/interview-james-wan-is-the-man-who-made-horror-personal-again/. Accessed 9 May 2022.

___. "Interview: James Wan Talks 'Insidious: Chapter 2,' 'The Conjuring,' and Defying the Industry's Expectations." Interview by Matt Barone. *Complex*, 6 Aug. 2013, www.complex.com/pop-culture/2013/08/james-wan-interview. Accessed 12 May 2022.

___. "James Wan Interview: *The Conjuring 2*, Fast 7, Statham." Interview by Duncan Bowles. *Den of Geek*, 13 June 2016, www.denofgeek.com/movies/james-wan-interview-the-conjuring-2-fast-7-statham/. Accessed 9 May 2022.

___. "James Wan on 'Malignant,' Why He Calls the Film a 'Genre Blender,' and How He

Brought Gabriel to Life." Interview by Steve Weintraub. *Collider*, 17 Sept. 2021, collider. com/james-wan-malignant-interview/. Accessed 9 May 2022.

Wan, James, and Leigh Whannell. "Interview: James Wan, Leigh Whannell Talk 'Insidious' and Classic Horror." Interview by Rob Frappier. *ScreenRant*, 13 Mar. 2011, screenrant.com/insidious-movie-interviews-james-wan-leigh-whannell/. Accessed 12 May 2022.

___. "*Saw* Creators Leigh Whannell and James Wan." Interview by Scott Tobias. *A.V. Club*, 29 Oct. 2010, www.avclub.com/saw-creators-leigh-whannell-and-james-wan-1798222299. Accessed 9 May 2022.

SELECTED WORKS

Saw, 2004; *Dead Silence*, 2007; *Death Sentence*, 2007; *Insidious*, 2010; *The Conjuring*, 2013; *Insidious: Chapter 2*, 2013; *Furious 7*, 2015; *The Conjuring 2*, 2016; *Aquaman*, 2018; *Malignant*, 2021

—*Joy Crelin*

Josh Wardle

Born: Mid-1980s
Occupation: Software engineer and inventor

In 2021, software engineer and inventor Josh Wardle completed a new project, a word game named Wordle that he created for his word game–loving partner. Soon afterward, he made the game freely available on his personal website, attracting a small but dedicated following. The number of Wordle players soon skyrocketed, its popularity spread mostly by word of mouth, and by late January 2022, more than ten million individuals were playing the game each day. "I'd be lying if I said this hasn't been overwhelming," Wardle said in a statement, as reported by Steven Morris for the *Guardian* (1 Feb. 2022). "After all, I am just one person, and it is important to me that, as Wordle grows, it continues to provide a great experience to everyone." While Wardle had previously played a key role in the development of the Reddit April Fool's Day projects Place and The Button—social experiments with an artistic flair—the success of Wordle drew far more media attention to Wardle himself, in addition to offers of funds from venture

capitalists. Wardle ultimately decided to sell the game to the *New York Times* in early 2022, removing himself from the day-to-day responsibilities associated with Wordle while ensuring the survival of his creation, in which he continued to take pride. "I made something that I would like to exist on the internet," he explained to Karl Vick in an interview for *Time* (1 Feb. 2022).

EARLY LIFE AND EDUCATION

Joshua Wardle was born in the mid-1980s. The youngest of three sons, he grew up in the village of Llanddewi Rhydderch, in southeastern Wales. His parents, Tessa and Christopher, operated an organic livestock farm, where they raised sheep and cattle. After completing school in the nearby town of Abergavenny, Wardle enrolled in Royal Holloway, University of London, to study media arts.

A creative person by nature, Wardle enjoyed studying art and other subjects that would enable him to delve into a variety of creative projects, regardless of whether they would be potentially lucrative. "My background is in art, and I'm just interested in making interesting things," he later told Ingrid Lunden and Amanda Silberling in an interview for *TechCrunch* (12 Jan. 2022). "The business side of things is not super interesting to me at all." After earning his bachelor's degree from Royal Holloway in 2006, Wardle traveled to the United States to study digital arts at the University of Oregon. He completed his Master of Fine Arts (MFA) degree in 2011.

CAREER IN SOFTWARE ENGINEERING

In late 2011, after completing his MFA, Wardle took an artist position with the website *Reddit*. He remained with the company for the next several years, rising to the position of senior product manager and working with the site's community engineering team. In that role, Wardle was responsible for helping to implement or improve the site's features, including its messaging and email notification functions. However, he became perhaps best known for his work on a number of creative projects introduced as special, limited-time April Fools' Day events. In 2015, Wardle contributed to a "subreddit," or subsection of the website, called The Button, a mysterious button that, when pressed, caused a countdown clock to reset. Each Reddit user could press the button only once, and users began to collaborate and make strategic use of their individual button presses to prevent the countdown clock from hitting zero.

The following year, Wardle worked on the April Fools' Day project Robin, which randomly placed pairs of Reddit users in a chatroom together. The two could decide whether to end the chat completely, remain in the chat, or combine the chat with another chat. Combined chatrooms could continue to combine with others of similar size, creating larger and larger groups of Reddit users. Much like The Button and Wardle's later projects at Reddit, Robin represented an intriguing social experiment. "It was like really useful to think about what responsibility you have when you create a space for people [to] interact," he told Vick. "You actually make a ton of decisions that impact the way that they interact with one another. And humans interacting is very, very complicated. Humans are very, very complicated."

For the 2017 April Fools' Day event, Reddit introduced Place, a temporary feature that presented users with a blank canvas on which they could draw by placing individual pixels of color. Each user could place only one pixel at a time and was required to wait a set duration before placing another. This encouraged users to work together to draw pictures or write messages. "There were a lot of internet culture references and memes, but also it reflects the kind of collaborative nature of the internet," Wardle told *CBC Radio* (13 Apr. 2017) about the project. "We saw country flags and these different groups working together. . . . Overall, it's like a super positive depiction of the internet." More than one million users participated in the event, which began on March 31 and lasted for seventy-two hours. Place received a great deal of media attention at the time, and Reddit would later revive Place for April Fools' Day in 2022.

Wardle left his project management position in 2017, but remained affiliated with Reddit in an advisory capacity for some time afterward. He subsequently took a software engineer position with the website *Pinterest*, for which he worked between early 2018 and early 2020. Wardle returned to Reddit in 2020 and remained there until late 2021, when he took a job with the art collective MSCHF.

WORDLE

In early 2021, Wardle set out to develop a word game for his partner, Palak Shah, who had spent time playing such games throughout the coronavirus disease 2019 (COVID-19) pandemic. "I wanted to come up with a game that she would enjoy," he recalled to Daniel Victor for the *New York Times* (3 Jan. 2022). Building upon a prototype game he had begun working on in 2013 but ultimately abandoned, Wardle developed a game that he called Wordle, a clever play on his own name, which he initially made available to Shah and a selection of their friends and relatives.

In its final form, Wordle was available to play once per day. The player is tasked with guessing a mystery word that is five letters in length and is drawn from a curated list of roughly 2,500 words. The player has six tries to guess the word, and each time they guess a letter correctly, the game will inform them of whether the letter is in the correct place or whether it falls elsewhere in the word. As Wardle himself discovered, the game can be surprisingly challenging. "I feel smart when I get a Wordle, even though I made the game," he told Lunden and Silberling. Having kept the game private for a time, Wardle made it available online in October 2021, hosting Wordle on a page of his personal website.

Though once confined to a small group of players, Wordle began to attract players quickly following its internet debut. Between the beginning of November 2021 and the end of January 2022, the number of daily users increased from less than one hundred to well over one million. "I think people kind of appreciate that there's this thing online that's just fun," Wardle told Victor about the game's appeal. "It's not trying to do anything shady with your data or your eyeballs. It's just a game that's fun." After a player in New Zealand began sharing their puzzle results with others, Wardle developed a tool that enabled players to share their results easily on social networks such as *Twitter* and *Facebook*. This not only stoked competition among existing players but also served effectively as an advertisement for Wordle, helping the game attract new players.

Alongside providing daily entertainment to its users, Wordle set in motion a wave of development of new once-a-day games, including variants on the Wordle formula that challenged players to solve multiple word puzzles at once, such as Quordle and Octordle. Other games that emerged included Semantle, which tasked users with guessing a word based on its semantic similarity to other words; the music-identification game Heardle and a host of variants dedicated to specific artists; the history game Yeardle; the geography game Worldle; film-related games such as Actorle; and many others.

SELLING WORDLE

As Wardle often mentioned in interviews, a particularly noteworthy characteristic of Wordle was its lack of monetization. Unlike many other online games, it was free to play, and the website on which it was hosted did not include any advertisements. "That was never the goal, really, to make money," Wardle told Vick. "The goal was to make a game that my partner would enjoy playing. What's interesting is, people ask me all the time about the monetization stuff. . . . None of that really appeals to me." While venture capitalists also contacted Wardle to discuss the game, he was not interested in transforming the game, which had originated simply as a fun personal project, into a profit-oriented business. "If I'd been trying to make a viral game I think it would be very different," he explained to Vick.

Though disinterested in monetization, Wardle was not averse to the idea of selling Wordle entirely, particularly after the rapidly increasing popularity of the game made the experience of owning it somewhat overwhelming. "I made this game but I had no [interest in] running a game business," he explained at the 2022 Game Developers Conference, as reported by Alissa McAloon for *Game Developer* (25 Mar. 2022). "I think of myself as an artist, I really enjoy creating things. Running a game business is not interesting to me." In late January 2022, Wardle sold Wordle to the *New York Times*, which sought to add the game to its existing slate of word games, including Spelling Bee—the game that sparked Wardle and Shah's love of online word games. While the newspaper announced that the game would initially remain free to play, some speculated that the company would eventually limit access to subscribers or to users of the *New York Times Games* app. Wardle, however, expressed his satisfaction with the sale of Wordle, which reportedly cost the *New York Times* more than one million dollars. In May 2022, Wardle was included in *Time* magazine's list of that year's one hundred most influential people in recognition of his work on the game, even though he was no longer Wordle's owner by the time of the list's publication.

PERSONAL LIFE

Wardle lived in Oakland, California, for several years after completing his master's degree but later moved to Brooklyn, New York, where he lives with Shah. An avid fan of the sport Ultimate Frisbee, also known simply as Ultimate, he played that sport for the UK–based team Clapham Ultimate between 2006 and 2008 and subsequently played for the University of Oregon, which he had chosen to attend in part because of its strong Ultimate program. Wardle also enjoyed playing the related sport, Goaltimate, and was a member of the local team Try Hard in Oakland. With a partner, Wardle cofounded Next Gen Network, a web platform for livestreaming Ultimate competitions, in 2012.

SUGGESTED READING

"How More Than 1 Million People Came Together and Created Reddit's 'Place' Masterpiece." *CBC Radio*, 13 Apr. 2017, www.cbc.ca/radio/asithappens/as-it-happens-thursday-edition-1.4069634/how-more-than-1-million-people-came-together-and-created-reddit-s-place-masterpiece-1.4069640. Accessed 12 Sept. 2022.

McAloon, Alissa. "Josh Wardle Reflects on the Unconventional Road to Wordle's Success." *Game Developer*, 25 Mar. 2022, www.gamedeveloper.com/gdc2022/josh-wardle-reflects-on-the-the-unconventional-road-to-wordle-s-success. Accessed 12 Sept. 2022.

Morris, Steven. "'Incredible': From Wordle's Welsh Beginnings to the New York Times." *The Guardian*, 1 Feb. 2022, www.theguardian.com/media/2022/feb/01/incredible-wordles-welsh-beginnings-to-the-new-york-times. Accessed 12 Sept. 2022.

Sherrill, Cameron. "The Life and Death of r/Place, Home to the Internet's Greatest Art War." *Esquire*, 6 Apr. 2022, www.esquire.com/lifestyle/a39636815/what-is-r-place-explained/. Accessed 12 Sept. 2022.

Victor, Daniel. "Wordle Is a Love Story." *The New York Times*, 3 Jan. 2022, www.nytimes.

com/2022/01/03/technology/wordle-word-game-creator.html. Accessed 12 Sept. 2022.

Wardle, Josh. "How Wordle's Creator Feels About Selling His Viral Game." Interview by Karl Vick. *Time*, 1 Feb. 2022, time.com/6143715/wordle-sale-josh-wardle-interview/. Accessed 12 Sept. 2022.

___. "Wordle Founder Josh Wardle on Going Viral and What Comes Next." Interview by Ingrid Lunden and Amanda Silberling. *TechCrunch*, 12 Jan. 2022, techcrunch.com/2022/01/12/josh-wardle-interview-wordle/. Accessed 12 Sept. 2022.

—*Joy Crelin*

Roberta Washington

Born: 1947
Occupation: Architect

When Roberta Washington was in eighth grade, a school assignment changed the trajectory of her life forever. Tasked with interviewing a working professional about their career, she interviewed a local architect whose insights about his field sparked Washington's own interest in a career in architecture. "It changed my life because until then I had never even heard of architects much less met one," she recalled to Sarah K. Filkins for the Women Who Are Architects Oral History Project (2 July 2020). "And here was one who was so convincing that this was a career for people who maybe wanted to create things that looked good but also there was an opportunity to in some way serve society." After earning degrees in architecture from Howard University and Columbia University, Washington went on to do just that, working on projects that included health-care facility designs for a public works department in Mozambique.

Following her return to the United States, in 1983 Washington founded her own architecture firm, Roberta Washington Architects, becoming one of the first Black American women to do so. Over the next several decades, Roberta Washington Architects established itself as a prominent architectural voice in New York City and beyond, designing structures ranging from housing for homeless New Yorkers to environmentally friendly school buildings to historically meaningful tourist attractions. All the while, Washington sought to engage with and draw from the groundbreaking women and Black Americans who preceded her in her field, as well as from the communities around her. As she told Asad Syrkett, Tanay Warerkar, and Patrick Sisson for *Curbed* (22 Feb. 2017), "When you look at others, you can see the strength in them."

EARLY LIFE AND EDUCATION

Roberta Devon Washington was born in Goldsboro, North Carolina, in 1947. She spent her childhood in Greensboro, North Carolina, where she attended segregated schools. Long drawn to the visual arts, Washington first developed an interest in architecture when she was in eighth grade. Tasked with interviewing working professionals for a school project, she set out to interview the tenant of the property next door, an architect who was teaching at a local college. The architect emphasized that architects not only create buildings with artistic appeal but also are capable of helping others with their designs, a revelation that intrigued Washington and sparked her desire to pursue a career in that field. While some adults in Washington's life sought to dissuade her from that career path, her mother, who worked as a maid, encouraged her to pursue her dreams. "She had had other aspirations and hadn't been able to achieve them and so she was especially concerned that her daughters should not follow her, in her footsteps, and so whatever we were interested in she supported us like a hundred percent," Washington told Filkins.

After graduating from high school, Washington enrolled at Howard University to study architecture. "The first year was really rough just because I came from a high school where girls did not take drafting courses," she recalled to Filkins about the experience. "I'd never been in a drafting room or touched anything that had to do with drafting although guys at my high school had. And so I felt like I was starting from behind on day one." Nevertheless, Washington soon mastered the key skills needed by architects and also gained work experience serving as an assistant to a health facilities planner in the Department of Health during the summers.

EARLY CAREER

After graduating from Howard, Washington moved to Detroit to work for an architecture firm that was designing a new hospital building

Photo via Library of Congress/loc.gov
[Public domain]

to be constructed on Howard's campus. Although the job gave her important experience in an actual professional architecture capacity, she soon grew frustrated with both her limited role and her work environment. "I did tons of bathroom designs and I did designs here and there, on every floor, and I was getting really very fed up with it," she told Filkins. "It was a huge firm. I think it was like five hundred people in one building or something." She eventually expressed her dissatisfaction to a supervisor, arguing that she was capable of more important work. The supervisor recommended that she pursue further education in hospital design. Washington went on to enroll in the hospital and health facility design program at Columbia University, from which she earned a master's degree in 1971.

After leaving school Washington worked for a number of different companies. However, she struggled to find a long-term position, as the economic recession underway at the time caused a number of the firms at which she worked to close. Meanwhile, she obtained her architecture license in 1975 and also developed an interest in Africa and the African independence movements then underway. In 1977 she relocated to Mozambique, which had gained independence from Portugal only two years before. Living in the province of Maputo, Washington took a position with the Provincial

Office of Public Works, for which she designed a number of healthcare, education, and housing facilities. She remained in Mozambique until late 1981, when she returned to the United States.

ROBERTA WASHINGTON ARCHITECTS

While Washington had gained further valuable experience during her years in Mozambique, she did not immediately consider establishing her own architecture firm upon her return to the United States. Instead, she took a series of positions with existing companies, again focusing on hospital design. "I think my desire, my intent was just to work in those firms forever," she told Filkins. "I could have just worked there forever. I didn't really think about starting a firm." Soon, however, she grew frustrated with the lack of advancement opportunities available to her and began to consider striking out on her own. She ultimately founded the firm Roberta Washington Architects, PC in 1983, becoming one of just a few Black American women operating their own architecture firms. Washington served as the firm's principal architect throughout the next several decades, during which the firm also employed other professionals as needed. It generally remained a small operation, with just a handful of employees assisting Washington.

Based in the Harlem neighborhood of New York, Roberta Washington Architects forged close ties with that neighborhood and the wider city, focusing on projects in New York. "In local communities, if they know that you exist, there is power there," Washington explained to Anjulie Rao for *Architect* magazine (20 Oct. 2021). The firm's first project, which she accepted even before her practice was fully set up, was a residential hotel intended to house New Yorkers experiencing homelessness. This led to involvement with several other local housing initiatives, including the CityHomes affordable housing project. Early on, Washington found her firm was often contracted by bigger companies who could then benefit from programs designed to support minority-owned businesses, but ultimately gave her little credit in the end result. However, thanks to her constant networking efforts, she built up a professional reputation on her own terms and found a steady stream of work.

Washington remained closely tied to the community, for example serving as chair of the Central Harlem Housing Committee and cochair of its Land Use Committee. Other major projects over the years included a mixed-use building at 1400 Fifth Avenue in Harlem, which notably incorporated a substantial percentage of recyclable building materials and was designed to maximize its energy facility. Following its completion, the building was reported to be the first residential building in Harlem to receive Leadership in Energy and Environmental Design (LEED) certification from the US Green Building Council. In keeping with Washington's longtime interest in hospital design, Roberta Washington Architects contributed to a number of healthcare–related projects, including medical facilities in Brooklyn. The firm was also responsible for the design of the Interpretive Center of New York's African Burial Ground National Monument, which opened in 2010.

Alongside the firm's work in New York, Roberta Washington Architects took on a number of significant projects outside of that city and state. For example, the firm worked on the renovation and expansion of the Barnard Environmental Magnet School (later known as the Barnard Environmental Science & Technology School) in New Haven, Connecticut, an environmentally friendly building that earned LEED Gold certification following its renovation in 2008. Washington also contributed to the design of the Museums at 18th & Vine in Kansas City, Missouri, which include the American Jazz Museum and the Negro Leagues Baseball Museum.

INDUSTRY LEADER

In addition to her design work, Washington cultivated a deep interest in the history of architecture and American architects. "In this profession, you always are looking for inspiration," she explained to Syrkett, Warerkar, and Sisson. "That's part of the reason I'm interested in the history of African Americans in architecture and the history of women in architecture in this country." As a writer, Washington published biographies of notable earlier architects in a number of publications, including the *Biographical Dictionary of African American Architects, 1865–1945* (2004). She advocated for the preservation of historic buildings and served as a member of New York's Landmarks Preservation Commission between 2007 and 2015. Reflecting her respected position in the architectural community, Washington was named fellow of the American Institute of Architects in 2006 and served as the 2011 James E. Silcott Endowed Chair in the Howard University School of Architecture and Design.

Along with working to recognize historical trailblazers in diversifying architecture, Washington also long sought to call attention to the work of contemporary Black women architects and to the systemic racism and sexism that they often must overcome. "If you are black and female, then you already know that you belong to a group that, in the eyes of some, has a demeaned spot in history. But if there's something that you want to do, you just look past it. I've encountered racism and sexism, but to succeed, I can't focus solely on that," she told Syrkett, Warerkar, and Sisson. "At the same time, I think there are places—whether it's women in architecture groups or the National Organization of Minority Architects [NOMA]—where you can turn for support and talk about how others did it." Washington herself attended her first NOMA conference in 1991, was elected NOMA's president for 1997, and maintained a strong affiliation with the organization over the subsequent decades. Her work was featured in the SAY IT LOUD—NOMA 50th Exhibition at the Detroit Historical Society's Robert and Mary Ann Bury Community Gallery, which opened in October 2021.

PERSONAL LIFE

Washington settled in New York City, in part because of her passion for the city's architecture. "Before New York City, most of my life happened in a town where the tallest building downtown was eighteen stories high and the second tallest was four stories. Once in New York, I was first struck by the heights, the congestion, and the muted-color palette. And then by how close in proximity buildings of different heights, styles, and ages seemed to live in peace with each other," she told Steve Cimino for *AIA Architect* (7 June 2018). "New York's architecture was a draw for coming, and remains a prime reason for staying."

SUGGESTED READING

Cimino, Steve. "New York City, Briefly." *AIA Architect*, 7 June 2018, www.architectmagazine.com/aia-architect/

aiafeature/new-york-city-briefly_o. Accessed 7 Feb. 2022.

Mathur, Chitvan. "Roberta Washington Architects—15 Iconic Projects." *Rethinking the Future*, www.re-thinkingthefuture.com/know-your-architects/a1510-roberta-washington-architects-15-iconic-projects/. Accessed 7 Feb. 2022.

Rao, Anjulie. "The Pursuit and Promise of Equity in Architecture." *Architect*, 20 Oct. 2021, www.architectmagazine.com/practice/the-pursuit-and-promise-of-equity-in-architecture_o. Accessed 7 Feb. 2022.

"Roberta Washington." *The Network Journal*, 26 June 2009, tnj.com/roberta-washington/. Accessed 7 Feb. 2022.

Syrkett, Asad, et al. "16 Architects of Color Speak Out about the Industry's Race Problem." *Curbed*, 22 Feb. 2017, archive.curbed.com/2017/2/22/13843566/minority-architects-diversity-architecture-solutions-advice. Accessed 7 Feb. 2022.

Washington, Roberta. "Washington, Roberta Devon, FAIA Oral History Interview." Interview by Sarah K. Filkins. *Women Who Are Architects*, 26 July 2020, tile.loc.gov/storage-services/service/afc/afc2019031/afc2019031_06000/afc2019031_06000_ms01.pdf. Accessed 7 Feb. 2022.

Weber, Cheryl. "Diversity How?" *Architect*, 11 Aug. 2006, www.architectmagazine.com/practice/diversity-how_o. Accessed 7 Feb. 2022.

—*Joy Crelin*

Jessica Watkins

Born: May 14, 1988
Occupation: Astronaut and geologist

"The thing about human spaceflight," astronaut and geologist Jessica Watkins told Ker Than for the website of Stanford University's Doerr School of Sustainability (13 Feb. 2018), "is that it pushes us to the limits of our capabilities on all different levels. It pushes the limits of our technological, scientific, psychological, and physical capabilities." As a member of the 2017 class of National Aeronautics and Space Administration (NASA) astronaut candidates, Watkins was ready and willing to test those limits—including, potentially, on the surface of a celestial body other than Earth. In addition to working on more typical NASA projects, she

was one of the astronauts selected as potential candidates to perform missions as part of the Artemis Program, which had set goals to return astronauts to the moon as soon as possible and, eventually, to develop the technology necessary to send humans to Mars. "As long as there's a ride back, sign me up," she told Marina Koren for *The Atlantic* (15 June 2017). "I have too many loved ones and too much work to do back here to go for a one-way trip." While a potential lunar mission remained far off at that juncture, in April 2022 Watkins had the opportunity to travel into space for the first time. A member of NASA's Expedition 67, she was set to spend about six months aboard the International Space Station (ISS), becoming the first Black woman to complete an extended stay on the ISS and a core member of the expedition's small crew.

EARLY LIFE AND EDUCATION

Jessica Andrea Watkins was born on May 14, 1988, in Gaithersburg, Maryland. Her mother, Carolyn, was a financial manager while her father, Michael, worked in management consulting. The family eventually resettled in Lafayette, Colorado, which Watkins came to consider her hometown, and she attended Fairview High School in Boulder. Interested in space travel from an early age, particularly as she was introduced to the legacy of astronaut Judith Resnik as an elementary schooler, she aspired to become an astronaut one day and worked toward that career with the encouragement of her parents. "I definitely wouldn't be here without their continual support," she told Than after later achieving her goal. "They've been on this journey with me throughout the entire process, so in a lot of ways it's a dream come true for them as well."

After graduating from Fairview High in 2006, Watkins enrolled at Stanford University and soon transitioned from a mechanical engineering focus to studying geological and environmental sciences. "It was a way for me to study space and keep my eyes on the stars while staying within the framework that would make me eligible to be an astronaut," she explained to Than. In addition to attending college, she completed a research internship at the Ames Research Center, a NASA facility in northern California, in 2008. It was there, in addition to her participation in other programs, that she was given firsthand exposure to NASA research and efforts related to Mars.

Photo via NASA/Wikimedia Commons.
[Puublic domain]

Alongside her academic career, Watkins was heavily involved in sports at Stanford as well, playing on the school's basketball and soccer club teams. She was also a prominent member of the Stanford women's rugby team, with which she claimed a national championship in 2008. For Watkins, participating in collegiate sports was a valuable experience that would benefit her in her career as an astronaut. "Being a team player is a really important part of what we do and I learned the best from the Stanford women's rugby team," she explained to Kristel Tjandra for the website of Stanford Club Sports (22 Apr. 2022). In fact, Watkins was not the first future astronaut to play for Stanford's women's rugby team; astronaut Sally Ride, the first American woman in space, had been an original member of the team upon its establishment in 1977. In addition to competing for Stanford, Watkins represented the United States on the international level in rugby sevens, a form of the sport with fewer players and shorter games than the standard rugby union format.

GRADUATE EDUCATION AND EARLY CAREER

Following her graduation from Stanford with a bachelor's degree in 2010, Watkins enrolled at the University of California, Los Angeles (UCLA), where she pursued doctoral studies in geology. While attending the university, she coauthored several peer-reviewed papers that went on to be published in periodicals such as the *Astrophysical Journal*. She served as a teaching assistant in the Department of Earth, Planetary and Space Sciences and completed several internships with the NASA Jet Propulsion Laboratory. The recipient of a graduate research fellowship from the National Science Foundation (NSF), she also received several awards from UCLA, including the 2010 Chancellor's Prize.

Watkins earned her doctorate in 2015, having completed the thesis "Tectonic and Aqueous Processes in the Formation of Mass-Wasting Features on Mars and Earth." From there, she took a postdoctoral fellowship at the California Institute of Technology (Caltech), where she worked in the Division of Geological and Planetary Sciences on projects related to NASA's Mars rover *Curiosity*. At the same time, she remained active in sports during that period, serving as a volunteer coach for Caltech's women's basketball team.

ASTRONAUT TRAINEE

In June 2017, NASA selected Watkins as a member of its 2017 class of astronaut trainees. "We knew we were going to receive a phone call that day, and it was going to be either 'yes' or a 'no,'" she told Than about the day she received that news. "I answered the phone, and [NASA Johnson Space Center Flight Operations Director] Brian Kelly was on the line. He said, 'How are you doing, Jessica?' I said I was feeling a bit under the weather and he said, 'Maybe we can help with that.' That's when I knew it was a positive call." In August of that year, she traveled to Houston, Texas, to begin her astronaut training, an extensive process in which aspiring astronauts complete physical training that will prepare them to undertake activities such as spacewalks, learn to use crucial space-related technology, and much more.

In addition to representing the accomplishment of Watkins's lifelong goal, her selection as an astronaut was significant because of the limited numbers of women and African Americans serving as astronauts. "It's something that I don't take lightly, and something that I know is an important responsibility," she told Koren about her status as a role model. "I'm excited about that opportunity, to be that kind of representative, to be able to be somebody that people can look to and see doing cool things, like going to space, and hopefully they will be able to see that that's something that they can do, too."

Two years after her selection as an astronaut trainee, Watkins served as one of the participants in the NASA Extreme Environment Mission Operations (NEEMO) 23 mission. During that mission, a crew of six, consisting of four "aquanauts" and two support technicians, spent nine days at Aquarius Reef Base, an underwater research station located in the ocean off the coast of Florida and operated by Florida International University. NEEMO missions are designed to help prepare astronauts for space, effectively simulating space missions and readying them for future spaceflight. In addition, NEEMO missions provide the participating aquanauts with opportunities to conduct underwater research relevant to spaceflight as well as research initiatives in other fields.

ARTEMIS PROGRAM

In late 2020, Watkins became one of the astronauts selected for the Artemis Team, a group of potential candidates for missions implemented as part of the Artemis Program. "We are a team that we all come with different strengths, different skill sets and it's really the combination of all those skill sets that's going to allow us to be successful and accomplish the goals we want to with Artemis," she told David Mullen for Colorado Springs's *The Gazette* (24 Jan. 2022) about the group. Established several years prior, the Artemis Program was designed to oversee the process of sending astronauts back to the moon, which humans had not visited since 1972.

Among other parts of the project, NASA and that agency's partners hoped to build a space station in orbit around the moon as well as a base camp on the moon's surface. The prospect of landing on the moon was particularly compelling for Watkins. "I did a lot of my graduate work on the geology of other surfaces, so to be able to go and actually put boots on those surfaces would be a dream come true," she explained to Mullen. Early Artemis Program missions included Artemis I, an uncrewed flight to the moon that was scheduled to launch in August 2022 but was subsequently postponed. Like other NASA initiatives, the exact timing of the ultimate return to the moon depended

on several technological, environmental, and human factors.

EXPEDITION 67

While a potential mission to the moon remained distant in the early 2020s, Watkins at last had the opportunity to travel into space in April 2022. On April 27, she served as a mission specialist aboard the SpaceX Crew-4 mission, which transported Watkins to the International Space Station (ISS). She was joined on that spaceflight by NASA astronauts Kjell Lindgren and Bob Hines as well as European Space Agency astronaut Samantha Cristoforetti, who had previously been part of the NEEMO 23 mission with Watkins. Upon arriving at the ISS, they joined the astronauts and cosmonauts already on board and began their work there, which included performing maintenance on the station and conducting research. "We can use Earth as an analog or laboratory to explore and understand surfaces of other planets," she explained to Tjandra about her work. "We can look at features and landforms and processes that happen on the Earth and then be able to apply that to other planetary bodies. So to be able to do that from [the] ISS is really exciting." A flight engineer for ISS Expedition 67, Watkins was set to remain aboard the ISS for six months and was widely noted as the first Black woman to achieve an extended stay on the station.

PERSONAL LIFE

In addition to focusing on astronaut training and her scientific work, Watkins remained an avid fan of rugby. She has also expressed interest in other sports and outdoor activities, including basketball and skiing. Watkins relocated to Houston upon joining NASA in 2017.

SUGGESTED READING

Adams, Char, and Donna M. Owens. "NASA Astronaut Jessica Watkins Celebrates 'Milestone' for Diversity in Space Industry." *NBC News*, 28 Apr. 2022, www.nbcnews. com/news/nbcblk/nasa-astronaut-jessica-watkins-celebrates-milestone-diversity-space-in-rcna25378. Accessed 12 Sept. 2022.

Aubourg, Lucie, and Antoine Boyer. "US Astronaut Jessica Watkins Sets Sights on Moon . . . and Mars." *Phys.org*, 13 Aug.

2022, phys.org/news/2022-08-astronaut-jessica-watkins-sights-moon.html. Accessed 12 Sept. 2022.

Koren, Marina. "The Millennial Astronaut Who Wants to Go to Mars." *The Atlantic*, 15 June 2017, www.theatlantic.com/science/archive/2017/06/mars-astronaut-jessica-watkins/530373/. Accessed 12 Sept. 2022.

Mullen, David. "Colorado Astronaut Jessica Watkins: A Dream Unexpectedly Comes True." *The Gazette*, 24 Jan. 2022, gazette.com/news/colorado-astronaut-jessica-watkins-a-dream-unexpectedly-comes-true/article_b6c5d6d0-3c9e-11eb-a74d-6fbd16da7a75.html. Accessed 12 Sept. 2022.

"NASA Astronaut Jessica Watkins Holds a Q&A from Space." *Caltech*, 18 Aug. 2022, www.caltech.edu/about/news/nasa-astronaut-jessica-watkins-holds-a-qa-from-space. Accessed 12 Sept. 2022.

Than, Ker. "Stanford Earth Graduate May Be Mars Bound." *Doerr School of Sustainability*, Stanford University, 13 Feb. 2018, earth.stanford.edu/news/stanford-earth-graduate-may-be-mars-bound#gs.at3h9g. Accessed 12 Sept. 2022.

Tjandra, Kristel. "Jessica Watkins '10 to Become First Black Woman on Extended ISS Mission." *Stanford Club Sports*, Stanford University, 22 Apr. 2022, stanfordclubsports.com/news/2022/4/22/womens-rugby-jessica-watkins-10-to-become-first-black-woman-on-extended-iss-mission.aspx. Accessed 12 Sept. 2022.

—*Joy Crelin*

Rosa Whitaker

Born: ca. 1960
Occupation: Chief executive officer

Rosa Whitaker was the first assistant US trade representative for Africa ever appointed. She was appointed by President Bill Clinton, a Democrat, in 1997 and went on to serve the administration of President George W. Bush, a Republican. She was a major architect of the African Growth and Opportunity Act (AGOA) of 2000, which was responsible for allowing African-made products to come into the country on a duty-free basis. Before AGOA, Whitaker told Stephen Williams in an interview for *African Business* (10 Mar. 2017), "the US did not have a trade policy for Africa. The US policy was to view Africa as a charity case, the beneficiaries of aid." Her goal at the State Department was to rid the relationship between the United States and Africa of that strong strain of paternalism, replace it with a true partnership model, and ensure that Africa did not get left behind economically as the world grew increasingly globalized.

While serving as the assistant US trade representative for Africa, Whitaker displayed in her office a Portuguese-language map of Africa, dating from 1590, as a symbol of her mission. "It's a reminder of the slave trade," Whitaker told Peter Alan Harper for *The Wichita Eagle* (30 Aug. 1998). "This is where Africa was under the rule of colonial masters. I look at it as a source of pride, . . . a reminder of Africa's history, historically, how far it's come, though it still suffers from global economic apartheid."

Since 2003, Whitaker—who came to feel that she could facilitate progress better as a member of the private sector—has been president and CEO of The Whitaker Group (TWG), a consultancy with offices in Washington, DC, and Accra, Ghana. From 2018 to 2021 she served as the president of Mercy Ships, a nonprofit organization that offers free surgical and health-care services in sub-Saharan Africa.

EARLY YEARS AND EDUCATION

Rosa Whitaker was born around 1960 in racially segregated Washington, DC, which had become the first major US city with a Black majority in 1957. Her parents, who later divorced, both worked for the US Postal Service, and money was often in short supply. "I grew up in a home full of love and encouragement but it definitely was not a home of privilege and comfort," she recalled to Roland S. Martin in an interview for the magazine *The Intelligent Lady* (Sept./Dec. 2017). "Education was highly valued in our home as a great equalizer that would ultimately balance the 'lack' in our lives with promise and opportunity. . . . My parents and elders often reminded us that as African Americans, a high price was paid to secure our right to receive an education."

Among the elder relatives advising Whitaker and her three siblings was their great-great-great-aunt Barbara Simmons, who lived to be 106. Simmons gave the Whitakers "firsthand

Photo by Sokwateng,
via Wikimedia Commons

accounts of [relatives born into slavery], and you can't be exposed to that and not have that impact you personally," Whitaker told Harper. "These discussions, the stories she shared, had a lot to do with my values, how I was shaped."

At thirteen, Whitaker joined the successful campaign for the District of Columbia Home Rule Act of 1973, which gave District residents more control over local affairs, and at fifteen she was elected youth chair of a neighborhood planning council. The following year, when she was sixteen, Whitaker made the decision to leave home and join a domestic exchange program aimed at fostering understanding between Black people and White people. For a year, she lived with a White family in Wisconsin. The school there had so many more resources than the schools she attended in DC and was so academically rigorous that she was able to skip her senior year of high school and graduate early. Although she had not yet formulated a specific career plan, she knew it would involve public service of some type. "From childhood, I knew that I wanted to make a difference in the lives of people that were disadvantaged by poverty and/or inequality," she explained to Martin. "I understood that I was burdened by economic injustice. Even at a very young age, I used to compare the lives of the people in my community to the lives of those I saw on television and often wondered what was wrong.

Eliminating poverty and all that comes with it has been the driving motivation pushing me into action for most of my life."

In 1977, Whitaker entered American University, in Washington, DC, where she earned a bachelor's degree in political science (1981) and a master's in public administration (1983). An active student, she helped found the South African Divestment Committee, which opposed South African apartheid; interned for the Congressional Black Caucus; and was a member of student government. She also studied abroad in Italy and London.

Whitaker's semester in London coincided with the Lancaster House negotiations on the future of Zimbabwe, formerly the British colony of Rhodesia, and she was subsequently inspired to volunteer there. "I was supposed to live in a rural village, but they didn't think I would make it," she recalled to Williams. "So my Zimbabwean friend invited me to live with her family. Her uncle was Edson Zvobgo, Zimbabwe's justice minister. That experience awoke a passion in me. I just knew that there was no turning back and Africa would be my life."

LAUNCHING A CAREER

Upon graduating from American University with her master's degree in 1983, Whitaker spent the next few years working at a social service agency. In 1986 she became director of Washington's Office of International Business, which was responsible for attracting foreign investment to the District, among other goals.

Whitaker was eager to join the US State Department but would not accept a job until she could be sure she would be stationed in Africa. In 1993 a position opened at the US Embassy in Côte d'Ivoire, as deputy chief of the economic section. In that capacity she negotiated with the country's officials, attempting to convince them of the benefits of joining the newly developed World Trade Organization (WTO). She admitted to Martin that she found her mission challenging. "How could I possibly motivate government officials that international trade would work for their country? Africa was not even integrated well into the world trading system." While in Africa, Whitaker met Mike Williams, an aide to Representative Jim McDermott, a Republican from Washington. With Williams, she brainstormed solutions, and the outline of what would eventually become the AGOA began to take shape.

In 1995, Whitaker returned to Washington to work in the Office of International Energy Policy. Among the high points of that post was accompanying President Clinton's commerce secretary, Ronald H. Brown, on one of his trips to Africa, which he viewed as a region of great beauty and untapped economic potential. When Brown was killed in a plane crash in 1996, his friend and colleague Representative Charles Rangel, a Democrat from New York known as the "Lion of Harlem," vowed to carry on Brown's efforts to boost Africa's economy. Whitaker took a sabbatical from the State Department to serve as Rangel's senior trade advisor.

AGOA

As part of Rangel's team, Whitaker revisited the AGOA, which had gotten stalled in the US House. The act was unpopular with labor unions, and many nongovernmental organizations characterized it as a cynical means to stop sending aid to Africa. Whitaker revised it repeatedly as it made its way through committee, and thanks in part to her charm and powers of persuasion—as well as the backing of Rangel, who would later become the first Black chair of the House Ways and Means Committee—it was enacted in 2000. The act—which bettered existing US trade programs by expanding duty-free benefits if a country could prove that it was working to improve its rule of law, human rights record, and respect for labor standards—was extended by President George W. Bush until 2025.

Meanwhile, in 1997, Clinton tapped Whitaker as assistant US trade representative for Africa—the first time that region had a dedicated emissary within the Office of the US Trade Representative. In that capacity, Whitaker negotiated trade agreements and spearheaded a series of initiatives meant to boost cooperation, investment, and equal partnerships between African nations and the United States.

THE WHITAKER GROUP

While gratified that AGOA had been enacted, Whitaker felt some frustration at the slow pace of progress. In 2003 she left government service to launch her own firm, The Whitaker Group (TWG), believing that it would be a more effective way of addressing the problems plaguing Africa. "Our mission is quite simple: utilising enterprise solutions to address poverty," she told Williams. "My interest is in justice, and infrastructure is one of our pillars."

Some observers were suspicious that Whitaker was leveraging the relationships she had made as a government official with African leaders for what they saw as personal gain. "It is hardly unusual for high-level government executives here to leave their positions for lucrative jobs in the private sector," Ken Silverstein wrote for the *Los Angeles Times* (2 Mar. 2004). "But the case of Rosa Whitaker stands out as an example of why Washington officials are increasingly debating what constitutes a conflict of interest in such comings and goings." Among the transactions watchdogs questioned was a $300,000-a-year contract to advise Uganda on how best to benefit from AGOA, and a similarly lucrative agreement with Ghana. Whitaker has maintained that her consulting activities were above reproach and had been approved by the trade representative's office. She has touted the number of initiatives she has facilitated since opening TWG. These have included agricultural and health-related projects, infrastructure development, technology adoption, and investment in energy. In 2010, she was named one of *Foreign Policy* magazine's Top Global Thinkers of the year in recognition of her work with TWG.

Whitaker is a prolific writer of op-eds and has commented publicly on topics related to Africa, trade, and more. In one piece that appeared in *Newsweek* (25 May 2021), she reminded readers that despite the gains made possible by AGOA, US "economic policy toward Africa is faltering primarily because we continue to welcome and build a dysfunctional network of aid peddlers instead of properly incentivizing trade and investment—proven catalysts for job creation and income expansion on the ground where it is needed most."

PERSONAL LIFE

Whitaker, who is also known as Lady Rosa Whitaker Duncan-Williams, is married to Archbishop Nicholas Duncan-Williams, known as a pioneer of the Charismatic movement in Ghana. In 2015, the *Washingtonian* reported that Whitaker had purchased a 19,000-square-foot mansion with two pools in Reston, Virginia, for $2.3 million.

SUGGESTED READING

Harper, Peter Alan, Associated Press. "Driven to Make a Difference: Rosa Whitaker Is the First Assistant U.S. Trade Representative for Africa." *The Wichita Eagle*, 30 Aug. 1998, p. 2B.

Silverstein, Ken. "Connections Work for Ex-Trade Official." *Los Angeles Times*, 2 Mar. 2004, www.latimes.com/archives/la-xpm-2004-mar-02-na-whitaker2-story.html. Accessed 3 Feb. 2022.

Whitaker, Rosa. "Interview with Lady Rosa Whitaker Duncan-Williams." Interview by Roland S. Martin. *The Intelligent Lady*, Sept./Dec. 2017, p. 18.

—. "Lobbying: Africa Needs a Unified Agenda—Rosa Whitaker." Interview by Patrick Smith. *Africa Report*, 1 Dec. 2014, www.theafricareport.com/3667/lobbying-africa-needs-a-unified-agenda-rosa-whitaker/. Accessed 3 Feb. 2022.

—. "President Biden Needs to 'Build Back Better' on Africa." *Newsweek*, 25 May 2021, www.newsweek.com/president-biden-needs-build-back-better-africa-opinion-1594283. Accessed 3 Feb. 2022.

—. "'We Were Able to Substitute Paternalism with Partnership,' Says Rosa Whitaker." Interview by Stephen Williams. *African Business*, 10 Mar. 2017, african.business/2017/03/economy/able-substitute-paternalism-partnership-says-rosa-whitaker/. Accessed 3 Feb. 2022.

—*Mari Rich*

Mike Winkelmann

Born: June 20, 1981
Occupation: Digital artist

In March 2021 Mike Winkelmann, also known by the name Beeple, unexpectedly became one of the world's highest-valued living artists when the storied auction house Christie's sold his digital work *Everydays: The First 5,000 Days* for $69 million. That piece consists of a collage of five thousand images from his ongoing project "Everydays," launched in 2007, which features a new piece of art posted online every single day. These images are often grotesque, incorporating imagery from science fiction and tending toward a surreal, violent, hyper-sexualized vision of American society. They revel in the disturbing side of popular culture,

colliding public figures and cartoons to create nightmarish scenes: humans suckle at the multiple breasts of a chained robotic Mickey Mouse creature, Abraham Lincoln spanks an infant Donald Trump, and so on. Many commentators noted that the unassuming Winkelmann, who also created video art for many high-profile music acts, seemed an unlikely creator of such provocative works, but he himself sought to avoid overthinking or analyzing his output. "I don't know where the hell that sh—'s coming from," he told Mickey Rapkin for *Esquire* (17 Feb. 2021) of his more bizarre imagery. "I try to listen as closely as possible to that tiny voice of, like, What is the picture I most want to make today?"

The Beeple style—and especially his nontraditional digital format—made Winkelmann a controversial figure in the art world. Most notably, he became a leading figure in the rise of NFTs, or non-fungible tokens, in which blockchain technology is used to confirm unique ownership of a piece of digital media. In this system, anyone can view a Beeple work online, but the true ownership rights can be bought and sold just like a physical artwork. The potential of NFTs drove a frenzy of investment in the early 2020s, and while some observers dismissed it as a fad or bubble, the lucrative sales of Beeple works hinted at how the technology could reshape the art market and beyond. "It's a bit of a paradigm shift," Winkelmann told Kara Swisher for her *New York Times* podcast *Sway* (22 Mar. 2021). "I really feel like it's such a blank slate technology that you are going to see this with everything."

EARLY LIFE AND EDUCATION

Michael Joseph Winkelmann was born on June 20, 1981, and grew up in Fond du Lac, Wisconsin, a small town outside of Milwaukee. His father, Peter, worked as an electrical engineer, and his mother, Dottie, was the director of the Fond du Lac senior center. Winkelmann had a creative side from an early age, though from the beginning he showed more aptitude for the burgeoning field of computer technology than traditional artistic skills. "Growing up, Mike loved to draw but he still isn't good at drawing," his mother told Sharon Roznik for the Fond du Lac *FDL Reporter* (15 Mar. 2021). "He would also write and direct fun movies with his friends. He was always on the computer."

As a teenager Winkelmann found a particular inspiration in electronic music, especially the artist Aphex Twin. "What can one person and a computer do?" he remarked to Kyle Chayka for the *New Yorker* (22 Mar. 2021). "That has always been a really cool concept to me, because it's the equalizer, in a way."

Winkelmann studied computer science at Purdue University and graduated in 2003. He was bored by programming, however, and more interested in making short films and teaching himself digital design. Though he took a regular job as a website designer, he continued his artistic endeavors on the side, mostly for his own amusement.

BECOMING BEEPLE

After discovering the work of British video artist Chris Cunningham, Winkelmann was inspired to create animated video loops that he paired with his electronic music experiments. He described these early efforts to Swisher as "very abstract audio visual, tightly synched audio and video," noting that he was interested in the "interplay between light and sound." That interest led him to adopt the name Beeple, taken from a furry 1980s toy that makes noise in reaction to changes in light. Soon he began to post his work online.

Inspired by the daily sketches of UK artist Tom Judd, on May 1, 2007, Winkelmann began a project called "Everydays," in which he vowed to post a new drawing on his website each day. "I think I thought that was a cool way to sort of incrementally improve," he explained to Swisher. After about a year, he realized he could use the project to teach himself 3D animation. He described one of his main tools, a program called Cinema 4D, to Swisher as "a 3D world where you can place any sort of objects or build any sort of objects." He also explained how he developed a collage-like style, relying on pre-made digital models that he could purchase and then manipulate in the program: "I'm taking these assets that I had not built and sort of putting them together in sort of a bunch of different ways."

The "Everydays" practice helped sharpen his skills, but Winkelmann initially began to garner attention for his increasingly elaborate animated music videos. Several of these attracted a following on video-sharing platforms, including *Instrument Video Nine*, which was featured on the Vimeo site in 2010.

Photo courtesy of Mike Winkelmann via Wikimedia Commons

His animations also proved popular for reuse by DJs and other artists. The work was not lucrative, however. "My personal work is my personal work," Winkelmann told Peter Kirn for the digital music site *CDM* (5 Mar. 2010). "I've made very, very little money from it and I don't see that changing anytime soon." Yet little did he know, such change was right around the corner.

Later in 2010 Winkelmann was hired to create an animated music video for "Kill Your Co-Workers," a song by the electronic musician Flying Lotus. The resulting work earned praise for its juxtaposition of playfulness and gore, enhanced by the rudimentary animation style. Winkelmann noted to Ryan Dombal for *Pitchfork* (5 Nov. 2010) that that style was, in fact, largely due to his limitations, both in skill and patience: "By having a simplified look, I can do stuff really quick. If I was doing a Pixar-level animation, I could spend three weeks just modeling one character. But with this grittier style, I can model three buildings and six characters and an octopus in four hours and animate it." The successful collaboration led to more projects in music, including postproduction work on the 2011 Erykah Badu music video "Gone Baby, Don't Be Long." Winkelmann began freelancing for companies producing live events and concerts, eventually designing animations for major acts such as Justin Bieber and events such as the MTV Video Music Awards and the Super Bowl. As his portfolio grew, he also did work for corporate clients like Apple and SpaceX.

SIGNATURE STYLE

Meanwhile, Winkelmann faithfully continued his "Everydays" project. Over the years his daily images tended to become more pointedly political, though, as Chayka noted, Winkelmann's sensibility "was established early on" and includes a clear "desire to provoke." Critics would later note that some examples verge into crude stereotypes, including racial caricature and sexism, though typically couched in an air of irony and absurdism. The signature Beeple style came to combine sci-fi imagery with ironic meme culture satirizing virtually every side of society.

Often individual works in the "Everydays" series include themes drawn straight from that day's headlines, informed by Winkelmann's practice of keeping two TVs in his workspace continually tuned to CNN and Fox News. His work often skewers famous figures; popular subjects from the first decade of "Everydays" include politician Hillary Clinton, North Korean dictator Kim Jong-un, and Mickey Mouse. As the project gained increasing attention during the cultural upheaval following the 2016 election of President Donald Trump, naturally Trump himself became a frequent focus. And while Winkelmann characterized himself as anti-Trump, some critics noted a symbiosis between the social-media fueled culture that gave rise to the reality television star president and the Beeple style. For example, Chayka described "Everydays" as "a digital time capsule, a hieroglyphic record of the overstimulated yet undernourished online hive mind."

Another defining aspect of the fully realized Beeple aesthetic in the "Everydays" series is that the images are often gory or sexually explicit. Trump, for example, is typically shown in an exaggerated or grotesque nakedness. Sometimes he is depicted with a woman's body or an infant's body, emphasizing the surreal atmosphere. Other elements of body horror and bloody violence are also common, further underscoring Winkelmann's bleak and unsubtle take on political satire. While critics were often divided over the artistic and social commentary merits of his work, a common

interpretation was that Winkelmann depicted American culture as reliably saturated in meaninglessness, violence, and greed.

NFT BREAKTHROUGH

In the late 2010s Winkelmann earned extensive mainstream attention for "Everydays." In 2018, the fashion house Louis Vuitton paid him to include some of the images on a clothing collection released the following year. In 2019, he was given a prominent shoutout by popular podcast host Joe Rogan, among others, and his Instagram account soon reached almost two million followers. Yet while the provocative Beeple art was gaining fans, it remained mostly a passion project for Winkelmann, who made his living from his video work instead. This was in part due to the difficulty in selling digital art, which by its nature can usually be easily copied and reproduced by anyone with a computer.

In 2020, Winkelmann was introduced to the concept of NFTs, which apply blockchain technology (as popularized by cryptocurrency) to digital media, giving incontrovertible proof of ownership even if the digital file is shared or reproduced widely. Some artists were beginning to use NFTs to monetize their works, leading to a fledgling "crypto art" market. Like many people, Winkelmann was initially skeptical of the idea: "Why would you spend $5,000 on an MP4?" he reflected to Rapkin. "The difference between owning it and not owning it was just an email that said, 'You won.' I can see how you would call bullsh— on that." Nevertheless, he decided to give it a try, listing three works for auction on Nifty Gateway, an online NFT marketplace. The sale was a resounding success, with interest so high that bidding crashed the site. One piece, a short 2020 election–themed animation called "Crossroads," sold for $66,666.66.

Winkelmann and Nifty Gateway held another auction in December 2020, including physical rewards like a custom digital picture frame for each sale. Demand was again high, with a few dedicated NFT investors and crypto art enthusiasts leading the way. The piece *Complete MF Collection*, which included an array of "Everydays" images, sold for $777,777, setting a record for an NFT at the time. In just a few months, Beeple had become one of the most in-demand contemporary artists at work. Duncan Cock Foster, cofounder of Nifty Gateway, told Rapkin that the sale marked a major milestone for the crypto art market. "We all felt like we were witnessing history," he said of watching the prices soar online. "This is one of the things, in retrospect, where people will say: How did we miss this?"

Further proof of Winkelmann's skyrocketing status in the art world came in March 2021, when the famed auction house Christie's hosted an online sale of his piece *Everydays: The First 5,000 Days*, a digital collage of every image in the ongoing daily Beeple project to that point. Stunning observers, the piece was sold for a record-breaking $69.3 million, the highest amount ever paid for a piece of digital art and the third-highest auction price for a work by a living artist, placing Winkelmann in the company of David Hockney and Jeff Koons. Beeple himself referenced his growing fame—and the building controversy over the artistic merits of NFTs—in a typically satirical fashion on his website, as quoted by Rapkin: "Not stopping until I'm in the MoMA . . . then not stopping until I'm kicked out of the MoMA, lol."

In November 2021 Winkelmann had another successful Christie's auction, with the video sculpture (and corresponding NFT) *Human One* selling for over $28.9 million. The physical part of the piece consists of a seven-foot-tall box with four LED screens, featuring an astronaut walking through various dystopian environments. Innovatively, the work was coded in such a way that Winkelmann could control the picture on the screens remotely, changing them at his whim.

PERSONAL LIFE

Winkelmann and his wife, Jen Winkelmann, a teacher, have two children together. In 2017, the family moved from Wisconsin to Charleston, South Carolina. Interviewers have often commented on Winkelmann's unassuming, "average dad" appearance and middle-class suburban lifestyle in contrast to his edgy artwork.

SUGGESTED READING

Chayka, Kyle. "How Beeple Crashed the Art World." *The New Yorker*, 22 Mar. 2021, www.newyorker.com/tech/annals-of-technology/how-beeple-crashed-the-art-world. Accessed 9 Jan. 2022.

Kastrenakes, Jacob. "Beeple Sold an NFT for $69 Million." *The Verge*, 11 Mar. 2021, www.theverge.com/2021/3/11/22325054/beeple-christies-nft-sale-cost-everydays-69-million. Accessed 18 Jan. 2022.

Rapkin, Mickey. "'Beeple Mania': How Mike Winkelmann Makes Millions Selling Pixels." *Esquire*, 17 Feb. 2021, www.esquire.com/entertainment/a35500985/who-is-beeple-mike-winkelmann-nft-interview/. Accessed 10 Jan. 2022.

Roznik, Sharon. "Artist 'Beeple' Who Sold $69 Million Digital Artwork Hails from North Fond du Lac." *FDL Reporter*, 15 Mar. 2021, www.fdlreporter.com/story/news/2021/03/15/beeple-artist-69-3-millions-sale-hails-north-fond-du-lac/4699856001/. Accessed 9 Jan. 2022.

Winkelmann, Mike. "Director's Cut: Flying Lotus." Interview by Ryan Dombal. *Pitchfork*, 5 Nov. 2010, pitchfork.com/news/40564-directors-cut-flying-lotus/. Accessed 9 Jan. 2022.

—. "Shared Inspiration: Beeple Talks Process, 3D Sound Robots, Work to Watch." Interview by Peter Kirn. *CDM*, 5 Mar. 2010, cdm.link/2010/03/shared-inspiration-beeple-talks-process-3d-sound-robots-work-to-watch/. Accessed 9 Jan. 2022.

—. "What the Heck are NFTs? Let's Ask Beeple." Interview by Kara Swisher. *Sway*, 22 Mar. 2021. *The New York Times*, www.nytimes.com/2021/03/22/opinion/sway-kara-swisher-beeple.html?showTranscript=1. Accessed 9 Jan. 2022.

SELECTED WORKS

"Everydays," 2007– ; *The Complete MF Collection*, 2020; "Crossroads," 2020; *Everydays: The First 5,000 Days*, 2021; *Human One*, 2021

—*Molly Hagan*

Siyabulela Xuza

Born: 1989
Occupation: Scientist and entrepreneur

In 2007, rising engineering star Siyabulela Xuza had the distinction of having an asteroid named after him. The Massachusetts Institute of Technology (MIT) Lincoln Laboratory presented him with this honor for his work in creating a safer, more energy efficient rocket fuel at that year's Intel International Science and Engineering Fair, the world's largest precollege science competition. It came a year after Xuza's invention claimed top prize at the Eskom Expo for Young Scientists, the oldest and most prestigious science fair in his native South Africa.

Xuza's early fascination with rocket science, which began after catching his first glimpse of a Cessna plane, eventually led to a scholarship at Harvard University, where he worked on developing micro fuel cells with advanced energy-storing capabilities. His innovative research has earned him comparisons to Elon Musk and garnered him the attention of several high-profile figures, including Mark Zuckerberg, Bill Gates, and former First Lady Michelle Obama. Since graduating from Harvard, Xuza has focused his energy-engineering expertise on harnessing Africa's energy potential and making it cleaner and more affordable. Xuza's personal story is the subject of a film that began filming in 2022.

EARLY LIFE AND EDUCATION

Siyabulela "Siya" Lethuxolo Xuza was born in 1989 in Mthatha, a small, rural township in the Eastern Cape province of South Africa. His first name means "Thank you" in Xhosa, one of South Africa's official languages. Xuza initially developed an interest in aeronautics at the age of five, when he spotted a Cessna aircraft flying over his town and scattering election pamphlets for the country's first multiparty democratic elections, held in 1994. That fascination only grew after his family moved from Mthatha to Johannesburg in 1997. By age twelve, Xuza was formulating homemade rocket fuel in his mother's kitchen, using sugar and chemicals from the local pharmacy. "While growing up I was a pain, because I was always curious, breaking things apart and putting them back together. I was just restless," he shared with Suthentira Govender for *Sunday Times* (19 Jan. 2014).

Xuza became equally enthralled with building rockets, after watching South African tech entrepreneur Mark Shuttleworth travel to space on a live television broadcast in late April 2002. Xuza's first attempt at launching a homemade missile exploded on the launchpad. He had better luck in 2003, successfully launching a rocket, *The Phoenix*, that not only reached an altitude of more than one kilometer—a South African amateur altitude

record—but was also powered by safer, affordable, and more energy-efficient rocket fuel that he invented. Xuza's experimentation earned him a scholarship to attend St. John's College, a well-regarded private secondary school in Johannesburg and one of the country's oldest educational institutions. It also became the basis of "African Space: Fueling Africa's Quest to Space," the gold medal-winning research project he unveiled in October 2006, at the Eskom Expo for Young Scientists, a prestigious national science-fair competition.

For his efforts, Xuza received the Dr. Derek Gray Memorial Award, as well as an all-expensepaid trip to Sweden to attend the Nobel Prize ceremony and the Stockholm International Youth Science Seminar in December 2006. The following May, Xuza was invited to represent his country as part of Team South Africa in the world's largest high-school research competition, the 2007 Intel International Science and Engineering Fair, held in Albuquerque, New Mexico. In addition to claiming two prizes, Best of Category and First Award, in the energy and transportation division, Xuza was the recipient of an $8,000 prize from the New Mexico Oil and Gas Company, as well as a high-performance laptop, courtesy of Intel and MIT, one of the world's top engineering schools.

HARVARD SCHOLARSHIP

Following Xuza's success at Intel, scientists from the MIT Lincoln Laboratory renamed the asteroid 23182 Siyaxuza, after the budding engineer. The small celestial body, located in the asteroid belt near Jupiter, had been discovered in July 2000 by astronomers with the Lincoln Near-Earth Asteroid Research, or LINEAR. After matriculating from St. John's College in 2007, Xuza, who had originally planned to attend the University of Cape Town to study chemical engineering, became one of nearly two thousand students to gain admission to Harvard University.

In addition, Xuza was awarded a scholarship from Harvard to pursue a degree in engineering sciences. "This achievement showed that South Africans, whether you're black, white, male or female, are equally capable of global innovation and excellence," he told Anton Pretorius for *Impumelelo Top Empowerment* (5 Nov. 2019), a South African publication that identifies the country's leading figures and highlights Black-owned and managed companies.

FOCUS ON ENERGY

When Xuza arrived on campus in September 2008, he faced the challenge of adjusting to his new surroundings. Rather than simply focusing on his passion for energy, he stepped outside of his comfort zone, exploring a wide variety of subjects, including Mandarin, world music, and economics. "I truly believe that people cannot rely on purely engineering to develop the world; they need to understand art and understand society in order to put a context to whatever invention they are developing," he shared with Joseph Simon for *Leadership Magazine* (Mar. 2014). "To be a great engineer, you have to be creative. I believe that people shouldn't be pigeon-holed into one category or another."

As an energy-engineering major, Xuza focused on finding an energy storage system for cellphones that serves as a clean, affordable alternative to batteries. "I realised that storage and not the generation of energy is where the opportunity lies, and I thought that is where I needed to put in the most innovation," he recalled to Govender. While conducting his thesis research at the Harvard Center for Nanoscale Systems and MIT's Microsystems Technology Laboratories, he experimented with micro fuel cells (MFCs) due to their high energy efficiency and higher energy density, which gives them the ability to store energy for longer periods of time. Another advantage of MFCs: as long as there is a continuous source of fuel and oxygen, they can produce electricity on a continual basis and do not need to be recharged.

Another focus of Xuza's innovative research involved designing an affordable, efficient solar-based system that could collect and generate energy through a storage platform that was smaller in size and not bound to a centralized grid. His goal: to capitalize on Africa's solar, wind, and fossil resources. "No one has personalized energy yet. The current energy model is large-scale and grid-tied," Xuza told Farah Abdurahman and Steve Rosenberg for *Beyond Sustainability Quarterly* (June 2011). "The traditional model, taking a huge land mass and building large-scale energy collection and generation and then transmitting it just won't work in the African context . . . . Solar technology is still expensive and fairly inefficient."

FUTURE LEADER

Xuza's groundbreaking work did not go unnoticed. In 2010, he was tapped to be a fellow at the African Leadership Network (ALN), a collaborative space aimed at developing Africa's emerging future entrepreneurs and leaders. The Kairos Society, a student-run nonprofit organization that recognizes the world's most promising entrepreneurs and innovators under the age of twenty-six, awarded him a 2011 fellowship. Xuza was also the guest of honor at the final launch of the National Aeronautics and Space Administration (NASA) space shuttle *Endeavour* in May 2011.

Following four years of exhaustive research, Xuza developed butane-powered fuel cells for his undergraduate thesis project, after determining that butane was capable of delivering power for up to two weeks. Xuza also determined that by employing circular conducting membranes he would be able to increase the power output of the micro fuel cells due to the increased surface area. After graduating from Harvard's School of Engineering and Applied Sciences in 2012, he and his classmates Kian Kerman and Shriram Ramanathan coauthored an article about this research that was published in the *Journal of Electroceramics*, a peer-reviewed scientific publication.

Xuza subsequently returned to his homeland and embarked on the motivational speaking circuit, sharing his personal story and addressing the potential for Africa to foster sustainable development. In 2014, he served as a guest speaker at the South African (SA) Innovation Summit, the Success Summit, the Green Building Convention, the Power and Electricity World Africa Conference, and the Southern Africa Telecommunication Networks and Applications Conference (SATNAC).

ACCOLADES

Audi South Africa also tapped Xuza to be one of its 2014 brand ambassadors; Xuza promoted the A4 2.0T Quattro, a fuel-efficient version of the A4 sedan. In 2015, he spoke at the African Leadership Academy in Johannesburg and was named energy ambassador for French-based oil and gas giant Total South Africa. *The South African*, an independent, English-language online news publication, included Xuza on its 2015 list of South Africa's top ten young entrepreneurs to watch. The following year,

Xuza was honored as part of the documentary-style series *21 Icons*, which highlighted South African visionaries shaping the country's future. "I am an example of what happens when you give young South Africans opportunities," he told Bill Suter for the Durban, South Africa–based publication *The Mercury* (4 Feb. 2016). "When you follow your passion, shut out noise that can distract you, and you are true to yourself, you achieve greatness."

In 2017, South African President Jacob Zuma bestowed Xuza with one of the country's highest honors, the Order of Mapungubwe in Silver, in recognition of Xuza's contributions to scientific innovation. He also received the 2017 Youth Diplomacy prize at the Ubuntu Awards, hosted by South Africa's Department of International Relations and Cooperation (DIRCO). Xuza continued to maintain a high profile as the CEO and founder of Galactic Energy Ventures, a venture capital firm he started in February 2018 for developing and investing in advanced energy storage solutions for the more than 600 million Africans, aged eighteen to thirty-five, who are unemployed and do not have access to electricity. He expects the global energy storage market to double six times by the year 2030 and envisions a future with personalized energy systems that would combine cheap storage systems with affordable and efficient solar panels.

PERSONAL LIFE

Xuza, a highly skilled Xhosa praise singer, performed for former South African President Nelson Mandela (1918–2013) in 2003.

SUGGESTED READING

Abdurahman, Farah, and Steve Rosenberg. "South Africa's Unsung Rocket Scientist Superhero: Siyabulela Xuza." *Beyond Sustainability Quarterly*, no. 11, June 2011, issuu.com/beyondpublishing/docs/issue11. Accessed 11 Jan. 2022.

Govender, Suthentira. "Young, Driven and Rocketing to Success." *Sunday Times*, 19 Jan. 2014, www.pressreader.com/south-africa/sunday-times-1107/20140119/281651072967065. Accessed 11 Jan. 2022.

Pretorius, Anton. "The South African NASA Named a Planet After." *Impumelelo Top Empowerment Companies*, 5 Nov. 2019, issuu.com/topcomedia/docs/topemp1019_full_book_issuu_latest. Accessed 11 Jan. 2022.

Simon, Joseph. "Rising Star." *Leadershipship*, no. 346, Mar. 2014, mags.capemedia.co.za/leadership/346/html5/index.html. Accessed 11 Jan. 2022.

Suter, Bill. "A Rocket Scientist and an 'Icon.'" *The Mercury*, 4 Feb. 2016, www.pressreader.com/south-africa/the-mercury-south-africa/20160204/282243779628715. Accessed 11 Jan. 2022.

"The World Revered Scientist: Siyabulela Lethuxolo Xuza." *Student Africa Magazine*, 24 Feb. 2015, issuu.com/studentafricamagazine/docs/sam_magazine_jan_march_issue_2015. Accessed 11 Jan. 2022.

Xuza, Sibulela. "My Journey to Harvard." *eJournal USA*, vol. 14, no. 8, 2009, Bureau of International Information Programs, US Department of State, www.yumpu.com/en/document/read/11596683/campus-connections-us-department-of-state. Accessed 11 Jan. 2022.

—*Bertha Muteba*

Halimah Yacob

Born: August 23, 1954
Occupation: Politician

Halimah Yacob began serving as the eighth president of the Republic of Singapore after being sworn in on September 14, 2017. She became the nation's first female head of state and the second person from the Malay ethnic minority to hold the office. Prior to the presidency, from 2013 to 2017, she broke ground as the first woman to serve as Speaker of the Singapore Parliament.

President Halimah has long been a vocal proponent of equal rights and social equity. She entered politics after more than thirty years as an attorney and labor advocate at Singapore's National Trades Union Congress (NTUC). While discussing her impetus to run for office, she explained to *LawLink* (Dec. 2021), an alumni magazine published by the National University of Singapore Faculty of Law, "One of my tasks in NTUC was to persuade younger women to take up leadership positions in their own unions or in NTUC. . . . Having spent time cajoling and persuading women to step up and be prepared to sacrifice for a higher purpose, I felt that I should practice that myself."

Although many Singaporeans were happy with Halimah becoming president, her election to the office proved controversial, with some claiming that she had been "selected," rather than "elected." That complaint stemmed from the fact that she had been the only candidate deemed eligible and had run without opposition. Despite the less-than-optimal circumstances surrounding her ascension to the presidency, Halimah expressed no regrets about running and promised to work to the best of her ability to further Singapore's status as a fair and equitable society.

EARLY YEARS AND EDUCATION

Halimah Yaacob was born in Singapore, at her family's home on Queen Street, on August 23, 1954. Her father was from India, and her mother was a Malay, a minority ethnic group that, in Singapore, includes Indigenous people from the Malay Peninsula and Indonesia. When Halimah was born, Singapore was still a British trading colony. While she was growing up, Singapore joined the fourteen-state Malaysian Federation in 1963. In 1965, following race riots between Singaporean Malays and Singaporean Chinese, who were and still are the majority ethnic group, Singapore became an independent nation. According to 2020 estimates, some three-quarters of the country's population are Chinese, while Malays comprise less than 14 percent and Indians about 9 percent.

It was in this sociopolitical milieu that Halimah's father scraped together a living as a security guard. When she was eight years old, he died of a heart attack, forcing her mother to raise Halimah and her four older siblings alone. Her mother managed to earn a meager income running a rudimentary food stall. Halimah could often be found alongside her, helping to keep the stall clean and serve customers.

When Halimah began her political career in 2001, journalists often requested childhood or family pictures, but she had none to offer; her early life was devoid of birthday celebrations and other such events, and no one in their impoverished neighborhood would have owned a camera. "I have no regrets though, as deprivation and hardship taught me very valuable lessons that stood me in good stead when I went to work and entered politics," she

Photo via Wikimedia Commons
[Public domain.]

told *LawLink*. "It taught me resilience, the ability to bounce back and not let setbacks and difficulties overcome me and define who I am."

Intent upon getting an education, Halimah attended Singapore Chinese Girls' School and Tanjong Katong Girls' School. Given a choice between training as a teacher or a lawyer, she chose law, believing the field would allow her to protect and seek justice for vulnerable or marginalized communities. She attended the National University of Singapore, where she earned a Bachelor of Laws (LLB) degree in 1978. She was called to the Singapore Bar in 1981. She would go on to earn a Master of Laws (LLM) degree from the university in 2001, and an honorary doctoral degree in 2016.

CAREER IN LABOR ADVOCACY

In 1978, Halimah opted not to enter private practice or seek out a lucrative post with a bank or other organization but instead accepted a job as an in-house attorney at the NTUC, a national confederation of trade unions whose mission was to advocate for workers and support working families. Many of her classmates, headed to more glamorous jobs, were surprised at the path she chose, but she was confident that she would be doing important work, giving voice to the concerns of workers and fighting for their rights. "I witnessed how little power and voice those without resources have," she said, as quoted by *LawLink*. Her role, as she saw it, was to even the balance of power between the unions and wealthy, well-resourced employers. She also felt that she was filling a valuable niche, as few students cared to pursue the specialty, and the University of Singapore eventually stopped including labor law in its curriculum.

During her thirty-three years at NTUC, Halimah held various roles, including director of its Legal Services Department, head of the Women's Development Secretariat, executive secretary of the United Workers of Electronics and Electrical Industries, and, ultimately, NTUC deputy secretary general. In 1999, she also began directing the Singapore Institute of Labour Studies, a leadership-development school later renamed the Ong Teng Cheong Institute of Labour Studies, after a former NTUC head. The following year she became the first Singaporean to be elected to the governing body of the International Labour Organization (ILO), a United Nations agency that brings together the governments, employers, and workers of its member states to develop policies and set fair standards. She regularly served as workers' spokesperson on various standard-setting committees, and she has described her role in the 2011 passage of the ILO Convention on Domestic Workers as being among her proudest accomplishments.

ENTRY INTO POLITICS

In 2001, Halimah was elected to Parliament to serve the Jurong Group Representation Constituency, a small area in the western part of the country. She later represented Marsiling–Yew Tee. Initially a back-bencher, a member of Parliament who does not hold office in the government or opposition, in 2011 she was appointed to the Ministry of Social and Family Development, and in that capacity, she advocated for additional services for older citizens and people with disabilities.

In 2013 Halimah was nominated by Prime Minister Lee Hsien Loong (son of Singapore's long-time first prime minister, Lee Kuan Kew) and elected by her fellow MPs as Speaker of Parliament, becoming the first woman in the country ever to hold the position. The position involves presiding when the MPs sit and ensuring that parliamentary business is conducted in an orderly manner.

PRESIDENCY

In August 2017, Halimah resigned from the People's Action Party (PAP)—Singapore's dominant political party—as speaker and MP for Marsiling–Yew Tee to run for the presidency. Although she was endorsed by Prime Minister Lee and presumed to enjoy the backing of the PAP, the election was controversial from the start. There had not been a Malay president in Singapore since Yusof Ishak, who served from 1965 to 1970—and there had never been a prime minister who was not a member of the Chinese ethnic majority. So, in the interest of ethnic equity, the government opened the 2017 presidential race only to Malay candidates.

There was immediate debate as to whether the government's decision violated the nation's tenets of meritocracy, but officials promised that the candidates would be held to the same high standards as in any election. That did nothing to quell complaints from Malays that because Halimah's father was Indian, Halimah should not consider herself Malay and should, therefore, be disqualified on the grounds that she was misrepresenting herself.

Criticism reached a crescendo when neither of Halimah's proposed opponents, businessmen Salleh Marican and Farid Khan, were deemed eligible according to Singaporean election laws: candidates from the private sector were required to have overseen a company with a minimum shareholder equity of $500 million, and the two had each missed the threshold. As a public servant, Halimah was exempt from that rule and was thus the only candidate to receive a certificate of eligibility from the elections board.

Running unopposed, Halimah was chosen in what was known as a "walkover" election and was sworn in on September 14, 2017, as the eighth president of Singapore. As head of state, Halimah plays a largely ceremonial and community-based role but does have the power during her six-year term to veto government budgets and certain public appointments. These expanded powers were the result of a 1991 change to the constitution meant to ensure that the government could not misuse the national reserves without oversight.

Halimah's inaugural speech focused on multiculturalism, meritocracy, and stewardship—all considered vital to Singapore's overarching goal of social cohesion. After taking office, she continued to promote causes that have long been important to her, including workers' rights, equal rights for women, services for older people and people with disabilities, and child health and welfare. While her official government page predominately featured photos of her opening public gardens, honoring World Autism Awareness Day, and other such activities, she has often been called upon to meet with international officials such as US Vice President Kamala Harris and Chinese President Xi Jinping.

In 2022, Channel News Asia (CNA) and the Institute of Policy Studies (IPS) reported that 82.2 percent of all Singaporeans they had surveyed in 2021 were comfortable with a Singaporean Malay as president—a jump from 65.5 percent of those surveyed by CNA and IPS in 2016. The researchers suggested that the rise could be a result of Halimah's tenure.

PERSONAL LIFE

Halimah, who is Muslim, has been married since 1980 to Mohammed Abdullah Alhabshee, a retired businessperson whom she first met at the National University of Singapore. They have five children.

Halimah is the patron of dozens of nonprofit organizations. Her advocacy and social-justice efforts have earned her numerous laurels, including *Her World* magazine's 2003 "Woman of the Year" honors and induction into the Singapore Women's Hall of Fame in 2014.

SUGGESTED READING

"Celebrating the Year of SG Women with Our Alumna: President Halimah Yacob '78 LLM '01 LLD '16." *LawLink: The Alumni Magazine of the National University of Singapore Faculty of Law*, Dec. 2021, law. nus.edu.sg/wp-content/uploads/2022/01/ LawLink-2021-online.pdf. Accessed 3 Apr. 2022.

"Halimah Yacob: First Woman President of Singapore." *Singapore Women's Hall of Fame*, 11 March 2021, www.swhf.sg/profiles/ halimah-yacob/. Accessed 3 Apr. 2022.

"HE President Halimah Yacob: President of Singapore." *The Muslim 500*, Royal Islamic Strategic Studies Centre, 2018, themuslim500.com/profiles/halimah-yacob/. Accessed 3 Apr. 2022.

Mahbubani, Kishore. "Opinion: Social Cohesion Must Be Engineered." *The Washington Post*, 17 Sept. 2018, www.

washingtonpost.com/news/theworldpost/ wp/2018/09/17/singapore/. Accessed 3 Apr. 2022.

"Singapore's Multi-Racial Society Open to Have Non-Chinese Leadership: Study." *Business Standard*, 2 Apr. 2022, www. business-standard.com/article/international/ singapore-s-multi-racial-society-open-to-have-non-chinese-leadership-study-122040200097_1.html. Accessed 3 Apr. 2022.

Wong, Tessa. "Why Singaporeans Aren't All Glad to Get the President They Wanted." *BBC News*, 13 Sept. 2017, www.bbc.com/ news/world-asia-41237318. Accessed 3 Apr. 2022.

Yuen-C, Tham. "President Halimah on Why She Became a Lawyer and Advocate for Gender Equality." *The Straits Times*, 5 Jan. 2022, www.straitstimes.com/singapore/ politics/president-halimah-on-why-she-became-a-lawyer-and-advocate-for-gender-equality. Accessed 3 Apr. 2022.

—*Mari Rich*

Bowen Yang

Born: November 6, 1990
Occupation: Comedian and writer

When Bowen Yang was a senior in high school, his fellow students voted him the most likely to appear on the famous, long-running sketch comedy show *Saturday Night Live* (*SNL*) one day. "That was just a fancy way of saying you're the funniest," he later recalled to Maureen Dowd for *The New York Times* (25 Jan. 2020). Informed in part by Yang's tenure as a member of his school's theater program and improvisational-comedy group, that superlative proved to be more accurate than most: Yang joined *SNL*'s writing staff in 2018, a decade after his high school graduation. He went on to make his on-screen debut on the show in a March 2019 episode.

Although Yang initially aspired to become a doctor, he changed course after graduating from New York University in 2012. Over the next several years he established himself as an up-and-coming performer in New York, participating in live comedy shows and in 2016 cofounding the humorous podcast *Las Culturistas*. His hiring at *SNL* proved to be a turning point of sorts, and he joined the on-screen cast as a featured player in late 2019 and became full-time member in September 2021. He also appeared in a number of additional projects, including the television series *Awkwafina Is Nora from Queens* and the fiction podcast *Hot White Heist*. "I don't think I'm saying yes to everything. I think it's just, like, timelines are synchronized in a fortuitous way," Yang told Jerry Portwood for *Rolling Stone* (21 June 2021) about his influx of new projects. "I think I'm just a beneficiary of good timing."

EARLY LIFE AND EDUCATION

Bowen Yang was born on November 6, 1990, in Brisbane, Australia. The second of two children born to Ruilin, a scientist, and Meng, a gynecologist, he spent his early childhood in Australia while his father pursued doctoral studies there. The family, originally from China, later moved to Canada and subsequently immigrated to the United States when Yang was nine years old, relocating to Aurora, Colorado. He and his older sister, Yang, spoke Mandarin at home. Although the experience of changing countries and schools was challenging at times for Yang, it also played a formative role in his development as a comedian. "I'd spoken French better than English. I thought, I'm dealing with a language barrier—what's the best way to get the kids to like me? It was about being broad and funny," he recalled to fellow performer Jean Smart in an interview for *Variety* (2021). "The comedic North Star for me at that time was Mr. Bean, because it doesn't matter if you spoke the language. Anyone could like Mr. Bean." Yang went on to attend Smoky Hill High School in Aurora, where he participated in the school's theater program and was a member of the improvisational-comedy troupe Spontaneous Combustion. He graduated from high school in 2008.

Following high school, Yang enrolled in New York University (NYU), where his older sister was already a student. A fan of *Grey's Anatomy*'s Doctor Cristina Yang (Sandra Oh), he aspired to become a medical doctor and majored in chemistry. Although he remained interested in comedy as an extracurricular activity, he did not consider pursuing a career in that field at the time. "I had tricked myself into thinking this is just a hobby. It's a little side gig, whatever," he explained to Tobin Low and Kathy Tu for the WNYC Studios podcast *Nancy* (10 Dec. 2018).

At his college graduation in 2012, however, Yang abruptly realized that he was following the wrong path. "I made a conscious choice not to sit with my other chemistry buds, my pre-med buds, and I sat with the arts kids because those were mostly my friends anyway from doing improv at school," he recalled to Low and Tu. "And then I just looked around and everyone was so happy. And everyone was so excited to go into this next chapter in their lives. And I was like, 'Oh no this is not how I feel at all.'" Although Yang had planned to enroll in medical school after completing his bachelor's degree, he chose not to, instead opting to enter the workforce and pursue opportunities in comedy.

EARLY CAREER

After graduating from NYU, Yang worked to establish himself as a comedian while holding a day job as a graphic designer for a furniture and design website. "They put up with so much of my crazy stuff, when I had to go to auditions on lunch breaks or leave early to do shows," he recalled to Dowd. In addition to performing in live comedy shows, Yang took on roles in a number of short comedy videos, including a CollegeHumor video short, and both wrote for and appeared in the 2013 web series *The Morning Announcements*. He would go on to appear in episodes of television comedy series such as *Broad City* and *High Maintenance*.

Among the most enduring projects of Yang's early career was the podcast *Las Culturistas*, which he created in collaboration with fellow NYU graduate Matt Rogers. Launched in 2016, *Las Culturistas* provides a humorous take on pop-culture topics and became known for the brief rant segment "I Don't Think So, Honey!" that concludes each episode. Yang and Rogers continued to record episodes of *Las Culturistas* into 2021 and hosted a number of events dedicated to the podcast, including live "I Don't Think So, Honey!" shows in which multiple comedians had the opportunity to air their pop-culture grievances. In addition to *Las Culturistas*, Yang gained notice beginning around 2018 for posting short videos to his social media accounts in which he would lip sync along to memorable clips from film and television. "I'll pick out a snippet of something and then basically will just sort of chunk it out by like 30, 20-second increments and just run those, run those, run those," he told Low and Tu about the process of creating the videos.

"I do like a hundred plus takes for each one, and 99 percent of them are terrible. And truly like I pick between two takes where I'm like, 'OK those are technically clean. I'd fix this and this and this, but you know what, not being too precious about it. Let's post.'" Major websites such as *Buzzfeed* and *Vulture* reported on Yang's lip sync videos, drawing further attention to his talents as a performer.

SATURDAY NIGHT LIVE

In 2018, Yang secured a position in the writers' room of the long-running sketch comedy show *Saturday Night Live* (*SNL*) after undergoing an extensive audition process that saw him demonstrate both writing and acting skills as he performed impressions and embodied a variety of characters. He officially joined the show's writing staff in the fall of 2018 and soon came to recognize the unique role his fellow writers played in developing the show's sketches. "They basically produce the sketches as soon as they get pitched," he explained to Julie Miller for *Vanity Fair* (3 June 2020). "They make decisions about set design, costuming, wigs, props, and give cast members and the host notes. There are so many granular creative decisions they make on the fly that are beyond the scope of what a writer does anywhere else." In addition to writing for the show, Yang made an on-screen appearance on March 30, 2019, portraying North Korean leader Kim Jong-un in an episode hosted by Sandra Oh. Alongside *SNL's* other writers, he was nominated for the 2019 Emmy Award for Outstanding Writing for a Variety Series.

Moving beyond the writers' room, Yang joined the on-screen cast of *SNL* as a featured player prior to the start of the show's forty-fifth season, making his official debut as a cast member on September 28, 2019. He became a key member of the show's cast over the next seasons, performing impressions of real-world figures such as presidential candidate Andrew Yang and portraying a host of original characters. Some of his roles, such as the iceberg responsible for the sinking of the Titanic, became the subject of widespread public attention after the sketches in which they appeared went viral. In recognition of his work, Yang was nominated for the 2021 Emmy Award for Outstanding Supporting Actor in a Comedy Series. He was promoted from featured player to member of the show's

repertory cast in September of 2021, in time for the show's next season.

OTHER PROJECTS

In addition to working on *SNL*, Yang appeared in the television comedy series *Awkwafina Is Nora from Queens* beginning in January 2020, when the series premiered on the channel Comedy Central. Yang portrays the protagonist's cousin in the series, which had begun development prior to his *SNL* career. A second season of *Awkwafina Is Nora from Queens* aired in 2021. Yang likewise took on a lead role in the 2021 fiction podcast *Hot White Heist*, an original production of the audiobook- and podcast-focused company Audible. Although he was an experienced podcaster thanks to his years of work on *Las Culturistas*, the world of fiction podcasts was an unfamiliar one for Yang. "*Las Culturistas* is so unstructured and loose," he told Portwood. "There's no preparation that goes into it. It's just about plugging in and playing. So for this Audible series, it was really about tracking character arcs. It was like doing a play or TV series." Yang also appeared in episodes of television series such as *Girls5eva* and *The Other Two* throughout that period.

Alongside his acting work, Yang remained active as a writer outside of *SNL*. For example, he contributed to the script for the 2019 Golden Globe Awards and cowrote a 2021 episode of the television series *Schmigadoon!*. Though his ongoing projects kept him busy, he remained focused on the importance of continually exploring new opportunities. "This is a business where not everything is handed to you, and you have to make your own work," he told Miller. "I'm not setting too many expectations for myself. I'm just trying to create opportunities for something interesting."

PERSONAL LIFE

Yang was outspoken in interviews about his experience as a teen who went through therapy to attempt to change his sexual orientation, which took place after his parents realized that he was gay. He told Emily Strohm for *People* (25 June 2021) that the situation was the result of "a huge chasm of misunderstanding" between him and his parents that "led to very dangerous situations overall," though he was able to maintain a positive relationship with his parents afterward. Yang likewise spoke out against the increasing prevalence of hate crimes against Asian Americans that started during the coronavirus disease 2019 (COVID-19) pandemic. During his March 27, 2021, appearance in the "Weekend Update" segment of *SNL* he urged viewers to take an active role in combating racism in their everyday lives.

SUGGESTED READING

Dowd, Maureen. "Bowen Yang of 'S.N.L.' Is a Smash. And a Mensch." *The New York Times*, 25 Jan. 2020, www.nytimes.com/2020/01/25/style/bowen-yang-snl.html. Accessed 12 Nov. 2021.

Miller, Julie. "*Saturday Night Live*'s Bowen Yang Shares a Spiritual Connection with Sandra Oh." *Vanity Fair*, 3 June 2020, www.vanityfair.com/hollywood/2020/06/saturday-night-live-bowen-yang. Accessed 12 Nov. 2021.

Strohm, Emily. "*Saturday Night Live*'s Bowen Yang Opens Up about Being Put in Gay Conversion Therapy as a Teen." *People*, 25 June 2021, people.com/tv/bowen-yang-opens-up-about-being-put-in-gay-conversion-therapy-teen/. Accessed 12 Nov. 2021.

Yang, Bowen. "Bowen Yang: 'My Only Job Is to Tell the Truth.'" Interview by Jerry Portwood. *Rolling Stone*, 21 June 2021, www.rollingstone.com/culture/culture-features/bowen-yang-snl-podcast-audible-1186653/. Accessed 12 Nov. 2021.

—. "Bowen Yang Isn't Here to Check a Box for Representation." Interview by Maxine Wally. *W Magazine*, 13 Oct. 2021, www.wmagazine.com/culture/bowen-yang-interview-2021. Accessed 12 Nov. 2021.

—. "Bowen Yang Was Fooled by *Grey's Anatomy*." Interview by Tobin Low and Kathy Tu. *Nancy*, 10 Dec. 2018, www.wnycstudios.org/podcasts/nancy/episodes/bowen-yang-was-fooled-by-greys-anatomy. Accessed 12 Nov. 2021.

—, and Jean Smart. "Jean Smart and Bowen Yang Discuss the Genius of '*Hacks*' and the Adrenaline Rush of Working at '*SNL*.'" *Variety*. Edited by Daniel D'Addario, 2021, variety.com/2021/tv/actors/actors-on-actors-bowen-yang-snl-jean-smart-hacks-mare-of-easttown-1234996536/. Accessed 12 Nov. 2021.

SELECTED WORKS

Las Culturistas, 2016– ; *Saturday Night Live*, 2018– ; *Awkwafina Is Nora from Queens*, 2020– ; *Hot White Heist*, 2021

—*Joy Crelin*

Jia Lynn Yang

Born: ca. 1982–83
Occupation: Journalist, author

As national editor at *The New York Times*, often called the nation's paper of record, journalist Jia Lynn Yang looks for the human faces behind the story. As she told Jackie Mansky for *Zócalo Public Square* (21 Apr. 2021), "For me, a great story needs people in it that you relate to." Her first book, *One Mighty and Irresistible Tide: The Epic Struggle Over American Immigration, 1924–1965* (2020), was longlisted for the 2021 Andrew Carnegie Medal for Excellence in Nonfiction, given by the American Library Association. Yang's debut book also was the recipient of the eleventh annual Zócalo Book Prize. The honor, which included a stipend of $10,000, is given to a work that focuses on social cohesion and community. Commenting on the award, Yang told Sarah Rothbard for *Zócalo Public Square* (21 May 2021), "My wildest dream of my book was that it would foster a sense of community. Thank you for seeing that spirit in my work."

In *Irresistible Tide*, Yang examines efforts to replace the United States' racist and xenophobic immigration policies of the 1920s with the more inclusive Immigration and Nationality Act of 1965. As she explained to Anna Diamond for *Smithsonian Magazine* (19 May 2020), "We often think of nationalism and immigration as opposing ideas and forces. The really interesting political turn in the '50s is to bring immigrants into this idea of American nationalism. It's not that immigrants make America less special. It's that immigrants are what make America special." Her initial inspiration for the book came in part out of wondering how US immigration laws had impacted her family's experience as Chinese immigrants.

EARLY LIFE AND EDUCATION

Jia Lynn Yang's parents were both able to immigrate to the United States under the 1965 Immigration and Nationality Act. Her mother, Mei-Shin, was born in Taiwan; because she had a background in microbiology, her odds for permanent residency in the United States increased. In 1976 she received word from the US Justice Department that her petition for a permanent residency visa had been granted. Born in Shanghai, Yang's father, Ed, came to the United States for graduate school and was able to remain as part of US policy to reunite families.

Yang's parents eventually settled in Virginia to raise a family. Yang was born and raised in Alexandria, Virginia, but spent summers with extended family in Los Angeles. While a student at Yale University in Connecticut, she fell in love with journalism by way of working on the *Yale Daily News*. She also wrote several research articles for the Washington, DC–based *National Journal* before she graduated, including one in 2003 on the civil service. Yang graduated in 2004 from Yale with a bachelor's degree in philosophy.

THE WASHINGTON POST

Yang worked as a staff writer for the business magazine *Fortune* from 2005 to 2010, when she was hired by *The Washington Post* as a business and economics reporter and editor. There, she focused on the overlap of policy and business and worked on the newspaper's Wonkblog. While at the *Post*, Yang occasionally reported from China. One of her articles, reported from Hong Kong in 2013, concerned Edward Snowden, who had leaked material from the National Security Agency (NSA), and his subsequent escape to China.

In 2015 Yang was promoted to the role of deputy national security editor, following a national search. As Peter Finn and Scott Wilson said of Yang's promotion in a public relations release for *The Washington Post* (27 July 2015), "She has shown a talent for insightful digital storytelling—a sensibility she will bring to our national security coverage. She is also an accomplished editor of long-form work." In 2018, Yang and her team shared a Pulitzer Prize with *The New York Times* staff for their coverage of Donald Trump, his transition team and administration, and Russian influence on the 2016 presidential election.

THE NEW YORK TIMES

Yang joined *The New York Times* staff in 2017 and emerged as one of the paper's leading editors for the National desk, working on major stories and investigations including those covering US political divisions during the presidency of Donald Trump, Supreme Court Justice Amy Coney Barrett, and the novel coronavirus 2019 (COVID-19) pandemic. One of the investigations she edited focused attention on sexual allegations against Cardinal Theodore McCarrick; he resigned his office twelve days after her article appeared, the first Catholic cardinal to do so because of alleged sexual abuse. She continued to report important stories from China and Taiwan as well.

In February 2021, Yang was promoted to lead *The New York Times*'s National desk. As National editor, she directed the work of about fifty editors and reporters who were responsible for news within the nation, excluding Washington, DC, and metro New York City. Her work, as she told Alex Traub for *The New York Times* (28 Oct. 2021), involved "spend[ing] a lot of time reading the stories we already have to ask: Is this what we envisioned? What else does it need? I enjoy the challenge of figuring out ideas for stories."

ONE MIGHTY AND IRRESISTIBLE TIDE

In 2016, while working for *The Washington Post*, Yang visited the Lyndon Johnson Presidential Library, where she saw an exhibit on Johnson's signing of the Immigration and Nationality Act of 1965. She wondered if the act, which banned immigration quotas, had benefited her family, and discovered that it had. Thus began four years of research that culminated in her book, *One Mighty and Irresistible Tide: The Epic Struggle Over American Immigration, 1924–1965* (2020). The title comes from remarks Johnson made when signing the act. As Yang told Mansky, "Migration is not a thing you can stop. As much as governments try to create borders, freedom of movement is a fundamental aspect of being human."

Yang has explained to reporters that though lawmakers had made more targeted attempts to restrict immigration to the United States, such as the 1882 Chinese Exclusion Act, the 1924 Johnson-Reed Act was the first US immigration law to impose broad restrictions on immigration, including on Jews, nearly all

Asians, and most people from Eastern and Southern European countries. The law would remain in effect until Johnson signed the 1965 Immigration and Nationality Act.

Yang's book explores the evolution of American national identity and immigration policy over the decades between the two acts, tracing the idea that the United States is a nation of immigrants to historian and activist Oscar Handlin, a first-generation citizen of Jewish immigrant parents. Handlin wrote the influential, Pulitzer Prize-winning book *The Uprooted* (1951) with the goal of ending the quota system. Yang credited Handlin's book with inspiring President John F. Kennedy's own book, *A Nation of Immigrants* (1964), as well as Kennedy's unsuccessful push for legislation to remove immigration quotas for various ethnic groups. Following Kennedy's assassination, President Lyndon B. Johnson wanted to continue his predecessor's work and Yang explores the ways that Johnson connected civil rights to immigration rights. As she told Diamond, "You've got people talking about racial equality. We're going to be getting rid of Jim Crow laws, so we should also look at our immigration laws in the same way. They have a similar kind of racial and discriminatory problem to them."

ADDITIONAL INSIGHTS

As Yang looked further into the driving forces of immigration laws, she noted that in polls, "you hardly ever see Americans clamoring for more immigrants," she told Diamond. "The people who want to change [immigration policy] are often presidents who are dealing with the foreign policy [consequences of the 1924 law]. That's one thing that really surprised me in my research, is how immigration was driven by foreign policy concerns."

Yang's research for and work on *Irresistible Tide* overlapped with her work for *The New York Times*. For example, in a piece titled, "Who Belongs in America?" (25 Apr. 2020), she wrote about her research on immigration policy and American identity for the book and tied it to her personal understanding of her family's experiences as Chinese American immigrants, particularly in the wake of increasing anti-Asian hate crimes in the United States during the COVID-19 pandemic. "The harassment has been a stunning reminder that, regardless of how long you have been in this country or

whether you were born here, your face can still mark you as foreign," she wrote in that article.

PERSONAL LIFE

Yang lives in Brooklyn with her husband, Zachary D. Carter, who is also a journalist and author, and their daughter. Yang begins her day checking the news to see what she missed while asleep. When asked what her typical workday was like, she told Traub, "I read the Morning newsletter, what's up on our site and on other big news sites. I have a very tiny window before my 2-year-old wakes up." Yang enjoys hiking; her favorite national park is Zion in Utah.

SUGGESTED READING

Diamond, Anna. "The 1924 Law That Slammed the Door on Immigration and the Politicians who Pushed It Back Open." *Smithsonian Magazine*, 19 May 2020, www.smithsonianmag.com/history/1924-law-slammed-door-immigrants-and-politicians-who-pushed-it-back-open-180974910/. Accessed 25 May 2020.

Finn, Peter, and Cameron Barr. "Staff News: Jia Lynn Yang Named Deputy National Security Editor." *The Washington Post*, 27 July 2015, www.washingtonpost.com/pr/wp/2015/07/27/staff-news-jia-lynn-yang-named-deputy-national-security-editor/. Accessed 21 May 2022.

Manksy, Jackie. "Journalist Jia Lynn Yang Wins the 11th Annual Zócalo Book Prize." *Zócalo Public Square*, 21 Apr. 2021, www.zocalopublicsquare.org/2021/04/21/jia-lynn-yang-one-mighty-and-irresistable-tide-book-prize/inquiries/prizes/. Accessed 21 May 2022.

Rothbard, Sarah. "This Radical, Revolutionary Nation of Immigrants." *Zócalo Public Square*, 21 May 2021, www.zocalopublicsquare.org/2021/05/21/jia-lynn-yang-one-mighty-and-irresistable-tide-zocalo-public-square-book-prize/events/the-takeaway/. Accessed 26 May 2022.

Traub, Alex. "Leading the News Coverage of 'This Big, Messy World of Ours.'" *The New York Times*, 28 Oct. 2021, www.nytimes.com/2021/10/28/insider/jia-lynn-yang-national-editor.html. Accessed 18 May 2022.

Yang, Jia Lynn. *One Mighty and Irresistible Tide: The Epic Struggle Over American*

Immigration, 1924–1965. W.W. Norton, 2020.

___. "Who Belongs in America?" *The New York Times*, 25 Apr. 2020, www.nytimes.com/2020/04/25/us/coronavirus-immigration-china-book-yang.html. Accessed 18 May 2022.

—Judy Johnson

Steven Yeun

Born: December 21, 1983
Occupation: Actor

When Academy Award nominations were released in March 2021, most who had been following Steven Yeun's career over the years were not surprised to see his name included in the running for Best Actor in a Leading Role. Such recognition, in this case for his role in the drama *Minari* (2020), seemed overdue for someone whose work had often drawn praise as inspired and wide-ranging. After breaking into television and film in 2010 with his performance as Glenn Rhee on the AMC hit series *The Walking Dead* (2010–16), Yeun went on to play parts as diverse as a psychopathic playboy and a struggling immigrant farmer in the fallow fields of Arkansas.

Yeun, who immigrated to the United States from South Korea as a young child, was pleased that his stereotype-defying performances made a positive impact on the entertainment industry and American society. Yet this outcome was not his primary motivator when selecting roles. In interviews he explained his concerns about being restrictively categorized rather than considered purely based on his acting, and his desire for characters to be seen as individuals contributing meaningfully to the story regardless of race. In a conversation with Matt Donnelly for *Variety* (2020), he stated, "I'm happy to serve a larger moment for the community. And I'm happy to push narratives and show who we are because I am that, too. I am an Asian American and the pride I have for that is immense. But also, for me, it's really about carrying my space and myself through this life and making sure that I tell it true from my perspective."

EARLY LIFE

Steven Yeun was born Yeun Sang-yeop on December 21, 1983, in Seoul, South Korea. His earliest years in South Korea were happy ones. He was adored by his large extended family, and his father was a successful architect.

Yeun's father developed an affinity for the North American landscape after traveling there for work, and decided to relocate the family. They immigrated in 1988 to the town of Regina, in the Canadian province of Saskatchewan. Soon after, they resettled in Taylor, Michigan. The transition was extremely difficult for Yeun, who did not speak English and was treated like an outsider for the first time in his young life. As a first grader, he came home one day and asked his parents what the English phrase "don't cry" meant in Korean, because teachers and students kept saying it to him. Around the mid-1990s, his family moved to Troy, Michigan, where his parents operated a store selling beauty supplies in nearby downtown Detroit. During these formative years, he was an athlete who enjoyed music and spent a fair amount of time in front of the television.

As a teenager Yeun divided his time between school, where he had an eclectic group of

Photo by Gage Skidmore,
via Wikimedia Commons

social acquaintances rather than close friends, and his parents' Korean church, where he connected with his faith and community while indulging in his passion for singing and guitar as part of the praise group's band. He developed a bifurcated identity of being both Korean and American, which often led to feelings of frustration and anger and a sense of needing to "perform" differently within various areas of his life. "When I was in school, I was playing within a persona," he reflected in a discussion with Jay Caspian Kang for *The New York Times Magazine* (3 Feb. 2021). "I'm going to be quieter, nicer, friendlier. But when I'm at church, I'm going to be me. When I'm at home, I'm going to be me. And sometimes I think I was putting up such a mask and a wall when I was at school that I had no patience for anything when I was at home."

HIGHER EDUCATION

After graduating from Troy High School in 2001, Yeun attended Kalamazoo College, where he studied psychology and neuroscience with the plan of going to medical school—in large part due to his parents' wishes. Everything changed, however, during his freshman year, when a friend brought him to sit in the audience for Monkapult, the school's improv team that her brother belonged to. The brother, Jordan Klepper, would become a mentor to Yeun and later a correspondent for *The Daily Show.*

Monkapult's show that night proved to be a life-altering moment for Yeun, who definitively realized that he, too, wanted to be involved in this kind of freeing expression of performance. He explained why improv especially caught his interest to Julie Hinds in a discussion for *Detroit Free Press* (13 Feb. 2016): "I think, for me, it was probably a combination of growing up naturally being in a household that was funny. My dad is a very funny person and he tells stories very well." He went on to add, "For me, the charm of improv is it forces you to live in that scene."

Yeun spent the rest of his college career seeking out as many performance opportunities as possible. Taking improv classes with the head of the theater department, he landed a spot in Monkapult and also acted in campus plays. However, when his mother came to see him in the production *Balm in Gilead*, she reluctantly told him that his performance was not very good. He decided to use her criticism

as inspiration to work harder. "I thought, 'Okay if I want to do this, even for fun, I've really gotta step my game up,'" he told Oliver Singer for *Interview* (13 May 2011). "So for the rest of school, I worked at it. I got a little better, a little better, and by the time I graduated, I knew I wanted to continue onward."

EARLY ACTING CAREER AND BREAKING THROUGH TO TELEVISION

After graduating from Kalamazoo in 2005, Yeun initially continued going through the motions of pursuing a more typical professional career, applying to work for Teach for America and considering the MCAT and LSAT tests. However, he realized that what he really wanted to do was follow Klepper's lead and relocate to Chicago to hone his craft on the city's renowned improv scene. Although his parents were wary of his decision, they were supportive and told him he had two years to make it work. Once in Chicago, he began taking classes at the Second City—the esteemed training program that gave rise to comedy stars like Bill Murray and Tina Fey. Soon, in addition to performing with Stir-Friday Night!, an all–Asian American sketch comedy troupe, he was part of the Second City Touring Company.

In 2009, with years of improv experience under his belt, Yeun knew it was time to expand his opportunities and make another move, this time to Los Angeles. Wasting no time in venturing out to auditions once there, he quickly landed three commercials and was put up to play a character on an ABC sitcom pilot. Although he was disappointed when he did not get that part, the casting director liked his performance enough to offer him a small role on the show *The Big Bang Theory* in 2010. In his conversation with Singer, he noted some creeping doubt upon getting the rejection call, as he thought, "I had one chance, and I screwed it up. Maybe this isn't going to work out." Soon afterward, however, he auditioned for a show in development called *The Walking Dead* and was offered a part. Where it often takes newer actors years on the LA audition circuit to land a lead role in a television show, Yeun had done it in about six months.

The Walking Dead debuted on AMC on October 31, 2010. A drama sourced from a comic book series of the same name, the show follows a group of strangers forced to live and work together to survive a zombie apocalypse.

Yeun played one of the main characters, Glenn Rhee, a young man forced to turn from a life delivering pizzas to one as a skilled zombie fighter. By its second season, *The Walking Dead* had become a cultural phenomenon, with millions of people tuning in each week to watch the characters played by Yeun and his costars as they overcame myriad physical and moral obstacles. The show's enormous success proved to be a pleasant surprise for Yeun. "I had no clue," he told Hinds, "I was just along for the ride. I was there to work and was so happy to be working in general."

Yeun's tenure on *The Walking Dead* lasted until the beginning of its seventh season in 2016. Throughout, he was lauded for his acting and the depth he brought to the character of Glenn, whose selfless and brave nature made him a fan favorite. Meanwhile, he also had a number of other television credits, including some voice-acting roles on animated works.

BURNING

Though Yeun was grateful for the professional experience of *The Walking Dead*, he explained in interviews following his departure that he also embraced the opportunity to select roles that allowed him to be truer to his own voice rather than just a narrative. This meant turning down some parts, even if they were leads, if he did not feel they were right for him. "I read more and asked, '*Does this speak to me, [to] who I am?*' and I said, 'No.' So I didn't do it. . . . Life as an artist isn't about being a martyr; it's about doing *you* really well," he told E. Alex Jung for *Vulture* (July 2017).

Adhering to this authenticity principle led him to portray a character written for him by director Bong Joon-ho in the 2017 film *Okja*, which received applause upon its premiere at that year's Cannes Film Festival. In 2018 Yeun was part of the cast of the black comedy *Sorry to Bother You* and costarred in the Korean psychological thriller *Burning*. Based on the Haruki Murakami short story "Barn Burning" (1992), the latter film follows a young man in Seoul dreaming of being a writer who gets pulled into the orbit of a wealthy Korean man with dark secrets named Ben (Yeun). The film, also premiered at Cannes, was met with overwhelming praise and was deemed one of the best films of 2018 by numerous critics.

For Yeun, the opportunity to play the darkly mysterious character of Ben was an exciting departure. Furthermore, he learned from working on a Korean-language film with a Korean director that he could just perform rather than worry about how he was being perceived by White audiences. He explained this to Jacob Stolworthy in an interview for the *Independent* (31 Jan. 2019), stating, "If you go to Korea, the characters are just humans because they're not thinking about it like that. That's something that I was made aware of [with *Burning*], which was really wonderful for me to know. I didn't have to represent all Asians. I could just represent myself."

MINARI

When Yeun received the script for *Minari* (2020), he immediately knew that he wanted to do everything in his power to see the film produced. "It was so honest and so truthful and so confident in its own point of view, I really loved it," Yeun told Anne Thompson for *IndieWire* (3 Mar. 2021). "It was unwavering in its own self, it didn't require a juxtaposition to anything else for its own existence."

Yeun committed to serving as an executive producer of *Minari*, a Sundance Film Festival standout, as well as one of the film's lead characters. His performance as Jacob Yi, a Korean immigrant who takes his family from California to rural Arkansas in the 1980s to try to make it as a farmer, ultimately earned him an Oscar nomination. It was beloved by critics and audiences alike for its heartfelt, authentic portrayal of the struggles that many immigrants endure trying to achieve their own versions of the "American Dream." For Yeun, the film was an homage to his father, who, like the character of Jacob, had also been a young Korean man trying to make a life for his family in America despite not speaking English. "Every time I talk about it, I'm just, like, crying about it, you know?" Yeun told Kang. "Because I think my dad felt seen."

In late 2021, Yeun's next big-screen appearance came as part of the cast of the film adaptation of the award-winning play *The Humans*. He also continued to take television roles, including voicing the lead character in the animated superhero series *Invincible*, which premiered that same year to strong reviews.

PERSONAL LIFE

Yeun married photographer Joana Pak, whom he had first met when he lived in Chicago, in 2016. After having a son together in 2017, the couple also welcomed a daughter in 2019. Yeun lives with his family in California.

SUGGESTED READING

Donnelly, Matt. "Steven Yeun on the Honesty of 'Minari' and His Eclectic Career: 'I Never Want to Lose That Sense of Wonder.'" *Variety*, 2020, variety.com/2020/film/news/steven-yeun-minari-the-walking-dead-lee-isaac-chung-1234867928/. Accessed 8 Feb. 2022.

Hinds, Julie. "Michigan's *Walking Dead* Star on Life before, after Glenn." *Detroit Free Press*, 13 Feb. 2016, www.freep.com/story/entertainment/2016/02/13/steven-yeun-walking--dead-amc-network-zombie-drama/80197832/. Accessed 3 Feb. 2022.

Kang, Jay Caspian. "The Many Lives of Steven Yeun." *The New York Times Magazine*, 3 Feb. 2021, www.nytimes.com/2021/02/03/magazine/steven-yeun.html. Accessed 3 Feb. 2022.

Yeun, Steven. "Awards Spotlight: For *Minari*, Steven Yeun Channeled His Father and 'Existential, Isolated Loneliness.'" Interview by Anne Thompson. *IndieWire*, 3 Mar. 2021, www.indiewire.com/video/steven-yeun-minari-interview-1234618138/. Accessed 4 Feb. 2022.

—. "*Burning* Actor Steven Yeun Interview: 'I Feel Like a Man with No Country.'" Interview by Jacob Stolworthy. *Independent*, 31 Jan. 2019, www.independent.co.uk/arts-entertainment/films/features/steven-yeun-burning-the-walking-dead-interview-glenn-rhee-harry-styles-andrew-lincoln-a8756391.html. Accessed 3 Feb. 2022.

—. "On the Road with Steven Yeun." Interview by Oliver Singer. *Interview*, 13 May 2011, www.interviewmagazine.com/culture/steven-yeun-walking-dead. Accessed 3 Feb. 2022.

—. "Steven Yeun Finds Life after Glenn." Interview by E. Alex Jung. *Vulture*, July 2017, www.vulture.com/2017/07/steven-yeun-interview-okja-walking-dead.html. Accessed 8 Feb. 2022.

SELECTED WORKS

The Walking Dead, 2010–16; *Okja*, 2017; *Burning*, 2018; *Minari*, 2020; *The Humans*, 2021; *Invincible*, 2021–

—*Emily Turner*

Yoo Jae-suk

Born: August 14, 1972
Occupation: Comedian and television personality

After making his debut in the early 1990s, Yoo Jae-suk became so ubiquitous a presence on South Korean television that he earned recognition as the "nation's MC." He has appeared on shows for every major Korean network—including SBS, KBS, and MBC—many of them airing concurrently. "When flipping through the channels on the weekend, it seems like every program features Yoo Jae-suk," Park Shin-hong wrote in an interview for *Korea JoongAng Daily* (12 June 2013). Yoo has made a name for himself as the host of several variety shows, a type of television program that is particular to Korean culture. Such shows often feature participants competing in games, challenges, and other humorous "missions." Among his biggest hits have been *Infinite Challenge*, on which he appeared from 2005 to 2016, and *Running Man*, which debuted in 2010.

Yoo's broad appeal has been credited, in large part, to his relatable persona, gentle wit, and virtually unimpeachable public character. In monthly "brand reputation" rankings compiled by the Korean Business Research Institute, he consistently featured at or near the pinnacle, and in yearly polls conducted by Gallup Korea, he topped the list of entertainment broadcasters and comedians every year between 2005 to 2009 and from 2012 to 2022. (In 2010 and 2011, he earned the number-two spot.) He remained wary of gaining too much confidence, though. "Someday [people] will say that Yoo Jae-suk is old school," he explained to Park. "I'm ready for that moment. . . . As long as I pledge to do my best for as long as I can, there is nothing to be afraid of."

EARLY YEARS AND EDUCATION

The eldest of three siblings, Yoo Jae-suk was born on August 14, 1972, in Seoul, South

Korea. His father was a civil servant (some sources specify he worked as a postal worker), and his mother held a variety of jobs to help support Yoo and his younger sisters. During one period, she worked as a janitor at Yoo's school to pay for his tuition.

Yoo has told interviewers that he was shy as a young child—a characteristic he attributed to moving often because of his family's fluctuating financial situation and changing schools three times. Still, he gradually came to love making people laugh and gained a reputation as something of a class clown. "I was a very funny kid," he recalled to Park. "I performed lots of pranks, and I was in charge of entertainment whenever there were school events such as field trips or festivals."

Yoo graduated from a high school in Seoul in 1991. Because of his propensity for comedy, it seemed natural to pursue a career in television, and to that end, he enrolled at the Seoul Institute of the Arts, a highly regarded school in South Korea's Gyeonggi Province.

A SLOW START

Despite his instructors' advice to wait until he had more experience, Yoo entered the KBS College Comedy Festival as a first-year student at the Seoul Institute of the Arts in 1991. "I was arrogant," he admitted to Park. "I expected to be ranked [at the top]. Since people always told me how funny I was, I just expected that the comedy scene would be startled by my debut." When he ended up receiving the lowest award—the "encouragement prize"— he thought a mistake had been made. Trying to exhibit an insouciant, devil-may-care attitude, Yoo, who had written and performed a commercial parody during the festival, impolitely kept one hand in his pocket when striding to the stage to pick up his award. "I really didn't know what the real world was like," he continued to Park. "After I made it into broadcasting, other comedians did come to find me, but not for the reasons I expected."

Following that inauspicious debut, Yoo spent several years in relative obscurity. At one point, he joined the army, and when he left the service, he found work as a reporter on *Entertainment Weekly*. The experience was a painful one. Yoo continually flubbed lines—mishaps he says were due to extreme nervousness—and he was quickly fired. Guest stints on various other shows were also less than successful. "I didn't put in enough effort and I always blamed others," he told Park, explaining that he would later come to regret such behaviors.

One year, friends and fellow comics Park Su-hong and Kim Yong-man invited Yoo to perform on a variety show aired to celebrate Chuseok, a South Korean holiday that is sometimes compared to American Thanksgiving. Tasked with learning choreography mimicking that of the popular boy band New Kids on the Block, Yoo badly messed up the steps; videos of the broadcast show him stumbling and out of sync with his castmates. "I just started shaking when I was onstage in front of all these people I didn't know," he told Park. "I forgot my lines and didn't get the dance moves right at all. I felt burdened by my desire to really prove myself through that act."

HAPPY TOGETHER

Despite his stage fright—and a monthslong period of depression that followed the Chuseok program—Yoo persevered, and in the early 2000s he was invited to appear on a talk show hosted by popular performer Seo Se-won. While he remained nervous, he found, to his surprise, that viewers seemed to enjoy his bumbling delivery. He quickly found his career gaining traction, especially after actor Choi Jin-sil recommended him to producers of a new variety show called *Happy Together*, which he began hosting in 2003 and which won him the first of a long string of MBC Entertainment Awards. The program continued airing into the early 2020s with Yoo as its host, eventually becoming KBS's longest-running variety show.

In 2003, Yoo also began hosting the game show *X Man*, which also became one of the most-watched shows in South Korea during its four-year run. The show's premise involved dividing participants into two teams, with an unknown "X Man" embedded to thwart them in completing their assigned challenges. Almost equally popular was the variety show *Family Outing*, which Yoo starred in from 2008 to 2010 alongside seven other "family" members who competed in games and performed other tasks in assorted South Korean locations.

INFINITE CHALLENGE AND RUNNING MAN

Although Yoo hosted and starred in numerous shows during the early twenty-first century— including *Village Survival: The Eight* (2018–19), *Cool Kids* (2018–19), the Netflix whodunit *Busted!* (2018–21), *You Quiz on the Block*

(2018–22), and *Sixth Sense* (2020–21)—he has remained perhaps best known and most beloved for two long-running hits: *Infinite Challenge*, for which he served as chief host from 2005 to 2016, and *Running Man*, which began airing in 2010.

Infinite Challenge has been credited with being one of the first shows in South Korea to follow a model made popular in the United States and exemplified by such reality competition programs as *Survivor* and *American Ninja Warrior*. The show involves humorous competitions between popular South Korean entertainers "in scenarios that vary from pretending they're Ghostbusters to crash courses in competitive wrestling," as television critic Karen Han described in a piece for *Thrillist* (2 Oct. 2017). During its run, *Infinite Challenge* was perennially among the best-rated Saturday night programs on television. Many outlets began referring to it as "the nation's variety show," and it garnered a slew of laurels each year, including several top MBC Entertainment Awards. Praising its sincere and open-hearted displays, Han expressed bewilderment as to why the show was not better known outside South Korea, despite featuring some well-known Western personalities, including Jack Black and Stephen Curry. "The willingness to look silly without winking at the camera counteracts any embarrassment that would come out of it," wrote Han, explaining the show's lighthearted appeal. "Watching the show requires that same kind of good faith, too. It's a principle that holds not just for television programs, but for cultures on the whole."

Running Man premiered in July 2010. In the summer of 2021, the cast announced that it had officially become the longest airing South Korean variety show of all time with more than 560 episodes aired—a record that had previously been held by *Infinite Challenge*. As in Yoo's earlier program, teams on *Running Man* compete in various games and races, which are often held in historic or iconic locations throughout Korea. Many of the challenges hark back to childhood games such as hide-and-seek, while others involve more complex tasks such as freeing a cast member from a locked glass cube or buying ingredients and cooking a dish in the shortest possible time. The show has spawned a theme park, an animated cartoon, and versions filmed in other Asian countries.

MAKING MUSIC

In addition to his television work, Yoo has enjoyed some success as a singer, often as part of a challenge for his variety shows. He made a cameo appearance in the 2012 viral music video "Gangnam Style" by the Korean singer known as Psy, donning a bright yellow suit, wig, and glasses, and challenging Psy to a dance-off. Then, in 2016, he took center stage with the boy band EXO on the video for their single "Dancing King."

In 2019, Yoo released *Bbong for Yoo*, a three-track compilation of "trot" songs (a rhythmic subgenre of K-Pop). The album earned him best male newcomer honors at the 2019 MBC Entertainment Awards. Yoo joked to journalists about the irony of being deemed a newcomer after nearly thirty years in show business and stated his intention to hone his singing skills before making a second album.

In early 2020, as part of his MBC show *Hangout with Yoo*, the comedian announced that he and fellow performers Lee Hyori and Rain were forming a musical supergroup. In July of that year, the group, which they christened SSAK3, released its 1990s-inspired debut single, "Beach Again," which quickly climbed the South Korean pop charts. They also won the televised talent competition *M Countdown*, leading some observers to assert that their already-established fame gave them an unfair advantage.

PERSONAL LIFE

Yoo married MBC announcer Na Kyung-eun, whom he met on the set of *Infinite Challenge*, in 2008. They have two children: a son, Yoo Ji-ho, born in 2010, and a daughter, Yoo Na-eun, born in 2018.

Yoo is known for his generosity and philanthropic activities. Among his pet projects have been those supporting disaster relief, education initiatives, purchasing coal for the needy in the winter, and paying outstanding hospital bills for ill fans. He has avoided the controversies that plague many stars; in one notable exception, however, during an episode of *Hangout with Yoo* in early 2022, he expressed dissatisfaction with the ruling against Korean speedskater Hwang Dae-heon during the 2022 Winter Olympics held in Beijing, asserting that the Chinese judges had been biased. In response, his Chinese fan club, Yooniverse, disbanded.

SUGGESTED READING

Cadavillo, Ginyn. "Running Man's Yoo Jae-suk: Korea's 'National MC' Striking Out with Lee Hyori and Rain in K-Pop Supergroup SSAK3." *South China Morning Post*, 13 Aug. 2020, www.scmp.com/magazines/style/celebrity/article/3097106/running-mans-yoo-jae-suk-koreas-national-mc-striking-out. Accessed 30 July 2022.

Han, Karen. "What American TV, and Americans, Could Learn from Korea's Wildest Game Show." *Thrillist*, 2 Oct. 2017, www.thrillist.com/entertainment/nation/korea-infinite-challenge-best-game-show. Accessed 30 July 2022.

Lee, Si-jin. "Yoo Jae-suk's Chinese Fan Club Yooniverse Disbands." *The Korea Herald*, 22 Feb. 2022, www.koreaherald.com/view.php?ud=20220222000758. Accessed 30 July 2022.

Leung, Jenny. "10 Hilarious Korean Variety Shows You Should Be Watching." *Time Out Hong Kong*, 12 June 2022, www.timeout.com/hong-kong/film/best-funny-korean-variety-shows. Accessed 30 July 2022.

Park, Yuna. "After Struggles, Yoo Jae-suk in His Second Heyday." *The Korea Herald*, 1 Jan. 2020, www.koreaherald.com/view.php?ud=20200101000119. Accessed 30 July 2022.

Yoo, Jae-suk. "With Fame Comes Humility for Yoo Jae-suk." Interview by Park Shin-hong. *Korea JoongAng Daily*, 12 June 2013, koreajoongangdaily.joins.com/news/article/article.aspx?aid=2972986. Accessed 30 July 2022.

SELECTED WORKS

Happy Together, 2003–20; *X Man*, 2003–07; *Infinite Challenge*, 2005–16; *Family Outing*, 2008–10; *Running Man*, 2010–; *Busted!*, 2018–21; *Hangout with Yoo*, 2019–

—Mari Rich

Trae Young

Born: September 19, 1998
Occupation: Basketball player

Although point guard Trae Young had planned throughout his high school career and record-setting single season at the University of Oklahoma for a career in professional basketball, the excitement of being drafted into the National Basketball Association (NBA) and the fanfare surrounding his talent nevertheless came as somewhat of a surprise. "The NBA was always a lifelong dream, but everything just happened so fast that it felt like it was overnight," he told Keith Gordon for *Maxim* (14 Jan. 2019). "My whole life changed. . . . I don't think I ever got used to it." Debuting with the Atlanta Hawks in the 2018–19 NBA season, Young joined a struggling team in the midst of a major rebuild. These struggles continued through his rookie and sophomore seasons—but Young still established himself as an electric young player capable of scoring like a superstar. Franchise leadership and fans alike anointed him the new face of the Hawks, and many viewed him as one of the brightest talents in the NBA.

A turning point came in the 2020–21 season, during which Young and the Hawks suddenly found themselves among the top teams in the league. "We didn't have a lot of time to keep accepting losing, and we just needed a change in winning and we just need to win," Young explained to Robby Kalland for *UPROXX* (29 Apr. 2021). "I think everybody's mentality and everybody's mindset really has changed and everybody's really just has been locked in, in focusing on winning each and every day." Defying expectations, the rejuvenated Hawks reached the NBA playoffs and made it all the way to the Eastern Conference Finals, with Young leading the way. Though they then lost to the eventual NBA-champion Milwaukee Bucks, Young remained dedicated to his team, signing a five-year contract extension in August 2021.

EARLY LIFE AND EDUCATION

Rayford Trae Young was born on September 19, 1998, in Lubbock, Texas. He was the first of four children born to Candice and Rayford Young. A talented basketball player, Young's father was a member of the Texas Tech University basketball team at the time of his birth and later played basketball professionally in Europe, where the family lived for a time. They returned to the United States when Young was about four years old, settling in Norman, Oklahoma.

Young began playing basketball as a child and benefited significantly from his father's experience and knowledge of the game over

Photo by Alexander Jonesi
via Wikimedia Commons

the course of his early life. "There is no way I would be here today without my parents, and especially my dad. He has always been that shoulder I could lean on, and he's always given me enough space to figure things out on my own as well," he told Gordon. "His knowledge of playing, and his relationships with former NBA players, helped mold me as a kid." Having established himself as a skilled player throughout his childhood, Young joined the Norman North High School varsity basketball team as a freshman and went on to play four successful seasons with the team. His senior season was particularly strong, as he averaged an incredible 42.6 points per game.

Attracting national attention as a basketball prospect, Young represented the United States in international competition as a teenager. He earned a gold medal at the 2016 International Basketball Federation (FIBA) Americas Under-Eighteen (U18) Championship. Although his dazzling performances on the court gave him the opportunity to play for whatever college basketball program he chose, Young decided to remain close to home after high school, committing to attend the University of Oklahoma. "I wanted to represent my city and my state," he told Chris Stonebraker in a video interview for *MaxPreps* (15 Mar. 2018). Young graduated from Norman North High School in 2017.

PREPARING FOR THE NBA

Joining the University of Oklahoma Sooners basketball team for the 2017–18 season, Young continued to perform at an elite level. He averaged 27.4 points and 8.7 assists per game. He was the first National Collegiate Athletic Association (NCAA) Division I player to lead the country in both scoring and assists and to reach the 800-point and 250-assist marks in a single season. His performance earned him numerous accolades—including consensus All-American First Team honors, Big 12 Conference freshman and newcomer of the year recognition, and the Wayman Tisdale National Freshman of the Year Award—as well as increased attention as an NBA prospect. Although some around him encouraged Young to play an additional season with the Sooners, the athlete himself had other ideas. "When I got on campus, my family wanted me to be on a two-year plan. But in my mind it was make an impact right away and play [professionally] right away," he explained to Marc J. Spears for *The Undefeated* (21 June 2018). Confident that he had proven himself, Young chose to declare for the 2018 NBA Draft after his single college season.

Young received widespread sports media attention in the months leading up to the draft. Some analysts considered him among the most promising talents available, though others expressed considerable concerns about how he might develop, especially due to his relative lack of size and defensive skills. Many commentators speculated that he might be selected eighth or ninth overall. On the day of the draft, however, the Dallas Mavericks selected him as the draft's fifth overall pick—and, to Young's surprise, promptly traded him (and a future first-round pick) to the Atlanta Hawks for the rights to Luka Dončić, whom the Hawks had selected with the third overall pick. "I was surprised that they traded for me, because they already had a point guard and I had heard that they weren't going to draft one," Young recalled to Gordon. "But when I finally visited after draft night and met everyone in the organization, I was elated. I knew this was the right place for me. And I knew they would give me plenty of opportunities to succeed." Young signed a contract with the Hawks in July 2018.

ATLANTA HAWKS

Young made his debut with the Hawks on October 17, 2018, in a game against the New York Knicks. Although the Hawks lost the game, Young immediately showed flashes of the scoring touch that had made him a prized draft selection. He played in eighty-one games over the course of his rookie season, averaging a strong 19.1 points and 8.1 assists per game; his 653 total assists were the second-most in the NBA that season. He was named rookie of the month on four occasions and earned Eastern Conference player of the week honors for the first time in March 2019. In recognition of his performance during his first season in Atlanta, Young was named to the NBA All-Rookie First Team. Although the Hawks still finished in the lower tier of the standings with a 29–53 record, many observers noted the franchise had found hope for the future.

The 2019–20 season saw Young further develop into one of the NBA's top scorers. He averaged 29.6 points and 9.3 assists per game over the course of the season, ranking fourth and third in the league, respectively. He also made his first NBA All-Star Game. In March 2020, however, the NBA suspended play in response to the spreading coronavirus disease 2019 (COVID-19) pandemic, ending the Hawks' season early. While the NBA returned to play that July with a special, sequestered "bubble" playoff tournament, the Hawks did not qualify due to their 20–47 record. The resulting unusually long offseason was frustrating for Young, who hoped to match his individual success with team results. "My focus was not to be in that situation again," he told Kalland. "My thought process and my focus was to get us to the playoffs. I mean, I didn't care about anything else, I just wanted to be a part of the playoffs. Sitting at home . . . while everybody was in the bubble was really killing me."

PLAYOFF CONTENDER

Delayed due to the ongoing pandemic, the 2020–21 NBA season began in December 2020 and was compressed to seventy-two games. Young played in sixty-three games over the course of the regular season and again excelled, averaging 25.3 points and 9.4 assists per game despite being hampered by an ankle injury late in the season. He also led the league in total free throws, with 484. Meanwhile, though the Hawks again struggled during the first half of the season, resulting in the firing of coach Lloyd Pierce, the team improved dramatically under new coach Nate McMillan. They finished with a 41–31 record, good for fifth in the Eastern Conference, and earned a postseason berth for the first time since 2015.

Facing off against another surprise contender in the New York Knicks in the first round of the playoffs, Young made his postseason debut at the Knicks' legendary home arena, Madison Square Garden. "My first playoff experience, being in the Garden, against the fans there. It was the experience of a lifetime," Young told NBA TV after the first game in the series, as reported by Alek Arend for *The Spun* (27 May 2021). Thriving in the spotlight, he averaged 29.2 points per game as the Hawks beat the Knicks four games to one. Young was similarly dominant as the Hawks went on to upset the number-one-seeded Philadelphia 76ers in the Eastern Conference Semifinals in seven games.

Atlanta then faced the Milwaukee Bucks, led by superstar Giannis Antetokounmpo, in the Conference Finals. Young burst out of the gate in the first game, scoring an impressive 48 points as the Hawks continued to defy expectations with a 116–113 victory. However, he injured his ankle and foot during the third game of the series and was forced to miss the fourth and fifth games, during which the Bucks took a 3–2 lead. Young made it back on the court for Game 6 but was still bothered by the injury, and the Hawks lost both the game and the series. "For me, not being able to be out there for my team for two games, and then tonight just wanting to battle and try to fight through it as much as I could and try to be out there for my team, it's definitely frustrating not being healthy and not being able to give my full 100 percent," he told Tim Bontemps for *ESPN* (4 July 2021) right after his team was eliminated.

Committed to continuing his career with the Hawks, Young signed a five-year contract extension with the team in August 2021, worth $172 million guaranteed and as much as $207 million based on performance incentives. He and his team began the 2021–22 season hoping to build on their deep playoff run from the previous season. However, the Hawks struggled significantly early on, though Young remained a dangerous scorer.

PERSONAL LIFE

Although Young maintained close ties to his home state of Oklahoma, he enjoyed building a new home for himself in the city of Atlanta after joining the Hawks. "The way the city embraced me, the love I get out here from the fans, I definitely feel it," he told Tres Dean for *GQ* (30 Sept. 2021). "I always tell people I have two homes at heart: Oklahoma and Atlanta." Young drew inspiration from Atlanta's culture and geography for a 2021 collaboration with the athletic wear company Adidas, lending his name to a line of sneakers that included a peach-colored shoe inspired by the city's Peachtree Street.

SUGGESTED READING

Arend, Alek. "Trae Young Shares Feelings on 1st Playoff Games at MSG." *The Spun*, Sports Illustrated, 27 May 2021, thespun.com/nba/atlanta-hawks/trae-young-shares-feelings-on-1st-playoff-games-at-msg. Accessed 12 Nov. 2021.

Bontemps, Tim. "Atlanta Hawks' Trae Young: 'Frustrating' Not Being at 100 percent in Game 6 Loss." *ESPN*, 4 July 2021, www.espn.com/nba/story/_/id/31759167/frustrating-not-being-100-game-6-loss. Accessed 12 Nov. 2021.

Spears, Marc J. "Four Hours with Trae Young ahead of NBA Draft." *The Undefeated*, 21 June 2018, theundefeated.com/features/four-hours-with-trae-young-on-the-eve-of-nba-draft/. Accessed 12 Nov. 2021.

Young, Trae. "Before March Madness: Trae Young." Interview by Chris Stonebraker. *MaxPreps*, edited by Mitch Stephens, 15 Mar. 2018, www.maxpreps.com/news/GGKSVCNVnUiZUp_9GM3Nsw/before-march-madness--trae-young.htm. Accessed 12 Nov. 2021.

—. "How Atlanta Hawks Star Trae Young Became the NBA's Most Exciting Rookie." Interview by Keith Gordon. *Maxim*, 14 Jan. 2019, www.maxim.com/sports/how-trae-young-became-nbas-most-exciting-rookie-2019-1/. Accessed 12 Nov. 2021.

—. "Trae Young Has Reached Wrestling Villain Status." Interview by Tres Dean. *GQ*, 30 Sept. 2021, www.gq.com/story/trae-young-adidas-interview. Accessed 12 Nov. 2021.

—. "Trae Young on the Mentality Change That's Helped the Hawks Find Their Stride." Interview by Robby Kalland. *UPROXX*, 29 Apr. 2021, uproxx.com/dimemag/trae-young-hawks-interview-playoffs-injury/. Accessed 12 Nov. 2021.

—Joy Crelin

Charles Yu

Born: January 3, 1976
Occupation: Writer

An avid reader and writer since childhood, it seemed that Charles Yu's destiny as a writer was a given. Instead, he took a different, more unconventional path on his way to becoming an award-winning author, earning a law degree from Columbia University and obtaining a day job as a lawyer while devoting the night hours to fiction writing. Though his first collection of short stories, *Third Class Superhero* (2006), and his critically acclaimed debut novel, *How to Live Safely in a Science Fictional Universe* (2010), were products of his late-night work and indisputable talent, he still questioned his ability to write, fighting against an ever-present imposter syndrome.

It was not until Yu began work as a television writer for popular series, including HBO's *Westworld*, AMC's *Lodge 49*, and FX's *Legion*, that these doubts started to dissipate. His reputation was further sealed with the arrival of his second novel, *Interior Chinatown*, in 2020, which earned him not only widespread critical praise and the prestigious 2020 National Book Award but also gifted Yu with a newfound sense of confidence in his craft. Moreover, the novel, published amid widespread attention to issues of social justice and racism in the United States, placed the author at the forefront of discussions about Asian American stereotypes and representation in the arts. "It does for the first time in a long time feel like there are conversations happening that wouldn't otherwise be happening," he remarked in the *Columbia Law School* website (16 Nov. 2020). "If there is a larger idea to the book, it's that a distorted picture of race in America hurts all groups, not just Asians."

EARLY LIFE AND EDUCATION

Charles Chowkai Yu was born on January 3, 1976, in Los Angeles, California. He is the son of Taiwanese immigrants, who, three years after his birth, welcomed into the family a second son named Kelvin. Yu's mother, Betty Lin Yu, was an accountant, and his father, Jin-Chyuan Yu, worked as a mechanical engineer and also ran a Taiwanese language school for a time—the first American school of its kind. Taiwanese culture was particularly important to the family. Until he was around five years old, Yu spoke Taiwanese as his first language, learning English when he began elementary school. His parents were active members in the Taiwanese American Citizens League, and Yu often attended camps for Taiwanese American children that focused on the culture of Taiwan.

Yu developed a love for reading early on, favoring fiction narratives like the Choose Your Own Adventure book series by R. A. Montgomery and Edward Packard. When he was not reading, he was often watching *The Twilight Zone*, playing the video game *Street Fighter II*, or pondering existentialist questions. "I feel like I was an existentialist from the age of five," Yu said to Adam Sternbergh for *The New York Times* (22 Jan. 2020). "Even as a kid, I was always obsessed with these questions. Who am I? How did I get here? What am I doing in this place?"

While he had a comfortable childhood, Yu began to take notice of the existence of implicit racial prejudices as he grew older, prejudices that had the power to make him feel like an outsider even when he was surrounded by a large community of Asian Americans. By the time Yu reached high school—a public high school in Los Angeles, where about 30 to 40 percent of the student body were Asian American—he had incorporated track and wrestling into his repertoire, though reading was still a most cherished activity for him. He studied literature classics like *The Old Man and the Sea* by Ernest Hemingway and also wrote poems from an early age. A friend giving him his first copy of *Poetry* magazine as a senior in high school proved to be a catalyst moment for Yu, as it inspired him to explore the world of poetry more deeply.

Following his high school graduation in 1994, Yu enrolled at the University of California, Berkeley, where he majored in molecular and cellular biology and minored in creative writing. As part of his writing program, he continued shaping and honing his poetry by taking workshops with renowned poets like Thom Gunn and Ishmael Reed. He also tried his hand at fiction writing during this time,

Photo by Larry D. Moore, via Wikimedia Commons

though without success. "I wrote one short story in college. It was a disaster. I sent it to a workshop, and they did not accept me," he told Robert Birnbaum of *The Morning News* (1 Nov. 2012), before continuing to say, "I figured I had nothing to offer the world of fiction, so I just stopped."

LAWYER BY DAY, WRITER BY NIGHT

After completing his bachelor's degree in 1997, Yu took a year off before attending law school at Columbia University in New York City for three years. As his time at Columbia drew to a close—when he was studying for the bar exam, more precisely—he went back to reading fiction, immersing himself in the works of authors like A. M. Homes and Donald Barthelme. Soon, Yu started to write short stories again and, although at first he was met with rejection, he chose to persevere. "I got hundreds of rejections. I started posting them on a wall. But one in fifty stories would get published," he said to Sternbergh.

Yu graduated from law school in 2001, after which he found work as an associate at Sullivan & Cromwell and then as a corporate attorney at Bryan Cave Leighton Paisner—two prominent international law firms. He could not ignore his desire to write, however. While he worked typical office hours during the day as a corporate lawyer, he spent the night hours devoted to his writing. Even after he became the in-house counsel at Digital Domain, a visual effects and digital production company, he continued this arrangement. It paid off in 2006, when he published *Third Class Superhero*, an anthology of short stories in which he examined the science fiction genre, exploring identity, relationships, and the essence of time.

Despite *Third Class Superhero* receiving positive reviews upon its release and selling relatively well, Yu still believed he lacked the credentials to be a full-time writer. "Not having an MFA, having a day job, there was always a feeling like I came in through the back door, or at least the side door," he admitted to Sternbergh. "Even to this day, it all feels a bit DIY. It's like I don't play an instrument, I play a shoebox guitar I made in my garage." Fortunately for him, one review for *Third Class Superhero* came from Richard Powers—an acclaimed author whose novel *The Echo Maker* was awarded the 2006 National Book Award for Fiction—who selected Yu to be named by the National Book Foundation as one of its Five Under 35 most promising writers in 2007. This honor encouraged him to finish a novel he had been working on, titled *How to Live Safely in a Science Fictional Universe*, which was published in 2010.

Yu's debut novel, which centers on a son searching for his lost father by means of quantum physics and time-traveling, received critical praise and did well financially. In 2012, not wanting his creative momentum to slip away, Yu followed *How to Live Safely* with a second collection of short stories, this one entitled *Sorry Please Thank You*. The stories in the book examine an array of science and pop culture themes, including zombies, virtual warriors, and wizards, but did not earn positive reviews. This led him to struggle with impostor syndrome once more, succumbing to doubts of whether he was truly meant to be a writer or if it was time to forgo the idea for good.

TELEVISION WORK

As Yu faced this predicament, David Levine, the co-head of drama at the mammoth television network HBO, called and told him of his interest in hiring him as a writer for television. Yu, however, was dubious at best. "He was so self-deprecating," Levine recalled to Sternbergh. "He told me, I have this other life,

I'm never really going to be a writer, this was always a side career. Writing was still a middle-of-the-night business for him. I just said, Why don't you do it full-time?" Despite his doubts, Yu quit his day job in 2014 (at that time, he was working as a lawyer for Belkin International) to become a writer and editor for the dystopian neo-Western television series *Westworld*. The series premiered to critical praise in 2016.

Yu served as the story editor for several episodes of the first season of *Westworld*. He also cowrote the eighth episode of the season, "Trace Decay," and received two 2017 Writers Guild of America Award nominations. He next worked on another HBO series called *Here and Now*, a dark comedy about a family with adopted children, serving as the executive story editor for ten episodes during 2018 and also writing one episode. After his successful work for HBO, Yu landed another job as a TV writer, this time for AMC's comedy-drama series *Lodge 49*. He crafted episode six of season one, titled "The Mysteries," which aired in 2018. A year later, in 2019, he added the FX series *Legion* to his repertoire of teleplays, also working as a coproducer on that show. In 2020, Yu found work writing for *Flight 008*, a sci-fi podcast, and *Dream Corp LLC*, a comedy aired on the *Adult Swim* website. Additionally, he contributed fiction and nonfiction to magazines such as *The New Yorker*, *Harper's*, and *Wired* throughout this period, as well as book reviews to *The New York Times*.

NATIONAL BOOK AWARD WINNER

Although Yu enjoyed working for television and learned a great deal in the process, he found the work challenging. As Yu told Jonathan Hum for *The News Lens* (12 Jan. 2021), writing for television diverged from fiction writing, his preferred style. "I really needed to learn how to think visually, in images," he described to Hum. "Real people would have to say the words that I was writing, and I had to keep in mind the production designer would have to design the set, or the director would have to explain to actors or understand what it meant." Yu also lamented the lack of diversity found in the writers' rooms for TV shows, explaining to Hum that, out of six writing rooms, he had been "the only person of color."

Even as Yu was busy working on a myriad of television projects, he had a stalled second novel waiting for completion. In 2020, Yu published that novel, entitled *Interior Chinatown*, which follows the life of a struggling actor named Willis Wu. Adopting the narrative structure of a screenplay, Yu spins a tale in which Willis fights against stereotypes that make him feel like an outcast. The book won Yu the prestigious 2020 National Book Award and was longlisted for the 2021 Andrew Carnegie Medal for Excellence in Fiction.

The novel also helped bring attention to discrimination faced by Asian Americans. "Too often when we talk about race in America it's often about Black and white," Yu told Hum. "It's also important to remember that there are more races in America and that looking at things from a more 360 view, I hope, is helpful in fighting this struggle." In early 2021, Yu established a creative writing prize for young Taiwanese American writers, in partnership with the *TaiwaneseAmerican.org* website.

PERSONAL LIFE

Yu married Michelle Jue, who worked for the environmental nonprofit Healthy Child, Healthy World. They have two children together, Sophia and Dylan, and reside in Irvine, California.

SUGGESTED READING

"National Book Award Finalist Charles Yu '01 Skewers Asian Typecasting On and Off Screen." *Columbia Law School*, 16 Nov. 2020, www.law.columbia.edu/news/archive/national-book-award-finalist-charles-yu-01-skewers-asian-typecasting-and-screen. Accessed 6 Dec. 2021.

Sternbergh, Adam. "With His Fourth Book, Charles Yu Finally Feels Like a Writer." *The New York Times*, 22 Jan. 2020, www.nytimes.com/2020/01/22/books/charles-yu-interior-chinatown.html. Accessed 30 Nov. 2021.

Yu, Charles. "Charles Yu." Interview by Robert Birnbaum. *The Morning News*, 1 Nov. 2012, themorningnews.org/article/charles-yu. Accessed 30 Nov. 2021.

—. "For Author Charles Yu, 'Non-Writing Time Can Also Be Productive.'" Interview by Courtney Vinopal. *PBS NewsHour*, 16 Feb. 2021, www.pbs.org/newshour/arts/for-author-charles-yu-non-writing-time-can-also-be-productive. Accessed 30 Nov. 2021.

—. "One Foot in the World of Black and White: An Interview with 'Westworld' Writer Charles Yu." Interview by Jonathan Hum. *The News Lens*, 12 Jan. 2021, international. thenewslens.com/article/145878. Accessed 30 Nov. 2021.

SELECTED WORKS

Third Class Superhero, 2006; *How to Live Safely in a Science Fictional Universe*, 2010; *Sorry Please Thank You: Stories*, 2012; *Interior Chinatown*, 2020

—*Maria del Pilar Guzman*

Najwa Zebian

Born: April 27, 1990
Occupation: Activist and poet

Najwa Zebian is a Lebanese Canadian poet, speaker, and self-help author whose work first became popular through social media. She was born and raised in Lebanon before moving to Canada when she was sixteen. She studied microbiology and education, eventually working toward a doctorate in the latter and began working as a teacher in 2012.

Many of Zebian's students were refugees or immigrants who felt out of place in Canada, as Zebian herself once had. She used writing and poetry to connect with them, rekindling a passion she had set aside when she was a teenager. Zebian self-published two books of poetry—*Mind Platter* and *The Nectar of Pain*—in 2016. She began to garner a following on social media, which was accelerated by her contributions to the #MeToo movement starting in 2017. This was fitting considering the nature of her work, which has often been about seeking connection to overcome trauma and pain. To this end, she published her first book of poetic inspiration and self-help, *Welcome Home*, in 2021.

Zebian's writing did not garner significant critical attention upon its publication, but millions of readers soon connected with her words, allowing her to attain an uncommon level of success for poets in the twenty-first century. Speaking to Deborah Dundas for the *Toronto Star* (18 Apr. 2019), she expressed surprised that so many people related to her writing, because she thought of it as such a personal task. "The response that I get from people usually is, 'Thank you for putting into words what I've been trying to say for years,'" she told Dundas. "I believe . . . that my words offer them that 'me too' element where I'm saying I understand, you're not alone, someone else out there has experienced this or is experiencing this . . . [readers] feel as if they've been given permission to feel their feelings as well."

EARLY LIFE AND EDUCATION

Najwa Zebian was born in Lebanon on April 27, 1990. Her parents were both teachers who taught in Lebanon and Canada. For much of her early life, Zebian was raised by her grandmother in Lebanon. Her parents' travel between the two countries was destabilizing for the young Zebian, who sought comfort in writing poetry starting from the age of thirteen. "My parents were in constant motion, so my home was my journal," she told Rupert Hawksley for the Middle East *National* (1 Nov. 2018). "It was the only thing that was constant."

In 2006, when she was sixteen, Zebian moved with her parents to Canada, settling in London, Ontario. As she later recalled, she had initially only come to visit, but when war broke out in Lebanon in 2006, she was forced to stay in Canada. She had been bullied at school in Lebanon and suffered bullying again at her new school in Canada. To cope, she stopped writing, literally tearing her beloved journal to shreds. "I didn't want to feel anymore," she explained to Hawksley.

Zebian graduated from high school two months early, just shy of her seventeenth birthday. She studied microbiology at the University of Western Ontario in London, Ontario, earning her bachelor's degree in that subject in 2011. She then received a bachelor's degree in education in 2012 and a master's degree in education, with a focus on curriculum studies, multiliteracies, and multilingualism, in 2013. In 2015, she began working on her doctorate in education, which she completed in 2022.

TEACHING CAREER

Zebian began her teaching career at a private school in 2012, while she was working on her master's degree. She went on to teach in elementary and secondary grades in public schools.

Meanwhile, inspired by her students, she began writing again. "I had a group of young refugees in my class, and I started writing as a

Photo by Najwazeb,
via Wikimedia Commons

way to empower them," she told Hawksley. She never dreamed it would become her career. "I never thought of myself as an author," she said. "Writing was genuinely my only way of dealing with the world."

MIND PLATTER AND *THE NECTAR OF PAIN*

Zebian self-published *Mind Platter*, her first collection of poetry, in 2016. She self-published her second book, *The Nectar of Pain*, the same year. Her arresting verses about love, friendship, and identity soon found a large audience on social media.

Zebian garnered hundreds of thousands of followers on *Instagram*, where fans shared inspirational and thoughtful quotes like this one from *Nectar of Pain*: "These mountains that you are carrying / you were only supposed to climb." The line, which some fans got tattooed on their bodies, became one of Zebian's most quoted. She also benefited from celebrity endorsements, including country singer LeAnn Rimes, actor Hilary Swank, and actor Danielle Brooks. When these celebrities shared her words on their own accounts, her following grew.

#METOO

Zebian's career was given an unusual boost during the #MeToo movement, which began in October 2017 as hundreds of thousands of people, including Zebian, shared painful experiences of sexual harassment, assault, and trauma on social media.

On October 15, 2017, Zebian shared some feelings related to her own #MeToo own experience, written in verse and posted on *Twitter*: "I was blamed for it. / I was told not to talk about it. / I was told that it wasn't that bad. / I was told to get over it." Shortly afterward, her words appeared in a *New York Times* article covering the #MeToo movement, and she soon published these lines as part of a full poem, "To You, If You Are #MeToo." The poem is characteristic of Zebian; while some detractors felt her poems were overly simplistic, her direct way of speaking to readers became a balm for many. "I know they don't believe you," the poem begins. She goes on to write, "But let me tell you this. / I believe you. / I hear you. / I honour your story." The poem ends with Zebian's own #MeToo gesture, offering comfort in a shared pain. She adopted the syntax of the #MeToo movement's slogan, writing, "Because they blamed me for it, too. / Because they told me not to talk about it, too." She ends the poem with the lines, "Because they told me to get over it, too. / Just like they told you, too."

Zebian spoke briefly about her experience with Ann Marie McQueen for the Middle East *National* (8 Jan. 2018). She told McQueen that she was aggressively pursued by an older man, an important figure in her field, when she began teaching. She told McQueen that she felt he took advantage of her. "I didn't know what was happening," she said. "I was very innocent and naive about people . . . lack of experience, lack of knowledge of really anything about these kinds of issues. I perceived the experience differently from what it truly was." When she publicly named the man, she received fierce pushback but also support. She told McQueen that she thought the negative reactions were born of fear. "If they actually bring themselves to believe that something wrong happened to you, that means they need to change, there's something that they need to do, so they just say: 'No, something is wrong with you,'" she said.

SPARKS OF PHOENIX

Zebian's status as a public figure of the #MeToo movement helped raise her profile. During this period, she spoke at political rallies and gave a TEDx Talk called "The Power of 'Me

Too.'" The increased exposure brought her to the attention of Kirsty Melville of Andrews McMeel Publishing, a company best known for discovering Indian Canadian poet Rupi Kaur. Kaur had also found devoted readers through social media starting during the 2010s. When her books were officially published, starting with *Milk and Honey* in 2014, they sold so well that Kaur was credited, as Sue Carter wrote for *Quill and Quire* (12 Feb. 2018), "with a resurgence in the international popularity (and sales) of poetry."

In 2017, at a poetry slam in Bankstown, New South Wales, Australia, Melville saw similar potential in Zebian. "Her message was so powerful, and so important," Melville told Carter, "and her work really resonates with young women." Zebian worked with the publishing company to expand and revise her debut, *Mind Platter*; the new edition was published in 2018, as was a new edition of *The Nectar of Pain*.

Zebian released her third book, *Sparks of Phoenix*, in 2019; by that time, she had garnered more than one million *Instagram* followers. The book is divided into six parts and charts her journey of healing from abuse. She told Carter in an interview for *Quill and Quire* (8 Apr. 2019) that while she did not change her writing process, the experience of making *Sparks of Phoenix* felt different from her other books. She felt she had formed a new relationship to heartbreak. "For me to evolve from writing just about life to writing about love and pain and vulnerability and shame helped me grow," she said. "*Sparks of Phoenix* has allowed me to write about it from the place of somebody who's looking back at what they went through."

WELCOME HOME

In 2021, Zebian published her first book that was not poetry, *Welcome Home: A Guide for Building a Home for Your Soul*, which combines memoir, some poetry, and storytelling to offer readers words of inspiration about finding self-worth. Zebian had long been interested in the concept of home, which she had once defined to Dundas as not "a physical place" but "a place where our souls and hearts feel at peace." A reviewer for *Publishers Weekly* (1 Apr. 2021) expressed interest in Zebian's personal story—"how she came to value herself independently of the opinions of others, including dealing with rejection from a significant other and learning to 'not run away from labels' regarding her Muslim faith"—but was unimpressed by her more generic advice to readers. "There isn't anything revolutionary here," the reviewer wrote, "and the opening framing device—labeling those reliant on others' opinions as homeless people who need to create their own home within—will be offensive to some."

Despite reservations from some critics, the book helped Zebian launch a larger self-help brand. She began hosting an inspirational interview podcast called *Stories of the Soul* and selling a digital self-help toolkit called the *Soul Academy*. As part of this brand expansion, she also began to offer one-on-one "soul sessions" for $350 an hour.

Also in 2021, Zebian published *The Book of Healing*, a collection of some of her most popular poems and prose.

SUGGESTED READING

Carter, Sue. "Is Najwa Zebian Poised to Be the Next Rupi Kaur?" *Quill and Quire*, 12 Feb. 2018, quillandquire.com/omni/is-najwa-zebian-poised-to-be-the-next-rupi-kaur/. Accessed 7 Sept. 2022.

Dundas, Deborah. "Najwa Zebian on How Poetry Helps Her Define Home." *Toronto Star*, 18 Apr. 2019, www.thestar.com/entertainment/books/2019/04/18/najwa-zebian-on-how-poetry-helps-her-define-home.html. Accessed 7 Sept. 2022.

Hawksley, Rupert. "Najwa Zebian: Writing Was Genuinely My Only Way of Dealing with the World." *National*, 1 Nov. 2018, www.thenationalnews.com/arts-culture/books/najwa-zebian-writing-was-genuinely-my-only-way-of-dealing-with-the-world-1.786901. Accessed 4 Sept. 2022.

McQueen, Ann Marie. "Najwa Zebian: The Lebanese Poet Speaking Up about the #MeToo Movement." *National*, 8 Jan. 2018, www.thenationalnews.com/lifestyle/najwa-zebian-the-lebanese-poet-speaking-up-about-the-metoo-movement-1.693755. Accessed 7 Sept. 2022.

Review of *Welcome Home: A Guide to Building a Home for Your Soul*, by Najwa Zebian. *Publishers Weekly*, 1 Apr. 2021, www.publishersweekly.com/9780593231753. Accessed 7 Sept. 2022.

Zebian, Najwa. "Poet Najwa Zebian Rises Again with Sparks of Phoenix." Interview by Sue Carter. *Quill and Quire*, 8 Apr. 2019, quillandquire.com/omni/poet-najwa-zebian-rises-again-with-sparks-of-phoenix/. Accessed 7 Sept. 2022.

SELECTED WORKS

Mind Platter, 2016; *The Nectar of Pain*, 2016; *Sparks of Phoenix*, 2019; *Welcome Home*, 2021

—Molly Hagan

Ginger Zee

Born: January 13, 1981
Occupation: Meteorologist and TV personality

As chief meteorologist for the ABC television network, Ginger Zee has covered such major weather events as historic hurricanes, extreme heat in Death Valley, and wildfires in Colorado on both the weekend and weekday editions of the popular morning program *Good Morning America*. Before that position, Zee worked at several local NBC stations in the Midwest, including in Flint, Michigan, and Chicago, Illinois. Zee defined her role as a television meteorologist to Valparaiso University's *Valpo Magazine* (21 May 2014), saying, "When you're a scientist on television, you're an explainer. You have to take science and make it simple, while also teaching people something."

Despite her successes as a television personality, Zee has struggled with mental illness and abusive relationships, which she has detailed in her two memoirs published in 2017 and 2022. Explaining the importance of sharing such an honest portrayal of her life, she told Tracy Swartz for the *Chicago Tribune* (5 Dec. 2017): "People see me for thirty seconds at a time and they see someone who's got a hair and make-up team that put them together and they're looking all right in the world, but it's not. We don't all have perfect lives, even if they are seemingly so."

CHILDHOOD AND EDUCATION

Ginger Zee was born Ginger Renee Zuidgeest on January 13, 1981, in Orange, California. (Zee adopted the pseudonym Ginger Zee early in her television career.) She moved with her family to Michigan as a young child with her brother, Sean. Her mother, Dawn Zuidgeest, was a performer, and she also struggled with depression. In spite of her mental health issues,

Zee told Sarah Ellison in an interview for *The Washington Post* (11 Jan. 2022) that her mother was instrumental in teaching her "how to be vulnerable, how to be transparent, and how to constantly work on myself to be the best version of me." Her father, Bob Zuidgeest, moved to the United States from the Netherlands. After her parents divorced, her mother remarried a social worker, which gave Zee a sense of safety.

Seeing the storms on Lake Michigan, Zee became fascinated by weather. The 1996 film *Twister* also made an impression on Zee as an adolescent; she saw a possible future self in the protagonist, who was played by Helen Hunt and based on a real-life meteorologist who led a group of storm chasers.

Zee graduated from Rockford High School in Rockford, a suburb of Grand Rapids, Michigan, in 1999. She then attended Valparaiso University in Indiana, where she was part of the Storm Intercept Team, a club for people interested in weather. The students chased storms, sometimes even going to a nearby state if weather conditions were promising. During her freshman year, a professor encouraged her to try for an internship at a local news station in Birmingham, Alabama, which she received. It was the stepping stone to a career in front of a camera. As she told *Valpo News*, "When I came back from that internship, I had on-camera experience." As a result, she was able to secure a position as a meteorologist at a PBS station in Merrillville, Indiana, when she was just nineteen years old. Zee soon gained her bachelor's degree in meteorology with minors in Spanish and mathematics, graduating a semester early in 2002.

CAREER IN TELEVISION

After beginning her career as a meteorologist in Grand Rapids, Michigan, Zee worked for the NBC affiliate WEYI-TV in Flint, Michigan, from 2003 to 2005. She returned briefly to Grand Rapids before moving in 2006 to Chicago, where she remained until 2011 with the third largest television outlet in the nation, WMAQ-TV. While in Chicago, she began appearing on national broadcasts at MSNBC and the Discovery Channel, where she hosted episodes of *Storm Chasers*. Concurrently, from 2008 until 2011, she also worked as an adjunct professor at Valparaiso, where she designed and taught the first course on television forecasting to be offered at the university. She provided

Photo by Ray Chiarello, via Wikimedia Commons.

real-life examples from the industry to her students, including placing special emphasis on the criticism one receives as an on-air weather forecaster from the public, noting that TV meteorologists face significant scrutiny as both television personalities and scientists whom viewers expect to forecast accurately 100 percent of the time.

In 2011, Zee became the weekend weather anchor for *Good Morning America*, necessitating a move to New York City. Zee subsequently became the weekday weather anchor for the program in 2013. In December of that year, she was named chief meteorologist when her predecessor retired. The new role made her the first female chief meteorologist of a major broadcast network in history. Announcing her promotion, ABC News president Ben Sherwood praised Zee, as reported on *Mlive.com* (2 Dec. 2013), stating: "Ginger always rushes straight toward the eye of any storm and weaves cutting-edge science with human emotion to elevate our coverage."

During her time on *Good Morning America*, Zee covered such major weather events as the Moore, Oklahoma, tornadoes, Hurricane Matthew in 2016, and Hurricane Ida in 2021. She was nominated for an Emmy Award for her 2018 coverage of the historic floods in Houston, Texas, following Hurricane Harvey that she contributed to the news program

20/20. Zee also provided in-depth reporting on special stories, such as her 2021 report on oyster farming in New York, which shed light on how the overharvesting of oysters has contributed to the destruction of a natural reef in the harbor that provides protection from storm surges.

Zee has also branched out into other areas of television during her career. In 2016, she began voicing the character of Dr. Zephyr Skye, a storm-chasing alien, on the animated Disney Junior show *Miles from Tomorrowland.* Zee partnered with professional dancer Val Chmerkovskiy in 2016 for the twenty-second season of ABC's *Dancing with the Stars.* The couple took third place. She also filmed a series for the DIY network in 2017 called *Renovation Realities: Ben and Ginger*, in which she and her husband shared their adventures renovating a suburban fixer upper. In 2019, she began hosting the series *Hearts of Heroes*, which focuses on people who rescue victims from natural disasters.

REPORTING ON CLIMATE CHANGE

In late 2021, Zee announced that in addition to her role as chief meteorologist at ABC, she would become the chief climate correspondent and managing editor of a new unit at ABC News devoted to climate change. The new role was an example of the increasing responsibilities that have been placed on television weatherpersons during the twenty-first century, as threats from human-created climate change rise dramatically. "As a scientist and someone who understands the atmosphere, I have not only a passion but a true connection to climate science," Zee explained to Marc Tracy for *The New York Times* (29 Jan. 2022).

Zee began with a story on the air quality of ports such as Los Angeles/Long Beach, where container ships were backed up waiting to unload. Even though the National Aeronautics and Space Administration (NASA) had confirmed the reality of poor air quality, Zee faced some pushback on social media, especially among conservative viewers. Her colleagues were quick to defend her science and her skills.

In her new role, Zee began hosting title "It's Not Too Late," a recurring feature on climate change in which she reports on innovations and technologies that offer hope for the future, such as electric vehicles and the potential for wind and solar power. Asked why she chose to advocate specifically in this arena, she told Tracy, "I've always been in love with the atmosphere, considerate of it, respecting it. But, mostly, this is just science. At the end of the day, I'm just telling you the science."

PUBLISHED WORKS

In addition to her career as a television meteorologist, Zee has published several books, including a memoir in 2017 called *Natural Disaster: I Cover Them. I Am One.* Her original idea had been to write a book for babies about weather. As a person who had excelled in math and science, she never thought of herself as a writer. However, in speaking to an editor, the idea grew first into a chapter book for middle grade readers, and eventually into a memoir. In the book, Zee details her five years in Chicago, a period in her life that included bouts of depression and drinking. "It's not the city's fault because it's a wonderful city and I love it," she told Swartz. "It was just the time in my life and some of the circumstances and the choices that I made and then, obviously, the mental illness that I was battling."

In 2018, Zee returned to her plan to write for middle grade readers when she published *Chasing Helicity*, the first book in a fiction trilogy for middle graders featuring fourteen-year-old Helicity. She and her friends endure various extreme weather situations, including flash floods and a tornado in the first book. The following year, *Chasing Helicity: Into the Wind* (2019), in which the characters encounter a hurricane, was published. *Chasing Helicity: Through the Storm*, the final volume of the trilogy, was published in 2020.

Zee published a second memoir in 2021. *A Little Closer to Home: How I Found the Calm after the Storm* is a deeper memoir, exploring her experiences with date rape and abortion. "I have learned, through a decade of really intense focus therapy, that no matter your trauma, you can't delete it from your life, which is what I tried to do for the longest time with many events and traumas," she explained to Ellison. "Instead of deleting it, you have to process it, and move through it." She compared working with her therapist, whom she sees weekly, to seeing a physical therapist for bodily pain. She also finds help through journaling daily.

PERSONAL LIFE

Zee, who has been a storm chaser since college, is an aficionado of extreme sports. She has surfed, raced an ice boat, and skydived on *Good Morning America*, among other pursuits. In 2014, she married NBC news correspondent Ben Aaron. The couple has two sons, Adrian and Miles.

SUGGESTED READING

Kaczmarczyk, Jeffrey. "'Good Morning America' Names Grand Rapids' Ginger Zee as Weekday Weather Anchor." *Mlive.com*, 2 Dec. 2013, www.mlive.com/entertainment/grand-rapids/2013/12/good_morning_america.html. Accessed 11 Apr. 2022.

Pierson, Colleen. "Rockford's Ginger Zee Makes Her Debut on 'Good Morning America.'" *Mlive.com*, 12 Nov. 2011, www.mlive.com/entertainment/grand-rapids/2011/11/rockfords_ginger_zee_makes_her.html. Accessed 12 Apr. 2022.

Swartz, Tracy. "Meteorologist Ginger Zee Details Chicago Struggles in New Book." *Chicago Tribune*, 5 Dec. 2017, www.chicagotribune.com/entertainment/ct-ent-ginger-zee-book-natural-disaster-20171205-story.html. Accessed 16 Apr. 2022.

Tracy, Marc. "As Storms Intensify, the Job of TV Weather Person Gets More Serious." *The New York Times*, 29 Jan. 2022, www.nytimes.com/2022/01/29/business/meteorologists-storm-weather-climate-change.html. Accessed 19 Apr. 2022.

"Whirlwind Ascent." *Valpo Magazine*, Valparaiso University, Spring 2014, www.valpo.edu/geography-meteorology/whirlwind-ascent/. Accessed 13 Apr. 2022.

Zee, Ginger. "Transcript: Ginger Zee, ABC News Chief Meteorologist and Author, 'A Little Closer to Home: How I Found the Calm After the Storm.'" Interview by Sarah Ellison. *The Washington Post: Washington Post Live*, 11 Jan. 2022, www.washingtonpost.com/washington-post-live/2022/01/11/transcript-ginger-zee-abc-news-chief-meteorologist-author-little-closer-home-how-i-found-calm-after-storm/. Accessed 4 May 2022.

SELECTED WORKS

Natural Disaster: I Cover Them. I Am One, 2017; *Chasing Helicity*, 2018; *Chasing Helicity: Into the Wind*, 2019; *Chasing Helicity: Through the Storm*, 2020; *A Little Closer to Home: How I Found the Calm After the Storm*, 2021

—*Judy Johnson*

Zemfira

Born: August 26, 1976
Occupation: Indie rock musician

Known by some fans and music journalists as "Kurt Cobain in a dress," Zemfira is an indie rock musician who transformed the role that women play in the Russian alternative rock scene after releasing her debut album *Zemfira* in 1999. Her punkish style combined with her controversial lyrics made her a popular but divisive public figure in Russia—a country where it can be dangerous to be different, let alone discuss issues such as depression and sexuality as openly as Zemfira has.

Throughout her career, Zemfira's nonconformity has led the Russian press to regularly speculate about her private life. Such speculations have been sustained over time by the fact that she rarely grants interviews and many of her songs' lyrics are open to interpretation about the artist's sexuality and personal life. The singer's unwillingness to back down from openly expressing herself through her music, despite the political and personal risks that can involve, has led to the development of a loyal fanbase in Russia and other former Soviet republics. Not long after the wildly successful release of her debut album in 1999, Zemfira participated in one of the few formal interviews of her career with Lora Alentova for *Neo Novosti* (1 December 1999), a Russian language monthly youth publication included in the city of Vladivostok's newspaper *Yezhednevnye Novosti* [*Daily News*]. When discussing how much of her work is autobiographical, Zemfira told Alentova, "Some are written after real emotional experiences, and others are situations you can imagine finding yourself in."

EARLY LIFE AND EDUCATION

Zemfira Talgatovna Ramazanova was born on August 26, 1976, in Ufa, the capital city of the Russian republic known as Bashkortostan, at that time part of the Soviet Union. Her mother was a doctor, and her father was a history teacher. As a child, Zemfira was highly

Photo by Marina Zakharova,
via Wikimedia Commons.

creative and interested in many different artistic mediums. Reflecting on this in her 1999 interview with Alentova, she stated, "As a child, I was engaged in writing, but then I concluded that it was more interesting to read prose than to write."

Zemfira soon found other ways to express herself, developing a passion for music at an early age. Her parents enrolled her in a music school where she began studying singing and piano. By the time she was a teenager, however, she began moving away from classical music towards rock after her older brother Ramil introduced her to bands such as Queen and Black Sabbath.

This period in Zemfira's life came in the context of perestroika, the name for a number of social and political reforms during the 1980s and early 1990s that Mikhail Gorbachev instituted while General Secretary of the Communist Party of the Soviet Union. Before perestroika, Soviet rock bands formed an underground music scene that could only be discovered by word of mouth, and music lovers' options were largely limited to songs produced by Melodiya, the state-run record company, or expensive, pirated recordings of Western rock bands such as the Beatles. Soviet rock musicians often had to perform in secret and could face political persecution for their work. When Gorbachev legalized

rock and roll in 1985, artists were allowed more creative freedom and could have their songs played on the radio. This led to the rock and roll renaissance that Zemfira experienced throughout her adolescence.

By the mid-1990s the Soviet Union had officially dissolved, and Zemfira started to perform covers of songs by Kino, Nautilus Pompilius, and Aquarium—three Russian rock bands that embodied the spirit of the 1980s transitional era of Russian history. At the age of sixteen, she began performing in local nightclubs. Around this time, she became friends with many people who belonged to the alternative scene.

After graduating from high school with honors, Zemfira had to decide whether she would pursue a career in music or basketball; she was talented enough at that sport to become the captain of the Russian Girls Junior Team by the time she was fourteen. She opted to pursue music instead of athletics, enrolling in the Ufa College of Fine Arts, where she studied vocal performance. She continued to sing in bars and restaurants during this time, performing mostly jazz and rock and roll covers with friends who provided her with instrumental accompaniment.

EARLY CAREER

After graduating from college in the 1990s, Zemfira was hired by a local radio station as a sound engineer. She worked there for the next three years, creating advertisements for the station during the day and then using their computer to record her own songs at night. In 1998 Zemfira invited fellow musicians Rinat Akhmadiyev, Sergei Sozinov, Sergei Mirolyubov, and Vadim Solovyov to join her band. Soon they sent out demo tapes to producers, including Ilya Lagutenko from the popular Russian rock band Mumiy Troll. Lagutenko loved Zemfira and her band's sound and invited them to record their first album in Moscow.

In many ways Lagutenko's invitation was unusual, as women had typically been underrepresented in the Russian rock scene. The few Soviet female rockers who had preceded Zemfira included the eccentric Zhanna Aguzarova, the punk poet Yanka Dyagileva, and new wave performer Nastia Poleva. Although all of these women had an impact on Russian music, they were, to a certain extent, anomalies. In the 1990s, most prominent female musicians in Russia were pop singers who had to present themselves in oversexualized ways to get radio airtime. As such, Zemfira's "unfeminine" appearance and dark, edgy sound represented a groundbreaking shift.

"I know the first impression that is formed about me," Zemfira told Alentova. "I put myself in the place of people who encounter me for the first time. A street girl who looks like a boy. And upon closer inspection, it turns out that this is not a boy, not a girl. This is Zemfira. I am afraid that neither journalists, nor even listeners will ever be able to understand this."

ZEMFIRA

On May 10, 1999, Zemfira and her band released their self-titled debut album with DMI Records. It contained several songs that were promoted heavily on radio stations and proved popular, including "Why," "Scandal," and "AIDS." Many of these songs were considered controversial, especially "AIDS," which addressed the viral epidemic that had claimed tens of thousands of Russian lives by that point. Amid the often-homophobic climate in Russia, there was government pushback over the single, as some in the Russian government felt that any acknowledgement of the AIDS epidemic could be considered an acknowledgment, or even endorsement of, same-sex attraction. Speaking to Alentova, Zemfira acknowledged that she knew "AIDS" would be contentious, stating, "Only because no one has sung about this before. It's out there regardless . . . and music is a form of mass media."

The single "Snow" also proved to be scandalous and would come to define Zemfira as a public figure throughout her career. A love song, "Snow," uses feminine pronouns to describe the unnamed person Zemfira sings about, as evidenced by the lyrics, "I burst into your (hers) life, and you (she) were stunned. I wanted love, but you didn't want." The implied same-sex relationship described in these lyrics generated controversy, but this challenging of social norms also helped endear Zemfira to many of her fans.

Ultimately, the *Zemfira* debut album was considered a smash success and sold 700,000 copies. It became a cultural touchstone for a generation of young Russians who were grappling with how to define their place in the world almost a decade after the Soviet Union fell. Furthermore, Zemfira's defiant presence and sound began to open the door for other female Russian rock musicians.

WIDESPREAD POPULARITY

By the time Zemfira released her second album, *Forgive Me My Love* (2000), she had become a rock sensation, widely popular across Russia and other former Soviet republics. Multiple singles from the album, including "Searching" and "Forgive Me My Love," became hits, which helped launch her nonstop touring around Russia and Eastern Europe. *Forgive Me My Love* went on to become one of Zemfira's most popular albums and helped further establish her as the wildly popular queen of alternative rock music in Russia. When reflecting on her meteoric rise to fame, Zemfira told Alentova, "You know, my whole life I told my mother: "Mom, your daughter will be a star." And when it happened, she wasn't even surprised . . . I incurably infected her with my fatal confidence."

Zemfira's third studio album, *14 Weeks of Silence*, was released in 2002. Its softer, more polished sound included more keyboards and drew comparisons to the music of bands such as Radiohead. The album, *14 Weeks of Silence,* sold more than a million copies and led to the band taking a break from years of near-constant recording and touring.

On March 1, 2005, Zemfira released *Vendetta*. Although it sold fewer copies than her previous albums, it was still quite popular. She continued to regularly perform and tour in the years that followed, releasing live albums in 2006 and 2010, respectively. Her next studio album, *Thank You* (2007), was noted for being more "mature" and experimental as a result of her mixing rock with classical music and jazz. The album also marked a new chapter in her personal and professional life—the music video for "We Scatter" was directed by Russian actor Renata Litvinova, who would later become one of Zemfira's best friends and regular collaborators.

In 2008 Zemfira went on the *Déjà Vu* tour in a handful of smaller clubs and venues before concluding with a concert at the Green Theatre in Moscow. Litvinova filmed the entire tour, later releasing a film called *Green Theatre in Zemfira* (2008). On April 1, 2008, Zemfira gave a concert performance of the *Thank You* album at Moscow's Olympic stadium, which led to her winning Steppenwolf prizes for Best Performance and Best Album. Meanwhile, Litvinova's documentary won Best Musical Movie of the Year.

Zemfira continued to release albums and perform over the following years. In 2016 she performed concerts for her sixth album, *Little Man (Live)* (2016), including a show at Madison Square Garden in New York City.

Throughout the second half of the 2010s, Zemfira toured and performed less prolifically. On July 20, 2019, she performed a rare "interview" by succinctly answering dozens of fan's questions on the Russian social networking site VKontakte. When a fan asked how she spends her time, she replied, "I watch movies, read, play something, water the plants. I can go many days without leaving the house." Although she reiterated to her fans on VKontakte that she would never tour again, Zemfira headlined the Stereoleto festival in St. Petersburg, Russia, in 2020. The following year she released a new album, *Borderline*, to positive reviews.

UKRAINE ACTIVISM

On July 7, 2015, Zemfira made headlines for accepting and waving a Ukrainian flag during a concert in Tbilisi, Georgia. This gesture of support for Ukraine was widely viewed as a criticism of Russia's illegal annexation of the Ukrainian territory of Crimea, as well as a critique of the policies of Russian president Vladimir Putin's administration. Subsequently, many of Zemfira's concerts in Russia were canceled.

On February 24, 2022, Zemfira performed a concert in Moscow, then participated in a "No War" flash mob in response to the Russian invasion of Ukraine, which had begun earlier that day. The next day, in a post on VKontakte that was later deleted, Zemfira wrote, "They call me endlessly, they say the same thing: Zemfira, be careful, they listen to you, they follow you, like all public people. I'm hysterical . . . I don't want war. And I'm not a coward."

Amid increasing government repression of antiwar activists in Russia, Zemfira reportedly fled the country after speaking out against the war. As a protest against the conflict in Ukraine, she also removed all content from her Instagram page except for black squares with the words "No War" and "Don't Shoot" that included footage of the war in Ukraine and Russian antiwar protesters.

SUGGESTED READING

Kohen, Hilah. "Russian Rock Fans Celebrate 20th Anniversary of Zemfira's Now-Legendary Debut Album." *Meduza*, 10 May 2019, meduza.io/en/feature/2019/05/10/russian-rock-fans-celebrate-20th-anniversary-of-zemfira-s-now-legendary-debut-album. Accessed 8 Apr. 2022.

Nechepurenko, Ivan. "Zemfira to Live in Your Head for a Long Time." *The Moscow Times*, 16 Apr. 2013, www.themoscowtimes.com/2013/04/16/zemfira-to-live-in-your-head-for-long-a23327. Accessed 8 Apr. 2022.

"Russian Rock Star Zemfira Releases Anti-War Video." *The Moscow Times*, 21 Mar. 2022, www.themoscowtimes.com/2022/03/21/russian-rock-star-zemfira-releases-anti-war-music-video-a76998. Accessed 8 Apr. 2022.

Steinholt, Yngvar B. "You Can't Rid a Song of Its Words: Notes on the Hegemony of Lyrics in Russian Rock Songs." *Popular Music*, vol. 22, no. 1, 2003, pp. 89–108, www.jstor.org/stable/853558. Accessed 8 Apr. 2022.

Zemfira. Alentova, Lora. "Minus 140 and Eternal Summer." Interview by Lora Alentova. *Neo Novosti*, vol. 12, 1999, pp. 3-5, zemfyra.tripod.com/inter9.htm. Accessed 8 Apr. 2022.

Zilberman, Michael. "The Pink Scare." *Salon*, 29 Feb. 2000, www.salon.com/2000/02/29/zemfira/. Accessed 14 Apr. 2022.

SELECTED WORKS

Zemfira, 1999; *Forgive Me My Love*, 2000; *14 Weeks of Silence*, 2002; *Thank You*, 2007; *Small Man (Live)*, 2016; *Borderline*, 2021

—*Emily Turner*

OBITUARIES

Adolfo

Born: Havana, La Habana, Cuba; February 15, 1923
Died: New York, New York; November 27, 2021
Occupation: American fashion designer

Adolfo gained renown in the 1970s for his trend-setting introduction of such styles as midi skirts, maxi coats, harem pants, and bolero jackets, and he went on to dress many of the world's wealthiest and best-known women, including, most famously, First Lady Nancy Reagan.

The Cuban-born designer, whose birthname was Adolfo Faustino Sardiña, began his career as a hatmaker in Paris but moved to New York City in 1948. There, as the chief designer for Emme Millinery, he earned a Neiman-Marcus Award and a Coty Award for his bold, geometric creations, and in 1962 he set out to open his own salon. He received national attention when Lady Bird Johnson commissioned four of his designs for the 1965 presidential inaugural festivities, but, aware that many women were beginning to view hats as unnecessary or old-fashioned, he branched out into designing clothing.

One of his first private apparel clients was the socialite Gloria Vanderbilt, and that roster soon included public figures like Jacqueline Kennedy Onassis and the Duchess of Windsor. One of his longest-standing and highest-profile relationships was with Nancy Reagan, who first wore Adolfo designs when her husband, Ronald, was governor of California. When she became First Lady of the United States, Reagan regularly wore garments by Adolfo, often in bright red, a color that became something of a trademark for her.

In later years, Adolfo designed for Saks Fifth Avenue and other high-end retail stores. He retired in 1993 and spent much of his time attending daily mass and reading nonfiction. (He continued, however, to earn royalties from licensing his name to several clothing, perfume, and accessory manufacturers.) He died on November 27, 2021, at his home in Manhattan, at the age of 98. His companion of more than four decades, Edward C. Perry, had predeceased him in 1994.

See Current Biography 1972

Madeleine Korbel Albright

Born: Prague, Czech Republic; May 15, 1937
Died: Washington, DC; March 23, 2022
Occupation: American diplomat

Though Madeleine K. Albright had a rich career as a world affairs analyst and diplomat, she was perhaps most celebrated for being the first female U.S. secretary of state.

Albright was born Marie Jana Korbelová on May 15, 1937, in Prague. Her father, Josef Korbel, was a diplomat for the embassy of what was then Czechoslovakia. When he began receiving Nazi death threats, the family was forced to leave for England. Albright's early childhood years took place in the chaos of early World War II-era London. Though the Korbels were Jewish, the threat of a Nazi victory led them to convert to Catholicism in 1941. As Albright later recalled, her parents even recounted Catholic "memories" to her and her siblings, so that it would be many years before she learned about her true religious origins.

After the war, Josef briefly returned to his diplomatic career, and the Korbels spent some years in both Czechoslovakia and Yugoslavia. With the Communist occupation of Prague in 1948, however, they relocated to the United States, where they received political asylum in Denver. As a teenager, Albright's interest in diplomacy continued to develop, and at one point she founded an international relations club at the Kent School for Girls. She pursued a political science degree at Wellesley College, graduating in 1959 and becoming an American citizen along the way.

Albright earned a master's in international affairs and a certificate in Russian in 1968, and a doctorate nearly 10 years later, all at Columbia University. In 1972, she made her first foray into U.S. politics, mounting a senatorial campaign. Four years later, when Jimmy Carter won the presidency, Albright became the congressional liaison for the National Security Council. In 1997, she was appointed secretary of state under President Bill Clinton, a position she would hold until 2001.

Outside of her political career, Albright founded multiple businesses, taught at Georgetown University, and directed the Council on Foreign Relations. She wrote a collection of political books and memoirs, and collaborated on *Fascism: A Warning* (2018), a critique of Donald Trump. In 2012, Albright was awarded the Presidential Medal of Freedom by Barack Obama.

Throughout her career, Albright was well-known for her habit of wearing eye-catching brooches that subtly conveyed her opinions and goals—an arrow pin that looked like a missile while negotiating the Anti-Ballistic Missile Treaty with the Russians, for example, or a jeweled snake to poke fun at the Saddam Hussein regime's characterization of her as a serpent. She once lent more than 200 of her pieces to the Smithsonian for an exhibit.

Albright, whose marriage to journalist Joseph Medill Patterson Albright ended in divorce, died on March 23, 2022, in Washington, DC, reportedly due to complications from cancer. She was survived by her three daughters, Katherine, Anne, and Alice; and six grandchildren.

See Current Biography 2000

Christopher Alexander

Born: Vienna, Austria; October 4, 1936
Died: Sussex, England; March 17, 2022
Occupation: British-American architect

Christopher Alexander was renowned for his works of architectural theory. Famously preferring old-fashioned to modern architecture, he also believed that everyone, architect or not, should have a say in the design of their own homes and neighborhoods.

Born Christopher Wolfgang John Alexander on October 4, 1936 in Vienna, Austria, he was the only child of archaeologists Ferdinand and Lilly Alexander. He was just two years old when the Nazis began their occupation of the country, leading his family to relocate to Oxford, England. As a young man, Alexander earned a scholarship to study mathematics and architecture at Cambridge University. It was during his undergraduate years that he discovered his distaste for modern architecture, which at the time was officially considered the ideal of building design. This was only one of his eccentricities as a student; in addition to his main studies at Cambridge, he also hired a personal "aesthetics tutor," hoping to better understand and quantify beauty.

Alexander went on to earn a PhD in architecture at Harvard University, where his dissertation, "Notes on the Synthesis of Form," would become his first published work, winning the American Institute of Architects Gold Medal. In the same year, not yet 30 years old, Alexander earned a position as an architecture professor at the University of California, Berkeley.

Alexander became best known for his written works, publishing over 20 texts on architecture and city planning. His most widely recognized work, *A Pattern Language: Towns, Buildings, Construction* (1977), was the second installment in Alexander's Center for Environmental Structure Series, which was finished in 1995. Patterns were a recurring theme in Alexander's work—one of his later texts, *The Nature of Order Book 1: The Phenomenon of Life* (2002) focused on the geometric patterns that occur in natural phenomena such as wood fibers.

Though most famous for his writing, Alexander also engaged in more hands-on field work, helping to construct buildings for communities in places as far-flung as Latin America and India. He also created a building system involving concrete blocks that could be easily stacked, so that homeowners and families might construct their own dwellings.

On March 17, 2022, Alexander died at his home in Sussex, England from complications related to pneumonia. He was survived by his wife, Margaret Moore, and his daughters, Lily and Sophie.

See Current Biography 2003

Clifford Alexander

Born: New York, New York; September 21, 1933
Died: New York, New York; July 3, 2022
Occupation: First African American Secretary of the Army

Clifford Alexander spent his lengthy career as a leading advisor to multiple Democratic presidents. Although he also had stints as a lawyer, businessman, and even a talk show host, he is best known as the first Black Secretary of the Army.

Clifford Leopold Alexander, Jr., was born on September 21, 1933 in Harlem, New York. Both of his parents participated in city politics, especially his mother, who served as a civil rights advisor to multiple New York mayors. As a young man, Alexander pursued a degree in government at Harvard University, where he also became the first Black student council president. After graduating in 1955, he went to Yale to study law. In 1958, having obtained his law degree, Alexander returned to New York, where he spent some years working as an assistant district attorney, as well as the executive director of an organization to fight poverty among Harlem youth.

In 1963, Alexander began his career in Washington, DC, serving on the National Security Council under President John F. Kennedy. Soon after his arrival, he found himself unofficially advising the president on race relations. Following Kennedy's assassination, Alexander was appointed by the new president, Lyndon B. Johnson, as a liaison to the civil rights movement. He worked to increase political involvement and support within the African American community, while helping to open the door for future big-name Black politicians, such as Robert C. Weaver and Thurgood Marshall.

In 1967, Alexander was made chairman of the Equal Employment Opportunity Commission. He continued to facilitate communication between the Black community and the government, meeting with civil rights leaders in the midst of the violence following the assassination of Dr. Martin Luther King, Jr. After leaving the Commission, he was appointed secretary of the Army. Under President Jimmy Carter, Alexander aided the rise of many Black men from officer to general, as well as rebuilding and diversifying the Army following the Vietnam War. He held his post as secretary until 1981. Though this was his last official government job, Alexander continued to serve and advise future Democratic presidents.

Alexander died at his home in Manhattan due to heart failure on July 3, 2022. He was survived by his wife, Adele; their children, Mark and Elizabeth; and seven grandchildren.

See Current Biography 1977

Rahul Bajaj

Born: Calcutta (now Kolkata), India; June 10, 1938
Died: Pune, India; February 12, 2022
Occupation: Indian businessman; politician

One of the richest men in India and head of his family's business empire, which encompasses dozens of companies, Rahul Bajaj was known as a larger-than-life industrialist with great vision and acumen.

Bajaj's grandfather, Jamnalal, had founded the Bajaj Group in 1926, running the fledgling business on the moral principles espoused by Mahatma Gandhi. Initially consisting of a steel mill and a sugar mill, the enterprise soon expanded into the manufacturing sector and became known, in particular, for its exceptionally popular two- and three-wheeled scooters. Bajaj, who had earned an MBA at Harvard took over Bajaj Auto in 1972, and in 1994, upon his uncle's death, he became head of the entire business group.

Under his leadership, the Bajaj Group further diversified, buying controlling interests in financial-services companies, appliance manufacturers, and a wide variety of other entities.

A staunch nationalist who took great pride in empowering millions of average Indians by providing them with a convenient, affordable means of transportation, Bajaj also served from 2006 to 2010 in the Rajya Sabha (the upper house of the Indian parliament).

At the time of his death, on February 12, 2022, following a long illness, Bajaj, who had by then assumed the title chairman emeritus, was worth an estimated $8.2 billion. The recipient of the Padma Bhushan, one of the country's highest civilian honors, he was accorded a state funeral, a rarity for an Indian businessman. He was survived by two sons, Rajiv and Sanjiv, and a daughter, Sunaina Kejriwal. He was predeceased in 2013 by his wife of more than five decades, Rupa.

See Current Biography 2007

Jennifer Bartlett

Born: Long Beach, California; March 14, 1941
Died: Amagansett, New York; July 25, 2022
Occupation: American artist

A New York–based artist, Jennifer Bartlett was best known for "Rhapsody," her 153-foot collection of Conceptual paintings exhibited in 1976. The large-scale work became one of the defining pieces of the late-twentieth-century American art movement.

Bartlett was born Jennifer Ann Losch in Long Beach, California, on March 14, 1941. She took after her mother, a former fashion illustrator, developing an early interest in drawing and viewing museum exhibits. By the end of high school, she knew she wanted to be a painter.

Bartlett graduated from Mills College in 1964 and then entered Yale, where she pursued a graduate degree alongside many who would become the most notable artists of their generation. After graduating, she moved to New York, where she was inspired not only by the Conceptualist art movement, but by subway signs. Inspired by the durability of the signs, she began painting on steel plates instead of graph paper; these plates would become her "canvas" for the rest of her career.

"Rhapsody" was first displayed at a Manhattan gallery in 1976. A wide variety of artistic styles and patterns, the 987-plate painting received overwhelming praise, and would eventually be exhibited in the Museum of Modern Art (MoMA) nearly 30 years later. Bartlett's next large-scale project was "In the Garden" (1979–80), a collection of almost 200 drawings based on a garden in Nice, France, where she had spent a winter. The work would become a catalyst for Bartlett's future projects, which usually depicted her own everyday surroundings, namely her studios, homes, and gardens.

In the midst of this artistic productivity, Bartlett still found time to give interviews, redesign multiple New York residences, and even write an autobiographical novel, *A History of the Universe*. In 1983, she embarked on a 10-year marriage to German actor Mathieu Carrière, during which she lived half of the year in Paris.

In 2012, Bartlett produced one of her most stylistically different projects, "Hospital Paintings," 10 canvases interrupted by a single line of color. These were inspired by a lengthy hospitalization for an illness that was never diagnosed.

Bartlett died at her home in Amagansett on July 25, 2022. Though she had been suffering with dementia, the direct cause of death was leukemia. Survivors include her daughter, Alice, and two sisters, Julie and Jessica.

See Current Biography 1985

Aaron T. Beck

Born: Providence, Rhode Island; July 18, 1921
Died: Philadelphia, Pennsylvania; November 1, 2021
Occupation: American psychiatrist

Aaron T. Beck transformed the treatment of depression, anxiety, and other mental disorders, introducing the world to the concept of cognitive behavioral therapy and improving outcomes for countless patients.

A professor of psychiatry at the University of Pennsylvania School of Medicine in Philadelphia, Beck had initially trained in Freudian psychoanalysis. When dealing with patients, however, he found flaws in Freud's theories, which held that depressed individuals were driven by a subconscious need to suffer. Beck discovered, by contrast, that most patients were happy and grateful to have their suffering alleviated.

He came to believe that people could be trained to replace their negative internal dialogue with more positive, realistic, and mood-improving ways of thinking. His system represented a radical departure from the dominant Freudian psychoanalytic model of the day.

Rather than focus on childhood traumas and conflicts, as most Freudians did, Beck began advising his patients to consider the distorted thinking that arose in day-to-day situations. For example, when someone came to him unable to socialize without drinking heavily because they thought of themselves as awkward or inept, he instructed them to avoid drinking to observe what occurred, and to gather evidence that their assumptions were false. (A socially anxious drinker, for example, was likely to find that, contrary to their expectations, no one disparaged or shunned them when they were sober.)

Cognitive behavioral therapy (CBT), as the method was eventually dubbed, is meant to be effective within 12 to 16 weeks, and since the late 1950s, when Beck first formulated the idea, clinicians have greatly expanded its applications. CBT is now widely used to treat eating disorders, panic attacks, performance anxiety, obsessive-compulsive disorder, and other such conditions, and in his later years, Beck used it to effectively treat various marginalized groups, such as drug addicts and late-stage schizophrenics.

Beck, who wrote more than 20 books, died at his Philadelphia home on November 1, 2021, at the age of 100. He was survived by his wife, Phyllis, who has the distinction of being the first woman ever to serve on the Pennsylvania Superior Court; daughter Judith, his frequent co-author and the president of the Beck Institute for Cognitive Behavior Therapy; daughter Alice, who is also a judge; two sons, Roy and Daniel; and several grandchildren and great-grandchildren.

See Current Biography 1999

Teresa Berganza

Born: Madrid, Spain; March 16, 1933
Died: Madrid, Spain; May 13, 2022
Occupation: Spanish singer

A mezzo-soprano and contralto, opera singer Teresa Berganza was most famous for her performances in the works of Rossini, Mozart, and Bizet, in particular Bizet's Spanish-set *Carmen*.

Teresa Berganza Vargas, the youngest of three siblings, was born on March 16, 1933, in Madrid, on the brink of the Spanish Civil War. While her father was a left-wing atheist, her mother was a politically and religiously conservative Catholic who would encourage the young Berganza to become a nun. As a young woman, Berganza attended Madrid's Royal Conservatory of Music in the hopes of one day leading a choir or teaching music in a Catholic school. However, Lola Rodríguez

Aragón, a voice tutor who would become Berganza's lifelong mentor, suggested that rather than teaching, Berganza train to be a serious performer.

Berganza made her debut in Mozart's opera *Così Fan Tutte* in 1957 in Aix-en-Provence, France. The following year, she appeared at the famed Teatro alla Scala in Milan in Gioachino Rossini's *Le comte Ory*. It was the year after, in London, that she would originate one of her signature roles—that of Rosina in *The Barber of Seville*, also by Rossini. Yet one of Berganza's most iconic performances, the lead in Prosper Mérimée's *Carmen*, was also one of the most awaited, since for years she claimed that the role intimidated her. When she did agree to perform in Edinburgh, in 1977, she spent many weeks preparing, most notably through interviewing Gypsy women in southern Spain, embracing Carmen's identity as a Romani woman.

Berganza had three children with her first husband, Félix Lavilla, a pianist at the conservatory where she had first studied. Her second husband, the priest José Rifá, quit the clergy for her, though their marriage lasted only a decade.

Berganza was very protective of her voice, often refusing to speak or go out when preparing for a performance. She performed in her last opera at 57, a 1992 production of *Carmen* staged at the Teatro de la Maestranza in Seville; she continued singing in recitals through her 70s.

Berganza died in Madrid on May 13, 2022. Information about her survivors was not made public.

See Current Biography 1979

Robert Bly

Born: Madison, Minnesota; December 23, 1926
Died: Minneapolis, Minnesota; November 21, 2021
Occupation: American poet, lecturer, editor, critic, translator, and activist

Robert Bly wrote more than 50 volumes of poetry, translations, literary criticism, and social commentary, but he was equally known for spearheading a movement that called for men to reclaim their primal power.

Bly attended Harvard along with a group of other soon-to-be-famed young writers, including John Ashbery, Adrienne Rich, Frank O'Hara, and John Hawkes, and he first came to widespread attention in the 1960s, with free-verse diatribes against the Vietnam War. He donated the $1,000 he won as part of his National Book Award for the 1967 poetry collection *The Light Around the Body* to draft-resistance causes.

Over the course of the next two decades, Bly published numerous volumes of translated works, poetry, and essays, many touching on esoteric or mythological themes. His career reached new heights, however, in 1990, with the publication of *Iron John: A Book About Men*, which drew on legends, Jungian psychology, and myth to argue that American men had grown soft and needed to rediscover their primitive instincts. The book spent more than a year in total on *The New York Times* bestseller list, perching at number one for 10 weeks.

Although Bly went on to author numerous other books, *Iron John* remained his best known. Although it had many detractors, who derided it as self-indulgent and misogynistic, it jumpstarted a fledgling "men's movement" in the United States. Bly created something of a cottage industry for himself as a result, organizing men-only seminars and retreats that featured drum circles, poetry readings, and campfires.

Bly died on November 21, 2021, at his home in Minneapolis. He was survived by Bridget, Mary, Micah, and Noah--his children from his first marriage to fellow writer Carol McLean; his second wife, Ruth Ray, a Jungian therapist; a stepdaughter, Wesley; and nine grandchildren. A stepson, Samuel, predeceased him in 1984.

See Current Biography 1993

Peter Bogdanovich

Born: Kingston, New York; July 30, 1939
Died: Los Angeles, California; January 6, 2022
Occupation: American motion picture director, producer, and writer

Peter Bogdanovich became one of the biggest names in Hollywood on the strength of award-winning pictures such as *The Last Picture Show* (1971), based on a Larry McMurtry novel and set in small-town Texas; *What's Up, Doc?*

(1972), a screwball comedy that confirmed the box-office draw of Barbra Streisand and Ryan O'Neal; and *Paper Moon* (1973), starring O'Neal and his real-life daughter, Tatum, as a pair of Depression-era grifters.

Bogdanovich had been an avid movie buff since the age of 12, and he admired directors like George Cukor, John Ford, Alfred Hitchcock, and Howard Hawks. He originally trained as an actor, wanting to emulate the stars he loved most, including James Stewart and Cary Grant, but after a brief period of appearing in summer-stock productions and television shows, he instead began writing about film for such periodicals as *Esquire* and *The Saturday Evening Post*, forging a close relationship with the iconic director Orson Welles along the way.

Bogdanovich directed his first feature, *Targets*, a low-budget thriller produced by Roger Corman in 1968. Although Corman was known as a master of shlock, *Targets* won critical praise for its sensitive and evocative direction. That success led to his hiring by Columbia Pictures to co-write the screenplay and direct *The Last Picture Show*, which was nominated for eight Oscars, including best picture.

The Last Picture Show catapulted Bogdanovich into the top ranks of Hollywood, but it also led indirectly to ignominy; he left his wife and two young children for the movie's female lead, the 19-year-old Cybil Shepherd, and the two became near-constant fodder for the tabloid press over the next several years—even as *What's Up, Doc?* and *Paper Moon* met with critical acclaim.

The mid-seventies found Bogdanovich making a string of flops, some of which he had meant as star vehicles for Shepherd, from whom he separated at the end of the decade, only to enter into another tabloid-worthy romance, this one with the married Playboy model Dorothy Stratten, who was killed by her estranged husband in 1980.

By the mid-eighties, Bogdanovich, nearly destitute and addicted to drugs, had entered into a relationship with Stratten's 20-year-old sister, falling even further from grace among LA's elite as a result. While his 1985 feature *Mask*, starring Cher, was a relative success, he raised the ire of industry insiders by suing the studio for interfering with his creative vision, and most of his subsequent work came from television.

In later years, Bogdanovich rehabilitated his image to a great degree, publishing highly regarded books about film and taking on acting roles in such television hits as *The Sopranos* and *Law and Order*. He died of unspecified causes at his California home on January 6, 2022, and was survived by the daughters from his first marriage, Alexandra and Antonia; and three grandchildren.

See Current Biography 1972

Mike Bossy

Born: Montreal, Canada; January 22, 1957
Died: Montreal, Canada; April 15, 2022
Occupation: Canadian hockey player

Mike Bossy is best known for earning a place in the Hockey Hall of Fame after leading the New York Islanders to four consecutive wins in the Stanley Cup Championships.

Michael Dean Bossy was born in Montreal on January 22, 1957. He and his nine siblings were raised speaking French and English. Bossy learned to skate at age three on a makeshift ice rink made by his father, who would fill the backyard of their building with water. As a teenager, Bossy attended Laval Catholic High School, but he soon dropped out to play for the Laval Nationals of the Quebec Major Junior Hockey League in the 1972–73 season. During his four seasons playing for Laval, Bossy scored 309 goals.

In 1977, Bossy was chosen by the New York Islanders, a team considered an extension of the National Hockey League (NHL) in an amateur draft. He had been turned down by other teams, but was soon proving them wrong, winning the Calder Memorial Trophy in the 1977–78 season, and the Conn Smythe Trophy in the 1982 Stanley Cup Playoffs. Despite being slighter than most ice hockey players, and less willing to fight, he was soon being lauded as one of the league's fastest skaters, and he went on to score the Islanders 573 goals in 752 NHL games.

In 1986, however, Bossy's career was interrupted by the onset of chronic back pain, leading to 17 missed games and an injured knee. It was discovered that he was suffering from two injured discs that were unlikely to heal. In 1988, Bossy retired from hockey and returned to Canada in search of broadcasting work.

Bossy's name was added to the Hockey Hall of Fame in 1991. Yet he continued to feel that he and the Islanders had never received the recognition they deserved, especially compared with more famous players like Wayne Gretzky.

Bossy had a longtime career as a hockey analyst for the French-language TVA Sports channel. When he was diagnosed with lung cancer in fall of 2021, he went on leave from his job. He died on April 15, 2022, at his home in Montreal, at age 65. He is survived by his wife, Lucie, and their daughters, Josiane and Tanya.

See Current Biography 1981

Peter Brook

Born: London, England; March 21, 1925
Died: Paris, France, July 2, 2022
Occupation: British theater and film director

Avant-garde director Peter Brook was known for his creative, large-scale staging of older plays and texts.

Peter Stephen Paul Brook was born in London on March 21, 1925. (Jewish Latvian immigrants, his parents had Anglicized their name.) Brook, the younger of two sons, developed a very early interest in the arts, performing a four-hour version of *Hamlet* at age seven and aspiring to be a movie director. He was educated at private schools, where he endured frequent bullying from his peers. At 16, he was accepted into Oxford University, where he would begin the move towards theater, staging a production of Christopher Marlowe's *Doctor Faustus* to raise money for an Aid to Russia Fund.

After graduating, Brook was employed–and later fired–by an advertising company. He did, however, continue directing fringe theater productions throughout the 1940s, including an innovative staging of *Love's Labour's Lost* for a summer festival in Shakespeare's birth village.

As he gained recognition, Brook began a period in which he staged mainly commercial theater. In 1956, he directed the British premiere of *A View from the Bridge* by Arthur Miller, and went on to mount a number of Shakespeare's plays starring acting legends such as Vivien Leigh and Laurence Olivier. He won a Tony Award for his 1966 production of *Marat/Sade* by Peter Weiss, but his opera productions were less successful—after being appointed to direct at the Royal Opera House in 1947, he received complaints that the music suffered at the expense of the acting and set design. He would not return to opera until a 1983 version of Georges Bizet's *Carmen*, which by contrast received glowing reviews.

Some of Brook's most famous productions were the most lavish—his 1970 version of *A Midsummer Night's Dream* included acrobatics inspired by a Chinese circus, for example, and won him another Tony. In 1985, he created a nine-hour production of the Hindu epic the *Mahabharata,* which was staged in France and New York. A similarly daring play, *The Man Who* (1995), was a staging of a neurological case study. Still, one of Brook's later productions, a 2011 version of Mozart's opera *The Magic Flute,* was praised for its "pared-down" simplicity.

Brook died on July2, 2022. Though he had been based in Paris, the location of his death was undisclosed. He was predeceased in 2015 by his wife, Natasha Parry. He was survived by his two children Irina and Simon.

See Current Biography 1961

Frederick Buechner

Born: New York, New York; July 11, 1926
Died: Rupert, Vermont; August 15, 2022
Occupation: American minister and author

Frederick Buechner was best known for his insightful—and often humorous--novels, essays, and memoirs, which usually had strong religious themes.

Born in Manhattan on July 11, 1926, Carl Frederick Buechner grew up during the height of the Great Depression. His once-affluent parents were hit hard, and Buechner and his brother perpetually changed schools based on the sporadic employment of their father, a salesman who committed suicide in 1936.

Buechner began his writing endeavors early on, publishing his first poems in the literary magazine of the Lawrenceville School in New Jersey, where he studied as a teenager. He began pursuing an English degree at Princeton University in 1943, but it was interrupted when he was drafted into the Army for World War II. After the war, he completed his degree, graduating in 1948.

After five years working as a teacher at Lawrenceville, Buechner returned to New York to concentrate on his writing career. He was 23 when he published his first novel, the widely successful *A Long Day's Dying* (1950). The debut follows a widow, her mother, her lovers, and her college-aged son, and the conflicts that arise between each.

In 1952, soon after publishing his less popular second novel, *The Seasons' Difference,* Buechner found himself inspired by the sermon of a lauded Presbyterian pastor. Two years later, he entered Union Theological Seminary, where he studied for four years and was ordained as a Presbyterian evangelist in 1958. Though not an official church pastor, Buechner became a chaplain at a New Hampshire academy, where he taught English and religious studies until 1967.

Buechner's writing soon began taking on a more religious aspect. This was particularly prominent in his 1965 novel, *The Final Beast,* about a widowed minister entrenched in scandal, and much later, *Brendan* (1987), which follows the many journeys of a sixth-century Irish saint. Through his autobiographies such as *The Sacred Journey* (1982) and *The Eyes of the Heart* (1999), Buechner recalls his relationship with his parents and reflects on his sense of self. Although occasionally criticized as moralizing, Buechner's works generally found a largely positive reception for their demonstration of the power of faith.

Buechner died on August 15, 2022, at his home in Vermont. He was survived by his wife, Judith; their three daughters; and 10 grandchildren.

See Current Biography 1959

Ed Bullins

Born: Philadelphia, Pennsylvania; July 2, 1935
Died: Roxbury, Massachusetts; November 13, 2021
Occupation: American playwright

Ed Bullins created almost 100 plays over the course of his decades-long career—including an ambitious 20-play cycle depicting the evolving Black experience—and was widely acknowledged as not only a pivotal figure in the Black Arts movement of the 1960s and 1970s but one of the most important playwrights of the twentieth century.

As a young man, Bullins was attracted to gang life in his native North Philadelphia, and street fights left him with missing teeth and scars. Although he was a decent student, he dropped out of high school in 1952 to join the Navy, where he served for almost three years.

After his release, Bullins moved to Los Angeles, got a GED, entered a local college, and founded a small literary magazine. In the mid-1960s he moved to San Francisco, where he became part of a close-knit circle of Black writers. Influenced by LeRoi Jones (who later became known as Amiri Baraka), he turned his hand to playwriting. His first effort, *How Do You Do*, a one-act play about an encounter between middle- and working-class Blacks, was mounted in 1965 to good reviews.

For the rest of his career, Bullins alternated between the west and east coasts, serving as artist-in-residence at the New Lafayette Theater, in Harlem, during one especially prolific period, and later becoming a professor at Northeastern University in Boston.

Like others in the Black Arts movement, he sought to encapsulate the modern Black experience in works specifically meant for Black audiences. He was sometimes criticized for too freely spotlighting violence and harsh dialogue, but he nonetheless garnered acclaim for such works as the Obie Award-winning *The Fabulous Miss Marie* and *In New England Winter* and the New York Drama Critics' Circle top pick *The Taking of Miss Janie*.

Bullins, who had retired from Northeastern University in 2012 and suffered from dementia in the final years of his life, died on November 13, 2021, at his Massachusetts home. He was survived by his third wife, Marva; sons Ronald and Sun Ra; daughters Diane Bullins, Patricia Oden, and Catherine Room; and several grandchildren and great-grandchildren. He was predeceased by four of his children: Ameena, Darlene, Donald, and Eddie Jr.

See Current Biography 1977

James Caan

Born: Bronx, New York, March 26, 1940
Died: Los Angeles, California; July 6, 2022
Occupation: American actor

Over the course of his lifetime, actor James Caan took on many dramatic and comic roles in film and television. However, he would remain most famous for his interpretation of gangster Sonny Corleone in Coppola's hit film *The Godfather*.

James Edmund Caan was born on March 26, 1940 in the New York City borough of the Bronx, to parents of German Jewish origin. Soon after his birth, the Caans relocated to Queens, where James and his siblings were raised. As a young man, Caan had little interest in academia, and he dropped out of multiple high schools, though he managed to graduate at age 16. He briefly flirted with higher education at a variety of large universities and small colleges, though he never completed a degree. Still, college had sparked his interest in acting, and Caan ultimately enrolled in the Neighborhood Playhouse School of Theater in Manhattan, where he studied for five years.

One of the young actor's first notable films was the western *El Dorado* (1966), in which he played opposite John Wayne and Robert Mitchum. Even more successful was *Brian's Song* (1971), a television film based on a true story that follows the friendship between two teammates in a major football league, one Black and one white. For his interpretation of a young, cancer-stricken athlete, Caan was nominated for an Emmy Award.

Yet it was *The Godfather* (1972), directed by Francis Ford Coppola, which would define Caan's career and even his persona for years to come. Cast as short-tempered mobster Sonny Corleone, Caan played opposite Al Pacino his brother, Michael. Caan's performance was such a success that he was reputedly often mistaken for a gangster in real life. He, Pacino, and actor Robert Duvall all received Oscar nominations for their performances in the film, now considered a masterpiece of the genre.

Caan's career took off following Coppola's film, and he proceeded to be cast in a wide variety of roles. However, his professional life took an abrupt dive during the 1980s when he lost his sister to leukemia; Caan subsequently entered a rehabilitation facility for drug addiction and spent six years in debt. It was not until the end of the decade that he would begin working steadily again. His final screen role came in 2021, when he appeared in *Queen Bees*, a lighthearted comedy about a group of senior citizens.

Caan died on July 6, 2022, in Los Angeles and was survived by his five children and four grandchildren.

See Current Biography 1976

Pat Carroll

Born: Shreveport, Louisiana; May 5, 1927
Died: Cape Cod, Massachusetts; July 30, 2022
Occupation: American actor

Though perhaps best known for voicing Ursula in Disney's *The Little Mermaid* (1989), performer Pat Carroll was also a TV comedian, a Broadway singer, and a gender-bending stage actor.

Patricia Ann Carroll was born on May 5, 1927, in Louisiana, though she grew up in Los Angeles. As a young woman, she attended Immaculate Heart College in Los Angeles, before dropping out and switching to the Catholic University of America, in Washington, DC, to study drama. Ultimately, however, Carroll did not graduate from either, preferring to learn by experience. In 1947, she moved to Plymouth, Massachusetts, to work at the Priscilla Beach Theater, making her debut in the play, *A Goose for the Gander*, which starred Gloria Swanson. Soon after, Carroll relocated to New York, where she earned money working odd jobs while searching for employment as a performer.

This came most often in the form of comedy. During the early 1950s, Carroll performed frequently at nightclubs and on television and variety series. In 1957, she won an Emmy for the sketch show *Caesar's Hour*, on which she was a regular. Later, in the early 1960s, she appeared frequently on *The Danny Thomas Show*. She also began work on Broadway—first appearing in the 1955 revue *Catch a Star!*, and later, more famously, in the Leonard Bernstein musical *On the Town* (1959).

In 1979, Carroll covered new ground in her one-woman, off-Broadway play, *Gertrude Stein, Gertrude Stein, Gertrude Stein: A One-Character Play*, about the iconoclastic poet.

The play received widespread praise, winning Drama Desk and Outer Critics Circle awards in 1980, and a Grammy for a recording the following year.

Carroll voiced many cartoon characters, but was most famous for, and allegedly most proud of, her performance as the sea witch Ursula in *The Little Mermaid*. However, she also earned more serious roles in plays at the Folger Shakespeare Theater, in Washington, including *The Merry Wives of Windsor, Mother Courage and her Children*, and *Romeo and Juliet*, each of which won her a Helen Hayes Award for an outstanding lead actress. *The Merry Wives* (1990) was particularly groundbreaking, as Carroll played the male character of Falstaff.

Carroll died on July 30, 2022 at her home on Cape Cod, of complications related to pneumonia. She was survived by two daughters, Kerry and Tara, and one granddaughter.

See Current Biography 1980

Ashton B. Carter

Born: Philadelphia, Pennsylvania; September 24, 1954
Died: Boston, Massachusetts; October 24, 2022
Occupation: American government official

Working in the Barack Obama administration, former Secretary of Defense Ashton B. Carter, a physicist by training, was successful in making the U.S. military more progressive and its ranks more welcoming to nontraditional members.

Ashton Baldwin Carter was born in Philadelphia, Pennsylvania, on September 24, 1954, into a family that deeply valued education. Always a serious student, he earned undergraduate degrees in medieval history and physics from Yale before winning a Rhodes scholarship that allowed him to attend Oxford University. There he continued his exploration of physics, this time with a focus on its policy implications, and in 1984 he accepted a professorship at Harvard's John F. Kennedy School of Government.

Carter quickly became known in the nation's capital for his clearheaded, nonpartisan views on defense systems, and he became a trusted advisor to multiple policymakers. In the early 1990s, under President Bill Clinton, he was appointed Assistant Secretary of Defense for International Security Policy, with responsibility for international nuclear weapons policy, among other weighty matters. From 2009 to 2011, he served as Under Secretary of Defense for Acquisition, Technology and Logistics, and he next became Deputy Secretary of Defense, functioning, in effect, as the department's chief operating officer and overseeing a massive budget and more than three million civilian and military employees.

In 2014, Obama tapped him to head the Department of Defense, and after extensive studies, in 2016 Carter opened all military posts, including those involved in combat, to female military members; he also eventually decreed that transgender people be allowed to serve.

Carter—the five-time recipient of the Department of Defense Distinguished Service Medal, among other awards—stepped down from public service in 2017 and became the director of the Kennedy School's Belfer Center for Science and International Affairs. He died of a heart attack on October 24, 2022, at his Boston home. The author of almost a dozen books and more than 100 articles about physics and national defense, he was survived by his second wife, Stephanie; daughter, Ava; and son, Will.

See Current Biography 2001

Lauro Fred Cavazos

Born: Kingsville, Texas; January 4, 1927
Died: Concord, Massachusetts; March 15, 2022
Occupation: American educator and politician

Lauro Cavazos served as the U.S. secretary of education from 1988 to 1990, making hm the first Latino person in the nation to serve in a cabinet-level post.

Lauro Fred Cavazos, a sixth-generation Mexican American, was born on January 4, 1927, on the King Ranch—established in 1853 as the largest cattle operation in the state— where his father worked as a foreman. Like all the children of the ranch's employees, Cavazos attended a two-room schoolhouse on the property before moving on to the public school in nearby Kingsville.

Cavazos graduated from high school in 1945 and served in the U.S. Army during the final stages of World War II. Upon his discharge,

he entered Texas Tech University, earning an undergraduate degree in zoology in 1949 and a master's in zoological cytology two years later. In 1954, at Iowa State University, he earned a PhD in physiology.

Cavazos then embarked on a career in academia, teaching anatomy at the Medical College of Virginia, chairing the anatomy department at Tufts University's School of Medicine, and later serving as dean of the latter institution. In 1980, he was named president of Texas Tech—making the school the largest in the country to be led by someone of Latino descent—and in that capacity, he was praised for substantially increasing the numbers of Black and Hispanic students.

In mid-1988 President Ronald Reagan tapped Cavazos, who had no previous political experience, as education secretary, and he was confirmed by the Senate in September of that year, 94–0. When George H. W. Bush was elected president on November 8, 1988, he retained Cavazos as a member of his cabinet.

Serving under two Republican presidents, Cavazos, a registered Democrat, was pressed to contend with an educational system suffering several serious problems: the dropout rate in public schools was high, overall academic scores were dropping, and funding was difficult to secure. Notably, institutions of higher learning were debating the fairness and efficacy of race-based admissions policies, and in late 1990, after the Education Department was compelled to roll back a ruling that federal aid would be denied to any school awarding race-based scholarships—legislation that had been strongly decried by civil rights activists and many faculty members—a chastened Bush asked Cavazos to step down.

Following his 27-month tenure in federal government, Cavazos rejoined Tufts and taught public health and family medicine until his retirement. He died at his home in Concord, Massachusetts, on March 15, 2022, at the age of 95. He was survived by his wife of more than 60 years, the former Peggy Ann Murdock; their 10 children; 15 grandchildren; and two great-grandchildren.

See Current Biography 1989

Benjamin Civiletti

Born: Peekskill, New York; July 17, 1935
Died: Lutherville, Maryland; October 16, 2022
Occupation: American lawyer

Benjamin Civiletti served as attorney general in President Jimmy Carter's administration, during a period that found him playing a pivotal role in the Iranian hostage crisis.

Benjamin Richard Civiletti was born in Peekskill, a town in Upstate New York, on July 17, 1935. In 1957 he earned a bachelor's degree from Johns Hopkins University, and four years later, he was awarded a law degree from the University of Maryland.

In 1976, when Carter won the presidency, he tapped Civiletti, then a successful civil and criminal litigator in private practice, to join the U.S. Justice Department. Civiletti, who had worked as an assistant federal prosecutor in Baltimore as a young attorney, served first as chief assistant in the criminal division before moving on to the number-two post of deputy attorney general in 1978; the following year he was named attorney general.

Although Civiletti was celebrated for taking down drug traffickers and mafioso, he will perhaps be most remembered for his role in the events that transpired after November 4, 1979, when revolutionary fighters besieged the U.S. Embassy in Tehran and seized 52 American hostages.

Civiletti—who addressed the Hague to argue for the release of the hostages—urged restraint but obtained peacetime emergency-powers orders for Carter, who subsequently seized billions of dollars in Iranian assets and halted oil imports from that country. The morass led indirectly to Carter's failed reelection bid, and the hostages were not released until January 20, 1981, the day rival Ronald Reagan was inaugurated as president.

With Carter out of the White House, Civiletti returned to his law firm in Baltimore, remaining there until retirement in 2014. The recipient of American Lawyer's lifetime achievement award, he died of Parkinson's disease on October 16, 2022, at the age of 87, at his home in a suburb of Baltimore. He was survived by his wife of more than a half-century, Gaile; their children, Benjamin, Andrew, and Lynn; nine grandchildren; and three great-grandchildren.

See Current Biography 1980

Max Cleland

Born: Atlanta, Georgia; August 24, 1942
Died: Atlanta, Georgia; November 9, 2021
Occupation: United States government official

Despite losing both legs and an arm during the Vietnam War, Max Cleland went on to a noteworthy career that included stints as a state senator in his native Georgia, administrator of Veterans Affairs in the Jimmy Carter administration, secretary of state of Georgia, and two-term U.S. senator.

Cleland's father had fought in World War II, and inspired by his example, Cleland joined the Army in 1965, volunteering for Vietnam two years later. On April 8, 1968, towards the end of his tour, Cleland retrieved a grenade he believed had fallen off his own belt (he later learned from witnesses that it had been dropped by another soldier), and when it exploded, his right leg and arm were instantly blown off, and his left leg was so badly damaged it was amputated at a field hospital.

Awarded the Bronze Star and a Silver Star for meritorious service, he returned to Georgia after he had recuperated from his injuries and was elected to the state senate. At 28, he was the youngest person ever elected to that body.

Named the head of the Veterans Administration in 1977, he served in that capacity until the end of Carter's presidency. From 1982 to 1996 he was Georgia's Secretary of State, and when Democrat Sam Nunn announced his retirement from the U.S. Senate, Cleland successfully vied for the seat. As a U.S. senator he gained a reputation as a social liberal and fiscal conservative. Although he generally hewed closely to the Democratic agenda and was reluctant to send troops overseas, he regularly voted for increased military spending.

Cleland's bid for reelection in 2002 was hurt by the repeated attacks Republicans mounted against him, which included, in the wake of 9/11, television ads that questioned his patriotism and suggested he was soft on terror. He ultimately lost the race to Republican opponent Saxby Chambliss (who had, somewhat ironically, relied on deferments to avoid the Vietnam draft). The election loss, coupled with the launch of the Iraq war in 2003, re-triggered Cleland's post-traumatic stress disorder (PTSD), and he was hospitalized for a time at Walter Reed. He had admitted that it took more than a year and intensive therapy before he felt better.

Cleland later accepted a teaching post at American University, served briefly on the 9/11 Commission, and completed a four-year term on the board of the Export-Import Bank.

The author of multiple memoirs, Cleland (who also worked as a consultant on the 1978 film *Coming Home*, about a disabled vet) died on November 9, 2021, from congestive heart failure. He had no surviving family but was mourned by a large circle of close friends.

See Current Biography 1978

Coolio

Born: Monessen, Pennsylvania; August 1, 1963
Died: Los Angeles, California; September 28, 2022
Occupation: American rapper

Coolio will perhaps be most remembered for the chart-topping 1995 hip-hop anthem "Gangsta's Paradise," which featured a memorable opening line based on Psalm 23: "As I walk through the valley of the shadow of death, I take a look at my life and realize there's nothin' left." The song was featured prominently in the film *Dangerous Minds*, earned a Grammy as best rap solo performance, was named the number-one hit of the year by *Billboard*, and was ultimately certified triple platinum, thanks in large part to it haunting minor-key backup track and compelling syncopation.

The rapper was born Artis Leon Ivey, Jr., on August 1, 1963, in Monessen, Pennsylvania. The family later moved to Compton, an urban area in California renowned for producing several successful recording artists, including Kendrick Lamar, N.W.A., and Dr. Dre. After his parents divorced, he was raised by his mother, Jackie, a factory worker. A bright student who suffered badly from asthma, he joined a gang in his early teens in an attempt to fit in, and at 17 he was jailed for several months on charges of theft. At one point—during a time when he was attending a local community college and attempting to get a rap career off the ground—he became addicted to cocaine and was forced to undergo rehab.

Upon his release, he became a volunteer firefighter, and in his twenties he moved to San Jose, California, to live with his father.

There he found work fighting fires with the state's Department of Forestry and explored Christianity on a deeper level than he had ever done before. Clean and sober thanks in large part to his work and newfound faith, Coolio, as he began calling himself, also restarted his music career, which benefitted from the growing mainstream popularity of West Coast hip hop.

Although he became most celebrated for "Gangsta's Paradise," which he sometimes complained overshadowed his other accomplishments, Coolio, who was signed to Tommy Boy Records, compiled a string of hits, including "Fantastic Voyage," from *It Takes a Thief*, his 1994 debut album; "Rollin' with My Homies," which he wrote for the soundtrack to the 1995 teen comedy *Clueless*; "1, 2, 3, 4 (Sumpin' New)" and "Too Hot," from the sophomore album *Gangsta's Paradise*; and "C U When U Get There," from 1997's *My Soul*.

Coolio's last album, *From the Bottom 2 the Top*, was released in 2009; by that time in his career, he had begun to take on occasional television and film work, including the 2008 reality show *Coolio's Rules*, which focused on his love life, and a 2009 web series, *Cookin' with Coolio*, which was released in connection with a cookbook.

Coolio was found unresponsive at a friend's Los Angeles home on September 28, 2022, and pronounced dead at the scene. He was said to be survived by 10 children, four of them with ex-wife Josefa Salinas.

See Current Biography 1998

George Crumb

Born: Charleston, West Virginia; October 24, 1929
Died: Media, Pennsylvania; February 6, 2022
Occupation: American composer and educator

George Crumb's daring effects and haunting sonorities earned him a 1968 Pulitzer Prize (for the composition *Echoes of Time and the River*), as well as characterization as a "musical dramatist."

Born to a clarinetist father and cellist mother, both of whom played professionally, Crumb began composing at the age of 10. He studied as a young man at the Mason College of Music, in Charleston, and the University of Illinois at Urbana-Champaign. He received a doctorate in composition in 1959 from the University of Michigan.

Among his best-known pieces is *Black Angels* (1970), which he composed for string quarter in response to the Vietnam War and which requires performers to employ unconventional techniques such as tapping their instruments' strings with thimbles. Other eclectic works include *Threnody I: Night of the Electric Insects* (1970), which was featured on the soundtrack of the horror film *The Exorcist*; *Vox Balaenae* (*Voice of the Whale*) (1971), which is performed by musicians wearing black masks; *Makrokosmos II* (1973), which is notated in the shape of a peace sign and which led to charges that Crumb was more concerned with gimmickry than artistry; and *Star-Child* (1977), set to Latin texts and featuring a youth choir.

A dedicated teacher, Crumb held posts at such schools as the University of Colorado and University of Pennsylvania, and his many notable students included Osvaldo Noé Golijov, Jennifer Higdon, and Christopher Rouse.

Crumb composed almost until the time of his death, and his 90th birthday was commemorated by the Chamber Music Society of Lincoln Center with the premiere of a new piece for percussion quintet.

He died on February 6, 2022, at the age of 92, in Pennsylvania, and was survived by his wife, Elizabeth May (Brown), a pianist; and sons Peter and David (the latter a fellow composer). His daughter, the performer Ann Crumb, died of cancer in 2019.

See Current Biography 1979

Raymond Damadian

Born: Queens, New York; March 16, 1936
Died: Woodbury, New York; August 3, 2022
Occupation: American physician and inventor

Raymond Damadian built the first magnetic resonance imaging (MRI) scanner, revolutionizing the diagnosis and treatment of cancer and other diseases by allowing clinicians to obtain unprecedently clear pictures of internal anatomy without exposing patients to harmful radiation, as in X-rays.

Raymond Vahan Damadian, who is of Armenian descent, was born on March 16, 1936, in New York City, and he grew up in Forest Hills, a middle-class section of the borough of Queens. He attended the University of Wisconsin, Madison, on a Ford Foundation scholarship, graduating in 1956 and then returning to New York to earn an MD at the Albert Einstein College of Medicine in the Bronx. It was later, while completing a fellowship in biophysics at Harvard, that he first learned of nuclear magnetic resonance technology, typically used to identify the chemical composition of substances in a lab.

He found that when body tissues from rats were bombarded with radio waves in a magnetic field, cancerous tissue could be differentiated from healthy tissue. He published those findings in 1971, and in 1974 he was awarded a patent for a new type of imaging device. In 1977, the first MRI scanner ever built was used on a test subject. (That machine is now in the Smithsonian Institution.) Fonar, the company he launched, sold its first commercial scanner in 1980.

While Damadian won numerous laurels throughout his life for his invention, including the National Medal of Technology and induction into the National Inventors Hall of Fame, he felt that he had been cheated out of the Nobel Prize, which instead went jointly in 2003 to Paul C. Lauterbur and Peter Mansfield, who refined the technology.

Enraged, Damadian paid for ads in several major newspapers decrying the Nobel Committee's decision. He also railed regularly against such companies as General Electric, Johnson & Johnson, and Hitachi, suing them (sometimes successfully) for patent infringement after they released their own versions of the now-ubiquitous scanner.

Despite his dissatisfaction with the course his invention had taken, Damadian remained active in the lab. He built the first open MRI machine (a boon to claustrophobic patients), and later in life he studied ways to effectively image cerebral spinal fluid.

Damadian died on August 3, 2022, of cardiac arrest, at his Woodbury, New York, home. He was predeceased in 2020 by his wife, Donna, and survived by his daughter, Keira; sons, Timothy and Jevan; and numerous grandchildren and great-grandchildren.

See Current Biography 2000

Midge Decter

Born: St. Paul, Minnesota; July 25, 1927
Died: New York, New York; May 9, 2022
Occupation: American journalist and author

Midge Decter was an influential thinker whose arguments against feminism, affirmative action, the gay rights movement, and other liberal movements helped give rise to neoconservatism in the 1970s.

Midge (Rosenthal) Decter was born on July 25, 1927, in St. Paul, Minnesota. Although she attended the University of Minnesota and the Jewish Theological Seminary of America briefly, she did not earn a degree.

After working for a time as a secretary, Decter married, had children, and became a full-time homemaker. When her children were older, she reentered the work world, serving variously as the managing editor of *Commentary* (a cultural and political magazine launched by the American Jewish Committee), editor at the Hudson Institute, *Saturday Review* book reviewer, and senior editor at Basic Books. From 1969 to 1971 she was the executive editor of the popular magazine *Harper's*.

She also penned such books as *The Liberated Woman and Other Americans* (1970), *The New Chastity and Other Arguments Against Women's Liberation* (1972), and *Liberal Parents, Radical Children* (1975), in which she set forth arguments against permissiveness, women's rights, and other phenomenon that she saw as detrimental to traditional social values and cultural standards.

She and her second husband, Norman Podhoretz, who edited *Commentary* from 1960 to 1995, joined such figures as Irving Kristol, Jeane Kirkpatrick, and Daniel Patrick Moynihan in promoting the ideology that came to be known broadly as neoconservatism: Kristol famously described proponents as former liberals "mugged by reality." Neoconservatism burgeoned throughout the 1980s, arguably reaching its height during the George W. Bush presidential administration.

The author of the 2001 memoir *An Old Wife's Tale: My Seven Decades in Love and War*, Decter died in New York City, on May 9, 2022, at the age of 94. She was survived by Norman Podhoretz; her daughters, Naomi and Ruthie; a son, John (now the editor of *Commentary*);

and numerous grandchildren and great-grandchildren.

See Current Biography 1982

Joan Didion

Born: Sacramento, California; December 5, 1934
Died: New York, New York; December 23, 2021
Occupation: American novelist, journalist, and screenwriter

Joan Didion was a seminal figure in the movement known as "New Journalism," characterized by a literary style and personalized perspective that made no pretense of objectivity. She was widely lauded for her insightful takes on postwar America, especially her native California, and her mordant views of modern culture, as expressed in numerous essay collections, novels, screenplays, and memoirs. In the public imagination, Didion's female protagonists owed much to her own persona: bright, sensitive, high-strung, and pessimistic.

Didion was a fifth-generation native of California's Sacramento Valley; she was famously descended from settlers who left the Donner party in 1846 and survived as a consequence. A dedicated writer since her teens, she won a college essay contest sponsored by *Vogue* and instead of accepting the prize trip to Paris, she wrangled a job at the magazine, where she worked her way up to associate features editor. By the early 1960s, she was well-established professionally, writing for such periodicals as *Mademoiselle* and the *National Review* and publishing a highly regarded debut novel, *Run, River* (1963), about a Sacramento family.

It was two essay collections—*Slouching Towards Bethlehem* (1968) and *The White Album* (1979)—that catapulted her to a prominent place in the literary world. In those volumes she explores Haight-Ashbury counterculture, the contemporary film industry, and the proclivities of rock bands like the Doors, among other topics. She also laid bare her own vulnerabilities: in *The White Album*'s title essay, she details the psychiatric evaluation she underwent at a California outpatient clinic.

Didion was also an astute political reporter, and she wrote extensively on hot-button topics like the civil war in El Salvador and Cuban immigration for *The New York Review of Books* and other publications. In addition to her almost 20 novels and collections of nonfiction essays and cultural criticism, she was a prolific screenwriter. Many of her screenplays, including those for *Panic in Needle Park* (1971), *Play It as It Lays* (1972), the Barbra Streisand/Kris Kristofferson remake of *A Star Is Born* (1976), and *True Confessions* (1981), were co-written with her husband, John Gregory Dunne, whom she had married in 1964.

In 2003 the couple's adopted daughter, Quintana Roo, became seriously ill with pneumonia that progressed to septic shock and was comatose in the hospital when Dunne died suddenly of a heart attack. Didion wrote about those events and her reactions to them in *The Year of Magical Thinking*, which was published in 2005, garnered that year's National Book Award for nonfiction, and was adapted for the stage in 2007. The acclaim with which the book was met was dimmed, however, by Quintana Roo's death from acute pancreatitis at the age of 39.

In addition to the National Book Award, Didion's many honors included election to the American Academy of Arts and Letters in 1981, the 1996 Edward MacDowell Medal, National Book Foundation's Medal for Distinguished Contribution to American Letters in 2007, honorary doctorates from Harvard and Yale, a National Medal of Arts presented by President Barack Obama in 2013, and a Lifetime Achievement Award from PEN Center USA in 2013.

Didion's final book, the essay collection *Let Me Tell You What I Mean*, was published in 2021, shortly before her death from the complications of Parkinson's disease on December 23 of that year, at her Manhattan home.

See Current Biography 1978

Robert J. Dole

Born: Russell, Kansas; July 22, 1923
Died: Washington, DC; December 5, 2021
Occupation: American politician

Robert (Bob) Joseph Dole spent a quarter century in the U.S. Senate, making him one of the longest-serving Republicans in that body. His political life was marked, however, by his high-profile defeats in the 1976 vice-presidential race, when he appeared on the losing ticket with incumbent President Gerald R. Ford, and in the 1996 presidential election, when he faced off against Bill Clinton.

The circumstances of Dole's childhood and young adulthood contributed greatly to his almost mythological stature as an American statesman. He grew up in the midst of the Dust Bowl in Kansas, facing all the deprivations and hardships of that place and time, and as an Army lieutenant in the 10th Mountain Division during World War II, he was wounded so seriously on an Italian battlefield that his compatriots left him for dead. Almost totally paralyzed, he was told he might never walk again, but after three years in Army hospitals and multiple surgeries, he recuperated fully, except for his right arm and hand, which remained immobile.

After leaving the hospital and finishing his college degree, Dole won election to the Kansas state legislature in 1951. After one two-year term as a legislator, he served four terms as the prosecuting attorney of Russell County, and in 1960, he easily won the general election to represent Kansas' Sixth Congressional District. He ultimately spent four terms in the House, generally hewing to a conservative agenda that found him regularly opposing safety-net programs like Medicare. His only major breaks from conservative ranks were his votes for the Civil Rights Act (1964) and the Voting Rights Act (1965).

When United States Senator Frank Carlson of Kansas announced his retirement in 1968, Dole won the Republican nomination to succeed him and the general election that followed. He gained prominence in the Senate sooner than most freshmen through his vocal defense of the policies of beleaguered President Richard Nixon.

Eventually, however, Dole gained a reputation as a pragmatist willing to reach across the aisle, and in 1976 President Gerald R. Ford—who was filling out the remainder of Nixon's second term as president—added him to the Republican ticket. After losing to Jimmy Carter and Walter F. Mondale, Dole returned to the senate, chairing the Finance Committee during the Reagan administration and serving as either minority or majority leader for almost a dozen straight years, from 1985 to 1996.

In 1996, Dole gave up his senate seat to make an ill-fated bid for the presidency, conducting what was widely seen as a disastrous campaign against the more charismatic Clinton. After having cast more than 12,000 votes during his senate tenure, Dole embarked on a career as a lobbyist, wrote a memoir, and appeared occasionally as a commercial pitchman for various products. He died on December 5, 2021, at the age of 98, shortly after being diagnosed with Stage 4 lung cancer. He was survived by his second wife, Elizabeth, and daughter, Robin.

See Current Biography 1987

Frank Donald Drake

Born: Chicago, Illinois; May 28, 1930
Died: Aptos, California; September 2, 2022
Occupation: American astronomer and astrophysicist

In his seminal 1962 book, *Intelligent Life in Space*, Frank Donald Drake asserted that "with almost absolute certainty, radio waves sent forth by other intelligent civilizations are falling on the earth." That belief inspired an ongoing project dubbed the Search for Extraterrestrial Intelligence, better known as SETI.

Born in Chicago, on May 28, 1930, Drake loved science from an early age. He graduated from Cornell University in 1952 with an undergraduate degree in engineering physics and, fulfilling the requirements of his ROTC scholarship, he subsequently spent three years as a Navy electronics engineer. In 1958 he earned a doctoral degree in astronomy from Harvard.

Drake next joined the staff of the National Radio Astronomy Observatory in West Virginia, where he was tasked with planning a research agenda for a powerful, new telescope. He decided to focus on two stars some 11 million light-years from Earth—Tau Ceti and Epsilon Eridani—and while he was not successful at picking up extraterrestrial radio waves as he had hoped, the project began to attract the attention of both the general public and scientists like Carl Sagan and Melvin Calvin. Drake, Sagan, and a handful of others later created the Golden Record, a 12-inch disc containing images and sounds representative of Earth and its inhabitants, including greetings in dozens of languages, music from various cultures, animal sounds, maps, nature pictures, and scientific diagrams; in 1977 the record was launched aboard the *Voyager 1* and *Voyager 2* spacecraft.

Drake spent much of his academic career at Cornell—where he led the National Astronomy and Ionosphere Center, which maintains a 300-meter antenna in Puerto Rico that serves as a vital component of SETI—and the University of California, Santa Cruz. He was also a longtime president of the nonprofit SETI Institute.

Drake devised an eponymous equation to estimate the number of extraterrestrial civilizations that could exist in our galaxy, but he came to accept that none might be found in his own lifetime, because, as he estimated, at least 10 million of the galaxy's 100 billion stars would have to be explored—a goal nowhere near completion. He died at his Aptos, California, home on September 2, 2022, at the age of 92. He was survived by his second wife, Amahl Shakhashiri; three sons, Steven, Richard, and Paul; two daughters, Nadia and Leila; and four grandchildren.

See Current Biography 1963

Charles W. Duncan Jr.

Born: Houston, Texas; September 9, 1926
Died: Houston, Texas; October 18, 2022
Occupation: American businessman and politician

During the Jimmy Carter administration, business magnate Charles W. Duncan Jr., headed the first cabinet-level Department of Energy ever established by a U.S. president—launched as the nation was in the midst of a dire oil shortage.

Charles William Duncan Jr. was born into a well-to-do Houston family on September 9, 1926; his father, Charles Sr., was vice president of an eponymous coffee company. In 1943, the younger Duncan graduated from Tennessee's Sewanee Military Academy and four years later earned a BS in chemical engineering from Rice University.

In 1948, after working for a time digging pipelines for an oil company, Duncan joined the family business, and by the time it was acquired by the Coca-Cola Company two decades later, it had grown in size and popularity to rival Maxwell House. He was subsequently retained by the Atlanta-based soft-drink giant and steadily climbed the corporate ladder there, becoming president in 1971. In that capacity, Duncan became friendly with Carter, then Georgia's governor, and after Carter ascended to the White House, he asked Duncan to become deputy secretary of defense.

Duncan was considered a visionary member of the Department of Defense, but in the summer of 1979 a worried Carter asked him to make a move to what was then the relatively new post of energy secretary. It was a tumultuous time: the shah of Iran had been overthrown, and formerly plentiful oil supplies were drying up. Panic ensued, and historically long lines began to appear at the gas pump. Duncan responded by shoring up relations with various oil-producing countries, advocating for more domestic energy production, and instituting subsidies for people unable to afford to heat their homes, among other measures, and the crisis gradually abated.

After leaving public service, Duncan became a trustee of his alma mater, and he chaired the Rice board for almost 15 years; Duncan College, a Rice residential school, was named in his honor.

Duncan died on October 18, 2022, at his Houston home, following a serious fall. He was survived by his wife of more than six decades, Anne; daughter, Mary Anne; and five grandchildren.

See Current Biography 1980

Barbara Ehrenreich

Born: Butte, Montana; August 26, 1941
Died: Alexandria, Virginia; September 1, 2022
Occupation: American author and political activist

Barbara Ehrenreich was best-known for the bestselling 2001 book *Nickel and Dimed: On (Not) Getting by in America*, for which she went undercover as a waitress and maid, among other jobs, in order to chronicle the difficulties of surviving in America on such low wages.

Barbara (Alexander) Ehrenreich was born on August 26, 1941, in Butte, Montana, to a homemaker mother and copper miner father—both heavy drinkers. In 1963 she earned an undergraduate degree from Reed College, and five years later she received a doctoral degree in cell biology from Rockefeller University.

Understanding that it was a privilege to hold a white-collar job, she embarked on a career in public policy and academia, but, inspired by the cultural upheaval of the 1960s, she decided to write instead. The first of her more than 20 books was *Long March, Short Spring: The Student Uprising at Home and Abroad* (1969), followed by *The American Health Empire: Power, Profits and Politics* (1970).

Although she published regularly, it was not until *Nickel and Dimed* that she came to mainstream public attention. Her detailed accounts of trying to make ends meet on the approximately $7 an hour she made as a store clerk, nursing home aide, and other such posts—as well as her tales of the indignities and disrespect she suffered—struck a chord with readers, who bought more than a million copies of the book and catapulted it onto the *New York Times* bestseller list, where it remained for more than two years. Ehrenreich's subsequent books included *Bait and Switch: The (Futile) Pursuit of the American Dream* (2005), *Bright-sided: How Positive Thinking Is Undermining America* (2009), *For Her Own Good: Two Centuries of the Experts Advice to Women* (2013), and *Natural Causes: An Epidemic of Wellness, the Certainty of Dying, and Killing Ourselves to Live Longer* (2018).

Ehrenreich died of a stroke on September 1, 2022, at a hospice facility in Alexandria, Virginia, not far from her home. Twice divorced, she was survived by her daughter,

Rosa, a professor of law; son, Ben, a writer; and three grandchildren.

See Current Biography 1995

Lee Elder

Born: Dallas, Texas; July 14, 1934
Died: Escondido, California; November 28, 2021
Occupation: American professional golfer

As the Professional Golfers' Association (PGA) of America admitted only white golfers until 1961, Lee Elder began his pro career in 1959 by joining the United Golfers Association (UGA), which has been compared to baseball's so-called "Negro leagues."

Elder first learned about golf while working as a caddie at an all-white club in Texas. Over the next few years, he won the UGA championship five times, and at one point, he racked up 21 wins in 23 consecutive tournaments. (Even that level of skill, however, did not translate into high earnings for Black players.)

In 1968, after rules had loosened thanks in large part to the Civil Rights movement, Elder began playing regularly on the PGA tour, and following his victory at the 1974 Monsanto Open at the Pensacola Country Club in Florida, he was invited to compete in the 1975 Augusta National Golf Club in Georgia, where he broke a major color barrier by being the first Black golfer to compete in the Masters Tournament, the most high-profile and prestigious competition in the sport. (His triumph in Pensacola was all the more satisfying because he had been refused entry to the clubhouse years earlier and had been forced to change clothes in the parking lot.)

While Elder did not perform as well as he had hoped during that initial outing, he went on to play in the Masters six times in total; he won four PGA Tour events and finished in second place numerous times before signing on to the PGA Senior Tour in 1984. As part of the PGA, Elder earned more than $2 million in prize money, and he later launched a foundation to help underprivileged youth.

The recipient of the 2019 Bob Jones Award for sportsmanship from the United States Golf Association, Elder died on November 28, 2021, in California. He was survived by his second wife, Sharon.

See Current Biography 1976

Elizabeth II (Elizabeth Alexandra Mary Windsor)

Born: London, England; April 21, 1926
Died: Aberdeenshire, Scotland; September 8, 2022
Occupation: Queen of the United Kingdom

The longest-ruling monarch in British history, Queen Elizabeth II ascended to the throne in 1952. Her reign spanned 70 years, 15 prime ministers (beginning with Winston Churchill), and periods of great social and political upheaval.

Elizabeth Alexandra Mary Windsor—the oldest daughter of Prince Albert, Duke of York, and Lady Elizabeth Bowes-Lyon—was born in Mayfair, London, on April 21, 1926. There was little anticipation that she would ever sit on the throne, but after her uncle, Edward VIII, unexpectedly abdicated in 1936, her father became King George VI, and she was his heir presumptive.

Educated at home by governesses and visiting teachers alongside her younger sister, Margaret, Elizabeth joined the Auxiliary Territorial Service during World War II. In 1947 she married Philip, Prince of Greece, a third cousin and officer in the Royal Navy.

The couple were on a tour of Kenya in 1952, when they received word that King George had died, making the young princess officially "Queen. Elizabeth II, by the Grace of God, of the United Kingdom of Great Britain and Northern Ireland and of her other realms and territories Queen, Head of the Commonwealth, Defender of the Faith."

She was crowned at Westminster Abbey on June 2, 1953, allowing the ceremony to be televised to an audience of more than 20 million people in an attempt to modernize the monarchy. To that end, she also engaged more with her subjects—visiting every country in the Commonwealth at least once and giving filmmakers unprecedented access for a documentary about her family life that aired in 1970.

Known for her commitment to duty, she was greatly admired in Great Britain, even by those who questioned the need for a modern monarchy. Criticism of the institution peaked in the 1990s, however, after a series of tabloid-worthy scandals involving her children, resulting in the divorces of her oldest son, Charles, Prince of Wales; and her second son, Prince Andrew. The situation worsened when Charles's ex-wife, the exceptionally popular Diana, died in a car crash in Paris in 1997, and the press tarred the royal family's response as cold and unfeeling.

Nonetheless, Elizabeth weathered those events and the vicissitudes of public opinion with characteristic stoicism, carrying on with her duties as she had always done. In June 2022 she marked her 70-year Platinum Jubilee, but the four-day celebration was marred by worry about her health, which had been in decline since the death of Philip in 2021.

On September 8, 2022, while at Balmoral, the royal estate in Scotland, Elizabeth, known throughout her life for her love of horses and corgis, died at the age of 96. The nation entered a 10-day period of mourning during which some people waited in line for more than 24 hours to view her lying in state. On September 19, following a funeral ceremony in Westminster Abbey, she was laid to rest in St. George's Chapel at Windsor Castle.

Elizabeth was survived by her oldest son, now King Charles III, and his wife, Camilla, now the Queen Consort; her daughter, Anne; her second son, Andrew; her third son, Edward, and his wife, Sophie, the Duke and Duchess of Sussex; eight grandchildren, the oldest of whom, Prince William, is now heir apparent; and 12 great-grandchildren.

See Current Biography 2002

Jason Epstein

Born: Cambridge, Massachusetts; August 25, 1928
Died: Sag Harbor, New York; February 4, 2022
Occupation: American editor and publishing executive

Jason Epstein made a lasting mark on the publishing world in 1952, when he founded Anchor Books, making parent company Doubleday the first-ever publisher of trade paperbacks. In addition to his business acumen, he was known for his discerning literary tastes, and over the course of his career he edited some of the most iconic authors of the era.

A graduate of Columbia University, where his classmates included Allen Ginsberg and Norman Podhoretz, Epstein was hired as a young man by Doubleday. His weekly salary of $45 did not allow him to buy as many books as he would have liked, and he hit upon the idea of publishing high-quality literature in inexpensive paperback form—a transformative idea during a time when paperbacks indicated lowbrow romance or adventure novels.

Doubleday agreed, and its new Anchor imprint volumes, selling for as little as 65 cents each and featuring works by D.H. Lawrence and Edmund Wilson, proved to be a massive hit. Despite his success there, Epstein left Doubleday when higher-ups refused to publish the controversial novel *Lolita*, by Vladimir Nabokov.

Epstein subsequently landed at Alfred A. Knopf, where he ran the paperback imprint Vintage, and then, in 1958, at Random House, where he edited works by literary lions like Philip Roth, Gore Vidal, and Norman Mailer. He served as the company's editorial director from 1976 to 1995, when he stepped down from that post but continued to be affiliated in other capacities.

In addition to launching what was known as the paperback revolution, Epstein is celebrated for conceiving the idea for *The New York Review of Books* in 1963, when a newspaper strike left readers needing a source of book-buying guidance. He is also credited with the idea for the Library of America initiative, which now consists of more than 300 volumes of classic literature, published with uniform and instantly recognizable covers.

Epstein died in Sag Harbor, New York, on February 4, 2022, of congestive heart failure. He was survived by his second wife, the writer Judith Miller; two children from his first marriage, Helen and Jacob; and three grandchildren.

See Current Biography 1990

Nicholas Evans

Born: Worcestershire, England; July 26, 1950
Died: London, England; August 9, 2022
Occupation: British author and journalist

Nicholas Evans was 43 years old when he wrote his first novel, *The Horse Whisperer*

(1995), which became a surprise bestseller in some 20 countries and shattered book-advance and film-rights records.

Nicholas Benbow Evans was born on July 26, 1950, in Worcestershire, a town in the West Midlands of England. He attended Oxford University, where he studied law before becoming a journalist and producer of television news programming. Deciding to transition into film, he made a handful of documentaries, but by the mid-1990s, with an awaited movie project stalled and several unsold screenplays piling up, he was discouraged and struggling financially.

Knowing that it was improbable to achieve success as a first-time novelist, he nonetheless decided to try his hand at writing a book. A fan of Westerns since childhood, he arranged to meet Tom Dorrance, Ray Hunt, and Buck Brannaman—cowboys with the seemingly preternatural ability to tame horses that other experts had deemed untrainable. The resulting novel, *The Horse Whisperer*, tells the story of a young woman, who, along with her beloved horse, is gravely traumatized after an accident: traveling to Montana with her mother to seek help from Tom Booker, the titular horse whisperer, they find both healing and romance.

The manuscript incited a bidding war among publishers, and Evans's North American advance of more than $3 million set a record for a debut novel; the movie rights were sold for a similar amount to Robert Redford's Wildwood Pictures, setting another record. With Redford at the helm and starring as the male lead, the movie hit theaters in 1998 and earned almost $200 million at the box office.

Evans continued to write novels that, while not the juggernauts that *The Horse Whisperer* proved to be, still sold well. These included *Smoke Jumper*, a 1999 book about wildfires and a man who fights them; *The Divide*, a 2005 thriller about ecoterrorism; and *The Brave*, a 2010 family saga involving Hollywood, the Old West, and murder.

Evans suffered various illnesses throughout his adulthood, including melanoma (a condition he initially hid from potential publishers) and kidney failure, which was caused by accidently eating poisonous mushrooms and which ultimately required transplant surgery. He died of a heart attack on August 9, 2022, at his London home. He was survived by his second wife, Charlotte, and four children: Finlay, Lauren, Max, and Harry.

See Current Biography 1998

Maria Ewing

Born: Detroit, Michigan; March 27, 1950
Died: Detroit, Michigan; January 9, 2022
Occupation: American opera singer

Maria Ewing performed numerous major soprano and mezzo-soprano roles at such iconic houses as the Metropolitan Opera and La Scala. Critics often commented on her dramatic presence, the result of closely studying actors and emulating them, as well as what they termed her "exotic" beauty. (Ewing was of mixed racial heritage, but rarely discussed her lineage publicly; it came to the fore when her daughter, actress and film director Rebecca Hall, appeared on a 2022 episode of the PBS show *Finding Your Roots* and was informed that her grandfather, despite claiming to be Native American, was, in fact, Black.)

Ewing hailed from a musically inclined family and grew up listening to classical recordings that her mother brought back with her from trips to her native Netherlands. She studied at the Cleveland Institute of Music and made her first noteworthy appearance, in the summer of 1973, at the Ravinia Festival, where she performed with the Chicago Symphony. After touring opera houses in Boston, San Francisco, and Cologne, among other cities, she made her Met debut in the fall of 1976, singing the role of Cherubino in Mozart's *Le Nozze di Figaro* (*The Marriage of Figaro*). Among her other early Met roles were Blanche in a 1977 staging of Poulenc's *Dialogues der Carmelites* and Dorabella in a 1982 production of Mozart's *Così Fan Tutte* (*All [Women] Are Like This*). She received widespread attention in 1986, when she performed in the title role of *Salome* in Los Angeles and other cities and ended the infamous Dance of the Seven Veils totally nude.

Ewing's highly regarded discography includes the Gramophone Award-winning *Don Giovanni* conducted by Bernard Haitink, as well as recordings of *Carmen*, *Salome*, Mozart's *Requiem*, Ravel's *Shéhérazade*, and Debussy's *La damoiselle élue*. She has also recorded song compilations by Rodgers and Hammerstein, Cole Porter, and George Gershwin, among other composers of popular music.

Ewing died of cancer on January 9, 2022, outside of Detroit. She was predeceased in 2017 by her ex-husband, the British theater director Peter Hall, with whom she often worked. She was survived by her daughter, Rebecca, who won acclaim in 2021 for directing *Passing*, a film revolving around two light-skinned Black women that she made, in some part, because of curiosity about her mother.

See Current Biography 1990

Paul Farmer

Born: North Adams, Massachusetts; October 26, 1959
Died: Butaro, Rwanda; February 21, 2022
Occupation: American physician; educator; organization founder; social activist; writer

The cofounder of the international nonprofit Partners in Health and one of the world's leading authorities on the treatment and control of tuberculosis, Paul Farmer devoted his life to bringing medical care to poor communities around the world.

Farmer first learned about Haiti while toiling alongside Haitian migrant workers picking oranges one summer in Florida. He became fascinated by the country, and after graduating from Duke University, he moved there. Dictator Jean-Claude Duvalier was still in power, and Haiti's hospital system was in dire condition, with even the most basic supplies difficult to get.

Inspired to be of practical help, he returned to the United States to attend Harvard, where he earned degrees in anthropology and medicine, returning regularly to Haiti to volunteer. He sometimes walked for hours to ensure that patients in isolated, rural villages were getting their medication.

In 1987 Farmer raised funds to cofound Partners in Health, which started with a single-room clinic and gradually expanded into a network of 16 major medical centers. Patients at the facilities, which feature modern equipment and well-stocked pharmacies, pay as little as $1.50 a day, even in the case of complex diseases like cancer.

Partners in Health is also active in Rwanda, which saw marked decreases in infant mortality and HIV infection following the initiative's launch, as well as in Peru, Russia, and Lesotho. In each locale, Farmer made it a mission to train and employ local medical personnel.

Farmer's many honors include a MacArthur Foundation "genius grant," the American Medical Association's Outstanding International Physician's Award, and the $1 million Berggruen Prize. He is the subject of the 2003 book *Mountains Beyond Mountains: The Quest of Dr. Paul Farmer, a Man Who Would Cure the World*, by Tracy Kidder, as well as a 2017 documentary, *Bending the Arc*.

Farmer died of a heart attack while working in Butaro, Rwanda, on February 21, 2022. He is survived by his wife, Didi, who works as a researcher at Partners in Health; and their three children, Catherine, Elizabeth, and Sebastian.

See Current Biography Illustrated 2004

Aaron Feuerstein

Born: Boston, Massachusetts; December 11, 1925
Died: Boston, Massachusetts; November 4, 2021
Occupation: Small-business owner

In 1995, business owner Aaron Feuerstein gained international attention when he refused to lay off workers at his textile plant after it was destroyed in a fire, then subsequently spent millions of dollars to rebuild it in order to keep them employed.

Malden Mills employed some 25,000 people at that time, and while that number was smaller than in previous decades, due to the ubiquity of cheaper textiles from overseas, Feuerstein had patented a propriety material, Polartec®, which was used by several major manufacturers of athletic apparel, and that kept the mill afloat, even as others closed their doors.

Then, on December 11, 1995, a boiler exploded, and the impact disabled the mill's sprinkler system. That, coupled with high winds that spread the fire to surrounding buildings in the complex, almost completely destroyed the mill. Rather than furlough workers, Feuerstein handed out holiday bonuses and ensured his employees that they would be paid until he could resume operations at the surviving buildings and replace the structures that had been lost in the blaze.

By the first weeks of 1996, hundreds of his employees were back at work, and within two years he reopened fully, in a complex that had cost him a reported $130 million. The story was widely publicized around the world, and Feuerstein became something of a folk hero, with many seeing him as a symbol of resistance to the waves of layoffs and the deindustrialization that had swept across the country in previous decades.

Despite the many feel-good stories published and honors bestowed on Feuerstein (including a front-row seat at the 1996 State of the Union address), the rebuilding efforts had left Malden Mills heavily in debt, and the company, which had been founded by his grandfather almost a century before, went bankrupt in 2001. In a subsequent restructuring plan, he was stripped of management duties, and in 2004 he left the company altogether.

Feuerstein, who was twice widowed, died of pneumonia on November 4, 2021, at a hospital in Boston. He was survived by his children, Daniel, Raphael, and Joyce; and six grandchildren.

See Current Biography 1997

James J. Florio

Born: Brooklyn, New York; August 29, 1937
Died: Voorhees, New Jersey; September 25, 2022
Occupation: American politician

In 1989, after a long stint in the U.S. House of Representatives, James Florio, known to friends and constituents as Jim, was elected governor of New Jersey, and he was awarded the John F. Kennedy Library Foundation's Profile in Courage Award in 1993, for his career achievements in the areas of education, gun control, and economic reform. He was denied a second gubernatorial term, however, by New Jersey voters angered at tax increases he instituted during his tenure.

James Joseph Florio was born into a working-class family in the New York City borough of Brooklyn, on August 29, 1937. He dropped out of high school to join the Navy,

earning a GED during his time in the service and distinguishing himself as an amateur boxer.

Florio, who later served in the Naval Reserves for almost two decades, subsequently returned to school, graduating from Trenton State College in 1962 and earning a law degree from Rutgers University five years later.

While practicing law, he became interested in politics, and during the 1970s he was a state assemblyman. He began his 15-year career in the House in 1974, unseating Republican John E. Hunt. Florio ran unsuccessfully for governor twice as a congressman—in 1977 and 1981; during that second bid he lost to Republican Tom Kean by a margin of only some 2,000 votes out of more than two million.

Florio fared better in 1989, billing himself as a moderate and promising to cut state spending and keep taxes in check. He took office, however, in the midst of an economic crisis that found New Jersey's deficit skyrocketing, and within months he had called for income and sales tax hikes of more than $2.5 billion.

Although his accomplishments included getting a ban on semiautomatic assault weapons passed, capping auto insurance costs, and cracking down on industrial polluters, voters never forgave him for reneging on his promise not to raise taxes, and in 1993 he lost his reelection bid to Republican opponent Christine Todd Whitman. Florio returned to his law practice after that defeat, but he reentered the political arena briefly in 2000, when he unsuccessfully vied for the Democratic nomination in a Senate race.

Florio died of heart failure on September 25, 2022, at a hospital in Voorhees, New Jersey. He was survived by his second wife, Lucinda; children, Chris, Gregory, and Catherine; seven grandchildren; and two great-grandchildren.

See Current Biography 1990

Emile Francis

Born: North Battleford, Saskatchewan, Canada; September 13, 1926
Died: West Palm Beach, Florida; February 19, 2022
Occupation: Ice hockey coach

Hall-of-Famer Emile Francis began his hockey career as a goaltender and went on to become one of the most popular coaches and general managers in the sport; he was especially celebrated for transforming the New York Rangers from NHL underdogs into a powerhouse team.

As a junior player in his native Saskatchewan, the 5-foot-6-inch Francis was known as "The Cat" for his relatively diminutive stature, quick reflexes, and nimble moves. He was signed to the Black Hawks, an NHL franchise, midway through the 1946–47 season and played in a total of 73 games before being traded to the Rangers in October 1948. He got time on the ice in only 22 games over the next four seasons, however, spending most of those years playing instead for New Haven and Cincinnati teams in the American Hockey League.

Francis retired from play after the 1959–60 season and began coaching in the Rangers' minor league organization. In 1962, he was named assistant general manager and promoted two years later to manager. He served in that capacity until 1976, and during his tenure, the Rangers made nine consecutive playoff appearances, reaching at least the semifinals from 1971 to 1974 and making it all the way to the Stanley Cup Final in 1972. He also took on coaching duties during 10 seasons, compiling a record of 342-209-103, with a franchise-topping 75 game wins and 34 playoff wins. Those stats are considered all the more remarkable by hockey aficionados given that when he first came on as GM, the Rangers had not finished first in a six-team league since 1942.

Francis was fired by the Rangers in 1976 and went on to become GM and coach for the St. Louis Blues, compiling a 46-64-14 record. During the final stage of his career, from 1983 to 1989 he served as a senior executive for the Hartford Whalers, who made the playoffs almost every year of his tenure.

Francis died on February 19, 2022; the Rangers announced the death but did not specify exact place or cause. He was survived by his sons, Bobby (an NHL coach) and Rick (a sports marketer), as well as by three grandchildren and a great-grandchild. He was predeceased by his wife, Emma, in 2020.

See Current Biography 1968

Charles Fuller

Born: Philadelphia, Pennsylvania; March 5, 1939
Died: Toronto, Ontario, Canada; October 3, 2022
Occupation: American playwright

When Charles Fuller won the Pulitzer Prize for drama in 1982 for *A Soldier's Play*, he became only the second Black playwright ever to garner that honor. The play—inspired by Herman Melville's *Billy Budd*—looks at the murder of a Black Army officer and the motivations behind it. While it was adapted for the big screen in 1984 (under the new title *A Soldier's Story*), winning Fuller an Oscar nod for his screenplay, it was not mounted on Broadway until 2020. Staged by the Roundabout Theater Company, that belated production earned two Tony Awards.

Charles H. Fuller, Jr. was born on March 5, 1939, in Philadelphia, Pennsylvania, in a neighborhood he described as violent and gang-ridden. He attended a local Catholic school, and a field trip to see a live production inspired him to consider a career in the theater. He attended Villanova University for a few semesters but then dropped out to join the Army; his time in the military, which included stints in South Korea and Japan, later informed *A Soldier's Play* and other works. Upon his discharge, he found work as a Philadelphia housing inspector and took night classes to complete his degree.

In 1968 he helped co-found the Philadelphia-based Afro-American Arts Theater, and that year his first play, *The Village: A Party*, was staged to mixed reviews. By the 1970s, Fuller had made New York his home base, and his plays began to be produced by the Negro Ensemble Company and Henry Street Settlement, among other organizations. These works included *In the Deepest Part of Sleep* (1974), about the effects of a mother's mental illness on a family; *The Brownsville Raid* (1975), which drew upon a true incident in which a group of Black soldiers are accused of a shooting in 1906 Texas; and the Obie-winning *Zooman and the Sign* (1980), about a father's search for justice after the murder of his daughter.

Fuller, who moved to Canada in the late 1980s, died in Toronto on October 3, 2022, at the age of 83. He was survived by his wife,

Claire; a son, David; four grandchildren; and three great-grandchildren.

See Current Biography 1989

Anne Garrels

Born: Springfield, Massachusetts; July 2, 1951
Died: Norfolk, Connecticut; September 7, 2022
Occupation: American broadcast journalist

Anne Garrels covered hotspots around the world, including Tiananmen Square, Bosnia, Chechnya, and Afghanistan. She won particular acclaim for her coverage of the 2003 war in Iraq, which garnered her the George Polk Award, the duPont-Columbia Award, and a Peabody Award—the latter two as part of a team at NPR, her longtime network.

Anne Longworth Garrels was born on July 2, 1951, in Springfield, Massachusetts. Her father's job as an executive at the Monsanto chemical company took the family to London when she was a child, and there she attended an all-girls' Catholic school. She returned to the United States for college, graduating from Middlebury College, in Vermont, in 1972 with a degree in Russian. By 1975 she was working at ABC News, ascending the ranks from researcher to Moscow bureau chief. In 1982, angered by her unflinching reporting on the hardships of life in the former Soviet Union, government officials expelled her.

In 1985, Garrels switched networks, joining NBC's Washington office to cover the U.S. State Department, and three years later she landed at NPR, which sent her for a time back to Moscow. She became renowned at NPR for her bravery and willingness to endure brutal physical conditions—qualities abundantly evident when she was stationed in Iraq during the bloody 2003 conflict there: at one point, she was one of just a dozen or so American journalists not embedded under the protection of U.S. troops to remain in Baghdad, and later, as bombing reached its peak, she was the only one to continue broadcasting from the epicenter of the violence.

Garrels retired as a full-time NPR correspondent in 2010, but continued to file occasional stories, most notably from Russia. In early 2022, as Vladimir Putin invaded Ukraine, she volunteered to travel there to provide coverage. By then, however, she was being treated for lung cancer, and the network declined her offer. In response, she launched a nonprofit that sent much-needed supplies to Ukrainian citizens.

The author of *Naked in Baghdad* (2003), a book about her time in that city, and *Putin Country: A Journey into the Real Russia* (2016), Garrels died at her Norfolk, Connecticut, home on September 7, 2022, at the age of 71, of lung cancer. She was predeceased in 2016 by her husband, James Vinton Lawrence, a onetime CIA operative who went on to become an illustrator. She was survived by her stepdaughters, Rebecca and Gabrielle.

See Current Biography 2004

Don Gehrmann

Born: Milwaukee, Wisconsin; November 16, 1927
Died: Madison, Wisconsin; July 23, 2022
Occupation: American runner

Don Gehrmann had a winning record as a runner, but he is perhaps best remembered for two anomalous incidents. The first occurred in 1950, during an annual race known as the Wanamaker Mile. Although Gehrmann was initially declared the winner, with a time of 4 minutes, 9.3 seconds, some of the judges disagreed, and the presumed second-place finisher officially protested. (The finish-line photo was of no use because someone had blocked the camera.) It took almost an entire year of wrangling among the authorities before Gehrmann's win was finally certified by the Amateur Athletic Union (AAU).

On another occasion, in 1952, he was resting in the stands enjoying a hotdog after breaking the world 1,000-yard outdoor record at an event in London. Suddenly, word reached him that the only American runner scheduled to take part in the quarter-mile race was pulling out because of an injury. Gehrmann gamely offered to run in his stead and ended up winning the race in 47.9 seconds.

Donald Arthur Gehrmann was born on November 16, 1927, in Milwaukee, Wisconsin, where he attended Pulaski High School; he has credited the school gym's slippery floor with honing his running ability. At the University of Wisconsin, he competed in races of up to two miles and won the vast majority of times.

He won almost 40 consecutive major races between 1948 and 1951, including multiple uncontested Wanamaker Miles, three NCAA 1,500-meter outdoor championships and two indoor AAU 1,000-yard titles. In 1950 he was voted best runner in the Big Ten since 1900, thanks to his dozen Big Ten titles.

His running career was relatively short, since at the time, professional track did not exist: the year after his unexpected quarter-mile victory in London he began focusing on making a living, embarking on a career in public relations and later teaching high school, coaching track, and working for the Wisconsin State government. He retired in 1985.

Gehrmann died at a Madison, Wisconsin, nursing home on July 23, 2022, at the age of 94. He was survived by his sons, Don, Tim, and Jim; two daughters, Kathy and Sue; 14 grandchildren; 22 great-grandchildren; and two great-great grandchildren. His wife of more than 70 years, Dolores, predeceased him in 2016.

See Current Biography 1952

Mikhail Gorbachev

Born: Privolnoye, Russia; March 2, 1931
Died: Moscow, Russia; August 30, 2022
Occupation: Russian politician

It is no exaggeration to call Mikhail Gorbachev a revolutionary or transformative leader. Over the course of his tenure, he oversaw the end of the Soviet Union's Cold War with the United States, launched a movement for political and economic reform known as *perestroika*, saw the dismantling of the USSR and the rejection of Communism in former Soviet republics, and instituted a new Russian policy of openness called *glasnost*.

Mikhail Sergeyevich Gorbachev was born on March 2, 1931, in Privolnoye, a Russian farming village, and he grew up in a humble home constructed of straw and mud. A member of the Komsomol—the Communist Party's youth organization—he earned the Order of the Red Banner of Labor and subsequently studied law at Moscow State University—an education that familiarized him with such political thinkers as Hobbes, Hegel, and Machiavelli.

Not long after graduating in 1955, Gorbachev was named first secretary of the Komsomol for the Stavropol region, beginning a steady rise up the political ranks that found him becoming regional party chief in 1970 and a full-fledged member of the Politburo (the USSR's major policy-making organization) in 1980. In 1985, upon the death of Konstantin Chernenko, Gorbachev ascended to the post of general secretary of the Communist Party of the Soviet Union.

In that new capacity, he immediately set out ambitious social and economic goals, calling for increased productivity among workers, a streamlined bureaucracy, and the adoption of modern technology in several sectors. In the late 1980s, under the policies of glasnost and perestroika, journalists enjoyed more freedom, citizens had more autonomy, and the government moved away from the totalitarian rule that had previously been the norm. Some multiparty elections began to take place, and a free-market system was encouraged.

Marking a new era of international cooperation, in 1987, Gorbachev and U.S. President Ronald Reagan agreed to destroy their stockpiles of medium-range nuclear weapons, and the following year the Soviet leader began the process of withdrawing troops from Afghanistan after an almost-decade-long occupation. The era also found several Eastern European nations ousting their communist regimes in favor of democratically elected leaders, and Gorbachev's strong support of them helped garner him the Nobel Peace Prize in 1990. With the USSR gaining more trust and respect on the international stage, Gorbachev took an even more reform-minded leap that year, draining the Politburo of power, eliminating the post of general secretary, and proposing the establishment of a presidency and council of advisers instead. The Central Committee approved the plan, and in March of 1990 Gorbachev was elected to the new presidential post, winning a majority of the vote in the recently instituted Congress of People's Deputies.

In 1991 Communist hard-liners unsuccessfully attempted a coup, and in the wake of that failed attempt, Gorbachev resigned from the Communist Party and eliminated its Central Committee. Soon, however, under the leadership of political rival and member of the Congress of People's Deputies Boris Yeltsin, the

Soviet republics formed a Commonwealth of Independent States. In response, on December 25, 1991, Gorbachev resigned the presidency, marking the formal dissolution of the USSR.

Five years later he again ran for president but received less than one percent of the vote. He remained in the public eye, however, giving lectures, participating in think tanks, and at one point purchasing an interest in the Russian newspaper *Novaya Gazeta*.

Gorbachev died in Moscow on August 30, 2022, at the age of 91. He was survived by his daughter, Irina; two grandchildren; and two great-grandchildren. His wife, Raisa, to whom he had been married since 1953, predeceased him in 1999.

See Current Biography 1996

Almudena Grandes

Born: Madrid, Spain; May 7, 1960
Died: Madrid, Spain; November 27, 2021
Occupation: Spanish novelist

Almudena Grandes is sometimes mentioned as one of the most important Spanish writers of her generation, and her work has been praised for shedding light on the lives of those on the sexual or socioeconomic fringes of traditional society.

Grandes first came to the attention of the literary world in 1989 with *Las Edades de Lulú* (*The Ages of Lulu*), a novel that traces a woman's sexual awakening against the backdrop of a post-dictatorship Madrid in the late 1970s. It sold more than a million copies and was made into a film notable for marking the screen debut of Oscar-winning actor Javier Bardem.

Grandes, who also wrote regularly for the newspaper *El País* (*The Country*), went on to author more than a dozen other novels, many tracing Spain's transformation in the aftermath of the civil war of the 1930s and during the Franco dictatorship. In addition to *Las edades de Lulú*, *Malena es un nombre de tango* (*Malena Is the Name of a Tango*; 1995) and *Los aires difíciles* (*The Wind from the East*; 2002) were also adapted for the screen.

Her more recent volumes include *El Corazón Helado* (*The Frozen Heart*), a dramatic, multigenerational family saga published in 2007; the award-winning *Inés y la alegría* (*Inés*

and Happiness; 2010), which relates the tale of a group of left-wing guerrillas fighting Franco's forces; *Los pacientes del doctor García* (*The Patients of Doctor García*), which was published in 2017 and won both the Jean Monnet Prize for European Literature and the Spanish cultural ministry's National Prize for Narrative; and *La madre de Frankenstein* (*The Mother of Frankenstein*), released in 2020.

The latter three are part of a series Grandes called *Episodios de una guerra interminable* (*Episodes in an Interminable War*), meant to highlight life in Spain during the first 25 years of Franco's dictatorship, from 1939 to 1964.

In 2020, not long after *La madre de Frankenstein* hit bookstore shelves, Grandes disclosed that she had been diagnosed with cancer. She died on November 27, 2021, at her Madrid home. She was survived by her husband, the poet Luis García Montero; their daughter, Elisa García Grandes; and two children from the couple's previous relationships, Mauro Caffarato Grandes and Irene García Chacón.

See Current Biography 2006

Lani Guinier

Born: New York, New York; April 19, 1950
Died: Cambridge, Massachusetts; January 7, 2022
Occupation: American lawyer; educator; writer

Lani Guinier was introduced to the general public in 1993, when President Bill Clinton nominated her as an assistant attorney general for civil rights. Her time in that spotlight was brief, because two months later, in the face of vociferous Republican opposition, he decided to withdraw her from consideration.

Guinier, then a professor at the University of Pennsylvania Law School, had been chosen by Clinton for her rigorous scholarship, reputation for innovative thinking, and leadership of the Voting Rights Project of the NAACP Legal Defense Fund in the 1980s. (In that post she notably won an acquittal for three Black civil rights activists who had been accused of voter fraud by Jeff Sessions, then a U.S. attorney.)

Despite her impressive résumé, conservative Republicans—and even some liberal Democrats—questioned her assertion that the Voting Rights Act had not gone far enough and that in a world where minorities were still badly marginalized, systems should be instituted to balance the scales. At one point, for example, she proposed that voters be granted a number of votes to use as they wished, theoretically allowing minority voters to throw their support behind a single candidate and increase their power as a bloc—a process known as cumulative voting.

After Clinton withdrew her nomination, Guinier returned to the University of Pennsylvania, and in 1998 she joined the faculty of Harvard Law School, where she became the first woman of color to be granted tenure and where she became known for her pioneering scholarship on topics such as implicit bias and merit hiring, which later entered mainstream discourse.

The author of several books, including *The Tyranny of the Majority: Fundamental Fairness in Representative Democracy* (1994), *Lift Every Voice: Turning a Civil Rights Setback Into a New Vision of Social Justice* (1998), and *Who's Qualified?: A New Democracy Forum on the Future of Affirmative Action* (2001), Guinier suffered from Alzheimer's in her later years, and at the time of her death, on January 7, 2022, she was residing in an assisted living facility in Cambridge, Massachusetts. She was survived by her husband, Nolan Bowie, a fellow legal scholar; her son, Nikolas Bowie, a law professor at Harvard; her stepdaughter, Dana Rice; and a granddaughter.

See Current Biography 2004

David Gulpilil

Born: Maningrida, Australia; July 1, 1953
Died: Murray Bridge, Australia; November 29, 2021
Occupation: Australian actor

When the National Aborigines and Islanders Day Observance Committee presented Australian actor David Gulpilil with a lifetime achievement award in 2019, the organization, which is dedicated to advancing Indigenous Australian communities, explained that his onscreen work had "revolutionized the way the world saw Aboriginal people."

David Gulpilil Ridjimiraril Dalaithngu was given his English first name by teachers at a government-run school he attended as a child in Arnhem Land, in Australia's Northern Territory. He was reportedly assigned, at random, the birth date of July 1, 1953, by Christian missionaries.

He began his acting career with a role in the film *Walkabout* (1971), the tale of an Indigenous teen who befriends two white children lost in the wilderness. (The British director Nicolas Roeg had come to Australia seeking Aboriginal cast members.)

Gulpilil's natural affinity led to other onscreen work, including regular appearances on the Australian police series *Boney* (1972–73); the miniseries *Luke's Kingdom* (1976); *Mad Dog Morgan* (1976), a film in which Dennis Hopper stars as an outlaw hiding out in the Australian Outback; and the miniseries *Timeless Land* (1980), a romanticized look at British exploration of the continent.

Gulpilil came to the attention of a much wider audience when he appeared in the hit comedy *Crocodile Dundee* (1980), in which he served as a foil to the main character, a wise-cracking poacher. In later years, Gulpilil became an increasing familiar face to audiences, often called upon to portray an Indigenous person forced to confront modern culture.

In 2014, at the arguable pinnacle of his career, he won a best-actor award at the Cannes Film Festival for his role in *Charlie's Country*, about an Aboriginal man who, distressed by life in an urban area of Australia, returns to the Bush to live.

Despite his relative professional success, Gulpilil had a troubled personal life; struggling with alcoholism, he was arrested numerous times for drunk driving, was convicted of domestic violence, and spent time in prison.

His final picture, released in 2021, was the autobiographical documentary *My Name Is Gulpilil*.

Gulpilil died of lung cancer on November 29, 2021, in Murray Bridge, in South Australia. Married multiple times, he is survived by a large extended family that includes seven children.

See Current Biography 2003

Bernard Haitink

Born: Amsterdam, The Netherlands; March 4, 1929
Died: London, England; October 21, 2021
Occupation: Dutch conductor

During his almost-three-decade tenure at the helm of Amsterdam's Royal Concertgebouw Orchestra, Bernard Haitink gained a reputation as an unassuming maestro, not given to dramatic, heavy-handed stylings and willing to let the orchestra itself shine.

He was, in fact, so unassuming that he almost let the chance to conduct the Royal Concertgebouw Orchestra pass him by when initially approached in 1956, fearful that he was not ready.

He ultimately changed his mind and agreed to step in as a replacement for an ill conductor, and when that performance went well, he became a regular guest conductor. He was appointed co-chief conductor in 1961 and chief conductor two years later.

In addition to his work with Concertgebouw, he was the music director of the Glyndebourne Opera from 1977 to 1988 and of London's Royal Opera from 1987 to 2002. Over the course of his career, he also conducted the London Philharmonic Orchestra, the Boston Symphony Orchestra, the Staatskapelle Dresden, and the Vienna Philharmonic, and in 2006 he became principal conductor of the Chicago Symphony Orchestra.

Throughout his years as a conductor, Haitink—who lived through Nazi occupation during World War II and oversaw the Netherlands Radio Philharmonic Orchestra as a young man—remained unafraid of standing up for his musicians. In 1982, for example, he threatened to boycott the Dutch stage altogether if the Concertgebouw's funding was cut, and in 1998 he resigned briefly from London's Royal Opera over similar concerns.

Haitink's recordings, done for various labels, include the complete symphonies of Mahler, Beethoven, Brahms, Tchaikovsky, and Shostakovich, among others. He did not retire until age 90, following an ambitious farewell tour of several European festivals.

Haitink died in London on October 21, 2021, at the age of 92. He was survived by his fourth wife, Patricia Bloomfield; Willem, Marianne, Robert-Jan, Ingrid, and Tessa (children from his first marriage); and several grandchildren.

See Current Biography 1977

Mustafa Ben Halim

Born: Cyrenaica, Libya; January 29, 1921
Died: United Arab Emirates; December 7, 2021
Occupation: Former premier of Libya; engineer

Mustafa Ben Halim was a Libyan politician who served as his country's third premier, from 1954 to 1957.

The United Kingdom of Libya, created under the auspices of the United Nations in late 1951, unites three North African territories: Tripolitania, Cyrenaica, and Fezzan. The territories had been taken from the Ottoman Empire by Italy in the Tripolitan War of 1911–12 and were occupied by the British and French at the end of World War II. The Emir Idris, hereditary religious leader of the Moslem brotherhood of Senussi, was proclaimed monarch by a Provisional Assembly in 1950.

According to varying sources, Ben Halim had been born in either Cyrenaica, on the eastern coast of modern-day Libya, or in exile in Alexandria, Egypt. He graduated from Alexandria University's civil engineering program and began his professional life at an Egyptian-based firm, but in 1950 he returned to Cyrenaica to help with the reconstruction of the country during its battle for independence. He was appointed Minister of Public Works, and in 1952 he was made Minister of the Province of Cyrenaica. In February 1954 he was asked to become Federal Minister of Communications but two months later he replaced Mohammed Saghisli as premier.

Ben Halim proved himself adept at diplomacy and negotiation, and in April 1955, when a new cabinet was formed, the King asked him to become minister of foreign affairs as well as premier. Ben Halim served as the king's private councilor from 1957 to 1958 and as the Ambassador to France from 1958 to 1960, when he left public service to launch his own business empire, which ultimately came to encompass construction, investment, manufacturing, and energy concerns. He was traveling during the 1969 coup in Libya, and, prevented from returning, he lived in exile for more than four decades, settling at different times in Lebanon and London. (During the early years of Muammar Gaddafi's dictatorship, he was tried in absentia for supposedly engaging in political corruption.)

In 1980, Ben Halim was appointed personal councilor to Crown Prince Fahd bin Abdul Aziz of Saudi Arabia, and in 2011, after Gaddafi's fall, he returned home.

Ben Halim died in the United Arab Emirates on December 7, 2021, at the age of 100. He and his wife, Yusra Kanaan, who was of Palestinian descent, had six children: Amr, an engineer and activist; Hany, a real estate developer; Tarek, a banker and philanthropist who died in 2009; Ahmed, an investment manager; Abir Challah; and Sherine Ben Halim Jafar, an author.

See Current Biography 1956

Darlene Hard

Born: Los Angeles, California; January 6, 1936
Died: Los Angeles, California; December 2, 2021
Occupation: American tennis player

Darlene Hard was the top-ranked American woman tennis player from 1960 to 1963, as well as being number two in the entire world in 1960 and 1961; over the course of her career, she won 21 Grand Slam championships.

She had been introduced to the game by her mother, a solid amateur player who instructed her on the public courts near her Los Angeles home. After graduating from high school, Hard became a presence on the amateur circuit, and in 1958 she won the first intercollegiate tennis championship ever mounted for women. (Famed player Billie Jean King, then a teen, has recalled looking up to her.)

Hard won U.S. amateur titles in 1960 and 1961 and the French title in 1960, making it to the prestigious Wimbledon finals in 1957 and 1959. She also won 13 Grand Slam championships in women's doubles and five in mixed doubles with a variety of partners. In the Wightman Cup, an annual competition between British and American players, she was a pivotal member of four winning teams.

Hard sometimes angered teammates and captains with her blunt, hard-charging style both on the court and off. Known for speaking her mind in often undiplomatic ways, she was written up by a team captain in 1962 for being "a disruptive element." (In 1957, before a Wimbledon final, she met Queen Elizabeth II and then, ignoring protocol, turned her back to the monarch to head to the locker room.)

Later in life, Hard taught tennis and owned two tennis shops. One of her tennis students, who worked at the University of Southern California, offered Hard an administrative job in 1981, and she remained there for almost four decades.

Hard died in Los Angeles on December 2, 2021, not long after retiring. Her death was announced by the International Tennis Hall of Fame, but no information was given on her survivors.

See Current Biography 1964

Orrin G. Hatch

Born: Homestead Park, Pennsylvania; March 22, 1934
Died: Salt Lake City, Utah; April 23, 2022
Occupation: American politician

Republican Orrin Hatch of Utah spent seven terms in the U.S. Senate: Over the course of his 42-year tenure, he worked under seven presidents and sponsored or co-sponsored approximately 12,000 pieces of legislation.

Orrin Grant Hatch's childhood has been described as "Dickensian." Born into a Mormon family in Homestead, Pennsylvania, on March 22, 1934, during the Great Depression, he grew up with eight siblings in a home with no indoor plumbing. After leaving high school to do missionary work, Hatch studied history at Brigham Young University (where he paid the tuition by working as a lathe operator), and earned a law degree from the University of Pittsburgh in 1962, thanks to a full scholarship. (While in law school, he lived with his wife and young children in a rebuilt chicken coop behind his parents' home.)

Following a stint in private practice, he decided to enter politics, disturbed by what he saw as the country's drift to the left and an erosion of traditional values. In 1977 he was elected to the Senate, where he was mentored by seasoned conservatives like Jim Allen and Strom Thurmond. Hatch went on to win reelection in 1982, 1988, 1994, 2000, 2006, and 2012.

Throughout that time, he burnished his conservative credentials, staunchly opposing abortion (his proposed "Hatch Amendment" asserts that there is no constitutional right to abortion), speaking out against social welfare programs, supporting tax cuts, serving as a booster for the wars in Afghanistan and Iraq, pushing tougher immigration policies, and trumpeting U.S. withdrawal from the Paris climate change accords, among other such stances.

As a member of the Senate Judiciary Committee, Hatch was also a major figure in getting conservative justices nominated to the U.S. Supreme Court. He was in the spotlight, for example, during Clarence Thomas's contentious but ultimately successful confirmation hearings, and he effectively blocked President Barack Obama's nomination of Merrick Garland, asserting that the confirmation process should wait until the next president was sworn in.

Hatch, who was awarded the Presidential Medal of Freedom by Donald Trump in 2018, died on April 23, 2022, in Salt Lake City, from complications of a stroke. He was survived by his wife, Elaine, to whom he had been married since 1957; his sons, Brent, Scott, and Jess; his daughters, Marcia, Kimberly, and Alysa; 23 grandchildren; and 36 great-grandchildren.

See Current Biography 1982

Anne Heche

Born: Aurora, Ohio; May 25, 1969
Died: Los Angeles, California; August 11, 2022
Occupation: American actor

Anne Heche was known for her roles in such films as *Donnie Brasco* (1997) and *Wag the Dog* (1997), as well as in television projects like *Ally McBeal* (2001), *Everwood* (2004–05), *Men in Trees* (2006–08), *Hung* (2009–2011), and *Chicago P.D.* (2018–19). She received equal attention, however, for her personal life: Heche openly entered into a romance with fellow entertainer Ellen DeGeneres in the late 1990s—an era in which same-sex relationships were often kept hidden in Hollywood—generating intense press coverage and impacting her career.

Anne Celeste Heche was born on May 25, 1969, in Aurora, Ohio. In a 2001 memoir, she revealed that her father, a closeted gay man, had sexually abused her as a child and her mother accused her of fabricating the accusation. After Heche's father died of AIDS in the early 1980s, her mother became a Christian-oriented therapist who advised clients to avoid acting on their same-sex attractions.

In 1987, after Heche graduated high school, she began appearing on the soap opera *Another World*, playing twins: one conventionally good and one evil. In 1991, she won a Daytime Emmy for her believable portrayal.

The 1990s found her acting in a succession of films opposite such stars as Johnny Depp (*Donnie Brasco*), Dustin Hoffman and Robert De Niro (*Wag the Dog*), Ed Harris (*Milk Money*), Demi Moore and Alec Baldwin (*The Juror*), and Harrison Ford (*Six Days, Seven Nights*). Her career suffered, however, after she and DeGeneres came out publicly as gay.

Gradually, the film industry—and society in general—became more accepting of same-sex relationships, and professionally, Heche rebounded somewhat, appearing frequently in television movies and series, as well as on the big screen in such pictures as *John Q* (2002), *What Love Is* (2007), *The Last Word* (2017), and *13 Minutes* (2021), which, while not blockbusters, drew modestly favorable notices.

She struggled on a personal level, however, and tabloids regularly reported on her drug use and mental health challenges, particularly after she and DeGeneres split, her subsequent marriage to a man ended in divorce, and she became embroiled in a messy custody battle.

On August 5, 2022, Heche, later proven to have cocaine in her system, was involved in a fiery car crash that left her brain-dead. On August 11, at a Los Angeles hospital, she was removed from life support and died. She was survived by her two sons, Homer Laffoon and Atlas Heche Tupper.

See Current Biography 1998

Hazel Henderson

Born: Bristol, Somerset, England; March 27, 1933
Died: St. Augustine, Florida; May 22, 2022
Occupation: Anglo-American environmentalist and economist

Hazel Henderson is credited with spreading the slogan "think globally, act locally," a call for more environmentally sustainable practices and policies.

Henderson was born Jean Hazel Mustard on March 27, 1933, in England, into a family that grew its own vegetables and raised chickens. After graduating from high school in 1950, she worked a series of odd jobs, including hotel clerk and telephone operator.

She had no interest in attending college, and after moving to New York City in 1957 with her first husband, a journalist, she became involved in the nascent environmental movement—spurred on when she found her young daughter regularly covered in soot and dirt spewing from the city's garbage incinerators. She soon helped found Citizens for Clean Air, which advocated for an air pollution index to be mentioned during daily weather reports.

Henderson also became known for her unconventional and forward-thinking economic views: she believed, for example, that gross national product (GNP) should include not just the value of goods and services but measurements of health, education, and other social factors. Asserting that CEOs and major shareholders should not profit at the expense of other stakeholders, she put forth the concept of ethical investing, founding the company Ethical Markets Media to promulgate her ideas.

Among her many books were: *The Politics of the Solar Age: Alternatives to Economics* (1981), *Building a Win-Win World: Life Beyond Global Economic Warfare* (1996), *Planetary Citizenship: Your Values, Beliefs and Actions Can Shape a Sustainable World* (2004), and *Ethical Markets: Growing the Green Economy* (2007).

Although she never earned a college degree, Henderson—the co-recipient of the 1996 Boston Research Center's Global Citizen Award—served as an adviser to such groups as the National Academy of Engineering and the National Science Foundation; held an endowed chair in conservation at the University of California, Berkeley; and lectured at the University of California, Santa Barbara.

Henderson died on May 22, 2022, at her St. Augustine, Florida, home from skin cancer. She was survived by her daughter, Alexandra, and a grandson. She was predeceased in 2016 by her second husband, internet pioneer Alan Kay.

See Current Biography 2003

Martha Henry

Born: Detroit, Michigan; February 17, 1938
Died: Stratford, Ontario, Canada; October 21, 2021
Occupation: American-born Canadian actress; theater director

Martha Henry was often called first lady of the Canadian stage, and she was especially celebrated for her decades of performances at the Stratford Festival of Canada.

Henry acted in public for the first time in a play put on by her childhood Brownie troop, which she had joined expressly for the chance to be on a stage. As a teen, she often traveled with her mother, who was part of a roving entertainment troupe, and she grew to love the backstage camaraderie.

In 1959 Henry graduated from what is now called the Carnegie Mellon University School of Drama, and the following year, she entered the National Theater School in Montreal, only to be told halfway through the three-year program that her instructors had taught her all they could, and she should be forging her professional career. She was immediately accepted into the company of the Stratford Festival and made her debut there as Miranda in a production of *The Tempest*.

She ultimately acted in more than 70 productions and directed 14 others at the festival, and among her most acclaimed roles were Isabella in Shakespeare's *Measure for Measure*, Beatrice in Shakespeare's *Much Ado About Nothing*, and Mary in Eugene O'Neill's *Long Day's Journey into Night*. Her final role in Stratford came in a 2021 production of Edward Albee's *Three Tall Women*. Ill with cancer, she used a walker during the first shows of the season in August, and by the time it closed, on October 9, she was performing from a wheelchair.

Henry died at her Stratford home just weeks later, on October 21. She was survived by her third husband, the actor Rod Beattie, and a daughter, Emma Rain, from her second marriage.

See Current Biography 2006

Dave Hickey

Born: Fort Worth, Texas; December 5, 1940
Died: Santa Fe, New Mexico; November 12, 2021
Occupation: American cultural critic; educator; writer; curator of exhibitions

Dave Hickey was considered one of the most divisive and iconoclastic cultural critics of his day.

He first came to widespread attention with the1993 book *The Invisible Dragon: Four Essays on Beauty*, considered incendiary as the term "beauty" had been deemed exclusionary and elitist by many critics in that decade. His follow-up, *Air Guitar: Essays on Art and Democracy* (1997), cemented his reputation as a free thinker, unafraid to buck the art establishment and its conventions. (He felt, for example, that there was little distinction between highbrow and lowbrow culture and that aesthetic judgments were purely subjective.) In 2016, he published *Wasted Words* and *Dust Bunnies*, both of which consisted of his thousands of social media posts and the collection *25 Women: Essays on Their Art*.

In addition to those books, Hickey wrote numerous exhibition catalogs, mounted gallery shows, and often lectured. He also taught at such schools as the University of Nevada and the University of New Mexico. Among his honors were a 1994 Frank Jewett Mather Award for art criticism and a 2001 "genius" grant from the MacArthur Foundation. (He claimed to have earmarked the MacArthur Foundation money to play poker in Las Vegas.)

At various times in his life, Hickey owned an art gallery, wrote country music in Nashville, served as the executive editor of the respected periodical *Art in America*, and wrote pieces for a variety of outlets, including *Rolling Stone* and the *Village Voice*.

Despite his professional accomplishments, there were periods in his life when Hickey was known for heavy drug use and partying with figures like Andy Warhol, the members of Aerosmith, and Waylon Jennings. He was given to pronouncements that would now be considered sexist or socially unacceptable but maintained a wide variety of friends.

Hickey died of heart disease on November 12, 2021, in Santa Fe, New Mexico, where he had settled with his wife, art historian Libby Lumpkin. She survives him, as does his brother, Michael.

See Current Biography 2007

A. Linwood Holton Jr.

Born: Big Stone Gap, Virginia; September 21, 1953
Died: Kilmarnock, Virginia; October 28, 2021
Occupation: Former governor of Virginia and lawyer

Abner Linwood Holton, Jr., a moderate Republican, served as governor of Virginia from 1969 to 1974 and was widely praised for his commitment to racial equality, attention to environmental concerns, and transformative tenure.

Holton, whose father owned a small coal-mine railroad, grew up in Big Stone Gap, a mining town in southwestern Virginia. After serving in the U.S. Navy during World War II, he studied law at Harvard, and when he graduated in 1949, he returned to Virginia to practice in Roanoke. He soon became active in the local Republican Party, which had little support in a state that was dominated by Democrats—including Harry F. Byrd, Sr., a white supremacist who had served as a governor and senator and who had been a driving force in Virginia politics for decades.

Holton held to the moderate conservatism embodied by Dwight D. Eisenhower, and he hoped that a Republican Party dedicated to racial equality and economic development would resonate with voters. Those hopes initially seemed fruitless; he was defeated in his 1955 and 1957 bids for a seat in Virginia's House of Delegates, and in 1965 he lost the gubernatorial race to an avowed segregationist.

Holton ran for governor again in 1969, and this time, with the support of Richard Nixon, the state's labor unions, and the Black community, he was elected. During his tenure, which lasted until 1974, Holton cleaned up Virginia's waterways, expanded access to abortion, and pushed for increased integration. (Even as many white parents sent their children to private schools in response to busing, Holton's children attended newly integrated public schools.) After leaving office, Holton served as the assistant secretary of state for congressional relations in the Nixon administration and then resumed his private law practice.

He died at his home in Kilmarnock, Virginia, on October 28, 2021, and was survived by his wife, Virginia ("Jinks"); their children, Anne, Woody, Dwight, and Tayloe; and several grandchildren.

See Current Biography 1971

bell hooks

Born: Hopkinsville, Kentucky; September 25, 1952
Died: Berea, Kentucky; December 15, 2021
Occupation: African American essayist, poet, and educator

The writer and feminist bell hooks, who preferred her name to be written in all lower case-letters, believed that mainstream feminism had marginalized the experiences of Black women and those from other underrepresented groups, and her writing did much to bring that issue to the fore and encourage change.

Although that is the topic for which she is best-known, thanks in large part to her seminal 1981 volume *Ain't I a Woman? Black Women and Feminism*, she also wrote widely about American history, economics, education, and relationships, and her oeuvre includes children's books, memoir, poetry, and literary criticism.

hooks, whose name at birth was Gloria Jean Watkins, grew up attending segregated schools in her small Kentucky town, and although she experienced racism firsthand, she drew solace from being part of a tightknit Black community.

While still an undergraduate at Stanford University, she began work on *Ain't I a Woman?*, although her first published work was the 1978 poetry collection *And There We Wept*. (It was then that she adopted her pen name, in homage to her grandmother Bell Blair Hooks.)

She went on to publish some 30 other books, including *Feminist Theory: From Margin to Center* (1984), *Yearning: Race, Gender, and Cultural Politics* (1990), *Teaching to Transgress: Education as the Practice of Freedom* (1994), the autobiographical *Bone Black: Memories of Girlhood* (1996), the children's book *Happy to Be Nappy* (1999), *Salvation: Black People and Love* (2001), *We Real Cool: Black Men and Masculinity* (2004), and *Writing Beyond Race: Living Theory and Practice* (2013).

hooks taught at such schools as the University of Southern California, Oberlin, and Yale, but she is most identified with her time at Kentucky's Berea College, which in about 2014 founded the bell hooks Institute in her honor.

hooks died on December 15, 2021, at her Berea home from end-stage renal failure. She was survived by four sisters and a brother.

See Current Biography 1995

William Hurt

Born: Washington, DC; March 20, 1950
Died: Portland, Oregon; March 13, 2022
Occupation: American actor

William Hurt enjoyed a heyday in the 1980s: he appeared in such big-screen hits as the steamy thriller *Body Heat* (1981); *The Big Chill* (1983), a heartwarming ensemble picture; *Children of a Lesser God* (1986), in which he plays a teacher at a school for the deaf; and the romantic comedy *Broadcast News* (1987), and he won an Academy Award for his portrayal of an imprisoned gay man in the 1985 film *Kiss of the Spider Woman*.

William McChord Hurt was born on March 20, 1950, in Washington, DC, where his father worked for the U.S. State Department. After his parents' marriage ended, his mother married Henry Luce III, the wealthy son of the founder of *Time* magazine, and Hurt was thus raised in relative privilege.

After studying acting at Juilliard, Hurt made a mark in the New York theater world, earning solid reviews for his work in a variety of plays, including *Henry V* in 1976, Lanford Wilson's *Fifth of July* in 1978, *Hamlet* in 1979, and *Childe Byron* in 1981. In 1985, he won a Tony for his role in the darkly comedic *Hurlyburly*.

By the time of that award, Hurt had also established himself as leading-man material in Hollywood. His first high-profile picture came in 1980, with *Altered States*, in which he portrays a scientist who experiments with mind-bending drugs and a sensory-deprivation tank.

A string of other hits followed, cementing Hurt's reputation as an intellectual and sexy presence on the screen. In addition to his Oscar for *Kiss of the Spider Woman*, Hurt received best-actor nods for *Children of a Lesser God* and *Broadcast News*—placing him in the spotlight during the awards ceremony for three consecutive years—and later, for *A History of Violence* (2005).

Hurt was introduced to a new generation of fans in 2016, when he played Secretary of State Thaddeus Ross in the big-budget Marvel picture *Captain America: Civil War*; he reprised the role in *Avengers: Infinity War* (2018), *Avengers: Endgame* (2019), and *Black Widow* (2021).

Hurt's final onscreen appearance was in the historical drama *The King's Daughter* (2022), and he could also be heard that year in multiple episodes of the animated television series *Pantheon*. He died at his home in Portland, Oregon, on March 13, 2022, from prostate cancer. He was survived by his sons, Alexander, Samuel, and William Jr.; a daughter Jeanne; and two grandchildren.

See Current Biography 1986

Nobuyuki Idei

Born: Tokyo, Japan; November 22, 1937
Died: Tokyo, Japan; June 2, 2022
Occupation: Japanese businessman

Nobuyuki Idei helmed the electronics and entertainment giant Sony from 1999 to 2005, a transformative period in which the company entered the Internet Age, embracing digital technology and transforming the world of video games.

Born on November 22, 1937, in Tokyo, Idei attended Waseda University, first studying photography but then switching to economics at the urging of his father, a professor in that field. Some sources also list his attendance at the London School of Economics and l'Institut des hautes études internationales in Geneva, Switzerland—stints that forced him to become proficient in English and French.

The daughter of Sony's co-founder was a college classmate, and in 1960 she arranged for him to interview at the Tokyo-based company, then trying to expand into Europe. Idei started out in the international division, helping to establish Sony France in 1968. In a steady rise through the corporate ranks, he began managing the audio division—home of Sony's enormously popular "Walkman" portable music player—in 1979 and the home video group in 1988.

A succession of top titles followed: the next year, he was named director of Sony Corp., and in 1994 he became managing director of the company. In early 1995, Idei ascended to the Sony presidency, and in June 1999 he stepped into the role of CEO, adding the chairmanship in 2000.

At the helm of the massive company, then valued at well over $100 billion, Idei pushed his engineers to be "Digital Dream Kids," entering into partnerships with companies like Intel and spearheading the development of interconnected devices and platforms. He also focused on global expansion, and the company's PlayStation games system quickly became an industry leader worldwide.

Despite his innovative ideas and solid stewardship, Sony went through periods of downturn, and Idei, who had been appointed to lead the Japanese government's IT Strategy Council in 2000, stepped down as CEO in 2005. He subsequently launched an independent management consultancy, and for several years he co-chaired the Japan Business Federation.

Idei died of liver failure on June 2, 2022, in Tokyo. He was survived by his wife, Teruyo, and their daughter.

See Current Biography 1997

Shintarō Ishihara

Born: Suma-ku, Kobe, Japan; September 30, 1932
Died: Ōta City, Tokyo, Japan; February 1, 2022
Occupation: Japanese author and politician

Shintarō Ishihara served as mayor of Tokyo from 1999 to 2012, earning a reputation as a contentious right-winger, eager to exert independence from and dominance over other nations.

Before becoming a politician, Ishihara was a writer whose debut novel, *Season of Violence* (1955), about a disillusioned and demoralized postwar Japan, won the prestigious Akutagawa Prize.

Although he continued to write (and eventually had numerous books and screenplays to his credit), in 1968 he entered politics, getting elected to Japan's parliament, the National Diet, as a member of the Liberal Democratic Party. He was elected mayor of

Tokyo in 1999 and served a total of four times. His accomplishments during that tenure included instituting regulations to cut carbon emissions, setting up loan programs for small businesses, and attracting the 2020 Summer Olympics to his city.

Ishihara drew the most attention, however, for his views on foreign policy, which involved pursuing aggressive action against China (often using derogatory language when he discussed that country), toughening Japan's relationship with the United States, and striving to build a strong nuclear-weapons program. After his tenure, he spent the next two years supporting right-wing causes and political parties but officially retired from politics in 2014.

Known for his misogynistic and racist views, Ishihara continued to write for at least an hour a day, almost up until the time of his death, on February 1, 2022, of pancreatic cancer. He was survived by his wife, Noriko, and sons, Nobuteru, Yoshizumi, Hirotaka, and Nobuhiro. He had once reportedly asserted to a journalist that he hoped that by the time he died he was hated by people for saying and doing exactly what he wanted to.

See Current Biography 2000

Morton L. Janklow

Born: Queens, New York; May 30, 1930
Died: Water Mill, New York; May 25, 2022
Occupation: American literary agent and lawyer

Morton Lloyd Janklow, one of the world's highest-profile literary agents, was known for negotiating multimillion-dollar book deals for novelists like Danielle Steel, Sidney Sheldon, and Judith Krantz, as well as for public figures like Pope John Paul II, and Presidents Richard M. Nixon, Jimmy Carter, and Ronald Reagan.

Janklow was born in the New York City borough of Queens on May 30, 1930. A high-achieving student, he graduated high school at age 16 and entered Syracuse University, where he studied political science and paid some of his tuition with poker winnings. He subsequently earned a law degree from Columbia Law School in 1953, joined the Army, and began practicing law in Manhattan upon his discharge.

Janklow entered the literary world after being approached by William Safire, a college

friend who had gone on to write speeches for Nixon; with Janklow's help, Safire negotiated a solid deal for his nonfiction book about the Nixon presidency, *Before the Fall*, which was released in 1975. When Safire wrote his first novel, *Full Disclosure*, Janklow arranged to sell the paperback rights to the 1977 political potboiler for more than $1 million.

That year, Janklow opened his own agency, and in 1980 he sold the paperback rights to Judith Krantz's *Princess Daisy* for a record-setting $3.2 million. His client list soon resembled a bestsellers list Who's Who, and it was not unusual to open *The New York Times* to find multiple books he had sold on its various lists. (In one notable example, in late 1989, Danielle Steel's *Daddy* perched at number one on the hardcover-fiction list, while Nancy Reagan held the same spot on the nonfiction list with *My Turn* and Sidney Sheldon dominated paperback fiction with the action-packed juggernaut *The Sands of Time*.)

Janklow—a tireless self-promoter who charged his clients 15 percent instead of the more customary 10 percent—was sometimes accused of coarsening the literary landscape by representing so many authors of formulaic, mass-market works. While he shrugged such criticism off, in 1988 he partnered with agent Lynn Nesbit, known for a more highbrow stable of authors, to form Janklow & Nesbit Associates, which has counted respected figures like Toni Morrison and Tom Wolfe among its clients.

Janklow died on May 25, 2022, at his Water Mill, New York home, of heart failure. He was survived by his second wife, the former Linda LeRoy; two children; and six grandchildren.

See Current Biography 1997

Mwai Kibaki

Born: Gatuyaini, Kenya; November 15, 1931
Died: Nairobi, Kenya; May 21, 2022
Occupation: Kenyan president

Kenya won independence from Great Britain in 1963, and in 2002 Mwai Kibaki became the nation's third president, following the tenures of Jomo Kenyatta (1964–78) and Daniel arap Moi (1978–2002). Kibaki's administration, which lasted until 2013, was tarred by accusations of corruption and political violence that sometimes overshadowed his accomplishments.

Born Emilio Mwai Kibaki on November 15, 1931, in the central Kenyan village of Gatuyaini, he studied history and political science at Uganda's Makerere University and later attended the London School of Economics. Once Kenya had won its independence, he joined the Kenya African National Union party, and from 1969 to 1981, he was appointed finance minister. During much of Moi's time in office, from 1978 to 1988, Kibaki was Kenya's vice president.

Not content to be second in command, Kibaki unsuccessfully challenged Moi in 1992 and 1997, and when term limits prevented Moi from running for another term, Kibaki again threw his hat in the ring. This time, he triumphed, and he began his tenure promising to fight the graft that had been rife under his predecessor. While he succeeded in revitalizing the Kenyan economy to some extent, introducing the idea of free primary school, improving the highway system, and expanding healthcare access, government corruption remained a major problem, and upper-echelon officials were regular sources of scandal.

After Kibaki won his hotly contested reelection bid in 2007, Kenya descended into violence and political chaos, and it took weeks—and the intervention of the U.N. — for him and his rivals to reach a power-sharing agreement. He subsequently helped draft a new constitution aimed at providing Kenyans with more freedoms and mitigating power imbalances; it was approved by a wide margin in 2010.

Kibaki served two terms as president, stepping down in 2013, when Uhuru Kenyatta took office. Kibaki died on May 21, 2022, in Nairobi, at the age of 90, and the nation entered an official period of mourning, with flags flown at half-staff. His wife, Lucy, had predeceased him in 2016; he was survived by his children, Judy, Jimmy, David, and Tony.

See Current Biography 2003

William Klein

Born: New York, New York; April 19, 1926
Died: Paris, France; September 10, 2022
Occupation: American photographer and filmmaker

William Klein was known for his experimental, iconoclastic approach to photography and for capturing a unique vision of street life in such major cities as New York, Paris, and Tokyo.

Klein was born in Manhattan on April 19, 1926, and was one of the few Jewish boys in a predominantly Irish enclave. His parents, immigrants from Europe, owned a clothing business, but it failed during the Great Depression, and Klein took solace in viewing the art in the city's many museums. He attended City College of New York, a public institution, but joined the Army before graduating.

Upon his discharge in 1948, he settled in Paris, where he had been stationed for a time, and there he studied with renowned artist Fernand Léger and rented a studio on the Left Bank. From the mid-1950s to the mid-1960s, he was under contract at *Vogue*, and in that capacity, he captured many of the cityscapes for which he became celebrated.

In addition to his photos, which he also published in book-length volumes, Klein turned to filmmaking, starting in 1966 with *Who Are You, Polly Maggoo?*, a spoof of the fashion world he had learned so well at *Vogue*. It was his documentaries, however, that captured the attention of film critics, particularly *Muhammad Ali, the Greatest*—a two-part 1969 film about the boxer and activist that was later retitled *Float Like a Butterfly, Sting Like a Bee*, after one of the heavyweight champ's catchphrases—and *Eldridge Cleaver, Black Panther* (1970), a progressively minded look at the controversial revolutionary.

His other movies included *Far from Vietnam* (1967), on which he collaborated with Jean-Luc Godard; *Mr. Freedom* (1968), a superhero satire; *Le couple témoin* (1977), a work of science fiction; *The Little Richard Story* (1980), a documentary about the rock-and-roll pioneer; the television movie *Made in France* (1985); and his final effort, *Messiah* (1999), about the Handel oratorio.

Klein died in Paris on September 10, 2022, at the age of 96. He was predeceased in 2005 by his wife, Jeanne, whom he had met his first week in Paris and married soon after. He was survived by their son, Pierre.

See Current Biography 2004

Leonid Kravchuk

Born: Velykyi Zhytyn, Poland (now Ukraine); January 10, 1934
Died: Munich, Germany; May 10, 2022
Occupation: Ukrainian politician

Following the collapse of the USSR, Leonid Kravchuk, a former Communist Party leader, became the first democratic president of Ukraine.

Leonid Makarovych Kravchuk was born on January 10, 1934, in Velykyi Zhytyn, a village in what was then Poland. His father, a farmer, had been killed during World War II. After studying Marxism and economics at Kiev T.H. Shevchenko State University, he embarked on a career in academia and joined the Communist Party. He subsequently rose steadily through party ranks, and by the 1980s, he had held positions of responsibility in the propaganda and ideology branches.

Kravchuk ascended to the post of Ukrainian Supreme Soviet chair in mid-1990, but watching the Communists fall out of favor in Moscow, he quit the party the following year and became a strong proponent of Ukrainian independence. In December 1991, he was elected by a wide margin as president of the newly independent nation.

Among his first actions as leader was signing a multinational agreement concerning the formal dismantling of the Soviet Union. Although Ukraine was then the third-biggest nuclear power in the world, directly behind the United States and Russia, he agreed to give up the country's stockpiles, in exchange for security guarantees. (Later, after Russian leader Vladimir Putin invaded Ukraine in early 2022, many political observers second-guessed that decision.)

In 1994, Kravchuk lost his reelection bid to Leonid Kuchma but remained an advocate for peace and independence. In 2020, he was appointed to represent Ukraine in the Trilateral Contact Group, alongside Russia and the Organization for Security and Cooperation in Europe.

In 2021, Kravchuk required heart surgery, and even after a long stint in intensive care, his health continued to deteriorate. He died on May 10, 2022, at a rehabilitation facility in Germany. He was survived by his wife, Antonina, a college professor; their son, Oleksandr; two grandchildren; and a great-grandchild.

See Current Biography 1993

Saul A. Kripke

Born: Bay Shore, New York; November 13, 1940
Died: Plainsboro, New Jersey; September 15, 2022
Occupation: American philosopher

Saul Kripke, the winner of the Royal Swedish Academy of Sciences Rolf Shock Prize (considered comparable in prestige to the Nobel), is considered among the most erudite and thoughtful philosophers of his era.

Saul Aaron Kripke was born into a religious Jewish family on November 13, 1940, in Bay Shore, a town on New York's Long Island. When he was a child, the family moved to Omaha, where his father, a rabbi, led a large congregation. Friends with the legendary financial whiz Warren Buffett, the elder Kripke had earned millions by the 1990s by following Buffett's advice.

Kripke was something of a prodigy, teaching himself Hebrew and reading the complete works of Shakespeare all before the age of 10. He graduated from Harvard in 1962—teaching a graduate class in logic at MIT during his sophomore year. Although he, himself, never earned a graduate degree, he took on a string of professorships at such schools as Rockefeller University and Princeton. In 2003, he joined the faculty of the City University of New York and was named a distinguished professor of philosophy and computer science. In 2007, the University's Graduate Center opened the Saul Kripke Center with the goal of collecting and disseminating his work, much of which had never been published, as he was known to deliver his lectures extemporaneously.

One notable exception was the seminal volume *Naming and Necessity*, drawn from a series of lectures he had given in Princeton in 1970 and published originally in 1972. The book, which has been reprinted more than a dozen times, introduced the term "rigid designator" to the philosophy world—indicating a term applied to the same object in *all* possible worlds and which thus must necessarily be true.

Kripke died on September 15, 2022, at the age of 81, while being treated for pancreatic cancer at a medical center in Plainsboro, New Jersey. His marriage to fellow philosopher Margaret Gilbert ended in divorce, and he was predeceased by his siblings, leaving no immediate survivors.

See Current Biography 2004

Guy Lafleur

Born: Thurso, Quebec, Canada; September 20, 1951
Died: Montreal, Quebec, Canada; April 22, 2022
Occupation: Canadian hockey player

Guy Lafleur, who helped the Montreal Canadiens win five Stanley Cup championships, is widely considered to be one of the greatest hockey players of all time.

Guy Damien Lafleur was born in Quebec on September 20, 1951, and fell in love with the game at an early age, avidly watching the Canadiens on television and sneaking into a local arena to practice whenever the rink was empty.

As a member of a junior team, he scored 103 goals during the 1969–70 season and topped that the following year with 130. As he had long dreamed, in 1971 the Canadiens made him their number-one pick in the NHL draft.

Lafleur had his breakout season in 1974–75, scoring 53 goals and establishing a reputation for bravado and self-assurance on the ice. Fans chanted his name during games, and so high did his profile rise that the team had to hire security for him during the 1976 playoffs, because he was receiving kidnapping threats. He faced a threat of another kind two years later, when the coach of the Boston Bruins encouraged his players to rough him up in an effort to stop him from scoring during a playoff game. (Even with the resulting head injury, he still recorded three goals and two assists.)

During Lafleur's 14 season with the Canadiens, the team won five Stanley Cups: in 1972–73, 1975–76, 1976–77, 1977–78, and 1978–79. With them, he became the first player in league history to make at least 50 goals and 100 points in six consecutive seasons. Despite his performance and star power, Lafleur went through a period of butting heads with the

team's general manager and coach, and midway through the 1984–85 season, he suddenly quit.

He did not remain off the ice long, however: in 1988 he joined the New York Rangers for a season and then returned to Canada to cap off his career by playing two seasons with the Nordiques. Among his career honors were induction into the Hockey Hall of Fame in 1988, three Art Ross Trophies (given to the player who leads the league in scoring for the season), and two Hart Memorial MVP Trophies.

Lafleur, a longtime smoker, died of cancer at a Montreal hospice on April 22, 2022. He was survived by his wife, Lise; his sons, Martin and Mark; a granddaughter; and his mother.

See Current Biography 1980

Moon Landrieu

Born: New Orleans, Louisiana; July 23, 1930
Died: New Orleans, Louisiana; September 5, 2022
Occupation: American lawyer and politician

Democrat Moon Landrieu served as the two-term mayor of New Orleans from 1970 to 1978. Known as a staunch proponent of integration, he notably earned the support of 99 percent of the city's Black voters in his first mayoral race.

He was born Maurice Edwin Landrieu on July 23, 1930, in a racially diverse neighborhood in New Orleans. (Moon was a childhood nickname that he legally adopted during his bid to lead the city.) The product of a Jesuit high school, he earned a baseball scholarship to Loyola University, graduating with a bachelor's degree in business administration in 1952 and a law degree two years later. After serving until 1957 in the Army's Judge Advocate General's Corps, he returned home to practice law.

Within a few years, Landrieu had entered the political arena, representing the city's Twelfth Ward in the State House from 1960 to 1966 and becoming known for his firm opposition to segregation—still an issue as the city worked to integrate schools and other public institutions. He then sat on the City Council as a member-at-large until mounting his mayoral campaign. (While on the Council, he led a push to remove the Confederate flag from its chambers.)

Landrieu easily won the Democratic primary in 1969, thanks in part to the backing of 90 percent of New Orleans's Black voters; in the general election, that figure jumped to almost 100 percent. As mayor, he appointed several Black officials to high-ranking positions, continued to push the integration of public facilities, and poured money into the revitalization of poor neighborhoods. Although he was sometimes criticized for his overly ambitious building and tourism-related projects, he easily won a second term in 1974 and served until 1978. Landrieu—who was also president of the United States Conference of Mayors from 1975 to 1976—was succeeded by the city's first Black mayor, Dutch Morial.

Landrieu's other high-level posts include U.S. Secretary of Housing and Urban Development under President Jimmy Carter (1979–81) and Louisiana State Appellate Judge (1992–2000). He died on September 5, 2022, at the age of 92, at his home in his native city. He was survived by his wife of more than six decades, Verna; daughters, Melanie, Melinda, Shelley, Madeleine, and Mary (who was a U.S. senator from 1997 to 2015); sons, Martin, Mark, Maurice, and Mitch (who was elected mayor of New Orleans in 2010 and, like his father, served two terms); 37 grandchildren; and 16 great-grandchildren.

See Current Biography 1980

Angela Lansbury

Born: London, England; October 16, 1925
Died: Los Angeles, California; October 11, 2022
Occupation: American actor

Over the course of her career, Angela Lansbury found success on the stage and the big screen, but she drew her biggest audiences playing mystery-novelist-turned-amateur-detective Jessica Fletcher in the television series *Murder, She Wrote*, which aired from 1984 to 1996.

Angela Brigid Lansbury was born into a well-respected family on October 16, 1925, in the Regent's Park section of London; her paternal grandfather, George, was a Labour Party official, and her father, Edgar, who died when she was nine years old, was a prominent politician and one-time mayor of the municipal borough of Poplar.

During World War II, her mother, Moyna, an actress, moved with Lansbury and her two younger brothers to the United States to escape the Blitz, the Germans' relentless bombing campaign. The family settled in Mahopac, New York, and Lansbury, who had begun studying at the Webber Douglas School of Singing and Dramatic Art in Kensington before the move, secured admission to the Feagin School of Dramatic Art in Manhattan.

Moyna soon moved with her children to Los Angeles, and there, Lansbury helped financially by working in a department store. An introduction to screenwriter John Van Druten led to a part in his 1944 film noir, *Gaslight*; that role—a scene-stealing Cockney maid—won her an Oscar nod in the category of best supporting actress and a contract with MGM.

Lansbury's other popular films included *The Picture of Dorian Gray* (1946), which earned her a second Academy award nomination; *The Three Musketeers* (1948); *The Manchurian Candidate* (1962); *Bedknobs and Broomsticks* (1971); *Death on the Nile* (1978); and the animated *Beauty and the Beast* (1991), in which she voiced the cheery Mrs. Potts. Concurrent with her big-screen career, Lansbury—who sometimes bemoaned that her cherubic, unconventional-for-Hollywood appearance relegated her to character roles—found varying degrees of success on the stage.

She made her Broadway debut in 1957 in the farce *Hotel Paradiso* and although other roles steadily followed, it was her turn in the title role of *Mame*—which opened in 1966 and ran for more than 1,500 performances—that made her a bona fide star. Her portrayal of a madcap socialite who mentors her orphaned nephew earned Lansbury a Tony, and some critics expressed puzzlement when the makers of the 1974 film version chose Lucille Ball to star instead. In addition to that first Tony, Lansbury took home statuettes for *Dear World* (1969), *Gypsy* (1975), *Sweeney Todd: The Demon Barber of Fleet Street* (1979), and *Blithe Spirit* (2009). In 2022, she was given a Lifetime Achievement Tony.

Throughout her decades in show business, Lansbury also appeared regularly on television, starting with the prestige "playhouse" series such as *Lux Video Theatre* and *General Electric Theater* so popular in the 1950s and moving on to guest roles on the hits of later decades, including *The Man from U.N.C.L.E.*, *Newhart*, and *Touched by an Angel*. She is indelibly associated, however, with *Murder, She Wrote* and the bicycle-riding sleuth who won the loyalty of legions of fans—despite producers' fears that viewers would not tune in to see a middle-aged widow solve crimes in a sleepy Maine town. The series aired for more than 260 episodes and was nominated for more than 40 Primetime Emmys, including several nods for Lansbury.

Lansbury died on October 11, 2022, at her Los Angeles home, at the age of 96. She was predeceased by her second husband, Peter Shaw, in 2003, and survived by sons, Anthony and David; daughter, Deirdre; three grandchildren; and five great-grandchildren.

See Current Biography 1967

Richard E. Leakey

Born: Nairobi, British Kenya; December 19, 1944
Died: Nairobi, Kenya; January 2, 2022
Occupation: Kenyan paleoanthropologist, conservationist and writer

Richard Leakey's discovery of ancient skeletons and fossils established him as an important figure in the world of paleoanthropology and contributed greatly to an understanding of humanity's roots in Africa.

The son of famed paleoanthropologists Louis and Mary Leakey, who had proved conclusively that Africa was the birthplace of man, Richard Leakey initially wanted to avoid that field and instead worked as a tour guide as a young man. He reconsidered, however, in 1967 while looking over Kenya's Lake Turkana and getting a strong gut feeling that important fossils could be found there.

That feeling turned out to be accurate: in 1972 he excavated a skull that helped scientists trace Homo erectus several million years earlier than had been possible before, and in 1984 he discovered a 1.6-million-year-old Homo erectus skeleton he dubbed "Turkana Boy."

In addition to his fossil finds, which led to regular appearances on magazine covers and television programs, Leakey was celebrated for his strong commitment to conservation and opposition to the ivory trade in Africa. He was so trusted a public figure that President Daniel Arap Moi chose him as a cabinet secretary and head of public service, partially to reassure international donors about the legitimacy of the Kenyan government. He also served at various

times as director of the National Museums of Kenya and chairperson of the Kenya Wildlife Service.

Leakey's many well-known books include *Origins* (1977), *Making of Mankind* (1981), *The Origin of Humankind* (1994), and *Wildlife Wars: My Fight to Save Africa's Natural Treasures* (2001).

Leakey suffered several devastating injuries and diseases throughout his life: he had a fractured skull as a youngster, crushed both legs severely in a plane crash, survived a kidney transplant, and skin cancer. He died of unspecified causes at his home outside of Nairobi on January 2, 2022, and was survived by his second wife, fellow paleoanthropologist Meave Leakey; their daughters, Louise and Samira; a daughter, Anna, from his first marriage, which ended in divorce; and three grandchildren.

See Current Biography 1995

John Leo

Born: Hoboken, New Jersey; June 16, 1935
Died: Bronx, New York; May 9, 2022
Occupation: American author and journalist

Readers of *U.S. News & World Report* and *Time* knew longtime columnist John Leo for his conservative streak, wit, and skepticism.

John Patrick Leo was born in Hoboken, New Jersey, on June 16, 1935. Because his mother was a Democrat and his father a Republican, he sometimes joked that theirs was a mixed marriage. (He later drew upon those circumstances for a *Time* magazine column called "Ralph and Wanda," which featured a staunchly conservative husband and his liberal wife.)

In 1957, Leo graduated from the University of Toronto, where he had edited the school paper and majored in philosophy and English. His first journalism job involved writing obituaries for the *Bergen Evening Record*, a New Jersey local.

He subsequently worked at the *Catholic Messenger* newspaper, the Catholic magazine *Commonweal*, and the *National Catholic Reporter*. Still relatively liberal, in 1967 he joined the staff of *The New York Times*, writing about the counterculture, antiwar protests, and other such issues. Immersed in that milieu, he gradually turned to the right, believing that liberals—particularly those on college campuses—were destroying traditional values and espousing empty pieties, as he viewed calls for affirmative action and politically correct speech.

Leo joined the staff at *Time* in 1974, covering mostly cultural and intellectual trends; he remained there until 1988 when he was hired by *U.S. News & World Report*, where his weekly columns—which regularly railed against pop-culture phenomenon like gangster rap or the elimination of the Western canon at elite universities—was syndicated to more than 100 newspapers.

Leo—the author of *How the Russians Invented Baseball and Other Essays of Enlightenment* (1989), *Two Steps Ahead of the Thought Police* (1994), and *Incorrect Thoughts* (2001) —retired in 2005. He subsequently served as a fellow at the Manhattan Institute, a conservative organization, and taught as a visiting scholar at Ralston College.

Leo, suffering in later years from Parkinson's disease, died on May 9, 2022, in the New York City borough of the Bronx. He was survived by his second wife, Jacqueline; his daughters, Alex, Kristin, and Karen; and three grandchildren.

See Current Biography 2006

Ramsey Lewis

Born: Chicago, Illinois; May 27, 1935
Died: Chicago, Illinois; September 12, 2022
Occupation: American jazz pianist and composer

Grammy-winning jazz artist Ramsey Lewis became known to even music lovers unfamiliar with the genre in 1965, when his instrumental version of "The 'In' Crowd" climbed the pop charts.

Ramsey Emmanuel Lewis, Jr. was born into a working-class Chicago family on May 27, 1935, and at the age of four, he began taking piano lessons. He quickly became skilled enough to perform during services at his church, and while still in high school, he joined the Clefs, a seven-piece band that played jazz at local venues. During World War II, four of the older members of the Clef were drafted, and the remaining three renamed themselves the Ramsey Lewis Trio.

In 1956 the trio released its debut, *Ramsey Lewis and His Gentle-Men of Swing*, kicking off a successful career that found its members regularly playing in Chicago clubs. They also recorded a steady stream of other albums, including *Ramsey Lewis and His Gentle-Men of Jazz* (1958), *Tribute to Clifford Brown* (1959), *In Chicago* (1960), *Never on Sunday* (1961), *Barefoot Sunday Blues* (1963), and *You Better Believe Me* (1964). Despite playing occasionally at such popular New York City venues as the Village Vanguard, as well as at the Newport Jazz Festival, Ramsey remained a relatively obscure figure outside the Chicago jazz scene.

That changed, however, in 1965, when he recorded the live album *The Ramsey Lewis Trio at the Bohemian Caverns*, which included "The 'In' Crowd," a song that had been a hit for singer Dobie Gray earlier that year. Lewis's version reached the number-five spot on the Billboard Hot 100, received frequent radio airplay, and earned the artist a Grammy. His subsequent covers of "Hang on Sloopy" and "A Hard Day's Night" proved similarly popular with mainstream music listeners.

Lewis remained active for decades: in 1995 he formed Urban Knights, a jazz supergroup that recorded several albums, and in 2007 the National Endowment for the Arts named him a Jazz Master. He died in Chicago on September 12, 2022, at the age of 87, and was survived by his wife, Janet; his daughters, Denise and Dawn; his sons, Kendall, Frayne, and Bobby; 17 grandchildren; and three great-grandchildren. He was predeceased by two other sons, Ramsey and Kevyn. His last album, *The Beatles Songbook*, was released posthumously.

See Current Biography 1996

Ray Liotta

Born: Newark, New Jersey; December 18, 1954
Died: Santo Domingo, Dominican Republic; May 26, 2022
Occupation: American actor

Ray Liotta was known for playing a variety of indelible characters in such enduring films as *Field of Dreams* (1989) and *Goodfellas* (1990).

Raymond Allen Liotta was born on December 18, 1954, in Newark, New Jersey, and raised by adoptive parents in the nearby town of Union. Banned from his high school basketball team for clashing with the coach, he serendipitously turned to the drama club.

Liotta studied acting at the University of Miami and later moved to New York, where he won a part on the popular daytime soap *Another World*, playing the fan-favorite character Joey Perrini from 1978 to 1981.

He first came to the widespread attention of filmgoers in 1986, when he played the ex-con husband of Melanie Griffith's character in the comedy *Something Wild*. His performance won rave reviews but threatened to pigeonhole him into playing mentally unbalanced or dangerous characters—a circumstance he fought against throughout his career. Liotta proved he could act against type in *Field of Dreams*, in which he portrayed the ghost of outfielder Shoeless Joe Jackson, who visits a baseball diamond built by Kevin Costner's farmer character in his cornfield. (The film popularized the phrase, "If you build it, they will come.")

Liotta's most iconic character, however, was arguably that of mobster Henry Hill in *Goodfellas,* one of director Martin Scorsese's most acclaimed films. The movie tells the real-life story of Hill, a member of the Lucchese crime family who later became a federal informant and entered the Witness Protection Program. Critics lavishly praised Liotta's masterly performance, and he went on to work steadily in a variety of projects both dramatic and comedic. These included: *Corrina, Corrina* (1994), *Operation Dumbo Drop* (1995), *Cop Land* (1997), *The Rat Pack* (1998), *Pilgrim* (2000), *Hannibal* (2001), *Wild Hogs* (2007), *The River Murders* (2011), *The Place beyond the Pines* (2012), *Muppets Most Wanted* (2014), and *The Many Saints of New York* (2021).

Liotta—who won a 2005 Emmy as outstanding guest actor in a drama for an appearance on the medical series *ER*—was filming a new movie when he died of unexplained causes on May 26, 2022, in his Dominican Republic hotel room. He was 67 years old. He was survived by a daughter, Karsen (from his former marriage to Michelle Grace, a fellow actor) and his fiancée, Jacy Nittolo.

See Current Biography 1994

James Lovelock

Born: Letchworth Garden City, England; July 26, 1919
Died: Dorset, England; July 26, 2022
Occupation: British environmental scientist

James Lovelock made pioneering scientific discoveries that catalyzed the environmental movement and became renowned for his Gaia theory, which captured the public imagination by stating, anthropomorphically, that Earth functioned as a living organism.

James Ephraim Lovelock was born on July 26, 1919, in Letchworth Garden City, just north of London. His father, a shopkeeper, encouraged a love of nature, and while he was an indifferent student early on, he enjoyed reading science fiction and history.

Granted conscientious objector status that allowed him to avoid serving in World War II, he graduated from Manchester University in 1941 and found work at the government-run Medical Research Council. He subsequently earned a PhD from the London University School of Hygiene and Tropical Medicine.

In the late 1950s, he invented an inexpensive portable device he called the Electron Capture Detector, capable of measuring toxic, manmade chemicals in the environment. Rachel Carson, the author of the seminal 1962 book *Silent Spring*, which helped launch the modern environmental movement, drew heavily upon his work, and the invention eventually prompted governments around the world to regulate the use of harmful compounds such as DDT and PCBs. Lovelock later studied chlorofluorocarbons, then widely used as coolants and aerosol propellants, and uncovered their role in making a hole in the planet's ozone layer.

In 1965, by then an expert on the chemical composition of Earth's atmospheres, he was working at NASA's Jet Propulsion Laboratory in California, when he developed the Gaia theory, which held that Earth was a self-regulating system, with the ability to maintain a healthy, comfortable climate and chemical composition. While his ideas initially met with skepticism from fellow scientists, after years of research-based evidence, the theory gained credibility and became key to the study of global warming.

Lovelock died on July 26, 2022, at the age of 103, at his home in the British county of Dorset. He was predeceased in 1989 by his first wife, Helen. He later married again, to Sandra Orchard, who survives him, as do his daughters, Christine and Jane; sons, Andrew and John; and grandchildren.

See Current Biography 1992

Loretta Lynn

Born: Butcher Hollow, Kentucky; April 14, 1932
Died: Hurricane Mills, Tennessee; October 4, 2022
Occupation: American country singer and songwriter

Loretta Lynn was among the most iconic and beloved country singers of her era. Immortalized in part in the lyrics of her 1970 hit "Coal Miner's Daughter," her life story captured the public imagination as much as her vast catalogue of music.

Born Loretta Webb on April 14, 1932, the singer was one of eight children. Raised in a cabin in Butcher Hollow, Kentucky, she never lost her deep Southern drawl. Her mother, who was of Cherokee and Scots Irish heritage, passed down her love of singing and storytelling, and the family often performed together at church. (One sibling, performing under the stage name Crystal Gayle, also later became a chart-topping singer.)

As a young woman, Lynn was uncertain about her level of talent, and she sang mainly in private, while doing household chores. Her husband, Oliver (usually known by the nicknames Doolittle or Mooney)—whom she married when she was 15–encouraged her, however, buying her a guitar and copies of music magazines. In 1960, after appearing on a televised talent show, Lynn signed with a small record label. One of her songs, "I'm a Honky Tonk Girl," received significant airplay on local radio stations, and she soon moved to Nashville and made her Grand Ole Opry debut.

Lynn recorded her first top-10 hit, "Success," in 1962, and she quickly amassed a string of hits. Many, like "You Ain't Woman Enough (to Take My Man)" and "Don't Come Home A-Drinkin' (With Lovin' on Your Mind)," both from 1966, were based on her husband's propensity for womanizing and drinking.

The 1970s marked something of a heyday for Lynn: The Academy of Country Music named her its artist of the decade, and in 1976 she published a bestselling memoir, titled, like her earlier hit song, *Coal Miner's Daughter*. (A big-screen biopic by the same name hit theaters in 1980, winning the actress Sissy Spacek an Oscar for her portrayal of the singer.)

Lynn was elected to the Country Music Hall of Fame in 1988, and in 2003 she received Kennedy Center Honors. In 2008 she was inducted into the Songwriters Hall of Fame, and two years later she garnered a Grammy for Lifetime Achievement. In 2013, President Barack Obama awarded her the Presidential Medal of Freedom.

Over the course of her career, Lynn—who wrote a second memoir, *Still Woman Enough*, in 2002—racked up more than 75 top-10 hits, with 16 of them perching atop the charts at number one.

Lynn died in her sleep on October 4, 2022, at the age of 90, at her ranch in Hurricane Mills, Tennessee, some 70 miles west of Nashville. Her husband of almost five decades predeceased her in 1996 as a result of congestive heart failure. One daughter, Betty Sue, and a son, Jack, also died before her.

She was survived by her daughters Patsy, Peggy, and Cissie; her son Ernest; 17 grandchildren; four step-grandchildren; and numerous great-grandchildren.

See Current Biography 1973

Birju Maharaj

Born: Uttar Pradesh (formerly Handia), India; February 4, 1937
Died: New Delhi, India; January 17, 2022
Occupation: Indian dancer

Birju Maharaj achieved star status in his native India for his contributions to Kathak, a style of traditional dance that can trace its origins back 2,000 years. Performed in royal courts, it became popular in both Hindu and Muslim cultures. (Kathak is one of eight regional, classical dance genres in India.)

Maharaj began dancing as a child under the tutelage of his father, the popular performer Acchan Maharaj, who had been a court dancer in the princely state of Rajgarh. At the age of seven, during a time when his country was still under British rule, Maharaj gave his first public performance. When he was 10, India gained independence, and Kathak began enjoying new popularity. Over the course of the next decade, Maharaj performed widely, and by the time he was in his 20s, he was known as one of India's best dancers—celebrated for his elaborate footwork and improvisational skill.

Having taught dance since the age of 13, he opened his own school in 1998. Concurrently, he was gaining renown as a choreographer of film dance scenes, including Satyajit Ray's classic *Shatranj Ke Khiladi* (1977) and the Bollywood hits *Devdas* (2002) and *Dedh Ishqiya* (2014). In 2015, he won a Filmfare Award for best choreography for his work on the film *Bajirao Mastani*.

Maharaj worked well into his 70s. He died in New Delhi on January 17, 2022, suffering cardiac arrest while undergoing dialysis. He was predeceased by his wife of more than five decades, Annapurna Devi, in 2008. They had two sons, Jaikishan and Deepak, both masters of Kathak; and three daughters, Mamta (also a leading Kathak dancer), Kavita, and Anita.

See Current Biography 2007

Lata Mangeshkar

Born: Sikh Mohalla, Indore, Madhya Pradesh, India; September 28, 1929
Died: Mumbai, Maharashtra, India; February 6, 2022
Occupation: Indian singer

Lata Mangeshkar was popularly known as the "nightingale of India," celebrated for her range, emotive abilities, and catalog of tens of thousands of songs.

Her father, Pandit Deenanath Mangeshkar, was a well-known musician active in Marathi-language theater, and Mangeshkar often sang with him in concert as a child. He died when she was 13, and to help support the family, she took a job with the Navyug Chitrapat Film Company and acted in Marathi- and Hindi-language films. She never cared much for acting, however, and in the late 1940s, after filmmakers began to hire professional singers to record the vocals for the onscreen actors, she found a new niche as a "playback singer," recording songs that would later be dubbed into the finished film.

Although playback singers generally remained anonymous, after her 1949 track "Aayega Aanewala" from the movie *Mahal*, got radio airplay, listeners clamored to know her name, and she shot to stardom. Over the course of her career, which spanned more than 70 years, Mangeshkar recorded some 25,000 songs in 20 different languages, and her music was featured in more than 1,000 films.

In 2001, she was awarded the Bharat Ratna, India's highest honor, in recognition of her vast contributions to Indian culture, which had won her fans throughout the entire subcontinent, as well as in the Indian diaspora.

Mangeshkar died in Mumbai on February 6, 2022, due to complications from COVID-19; following her death, the Indian government declared a two-day period of national mourning, with flags flown at half-staff, and she was given a formal state funeral.

See Current Biography 2003

Richard Marcinko

Born: Lansford, Pennsylvania; November 21, 1940
Died: Fauquier County, Virginia; December 25, 2021
Occupation: American writer, motivational speaker, CEO of Richard Marcinko Inc., and former military officer

Richard Marcinko, a much-decorated veteran of the war in Vietnam, was the founding commander of Navy SEAL Team 6, the elite unit that captured the public imagination and later conducted the raid that killed Osama bin Laden.

Marcinko dropped out of high school to enlist in the U.S. Navy in 1958. Deployed to Vietnam with SEAL Team 2 in 1967, he garnered a plethora of honors, including four Bronze Stars, a Silver Star, and a Vietnamese Cross of Gallantry. He completed two tours in Vietnam and served as head of SEAL Team 2 from 1974 to 1976.

When a 1980 mission to rescue American hostages seized in Tehran failed, Marcinko was charged with creating a SEAL unit that could respond quickly to terrorist crises. The name SEAL Team 6 was chosen in an attempt to convince enemies to believe the force was larger than it was; in reality, only two teams already existed. The members of the new unit—who cultivated a reputation as rogue combatants, willing to bend any rule to succeed in a mission—were trained to take on tasks too dangerous for other military units, including retrieving nuclear weapons that might fall into enemy hands. Their part in the 2011 killing of Osama bin Laden, the mastermind behind the terrorist attacks of 9/11, only strengthened that mythos in the public eye. Marcinko's 1992 autobiography, *Rogue Warrior*, was just one of the dozens of books and movies that kept the SEAL's image as the toughest fighting force on the planet alive.

After retiring from the Navy in 1989, Marcinko authored other books and found himself in demand as a motivational speaker and military consultant.

He died of a heart attack at his Fauquier County, Virginia, home on Christmas Day in 2021, at the age of 81. He was survived by his second wife, Nancy; four daughters, Brandy, Tiffany, Hailey, and Kathy-Ann; and two sons, Matthew and Ritchie.

See Current Biography 2011

Mary Alice

Born: Indianola, Mississippi; December 3, 1936
Died: New York, New York; July 27, 2022
Occupation: American actor

Mary Alice was equally adept acting in stage productions, television shows, and films, and her presence lent gravitas and dignity to many and varied projects.

Mary Alice Smith was born on December 3, 1936, in Indianola, Mississippi, and raised in Chicago. Adopting her parents' strong ethic, she sought out a career that would provide a solid, middle-class life and settled upon teaching. In 1965 she graduated from what was then known as Chicago Teachers College and accepted a job at a local elementary school. Still, she loved the escapism movies provided and dreamed of acting one day.

After two years of teaching, she moved to New York to study at the acclaimed Negro Ensemble Company, dropping her surname along the way. She was soon finding steady work, appearing in episodes of popular Black sitcoms (*Good Times* and *Sanford and Son*, for example), hourlong dramas (*Police Woman*),

and soap operas (*All My Children*); acting in films like *The Education of Sonny Carson* (1974) and *Sparkle* (1976); and winning acclaim for her theater performances (notably, a 1983 Yale Rep production of *Raisin in the Sun*).

That acclaim reached a peak in 1987, when she starred on Broadway in August Wilson's *Fences*, alongside James Earl Jones. The two each won a Tony Award for their portrayal of an embattled married couple in 1950s-era Pittsburgh. By the end of the 1980s, Mary Alice had also become a fixture on the small screen, amassing dozens of credits for roles in some of the most-watched sitcoms and miniseries of the day, including the Cosby spinoff *A Different World* and the Oprah Winfrey-backed *Women of Brewster Place*.

Mary Alice continued to work steadily throughout the 1990s and early 2000s. Among her highest-profile projects were *The Bonfire of the Vanities* (1990), *Awakenings* (1990), the series *I'll Fly Away* (on which she appeared in seven 1992 episodes, earning an Emmy), *Malcolm X* (1992), *The Wishing Tree* (1999), and *The Matrix Revolutions* (2003). Her final screen appearance came in a 2005 episode of the detective show *Kojak*.

Paramedics were called to Mary Alice's New York City apartment on July 27, 2022, and they discovered her dead. She was 85 and had no immediate survivors.

See Current Biography 1995

Lowry Mays

Born: Houston, Texas; July 24, 1935
Died: San Antonio, Texas; September 12, 2022
Occupation: American broadcasting executive

Lowry Mays turned a single radio station he acquired in the 1970s into the media behemoth Clear Channel Communications, revolutionizing the broadcast industry along the way.

Lester Lowry Mays was born in Houston, Texas, on July 24, 1935, and graduated from Texas A&M University with a degree in petroleum engineering in 1957. Rather than entering the workforce immediately, he signed up for the U.S. Air Force and was sent to Taiwan to manage the construction of a massive oil pipeline. Upon his discharge, he entered Harvard, earning an MBA in 1962 and launching a career in the investment sector. He opened his own firm in 1970 and soon found himself the co-owner of KEEZ, a floundering FM station whose original owners had backed out of their loan.

Despite having no knowledge of the radio business, two years later Mays launched the San Antonio Broadcasting Company, which was renamed Clear Channel in the mid-1970s. While consistently maintaining that he was in the business of selling products, not entertainment, Mays spent the next quarter-century acquiring additional radio and television stations, and after Congress loosened regulations in 1996, he accelerated his pace. By 2001, Clear Channel encompassed an estimated 1,200 stations, as well as live music venues, sports management firms, and billboard companies, among other entities, and revenues had reached $8 billion a year.

Mays was not without his detractors: artists often charged that he squeezed out competitors—and thus musical choice, and he was blamed in some quarters for the rise of conservative talk radio. Mays suffered a stroke in 2005. In 2006, he sold the company to a private equity firm for almost $18 billion. (It was later renamed iHeartRadio.)

Mays died in San Antonio, on September 12, 2022. He was predeceased in 2020 by his wife of more than 60 years, Peggy, who had helped him launch the Mays Family Foundation. He was survived by his sons, Mark and Randall; daughters, Kathryn and Linda; 16 grandchildren; and three great-grandchildren.

See Current Biography 2003

David G. McCullough

Born: Pittsburgh, Pennsylvania; July 7, 1933
Died: Hingham, Massachusetts; August 7, 2022
Occupation: American historian and biographer

David McCullough was known as a consummate chronicler of American history and its major statesmen, including John Adams, Harry S. Truman, and Theodore Roosevelt.

One of four sons, David Gaub McCullough was born on July 7, 1933, in Pittsburgh, Pennsylvania. Following a childhood he consistently described as loving and happy,

he entered Yale University, where he studied under such acclaimed figures as John O'Hara, Robert Penn Warren, and Thornton Wilder. Upon graduating in 1955 with an honors degree in literature, he joined the staff of *Sports Illustrated*, then a fledgling publication. He subsequently took jobs at the magazine *American Heritage* and at the U.S. Information Agency, which functioned as something of a public-relations arm of the government.

In 1968, when his first book, *The Johnstown Flood*—a volume about an 1889 dam failure he had spent nights and weekends writing—proved to be a success, he decided to devote himself fulltime to writing about history-related topics.

His books included *The Great Bridge* (1972), a detailed account of the construction of the Brooklyn Bridge; *The Path Between the Seas: The Creation of the Panama Canal* (1977), a recipient of a National Book Award; *Mornings on Horseback*, a National Book Award-winning look at a young Theodore Roosevelt; the Pulitzer Prize-winning *Truman* (1992), which remained on the *New York Times* bestseller list for more than ten months and inspired an HBO movie; *John Adams* (2001), which won a Pulitzer and was used as the basis for a television miniseries; *The Wright Brothers* (2015); and *The Pioneers: The Heroic Story of the Settlers Who Brought the American Ideal West* (2019).

In addition to his writing—which sometimes attracted criticism for its focus on the accomplishments of white men and exclusion of diverse points of view—McCullough frequently served as a narrator of historical films and television documentaries, including the Ken Burns series *The Civil War* (1990) and PBS's *American Experience* (1988–99).

The recipient of a 2006 Presidential Medal of Freedom, McCullough died on August 7, 2022, at his home in Hingham, Massachusetts, at the age of 89. He was predeceased in June of that year by his wife of several decades, Rosalee. He was survived by his daughters, Dorie and Melissa; three sons, David Jr., William, and Geoffrey; 19 grandchildren; and two great-grandchildren.

See Current Biography 1993

James A. McDivitt

Born: Chicago, Illinois; June 10, 1929
Died: Tucson, Arizona; October 13, 2022
Occupation: American pilot and astronaut

James A. McDivitt was the commander of Gemini 4, a 1965 NASA mission notable for being the first ever to include a spacewalk outside the capsule by an American astronaut.

James Alton McDivitt was born on June 10, 1929, in Chicago, Illinois, but was raised in Michigan. He completed a few semesters of community college but, fascinated by the thought of flying, he dropped out in 1951 to join the U.S. Air Force. During the Korean War, he flew almost 150 combat missions, and when that conflict ended, he entered the University of Michigan, where he earned top grades and a Bachelor's Degree in Aeronautical Engineering.

After graduating in 1959, McDivitt was sent to Edwards Air Force Base, in California, as a test pilot, and there he was chosen in 1962 as an astronaut candidate.

Gemini 4 launched on June 3, 1965, with the goal of determining whether astronauts could withstand long periods in space: the mission lasted four days and made history when crewman Ed White made a pioneering spacewalk of approximately 23 minutes. McDivitt's second command mission, Apollo 9, launched on March 3, 1969, and lasted 10 days, with the goal of testing a prototype lunar module.

Following those two flights, McDivitt became a manager of NASA's Apollo spacecraft program—a post he retained until retiring from the Air Force in 1972 with the rank of brigadier general. (By the time he retired he had helped oversee Apollo 12, 13, 14, 15, and 16.) He subsequently joined the private sector, serving variously as an executive with the Consumers Power Company, Pullman, and Rockwell International.

McDivitt—whose many honors included two NASA Distinguished Service Medals, a NASA Exceptional Service Medal, two Air Force Distinguished Service Medals, and four Distinguished Flying Crosses—died on October 13, 2022, at the age of 93, in Tucson, Arizona. He was survived by his second wife, Judith; children, Katie, Ann, Michael, and Patrick; stepsons, Joe and Jeff; seven grandchildren; five step-grandchildren; and six great-grandchildren.

See Current Biography 1965

Gerald McEntee

Born: Philadelphia, Pennsylvania; January 11, 1935
Died: Naples, Florida; July 10, 2022
Occupation: American labor leader

Gerald W. McEntee served from 1981 to 2012 as the president of the American Federation of State, County and Municipal Employees (AFSCME), one of the most influential labor unions in the nation, and the largest affiliated with the AFL-CIO.

Gerald William McEntee was born in Philadelphia, on January 11, 1935. His father, who drove a garbage truck for the city, helped organize his fellow sanitation workers. After McEntee graduated from La Salle University in 1956 and served briefly in the Army, he joined AFSCME while working for the Philadelphia Bureau of Traffic Engineering.

Soon after joining, McEntee joined the staff of the union's Philadelphia local council, and in 1973 he began heading the state council. In that capacity, he led an effective strike, one of the largest ever mounted in the U.S. by public employees, in response to state threats to cut back on health coverage.

In late 1981, following the death of longtime AFSCME president Jerry Wurf, McEntee was chosen to fill that top spot. He quickly became known as something of a political kingmaker, encouraging the union to pour millions into everything from state legislative races to presidential campaigns. In 1995, McEntee became chairman of the AFL-CIO's political committee, giving him even greater clout.

McEntee continually fought against proposed government cuts and attempts to privatize public services—generally by Republican officials, and he engaged in high-profile battles against President George W. Bush (whose efforts to privatize Social Security were unsuccessful thanks in some part to McEntee's activism) and other politicians.

McEntee—who won praise for his focus on pay equity and rights for workers from marginalized and underrepresented groups—died at his Florida home on July 10, 2022, at the age of 87. He was survived by his wife, Barbara; daughters, Patricia, Kathleen, and Kelly; 10 grandchildren; and five great-grandchildren.

See Current Biography 2000

Robert C. McFarlane

Born: Washington, DC; July 12, 1937
Died: Lansing, Michigan; May 12, 2022
Occupation: American presidential adviser

Robert McFarlane served as the national security adviser under President Ronald Reagan from October 17, 1983 to December 4, 1985, and during that period he became deeply embroiled in the Iran-Contra scandal. That incident involved a secretive plan to sell arms to Iran in exchange for the release of Western hostages; profits from those sales was then covertly sent to Nicaraguan rebels (known as Contras), who were trying to overthrow the Marxist in that country. Aid to the Contras and arms sales to Iran had been expressly prohibited by Congress, and in the wake of the scandal, McFarlane was found guilty of withholding important information, ending his government career and irrevocably tarnishing his reputation.

Robert Carl "Bud" McFarlane was born in the nation's capital on July 12, 1937; his father, William, was a Democratic congressman from Texas. At the Naval Academy in Annapolis, McFarlane was a top student, and upon graduating in 1959, he joined the Marines, leading early combat missions in Vietnam. While still in the military, he completed internships under national security advisers Henry Kissinger and Brent Scowcroft, and for a time he was a staff member at the U.S. State Department and the Senate Foreign Relations Committee.

Still, some insiders found it surprising when McFarlane—a quieter, less self-promotional figure than many of his predecessors—was tapped in October 1983 to become national security adviser, with responsibility for coordinating defense policy among various government departments.

When the Iran-Contra scandal became known, McFarlane was unique among the participants for accepting blame for his role and expressing remorse. He was sentenced to 200 hours of community service, which he filled by

working with the disabled and local youths. In 1987, a guilt-ridden McFarlane, believing he had let down the nation he loved, attempted to commit suicide by overdosing on valium. Discovered in time, he underwent intensive psychiatric treatment. After his release from Bethesda Naval Hospital, McFarlane resumed his non-government career as an international business consultant; the firm he founded was especially active in the energy sector. President George H.W. Bush formally pardoned him in 1992.

McFarlane was visiting friends in Michigan on May 12, 2022, when he died from a previously undiagnosed lung condition. He was survived by his wife, Jonda; three children, Lauren, Melissa, and Scott; and eight grandchildren.

See Current Biography 1984

Meat Loaf

Born: Dallas, Texas; September 27, 1947
Died: Nashville, Tennessee; January 20, 2022
Occupation: American singer and songwriter

Meat Loaf, born Marvin Lee Aday, was a bombastic singer whose 1977 debut album, *Bat out of Hell*, became one of the top recordings of all times, selling more than 40 million copies in the U.S. alone, despite mainly dismissive reviews from rock critics, who disdained his operatic campiness and Broadway-style belting.

He began his music career in a series of short-lived bands but had greater success when he was hired to perform in stage musicals like *Hair* in the late 1960s. It was while auditioning for the show *More Than You Deserve*, which ran in New York in 1973 and 1974 that he met composer Jim Steinman, and the two collaborated on *Bat out of Hell*, which yielded several hit singles, including the eight-and-a-half-minute-long "Paradise by the Dashboard Light," the ballad-like "Two Out of Three Ain't Bad," and the power-chord-filled "All Revved Up with No Place to Go."

In all, Meat Loaf recorded 12 studio albums, although none came close to the juggernaut status of *Bat Out of Hell* with the exception of *Bat Out of Hell II: Back into Hell*, (1993) which contained the Grammy-winning number-one single "I'd Do Anything for Love (but I Won't Do That)."

In addition to his recording, Meat Loaf enjoyed a successful career in the film industry, with such cult favorites as *The Rocky Horror Picture Show* (1975) and *Fight Club* (1999) to his credit.

He suffered from health problems throughout his life, some due to the excess weight that had prompted his choice of the name Meat Loaf, and he died on January 20, 2022, in Nashville, Tennessee, with his wife, Deborah, and his daughters, Pearl and Amanda, by his side.

See Current Biography 2006

Sue Mingus

Born: Chicago, Illinois; April 2, 1930
Died: New York, New York; September 24, 2022
Occupation: American band manager and record producer

When most people hear the name Mingus, it is bass player and composer Charles Mingus who comes to mind. But it was his wife, Sue Mingus, who was responsible, in large part, for promoting his work and ensuring his long-lasting legacy.

Born Susan Graham on April 2, 1930, in Chicago, she was raised in a musically minded family: her father was an amateur opera singer, and her mother played the harp.

Mingus studied history at Smith College, graduating in 1952 and then moving to Paris to pursue an editorial career. She subsequently lived for a time in Rome, and in 1958 she settled in New York City and found work at the New York Free Press, an alternative paper.

In 1964 she met Charles Mingus at the Five Spot Café, a downtown club where he regularly played. Immediately attracted to each other, they soon became a couple, and within years she had become indispensable to him, managing his bookings, negotiating his contracts, and, on a personal level, ensuring that he stayed clean and sober since he had battled addiction issues in his past.

Charles Mingus died in 1979, at the age of 56, after years of suffering with amyotrophic lateral sclerosis. His widow, determined to help cement his place among the era's jazz greats, planned two days of tribute concerts at Carnegie Hall and spearheaded the creation of Mingus Dynasty, a band devoted to keeping his music alive. She arranged for his compositions—many never performed—to be catalogued in the Library of Congress and hired more than 30 musicians to mount a production of a previously undiscovered orchestral work, *Epitaph*, at Lincoln Center in 1989.

Her efforts to keep him in the spotlight worked almost too well: unlawful recordings of his concerts were a hot commodity in the record stores of the eighties and nineties, and Mingus was known to march into those establishments to grab as many as she could carry in order to discard them. (One such incident resulting in a clerk calling the police on her.)

The author of *Tonight at Noon: A Love Story*, a 2002 memoir, Sue Mingus died in a Manhattan hospital on September 24, 2022, at the age of 92. She was survived by the children from her first marriage, Roberto and Susanna; four grandchildren; and two great-grandchildren.

See Current Biography 2008

Grace Mirabella

Born: Maplewood, New Jersey; June 10, 1929
Died: New York, New York; December 23, 2021
Occupation: American editor

Before founding an eponymous magazine, Grace Mirabella made her name at the helm of *Vogue*, making that iconic title a must read for career women in the 1970s and 1980s.

Mirabella began her career at *Vogue* in 1952, with an entry-level job verifying the store credits in photo captions. She left briefly in 1954 to work in public relations in Italy, but returned to the magazine the following year as shopping editor. She subsequently climbed the ladder at *Vogue*, and in 1971, when longtime editor Diana Vreeland was abruptly fired because publisher Condé Nast wanted to take the magazine in a different creative direction, Mirabella was tapped as her replacement.

In her new role at the helm, Mirabella added sections on topics like the arts and fitness instead of focusing solely on fashion, and the fashions she did feature were suitable for a new generation of women just entering the work world in force. Under Mirabella's direction, circulation tripled, from 400,000 in 1971 to more than 1.2 million in 1988. Despite that success, in the summer of 1988, Mirabella was ousted in much the same way Vreeland had been and replaced by an editor 20 years younger, Anna Wintour.

The following year Mirabella launched her own eponymous magazine, aimed at women who were interested in politics and business as well as beauty and fashion. She stepped down in 1996 to lecture and write, and without her in charge *Mirabella* floundered, shutting down four years later.

Mirabella died in her Manhattan home on December 23, 2021, at the age of 92. She was predeceased in 2001 by her husband, surgeon and anti-smoking activist William G. Cahan. She was survived by her stepsons, Anthony and Christopher; seven step-grandchildren; and three step-great-grandchildren.

See Current Biography 1991

Issey Miyake

Born: Hiroshima, Japan; April 22, 1938
Died: Tokyo, Japan; August 5, 2022
Occupation: Japanese fashion designer

Issey Miyake was among the first Japanese-born designers to make a splash in the fashion world; known for his embrace of technology, which made possible innovative fabrics and production processes, he was particularly celebrated for comfortable, iron-free clothing featuring myriad sharp pleats.

Born Kazunaru Miyake on April 22, 1938, in Hiroshima, he was seven years old when the United States infamously dropped an atomic bomb on the city. By the time he was 10, his mother had died from radiation poisoning, and he had developed bone-marrow disease that left him with a severe limp.

Miyake's love of clothing developed while reading his sister's fashion magazines, and as a young man, he enrolled at Tokyo's Tama Art University. Soon after graduating in 1963, he moved to Paris and became an apprentice at the Guy La Roche and Givenchy fashion houses. He founded an eponymous design studio in Tokyo in 1970. (He preferred the term design to fashion, believing that the latter indicated an ephemeral phenomenon.)

By the 1980s, he was among the most famed designers in the world: in addition to the usual socialites and trendsetters, workers at the electronics giant Sony wore uniforms

designed by him, and every day, the tech mogul Steve Jobs sported a Miyake-designed black turtleneck.

In the early 1990s he introduced Pleats Please, a line of clothing featuring thousands of micro-pleats, with no buttons, zippers, or constricting waistlines or armholes. Thanks to a proprietary heat treatment, the lightweight synthetic fabric never lost its shape and never required ironing. (That line remains among his most popular.) Among his other technological innovations was a process whereby a computer-programmed weaving machine could extrude a tube of fabric that would then be cut along pre-marked lines to instantly produce a dress or other article of clothing.

Miyake—whose work is in the permanent collection of New York City's Museum of Modern Art—died on August 5, 2022, at the age of 84, in Tokyo, from cancer of the liver. Although he was known throughout his life as a loyal friend and avid collaborator, he was an exceptionally private person, and no information was made publicly available about his survivors.

See Current Biography 1997

Luc Montagnier

Born: Chabris, France; August 18, 1932
Died: Neuilly-sur-Seine, France; February 8, 2022
Occupation: French virologist

Nobel Prize-winning researcher Luc Montagnier helped discover the virus that causes acquired immunodeficiency syndrome (AIDS), and while that work earned him a great degree of respect, later in life his image became severely tarnished because of fringe scientific views he developed.

Early in his career, Montagnier, who trained at the University of Poitiers and the Sorbonne, discovered the first double-stranded RNA virus, as well as a new method of culturing cancer cells. In 1972, he became the founding director of the Viral Oncology Unit at the Pasteur Institute, in Paris.

In 1983, he and his colleagues at the Institute examined a lymph node that had been removed from a man diagnosed with AIDS. At that point, clinicians had identified the syndrome but had no idea of its cause; many suspected that the culprit was a retrovirus, which invades its host cell's DNA and takes control of it.

Examining the tissue, Montagnier, an expert in retroviruses, discovered a never-before-seen example he dubbed L.A.V. (lymphadenopathy associated virus). Along with co-author Françoise Barré-Sinoussi, he reported that groundbreaking finding in a May 1983 issue of the peer-reviewed journal *Science*.

Controversy erupted the following year when American researcher Robert Gallo of the National Institutes of Health used a sample from the same patient to confirm the link between a retrovirus he called H.T.L.V.-III and AIDS. Even the nonscience press began reporting on the bitter rivalry and lawsuits that ensued as the two research teams fought over bragging rights and patents.

In 1986, H.T.L.V.-III and L.A.V. were given one official name, H.I.V., and shortly thereafter the governments of France and the United States agreed to jointly credit both Montagnier and Gallo and to share patent royalties. That year, the two men shared the Albert Lasker Medical Research Award: Montagnier for discovering the virus and Gallo for linking it to AIDS. In 2008, however, when the Nobel Prize for Medicine or Physiology was announced, Montagnier and Barré-Sinoussi were recipients, while Gallo was not mentioned. (The Nobel Committee asserted that the French scientists had made the initial discovery.)

In later years, Montagnier drew the ire of the scientific community by claiming that DNA emitted electromagnetic radiation, autism could be treated with antibiotics, and that COVID-19 vaccines were ineffective, among other controversial stances.

He died on February 8, 2022, in the French suburb of Neuilly-sur-Seine, at the age of 89. His immediate family included his wife, Dorothea; two daughters, Anne-Marie and Francine; and son, Jean-Luc. French newspapers reported that he was surrounded by his children at the time of his death.

See Current Biography 1988

Robert Morse

Born: Newton, Massachusetts; May 18, 1931
Died: Los Angeles, California; April 20, 2022
Occupation: American actor

Robert Morse was beloved by theater fans for his work in *How to Succeed in Business Without Really Trying* (1961), a show seemingly tailor-made for his brand of winsome charm. (He also appeared in the 1967 film version, which proved to be a similar hit.) He later became a familiar face to television viewers thanks to guest spots on such popular 1970s and 1980s shows as *Love, American Style*, *Fantasy Island*, *The Dukes of Hazzard*, and *Murder, She Wrote*, and he won over a new generation of fans with his turn in the series *Mad Men*, which ran from 2007 to 2015 and was among the most acclaimed shows of its era.

Robert Alan Morse was born on May 18, 1931, in Newton, Massachusetts, into a family at the periphery of the entertainment industry: his father managed a chain of movie theaters, and his mother was a pianist. An avowed class clown, he was mentored by a teacher who suggested he try acting. Morse moved to New York to try his hand at finding roles but ended up getting discouraged and joining the Navy in 1950 instead.

Upon his discharge in 1954, he revisited his dream, enrolling in the American Theater Wing. His first Broadway role was in the Thornton Wilder comedy *The Matchmaker*, with Ruth Gordon in the titular role. (Morse reprised his own role, a store clerk, in the 1958 film adaptation.) Other stage roles followed, and in 1961 he was hired to play J. Pierrepont Finch, a window washer at the Worldwide Wicket Company who dreams of climbing the corporate ladder, in *How to Succeed in Business Without Really Trying*. Thanks in large part to Morse's appeal and winning tunes by Frank Loesser, the show ran on Broadway for more than 1,400 performances and garnered the actor a Tony Award.

Morse's career rarely reached those heights after that: he bemoaned the fact that movie roles meant for short, funny men like him often went to rival actor Jack Lemmon. While he found steady work as a guest star on television, Morse often contended with depression, turning to alcohol to cope.

Things improved in 1989, when he mounted the one-man show *Tru*, in which he uncannily portrayed writer Truman Capote, capturing his subject's distinct high-pitched voice and mannered gestures so accurately that reviewers referred to him as Capote incarnate. Morse won another Tony for the role and snagged an Emmy for the 1992 television adaptation.

In later years, Morse found ample voiceover work, but it was *Mad Men* that brought him the most professional respect and acclaim towards the end of his career. In it, he played Bertram Cooper, an eccentric older partner at the ad agency that provides the setting for much of the series. (The title, *Mad Men*, is a nod to the many agencies that once lined Madison Avenue in New York.) That work earned him Emmy nominations in 2008, 2010, 2011, 2013, and 2014.

Morse—whose final acting job was a voiceover stint on the cartoon series *Teen Titans Go!* (2015–2021)—died on April 20, 2022, at the age of 90, in Los Angeles. He was survived by his second wife, Elizabeth, a teacher; his children, Robyn, Andrea, Hilary, Allyn, and Charles; and five grandchildren.

See Current Biography 1962

Thierry Mugler

Born: Strasbourg, France; December 21, 1948
Died: Vincennes, France; January 23, 2022
Occupation: French fashion designer, photographer, and perfumer

Designer Thierry Mugler enjoyed a heyday in the late 1980s and early 1990s, when he became known for his over-the-top, dominatrix-inspired fashions, which often involved leather and latex.

Mugler told interviewers that he was inspired by his mother's innate elegance, and at the age of 20 he left his home in Strasbourg to design fashions in Paris. In 1974, he launched his own brand, gradually gaining visibility and popularity, thanks in some part to ad campaigns shot by noted photographer Helmut Newton.

By the mid-1980s his fashion shows had become elaborate extravaganzas, featuring billowing clouds of smoke and choruses who sang as his models—who included the singer Grace Jones, the drag performers Joey Arias and Lypsinka, and socialite Ivana Trump—

strode along the catwalk. By the mid-1990s, however, Mugler's popularity had waned somewhat, a phenomenon that critics have blamed on his embrace of gay culture in the midst of the AIDS crisis.

Demand remained high, however, for Angel, a vanilla-and-patchouli-based perfume he had developed, and in 1997, beauty conglomerate Clarins purchased a controlling stake. Mugler retired from his brand in 2002 and went on to design a Las Vegas show for Cirque du Soleil and create fashions for stars like Beyoncé, Kim Kardashian, and Cardi B.

He later took up bodybuilding and caused a stir when he appeared nude in a 2019 issue of *Interview* magazine.

Mugler died of unspecified causes at his home in Vincennes, outside of Paris, on January 23, 2022.

See Current Biography 2010

Christopher Newton

Born: Deal England; June 11, 1936
Died: Unknown; December 20, 2021
Occupation: Canadian theatrical director; actor

Christopher Newton served as the artistic director of the Ontario-based Shaw Festival, which mounted works inspired by playwright George Bernard Shaw, from 1979 to 2002, and he is credited with revitalizing both the festival and interest in Shaw.

Newton, a native of England, was educated at Newton University of Leeds before coming to the United States to study at the University of Illinois. In 1961, he began touring with the Canadian Players, putting on plays by Shakespeare and Shaw in small venues across that country. Later, playing on the theater festival circuit, he came to the attention of director Mike Nichols, who invited him to work for a time in New York.

In 1968, Newton became the Founding Artistic Director of Theatre Calgary, and in 1976 he took over the Vancouver Playhouse, which flourished under his direction.

In 1979, he assumed leadership of the Shaw festival, then floundering badly. While it took several years, eventually, the company became one of the most celebrated in Canada thanks to Newton's savvy hiring and expert play curation. During his more-than-two-decade tenure, he directed many major works, including *Man and Superman, You Never Can Tell, Caesar and Cleopatra, Heartbreak House, Major Barbara, Pygmalion, Lady Windermere's Fan, Peter Pan,* and *After the Dance.*

Newton, an avid gardener in his later years, retired in 2002. Among his many laurels were the Order of Canada, the Governor General's Award, the Molson Prize, the Chalmers Award, and multiple Jubilee Medals.

He died on December 20, 2021, and was survived by his partner of 37 years, Nicholas MacMartin.

See Current Biography 1995

Olivia Newton-John

Born: Cambridge, England; September 26, 1948
Died: Southern California; August 8, 2022
Occupation: British-Australian singer and actor

Olivia Newton-John was one of the most popular recording artists of the 1970s and 1980s, with hits on both the pop and country charts to her credit. She also appeared on the big screen, most notably alongside John Travolta in the 1978 box-office sensation *Grease,* one of the highest-earning movie musicals of that or any era.

Olivia Newton-John, the youngest of three children, was born on September 26, 1948, in Cambridge, England. Her maternal grandfather was the physicist Max Born, a Nobel laureate, and her father was a World War II intelligence officer who later became an educator.

When Newton-John was six, she moved with her family to Melbourne, Australia, and there she formed her first singing group at age 14. She soon began appearing on local television and radio programs, and she recorded her first single, "'Til You Say You'll Be Mine," in 1966. Her debut solo album *If Not for You,* was released in 1971, followed by *Let Me Be There* (1973), the latter of which earned her a Grammy for best female country vocal performance in an era in which the lines between mainstream soft rock and country were blurred.

Newton-John won legions of new fans after appearing in *Grease.* Her character's arc, from virginal girl-next-door to seductress, seemed in some respects to mirror her real-life career trajectory; after the movie's release,

the singer's squeaky-clean image underwent a transformation that found her recording a 1978 platinum-selling album titled *Totally Hot,* whose cover featured her clad in skintight leather.

Among Newton-John's other hits was the soundtrack to the 1980 movie *Xanadu,* which went double-platinum and yielded the number-one song "Magic," despite the fact that the movie itself bombed at the box office. In 1981, she released the track "Physical," whose video involved her cavorting with barely clad men in a gym; "Physical" spent ten weeks at the number-one spot on the Billboard pop chart and its campy video garnered a Grammy. It was later called the song of the decade by some critics.

Although her career lost some of its luster after the mid-1980s, Newton-John continued to perform and record. In 1992, she was diagnosed with breast cancer, became an outspoken advocate for more research, and launched an eponymous foundation dedicated to finding alternative treatments.

In 2017, Newton-John, who had been honored with the Order of the British Empire at the height of her career, announced that her cancer had returned. She died on August 8, 2022, at her Southern California Ranch. She was survived by her husband, John Easterling; her daughter from her first marriage, Chloe Rose Lattanzi; her sister, Sarah; and her brother, Toby; as well as by several nieces and nephews.

See Current Biography 1978

Norodom Ranariddh

Born: Cambodia; January 2, 1944
Died: France; November 28, 2021
Occupation: Prince; former prime minister of Cambodia

The second son of the popular Cambodian monarch King Norodom Sihanouk and his first wife, Phat Kanhol, Prince Ranariddh was educated in France and began adult life as a teacher of constitutional law and political sociology at the University of Provence.

In 1983, at his father's behest, he left France to lead the National United Front for an Independent, Neutral, Peaceful and Cooperative Cambodia, a coalition of royalist forces that stood in opposition to the

Vietnamese-installed government. In 1992, known by the acronym FUNCINPEC, it became an official political party.

FUNCINPEC won the 1993 Cambodian general election and formed a coalition government with the Cambodian People's Party (CCP). Ranariddh became the First Prime Minister, and the CCP's Hun Sen was named the Second Prime Minister. The two engaged in a bitter rivalry, however, and in 1997 fighting broke out between their respective military forces. It ended with Ranariddh being ousted in a coup.

He returned to Cambodia in early 1998 to lead his party in that year's general election, which FUNCINPEC lost to the CPP. Ranariddh subsequently became President of the National Assembly, and while many hoped he would succeed his father on the throne, he renounced that right and remained in politics.

In 2006, Ranariddh was ousted from FUNCINPEC and responded by forming the Norodom Ranariddh Party (NRP). That effort was short-lived: convicted of embezzlement, he left Cambodia until pardoned in 2008, and upon his return he tried unsuccessfully to merge NRP with FUNCINPEC. In 2014, he founded the unpopular and ill-fated Community of Royalist People's Party, and the following year he rejoined FUNCINPEC and was elected party president.

In 2018 Ranariddh and his second wife, Ouk Phalla, were in a serious car accident. She was killed, and he suffered grave health effects. He died in France on November 28, 2021, and was survived by a daughter, Norodom Rattana Devi; four sons, Norodom Chakravuth, Norodom Sihariddh, Norodom Sothearidh and Norodom Ranavong; his half-brother King Norodom Sihamoni; and several other half siblings.

See Current Biography 1999

Claes Oldenburg

Born: Stockholm, Sweden; January 28, 1929
Died: New York, New York; July 18, 2022
Occupation: American sculptor

Claes Oldenburg is best-known for his massive sculptures of such everyday objects as clothespins and hamburgers. While his choice of subjects is considered mundane to some observers, he asserted that these types of items were instead the basis of much of society's mythological thinking and emotional resonance, citing the reverence and care with which they are depicted in advertising.

Claes Oldenburg was born on January 28, 1929, in Stockholm, Sweden, and he had a relatively peripatetic youth because of his father's diplomatic career. He spent most of his formative years in Chicago and studied at both Yale and the Art Institute of Chicago.

The sculptor, who drew comic strips as an employee of the City News Bureau of Chicago early in his career, became a U.S. citizen in 1953 and moved to New York City in 1956. There he participated in "happenings," events that involved visual and performance art with other forms. (He once, for example, rented a private pool, filled it with balloons, and had people swimming among them.)

His first large-scale sculpture—or "colossal monument" as he sometimes called such works—was "Lipstick (Ascending) on Caterpillar Tracks," a giant tube of makeup mounted on tractor wheels that was installed on the grounds of Yale in 1969.

Subsequent large-scale projects included a giant trowel placed at the Kröller-Müller Museum in the Netherlands in 1976, a soon-to-be-iconic clothespin mounted in Philadelphia in advance of the nation's bicentennial, a spoon holding a cherry installed at the Minneapolis Sculpture Garden in the mid-1980s, giant binoculars that were incorporated into a Frank Gehry building in California in 1991, a massive badminton shuttlecock that graced New York City's Guggenheim Museum in 1995, and a dropped ice cream cone atop the roof of a German shopping mall in 2001.

Many of his works were collaborations with his second wife, Coosje van Bruggen, and after 1981 her signature also appeared on the pieces. (She died in 2009, of breast cancer.)

Oldenburg died on July 18, 2022, in New York City, at the age of 93. In addition to van Bruggen, he was predeceased by his brother, Richard, a longtime director of New York's Museum of Modern Art (MoMA). He was survived by two stepchildren, Paulus and Maartje, as well as by three grandchildren. His work is part of the permanent collections at several major museums around the world.

See Current Biography 1970

Jacques Perrin

Born: Paris, France; July 13, 1941
Died: Paris, France; April 21, 2022
Occupation: French actor and filmmaker

Jacques Perrin enjoyed a long international film career—appearing in approximately 100 pictures and producing dozens more—but he was best-known to U.S. audiences for his role in *Cinema Paradiso* (1988).

He was born Jacques André Simonet on July 13, 1941, in Paris. His father managed the state-run theater Comédie-Française, while his mother was an actress. (He took her last name as a stage name.) Perrin studied at the Conservatoire National Supérieur d'Art Dramatique and soon began winning film roles.

Among his earliest pictures were the Italian drama *Girl with a Suitcase* (1961), in which he portrayed an earnest teen trying to save a naive woman from his loutish brother; *The Young Girls of Rochefort* (1967), a musical that starred Catherine Deneuve; and *Z* (1969), a political-assassination thriller directed by Greek filmmaker Costa-Gavras and produced by Perrin.

Perrin—whose other collaborations with Costa-Gavras included *State of Siege* (1972) and *Special Section* (1975)—did not become widely known to American audiences until 1988, when *Cinema Paradiso* was released. *Cinema Paradiso* tells the tale of Toto, an eight-year-old boy who becomes enamored of movies while growing up in a small Sicilian village and is befriended by the projectionist at his local theater; Perrin played the adult Toto, who has grown up to be a filmmaker, and while some critics characterized the movie as saccharine, it enjoyed significant success at the box office. *The Chorus* (2004), about a group of singing orphans who are mentored by Perrin's character, also proved to be a popular draw at U.S. arthouses.

Perrin also enjoyed a large measure of success as a producer of nature documentaries. A passionate environmentalist throughout his life, he was the force behind such pictures as *Microcosmos* (1996), about insects; *Oceans* (2009); and *Winged Migration* (2001), which tracks cranes, geese, and storks over the course of a year as they travel thousands of miles. *Migration* is considered by many critics to be a masterwork in the genre.

Perrin died in Paris, on April 21, 2022, the year in which his last film, the drama *Goliath*, was released. He was survived by his second wife, Valentine, and sons, Mathieu, Maxence, and Lancelot.

See Current Biography 2004

Wolfgang Petersen

Born: Emden, Germany; March 14, 1941
Died: Los Angeles, California; August 12, 2022
Occupation: German film director

Filmmaker Wolfgang Petersen was acclaimed in both his native Germany and Hollywood and was equally celebrated in both locales for the 1981 war picture *Das Boot*, which garnered six Oscar nods and became among the top-grossing German-language films ever released.

Petersen was born on March 14, 1941, in Emden, a town in Northern Germany. As a child in post-World War II Germany, he attended children's matinees at his local cinema and became particularly fond of Westerns with stars like John Wayne. At age 14, he received an eight-millimeter camera for Christmas and began making his own amateur films.

Excused from military service because of scoliosis, Petersen found work at a theater in Hamburg and later attended the German Film and Television Academy in Berlin, West Germany's first school of its type. His senior film project was purchased by a German television network, and he was subsequently hired to direct the popular crime series *Tatort* (*Crime Scene*).

By the time *Das Boot* was released, Peterson had directed some 20 German television films, miniseries and shorts. That acclaimed film, however, catapulted his career into an entirely new direction. The story of a group of sailors on a German U-boat, *Das Boot* won high praise for its historical verisimilitude and atmospheric staging, and it earned over $80 million in international box-office receipts. Its six Academy Award nominations set a record in the German film industry.

Now considered a Hollywood A-lister, Petersen spent much of his subsequent time in the United States, directing mainstream fare like the family-friendly fantasy *The NeverEnding Story* (1984); *In the Line of Fire* (1993), starring Clint Eastwood as a Secret

Service agent; the Harrison Ford vehicle *Air Force One* (1997); *The Perfect Storm* (2000) starring George Clooney as Captain Billy Tyne, based on a true story about commercial fisherman caught in the titular disaster; and *Troy* (2004), which starred Brad Pitt as Achilles.

Petersen's final film, the 2016 crime caper *Vier gegen die Bank* (*Four Against the Bank*), was also his first German-language work since *Das Boot*. He died of pancreatic cancer on August 12, 2022, at his home in the Brentwood section of Los Angeles. He was survived by his wife, Maria-Antoinette Borgel; a son, Daniel; and two grandchildren.

See Current Biography 2001

Sidney Poitier

Born: Miami, Florida; February 20, 1927
Died: Beverly Hills, California; January 6, 2022
Occupation: American actor and director

Sidney Poitier was widely acknowledged to be Hollywood's first Black leading man and credited with opening doors for future generations of Black actors.

Poitier was born in Miami, Florida, where his parents, tomato farmers from the Bahamas, had traveled to sell their crop. The youngest of nine children, he was raised in the Bahamas and at 12 dropped out of school to become a laborer. When he was a mischievous 14-year-old his parents sent him to Miami to live with an older brother.

There, in the American South, he first experienced segregation and racism. He later settled in New York City, where he found work washing dishes, digging ditches, and doing other unskilled labor. He was once shot in Harlem and often resorted to sleeping in public restrooms.

Lying about his age, he enlisted in the Army in 1943 and worked as an orderly at a Long Island veterans' hospital. Discharged two years later, he returned to the city and tried out unsuccessfully for the American Negro Theater. Stymied by his heavy Bahamian accent, he purchased a radio and began practicing his English relentlessly.

In 1946, he won a role in an all-Black production of *Lysistrata*, and other acting jobs gradually followed, including a role as a physician dealing with a racist patient in *No Way Out* (1950), a young priest in *Cry, the Beloved Country* (1962), a recalcitrant student in *Blackboard Jungle* (1955), and an escaped convict in *The Defiant Ones* (1958).

He broke new ground in 1963 when his work in the big-screen picture *Lilies of the Field*, which starred Poitier as a roving handyman who is coerced into helping a group of nuns build a chapel, made him the first Black performer ever to win an Academy Award in the best-actor category.

As the Civil Rights movement gained traction, Poitier found increasingly steady work, often portraying characters who faced injustice with poise and quiet dignity. In 1967 he appeared in three box-office hits: *In the Heat of Night* (opposite Rod Steiger), *Guess Who's Coming to Dinner* (alongside Spencer Tracy and Katharine Hepburn), and *To Sir, with Love* (whose theme song received heavy radio airplay).

As the pacifist Civil Rights movement gave way to the Black Power movement, films in which Black men repressed their anger and incited change in the hearts of racists with calm and reason fell out of favor. More popular were violent movies like *Shaft* (1971) and *Super Fly* (1972), which had no roles for someone of Poitier's restraint.

Although his star faded somewhat, Poitier had another box-office hit with the comedy *Uptown Saturday Night* (1974), in which he and Bill Cosby play friends who attempt to find a winning lottery ticket. While he never regained his former level of fame, he appeared with some regularity over the next decades in such projects as *A Piece of the Action* (1977), *Shoot to Kill* (1988), *Separate but Equal* (1991), *Sneakers* (1992), *A Good Day to Die* (1995), *The Jackal* (1997), and *The Last Brickmaker in America* (his final picture, released in 2001).

Poitier, who was awarded the Presidential Medal of Freedom in 2009 for his efforts to break down Hollywood's racial barriers, died on January 6, 2022, at his California home. He was survived by his second wife, Joanna Shimkus, and five of his six daughters.

See Current Biography 2000

Tina Ramirez

Born: Caracas, Venezuela; November 7, 1929
Died: New York, New York; September 6, 2022
Occupation: American dancer and director

Tina Ramirez was the founder of the New York-based Ballet Hispánico, launched in 1970 with the goal of providing Hispanic dancers with the chance to perform professionally and to introduce their culture to a broader audience. It is widely considered to be among the most respected and skilled dance companies in the world.

Ernestina Ramirez was born on November 7, 1929, in Caracas, Venezuela. Her father, José, was a famed bullfighter who used the name Gaonita in the ring. Her parents divorced when Ramirez was a child, and she moved to the United States with her mother, Gloria, who eventually remarried and became a community activist.

As a teenager, Ramirez began dancing professionally, touring with a show called *Rhythms of Spain*. She later began performing as a duo with her sister Coco, demonstrating flamenco at nightclubs throughout the United States and appearing in stage musicals that included Hispanic characters. (She was also featured in a television adaptation of *Man of La Mancha*.)

Ramirez, who lived in Spain briefly as a young woman, took lessons from flamenco dancer Lola Bravo, and in 1963 she took over management of Bravo's New York studio and began instructing her own students, many of whom came from poor families living in the surrounding Latino enclaves.

Savvy about the workings of local government thanks to her mother's community activism, Ramirez won funding from New York City's Office of Economic Opportunity in 1967 to start a summer arts program, and three years later, the New York State Council on the Arts awarded her a $20,000 grant to launch Ballet Hispánico, which drew some of its members from her summer arts-program graduates.

Occasionally, observers were confused by the group's name, expecting to see classical ballet, but gradually, Ballet Hispánico became part of the fabric of the city. By the time of Ramirez's death, on September 6, 2022, at the age of 92, the company had performed pieces from dozens of choreographers and had almost 100 works in its repertory.

Ramirez, who was survived by her sister Coco, was the recipient of a 2005 National Medal of Arts, and her other laurels included the NYC Mayor's Award of Honor for Arts and Culture (1983), the NYS Governor's Arts Award (1987), the Hispanic Heritage Award (1999), and an honorary Doctor of Fine Arts degree from Juilliard (2018).

See Current Biography 2004

Fidel V. Ramos

Born: Lingayen, Philippines; March 18, 1928
Died: Manila, Philippines; July 31, 2022
Occupation: Filipino politician and police chief

Fidel Valdez Ramos served as president of the Philippines from 1992 to 1998, overseeing a period of relative peace, stability, and economic growth.

Ramos was born on March 18, 1928, in Lingayen, north of Manila. His family was esteemed in Filipino society; his father, Narciso, served as an envoy and foreign minister, and one of his sisters was a diplomat and senator.

Ramos attended West Point Military Academy, graduating in 1950. He later earned a master's degree in civil engineering from the University of Illinois. After serving alongside U.S. troops in the Korean War and commanding a Philippine unit in Vietnam, he returned to his native country, then under the rule of President Ferdinand Marcos—who happened to be his second cousin. Ramos joined the Marcos regime, becoming one of the leader's "Rolex 12," so-called because of the expensive watches they were given. Marcos named him head of a ruthless national constabulary charged with fighting terrorism.

In 1972 Marcos, increasingly embattled, imposed martial law and arrested several political opponents, including Senator Benigno Simeon Aquino Jr., who was imprisoned and then exiled for years. Upon his return in 1983, Aquino was assassinated, thrusting his widow, Corazon, into the public eye. When she was elected as president in 1986, Ramos, then chief of the Filipino armed forces, threw his support behind her, surprising those who believed he would remain loyal to Marcos.

Corazon Aquino retained Ramos as armed forces chief and later named him defense minister, and in 1992, when he threw his hat in the ring for the presidency, she backed him. He vowed to continue strengthening democracy in the Philippines, and his accomplishments over his six-year tenure included quelling two longstanding guerilla insurgencies, purging the police force of corruption, cracking down on crime, and boosting private enterprise and foreign investment.

Suffering from dementia and heart problems, Ramos died at the Makati Medical Center in Manila, on July 31, 2022. He was survived by his wife of almost seven decades, Amelita; and four daughters, Angelita, Carolina, Cristina, and Gloria. He was predeceased in 2011 by a fifth daughter, Josephine.

See Current Biography 1994

Dan Reeves

Born: Rome, Georgia; January 19, 1944
Died: Atlanta, Georgia; January 1, 2022
Occupation: American football coach and player

Dan Reeves coached his teams to four Super Bowl appearances but did not triumph in any of them.

Reeves joined the Dallas Cowboys in 1965, after graduating from the University of South Carolina, where he had been a quarterback; during the eight seasons he played with the Texas-based team, which made him a running back, he recorded 1,990 rushing yards. In 1970, he assumed backfield coaching duties, and he later became an offensive coordinator under famed Coach Tom Landry.

With that experience under his belt, in 1981 Reeves became head coach of the Denver Broncos, who reached the Super Bowl in 1987 (against the New York Giants), 1988 (against the Washington Redskins), and 1990 (against the San Francisco 49ers). The Broncos lost each of those games by wide margins, and in 1992, team owner Pat Bowlen fired Reeves, citing intractable differences in personality and style.

Despite the streak of Super bowl losses behind him, Reeves was hired by the Giants the following year. The Giants lost to the 49ers, 44–3, in a 1993 divisional playoff game and did not even make the playoffs over the next three seasons; as a result, in 1996 he was summarily dismissed.

He was, however, quickly snapped up by the Atlanta Falcons—a team that was soon being considered among the best in the league under his direction. The following year, however, just as the Falcons were in the middle of a winning streak, Reeves was forced to undergo emergency quadruple bypass surgery. He returned to work in time to watch them play in the Super Bowl against the Broncos but then had the disappointment of seeing the rival team win, 34–19.

That defeat seemed to kick off several losing seasons for the Falcons, and Reeves was once again fired, in 2003, with just a handful of games left in the season. Despite his checkered record, the Associated Press named him coach of the year twice.

Reeves, suffering from dementia, died at his Atlanta home on January 1, 2022. He was survived by his wife, Pam; children, Lee, Laura, and Dana; and several grandchildren.

See Current Biography 2001

Régine

Born: Etterbeek, Belgium; December 26, 1929
Died: France; May 1, 2022
Occupation: French singer and nightclub owner

The impresario known as Régine is credited with launching the world's first discotheque in the late 1950s, setting off a craze that had become ubiquitous by the 1970s and changing nightlife forever.

Régine was born Rachelle Zylberberg on December 26, 1929, in Etterbeek, Belgium. She never knew her mother, who abandoned the family soon after her daughter's birth. Her father, an alcoholic Polish immigrant, ran a small restaurant near the Parisian neighborhood of Montmartre, where Régine—who had a brother, Maurice, and a half sister, Evelyne—waited on tables as a child. When the Nazis invaded Paris in 1940, her father was sent to a prison camp, and Régine hid in a convent, bullied by the other girls for being Jewish.

For a time after the war, she peddled undergarments on the streets of Paris, all the while dreaming of fame and fortune. In 1957, she borrowed money and opened a small nightclub in a basement space off a Parisian alley. Noticing a lag in activity when the jukebox was between songs, she installed two turntables so that the music played continually. That innovative and wildly successful establishment is generally considered the first-ever discotheque, and by the 1970s Régine—who also recorded a handful of albums and appeared in occasional films—had opened almost two-dozen clubs in cities around the world, including Rio de Janeiro, Saint-Tropez, London, Cairo, Los Angeles, and Miami, as well as an eponymous nightspot in New York City that attracted a steady stream of celebrities like Joan Collins, Mick Jagger, Andy Warhol, and Brooke Shields.

By the 1990s, however, Régine's $500 million business empire had dwindled thanks to a burgeoning new generation of popular clubs. She spent her later years living in Paris, doing charitable work, and throwing occasional parties. Still known as the "Queen of the Night," she published a memoir, *Mes Nuits, Mes Rencontres* (*My Nights, My Encounters*) in 2015.

Régine's two marriages ended in divorce. She died in France (some French-language sources specify in a region of Paris) on May 1, 2022, at the age of 92. She was predeceased by her son, Lionel, in 2006, and no information about other survivors was made publicly available.

See Current Biography 1980

Harry Reid

Born: Searchlight, Nevada; December 2, 1939
Died: Henderson, Nevada; December 28, 2021
Occupation: American politician

Harry Reid, a Democrat who served as Senate Majority Leader from 2007 to 2015, was largely responsible for the 2010 passage of Barack Obama's Patient Protection and Affordable Care Act, which extended health care coverage to tens of millions of previously uninsured Americans and prevented insurance companies from turning away those with preexisting conditions.

Reid's youth was often described as "Dickensian." One of four boys, he was born in a small Nevada mining town and lived in a home with no indoor plumbing. His father, a miner, suffered from depression and drank heavily, and his mother took in laundry from local brothels to help keep the family fed. Reid, who worked in the mines and at a local

gas station as a teen, hitchhiked to the nearest large town, Henderson, each Monday and stayed with relatives until Friday in order to attend high school.

Despite those hardships, he was a bright and popular student, and thanks to athletic scholarships he won as a boxer, he later earned degrees from Utah State University (1961) and the George Washington School of Law (1964). He worked as Henderson city attorney from 1964 to 1966, Nevada's lieutenant governor from 1970 to 1974, and chair of the Nevada Gaming Commission—a post that put him in the crosshairs of organized crime bosses—from 1977 to 1981.

In 1982 Reid, who had converted to Mormonism, was elected to the U.S. House of Representatives, where he served until winning election to the Senate in 1986. As a relatively conservative Democrat, he soon gained a reputation for not hewing strictly to party lines. For example, he supported a Republican-led ban on burning the American flag and was known to side with the mining industry in its conflicts with environmentalists.

In late 2004 Reid was named Senate Minority Leader, and when the Democrats triumphed in the midterm elections of 2006, he became Majority Leader. He won praise from many quarters for challenging George W. Bush's stance on the Iraq War, and in 2009, he kept his leadership post when Obama stepped into the presidency.

A key supporter of Obama's efforts to improve health care for Americans, Reid also became well known for his efforts to reach bipartisan agreement on raising the debt ceiling while instituting spending cuts in order to balance the budget.

The Republicans regained control of the Senate in the 2014 midterms, and Reid, now Minority Leader, announced he would not be seeking reelection in subsequent elections; his decision was due in some part to losing much of his vision in a 2015 accident.

Reid left the Senate in 2017. He was suffering from pancreatic cancer when he died on December 28, 2021, at his Henderson home. He was survived by his wife, Landra; their children, Rory, Lana Reid Barringer, Leif, Josh, and Key; and 19 grandchildren. Shortly before his death, the Las Vegas airport had been renamed in his honor.

See Current Biography 2003

Ivan Reitman

Born: Komárno, Czechoslovakia (now Slovakia); October 27, 1946
Died: Montecito, California; February 12, 2022
Occupation: Czech-born film director and producer

Many of Ivan Reitman's films became the cultural touchstones of their day, including *Animal House* (1978), whose frat-boy protagonists made "toga party" and "food fight" into unavoidable catchphrases, and *Ghostbusters* (1984), a juggernaut supernatural comedy whose theme song and tie-in merchandise were inescapable the year of its release.

Reitman's parents had survived the Nazis, and in 1950, when he was a preschooler, they fled their native Czechoslovakia to escape communism and settled, virtually penniless, in Canada. They had made part of the trip hidden under the floorboards of a tugboat for five days and had given Reitman tranquilizers to keep him quiet.

The family ultimately founded a successful dry-cleaning business, and Reitman attended McMaster University, in Ontario, thinking initially that he would study music as he had been in a folk band in high school. His goals changed, however, after he happened to take a film course.

His early efforts did not bode well for his future as a mainstream filmmaker; one picture, *The Columbus of Sex*, made shortly after he graduated, got him fined $300 in 1969 under the obscenity provisions of Ontario's Criminal Code.

Still, he began to sign on to produce various projects, including *The Magic Show* (1974), a Broadway extravaganza starring Doug Henning and the David Cronenberg horror film *Shivers* (1975).

In 1978 Reitman co-produced *Animal House*, which remained one of the signature films of his career and made a star of John Belushi. Reitman long maintained that he wished he had directed the iconic picture instead of just co-producing it. He did get to direct his next project, however: *Meatballs* (1979), a madcap comedy starring Bill Murray. He and Murray developed a fruitful working relationship; the comedian also starred in *Stripes* (1981) and *Ghostbusters* (1984).

Reitman's many other popular pictures include the Robert Redford vehicle *Legal Eagles* (1986); *Twins* (1988), which featured the unlikely pairing of Arnold Schwarzenegger and Danny DeVito; *Kindergarten Cop* (1990), which also placed Schwarzenegger, previously known as an action hero, in comic situations; the political comedy *Dave* (1993); *Six Days Seven Nights* (1998), which features Harrison Ford and Anne Heche as nemeses who must survive together after their plane crash lands in a remote area; and football drama *Draft Day* (2014).

Reitman died at his home in Montecito, California, on February 12, 2022, of unspecified causes. His children, Jason, Catherine, and Caroline made the announcement.

See Current Biography 2001

Peter Robinson

Born: Yorkshire, England; March 17, 1950
Died: Toronto, Ontario, Canada; October 4, 2022
Occupation: Canadian crime novelist

Inspector Alan Banks, the protagonist of almost 30 crime novels, was the creation of beloved author Peter Robinson. The books were translated into 20 languages, sold some nine million copies worldwide, were adapted into a popular television series that aired from 2010 to 2016, and won Robinson dozens of writing prizes.

Peter Robinson was born in West Yorkshire, England, and grew up in a working-class section of Leeds. He studied English literature at the University of Leeds, graduating with honors in 1974 before moving to Canada. In his adopted country, he entered the University of Windsor, where he took classes with acclaimed author Joyce Carol Oates and earned a master's degree in 1975. He later returned to school to work towards a PhD, which he received at York University in 1983.

Robinson, homesick for his native Yorkshire, decided to base the setting of his first novel, *Gallows View* (1987), on towns he was intimately familiar with like Richmond and Ripon. The fictional Eastvale, as he called it, was larger than its real counterparts, however, because, as the author joked to journalists, no reader would ever believe so many murders could occur in a place too small.

Gallows View, which garnered Robinson the first of many Arthur Ellis Awards from Crime Writers of Canada, introduced the character of Banks, a skilled detective with an unrelenting dedication to fairness and justice, a complex romantic life, and a love for rock music. Robinson went on to write 28 more Banks novels, as well as stand-alone novels like the psychological thriller *Caedmon's Song* (1990), and short-story collections like *Not Safe after Dark* (1998) and *The Price of Love* (2009).

In addition to its Arthur Ellis Awards, the organization Crime Writers of Canada honored Robinson with the 2010 Derrick Murdock Award for his contributions to the genre and in 2020 named him a "Grand Master" for his body of work. His international laurels included an Edgar Award from the Mystery Writers of America, the Le Grand Prix de Littérature Policière in France, and the Dagger in the Library, an annual prize given by the British Crime Writers' Association.

Robinson, who taught at the University of Windsor and other schools on occasion, died in Toronto on October 4, 2022, from what his publisher described as a brief illness. He was survived by his wife, Sheila. His final novel, *Standing in the Shadows*, will be published posthumously in early 2023.

See Current Biography 2007

Magdalena Ruiz Guiñazú

Born: Buenos Aires, Argentina; February 15, 1935
Died: Buenos Aires, Argentina; September 6, 2022
Occupation: Argentine writer and journalist

Magdalena Ruiz Guiñazú was among the most prominent Argentinean journalists of her day. A ubiquitous presence on her country's televisions and radios, she was given a lifetime achievement award by the International Women's Media Foundation in 2003, adding to a long list of laurels that included 14 Martín Fierro Awards from the Association of Argentine Television and Radio Journalists, a Legion of Honor from the government of France, and the Italian Order of Merit.

María Magdalena Teresa Ruiz Guiñazú was born on February 15, 1935, in Buenos Aires. (Some sources say 1931.) Her mother, María Celina Cantilo Ortiz Basualdo, hailed from a wealthy family, and her father, Enrique Ruiz Guiñazú, was a career diplomat who at one time served as Argentina's foreign minister. Against that privileged backdrop, she became fluent in English, Italian, and French, and as a teen she decided upon a career in journalism.

She began working at a woman's magazine in the 1960s, and in the 1980s, she was hired by one of the few private radio stations allowed to operate during the brutal military dictatorship of General Jorge Rafael Videla, who had assumed control over Argentina in 1976. The period from 1976 to 1983 is generally called the "dirty war," during which thousands were kidnapped, tortured, or killed—many simply disappeared with no trace. Ruiz Guiñazú could frequently be heard on the air in those years, and her byline appeared regularly in *La Nación*, a widely read newspaper.

In 1983, once Raúl Alfonsín became the first democratically elected president of Argentina in more than 20 years, he established a National Commission on the Disappearance of Persons, and Ruiz Guiñazú was appointed as one of its members. The Commission was later instrumental in bringing many of the dirty war's perpetrators to justice.

In 1987 Ruiz Guiñazú moderated Argentina's first televised political debate, and that year she began hosting a morning radio show, *Magdalena Tempranisimo*, that became known for its unflinching look at current events. (Her willingness to probe politically sensitive topics sometimes resulted in death threats.) The show aired on Radio Mitre for more than 20 years.

Concurrently, she appeared frequently on television; wrote several books, including a novel and a collection of her newspaper columns; and founded Asociación Periodistas, an organization dedicated to advancing press freedom.

Ruiz Guiñazú's marriage produced four children before ending in divorce. Later, for more than 25 years, she was involved with Argentine equestrian Sergio Dellacha, but the pair never wed. Ruiz Guiñazú died in Buenos Aires on September 6, 2022.

See Current Biography 2004

Bill Russell

Born: Monroe, Louisiana; February 12, 1934
Died: Mercer Island, Washington; July 31, 2022
Occupation: American basketball player and sportscaster

Basketball Hall of Famer Bill Russell helped the Boston Celtics win 11 NBA championships—including eight consecutively, from 1959 to 1966. Named an All-Star a dozen times and the NBA's MVP five times over the course of his 13-year pro career, he also held the distinction of being the first Black head coach in that or any major U.S. sports league.

William Felton Russell was born on February 12, 1934, in Monroe, Louisiana. He often described to interviewers the racism his family experienced: his father was sometimes denied service at local establishments, for example, and his mother was harassed by police for wearing clothes considered too stylish for her station. When Russell was nine, the family moved to California, where his father opened a trucking business.

Russell, whose mother died when he was 12, earned a basketball scholarship to the University of San Francisco, where he played three varsity seasons and helped lead the team to NCAA championships twice. He subsequently played on the U.S. Olympic team and is widely credited for bringing home a gold medal from the Melbourne Games in 1956.

Later that same year, he joined the Celtics, playing in 48 rookie games and helping the Boston franchise win its first-ever NBA championship. Every year from 1959 to 1966, the Celts repeated that feat, but 1967 found them facing off unsuccessfully against the Philadelphia 76ers—a team that included Wilt Chamberlain, a career-long rival of Russell's.

In Russell's last two seasons—a period in which he both played and coached—the team regained the championship, with the 1969 triumph providing a particular vindication as that matchup was against the Los Angeles Lakers, which had signed Chamberlain.

By the end of his playing career, Russell had recorded 21,620 rebounds, averaging more than 20 a game, making him the number-two rebounder in league history. (Chamberlain was number one, but observers have pointed out that the playing field was not level, as he was several inches taller than Russell.)

After leaving the court, Russell served for a time as an ABC sports commentator, and he subsequently returned to coaching, signing on with such teams as the Seattle SuperSonics and Sacramento Kings. Later in life, he made occasional commercials, appeared on the motivational-speaking circuit, and attended fan conventions to sign autographs.

An outspoken advocate of civil rights throughout his life, he was awarded the Presidential Medal of Freedom in 2011.

Russell died on July 31, 2022, at the age of 88. Although his family did not disclose details, some sources list his place of death as Mercer Island, Washington. Russell had been married four times and had three children, but no information was made publicly available about his survivors. The annual Bill Russell NBA Finals Most Valuable Player Award has been named in his honor since 2009.

See Current Biography 1975

Nafis Sadik

Born: Jaunpur, India; August 18, 1929
Died: New York, New York; August 14, 2022
Occupation: Pakistani physician and United Nations official

Nafis Sadik, a former executive director of the U.N. Population Fund, was known for her staunch belief that women should have control over their reproductive choices and her advocacy for curbing global population growth.

Sadik was born Iffat Nafis Shoaib on August 18, 1929, in Jaunpur, India. Her father, Muhammad, an executive of the World Bank, was at one time the finance minister of Pakistan. From an early age, she expressed interest in a career that would have an impact on the world—despite the fact that such ambition was then considered unusual for a girl from a Muslim family.

Sadik ultimately decided to pursue medicine. She attended a convent school in the city then known as Calcutta before earning a degree from Pakistan's Dow Medical College, in Karachi. She then traveled to the United States to study at the Johns Hopkins University School of Medicine and complete an internship at Baltimore City Hospital.

Returning to Pakistan, Sadik found work at hospitals run by the Pakistani military, most often being assigned to wards devoted to women and children. She began overseeing a governmental health commission in 1964 and was soon named to Pakistan's Central Family Planning Council. In 1970, she was tapped to serve as the council's director.

The following year, Sadik joined the U.N. Population Fund, an agency dedicated to sexual and reproductive health in countries around the globe. (Its aims include ensuring reliable access to contraception, training birth attendants, preventing gender-based violence, and discouraging female genital mutilation.) She was named assistant executive director in 1977 and executive director a decade later.

In the latter post, Sadik was largely responsible for the "Program for Action," a plan to mitigate world population growth. The plan, meant to be transformative and considered revolutionary by many observers, stressed that women must have control of their health and reproductive choices. Despite facing staunch opposition from the Catholic Church and other such groups, the program was adopted by almost 200 countries in 1994, at a U.N. conference in Egypt.

Sadik retired from the U.N. in 2000. She died at her home in New York City on August 14, 2022, at the age of 92. She had been predeceased by her husband, Azhar, an energy-sector executive. One daughter, Mehreen, also predeceased her, in 2015. She was survived by a son, Omar; three daughters, Ambereen, Wafa, and Ghazala; ten grandchildren; and four great-grandchildren.

See Current Biography 1996

Mort Sahl

Born: Montreal, Canada; May 11, 1927
Died: Mill Valley, California; October 26, 2021
Occupation: Canadian comedian

In an era when many performers relied upon mother-in-law jokes and gentle observational humor, Mort Sahl's biting stand-up comedy and irreverent social commentary paved the way for others such as Lenny Bruce, George Carlin, and Richard Pryor.

Sahl pushed back against authority even as a young man serving in the military on an Alaska base; during his time in the service, he edited a satiric newspaper called *Poop from the Group* that often earned him mess-hall duty.

Following his discharge, he earned a degree in urban management from the University of Southern California, moved to the San Francisco area, and began performing his comedy at the hungry i, a nightclub that soon became nationally known thanks in some part to him.

His targets included establishment figures like Joseph McCarthy and Dwight D. Eisenhower, and as his popularity grew, he played packed college auditoriums, appeared on the television talk shows of the era, and recorded multiple best-selling albums, including *At Sunset*, which he made in 1955 and which the Library of Congress cites as being among the earliest examples of modern stand-up comedy on record.

Sahl was hired by the John F. Kennedy campaign to write jokes for the candidate, but after JFK was elected, he made the popular, new president the object of his barbs. It was a misstep in the public eye, and Sahl's star dimmed considerably and never fully recovered. (His career was not helped by what some considered an unseemly fascination with the Kennedy assassination and the faults he found in the Warren Commission report.)

Sahl took some pride in skewering people on both the left and right, and throughout his life, he often expressed bitterness about how progressives had turned away from him.

He died on October 26, 2021, at his home in Mill Valley, California. Married and divorced four times, Sahl had one son, who died of a heroin overdose in 1996.

See Current Biography 1960

Manuel Santana

Born: Madrid, Spain; May 10, 1938
Died: Marbella, Spain; December 11, 2021
Occupation: Spanish tennis player

Manuel Santana was considered one of the greatest tennis players Spain has ever produced.

Born Manuel Santana Martínez, the player got his start as a ball boy at Madrid's Velázquez tennis club, using his tips to help support his struggling family. At 13, he won a ball boys' tournament and was officially admitted to the club as a member, and in 1955 he won the Spanish junior championship.

In 1961, in Paris, he won his first Grand Slam, playing on a clay court and trouncing Italy's Nicola Pietrangeli, whom he beat again in the French Open in 1964. (He was the first Spaniard ever to win a Grand Slam event.) In 1965, although he disliked playing on grass, he became the first European in almost 40 years to win at Forest Hills (later renamed the U.S. Open). He racked up a win at Wimbledon the following year, cementing his reputation as a world-class player.

Over the course of his career Santana won 72 tournaments and inspired such Spanish tennis greats as Manuel Orantes, Conchita Martínez, and Rafael Nadal. (At the time of Santana's death, only Nadal had won more Grand Slams.)

In addition to his four Grand Slam triumphs (Forest Hills, Wimbledon, and the French Open twice), Santana represented Spain at the 1968 Olympic Games in Mexico City, winning gold in singles and silver in doubles. After retiring from competition, Santana captained Spain's Davis Cup team from 1980 to 1985 and again from 1995 to 1999. He also served as manager of multiple tennis clubs and directed the Mutua Madrid Open tournament for several years.

Santana, who had been diagnosed with Parkinson's disease, died of an apparent heart attack in Marbella, on December 11, 2021. He was survived by his fourth wife, Claudia, and his five children: Beatriz, Manolo, Borja, Bárbara, and Alba.

See Current Biography 1967

Maarten Schmidt

Born: Groningen, Netherlands; December 28, 1929
Died: Fresno, California; September 17, 2022
Occupation: American astronomer

In 1963, Maarten Schmidt gained renown in the scientific world for his groundbreaking identification of a quasar—an exceptionally bright object powered by an enormous black hole. Billions of light-years away, quasars were the most-distant objects ever identified in the universe to that date, and his work caused astronomers to rethink their conventional concepts of the cosmos.

Maarten Schmidt was born on December 28, 1929, in Groningen, a city in The Netherlands. His uncle, an amateur astronomer, encouraged his youthful interest in science and helped him build a rudimentary telescope, using the tube from an empty roll of toilet paper. During World War II, when Groningen residents were ordered to extinguish all lights in order to hinder German bombing attempts, he found his stargazing activities even more fruitful.

Schmidt attended the University of Groningen, where he studied math and physics, earning an undergraduate degree in 1949 and a master's degree in 1950. He received a PhD from Leiden University six years later. After spending time in the United States as a Carnegie Fellow, in 1959 he joined the faculty of the California Institute of Technology, in Pasadena.

By that time, astronomers had discovered a way to harness the power of radio technology in their studies, but they were puzzled by invisible objects they dubbed "quasi-stellar radio sources" or "quasars," which emitted discernable radio signals but were difficult to categorize. In 1963, Schmidt, using the powerful telescope at San Diego's Palomar Observatory, was able to pinpoint one such object that appeared to be moving swiftly away from Earth. When he measured its speed (an astonishing 30,000 miles a second), he discovered that it was 2.4 billion light years away—one of the most distant objects in the universe from Earth.

Schmidt published his findings in the journal *Nature* and spent much of the rest of his career studying quasars—work that earned him the inaugural Kavli Prize in Astrophysics in 2008.

After serving, variously, as head of Caltech's Division of Physics, Mathematics and Astronomy and director of its Hale Observatories, Schmidt retired in 1996, with the title of Francis L. Moseley Professor Emeritus of Astronomy.

He died on September 17, 2022, at his Fresno home at the age of 92. He was predeceased by his wife, Cornelia, and survived by their children, Anne, Elizabeth, and Marijke; four grandchildren; and five great-grandchildren.

See Current Biography 1966

Vin Scully

Born: Bronx, New York; November 29, 1927
Died: Los Angeles, California; August 2, 2022
Occupation: American sportscaster

Vin Scully spent nearly seven decades as the announcer for the Dodgers, initially in Brooklyn and then, when the franchise moved to the West Coast in 1958, in Los Angeles. Known for his accurate play-by-play and engaging stories, he won a spot in the Baseball Hall of Fame in 1982 and garnered a lifetime-achievement Emmy Award in 1995.

Vincent Edward Scully was born in the New York City borough of the Bronx on November 29, 1927, to parents who had immigrated from Ireland. As a boy, he loved listening to broadcasts of college ballgames, and he played the outfield while in high school. Later, at Fordham University, he hit only one home run his entire two-season college career, but he excelled on the air as a sports commentator for WFUV, the university's station.

Scully graduated in 1949 and found work as a fill-in reporter at a CBS affiliate in Washington, DC. While there, he met Red Barber, who headed sports coverage for CBS Radio and also announced Dodgers games. Barber assigned Scully, then 22, to announce a game at Ebbets Field, and impressed by his performance, signed the young sportscaster the following year to a spot as number-three announcer for the Dodgers. In 1954, Scully ascended to the number-one spot, and four years later, when the iconic team moved to Los Angeles, he went with them.

Known for asking listeners to "pull up a chair," Scully was behind the microphone during some of baseball's most enduring moments: when the Dodgers, then still in Brooklyn, clinched the 1955 World Series; when Sandy Koufax pitched shutouts in games five and seven, helping win the 1965 World Series in a best-of-seven matchup against the Minnesota Twins; when Hank Aaron of the opposing Braves hit his 715th home run, shattering Babe Ruth's record; and numerous others.

In addition to his duties with the Dodgers, Scully offered commentary on football and golf for CBS during portions of his career, and as a member of the sports team at NBC, he could be heard during baseball's Game of the Week, All-Star Games, the playoffs and the World Series. He stepped down from the networks in 1998 but continued to announce local games until 2016; his final time in the booth came on October 2 of that year, during a game that saw the Dodgers unsuccessfully face off against the San Francisco Giants.

Scully—who was named the number-one sportscaster of all time by the American Sportscasters Association in 2009 and received the Presidential Medal of Freedom in 2016—died at his Los Angeles home on August 2, 2022, at the age of 94. The twice-widowed Scully was survived by three daughters (Erin, Kelly, and Catherine); two sons (Kevin and Todd); and more than 20 grandchildren and great-grandchildren. He was predeceased in 1994 by one son, Michael.

See Current Biography 2001

Bernard Shaw

Born: Chicago, Illinois; May 22, 1940
Died: Washington, DC; September 7, 2022
Occupation: American journalist

Shaw was a familiar face to CNN viewers; as a prime-time anchor for two decades, he provided a calm, authoritative voice during troubling times and periods of violence, including the Persian Gulf War and the Tiananmen Square protests.

Bernard Shaw was born into a working-class Chicago family on May 22, 1940. Fascinated from a young age by the daily newspapers his father brought home and a fan of the legendary journalist Edward R. Murrow, Shaw dreamed of forging his own reporting career. That ambition was cemented in 1961, after he met and befriended CBS anchor Walter Cronkite while serving in the Marines.

After leaving the military, Shaw attended the University of Illinois, Chicago, graduating in 1966 with a degree in history. He then embarked on a succession of jobs at local media outlets, and in 1971 he became a political reporter at CBS. A few years later, he accepted a post as Latin American correspondent at ABC. During his stints at those major networks, he covered numerous history-making events, including Watergate and the Jonestown Massacre.

In 1980, when media mogul Ted Turner launched CNN (Cable News Network), aiming to present 24 hours of news coverage each day—a stark contrast to the 30-minute news shows that ran on the major networks—Shaw became one of the first Black primetime anchors in television history.

Shaw remained at CNN until his retirement in 2001, winning widespread praise for his coverage from Baghdad during the bloody conflict there, his unruffled demeanor after the attempted assassination of President Ronald Reagan, and his fact-filled reportage during the government's establishment of martial law in Beijing. On at least one occasion, however, he faced negative criticism; while moderating a 1988 presidential debate between Democrat Michael Dukakis and incumbent Republican George H.W. Bush, Shaw asked Dukakis if he would be tougher on crime if his own wife were raped or murdered—a line of questioning that many viewers found distasteful and unprofessional.

Shaw died of pneumonia at a Washington, DC hospital on September 7, 2022. He was survived by his wife, Linda; daughter, Anil; and son, Amar.

See Current Biography 1995

Mark Shields

Born: Weymouth, Massachusetts; May 25, 1937
Died: Chevy Chase, Maryland; June 18, 2022
Occupation: American political commentator and columnist

Mark Shields was a Democratic political consultant who switched, mid-career, to working as a newspaper columnist and television commentator, most notably on the CNN show *Capital Gang* and *PBS NewsHour*, on which he attracted equal measures of praise and opprobrium for his staunchly liberal views.

One of four children, Mark Stephen Shields was born in Weymouth, Massachusetts, on May 25, 1937. He sometimes joked to interviewers that in his Irish-Catholic family, you were a Democrat and Red Sox fan from birth. (Among his most indelible childhood memories was of venturing out with his parents at five in the morning to watch President Harry S. Truman pass through town.)

Shields graduated in 1959 from the University of Notre Dame, and the following year he enlisted in the U.S. Marines. He spent two years in the service and then secured a job as an aide to Wisconsin senator William Proxmire. Following that stint, he embarked on a career as an independent campaign strategist. Although he worked on numerous failed national campaigns, including those of Robert F. Kennedy, Sargent Shriver, Mo Udall, and Edmund Muskie, he also had regular successes. He was instrumental, for example, in John J. Gilligan's 1970 Ohio gubernatorial win and Kevin H. White's Boston mayoral bid in 1975.

By the end of the 1970s, he had decided to follow a different trajectory, and he found work at *The Washington Post*—first as an editorial writer and then a weekly syndicated political columnist. From 1988 to 2005 he appeared on the CNN talk show *Capital Gang*, facing off against his conservative counterparts. Starting in 2007, he also performed a similar function on the show *Inside Washington*, which aired on PBS and ABC until going off the air in 2013.

In what was arguably his highest-profile assignment, he served as a regular commentator on PBS NewsHour for more than three decades, from 1987 through 2020. Shields, who taught at the University of Pennsylvania and Harvard in addition to his media duties, retired at the age of 83.

Two years later, on June 18, 2022, Shields died at his home in Chevy Chase, Maryland, due to kidney failure. He was survived by his wife of more than five decades, Anne, a lawyer and administrator at the U.S. Department of the Interior; their daughter, Amy; and two grandchildren.

See Current Biography 2005

Jô Soares

Born: Rio de Janeiro, Brazil; January 16, 1938
Died: São Paulo, Brazil; August 5, 2022
Occupation: Brazilian actor and humorist

Jô Soares is best known for his work as a humorist and a television talk show host.

Jô Eugênio Soares was born on January 16, 1938 in Rio de Janeiro, Brazil. He originally aimed to become a diplomat like his grandfather, and as a child he learned to speak English, French, Italian, and Spanish in addition to his native Portuguese. He developed an interest in theater as a student in Switzerland during his teenage years and began studying acting once he returned to Brazil.

Soares first appeared onscreen in a 1954 musical film and had his television debut four years later, when he began writing and performing comedy sketches on the Brazilian station TV Rio. His writing soon developed a characteristic style of ironic humor notable in the show's characters. In 1988, he began hosting the talk show *Jô Soares Onze e Meia* ("Jô Soares at Eleven-Thirty") on the station SBT. Soares also published some of his humor in newspaper columns and later, books. Soares wrote four novels, but is perhaps best known for his first, *O Xangô de Baker Street* ("A Samba for Sherlock"), a historical mystery-comedy published in 1995 and made into a film in 2001.

In 2000, Soares moved to Rede Globo, where he hosted a talk show, *Programa do Jô*, until 2016 and quickly gained fame for its hundreds of celebrity guests and Soares's humorous catchphrases.

Soares's other achievements include producing several plays, releasing various jazz albums, and appearing in Brazilian sketch comedy series throughout the 1970s and 1980s, including such titles as *Faça Humor, Não Faça Guerra* ("Make Humor, Not War") and *Viva o Gordo* ("Long Live the Fat Man").

Soares had one son, Rafael, from his marriage to the actress Therezinha Millet Austregésilo (to whom he was married from 1959–79). Rafael died in 2014 at the age of 50, leaving his father without any surviving relatives. Soares died at age 84 on August 5, 2022, in the Sirio Libanes hospital of São Paulo, where he had been suffering from pneumonia since July 28.

See Current Biography 2002

Stephen Sondheim

Born: New York, New York; March 22, 1930
Died: Roxbury, Connecticut; November 26, 2021
Occupation: American composer and lyricist

Stephen Sondheim was one of the most celebrated and creative figures in the theater world, setting the bar high for the American stage musical.

When he was a child, Sondheim was deeply influenced by lyricist Oscar Hammerstein, a family friend, and he became determined to pursue a similar path. The launch of his musical career was inauspicious, however: while in his early 20s he wrote lyrics and music for a show titled *Saturday Night*, but the producer died before raising the money to mount it. (The musical was not presented to the public until 1997.)

Sondheim fared better later in the 1950s, when he wrote the lyrics for the hit shows *West Side Story* and *Gypsy*, which earned him a reputation on Broadway as someone able to write character-driven lyrics capable of revealing salient truths and advancing the story. In 1962, he wrote the music and lyrics for *A Funny Thing Happened on the Way to the Forum*, which won a Tony Award for best musical and ran on Broadway for more than two years.

His subsequent shows included *Company* (1970), which won six Tonys; *Follies* (1971), directed by regular Sondheim collaborator Harold Prince; *A Little Night Music* (1973), which featured what was arguably his most famous song, "Send in the Clowns"; the comically macabre *Sweeney Todd* (1979); *Merrily We Roll Along* (1981), based on a 1934 play of the same name by George S. Kaufman and Moss Hart; *Sunday in the Park with George* (1984), which won a Tony nod as best musical, along with the 1985 Pulitzer Prize for Drama and a slew of other honors; the fairy tale-inspired *Into the Woods* (1987); and *Assassins* (1990), based on the lives of a group of murderous historical figures, including John Wilkes Booth and Lee Harvey Oswald.

Over the course of his storied career, Sondheim wrote both the music and lyrics for a dozen shows (as well as for a handful of revues, including *Side by Side by Sondheim* and *Sondheim on Sondheim*.) In all, he won five Tony Awards for best musical, and six for best original score. Among his other laurels were Kennedy Center Honors for lifetime achievement in 1993, a Tony award for lifetime achievement in 2008, and a Presidential Medal of Freedom presented by Barack Obama in 2015. In 2010, a Broadway theater was named in his honor.

Sondheim maintained a townhouse on East 49th Street in Manhattan, as well as a home in the western Connecticut town of Roxbury. He was in Roxbury when he died on November 26, 2021, of cardiovascular failure. He was survived by his husband, Jeffrey Romley, as well as by a half-brother, Walter.

See Current Biography 1973

Pierre Soulages

Born: Rodez, Occitania, France; December 24, 1919
Died: Sète, France; October 26, 2022
Occupation: French painter and printmaker

Soulages was one of the most respected artists of post-World War II Europe, celebrated, especially, for his abstract explorations of the color black in all its variations.

Pierre Jean Louis Germain Soulages was born in Rodez, a town in the south of France, on December 24, 1919. Raised by his mother and older sister from the age of five, following the death of his father, Soulages developed an early interest in art. After being admitted to Paris's École des Beaux-Arts, however, he became disillusioned by its traditional curriculum and dropped out.

He was drafted during World War II, and when France fell in 1940, he entered a school of fine arts in Montpellier—a city that the Nazis subsequently occupied. Knowing that he was subject to arrest and forced labor, Soulages obtained false papers that enabled him to work in a vineyard.

After the allied victory, he returned to Paris to paint, and he soon attracted attention with a series of somber works that made use of dark walnut stain or tar. He continued experimenting with the color black, often using wide swaths of paint that caught the light in interesting ways. His work was featured at the prestigious Venice Biennale in 1952, and New York galleries vied to represent him. (In 1954 he signed with the Samuel Kootz Gallery, a pioneering champion of Abstract Expressionists.)

In 2014 Soulages donated several hundred works to launch an eponymous museum in his hometown, and five years later, he celebrated his 100th birthday with an exhibition, "Pierre Soulages: A Century," at the Lévy Gorvy gallery in New York City.

Soulages died on October 26, 2022, at the age of 102, at a hospital in Sète, a city in the south of France. He was survived by his wife of several decades, Colette, who helped manage his career.

See Current Biography 1958

Antonietta Stella

Born: Perugia, Italy; March 15, 1929
Died: Rome, Italy; February 23, 2022
Occupation: Italian opera singer

Antonietta Stella performed in opera houses around the world, becoming known for her rich vocalism and expressive acting.

After she began learning the arias she heard on the radio, at age 10 Stella embarked on singing lessons, and she ultimately studied at the Conservatory of Perugia and at the Accademia Nazionale di Santa Cecilia in Rome. She won first prize in the Spoleto Operatic Festival in 1949 and made her professional debut, at the Rome Opera House, on January 27, 1951, singing the role of Leonora in Verdi's *La Forza del Destino* (*The Force of Destiny*).

In 1954, Stella made her debut at the famed Teatro alla Scala in Milan, singing the leading role of Desdemona in Verdi's *Otello* and garnering international attention. She regularly performed at La Scala after that, singing such parts as Violetta in *La traviata* (*The Fallen Woman*), the title roles in *Aida* and *Tosca*, Mimi in *La bohème* (*The Bohemian*), and Cio-Cio-San in *Madama Butterfly*.

The year 1955 was an auspicious one for her, marking her debuts at the Wiener Staatsoper, London's Royal Opera House, the Paris Opera, and the Lyric Opera of Chicago. She made her Metropolitan Opera debut the following year, in *Aida*, and over the course of her career she would perform more than 70 times on the Metropolitan stage. She was also active in the recording studio, releasing well-reviewed versions of *Il trovatore* (*The Troubadour*), *Tosca*, *La traviata*, *Don Carlo*, and *Andrea Chenier*, among other works.

Most associated with operas by Puccini and Verdi, Stella was known by the end of her career as one of the most skilled spinto sopranos ever to perform. (A spinto can reach the high notes of a lyric soprano but is also capable of pushing her voice further.)

Stella died in Rome, on February 23, 2022, at the age of 92.

See Current Biography 1959

was survived by his wife, Joy, and two children, Austin and Sophie.

See Current Biography 1991

Dean Stockwell

Born: Hollywood, California; March 5, 1935
Died: Hollywood, California; November 7, 2021
Occupation: American actor

Over the course of his decades-long-acting career, Dean Stockwell was featured in more than 200 film and television projects, ranging from childhood appearances on the big screen alongside icons like Gene Kelley and Gregory Peck to his stint in the audience-favorite science fiction series *Quantum Leap* (1989–93).

The son of actor Harry Stockwell, who provided the voice of Prince Charming in Walt Disney's *Snow White and the Seven Dwarfs*, Dean Stockwell appeared on Broadway in 1943, at age seven and was immediately signed by a Hollywood talent scout. He kicked off his movie career in 1945, appearing in the big-budget pictures *The Valley of Decision* and *Anchors Aweigh*. By the time he graduated from high school at 16, he had made almost 20 films.

Stockwell had never really enjoyed acting, and he resolved to find a different career path. By age 20, however, he realized he was trained for little else and began to accept additional roles in such films as *Compulsion* (1959), *Sons and Lovers* (1960), and *Long Day's Journey into Night* (1962). Despite being in demand, he remained unhappy with the profession, and he often took breaks, fading from the public eye from time to time.

In 1984, he accepted roles in David Lynch's sci-fi epic *Dune* and in the drama *Paris, Texas*, and those appearances marked something of a career revival for him. He garnered an Academy Award nomination as Best Supporting Actor for his performance as a capo in *Married to the Mob* (1988) and went on to join the cast of the popular television series *Quantum Leap*, which earned him multiple Emmy nominations as well as a Golden Globe. His final role came in 2015, in the little-seen film *Entertainment*.

Stockwell died on November 7, 2021, of natural causes in Hollywood, California. He

Peter Straub

Born: Milwaukee, Wisconsin; March 2, 1943
Died: New York, New York; September 4, 2022
Occupation: American novelist and poet

Although he often claimed to be beyond categorization, Peter Straub's novels were praised as having revived the horror genre, and during the 1970s and 1980s, he became known as one of the top names in that realm, ranking alongside Stephen King and Anne Rice.

Peter Francis Straub was born on March 2, 1943, in Milwaukee, Wisconsin. His childhood was marked by a near-fatal car accident when he was seven years old. The incident left him with a notable stutter, though he managed to overcome the most major physical impacts and learn how to walk again. As a young man, Straub graduated from the University of Wisconsin-Madison with an English degree in 1965. He continued pursuing this field through a master's program at Columbia University, before returning to his birthplace of Milwaukee to become an English teacher.

He first published works of poetry in the early 1970s, but did not gain true fame until the release of his third novel, *Julia* (1975), a ghost story about a grieving woman haunted by what may be the spirit of her dead daughter. A film adaptation, *Full Circle*, would be made in 1977. Straub went on to publish *If You Could See Me Now* (1977), a psychological horror novel following a teacher returning to his home after 20 years to find it changed for the worse, and *Ghost Story* (1979), about four men haunted by a dark crime committed in their youth. A film adaptation of *Ghost Story* would come out in 1981. Straub remained a prolific writer up through the 2010s, producing short stories, novellas, and nonfiction in addition to his more famous novels.

Straub was friends with the well-known horror author Stephen King, who had written a blurb for *Ghost Story* and who later collaborated with Straub on the novel *The Talisman* (1984). The book tells the story of a boy who enters an alternate universe to cure his mother's cancer.

Later, in 2001, Straub and King published a sequel, *Black House*.

Straub died in New York City of complications related to a broken hip on September 4, 2022. He is survived by his wife, Susan, his brother, John, his children, Emma and Benjamin (a novelist and film producer, respectively), as well as by three grandchildren.

See Current Biography 1989

André Leon Talley

Born: Washington, DC; October 16, 1948
Died: White Plains, New York; January 18, 2022
Occupation: American fashion editor

André Leon Talley rose to the top of the elitist and thinness-obsessed world of glossy fashion magazines despite being a large, Black man who had grown up in the Jim Crow South.

Talley was raised by his grandmother, a maid, in the college town of Durham, North Carolina, and he has recalled students throwing rocks at him when he cut across campus.

Early on, he became fascinated by fashion and travel—symbols of escape from his provincial milieu—and he majored in French studies at North Carolina Central University and earned a master's degree from Brown University before decamping to New York City, where he volunteered at the Metropolitan Museum of Art's Costume Institute. There, he met Diana Vreeland, the director of the Institute and a former *Vogue* editor, who took him under her wing. Thanks to her letters of recommendation, he found work as a writer and receptionist at Andy Warhol's *Interview* magazine, where he met other fashion-industry figures like Diana Vreeland and Karl Lagerfeld.

Talley soon became a fixture on the city's social scene, instantly recognizable thanks to his height (6' 6") and flamboyant outfits. He moved to Paris after becoming that city's bureau chief for *Women's Wear Daily*, and in the 1980s, he began his association with Anna Wintour, the iconoclastic editor of *Vogue*. He served variously as fashion-news director, creative director, and editor-in-large of the magazine, and in the process, he encouraged Wintour to feature increasing numbers of Black models at a time when few high-fashion magazines were doing so.

In addition to his work at *Vogue*, where he remained until 2013, Talley served as First Lady Michelle Obama's stylist, appeared as a judge on the reality television show *America's Next Top Model*, and wrote multiple memoirs. He suffered from several health problems in his later years and died on January 18, 2022, at his home in White Plains. Although he was openly gay, he had no serious romantic partner and left no immediate survivors.

See Current Biography 2003

Alain Tanner

Born: Geneva, Switzerland; December 6, 1929
Died: Geneva, Switzerland; September 11, 2022
Occupation: Swiss film director

Filmmaker Alain Tanner was an important figure in the Swiss New Wave, a cinematic movement that had its genesis in Geneva during the 1970s.

Tanner was born in Geneva, on December 6, 1929, into an artistic family: his father was a writer and his mother a painter. Raised in a French-speaking region in the west of Switzerland, Tanner loved movies from an early age, and while he studied economics at the University of Geneva, he dreamed of a career as a filmmaker. Upon graduating, he joined the Merchant Marines, and in the mid-1950s he moved to London, where he worked subtitling movies and organizing the British Film Institute archives. He also became interested in making documentaries, and in 1957 he co-directed a short experimental film about Piccadilly Circus that won a prize at that year's Venice Film Festival.

After moving back to Switzerland, he began directing television projects and in 1968 helped form what became known as the Group of 5; besides Tanner, it included the filmmakers Michel Soutter, Claude Goretta, Jean-Louis Roy, and Jean-Jacques Lagrange. His first feature-length picture, *Charles Dead or Alive*, about a philosophical young watchmaker navigating family relationships and romantic entanglements, won first-place honors at the 1969 Locarno Film Festival.

His subsequent films included *The Middle of the World* (1974), which examines the affair between a waitress and a married politician; *Jonah Who Will Be 25 in the Year 2000* (1976), which listens in to a group of friends as they ponder politics, sex, and philosophy; *Light Years Away* (1981), which won the jury's special grand prize at Cannes; *The Diary of Lady M* (1993), about a passionate, young actress; and *Fleurs de sang* (2002), about a 14-year-old who murders her middle-aged lover. These and others (some 21 feature-length movies in all) earned Tanner a reputation for having a willingness to probe uncomfortable topics, ability to evocatively trace a character's personal growth, and iconoclastic worldview.

Tanner died at a Geneva hospital on September 11, 2022, at the age of 92. He was survived by his wife, Janine; daughters, Nathalie and Cécile; and three grandchildren.

See Current Biography 1990

Wayne Thiebaud

Born: Mesa, Arizona; November 15, 1920
Died: Sacramento, California; December 25, 2021
Occupation: American artist and educator

Wayne Thiebaud's depictions of mid-century Americana were considered by some critics to be exemplars of twentieth-century Pop Art—although others asserted that he defied such neat characterization.

Thiebaud grew up in a farming family in Utah, and he credits his early interest in art to an amateur cartoonist uncle who sketched as a way to entertain him as a child. He studied commercial art in high school and later worked as a sign painter and cartoonist. He also became an apprentice animator at the Disney studios and created movie poster illustrations.

Drafted during World War II, he created illustrations for an Air Corps newspaper, and after the war he was hired to work on an in-house magazine published by Rexall Drugs. Thiebaud soon came to the realization that he wanted to pursue a more serious art career, and by the early 1960s he was exhibiting his work at New York galleries. Although his colorful renderings of cakes, gumball machines, candy apples, and pinball machines led critics to refer to him as a Pop artist, he, himself, was uncomfortable with the term, feeling it implied a cynicism that he did not possess. He later became associated with a group on the West Coast known as Bay Area Figuratives. Thiebaud's paintings have

sold at auction for millions of dollars, with the 1962 painting "Four Pinball Machines" selling for a record $19.1 million in 2020.

Thiebaud, who taught for decades at the University of California, Davis, died at his Sacramento, California, home on December 25, 2021, at the age of 101. He was predeceased in 2015 by his second wife, Betty Jean, and in 2010 by one son, Paul. He was survived by daughters Twinka and Mallary Ann; another son, Matthew; and six grandchildren.

See Current Biography 1987

Franklin A. Thomas

Born: Brooklyn, New York; May 27, 1934
Died: New York, New York; December 22, 2021
Occupation: American foundation official and lawyer

Ford Foundation president Franklin A. Thomas was the first Black person ever to head a major philanthropic organization in the United States.

Thomas grew up in the Bedford-Stuyvesant section of Brooklyn, within a close extended family of immigrants from Barbados. His father, a security guard and laborer, died when Franklin was 11, and his mother supported the family as a waitress and housekeeper. Watching how she was looked down upon and dismissed by others ignited a passion in him for social justice.

Thomas earned an academic scholarship to Columbia University, where he became the first Black captain of an Ivy League basketball team. After earning his undergraduate degree, he enlisted in the Air Force but subsequently returned to Columbia to study law.

After President Lyndon B. Johnson's Great Society legislation led to the formation of the Bedford-Stuyvesant Restoration Corporation in 1967, Thomas became its first president, and he spent the next decade overseeing economic development and housing, healthcare, and other programs.

He gained a reputation for calm, pragmatic leadership, and in 1979 the Ford Foundation tapped him to succeed McGeorge Bundy as its president. At the time, the organization was floundering; its endowment had dropped from $4.1 billion in 1973 to $1.7 billion because of overspending, and grant recipients were feeling the pinch of the era's rampant inflation. Thomas responded by trimming the staff; shuttering several foreign offices; and refocusing on six core areas of need, including education and urban poverty. The strategy proved successful: by the time Thomas stepped down in 1996, the Foundation's endowment had reached $7 billion.

After he left the organization, Thomas—who was romantically involved at one point with feminist leader Gloria Steinem—devoted much of his time to anti-apartheid activities in South Africa. He died on December 22, 2021, at his home in Manhattan. He was survived by his second wife, Kate Whitney; his children, Kyle, Keith, Kerrie, and Hilary; his stepchildren, Andrea, Lulie, and Laura; 16 grandchildren; and four great-grandchildren.

See Current Biography 1981

David Trimble

Born: Belfast, Northern Ireland; October 15, 1944
Died: Belfast, Northern Ireland; July 25, 2022
Occupation: British political leader

The recipient of numerous political honors and a Nobel Peace Prize, Northern Irish unionist politician David Trimble grew famous for his efforts to unite conflicting parties during his time in high office.

William David Trimble, the second of three children, was born into a Presbyterian family in Belfast, with both his parents holding low-level positions in the Ministry of Labor. He grew up and was educated in the nearby town of Bangor, before beginning a position as a civil servant. Eventually, he received a first-class honors degree in law at Queen's University in Belfast.

In the early 1970s, Trimble began his political career with connections to the radical right-wing Vanguard Unionist Progressive Party, which had paramilitary connections. The party's platform rested on the belief in Irish loyalty to the British Crown (as opposed to the nationalists, who believed that Northern Ireland should be its own sovereign state). Though in the future, Trimble would promote strategies for peace, he tended to oppose peace settlements earlier in his career. By this time, the violent period of Ireland's recent history known as the "Troubles" had reached its peak,

England having sent troops to restore its direct power in Northern Ireland in 1972.

In 1978, Trimble joined the more mainstream Ulster Unionist party and was elected to the British Parliament, where he would hold a seat until 2005. Five years later, he was chosen as the leader of the Ulster party and started on a more moderate, bipartisan path, working to bridge the gap between unionists and nationalists, and Catholics and Protestants. In 1998, Trimble and the nationalist John Hume jointly won the Nobel Peace Prize for their contribution to the Good Friday agreement, a compromise that brought an end to three decades of the Troubles. In accordance with the agreement, Trimble became the first minister of Northern Ireland.

In 2019, Trimble supported the United Kingdom's decision to separate from the European Union (EU). However, he disapproved of what is known as the Northern Irish Protocol, which allows Northern Ireland, unique among other regions of the United Kingdom, to retain a partial connection to the EU.

On July 25, 2022, Trimble died following a brief illness. He is survived by his second wife, Daphne Elizabeth Orr, and their four children, Richard, Victoria, Nicholas, and Sarah.

See Current Biography 2000

Jean-Louis Trintignant

Born: Piolenc, France; December 11, 1930
Died: Southern France; June 17, 2022
Occupation: French actor

Jean-Louis Trintignant is best known for his subtle but memorable presence in many celebrated European films during the latter half of the mid-twentieth century.

Jean-Louis Xavier Trintignant was born on December 11, 1930, in Piolenc, France. Trintignant's wealthy, southern French family had no background in theater—his father was an industrialist and local politician, and both of his uncles drove racecars. He first considered following in their footsteps and becoming a racer himself; he then instead turned his focus to law school, but finally set off on a new trajectory after he saw a performance of *The Miser* by the playwright Molière and moved to Paris to study acting. He appeared in his first play at the age of 20.

In 1956, Trintignant had his breakout role in Roger Vadim's film *And God Created Woman*, starring opposite Vadim's wife, Brigitte Bardot. This was followed in 1959 by Vadim's *Les Liaisons Dangereuses* ("Dangerous Liaisons"), based on the eighteenth-century novel of the same name, in which Trintignant took on a minor but romantic role.

Trintignant's most romantic role, however, was in the 1966 international hit film *A Man and a Woman*, as a racecar driver. He told interviewers he had been inspired in his performance by his early interest and familial background in the sport.

Though more often playing a supporting rather than a lead role, Trintignant spent the next three decades constantly working, appearing in about three films a year, as well as continuing to dabble in theater. One of his few leading roles was in the 1994 Polish film *Red*, in which he played a suspicious judge using surveillance equipment on his neighbors.

Trintignant never fully lost his passion for racing. As an older man he participated in various sports-car events, such as the 24 Hours of Le Mans (1980) and the Monte Carlo Rally (1984).

Tragedy struck Trintignant's life in 2003, when his daughter, Marie, one of his three children with the actress Nadine Marquand, was found beaten to death in Lithuania, at the age of 41. The murderer was later discovered to have been Bertrand Cantat, a famous rock star and Marie's boyfriend at the time.

Trintignant suffered from depression following his daughter's death and spent over a decade away from the film world, until agreeing to appear in the Oscar-winning *Amour* (2012). In this film, Trintignant played an elderly man looking after his dying wife.

Trintignant died at his home in southern France from complications related to prostate cancer, on June 17, 2022. He is survived by his third wife, the racecar driver Marianne Hoepfner Trintignant.

See Current Biography 1988

Desmond Tutu

Born: Klerksdorp, Witwatersrand, South Africa; October 7, 1931
Died: Cape Town, South Africa; December 26, 2021
Occupation: Anglican prelate and social activist

Desmond Tutu was a towering figure in the fight against the system of racial discrimination known as apartheid in South Africa; in 1984 he received the Nobel Peace Prize for his efforts.

Although Tutu, who is of Xhosa and Tswana descent, initially wanted to pursue a medical career, he was unable to afford the necessary training and instead became a teacher. He changed courses in 1957, when he entered St. Peter's Theological College in Johannesburg. He was ordained as an Anglican cleric in 1961 and served in various local churches. From 1972 to 1975, he was the associate director for the World Council of Churches and was next appointed dean of St. Mary's Cathedral in Johannesburg, he had the distinction of being the first Black South African ever to hold that post. From 1976 to 1978, he also served as bishop of Lesotho.

In 1978, Tutu accepted an appointment as the general secretary of the South African Council of Churches, and he used his pulpit to speak against the injustices of apartheid. His moving rhetoric and persuasive arguments soon made him a leading spokesperson, as he espoused nonviolence and economic sanctions as the best way to deal with the South African government. His 1984 Nobel Prize sent a strong message to government leaders that the eyes of the world were upon them.

In 1985, Tutu was named Johannesburg's first Black Anglican bishop, and in 1986 he was made the first Black archbishop of Cape Town. The latter post made him spiritual leader to the 1.6 million members of his country's Anglican church.

In 1995, with apartheid dismantled, South African President Nelson Mandela appointed Tutu to head the Truth and Reconciliation Commission, charging him with investigating the many human rights abuses that had occurred during the apartheid era. The following year he became archbishop emeritus, and in 2010 he retired from public life altogether.

In addition to his Nobel Prize, Tutu—a prolific writer who published multiple memoirs, essays, and collections of sermons—was the recipient of such international laurels as the U.S. Presidential Medal of Freedom (2009) and the Templeton Prize (2013).

He died in Cape Town, on December 26, 2021, at the age of 90. He had been battling cancer for years. He was survived by his wife of more than six decades, Nomalizo Leah Shenxane; a son, Trevor Thamsanqa Tutu; and three daughters, Theresa Thandeka Tutu, Naomi Nontombi Tutu, and Mpho Andrea Tutu van Furth; as well as seven grandchildren.

See Current Biography 1985

Vangelis

Born: Agria, Greece; March 29, 1943
Died: Paris, France; May 17, 2022
Occupation: Greek composer

The composer and musician professionally known as Vangelis gained much of his fame for creating the score of the hit film *Chariots of Fire* (1981).

Born Evangelos Odysseas Papathanassiou in Agria, Greece, on March 29, 1943, Vangelis grew up in Athens and started playing piano at age four. He performed in public for the first time two years later. Though he had little formal training and never learned to read music, he went on to play the organ with the Greek rock band the Forminx and become the founder of the band Aphrodite's Child, which earned Europe-wide fame. He would become particularly distinguished in the music world for his vast array of synthesizers and his New Age style of music.

Vangelis left Greece for Paris after the military coup in 1967 and then moved from Paris to London when Aphrodite's Child broke up. In England, he began composing for television shows, most notably the French documentary series *L'Apocalypse des Animaux* (1973). At the same time, he produced solo albums and film projects, shortening his given name when told that it was too long to fit on a record sleeve and difficult to pronounce.

Chariots of Fire, a film about two British runners in the 1924 Summer Olympics, was arguably Vangelis's first major film score. He went on to compose for the iconic science fiction film *Blade Runner* (1982), followed by such successes as *Antarctica* (1983); *The Bounty* (1984); which starred Anthony Hopkins and Mel Gibson; *Alexander* (2004) starring Colin Farrell, and the Greek film *El Greco* (2007), about the famed Renaissance artist. Vangelis also composed the music for large-scale sporting events such as the 2000 and 2004 Olympics and the World Cup of 2002.

One of Vangelis's most notable recent compositions was *Mythodea* (2001), a choral symphony recorded at the Temple of Zeus, in Athens, meant as a commemoration of NASA's Odyssey spacecraft mission to Mars.

Vangelis died of heart failure in Paris, on May 17, 2022. He had no biological children, but is survived by his partner, Laura, and her daughter, Melia.

See Current Biography 2003

Emi Wada

Born: Kyoto, Japan; March 18, 1937
Died: Unknown; November 13, 2021
Occupation: Japanese costume designer

Emi Wada (born Emiko Noguchi) is best known as the designer of the more than 1,000 costumes worn in *Ran*, Akira Kurosawa's 1985 masterwork. She worked for more than three years on the film, which transposes the action of Shakespeare's *King Lear* to ancient Japan—weaving fabric from threads she had hand-dyed and calling upon inspiration from varied sources, including Botticelli and traditional Noh theater. That effort paid off with an Academy Award, the only one ultimately awarded to the film.

Wada, who earned a degree from the Kyoto City University of Arts, had ambitions of becoming a painter. She switched courses after marrying Ben Wada, a television director, and agreeing to collaborate with him on costuming for his projects. Her work made its big-screen debut in 1973, in *Marco*, a comedy starring Desi Arnaz and Zero Mostel.

It was her work on *Ran*, however, that put her at the forefront of her field. Her subsequent films included *The Hall of the Crying Deer* (1986), *Princess from the Moon* (1987), *Rikyu* (1989), *Dreams* (1990), *The Bride with White Hair* (1993), *Prospero's Books* (1991), *The Pillow Book* (1996), *Hero* (2002), *House of*

Flying Daggers (2004), *The Go Master* (2006), and *The Warrior and the Wolf* (2009). Her final film was *Love After Love* (2020).

In addition to her work with such revered filmmakers as Kon Ichikawa, Hiroshi Teshigahara, and Peter Greenaway, Wada often designed costumes for the opera stage, and in 1993 she won a Primetime Emmy for her work on the PBS *Great Performances* broadcast of Stravinsky's opera *Oedipus Rex*.

Throughout her career, Wada was known for her exacting standards: one widely circulated story holds that while working on *Hero*, she ordered truckloads of various mineral waters, seeking to create the exact shade of red dye she had envisioned. She reportedly refused to work on the eagerly anticipated 2005 film *Memoirs of a Geisha*, on the grounds that it depicted an unrealistic, westernized version of Japan.

Wada died on November 13, 2021. Her husband had predeceased her in 2011.

See Current Biography 2007

Fred Ward

Born: San Diego, California; December 30, 1942
Died: San Diego, California; May 8, 2022
Occupation: American actor and producer

Appearing in various well-known films of the late twentieth century, the actor Fred Ward was recognized for his range and versatility. While he more often had a supporting rather than a leading role, Ward became famous for his ability to disappear inside his characters, particularly in the film *Henry and June* (1990) in which he played mid-century novelist Henry Miller.

Born on December 30, 1942, in San Diego, California. Frederick Joseph Ward grew up in 1940s-era California and Texas, raised alternately by his grandmother and mother, who supported her son by working as a bartender. The Wards moved frequently: circumstances Ward came to believe contributed to his own restlessness as an adult. After a period serving with the U.S. Air Force directly out of high school, Ward moved to New York and began taking acting classes at the Herbert Berghof Studio. Ward's first few films were minor, however, and he made more money from taking on blue-collar jobs throughout the country; he eventually managed to fund a trip to Europe and Morocco in that way.

Ward gradually won more substantial roles, starting with *Escape from Alcatraz* (1979), in which he played a convict alongside Clint Eastwood, and followed a few years later by *Silkwood* (1983), playing opposite Meryl Streep. Yet, he was not fully recognized by Hollywood until the 1983 film *The Right Stuff*, based on the book by Tom Wolfe, which follows the astronauts chosen to fly the spacecraft for the Mercury Project, known as the Mercury Seven. Seven years later, Ward was cast in *Henry and June*, which told the story of Miller's love triangle with his wife, June, and erotic writer Anaïs Nin. Ward was both praised and criticized for his carefully studied "impersonation" of Henry Miller.

Ward had trouble equaling the successes of *The Right Stuff* and *Henry and June*. Following these two films, he appeared in a variety of other projects and had a hopeful appearance in the film *Remo Williams: The Adventure Begins* (1985). Intended to become a successful franchise, the film did poorly at the box office, and no sequels were made.

Ward died of undisclosed causes on May 8, 2022. (According to some sources, his place of death was San Diego.) He is survived by his third wife, Marie-France, and his son, Django.

See Current Biography 2001

Shane Warne

Born: Ferntree Gully, Victoria, Australia; September 13, 1969
Died: Thailand; March 4, 2022
Occupation: Australian cricket player

Those familiar with cricket generally consider Shane Warne the greatest spin bowler the sport has ever produced. (Spin bowling is a technique in which the player bowls the cricket ball so that it rotates rapidly and deviates from its normal straight path after bouncing on the pitch, making it difficult for the batsman to get a clean shot.)

Spin bowling requires superior upper-body strength—an attribute Warne began to develop after breaking both legs as a child and having to push himself around on a cart. Although not a motivated student, at 15 he won an athletic scholarship to Mentone Grammar School in Melbourne, where he distinguished himself at tennis, Australian rules football, and swimming, as well as cricket.

In 1984, he joined St Kilda Cricket Club, where he climbed the ranks from the under-19 team to the reserves team. In 1990, he began training at the Australian Cricket Academy in Adelaide, and he later moved to England, where he joined the pros as a member of the Lancashire League's Accrington Cricket Club.

He made his international debut in 1992 and after returning to Australia, he gradually developed into a force to be reckoned with: he was said to take special pleasure going up against England and South Africa, and in Test cricket (considered the highest form of the game), 325 of his 708 career wins were against those countries.

Warne's playing prowess was sometimes overshadowed in the press by his personal foibles; In February 2003, for example, right before the start of the World Cup, Warne was disqualified for taking a banned diuretic. Other drug scandals sometimes occurred, as did controversies surrounding his gambling. Still, the public forgave those incidents in light of his performance on the pitch: In 2005, Warne became the first bowler in cricket history to take 600 Test wickets—the same year in which he broke the record for number of wickets in a single calendar cycle, with 96.

Warne retired from cricket in 2013 to run an eponymous foundation devoted to helping ill and underprivileged children. He died on March 4, 2022, of an apparent heart attack while vacationing in Thailand and was survived by three children born of his marriage to ex-wife Simone Callahan: Summer, Jackson, and Brooke.

See Current Biography 2005

Open Golf Championships in Toledo. By high school, Weiskopf was leading his school's golf team to the Cleveland city championships. Eventually, he was recruited to Ohio State University's golfing team. Weiskopf officially went professional in 1964 and would go on to participate in the PGA Tour from 1968 to 1982.

One early significant PGA-related event in Weiskopf's career came during the Tour of 1973, in which he won five games, most notably at the British Open, and was praised for his distinctive swing. After his victory, Weiskopf paid tribute to his late father. He then went on to win runner-up four times in the Masters Tournaments and first place in the Canadian Open in both 1973 and 1975. It was at this last game that he defeated champion Jack Nicklaus, who had also been on the golf team at Ohio State.

In 1983, Weiskopf took a break from playing and instead began designing golf courses, both in the United States and overseas. He also began working as a golf analyst for CBS Sports, covering the Masters; he also assisted with the coverage of the British Open on the networks ABC Sports and ESPN.

Weiskopf later joined the Senior PGA Tour, later renamed the Champions Tour, as well as participated in the 1995 U.S. Senior Open, where he defeated Jack Nicklaus once again.

Weiskopf died of complications related to pancreatic cancer, at his home in Montana, on August 20, 2022. News of the death was released by the PGA Tour. He is survived by his second wife, Laurie, and his children, Heidi and Eric.

See Current Biography 1973

Tom Weiskopf

Born: Masillon, Ohio; November 9, 1942
Died: Big Sky, Montana; August 20, 2022
Occupation: American golfer

Tom Weiskopf was the winner of 16 events on the Professional Golfing Association (PGA) Tour, most famously the British Open.

The oldest of three children, Thomas Daniel Weiskopf was born on November 9, 1942, to parents who had both previously participated in Ohio sporting tournaments. Weiskopf's father, a railroad worker, sparked his son's interest in golf in 1957, when he brought him to the U.S.

Lina Wertmüller

Born: Rome, Italy; August 14, 1928
Died: Rome, Italy; December 9, 2021
Occupation: Italian film director

Lina Wertmüller, the auteur responsible for such provocative films as *The Seduction of Mimi* (1972) and *Swept Away* (1974), was the first woman ever to be nominated for an Oscar as best director—an honor she received for her 1975 work *Seven Beauties*.

Wertmüller, a native of Rome, attended a Stanislavski-based drama school there and spent the 1950s touring with a puppet troupe, writing for television, and taking on small stage roles. A stint as an assistant director on Federico Fellini's 8½ incited a desire to make films herself, and her first effort was *The Lizards* (1963), who sensibilities were deeply influenced by Fellini's work. She enjoyed a heyday in the 1970s by examining the changing sexual mores of the era and Italy's chaotic political scene.

The Seduction of Mimi—about a philandering Sicilian laborer (Giancarlo Giannini) and his wife—was chosen as an official entry at Cannes and marked her as a filmmaker to watch. She followed with *Love and Anarchy* (1973), which starred Giannini as a hapless would-be assassin; the social satire *All Screwed Up* (1974); *Swept Away* (1974), in which Giannini plays a deckhand dealing with an imperious passenger after a shipwreck; and *Seven Beauties* (1975), a controversial picture about a Neapolitan deserter who seduces the sadistic female commandant of a Nazi concentration camp.

Wertmüller enjoyed greater popularity in America than in Europe, but even in the United States critical opinion was divided, with many seeing her work as affected and pretentious. She became an object of some derision for her film titles, which gradually got longer and more convoluted; her 1978 film *Un fatto di sangue nel comune di Siculiana fra due uomini per causa di una vedova: Si sospettano moventi politici. Amore-Morte-Shimmy Lugano belle Tarantelle. Tarallucci e vino* holds a Guinness record for the length of its full title. (It is also known as *Blood Feud or Revenge*.)

Her final film was a 2014 documentary short, *Roma, Napoli, Venezia . . . in un crescendo rossiniano* (*Naples, Venice . . . in a Rossinian Crescendo*), in which composer Gioachino Rossini discusses the influence each of those cities had on his work.

Wertmüller, who was given an honorary Oscar for her body of work in 2019, died at her home in Rome on December 9, 2021. She is survived by Maria Zulima Job, her then-husband's child with another woman, whom she adopted shortly after birth.

See Current Biography 1976

Av Westin

Born: New York, New York; July 29, 1929
Died: New York, New York; March 12, 2022
Occupation: American television producer and director

Av Westin is best known for his role in the success of the ABC entertainment show *20/20*, which had won more than 30 Emmy Awards at the time of his death.

Avram Robert Westin grew up in Manhattan and attended New York University, first as a pre-med student; he later switched to English and history, however, after working for CBS Broadcasting in 1947. He graduated in 1949 and continued to work for CBS for almost two decades as a writer, director, reporter, and producer. It was there that Westin won an Emmy for the documentary *The Population Explosion* (1960).

In 1969, after two years as the executive director of the Sunday-night news show *Public Broadcasting Laboratory*, Westin switched to ABC News. Westin became executive producer of ABC's evening newscast, which had not yet gained its present fame. He had ambitions to increase the network's popularity and prestige. Though he left for two years due to disagreements with ABC's president, Westin returned to the program in 1969. In 1978, together with Roone Arledge, a broadcasting executive and then-president of ABC Sports and ABC News, Westin revamped the program into *World News Tonight*. The new show was faster and more visually oriented, helping ABC rise in competition with NBC and CBS. Even so, Arledge and Westin occasionally clashed, with Arledge sometimes removing certain news segments of Westin's that he dismissed as unimportant.

In 1979, Arledge moved Westin to *20/20*, an entertainment show that under Westin's management would combine investigative journalism with lifestyle, celebrity, and artist features. The 1980s saw *20/20*'s rise to respect and fame, thanks in large part to hosts Barbara Walters and Hugh Downs and a variety of A-list correspondents. In 1987, however, Westin was suspended from *20/20* after criticizing ABC News' procedures and efficiency, apparently at the request of another executive of the company.

Westin continued to produce some programs within ABC before finally leaving the network in 1989. He then went on to executive produce for several other networks, including King World Productions, Time Warner, and the National Academy of Television Arts Sciences' Foundation.

On March 12, 2022, Westin died of cardiac arrest in a hospital in Manhattan, the city where he had spent his life. He is survived by his third wife, Ellen, and a son, Mark.

See Current Biography 1975

Betty White

Born: Oak Park, Illinois; January 17, 1922
Died: Los Angeles, California; December 31, 2021
Occupation: American actor

Betty White's career spanned more than 70 years—during which time she received five Primetime Emmys, a Daytime Emmy, and multiple lifetime achievement awards. In 2014, the *Guinness Book of World Records* certified her as the longest-working female entertainer ever.

White, who often appeared in student productions at Beverly Hills High School, served during World War II in the American Women's Voluntary Services, driving supplies to government encampments in the Hollywood Hills.

After the war, she became active in the Bliss-Hayden Little Theater and quickly caught the eye of agents who found her roles in the radio shows popular in the 1940s. She broke into television work in 1949 on the talk show *Al Jarvis's Hollywood on Television*, eventually replacing Jarvis as host. She became a fixture in the 1950s, appearing on sitcoms and variety shows, and during the 1960s she remained a familiar face, especially to fans of game shows like *To Tell the Truth*, *Match Game*, and *Password*, on which she appeared regularly.

She is most celebrated for two later roles: Sue Ann Nivens and Rose Nylund.

Sue Ann—a character on *The Mary Tyler Moore Show* (1973–77), a sitcom about an off-beat newsroom—was the nymphomaniacal hostess of a household hints show, who often popped cheerily into the newsroom to flirt and tell tales of her sexual exploits.

Rose was one of the four older female characters who shared a home in Miami in *The Golden Girls*, which ran originally from 1985 to 1992. Dimwitted but loveable, Rose became known for her innocent malapropisms, and the authenticity White brought to the role earned her another Emmy.

White was introduced to an entirely new generation of viewers when she hosted *Saturday Night Live* in May 2010 at the behest of fans who had started a lively and unironic social-media campaign. During the show, she enthusiastically participated in off-color and irreverent sketches, cementing her reputation as a good-natured yet bawdy trouper and earning yet another Emmy.

White, who had been inducted into the Television Academy Hall of Fame in 1995, later appeared on the sitcom *Hot in Cleveland* (2010–15); starred in and produced the reality show *Betty White's Off Their Rockers*, which featured senior citizens playing pranks on younger people; and filmed guest spots on such television programs as *Ally McBeal*, *Boston Legal*, and *That '70s Show*. She acted well into her 90s; her last screen credits came in 2019, when she voiced characters for the animated films *Toy Story 4* and *Trouble*.

A committed animal-welfare activist for much of her life, White died peacefully in her sleep from a stroke on December 31, 2021, at the age of 99. She was survived by three stepchildren (David, Martha, and Sarah) from her marriage to her third husband, the game-show host Allen Ludden, who had predeceased her in 1981.

See Current Biography 2010

Maury Wills

Born: Washington, DC; October 2, 1932
Died: Sedona, Arizona; September 19, 2022
Occupation: American baseball player

Maury Wills, a shortstop for the Los Angeles Dodgers, was known for his enviable ability to steal bases; in 1962 alone, he stole 104, breaking a record set by the legendary Ty Cobb almost 50 years before.

Maurice Morning Wills was born on October 2, 1932, in the nation's capital. He was one of 13 children in his churchgoing, working-class family. A star football and baseball player while in high school, he joined the Dodgers' franchise as an infielder in 1951 and played in the minors until mid-1959.

By the end of 1960, his first full season, he had established himself as a major-league player to watch, stealing 50 bases and winning the National League's base-stealing title—an honor he garnered in 1961, '62, '63, '64, and '65 as well. He was also named the 1962 MVP, thanks to his record-breaking 104 steals that year.

Wills remained with the Dodgers until the end of the 1966 season, when he was traded to the Pittsburgh Pirates. During his time in LA, the team won the World Series during his rookie season, 1963, and 1965; and captured a pennant in 1966.

After a short stint in Pittsburgh and another in Montreal with the Expos, in 1969 Wills returned to the Dodgers, capping off his pro career with them in 1972. In all, he had stolen 586 bases, recorded a career batting average of .281, been an All-Star five times, and garnered Golden Glove Awards twice.

Later in the 1970s, Wills worked as a television baseball analyst, and for a time he managed the Seattle Mariners—a stint that ended ignominiously in 1981, after he was caught illegally ordering the batter's box extended to give the team an unfair advantage.

Wills died on September 19, 2022, at his Arizona home, at the age of 89. He was survived by his third wife, Carla; two sons, Barry and Bump (the latter also a pro baseball player); four daughters, Mauricia, Anita, Wendi, and Susan; seven grandchildren; and eight great-grandchildren.

See Current Biography 1966

Edward O. Wilson

Born: Birmingham, Alabama; June 10, 1929
Died: Burlington, Massachusetts; December 26, 2021
Occupation: American entomologist and sociobiologist

Edward O. Wilson's pioneering (and at times iconoclastic) work on biodiversity won him two Pulitzer Prizes, as well as both respect and opprobrium in the scientific community.

As a child, Wilson spent a great deal of time in the wooded area and tidal pools of Alabama. He developed an obsession with ants, and while in high school, he discovered the first colony of imported fire ants ever found in the United States.

In 1953, while in graduate school at Harvard, he embarked on a trip to Cuba, Mexico, New Guinea, and the South Pacific to study ants. After earning his doctoral degree, Wilson joined Harvard's faculty of biology and zoology in 1956. In 1961, he began collaborating with University of Pennsylvania biologist Robert MacArthur. The two developed general equations to predict how many species a given island could support, and in 1967 they published *The Theory of Island Biogeography*, considered a seminal work of ecology as their findings could be used to make predictions about the biodiversity of a wide range of ecosystems.

In 1975, Wilson published *Sociobiology: The New Synthesis*, in which he controversially asserted that human behaviors might be the result of a natural selection process. Praised in some quarters, he was accused of dredging up old theories of biological determinism that had led to racist attitudes and policies.

In the 1980s, with that controversy behind him, he took up the mantle of environmental activist, stressing that numerous species were headed towards extinction because of the destruction of their habitats. His 1992 book on the topic, *The Diversity of Life*, became a best-seller. (His Pulitzers were given for two other popular volumes, *On Human Nature* in 1979 and *The Ants* in 1991.)

Wilson retired from Harvard in 2002 but continued to remain active. He subsequently wrote more than a dozen other books; launched an online "Encyclopedia of Life," with the goal of including information on every known species; and started an eponymous foundation dedicated to biodiversity.

Wilson died on December 26, 2021, in Burlington, Massachusetts. He was predeceased earlier that year by his wife, Irene. He is survived by their daughter, Catherine.

See Current Biography 1979

Larry Woiwode

Born: Carrington, North Dakota; October 30, 1941
Died: Bismarck, North Dakota; April 28, 2022
Occupation: American writer

A literary icon of 1970s New York, Larry Woiwode (WHY-woody) was known for the themes of family, faith, and home threaded throughout his poems, novels, short stories, and essays, most of which were set in the American West.

Larry Alfred Woiwode was born in Carrington, North Dakota, on October 30, 1941 and moved between that state and Illinois during his youth. Woiwode, whose mother died when he was not yet ten, studied acting and literature at the University of Illinois Urbana-Champaign and relocated to New York at the age of 24. He would eventually have as a mentor the editor William Maxwell, who had also coached such writers as John Cheever, J.D. Salinger, and John Updike. Woiwode's first novel, *What I'm Going to Do, I Think* (1969) was a success, garnering the William Faulkner Foundation Award for the best first novel of the year, and becoming a finalist for the National Book Award. The novel follows a young couple on their honeymoon at a Michigan lake house and their inner emotional dilemmas.

Woiwode's 1975 novel, *Beyond the Bedroom Wall*, gave him newly classic status, and he was compared by many critics to authors such as Dickens and Tolstoy. The ambitious 600-page saga, which had taken Woiwode five years to write, centers on four generations of a farming family in North Dakota.

In 1978, Woiwode returned with his family to his home state of North Dakota, where he bought a 160-acre farm that the Woiwodes cultivated themselves while homeschooling their four children. Woiwode was a devout Presbyterian, and he wrote frequently about how his faith had shaped his life.

As well as producing many novels, short-story collections, memoirs, and poems, Woiwode taught creative writing and literature at several universities, and was named the poet laureate of North Dakota in 1995.

Woiwode died in a Bismarck hospital of unknown causes on April 28, 2022. His many survivors include his wife and children, three siblings, ten grandchildren, and two great-grandchildren.

See Current Biography 1989

Vladimir Zhirinovsky

Born: Almaty, Kazakhstan, April 25, 1946
Died: Moscow, Russia; April 6, 2022
Occupation: Russian politician and lawyer

The former leader of the Liberal Democratic Party of Russia, Vladimir Zhirinovsky was known for his inflammatory rhetoric and ultranationalist, imperialist views.

Zhirinovsky was born Vladimir Volfovich Eidelshtein in what was then the Kazakh Soviet Socialist Republic. Though his speeches as a politician would later be marked by anti-Semitic accusations, his own father was a Polish Jew, a fact that Zhirinovsky would try to conceal for many years, eventually changing his surname to that of his mother's first husband. Zhirinovsky publicly spread the rumor that he had lost his father at an early age to a car accident, but in actuality the older man had been deported to Poland and is thought to have ultimately settled in Israel.

Zhirinovsky left Kazakhstan for Moscow State University, where he obtained degrees in Turkish and literature. At the Institute of Marxism-Leninism, he also pursued studies in international relations and law, originally intending to be a lawyer. However, once the Russian political system became more accessible under leader Mikhail Gorbachev in the 1980s, Zhirinovsky decided to try his hand at politics. He attempted to join virtually every existing political party but was turned down by many, including the Communist Party. He subsequently started his own Liberal Democratic Party (LDP).

Zhirinovsky unsuccessfully ran for president six times and never managed to gain substantial popularity for the LDP. However, he was very influential in establishing the political tone for the coming decades, and often correctly predicted some of the more extreme changes to come in Russian politics during the 2010s. After Vladimir Putin won the presidency in 2018, Zhirinovsky anticipated the lifting of the two-term limit, which the Kremlin did soon after. In a speech in December 2021, he suggested that a turning point for the country would come in 2022, which indeed occurred in the form of Russia's invasion of Ukraine.

Zhirinovsky was an ardent supporter of similarly populist politicians, including Donald Trump and Putin, though he lost to the latter in multiple elections. He often professed his hopes for Russia to expand its territory, a platform that had once been unpopular but became mainstream with the Ukraine invasion.

While Zhirinovsky did gain some earnest followers, he was also criticized for his racist and misogynistic onslaughts, and he had a known history of sexual assault. On April 6, 2022, Zhirinovsky died in a Moscow hospital after a two-month long battle with Covid-19. Information about his survivors was not made available in the Western press.

See Current Biography 1995

CLASSIFICATION BY PROFESSION

ACTIVISM
William J. Barber II
Liz Chicaje
Elisa Loncón
Pidgeon Pagonis
Najwa Zebian

ARCHITECTURE
Anna Heringer
Rozana Montiel
Roberta Washington

ART
Rocío Caballero
Aaron Gilbert
Martine Gutierrez
Yaya Han
Shamsia Hassani
Thomas Heatherwick
Bharti Kher
Angelbert Metoyer
Joe Ollmann
Lincoln Pierce
Mike Winkelmann

BUSINESS
Ime Archibong
Maverick Carter
Patrick Collison
Ellen Davis
Cathy Engelbert
Jim Fitterling
Michele Thornton Ghee
Patrick Gottsch
Tony Khan
Anthony W. Marx
Myron Mixon
Ronaldo Mouchawar
Kunle Olukotun
Chamath Palihapitiya
Azim Premji
Catherine Raîche
Shahrzad Rafati
Hayat Sindi
Katrina Spade
Dhivya Suryadevara
Adi Tatarko
David Thompson
Rosa Whitaker
Siyabulela Xuza

COMEDY
Quinta Brunson
Mort Sahl
Bowen Yang

COMPUTER SCIENCE
Fei-Fei Li
Francesca Rossi
Josh Wardle

CONSERVATION
Shelton Johnson

DANCE
Tamara Rojo

ECONOMICS
Akinwumi Adesina

EDUCATION
Norma Dunning
Ross Gay
Robin Wall Kimmerer
Cato T. Laurencin
Elisa Loncón
Rainbow Rowell
Leni Sorensen

ENGINEERING
Katie Bouman

ENTERTAINMENT
Alison Roman
Yaya Han

FASHION
Halima Aden
Isabella Springmühl
Tejada

FICTION
Karen Bender
Liu Cixin
David Diop
Norma Dunning
Owl Goingback
Katie Kitamura
Kieran Larwood
Emily St. John Mandel

Damodar Mauzo
Mohamed Mbougar Sarr
Sigrid Nunez
Victor Pelevin
Lincoln Pierce
David Treuer
Charles Yu
Najwa Zebian

FILM

Jonathan Bailey
Radha Blank
Elizabeth Debicki
Ariana DeBose
Carolina Gaitán
Michael Greyeyes
Luke Grimes
Kathryn Hahn
Ryusuke Hamaguchi
Emily Hampshire
Siân Heder
Matthew Heineman
Alfonso Herrera
Moses Ingram
Troy Kotsur
Simu Liu
Anthony Mackie
Regé-Jean Page
Pidgeon Pagonis
Evan Peters
Fatima Robinson
Olivia Rodrigo
Michaela Jaé Rodriguez
Shahrbanoo Sadat
Hiroyuki Sanada
Hailee Steinfeld
Iman Vellani
James Wan
Steven Yeun

FOOD

Myron Mixon
Alison Roman
Leni Sorensen

GOVERNMENT

Lina Khan
Kathleen Hicks
Zahid Quraishi

GRAPHIC NOVELS

Joe Ollmann
Rainbow Rowell

JOURNALISM

Nikole Hannah-Jones
Mina Kimes
Hannah Reyes Morales
Jia Lynn Yang

LAW

Lina Hidalgo
Ketanji Brown Jackson
Lina Khan
Barbara Lagoa
Mia Mottley
Zahid Quraishi

LITERATURE

David Diop
Ross Gay
Owl Goingback
Damodar Mauzo
Mohamed Mbougar Sarr
Sigrid Nunez
David Treuer

MATHEMATICS

Ana Caraiani

MEDICINE

Laurent Duvernay-Tardif
Ashish Jha
Rachel Levine
Vivek Murthy

MUSIC

Nancy Ajram
Raúw Alejandro
Anitta
Gord Bamford
Max Barskih
Jon Batiste
Black Pumas
Jessie Buckley
Eric Burton
Sharon D. Clarke
Colt Ford
Carolina Gaitán
Johnny Gandelsman
Leela Gilday
Asmki Grigorian
Mickey Guyton
Alfonso Herrera
Yoo Jae-suk
Wissam Joubran
Jonathan McReynolds

Leon Michels
Kim Petras
Adrian Quesada
Toshi Reagon
Roddy Ricch
Olivia Rodrigo
Sinach
Hailee Steinfeld
Susanne Sundfør
Zemfira

NONFICTION
Quinta Brunson
David Diop
Robin Wall Kimmerer
Emily St. John Mandel
Sigrid Nunez
Imani Perry
Alison Roman
Jay Shetty
David Treuer
Jia Lynn Yang
Ginger Zee

PERFORMING ARTS
Thomas Forster
Fatima Robinson

POETRY
Ross Gay

POLITICS, FOREIGN
Gabriel Boric
Tony Briffa
William Katonivere
Fiamē Naomi Mata'afa
Mia Mottley
Rodrigo Chaves Robles
Claudia Sheinbaum
Mary Simon
Halimah Yacob

POLITICS, U.S.
Eric Adams
Colin Allred
Justin Bibb
Spencer Cox
Kathleen Hicks
Lina Hidalgo
Gina Ortiz Jones
Hersey Kyota
Rachel Levine
Sarah McBride

Jonathan Nez
Burgess Owens
Nsé-Ufot

SCIENCE
Asha de Vos
Lauren Esposito
George F. Gao
Dominique Gonçalves
Timnit Gebru
Tristan Harris
Cato T. Laurencin
Kunle Olukotun
Gay Jane Perez
Thalappil Pradeep
Rudy Putra
Hayat Sindi
Shakuntala Haraksingh Thilsted
Rochelle Walensky
Jessica Watkins
Siyabulela Xuza
Ginger Zee

SOCIOLOGY
Oyèrónké Oyěwùmí

SPORTS
Colin Allred
Pete Alonso
Tijana Bošković
Toni Breidinger
Joe Burrow
Lisa Byington
Jasmine Camacho-Quinn
Patrick Cantlay
Maia Chaka
Jon Cooper
Caeleb Dressel
Laurent Duvernay-Tardif
Natalie Geisenberger
Mikyla Grant-Mentis
Kendra Harrison
Jonathan Huberdeau
Lee Kiefer
Mikaël Kingsbury
Carissa Moore
Francis Ngannou
Burgess Owens
Artemi Panarin
Fiann Paul
Marie-Philip Poulin
Christian Pulisic
Quinn
Seiya Suzuki

Classification By Profession

Elaine Thompson-Herah
Stefanos Tsitsipas
Tai Tzu-ying
Kevin VanDam
John R. Velazquez
Trae Young

TECHNOLOGY
Fei-Fei Li
Francesca Rossi
Josh Wardle

TELEVISION
Anitta
Jonathan Bailey
Jon Batiste
Radha Blank
Quinta Brunson
Jessie Buckley
Sharon D. Clarke
Ariana DeBose
Carolina Gaitán
Michael Greyeyes
Luke Grimes
Kathryn Hahn
Emily Hampshire
Alfonso Herrera
Moses Ingram
Yoo Jae-suk
Troy Kotsur

Simu Liu
Andrew Mackie
Myron Mixon
Regé-Jean Page
Evan Peters
Michaela Jaé Rodriguez
Fatima Robinson
Olivia Rodrigo
Hailee Steinfeld
Iman Vellani
Bowen Yang
Steven Yeun
Ginger Zee

THEATER
Jonathan Bailey
Jessie Buckley
Sharon D. Clarke
Ariana DeBose
Michael John Garcés
Moses Ingram
Troy Kotsur
Hannah Moscovitch
Regé-Jean Page
Michaela Jaé Rodriguez

VOICE ACTING
Emily Hampshire
Steven Yeun

LIST OF PROFILES

List Of Profiles

List Of Profiles

List Of Profiles